Encyclopedia of
Great Popular Song Recordings

Steve Sullivan

Volume 2

THE SCARECROW PRESS, INC.
Lanham • Toronto • Plymouth, UK
2013

Published by Scarecrow Press, Inc.
A wholly owned subsidiary of The Rowman & Littlefield Publishing Group, Inc.
4501 Forbes Boulevard, Suite 200, Lanham, Maryland 20706
www.rowman.com

10 Thornbury Road, Plymouth PL6 7PP, United Kingdom

British Library Cataloguing in Publication Information Available

Library of Congress Cataloging-in-Publication Data

Sullivan, Steve, 1954–
    Encyclopedia of great popular song recordings / Steve Sullivan.
        volumes cm
    Includes bibliographical references and index.
    ISBN 978-0-8108-8295-9 (cloth : alk. paper) — ISBN 978-0-8108-8296-6 (ebook)
    1. Popular music—Discography. 2. Popular music—History and criticism. I. Title.
    ML156.4.P6S87 2013
    016.78164026'6—dc23   2012041837

∞™ The paper used in this publication meets the minimum requirements of American
National Standard for Information Sciences—Permanence of Paper for Printed Library
Materials, ANSI/NISO Z39.48-1992.

Printed in the United States of America

Contents

Playlist 6

Hot Time in the Old Town, 1893–2008

After the Ball (1893)—George J. Gaskin (written by Charles K. Harris)

Recorded for New Jersey label in early 1893; #1 record of 1893 in *Pop Memories* (*Trad-#188*)

The 1890s was a golden decade for sentimental ballads, and *After the Ball* was the one that set the standard for all that followed in its massive wake. Born in Poughkeepsie, New York, on May 1, 1867, Charles K. Harris loved minstrel show songs as a boy, constructed his own banjo to help perform them, and began writing songs at sixteen. His first song was published by M. Witmark and Sons, the firm that was more responsible than any other for making music publishing a booming business since its establishment in 1886. But since writing songs for a publisher earned the writer little money, Harris decided to launch his own publishing firm, starting with a one-room office in Milwaukee. One song was to make the Charles K. Harris Company a giant in the industry.

The story goes that Harris wrote *After the Ball* after personally witnessing an incident during a brief visit to Chicago where, at a dance, he noticed a young couple argue and separate. This triggered the thought: "Many a heart is aching after the ball." He wrote the words and music after returning to Milwaukee, fashioning an intricate narrative of mistaken identity. An old man explains to his little niece why he never married. Many years ago after the ball, he explained, he saw his sweetheart kiss a strange man. Believing her to be unfaithful, he ended their relationship, and only years later discovered that the strange man was the girl's brother. Vaudeville superstar May Irwin was so struck by the tune that she interpolated it in her burlesque production *Poets and Puppets* at New York's Garden Theatre. Harris copyrighted the number on November 12, 1892,[1] and paid a well-known performer, J. Aldrich Libbey, $500 plus a percentage of sheet music royalties to include it in his San Francisco extravaganza *A Trip to Chinatown*. (Irwin and Libbey each made public claims to have been the first introduce the hit, a debate covered in *The Music Trades* in 1907; Harris settled the matter in his late-1906 autobiography by saying that Irwin sang it first, but Libbey's performances were crucial to its success.) The song received a tumultuous reception; a few days after Libbey sang it, Harris received one order for 75,000 copies of the sheet music, and from there additional orders flooded in, particularly after John Philip Sousa performed the ballad at the World Exposition of 1893.[2] In his 1926 memoir, Harris gave Sousa much credit: "There were thousands of visitors to the World's Fair who heard Sousa's band play it as only he could render it. They would then invariably buy copies in Chicago's music stores to take back home with them, to show the home folks the reigning song success of the World's Fair. That was one of the reasons why the song spread throughout the world as no ballad of its kind had ever done before."

Eventually the melancholy waltz-time ballad is often said to have sold more than five million copies, a staggering and perhaps unprecedented total if true. (Higher figures have been claimed for *Old Folks at Home* and *Listen to the Mockingbird*, but with less credibility. And contemporaneous reports in *The Music Trades* based on Harris's own claims, such as the May 25, 1907, issue, gave the sales figure as "only" 1.5 million, a figure made more specific as 1,520,000 in the February 8, 1908, edition.) Indeed, according to an article in the December 1, 1906, *Music Trades*, the word "hit" first came into wide usage in the United States with regard to popular songs to describe the *After the Ball* phenomenon. Harris stated in his autobiography that the song earned him more than ten million dollars; however, the February 1932 *Metronome*

1. Fuld, *Book of World-Famous Music*, p. 87.

2. David Ewen, *All the Years of American Popular Music*, p. 105–6.

said it earned him "only" $200,000, so the true figure is presumably somewhere in between. The song's enduring popularity was extended by its use in multiple Broadway and movie productions of *Show Boat*.[3]

George Jefferson Gaskin, "the Silver-Voiced Irish Tenor," was born on February 16, 1863, in Belfast, Ireland, and came to the United States as a youth. He made his recording debut for Thomas Edison's North American Phonograph Company in August 1891; two of his first big successes for the company were *Drill, Ye Tarriers, Drill* and *Slide, Kelly, Slide*. With a repertoire that ranged from sentimental pop and Irish tunes to sacred, comic, and patriotic, he was perhaps the most popular singer on record during the 1890s, making cylinders for virtually every major company then doing business. His rendering of *After the Ball* was perhaps the biggest recording of 1893 (the other hit version of the song was by "artistic whistler" John York Atlee). Gaskin remained a top-level star until he largely left recordings in 1904.[4] Samples of Gaskin's recordings can be found on the Archeophone CDs *The Phonographic Yearbook: The 1890s* (Volumes 1 and 2), and the tinfoil.com CD *Brown Wax Cylinder Recordings: 24 Popular Selections from 1895–1897*.

After the Ball was "a defining moment in the creation of the new musical culture," declares David Suisman in *Selling Sounds: The Commercial Revolution in American Music*. Before 1893, most popular songs had been regional successes that gradually spread by word of mouth. Harris' breakthrough by utilizing an aggressive national promotion opened eyes throughout the publishing business, and would become the new industry standard. "*After the Ball* changed the social geography of American music and the basic relation between music and business."[5]

Daisy Bell (1894)—Edward M. Favor (written by Harry Dacre)

Edison 1058

Bicycling was an American craze during the 1890s, and romance is eternal; the two were joined to create one of the decade's most enduring songs, *Daisy Bell*.

Although bicycling had been growing in popularity in the United States ever since the 1870s, it was the advent of the "safety bicycle" in the 1890s with two wheels of equal size, plus a roller chain geared transmission—that made it the era's most popular mode of transportation,

as well as recreation. David Ewen recounted that the seeds of *Daisy Bell* were planted when popular British composer Harry Dacre (born Henry Decker) first came to the United States and was charged a duty for his bicycle. A friend, American songwriter Billy Jerome, remarked lightly, "It's lucky you didn't bring a bicycle built for two, or you'd have to pay double duty."[6] (Sigmund Spaeth in *A History of Popular Music in America* found this tale "a little too pat to be true.") After New York publishers turned it down, the song resulting from that purported remark was introduced in a London music hall by Katie Lawrence, and then became an American success when performed in early 1892 by Jennie Lindsay at the Atlantic Gardens on New York's Bowery and the Winter Garden on Union Square. Spaeth remarked that the song "has the great virtue of not taking itself seriously," enabling it to stand out in the musically maudlin 1890s.[7]

Daisy Bell was introduced on record by Dan Quinn, who enjoyed a major hit with it in late 1893. But perhaps the finest version on record came shortly thereafter by Edward M. Favor. Born Edward M. Le Fevre in 1856 in New York City, he began his stage career in the 1880s, became well known in the early 1890s in the Broadway musical comedy *1492*, and in 1893 he became perhaps the first original-cast artist to record a song he had introduced on the New York stage, with a selection from that show, *The Commodore Song*. A pleasant-voiced tenor, Favor recorded extensively for Edison, North American, Columbia, Victor, and other labels until his final issued performances in 1914, specializing in Irish songs but covering a wide range of material. Favor and his wife, Edith Sinclair, were vaudeville headliners, and starred together in musical comedies. He continued to work regularly in theater productions through the early 1930s, and died in 1942.[8]

Favor's recording of *Daisy Bell* (available on the tinfoil.com CD *Brown Wax Cylinder Phonograph Recordings, 1888–1894*) is a thoroughly charming performance of the waltz song, accompanied by piano. Movie aficionados will recall that this was the song programmed into the HAL 9000 computer and "sung" as its dying words in *2001: A Space Odyssey*. "Daisy, Daisy, give me your answer, do / I'm half crazy, all for the love of you . . ."

A Hot Time in the Old Town (1897)—Len Spencer with Vess Ossman (written by Theodore Metz & Joe Hayden)

Columbia 7266

Recorded in early 1897 in New York (brown wax cylinder); Spencer later recorded song for Berliner 0163

3. Harris enjoyed many other hits, nearly all in the tear-jerking ballad category, such as *Break the News to Mother* (1897). They were easily mocked—Sigmund Spaeth (*History of Popular Music in America*, p. 259) called the story told by *After the Ball* "absurd"—but he remained one of America's most renowned songwriters and publishers for over thirty years.

4. "He stands unrivaled in his class," proclaimed an 1894 New Jersey Phonograph Company catalog of Gaskin.

5. Suisman, p. 28–30.

6. *The Life and Death of Tin Pan Alley*, p. 77–78.

7. Spaeth, p. 264–65. The song was published by November 30, 1892 (Fuld, *Book of World-Famous Music*, p. 189).

8. Gracyk, *Popular American Recording Pioneers*, p. 108–11.

One of the defining songs of the Gay Nineties, *A Hot Time in the Old Town* is best known to modern listeners through Bessie Smith's enjoyable 1927 recording backed by a stellar band that included Coleman Hawkins and Fletcher Henderson. But a song so indelibly linked to an era is best experienced in its original form, and hearing the performance that helped introduce *Hot Time* to the world pulls back the curtains on a lost age.

According to legend, Theodore Metz (born in Hanover, Germany in 1848) wrote the song in 1886 while working at a minstrel show, after watching a fire as his train stopped in Old Town, Louisiana. Old Town, also known as Marion, was located about twenty-five miles up the Calcasieu River from Lake Charles. Someone purportedly remarked, "They're certainly having a hot time in the Old Town tonight." (Bessie Smith—quite familiar with the fact that Old Town was a distinct place—sang the lyrics as "there's a hot time in Old Town tonight"; rather than "the old town.")[9] Metz used the phrase as the title for a new march he had written for the show, and it served as an instrumental piece for several years. After he persuaded one of the troupe's singers, Joe Hayden, to add some words, the number was finally printed under the title *In Old Town To-night* in February 1896, with words and music credited to Cad L. Mays of the minstrel team Hunter & Mays, and copyrighted that July under its more famous title by Willis Woodward & Co., this time credited to Metz.[10] It was popularized at the St. Louis bordello/variety theater the Castle Club (located at 212 South 6th Street) by a celebrated street singer and "voodoo priestess" known as "Mama Lou" (real name Letitia Lula Agatha Fontaine); Mama Lou had also helped introduce such hits as *Ta-ra-ra Boom-de-ay* and *Mr. Johnson, Turn Me Loose*.[11]

Showcasing the song at a bawdy house was appropriate considering the implications of its lyrics, notes Nicholas E. Tawa. Ostensibly about a religious meeting, the lyric's second verse refers to the ample supply of sexually attractive young women, one of whom is "dressed all in red"—a tipoff that she has no moral restraints, as she promises the male visitor a hot time that evening. The song's tempo was described on the sheet music cover as both a march and a "Schottische"; the latter was a duple-time, rhythmic dance familiar in the U.S. since around 1850, and a strong influence on ragtime.[12] The number was first recorded in late 1896 by Dan Quinn. It was just a matter of weeks later that Spencer and Ossman laid down the classic version.

Leonard Garfield Spencer, one of the fabulous characters of the pioneer recording era, was born on February 12, 1867, in Washington, D.C.; his mother was a renowned suffragist and political activist, and his grandfather Platt Rogers Spencer a famous educator who developed the "Spencerian" method of penmanship long taught in schools. Len became an instructor at the Spencer Business College, which just happened to be one of the first users of the "office graphophone" or Dictaphone. Very soon after the Columbia Phonograph Company opened in the nation's capital in 1889, Spencer paid a visit, was intrigued, and the following year began his recording career there. Dubbed "the Orson Welles" of the early recording era by *Hobbies* magazine columnist Jim Walsh, Spencer became one of the recording industry's first nationally known stars, doing everything from novelties, ballads, and rhythm numbers to comic duets (most notably with Ada Jones) utilizing his skill at playing a variety of ethnic roles, and also many dramatic recitations and even auctioneer records. He remained a prolific performer (and also sketch writer and booking agent for other artists) until not long before his death in 1914.[13]

Banjo king Vess Ossman was one of Spencer's favorite recording partners during the 1890s, and his presence is crucial to the appeal of this performance (available on the Archeophone CD *The 1890s, Vol. 2*). Ossman was the first artist to put the ragtime-styled syncopation on record. Ossman introduces the familiar theme to set the stage for Spencer's vocal, done in minstrel style (Spencer would later make a number of minstrel records with his own studio troupe). He was a better actor than singer, but that thespian skill provides just the juice needed for this vigorous rendition. *Hot Time* would be immortalized as the song that supposedly accompanied Theodore Roosevelt's Rough Riders in their Spanish-American War charge up San Juan Hill, although after he became president, Teddy renounced the tune for its constant repetition at his public appearances.[14] Indeed, when Roosevelt

9. Some early citations of the song, as in the June 19 and September 11, 1897, issues of *Music Trade Review*, gave the title without "the" in the middle.

10. Fuld, *The Book of World-Famous Music*, p. 278. The September 11, 1896, *Music Trade Review* (p. 13) printed a letter from publisher Joseph Flanner, which asserted that the Metz song was "an exact transcript of my song, *In Old Town To-night*, with different words to it." Flanner said he had published the composition, written by Cad L. Mays, on January 20, 1896, and was prepared to file suit under the copyright law. It was later determined that the melody of the chorus to the song we know was indeed by Mays (its copyright filing described it as "An Up to Date Hot Stuff Coon Song"), with different lyrics and arrangement; the two publishers finally combined their editions, with sole credit to Metz and Hayden.

11. According to its publisher (in an article by Carroll Fleming reprinted in the September 29, 1900, *Music Trade Review*), *Hot Time* sold 750,000 copies of sheet music, generating $30,000 in royalties.

12. *The Way to Tin Pan Alley: American Popular Song, 1866–1910*, p. 183.

13. Tim Gracyk with Frank Hoffman, *Popular American Recording Pioneers 1895–1925*, p. 314–19. Also see Jim Walsh's articles on Spencer in *Hobbies*, May through August 1947 issues.

14. The August 6, 1898, *Music Trade Review* quoted one military officer on *Hot Time* as heard during the Santiago campaign: "It is defiant, full of hope, prophetic, American in its flippant, reckless, slangy dash . . .

asked the Library of Congress to make a collection of the great battle songs in U.S. history, *Hot Time* was specifically barred because it was ragtime, even though (as the January 25, 1908, *The Music Trades* stated) it "was the battle song of the entire Spanish War, sung in camp and field, and hospital and on shipboard. The soldiers sang it from one end of the Philippines to the other . . ." The song's renown was so powerful that a professor at Northwestern University declared in 1903 that it was destined to become the national anthem.[15]

Smoky Mokes (1904)—Peerless Orchestra (written by Abe Holzmann)
Edison 712; recorded in 1904

Smoky Mokes is an exciting cakewalk—a syncopated dance piece just one step removed from ragtime—that marks an important step on the road to the birth of jazz. It was first recorded in 1899 by the Columbia Orchestra, but cylinder preservationist Glenn Sage remarks that "the syncopation may have been too much for the pianist and orchestra to handle," as they seem out of sync for the first half of the record. (Banjo wizard Vess L. Ossman, an accomplished pro at syncopation, recorded much better versions for Berliner and Columbia in 1899 and 1900.)[16] However, five years later, the Peerless Orchestra nailed the song in memorable fashion. The fame of composer Abe Holzmann was such that (as reported in the May 26, 1906, *Music Trades*) a letter with his photograph on the envelope and no address other than "New York" was promptly delivered to him at the office of his publisher Leo Feist.[17]

David Wondrich writes in *Stomp and Swerve: American Music Gets Hot, 1843–1924* that this performance "rips out of your speakers with an urgency that ten decades have done nothing to abate."[18] A "moke," it should be noted, is a person of color. The record gets off to a flying start with a vigorous main theme, which yields to a somewhat mellower, contrasting B theme before returning. The pace never flags; clocking in at just two minutes and five seconds, every second is crackling with energy. It's available on the tinfoil.com CD *The Black Wax Sampler, 1902–1912* (part of the *Brown Wax Cylinder* collection).

(The personnel of the Peerless Orchestra is unknown; it is not to be confused with other bands of the same name which recorded extensively for the Zon-o-Phone label in London during the first two decades of the century.)

Cuddle Up a Little Closer, Lovey Mine (1908)—Ada Jones & Billy Murray (music by Karl Hoschna, lyrics by Otto Harbach)
Victor 5532
Recorded c. July-Aug. 1908 (the duo also recorded it for Edison 9950, Zon-o-Phone 5175, & Indestructible 876) *Pop Memories* debut Sept. 12, 1908 (5 weeks at #1)

What was it about the teaming of Ada Jones and Billy Murray that made them the premier vocal duet pairing of the pre-1920 recording era? Murray was the age's unsurpassed male recording star, his clear tenor voice, ability to navigate rapid-fire lyrics and handle a variety of ethnic accents and musical styles making him incredibly prolific whether in solo, duet, or group formats. Contralto Ada Jones was similarly versatile. Individually, they were wonderful. But together—suffice to say that the very essence of musical chemistry can be found in the several dozen sides Ada and Billy did together from late 1906 to 1922. More than anything else, it is the palpable sense one gets that these two people immensely enjoyed one another's company; they not only fed off each other musically, trading off lines with dexterity or melding their voices together, they radiated a sense of warmth that still makes listeners smile a century later.

Biographers Frank Hoffman, Dick Carty, and Quentin Riggs: "Two particular roles reprised by Murray time after time will serve to illustrate his affinity for Everyman's outlook: the perpetual victim of love, and the travails of the drinking man. While Murray sang his share of love songs, particularly in his duets with Ada Jones, he was without peer in projecting an ironic sense of heartache with which his listeners could readily identify."[19] The recording was made late in a "trade depression" for the national economy and the music industry that had begun with a financial panic in October 1907. The *Edison Phonograph Monthly* in March 1908 acknowledged: "The volume of every business has, in the past few months, undergone a shrinkage that in the aggregate is large." Fortunately, by the time *Cuddle Up* was released, conditions had begun to improve and fans could more easily enjoy their favorite duo.

Cuddle Up a Little Closer, the first of Otto Harbach's many pop hits, was originally intended for a vaudeville sketch, but was introduced in the New York show *Three*

So far as the music is concerned, *A Hot Time* is immeasurably superior to *The Star Spangled Banner* for the purposes of a national anthem."

15. July 11, 1903, *Music Trades*. The July 1, 1911, issue reported that some 3,500 singers from around the country performed it at the North American Saengerbund in Milwaukee.

16. The March 17, 1900, *Music Trade Review* called *Smoky Mokes* "a 'hit' second to none."

17. This was one of the crucial early hits that established Feist (whose firm was founded in 1897) as one of the leaders among Tin Pan Alley publishers.

18. Wondrich, p. 67.

---

19. Hoffman, et al., *Billy Murray*, p. 202. *Three Twins* was the fourth show written by Hoschna and Harbach, but the first major success.

Twins, which opened on June 15, 1908.[20] Just weeks later, Ada and Billy cut the record that would sweep the country. It's a simple little number that would seem corny in the wrong hands; as performed by the peerless duo, it is just enormously sweet and charming.

Ada is presented as a symbol of the changing role of women in American society by William Howard Kenney in *Recorded Music in American Life: The Phonograph and Popular Memory, 1890-1945*, citing in particular her many depictions on record of girls from modest circumstances making their own way apart from their families in cities like New York and Chicago. "Ada Jones's portraits of urban working-class women emphasized their buoyant independence and unsentimental freedom from Victorian propriety." Turning around a phrase of the era, he suggests, "Ada Jones made records for the masses, not the classes."[21]

Whipped Cream (1913)—Fred Van Eps (written by
 Percy Wenrich)
Columbia 1294
Recorded on Feb. 6, 1913 (released in May)[22]

The successor to Vess Ossman as the recording industry's top virtuoso on the five-string banjo, Fred Van Eps (born December 30, 1878, in Somerville, New Jersey) studied Ossman's early cylinder recordings before launching his own solo career in 1897 on Edison cylinders. Particularly from 1910–1920, he was working prolifically for Victor and Columbia, usually in a trio format (most often with brother Bill Van Eps on second banjo, and Felix Arndt on piano). Even after his long recording career finally trailed off in the 1920s, he continued to pay sporadic visits to the studio as late as the 1950s, played for years with the NBC Radio Orchestra, and also developed several technical devices used by the recording industry. His son George was a guitarist with Ray Noble's orchestra (with a recording career extending from the 1920s to the 1990s), and three other sons were also successful musicians.[23] Van Eps died at eighty-one in 1960.

Written by Percy Wenrich (composer of such hits as *Put On Your Old Gray Bonnet*), *Whipped Cream* is a vigorous syncopated number with Van Eps soloing with orchestra accompaniment. This is ragtime through and through, as the banjoist hits some exciting peaks climbing the scales. It's included on the Archeophone CD *Real Ragtime: Disc Recordings From Its Heyday*.

Snake Rag (1923)—King Oliver's Creole Jazz Band
 (written by Joe Oliver)
Gennett 5184
Recorded on April 6, 1923 (*Jazz-#136*)

Among the nine selections completed by King Oliver's Creole Jazz Band during its historic two-day first recording sessions at the Starr Piano Company's studios in Richmond, Indiana, in April 1923, *Dipper Mouth Blues* is the acknowledged masterpiece, but not too far behind is the spectacular *Snake Rag*. After reigning at its home base of Chicago's Lincoln Gardens until late February, the group did a tour of the Middle West, then arrived in Richmond.

Gennett's recording studio opened in 1920; Starr was turning out 15,000 pianos, three million records, and 3,000 phonographs a year (pressing records for other labels), so owner Henry Gennett decided their own studio was the next step—even if it was in a warehouse that was a five-hour train ride southeast of Chicago. As described by Armstrong biographer Laurence Bergreen, the studio was an "acoustic nightmare": 125 feet by 30 feet, with minimal soundproofing to the point where musicians routinely complained they couldn't hear one another when they played.[24] Yet seven black musicians created magic in this room that was also used as the regular recording site for the Ku Klux Klan on the private "KKK" label (with a burning cross on the records, such as *Why I Am a Klansman* by the "100% Americans Orchestra"); Indiana was said to have the largest KKK membership of any state, including several thousand in Richmond. Because it would not have been safe for them to stay in Richmond overnight, they rode the train out of town to a "safe haven" after finishing work April 5 before returning to the studio the next day.

The King Oliver band during the 1922–1924 period was most famous for the dazzling double-cornet breaks that Joe Oliver and young Louis Armstrong worked out, and *Snake Rag* is one of the best available representations of this innovation. This is a thrillingly uptempo, fun, high-energy performance possessing a relentless quality, with a remarkable seven double-cornet breaks, the two hottest saved for the end. William Howland Kenney cites the piece's "slithering, muted-cornet-to-sliding-trombone effects" as crucial to its impact.[25] The band recorded the number again for Okeh 4933 in Chicago two months later, nearly as superb, but the Gennett original is regarded as the classic. Dan Morgenstern: "Though

20. Discussing the song's popularity and romantic influence, the September 26, 1908, *Billboard* suggested that according to the New York City marriage license bureau, "matrimonial ventures have been on the increase" since the tune was introduced.

21. Kenney, p. 36–37.

22. The record's B side was another rag-flavored instrumental, accordionist Guido Deiro with Irving Berlin's *Everybody's Doing It Now*.

23. See Jim Walsh's series on Van Eps in *Hobbies* from January through August 1956.

24. Bergreen, *Louis Armstrong: An Extravagant Life*, p. 216–17.

25. William Howland Kenney, *Chicago Jazz: A Cultural History, 1904–1930*, p. 132.

they seemed purely spontaneous to the listeners, these breaks were in fact worked out in a most ingenious way: at a given point in the preceding collective band chorus, Oliver would play what he intended to use as his part in the break, and Armstrong, lightning quick on the uptake, would memorize it and devise his own second part—which always fit to perfection." Duke Ellington's 1926 piece *The Creeper* quotes (at the record's conclusion) from one of the cornet breaks in *Snake Rag* (specifically from the Gennett version), and so does the delightful *Come On and Stomp, Stomp, Stomp* (1927) by Johnny Dodds' Black Bottom Stompers—Dodds having played clarinet (along with brother Baby Dodds on drums) on the original *Snake Rag*.

Old Dan Tucker (1925)—Uncle Dave Macon
Vocalion 15033
Recorded on April 13, 1925

This is where American music begins. The American minstrel movement was launched in 1843 by Daniel Decatur Emmett, leader of the Virginia Minstrels, and *Old Dan Tucker* was the most important Emmett original—putting lyrics to an existing folk tune—to entertain generations of minstrel fans.[26] [27] David Wondrich writes in *Stomp and Swerve*: "The Virginia Minstrels were the first truly American band, playing American music—or at least the first to be publicly recognized as such. When Billy Whitlock added his percussive banjo to Dan Emmett's fiddle, he was doing something new and dangerous, at least for white folks. Before the Virginia Minstrels, white performers kept the (white) fiddle and its music segregated from the black banjo and its music." *Dan Tucker* was on the program for the historic first full-length 'Ethiopian concert' by the Virginia Minstrels at Boston's Masonic Temple on March 7, 1843.[28]

After some seventy years as an all-American favorite, *Old Dan Tucker* was given its first commercial recording on March 16, 1916, by Harry C. Browne for Columbia.

---

26. Vance Randolph, "The Ozark Play-Party," July–Sept. 1929 *Journal of American Folklore*, Vol. 42. According to Newman White (*American Negro Folk Songs*), it may have been used on stage as early as 1841. The very similar *Get Out of the Way, Old Johnny Tucker* was published in 1850 (*Negro Minstrel's Song Book*, see Newman White, *American Negro Folk Songs*).

27. Y. N. Nathanson, in an article for the January 1855 *Putnam's Monthly* (as referenced by Newman White, *American Negro Folk Songs*) whose authorship was only revealed later, remarked that the song offered "a series of vivid pictures, disconnected in themselves, varying as rapidly as the changes in a kaleidoscope, and yet presenting to us the character of the hero, as a most artistic whole." Robert Cantwell in *Bluegrass Breakdown: The Making of the Old Southern Sound* (p. 124), notes that this is "precisely the poetic form of oral-formulaic song and a characteristic of all Afro-America folksong."

28. David Wondrich, *Stomp and Swerve: American Music Gets Hot, 1843–1924*, p. 22.

That was followed by hillbilly pioneer Fiddlin' John Carson's 1924 rendition. The third—by Uncle Dave Macon—was the finest.[29]

Uncle Dave Macon personifies better than anyone else the deeply rooted traditions of old-time country or hillbilly music in the 1920s. Born David Harrison Macon on October 7, 1870, in Smart Station, Tennessee, he moved in 1873 with his family to Nashville where his parents opened a boarding house that catered to theatrical people. There he learned (writes Bill Malone) "songs, stories, and instrumental techniques from the colorful vaudeville and circus personalities who passed through the city." One circus comedian and banjoist in particular made him resolve to become an entertainer. After marriage in 1900, he moved to a small farm and ran a mule and wagon transportation business for twenty years, while playing music on the side. In 1918 a talent scout for the Loew's Theatre Circuit saw him performing at a party and signed him up for minstrel and vaudeville bookings all over the South. Macon began his recording career in 1924 at age fifty-three, and two years later joined the still fledgling Grand Ole Opry, where he quickly became one of the most beloved stars. A brilliant banjoist whose rich storytelling abilities were based on a thorough knowledge of Southern folk traditions and tales, he helped establish the Opry's early identity, and remained with it until his death in 1952. Ralph Rinzler: "With the exception of the Carter Family, Uncle Dave preserved more valuable American folklore through his recordings than any other folk or country music performer."[30]

Macon opens the record with a spoken introduction, offers some nifty variations on *Casey Jones* on his five-string banjo, then launches into *Old Dan Tucker* with enormous gusto.[31] This is pure hillbilly entertainment with no holding back, furious banjo thrashing and enthusiastic vocal: "Get out the way, old Dan Tucker, you're too late to get your supper . . ." One imagines it's not too different from the way Dan Emmett and the Virginia Minstrels put the number over generations earlier. The performance is included on the Archeophone CD *Stomp and Swerve: American Music Gets Hot*.

East St. Louis Toodle-Oo (1927)—Duke Ellington & His Kentucky Club Orchestra (written by Bubber Miley & Duke Ellington)
Vocalion 1064, recorded on Nov. 29, 1926

---

29. Meade, *Country Music Sources: A Biblio-Discography of Commercially Recorded Traditional Music*, p. 757.

30. Bill Malone, *Country Music, U.S.A.* (2nd revised ed.), p. 72–74.

31. "It ain't so much what you got," Macon liked to say, as quoted by Charles K. Wolfe (*Classic Country*, p. 252–53). "It's what you can put out. And boys, I can put out."

Also recorded for Brunswick 3480 on March 14, 1927, and for Columbia 953 (as "Duke Ellington & His Washingtonians") on March 22, 1927[32] (*Jazz-#109*)

A collaboration between Duke Ellington and his trumpet star Bubber Miley, *East St. Louis Toodle-Oo* was originally titled "East St. Louis Toad-low," and referred to an old man so bent with age that he walked as low as a toad. Additionally, the song was meant to evoke a popular ragtime dance called the todolo. The latter was discussed by O. M. Samuels in the July 1, 1911, *Variety* as one of the "erotic" dances (along with the turkey trot and the Grizzly Bear) then widely popular and which, he said, had originated in New Orleans about fifteen years earlier.[33] *East St. Louis* happened to be the title of a song that W. C. Handy heard two guitarists play in 1892—"I walked all the way from old East St. Louis and I didn't have but one po' measly dime" "—serving as an early inspiration to "The Father of the Blues."

This was one of a group of four songs that were the first Ellington compositions copyrighted and published, and one of the first two Duke originals that he was allowed to record. All three of the song's 1926–1927 performances are dominated by Miley's forceful trumpet playing. "Miley's urgent solo and the somber, almost weeping figure Ellington scored for the reeds and tuba combined to introduce a new sound in American music," declares Gary Giddins.[34] *East St. Louis Toodle-Oo* became the band's first theme song. On December 4, 1927, just days after the Brunswick recording, the Ellington band began its historic run at Harlem's Cotton Club that would extend until early 1931.

James Wesley "Bubber" Miley was born on April 3, 1903, in Aiken, South Carolina, grew up in New York, and in the early 1920s toured with Mamie Smith among other artists. In 1923 he joined the Washingtonians led by Elmer Snowden, and remained when Duke Ellington took over in 1924. His growling trumpet style became widely influential, using both the growl and the plunger to create the "jungle" effects for which the early Ellington band was known. He left Ellington in early 1929, and after three more years working with various other bands died of tuberculosis in 1932. "The theme of *East St. Louis Toodle-Oo* shows Miley at his melodic best," writes Giddins. "The melodic line is so disarmingly simple that, except for the use of the mute and growl, it would sound like pure folk song." Underneath Miley's trumpet, El-

lington fashioned a "moaning" passage that provided a striking contrast to the soloist. Thomas Brothers in *Louis Armstrong's New Orleans* remarks that Miley's soloing on this record stands in stark and compelling contrast to Duke's ragtime-styled playing, because Miley "is free and fluid in his quarter-tone inflections, vocalized timbres, speech-like rhythms," and "dragging slightly behind the beat to create a feeling of detachment from the underlying pulse."[35] In other words, Bubber is playing the blues.

As Ellington continued to play with the piece after Miley's departure, he made perhaps its finest recording for Master in March 1937, featuring Cootie Williams on plunger-muted trumpet and Barney Bigard on clarinet, with a more significant contribution by Duke on piano (his role had been secondary in the 1926–1927 versions). Samuel A. Floyd, Jr., (*The Power of Black Music*) writes that the 1937 version "is technically more advanced and the arrangement is more elaborate, containing more sophisticated and varied articulations, more inner parts, more part-harmony, many harmonized doo-wahs, and more striking use of the capabilities of the full ensemble." As a result, even though the tune is taken at a slower tempo than a decade earlier, the performance swings with greater confidence. Ralph Ellison: "During the Depression whenever his theme song *East St. Louis Toodle-Oo* came on the air, our morale was lifted by something inescapably hopeful in the sound. Its style was so triumphant and the moody melody so successful in capturing the times yet so expressive of the faith which would see us through them."[36]

Stardust (1927)—Hoagy Carmichael & His Pals
Gennett 6295[37]

Recorded in Richmond, Indiana on Oct. 31, 1927, released on Jan. 1, 1928 (*Trad-#9, NPR-100, Jazz-#29, RIA-#40, DMDB-#43, GHF, BBC-#2, ASCAP*)[38]

The premiere performance of America's greatest pop ballad, the Halloween 1927 rendition of *Stardust* by a small combo led by its composer Hoagy Carmichael, is a revelation. It punctures two long-held myths about the song, the melody of which was inspired by his friend and musical hero, Bix Beiderbecke.

32. Vocalion version reissued in March 1943 as part of Victor album "A Duke Ellington Panorama"; one month later, Brunswick version included on Decca album "Ellingtonia."

33. Lawrence Gushee, "The Nineteenth-Century Origins of Jazz," *Black Music Research Journal* (Spring 1994), p. 20.

34. *Visions of Jazz*, p. 108–9.

35. Brothers, p. 68.

36. From "Homage to Duke Ellington on His Birthday," Washington, D.C., *Sunday Star*, April 27, 1969; reprinted in *Living With Music: Ralph Ellison's Jazz Writings*, p. 81.

37. It was released on Gennett's Electrobeam black label, apparently to emphasize that it was electrically recorded.

38. *Stardust* was also voted the #1 Tin Pan Alley song of all time in a February 1937 *Down Beat* poll of forty top musicians including Louis Armstrong and Duke Ellington.

One myth, that the song's famous opening verse (the melody that would later be associated with the words "And now the purple dusk of twilight time steals across the meadows of my heart") did not exist until 1930 and may not have even been written by Carmichael, is utterly dispelled because, after a brief guitar introduction (by Don Kimmel), trumpeter Byron Smart introduces the haunting verse melody that the world would come to know so well. Carmichael biographer Richard Sudhalter remarks that Smart plays in a "heraldic, Bix-like manner." Structurally the melody is a standard 32 bars, in ABAC form; "but its essence lies in a phrase-building technique often found in Bix's solos. A brief phrase of one or two bars is set out, followed by a similar companion phrase, expanding or complementing it; a third phrase then sums up, often incorporating material from the first two." It's "not hard to imagine Hoagy Carmichael, as a fledgling composer dazzled by Bix, seizing on it as a way of constructing songs." The high spot of this original *Stardust* recording was Hoagy's full-chorus piano solo, "its chordal devices clearly echoing Bix's fascination with the Impressionists and such 'moderns' as Igor Stravinsky."[39]

The second myth is perhaps not quite a myth but a somewhat misleading impression: It is true that the early recordings of *Stardust* were taken at dance tempos—just like virtually all other 1920s instrumentals by bands—until Victor Young's 1930 arrangement for the Isham Jones orchestra established it as a ballad. But the Carmichael recording features a medium dance tempo that can be called gentle, and the composer's lovely full-chorus piano solo is unmistakably meditative in mood; it is one small step removed from being a ballad. Will Friedwald writes in *Stardust Melodies* that from the very start, "*Stardust* was always essentially a reflective, contemplative tone poem." Most important of all, it is a wonderful performance.

For the historic recording session, Carmichael recruited a group of musicians who usually played with pianist Emil Seidel's dance band. It's a different group from the "Hoagy Carmichael and His Pals" who had recorded at Gennett (whose Richmond studio was a short drive from the composer's alma mater, Indiana University, where he continued to spend much time) four days earlier, as that group included Tommy and Jimmy Dorsey and cornet standout Andy Secrest. The combo for *Stardust* included no stars other than Hoagy, but the musicianship is nonetheless outstanding. Following the guitar intro and Smart's statement of the verse, the song's primary melody is introduced on alto sax by either Gene

Woods or Dick Kent. Carmichael's piano solo (literally so as he is completely unaccompanied) immediately sets up, in Friedwald's words, "a brilliant set of variations on the song."[40]

In November 1922, a young Bix Beiderbecke had the opportunity to sit in with the Original Dixieland Jazz Band at a Chicago engagement, and group leader Nick LaRocca recalled that when they played the melody of pianist J. Russell Robinson's recent composition *Singin' the Blues*, Bix responded with a countermelody that Carmichael found quite striking. In their Beiderbecke biography, Sudhalter and Philip Evans note that the verse of *Stardust*, when played at about the same tempo as the legendary 1927 Bix Beiderbecke–Frankie Trumbauer recording of *Singin' the Blues*, "takes on the melodic shape of a characteristic Bix solo." Also, the refrains of two songs "begin in the same chordal position; this, coupled with Bix's affinity for both songs, makes more than likely a countermelody to *Singin' the Blues* incorporating elements of either Hoagy's verse or chorus—or both." And Carmichael always acknowledged Bix as the ballad's chief inspiration.

Sudhalter in his Carmichael biography points out that the song's melody was "partly inspired by Bix's improvisations and his admiration for the now almost forgotten American composer Eastwood Lane." The solo amounted to a "melodic paraphrase" that generally follows the song's harmonies with some inventive interpolations; "far from a random improvisation, but as lovingly worked out . . . as the *Stardust* melody itself." The several other records of the tune made from 1927 to early 1930 would follow the basic format of this arrangement. "Yet there's something in this first performance that arrests attention: a sense of moment, something more important going on than just a pop melody . . . this *Stardust* (notably the Carmichael piano solo) . . . suggests a musical landscape alive with possibility and evocative potential."[41]

Statesboro Blues (1928)—Blind Willie McTell
Victor 38001
Recorded in Atlanta on Oct. 17, 1928 (*Blues-#41, RHF*)

Perhaps the finest of all blues twelve-string guitarists, Blind Willie McTell was also a singularly gifted composer and synthesizer, piecing together original and traditional melodic and lyrical elements into powerful musical entities. *Statesboro Blues* was his most enduring creation. Born William Samuel McTier on May 5, 1901, in Thomson, Georgia, near Augusta, his family was highly musical (both his mother and father played guitar),

---

39. Sudhalter, *Stardust Melody: The Life and Music of Hoagy Carmichael*, p. 108–11.

40. Friedwald, *Stardust Melodies*, p. 5–6.
41. Sudhalter, p. 108–11.

and he was also related to Georgia Tom Dorsey (a blues powerhouse of the 1920s before he turned to gospel as Thomas A. Dorsey). He was nearly blind from birth, but with exceptional hearing and sense of touch, this impediment was minimized.

Having played standard six-string guitar from childhood, by the mid-1920s he switched almost exclusively to the twelve-string. The twelve-string "is a potent musical tool able to achieve tones and timbres no six-string could reach," explains Robert Santelli. "And it can mime certain human feelings that simply sound better and warmer coming from a guitar with twice as many strings." Barbecue Bob and Huddie Ledbetter (Leadbelly) were outstanding on the jangly, ringing twelve-string. "But the best of them all was Blind Willie McTell." After studying at schools for the blind in Macon and New York City, McTell hoboed along the East Coast singing and playing guitar, and worked medicine shows and carnivals. His first Atlanta recording session for Victor was in October 1927. A year later almost to the day came his second session for Ralph Peer's field recording unit, which yielded *Statesboro Blues*, named after the Georgia town where he lived for a time. It's built on the foundation of a song Barbecue Bob recorded a few months earlier, *Going Up the Country*. The song demonstrates his power as a storyteller, based on his experiences as a blind hobo. McTell was an effective if not distinctive singer, but could unfold a narrative beautifully. "With a nasally whine," writes Santelli, "McTell cut a musical vignette about growing up amid family strife, economic hardship, and boredom."[42] Samuel Charters: "He seemed to be almost crying to himself, half singing, half chanting the irregular verses."[43] Combined with his "extraordinary slide guitar work in which McTell uses the riffs he creates as part of the story's dialogue" (as described by Santelli), the overall impact was indelible. The performance exemplifies author Ralph Ellison's description of the blues as "an autobiographical chronicle of personal catastrophe expressed lyrically."[44]

The structure of the early blues, writes Luc Sante, "with its two-line reiteration followed by a lapidary summation line . . . could have been almost consciously designed to frame a view of the world that is fatalistic, expecting the worst, armored against fresh injury—yet by the same token indestructible, eternally renewable. Its compact shell, enclosing volumes, holding volatile emotions to a ground, was well suited to the guardedness and self-containment of African-Americans in the Jim Crow

era. It is equally ideal for songs of endurance, of suffering, of deflected aspiration, and of deeply concealed resistance."[45]

McTell recorded as "Blind Sammie" for Columbia, as "Georgia Bill" for Okeh, and as "Blind Willie" for Vocalion, had a memorable Library of Congress recording session in 1940, and cut fifteen songs for Atlantic nine years later. After returning for one album in 1956, he left music to serve as a preacher at Mount Zion Baptist Church in Atlanta, and died two years later. *Statesboro Blues* was introduced to a rock audience through the Allman Brothers Band, and McTell's original was inducted into the Rock & Roll Hall of Fame in 1995. As Bob Dylan declared in his classic musical tribute, "nobody can sing the blues like Blind Willie McTell."

Careless Love (1928)—Lonnie Johnson
Okeh 8635
Recorded in New York on Nov. 16, 1928 (*Blues-#133*)

Crossing musical boundaries between blues, jazz, and soul balladry with the same ease with which he mastered multiple instruments and spanned four decades of music, Lonnie Johnson was a colossus of talent matched by few others in his time. He made many important recordings in his long career; *Careless Love* stands out among them for being a definitive performance of what may have been the very first great blues standard.

Born in New Orleans on February 8, 1889 (although Johnson indicated in latter-day interviews that his year of birth may have been as late as 1899, a possibility that cannot be ruled out based on the documented facts of his life), Alonzo (Lonnie) Johnson got his start playing violin in a string band led by his father, played guitar and violin in cafes and theaters as a teenager, did a theater tour of Europe in 1917–1918, played in Mississippi riverboat bands from 1920–1922 (including Fate Marable's band that for a time included a young Louis Armstrong), then settled in St. Louis. After winning a contest, he began recording for the Okeh label in November 1925, and quickly established himself as one of the era's guitar virtuosos. He played with Armstrong on some Hot Five classics (including *Hotter Than That* in 1927); guested with Duke Ellington (*The Mooche* in 1928), made some sensational duets in 1928–1929 with white guitarist Eddie Lang (who adopted the pseudonym Blind Willie Dunn to disguise the interracial pairing), and recorded with other jazz notables such as Johnny Dodds, James P. Johnson, and Clarence Williams. On his own records, Johnson also emerged as a first-rate blues vocalist, and the handful of records on which he played violin (such as *Violin Blues* with the Johnson Boys in 1928) are cherished by collec-

42. Santelli, *The Best of the Blues*, p. 224–27.
43. *The Country Blues*, p. 94.
44. Originally from Ellison's article "Richard Wright's Blues" in *The Antioch Review* (summer 1945); reprinted in *Living With Music: Ralph Ellison's Jazz Writings* (p. 103).
45. *A New Literary History of America*, p. 478–82.

tors. After a few years out of music during the Depression, he resumed recording in 1937, and scored a surprise #1 R&B smash in 1948 with the ballad *Tomorrow Night*. That led to another round of recordings, and he reached a new audience with the folk/blues revival of the early 1960s until his death in 1970.

Johnson, writes Francis Davis, sang "beautifully, in that fluttering way of his, marking the ends of choruses with elegant, flatpicked arpeggios, phrasing his guitar one jump ahead of the beat, or one step behind . . . His rhythm and harmonic sense were fanciful and unerring, and he was probably the first improvising guitarist to base his style on cleanly articulated single-string lines rather than heavily strummed chords—the first guitarist to phrase like a horn, a full decade before [Charlie] Christian."[46] Rudi Blesh (*Shining Trumpets*) noted that the finest early blues treatments of *Careless Love* "have taken this dark and passionate song of the Kentucky mountains into one of the most beautiful of all blues, a song that strikes deep and straight to the heart . . . it is an expression of the utmost sadness, a bitter song and a sweet song. In its unavailing, bitter regret there lingers unforgotten love, faintly and warmly sweet."

Careless Love, copyrighted as *Loveless Love* in 1921 by W. C. Handy, was rooted in a traditional folk blues that Handy recalled learning and playing for dancers in Bessemer, Alabama, in 1892. It's said to have been played by the Buddy Bolden band around 1900–1905.[47] Folk-song collector Howard Odum reported it in 1911 in the *Journal of American Folklore* as "Kelly's Love" (his misunderstanding of his black informant's diction).[48] In 1915, Eber C. Perrow printed a version collected from country whites in Mississippi. Portions of the lyric are similar to the words of the traditional British songs *O Waly, Waly* and *I Wish, I Wish*. In 1947's *Folk Song USA*, John and Alan Lomax called it "one of the earliest, if not actually the first, blues," suggesting that it may be of white origin but "has changed hands across the race line so frequently that it has acquired a pleasant coffee color."[49] Noble Sissle was the first to record Handy's treatment as *Loveless Love* in 1921, followed by Alberta Hunter in February 1923. According to discographers Gus Meade, Jr., and Dick Spottswood, its first recorded version as *Careless Love* was by Oscar "Papa" Celestin's Original Tuxedo Jazz Orchestra for January 1925 for Okeh; four months later came Bessie Smith's classic rendition. There were country recordings of the song in 1926 (Lester McFarland and Robert A. Gardner for Vocalion)

and 1927 (Johnson Brothers), and blues versions in 1928 by Eva Parker, and Lulu Jackson.

Lonnie Johnson's rendition is a powerful solo vocal with guitar, using particularly vivid lyrics. We know the familiar "love, oh love oh careless love" refrain, but Johnson underlines the emotions behind it by singing: "You have robbed me out of my silver, and out of all my gold / I'll be damned if you rob me out of my soul!"[50] Samuel Charters in *The Country Blues* declared it "one of his finest achievements." The bitterness of Johnson's revised lyrics, in which he "blamed love for an entire life of troubles," reaches a peak when he cries, "Damn you, I'm going to shoot you / Shoot you four, five times / Then stand over you until you finish dying." *Careless Love* was to become closely associated with Johnson, and he recorded it again at his final session nearly forty years later.

I Can't Give You Anything But Love (1929)—Louis Armstrong (music by Jimmy McHugh, lyrics by Dorothy Fields)[51]
Okeh 8669 & 41204
Recorded on March 5, 1929 (released on April 5); reissued on Columbia 38052 in Dec. 1947 (*TG*)

Already the pre-eminent jazz god by 1929, Louis Armstrong crossed over to a new realm with his performance of one of the Depression era's best-loved songs. Black vocalists had recorded standard pop songs before, most notably Ethel Waters, but nothing quite like what Satchmo did with *I Can't Give You Anything But Love*. From this point onward, he was clearly in the top echelon of vocal giants in addition to his instrumental mastery.

Originally written for the 1927 show *Harry Delmar's Revels* but dropped from its score, the song was introduced on Broadway the following year by Aida Ward in *Blackbirds of 1928*. Cliff "Ukelele Ike" Edwards brought it to a mass audience with his best-selling July 1928 recording for Columbia. Five months later, singer Lillie Delk Christian recorded the song, with accompaniment led by Armstrong, so Louis was quite familiar with the piece before he tackled it himself.

As Dan Morgenstern describes it, the "first great jazz ballad record" opens with Armstrong's muted trumpet solo (one of the relatively few occasions in the 1920s on which he used a mute), backed by chords from the band, "then sings a passionate vocal and, after a trombone

46. Davis, *The History of the Blues*, p. 144–45.
47. Marquis, *In Search of Buddy Bolden*, p. 107.
48. *Journal of American Folklore* (July–September 1911), p. 256, 286.
49. John and Alan Lomax, *Folk Song USA*, p. 39.

50. This stanza echoes similar lines in the traditional *Jack O' Diamonds*.
51. David Jasen and Gene Jones: "For years, the rumor circulated" that Fats Waller and Andy Razaf had actually written this song and sold it outright for a flat fee, relinquishing author credits, as they were known to sometimes do in the late 1920s. Credited composer Jimmy McHugh was professional manager of Irving Mills' publishing house, which was a regular stop on Waller and Razaf's Tin Pan Alley "selling sprees," and which published *Anything But Love*. (*Spreadin' Rhythm Around*, p. 208–9.)

break [by J. C. Higginbotham], constructs an aria-like open horn solo, ending with a climb to the top."[52] Andre Hodeir in *Jazz: Its Evolution and Essence* remarked that in his vocal chorus, Armstrong "treats the vocal as a kind of countermelody to the principal one," replying to the saxophones' recapitulation of the main theme, and establishing "a kind of reciprocal relationship between the theme and its simultaneously expressed variation." In his final trumpet solo, he paraphrases the melody's principal motif, then spreads the parts out with long rests and the addition of some extra notes, creating "a beautiful effect."[53] His vocal improvisation made such an immediate impact that Ethel Waters' 1932 recording of the song copied it almost exactly.

Phil Schaap, in liner notes for Sony's 2000 reissue of Armstrong's Hot Five and Hot Seven–related recordings, remarks that this performance "gives us Armstrong the man who used the rhythms, harmonies, and improvising techniques of the blues to energize and re-create pop song material." The piece demonstrates how "his vocal music was an extension of his horn work: the voice's anything-can-happen improvising against the melody of *I Can't Give You Anything But Love* recalls the genius's work on the horn." Although billed on the label as Armstrong with his Savoy Ballroom Five, it's actually a big-band performance.

Hodeir suggested that Armstrong's 1938 recording of the song for Decca contains a trumpet chorus that is "not only the most beautiful solo Armstrong ever recorded but also one of the most successful feats in the history of jazz." He compares the differences between "the vehement improvisation of the first version and the admirable line" of the 1938 rendition to the differences between the early organ works of Bach. The rhythmic transformation he achieves in the solo is "an absolute work of genius." "In less than ten years, the great trumpeter not only moved toward a purity of expression that is the most certain sign of an artist's maturity, but actually reached it."[54]

(Personnel includes Albert Nicholas on alto sax, Teddy Hill on tenor sax, Luis Russell on piano, Lonnie Johnson on guitar, Eddie Condon on banjo)

Soldier's Joy (1929)—Gid Tanner & His Skillet Lickers

Columbia 15538

Recorded in Atlanta on Oct. 29, 1929 (*Folk-#66, C&W-#83*)

When it came to red-hot fiddling with the old-time country hoedown sound, there was no one quite like Gid Tanner and the Skillet Lickers. James Gideon Tanner was born on June 6, 1885, in Thomas Bridge, Georgia. He began playing fiddle around 1900, and by 1913, while working as a chicken farmer, was a frequent winner at Atlanta fiddling conventions. The Skillet Lickers were formed in Atlanta in 1926 by Columbia Records' artists and repertoire man Frank Walker, teaming Tanner and blind guitarist-singer Riley Puckett (his frequent contest partner) with younger fiddling phenom Clayton McMichen and banjo player Fate Norris; the Skillet Lickers quickly became the foremost string band in the still-young world of hillbilly music.

Soldier's Joy is a Scottish/British fiddle tune that dates back to at least 1778 (included in Joshua Campbell's *A Collection of the Newest and Best Reels and Minuets*), and may go back still further.[55] By 1784–1785 it was so well known that Robert Burns wrote a song to the tune as the opening selection in his *Beggars Cantata*, later known as *The Jolly Beggar*. Folklorists report that *Soldier's Joy* appears in virtually every sizable collection of fiddle tunes from the late 1800s onward. And its renown extended well beyond the U.K. and America: Musicologist Dick Spottswood has turned up a 1914 cylinder recording of the song made in rural Sweden by Lars Johan Sundell, with two fiddlers, under the title *Visslarepolska fran Ydre harad* (which translates to "Whistler's Polka"), which he included on the Rounder CD compilation *Raw Fiddle*. Alan Jabbour, in liner notes for the 1971 Library of Congress album *American Fiddle Tunes*, remarked that the melodic structure suggests that "the tune may originally have been conceived as a hornpipe, but in America, at least, it is generally used for reels, square dances," and other group dances.

In the United States, *Soldier's Joy* was first recorded in 1917 by the Victor Band (on Victor 18331); the first country version was in 1924 as *I Am My Mama's Darling Child* by Samantha Bumgarner and Eva Davis (violin and banjo) and Uncle Dave Macon, and by other artists during the next few years including Fiddlin' John Carson (1925).[56] Clayton McMichen (born in Allatoona, Georgia, on January 26, 1900, a fiddle contest winner at the precocious age of fourteen, and regarded by some as the era's foremost virtuoso on his instrument) waxed it in 1927 as part of his solo *Fiddlin' Medley*, so he knew the tune well by the time he recorded it with Tanner two years

52. *Living With Jazz*, p. 30. At the suggestion of his manager Tommy Rockwell, Armstrong, to provide a contrast to the singers who had been performing the tune in a cheerful manner, gave it a more nuanced approach, "like life really is." (Teachout, *Pops*, p. 130–31.)

53. Hodeir, p. 162–64.

54. Hodeir, *Jazz: Its Evolution and Essence*, p. 164–68. The year 1938 also happened to feature one of the most fondly remembered uses of *I Can't Give You Anything But Love*, as the song is rendered several times by Cary Grant and Katharine Hepburn to soothe an escaped leopard in the comedy classic *Bringing Up Baby*.

55. *The Soldier's Joy* is a single-sheet song with music issued between 1755 and 1760 with militaristic lyrics reflecting tensions between England and France.

56. Meade, *Country Music Sources*, p. 713.

later. Billy Altman writes that this performance "neatly captures the group's energy and barn dance-ready spirit." After Gid's brief spoken introduction ("Well, folks, here we are again, the Skillet Lickers, hot and rarin' to go . . ."), the three fiddles (the brilliant Lowe Stokes being the third) launch into it with ferocious verve, with some simple old-timey lyrics sung by Puckett.[57]

Robert Cantwell, hailing this "joyous" performance, remarks that in the Skillet Lickers, "we hear the raucous, brilliant, and spontaneous sound of southern mountain musicians who understood that in the recording studio they were at liberty to play as they might after the dancers had gone home—that is, with a heightened vitality and energy, taking immense pleasure in their own music, communicating that pleasure to an audience who could attend more closely to the music than actual dancers and who could *imagine* a dance more gay and wonderful than is usually possible for ordinary self-conscious mortals, even in the north Georgia hills."[58] A "shave and a haircut, two bits" fiddle coda brings it to a conclusion. Tanner's group would record the song again in 1934 for Bluebird, and McMichen did it once more for Decca in 1939. The Tanner original is included on the Sony boxed set *Can't You Hear Me Callin': Bluegrass: 80 Years of American Music.*

Two Step D'Eunice (1929)—Amédé Ardoin & Dennis McGee

Columbia 40511-F
Recorded in New Orleans on Dec. 9, 1929 (*World-#23*)

The early years of Cajun commercial recording were filled with outstanding artists, but there can be little doubt about who was the most intense, passionate, and accomplished performer. Amédé Ardoin,[59] the first great black Louisiana Creole musician, was born around 1896–1897 in L'Anse des Rougeau, a small farming community between Eunice and Mamou. He and white fiddler Dennis McGee (born January 26, 1893) met as sharecroppers, and in 1921 they began performing together for house dances in the neighborhood. Michael Doucet: "Amédé had already developed his own unique style of playing the newly introduced accordion. Dennis added the ancient sounds of French and Celtic music on the fiddle. Together the descendant of African slaves and the descendant of Acadian exiles created a new sound that helped form the basis for what is now called Cajun music."[60]

After the tremendous (at least in south Louisiana) response to the April 27, 1928, Cajun debut recordings of Joseph Falcon and Cleoma Breaux for Columbia, record labels began to seek out other French Louisiana performers to meet the local demand. On October 2, 1929, Douglas Bellard and Kirby Riley became the first rural Afro-Creoles from southwest Louisiana to record, including the Cajun standard *Les Flammes d'Enfer* (The Flames of Hell). Two months later, Amédé Ardoin got his opportunity. Ryan Andre Brasseaux: "These Afro-Creole recording artists' extensive use of blue notes, highly syncopated melodic phrasing, crying vocal, and repertoire diversified the Cajun portfolio by generating a sort of race record subgenre under the auspices of the commercial Cajun umbrella."[61]

At the December 9, 1929, debut session for Ardoin (McGee had first recorded on March 5, 1929, with Sady Courville), the combination of Ardoin's fervent vocals pushed to the upper limits of his vocal range and fiery accordion style, with McGee's sympathetic fiddle accompaniment, made *Two Step d'Eunice* an instant Cajun classic. Like nearly all early Cajun songs, the lyrics (as translated from the French) are simple, but Ardoin convinces us that he feels the words—about a man agonizing when his girl decides to marry another man—down to his bones: "Oh, why, Joline? Why is that you abandon me? / What am I going to do, little girl, Joline? You are hurting me." Doucet notes that his vocal "eloquently expressed his tragic love/hate relationship with Joline, the ever-present character in the world of his songs. Joline represents Amédé's concept of woman in a life of unrequited love. She is such a durable persona that many Cajun performers after him, especially Iry LeJeune, kept the name and the motif alive in their recordings." This performance was included in the Library of Congress compilation *Folk Music in America* (Vol. 14, "Solo and Display Music," 1978).

The diatonic button accordion was introduced to Louisiana in the mid-1800s (one of the earliest printed accounts dates from 1871).[62] But Cajun music continued to be primarily fiddle music, often accompanied by harmonica or guitar, into the early twentieth century. The introduction around 1908 of accordions in the keys of C and D (previous accordions had been in different keys that made it extremely difficult to accompany a fiddler with both instruments remaining in tune) was the crucial step that made the accordion-and-fiddle combination the new standard in Cajun music.[63]

57. While Stokes lacked the fame of Tanner and McMichen, country music scholar Tony Russell regards him as the finest of all the era's Georgia fiddlers (Spring 1972 *Old Time Music*, "Georgia String Bands").

58. Cantwell, *Bluegrass Breakdown*, p. 52.

59. His first name has sometimes been spelled "Amédée."

60. Michael Doucet (leader of Beausoleil and Cajun music historian), liner notes for the Arhoolie album *Amédé Ardoin: His Original Recordings 1928–1938.*

61. *Cajun Breakdown*, p. 56.

62. Brasseaux, *Cajun Breakdown*, p. 18–20.

63. Barry Jean Ancelet, liner notes for Arhoolie album *Pioneers of Cajun Accordion 1926–1936*; Ann Allen Savoy, *American Roots Music*, p. 110. The Sterling and Monarch companies made such fiddle-compatible accordions even more widely available in the early 1920s.

Both Ardoin and McGee went on to make many other fine recordings, although Ardoin suffered failing health in the late 1930s and died in 1941, while McGee reaped the benefits of the Cajun revival of the 1970s to become a living symbol of the music's rich legacy, serving as a mentor to a new generation of artists such as Michael Doucet. The early recordings of the two men were jointly inducted into the National Recording Registry by the Library of Congress in 2003. Ann Allen Savoy writes that Ardoin's music "laid the groundwork for Cajun music as we know it today."[64]

Worried Man Blues (1930)—Carter Family
Victor 40317
Recorded in Memphis on May 24, 1930

The original recording of one of the great folk/country standards, *Worried Man Blues* was one of the first genuine blues releases by the Carter Family; its flip side was another winner, *The Cannon Ball*. A. P. Carter is believed to have learned the song from an itinerant black musician. Greil Marcus noted that the Junior Parker blues hit *Mystery Train*, which was subsequently Elvis Presley's greatest Sun Records classic, borrowed its central train image from this Carter Family record. "*Worried Man* is the story of a man who lays down to sleep by a river and wakes up in chains. The Carters don't tell you if the man is black or white, or if he killed someone, stole a horse, or did anything at all . . . You would have to go a long way to match that as an image of the devil in the dream, or as the plain symbol of a land whose profound optimism insures that disaster must be incomprehensible."[65] Another early country record describing a man falling asleep and awakening to find shackles on his feet is *Steamboat Whistle Blues* by Roy Acuff in 1936. In 1940, *Worried Man Blues* was one of ten performances included in Victor's multi-78 album *Smoky Mountain Ballads* (assembled by John Lomax), the first major reissue album of vintage hillbilly/folk recordings; this historic collection was itself reissued in 1964 as part of the label's Vintage Series.

"There is no protest in the song, no revolt, only an absolute, almost supernatural loneliness: a bewilderment that is all the more terrifying because it is so self-effacing and matter-of-fact." Like the rest of the song, writes Marcus, its description of riding a train sixteen coaches long "simply defines the singer's world, and there is no way out, save for the death the man promises will someday save him from his song." John Cohen notes in *The New Lost City Ramblers Song Book* that fragments of the song were in oral tradition before the Carters put them

together. In particular, the "train I ride" line has a precedent in Texas blues great Blind Lemon Jefferson's 1927 record *Right of Way Blues*, in which he sings: "The train I ride, 18 coaches long." Ida Cox sang "Lord I'm worried now, but I won't be worried long" in *Southern Woman's Blues* (1925), and the phrase quickly became ubiquitous in the blues. Similar lines were offered by Blind Blake on *Blake's Worried Blues* (1926), Jennie Clayton on the Memphis Jug Band's *State of Tennessee Blues* (1927), John D. Fox on *The Worried Man Blues* (1927), Ishman Bracey on *Saturday Blues* in 1928 ("Now I'm worried now, but I won't be worried long / It takes a worried woman, now, sing a worried song"), and Charley Patton on *Green River Blues* (1929), among numerous others.

Carter Family biographers Mark Zwonitzer and Charles Hirshberg: The song "spoke a simple unjustifiable truth: Some men were born to the poor and lonesome class in America, and despite the national promise, that class was hard to escape. Even if somebody did, the hellhounds stayed on his trail. Having come up in Poor Valley, A. P. had to know deep down his own good fortune could vaporize, and without reason."[66]

Carter Family, courtesy of Library of Congress (American Folklife Center, Corporate Subject file).

64. Ann Allen Savoy, *Cajun Music: A Reflection of a People*, p. 13.
65. Marcus, *Mystery Train: Images of America in Rock 'n Roll Music*, p. 171–72.

66. *Will You Miss Me When I'm Gone?*, p. 138.

I'm So Glad (1931)—Skip James

Paramount 13098

Recorded c. Feb. 1931 in Grafton, Wisconsin (*Blues-#101*)

"Blues do not promise that people will not be unhappy, but that unhappiness can be transcended, not by faith in God, but by faith in one's own ability to accept unhappiness without ever conceding oneself to it," remarked author Gerald Early. One can hardly imagine a better example of this principle than *I'm So Glad*, blues master Nehemiah "Skip" James' bold reinvention of a pop tune by crooner Gene Austin, *So Tired*. The Austin record (recorded on March 27, 1928, for Victor) was a bit bland; considerably more interesting thanks to stellar guitar work was bluesman Lonnie Johnson's variation, *I'm So Tired of Living All Alone* (actually recorded before Austin on March 9, 1928, for Okeh). The Dallas String Band covered Johnson's version that December. James' adaptation (from the same sessions that produced his masterpiece *Devil Got My Woman*) soared far beyond its predecessors.

Asked at the Grafton, Wisconsin, recording session how fast he could play, James' response was to launch into *I'm So Glad*, starting it in 16th notes, then accelerating to 32nds. "Oh, no, that is too fast!" he was told, and he moderated the tempo to the version we know today. "So tired of sighing, so tired of crying, I'm so tired of living all alone," Lonnie Johnson had sung. James begins with the same sentiments, but then breaks free of despair into jubilation: "I'm tired of weeping, tired of moaning, tired of groaning for you / I'm so glad, I'm so glad, I'm so glad, I don't know what to do." And indeed he sounds emotionally transported—perhaps by religious ecstasy, as the Bentonia, Mississippi, native's twenty-six recordings in 1931 included gospel numbers, and he would leave the blues for a Texas Baptist seminary and then the Southern gospel revival circuit after 1931. Ted Gioia: "James sings like a man possessed, but the bliss he celebrates has the queasy tone of a bipolar up cycle that will soon come crashing down into the depths of despair."[67] What makes this recording a classic, above all, is his scintillating, lightning-fast guitar virtuosity. David McGee calls his mastery of both guitar and piano "breathtaking": "His intricate fingerpicking style influenced folk, bluegrass and country-blues artists alike, his [latter-day] disciples including virtuosos such as John Fahey and Leo Kottke."[68] It is sobering to consider that only two copies of this Paramount 78 are known to survive, and all CD transfers are from one of these two scratchy 78s; had they not survived, the loss to music history would have been incalculable.

Biographer Stephen Calt: "What enabled him to outplay rivals was his development of a three-finger picking technique, itself unusual in the realm of blues guitar. Whereas James used his index and middle fingers to pick the top three strings, most blues guitarists used only an index finger."[69] Charley Patton, Bo Carter, and Mississippi John Hurt were among the few who shared this approach. "The fluency it provided was ultimately responsible for *I'm So Glad*, a tour de force of fingerpicking that could not have been emulated by a one-digit treble picker." In this performance, James "used ascending instrumental breaks to create crescendo effects . . . leaping an octave above his open top string in the process." The result was "one of the most extraordinary examples of fingerpicking found in the realm of guitar music, one that is virtually impossible to improve upon."[70]

It's not surprising that the phrase "I'm so glad" is frequently heard in religious songs. *The Story of the Jubilee Singers* (1880) described a spiritual by that title performed by the Fisk University Jubilee Singers: "I'm so glad, I'm so glad, I'm so glad / There's no dying there / I'll tell you how I found the Lord, no dying there . . ." A possible offshoot of that song which may have had an influence on James' performance is *Glad I've Got Religion* (reported by Howard W. Odum in 1909).[71] The refrain: "I'm so glad, so glad, I'm so glad, so glad / Glad I got religion, so glad . . ."

After James' rediscovery in 1964 followed by new live and studio performances, Eric Clapton and Cream included a version of *I'm So Glad* on their million-selling 1967 debut album *Fresh Cream*. Clapton made sure that royalties went to James, and this income (about $6,000, according to Peter Guralnick) helped carry him through hospitalizations and then paid for his funeral after his death in 1969.

Creole Rhapsody (1931)—Duke Ellington & His Cotton Club Orchestra

Brunswick 6093 (both sides, as "The Jungle Band")

Recorded on Jan. 20, 1931; also recorded for Victor 36049 (both sides) on June 11, 1931 (*Jazz-#143*)

As Duke Ellington's reputation expanded during 1930, highlighted by the band's autumn two-week engagement at Broadway's Paramount Theatre—the first time a black orchestra had played there—he set out to compose his first large-scale piece beyond the confines of a three-minute ten-inch record. The six-and-a-half-minute *Creole Rhapsody* was a momentous achievement, released

67. Gioia, *Delta Blues*, p. 142.
68. *Rolling Stone Jazz and Blues Album Guide* (1999), p. 359.

69. *I'd Rather Be the Devil: Skip James and the Blues*, p. 92.
70. Calt, p. 151.
71. July 1909 *American Journal of Religious Psychology and Education*, "Religious Folk-Songs of the Southern Negroes" (p. 309). John Wesley Work discussed a similar song in *American Negro Songs* (1940), p. 142.

on both sides of a 78 by Brunswick, and in an expanded new recording by Victor (running over eight minutes, requiring it to occupy both sides of a 12-inch record) five months later.[72] In his memoir *Music Is My Mistress*, Ellington said he dashed off the composition overnight, writing "so much music that we had to cut it up and do two versions."[73]

The groundbreaking nature of extended works by a mere "popular" orchestra "upset those segments of society that insisted on strict pop/classical segregation," notes biographer Harvey Cohen. Songs requiring the listener to turn the record over to hear the piece in its entirety also represented a commercial obstacle. But in musical terms, the departure from the norm was more than justified. "With their shifting tempos and unpredictable transitions, these pieces represented a musical adventure," writes Cohen not just of this work but Duke's future long-form compositions such as *Reminiscing in Tempo* and *Diminuendo and Crescendo in Blue*. "They were and remain examples of the kind of emotional and carefully plotted-out music that reward repeated listenings and careful attention . . . In these longer works, Ellington demonstrated the myopia of segregation in the area of music."[74]

Gunther Schuller in *Early Jazz* writes that for all the innovations of the original Brunswick version—most notably asymmetrical phrase lengths and perhaps the first recorded jazz trombone duet—the Victor version is superior because of the musicians' better performances.[75] (When the Brunswick version was reissued in 1944, *Metronome* called it "a splendid combination of well-linked themes and brilliant solos" including those by Johnny Hodges and Barney Bigard, with "an exciting climax.") After the Brunswick recording, Ellington apparently decided the piece would work better if the two sections were played at different tempos, and during the intervening time his men had more thoroughly learned to play the intricate composition. "The ensemble work is immeasurably improved, and the tempo changes—then as well as now a rarity in jazz—come off surprisingly well." Also, Ellington scrapped most of the original second section, and for the Victor performance replaced it with new material "in the dreamy, lyrical vein of *Mood Indigo*." Schuller singles out for praise "an incredibly creamy blend of saxophones and muted valve trombone" (the latter by Juan Tizol). The three saxophones accompanying Arthur Whetsol on trumpet "achieve a sound, in terms of both tone quality and voice-leading, that Ellington only approached" on his 1940 classics such as *Warm Valley*. Ellington would build on the lessons learned in his experimentation here with his subsequent long-form pieces such as *Diminuendo and Crescendo in Blue*.

About two weeks after this recording, the band ended the thirty-eight-month run at Harlem's Cotton Club that had helped establish its national reputation, entering a new phase of the Ellington saga. In January 1933, the New York School of Music presented its award for best composition of the year to *Creole Rhapsody*, "because it portrayed the Negro life as no other piece had."

I Gotta Right to Sing the Blues (1933)—Louis Armstrong & His Orchestra (music by Harold Arlen, lyrics by Ted Koehler)

Victor 24233

Recorded on January 26, 1933 (released in April)

Composer Harold Arlen and lyricist Ted Koehler wrote *I Gotta Right to Sing the Blues* for the tenth edition (and the shortest-running) of the *Earl Carroll Vanities*, in which it was performed by Lillian Shade. Ethel Merman was the first artist to record the song, just two days after the show opened in September 1932. Louis Armstrong took full possession of the number in this performance; he's in top vocal form, and his final trumpet chorus, writes Martin Williams, "is one of his most eloquent and grandiose transformations of a popular song. It is in a mature ballad style, free of almost all his rhythmic embellishments and ornamentations. It seems to float above the tempo, above the time, above the piece itself."[76] Biographer John Chilton calls the song's introduction "a breath-taking example of instant composition. Louis begins his solo by filling the break-space with a single low-register note, and this quiet beginning heralds the climactic improvising that follows."[77] Pianist Teddy Wilson and clarinetist Budd Johnson are also in the ensemble. Later in 1933, singer-trombonist Jack Teagarden turned in another superb rendition of the song that would become one of his trademarks. Citing this performance as one of Armstrong's greatest, jazz essayist Whitney Balliett remarked that, "moving into the upper register, he perfected a soaring lyricism, full of swoops and falls and stately long notes." Balliett also notes that as a vocalist, "he handles a song with matchless sensitivity."[78]

72. These appear to be among the earliest jazz recordings released as two-parters. Jazz scholar Rob Bamberger points out at least one predecessor, the two-part *Dreamland Blues* recorded by Troy Floyd & His Shadowland Orchestra in June 1929. A number of blues numbers (by artists including Bessie Smith, Ma Rainey, and Charley Patton), and Mexican-American corridos, had been issued on both sides of a 78 in the 1920s. Ellington later recalled that his insistence to Brunswick on releasing it in two parts "just about got [us] thrown off the label." In 1935 Ellington did an even more expansive four-part opus across both sides of two 78s, *Reminiscing In Tempo*.

73. *Music is My Mistress*, p. 82.

74. Cohen, *Duke Ellington's America*, p. 76.

75. Schuller, p. 352–54. Thomas Hischak (*Tin Pan Alley Song Encyclopedia*, p. 158) points out how the notes cascade downward on the lyric "down around the river."

76. Liner notes, *Smithsonian Collection of Classic Jazz*, p. 21.

77. Chilton, from *Louis: The Louis Armstrong Story*, p. 240.

78. *Collected Works: A Journal of Jazz*, p. 35.

Joaquin Murrieta (Parts 1 & 2) (1934)—Los Madrugadores

Decca 10036

Recorded on Sept. 11, 1934 (*World-#55*)

"The *corrido* century"—Texas scholar Americo Paredes' characterization of the classic period for the narrative ballads of the Texas-Mexican border—ran from 1836 to the late 1930s. He placed the starting point at 1836 because civil war, Indian raids, and the English-speaking "invasion," in his view, all began along the Rio Grande border that year, and these became three of the primary topics of the emerging musical genre. Commercial recordings of Mexican music began around the turn of the twentieth century (Edison made 300 records of Mexican national airs and marches in 1904 alone), but it was not until the early 1920s that folk-based corridos—story songs describing in detail actual border-region events and personalities in vivid journalistic manner, albeit with a definite Mexican point of view—appeared on record. A noteworthy early example is *Heraclio Bernal* by Trio Nava in 1921 (an account of an alleged cattle rustler in the state of Sinaloa who was captured and killed in 1892). The most prolific period for recorded corridos was 1928–1936, and among the greatest artists of the genre was the combo known as Los Madrugadores; their most celebrated performance was *Joaquin Murrieta*.

Joaquin Murrieta, according to the research of Richard G. Mitchell, was a Sonora, Mexico, native who came to California hoping to strike it rich gold mining, and when that didn't work out became the leader of a band of highwaymen, carrying out horse stealing and murders. When the 1852 killing of General Josh Bean, older brother of Roy Bean (later an infamous Texas judge) was said to have been planned by Murrieta, the bandit was tracked down by posses and executed. According to unverified legend (and myth is as much a part of corridos as fact), Ranger Harry Love brought back what was said to be Joaquin's head, which was preserved in alcohol in a San Francisco saloon until fire and earthquake destroyed it in 1906.[79]

The founder of Los Madrugadores, Pedro J. Gonzalez, left Mexico after the Revolution when he fought with Pancho Villa, and took part in a New Mexico raid in 1916. He settled in Los Angeles, worked for a time as a longshoreman, and in 1928 started the first Spanish language radio program on the West Coast. In 1930 he teamed with two gifted singers and guitarists, the Sanchez brothers: Jesus (born February 6, 1906, in Guadalupe de los Reyes, Sinaloa), and Victor (born December 7, 1907, in Magdalena, Sonora). The brothers came to the U.S. as youngsters, and to California by 1927. Billed as Los Hermanos Sanchez and Gonzalez, they had a program over station KMPC six mornings a week from 5 to 6 a.m. (in 1931 they moved to KELW in Burbank and their show expanded from 4 to 6 a.m. seven days a week); that schedule soon earned them the name Los Madrugadores, the Early Risers. Before long, reports Philip Sonnichsen, the group name "became a household word in practically every Spanish-speaking home." In 1933 they began making records, expanding their fame nationwide. In 1934 Gonzalez was sentenced to San Quentin prison on rape charges, and served six years even though the woman he was accused of raping admitted after the trial that she had been coerced by authorities to lie under oath (perhaps due to his political activism on behalf of Mexican-Americans). He resumed performing after his release; Jesus Sanchez died in 1941. But Los Madrugadores carried on, usually featuring the Sanchez brothers but also in various other configurations employing the same musical style; between 1933 and 1941, the group recorded over 200 selections.

Victor Sanchez heard *Joaquin Murrieta* as a child in Mexico and later in Arizona, and when the group began performing on radio it became one of their most requested numbers. By the time they recorded it for Decca, Gonzalez had left, and they were joined by Fernando Linares as the third voice (with the two brothers on guitars). Because the standard practice for corrido recordings was to stretch the tale across both sides of a 78, three or four verses were added to the traditional tune. Murrieta is portrayed heroically as a Mexican Robin Hood:

Los Madrugadores, courtesy of Library of Congress, Arhoolie Records.

---

79. See liner notes by Philip Sonnichsen for Arhoolie's *Texas-Mexican Border Music, Vols. 2 &3.*

"From the greedy rich, I took away their money / With the humble poor, I took off my hat." As dramatized here, he becomes a highwayman only after his wife was killed by an American, and finally a rampaging avenger who kills over a thousand perceived enemies. "I am the one who dominates even African lions," he boasts, depicting himself as invincible. Viewing California as a possession of Mexico (as it had been until the Treaty of Guadalupe Hidalgo in 1848 transferred it to the United States), he reigns there with pistol ready at hand. "I am that Mexican named Joaquin Murrieta," he cries. The epic is found on the Arhoolie/Folklyric collection *Corridos & Tragedias de la Frontera*.

Manuel Pena describes the *corrido* as a "quintessentially Mexican genre, deeply rooted in norteno culture" (northern Mexico near the Texas border). It has played "a crucial role in reinvigorating Mexican culture in the Hispanic Southwest, especially as it is counterposed against the power of an invasive Anglo culture that threatens constantly to efface its presence from the region. In the face-off between the two antagonistic cultures, the corrido stakes out a Mexican position that does not easily yield to a hegemonic Anglo culture."[80]

What a Little Moonlight Can Do (1935)—Billie Holiday/Teddy Wilson & His Orchestra (written by Harry Woods)

Brunswick 7498

Recorded on July 2, 1935 (released in mid-Sept.); reissued by Columbia as part of Holiday-Wilson album in late July 1941

In the latter-day mythology surrounding Billie Holiday, emphasis is almost invariably placed on Lady Day as tragic figure, singing sad laments while symbolizing victimization by a cruel society. While not untrue, this portrait is incomplete; all too often it is forgotten that the young Billie Holiday was also capable of conveying joy. Never was that more true than on the standout song from her very first recording date with Teddy Wilson and the second session of her budding career, *What a Little Moonlight Can Do*.

In its original incarnation, *Moonlight* was a rather nondescript little number from an obscure British movie, *Roundhouse Nights*. Its Massachusetts-born composer, Harry Woods, also wrote such 1920s hits as *When the Red Red Robin Comes Bob-Bob-Bobbin' Along* and *Paddlin' Madelin' Home*, plus 1930s successes including *Try a Little Tenderness*. Based on the original British

rendition (as cornily recorded by Jack Hulbert), there was every reason to believe the song, with a simple melody reminiscent of *Baby Face*, would quickly be forgotten. But in the hands of the eager young vocalist (only recently turned twenty) possessing a gift for handling lyrics like none before her, and the seven-piece pickup band that just happened to include an array of future jazz legends, this paper-thin composition is transformed into pure magic. Producer John Hammond (who had discovered Billie two years earlier at Monette Moore's club on 133rd Street in Harlem, and "decided that night that she was the best jazz singer I had ever heard") created an informal jam-session atmosphere, arranging for the session to begin in late afternoon, and Holiday biographer John Chilton wrote that "his strategy paid rich dividends. It was the type of accompaniment that Billie might have gotten at a Harlem party, or at her club when top-class visiting musicians sat in."[81]

This was an assemblage of jazzmen on the cusp of greatness. Leader/pianist Teddy Wilson was twenty-two and just beginning to build his reputation; this was his first date as a leader. Benny Goodman on clarinet, twenty-six, was right on the verge of his breakthrough as the King of Swing. Trumpet virtuoso Roy Eldridge, twenty-four, and stellar saxophonist Ben Webster, twenty-six, had their careers as headliners still ahead of them. "It astonishes me, as I look back, at how casually we were able to assemble such all-star groups," Hammond recalled in his autobiography. "It simply was a Golden Age; America was overflowing with a dozen truly superlative performers on every instrument. And yet business wasn't that good." Therefore, they were happy to work for union scale.[82]

"Billie's relaxation in this exalted company is apparent," writes Chilton. The combo rips into *Moonlight* (the second song at the session) at a torrid tempo and with thrilling solos (with Goodman's solo kicking things off following Wilson's brief piano intro), and Billie is right there with them. "Ooh, ooh, ooh, what a little moonlight can do," she sings with gusto and assurance, and as she speaks of tongue-tied lovers who can only utter the words of love when a little moonbeam comes peeping through, a world of romantic promise seems to explode through the vinyl. Donald Clarke: "This one was taken at a crackling pace, as quick a beat as Billie ever sang over, but of course Goodman and Billie made it sound easy."[83] Her treatment of the song, observed Michael Brooks, "is both a sexual celebration and a verbal revelation of the cosmic link between man and nature. This is what Harry Woods

---

80. *A Texas-Mexican Cancionero: Folksongs of the Lower Border*, p. xxvii–xxix. In *The Mexican American Orquesta: Music, Culture, and the Dialectic of Conflict* (p. 316), Pena describes the song as "something of an enigma," because, while it documents an outlaw's exploits of the 1840s and 1850s, it was apparently not composed until a half-century or more later. It was widely sung during the 1910 Mexican Revolution.

81. John Chilton, *Billie's Blues: The Billie Holiday Story* (paperback ed.), p. 23–24.

82. *John Hammond on Record: An Autobiography*, p. 147–48.

83. *Billie Holiday: Wishing On the Moon*, p. 92–93.

and others less talented were trying to say . . . and Billie with the skill of a surgeon cuts through all the fumbling verbiage and gets to the heart of the matter."[84] For the moment at least, Billie Holiday was young, happy, and all things were possible; that is the emotion that makes this an unforgettable recording.

(Personnel: Teddy Wilson; Roy Eldridge; Benny Goodman; Ben Webster; John Trueheart on guitar; John Kirby on string bass; Cozy Cole on drums)

Pennies from Heaven (1936)—Bing Crosby (music by Arthur Johnston, lyrics by Johnny Burke)
Decca 947
Recorded in Hollywood on July 24, 1936; chart debut Nov. 28, 1936 (#1 for 10 weeks in *Pop Memories*) (*Trad-#46, MEM-#52, GHF, RIA, BBC*)

Bing Crosby's biggest smash single before *White Christmas, Pennies from Heaven* is an enormously engaging pop tune with precisely the optimistic, things-are-brightest-just-when-they-look-darkest viewpoint that people desperately wanted to hear and believe in the midst of the Great Depression. Will Friedwald writes that this performance "exemplifies lyric interpretation at

Bing Crosby, courtesy of Library of Congress, LC-USZ62-126066.

its finest. Crosby, at his most soothing and reassuring, sings thought by thought rather than word by word. He and lyricist Burke make *Pennies from Heaven* not only practically the finest of all depression songs [in both the capitalized and uncapitalized meanings of the word], but one of the cornerstone concepts of the country's collective consciousness."[85] It was Crosby who hired Burke to put words to Johnston's melody, after Burke had won the 1934 ASCAP award for *The Beat of My Heart*. The lyricist would become a big part of Bing's career, co-writing many future hits for him including *What's New, Moonlight Becomes You,* and *Swinging On a Star.*

Georgie Stoll directs the orchestra, including Joe Sullivan on piano and Bobby Sherwood on guitar, and the arrangement is by John Scott Trotter, indeed serving as the first of his many charts for Bing.

Steel Guitar Rag (1936)—Bob Wills & His Texas Playboys
Vocalion 03394
Recorded in Chicago on Sept. 29, 1936 (*C&W-#78, NPR-300, GHF*)

"Take it away, Leon!" Bob Wills' encouraging cry to his steel guitar virtuoso Leon McAuliffe—country music's three-decades-earlier counterpart to James Brown shouting out "Maceo!" to his saxophonist sideman Maceo Parker—became a universally known exhortation thanks to this Texas Playboys instrumental classic. Black guitarist Sylvester Weaver had originated *Guitar Rag* in 1923 (no "steel" back then), and the piece had subsequently been recorded under that title by the duo of Roy Harvey and Jess Johnston in 1930. But none of those artists could match the brilliance of William Leon McAuliffe, born in Houston on January 3, 1917. He began playing guitar at fourteen, played with the Light Crust Doughboys starting in late 1933, and soon thereafter met Milton Brown's great guitarist Bob Dunn, who taught him how to electrify his National resonator guitar. McAuliffe admitted modestly that he could never match the jazz played by Dunn, offering instead his own unique stylings, usually playing melody even given a solo chorus.[86]

The unamplified steel guitar was introduced to country music by Ellsworth T. Cozzens on three 1928 sessions with Jimmie Rodgers that included *The Brakeman's Blues* and *In the Jailhouse Now.* Dick Spottswood reports that the first known recording of an electronically amplified guitar—or indeed of any electronically amplified instrument—was a February 22, 1933, single by Noi Lane's Hawaiian Orchestra coupling the foxtrot *Alekoki* and the waltz *Hawaiian Love,* a vocal and an instrumen-

84. Brooks, liner notes for the 1991 Columbia compilation *Billie Holiday: The Legacy.*

85. *Biographical Guide to the Great Jazz and Pop Singers*, p. 120.
86. Charles R. Townsend, *San Antonio Rose*, p. 126.

tal serving as Hawaiian guitar showcases for Sam Koki.[87] The first use of an amplified steel guitar other than a Hawaiian or slide guitar on record was by McAuliffe on Bob Wills' first studio session on September 23, 1935.[88] McAuliffe attached a pickup from the amplifier to his acoustic steel guitar.[89]

In March 1935 the eighteen-year-old McAuliffe joined Wills' band, and he quickly became one of the focal points of the pioneering Western Swing ensemble. The guitarist said he'd never heard the Weaver original, but had learned the song from a friend, and added a bit of the pop tune *On the Beach at Waikiki*. Bill Malone writes that this performance of *Steel Guitar Rag*, a perfect symbol of Wills' fusion of country, blues, and jazz, did more than any other recording to popularize the electric guitar with a national audience "and was a portent of that instrument's coming dominance in country music."[90] By year's end, Gibson and other guitar manufacturers were introducing their own electric models, and mail-order catalogs began advertising guitars that included built-in pickup devices and volume controls.

They Can't Take That Away from Me (1937)—Fred Astaire (written by George Gershwin & Ira Gershwin)
Brunswick 7855
Recorded on March 14, 1937; *Pop Memories* debut Apr. 17, 1937 (1 week at #1)[91] (*Trad-#35, NPR-300, APS, 1001, BBC, DMDB*)

It is fortunate indeed that George and Ira Gershwin had the opportunity to complete the score of the film *Shall We Dance?* for Fred Astaire before George's death of a brain tumor at age thirty-eight in July 1937. The score includes several enduring standards, of which the finest is *They Can't Take That Away from Me*. The song is "etched like acid into my memory bank," wrote Alec Wilder in *American Popular Song*. Wilder said the song's ending achieves "a calm pastoral resolution in the face of

the lyric's refusal to be separated from all [of the loved one's] qualities. A beauty!"[92]

Biographer Deena Rosenberg calls it "one of the Gershwins' most haunting songs" whose "very simplicity makes it both poignant and great . . . In songs like this, the Gershwins capture, in miniature, very specific emotional moments. Each song is a personal and original expression of a universal feeling, mood or frame of mind—a description that probably applies to all great art."[93]

"The song is a masterpiece in every sense of the word and another unsurpassed argument for [the theory] that melody and rhythm are inseparable," remarks James R. Morris. "The lyric is witty and urbane, the music concise and compact; both are lean and balanced, without a note or a rhythmic emphasis wasted." Astaire's performance "is extremely graceful. His sense of space and his sensitivity to the subtlety of musical gestures are hallmarks of both his dancing and his singing."[94]

Boogie Woogie (1938)—Tommy Dorsey & His Orchestra
Victor 26054
Recorded on Sept. 16, 1938; chart debut Oct. 22, 1938 (#3 peak); returned to chart on Jan. 16, 1943 (reached #5) (*BB Juke-#6*)

Clarence "Pine Top" Smith had captivated blues and jazz lovers with his December 1928 recording of *Pine Top's Boogie Woogie*, an irresistibly funky piano solo with his spoken dance calls and self-commentary. A vastly wider audience of big-band fans was introduced to the song through Deane Kincaide's enormously inventive rearrangement for Tommy Dorsey. A big hit in 1938, it actually sold even more copies when re-released over four years later, in the midst of the musicians' union's recording ban.

We can probably thank Meade Lux Lewis. His 1927 piano solo *Honky Tonk Train Blues* was a marvel heard by relatively few due to limited distribution (it actually wasn't released by Paramount until 1930), but when he re-cut the piece for Victor in April 1936, a new vogue for the African-American tradition of boogie woogie piano (described by Ted Gioia as "insistent left-hand patterns based on blues chord progressions, underscoring syncopated melody lines or block chords in the right hand") was launched. Saxophonist Kincaide's arrangement of *Boogie Woogie* features pianist Howard Smith, but also gives plenty of space for the full band to riff away madly,

87. The Lane Hawaiians record was issued on Victor 24306, in the midst of pop releases by Ray Noble and Eddy Duchin. Dunn's love for Hawaiian music helped shape his early prowess on steel guitar. The January 1935 Brown instrumental *Taking Off* became, noted Kevin Reed Coffey in the *Journal of Country Music*, Vol. 17 #2 (1995), "country music's first steel guitar classic."

88. Eddie Durham began playing amplified guitar on record on September 23, 1935 (the same day as McAuliffe) with Jimmie Lunceford's band including the celebrated *Hittin' the Bottle*, although he used an acoustic guitar amplified by an aluminum resonating disc. Electric guitars in the modern sense became big-band staples in 1939, most notably Floyd Smith with Andy Kirk's band, T-Bone Walker with Les Hite, then Charlie Christian with Benny Goodman.

89. Wills had wanted to record *Guitar Rag* at the band's debut session, but Vocalion's A&R man Art Satherley vetoed it as uncommercial. By the following year, Bob had enough clout to get his way.

90. *Country Music, U.S.A.* (2nd revised edition), p. 158.

91. Cited as Brunswick's #1 best seller in the April 17 and 24 *Billboard*s.

92. Wilder, p. 156–57.

93. *Fascinating Rhythm: The Collaboration of George & Ira Gershwin*, p. 344–47.

94. Liner notes for the Smithsonian's *American Popular Song*, p. 54–55. Astaire and Rogers reprised the song in their final picture together a dozen years later, *The Barkleys of Broadway*.

including Dorsey's soloing on trombone.[95] Biographer Peter Levinson calls Dorsey's bluesy solo on the last chorus "one of the outstanding solos of his entire career."[96] Unfortunately, Pine Top Smith was no longer around to reap the benefits of his composition's revival; he was shot to death in 1929. The Dorsey record was voted the #6 all-time favorite record in combined *Billboard* polls of disc jockeys from 1949–1961.

Precious Lord (Take My Hand) (1939)—Golden Gate Quartet
Victor 20-3159 (also issued as Bluebird B-8160); released under the title *Precious Lord*

Recorded at Andrew Jackson Hotel in Rock Hill, South Carolina on February 2, 1939 (*GOSP-#61*)

Thomas A. Dorsey, the father of modern gospel music, got his start under the name "Georgia Tom" as pianist, singer, and songwriter on some of the bawdiest blues 78s of the late 1920s, performing with Tampa Red as the Hokum Boys and accompanying blues greats such as Ma Rainey. When he switched to sacred music, he began creating a succession of classics that became among the best-loved hymns of both the black and white churches. *Precious Lord, Take My Hand* has over the years touched more listeners than any of his compositions; Horace Clarence Boyer calls it second only to *Amazing Grace* in popularity in the African-American community.[97] Sallie Martin (accompanied by Dorsey on piano) publicly introduced (but did not record) it in 1932, Elder Charles Beck put it on record for the first time in 1937, and Mahalia Jackson's 1956 recording is perhaps definitive. But the first version to reach a broad national audience was the 1939 version by the mighty Golden Gate Quartet of Norfolk, Virginia. It was made a year and a half after the Gates, at their debut recording session, cut an early treatment of Dorsey's classic *(Standing By the) Bedside of a Neighbor*. With tenors Henry Owens and William Langford, baritone Willie Johnson, and bass vocalist Orlandus Wilson, this a cappella rendition—prominently featuring a skillful Mills Brothers–like vocal impersonation of a muted horn—is haunting and powerful.

All the Things You Are (1939)—Tommy Dorsey & His Orchestra (music by Jerome Kern, lyrics by Oscar Hammerstein II)

Victor 26401

Recorded on Oct. 20, 1939; chart debut Dec. 16, 1939 (2 weeks at #1 in *Pop Memories*)[98] (*NPR-300*)

Regarded by some as Jerome Kern's masterpiece, *All the Things You Are* is a ballad of exquisite beauty but also such melodic complexity that Kern himself confessed to being amazed that it became a huge popular hit. "It is not only very ingenious, but very daring," wrote Alec Wilder in *American Popular Song*. Like Harold Arlen's *Blues in the Night*, he suggested, it proved the adage that "if the opening measures of a song are singable, it doesn't matter how complex the rest of it is."[99] Indeed, Kern himself initially felt that it was so musically sophisticated that he almost took it out of the show for which it was designed because the public wouldn't get it. Wilfrid Sheed, in *The House That George Built*, remarks that "its sheet music is the most formidable I've seen so far, outside of Gershwin's own arrangements. Listening to it, I can only marvel at how it gets from here to there." When the song became an immediate pop standard, "[t]his was surely a great moment in our history and perhaps the public's finest hour."[100]

The song was written for Kern's final Broadway show, *Very Warm for May*—and despite this classic and some other fine songs, the show was a flop, closing after fifty-nine performances. *All the Things* would become the ninth most-recorded song of the entire pre-1955 era; that intricate, lovely melody is matched by the gentle poetry of its lyrics. ("You are the promised kiss of springtime / That makes the lonely winter seem long. / You are the breathless hush of evening / That trembles on the brink of a lovely song . . .") Kern biographer Gerald Bordman remarks that in addition to an unconventional key change in the verse (from A to G flat), there were also "unexpected notes and harmonic progressions that for all purposes represented hidden key changes throughout the song." Even fellow composer Arthur Schwartz had initial doubts about the song's demanding nature, but he later came to regard it as "the greatest song ever written."[101] Lyricist Oscar Hammerstein, Kern's frequent partner for over a dozen years, wrote just a few more songs with him (including *The Last Time I Saw Paris*) before moving on to his new teaming with Richard Rodgers.

Tommy Dorsey's orchestra was hot in 1939, rivaled in popularity only by Artie Shaw and up-and-coming Glenn Miller, and *All the Things You Are* provided a strong conclusion for the year. It was also the last big hit for vocalist Jack Leonard, who left the band in November just weeks after recording it; his successor would be a fellow

95. Kincaide had recently come over from Bob Crosby's band; his other best-known charts for Dorsey would include *Hawaiian War Chant* and a two-part version of *Milenberg Joys*.

96. Levinson, *Tommy Dorsey: Livin' In a Great Big Way*, p. 99–100.

97. *How Sweet the Sound*, p. 61. The song's great "crossover" popularity among white Christians is suggested by a 1953 poll of 10,000 people asking their favorite hymns conducted by a Seventh Day Adventist radio program in California, the results published by *The Christian Century*. *The Old Rugged Cross* ranked #1, and *Precious Lord* placed #6, ahead of *Rock of Ages*.

98. Reached #1 on *Billboard*'s sheet music and radio airplay charts.

99. Wilder, p. 77–79.

100. Sheed, p. 139–40.

101. Bordman, *American Musical Theater*, p. 383.

named Sinatra. Victor in early 1944 reissued Dorsey's and Artie Shaw's versions of the song on opposite sides of the same 78.[102] George Simon writes in *The Big Bands* that although several other bands could match Dorsey's in the potency of their swing, "none could come close to Tommy's when it came to playing ballads." The trombonist "was a master at creating moods—warm, sentimental and forever musical moods—at superb dancing and listening tempos."[103]

When You Wish Upon a Star (1940)—Cliff Edwards
(music by Leigh Harline, lyrics by Ned Washington)
Victor 26477
Recorded in Oct. 1939; *Pop Memories* debut Feb. 17, 1940 (peak position #10)[104] (*AFI-#7, Trad-#23, RIA-#55, GHF, BBC, DMDB*)

One of the most beloved songs in movie history, *When You Wish Upon a Star* represented a wonderful comeback by a 1920s pop superstar who had fallen on hard times. A decade after his run of hits had ended, Cliff Edwards, the man known as "Ukulele Ike," enjoyed his finest hour.

Born on June 14, 1895, in Hannibal, Missouri, Edwards made his performing debut in his teens in St. Louis saloons, moved into Chicago nightclubs in 1918 (by which time his choice of simple instrumental self-accompaniment provided his stage name), then entered the New York vaudeville circuit. After making his first commercially issued recordings for Gennett in 1922, Edwards generated a big stir with his work for the Pathé label starting a year later; in addition to the genial warmth of his vocals, the novelty of his one-man band approach (also playing kazoo), he was one of the first singers to introduce what became known as scatting on record (the very first was probably Gene Greene on his 1911 recording of *King of the Bungaloos*), and certainly the first to do it on a regular basis, breezily twisting and dancing around the lyrics. Seeking (as Will Friedwald writes) to "get as many different kinds of musical textures out of his voice as possible," he used a combination of sound effects, verbal nonsense, and improvisational ingenuity.[105]

A top attraction on Broadway including *Lady Be Good* (1924) and *Ziegfeld Follies* of 1927, Edwards transferred his stardom to movies with the dawn of the sound era, appearing in twenty-three films from 1929–1931, most notably *Hollywood Revue of 1929* in which he introduced

(and had the biggest hit record with) *Singin' in the Rain*. While continuing to appear in movies thereafter, he had become largely a forgotten figure to the general public until Walt Disney made him the singing and speaking voice of Jiminy Cricket in the 1940 animated classic *Pinocchio*. Perhaps no one else could have given *When You Wish Upon a Star* such an aura of sweet optimism, and his performance helped it win the Oscar for best song in a motion picture. He went on to make contributions to other Disney films such as *Dumbo* (as a black crow), returned as Jiminy Cricket in *Fun and Fancy Free*, and in the 1950s made frequent appearances on TV's *Mickey Mouse Club*.

Named the #7 greatest movie song ever by the American Film Institute in its 2004 TV special "100 Years, 100 Songs," it was ranked as the #55 Song of the Century by the Recording Industry of America in 2001.

Tuxedo Junction (1940)—Glenn Miller & His Orchestra (written by Erskine Hawkins, Buddy Feyne, William Johnson & Julian Dash)
Bluebird 10612
Recorded on Feb. 5, 1940; chart debut Feb. 24, 1940 (9 weeks at #1)[106] (*MEM-#71*)

Erskine Hawkins' band introduced the enormously engaging, easy-loping instrumental *Tuxedo Junction* with a July 1939 recording featuring a classic muted trumpet solo by Wilbur "Bud" Bascomb. Born July 26, 1914, in Birmingham, Alabama, trumpeter Hawkins formed his band in 1936; its other most acclaimed record was *After Hours* (1940).[107] Glenn Miller had heard Hawkins play the song on the night the two bands had performed on Christmas Eve at Harlem's Savoy Ballroom, and noted the crowd's enthusiastic reaction. Chummy MacGregor told Miller biographer George T. Simon that Hal McIntyre obtained a lead sheet for the tune from one of the saxists in Hawkins' band, and Jerry Gray brought in a simple sketch of the song to an early-morning rehearsal.[108] The revised chart, reports John Flower in his bio-discography of the Miller civilian band, "added brass figures, plungers, and pedal note pauses for the trombones and the build-up at the finish."[109] Simon: "The guys liked playing it and they began contributing their own ideas, so what eventually emerged was a conglomerate creation, known in musicians' parlance as a 'head arrangement.'"

102. Victor had done the same thing in 1936 with the original release of competing *Stardust* versions by Benny Goodman and Tommy Dorsey on the same disc.

103. Simon, p. 159–60.

104. *When You Wish* reached #1 on both the *Billboard* sheet music and radio charts.

105. Friedwald, *Biographical Guide*, p. 543–46. Friedwald notes that Edwards was creating "full-blown scat solos" from the very start of his recording career, more than three years before Louis Armstrong more famously did so on *Heebie Jeebies*.

106. *Junction* was #1 for 9 weeks on the *Billboard* "Record Buying Guide" (measuring jukebox activity), and was a big retail seller, while making little impression on the sheet music or radio airplay charts, and being omitted entirely by *Your Hit Parade*.

107. Dud Bascomb told Stanley Dance (*The World of Swing*, p. 197) that saxophonist Bill Johnson was the song's primary composer. The song's title references an area of the Birmingham black community where residents would get dressed up for a night out on the town.

108. Simon, *Glenn Miller & His Orchestra*, p. 204.

109. Flower, p. 128–29.

Miller's record sold a strong 115,000 copies in its first week, and kept going to become one of his biggest hits. The featured soloists are Dale McMickle on muted trumpet, Clyde Hurley on open horn, and Chummy Mac-Gregor on piano. In composite *Billboard* disc jockey polls from 1949–1961, it was voted the #21 all-time favorite record.

Night and Day (1942/1957)—Frank Sinatra
Recorded on Jan. 19, 1942 for Bluebird 11463 (first released in early March 1942
Chart debut March 28, 1943, #16 peak);[110] most famous later version for the Capitol album *A Swingin' Affair!* (recorded on Nov. 26, 1956, chart debut May 27, 1957, peak position #2) (*Trad-#163*)

Frank Sinatra and Cole Porter's *Night and Day* share a long and very interesting history. It was the song that helped Sinatra earn his first big break—being hired by Harry James in early 1939. The trumpeter-bandleader had driven from New York City to the Rustic Cabin in Englewood Cliffs, New Jersey, to see the young singer. "This very thin guy with swept-back hair . . . climbed on the stage," James recalled to his biographer Peter Levinson. "He'd sung only eight bars of *Night and Day* when I felt the hairs on the back of my neck rising." The song was part of Sinatra's very first recording session as a solo artist three years later (while he was still with Tommy Dorsey). He selected it as his only number in his first post-Dorsey film appearance later that year, *Reveille with Beverly*, and then used it as his radio theme song in the late 1940s. In subsequent years he "sang it in every way that it was conceivable for Frank Sinatra to sing any song, and that was quite a few," writes Will Friedwald in *Stardust Melodies*. As a result, next to Fred Astaire for his original 1932 recording, no other singer is more closely linked to the Porter masterpiece than the Chairman.

In his Sinatra biography *The Song Is You*, Friedwald describes Axel Stordahl's "great" danceable ballad arrangement which introduces his "equally classic countermelody, which pivots on a five-note phrase that the arranger repeats at various intervals and rhythmic durations, generally on the strings." (A harp is part of the string ensemble.) As Sinatra's radio theme, "Stordahl's original contrapuntal line became as familiar to listeners as Porter's central melody." Many of the "trademarks of Sinatra's mature Columbia period are already here: the long phrasing—often eight or even sixteen bars to a breath—the tenuous, breathlessly romantic sound, and

the deeply felt and communicated recital of the lyrics. He achieves this partly with the aid of slight alterations, at once jazzy and incredibly personal, making the decade-old song sound spontaneous." The concluding chorus of his 1942 performance added bits of "word painting" that Sinatra would retain in latter-day renditions, such as "way down inside of me" and "this torment won't ever be through." The recording's other innovation comes at the end, when Sinatra sings the final "night and day" on three different notes in a descending pattern (instead of singing the three words on the same note, as Porter wrote).[111]

Although Sinatra's Bluebird recording of *Night and Day* was only a mild chart success, it left a lasting impression on disc jockeys, who voted it the #11 all-time favorite record in combined 1949–1961 *Billboard* polls. However, more renowned among general listeners was his 1956 Capitol recording with arrangement by Nelson Riddle. This one is a swinger, although Friedwald notes that it's actually only a marginally faster tempo than 1942's ballad treatment. It opens with an orchestral fanfare, Sinatra singing "night and day," "and then the orchestra re-entering with a POW!" before Sinatra gets to the next line ("you are the one!"). Valve trombonist Juan Tizol, famous for his long association with Duke Ellington, offers a Middle Eastern-flavored solo in the midsection. Riddle, writes Friedwald, "re-employs the same kind of bouncing brass, swinging strings, and overall orchestral coloration that he had pulled off so spectacularly" with Sinatra just months earlier on *I've Got You Under My Skin*. The singer achieves a big ending by stretching out the final note for dramatic effect.

Some Sinatra aficionados argue that his greatest *Night and Day* of all came in a pair of 1959 concerts (March 31 and April 1) in Australia with the Red Norvo Quintet plus Bill Miller on piano, made available on CD decades later. (Exactly twenty years earlier, Norvo had tried to hire Sinatra as male vocalist for his band, but Frank had already just agreed to go with Harry James.) Using the Riddle arrangement as a point of departure, the small combo offers brilliant soloing, especially by vibraharpist Norvo as he improvises over the chords. Whereas in his earlier recordings of the song Sinatra did one-and-a-half choruses, in Australia he sang two full choruses, generating great momentum with (in Friedwald's phrase) "contagious euphoria," shooting notes back and forth with Norvo.

And then there were Sinatra's Latin-flavored 1954 version of the song, his slow-with-strings 1962 arrangement—and, God help us, even a disco version cut in 1977. We'll stick with the above three.

---

110. The record was given a glowing review in the March 7, 1942 *Billboard*, noting that it "proves that he can hold his own quite well" as a romantic balladeer. In the April 11 issue, it was reported as the #9 biggest seller on the West Coast.

---

111. *The Song Is You*, p. 42–54.

Oh, What a Beautiful Mornin' (1943)—Alfred Drake & Original Cast of *Oklahoma!* (music by Richard Rodgers, lyrics by Oscar Hammerstein II)

From Decca's Broadway cast recording of *Oklahoma!*, chart debut Dec. 18, 1943 (spent 4 weeks on *Billboard* pop singles chart as package of 78s; 24 weeks on newly-created album chart starting March 24, 1945; another 9 weeks in 1950 reissue)[112] [113] (*NPR-100, Trad-#85, GHF, RIA*)

Oklahoma! was the musical that officially ushered Broadway into the modern era. *Oh, What a Beautiful Mornin'* provided its irresistibly warm opening number.

As the 1940s began, recounts Ethan Mordden in *Beautiful Mornin': The Broadway Musical in the 1940s*, the genre of musicals on the Great White Way "was deeply vexed. Depression economics had all but banned the daring or even mildly unusual show, and the seasonal tally of new shows was down from an average of about forty-five in the 1920s to about fifteen." Hollywood had lured away many of its top performers and composers. Most of the top shows of 1938–1942 were "decrepit genre, junk about nothing." But conditions for a possible revival were in place. Theatergoing was on the rebound by the early 1940s. A "huge audience was awaiting a long overdue revolution in the writing and staging of musicals . . . 1943 was about as late as the revolution could happen if the musical was to survive."[114]

Richard Rodgers (born June 28, 1902, in New York City) and Lorenz Hart had been one of Broadway's most brilliant songwriting teams since 1925, with a succession of hit shows, and song classics including *Isn't It Romantic, Lover, Blue Moon, The Lady Is a Tramp*, and *Where or When*. But by 1942 Hart was physically and spiritually worn out. When the Theatre Guild approached the team with the proposal to adapt its 1931 play *Green Grow the Lilacs* (written by Lynn Riggs) as a musical, he suggested that Rodgers find another lyricist for the project. Rodgers turned to Oscar Hammerstein II, Jerome Kern's partner on many hit shows since the 1920s—above all the classic *Show Boat*—but now available since Kern had left Broadway behind to focus on Hollywood.

Green Grow the Lilacs was based on the opening of the Oklahoma territory in 1889 and its aftermath with tensions between farmers and cattlemen until they dis-

covered common ground in the founding of a new state. Inspired by the classically American story line, Rodgers and Hammerstein set out to create a show in which every song, and every dance, served a function in carrying the narrative forward. Before, notes Mordden, "songs tended to block the action, stop it dead. *Oklahoma*'s songs convey it." In his partnership with Hart, Rodgers had generally written the melody first, sometimes based on a title or lyrical hook. For this show, Hammerstein persuaded the composer to let him initiate an entire lyric for each number, "and perhaps this inverted procedure is what called up an entirely new sound in Rodgers."

For the opening song, Hammerstein took as his inspiration Lynn Riggs' original stage instructions for the first scene of *Lilacs*: "It is a radiant summer morning several years ago, the kind of morning which, enveloping the shapes of the earth—men, cattle in the meadow, blades of the young corn, streams—seems to make them exist now for the first time, their images giving off a visible golden emanation that is partly true and partly a trick of the imagination, focusing to keep alive a loveliness that may pass away."[115]

Expanding upon these images, Hammerstein completed the song's lyric in three weeks. When he took it to Rodgers, the composer was so affected by its simple but touching quality that he was driven to create its lovely, lazy melody in less than ten minutes. *Oh, What a Beautiful Mornin'* is sung by the cowboy Curly as he comes loping through the field in search of the object of his affections, Laurey, on a sun-drenched morning.[116]

Alfred Drake, a New York City native (born Alfred Capurro on October 7, 1914), made a perfect Curly. Blessed with a strong, authoritative baritone, he made his New York stage debut in 1933, and had increasingly significant roles in a number of shows until *Oklahoma!* became his breakthrough. Drake later co-starred in the hits *Kiss Me, Kate* (1949) and *Kismet* (1953), along with three Shakespeare productions and numerous TV roles.

Opening at the St. James Theater on March 31, 1943, *Oklahoma!* obliterated every previous record for popularity in the American musical theater, running on Broadway for an unprecedented 2,212 performances—five years and nine months. Its national tour lasted so long that it came back to New York in 1953 after ten years on the road, as the show's first of several Broadway revivals. It was the first Broadway cast album to make the *Billboard* charts, placing on the singles chart

---

112. A week before its chart debut, a front-page story in the December 11, 1943, *Billboard* reported that the *Oklahoma!* cast album was "making disk sales history," selling more quickly than any previous Broadway set. *Beautiful Mornin'* reached #2 on the *Billboard* sheet music chart

113. Based on the approximately eighty weeks in the Top Ten it would have accumulated if the *Billboard* album charts had begun by late 1943, it stands as the third biggest album of the decade behind the *South Pacific* cast album (1949) and the 1945 Glenn Miller hits collection.

114. Mordden, p. 3–4, 70–71.

115. Hugh Fordin, *Getting to Know Him: A Biography of Oscar Hammerstein*, p. 187–89.

116. As the number ended, an opening-night observer recalled, "it produced a sigh from the entire house that I don't think I ever heard in the theater. Just, 'Aaaah!'" (Larry Stempel, *Showtime*, p. 302.)

because a separate album chart wouldn't exist for another year and a half.

Oklahoma! was one of the first eleven inductees to the Grammy Hall of Fame (1976), and named one of the 100 most important American musical works of the century by National Public Radio. Like no major show before it, Stephen Sondheim would later say admiringly, the story is "told *through* its songs, not just *with* its songs."[117] "The very title of the show," declares Morddens, "has become a summoning term meaning 'the work that changed the form.'"

Opus No. One (1944)—Tommy Dorsey & His Orchestra (written by Sy Oliver)

Victor 20-1608

Recorded on Nov. 14, 1944; chart debut March 3, 1945 (#12 peak)

Sy Oliver, a key ingredient in the success of the Jimmie Lunceford band in the 1930s, joined Tommy Dorsey as arranger and composer in 1939, and (writes Gunther Schuller) gave the band, for the first time, "a distinctive jazz-oriented sound and style. Oliver's great talent . . . burst upon the Dorsey band like a series of grand musical detonations" with some of the 1940s' finest big-band performances.[118] One of the best was *Opus No. One*, recorded at Dorsey's first Victor session after the company finally reached a settlement with James Petrillo's musicians' union to conclude the union recording ban that had begun over two years earlier.

Melvin James "Sy" Oliver was born on December 17, 1910, in Battle Creek, Michigan, grew up in Ohio, and was already playing trumpet professionally while in high school. He joined Lunceford in 1933, and his distinctive arrangements on *For Dancers Only*, *Organ Grinder's Swing*, *T'ain't What You Do*, and others helped forge Lunceford's reputation. With Dorsey, he also became an important songwriter, his biggest hits including *Yes Indeed* (1941) and *Well, Git It!* (1942). "I have never encountered as dramatic impact on an orchestra by just one individual as in the case of Sy Oliver with Tommy Dorsey's orchestra," declares Schuller. "Instantly, under Oliver's leadership, the band plays with a deep open-spaced swing and beat, feeling rather than reading the music. And the instrumental colors are now strong prime colors, blues-saturated." One of his crucial changes was introducing a baritone saxophone to the ensemble, which "added a much-needed depth and fullness to the band's sound."

Opus No. One is a delightfully swinging number with featured solos by Buddy DeFranco on clarinet, Milt Golden on piano, Bruce Branson on baritone sax, and Buddy Rich on drums. Dorsey biographer Peter Levinson calls Oliver's arrangement "miraculous."[119] DeFranco's solo was such a thing of perfection that Dorsey insisted that he play it exactly the same way at every performance; when he tried to introduce some bebop-inspired variations, the leader fired him. Dorsey's trombone is complemented by young trombonist and future arranger Nelson Riddle. Strings had been added to the band by this time, and Schuller notes that Oliver gives the strings a counter-melody (one that suggests Ray Noble's *Cherokee*) "that enhances the drive generated by the brass and the saxes." Adding to the appeal of the record was its B side, a potent new treatment of *On the Sunny Side of the Street*. *Opus No. One* was voted the #26 all-time favorite record in combined *Billboard* disc jockey polls from 1949–1961, and included on the Smithsonian's boxed set *Big Band Jazz*.

Now's the Time (1945)—Charlie Parker's Re-Boppers (written by Charlie Parker)

Savoy 573

Recorded on Nov. 26, 1945 (*Jazz-#139*)

Charlie Parker's historic first session as a leader on the Savoy label, which produced the immortal *Ko Ko*, also gave us another indelible Bird gem, *Now's the Time*. The second number completed that day (right after the song that served as its flip side, *Billie's Bounce*), it's a fundamentally simple riff tune, a blues in F major, based on the repetition of a six-note lick; it is Parker's earthy alto saxophone soloing that makes it (in Carl Woideck's words) "a concise masterpiece."[120] Young Miles Davis is on trumpet, Dizzy Gillespie on piano, Curly Russell on bass, and Max Roach on drums. Miles at this point, writes Ingrid Monson, "sounded tentative and technically subpar, but his understated presence seems to have allowed Parker greater musical and psychic space" in comparison to his classic work earlier in the year with Dizzy Gillespie.[121] The words of Francis Davis, in analyzing Parker's significance to jazz history in relation to Gillespie's, could be applied to this performance: "Unmatched among modernists as a blues player, Parker brought a human cry to bebop's experimentalism—ultimately as crucial an element to the music's acceptance as Gillespie's showmanship."[122]

"Bebop's embracing of the blues and its re-establishing of the primacy of rhythm in jazz revealed its developers' commitments to their [African-American] heritage

117. Stempel, p. 305.
118. *The Swing Era: The Development of Jazz, 1930–1945*, p. 686.

119. Levinson, *Tommy Dorsey: Livin' in a Great Big Way*, p. 185.
120. *Charlie Parker: His Life and Music*, p. 112, 114.
121. *A New Literary History of America* (p. 775)
122. Davis, August 8, 1999, *New York Times*, review of Shipton's Dizzy Gillespie biography *Groovin' High*.

and their realization that a successful revolution lay in the power of that heritage," declares Samuel A. Floyd, Jr., in *The Power of Black Music*. Its players "did what the turn-of-the-century and Harlem Renaissance modernists refused or were not able to do: they merged rationality and myth—with musically significant results—and they accomplished this by focusing on the blues and on rhythm . . . Bebop reflected—and its practitioners exulted in—not only the pleasure and excitement of musical discovery and achievement, but also the joy and exuberance of myth and ritual."[123]

In one of the most notorious musical ripoffs of the era, Parker's utterly infectious central riff for *Now's the Time* was appropriated to become a huge chart-topping early-1949 R&B hit for saxophonist Paul Williams, using an original tune for its A section and Parker's theme for the B section (covered successfully for the pop market by Tommy Dorsey's band), *The Hucklebuck*; Bird, of course, didn't get a dime.[124]

(Get Your Kicks on) Route 66 (1946)—King Cole Trio
(written by Bobby Troup)
Capitol 256
Recorded in Los Angeles on March 15, 1946; chart debut June 8, 1946 (reached #3 on R&B chart, #11 pop) (*Jazz-#52, Trad-#57, GHF, NPR-300, R&B-#103, 1001*)

John Steinbeck called Route 66 "the mother road" in his 1939 classic *The Grapes of Wrath*. Commissioned in 1926 as one of the nation's principal east-west arteries, it started with a patchwork of existing roads from Chicago to Los Angeles (of which only 800 miles were then paved), linking them together with new stretches of highway built by thousands of unemployed young men from 1933 to 1938 hired by the Works Progress Administration, and by the end of 1938 the road was confirmed as "continuously paved." Hundreds of thousands of migrants traveled west on Route 66 seeking a better life in the midst of the Depression. The nation's epic wartime manpower mobilization would have been infinitely more difficult without the road dubbed the "Main Street of America." And with the new prosperity and mobility Americans would enjoy after the war, mighty 66's status as a symbol of personal freedom was deepened. Bobby Troup's *Route 66* is a celebration of that legacy, created right at its peak.

Born on October 18, 1918, in Harrisburg, Pennsylvania, pianist-composer Troup burst on the pop music scene in 1941 as composer of the Sammy Kaye hit *Daddy*, and

was an arranger for Tommy Dorsey before his World War II service. It was not too long after receiving his discharge papers that he and his wife Cynthia drove in their 1941 Buick convertible from Lancaster, Pennsylvania, to Los Angeles to help restart his career, following the Pennsylvania Turnpike (just opened the previous year as the first full American superhighway) to U.S. 40, and then picking up Route 66 in St. Louis for the final 1,800 miles of the trip (a trek detailed by Arthur Krim).[125] During the seven-day drive west, Cynthia suggested that he write a song about highways, and offered the rhyme, "get your kicks on Route 66," which happened to offer a hint of sexual invitation along with its lure of the open road. Bobby sketched the outlines of the song as they traveled the highway, reaching their destination of Sunset Boulevard and Hollywood on February 15, 1946.

Nat "King" Cole and his trio were working at the posh Trocadero nightclub on Sunset Boulevard when Troup arrived several days later to pitch him some songs. *Route 66* wasn't yet completed, but it impressed Cole enough that he urged the songwriter to put on the finishing touches. (The singer's own travels on Route 66 from Chicago to Los Angeles before the war may have made him particularly receptive to the subject matter.) Troup completed the piece in late February, and Cole first performed it on radio for the March 13 CBS *Old Gold* program hosted by Frank Sinatra. Two days later, the King Cole Trio recorded it at the Capitol studios. The record was released on April 22, and immediately attracted dueling cover versions by Georgie Auld's orchestra (on April 30) and Bing Crosby with the Andrews Sisters (May 10). The latter was particularly tough competition, but Cole's original would emerge supreme. The trio—Nat on piano and vocals, Oscar Moore on guitar, and Wesley Prince on bass—had taken the country by storm during the previous two years, and with three classic hits issued in rapid succession during the last half of 1946—*Route 66, (I Love You) For Sentimental Reasons*, and *The Christmas Song*—Cole was fully elevated into the Crosby-Sinatra realm of the foremost pop singers. [126]

Troup's instant classic accurately described the trail followed by the 2,448-mile highway: south from Chicago to St. Louis, veering southwest through Tulsa and Oklahoma City, then straight west to Amarillo and Albuquerque, and finally through Arizona before concluding in Santa Monica outside Los Angeles. Cole's vocal is hip and swinging, and the telepathic interplay between his piano and his Trio partners adds to the

123. Floyd, p. 142–43.
124. Incredibly, the Williams record that failed to credit Parker was issued by Savoy (indeed, the discs even shared the same producer, Teddy Reig), meaning that Bird was robbed by his own label.
125. "Get Your Kicks on Route 66! A Song Map of Postwar Migration," in the book *The Sounds of People and Places: A Geography of American Music from Country to Classical and Blues to Bop*, p. 137–45.
126. Leslie Gourse, *Unforgettable: The Life and Mystique of Nat King Cole*.

sense of infectious fun. A young Jack Kerouac heard the tune on the juke box in New York, and was inspired to plan a California trip on Route 66 to Denver and San Francisco for the summer of 1947, which he would chronicle in *On the Road*.[127]

In the mid-1950s Troup would help launch the career of sultry songstress Julie London, whom he married, and with whom he appeared in the 1970s TV series *Emergency*, which followed a number of other movie and TV roles. As for Route 66, it fueled westward tourism for a generation, was further immortalized by the 1960–1964 hit TV series, and was gradually bypassed by a modern four-lane highway; the final section of the original road was succeeded by Interstate 40 at Williams, Arizona, in 1984. But even though it no longer appears on maps, portions of the road are still there to be driven by its devoted partisans. In 2003, the Smithsonian Institution's exhibition on travel, "America On the Move," devoted a major section to the Route 66 of song, story, and national mythology. The 2006 Disney/Pixar animated film *Cars*, which partly took place on the mighty roadway, had a sweet obsession with Troup's song, using multiple versions on the soundtrack. *Route 66*, declares Krim, "serves as an Homeric ballad for a geography of the Southwest in the postwar migration to California."

Dark as a Dungeon (1947)—Merle Travis
Recorded in Hollywood on Aug. 8, 1946
From the Capitol album *Folk Songs of the Hills* (released on June 9, 1947) (*Folk-#35, C&W-#99, NPR-300*)

Dark as a Dungeon was, along with *Sixteen Tons*, a classic song of the coal mining life written in 1946 by Merle Travis based on memories of his father laboring in the mines of Muhlenberg County in western Kentucky.[128] It was precisely the soul-deadening work that Travis successfully avoided by becoming a virtuoso guitarist and hit-making singer/writer. The song, writes Bill Malone, "recalled not only the dangers involved in coal mining but also the curiously intoxicating appeal that such labor had for many miners." These workers were addicted to coal labor, Travis remarked, "like a fiend for his dope, and a drunkard his wine."[129]

He wrote the piece (as related to Archie Green) shortly before the recording session for the album. Re-

turning home from a Redondo Beach, California, date with his girlfriend, reminiscing about his childhood sparked the idea for the song; he pulled the car up under a street lamp and scribbled the words on the back of an envelope. Despite the great success Travis had already enjoyed in 1946 and early 1947 with seven Top Five country hits including two that held the #1 position for a combined twenty-eight weeks, *Folk Songs from the Hills* was not a big seller at first, and was deleted from Capitol catalogs when the label converted from 78s to LPs.[130] *Dungeon* reached its widest original audience through a wonderful 1948 performance by the Maddox Brothers and Rose, an emotionally affecting rendition (featuring the great Rose Maddox);[131] Travis' frequent musical partner Grandpa Jones also waxed splendid 1950 and 1956 versions with his wife Ramona. In later years Johnny Cash was just one of many performers who did full justice to it.[132]

But there can be no substitute for Travis' original, which includes a powerful verse typically left out of cover versions (the "fiend with his dope" section). Travis also wrote another verse that even he did not perform initially because it was thought to be too "scary" for children: "The midnight, the morning, or middle of the day / Is the same to the miner who labors away / Where the demons of death often come by surprise / One fall of the slate and you're buried alive."[133] His strong, sturdy baritone conveys an authority that's perfect for his composition. *Dark as a Dungeon* was included in the Library of Congress Bicentennial fifteen-record collection *Folk Music in America*.[134]

Tenderly (1947)—Sarah Vaughan
Musicraft 504
Recorded July 2, 1947; chart debut Nov. 15, 1947 (reached #27); also recorded for MGM 10705 in 1950 (*Trad-#106*)

The first commercially recorded version of the gorgeous Walter Gross–Jack Lawrence ballad was that of Sarah Vaughan,[135] and it's a ravishing rendition that

---

127. The enduring stature of *Route 66* is wittily suggested by Wilfrid Sheed in *The House That George Built* (p. 96), saying that Hoagy Carmichael's *Georgia On My Mind* "on my occasional travels seems to take turns with *Route 66* as our real national anthem."

128. Travis' father and two brothers worked for the Beech Creek Coal Company, his dad laboring there until age seventy. They were more fortunate than his brother-in-law, who died after contracting black lung disease (interview in May–June 1976 *Sing Out!*).

129. *Don't Get Above Your Raisin': Country Music and the Southern Working Class*, p. 43.

130. The album was reissued, with four additional songs to fill a 12-inch LP, in December 1957 retitled *Back Home*. (Green, *Only a Miner*, p. 279–94.)

131. In 1949, B. A. Botkin included the song in *A Treasury of Southern Folklore*. Four years later, John Greenway included it in *American Folksongs of Protest*.

132. Another important early version was by Cisco Houston on his 1951 Folkways album *This Land Is My Land*.

133. This stanza was included in the version of the song received by the U.S. Copyright Office on February 27, 1956, but retroactively identified with the June 1947 album release date; the song had been legally unprotected for nearly a decade (Green, *Only a Miner*, p. 290).

134. Volume 8, "Songs of Labor and Livelihood."

135. The next earliest versions cited in *Popular Recordaid* were a few months later in 1947 by the orchestras of Randy Brooks (for Decca) and Charlie Spivak (for Victor); in 1948 singer Clark Dennis did it for Capitol.

helped to define the song until Rosemary Clooney's classic 1951 recording.[136]

The lady known as "The Divine One" was born on March 27, 1924, in Newark, New Jersey. After winning an amateur contest at New York's Apollo Theatre, she sang with the Earl Hines band in 1943, then started a longtime alliance through her 1944–1945 stint with Billy Eckstine's ground-breaking ensemble (indeed, it had been Eckstine who'd encouraged Hines to hire her). It was her shimmering 1945 performance of *Lover Man* with Dizzy Gillespie that helped establish her reputation; following 1945–1946 work with John Kirby, "Sassy" launched a solo career that would earn her acclaim as one of the all-time great jazz vocalists.[137] *Down Beat* honored her as the most popular female singer, and she also won the *Esquire* New Star Award for 1947.

Will Friedwald in *Jazz Singing* notes Sarah's "incredible musicianship" possessing such a vast range that "she could probably sing half the piano if she wanted," with an ease in jumping up and down the octaves, and a vibrato that was hers alone.[138] In her 1940s recordings, remarks David McGee, "the young, feathery-voiced Vaughan demonstrates an uncanny knack for investing a lyric with precisely the proper emotion . . . Moreover, one is struck by her innate musicality at this early stage." This wonderful performance of *Tenderly* was matched by the one she waxed on November 12, 1954. "You took my lips, you took my love, so tenderly . . ."

(George Treadwell's orchestra, large ensemble with four trumpets including Emmett Perry and Hal Mitchell, three trombones, two alto saxes, two tenors including Budd Johnson, baritone sax, piano, bass, drums)

It's Mighty Dark to Travel (1947)—Bill Monroe & His Bluegrass Boys

Columbia 20526

Recorded in Nashville on Oct. 27,1947 (released on Dec. 27, 1948) (*C&W-#136*)

One of the defining performances of early bluegrass, *It's Mighty Dark to Travel* shows the most extraordinary working band in the genre's history at the peak of its powers.

Bill Monroe's band already had few rivals for musicianship and creativity when Lester Flatt came aboard in March 1945 after leaving the band of Bill's brother Charlie Monroe. Flatt's prowess at high-lonesome vocals was comparable to Monroe's own, and his gifts as a songwriter were actually more advanced at this stage. It was later that year that the final element of the ensemble's greatness fell into place when twenty-one-year-old North Carolina banjo virtuoso Earl Scruggs auditioned and was quickly hired. Monroe biographer Richard D. Smith relates that right from the start of his tenure with the band, "Earl Scruggs electrified audiences."[139] Monroe was quick to showcase the newcomer as featured soloist.

The story goes that one day Monroe struck up a conversation with a black man in a barber shop, and when he asked how the man was doing, he replied sadly, "oh, it's mighty dark to travel." Sensing a song idea in the remark, Monroe related the conversation to Lester Flatt, and the two worked out the piece from there. Bill Malone: "All the 'classic' ingredients of bluegrass are here: the hard-driving song full of the lonesome imagery that Monroe so favored; the interplay among the acoustic instruments—the syncopated, three-finger-style banjo of Earl Scruggs; the smooth, blues-tinged fiddling of Chubby Wise; the solid string bass underpinning of Howard Watts; and, of course, the inimitable mandolin of Monroe—and the duet singing of Flatt and Monroe."[140]

The band's September 16 and 17, 1946, sessions—the first recordings with Flatt and Scruggs—had established the foundations of the classic bluegrass sound, and Robert Cantwell writes that this session a year later brought the new style to its peak. "Here the hounds of syncopation—an emphatic backbeat and a driving, unflagging banjo roll—have been let loose, flushing the rhythm out of the [old 2/4] meter and opening a wide antiphonal frontier" where Monroe's "parallel harmony lines become, by a kind of rhythmic infraction, improvised countermelodies playing around the beat and welling up between lead phrases in patterns built on the call-and-response plan of Afro-American music. The rhythm no longer bounces but floats, like a jazz rhythm, while all the musicians drive it forward, like jazz musicians cooperating to fill in all the spaces with licks and runs contrived to sustain a balanced structure of opposing rhythms . . . the music is suddenly deeper, richer, more complex and powerful."[141]

Bill Friskics-Warren notes that Scruggs is in full overdrive on this performance. Flatt "might be singing about being lost on a dark gravel road since his baby left him, but from the fevered breakdown Scruggs and company are laying down behind him, you'd swear he was racing along just fine." He also emphasizes the strong black in-

136. One of Jack Lawrence's other best-known songs, the lilting ballad *Linda*, was written for the young daughter of his lawyer, Lee Eastman, and was a hit for Buddy Clark. The little girl grew up to marry Paul McCartney, and McCartney would later purchase Lawrence's song catalog for over $500,000.

137. She began working with orchestra leader George Treadwell in 1946, and he would manage her career from that point on. (Gourse, *Sassy: The Life of Sarah Vaughan*, p. 48–49.)

138. Friedwald, p. 272.

139. Richard D. Smith, *Can't You Hear Me Callin'?: The Life of Bill Monroe, Father of Bluegrass*, p. 89.

140. Liner notes, *The Smithsonian Collection of Classic Country Music*, p. 47.

141. Robert Cantwell, *Bluegrass Breakdown: The Making of the Old Southern Sound*, p. 106–7.

fluence on the Monroe sound as exemplified by this number: "from Bill's soulful high tenor, to the galvanizing effect of the African-derived banjo, to the story behind this song, the influence is undeniable."[142] [143] There are three surviving takes of the song, and the one that finally saw the light of day in a 1992 compilation is regarded as perhaps the finest of all. More than sixty years after the original, Earl Scruggs played *It's Mighty Dark to Travel* again as a member of Ricky Skaggs' star-studded ensemble on the 2008 album *Honoring the Fathers of Bluegrass*.

Amazing Grace (1947)—Mahalia Jackson
Apollo 194
Recorded on Dec. 10, 1947 (*GOSP-#20*)

Mahalia Jackson recorded *Amazing Grace* at her third session for Apollo, three months after her career-transforming waxing of *Move On Up a Little Higher*, but before that record had been released and assured her future course. It was a song she had been singing since the very outset of her career as a teenager in the late 1920s.

The earliest recordings of the song by black performers seem to have been by the Rev. H. R. Tomlin (assisted by the Rigoletto Quintette of Morris Brown University) on August 19, 1926, for Okeh, and two September 1926 renderings by the Rev. J. M. Gates (introducing the song as "one of the good old familiar hymns") for Perfect and Victor. The Library of Congress was the venue for two noteworthy 1940 interpretations by Blind Willie McTell and Huddie Ledbetter (aka Leadbelly).

Steve Turner writes in *Amazing Grace: The Story of America's Most Beloved Song* that gospel singers have "tended to omit from rather than add to stanzas" of the song, and this is certainly true of Mahalia's rendition. Indeed, on her Apollo recording she omits all the stanzas, singing only the familiar chorus accompanied by organ, slowly and with all her customary power and beauty. Turner: "Mahalia spent so much time savoring each word and exploring the layers of possible meaning that it took her over two minutes to get through the [chorus]. The first word took her thirteen seconds to enunciate."[144] On her subsequent 1954 version for Columbia she sang the first stanza twice, "but between them she 'moaned' out a verse in exactly the same way" that Reverend Gates had done.[145]

For Mahalia, *Amazing Grace* "was more Baptist than Sanctified because it was slow and moving, dependent on subtle emotional inflections rather than energetic twists and turns, and it took her back to her roots in New Orleans."[146]

I've Got My Love to Keep Me Warm (1948)—Les Brown & His Orchestra (written by Irving Berlin)
Columbia 38324
Recorded in Hollywood on Sept. 16, 1946; chart debut Dec. 25, 1948 (1 week at #1)

Irving Berlin wrote *I've Got My Love to Keep Me Warm* for the 1937 film *On the Avenue* (starring Dick Powell and Alice Faye), and it was recorded memorably by Billie Holiday among many other artists. Les Brown's orchestra recorded a deliciously easy-swinging instrumental arrangement by Skip Martin in September 1946, just as the big-band business was going into a swoon, with many top bands folding at year's end. The ultra-smooth, gently swinging instrumental performance sat on Columbia's shelves for over two years. As Brown recalled for George Simon (*The Big Bands*), one night in 1948, "when we were running out of tunes" performing on the air with Bob Hope, the band pulled out the number, and it drew an enthusiastic audience response. Columbia immediately wired Brown "telling us to get into the studio the next day and record it. I wired back, 'Look in your files.'"[147] When they finally released it in late October, the record reawakened many listeners' warm feelings for the swing era, and the song—completed by the Brown ensemble in just fifteen minutes—became a surprise smash. Combined *Billboard* polls of disc jockeys from 1949–1961 voted it the #18 all-time favorite record.

The Death of Ellenton (1951)—Johnson Family Singers
Columbia 20895
Recorded in Nashville on May 7, 1951

May 1951 was not a time in American history when social protest was welcomed. The Korean War had been raging for exactly one year; Gen. Douglas MacArthur had been relieved of command one month earlier; the Cold War and McCarthyism were triggering fear and mistrust; anyone questioning authority was at risk of being called a traitor. But in the midst of this stifling atmosphere, an all-American family group from North

---

142. *Heartaches By the Number: Country Music's 500 Greatest Singles*, p. 62–63.

143. Mac Martin, in a September 1996 *Bluegrass Unlimited* feature on "The Recordings That Defined Bluegrass," remarks that Scruggs developed his trademark three-finger banjo roll only gradually during these sessions. It was not until the release of this performance, eighteen months after *Will You Be Loving Another Man?*, that a second recording with this banjo break reached the market.

144. *Turner*, p. 157–58.

145. This approach to religious singing apparently crossed racial lines in the South; according to Pete Seeger, his Arkansas-born Weavers

partner Lee Hays taught him *Amazing Grace* sung in "long-meter" style, so slow that it could take up to two minutes to get through a single verse (September–October 1976 *Sing Out!*).

146. Horace Clarence Boyer shares the view that Jackson's approach to this song was an exception to her generally Pentecostal-flavored style, taking *Grace* in the older Baptist "lining-hymn" tradition. (*How Sweet the Sound*, p. 87.)

147. Simon, p. 105.

Carolina best known for its religious hymns (in the style of the Chuck Wagon Gang)[148] hurled a protest song that would have made Woody Guthrie proud; it was nothing less than extraordinary for its time, particularly for its explicit condemnation of the military.

The Death of Ellenton is the account of the Atomic Energy Commission uprooting (on just five weeks' notice) the entire rural community of Ellenton, South Carolina—along with the nearby towns of Jackson, Dunbarton, and Snelling—to construct an atomic energy plant along the banks of the Savannah River in Aiken County. The action was authorized by President Truman on November 28, 1950. "The local residents were stunned," writes Holly C. Baker. Residents "had to leave the land their families had occupied since the eighteenth century. Approximately 8,000 people in the area were displaced; every building not relocated was razed." "New Ellenton" was built to replace the town thirty miles upstream. Despite financial benefits such as job preference for former residents in the new facility, some native Ellentonians and their brethren called themselves the "first displaced persons of World War III."[149] (New Ellenton, located in western South Carolina twenty-four miles from Augusta, is a small town with 2,250 residents as of 2000.) Jesse "Pa" Johnson (the group's leader) is credited as co-writer of the song with a "D. Smith." Young Betty Johnson's pure soprano leads the group's harmonies, describing the death of a town with sorrow and concealed anger; they're accompanied only by guitar. One of Pa Johnson's sons who performed with the group, Kenneth M. Johnson, wrote a memoir of the family's experiences, *We Sang for Our Supper*. Betty Johnson was still making occasional recordings, her voice still lovely, as recently as 2008.

"Alone among country songs I know, this treats the devastation wrought by the bomb not abroad, not as a religious bit of imagery, but as an industrial reality" in America, remarked Robert Coltman.[150] Its contrast from the several postwar country songs dealing with the atomic bomb as a weapon of God's power and wrath foreshadowing the Day of Judgment (such as Fred Kirby's *Atomic Power* written immediately after Hiroshima, and the Louvin Brothers' *Great Atomic Power* five years later) could hardly have been more vast.[151] In 1978 this performance was included in the Library of Congress compilation *Folk Music in America*.[152] Holly Baker, in liner notes for the set, reports that within a week of Truman's announcement in 1950, a sign appeared tacked to the name and population marker on the outskirts of Ellenton: "It is hard to understand why our town must be destroyed to make a bomb that will destroy someone else's town that they love as much as we love ours. But we feel that they picked not just the best spot in the U.S. but in the world. We love those dear hearts and gentle people who live in our home town."

My Babe (1955)—Little Walter & His Jukes (written by Willie Dixon)
Checker 811
Recorded on Jan. 25, 1955; chart debut March 12, 1955 (#1 for 5 weeks R&B) (*Blues-#75, AL*)

After establishing himself as the unparalleled master of blues harmonica (first with Muddy Waters' band and then on his own), Little Walter Jacobs also proved to have an engaging, easy-flowing vocal style. He scored his biggest vocal hit with *My Babe*, Willie Dixon's reworking of the old spiritual *This Train (Is Bound for Glory)*. Dixon had given the number to Walter because it fit his performing style, but remarked in his autobiography, *I Am the Blues*, that "it took damn near two years for him to record it." Indeed, Walter's band first tried recording the number on July 1, 1954, but the arrangement hadn't been properly worked out yet. Six months later, they were ready.

Little Walter's biographers Tony Glover, Scott Dirks, and Ward Gaines report that immediately before Walter's January 25 session, Dixon took part in a gospel session with pianist Reverend Ballinger that included *This Train*, which (they note) "is the direct source for Dixon's chorus, rhythm and melody" for the song.[153] Dixon suggested to Walter to use a bouncier arrangement of the song than the one that hadn't worked back in July, a tempo closer to the spiritual from the preceding session. That did the trick, although Walter kept the band doing take after take that night until he was satisfied. "From the opening drum hit and walking bass guitar line, the tune has 'hit' written all over it. Walter sings with energy and conviction, and his lively, swinging two-chorus harp solo is a nice controlled power surge."[154]

David Evans and Colin Escott note that the basic structure of *My Babe*—four lines with a "compound

148. The Johnson Family Singers got their first regular radio job in the early 1940s at WBT in Charlotte, North Carolina. They developed their style at the music schools run by the Stamps-Baxter and James D. Vaughan publishing companies, which emphasized traditional Southern shape-note hymn singing.

149. From liner notes, Library of Congress, *Folk Music in America*, Record 12: "Songs of Local History and Events."

150. May 1978 *Journal of Country Music*.

151. See Charles Wolfe article "Nuclear Country: The Atomic Bomb in Country Music," in January's *Journal of Country Music*, Vol. 6 #4 (1978).

152. *Folk Music in America*, Volume 12, "Songs of Local History and Events". The song's music and lyrics were printed in the January 1969 *Sing Out!*, although the headnote simply called it "traditional."

153. Sister Rosetta Tharpe was the gospel star most closely identified with *This Train*; her biographer Gayle Ward notes that Dixon replaced the traditional lines about the procession of saints in heaven with his tale of a woman who won't tolerate her man's cheating ways.

154. Glover, et al., *Blues with a Feeling*, p. 141.

third line"—can be found in many blues of the 1920s, and probably dates back to the pre-1900 era. The song is utter simplicity itself, but the performance is irresistibly funky and deeply sensual, with Walter's voice and harmonica accompanied by Dixon on bass and backing vocals, Robert "Junior" Lockwood on guitar, and Fred Below on drums. Gerard Herzhaft relates that Walter, a demanding leader, "worked for weeks on a piece with his accompanists before recording. This gave his records a perfection and cohesiveness that was seldom equaled."[155] "My babe, she don't stand for no foolin', my babe . . . When she's hot, there ain't no coolin' . . ."

A Satisfied Mind (1955)—Porter Wagoner (written by
    J. H. "Red" Hays & Jack Rhodes)
RCA Victor 6105
Recorded Sept. 11, 1954; chart debut May 28, 1955 (#1
    for 4 weeks C&W) (*HBN-#39, C&W-#106*)

The second charted song for the man from West Plains, Missouri (born on August 12, 1927), a touching statement of discovering life's true values only after losing everything, proved to be the defining hit of his long career. After getting his start singing on local radio, Wagoner was recruited for the *Ozark Jamboree* national TV show, which led to a recording contract with RCA Victor. His 1952–1954 singles flopped until *Company's Comin'* provided his first hit in 1954, paving the way for his breakthrough. Wagoner would churn out scores of C&W hits for the next quarter century, including his duet partnership with Dolly Parton; this is the song for which he'll be best remembered.

A Satisfied Mind was first recorded in 1954 in Houston by its co-writer Red Hays for the Starday label. Hays was inspired by the sayings of his mother, with the title image provided by his father-in-law. Wagoner biographer Steve Eng remarks that it was an "unlikely" hit as a "tranquil, yet thoughtful song" with a somewhat abstract message. However, it possesses "the same whimsically enduring qualities" of Thomas A. Dorsey's *Peace in the Valley*, which had been a giant hit for Red Foley. Song publisher Si Siman (Earl Barton Music), convinced of the song's potential, tried unsuccessfully to get Wagoner and Foley among others to record it, until Porter finally came around. It was recorded at the Springfield, Missouri, station KWTO, accompanied by Don Warden on steel guitar, Speedy Haworth on rhythm guitar and harmony vocals, and Buster Fellows on fiddle. At the time of the recording, his RCA contract had actually expired, with his future uncertain. Because the track was basically designed as a demo—its total budget of 40 dollars paid for by the artist—to impress RCA, Wagoner produced

the session himself (he would produce most of his later sessions as well). But RCA A&R man Steve Sholes realized that the "demo" was good enough to release. Foley recorded it on April 6, 1955, for Decca, followed five days later by Jean Shepard for Capitol.[156] That same month, RCA released Wagoner's seven-month-old version, which broke out in Houston and hit the national charts a few weeks later (Shepard's treatment charted in June and reached #4 C&W).

Richard A. Peterson cites the song as an example of class consciousness in country music with its look at wealth and poverty and the observation, "It's hard to find one rich man in ten with a satisfied mind."[157] Gospel great Mahalia Jackson recorded *A Satisfied Mind* very shortly after it became a hit (in August 1955), and it has been covered in subsequent years by Joan Baez, Bob Dylan, and the Byrds among others. "There is a mournfulness to this recording," writes David Cantwell, ranking it #39 in *Heartaches By the Number: Country Music's 500 Greatest Singles*, "a palpable sense of frustrated yearning that emphasizes the circular nature of the song's advice—the path to satisfaction, Wagoner says, is to have a satisfied mind. But how do you achieve that?" Wagoner's not telling. "Probably because he doesn't know." And that, he notes, is what makes the performance so melancholy.[158]

**Sophisticated Lady (1956)—Rosemary Clooney with
    Duke Ellington & His Orchestra** (music by Duke
    Ellington, lyrics by Mitchell Parish)
Orchestra recorded on Jan. 23, 1956, vocal recorded dur-
    ing Jan. 23–27 in Los Angeles, for the album *Blue
    Rose*; released as a single on Columbia 40701[159]
    (*Trad-#187, APS*)

One of Duke Ellington's greatest ballads, *Sophisticated Lady* was a hit instrumental for his orchestra in 1933; when Mitchell Parish added lyrics later that year, it became an enduring standard for vocalists. James R. Morris: "Intense harmonic textures are *Sophisticated Lady*'s identifying trademark: rich chromatic tonalities which color the melody unforgettably . . . In the final A section, a remarkable number of chromatic, dissonant harmonic possibilities are explored."[160]

155. *Encyclopedia of the Blues*, p. 207.

156. *A Satisfied Mind: The Country Music Life of Porter Wagoner*, p. 95–102. The record is believed to have sold 200,000 copies.
157. *You Wrote My Life: Lyrical Themes in Country Music*, p. 48.
158. *Heartaches*, p. 24.
159. William Brown's Columbia Records discography lists the recording date for the single as January 23, 1956, which agrees with other sources for the date of the orchestra's recording. Hajdu writes that Clooney's part was completed by January 27.
160. Annotation for Smithsonian box set *American Popular Song*, p. 85–86. William Zinsser in *Easy to Remember: The Great American Songwriters and Their Songs* (p. 117) similarly praises the melody's "chromatically descending half-tones" which by themselves define the song's title.

The song originated with a practice riff being played by Lawrence Brown, to which fellow trombonist Sam Nanton also contributed. Ellington built the piece from there, paying his two musicians fifteen dollars each for their contributions. The band's original May 16, 1933, recording of the song (issued on Brunswick 6600, with a renowned instrumental performance of *Stormy Weather* on the B side) featured solos by Toby Hardwick on tenor sax, Barney Bigard on clarinet, Brown, and Duke. One of the song's early admirers was George Gershwin, who was particularly taken by its melodic bridge. A 1945 waxing of the song was followed by an eight-minute rendition (including brief vocal by Yvonne Lanauze) in late 1950 for *Masterpieces by Ellington*, the first 12-inch jazz LP.

There have been many exceptional versions over the years, but it's impossible to top Rosemary Clooney's with the Ellington band itself. They had planned to record the album *Blue Rose* in the studio together—Duke's first full-length collaboration with any vocalist—but her advanced pregnancy with her fourth child made it impossible for her to travel. (She was also fed up with producer Mitch Miller's intrusive ways, and had resolved not to record again under his direction in New York.) So the Ellington orchestra recorded its part in New York at Columbia's East 30th Street studio in January; then Rosemary performed her vocals at the Radio Recorders studio in Los Angeles near her home, listening to the pre-taped backing tracks on headphones, supervised by Duke's collaborator Billy Strayhorn, who flew back and forth with lead sheets. David Hajdu: "Accustomed to working with a live orchestra surrounding her rather than with frozen accompaniment squeaking through a set of headphones, Clooney was jittery." But Strayhorn gently helped her through it.[161] She recalled in her autobiography: "We never laid our eyes on each other the whole time. But I felt like I was right in the middle of that band."[162]

The results were magical; the Ellingtonians are in top form, and Rosemary gives her trademark warmth to the melancholy lyrics. Will Friedwald, noting that "Clooney's darker tone" perfectly suited Ellington (who preferred deeper-toned singers more than other bandleaders), also praises Strayhorn's "mastery of the art of orchestration" as evidenced here. "The lyrics [to] Strayhorn and Ellington have never received a better hearing" than on this album.[163] Trumpeter Clark Terry recalled for Hajdu that he told Strayhorn: "That chart we just played"

of *Sophisticated Lady* "is really the most fantastic chart I have heard in a long time. And he said to me, 'Did you enjoy your part?' I'll never forget that . . . The man was always thinking about *you*."[164]

(Personnel: Cat Anderson, Willie Cook, & Clark Terry on trumpets; Ray Nance on cornet; Britt Woodman, John Sanders, & Quentin Jackson on trombones; Jimmy Hamilton on clarinet/tenor sax; Russell Procope on clarinet/alto sax; Johnny Hodges on alto sax; Paul Gonsalves on tenor sax; Harry Carney on baritone sax; Duke Ellington on piano; Jimmy Woode on bass; Sam Woodyard on drums)

Touch the Hem of His Garment (1956)—The Soul Stirrers (written by Sam Cooke)
Specialty 896
Recorded on February 2, 1956 (*GOSP-#23*)

For many Sam Cooke admirers, the most glorious singing of his too-short life came while singing gospel with the Soul Stirrers. Listening to the extraordinary performance on *Touch the Hem of His Garment* that showcases his soaring tenor to maximum effect, one can readily understand the basis for this conviction.

Cooke had joined the already-legendary group at age nineteen in late 1950 when its longtime lead singer R. H. Harris left, and by 1956 was one of the shining lights in the gospel world—not only as a singer with few equals in gospel history, but also as a brilliant songwriter, and a dazzlingly charismatic stage presence. According to legend, the group was driving to a recording session that February day, with Sam in the back clowning around, when S. R. Crain turned around and told him to cut it out, they needed another song for the session. Sam grabbed a Bible, began thumbing through it until he found something suitable in the book of Matthew, and began devising a song around the story with a borrowed guitar. By the time they arrived at the studio, he had completed *Touch the Hem of His Garment*. Producer Bumps Blackwell described the incident as evidence of "a God-endowed gift."

The song is based on an episode in Matthew 9:20 and 9:22 in which Jesus is walking in a crowd, and a sick woman comes up behind him and touches his robe. "If I only touch his cloak, I will be healed," she says to herself. Jesus assures the woman that her faith will make her whole, and she is miraculously healed. Cooke biographer Daniel Wolff cites the song's two-part narrative climaxing when Jesus turns and asked who touched him. "The song hinges on this moment of revelation, and when Sam sings 'It was I,' he holds the 'I' through a clear, sustained

161. Hajdu detailed the collaboration in his Strayhorn biography *Lush Life* (p. 146–49). With her husband José Ferrer in England directing and starring in a film, Strayhorn stayed at her home for a week, caring for her and even making her breakfast in bed in between their recording sessions.

162. *Girl Singer: An Autobiography*, p. 153.

163. *A Biographical Guide to the Great Jazz and Pop Singers*, p. 96. Gary Giddins agreed, calling this performance "one of the finest versions of

Sophisticated Lady on record." (Second annual *Oxford American Southern Music Issue* (1997), p. 149)

164. *Lush Life*, p. 146–49.

yodel that extends the moment, jacking up the tension and underlining how scared and determined the woman must have felt. The moment of identification—'I did it, I!'—works on another level, too. This 'I' could only be [Sam Cooke]; no one else turned a note like that; no one else stopped time in quite that way." In the chorus, his trademark "becomes the song: Sam curlicues, the rest echo. The remarkable thing is that it isn't just a mannerism: the yodel pushes the narrative forward, pulling us into the miracle itself."[165] Barely two minutes long, the performance is utterly riveting.

With sales of more than 27,000 copies according to Specialty data, *Touch the Hem* was one of Cooke's biggest successes with the Soul Stirrers, and served as a prelude for his move to pop one year later. Not until his masterpiece *A Change Is Gonna Come* would he fully match the power and emotion he achieved here. "The twists and turns of Cooke's phrasing" on this song, wrote Anthony DeCurtis, "create a shattering impact." Wolff: "When Sam took hold of a note . . . it wasn't the traditional nonverbal moan that Holiness congregations were used to. It wasn't a cry of pain. Instead, he decorated the note, embellishing the melody till it hung, fragile as lace, in the air over the congregation."[166]

Hound Dog (1956)—Elvis Presley
RCA 47-6604
Recorded on July 2, 1956; chart debut Aug. 4, 1956 (11
 weeks at #1, #1 for 6 weeks R&B)[167]; #2 in U.K.
 (*GHF-#53, NPR-100, RS-#19, Juke-#1, DMDB-#25,*
 RIA-#68, 1001, BBC-#46, ACC-#76, DM, TC, DET)

It shouldn't have worked. Jerry Leiber and Mike Stoller had written *Hound Dog* for blues belter Big Mama Thornton on her massive #1 R&B hit in 1953, and the lyrics just didn't make a lot of sense coming from a male perspective. After all, it's a number about a woman commenting disparagingly about a horny male suitor pawing at her door like a dog. But Elvis Presley not only made it work (albeit with changes in the lyrics that he only partially remembered from the original, and a modified melody), but made it one of the biggest smash singles of the rock era.

The idea for doing the song came during Presley's disastrous two-week engagement in Las Vegas starting at the end of April 1956. While there, relates biographer Peter Guralnick, Elvis went to catch the lounge act at the Sands, the white group Freddie Bell and the Bellboys, and was struck by their show-stopping arrangement of

Hound Dog (considerably faster than the original version and with a few new lyrics, most notably "you ain't never caught a rabbit and you ain't no friend of mine"); immediately, Elvis resolved to record it. "We stole it straight from them," confessed the King's lead guitarist Scotty Moore.[168] Presley already knew the song from Thornton's record, and was certain he could take it in a new direction. He and the band performed it live for two months (including a scandalously pelvis-thrusting, exuberant rendition on Milton Berle's TV show on June 5) before cutting it in the studio. They recorded it one day after Steve Allen had a self-conscious Elvis sing the number in tuxedo to a basset hound on his program.

Despite their experience with the number, as they led off the session with *Hound Dog*, seventeen takes had still not produced a satisfactory master. The drums weren't working right, Moore wasn't quite nailing his guitar part, and boogie pianist Shorty Long was having problems. But Presley never lost his concentration. Finally, on the eighteenth take, it began to come together: drummer D. J. Fontana's furious assault, Scotty's exciting solo, and Elvis cutting loose. Determined to achieve perfection, they kept going through thirteen more takes before producer Steve Sholes called a halt and suggested listening to playbacks. Al Wertheimer recalled that Presley crouched on the floor listening intently to the thirty-first take. "At the end of the song he slowly rose from his crouch and turned to us with a wide grin, and said, 'This is the one.'" After two hours devoted to recording one song, in the middle of summer with the air conditioner turned off due to the noise, they had a rock classic.

While Elvis' *Hound Dog* was soaring up the American charts, Mike Stoller was, along with 128 other passengers, aboard the Italian ocean liner the Andrea Doria. Returning home from a belated honeymoon in Europe, Stoller was caught up in the drama of the liner's collision with the Stockholm and its sinking in deep fog sixty miles south of Nantucket. When the songwriter was returned safely to New York on July 26, 1956, a relieved Jerry Leiber greeted him with the news of the unexpected smash cover version.[169] Leiber & Stoller, as blues purists, hated his light-hearted approach to their song, only

165. Wolff, *You Send Me*, p. 125–26.

166. Wolff, p. 99–100.

167. Presley had reached #3 on the R&B chart with his two previous singles; *Hound Dog* was his first of six #1 R&B hits over a three-year period.

168. Bell's group released *Hound Dog* as their debut single in 1955 on Teen 101; several months before Elvis' hit, the group was seen in the film *Rock Around the Clock*. There was also another link in the chain between the Thornton original and Elvis: George Moonoogian found a stylistic similarity between Frank Motley's 1954 sequel number *Mr. Hound Dog's in Town*, on the Big Town label, and the Freddie Bell record. (Article "Ain't Nothin' But a Hound Dog" by Moonoogian and Roger Meedem, June 1984, *Whiskey, Women, and . . .*)

169. When Presley decided to record *Hound Dog*, Hill & Range Songs, on behalf of Elvis Presley Music, bought half the publishing rights from Don Robey's publishing firm. Johnny Otis held part of the copyright through another publishing firm, Valjo, which filed suit against Elvis Presley Music and Leiber & Stoller, accusing them of conspiring to deprive Valjo of the song's publishing rights.

warming up to Elvis through their subsequent work together on the 1957 *Jailhouse Rock* soundtrack.

Named by the Amusement and Music Operators Association (AMOA) as the #1 juke box hit of all time in 1988 (with its flip side *Don't Be Cruel*), *Hound Dog* became the fourth rock & roll record inducted into the Grammy Hall of Fame in 1988.

Prelude to a Kiss (1957)—Duke Ellington & His Orchestra

Original issue on Brunswick 8204 (recorded on Aug. 9, 1938)[170]

Greatest version recorded in Oct. 1957 for the Columbia album *Ellington Indigos*; released in late Feb. 1958[171]

Prelude to a Kiss is one of the (in Ted Gioia's phrase) "meditative tone poems" that were a hallmark of Duke Ellington's work during the 1930s, alongside *Mood Indigo* and *Solitude*. He was "able to incorporate disparate stylistic devices into these mood pieces—plaintive blues calls, impressionistic harmonies, overtones of romantic ballads—without destroying the overall unity of the performance."[172] *Prelude to a Kiss*—particularly in its extraordinary 1957 Columbia version—is one of the most overwhelmingly romantic recordings ever made.

Johnny Hodges, the focal point of *Prelude*, was born in Cambridge, Massachusetts, on July 25, 1906. Mid-1920s stints with Willie "The Lion" Smith, Sidney Bechet, and (in 1926–1927) Chick Webb preceded his hiring by Ellington in 1928 (debut record session on June 5). Within a few years he was regarded as one of the foremost alto saxophonists in jazz and, as Duke lavished solo features on him, would be seen by many as second on the instrument only to Charlie Parker. After leaving Ellington to lead a small group from 1951–1955, he returned to remain an almost constant presence in the matchless ensemble until his death in 1970. Gioia writes that "no other player of his generation forged such a distinctively stylized approach to the saxophone . . . Hodges produced a tone so rich that even a single note could resonate with a universe of emotion."

Due to the very fortunate fact that many of Ellington's musicians stayed with the band for many years, they were able to so totally inhabit Duke's music that it became a part of their genetic makeup. Hodges had been the featured soloist on the original 1938 waxing of *Prelude* (playing the soprano instead of his customary alto) along with trombonist Lawrence Brown, and made it an imme-

diate Ellington standard. Gunther Schuller in *The Swing Era* calls it "one of Ellington's finest ballads, although too sophisticated in its weaving melody and chromatic harmonies to gain wide public acceptance."[173] But it was on the Columbia album *Ellington Indigos* nineteen years later that Hodges nailed the song like never before in an arrangement totally built around him. He soars, he plunges, he throbs, all but pouring out of the disc with passion, the very essence of swooning romance. If this is merely the prelude to a kiss, one wonders if what follows could possibly match it.

Peggy Sue (1957)—Buddy Holly

Coral 61885

Recorded in July 1957; chart debut Nov. 11, 1957 (#3 peak); reached #2 on R&B chart;[174] #4 in Canada, #6 in England (*NPR-100, RHF, GHF, PW, Juke-#37, ACC-#106, RS-#197, AHR, TC, DMDB*)

Hot on the heels of his breakthrough smash *That'll Be the Day* (but recorded before that song had hit the charts), Buddy Holly solidified his status with *Peggy Sue*. This one is defined from the opening seconds by its relentless, pounding beat that carries throughout the song, almost evoking an African jungle feeling and having a trance-like effect. Amazingly, this is a two-man performance: Holly on vocal and guitar, and Jerry Allison on drums. Thomas Ryan observes that Allison's "rolling sixteenth-note paradiddles (a standard drum exercise) are drenched in a rhythmic echo that propels the song while Holly sings about Peggy Sue, invoking her name over and over with dozens of varying inflections."[175] Originally titled "Cindy Lou," it was renamed (at the drummer's request) for Allison's girlfriend who would become his wife, Peggy Sue Gerron; the couple had just broken up, and Jerry wanted to woo her back. (The beautiful blonde had also been a friend of Holly's since high school.) The lyrics are childlike in their simplicity and repetition, but Holly belts them out with such conviction and sensuality that no one can doubt his intense ardor for this woman.

Holly had initially tried the song with a Latin or calypso tempo, which hadn't worked at all. Then Allison switched to the unbroken drumming sound, using a snare drum with the snares off. "When they tried the new beat, the song was completely transformed," writes biographer Ellis Amburn. Initially, it threw Holly off: "When the time came for the lead break, he discovered it was physically impossible to switch from the rhythm position to the lead position on his Fender Stratocaster." He solved

170. Another version of *Prelude*, this time with a vocal by Mary McHugh, was recorded two weeks later under Hodges' leadership.

171. Album reviewed in the March 3, 1958, *Billboard*.

172. Gioia, *History of Jazz*, p. 121, 184. Saxophonist Otto Hardwick is credited with contributing to the melody.

173. Schuller, p. 101–2.

174. The strong R&B chart performance of both *That'll Be the Day* and *Peggy Sue* reflected the records' appeal to black audiences; that's why the Crickets were booked onto an otherwise all-black tour in 1957.

175. *American Hit Radio*, p. 26–27.

Buddy Holly, courtesy of Library of Congress, LC-USZ52-125028.

the problem by instructing Niki Sullivan to kneel at his feet and throw the switch of his Strat the instant Buddy nodded.[176] [177] Jimmy Guterman calls Holly's playing on this record (consisting of nothing but downstrokes) "the greatest rhythm guitar solo in all rock 'n roll."[178] Producer Norman Petty (describes Amburn) jiggered the volume on Allison's mike, which gave the record "its erotic throbbing sensation." As he had done on *That'll Be the Day*, Petty claimed part songwriting credit, although by all other accounts but his own he had nothing to do with its writing.[179] The singer's drawn-out phrasing here, suggest David Dalton and Lenny Kaye, "is so enmeshed with the guitar it almost sounds as if his heart strings are literally being plucked."[180]

"With the mention of desire, the song breaks open," writes Paul Williams in *Rock and Roll: The 100 Best Singles*. "Hunger can be heard in the vocal, and Buddy goes into his lead guitar break, which is entirely and unforgettably a celebration of wanting . . . Intense." There

is, he writes, "something perfect about the sound of this song. It gets into the blood."[181]

All I Have to Do Is Dream (1958)—Everly Brothers
(written by Boudleaux & Felice Bryant)
Cadence 1348
Recorded in March 1958; chart debut Apr. 21, 1958 (5 weeks at #1 on pop chart; #1 for 3 weeks C&W; #1 for 5 weeks R&B) ; #1 for 7 weeks in U.K., #1 (5 weeks) in Canada (*GHF, RHF, PW, BMI-#33, DMDB-#91, RS-#142, DM, 1001, ACC*)

"This song has been running through my head for years and years," admits Paul Williams, including *All I Have to Do Is Dream* in his book *Rock and Roll: The 100 Best Singles*. "It's so pretty, so evanescent, so—dreamlike." He cites Richard Meltzer's term "heaven rock" to describe certain songs that are "immensely powerful, monstrously forceful and affecting, precisely because of [their] unearthly, mysterious lightness."[182] Phil and Don Everly's greatest ballad, from the prolific pens of the husband and wife team the Bryants who provided eleven of their hits from 1957–1960, became the angelic-voiced duo's biggest hit of all.

Felice was working as an elevator operator at a Milwaukee hotel when Boudleaux Bryant played there with a jazz band at their first encounter. She said she recognized his face immediately—for she had somehow seen him in a dream when she was eight years old. So the subject matter of dreams had a particular resonance in their lives. They wrote *All I Have to Do Is Dream* in just fifteen minutes.

Like all of the Everlys' best work on Cadence, this recording represents great beauty by careful design. The Everlys typically rehearsed their vocals for two or three days in advance of a session. They had access to the finest musicians in Nashville, often including Chet Atkins on guitar (featured on the unforgettable, tremulous intro here) and Floyd Cramer on piano.[183]

The brothers' "vocal texture combined with this subject matter (dreaminess, impotence, desire as a possession, longing, precious pleasurable sweet sadness) is so remarkable, so mysterious, so immediately familiar, so penetrating," exclaims Williams, that it probes straight to the heart. He points out that after the song's opening tremolo guitar chord by Atkins, it presents vocals all the way to the finish with no instrumental break. "Every

176. *Buddy Holly: A Biography*, p. 78–79.

177. In Bill Griggs' September 1978 *Goldmine* interview with Niki Sullivan, the "forgotten Cricket," Sullivan explained that he initially played rhythm guitar on *Peggy Sue* in unison with Holly. But because of Buddy's problem in getting his hand down to the switch to change from the song's bridge to the chorus while strumming rapidly, Sullivan stopped playing so he could move the switch for the singer, making it a two-man performance.

178. Guterman quoted by Amburn, *Buddy Holly: A Biography*, p. 79; see footnote 176.

179. Petty is negatively portrayed by Amburn, but Colin Escott, in the *Journal of Country Music*, Vol. 18 #1 (1996), p. 57, suggests that he deserves better. *Peggy Sue* "was every bit as much Petty's triumph as Holly's; Petty rides the fader on the drum microphone in time with the drumming, giving the record its hypnotic ebb and flow."

180. *Rock 100: The Greatest Stars of Rock's Golden Age*, p. 28.

181. Paul Williams, p. 35–36.

182. Williams, p. 41–42.

183. Cadence owner Archie Bleyer produced the session. However, by Don Everly's account (*Journal of Country Music*, Vol. 15 #2 (1993), constant arguments between Bleyer and Wesley Rose (head of Acuff-Rose publishing) meant that the Everlys, Chet Atkins, and Boudleaux Bryant effectively ran most of their sessions.

phrase leads into another, and always that wonderful trembling reading of 'dream' . . . God, I love it."

Solitude (1958)—Tony Bennett

Recorded on Dec. 30, 1958 with Count Basie & His Orchestra; originally from the Columbia album *In Person! With Count Basie*

Tony Bennett has always had a special love for the music of Duke Ellington, so it's appropriate that he turned in perhaps the definitive version of one of Duke's greatest ballads. *Solitude* was originally a big instrumental hit for the Ellington band as recorded on January 10, 1934; lyrics were subsequently added by Edgar DeLange and Irving Mills. This was the first of two albums he did with the mighty Basie band (the Count is conducting only, with Ralph Sharon taking his place at the keyboard and also arranging), including Thad Jones on trumpet and saxophonists Frank Foster and Frank Wess.[184] [185] Although the quality of the lyric falls short of Duke's melody (David Jenness and Don Velsey, in *Classic American Popular Song: The Second Half-Century, 1950–2000*, mocking the phrase "I sit in my chair / I'm filled with despair," suggest that the song should have remained an instrumental), Bennett delivers it with such emotional conviction that all doubts are swept aside. It was included on the Bennett compilation CD *Jazz*.

(Our) Love Is Here to Stay (1959)—Ella Fitzgerald

(written by George & Ira Gershwin)

From the Verve album *Ella Fitzgerald Sings the George and Ira Gershwin Song Book* (recorded on Jan. 5, 1959); *Cash Box* chart debut Dec. 19, 1959 (#44 peak)

As the Ella Fitzgerald *Song Books* series of albums provided vocal jazz with some of its most enduring classics starting with the 1956 Cole Porter set, the only criticism frequently heard was directed at Buddy Bregman's arrangements. But when Verve founder Norman Granz was able to recruit the foremost arranger in popular music, Nelson Riddle, for the wildly ambitious five-record George Gershwin songbook, the last reservation was wiped away: great singer and songs were finally given arrangements to match. Gary Giddins writes that Riddle "did some of his finest work" on this album,[186] and with Ella at the peak of her vocal powers, the result was magic. One of its many highlights was her warm, glow-

ing treatment of George Gershwin's last completed song, *Our Love Is Here to Stay.*

This is the ultimate version of the classic ballad to which Ira Gershwin crafted lyrics only after George's death in July 1937; Vernon Duke (composer of *April in Paris* among other songs) polished the finished product from Gershwin's own sketches and *American in Paris* co-star Oscar Levant's recollections of hearing Gershwin perform it in private gatherings. Gershwins biographer Deena Rosenberg notes that the melody "helps emphasize the stability, fulfillment, and permanence of love" against the background of a rapidly-changing and darkening world.[187] Introduced in the 1938 film *The Goldwyn Follies* by Kenny Baker, the song's most significant early recording was by Mildred Bailey with Red Norvo's band. Its most universally known version from that point until Ella was Gene Kelly's for the 1951 soundtrack of *An American in Paris*. Ella also did another wonderful version teaming with Louis Armstrong in 1957.

Tad Hershorn explored the genesis of the Song Book series in *Norman Granz: The Man Who Used Jazz for Justice*. Granz had become Ella's manager in 1953, and after clearing up her financial affairs, got her a series of prestigious engagements earning the singer the biggest paydays of her career to date. It was his involvement with the soundtrack for *The Benny Goodman Story* in 1955 that provided the opportunity for his longtime goal of recording Ella on his own label. Decca wanted to use Goodman veterans Teddy Wilson and Gene Krupa on the soundtrack, plus Stan Getz, all of whom were under contract to Granz. "Ever the wily bargainer, he knew he held all the cards." Granz offered to make the artists available in return for Decca releasing Ella from her contract (she'd been on the label from the start of her career with the Chick Webb band in 1936, and sold 22 million records there). The deal was made, and Ella's landmark series of albums devoted to the work of America's greatest songwriters began on Granz's Verve label (indeed the creation of the new label—which succeeded his previous labels such as Clef—was announced almost as soon as she left Decca).[188] With these eight albums, remarks Will Friedwald, "Fitzgerald left a definitive record of virtually every song that anybody would ever sing—and to a vast extent defined the parameters of what was becoming recognized as the Great American Songbook."[189]

(Nelson Riddle & His Orchestra: Don Fagerquist, Mannie Klein, Dale McMickle & Shorty Sherlock on trumpets; Milt Bernhart, Dick Noel & Tommy Pederson

---

184. Basie recorded for a different label, so a tradeoff was arranged: the *In Person* album was issued on Columbia, and *Bennett-Basie: Strike Up the Band* on Roulette.

185. Bennett recalls that Columbia taped him and the band in mono at the Latin Casino in Philadelphia, but when it was decided to do the album in stereo, he re-recorded the songs in the Columbia studio with a small crowd. (Friedwald, *Biographical Guide*, p. 44.)

186. Giddins, *Visions of Jazz*, p. 203.

187. Rosenberg, *Fascinating Rhythm*, p. 364–65.

188. Hershorn, *Norman Granz: The Man Who Used Jazz for Justice*, p. 215–16, excerpted in September 2011 *Jazz Times*.

189. Friedwald, *Biographical Guide*, p. 175. He calls Ella the possessor of "the loveliest voice in popular music."

on trombones; Karl DeKarske on bass trombone; Vincent DeRosa on French harp; Ted Nash on tenor sax; Buddy Collette, Harry Klee, Joe Koch & Champ Webb on woodwinds; Paul Smith on piano; Kathryn Julye on harp; Herb Ellis on guitar; Joe Comfort on bass; Frank Flynn & Alvin Stoller on drums)

Since I Don't Have You (1959)—The Skyliners (written by Joe Rock, Lennie Martin, James Beaumont, Janet Vogel, Walter Lester, Joe Verscharen, & John Taylor)

Calico 103

Recorded Dec. 3, 1958; chart debut Feb. 16, 1959 (#3 R&B, #12 pop)[190] (*DM-#36*)

Doo-wop heartbreak ballads just don't come any more richly romantic than this one. Formed as the Crescents in Pittsburgh (members were added from two other local groups, the Montereys and the El Rios), the Skyliners selected their new name after the Charlie Barnet big-band hit of the 1940s, and began auditioning for record labels. A demo tape with *Since I Don't Have You*, written by the group's members along with their manager Joe Rock,[191] was rejected by more than a dozen companies before finding a home at the tiny Pittsburgh-based Calico label. After the Skyliners performed it on *American Bandstand*, the record took off (within three days of the broadcast it had sold 100,000 copies). Although the group was white, the record was a bigger R&B smash than it was in the pop market, perhaps because it recalled some of the best black balladeers such as the Platters.

A love song filled with desperate yearning, *Since I Don't Have You* is a gorgeous composition that is exceeded only by the power of its performance here. Lead singer Jimmy Beaumont is exceptional—just savor his swooping leaps into falsetto on the line "I-I-I don't have anything"—and soprano Janet Vogel brings the song to a spectacular conclusion with what Bob Hyde calls "the astonishing high-C finale."[192] The group is accompanied by Lenny Martin's orchestra, with some eighteen musicians, a remarkably lush production for a small company. The Skyliners had a few subsequent hits, including *This I Swear* and a doo-wop cover of *Pennies from Heaven*, Beaumont recorded as a solo act, and he formed a revamped version of the group in the 1970s.

My Funny Valentine (1959)—Tony Bennett (music by Richard Rodgers, lyrics by Lorenz Hart)

Recorded on Oct. 28, 1959 for the Columbia album *Tony Sings for Two* (*APS*)

For a number that's long been accepted as one of the great American love songs, *My Funny Valentine* is a savagely dark piece of lyric writing by Lorenz Hart, providing an edginess that's a fascinating counterpoint to the loveliness of Richard Rodgers' melody. Hart, deeply insecure due to his short stature (just under five feet) and his outsider status as a bisexual, channeled his insecurities into some of the most biting, and superbly crafted, lyrics ever penned, and *Valentine* holds a lofty place among them. The warm sentiment of love expressed late in the song, remarked Stephen Holden, "doesn't really make up for the stinging criticisms preceding it. *My Funny Valentine* is a wounding love song."[193]

It was written by Rodgers and Hart for the Broadway musical *Babes in Arms*, which opened in April 1937 and was an immediate hit. The show's lead character was Val Le Mar—short for Valentine; after the composers finished the song, writes Will Friedwald, "they decided it was so strong it could further tie the plot to the score if the lead character happened to be named Valentine." Mitzi Green introduced it in the show, but while *Where or When* and *The Lady is a Tramp* became the production's big hits, *Valentine* didn't really emerge on its own until after World War II. Mabel Mercer made it a staple of her New York cabaret act, Margaret Whiting became the first major vocalist to record it by 1950, and then Frank Sinatra ensured its status as an important standard by making it the opening track for his 1954 Capitol album *Songs for Young Lovers*.

Alec Wilder writes in *American Popular Song*: "This song must have meant a great deal to both writers. The lyrics show Hart's ability to keep his detachment and sympathy in perfect balance." He calls the climax "remarkable," as Rodgers carries the melody an octave higher, "with fuller harmony and fitting the climax of the lyric, 'stay, little Valentine, stay!'"[194] Friedwald made it one of the twelve great songs he examined at length in his book *Stardust Melodies*.[195] He singles out for praise its harmony line, which "is so strong it's practically another melody, giving the song an almost contrapuntal feeling. Essentially, the harmony line for the central part of the melody is a chromatically descending line"; the song's three sections are in minor, with an occasional major chord thrown in for variety.

190. It reached #1 on the *Cash Box* R&B chart, the first white group to achieve that.

191. According to Jay Warner (*Billboard Book of Singing Groups*, p. 293), Rock wrote the lyric about a girl who had just left him, and Beaumont came up with the music the next night.

192. *Doo Wop Box* annotation, p. 62. Tenor Wally Lester was only fourteen at the time of the recording; the others were all sixteen or seventeen.

193. Holden, April 30, 1995, *New York Times*, p. H-36.

194. Wilder, p. 205–7.

195. Friedwald, p. 349–73.

"Rodgers' harmonic ambiguity is directly reflected in Hart's melancholy, but not bleak, lyric," he continues. "What makes the whole thing so remarkable is the happy/sad nature of the lyric, brilliantly mirroring the major/minor nature of the music." The craftsmanship of Hart's lyric "is impeccable—as in the famous rhyme of 'laughable' and 'unphotographable'—who but Hart would have come up with a musical comedy love song in which the declaration of love is conveyed as a list of the other person's faults? The message is that love doesn't exist despite these failings but perhaps because of them; these touches of humanity are, in the end, what endear the other to us."

Perhaps the finest of the many outstanding renditions of *My Funny Valentine* was offered by Tony Bennett, accompanied only by his longtime pianist, Ralph Sharon. The slow, stripped-down arrangement brings out the song's sterling qualities (although Bennett softens the bite by excluding the verse). Friedwald notes that with the song in F major, "we expect Bennett to go up to high E on the second 'stay'; instead, he surprises us by shooting a third higher and hitting high G." The duet ends as Sharon throws in a brief quote from *Greensleeves*.

Sweet Sixteen (1960)—B.B. King

Kent 330

Recorded in Los Angeles on Oct. 26, 1959; chart debut Jan. 18, 1960 (#2 R&B) (*Blues-#129*)

This impassioned, revised performance of a song first recorded by Walter Davis with Big Joe Williams in 1935 is one of B.B. King's undeniable classics, split into two parts for its single release. It was also a #3 R&B hit for Joe Turner in 1952, and the song had belonged to him until King took it to an entirely higher level. Biographer Sebastian Danchin sums up this performance: "Nostalgia for the first moments of love, a woman's failure to understand, a man's surrender, wounded male pride that feels it must protest, family break-up and loneliness: in a few simple words, *Sweet Sixteen* draws a picture of the sociology of black America . . ."[196] Charlie Gillett: The record "used a strong blues riff behind King's voice and guitar and built up into one of the most dramatic blues performances ever recorded, with gospel inflections dominating King's singing at the end of the two-part performance."[197]

"Imagine the history of blues guitar-playing as a railroad map, criss-crossed with lines of development and influence, B.B. King is a major junction, the Grand Central

Station of post-war blues," declares Tony Russell. "Here the West Coast tracks of T-Bone Walker and Lowell Fulson meet the Chicago blues of Buddy Guy and Magic Sam and the Southern railway that stretches north from Memphis and Mississippi, carrying the musical freight of Elmore James and Muddy Waters."[198]

Rank Strangers (1960)—Stanley Brothers (written by Albert E. Brumley)

Starday 506[199]

Recorded in Jacksonville, Florida c. March 1960;[200] released in Aug. 1960 (*HBN-#9, C&W-#42, DM-#99, RR*)

Albert E. Brumley was one of the best-loved writers of sacred and sentimental songs during the early decades of country music; Carter and Ralph Stanley were rivaled only by Bill Monroe and Flatt & Scruggs among the royalty of bluegrass music. When these two musical forces came together on *Rank Strangers*, the result was a classic recording.

The Brown's Ferry Four (Grandpa Jones, Alton and Rabon Delmore, and Merle Travis, with Travis later succeeded by Red Foley) were more responsible than anyone else for making Albert Brumley songs a standard part of country music repertoire, with their late-1940s recordings of *I'll Fly Away, I'll Meet You In the Morning, Jesus Hold My Hand*, and *If We Never Meet Again*, among others. During the pre-1950 era, the main counterpart to *I'll Fly Away* as Brumley's best-known song was *Turn Your Radio On*, which he wrote especially for the Dallas group the Stamps Quartet. Brumley's songs (writes Bill Malone) "equated home and Christian morality, and they cautioned against straying too far afield from the values and moral strength of the old homestead . . . These nostalgic but potent visions of a celestial antidote to a decaying rural society, combined with the hope for security and reconciliation beyond the grave, made Brumley's songs irresistible to thousands of people in the Depression and World War II–era South."[201]

Rank Strangers, written in 1942,[202] is a stark, harrowing account of a man who spent years away from his

---

196. Sebastian Danchin, *Blues Boy: The Life and Music of B.B. King*, p. 50–51.

197. *The Sound of the City: The Rise of Rock and Roll*, p. 173.

198. Russell, *The Blues: From Robert Johnson to Robert Cray*, p. 74.

199. Starday 506 listed the song's title as *Rank Stranger* (singular), and Ralph Stanley's autobiography also uses the singular. But the term is pluralized in the lyrics, and it is generally known with the plural title. The release date was provided by the online Bluegrass Discography.

200. Recording date according to Sony boxed set *Can't You Hear Me Callin'?: Bluegrass: 80 Years of American Music*, p. 37.

201. Bill Malone, *Don't Get Above Your Raisin': Country Music and the Southern Working Class*, p. 99.

202. The song was never copyrighted (indeed, despite his great output, Brumley is mostly absent from records in the Copyright Office of the Library of Congress). More surprisingly, *Rank Stranger* does not appear in any of the several compilations of religious songs that he published from

mountain home, finally returning to find that everything had changed, and everyone a stranger, with all their loved ones gone. What happened? Bill Friskics-Warren in *Heartaches By the Number* (ranking it as the #9 greatest country single) suggests that perhaps, given the strip-mining that had ravaged the Carters' Clinch Mountains, the brothers' friends and kin had moved away in search of arable land elsewhere, or perhaps it even describes life during nuclear winter. But this doesn't account for "how the people and places haven't just changed, how they haven't merely aged or been disfigured by some cataclysmic upheaval, but are different—fundamentally altered. The feeling of spiritual alienation the Stanleys convey, estrangement akin to that of Robert Johnson's *Stones in My Passway* or Blind Willie Johnson's *Dark Was the Night, Cold Was the Ground*, is stone cold absolute."[203]

Friskics-Warren offers an alternative, that "the dystopia depicted in *Rank Strangers* isn't so much a physical place (although it's certainly that) as a moral condition." This makes the record a counterpart to the Monroe Brothers' 1936 classic *What Would You Give In Exchange for Your Soul*. Ralph Stanley opens the chorus in "a piercing, unearthly tenor," before Carter picks up the vocal, and Curley Lambert's mandolin "keens inconsolably" in the background.[204] The stranger informs them that "their loved ones have gone on to their homes in glory. The stranger trusts he'll also reach that beautiful place by and by, but whether the Stanleys will join him there isn't clear. Adrift in some internal limbo, Ralph's aggrieved wailing floats, untethered, on the chorus, making it plain that, for now, the brothers are stuck in a living hell."

Having recorded for Rich-R-Tone, Columbia, and Mercury before signing with Starday in 1958, the Stanleys left the latter label after this final session,[205] and went on to record fifteen albums for the King label until Carter's death in 1966.

The Library of Congress inducted the record into the National Recording Registry in 2008.[206] "Schematically, *Rank Strangers* is a folk tale, with an air of legend and miracle, the ashes and dust from which the Ur-myth

of rock and country and soul wanderlust is fashioned," muses Dave Marsh. "The returning native in *Rank Strangers* represents many things—a Christian adrift in the temporal world, a sinner trying to storm the gates of heaven." The song is "a gorgeous example of how the most elementary kinds of American music came to life in those postwar years, an elegantly composed metaphor for the psychic stress that people not only endured but used to craft into something approaching art in those days of cultural turmoil."[207]

Will You Love Me Tomorrow? (1960)—The Shirelles
(music by Carole King, lyrics by Gerry Goffin)
Scepter 1211 (originally issued under the title "Tomorrow")
Chart debut Nov. 21, 1960 (2 weeks at #1 on pop chart; #2 for 4 weeks R&B); reached #2 in Canada, #4 in England (*R&B-#43, RHF, GHF, DM-#105, ACC-#110, RS-#125, RIA-#179, 1001, DMDB*)

Called "an astonishingly honest (for 1960) restatement of the old 'will you still respect me in the morning' theme,"[208] *Will You Love Me Tomorrow* is one of the era's shining pop music gems. The song demonstrated that even as the songsmiths of New York's Brill Building served as an assembly line of tunes for teenagers, very real issues could be touchingly addressed within the pop framework.

The Passaic, New Jersey, quartet of Shirley Owens, Beverly Lee, Doris Kenner, and Addie "Micki" Harris were inseparable girlfriends who came together in junior high school as the Poquellos, and first recorded as the Shirelles for Tiara in 1958. Managed by Florence Greenberg, who ran the small Scepter label that she had founded (just as she had launched Tiara) and was the mother of a classmate, the girls had a minor hit in 1958 with *I Met Him On a Sunday*, first cracked the Top 40 two years later with *Tonight's the Night*, and then scaled the pop stratosphere with this record. Greenberg was the only female head of a significant record label at the time, and was known for fighting "tooth and nail" on behalf of her artists.

Carole King had recorded a few songs as a teenager in 1958–1959, but she and Gerry Goffin were still getting established as songwriters at the Brill Building, working at Aldon Music under Don Kirshner, when *Will You Love Me Tomorrow* became their first smash not long after they were married. (Technically, the Aldon publishing firm, like some of the other songwriters popularly associated with the Brill Building name, was located at 1650 Broadway, the Music Building, across the street from

1946–1953. It also appears that no one had recorded the song before the Stanleys.

203. *Heartaches By the Number: Country Music's 500 Greatest Singles*, p. 7–8.

204. Ralph Mayo is on guitar.

205. The session was held at Magnum Records, a small studio in Jacksonville, utilizing an Ampex 400 reel-to-reel tape recorder. Its makeshift echo chamber (as described by Magnum partner Tom Rose in the July 2000 *Bluegrass Unlimited*) was a large tank, formerly used as a storage unit at a gas station, with the sound funneled through a speaker mic inside. Thanks to engineer Tom Markham, the sound quality and effects were impeccable.

206. Ralph Stanley offered the pointed comment in *Man of Constant Sorrow: My Life and Times* (p. 195) that this selection was "quite an honor, especially when you consider that the Stanley Brothers still ain't in the Country Music Hall of Fame."

207. *The Heart of Rock & Soul*, p. 70–71.

208. Greg Shaw, *Rolling Stone Illustrated History of Rock & Roll*, p. 124.

the Brill Building's famous 1619 Broadway address.) Scepter happened to also have its headquarters at 1650 Broadway. The story goes that Luther Dixon, who served as the Shirelles' producer, owed King and Goffin a favor and offered them the opportunity write a song for the group. Carole's melody inspired Goffin; the night before the scheduled session he swiftly completed the lyrics, and shortly after midnight they finished the song's bridge together. The songwriters said they were influenced by the Drifters' *Save the Last Dance for Me*; although the songs are quite different melodically, they have similar chord structures. Dixon had written *Tonight's the Night*, and that song's story line was carried forward with *Will You Love Me Tomorrow*. Oddly enough, Shirley Owens hated Carole's voice/piano demo of the song, which she thought sounded too country & western, and the group was also concerned that its story line might be too suggestive for radio; she had to be virtually coerced into recording it. With Shirley's fervently earnest lead vocal and a lush string arrangement crafted by King and conducted by Dixon, the song struck an immediate chord, and became the first girl-group record to top the charts in over five years, and the first #1 by a black girl group. The record's B side, *Boys*, was later covered by the Beatles. The Shirelles went on to enjoy a string of twelve Top 40 hits through 1963 including *Dedicated to the One I Love*, *Baby It's You*, and *Soldier Boy*, and continued recording into the 1970s.

"The quaver in Shirley Owens's lead vocal and the dramatic ironies and deliberate contradictions in Goffin's lyrics create a tension that aches to the point of excruciation," writes Ken Emerson.[209] The narrative was based in large part on the couple's own experience: King became pregnant in the summer of 1959, and, aged seventeen and twenty, they were married on August 30. She dropped out of college and worked as a secretary until late in her pregnancy, and Goffin worked at a chemical plant; they wrote songs at night. Therefore the dilemma of teenage sex, pregnancy, and commitment was not merely the pretext to a song, but central to their own lives. When it soared to the top, Kirshner and King took a limousine to Goffin's chemical plant, presented him with a $10,000 check, and told him he didn't have to work there anymore.

Dave Marsh suggests that it is perhaps the King-Goffin song most likely to endure longest, "not only for its beautiful melody . . . but because its lyric defines a certain stage of female teenage sexuality, a subject difficult to put into song without pandering and almost impossible to render with this much pathos." He praises Dixon's arrangement with riffing strings generating a churning

pizzicato that "exquisitely" sets up Owens' "guileless" vocal, her best performance ever.[210] Thomas Ryan called the record "the salvo shot that signaled the arrival of a feminine perspective in rock and roll music."[211]

Susan J. Douglas dedicated the title of a chapter to the group ("Why the Shirelles Mattered") in her book *Where the Girls Are*. "Even though this song was about sex, it didn't rely on the musical instrument so frequently used to connote sex in male rockers' songs, the saxophone. Saxes were banished, as were electric guitars; instead, an entire string section of an orchestra provided the counterpoint to Shirley Owens's haunting, earthy, and provocative lead vocals." While her voice "vibrated with teen girl angst and desire, grounding the song in fleshly reality, violin arpeggios fluttered through like birds, and it was on their wings that [our] erotic desires took flight and gained a more acceptable spiritual dimension. It was this brilliant juxtaposition of the sentimentality of the violins and the sensuality of the voice that made the song so perfect, because it was simultaneously lush and spare, conformist and daring, euphemistic yet dead-on honest." Not only was it about longing and desire, "it was about having a choice. For these girls, the decision to have sex was now a choice, and *this* was new. This was, in fact, revolutionary. Girl group music gave expression to our struggles with the possibilities and dangers of the Sexual Revolution."[212]

The Lion Sleeps Tonight (1961)—The Tokens (adapted/written by George David Weiss, Hugo Peretti, Luigi Creatore, & Albert Stanton)
RCA 7954
Chart debut Nov. 13, 1961 (3 weeks at #1); #1 in Canada, #11 in England[213] (*RIA-#159, DM-#309, AHR, WASH-#58, Folk-#63, DMDB*)

When the Brooklyn-based doo-wop group the Tokens scored a massive #1 hit in 1961 with *The Lion Sleeps Tonight*, it was well known that they were adapting a folk tune with African roots recorded a decade earlier by the Weavers known as *Wimoweh*. Few realized at the time that the song had originated in 1939 as a song entitled *Mbube* by the South African group of Zulu tribesmen Solomon Linda and the Original Evening Birds, or that Linda's hauntingly lovely record—which Pete Seeger of the Weavers had acquired and reworked for his group in 1952—had been the biggest hit in black Africa prior to 1950, selling some 100,000 copies. South African native Miriam Makeba also recorded the song in 1952.

209. *Always Magic in the Air: The Bomp and Brilliance of the Brill Building Era*, p. 90–91.

210. *The Heart of Rock & Soul*, p. 76–77.
211. *American Hit Radio*, p. 68.
212. *Where the Girls Are: Growing Up Female with the Mass Media*, p. 84–85.
213. #1 in New Zealand, #6 in Belgium.

The Tokens were formed under the name the Linc-Tones at Lincoln High School in Brooklyn in 1955, two of the members being Hank Medress and future pop star Neil Sedaka, and they recorded a single as the Tokens for the Melba label in 1956. Following its breakup in 1958, Medress formed Darrell & the Oxfords, then launched a new Tokens in 1960 with lead singer Jay Siegel and brothers Phil and Mitch Margo, and began recording for Warwick. Their delightful doo-wop number *Tonight I Fell in Love* was a Top 15 hit in early 1961.

Because the group (and Siegel in particular) had loved the Weavers record (Siegel brought that group's Carnegie Hall concert album to one of their rehearsals),[214] their producers Hugo Peretti and Luigi Creatore hired George Weiss (co-writer of Elvis Presley's *Can't Help Falling in Love*) to write new English lyrics, and together they crafted a fresh arrangement. According to the official account, Weiss had no idea that "mbube" is the Zulu word for "lion," that Solomon Linda was singing "Hush! Hush! . . . If we're all quiet, there'll be lion meat for dinner," and came up on his own with the tale of the lion slumbering in the village. For the recording session, operatic soprano Anita Darien was added to double the sax solo at the top of her range; but the primary virtuosity here is the soaring falsetto of Jay Siegel, with the group's finely-honed backing harmonies.

Medress formed his own label B. T. Puppy in 1964, and—with the group having gained valuable experience by producing *The Lion* themselves—produced hits by the Chiffons (*He's So Fine*), and the Happenings (including *See You in September* and *I Got Rhythm*) that were noteworthy for their creative vocal arrangements, also producing records by other artists. After the Tokens scored their last chart hit in 1970, the group stayed busy recording TV commercial jingles. Medress produced Tony Orlando & Dawn, and left the Tokens, which continued as the duo of the Margo brothers under the name Cross Country and landed a Top 30 hit in 1973 with their remake of *In the Midnight Hour*. The Tokens' original hit recording of *The Lion* hit the singles chart again in 1994 following its inclusion in the blockbuster soundtrack for the Disney animated classic *The Lion King*.

Can't Help Falling in Love (1961)—Elvis Presley (written by George David Weiss, Hugo Peretti & Luigi Creatore)[215]
RCA 47-7968

Recorded at Radio Recorders in Hollywood on March 23, 1961;[216] chart debut Dec. 4, 1961 (#2 peak); 4 weeks at #1 in England (with its flip side *Rock-a-Hula Baby*); #1 (5 weeks) in Australia;[217] from the soundtrack album *Blue Hawaii* (20 weeks at #1); (*RS, DM, WASH-#13, BBC, DMDB*)

Rivaled only by *Love Me Tender* and *Are You Lonesome Tonight?* as Elvis' definitive snuggle-up-close love ballad, *Can't Help Falling in Love* was adapted from the eighteenth century melody *Plaisir d'Amour* (by Italian composer Giovanni Martini) to become the theme from Presley's biggest movie soundtrack, *Blue Hawaii*. The closing number in just about every Elvis concert from 1969 to the end, it was ranked as the #4 all-time favorite oldie in combined 1973–1980 listener surveys by WASH-FM, and the #7 favorite oldie in eleven combined surveys (1994–2004) by WBIG-FM, both in Washington, D.C.

Here, writes Dave Marsh, "Elvis fashioned one of the great ballad performances of his career, singing with such gentle insistence ('Shall I stay' pronounced as if the words are fragile as crystal) that the corniness of the arrangement, with the Jordanaires mixed too high in the background and a steel guitar intruding on everything, makes little or no difference." The song emerges as "a confession of Presley's complete surrender to the whims of forces greater than he can comprehend. 'Like the river flows, surely to the sea / Darling so it goes, some things are meant to be' is not a declaration of devotion, but an acknowledgment of powerlessness. Whether true or not, this is what Elvis Presley believed and that is why he renders the song with such tremendous conviction."[218]

So Much In Love (1963)—The Tymes (written by Roy Straigis, William Jackson & George Williams)
Parkway 871
Chart debut June 1, 1963 (1 week at #1 on pop chart, #4 R&B); #13 in Canada, #21 in England[219] (*RIA-#215, DM*)

It opens with the sound of waves rolling gently onto a beach, birds chirping, and fingers snapping, and the Tymes' *So Much In Love* builds from there as a gorgeous street-corner harmony ballad harking back to the golden age of doo-wop.

The Philadelphia quintet began in 1956 as the Latineers with tenors George Hilliard and Albert Berry, baritone Norman Burnett, and bass Donald Banks. George Williams came aboard as lead singer in 1961 with a

214. Warner, *Billboard Book of American Singing Groups*, p. 466.
215. Weiss' long list of co-writing credits ranges from Kay Starr's chart-topping *Wheel of Fortune* and the English adaptation of *The Lion Sleeps Tonight* to Louis Armstrong's *What a Wonderful World*. Hugo Peretti and Luigi Creatore, who collaborated with him on *The Lion*, were best known as pop producers for artists including Sam Cooke.
216. His backing band for the session includes Scotty Moore and Hank Garland on guitars and Bob Moore on bass.
217. #1 in South Africa, #2 in New Zealand.
218. Marsh, *The Heart of Rock & Soul*, p. 489–90.
219. #5 in New Zealand.

sweetly supple tenor strongly reminiscent of Johnny Mathis (a lovely revival of Mathis' hit *Wonderful, Wonderful* would be their second single), and they became the Tymes. The Philly-based label Parkway signed them in April 1963 after the group performed at a talent show sponsored by radio station WDAS. They made enough of an impression that they were directed to Billy Jackson, A&R director at Cameo-Parkway. Williams had written the melody and first verse of a romantic number he called *The Stroll*.[220] Producer Jackson and arranger Roy Straigis finished the song; it was Jackson's idea to add the seashore sounds, and to change the title. Released right at the start of summer, *So Much In Love* became a perfect seasonal pleasure for all the lazy Augusts of our mind.[221]

Since I Fell for You (1963)—Lenny Welch (written by Buddy Johnson)
Cadence 1439[222]
Recorded on Aug. 13, 1963; chart debut Oct. 26, 1963 (#4 peak)[223]

In its original incarnation, *Since I Fell for You* was performed by Buddy Johnson's big band on November 7, 1945, (on Decca 48016) as a ballad vehicle for his sister and primary vocalist, Ella Johnson. Although Ella was an intriguing and offbeat singer who had a devoted following, her voice was modest at best and that recording rated as pleasant but not truly memorable. Annie Laurie with Paul Gayten's combo scored a #3 R&B hit with it in 1947, and it was a favorite of doo-wop groups, including the Harptones (1954) and the Spaniels (1956). Buddy's tune finally became one of the all-time ravishing, swooning love ballads as masterfully rendered by Lenny Welch.

Born on May 15, 1938, in New York City and raised in Asbury Park, New Jersey, Welch was signed at nineteen by A&R man/bandleader Archie Bleyer, made his recording debut in 1958 for Decca, and just one of his first seven singles for Cadence (the haunting country ballad *You Don't Know Me* in 1960) made the charts by mid-1963. *Since I Fell for You* changed his fortunes in a hurry. Welch's big, soaring tenor was perfect for this emotionally anguished musical valentine of unrequited passion, wrapped up in ultra-lush orchestration that seems not at all excessive but tailor-made for the occasion. When he chokes up on the line, "But what can I do, I'm still in love with you," you absolutely believe he's the most des-

perately lovesick guy on the planet. The emotions of the song proved unexpectedly resonant as it dominated the airwaves during the weeks after the JFK assassination.

Welch scored a few subsequent hits using the same approach of reviving smoochy love ballads, most notably *Ebb Tide* (1964) and a vastly slowed-down arrangement of Neil Sedaka's *Breaking Up Is Hard to Do* (1970) that would be borrowed several years later by Sedaka himself. He has pursued a side career as an actor (including appearances on *General Hospital*), and remained an active performer (ranging from shows in Radio City Music Hall and Las Vegas to singing in TV ad campaigns) well into the 2000s.

Twist and Shout (1964)—The Beatles (written by Bert Berns)
Tollie 9001
Recorded Feb. 11, 1963; chart debut March 14, 1964 (4 weeks at #2);[224] from the album *Introducing The Beatles* (chart debut Feb. 8, 1964, spent 9 weeks at #2); reissued on Capitol 5624 to chart again on Aug. 9, 1986 (#23 peak) (*DM-#177*)

At 10 p.m. on that February 1963 evening, near the conclusion of a marathon recording session for the Beatles' U.K. debut album *Please Please Me*, the boys still needed one more song. The Isley Brothers' 1962 hit *Twist and Shout* had been a part of the quartet's live show for months, so it was a natural choice. John Lennon—nursing a sore throat after spending nearly all day in the studio—took some medication and found the energy for two all-out assaults on the song, stripped to the waist.[225] After the album was released in the U.K. in late March, the Tremeloes hit #4 on the British chart with their own cover version. Almost simultaneously, the Beatles released their first extended play album, with *Twist and Shout* the title number and including three other songs; it too got to #4.

When Beatlemania hit America the following January, Vee Jay Records included *Twist and Shout* on their album *Introducing the Beatles*. The frenzied crowd response greeting the group's performance of the song on their third *Ed Sullivan Show* performance on February 23 led Vee Jay to release it as a single on its Tollie label; it shot swiftly to #2 and reportedly sold a million copies within three weeks.

Producer George Martin recalled that this was one number that "always caused a furor" in the group's performances at Liverpool's Cavern Club. "John absolutely screamed it. God alone knows what he did to his larynx each time he performed it, because he made a sound

220. Warner, *Billboard Book of American Singing Groups*, p. 470.

221. After the hits ran dry following a 1968 Top 40 version of *People*, the Tymes returned in a more strongly R&B vein with the 1974 hit *You Little Trustmaker*.

222. Columbia acquired the Welch master from Cadence, and reissued it in January 1967 on Columbia 44007 (William Brown, *The Columbia Records (U.S.) 35000–40000 Series: Popular Singles Discography, 1939–1974*).

223. #2 in New Zealand, #19 in Canada.

224. #2 in New Zealand, #5 in Canada, #7 Norway, #10 Germany. *Twist and Shout* was not issued as a single in England.

225. McDonald, *Revolution in the Head*, p. 76.

rather like tearing flesh."[226] At least one writer has suggested that Lennon's intensity in turning the song into a "shrieking catharsis" can be seen as a prelude to his subsequent embrace of psychologist Arthur Janov's "primal scream" therapy.[227]

Bert Berns, a Bronx-raised son of Russian Jewish immigrants, wrote *Twist and Shout* under the dual pseudonyms of Bert Russell and Phil Medley. Berns also wrote or co-wrote such other hits as *Cry Baby, Hang On Sloopy*, and *Piece of My Heart*, and co-founded the record labels Bang (where Neil Diamond got his start) and Shout, before his untimely death in December 1967.

Dave Marsh notes that the ferocious excitement of Lennon's vocal—which makes the Isleys' original "seem absolutely tame" by comparison—is only part of the record's appeal. "There's a lightness in the harmonies and in the guitar parts that bespeaks the complete empathy" of men who had grown up together and thought as one. And anyone who can resist those exuberant Lennon-McCartney 'ahhh's' just plain doesn't like rock and roll."[228]

The featured role that *Twist and Shout* played on the soundtracks of the comedies *Ferris Bueller's Day Off* and Rodney Dangerfield's *Back to School* gave the song yet another life with a hit reissue.

Chimes of Freedom (1965)—The Byrds (written by Bob Dylan)
Recorded in March 1965
From the Columbia album *Mr. Tambourine Man* (chart debut June 26, 1965, reached #6)[229]

Chimes of Freedom, writes Oliver Trager, "is a jewel in Dylan's poetic crown. Employing all the pigments available on his ample poetic palette, Dylan utilizes a triple-whammy of the alliterative inscape of Gerard Manley Hopkins, the organic vision of William Blake, and Shakespeare's violent sense of drama in his creation of this powerfully compassionate paean to the downtrodden with a romantic sweep of language and universality. In his mixed-sensorial suggestion that freedom's chimes flash, Dylan dangles the notion that humanity has yet to grasp the promises of liberty floating just out of reach, like a feather caught by the wind."[230]

The song "depicts a world where the bells are tolling amid great changes and upheaval across the globe, evocative of Native America's vision of 'A Great Cleansing,'" says Trager. Its opening seems to foreshadow a time of darkness. "But the sun slowly rises over the course of the song and his hope here is nothing short of all the world's people rising as one to proclaim their survival . . . after another tough night on history's dangerous road; as the sounds of chiming church bells fill the air, the storm clears and dawn breaks."

Dylan included it on his fourth album *Another Side of Bob Dylan*. Even before The Byrds carried the composer's *Mr. Tambourine Man* to chart-topping glory in mid-1965, the group began recording its debut album, and *Chimes* was one of its centerpieces. As with all of the Byrds' recordings of Dylan songs, it features a rich and inventive arrangement, Roger McGuinn's emotionally searching lead vocal and riveting twelve-string Rickenbacker guitar solos, and the lush, shimmering harmonies of David Crosby, Gene Clark, Chris Hillman, and Michael Clarke.

When Bruce Springsteen led an Amnesty International tour promoting the cause of human rights for all in 1988, its theme song was *Chimes of Freedom*, used as the climax of each show with all the performers coming together and trading verses. In its cry on behalf of political prisoners, "the aching ones whose wounds cannot be nursed," and ultimately "every hung-up person in the whole wide universe," a more perfect ode to freedom cannot be imagined.

The Tracks of My Tears (1965)—The Miracles (written by Smokey Robinson, Warren Moore & Marvin Tarplin)
Tamla 54118
Chart debut July 10, 1965 (#2 on R&B chart, #16 pop)[231] (*R&B-#21, DM-#46, RS-#50, RHF, GHF, RR, RIA, ACC-#44, 1001, DMDB*)

"Life's illusions and contradictions are at the heart of Smokey Robinson's best songs," wrote *Rolling Stone* in ranking this song #12 among the 100 best songs of the past twenty-five years in 1988. "*The Tracks of My Tears* stands alone as the finest example of Robinson's ability to create tales of exquisite love and sadness, and as his most heartfelt vocal performance."[232]

The song was created at Robinson's Detroit home with Smokey, fellow Miracle Warren Moore, and the Miracles' guitarist Marv Tarplin. As Tarplin played licks

226. Martin, *All You Need Is Ears*, p. 131.
227. Tim Riley, *Tell Me Why*, p. 59–60: As the band relentlessly builds momentum and roars into the final verse with hysterical screams, it's "the musical equivalent of an orgasm, and it counts among the most exciting moments in all their music."
228. Marsh, *The Heart of Rock & Soul*, p. 122.
229. The album was voted #178 for all time in a poll of some 100,000 fans and critics by Virgin (1998), and selected as #232 best ever by *Rolling Stone* in 2003.
230. *Keys to the Rain*, p. 104–5. Robert Shelton agrees: "In language, sweep, universality, and compassion, one of his most profound song-poems." (*No Direction Home*, p. 157.)

231. The single didn't chart in its original British release, but reached #9 in a 1969 reissue. *Tracks of My Tears* was reissued again in the U.S. in 1987 in connection with its use in Oliver Stone's film *Platoon* (April 18, 1987 *Billboard*).
232. September 8, 1988 *Rolling Stone*, p. 78.

on his Les Paul custom instrument, they began tossing around musical ideas. Tarplin told writer Bob Gallagher that, odd as it seems, the song's melody was inspired by Harry Belafonte's *Banana Boat Song (Day-O)*. "It's basically the same changes, but at another tempo with another type of feeling."

"I had that track for a while, but I really couldn't think of anything to fit it, because it was such an odd musical progression," Robinson recalled. For weeks he re-listened to the tape of the rough instrumental track, and tried out a myriad of lyrical ideas. "Finally, the chorus came to me. No one had ever said 'tracks of my tears.' The whole thought of tears was to wipe them away so no one could tell you've been crying. To say that I can't wipe them away because they've left these tracks . . . I thought was a good idea."[233] The group headed for the studio as soon as the song was done, with Robinson as producer and arranger, and pianist Earl Van Dyke leading the Motown session band.

The song opens with a melancholy guitar introduction by Tarplin, with two other guitarists, Robert White and Eddie Willis, in quiet support. Motown founder Berry Gordy remarked in his memoir that this record "brought out something about Marv Tarplin and Smokey working together that always touched a dramatic chord with me. It became my favorite song of theirs . . . a masterpiece."[234]

Before this record, the Miracles had hit the Top 40 of the pop chart ten times, including the smashes *Shop Around* and *You've Really Got a Hold on Me*, and Robinson had made his mark as one of the supreme writers and producers, as during the previous twelve months in which he hit the top with Mary Wells' *My Guy* and the Temptations' *My Girl*. *Tracks of My Tears* demonstrated that he could achieve the same level of greatness as a performer.

"With its crying lead and doo-wopping background, *The Tracks of My Tears* is a throwback" to smooth 1950s R&B ballads, writes Dave Marsh, ranking it #46 in *The Heart of Rock & Soul*. "What brings it up to date are the details: huge drums, a lovely guitar line by [Tarplin], sharp horns, hi-fi dynamics. The lyrics might be flimsy if their rhyme scheme weren't so intricate. 'My smile is my makeup I wear since my breakup with you' is tremendous not for what it says but because it sings. If you're going to be the coolest crooner around, it helps to know how to craft such material. Only one guy did."[235] Craig

Werner suggests that there are multiple levels of meaning to the song: "Responding to *The Tracks of My Tears* as a profound expression of the psychological cost of black masking [blacks concealing their true selves from white society] didn't keep you from singing it when you saw your lover with somebody else."[236]

"Of his countless great songs, Smokey's masterpiece is *The Tracks of My Tears*," writes Nelson George, "a song so compelling, so resilient," that no amount of inferior remakes could ever diminish it. George notes that in addition to the touching lyrics, the song "possesses a wonderfully wistful melody and a brilliant production."[237] The song's success, noted *Rolling Stone* in 2000, "was also due in no small part to Robinson's crystal falsetto, which perfectly conveyed the tune's pathos and agony. For Robinson, it was an unmatched artistic summit."[238]

Do You Believe in Magic? (1965)—Lovin' Spoonful
(written by John Sebastian)
Kama Sutra 201
Chart debut Aug. 21, 1965 (reached #4 in *Record World*, #9 in *Billboard*); #3 in Canada (*Folk-#77, RHF, GHF, RS, DM, AHR*)[239]

Pure love of music no matter what its form; the unshakable conviction that music has the power to turn sadness into joy, and to make life worth living. This is the feeling behind the Lovin' Spoonful's breakthrough hit *Do You Believe in Magic?*, one of the happiest records ever made and one that sums up the sunny side of the 1960s like few others.

The Lovin' Spoonful was formed at the end of 1964 by John Sebastian (born on March 17, 1944, in New York City), a Greenwich Village folk music veteran who'd played harmonica on albums by Judy Collins, Tom Rush, and other folkies, and guitarist Zal Yanovsky, a former member of the folk-rock group the Mugwumps (alongside future Mamas & Papas Cass Elliot and Denny Doherty). With Steve Boone on bass and Joe Butler on drums, they named their group from a line in the song *Coffee Blues* by the great bluesman Mississippi John Hurt, with whom Sebastian had played in the Village.

In addition to folk and rock, jug band music (particularly Jim Kweskin's band) was a key influence on the group, and very evident on their debut hit. "The element that they brought that was different from other folk influences was that they tended to not only put a lighthearted

233. Nelson George, *Where Did Our Love Go? The Rise & Fall of the Motown Sound*, p. 68. In his autobiography *Smokey: Inside My Life* (p. 119–20), Robinson expanded the time frame, saying Tarplin's track "haunted me for months" until he came up with the verses. He credits Gordy with the critique that "you buried your hook," and the commercially savvy suggestion that they repeat the central line ("it's easy to trace . . .") "until you wear it out."

234. Gordy, *To Be Loved*, p. 223.

235. Marsh, p. 36.

236. *A Change Is Gonna Come: Music, Race, & the Soul of America*, p. 27.

237. George, *Where Did Our Love Go?*, p. 68.

238. December 7, 2000, *Rolling Stone*, p. 88, ranking it the #46 "greatest pop song."

239. *Magic* has accumulated over three million broadcast performances as certified by BMI, placing it just slightly below the organization's all-time top 100.

spin on their music, but they also adapted really odd instruments to use in the studio," Boone told Richie Unterberger in *Turn! Turn! Turn! The '60s Folk-Rock Revolution.* "We were one of the few folk-rock bands that played on all our records . . . no studio musicians involved."[240]

Sebastian's *Do You Believe In Magic?* was recorded in early 1965 before the Spoonful had a recording contract, although the folk-oriented Elektra label had expressed an interest.[241] Philles records owner Phil Spector fell in love with the song—biographer Dave Thompson says the demo "was seldom off the Philles office turntable"—but disliked the group's name and never got in touch. The tape was shopped around to almost every record label until Kama Sutra, a new label distributed by MGM, agreed to release it.[242]

A big element in the song's appeal is Sebastian's autoharp—an instrument beloved in traditional country music (as played by Mother Maybelle Carter and Ernest "Pop" Stoneman among others) and occasionally heard on folk albums, but largely unknown in rock. "By placing a ukulele contact mike on the back of it and plugging the mike into an amplifier, he'd made the autoharp into a rock instrument," noted Unterberger. (Through multi-tracking, the singer also played an acoustic Gibson guitar whose face was sanded down "so it was really loud." The piano part is played by the Modern Folk Quartet's Jerry Yester.)[243] "It just suddenly fit for one of the things I was writing, and we had something that was a little different," Sebastian recalled. "Nobody else could play the damn thing!"

The combination of that autoharp and Yanovsky's electric guitar over a buoyantly upbeat shuffle rhythm was nothing short of magical. Sebastian's melody, he later said, was rooted in Motown chord progressions. As he breezily, jubilantly sings about listening to rock, rhythm & blues, or jug band music, and describes the smile that "won't wipe off your face no matter how hard you try," you believe every word. Listening to *Do You Believe in Magic?* and not feeling a spiritual uplift is almost a physical impossibility.

In My Life (1966)—The Beatles
Recorded Oct. 18 & 22, 1965; from the Capitol album *Rubber Soul* (chart debut Dec. 25, 1965, #1 for 6 weeks) (*RS-#23, ACC, TC, DMDB*)[244]

As he went through a period of introspection in 1965–1966 coming to grips with the pressures of having every move analyzed by rabid fans and critics, John Lennon reached down to create one of his most moving and enduring songs. *In My Life* looks back on the cherished places of childhood, loved ones, and friends, and tries to gain perspective on what he values most as he searches for ways to tell his lover how much she means to him. It is a deeply reflective ballad with a warm and generous spirit; a song capable of giving comfort in times of personal loss.

"It was the first song I wrote that was consciously about my life," said Lennon. Starting as a description of a bus journey from his boyhood home into Liverpool, "it wasn't working at all. But then I laid back and these lyrics started coming to me about the places I remember. Paul [McCartney] helped with the middle eight. It was, I think, my first real major piece of work." McCartney's memory is that after John showed him the words, "I recall going off for half an hour and sitting with a Mellotron he had, writing the tune. Which was Miracles-inspired, as I remember."[245] After the group had recorded the basic track, Lennon asked producer George Martin to "add something baroque-sounding" in the middle. Martin's response was to design and record a Bach-flavored piano part at half speed, then playing it back at full speed, thus convincingly simulating the sound of a harpsichord.

"A meditation on his past and the mixed pleasures of recollecting it, *In My Life* strikes a deeper note than previous Beatles lyrics, embracing thoughts of death without stylizing them," remarks Ian MacDonald.[246] Like

240. Unterberger, p. 173–75.

241. As discussed in the Elektra Records history *Follow the Music* (p. 123–24), Sebastian had been a regular session musician for Elektra artists, and he was close to both label founder Jac Holzman and producer Paul Rothchild. Holzman loved *Do You Believe in Magic?*, "a song that echoed my own feeling about music, about being young with all the possibilities open before you." But the band wanted a $10,000 advance, and by the time he agreed to pay it, they had already committed to Kama Sutra.

242. The inspiration for *Magic*, as Sebastian recalled in *Off the Record: Songwriters on Songwriting*, was looking into the audience at the Night Owl Café in Greenwich Village and seeing a beautiful sixteen-year-old girl dancing happily, symbolizing for him and Yanovsky that "our audience . . . had finally found us. I wrote [the song] the next day."

243. Tony Fletcher, *All Hopped Up and Ready to Go: Music from the Streets of New York, 1927–77*, p. 217. Fletcher emphasizes the role of producer Erik Jacobsen, a young bluegrass banjo player who'd become a close pal of Sebastian's in Greenwich Village; the group insisted on using him as producer, and he justified their faith. "Run through an amplifier, these components [autoharp and the other instruments] were all arrayed sonically so that listeners would hear them as a unique whole. Jacobsen's studio tricks served to elevate *Do You Believe in Magic?* above the usual limitations of the pop single."

244. *In My Life* ranked as the #19 favorite oldie in eleven combined listener surveys by Washington, D.C.'s WBIG-FM (1994–2004).

245. Jonathan Gould partially agrees in *Can't Buy Me Love: The Beatles, Britain, and America* (p. 303), saying that the song "owed a conscious debt" to Smokey Robinson's *The Tracks of My Tears*—but not in its melody, which is quite different, but in the "vocal delivery and instrumental texture." *Rolling Stone*, in its 2010 special edition *The Beatles: 100 Greatest Songs* (p. 22), notes that this is one of only a handful of Beatles songs in which Lennon and McCartney strongly disagreed over who wrote what. Lennon insisted that the lyrics were entirely his own, while McCartney says the opening verse was John's and thereafter he rewrote Lennon's original version, making the references less specific and more universal. Lennon's nod to the late Stu Sutcliffe, the group's former bassist, in "some are dead and some are living," remained.

246. MacDonald, *Revolution in the Head: The Beatles' Records and the Sixties*, p. 169–70. He suggests that melody's "angular verticality, spanning an octave in typically—and difficult—leaps," shows more of

so many Beatles' classics, it's all about the details. Tim Riley: "The opening melody distills the singer's experience into a poignant guitar line played with stirring restraint. Ringo's irregular drumbeat adds a perpetual hesitancy, backing Lennon's soulful vocal performance with stop-and-start timidity. For all the certainty of the singer's devotion, he sings from a place of discomfort—the discomfort implicit in love itself." Martin's classically styled keyboard "links the popular idiom up with the history of music in the same way that the lyrics link the present love affair up with past involvements. (This is all done with astonishing aplomb.) The caesura ending, where the band stops and Lennon sings the final title line in dreamy falsetto, ranks with the ending of *God* on his first solo as the most beautiful singing of his career."[247] Jonathan Gould in *Can't Buy Me Love* admires how "the lyric strikes a delicate balance between a sense of longing and a sense of fulfillment."

In My Life is the most indelible song from the album voted #20 by some 200,000 fans in Virgin's 1998 "All-Time Top 1,000 Albums" poll, and ranked the #5 album ever by *Rolling Stone* in 2003. It was also called the #63 best pop song by *Rolling Stone* and MTV in December 2000, and voted the #19 all-time favorite song in ten combined 1994–2003 WBIG-FM listener surveys in the Washington, D.C., area.

Hold On! I'm Comin' (1966)—Sam & Dave (written by Isaac Hayes & David Porter)
Stax 189
Chart debut Apr. 23, 1966 (#1 for 1 week R&B, #21 pop)
    (*DM-#23*)
Sam Moore (born on October 12, 1935, in Miami) and Dave Prater (born on May 9, 1937, in Ocilla, Georgia) started as gospel singers, and used that training for some of the most exciting call-and-response soul classics of the 1960s. The duo first teamed in 1961 and recorded some unsuccessful singles for the Roulette label before Jerry Wexler signed them to Atlantic's Stax subsidiary and teamed with its fabulous house band, the MGs (guitarist Steve Cropper, bassist Duck Dunn, and drummer Al Jackson). Their first release on the label was a hit, *You Don't Know Like I Know*; the second, *Hold On! I'm Comin'*, was pure musical dynamite exploding over radio airwaves.

"The use of two voices answering each other in a rapid dialogue at times, echoing each other's phrases at others, and singing harmony in the choruses was a standard device of . . . church-based gospel singing," and had been used by several other black vocal groups in the previous decade, noted Charlie Gillett in *The Sound of the City.* "But with Stax, Sam and Dave made records that surpassed the excitement of earlier duo performances because they were answering not only each other but the encouraging riffs of the band."[248] And what a band it was. Wexler was thrilled with the duo's talent, as discussed in his autobiography: "I put Sam in the sweet tradition of Sam Cooke or Solomon Burke, while Dave had an ominous Four Tops' Levi Stubbs–sounding voice, the preacher promising hellfire."[249]

The record's opening ascending horn line, according to Rob Bowman's Stax boxed set liner notes, was borrowed from an unsuccessful earlier session for another song. Steve Cropper's guitar work was James Brown–inspired. Jackson's drum part on the verses was an uptempo version of the drum line on the Lee Dorsey record *Get Out of My Life, Woman.* Sam Moore, writes Bowman, "begins at full steam and becomes more apocalyptic as he goes on." He points out that Sam & Dave immediately repeat the second chorus, catching Wayne Jackson by surprise and causing him to miss the first trumpet response; but because the intense feeling of the performance was dead-on, Stax (true to its improvisational spirit) left in the mistake.[250] In the oral history of the duo, Sam recalls that it took two-and-a-half hours to record the number, so long that "they almost gave up on it."[251] Weirdly, Moore said he hated the song when Hayes and Porter first presented it to them, and the duo's fiercely aggressive vocals stemmed from their initial anger at being forced to record it. (Hayes is present here on piano.) He changed his mind, of course, upon hearing the finished product.[252]

Dave Marsh, ranking this at #23 in *The Heart of Rock & Soul,* remarks that "if you know a greater statement of sexual urgency, keep it to yourself because it probably . . . is illegal."[253] This record, writes Peter Guralnick in *Sweet Soul Music,* "epitomized the very formula that [Stax co-founder] Jim Stewart had been groping for ever since he had first heard Ray Charles and started recording rhythm and blues."[254]

McCartney's touch than Lennon's. "On the other hand, the chromatic descent, via the minor subdominant, in the second half of the verse suggests Lennon. Perhaps McCartney did the first half of the verse, Lennon the second?"
    247. Riley, *Tell Me Why*, p. 166–68.

248. Gillett, p. 238–39.
249. Wexler, *Rhythm and the Blues*, p. 177–78. Wexler had first heard the duo at a Miami nightclub a few years earlier.
250. Stax seldom bothered to correct such minor mistakes, notes Bowman. "If a given take had that gospel-infused sanctified feeling, it was a keeper."
251. Moore and Dave Marsh, p. 75. The record was initially distributed to radio stations as simply "I'm Coming"; some stations protested that it sounded dirty, so it was pulled and quickly issued to the full market under the longer title.
252. See Bowman's description of the session in *Soulsville U.S.A.: The Story of Stax Records*, p. 91–92.
253. Marsh, p. 23.
254. Guralnick, p. 159–60.

Wouldn't It Be Nice? (1966)—The Beach Boys (written by Brian Wilson & Tony Asher)

Capitol 5706

Chart debut July 30, 1966 (reached #5 in *Record World*, #8 in *Billboard*); #4 in Canada;[255] from the album *Pet Sounds* (chart debut May 28, 1966, #10 peak) (*RR & GHF* for album; *AHR*)

Brian Wilson was a young man in mental turmoil during much of the 1960s through psychological problems deepened by drug use and family complications. Yet he wrote some of the sunniest, happiest songs of the decade, none more so than *Wouldn't It Be Nice*. This is one of the most blissfully joyous songs about new love ever written, its sheer wide-eyed innocence and hope (carried along by a gorgeous melody and performance) genuinely touching. It was the biggest hit from the Beach Boys' masterpiece, *Pet Sounds*, voted the #6 album ever in Virgin's 1997–1998 survey; in December 2003 *Rolling Stone* ranked it the #2 best album ever. And its pairing with B side *God Only Knows* made this one of the all-time great double-sided singles.

The song's evolution was described by Charles Grenata. Wilson had been working assiduously on the melody, and refused to play it for writing partner Tony Asher until it was done. Then, with both men sitting at the piano, Asher began crafting the lyrics, with Wilson taking apart every lyric suggestion. Finally, he agreed to let Asher take a tape of the melody home to do the lyrics on his own without the micromanagement. "It's a song that people who are young and in love can appreciate and respond to," Asher told Grenata. "When we were writing, I was aware of the intricate rhythms that Brian had accomplished musically. There are changes in tempo and legato parts that make it very interesting."[256] Group historians Andrew Doe and John Tobler, after citing the accordion-driven track of "impressive complexity" cushioned by those luscious harmonies, note that "the lyrical hints at immortality in the first two verses are allayed by the matrimonial hopes of the bridge."[257]

Thomas Ryan remarked that the song "fit neatly into the 'escapist fantasy' category, and three decades later its lyrics have lost none of their artful significance. Innocently and deliberately, the song conveys the fanciful desire of a youthful couple to 'say goodnight and stay together.' The love is pure, and the desire is reasonable. The most beautiful and touching line comes in the refrain: 'Maybe if we think and wish and hope and pray, it might come true.' . . . The spiritual beauty of 'Wouldn't It Be Nice' lies in its blend of youthful optimism and in

its childish impatience. Best of all, it captures the singular moment in which the promise of a happy future and the desire of the present make these traits not only appropriate, but enviable."[258]

God Only Knows (1966)—The Beach Boys (music by Brian Wilson, lyrics by Tony Asher)

Capitol 5706; chart debut Aug. 13, 1966 (#39 peak)

B side of Top Ten hit *Wouldn't It Be Nice*; #2 in England, #4 in Canada;[259] from the album *Pet Sounds* (*RS-#26, RHF, GHF for album, ACC-#43, BBC-#59, Time, 1001, AHR, TC, DMDB*)[260]

One of the most sumptuously gorgeous ballads to ever spring from the pen of troubled genius Brian Wilson, *God Only Knows* was among the key songs that helped establish the Beach Boys' *Pet Sounds* as a pop album masterpiece. Little wonder that Paul McCartney has called it one of his all-time favorite songs (he and John Lennon were inspired to write *Here, There and Everywhere* the night they first heard *Pet Sounds*), and Wilson himself has declared it his best work. It "helped to broaden the definition of soul because of its soul-baring honesty," writes Thomas Ryan. "The . . . sense of satisfaction that lies on the surface of the song is counterbalanced with an insecurity that prevents the lyrics from resolving themselves. This lack of resolve guarantees the song its lasting strength. The emotion it captures is akin to a seesaw that is precariously balanced on a fulcrum . . . Whatever dangles eventually drops, and the sadness inherent in the lyric is one of recognition. In the present, it celebrates satisfaction and a sense of wonder, but it is also sad in that it simultaneously recognizes the fallibility of love. The French horns also add to the lonely undertow."[261]

Charles Grenata calls *God Only Knows* the "zenith" of the writing collaboration between Wilson and Asher.[262] It is "an essential work of art that might just be the most inspiring song in all of rock 'n roll music." By adding a contrasting vocal interlude to the bridge and a round-style vocal tag to the ending to the song's 32-bar pattern, "Brian uses the breaks to highlight some spectacular vocal harmony effects, which augment the tune's rarefied tone." The "unconventional vocal embellishments integrated into the arrangement (for example, the complicated in-and-out vocal round at the song's end) were far more sophisticated than anything the Beach Boys—or

255. In England, it was the uncharted B side of the #2 smash *God Only Knows*.

256. *Wouldn't It Be Nice: Brian Wilson and the Making of the Beach Boys' Pet Sounds*, p. 90–91.

257. Doe and Tobler, *Brian Wilson and the Beach Boys*, p. 48.

258. Ryan, *American Hit Radio*, p. 233–34.

259. #6 in Norway.

260. Named by VH1 in 2000 as one of the 100 Greatest Songs of Rock & Roll.

261. *American Hit Radio*, p. 234–35.

262. Asher had been a jingle composer and advertising copywriter when he was introduced to Wilson, but was able to capture Brian's psychological fragility in a lyric based partly on Wilson's love for—but emotional distance from—his wife Marilyn. Toby Creswell in *1001 Songs* (p. 97): "It's the song of a man barely hanging on, and in a few years he would be over the edge."

any other modern pop vocal group—had done before. There is also the fine interplay between the vocal and melodic portions of the song; a subtle musical contrast that tempers the tune's celebratory melody with the bittersweet irony of its lyrics—an effect that appreciably strengthens the song's emotional impact."[263]

Lyricist Tony Asher was so moved by the beauty of Brian's melody that he was especially anxious to craft words of matching quality. "How many love songs start off with the line, 'I may not always love you?'" he remarked to Grenata. "I liked that twist, and fought to start the song that way." Of course, by song's end it is clear that the singer's love is total. But there is an intriguing lyrical complexity beneath the surface. "Although one could reasonably conclude that the central character is asserting that if the couple's love dies, he will die, within his declaration of unconditional love lies a daunting subtext: 'I love you now, but if we ever part, life will go on. I will survive in spite of you.'"

Carl Wilson sings his brother's composition with aching beauty in soaring falsetto. On early takes of the song, Brian sang lead; one of these is included on *The Pet Sounds Sessions*, and it sounds just about as wonderful as the version we know. "After hearing a rough mix of the record, however, Brian decided that Carl's voice was better suited for the reverential tone he desired."[264] Songwriter Jimmy Webb: "I love *God Only Knows* and its bow to the baroque that goes all the way back to 1740 and J. S. Bach. It represents the whole tradition of liturgical music that I feel is a spiritual part of Brian's music. And Carl's singing is pretty much at its pinnacle—as good as it ever got."[265]

Gimme Some Lovin' (1967)—Spencer Davis Group
(written by Steve Winwood, Muff Winwood & Spencer Davis)
United Artists 50108
Chart debut Dec. 31, 1966 (peak #7 in *Billboard*, #5 *Record World*); reached #2 in England, #1 in Canada (*RHF, GHF, PW, DM-#169, RS, AHR, TC, ACC, DMDB*)
Called by Ken Emerson "one of the most excited and exciting vocals ever recorded by a white man,"[266] *Gimme Some Lovin'* introduced the world to an eighteen-year-old blue-eyed soul dynamo named Steve Winwood.[267] The intensity of this performance, describes Paul Williams in

Rock & Roll: The 100 Best Singles, "resonates in shimmering waves from Winwood's voice, in a joyous, unresolved, unresolvable tension, building to a fever pitch through every verse," in the pounding bass drums and rhythm guitar "acting as one," and in "the relationship between the riff and the equally driving organ chords [by Winwood] that sustain and sustain and sustain, building in pitch along with the vocal and straining every muscle against the rhythmic figure's implicit restraints."[268]

The Spencer Davis Group was formed in 1963 with Spencer Davis on guitar, Steve Winwood (born on May 12, 1948, in Birmingham, England) on organ and vocals, his brother Muff Winwood on bass, and drummer Peter York. Signed by producer Chris Blackwell, they had three singles scrape the lower levels of the U.K. charts in 1964–1965 before *Keep On Running* was released in December 1965 and went to #1, and *Somebody Help Me* did the same a few months later. But *Running* was only a minor U.S. chart single, and its successor went nowhere, leading Atco (distributed by Atlantic) to drop the group. *Gimme Some Lovin'* broke them Stateside with a vengeance after switching to United Artists.

Inspired by Junior Walker & the All-Stars' 1965 smash *Shotgun*, *Gimme Some Lovin'* was written during the group's rehearsal at London's Marquee Club. The singer later recalled for author Timothy White that the song was also inspired by Muff's love for a bass riff from a record by Stax songwriter Homer Banks called *Whole Lotta Lovin'*. After Muff came up with the vigorous bass lick, Davis responded with a guitar line that played off Ravel's *Bolero*; and Winwood took it from there. *Rolling Stone*, ranking it the #26 single of the past twenty-five years in 1988, noted that Winwood's introductory organ passage sounds as if he were "standing on the keys," and after he cries out "Hey!" Steve "pleads for lovin' with all the fervor of a teenager in heat."[269] The phenom was known for doing a potent Ray Charles impression, and sounds as if he's channeling Brother Ray. He soon left Davis to co-found Traffic, and came back to score an impressive run of solo hits in the 1980s (including the chart-topping *Roll With It* that was virtually a musical sequel to the steamy spirit of this breakthrough).

My Back Pages (1967)—The Byrds (written by Bob Dylan)
Columbia 44054
Chart debut Apr. 1, 1967 (#30 peak in *Billboard*, #26 in *Cash Box*);[270] from the album *Younger Than Yesterday*

263. Grenata, *Wouldn't It Be Nice*, p. 99–103.
264. The nine-minute session track for the song in *The Pet Sounds Sessions* also includes, write Andrew G. Doe and John Tobler in *Brian Wilson and the Beach Boys: The Complete Guide to Their Music* (p. 50) "an awesome and previously unheard vocal tag of immense complexity and beauty. Why this was consigned to the vaults remains a complete mystery."
265. Webb quoted by Grenata, *Wouldn't It Be Nice*, p. 99.
266. *Rolling Stone Illustrated History*, p. 283.
267. Similarly, rock artist Al Kooper called the youngster "the finest white blues singer I have ever heard, regardless of age or environment."
268. Williams, p. 107–8.
269. September 8, 1988 *Rolling Stone*, p. 98. The session was produced by Chris Blackwell, who became best known for his work with Bob Marley & the Wailers.
270. Reached #3 in Puerto Rico.

No one covered Bob Dylan songs more masterfully than the Byrds, and this is one of their most richly satisfying Dylan interpretations of all. *My Back Pages* was originally from the 1964 album *Another Side of Bob Dylan*, but a less than vibrant original performance—it was recorded in the early hours of the morning when Dylan sounded tired—led many to overlook it until Roger McGuinn & Co. brought out the song's full potential (excising two of Dylan's stanzas).

It's a confession by a young man who had been aflame with the ideological passions of youth that the world is not as black and white as he had imagined. It was a renunciation of politics and "finger-pointing" to focus on introspection, although of course Dylan would continue to return to social concerns in years to come. Dylan biographer Robert Shelton saw the piece in classical poetic terms: "From Blakean 'Experience,' Dylan has moved back toward 'Innocence,' which will keep him forever young. This song of self-discovery returns to a child's openness."[271] With vivid lyrics, the reedy McGuinn voice and jangly twelve-string Rickenbacker guitar, and those timeless group harmonies in full glory, this is an undeniable classic.

The Byrds, notes Richie Unterberger, took Dylan songs and made them a "gorgeous listening experience. The Byrds were not copyists, and somehow transformed the sluggish pound of Dylan's acoustic guitars into danceable tempos. McGuinn introduced spellbinding twelve-string riffs, particularly at the opening and closing of the arrangements, that were wholly of his own invention, while the Byrds' harmonies imbued the songs with an uplifting joy largely missing from Dylan's own work."[272]

A late-1965 essay on Dylan by Maurice Capel (before the Byrds had recorded the song) offered this analysis: "His aim is to remain an individual against the twin pressures of conformism and of a purely abstract revolt, to define and to hold a middle ground between social lies and self-deception, acquiring thus a permanently questioned and constantly renewed concrete identity. The dialectics of change and movement—from the private to the outside world and back again—enrich and resolve his individuality. In *My Back Pages*, Dylan describes aging as the need to see the world in black and white (with the old on the side of the angels), and

to believe one has 'something to protect'—segregating oneself from the unprotected."[273]

Somebody to Love (1967)—Jefferson Airplane (written by Darby Slick)
RCA 9140
Chart debut April 1, 1967 (#5 peak); reached #4 in Canada;[274] from the album *Surrealistic Pillow* (#3 peak) (*RHF, RS-#279, ACC, DMDB*)

Few singles in rock history have such a jet-propelled opening as the Jefferson Airplane's *Somebody to Love*: The needle hits the groove (in those old vinyl days), and from out of the silence explodes Grace Slick's ferocious soprano, belting out the words, "When the truth is found to be lies / And all the joy within you dies . . ." behind a driving beat. Once the listener recovers from the shock of the zero-to-90 miles per hour vroom! introduction, you're further riveted by the power and no-holds-barred quality of Slick's voice, and the emotional urgency behind her tale. Not a bad way for pop music to be introduced to a band that had been struggling for nearly two years until this breakout hit.

Singer-songwriter Marty Balin formed Jefferson Airplane in San Francisco in 1965 with guitarist/singers Paul Kantner and Jorma Kaukonen, bassist Jack Casady, drummer Skip Spence, and lead singer Signe Anderson. RCA signed the Airplane, but their 1966 debut album *Jefferson Airplane Takes Off* never reached flying altitude, leading to the departures of Anderson and Spence. Spencer Dryden became the new drummer. To replace Anderson, the band recruited Grace Slick (born on October 30, 1939, in Chicago), lead singer of another Bay-area group, the Great Society.

Somebody to Love was written by Slick's brother-in-law Darby, and had been included in the Great Society's little-noticed debut album.[275] As reworked by the Airplane, it became much faster-paced than in its original version, which served to further accentuate Slick's hell-bent-for-leather quality; this was a chick who knew exactly what she wanted and wasn't the least bit shy about letting the whole world know. Before Slick, only a few female singers (such as rockabilly turned country dynamo Wanda Jackson) had that fierce, abandoned quality; after Slick, many would at least attempt to follow that approach, although most couldn't pull it off like she did. Jorma Kaukonen offered an exciting, feedback-drenched guitar solo, using an Echoplex. Steve Futter-

---

271. *No Direction Home*, p. 158. The song's central refrain suggests death and rebirth.

272. *Turn! Turn! Turn! The '60s Folk-Rock Revolution*, p. 137. David Crosby raised an initial objection to the group covering another Dylan tune, feeling it could be seen as a step backward. (Crosby had also strongly opposed recording the career-making *Mr. Tambourine Man*, so his judgment regarding Dylan was dubious.) (Rogan, *Timeless Flight Revisited: The Sequel*, p. 201–2.)

273. Essay included in *The Dylan Companion*, p. 102–16.

274. #1 (1 week) in Philippines, #3 in Holland (1970).

275. Under the title *Someone to Love*, it had been released as a single on a small label (North Beach 1001). The November 1966 *Crawdaddy* called Slick "the single most talented woman in San Francisco's performing rock scene," but said the single was no longer available.

man calls it "one of the most intense performances to ever break the Top Ten."[276]

Darby Slick remarked to *Rolling Stone* that the song was all about "doubt and disillusionment." The magazine, including it among the best 100 singles of the past twenty-five years in 1988, remarked that "the focused energy of the music, the unflinching honesty of the words and the power of the performance came together in a song that announced the Jefferson Airplane and the San Francisco sound to the world with a roar."[277]

Born Under a Bad Sign (1967)—Albert King (written by Booker T. Jones & William Bell)
Stax 217
Recorded on May 17, 1967; chart debut Aug. 26, 1967 (#49 R&B); from the album *Born Under a Bad Sign* (*Blues-#20, RHF, GHF, DM*)

"If it wasn't for bad luck, I wouldn't have no luck at all." Blues lyrics just don't come any pithier than that, and when added to the powerful guitar and strong vocals of Albert King, backed by three-quarters of Booker T. and the MGs, it makes *Born Under a Bad Sign* one of the undisputed blues gems of the 1960s.

Born Albert Nelson on April 25, 1923, in Indianola, Mississippi (he changed his surname in honor of B.B.), King sang with the Harmony Kings gospel group from 1949–1951 before launching his career as one of the modern era's greatest blues guitarist/singers in 1953. King's 1950s recordings were not widely heard, but his early 1960s singles began earning a strong following—leading to his 1967 breakthrough with *Bad Sign* (both the title song and comparably outstanding album). Robert Palmer declared the album "probably the most important and certainly the most stirring hard blues LP of the 1960s."[278] From that point on, King was a god to serious blues lovers, both for his incredible string-bending guitar style—designed in part because he played left-handed and preferred not to re-string his instrument—and his superb original songs (he wrote or co-wrote most of his pre-1972 songs). An imposing physical presence, King stood 6 foot 4 and 250 pounds, and showed stage flair with his "flying U" guitar. Having appeared on the first Fillmore East concert bill in 1968 (with such rockers as Big Brother & the Holding Company), he also played at the hall's closing concerts three years later.

Organist Booker T. Jones wrote *Bad Sign* with one of Stax's crucial singers and songwriters, William Bell. It was Bell's idea to create a song based on astrology,

which was then trendy, and told Stax historian Rob Bowman that he came up with the song's signature riff while fooling around on guitar.[279] Jones is joined here by fellow MGs Donald "Duck" Dunn on bass and Al Jackson on drums (plus Wayne Jackson of the Memphis Horns on trumpet); only guitarist Steve Cropper is absent, for the obvious reason that Albert's ax is quite sufficient. Dave Marsh remarks that King's "unique" guitar work, coupled "with a song so classic it sounds like it must have been unearthed rather than written, the result is virtually timeless."[280]

(Your Love Keeps Lifting Me) Higher and Higher (1967)—Jackie Wilson (written by Carl Smith, Raynard Miner, Gary Jackson & Billy Davis)
Brunswick 55336
Recorded on July 7, 1967; chart debut Aug. 26, 1967 (#1 for 1 week R&B, #6 pop) (*R&B-#53, RHF, GHF, PW, BMI-#39, DM-#168, RS-#248, 1001, AHR, ACC, TC, DMDB*)

The man known as Mr. Excitement for his incendiary stage performances scored the most unforgettable hit of his career with the record that became the last of his thirteen Top-20 pop hits. Born on June 9, 1934, in Detroit, Wilson was briefly a professional boxer and then a solo performer before exploding on the music scene as the successor to Clyde McPhatter singing lead tenor with the Dominoes when they were one of the top acts in R&B in 1953 (that year's *Rags to Riches* was his best-known record with the group). Wilson went solo in 1956, and when Elvis Presley caught his act in Las Vegas, he was so impressed (reports James Miller) that he went back to see him four nights in a row. Wilson's overpowering tenor with an operatic range, and acrobatic dance moves on stage, could drive any audience into a frenzy.

It was young Detroit songwriter and soon-to-be Motown founder Berry Gordy who provided Wilson with his breakthrough solo hit in 1957, *Reet Petite*, and it was quickly followed by a series of pop and R&B successes, including the Top Ten smash *Lonely Teardrops*. He had managed only one Top 40 pop hit in three-and-a-half years when his star was briefly returned to supernova status by *Higher and Higher*, which had first been recorded in early 1967 by the Dells; one of its co-writers, Billy Davis, had co-written *Petite* and *Teardrops* with Gordy. Before the group's version was even released, producer Carl Davis heard an advance copy and decided it was perfect for Wilson. Gary Jackson (who had not been involved in the song's original creation) did a slight rewrite with some lyric changes.

---

276. August 31, 2003, *Washington Post*, p. N-27.
277. September 8, 1988, *Rolling Stone*, p. 132.
278. In *Deep Blues* (p. 246), Palmer praises the track's "bulldozer" rhythm, and remarks that Cream's cover version and *Strange Brew* "were practically Albert King parodies."
279. *Soulsville U.S.A.*, p. 126–27.
280. Marsh, *The Heart of Rock and Soul*, p. 388.

Wilson unleashed one of his most high-powered performances on record, and he had a lot of help. Bassist James Jamerson, guitarist Robert White, drummer Richard "Pistol" Allen, and keyboardists Earl Van Dyke and Johnny Griffith—the core of Motown's legendary "Funk Brothers"—laid down a devastatingly infectious groove for the cooking uptempo number, which was recorded at the Columbia studios in Chicago under the guidance of Carl Davis. The session's arranger, Sonny Saunders, recalled that after a half hour of trying the piece wasn't quite working, until Allen launched into a double-timing of the rhythm that proved the key.[281]

Paul Williams calls the rhythm track "joyous unrelieved tension all the way . . . hypnotic, riveting," and writes of Wilson's "transcendent" performance, "so awake, so alive" that it brings listeners to "a state of heightened awareness."[282] The song was ranked as the #39 most-played number since 1940 by Broadcast Music, Inc. (BMI). Wilson suffered a stroke while performing on stage in 1975, and died in 1984. "Now, with my lovin' arms around you, I can stand up and face the world . . ."

Wichita Lineman (1968)—Glen Campbell (written by Jimmy Webb)
Capitol 2302
Chart debut Nov. 2, 1968 (#1 for 2 weeks C&W, #3 pop); #3 in Canada, #7 in England; from the album *Wichita Lineman* (chart debut Nov. 16, 1968, #1 for 5 weeks on pop chart)[283] (*GHF, C&W-#53, ACC-#176, HBN-#187, RS-#195, AHR, DMDB*)

After Glen Campbell scored a 1967 hit with Jimmy Webb's song *By the Time I Get to Phoenix*, the young composer invited him to his Hollywood home, where he played *Wichita Lineman*. Webb had seen a lineman on the Kansas-Oklahoma border high atop a telephone pole, with plenty of time to think, and it inspired what became Campbell's finest recording. *Country America* readers selected it as one of the top 100 C&W songs of all time, and Thomas Ryan cited Webb's lyrics as "an eloquently plain yet poetic way of expressing this overwhelming desire."[284]

Campbell was so knocked out by the song that he immediately cut a demo recording. Because he loved the sound of Webb's huge, unwieldy electric church organ,

he arranged to have the instrument hauled into the studio for the session.[285] The organ furnished the chiming sound at the fadeout, signifying telephone signals. Carol Kaye (whom Campbell got to know while both worked as session musicians on Phil Spector productions) opens the record with her distinctive bass lines, and Glen serves as the guitar soloist; the track took just ninety minutes to record. Toby Creswell: "The imagery here is so clear and simple that it only takes two verses to break your heart." Campbell's vocal is "flawless . . . his voice quavering and cracking with sadness and resignation and desire."[286]

Songwriter Diane Warren: "All of Jimmy Webb's songs, especially *Wichita Lineman*, touch me so deeply . . . you can see the whole picture: the guy up on the telephone pole; the lonely, empty, desolate road; the trucks going by. It's one of those songs that talks to me, and that's the reason it endures."[287] Bill Friskics-Warren pays tribute to producer Al DeLory's skillful arrangement. "There's the crystalline wash of strings early on, a moment of clarity akin to what the song's pole-sitting protagonist must feel, his head above the wires, surveying the horizon. The dark rumblings that follow the words 'overload' and 'strain,' however, suggest pressure on the lines—and stormy times at home. Then there's the way the violins echo the whine of his lover's siren call as it surges through the telephone lines; the repairman's desire positively smolders in the loud, lusty guitar tones on the break."[288]

Both Sides Now (1968)—Judy Collins (written by Joni Mitchell)
Elektra 45639
Recorded on Sept. 28, 1967; chart debut Nov. 9, 1968 (#8 peak); reached #3 in Canada, #14 in U.K.; from the album *Wildflowers* (chart debut Jan. 6, 1968, #5 peak)[289] (*Folk-#50, GHF*)

Joni Mitchell wrote *Both Sides Now* in March 1967 under the influence of Saul Bellow's book *Henderson the Rain King*. As related by biographer Karen O'Brien, the passage in the book that especially resonated with Joni found its "hapless anti-hero" Eugene Henderson peering down from an aircraft window high above the Egyptian countryside and reflecting on what he saw below him:

281. Nelson George, in *Where Did Our Love Go? The Rise & Fall of the Motown Sound* (p. 108), noting the perfection of Wilson's soaring voice matched with the mighty Motown groove: "It is one of the sad injustices of pop history that, because of contractual obligations to Brunswick, Wilson was never able to benefit on an ongoing basis from a sound that his voice and success helped to create."

282. Paul Williams, *Rock and Roll: The 100 Best Singles*, p. 124–25.

283. Campbell was an all-dominant force on the *Billboard* country album charts during this period. On October 19, 1968, he stood at #1, #2, #4, #5, and #8. When *Lineman* hit #1 on November 30 (where it would remain for twenty weeks), he had six of the top sixteen country LPs.

284. *American Hit Radio*, p. 332–33.

285. *Rhinestone Cowboy: An Autobiography*, p. 76. "I hadn't done any manual labor in years, and Hammond organs are heavy," but it was worth it.

286. Creswell, *1001 Songs*, p. 389.

287. May 1997 *Musician* magazine, p. 30. In Campbell's words: "I think Jimmy Webb writes probably the best melodies and chord progressions of anybody that I've ever heard, including the greats. He's my very favorite writer of all time." (*Billboard Book of Number One Country Hits*, p. 17.)

288. *Heartaches By the Number: Country Music's 500 Greatest Singles*, p. 97–98.

289. In a case study of the impact a hit single can have on album sales, *Wildflowers* had been a solidly steady seller for months but had peaked at #36 in July and then dropped down; after the single hit, it soared into the Top Ten in December.

"I dreamed down at the clouds, and thought that when I was a kid I had dreamed up at them, and having dreamed at the clouds from both sides as no other generation of men has done, one should be able to accept his death very easily. However, we made safe landings every time . . . I kept thinking, 'Bountiful life! Oh, how bountiful life is!'"

Sheila Weller in *Girls Like Us* suggests that the song was also a reflection of Mitchell being on the "cusp" of estrangement from her husband Chuck Mitchell, and was "undeniably tied to her turmoil" about the baby daughter they had recently given up for adoption. "*Both Sides Now*'s theme of thoughtful indecisiveness and the shifting, illusory nature of truth suggests it was unconsciously autobiographical."[290]

Tom Rush, the first established performer to believe in Mitchell's talent, had tried to get other artists to record her songs, including Judy Collins, but said "I couldn't 'sell' her tunes to Judy at first." It was musician Al Kooper (who had been a friend since she moved to New York) who called her at three in the morning in mid-1967 to tell her "he had met a great songwriter and wanted me to hear her sing an amazing song. He put Joni Mitchell on the phone . . . After Joni sang me *Both Sides Now*, I put the phone down and wept. I had never heard a song that I felt was so beautiful, and it would change both our lives."[291] [292] Judy included *Both Sides Now* (which was also cut under the title *Clouds* by Dave Van Ronk for his early-1968 album *Dave Van Ronk & the Hudson Dusters*) on her album *Wildflowers*.[293] Because both Collins and her label Elektra were not at all singles-oriented, nearly ten months would pass following release of the album before the company issued *Both Sides Now* as a 45, to sensational success.[294] [295]

Born on May 1, 1939, in Seattle and raised in Denver, Judy Collins was a piano prodigy and gave her debut performance at thirteen with the Denver Businessmen's Symphony. She switched from classical to folk music, became part of the Greenwich Village scene in New York, and Elektra issued her debut album *Maid of Constant Sorrow* in 1961. By mid-decade, she was one of the most admired performers in folk, and soon began branching out to feature theater and art songs, larger arrangements, and some of her own compositions. *Wildflowers* (her seventh LP, also including her haunting original ballad *Since You Asked*) presents Judy at her peak, and it proved the biggest album of her career.

After doing a couple of Joshua Rifkin arrangements on a previous album, *Wildflowers* was Collins' first album that was entirely orchestral—indeed, perhaps the first fully orchestrated album by any acoustic artist, "not a folk guitar on it," as she noted. Prior to his work with Collins, Rifkin had been the driving force at Elektra's Nonesuch classical imprint, including a best-selling album of baroque Beatles orchestrations in 1965. *Wildflowers* was also one of the earliest pop albums to use the new Dolby noise reduction system, providing sonic clarity considered exceptional for the time.[296]

With simple yet touching childlike imagery, a beautifully lilting melody, a smoothly flowing arrangement by Rifkin (who also conducts and plays harpsichord here),[297] the expert production of Mark Abramson, and Judy's crystalline soprano, *Both Sides Now* is an enchanting slice of pop music, capturing idealized youthful notions of life and love as they begin to bump up against more complicated adult realities.

Proud Mary (1969)—Creedence Clearwater Revival
(written by John Fogerty)
Fantasy 619
Chart debut Jan. 25, 1969 (3 weeks at #2 in *Billboard*, reached #1 in *Record World*); #2 in Canada, #5 in Germany, #6 in Australia, #8 in England;[298] from the album *Bayou Country* (#7 peak) (*RHF, GHF, BMI-#24,*[299] *Juke-#26, DMDB-#54, RIA-#115, DM-#125, RS-#156, AHR, DMDB*)

290. Weller, *Girls Like Us: Carole King, Joni Mitchell, Carly Simon, and the Journey of a Generation*, p. 221–22.

291. Collins, *Sweet Judy Blue Eyes*, p. 215–20. "When I began to sing *Both Sides Now*, I felt I had lived through the song. Joni had written a great song, perhaps one of the greatest ever written. *Both Sides Now*, as a composition, has everything: sweep and tenderness, specificity as well as breadth. It speaks to everyone who might hear it, a perfect jewel of a song."

292. In her first memoir (*Trust Your Heart: An Autobiography*, p. 149–50), Collins had credited Rush with putting Mitchell on the phone to sing her *Both Sides Now*, before shifting the credit to Kooper in the later book. She describes having dinner at Joni's New York apartment a few months after the recording, and being brought to tears by Mitchell's performance of another new song. "You can break my heart anytime you like. Just open your mouth and sing" (*Trust Your Heart*, p. 151).

293. Karen O'Brien, *Shadows and Light: Joni Mitchell: The Definitive Biography*, p. 55, 58–59.

294. Prior to the debut album by The Doors in early 1967, Elektra had always regarded singles as an afterthought designed only to draw a bit of extra attention to an album. Jac Holzman said he immediately saw *Both Sides Now* as a potential single, "but I wasn't sure about the timing." When rumors surfaced that the Irish folk-rock group the Johnstons was planning to issue a cover version, he hustled the principals back into the studio to remix the song for single release. The Johnstons' single did come out first, but only reached #128.

295. The single's B side was one of the earliest treatments of Sandy Denny's folk classic *Who Knows Where the Time Goes*. It's a different

version than the one Judy would use as the title song of her end-of-1968 album.

296. Holzman (as discussed in his memoir *Follow the Music*, p. 216–19) had acquired the "Dolby boxes" in England, and his engineers led by John Haeny had to learn how to use them. "If ever an artist and a technology were made for each other," remarked Haeny, "it was Judy and Dolby." The album was recorded at the lavish Studio One at United Western Recorders in Los Angeles. Everything was recorded live; the best vocal and orchestra performances were then spliced together individually.

297. Rifkin would gain still greater renown a few years later through recording and re-popularizing the ragtime music of Scott Joplin.

298. #3 in New Zealand, #4 in Switzerland, #6 Norway.

299. Certified with over five million broadcast performances.

An American classic set against a richly nostalgic Mississippi River background was written by a man who at the time had never set foot in the South. "From the time I was a kid, I was drawn to that mythical world of Mark Twain," *Proud Mary* composer and singer John Fogerty said in a 1997 interview. "Stephen Foster, Howlin' Wolf . . . The South seemed to exist in another time—a slower, more leisurely time. It seemed exotic as if it were someplace far away, and yet very American at the same time. It seemed more American than where I was."[300]

Berkeley, California, was John Fogerty's birthplace on May 28, 1945. John's older brother Tom formed the Blue Velvets in the late 1950s in El Cerrito across the bay from San Francisco, and by the mid-1960s the group, with Tom as lead singer and John on guitar, released some obscure singles as the Golliwogs. It was only when John stepped forward as singer, songwriter, and producer that the group, renamed Creedence Clearwater Revival, changed their fortunes. A psychedelic remake of the 1950s rock standard *Suzie Q* became a hit in 1968, but when a similar remake, *I Put a Spell on You*, didn't fare as well, they knew it was time to step up with something original. John's response to the challenge was *Proud Mary*.

It was one of several songs Fogerty wrote in his little El Cerrito apartment in 1968, usually late at night when unable to sleep. Having already finished the title song, he decided to make the album *Bayou Country* a suite of songs relating to the South, drawing equally on the nineteenth century antebellum South and the twentieth century blues, rock, and gospel he loved. In the notebook he maintained with ideas for lyrics, *Proud Mary* was his first entry as a possible song title, but originally thought it might be a piece about a maid in a household of rich people. Then, while in a hotel room on the road watching an episode of the TV show *Maverick* featuring Mississippi River gambling boats, the song began to take shape in his mind.

As related in the Creedence biography by Hank Bordowitz, Fogerty had just gotten his honorable discharge from the Army Reserves. After happily turning cartwheels outside his home, he went back inside, "picked up my guitar and started strumming. 'Left a good job in the city' and then several good lines came out of me immediately. I had the chord changes, the minor chord where it says, 'Big wheel keep on turnin' / Proud Mary keep on burnin' . . . By the time I hit 'Rolling, rolling, rolling on the river,' I knew I had written my best song. It vibrated inside me."[301] [302]

A one-hit wonder no longer, Creedence used the launching pad of *Proud Mary* to begin an amazing run of memorable hits. No less than Bob Dylan declared it his favorite song of the year. In fact, it was Dylan who talked Fogerty into doing the song again on stage in 1987 at a time when John was refusing to perform old Creedence numbers due to a bitter legal dispute with his former label. He's sung it with a smile ever since. Ike & Tina Turner's Top Ten remake of the song in 1971 is fun, but the song will always belong to Creedence and Fogerty.

The Amusement and Music Operators Association (AMOA) in 1988 called it the #26 biggest juke box hit ever, and just about every radio listener survey of favorite oldies includes it in the Top 100. Dave Marsh notes that Fogerty "came up with a riff and a rhythm that roll along as mighty as the Mississippi itself. The surging flood of guitar and drums, the bass line's undertow and the liquid guitar solo justify every vocal and lyric affectation."[303] *Rolling Stone* called it the #52 top single of the past twenty-five years in 1988; in 2000 the magazine ranked it as the #41 best pop song. Asked if he's proud of the song, Fogerty replied: "Put it this way: I felt compelled to sing it about ten years ago when I got married. I sang *Proud Mary* at my wedding because so many others had it sung at their wedding. I was proud I could do it with a little extra credential."

Jay Cocks wrote of Fogerty in *Time* magazine: "He can do what only the greatest American songwriters can: make music that sounds, even when you first hear it, as if you've known it forever. Music that's more than something you grew up with—music that's a birthright."[304]

Suspicious Minds (1969)—Elvis Presley (written by Mark James)
RCA 47-9764
Recorded on Jan. 22, 1969; chart debut Sept. 13, 1969 (1 week at #1); #1 (3 weeks) in Australia, #1 (2 weeks) in Canada, #2 in England[305] (*RHF, GHF, BMI-#30, ACC-#56, DMDB-#77, RS-#91, 1001, DM*)

The Great Comeback—the NBC Christmas special that had re-established Elvis Presley's credentials as The King after years of sliding into irrelevancy in Hollywood—had occurred just nine months earlier, confirmed by the spring 1969 smash *In the Ghetto*. *Suspicious Minds* not only returned Elvis to the #1 spot on the charts for the first time in seven years, it swept aside all remaining doubts: he was back, with a vengeance, as a contemporary artist with renewed fire and hunger.

300. September 19, 1997, *Washington Post*, Weekend section, p. 15.
301. Bordowitz, *Bad Moon Rising*, p. 53–54.
302. Fogerty's guitar solo here 'was sort of me doing Steve Cropper.' See commentary on *Proud Mary* in *Up Around the Bend: The Oral History of Creedence Clearwater Revival* by Craig Werner, p. 82–84.

303. Marsh, *The Heart of Rock & Soul*, p. 89.
304. Cocks, June 2, 1997, *Time*.
305. #1 (6 weeks) in South Africa, #1 in Belgium and New Zealand, #2 in Denmark and Sweden, #3 in Malaysia, #4 in Holland, #5 in Spain, #6 in France, #8 Germany.

Mark James, a talented young writer for producer Chips Moman, had recorded his composition *Suspicious Minds* for the Scepter label in 1968 (the same year his song *Hooked On a Feeling* was a smash for B. J. Thomas), but the record was not a hit. Moman believed in the song, and given the opportunity to produce Elvis at Moman's American Recording Studios in Memphis (the first time the singer had recorded in Memphis since 1955, in sessions that produced thirty-five tracks), he took the exact same arrangement and poured everything into what he was certain would be a blockbuster. The producer's house ensemble, known as the 827 Thomas Street Band, is crackling with soulful power (including the Memphis Horns and the Sweet Inspirations featuring Cissy Houston on gospel-fired backing vocals), freeing Elvis to really cut loose. Reggie Young sets the pace on electric guitar (actually Scotty Moore's old Super 400 blond Gibson guitar, which the ex-Presley bandmate had given to Moman), with Mike Leech on bass and Gene Chrisman on drums.[306] As publisher of the song, Moman refused to give away a share of the rights to Presley—as had been the kickback-like custom for songwriters ever since Elvis became Elvis in 1956—but fortunately Presley loved the song so much that this didn't stop him from recording it.[307] This tale of infidelity was exactly the kind of mature, adult theme he wanted to forge a fresh image for a new generation, and judging from this performance (two years after his marriage to Priscilla) it clearly touched something in him emotionally.

Biographer Peter Guralnick writes that Elvis's "singing achieves the same remarkable mixture of tenderness and poise that it did on *In the Ghetto*, with one significant element added—"an expressive quality somewhere between stoicism (at suspected infidelity) and anguish (over impending loss)." Everyone in the studio knew that this was the song. An atmosphere of excitement and anticipation runs all the way through its recording," which was completed in just four full takes.[308] Alan Light: "*Suspicious Minds* presented an emotional complexity, a rendering of an adult struggle with an adult situation, that was unprecedented in the Presley canon."[309]

Something (1969)—The Beatles (written by George Harrison)
Apple 2654
Recording completed Aug. 15, 1969; chart debut Oct. 18, 1969 (#3 peak); reached #4 in England, #1 (5 weeks) in Australia, #1 (5 weeks) in Canada, #1 (2 weeks) in W. Germany;[310] from the album *Abbey Road* (#1 for 11 weeks) (*GHF, BMI-#17*,[311] *RS, AHR, BBC, DMDB*)[312]

Even casual Beatles fans knew that George Harrison was developing into a first-rate songwriter with stellar contributions like *While My Guitar Gently Weeps* to the group's albums, but the release of *Abbey Road* proved that "the quiet one" had fully come into his own. Two of the album's three best songs (John Lennon's *Come Together* being the other) were Harrison compositions: *Here Comes the Sun*, and the ballad that Frank Sinatra (with a bit of hyperbole) would call the finest love song written in the past fifty years: *Something*.

George wrote the chords and melody at the piano during a break in making the group's *White Album* in 1968, taking his initial inspiration from the title of a song on James Taylor's debut album on the Beatles' Apple label released in December 1968, *Something in the Way She Moves*. It took him awhile to work out the lyrics, but Harrison proudly noted that it's "probably the nicest melody line I've ever written."[313] It was too late to be included on the album, so he gave the song to Joe Cocker; as it happens, Cocker's version (on his second album) was released just a few weeks after *Abbey Road*. George then recorded it with backing by twelve violas, four violins, four cellos, and a string bass. But the song was more than just George and an orchestra, as Tim Riley emphasizes: "The interplay between Paul McCartney's bass and George's guitar during the guitar solo . . . is one of the best things about the song itself—Paul comes close to stealing the show."[314]

---

tryouts of the number that Elvis returned to the studio in the first week of August to overdub the rise-and-fall coda (not a part of the original January recording) that became a highlight of the issued record.

310. *Something* was also #1 in New Zealand, Norway, and Singapore, and #3 in France.

311. BMI honored *Something* in 1989 for not only reaching the milestone of four million total broadcasting performances, but also as one of the twenty most-played songs for the twelve months ending in September 1988, the only one of the Top 20 dating from before the 1980s (September 30, 1989, *Billboard*).

312. An Internet tabulation of the top 10,000 hits of 1955–2000 (based on sales, radio airplay, etc.) ranked it #49 for the modern era. In the *Zagat Survey Music Guide* (2003), over 10,500 participants voted *Abbey Road* the #2 album of all time.

313. Harrison told Timothy White that, despite popular belief, the song was not specifically inspired by his then-wife Patti. When he wrote it, "I had Ray Charles in my head. I always imagined Ray singing it, and eventually he did record it." (July 4, 1992, *Billboard*).

314. Riley, *Tell Me Why*, p. 315–17.

---

306. Leech's "incredible bass line," intricate and jazzy, is called one of the record's highlights according to Roben Jones.

307. Roben Jones elaborates in *Memphis Boys: The Story of American Studios* (p. 212–13). Two representatives of Hill & Range, Presley's publisher, backed Moman up "like a cornered animal," demanding a piece of the song. "In what may have been his finest hour at American," Chips adamantly refused before storming back into the control room, and after a tense few moments, Elvis went ahead with the session.

308. *Careless Love: The Unmaking of Elvis Presley*, p. 335.

309. Feature on Presley's 1969 comeback, *Oxford American Southern Music Issue* (Summer 2005), p. 136. His performance of the song at the Las Vegas Hilton on August 24, 1969, before the single's release (finally issued in the 2001 boxed set *Elvis: Live in Las Vegas*), a six-and-a-half-minute rendition with multiple crescendos, was "thrilling"; upon its conclusion, "his—and our—excitement is palpable." It was only after such early live

From its fetching melody and elegantly simple lyrics, to Harrison's warm vocal and impeccable guitar solos, *Something* was his masterpiece. David Segal writes of his guitar solo here that it "starts in an almost casual whisper, then slowly builds to a series of insistent squiggles."[315] Broadcast Music, Inc., (BMI) ranks it as the #17 most-played song from 1940 onward.

Thomas Ryan: "*Something* moves at a languid, slow-as-molasses pace that is both self-assured and romantic. The atmosphere resonates with the peace of mind and satisfaction that comes after making love . . . none [of the cover versions] has come close to the ethereal feeling of the original."[316]

Come Together (1969)—The Beatles
Apple 2654
Recorded July 21–30, 1969; chart debut Oct. 18, 1969 (#1 for 1 week); #4 in England (as B side of *Something*);[317] from the album *Abbey Road* (*GHF, RS-#205, AHR, TC, DMDB*)

Digging one of the hardest-rocking blues grooves of any Beatles single, John Lennon began writing *Come Together* as a possible campaign song for Timothy Leary for governor of California (a notion shot down when Leary was imprisoned for advocacy of drugs). His opening line was borrowed from Chuck Berry's *You Can't Catch Me* ("Here comes old flat top"), which led the copyright holder to sue Lennon (a case resolved when Lennon later agreed to record that Berry number); but the rest of the song is unmistakably from the darker recesses of his psyche. Thomas Ryan: "He sounds bitter, resentful, and paranoid, and his detached expression adds to the overall impact . . . Bleak and flippant, moody and taunting, Lennon's lyrical shell game tests his audience's faith, tempting them to follow him and interpret the meaning of his confusing self-portrait. In that sense, *Come Together* is a Rorschach test, an invitation to wade through this aural cubist portrait to see Lennon as he saw himself."[318] Tim Riley sees the piece as a skillful exercise in "unraveling separate strands of identity crouched in contradictions and cryptic asides."[319]

Besides the potent quality of the song, the group's performance here—putting behind them the sloppiness of their January 1969 sessions whose music had to be

shelved for a year—is Grade A. Lennon, seldom generous in praising his bandmates, complimented Paul McCartney on the "swampy and smoky" piano lick he worked out for the song. Mark Hertsgaard writes that the song "was a prime example of how tight and powerful a musical unit all four Beatles continued to be during the *Abbey Road* period. There is as much inventiveness and life in the first three seconds of *Come Together* as is found on whole albums by many other musicians."[320]

Moondance (1970)—Van Morrison
From the album *Moondance* (chart debut March 14, 1970, #29 peak)
Later reissued as a single on Warner 8450, chart debut Nov. 19, 1977 (#92 peak) (*RHF, GHF, RS-#231*)

Dreamy and giddily romantic, *Moondance* is a jazz-inflected ballad that Van Morrison felt could be perfect for Frank Sinatra, but not even the Chairman could have matched the inspired vocal adventure on which Van takes us in this timeless performance. His previous album *Astral Weeks*—critically beloved but commercially unsuccessful—had been the result of creative inspiration for Morrison, while by contrast (describes biographer Steve Turner) *Moondance* "was the result of perspiration." "The apparent effortlessness of the title track was achieved only after repeated attempts throughout 1969 to tape a version that satisfied him." At least six New York sessions revolved around the song.[321] But persistence paid off with a classic. *Rolling Stone*, in ranking the album #65 for all time in 2003, writes that as Morrison turns words over in his mouth, he is "not scatting so much as searching for the sound of magic."[322] A terrific band provides impeccable support, providing him on this album with the freedom "to swing from Stax-like soul to cocktail-bar jazz and country blues."

(Album personnel: Jack Schrorer on alto & soprano sax, Collin Tillton on tenor sax & flute, Jeff Labes on keyboards, John Platania on lead & rhythm guitars, John Klingberg on bass, Garry Malabar on drums & vibes, Guy Masson on congo drum; produced by Morrison, with executive producer Lewis Merenstein)

Black Magic Woman (1970)—Santana (written by Peter Green)
Columbia 45270
Recorded on June 4 & 5, 1970; chart debut Nov. 14, 1970 (peak position #4); reached #1 in France, #2

---

315. Jonathan Gould in *Can't Buy Me Love* (p. 576–77) points out that the tune in the verse "is actually very narrow, moving in a range of five notes, which allows George to sing it with great relaxation and force. What gives the song its melodic flavor is the pining electric guitar riff that introduces the verse and the bridge (and whose effect is amplified as the song progresses by George Martin's unobtrusive arrangement for strings)."

316. *American Hit Radio*, p. 360–61.

317. *Come Together* was also #1 in New Zealand and Switzerland, #2 in Canada, and #4 in Japan and Spain.

318. *American Hit Radio*, p. 359–60.

319. Riley, *Tell Me Why*, p. 312–15.

---

320. Hertsgaard, *A Day in the Life*, p. 295–97. Ian MacDonald (*Revolution in the Head*, p. 358–59) sees it as "a call to unchain the imagination and, by setting language free, loosen the rigidities of political and emotional retrenchment."

321. *Van Morrison: Too Late to Stop Now*, p. 98, 101.

322. December 11, 2003, *Rolling Stone*, p. 113.

in Canada; from the album *Abraxas* (6 weeks at #1) (*RHF, GHF, DM*)

With roots in Latin and African musical traditions as well as rock, blues, and jazz, Santana—the band and its leader Carlos Santana—carved out a niche all their own in the psychedelic scene of San Francisco after its formation in 1966. Born on July 20, 1947, in Autlan de Navarro, Mexico, the son of a Mariachi violinist, Carlos Santana and his ensemble made a crucial connection with promoter Bill Graham, signed with Columbia, and created a sensation at the Woodstock festival in August 1969. That perfectly coincided with the release of their debut album, which became a smash thanks largely to the leader's distinctively fiery yet always relaxed guitar sound that could be mistaken for no one else's.

Black Magic Woman began as a cut from the early-1969 Fleetwood Mac album *English Rose*, written by the group's then-leader Peter Green. As an extended cut from the second Santana album *Abraxas*, it provided a dazzling showcase for Carlos' guitar pyrotechnics, and the song was combined with Hungarian jazz guitarist Gabor Szabo's *Gypsy Queen*. Edited for single release, it soared to the Top Five and helped drive the chart-topping album to sales exceeding five million. Gregg Rolie's vocal provides just the right aura of mystery to the supernatural-tinged lyrics (his organ further adds to the song's sense of atmosphere) as Santana's guitar soloing weaves over, under, and around him.

The band decided to record the song after Rolie started to sing it at a soundcheck in Fresno, Carlos Santana said. "If you'll listen to Fleetwood Mac's, it's very different than ours, even though it is the same song. We arranged it differently and put our own fingerprints on it."[323] A key element in the sound of *Abraxas* was the band's addition of veteran jazz engineer Fred Catero as co-producer. Dave Marsh notes the extent of the ethnic fusion at work here, with "a Mexican-American guitar player steeped in the salsa of the Eastern Caribbean playing a black blues song written by a British/Jewish guitarist turned fundamentalist Christian. What's amazing is how well the smoldering power of Santana's guitar and the husky yearning" of Rolie's vocal have held up.[324] And the musical power of Carlos Santana held up so well that he scored the most phenomenal hit of his career after years out of the limelight with the 1999 album *Supernatural*, which sold over 14 million copies and swept the Grammies.

America the Beautiful (1972)—Ray Charles
ABC/TRC 11329 (uncharted B side of *Look What They've Done to My Song, Ma*)

From his album *A Message from the People* (chart debut Apr. 29, 1972); new version issued as CrossOver 985 (chart debut Apr. 17, 1976, #98 R&B) (*GHF, DM*)

Next to Woody Guthrie's *This Land Is Your Land*, perhaps no patriotic American anthem is more powerful and moving than *America the Beautiful*. Nearly eighty years after its creation, the song received its definitive rendition in the magnificently soulful performance of Ray Charles. Katharine Lee Bates was inspired to write *America the Beautiful* by a train trip she made to Colorado in 1893. Traveling through the Midwest inspired her lines about fruited plains and purple mountains; along the way she stopped in Chicago for a 400th anniversary exposition on Columbus coming to America, and its so-called "white city" of fourteen brilliantly illuminated buildings inspired the "alabaster cities" of the last verse. At the conclusion of her trip, it was her July 22, 1893, mule ride to the top of Colorado's Pikes Peak that inspired her opening lines: "O beautiful for spacious skies / For amber waves of grain . . ."

Her words were first published in *The Conregationalist*, a Boston church weekly, on July 4, 1895. A melody by New Jersey church organist Samuel Augustus Ward, originally titled *Materna* (1882), was first wed to Bates' words in 1904.[325] Bates continued revising the poem, publishing the final version in 1911, according to a 2001 book by Bates' great-niece, *America the Beautiful: The Stirring True Story Behind Our Nation's Favorite Song*.[326] There was an effort to have it declared the national anthem in the 1920s, before Congress finally gave that distinction to *The Star-Spangled Banner*.

In the wrong musical hands, this is a song that (like most patriotic odes) can seem positively cornball. But Ray Charles believed in the ideals it represented, and he sang it with passion and gospel-fired organ and piano, backed by a choir, and in so doing transformed, broadened, and elevated its meaning. After Charles first recorded the song in 1972, four years later a new version was issued to coincide with the Bicentennial. Then, after the horrible events of September 11, 2001, his recording began to receive massive radio airplay (as it had never received before) as a numbed nation struggled to recover its spirit; Ray performed it at the World Series and other events around the country. If any single song can be said to have helped (in some small way) to heal a nation, Charles performed that service with *America the Beautiful*.

323. Craig Rosen, *Billboard Book of Number One Albums*, p. 126.
324. Marsh, *The Heart of Rock & Soul*, p. 537–38.

325. The poem and this music were first printed together in a YMCA hymnal published October 25, 1910 (Fuld, *Book of World-Famous Music*, p. 96).
326. The first major recording of the song was in 1925 by longtime Metropolitan Opera star Louise Homer.

After Charles' death in 2004, black *Washington Post* columnist William Raspberry noted how "his prayerful exaltation of America has become the virtual theme song of the Fourth of July . . . Charles transformed the holiday for me—from the Norman Rockwell tableaux that never seemed to include anyone who looked like me—to a holiday for all Americans." Brother Ray accomplished that because "he had a way of cutting through the confusions and mixed emotions and preconceptions, and reaching us at our very core. The genius that made it possible for him to universalize the blues and spirituals and country—anything he touched—made it possible for him to universalize patriotism, too." When Charles subtly changed Bates' lyrics to sing "God done shed his grace on thee! He crowned thy good, yes he did, in a brotherhood," the singer didn't merely shift to black vernacular, but (Raspberry suggested) changed the meaning, by passionately affirming that American brotherhood and sisterhood, across all racial and other differences, is a divine dispensation. And if that allows people to "believe that their nobler instinct represents their 'true' self—that it is their greed, their envy and their bigotry that are the aberration"—well, that's not a bad thing at all.[327]

Drift Away (1973)—Dobie Gray (written by Mentor Williams)
Decca 33057
Recorded on Jan. 5, 1973; Chart debut Feb. 24, 1973 (#5 peak in *Billboard*, reached #4 in *Record World*);[328] #4 in France, #13 in Canada (*DM-#145, AHR*)

A classic statement of the power of music to envelop one's being and at least momentarily sweep troubles aside, *Drift Away* is timeless.

Born Lawrence Darrow Brown on July 26, 1940, in Brookshire/Simonton, Texas,[329] Dobie Gray came to Los Angeles in 1960 and recorded under a variety of names before breaking through with his 1965 hit *The In Crowd*. His followup singles went nowhere, until *Drift Away* became the defining song of his career. Gray had been recording demos for songwriter Paul Williams in the early 1970s, and this is what introduced him to Paul's brother, songwriter-producer Mentor Williams. Mentor helped him land a new contract with MCA, and in Nashville produced the album that included this classic, with an elegant string arrangement by Mike Leech. Beyond its exceptional quality, the record also earned a footnote in pop music history as the final single release on the original Decca label.[330] The classic provided quite a finale after a history dating back to 1934. The striking Williams-penned ballad *Loving Arms* deserved to be a comparably big sequel but fell short of hit status, and Gray had just one more Top 40 hit five years later, *You Can Do It*. But in 2004, when the rock group Uncle Kracker cut a faithful remake of *Drift Away*, Gray was invited to sing the final chorus on the song that he had called "my salvation" three decades earlier[331], and it returned him to the upper reaches of the pop chart one more time.

Dave Marsh: "Gray sang on the raspy side of easeful, which made him perfect for [the song's] complex message in which the desire to rock out is presented as the desire to dream, the longing to bop is equated with the longing to be soothed . . . *Drift Away* makes the music seem bigger simply by restating its finest accomplishment—the degree to which it sank into the hearts of men."[332] "When times are hard," writes Thomas Ryan, "music is a means of escape, helping us ease our worries by transcending them. This is no small matter, and the beauty of *Drift Away* is that it enacts exactly what it is celebrating. When it comes on, we drift away."[333]

(The all-white Nashville backing band for the album includes David Briggs—best known for producing Neil Young's album *Everybody Knows This Is Nowhere*—on keyboards, Reggie Young on guitar, Mike Leech and Troy Seals on bass, and Kenny Malone on drums.)

The Way We Were (1973)—Barbra Streisand (music by Marvin Hamlisch, lyrics by Alan & Marilyn Bergman)
Columbia 45944
Chart debut Nov. 24, 1973 (3 weeks at #1); #1 (1 week) in Canada, #6 in Australia, #31 in England (*GHF, AFI-#8, WASH-#21,*[334] *Trad-#41, BBC-#89, DMDB-#98, RIA, ASCAP*)

Barbra Streisand's first chart-topping single after a decade as one of the biggest-selling female recording artists ever, *The Way We Were* also provided the perfect theme song for one of the era's most fondly remembered movie romances.

Born Barbara Joan Streisand on April 24, 1942, in Brooklyn (she would later change the spelling of her first name to make it more distinctive), the legendary diva got her professional start singing in a Greenwich

---

327. Raspberry, July 5, 2004, *Washington Post*, p. A17.

328. Only reached #42 R&B.

329. Gray was one of eight children in a family of sharecroppers scuffling to make a living on frequently arid Texas soil. His first professional break came answering an ad placed by Sonny Bono, then A&R man for the Specialty label.

330. Michael Ruppli, *The Decca Labels: A Discography*. The company had been acquired in 1969 by MCA Communications Group, and after *Drift Away* the corporation discontinued the Decca name so that all new recordings and reissues came out under the MCA imprint.

331. Interview, March 27, 1974, *New Musical Express*.

332. *The Heart of Rock & Soul*, p. 100–101.

333. *American Hit Radio*, p. 457.

334. Ranked as the #6 favorite song in eight combined 1973–1980 listener surveys by WASH-FM in Washington, D.C.

Village club and then New York's famous Blue Angel. Producer David Merrick saw her there, cast her in the 1962 Broadway musical *I Can Get It for You Wholesale*, and her huge voice and potent stage presence made an immediate impression. Her 1963 debut album for Columbia won the Grammies' top honor as Album of the Year and stayed on the *Billboard* chart for 101 weeks. Streisand proceeded to triumph on Broadway portraying Fanny Brice in 1964's *Funny Girl*, and four years later co-won the Academy Award as best actress in the movie version, launching a decades-spanning career as actress and later director.

The Way We Were cast her as a gawky Jewish leftist political activist who fell in love with her polar opposite, Robert Redford as a dapper WASP apolitical writer, depicting their unlikely romance from college and into marriage and divorce. One of Streisand's favorite song-writing teams, husband and wife Alan and Marilyn Bergman, teamed with composer Marvin Hamlisch to produce a title song capturing the arc of the characters' romance with all its bittersweet qualities.[335]

They wrote the first version of the song while filming was still underway, and reactions to it were positive, but they decided to try an alternate approach. So Hamlisch composed a different melody, and the Bergmans a new lyric; as Alan explained it, "to function the same way that song worked in the movie, as a corridor back into time," but in a "more cerebral" way. Streisand and director Sydney Pollack loved both songs; to decide which one to use, Barbra recorded both, and they were compared in terms of how each worked against the images in the film. "And the first one we wrote—which became the big hit—worked with the images, and the other one didn't." The alternate version was released years later on a Streisand retrospective album, cheekishly titled *The Way We Weren't*.[336] David Jenness and Don Velsey note that the hit tune is "adored by singers for its romantic sweep. The way the melody wreathes itself" around one point in the chord structure is "memorable."[337] The Bergmans, whose previous songs had included the gorgeous *What Are You Doing the Rest of Your Life?*, would re-team with Barbra for her 1983 film *Yentl*.[338]

The Grammy winner as Song of the Year and also Academy Award winner as best song, *The Way We Were* was selected as the #8 greatest movie song ever in 2004 by the American Film Institute.

What Made America Famous (1974)—Harry Chapin
Elektra 45893
Cash Box chart debut July 6, 1974 (#87 peak); from the album *Verities & Balderdash* (chart debut Sept. 7, 1974, #4 peak)

Just in time for the 4th of July, Harry Chapin unleashed this epic parable about the heart of America—after first taking us through a horrific tale that also showed the darker side of the national character. One Los Angeles radio station made *What Made America Famous* the only current record it played on the 1974 Independence Day oldies weekend.

The specific inspiration for the song was the town of Point Lookout, New York, an extremely conservative community in which Chapin was living while working on the 1970 re-election campaign of Congressman Allard Lowenstein. Because he was a shaggy-haired activist and folk singer who sometimes performed at a coffeehouse he'd set up in the town, Chapin was resented by some fellow residents. The central incident in the piece was based on fact: a suspicious fire at one of the few places in town where many black families lived; it took the volunteer fire department two hours to answer the call. He dubbed *What Made America Famous* his "farewell document" when he moved away two years later.

More broadly, the song was also an outgrowth of the passionate social activism that had become a major part of Chapin's life during the preceding year, above all his deep involvement in the world hunger issue to which he would devote literally hundreds of benefit concerts to the end of his life. "I cared almost too deeply for that song," Chapin remarked a few years later. "I loved it. I wanted it to be a hit more than anything I ever wrote." "He felt the song made an important statement about America and the American dream, which embodied everything Chapin had learned to become, a social activist and humanitarian," writes Chapin biographer Peter M. Coan, "To him, America seemed to have forgotten the passion for life it had in the Sixties . . . Chapin felt it was time to reintroduce some hope into that great dream of ours."[339] The original version of the song had a bleak ending in which the bigoted firemen allow the hippie kids and welfare families to die, but fortunately he decided to have one of the firemen rise above his prejudices and come to the rescue, serving as a symbol of hope.

335. The Bergmans had first met Streisand in 1962 before her Broadway breakthrough. "I'd never heard anyone like her in my life," recalled Marilyn. (William J. Mann: *Hello, Gorgeous: Becoming Barbra Streisand*, p. 241–42.)

336. Bishop, *Songs in the Rough*, p. 80.

337. *Classic American Popular Song: The Second Half-Century, 1950–2000*, p. 246–47.

338. While *The Way We Were* was still riding high on the charts, Hamlisch scored a Top Ten single of his own with the Scott Joplin piano instrumental *The Entertainer* from the score of *The Sting*, and a year later his Broadway epic *A Chorus Line* became the longest-running musical in history to that time, with over 6,000 performances from 1975 until it finally closed in 1990.

339. Coan, p. 293–94.

Less than a year later, Chapin made it the centerpiece of his Broadway musical *The Night That Made America Famous*, in which he starred, with his original songs set against the general theme of America's journey from the idealism of the Kennedy administration through the disillusionment of assassinations, Vietnam, and Watergate. Opening on February 26, 1975, at the Ethel Barrymore Theater, produced by Edgar Lansbury and Joseph Beruh of *Gypsy* and *Godspell* fame, and directed by Gene Frankel (already the winner of three Obies for his celebrated off-Broadway productions), the show ran for seven weeks and forty-five performances, although it was nominated for two Tony Awards. In the song's sprawling tale we see small-town prejudice and injustice, but also courage and compassion. And his central question slices to the essence of what a great country should be: "Something's burning somewhere. Does anybody care? Is anybody there?"

Bohemian Rhapsody (1976)—Queen (written by Freddie Mercury)

Elektra 45297

British chart debut Nov. 8, 1975 (EMI 2375, 9 weeks at #1); U.S. chart debut Jan. 3, 1976 (peak position #9); #1 (5 weeks) in Australia, #1 (2 weeks) in Canada[340]; returned to chart on March 21, 1992 (peak position #2); returned to #1 (5 weeks) in U.K. in Dec. 1991 (*GHF, RHF, UK-#4, DMDB-#17, BBC-#18, Time, RS-#166, 1001, TC*)

Queen guitarist Brian May told *Rolling Stone* that everyone in the band was bewildered when lead singer/songwriter Freddie Mercury brought them a draft of the four-part suite *Bohemian Rhapsody*—even before he told them, "That's where the operatic parts come in!" A pop song like no other, it became Britain's biggest-selling record in history to that point,[341] and sixteen years after hitting the American Top Ten, soared still higher after being featured in the Mike Myers comedy *Wayne's World*.

Queen was formed in London in 1971, merging hard-rocking drive with elements of British music hall and plenty of bombast. Elektra's Jac Holzman was knocked out by the group's demo tape, and got into an intense battle with Columbia to sign the band; as Holzman recalled in his memoir, "this was going to be Harry Chapin times two, Clive Davis and me duking it out again."[342]

Killer Queen, from their third album at the end of 1974, was their first major hit, introducing most listeners to Mercury's charismatic vocal style and the band's multi-layered guitars and overdubbed vocals. A year later came *Bohemian Rhapsody*.

A wild six-minute montage of pseudo-opera and heavy metal, it had a vast sound that was unlike anything that came before, spinning a tale of a young man who's set to die for committing murder.[343] The band started recording the album on August 24, 1975, at Rockfield's Studio 1 in rural Wye Valley; for the pseudo-opera section, producer Roy Thomas Baker drew upon his experience helping to record the D'Oyly Carte Opera Company for Decca.[344] It was all campy and over-the-top, yet quite irresistible; even if one couldn't take it too seriously, the furious craft that went into the song was remarkable. *Rolling Stone*: "Recording technology was so taxed by the song's multi-tracked scaramouches and fandangos that some tapes became virtually transparent from being overdubbed so many times."[345] While many were overwhelmed upon hearing the insanely ambitious six-minute track, others, notes biographer Mark Blake, asked them in essence, "Are you out of your mind?" But the band formed a united front behind Mercury's insistence that it should be the leadoff single from *A Night at the Opera*, with historic results.

Queen ran up a long string of hits into the 1980s including *We Are the Champions* and *Crazy Little Thing Called Love*. After Mercury's death from complications due to AIDS in late 1991, an all-star memorial concert at Wembley Stadium was broadcast to an international audience of a billion people.

The Wreck of the Edmund Fitzgerald (1976)—Gordon Lightfoot

Reprise 1194

Chart debut Aug. 28, 1976 (spent 2 weeks at #2); #1 (1 week) in Canada; #40 in England;[346] from the album *Summertime Dream* (*Folk-#112*)

On November 10, 1975, extending to early November 11, a horrendous storm ranking among the worst ever since commercial shipping began on the Five Great

---

340. #1 for 7 weeks in Belgium, 4 weeks in Holland, #1 in Yugoslavia. It's reported to have sold over three million copies worldwide.

341. Even as of 2011, it ranked as the third biggest-selling British single ever (over two million copies), and the second top record ever on the U.K. charts.

342. *Follow the Music*, p. 380–82. As in Chapin's case, Queen and its manager Jack Nelson were won over by Holzman's personal belief in the group's music, overriding Columbia's superior resources. And as with Chapin, Queen's trademark song was epic-length and vastly more complex than the Top 40 norm.

343. Mercury used, as a point of departure, a variation on the opening line ("Mama just killed a man") of an unfinished number he did with Chris Smith from 1968, *The Cowboy Song*.

344. Blake, *Is This the Real Life?*, p. 167–75. Baker's other top successes as producer were the first four albums by The Cars, and Journey's first two hit LPs.

345. *Rolling Stone 500 Greatest Songs* (2010), p. 63. Blake: "In the pre-digital age, Queen had just twenty-four analog tracks to work with. However, to complicate the process, they then had to record the backing vocals before the lead vocal." As Mercury tacked on more "Galileos" and the new vocal harmonies were "bounced" onto existing tracks, the total overdubs for the song are said to have totaled up to 180.

346. #3 in France.

Lakes in 1913 sank the giant ore freighter the SS *Edmund Fitzgerald* (at 729 feet the length of two football fields) on Lake Superior, killing all twenty-nine men on board. The ship's radars went out as the ship began filling with water and then listing to one side. As the storm grew in ferocity, with waves thirty feet high, several coast guard stations shut down, communications towers were evacuated, and finally all power in Sault Ste. Marie went out. The ship *Arthur M. Anderson*, which accompanied the *Fitzgerald* across the lake, turned around and headed back into the storm in a desperate but futile effort to save the doomed men. Just months after the tragedy, Ontario-born folk troubadour Gordon Lightfoot ensured that the men would not be forgotten by creating this classic narrative ballad.

Not mentioned in the song is an eerie historical fact: On November 11, 1913, 254 lives were lost when eighteen ships (twelve of them on Lake Superior) went down in another devastating storm (the so-called "Great Lakes Storm" that had begun on November 7). Also, a November 11–13, 1940 storm on Lake Michigan killed fifty-seven men on three freighters. As Lightfoot sings, based on an old sailor's tale, Superior "never gives up her dead," because of the low temperature of the water, causing bodies to sink and never surface.[347]

Lightfoot (born on November 17, 1938, in Orillia, Ontario) created his epic atop a long, British-derived tradition of folk tunes about maritime disasters including on the Great Lakes. Carl Sandburg's *American Songbag* (1927) features one, *Red Iron Ore*, with a detailed narrative structure much like the *Edmund Fitzgerald*. "It is a log, the diary of a ship and its men on one cruise," writes Sandburg. Riding up Lake Michigan, the two vessels traveling from Chicago to Cleveland "passed through death's door" as the storm howled furiously. Unlike the doomed men of the *Fitzgerald*, the men of *Red Iron Ore* lived to tell the tale.[348]

Ever since he first emerged on the Canadian folk scene a decade earlier, Lightfoot had made vivid story songs one of his stocks in trade, such as his *Canadian Railroad Trilogy* recalling the heroes who helped forge a path across the nation.[349] In *Edmund Fitzgerald* (the freighter, incidentally, was named after a former presi-

dent of Northwestern Life Insurance Co., which owned the vessel) he traced the tragedy from start to finish with documentary-like detail.[350] Like Henry Wadsworth Longfellow in *The Song of Hiawatha*, he used the Indian name for Lake Superior ("On the shores of Gitche Gumee . . . Dark behind it rose the forest, rose the black and gloomy pine trees"). A six-and-a-half-minute ballad with no melodic bridge, spinning a tale of death, hardly seemed a likely candidate for pop success. Yet the story gripped everyone who heard it, aided by a stately, somber electric guitar line that serves as the musical hook. It became the second biggest hit of his career (after the 1974 chart-topper *Sundown*).

Lightfoot himself had gone sailing on Lake Superior, and, notes biographer Maynard Collins, "knew what it was like to confront its viciousness when winds were at gale-force." He resolved to make the song "a memorial" to the ship's crew. With some understandable hyperbole, Collins called this "a song which resonated within the unconsciousness of the nation, a story which millions . . . found so compelling" that listening to it on the radio became not mere entertainment, but "more in the nature of a religious experience . . ."[351]

Isn't She Lovely? (1976)—Stevie Wonder
From the Tamla album *Songs in the Key of Life* (chart debut Oct. 16, 1976, 14 weeks at #1)[352] (*GHF for album*)

One would be hard pressed to find a more emotionally touching song about the joys of new parenthood than Stevie Wonder's *Isn't She Lovely*. From the moment his epic two-and-a-half-disc album *Songs in the Key of Life* hit stores after months of anticipation, this was the song that generated the most requests and touched the deepest chords. Even though never released as a single, it ranks alongside his chart-toppers as one of his most enduring works.

After three consecutive classic albums—*Talking Book* (November 1972), *Innervisions* (1973), and *Fulfillingness' First Finale* (1974)—the latter two both Grammy winners as album of the year—the world anxiously awaited his next offering. But as he plunged into a series of marathon sessions that sometimes kept him in the studio for forty-eight hours straight without sleep, the scheduled release date for the new album kept getting pushed back. After laying down a rough instrumental track on electric piano or drums and an outline of his vocal, he would call his musicians at all hours of the day or night so he could seize the time of musical inspiration. At one

347. The thirty-fifth anniversary of the tragedy in November 2010 brought press accounts of the continuing mystery over how the sinking happened. The lingering uncertainties caused Lightfoot to slightly alter his lyrics that year after watching a documentary that suggested a "rogue wave" was to blame; he eliminated a reference to a hatchway failure and the suggestion of human error. The *Edmund Fitzgerald* wreckage still sits 530 feet below Lake Superior's surface.

348. Sandburg, p. 176.

349. His four albums for United Artists starting in 1966 were packed with songs later recorded by other artists, including *Early Morning Rain* (popularized by Peter, Paul, & Mary), until he made his own breakthrough as a hit-making artist with *If You Could Read My Mind*.

350. He got the idea for the song from a *Newsweek* account of the disaster.

351. Collins, *Lightfoot: If You Could Read His Mind*, p. 191–94.

352. It was #1 for 20 weeks on the R&B chart, and placing it #5 for all time (*Joel Whitburn's Top R&B Albums*).

point in early 1976 a full-scale press listening party had been scheduled before Wonder abruptly cancelled it to work on the music some more. More than just evidence of his perfectionism, it was as if he wanted to pour his entire life essence into this one album.

Finally, the wait was over, and *Songs in the Key of Life* met every expectation. Craig Werner writes in *Higher Ground* that the album "weaves the threads of gospel, jazz, and the blues into a tapestry that defines the breadth and depth of the African American tradition as clearly as any record ever made."[353] The album was the longest-running #1 smash of his career, and became his third consecutive release to win Album of the Year honors from the Grammies.

Isn't She Lovely? was Stevie's gift—biographer Mark Ribowsky calls it a "three-chord sonata"[354]—to his daughter Aisha Zakia (the African words for "strength and intelligence"). Aisha was born on April 7, 1975, the product of his relationship with Yolanda Simmons following his divorce from Syreeta Wright. A father for the first time, Wonder—after years of living on the run without a fixed address, going from hotel rooms to studios—bought homes in California and New York City to try and provide a stable family life. However, the obsessive process of creating the album kept him away from home as much as ever despite his best efforts.

The song begins with the actual recording of a newborn baby's first cry (they made the rounds of Los Angeles maternity wards to capture just the right sound), and then launches into a sweet, warm melody with a brisk medium tempo and a vocal radiating pure joy and happiness. His harmonica solo here, writes biographer John Swenson, "is one of the best things Stevie ever recorded."[355] The lyrics are simple and unaffected, perfectly expressing the emotions of the occasion. When he sings, "I can't believe what God has done, through us he's given life to one," you don't doubt for an instant the words come from the heart. Late in the song, the repeat choruses are accompanied by the sound of Stevie giving Aisha a bath.

Songs in the Key of Life is one of only nineteen recordings ever inducted into the Grammy Hall of Fame in its first year of eligibility (2002). Called the #56 top album ever by *Rolling Stone* in 2003, it was ranked as the #7 greatest album by VH1 the same year.

Until the Night (1978)—Billy Joel
From the Columbia album *52nd Street* (chart debut Oct. 28, 1978, 8 weeks at #1); song released as a single in England (reached #50, April 1979)

Long Island–born Billy Joel (born May 9, 1949, in the town of Hicksville), whose hit-making career was launched by 1974's *Piano Man*, was on an incredible roll from 1977–1980, running off three consecutive albums that would have combined sales of more than 24 million. The centerpiece of this hot streak—and the Grammy winner as Album of the Year—was *52nd Street*. A potent and diverse collection that encompassed ballads and rockers, plus Latin and jazz-inflected pieces, the album included the hits *My Life* and *Big Shot*, but perhaps its finest song was Joel's fabulous musical tribute to the sounds of Phil Spector and the Righteous Brothers, *Until the Night*.

A tale of an Everyman trying to get through the day and to overcome his insecurities until he can truly come alive at night alongside his woman, *Until the Night* achieves musical melodrama in the Spector tradition of moving from soft and subtle to steadily mounting orchestration and emotion. The piece builds relentlessly, with Joel singing multi-tracked baritone-tenor harmonies with himself to evoke Bill Medley and Bobby Hatfield, until it becomes a soaring epic. (Joel biographer Hank Bordowitz notes that the blue-eyed soulsters and Spector had been, along with the Beatles and R&B, among the artist's strongest musical inspirations.)[356] A passionate saxophone solo by Richie Cannata sends the temperature escalating still higher before the singer brings it all home in the final chorus with a stirring climax that richly satisfies all the mounting anticipation. Credit for the song's

Billy Joel, PhotoFest.

353. Werner, p. 226.
354. Ribowsky, p. 264.
355. Swenson, *Stevie Wonder*, p. 114.

356. Bordowitz, *The Life and Time of an Angry Young Man*, p. 17.

horn and string orchestration goes to Robert Freedman, with concertmaster David Nadien, and Phil Ramone as album producer. It could only have been created by an artist with a deep love for pop traditions, and the consummate skill to equal the men who had inspired him. Even *Rolling Stone*, seldom a Joel partisan, declared this performance "vast and romantic."[357]

Redemption Song (1980)—Bob Marley & the Wailers
Island 49636 (single released in 1980)
From the Island album *Uprising* (chart debut Aug. 9, 1980, #45 peak) (*RS-#66, World-#19, 1001*)

Virtually unique among Bob Marley's major songs, *Redemption Song* is a solo performance, just voice and acoustic guitar. That stripped-down presentation does not diminish its impact as one of the reggae king's most stirring freedom anthems. When Island Records producer Chris Blackwell first heard the tapes for *Uprising*, he told Marley something more was needed. The next day, the artist returned with two new compositions, including *Redemption Song*. He first recorded it with the Wailers, but Blackwell suggested he try it as an acoustic folk song, and the number became the final track on his final album.[358] Biographer Timothy White calls it a "plaintive, almost Dylanesque acoustic spiritual, devoid of any trace of reggae." In it, his voice "bore the authority of a Biblical patriarch."[359] Inspired by the writings of black nationalist Marcus Garvey, it is a potent symbol of the classic Rasta themes: looking back to slavery days in decrying injustice, but, with faith in the Almighty and the shared commitment of the people, predicting ultimate victory over tyranny. "None but ourselves can free our minds," he sings; it is up to each man and woman to remove their mental shackles. Barely nine months after its release, Bob Marley was dead of cancer.

Redemption Song is, declares Kwame Dawes, "a tight fist of a song. Its efficiency is remarkable . . . In four minutes, Marley tells of a history that spans 400 years." The "pirates" described in the first verse are slave merchants. After outlining the horrors of the middle passage until slavery ended in Jamaica in 1838, "he also speaks of the transcendence out of the mire of the system through the 'hand of the Almighty.'" In the modern world, he cautions, we must emancipate ourselves from enslavement of the mind. The song "would confirm Marley's commitment to the task of teaching and leading his people out of the world marked by oppression and hopelessness into a place of survival."[360]

The River (1980)—Bruce Springsteen
From the Columbia album *The River* (chart debut November 1, 1980, 4 weeks at #1); title song released as single in England (reached #35, June 1981)[361] [362] (*TC*)

Ten months after the release of Bruce Springsteen's fourth album *Darkness on the Edge of Town*, sessions for its successor began in early April 1979. As before, the artist's vast array of new material and obsessive perfectionism made the process a marathon; biographer Christopher Sandford cites examples during this period in which Springsteen sat in the studio meticulously deconstructing twenty or more mixes of a three-minute song. He and the E Street Band tried their hand at recording some ninety tracks during the next sixteen months (170 days of studio time typically running from 7 p.m. to 6 a.m.) before finally whittling them down to the twenty songs on the two-record album *The River*.[363] A diverse and powerful collection, arguably its high point was the title song.

Having listened to a lot of Hank Williams and early Johnny Cash during the previous couple of years, Springsteen drew upon their influences in crafting the stark, stripped-down, intense narrative of *The River*. Eric Alterman reports that while living on his farm in Holmdel, New Jersey, he had also been watching old John Ford movies and American film noir of the immediate post–World War II period, and something of their influence can also be heard in the song's beautiful bleakness and quiet desperation.[364] He first publicly performed the song at the September 1979 *No Nukes* concert at Madison Square Garden.

Dave Marsh, writing of the album in general but in words specifically applicable to the title track, calls it "a record about inescapable realities, including the reality of always trying to escape and always falling back . . . Time is always running out" on the characters. "These songs are filled with ghosts and corpses." The heroes of his early albums felt that faith and passion made all things possible; here, faith "will only get you so far, and not a step more."[365] The protagonist here is a working-class kid who gets his girlfriend pregnant, and is forced to settle for a dreary, hard-scrabble life that makes a mockery of his youthful dreams. (The girl is a representation of Springsteen's older sister, who married as a teenager.)[366] "Is a dream a lie if it don't come true?" he asks. The

---

357. Paul Evans, *Rolling Stone Album Guide* (1992), p. 371.
358. In live performance Marley almost always performed this song solo, including his last concert in Pittsburgh in 1980.
359. *Catch a Fire*, p. 306.
360. Dawes, p. 308–12. Nobel Laureate Derek Walcott admired the song for its ability to say so much in a short space.

361. It took awhile for Springsteen to crack the British singles market, and this was actually his highest-charting song until *Dancing in the Dark* in 1984.
362. *The River* sold over five million copies, was Springsteen's first album to hit #1, and was selected as the second-best album of the year in the *Village Voice* critics' poll.
363. Sandford, *Springsteen: Point Blank*, p. 167–69.
364. *It Ain't No Sin*, p. 116.
365. *Two Hearts*, p. 229.
366. "I based the song on the crash of the construction industry in late 1970s New Jersey and the hard times that fell on my sister and her family,"

river itself is both a physical symbol of carefree youth as the place where he and Mary would once go to escape, and finally as a metaphor for what has been lost, as the river—like his life—has gone dry. The music is as haunting as the lyrics, with a yearning vocal and a ghostly quality, and in this brooding, deeply introspective work one hears the sound of a great artist reaching maturity. "A breakthrough song for me," the artist would call it in liner notes for his *Greatest Hits* CD. "It was in the detail. One of the first of my story songs that eventually led to [the album] *Nebraska*."

New Year's Day (1983)—U2
Island 99915
Chart debut Apr. 2, 1983 (#53 peak); reached #10 in England;[367] from the album *War* (chart debut March 19, 1983, #12 peak) (*PW, RS, ACC*)

Written against the background of rising tensions in Eastern Europe with the Solidarity movement challenging the Communist government of Poland and the December 1981 imposition of martial law resulting in the arrest of Solidarity leaders, *New Year's Day* contemplated love in the aftermath of war. Adam Clayton had come up with what Bono called "a killer bass line" at a soundcheck, and The Edge had further developed the melody on piano. Bono struggled with the lyrics, and tensions were rising in the studio; the group was on the verge of a breakthrough after two albums, and much was riding on the third (including a big debt owed to Island Records). Finally Bono improvised the lyrics on the fly, partly inspired by his new wife Ali, and it all came together.[368] The "impressionistic political backdrop infused the track with a sense of separation and longing that

U2, PhotoFest.

gives it its distinctive resonance," relates Niall Stokes. "Subconsciously I must have been thinking about Lech Walesa being interned and his wife not being allowed to see him," recalled Bono. "Then, when we'd recorded the song, they announced that martial law would be lifted in Poland on New Year's Day. Incredible."[369]

Pink Houses (1983)—John Mellencamp (written by John Mellencamp)
Riva 215
Chart debut Dec. 10, 1983 (peak position #8); from the album *Uh-Huh* (chart debut Nov. 5, 1983, reached #9, sold 3 million copies) (*RS, DM, AHR, TC*)

Great songs sometimes spring from simple beginnings. According to John Mellencamp, *Pink Houses* was inspired while driving home to Bloomington from the Indianapolis airport by spotting an old man "sitting on the porch of his pink shack. He waved, and I waved back. That's how the song started." Whereas Mellencamp's earlier hits (such as *Hurts So Good* and *Jack & Diane*) had been self-absorbed, here the maturing artist turned his gaze outward to take a populist stand on behalf of the common man's aspirations in the face of many obstacles. Thomas Ryan: "*Pink Houses* is a simple metaphor for the American dream, stripped down to its most basic form . . . Mellencamp seems awed by the resilience of people who survive in tough times." Maybe fame and fortune are out of reach, "but a little pink house is a perfectly respectable goal to strive for." The artist "sees the beauty of millions of people struggling individually to claim a small slice of fulfillment. The most astonishing thing about his lyrical personification is how . . . Mellencamp turns individual lives into a microcosm of the American experience."[370]

The number was recorded in about a day by the Indiana-born artist in a farmhouse in Brownstown, Indiana.[371] An oblivious Ronald Reagan campaign tried to use the song for a 1984 re-election campaign ad (until the singer shot down the idea), "not noticing the bitter heartland rage under the cheery chorus," *Rolling Stone* noted. A quarter century later he performed *Pink Houses* (backed by a sixty-member Baptist choir) before 400,000 people at the Lincoln Memorial on January 18, 2009, for the "We Are One" concert preceding Barack Obama's inauguration. Dave Marsh remarks that the piece opens with chords lifted from the Rolling Stones' *Salt of the Earth*

Springsteen related in *Songs* (p. 100–101). "When my sister first heard it, she came backstage, gave me a hug, and said, 'That's my life.'"

367. #6 in France, #9 in Norway.

368. As he described in *U2 by U2* (p. 166–67), Bono came up with five or six verses "completely on the mike," with nothing written down, and producer Steve Lillywhite chose the best ones for the record.

369. *U2: Into the Heart*, p. 41

370. Ryan, *American Hit Radio*, p. 530–32.

371. "The Shack," as it was dubbed, had a control room "so small you literally couldn't turn around," using mobile equipment flown in by the Miami-based Criteria Studios. As described by biographer Heather Johnson (p. 61–64), the song was cut live with all the musicians together, "their instruments bleeding into one another, which only added to the album's raw, natural sound."

(or perhaps *Tumbling Dice*), and acknowledges that "the defeated stick with the very hopes that the cynical have pushed aside for fear their hearts will break."[372]

Centerfield (1985)—John Fogerty
Warner 29053
Chart debut May 25, 1985 (#44 peak); from the album
    Centerfield (chart debut Jan. 26, 1985, 1 week at #1)

For nearly ten long years after his second solo album in 1975, John Fogerty was absent from the pop music scene. Enmeshed in a bitter legal battle with his former label Fantasy and reclusive by nature, the former Creedence Clearwater Revival leader seemed to have vanished into the shadows. Then came *Centerfield*—and suddenly, it seemed like 1970 all over again. That one-of-a-kind raspy voice, that chooglin' guitar style, and above all the distinctive narrative voice as songwriter were all delightfully intact. The album's leadoff single, the very Creedence-like rocker *The Old Man Down the Road*, helped drive the album to #1, but still better was the title song, merely one of the most perfect songs ever written about our National Pastime.

"I was never good enough to play ball," Fogerty told Scott Isler as quoted in the Creedence biography *Bad Moon Rising*, "like twenty million frustrated centerfielders. I packed several images into *Centerfield*. I really do love baseball, so I didn't have to research it . . . When I sing, 'And you can kiss that one good-bye,' I'm quoting former Giants and A's announcer Lon Simmons. I decided that the concept of playing in center field in the manner that a twelve-year-old or younger boy might feel about playing center field in Yankee Stadium would be symbolically a nice metaphor for my first comeback album."[373]

He began recording the album shortly after attending baseball's 1984 All-Star Game at Candlestick Park in his native San Francisco, playing all the instruments himself in his home studio. After completing six songs, he played the tape for the head of his new label, Warner; the reaction was ecstatic. When *Centerfield* came out in January 1985, writes biographer Hank Bordowitz, "it was like D. B. Cooper had emerged from the north woods with hundred dollar bills for everyone."

Just as in Creedence classics like *Green River* and *Down on the Corner*, Fogerty took us back to childhood days with timeless images, and not only gave us one of those delicious little guitar hooks (opening the song), but also an infectious, hand-clapping refrain ("I'm ready to play"—clap, clap-clap—"today!"). As it hit the top of the charts, *Centerfield* was called the #10 best album of 1985 in the *Village Voice* critics' poll, which also called the title song the year's #13 best single. With warm memories of fictional characters ("Casey At the Bat"), Chuck Berry (*Brown Eyed Handsome Man*), and real heroes (Willie Mays and Joe DiMaggio), along with a boundless sense of happy possibility, it's become almost as ubiquitous in baseball games as *Take Me Out to the Ball Game*. *Centerfield* is not just about getting in the game; it's about getting off the bench and throwing yourself into life, ready to relish "a moment in the sun." "Put me in, coach . . ."

Sun City (1985)—Artists United Against Apartheid
    (written by Steven Van Zandt)
Manhattan 50017
Chart debut Nov. 2, 1985 (reached #38 on pop chart, #21
    R&B); #21 in England;[374] (*VIL-#22, DM, 1001*)

From the comfort of today's perspective it may seem as if it was historically inevitable that the abomination of apartheid—South Africa's policy of racial segregation— would crumble, but this outcome was hardly a certainty in 1985. The awful laws had been national policy since 1948 and had been enforced with particular brutality since the early 1960s, not only denying the country's overwhelming black majority the right to vote but also stripping them of full citizenship, legal rights (for education, health care, jobs, etc.), and human dignity. And some of the nation's most respected black leaders, above all Nelson Mandela, had languished in prison for decades. Even in the face of international revulsion and economic sanctions, the South African government seemed prepared to defy the world indefinitely. One of their devices to attract foreign dollars and respectability (and to get around sanctions) was to hire Western pop entertainers for lavish concerts at a luxury resort location known as Sun City, which it designated as not technically a part of South Africa, although everyone recognized this as a convenient fiction.

Rocker Steven Van Zandt (born Steven Lento on November 22, 1950, in Winthrop, Massachusetts, and raised in New Jersey), famous for his early role as guitarist/ backing singer in Bruce Springsteen's E Street Band and later with his own albums as Little Steven, responded to the situation by organizing a remarkable all-star project, Artists United Against Apartheid. He wrote and produced *Sun City*, a musically propulsive, emotionally urgent rocker whose array of participants came very close to matching the star power of USA for Africa (*We Are the World*) a few months earlier, but wider in its musical scope including a hefty role for rappers and

---

372. *The Heart of Rock & Soul*, p. 228–29.
373. Bordowitz, p. 198–99.

374. #3 in Holland and Sweden, #4 in Belgium, #5 in Sweden, #10 in France.

world-music figures. And beyond question the fierce anger and explicit desire for political change at the heart of the record was quite different from the brotherly-love approach of the earlier project.[375] Dave Marsh: "Having Bruce Springsteen, Miles Davis, Bobby Womack, Ruben Blades, the Ramones, Pete Townshend, and Run-DMC on one track isn't just an eclectic coup, it's a remarkable breakthrough in artistic unity, at least within what had been pop music's own kind of apartheid." Van Zandt made sure that black performers took the lead, from jazz legend Davis' introductory trumpet soloing onward. "Yet the thing that assures that *Sun City* will last," continues Marsh, "is its stature as one of the most inventive hip-hop records extant, as well as a scorching example of how combustible things can really get when dance-pop and rock are brought together full-bore . . . [this is] an actual left-wing anthem that not only can but must be danced to."[376] The *Village Voice* critics' poll agreed, voting *Sun City* the #1 best single of 1985. Apartheid finally began to collapse through 1990–1993 negotiations, before full democracy arrived with all-races elections in 1994 resulting in Nelson Mandela becoming the first president of all South Africans.[377] Van Zandt carved out a new acting career playing Silvio Dante on HBO's *The Sopranos*, hosted his own syndicated radio show *Little Steven's Underground Garage*, and found time to resume performing with the E Street Band.

The Living Years (1989)—Mike & the Mechanics
(written by Brian Robertson & Mike Rutherford)
Atlantic 88964
Chart debut Jan. 7, 1989 (1 week at #1); #1 (1 week) in Australia, #2 in England, #4 in Canada[378]

During down time between albums by his group Genesis, British guitarist-bassist-songwriter Mike Rutherford (born October 2, 1950) formed the side venture Mike & the Mechanics, which became quite a successful entity in its own right. Rutherford had been one of the founding members of Genesis in 1967, which steadily grew to become a hit-making machine by the 1980s. But as Genesis singer Phil Collins also pursued a simultaneous solo career, the time between albums lengthened; Mike & the Mechanics debuted with the Top Ten hits *Silent Running* and *All I Need Is a Miracle* during the three-year period after the 1983 *Genesis* album; and the five-and-a-half-

year time that followed the 1986 Genesis LP *Invisible Touch* provided the opening for Mike & the Mechanics' biggest hit, *The Living Years*. The group's other key member, Paul Carrack, was born on April 22, 1951, in Sheffield, Yorkshire, England, and served as lead singer of Ace (1975 smash *How Long*), Squeeze (1981 album-rock favorite *Tempted*), also had seven chart hits on his own during the 1980s and 1990s, and enjoyed his greatest success with the Mechanics. The first single from the group's second album in late 1988 got no higher than #63; then came the big one.[379]

Scottish-born Brian (B. A.) Robertson had written the first verse of the song about losing one's father without having the chance to speak from the heart, before his father passed away in 1986. Fred Bronson in *The Billboard Book of Number One Hits* recounts that Robertson was at Rutherford's house when the news came. Rutherford's father had also died that year. They wrote the music around the first verse, and only the second verse was completed when the time came for the recording session. Robertson came up with the emotion-packed final verse shortly before Carrack had to record the vocal.[380] The addition of a children's choir (on the "say it loud, say it clear" chorus) behind Carrack—in his finest performance ever—provided an extra dimension for the song to really pack a wallop. This is a song that expresses important truths in an eloquent, moving way without succumbing to mawkishness. As long as there are parents and children who find it difficult to express shared feelings, *The Living Years* will have meaning.

Tum Agar Yuhi Nazren (c. 1988–1992)—Nusrat Fateh Ali Khan
Included on the Real World CD *The Supreme Collection, Vol. 1.* (did not chart)

The foremost legend of Pakistani music was born on July 12, 1948, in Lyallpur (later renamed Faisalabad), Pakistan. J. Poet: Nusrat "made qawwali—a Sufi devotional music that sings the praises of Allah and was almost unknown outside the Pakistani community—into one of the most exciting genres of world music. A qawwal is known for his vast knowledge of mystic poetry and his ability to weave these texts into a trance-inducing performance. Like Native American and African shamans, qawwals often use repetition and vocables—meaningless syllables and shouts of joy—to express the inexpressible ecstasy of communion with Allah. Nusrat was one of the great qawwals, and perhaps the most expressive singer, in any genre, of the late twentieth century. He often moved audiences to tears, even those who spoke no Arabic or

375. The November 29, 1986, *Billboard* reported that the *Sun City* project donated nearly $400,000 to a United Nations' Africa Fund benefiting political prisoners and their families.

376. *The Heart of Rock and Soul*, p. 444–45.

377. Van Zandt led a performance of *Sun City* at a Mandela tribute concert before 72,000 at Wembley Stadium in 1988. To his disgust, the Fox television network, in its broadcast of the performance, edited out every statement against apartheid, defeating the very purpose of the concert.

378. #1 in Ireland and Japan, #6 in Sweden, #7 Poland, #8 on Pan-European.

379. A key addition to the group for this album was guitarist Tim Renwick, best known for his work with Al Stewart (*Year of the Cat*).

380. Bronson, p. 723.

Farsi, with the sheer emotional power of his voice."[381] Discovered by the West after Peter Gabriel invited him to sing on the soundtrack of *The Last Temptation of Christ* (1988), Nusrat died on August 16, 1997. The late Jeff Buckley: "His voice is velvet fire, simply incomparable . . . There is a pure devotion and a fierce virtuosity to grow wings and soar through music."[382]

On this performance, a chorus of ten voices is led by Nusrat's intense and exceptionally flexible instrument, backed by tabla rhythms and synchronized handclaps, and a melody carried by harmoniums. He scats skillfully in trance-like segments, and sustains a remarkable level of passion across more than eighteen minutes. After Khan's death in 1997, Gabriel declared: "I have never heard so much spirit in a voice. My two main singing inspirations, Nusrat and Otis Redding, have been the extreme examples of how far and how deep a voice can go in finding, touching, and moving a soul."[383]

Louisiana 1927 (1991)—Aaron Neville (written by Randy Newman)

From the A&M album *Warm Your Heart* (chart debut June 29, 1991)

The most gorgeous pop song to spring from the fertile mind of New Orleans native Randy Newman, *Louisiana 1927* is an account of a disastrous flood of the Mississippi delta that also inspired Charley Patton's 1929 two-part blues classic *High Water Everywhere*, and Newman's imagining of President Hoover's visit to the site. Many communities from Illinois and Iowa down to Mississippi and northern Louisiana were destroyed by the April 1927 flood, which submerged some 30 million acres, killed more than 500 people, and left some 700,000 homeless. The Red Cross supervised 154 relief camps, housing and feeding more than 325,000 refugees. (Plaquemine, mentioned in the song, is a town some eighty miles upriver from New Orleans.) Those who lived through it regarded it as a flood of Biblical proportions; folks saw Mississippi catfish swim across the streets of Louisiana towns. William Faulkner would write a book about it, *The Wild Palms*.[384]

The song appeared on Newman's acclaimed 1974 album of pieces about the South, *Good Old Boys*. His limited vocal couldn't detract from the stunning melody (Newman would later borrow elements of it for his clas-

sic 1984 motion picture score for *The Natural*), and rich orchestration; in 1989 it was used memorably under the closing credits of the Louisiana-set film *Blaze*. But this was a song crying out for a great voice to do it full justice. That voice belonged to New Orleans–born (on January 24, 1941) Aaron Neville.

Neville began performing with his brothers in the 1950s, and recorded a series of fine singles for the Minit label starting in 1960 that won a local following but never rose to the national level. His miraculous, multi-octave tenor was brilliantly showcased on his 1966 #2 smash *Tell It Like It Is*, but followup records didn't sell, and for years he returned to being a Crescent City favorite. The Neville Brothers scored wide attention for several outstanding albums starting in 1981, and then Aaron returned to the pop mainstream in 1989 courtesy of Linda Ronstadt, who featured him on her Top Ten album *Cry Like a Rainstorm, Howl Like the Wind*. That success led to a new solo record deal, and Linda co-produced the first album, *Warm Your Heart*. Britt Robson writes that in appearance, Neville—with a huge bodybuilder's physique, earring, and black birthmark over his right eye—has a "look that exudes power with a hint of danger. But when Neville starts to sing in his inimitable falsetto, it's as if angels have unfurled their wings and are hovering beatifically in the heavens."[385]

A longtime friend of Newman's, Ronstadt knew that *Louisiana 1927* was an absolutely perfect vehicle for Neville's one-of-a-kind voice. Wisely, they used the exact same orchestral arrangement as Newman's original. The result is magnificent. In September 2005, in the wake of the human tragedy wrought by Hurricane Katrina across coastal Louisiana and Mississippi—killing some 1,600 people, displacing over a million more, and all but wiping out much of New Orleans as we had known it—Randy Newman led off a nationally televised benefit program by singing his classic, and Aaron Neville performed it at a separate televised benefit for the victims.

Steve Erickson, noting that the song's melody has much in common with that of *Sail Away*, suggests: "*Sail Away* is great in its singularity, although it has the sense of a fable that presumes to speak universal truths, while *Louisiana 1927* is great in its universality, although it has a sense of specificity that fixes it to an exact geography and page of calendar . . . Newman easily assumes the voice of both slaver and farmer, the first in its easy bravado and the second in its plainspoken pathos, while both still share a common American naivete."[386] Anthony Walton: "With this song, which I nominate as the most

---

381. J. Poet, *MusicHound World*, p. 380.

382. Liner notes to *The Supreme Collection, Vol. 1.*

383. August 30, 1997 *Billboard*, p. 10.

384. The cataclysm also inspired contemporary recordings by black preachers such as *The 1927 Flood* (recorded in 1928) by Elder Lonnie McIntorsh, discussed by Paul Oliver in *Songsters and Saints* (p. 195). McIntorsh's tone implied reproach and justification for God's retribution on the sinful: "For the people had got so wicked / They wouldn't hear God's command . . . he poured out his flood upon the land."

385. February 23, 2003 *Washington Post*, p. G-2.

386. Steve Erickson chapter on the two Newman songs in *The Rose and the Briar: Death, Love and Liberty in the American Ballad*, p. 307–14.

beautiful ever written by an American, Newman reaches a level that few, if any, songwriters have attained."[387]

Tears In Heaven (1992)—Eric Clapton (written by Eric Clapton & Will Jennings)
Reprise 19038
Chart debut Feb. 8, 1992 (4 weeks at #2); #1 (2 weeks) in Canada, #5 in England;[388] live version featured on the Duck album *Unplugged* (chart debut Sept. 12, 1992, 5 weeks at #2) (*GR, RS, DM, DMDB*)

"It's one of the great songs about loss," said Russ Titelman, producer of the soundtrack to *Rush*, which introduced Eric Clapton's shattering acoustic ballad *Tears In Heaven*. The legendary guitarist's four-year-old son Conor had died in March 1991 in a fall from the window of his New York high rise. When Clapton was given the assignment that year of scoring *Rush*, director Lili Zanuck suggested that he re-record his Derek & the Dominos song *I Am Yours* for an emotionally important scene in the picture. But the artist wanted to use something new, so he played her the demo of the song he had written as an elegy for Conor. She was stunned by its quiet power, and so was everyone else when the piece was released as a single. It became a million-seller and his biggest hit since *I Shot the Sheriff* eighteen years earlier. *Tears In Heaven* served as the centerpiece of Clapton's MTV *Unplugged* album, which sold over 10 million copies and won the Grammy for Album of the Year; *Tears* was named both Record and Song of the Year. In 2000 *Rolling Stone* ranked it as the #45 greatest pop song.

"Musically, I had always been haunted by Jimmy Cliff's song *Many Rivers to Cross* and wanted to borrow from that chord progression," writes Clapton in his memoir, "but essentially I wrote this one to ask the question I had been asking myself ever since my grandfather had died. 'Will we really meet again?'" The birth and development of such songs "is what kept me alive through the darkest period of my life." It's one of the songs never meant for public consumption; "they were just what I did to stop from going mad." When he hesitated before placing this intensely personal piece in the film, Zanuck argued that "it might in some way help somebody, and that got my vote."[389]

Passionate Kisses (1992)—Mary Chapin Carpenter (written by Lucinda Williams)
Columbia 74795

Chart debut Dec. 26, 1992 (reached #4 on C&W chart, #57 pop); from the album *Come On, Come On* (chart debut July 18,1992, sold 5 million copies)

Lucinda Williams' anthem of wanting the simple good things in life (from her 1988 album *Lucinda Williams*) becomes an exhilarating cry of independence in Mary Chapin Carpenter's full-tilt performance, joined by Shawn Colvin on the chorus. Wisely, she uses exactly the same arrangement as Williams' original, albeit with stronger vocals, a harder-driving band, and a heightened sense of exuberance. This was a double Grammy winner for best C&W song and best country female vocal.

Born in Lake Charles, Louisiana, on January 26, 1953, Williams grew up immersed in country and folk music, moved to Houston where she began performing in clubs, and recorded two 1979–1980 albums for Smithsonian/Folkways.[390] After relocating to Los Angeles, her 1988 album won raves (including some "ten-best-of-the year" plaudits) and provided material for Patty Loveless and Emmylou Harris in addition to Carpenter, although the Rough Trade label soon folded.[391] Bob Bradley, noting that poetry was central to Williams' background, remarks that *Passionate Kisses* is in part "a catalog, an inventory" of everyday objects of desire, utilizing a technique that dates back to Walt Whitman.[392] The combination of her 1992 Polygram album *Sweet Old World*, and Carpenter's hit cover, put Lucinda on the road to becoming one of her generation's most respected singer-songwriters with a gift for vivid storytelling and soaring melodies, and a symbol of the rootsy, genre-crossing alt-country movement.

(Personnel: John Jorgenson on electric guitars, Carpenter on acoustic, Bob Glaub on bass, Matt Rollings on piano, Andy Newmark on drums)

Everybody Hurts (1993)—R.E.M.
Warner 18638
Chart debut Sept. 11, 1993 (#29 peak); reached #7 in U.K.;[393] from the album *Automatic for the People* (chart debut Oct. 24, 1992, peak position #2) (*TC, DM*)

A response to concerns over teenage suicides, *Everybody Hurts* is an acoustic ballad of profound empathy.

387. Walton, feature on Newman in July–August 2000 *Oxford American Southern Music Issue*, p. 88.
388. #1 (5 weeks) in New Zealand, #1 in Ireland and Poland, #2 in Japan.
389. *Clapton: The Autobiography*, p. 250–52.
390. She learned about writing from her father, Professor Miller Williams, author of many volumes of poetry and criticism, and editor of the University of Arkansas Press.
391. Although Williams' album wasn't initially a strong seller, to help further expose her work, Rough Trade in 1989 released an EP of *Passionate Kisses* that also included three live tracks.
392. *Journal of Country Music*, Vol. 18 #2 (1996), p. 37. "There are no vague generalities; these are the things she desires, and they are hard, fast specifics. She knows the odds of her request," and she poses it "with panache and flourish."
393. #1 in Poland, #4 in Holland, #9 in Sweden.

The song began with a "rehearsal-room noodle" on electric piano by drummer Bill Berry, to which Michael Stipe wrote lyrics. Stipe's evocative falsetto tenor expresses understanding of psychological pain, with gentle encouragement to embrace life. It was the standout song from the Georgia-based group's album that followed its breakthrough classic *Losing My Religion.*

Everybody Hurts was "the ballad R.E.M. had always had in them but had never dared attempt," writes Tony Fletcher. Opening with a gentle acoustic guitar and softly stated electric piano chords, the piece opens up into Stipe's vocal, "as far forward in the mix as it had ever been, as keenly enunciated and as emotionally empowered, and his lyric left no hint of ambiguity . . . It was a song of sympathy and a show of solidarity for everyone weighed down by life, for anyone who might be considering ending it all."[394] The arrangement was designed to underline and build the emotion, moving from the sparsely accompanied first two verses, with Stipe's gradually more intense (and overlapping) vocals, to the entry of the electric guitar and violins in the bridge, and a return to simplicity for the concluding section.

Elizabeth Wurtzel compares the song to *Bridge Over Troubled Water* in both its anthemic quality and Stipe's near-falsetto vocal. "*Everybody Hurts* is unique for R.E.M.'s body of work in that it offers one of the rare moments where Stipe seems to lose control, seems to be stretching his voice to allow emotion (as opposed to rumination) to get the best of him."[395] In 1998, a poll of close to 200,000 British and American fans for Virgin All-Time Top 1,000 Albums voted *Automatic for the People* the #7 album ever. The British magazine *Q*, in ranking *Everybody Hurts* as the #31 song of all time in December 2003, remarked that it "cuts so deep into the heart you think you might never recover . . . Three bars in, tears flow."

I Swear (1994)—All-4-One (written by Frank J. Meyers & Gary Baker)
Blitzz/Atlantic 87243
Chart debut Apr. 23, 1994 (11 weeks at #1); #1 (9 weeks) in Germany, #1 (5 weeks) in Australia, #1 (3 weeks) in Canada, #2 in England[396] (*BILLB-#24, DMDB*)

The Los Angeles-based interracial vocal group All-4-One (Jamie Jones, Delious Kennedy, Alfred Nevarez, and Tony Borowiak) capitalized on the success of Boyz II Men by scoring big on the charts with melodic, doo-wop flavored romantic ballads that harkened back to a more

innocent time. *I Swear* was the first songwriting collaboration between Gary Baker (who had penned country hits for Alabama among other artists) and Frank J. Meyers (author of the Eddie Rabbitt–Crystal Gayle smash *You and I*). Amazingly, after they shopped the song around, it was five years before anyone recorded it. John Michael Montgomery took the ballad to #1 on the country chart for Atlantic in February 1994. Realizing the song's crossover potential, the label wanted to record a pop version, and matched it with their hot new group. All-4-One had just taken their revival of the Tymes' 1963 ballad classic *So Much In Love* to the Top Ten, and was already in the studio working on its first album when the call came to add the Montgomery song. In two days under the production of David Foster, the song was completed, a classic harmony ballad performance conveying deep romantic devotion, and rush-released as a single. Soaring to #1 in just a month, it became only the fourth record since 1960 to hold the top spot for ten or more weeks.

One Sweet Day (1995)—Mariah Carey & Boyz II Men (written by Mariah Carey, Michael McCary, Nathan & Wanya Morris, Shawn Stockman, & Walter Afanasieff)
Columbia 78074
Chart debut Dec. 2, 1995 (16 weeks at #1);[397] #1 (2 weeks) in Canada, #2 in Australia, #6 in England[398] (*BILLB-#1, DMDB*)[399]

The longest-running Number One single on the *Billboard* chart since Francis Craig's *Near You* all the way back in 1947, *One Sweet Day* transcended the superstar teaming of two of the 1990s' foremost hit-making acts to stand on its own merits as a classic pop single.

Born in New York City on March 27, 1970, Mariah Carey used her combination of a remarkable multi-octave voice, songwriting prowess, and dazzling biracial beauty (white mother, black father)—plus an all-out promotional campaign by Columbia—to achieve immediate superstardom with her 1990 debut album, which sold nine million copies; her first six albums through 1995 sold over 40 million copies in the U.S., and even before this record had generated nine #1 singles. Her knack for mixing soaring pop ballads with dance-pop numbers made her a natural match with the Philadelphia R&B ballad kings Boyz II Men, who from 1992–1994 had accumulated a remarkable thirty-three weeks at #1 with three chart-topping singles.

394. Fletcher, *Remarks/Remade: The Story of R.E.M.*, p. 214–15.
395. *The Oxford American Book of Great Music Writing*, p. 291.
396. #1 (6 weeks) in New Zealand; #1 in Austria, Holland, Spain, Switzerland; #2 in Belgium, Norway; #3 in Sweden.

397. #2 for 9 weeks on R&B chart, kept out of #1 by Whitney Houston's *Exhale (Shoop Shoop)*.
398. #1 in Brazil and New Zealand, #2 in Holland, #6 on Eurochart, #6 in Japan and Norway.
399. *Joel Whitburn's Top Pop Singles 1955–2008*, 12th edition, p. 1314.

According to Fred Bronson, Mariah had written one verse before she and co-writer Walter Afanasieff did the chorus, and then they arranged to meet with the group to discuss a collaboration. Nathan Morris of Boyz II Men was impressed by what he heard and told her about a song he had written two months earlier in the same vein. Afanasieff recalled that they "merged the two songs together lyrically and a bit melodically," and despite chaotic conditions in the studio it all worked. Carey said the song was not inspired by the loss of one specific person in her life but by several people she knew. (According to Sony Music president and her then-husband Tommy Mottola, the lyric reflected the death of one of her producers, David Cole, and the death of a road manager to Boyz II Men.)[400] The fact that the record was released during a period of high public awareness of the death toll from AIDS (which seemed to be suggested by the line "like so many friends we've lost along the way") made the emotional impact of the song all the more potent.[401]

Don't Know Why (2002)—Norah Jones (written by Jesse Harris)
Chart debut as album cut Sept. 28, 2002 (reached #30, 27 total weeks);[402] From the Blue Note album *Come Away With Me* (chart debut March 16, 2002, 4 weeks at #1, sold 10 million copies)[403] (*2000s-#78*)

No one could have predicted it. A gentle album of reflective piano-based ballads by an unknown artist, with just one established pop standard and no guest stars, and issued on a jazz record label, could be expected to generate respectful notices and perhaps sell a couple of hundred thousand copies at best. But after a suitably quiet start, something about Norah Jones' album *Come Away with Me* struck a chord with listeners, especially one thoroughly ingratiating song, *Don't Know Why*. As it grew into a phenomenon, it came to represent (as one critic noted) "a low-volume refuge in a high-pitched pop world." True, but not only that; Norah Jones is a singer and pianist of great warmth, and the disarming appeal of the song is timeless.

Born on March 30, 1979, in New York City and raised in Dallas by her mother (her father is legendary sitar player Ravi Shankar), Norah attended an acclaimed Dallas school for performing arts that honed her skills as a pianist, and after starting to sing as well was a two-time winner of *Down Beat* magazine's Student Music Awards

for best jazz vocalist. After graduation she was a jazz piano major at University of North Texas, after two years ventured to New York, and being spotted performing in clubs, was signed by Blue Note. But between the time of her signing and the recording of her debut album, she had moved from her jazz-standards phase to a more diverse repertoire that ranged to country and folk along with sprinklings of jazz and pop. With that stylistic shift, veteran producer Arif Mardin, who had worked with a vast range of artists over the previous four decades from Aretha Franklin on down, came aboard and helped guide Jones to a remarkable triumph. Along with her vocal and piano stylings, Jones' combo was also a big asset, with guitarists Jesse Harris (composer of *Don't Know Why* and most of the album's other songs) and Adam Levy, bassist Lee Alexander, and drummer Dan Reiser. There's a subtle sensuality in *Don't Know Why*, a hushed intimacy—with that hypnotic, "creamy-cool" voice—that pulls in the listener and won't let go.[404] When she walked away with a staggering eight Grammy Awards on February 23, 2003, including the big three of album, record, and song of the year, the triumph was complete. The album held the #1 spot on the *Billboard* Contemporary Jazz chart for a staggering 142 straight weeks. Jones has continued to broaden her repertoire in subsequent years and co-writes much of her material (such as her 2004 followup set *Feels Like Home*, and 2012's *Little Broken Hearts*), while remaining a tremendous force on the album charts.

Ain't Talkin' (2006)—Bob Dylan
From the Columbia album *Modern Times* (chart debut Sept. 16, 2006, 1 week at #1)[405]
"There is no precedent in rock & roll for the territory [Bob] Dylan is now opening," declared Joe Levy in *Rolling Stone*. Starting at age fifty-six with 1997's *Time Out of Mind*, continuing with 2001's *Love and Theft*, and finally at sixty-five with *Modern Times*, the man who had revolutionized pop music in his youth created three consecutive masterpieces, leaving in the dust nearly all the artists young enough to be his children and grandchildren just as he had surpassed those in his own generation. *Ain't Talkin'*, the concluding track on Dylan's first album to hit #1 in thirty years, thrillingly showed the genius still at the top of his game. A dark, quietly brooding acoustic narrative that, across almost nine minutes, slowly and relentlessly builds in power, demonstrated again that no one can envision an apocalypse like Dylan. "The tune

400. Mottola, *Hitmaker*, p. 289. He notes that "the inspiration, the lyrics, and the 'see you in heaven' message were so personal," helping to make it an instant classic.

401. *Billboard Book of Number One Hits*, p. 823.

402. #4 in Poland.

403. The album's worldwide sales exceed 18 million. As of December 2012, according to Nielsen SoundScan, its U.S. total stood at 10.9 million, making it the eleventh biggest seller from 1991 onward.

404. Her piano style draws on the casual approach of Floyd Cramer, a mainstay of the 1960s "Nashville Sound" including his own smash *Last Date* and Patsy Cline's *Crazy*.

405. The album debuted at #1 (selling nearly 200,000 copies in its first week), making Dylan the oldest artist to have a chart-topping debut. It also hit #1 in seven other countries.

coldly describes an evil spirit roaming the earth, seeking revenge," describes Pat Gilbert in *Entertainment Weekly*. Levy writes that it "has the hard-boiled moralism of a Raymond Chandler novel."[406] *Modern Times* was voted the #1 best album of 2006 in the *Village Voice* critics poll, and won the Grammy for best contemporary folk/Americana album.

Starting in the Mystic Garden, Dylan's protagonist finds himself in a godless place "where the cities of the plague run with hog-eyed grease," and one man sets out to avenge his father's death while seeking his mother's guidance. "I'm tryin' to love my neighbor and do good unto others / But, oh mother, things ain't going well," he laments with foreboding. The title refrain "Ain't talkin', just walkin'" provides a powerful mantra for the laconic agent of retribution. "The suffering is unending," he sings. "Every nook and cranny has its tears."

The initially weird "toothache in my heel" line is actually an homage to one of the earliest quintessentially American songs, *Old Dan Tucker*, originated by Dan Emmett for his minstrel troupe in 1843. One version of the ancient tune has this stanza: "Old Dan Tucker's a fine old man / Washed his face in a frying pan / Combed his head with a wagon wheel / And died with a toothache in his heel." The reference to a "hog-eyed man" is an oblique reference to another venerable song (with variants traced back to at least 1849 during the California Gold Rush), *The Hog-Eyed Man*, collected by Cecil Sharp in *English Folk Songs from the Southern Appalachians*. Carl Sandburg, including this song in *The American Songbag* (a very important collection to the young Dylan) as *The Hog-Eye Man*, explained that a "hog-eye" was "sailor slang in the 1850s for a barge that cruised around Cape Horn to San Francisco where a dirty, tumultuous little Babylon met all newcomers and offered them a 'good time.'"

Sean Wilentz calls *Ain't Talkin'* "an arresting mystery that told of the yearning that does not disappear with age, and that also, to my ear, sounded at one level like a nar-

rative of Christ's last days."[407] "He's a weary traveler, a bluesman and a pilgrim, on a dark and unforgiving road," remarked Jon Pareles in the *New York Times*.[408] By the chilling conclusion, having carried out his mission, he walks up the road, around the bend, headed for "the last outback, at the world's end."

Viva La Vida (2008)—Coldplay

Capitol track, chart debut May 24, 2008 (1 week at #1, 51 total weeks); #1 (1 week) in England;[409] From the album *Viva la Vida or Death and All His Friends* (#1 for 2 weeks) (*GR, 2000s-#11, 1001*)

Building momentum with every album, Coldplay soared to new commercial heights with its fourth studio release, and its first collaboration with super-producer Brian Eno generated the band's first chart-topping single, *Viva La Vida*.[410] Although the album as a whole had what *Rolling Stone* called an "art-school weirdness," the single was a pure-pop gem bursting with (in Will Hermes' phrase) the "stadium-scale melodies" and singalong choruses for which they're best known. The title (translating as "Long Live Life") was inspired after Martin saw the phrase on a painting by Frida Kahlo. The fact that Eno had co-produced U2's *The Unforgettable Fire* and *The Joshua Tree* made him a perfect fit for a British band that had long done its best to emulate Bono & company. As Chris Martin leads the soaring chorus— "I hear Jerusalem bells a-ringing, Roman cavalry choirs are singing"—it "feels like a rallying cry for a Christian empire."[411] The album became the biggest worldwide seller of 2008, and *Viva La Vida* earned top Grammy honors as Song of the Year.

---

406. August 14, 2006 *Rolling Stone*.

407. *Bob Dylan in America*, p. 314.
408. August 20, 2006, *New York Times*.
409. #1 in European radio airplay, Holland, Italy, and Spain; #3 in Belgium, #4 in Canada, #5 in Germany, Norway and Switzerland, #7 France and Sweden.
410. Surprisingly enough, this was only the band's second U.S. Top Ten single, following *Speed of Sound* (2005).
411. June 26, 2008, *Rolling Stone*, p. 73. Hermes credits Jonny Buckland's guitar work as one of the album's highlights.

Playlist 7

Fascinating Rhythm, 1891–2008

One Minute Too Late (1891)—(Voss') The 1st Regiment Band

Recorded on Oct. 2, 1891 for North American Phonograph Co. at Thomas Edison's studio in Orange, New Jersey

Twelve years after Thomas Alva Edison invented the phonograph in 1877, he founded the Edison Talking Machine Company, which made its first known records on May 24, 1889. (After numerous instrumental solos and duets were recorded during the next three months, the initial band performances, by Duffy & Imgrund's 5th Regiment Band, were captured on brown wax cylinder on August 19, 1889.) Because of the severe limitations in early recording technology which made it difficult to properly record certain instruments or types of voices, military-style bands, whose full-bodied sound could be easily captured by the crude recording horns, were especially popular. One of the first bands to record extensively for Edison was the 1st Regiment Band, soon to be known as Voss' 1st Regiment Band.[1]

---

1. The status achieved by the band is reflected by this comment in an 1895 United States Phonograph Co. catalog: "To say that we expect to make Voss' Band records as long as we remain in the business is only another way of stating that the popularity of the records does not wane."

Graphophone recording (1889), courtesy of Library of Congress, LC-USZ62-107098.

Theodor E. Wangemann (born in Berlin, Germany, on February 13, 1855) was the chief recording engineer for Edison until his death in a 1906 accident, and thanks to his brilliance in the studio, some of the early Edison recordings possess a sharp fidelity that would be unequalled until the advent of electrical recordings nearly three-and-a-half decades later.[2] The 1st Regiment Band's recording of *One Minute Too Late* is the definitive example. A briskly uptempo "gallop," it features the horn and woodwind sections trading off passages with vigorous energy. Bright and thoroughly pleasant, its sound—as heard on the CD *Brown Wax Cylinder Phonograph Recordings, 1888–1894* issued by tinfoil.com—is astonishingly clear and crisp. The Voss band would continue to record for Edison through the end of the 1890s.

A Bunch of Rags (1899)—Vess L. Ossman
Columbia 3861
Recorded c. Jan. 1899 (later recorded for Edison 7305)

The man who was responsible for arguably the very first, no-doubt-about-it ragtime recording—*Rag Time Medley* in August 1897 (one of nearly seventy discs that he made for Berliner from 1897–1900)—produced his own exceptional ragtime composition just seventeen months later. Banjo virtuoso Ossman is all by himself on this delightfully bright, brisk solo performance, very dance-like and melodic. It can be heard on the tinfoil. com CD *Brown Wax Cylinder Phonograph Recordings: 24 Popular Selections from 1899.*

Vess L. Ossman and son, courtesy of Library of Congress (Jim Walsh collection), LC Recorded Sound Division.

---

2. Jim Walsh offered a mini-profile of Wangemann in the April 1953 *Hobbies*.

In addition to his historic role in American recordings, Ossman helped popularize ragtime banjo abroad with his triumphant 1900 tour of England. The banjo duo of Cadwallader Mays and Parke Hunter had played some rag selections when they came to England in 1897, but caused nothing like the stir generated by Ossman. "After his opening selection of *A Bunch of Rags*," declared a London newspaper account, "one can well say that no banjoist ever received such an ovation . . ."

Bill Bailey, Won't You Please Come Home (1902)—
     Arthur Collins (written by Hugh Cannon)
Columbia 872
Recorded in May 1902 (also recorded in Sept. for Edison
     8112); *Pop Memories* debut July 12, 1902 (#1 hit)[3]
     (*MEM-#119, DMDB*)

One of the most prolific and popular performers of the pioneer recording era, Philadelphia-born Arthur Collins began his recording career for Edison in May 1898, and within a matter of months was one of the most in-demand of all performers, including work for the Berliner and Zon-o-Phone labels, and then Victor and Columbia. His 1899 recordings of *I Guess I'll Have to Telegraph My Baby* and *Hello, Ma Baby* helped establish the songs, among the biggest of their time. So it was appropriate that he had the definitive original version of the ragtime-styled *Bill Bailey*; it's a brisk, enjoyable rendition of the future standard, with only piano accompaniment, and is included in the boxed set *American Pop: An Audio History: From Minstrel to Mojo: On Record, 1893–1946.* Ragtime pianist and composer Hugh Cannon (born in Detroit on April 9, 1877) had his one giant popular success with the number, which was first publicly performed by John Queen in a musical pastiche, *Town Topics*, in Newburgh, New York.[4]

A number of prior popular songs, including 1901's *Ain't Dat a Shame*, made references to a Bill Bailey; *Shame* is credited to Cannon's friend John Queen and accomplished songsmith Bert Leighton, although Leighton later claimed sole authorship. Peter C. Muir calls the tune "basically a prequel" to the *Bill Bailey* we know. For example, in Cannon's song, Mrs. Bailey begs her husband to return, regretting their original separation, when she wouldn't allow him back into their home; *Ain't Dat a Shame* concerns the original argument. Muir also sees the melodies for both songs as variants of the *Frankie and*

---

3. In 1972 *Bill Bailey* was one of ten songs given special citations by the Songwriters Hall of Fame as historic standards.
4. The song was first reported as a hit (as performed in vaudeville) in the July 5, 1902, *Music Trades*; on September 6, the publication cited it as the second biggest seller for publisher Howley, Haviland & Dresser behind only *In the Good Old Summer Time*. The Jan. 3, 1903, issue noted that it was being performed by "William Murray" with the Al G. Field Minstrels—the same Billy Murray who would begin his reign as the era's #1 pop recording star later that year.

Johnny tune family, and suggests that both may derive in part from folk sources. Specifically, he cites a transcription of a folk ballad, *I Went to the Hop-Joint*, that has a comparable *Frankie & Johnny*–like melody, and whose lyrics discuss a Bill Bailey with the refrain "why don't you come home," although it's unclear whether *Hop-Joint* or *Bailey* came first.[5] According to a series of 1966 newspaper articles by Don Durst, the immediate inspiration for both numbers may have been Willard Godfrey "Bill" Bailey, a trombonist and music teacher (and apparently an acquaintance of Cannon's) from 1894–1907 in Jackson, Michigan, where it is believed to have been composed.[6] After it became a smash, the market was flooded with what David Ewen called a "rash" of other Bill Bailey songs by various composers, all quickly forgotten while the original has endured.

Cannon, typically dismissed by music historians as a one-hit wonder who soon sank into alcoholism and poverty well before his death in 1912, is celebrated by Muir as perhaps the first popular composer whose career (however brief) was based primarily on songs containing the crucial elements of folk-based "proto-blues" that would within a decade blossom fully into the blues.[7]

Nicholas T. Tawa offers an intriguing analysis of the song's philosophy. The title character is living like a king while exploiting his girlfriend until she throws him out of the house, but then he finds other women to prey upon, enabling him to maintain his lavish lifestyle. Nevertheless, his original girlfriend pleads for him to return, promising to be at his beck and call and to pay the rent. Tawa remarks that the song presents a survival-of-the-fittest worldview, with moral rightness being superseded by the goal of prevailing by any means possible.[8]

In My Merry Oldsmobile (1905)—Billy Murray (music by Gus Edwards, lyrics by Vincent P. Bryan)[9]
Victor 4467[10]

Recorded Aug. 8, 1905 in Philadelphia; *Pop Memories* debut Oct. 10, 1905 (reached #1)[11] (*DMDB*)

Inspired by one of the first trans-continental automobile races from New York City to the Lewis & Clark Exposition in Portland, Oregon, between two Oldsmobiles from April to June 1905,[12] *In My Merry Oldsmobile* paved the way for the many automobile songs that would flood popular culture in the years to come.[13] The lyric takes the form of a marriage proposal, with Johnny envisioning their drive to the church where they'll be wed. It was a natural for Billy Murray, a few months after he had celebrated another mode of travel in *Come Take a Trip in My Airship*. Years later the song would be used in commercials for Oldsmobile. Murray had a personal love for automobiles, attending some races (possibly including the Indianapolis 500) with his friend Jimmy Martindale,[14] and would later record many other car-related songs, including *Take Me Out for a Joy Ride* (1909), *He'd Have to Get Under—Get Out and Get Under (to Fix Up His Automobile)* (1914) and *The Little Ford Rambled Right Along* (1915). "Come away with me Lucille, in my merry Oldsmobile / Down the road of life we'll fly automobubbling, you and I . . ."

Auld Lang Syne (1907)—Frank C. Stanley
Columbia 3731

Pop Memories chart debut Dec. 14, 1907 (reached #2) (*RIA-#73, Trad-#159*)

One of the most ancient still-familiar songs in Western popular music, *Auld Lang Syne* is a traditional Scottish melody first published in 1687. The phrase "auld lang syne" appeared in print in Scotland at least as early as 1694, and the earliest version of the poem with that title was included in James Watson's *Scots Poems* in 1711. Poet Robert Burns set down the words we've come to know in 1788, which were not published until six months after his death in 1796. The words "auld lang syne" means "old long since," the equivalent of "good old days."[15] One of the first and possibly the finest early recording of the standard was by Frank Stanley.

---

5. Muir, *Before "Crazy Blues": Commercial Blues in America, 1850–1920.*

6. However, Muir casts doubt on the Michigan trombonist as the inspiration for Cannon's song, pointing out that the composer didn't move to Michigan until around 1904, two years after his big hit. It's more likely, he suggests, that the character was derived from oral tradition. Muir also says it's possible that after the success of *Ain't Dat a Shame*, Queen may have suggested to Cannon the idea of a sequel.

7. The trade press of the time was quite harsh in describing Cannon's downfall into drink and poverty, including accounts in the August 22, 1908, and in the January 29 and February 5, 1910, *Music Trades*; he died "Friendless and Broke," as the headline proclaimed in the June 29, 1912, issue.

8. *The Way to Tin Pan Alley: American Popular Song, 1866–1910.*

9. Edwards was one of the foremost pop composers of the era; lyricist Bryan's other best known song was *In the Sweet Bye and Bye*, and Murray did well with some of his other numbers, such as *He Goes to Church on Sunday*.

10. Also recorded by Murray for Columbia 491; Columbia 2-minute cylinder 33061; Kalamazoo 6965; and Oxford 3564; additionally issued on Harmony 491, Standard 491, United 491, Silvertone 3564, & Standard 3564; reissued on Victor 16248.

11. The song was copyrighted on June 12, 1905 (Fuld, *Book of World-Famous Music*, p. 299), and Murray recorded it shortly thereafter.

12. The 7-horsepower Olds Runabouts in the 1905 race were the first motorized vehicles to cross the United States from east to west (a 1903 transcontinental automobile trip from San Francisco to New York—it was not a race—went the opposite direction), and the first to cross the Cascade Mountain range.

13. Dwight B. Huss was the winning driver. Prior to that, the first transcontinental road race was completed on August 21, 1903, the victorious Model F Packard taking fifty-one days. That was topped a year later by L. L. Whitman, who crossed the country in a Franklin in thirty-three days. The rapidly growing appeal of the automobile was demonstrated by a Madison Square Garden Auto Show on January 20, 1905, at which more than 100 motorcars were shown.

14. Hoffman, Carty, and Riggs, *Billy Murray: The Phonograph Industry's First Great Recording Artist*, p. 184.

15. Fuld, p. 115–17. "The exact extent of Robert Burns's responsibility for the words and/or music of *Auld Lang Syne* has always been a point of

Born William Stanley Grinsted on December 29, 1868, in Orange, New Jersey, he recorded at least a dozen cylinders under his real name as a solo banjoist for the North American Phonograph Company in 1891–1893 (none have survived), then resumed working full time at an Orange bank until finally putting his deep baritone voice (sometimes characterized as a bass) to work as a singer starting in 1898 under the name Frank C. Stanley. He adopted the pseudonym because he didn't want his work on phonograph records to detract from his singing with church choirs and in concerts under his real name. (He also recorded a few banjo accompaniments to singer Arthur Collins in 1900–1902 under the name George S. Williams.) Recording for each of the big three companies (Edison, Victor, and Columbia), Stanley was used most frequently in duets, most notably with Byron Harlan, Corinne Morgan, Henry Burr, Elise Stevenson, and starting in 1905 did an increasing number of solos. But it was his work as leader of the hugely popular Peerless Quartet (also including Burr) from 1906–1910 that provided Stanley's greatest fame. He also found time to be elected alderman and public school commissioner of Orange, and served on the city's Common Council at the time of his death.[16]

Stanley's rendition of *Auld Lang Syne*, as heard on the Archeophone CD *1907: Dear Old Golden Rule Days*, shows off the resonant, rumbling power of his voice, and remained in Columbia catalogs for many years thereafter. The song was being used by revelers to usher in the new year in both America and Britain by at least the 1890s; Guy Lombardo & the Royal Canadians institutionalized that usage with his annual New Year's Eve radio broadcasts starting in 1929. "We'll take a cup of kindness, dear, for auld lang syne . . ."

Come, Josephine, in My Flying Machine (1911)—Ada Jones & Billy Murray with Chorus (music by Fred Fisher, lyrics by Alfred Bryan)
Edison 10505 & Edison Blue Amberol 1949
Released in July 1911 (*DMDB*)

Seven years after Billy Murray had celebrated the Wright Brothers' Kitty Hawk flight with *Come Take a Trip in My Airship*, *Come, Josephine, in My Flying Machine* was introduced in vaudeville by Blanche Ring, and given its most unforgettable rendition by Murray and his favorite duet partner, Ada Jones. Ada & Billy's original giant hit version of *Josephine* had been recorded with his group the American Quartet for Victor in November

1910, but their duet (also accompanied by that group) is impossible to top—particularly the four-minute and eighteen-second version on Blue Amberol that allows for extra verses and choruses. Born on September 30, 1875, in Cologne, Germany, to American parents, composer Fred Fisher came to the U.S. in 1900 after serving in the German navy and the French Foreign Legion, began writing songs, and after a few minor hits *Josephine* was his first giant success. He went on to enjoy a long and prolific career, including *Peg o' My Heart* (1913), *Dardanella* (1919), and *Chicago* (1922). Coming two years after the first successful flight over the English Channel in July 1909, *Josephine* captures the innocent romance and wonder with which early air travel was viewed. In 1997, Leonardo DiCaprio would happily sing a few lines of the song to Kate Winslet while they were aboard another new amazing creation of man, in *Titanic*.

Nicholas Tawa cites *Josephine* among a group of songs exemplifying a shifting tide away from the conservative, rural/small-town orientation that reinforced trust in family and traditional values, and toward a modern, urbanized approach that questioned the old ways. "The essence of the new popular song was the depiction of

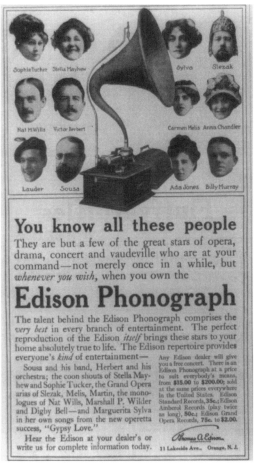

Edison Phonograph (1912), courtesy of Library of Congress, LC-USZ62-99979.

---

controversy," he notes. But it's generally agreed that he did not compose the words of the first, and most familiar, verse, although he may have revised them.

16. Gracyk and Hoffman, *Popular American Recording Pioneers*, p. 325–32.

sensations over which the individual had little or no control [such as violence or passion] and the situations, even predicaments, in which they placed the individual. At a critical point in America's cultural history, popular song reached the decisive climax toward which it had been moving during the [1870s and] eighties. Vivid emotional experiences were now portrayed. In a majority of instances they predicated an unfriended individual, a powerless or ineffective God, or a society characterized more and more by amorality."[17]

Ada Jones, notes William Howard Kenney, interpreted the phonograph as the voice of the people. In an article for the February 1917 *Edison Amberola Monthly*, she declared: "I believe that the world is enriched by the melodies and sentiments that come from the masses. Only a fragmentary portion of either classical or popular music becomes immortal, and fully as much 'popular' music survives as does classical. I like ragtime because I feel that it is typically American. It is alive, virile, dashing, and stimulating."[18]

Moonlight Bay (1912)—American Quartet (music by Percy Wenrich, lyrics by Edward Madden)
Victor 17034
Recorded Dec. 15, 1911; *Pop Memories* debut March 9, 1912 (reached #1); group also recorded song as Premier Quartet for Edison 10550 & Edison Amberol 962 (*MEM-#112, DMDB*)

"We were sailing along on moonlight bay . . ." Just that opening line conjures up an entire lost era of a slower-paced America that (in our mind's eye, at least) had plenty of time for gentle spooning in an unspoiled natural setting. Composer Percy Wenrich was one of the era's specialists in sentimental ballads, with other credits including *Put on Your Old Grey Bonnet*, *Silver Bell* and *When You Wore a Tulip (And I Wore a Big Red Rose)*. Lyricist Edward Madden also penned the words to *By the Light of the Silvery Moon*. With Billy Murray in the lead and the harmonies of John Bieling, Steve Porter, and William F. Hooley, authentic barbershop-style singing doesn't come much sweeter than this. "We could hear the voices ringing, they seemed to say / 'You have stolen her heart' 'Now don't go 'way' / As we sang love's old sweet song on Moonlight Bay . . ."

William Howland Kenney, in *Recorded Music in American Life: The Phonograph and Popular Memory, 1890–1945*, cited the findings from a 1921 survey of over 2,600 Americans by Thomas A. Edison, Inc., in confirming that "the phonograph had become a mass-produced

'private' shrine at which to summon forth spirits that allowed listeners momentarily to escape from the ravages of time into a domain in which dead loved ones seemed to live once again."[19] The deeply nostalgic qualities of *Moonlight Bay* embody this idea.

Toots (1914)—Dr. Clarence J. Penney (written by Felix Arndt)
Victor 17694
Recorded on Aug. 31, 1914 (released in March 1915)

This obscure but wonderful recording is a high-energy mandolin performance by Penney (of whom very little is known), accompanied by the song's composer, Felix Arndt, on piano. The mandolin began to turn up on commercial recordings by the turn of the twentieth century. Samuel Siegel made numerous mandolin solos and duets with piano or harp-guitar, starting with six solos for Victor on October 20, 1900; he subsequently recorded as well for Edison and Columbia. Some of the first truly memorable records featuring the instrument were made in 1906–1907 by the Ossman-Dudley Trio (banjoist Vess Ossman accompanied by mandolin and harp-guitar). Clarence Penney first turned up as composer of *Ingomar (Intermezzo)*, a bells solo recorded by Chris Chapman in 1905 that Victor rejected. Arndt was an outstanding pianist-composer with a strong feeling for ragtime and proto-jazz, most notably his 1914 piece *Desecration Rag*; his biggest hit was *Nola*. A frequent partner on records to banjoist Fred Van Eps, he died during the flu epidemic in 1919.

Toots has a very appealing dance-like quality suitable for the one-step; the melody is intricate but immensely catchy. David Jasen, who included this performance on the 1973 RBF Records LP *Ragtime Entertainment*, remarked that it is "a delightful and charming rag, and this is its only recorded version." The recording was made two months before the tune was copyrighted. The flip side is another Penney-Arndt duet, *Indianola Patrol*; the duo also did another title on this date that was unreleased, the Penney original *Le Trousseau*. The mandolinist's only other known performances were *Azalea Waltz* (Victor 17643, cut one week later), and a semi-classical number in November that was left on the shelf, both also with piano. *Toots* is also included on the Timeless Holland CD *From Ragtime to Jazz, 1902-1923*.

James Weldon Johnson remarked in *The Book of American Negro Poetry* (1922): "Anyone who doubts that there is a peculiar hell-tickling, smile-provoking, joy-awakening, response-compelling charm in Ragtime needs only to listen to its bizarre harmonies, its audacious resolutions often consisting of an abrupt jump from one

---

17. *The Way to Tin Pan Alley: American Popular Song, 1866–1910*, p. 139–40.

18. *Recorded Music in American Life: The Phonograph and Popular Memory, 1890–1945*, p. 37.

19. Kenney, p. 7–12.

key to another, its intricate rhythms in which the accents fall in the most unexpected places but in which the fundamental beat is never lost, in order to be convinced. I believe it has its place as well as the music which draws from us sighs and tears."

Steal Away to Jesus (1915)—Fisk University Male Quartette

Columbia 2803

Recorded on Oct. 21, 1915[20] (*GOSP-#130*)

Steal Away to Jesus was one of the spirituals (like *Swing Low, Sweet Chariot* and *Follow the Drinking Gourd*) sung by slaves as a secret language to convey not merely the hope that they were going to escape to freedom, but the specific message that the time had come for escape via the metaphorical Underground Railroad. "When they heard a voice call out 'Steal away to Jesus, I ain't got long to stay here,' slaves knew that Harriet Tubman used the song as a summons" to flee toward freedom, writes Craig Werner in *A Change Is Gonna Come: Music, Race, & the Soul of America*.[21] Following the Civil War, its fame was spread internationally by the choir founded by the all-black Fisk University in Nashville, which in 1871 began touring around the U.S. and abroad to raise funds for the first institution created to educate newly freed slaves and their children. *Steal Away* was first recorded by the Dinwiddie Colored Quartet for the Victor Talking Machine Company on October 29, 1902. Its most renowned early performance was by the descendant of the same group that had made the song widely known, the Fisk University Male Quartet (formerly known as the Fisk University Jubilee Singers). Their performance is slow, hushed, and haunting.

I Love a Piano (1916)—Billy Murray (written by Irving Berlin)

Victor 17945

Recorded on Jan. 5, 1916; *Pop Memories* debut April 8, 1916 (1 week at #1) (*APS*)

Irving Berlin wrote *I Love a Piano* for the Broadway show *Stop! Look! Listen!*, which presented it as a production number with an immense keyboard running from one end of the stage to the other, before which six pianists pounded away on six pianos.[22] Its happy, breezy style made it well suited to the king of pre-1920 recording artists, Billy Murray, with Walter Rogers directing the backing orchestra that includes Rosario Bourdon on piano.

The song came out just as the piano had reached its zenith of popularity in American households. Craig Roell in *The Piano in America, 1890–1940* reports that from 1870–1890, piano production increased at a rate 1.6 times faster than population growth. This ratio increased to 5.6 times from 1890–1900, and 6.2 times the following decade. The industry's peak year in production was 1909, with over 364,000 pianos valued at $58.5 million. In 1914, 323,000 pianos were produced, valued at $56 million; also, mechanized player pianos became the rage in that decade, with some 800,000 player pianos reported to be in operation east of the Mississippi River alone in 1918.

As the flip side of Harry MacDonough's performance of *The Girl on the Magazine* (another song from *Stop! Look! Listen!*), this Victor record became the first double-sided #1 hit.[23] Both songs were introduced in the show by Harry Fox. *I Love a Piano*—which Berlin declared over four decades later was his personal favorite among his compositions—was included in the Smithsonian boxed set *American Popular Song*.

Tin Roof Blues (1923)—New Orleans Rhythm Kings (written by Paul Mares, Walter Melrose, Ben Pollack, Mel Stitzel, George Brunis, & Leon Roppolo)

Gennett 5105

Recorded in Richmond, Indiana on March 13, 1923

The sensational success of the Original Dixieland Jazz Band (ODJB) starting in 1917 inspired a legion of young white musicians to explore this exciting and mysterious new music. Among the first and best of their progeny were the New Orleans Rhythm Kings (NORK), who contributed an authentic jazz classic, *Tin Roof Blues*.

The heart of the Rhythm Kings lay in their three New Orleans–raised horn men: cornetist Paul Mares, clarinetist Leon Roppolo, and trombonist George Brunis. Gunther Schuller: "Compared with the ODJB, the Rhythm Kings played a better brand of jazz, and Leon Roppolo was considered the best white New Orleans musician. They not only improvised, but they had a different attitude, a humility toward jazz. Whereas [ODJB leader Nick LaRocca] would deny the Negro musical heritage of New Orleans, Paul Mares proudly claimed that he tried to emulate King Oliver's tone and style."[24] Schuller called them "the earliest and most authentic link" between the black New Orleans ensemble tradition represented by Oliver's Creole Jazz Band, and subsequent white emulators led by Bix Beiderbecke.

---

20. Curiously, while eight of the other Fisk recordings from October 1915–February 1916 were released during 1916, four titles, including *Steal Away*, were issued as late as 1920.

21. Werner, p. 7.

22. The show opened on December 25, 1915; *Piano* was introduced by Harry Fox and the ensemble. Despite its two big hits, it ran for a modest 105 performances.

---

23. Called "the big song hit" from the musical, the tune received a new lease on life, reported the September 16, 1916, *Music Trades*, when Berlin made it available as an independent number, increasing its appeal in areas where the show had not been seen.

24. *Early Jazz*, p. 186.

The band formed in Chicago in 1921; Roppolo had played in the backing group for vaudeville "Shimmy Queen" Bee Palmer on a Midwest tour that year; Paul Mares (cornet) and George Brunis (trombone) had played on riverboats working the upper Mississippi as far north as Minnesota. They first recorded as the Friars Society Orchestra (named after Mike Fritzel's Friar's Inn, a Chicago cabaret on South Wabash Street in the Loop where they regularly played) for Gennett in August 1922, including the original version of *Bugle Call Rag* (under the title *Bugle Call Blues*). Seven months later, in two days of sessions under their new identity, they debuted *Tin Roof Blues*. In July that year, the NORK made history with the first interracial jazz record session as they invited Jelly Roll Morton to man the keyboards for four numbers, including his own classic *Mr. Jelly Lord*.

Tin Roof Blues was a collective group original, credited to all five members plus the song's publisher Walter Melrose (it was part of the first significant group of jazz pieces issued on sheet music).[25] Some have suggested that elements of the tune were lifted from *Jazzin' Babies Blues*, written by the New Orleans–born, Chicago-based black pianist Richard M. Jones (best known as composer of *Trouble In Mind*) and recorded soon after this session by King Oliver, but even if true the NORK introduced significant new qualities to the melodic idea. It was Melrose who suggested that the tune needed a title evocative of New Orleans, so they named it after the Tin Roof Café on Baronne Street back home. Mares' cornet soloing on this performance deeply influenced Beiderbecke; Brunis on trombone is prominently showcased; and Schuller notes that the piece features "one of Roppolo's most poignant, expressive blues solos." William Howland Kenney: "At the time they recorded, few popular white groups had ever achieved this flowing and focused rhythmic impact. Unlike many of the white hotel and dance hall bands of that time, in which a rhythmic disjunction separated percussion from wind instruments, [the NORK] played with a shared rhythmic pulse."[26] [27] Richard Sudhalter called Roppolo "the first great jazz soloist to appear on records" (predating Louis Armstrong by eight months and Sidney Bechet by eleven), declaring that "there is something of phantasm, something wraithlike, in the very sound Rop-

polo produces. It is at its most ghostly in the altissimo concert F with [which] he begins the *Tin Roof* solo." He cites in particular the clarinetist's use of vibrato. "The very speed of Roppolo's vibrato lends it an expressive urgency comparable to that of the French chanteuse tradition later epitomized by Edith Piaf."[28]

The Original Memphis Five (on Victor) and the Original Indiana Five (on Perfect) recorded cover versions of *Tin Roof Blues* later that year, and it quickly became a standard part of jazz repertoire. Exactly thirty years later, lyrics were added to the venerable tune, and it became a #1 smash for Jo Stafford, *Make Love to Me*.[29]

(Other personnel: Mel Stitzel on piano, Ben Pollack on drums)

It Had to Be You (1924)—Marion Harris (music by Isham Jones, lyrics by Gus Kahn)
Brunswick 2610
Recorded in March 1924; *Pop Memories* debut July 26, 1924 (reached #3)

One of the most enduringly popular ballads of the 1920s, *It Had to Be You* was at the forefront of a flurry of wonderful songs co-written by Isham Jones in his peak year of 1924. Born on January 31, 1894, in Coalton, Ohio, Jones came to Chicago in 1915, playing tenor sax and leading a trio, soon became one of the city's best-known bandleaders, and began his prolific recording career for Brunswick in 1920. His original hits included *On the Alamo* (1922), *Swingin' Down the Lane* (1923), *Spain* and *The One I Love Belongs to Somebody Else* (both 1924), and *I'll See You in My Dreams* (1925). Gus Kahn (born on November 6, 1886, in Coblenz, Germany), a Tin Pan Alley veteran with credits dating back to 1906, provided lyrics for each of these songs, along with such other 1920s standards as *Carolina In the Morning, Yes Sir! That's My Baby*, and *Makin' Whoopee*. Jones recorded all of his songs as instrumentals; the greatest original vocal interpretation of *It Had to Be You* was by the superbly gifted Marion Harris, who had demonstrated ever since the start of her recording career in 1916 an equally keen gift for both blues and straight ballads. The song was first reported as "a real hit in Portland" in the June 21, 1924, *Music Trades*, with similar reports in the issues of August 2 (as a best-selling record in Green Bay), August 23 (big in Buffalo), August 30 (strong in Seattle), and September 6 (a hit in both Denver and Toledo). As late as November 8, it was cited among the top-selling records in Milwaukee.[30]

---

25. The Melrose Brothers Music Co. had an ongoing relationship with Gennett. As noted by the label's historian Rick Kennedy, starting in 1923 "jazz songs that debuted on the Gennett label were soon issued by the Melrose brothers . . . as stock orchestrations or in sheet music form," including King Oliver's *Chimes Blues* and most of Jelly Roll Morton's compositions (*78 Quarterly* #8 (1994), p. 43).

26. *Chicago Jazz: A Cultural History*, p. 129.

27. Attesting to the record's best-seller status, Henry C. Speir, a Jackson, Mississippi record seller renowned as a talent scout for blues artists including Robert Johnson, told Gayle Dean Wardlow that *Tin Roof Blues* was his biggest Gennett record of the decade, selling "thousands" at his store over the years (*78 Quarterly* #8 (1994), p. 24).

28. *Lost Chords*, p. 41.

29. E. H. Morris, the song publisher that owned the copyright for *Tin Roof Blues*, also published *Make Love to Me*, and made sure that the tune's 1922 composers were properly credited when the pop song's adapters initially neglected to do so (November 1975 *Songwriter Magazine*).

30. An article in the February 9, 1924, *Music Trades* described Jones' standard method of test-marketing all his new songs before he would allow

Sweet Georgia Brown (1925)—Ethel Waters (written by Maceo Pinkard, Kenneth Casey & Ben Bernie)
Columbia 379
Recorded on May 13, 1925; *Pop Memories* chart debut Sept. 19, 1925 (peak position #6) (*Trad-#161, APS*)

Universally known to the post–World War II generation as the theme song of the Harlem Globetrotters, *Sweet Georgia Brown* was introduced as an instrumental by Ben Bernie's orchestra (and co-credited to the leader), but the song received its most memorable recording just a short time later by the great Ethel Waters. Waters had been recording for other labels since 1921; this was just her second session for Columbia, and she's accompanied by a small combo featuring Joe Smith on cornet, Buster Bailey on clarinet, and Fletcher Henderson on piano; the first two in particular turn in nice solos. Ethel is in top form, taking the song at a brisk, swinging tempo. Richard Hadlock writes that her performance here "was fifteen years ahead of its time, despite the stodgy accompaniment."[31]

Alec Wilder in *American Popular Song* declared his astonishment that *Sweet Georgia Brown* became a standard "because it's so difficult." Set in the key of G major with the first four measures following the notes of the chord E-dominant seventh, the second four measures A-dominant seventh, and the third four measures D-dominant seventh, the piece is vocally demanding.[32] But Ethel makes it sound easy. "Fellas she can't get are fellas she ain't met / Georgia claimed her, Georgia named her, Sweet Georgia Brown . . ."

Fascinating Rhythm (1926)—Fred Astaire & Adele Astaire (music by George Gershwin, lyrics by Ira Gershwin)
Columbia 3969
Recorded in London on April 29, 1926 (*Trad-#33, RR-#72*)

The musical partnership of George and Ira Gershwin achieved a new level of ingenious artistry on *Fascinating Rhythm*. Deena Rosenberg: "This song has countless musical and lyrical subtleties; perhaps most notable among these is that the words describe exactly what the music is doing. In both verse and chorus, the rhythm is driving, the key unstable; the verse describes a persistent rhythm that 'pit-a-pats through my brain,' the hard vowel sounds sustaining the insistent image. When a musical phrase is frenzied, the verbal counterpart is short, breathless and equally frantic; when the music is broader and rhythmically more stable, the words form a longer, more

descriptive sentence. It is rare indeed for the words of a song to paint so vivid a picture of their musical counterpart." Ira's lyrics are packed with Jazz Age phrases like "on the go" and rhyming "a-quiver" with "flivver," a small, cheap 1920s car. What Ira achieved in the lyric was "a truly phenomenal feat," remarked composer Arthur Schwartz, "when one considers that . . . [he] was required to be brilliant within the most confining rhythms and accents."[33]

Fascinating Rhythm was written for *Lady, Be Good!*, which opened on Broadway December 12, 1924, ran through the following September,[34] then toured ten cities, winding up in London, a combined run of more than two years.[35] It was during the London engagement that the show's sibling stars Fred and Adele Astaire recorded the song, accompanied by George Gershwin himself on piano. Fred had begun his friendship with Gershwin a decade earlier, when George was working as a song plugger at Jerome H. Remick's. James R. Morris notes that while Adele's vocal style is rooted in nineteenth century traditions, Fred is more rhythmically adventurous, and the two are engagingly out of sync for a brief moment, "prophetic in their divergence."[36] Biographer Edward Jablonski writes that George's creation of "misplaced accents" posed a challenge to Ira. "It was a tricky rhythm for those days, and it took me several days to decide on the rhyme scheme," Ira later recalled. David Jenness and Don Velsey remark that in this "exceedingly tricky song," phrases "quite regular in themselves are set so that successive stresses fall on non-corresponding beats; the effect is that of constant syncopation."[37] "Oh, how I long to be the man I used to be! / Fascinating rhythm, oh, won't you stop picking on me?"

Will Friedwald makes the point that when great composers wrote specifically for him as they so often did, Astaire's style of vocal syncopation "helped to shape the songs and influence the way they would sound even before they were written." In the case of *Fascinating Rhythm*, there are certain interjections that probably would not have even been written had it not been Astaire who was to deliver them. He was, "after Armstrong and Crosby, the most important conduit for the concept of

them to be published. He would try out the number at Chicago's College Inn, observe the response of dancers, and listen to any comments. "If you can get the people to judge, you're pretty certain of a reliable verdict."
31. *Jazz Masters of the '20s*, p. 237.
32. Wilder, p. 461.

33. *Fascinating Rhythm: The Collaboration of George and Ira Gershwin*, p. 91–96.
34. On Broadway, the Astaires did *Fascinating Rhythm* with their co-star Cliff Edwards ("Ukulele Ike"), accompanied by the twin pianos of Arden and Ohman; Edwards' December 1924 recording of the song was one of his most acclaimed. The composer often provided accompaniment for the show's rehearsals, and Astaire recalled in his autobiography that "hoofer Gershwin" even suggested and demonstrated a key movement for the *Fascinating Rhythm* dance routine (*Steps In Time*, p. 134–35).
35. Fred and Adele had scored the biggest triumph of their careers to date with the London show *Stop Flirting* in 1923.
36. Annotation for Smithsonian's *American Popular Song*, p. 38–39.
37. *Classic American Popular Song: The Second Half-Century, 1950–2000*, p. 20–21.

jazz and syncopation into the American mainstream. In a sense, syncopation was a necessity for the dancer: He didn't have the operatic chops to hold every note for as long as it was written, so he broke notes up, and the rhythm along with them."[38]

Irving Berlin compared jazz to the "rhythmic beat of our everyday lives. Its swiftness is interpretive of our verve and speed and ceaseless activity." In commenting on this implication that jazz was linked to industrialization and the pace of urban life, Stephen Kern, in *The Culture of Time and Space*, offered the view that "the mixture of syncopation, irregularity and new percussive textures gave an overall impression of the hurry and unpredictability of contemporary life."[39] Kathy J. Ogren, in *The Jazz Revolution: Twenties America and the Meaning of Jazz*: "Jazz rhythms, in particular syncopation, joined mechanization as a cause of the hectic tempo of the Twenties."[40]

Sugar Baby (1927)—Dock Boggs
Brunswick 118
Recorded on March 9, 1927 (*HS*)

Recorded at the same session as Dock Boggs' immortal *Country Blues* and similar in style, *Sugar Baby* is another potent performance on vocal and banjo, accompanied by Hub Mahaffey on guitar. Coupled with *Down South Blues*, it was his first release on Brunswick. John Boggs, Dock's oldest brother, taught him the song. According to Jon Pankake, it is a traditional number in the Southern mountains, and may be a distant relation of the ancient ballad *The Lass of Roch Royal* (Child #76 as collected by Francis James Child, dating it back to at least a 1776 Scottish songbook), with which it shares a few lines. (The older song's refrain: "Oh, who will shoe your pretty little feet? / Who will glove your hand? / And who will kiss your sweet little lips / While I'm in a foreign land?") Under the title *Sugar Babe*, it was included (with mostly different lyrics than heard here: "shoot your dice and have your fun, sugar babe / Shoot your dice and have your fun, run like the devil when the police come, sugar babe") in Cecil Sharp's *Eighty English Folk Songs of the Southern Appalachians* (collected during 1916–1918 as song #245), and subsequently in Bascom Lamar Lunsford's 1929 song collection, and John and Alan Lomax's 1934 *American Ballads and Folk Songs*. Boggs' stark, plain-spoken vocal and equally fervent banjo carry a strongly bluesy feeling as he describes a husband considering leaving his wife and child behind: "I've got no sugar baby now. . . . Who'll rock the cradle, who'll sing the song / Who'll rock the cradle when I'm gone?"

Peter Muir, in his 2004 doctoral dissertation *Before 'Crazy Blues': Commercial Blues in America, 1850–1920*, suggested that *Sugar Baby* is a white Appalachian variant of the black folk tune *Sweet Thing*, which (just to make the web more intriguingly tangled) evolved by around 1890 as a descendant of *Mister Frog Went A-Courtin'* (aka *Froggie Went A-Courting*), an Anglo-American folk song—already more than three centuries old by that time—universally known among both blacks and whites in the South in the nineteenth century. *Sugar Baby* is also melodically related to another old Southern favorite, *The Crawdad Song* ("You get a line and I'll get a pole, we'll go down to the crawdad hole").[41]

The song was also recorded as *Going Back to Jericho* in 1926 by Doc Walsh, as *Honey Babe* by the Carter Family, as *Red Apple Juice* by Bascom Lamar Lunsford, and as *Red Rocking Chair* by Charlie Monroe (1949) and the Country Gentlemen (1961). Dock Boggs' entire original body of work was eight recordings in March 1927 and another four sides in 1929, until he was rediscovered during the folk revival in 1963, leading to three albums.

Greil Marcus writes that this is "real killer-inside-me stuff; Sugar Baby was what Boggs called his lover, who you weren't sure would survive the song."[42] Dock Boggs "was a singer and banjo player who sounded as if his bones were coming through his skin every time he opened his mouth; that was the sound that drew people to him." It was included on Harry Smith's *Anthology of American Folk Music*; in liner notes for the 1997 reissue of the classic compilation, guitarist/folklorist John Fahey admiringly described this as a "primitive and scary" performance.

James Alley Blues (1927)—Richard "Rabbit" Brown
Victor 20578 (issued as *James Alley*)
Recorded in New Orleans on March 11, 1927 (*HS, HBN*)

"I sometimes think *James Alley Blues* is the greatest record ever made," writes Greil Marcus.[43] It's a low-key but compelling blues ballad, with New Orleans artist Richard "Rabbit" Brown (a songster born in the early 1880s) on solo vocal and guitar. "I was born in the country," he sings, and his woman wanted to "hitch me to a wagon and drive me like a mule . . . If you don't want me, why don't you tell me so?" In this vivid account of a dysfunctional relationship, he wavers between loving her and wanting to see her dead: "Sometimes I think you're too sweet to die / Other times I feel like you should be

---

38. Friedwald, *Biographical Guide*, p. 16.
39. *The Culture of Time and Space*, p. 123–24.
40. Ogren, p. 144.

41. The ubiquitous melody also turned up in a host of other early country and blues songs, including the Carolina Tar Heels' *Ain't No Use Workin' So Hard*, Bill Cox's *NRA Blues*, and Blind Willie McTell's *Hillbilly Willie's Blues*. (*Old Time Music* #3 Winter 1971–1972).
42. September 2, 2001, *New York Times*; reprinted in *Bob Dylan by Greil Marcus: Writings 1968–2010*, p. 303.
43. *Mystery Train: Images of America in Rock 'n' Roll Music*, p. 200.

buried alive." "I done seen better days," he sings philosophically. "But I'm puttin' up with these."

James Alley "was twenty to thirty years ahead of its time," writes Bill Friskics-Warren in *Heartaches By the Number*. He notes that it anticipated Hank Williams' confessional songwriting, and served as a precursor for Bob Dylan's *Maggie's Farm* (along with the direct inspiration for that Dylan piece, the Bently Boys' *Down on Penny's Farm*).[44]

One of the few contemporary reviews of a blues record, by Abbe Niles in the July 1928 edition of a literary journal, *Bookman*, described Ralph Peer's field session on which Brown was recorded. "Rabbit Brown . . . sang to his guitar in the streets of New Orleans, and he rowed you out into Lake Pontchartrain for a fee and sang to you as he rowed." On this as on other Victor field sessions, Victor leased General Electric equipment and used two Western Electric condenser microphones, but (as Samuel Charters reported in *The Country Blues*) "in New Orleans it was so hot and the humidity was so high that the microphones shorted out. They had to use old-fashioned carbon microphones, but the heat made them 'sizzle' and hum while they were being used, so they had to pack the microphones in ice until they were ready to record."[45]

James Alley (actually Jane Alley) was a narrow street in a poor neighborhood (located in the turpentine distillery district) between Perdido and Gravier, just behind New Orleans' city jail, slightly southwest of Canal Street. Charters: "The prisoners can shout to anyone turning into the alley . . . The railroad tracks are just beyond the end of the alley." In the early days of New Orleans brass-band parading, "the section was called 'the battleground' because the gangs of boys that followed their favorite bands would meet at the boundaries and fight to see who would follow the music into disputed ground." Louis Armstrong was born on Jane Alley, and Rabbit Brown grew up there. (Jane Alley was wiped out around the late 1960s to make room for the city's Traffic and Municipal Court building.)[46] He made his living singing in bordellos and saloons in Storyville until that red-light district was closed in November 1917. Brown was in his late forties when the opportunity to record arrived in 1927; Victor's field unit was in town to record Louis Dumaine's jazz band.

According to Marcus, the opening notes of the song represent an ancient New Orleans theme that was heard again twenty-nine years later at the beginning of Shir-

ley & Lee's *Let the Good Times Roll*. Jeff Todd Titon in *Early Downhome Blues* suggests that it's part of the same basic tune family as Charley Patton's *Pony Blues*. *James Alley* was included on the Harry Smith folk music anthology, and the compilation *Times Ain't Like They Used to Be: Early American Rural Music, Vol. 2*. Dylan made it one of the first songs he recorded at an informal 1961 session. Brown has a clear, distinctively accented voice that's extremely appealing. He recorded only four other songs at this single session produced by Peer, one of them (the flip side of *James Alley*) the delightful *I'm Not Jealous*.

Luc Sante: "The blues was not a reaction or a spontaneous utterance or cry of anguish in the night, and it did not arise from the great mass of the people like a collective sigh. It was a deliberate decision arrived at by a particular artist through a process of experimentation, using materials at hand from a variety of sources. It was taken up by others and expanded to encompass anguish as well as defiance, humor, lust, cruelty, heartbreak, awe, sarcasm, fury, regret, bemusement, mischief, delirium, and even triumph. It grew to be the expression of a people, but not before it had become as diverse and complicated as that people."[47]

Guitar Rag (1927)—Sylvester Weaver
Okeh 8480[48]
Recorded on April 13, 1927 in New York, released on Aug. 5 (originally recorded song on Nov. 2, 1923) (*AL*)

The first black guitarist to make records under his own name (and also the first significant rural male bluesman to record), Sylvester Weaver was born on July 25, 1897, in Louisville, Kentucky, and made his recording debut on October 23, 1923, when he accompanied vaudeville blues singer Sara Martin on two numbers, the first time on record that a popular female singer was backed up only by guitar.[49] Weaver was also the first country bluesman to record for Okeh; one of the biggest companies in the race-music field, it had previously used only urban artists. Two weeks later on November 2, he cut the original version of his classic *Guitar Rag* backed by *Guitar Blues* (on Okeh 8109), both showing off his nimble-fingered dexterity on six-string guitar. However, due to the limitations of the acoustic recording process, these and

44. *Heartaches By the Number: Country Music's 500 Greatest Singles*, p. 112–13.

45. *The Country Blues*, p. 87. Charters provided the full lyrics to *James Alley* on p. 98–99.

46. Terry Teachout, *Pops: A Life of Louis Armstrong*, p. 391. Armstrong typically called it "James Alley" in interviews, so this seems to have been how it was colloquially known.

47. "The Invention of the Blues," article in *A New Literary History of America*, p. 482.

48. The flip side is another fine instrumental with a mysterious title, *Damfino Stump*.

49. Robert B. Winans' analysis of the WPA's ex-slave narratives from the 1930s, counting the number of references to playing musical instruments (from the 1840s to the Civil War), found only 15 references to the guitar, compared to 205 for fiddle, 106 for banjo, 75 for percussion, etc. Charles Wolfe saw this as "strong evidence of the guitar's late arrival in black folk music." (Fall 1980 *Black Music Research Newsletter*).

the four other solo sides he cut in May–June 1924 didn't have the proper fidelity to truly show what he could do. It was only three-and-a-half years later when he returned to record *Guitar Rag* electronically—and this time adding a new strain to his simple but irresistibly infectious main theme, about two minutes into the record—that the song truly emerged as a powerhouse. The uptempo, dance-like piece was indeed rooted in ragtime syncopations, but would soon be taken in new directions.

The Famous Hokum Boys—the formidable duo of guitarist Big Bill Broonzy and pianist Georgia Tom Dorsey on mostly spoken vocals (the same Thomas Dorsey later to become the greatest of gospel composers)—recorded two freewheeling versions of *Guitar Rag* in April 1930. Eight months later, Roy Harvey and Jess Johnston became the first white artists to record it; their acoustic guitar duet carried it close to the edge of what would become bluegrass a decade later. But the song would reach a far wider audience when electric steel guitar wizard Leon McAuliffe made it his personal virtuoso showcase with Bob Wills & His Texas Playboys as *Steel Guitar Rag* (recorded on September 29, 1936, for Vocalion). McAuliffe put his name on the record as composer, but this was Sylvester Weaver's creation, gussied up with some fresh touches.[50] Weaver recorded a total of thirteen guitar solos, two six-string banjo solos (on a standard banjo with a guitar neck), and eight guitar duets. His definitive performance can be found on the boxed set *American Pop: An Audio History, from Ragtime to Mojo.*

Weaver retired from music at the end of 1927 having recorded twenty-six sides under his name, returned home to Louisville, and died in unwarranted obscurity in 1960. Finally in 1992 the Kentucky Blues Society raised enough funds to place a headstone on his grave, and ever since has presented its Sylvester Weaver Award annually to "those who have dedicated their lives to presenting, preserving, and perpetuating the blues."

Lafayette (Allons à Lafayette) (1928)—Joseph F. Falcon

Columbia 15275-D

Recorded April 27, 1928; misspelled title on record label: *Lafayette (Allon a Luafette)* (*World-#10, Folk-#72, RR, 1001, ARM*)

Cajun music in French-speaking southwest Louisiana—dance tunes initially built around the fiddle and guitar, joined by the harmonica during the post–Civil War period, and by the early 1900s frequently using the accordion in place of the mouth harp—had been growing in regional popularity since the late nineteenth century. By the 1920s, the music's local popularity had reached a point where commercial record companies were finally taking notice. The one performance that firmly established Cajun music as an important force in the recording world was *Allons à Lafayette* by Joseph Falcon (born on September 28, 1900, in Rayne, Louisiana) and Cléoma Breaux.

The first Acadian refugees came from Canada to the Louisiana territory in 1764; after Louisiana entered the Union in 1812, the number of French speakers in the Bayou section of the state outnumbered English speakers by three to one. As outlined by Ryan Andre Brasseaux, an 1881 published account reported a prairie settlement there of some 150 Cajun families that included at least sixty fiddlers.[51] By the turn of the twentieth century, Afro-Creoles in south Louisiana had developed a distinctive syncopated sound using fast choppy rhythms featuring many rapid runs. Malcolm L. Comeaux: "It evolved into a style not found elsewhere in the world, and based on that style, probably first developed by black Creoles and then taught to Cajuns."[52] The word "Cajun" is a corruption of "Acadian." The cultural isolation of Louisiana Acadians was accentuated by prejudice: during the 1910–1930 era, speaking French became a punishable offense at public schools; children began dropping out in large numbers and working full time on family farms.

George Burrow, a popular local politician based in Rayne, Louisiana, saw the appeal of Cajun music, and in early 1928 decided to sponsor the trio of vocalist Leon Meche, accordionist Joe Falcon, and guitarist Cléoma Breaux (her brother was another of the top early Cajun artists, Amédée Breaux). He made a deal with the Columbia Record Company to do a recording session with the trio, under which he agreed to purchase 250 records to sell at house dances and dance halls. When the trio made the daylong journey on April 27, 1928, from Acadia Parish to Columbia's makeshift recording facility in a New Orleans hotel suite, the musicians' decidedly rustic appearance caused nervous Columbia officials to rescind the deal, until a confident Burrow wrote a check for 500 records. Based on that increased commitment, the label's engineers consented to issue one record if a test recording proved acceptable. At that point Meche, overcome by nerves before the microphone, suggested that Falcon take his place as vocalist, and so the session proceeded with Falcon and Breaux working as a duo. The initial test recording of the two-step number *Lafayette* quickly convinced the engineers that the pairing worked musically,

---

50. All the cover versions are based primarily on Weaver's 1923 original, which was apparently a better seller than his electrical remake (the latter turned up rather seldom in collections of 78s), and do not include his additional melodic strain.

51. Brasseaux, *Cajun Breakdown: The Emergence of an American-Made Music*, p. 16.

52. Comeaux, "Introduction and Use of Accordions in Cajun Music," *Louisiana Folklore Miscellany* 7 (1999), quoted by Brasseaux, p. 21.

so they proceeded to cut permanent versions of *Lafayette* and its 78 rpm companion piece, *The Waltz that Carried Me to My Grave.*

"Allowing for the volume of Falcon's accordion, engineers distanced the microphone from the performers, producing in the process a swollen sound rich with ambient echo," writes Brasseaux. "Falcon's warm vocal quivered under the strain of nerves and exertion, thus endowing the first Cajun record with a sense of urgency. Falcon and Breaux's debut session ignited a recording revolution in south Louisiana and marks Cajun music's entrance in America's musical marketplace."[53][54] Columbia's top competitor, Victor, made its first Cajun recordings in October 1928, and during the coming months and years, the music of French Louisiana became an established part of record companies' menu of ethnic offerings. Joe Falcon enjoyed a long career extending into the 1960s. Cléoma Breaux (whom he subsequently married) made a number of fine records on her own, as the first important female Cajun artist, until a tragic injury in December 1937 cut short her career and led to her death in 1941. Local consumption of Cajun records, notes Brasseaux, "all flowed from one source: the Falcon-Breaux debut *Lafayette* was the Cajun tributary into the mainstream where the local became a bona fide extension of the commercial American music project." In 2007 *Lafayette* was selected by the Library of Congress for the National Recording Registry.

How Long, How Long Blues (1928)—Leroy Carr
Vocalion 1191
Recorded on June 19, 1928 (released in Aug.) (*Blues-#31, GHF, SB*)

The evolution of the blues from its rural roots to a new urbanized style found one of its key transitional artists in Leroy Carr, born on March 27, 1905, in Nashville and raised in Indianapolis. He taught himself to play piano, worked with a traveling circus as a teenager, then in dance halls and parties across the Midwest. In 1928 he formed his great partnership with guitarist Scrapper Blackwell (real name Francis Hilman Blackwell, North Carolina–born and part Cherokee), and this record, from their debut session (cut by a Vocalion mobile unit at the radio station WFBM in Indianapolis), became not only a breakthrough hit but one of the biggest-selling blues records of the entire pre–World War II era. The two men had to be recalled to the studio three times to record a new master because the old one had worn out from numerous pressings. (It's even been claimed that it ultimately sold a million copies, surely an impossibility.)

"The song has a haunting sadness, carried by an evocatively persistent melody and Leroy's expressive, wistful voice," writes Giles Oakley in *The Devil's Music*, "and there was warmth, too, in his gently rolling piano accompaniment, which betrayed no bitterness, and no anger. Leroy Carr's blues were those of resigned regret; simple statements of sadness." Blackwell's contributions were equally crucial; his "strong, cutting incisiveness on guitar contrasted with the softness of Carr's restrained mood, bringing tension to the sound."[55] The song was an oft-cited favorite of author Ralph Ellison; Robert O'Meally, in *Living with Music: Ralph Ellison's Jazz Writings* suggested that Carr's central cry here echoes the Biblical lament "How long, O Lord" from Psalm 6:3 "and sounds, for all its secularity, an urgent yearning for wholeness, meaning, and inner peace."[56]

The influence of this record was massive and enduring. In *Escaping the Delta*, Elijah Wald asserts of the Carr performance and the 1928 Tampa Red–Georgia Tom hit *It's Tight Like That*: "Virtually all popular blues for the next twenty years can be seen as flowing directly from these two records . . . [Carr] was the blues world's most influential male singer, at least until the 1950s, and his impact extended well beyond the boundaries of what is normally considered blues."[57] Nat "King" Cole, Ray Charles, and Sam Cooke were just a few of the post-war performers who owed a significant stylistic debt to Carr. His relaxed, intimate crooning, possessing a wistful quality, found an ideal foil in Blackwell's attacking style. Mark A. Humphrey cites for this performance in particular the "insistent, doomy bass in Carr's left hand and Blackwell's heavy thumb."[58] Although the two men were quite different (Carr mellow, Blackwell combative), both shared a love of alcohol, and their partnership ran deep despite occasional flareups; when Carr died in late April 1935 after a long deterioration due to liver damage, Blackwell was crushed and seldom performed for the remaining thirty years of his life.

Jeff Todd Titon's analysis of the song in *Early Downhome Blues* found a close similarity both melodically and rhythmically with what he calls the *Crow Jane* "family" of two-line, approximately eight-bar blues, although the harmonic support is considerably different. W. K. McNeil writes that the melody is generally thought to be based on a 1925 Ida Cox record for Paramount featuring

---

53. Brasseaux, p. 49–52. A partial translation of the refrain: "Let's go to Lafayette, to change your name . . . you're too cute to act so naughty." It was a traditional tune Falcon had known since childhood, for which he created lyrics.

54. The diatonic accordion, limited to a range of twenty notes (ten each pushing and pulling), was, remarks Kevin Fontenot, "portable and easily heard in the loud dance halls of Louisiana." (*Ethnic and Border Music: A Regional Exploration*, p. 4–5.)

55. Oakley, p. 161.

56. *Living with Music*, p. xxv.

57. *Escaping the Delta: Robert Johnson and the Invention of the Blues*, p. 36–37.

58. *Nothing But the Blues*, p. 159–60.

Papa Charlie Jackson on banjo (*How Long Daddy, How Long*). Bob Koester in the February 1964 *Blues Unlimited* opined that Daddy Stovepipe (Johnny Watson), who began his recording career in 1924 for Gennett, introduced the song that may have served as its prototype, although Watson's song used a different melody. Although not offering another originator for the song, Dave Hatch and John Williams in the April 1965 *Blues Unlimited* argued that Carr was not its author, based on the tune's chord structure: his other piano blues consistently omitted flattened thirds and sevenths, which are quite prominent in *How Long Blues*. Wald suggests that the Carr melody is closely related to *East St. Louis*, which W. C. Handy recalled hearing in 1892. But Carr and Blackwell worked magic with the tune that no one else had done. "As a vocalist" (writes Robert Santelli), "Carr created a mood based on restraint and resignation, which was the perfect setting for Blackwell to exercise his guitar prowess."[59]

Wild Cat (1928)—Joe Venuti & Eddie Lang
Bluebird 10280[60]
Recorded in New York on June 21, 1928 (*AL*)

One of the great partnerships in early jazz, violin virtuoso Joe Venuti and guitar dazzler Eddie Lang worked together in a number of settings over more than a ten-year period, and never more memorably than in their duo and trio recordings that gave both soloists plenty of room to strut their stuff. *Wild Cat* was perhaps their hottest showcase of all.

Joe Venuti was born on September 1, 1904; for years he said he was born at sea while his Italian immigrant parents were en route to America, but it's generally believed he was born in Philadelphia. Eddie Lang was born Salvatore Massaro in Philadelphia on October 25, 1902. The two became early friends, and served as co-leaders of an Atlantic City combo in the early 1920s before launching their jazz careers. Lang first became known for his single-string guitar solos with the Mound City Blue Blowers in 1924–1925, and Venuti with the Jean Goldkette orchestra in 1924–1927 (Lang also played for a time with Goldkette), before they made their first duo recordings in 1926. Both men were featured with Roger Wolfe Kahn's band in 1927–1928, and with Paul Whiteman in 1929–1930. When Bing Crosby left Whiteman for a solo career, Lang became his regular accompanist and a close friend, until the guitarist's tragic death in March 1933 from complications after a tonsillectomy; Crosby's biographer Gary Giddins writes that Bing never quite got over Lang's passing. Venuti would remain an active jazzman for decades thereafter.

Wild Cat is a thrilling performance (accompanied by Frank Signorelli on piano) in which Venuti cuts loose with fire and intensity (classical violin great Jascha Heifetz was an avowed admirer of his virtuosity and a friend), matched step for step by Lang. After a brief respite in the ferocious tempo at mid-song, Venuti roars forward again to a breathless finish. Allen Lowe, including the song in his boxed set of classic 1893–1946 recordings (*American Pop*), calls it "an astonishing tour de force of Venuti's technical wizardry, and Lang's genius for parallel accompaniment."[61] The flip side of this 78 was another renowned Lang-Venuti workout, *Doin' Things*. Ted Gioia writes that Venuti and Lang played a key role in "defining the role of guitar and violin in the jazz idiom" with recordings that "went a long way toward forging a chamber-music style of jazz combo playing."[62]

I'm Thinking Tonight of My Blue Eyes (1929)— Carter Family
Victor 40089
Recorded on Feb. 14, 1929

A. P. Carter was a supremely skilled collector and reinterpreter of traditional songs, and this was one of his finest—a deeply touching, melancholy ballad about a love who is lost across the sea. Its roots were in British folk tunes; Sara Carter, A. P.'s wife, remembered hearing variations on the song as a child. But the Carters gave it a new emotional immediacy. "I'm thinking tonight of my blue eyes, who is sailing far over the sea / I'm thinking tonight of my blue eyes, and I wonder if he ever thinks of me. . . . A link in the chain has been broken, leaving me with a sad and aching heart . . ."

We learn in *Country Music Sources* (Meade and Spottswood) that the first recording of the song, albeit with quite different lyrics, was *Thrills That I Can't Forget* by Welby Toomey for the Gennett label in 1925. The irresistibly named Earl Johnson & His Clodhoppers did it two years later for Okeh as *In the Shadow of the Pines*; and then came two 1928 versions under still other titles, *I Can Never Forget* by Emry and Henry Arthur (Emry Arthur also had the distinction of making the first commercially issued recording of *I Am a Man of Constant Sorrow*), and *Broken Hearted Lover* by the Ernest Stoneman Family. Finally, the Carters gave it the performance for the ages four months after the Stonemans; they recorded it again for the ARC family of labels on May 10, 1935.

Roy Acuff would use the same melody with new lyrics in 1936 for his classic inspirational hit *The Great Speckled Bird*. And the durable melody had yet another life when it was used for Hank Thompson's 1952 smash, *The*

59. Santelli, *Best of the Blues: The 101 Essential Albums*, p. 61.
60. The duo had previously recorded the song in January 1927 for Okeh 40762.
61. Lowe, *American Pop*, p. 102. *Wild Cat* was also included in the boxed set *RCA Victor Jazz: The First Half-Century*.
62. Gioia, p. 88–89.

Wild Side of Life, and Kitty Wells' even bigger answer song that same year, *It Wasn't God Who Made Honky Tonk Angels*. Mark Zwonitzer and Charles Hirshberg: "It was as if the melody was so deeply encoded in country music's double helix of performer and audience that every time a singer sneaked it in under his or her own lyrics, the songs hit with the reflexive thump of recognition."[63]

Gregorio Cortez (Parts 1 & 2) (1929)—Pedro Rocha & Lupe Martinez (Trovadores Regionales)

Vocalion 8351
Recorded in October 1929 (*World-#20, RR-#73*)

The Mexican *corrido*, as described by Manuel Pena, "represents the antithesis to the whole process of cultural assimilation [of Mexicans who have emigrated to America]: it is a form of cultural resistance." Its significance is also broader than such other Mexican musical genres as the *orquesta* or the *conjunto*, he argues, because "it transcends class difference and involves the total ethnic group." The perfect illustration is the song that may constitute the definitive corrido, *Gregorio Cortez*. "No other Mexican-American corrido has been more widely known," reported Americo Paredes.[64]

The term corrido (notes Philip Sonnichsen) comes from the Spanish verb *correr*, meaning "to run" or "to flow"; "hence a corrido is, in effect, a running account of a particular story, a narrative ballad usually colored by the amount of information the corrido maker has at hand, his political views, his feelings about the circumstances surrounding a given incident, and his emotional attitude." The first true corrido is believed to have originated in 1808, but its modern development is generally traced from 1867 onward. Just as the classic era of original corridos was approaching its conclusion in the 1920s, the ballads began to reach commercial recordings, culminating in the "golden age of the recorded corrido" from about 1928–1936.[65]

In Karnes County, Texas, on June 12, 1901, Gregorio Cortez shot and killed Sheriff Brack Morris, who had just shot Cortez's brother. The sheriff was trying to arrest the Cortezes for an alleged horse theft that later investigations proved they had not committed. Cortez fled some 500 miles, mostly on horseback, while hundreds of men in multiple posses pursued him; en route to the Rio Grande, he killed another Texas sheriff, and was accused of the death of a constable. As the ballad dramatizes: "Then said Gregorio Cortez, with his pistol in his hand / 'Don't run, you cowardly *rinches*, from a single Mexi-

can!'" Finally, he was captured near Laredo. A three-year legal battle ensued, rallying Mexican-Americans behind his cause, at the end of which he was acquitted of two of the murders. However, he was sentenced to life imprisonment for the killing of Sheriff Robert Glover of Gonzales County. After eight years in prison, Governor O. B. Colquitt pardoned him in 1913 (he died three years later), and the corrido about him became (writes Pena) "a milestone in the Mexican-American's emerging group consciousness."[66]

Pedro Rocha (born on February 21, 1888, in Matehuala, Coahuila) and Lupe Martinez (born on January 15, 1901, in San Luis Potosi) both came to the United States before 1910, and began singing together in San Antonio in the 1920s, performing on the streets and then on early Spanish-language radio programs there and in Corpus Christi. Between March 1928 and 1937 they recorded over 200 selections, although after Martinez died in 1936, Rocha teamed with a new partner, Jose Angel Colunga; Rocha continued to make records into the 1950s.[67] *Gregorio Cortez* is a vigorous vocal and guitar duet, offered in two parts (covering both sides of the 78) like many corridos, totaling over five minutes.[68] It's included in several Arhoolie/Folklyric compilations. The performance was inducted into the National Recording Registry in 2004.

In ballads such as *Gregorio Cortez* and *Joaquin Murrieta*, asserts Pena, "Mexicans were mounting a sustained challenge to their subordination in the capitalist system that had emerged in the Southwest by the end of the 19th century." Paredes—who made the song the focal point, and its most famous phrase the title, of his book *With His Pistol In His Hand*—notes that many other corrido heroes had preceded him, "but in Cortez's life was epitomized the idea of the man who defends his rights *con su pistola en la mano*."[69]

Down on Penny's Farm (1929)—Bently Boys

Columbia 15565
Recorded on Oct. 23, 1929 in Johnson City, Tennessee (*Folk-#106, HS*)

American agriculture was hit with an economic depression starting in 1921 foreshadowing the Great De-

63. *Will You Miss Me When I'm Gone*, p. 122.

64. *A Texas-Mexican Cancionero: Folksongs of the Lower Border*, p. 30–31, 66–67.

65. Annotation for Arhoolie's *Corridos y Tragedias de la Frontera: The First Historic Recordings of Mexican-American Ballads*.

66. Manuel H. Pena, *The Texas-Mexican Conjunto: History of a Working-Class Music*, p. 38–40.

67. *Ethnic Music on Records*, Vol. 4, p. 2241–46.

68. John Storm Roberts in *The Latin Tinge* (p. 25) offers this as an example of the "pure" rural Mexican style, with an uneven 3/4 rhythm, simple accompaniment using runs similar to Anglo-American playing, and almost no pauses between verses.

69. *With His Pistol In His Hand*, Introduction, p. 1–2. Chapter II of Paredes' book traces "The Legend"—the colorful mythology that quickly grew around Cortez, providing the basis for the corrido. Chapter III is "The Man"—the actual documented facts of Cortez's life, and the events of 1901 leading to his arrest, trial, and incarceration. The remainder of the book examines the corrido itself, its historical antecedents, and the variations in the song as it evolved during subsequent years in oral tradition.

pression yet to come, but Southern farmers were little affected—because most were already struggling to survive.[70] By 1930, some 55 percent of all Southern farms were operated by tenants. This is the hardscrabble life depicted with startling vividness by the Bently Boys in *Down on Penny's Farm*, recorded just one day before Wall Street's Black Thursday (October 24, 1929).

The identities of this duo (banjo and guitar, with solo vocal) are unknown, although they're believed to be from North Carolina; it's one side of their only 78. Included on Harry Smith's *Anthology of American Folk Music*, this is a deeply bluesy account of the life of a sharecropper, indebted to both landlord (George Penny) and merchants. "A virtually unyielding cycle of crop mortgages, declining prices, rising freight rates, and limited educational opportunities perpetuated the system and ensured that the farmer's children and grandchildren would also become ensnared in its clutches," writes Bill Malone.[71] The song's origins date back many years earlier—it was described in the Smith anthology as a "regionalized recasting" of an earlier song called *Hard Times*—but it possessed a documentary-like accuracy for conditions in 1929. The record was also a bit ahead of its time in using the banjo as the lead instrument.

It was also recorded as *On Tanner's Farm* by Gid Tanner and Riley Puckett (accompanied by Ted Hawkins) in 1934, and John and Alan Lomax included the number in the 1941 book *Our Singing Country* (under the title *Hard Times in the Country*). Alan Lomax reissued the Tanner recording in August that year on the album *Smoky Mountain Ballads* for RCA Victor's Vintage series. Bascom Lamar Lunsford recorded another variant, *Down on Roberts' Farm*, for the Library of Congress in 1949, and said he learned it from North Carolina performer Claude Reeves; John Greenway subsequently included this piece in his book *American Folksongs of Protest*. Pete Seeger, having heard the Bentlys' record through Alan Lomax (who had rescued it from Columbia's out-of-print file), performed it on his first solo album, *Darling Corey* (1950).[72] The lyrics to *Down on Penny's Farm* were also printed in the May 1954 issue of *Sing Out!* One of Bob Dylan's earliest songs, *Hard Times in New York Town* (1961), was a virtual rewrite (as discussed by Todd Har-

vey), and a few years later Dylan used the Bentlys' classic as a point of departure for *Maggie's Farm*.[73]

Little Sadie (1929)—Clarence (Tom) Ashley
Columbia 15522
Recorded on Oct. 23, 1929 in Johnson City, Tennessee

The intense murder ballad *Little Sadie* is given an almost hypnotic feeling through Clarence Ashley's solo vocal and passionate five-string banjo playing.[74] Chilling in its blunt, straightforward description of his deed ("I met my little Sadie and I blowed her down"), and then describing his flight from the law, this is from the same remarkable session that also produced *The Coo Coo Bird*. Not one second is wasted in this fiercely paced, relentless performance; the wordless final 40 seconds alone could make one's hair stand on end.

Like many rural musicians of his time, Ashley—while he stayed busy with various ensembles including Byrd Moore & His Hot Shots and later the Carolina Tar Heels, and playing with other musicians including fiddler G. B. Grayson, in addition to his regular work in medicine shows—couldn't make a living solely through music. During the 1920s he farmed and worked at a sawmill; later he labored with furniture, coal, and lumber. Only with the folk revival of the 1960s could he pay the bills solely through his art.

Little Sadie (sometimes known as *Bad Lee Brown*, as in G. Malcolm Law, Jr.'s, *Native American Balladry*) was first recorded as *Penitentiary Blues* by Buddy Baker for Victor in 1928. Riley Puckett did it in 1934 for Bluebird as *Chain Gang Blues*; Hank Thompson offered a memorable variation in 1958 as *Cocaine Blues*; and Bob Dylan—inspired above all by Ashley's definitive treatment—recorded it in 1970.

Dancing in the Dark (1931)—Bing Crosby
Brunswick 6169
Recorded in New York on Aug. 19, 1931; *Pop Memories* debut Sept. 19, 1931 (#3 peak)

Talk about value for money: This Brunswick 78 pairing *Dancing in the Dark* with *Star Dust* offered two of the greatest ballads in all of American popular song, both brand new, performed by the man who was swiftly emerging as pop music's foremost star. *Dancing in the Dark* by Arthur Schwartz and Howard Dietz had just been introduced in the Fred and Adele Astaire Broadway musical *The Band Wagon*, and the lush, sensuous ballad was perfectly suited to both the voice and personal

70. Even while the United States as a whole was growing more wealthy in the years immediately after the Great War, the wealth census of 1922, as compared with that of 1912, showed that the money value of farm products "increased only slightly in the decade—really a loss in actual buying power for the farmer," summarizes Preston William Slosson in *A History of American Life* (p. 1102). The gulf between urban and rural America only grew wider during the next several years.

71. Malone, *Don't Get Above Your Raisin': Country Music and the Southern Working Class*, p. 31.

72. Josh Dunston and Ethel Raum, *Anthology of American Folk Music* (book analyzing the Smith collection). The Seeger album was cited in the August 1950 *Sing Out!*

73. Todd Harvey, *The Formative Dylan: Transmission and Stylistic Influences, 1961–1963*, p. 37.

74. Ashley used a G-modal banjo tuning that was popular in much of the Appalachian region.

style of Bing Crosby.[75] Odd as it may seem from today's perspective, the young Crosby (then twenty-eight) was regarded as a singer of genuinely erotic seductive powers, with a gift for achieving great intimacy through the microphone, and that can be clearly heard in this performance. The Crosby voice in 1931–1932 had a particularly husky quality due to nodes on his vocal cords that would soon heal, and to some aficionados this gave a special emotional edge to his recordings of the time.[76] Morris Dickstein found the song so evocative that he used it as the title for his "cultural history of the Great Depression," calling it "a song about a community of two surrounded by a great darkness, a moment of tenuous joy whose backdrop is impermanence and insecurity, 'the wonder of why we're here . . . and gone.'"[77]

Crosby, remarks Nick Tosches in *Where Dead Voices Gather*, was "the first singer to work the microphone as if it were a woman—not only singing to it as if were a woman, but taking it in his hands as such. Though overlooked and all but invisible to modern eyes, this was the most revolutionary move in the history of popular singing. Before Crosby, the microphone was regarded as an ill-favored object, a cold and ugly technological necessity whose presence was something to be overcome. He made of it a surrogate of desire, an instrument of physical as well as of vocal expression."[78] Will Friedwald notes that Bing "turns *Dancing in the Dark* into an example of Depression desperation that's culturally as well as sexually charged."[79]

In a slight idiosyncrasy heard in some other Crosby records of the period, Bing sings the verse *after* the first chorus. The studio orchestra (conducted by Victor Young) includes Tommy Dorsey on trombone, Jimmy Dorsey on clarinet, Benny Krueger on C-melody saxophone, and Bing's favorite accompanist, Eddie Lang, on guitar. Just one month after this recording, Crosby debuted as star of his own CBS radio program, and would shortly ascend to an entirely new level of multi-media success. "We can face the music together / Dancing in the dark . . ."

Tea for Two (1933/1939)—Art Tatum (written by Vincent Youmans & Irving Caesar)
Brunswick 6553

Recorded on March 21, 1933; Decca 2456, recorded on April 12, 1939 (*GHF-#64, Jazz-#78, DMDB-#82, Trad-#98*)[80]

"God is in the house." That's what Fats Waller said when he saw Art Tatum enter a New York club where he was working, stopped playing and announced, "I play piano, but God is in the house tonight!" His staggering technique at the keyboards was without equal, the almost superhuman dexterity of his fingers matched by his imagination. *Tea for Two* was his very first solo commercial recording, and six years later he dashed off an even more celebrated version of the standard.

Born on October 13, 1910, in Toledo, Ohio, blind in one eye and having only slight vision in the other, Tatum had several years of classical music studies, garnered a local reputation as a piano virtuoso from his mid-teens, began performing on radio in 1929, and came to New York in 1932 as accompanist for singer Adelaide Hall. From his March 1933 debut solo recording session, the Tatum legend was born. His large hands enabled him to easily cover the entire keyboard, his ear was pitch-perfect, and his grasp of both classical and popular repertoire gave him an almost unlimited range of musical possibilities. His lightning speed dazzled audiences, and utterly intimidated his fellow musicians.

Tea for Two, the hit from the 1924 Broadway musical *No, No, Nanette*, was to be a lifelong Tatum favorite, and made a perfect debut recording. Indeed, he had originally used the tune as his introductory piece in a 1932 Harlem nightclub showdown with established piano titans Fats Waller, James P. Johnson, and Willie "The Lion" Smith, blowing away the competition. "That Tatum, he was just too good," Waller later recalled. "He had too much technique . . . He sounds like a brass band." "When Tatum played *Tea for Two* that night," said Johnson, "I guess that was the first time I ever heard it really played."

Ed Kirkeby, who managed Waller, was present on that night, and colorfully described it in his book *Ain't Misbehavin'*. As Tatum launched into the tune, the "right hand was playing phrases which none of the listeners had imagined existed, while the left hand alternated between a rock solid beat and a series of fantastic arpeggios which sounded like two hands in one. His hands would start at opposite ends of the keyboard and then proceed towards each other at a paralyzing rate; one hand picking up the other's progression and then carrying it on himself, only to break off with another series of incredible arpeggios. Just when it seemed that he had surely lost his way, Tatum came in again with a series of quick-changing harmonies that brought him back smack on the beat."[81]

75. In *Easy to Remember: The Great American Songwriters and Their Songs*, William Zinsser calls *Dancing* and the best work of Schwartz and Dietz "grandly constructed songs, soaring at exactly the moment when they needed to take flight and then returning to earth, all musical issues resolved." (p. 67)

76. Giddins, *Bing Crosby, A Pocketful of Dreams: The Early Years, 1903–1940*, p. 269–70.

77. Dickstein, *Dancing in the Dark; A Cultural History of the Great Depression*, p. xix.

78. Nick Tosches, *Where Dead Voices Gather*, p. 157.

79. Friedwald, *A Biographical Guide to the Great Jazz and Pop Singers*, p. 118.

80. It was the 1939 Decca version selected for the Grammy Hall of Fame.

81. Kirkeby, Schiedt, and Traill, *Ain't Misbehavin': The Story of Fats Waller*, p. 148.

In his 1933 performance, remarks Dan Morgenstern, "we recognize two great influences: Fats Waller and Earl Hines—the former in the steady stride of the left hand and the rippling, calm arpeggios in the contrasting right, and the latter in the rhythmic suspensions and 'strange' harmonies of the breaks in the second chorus."[82]

Gunther Schuller in *The Swing Era* notes that while Tatum was sometimes criticized for being a showoff "acrobatic act," this 1933 performance takes the song at a relaxed, happy Waller tempo and mood, albeit with Art's patented flourishes.[83] Gary Giddins sharply disagreed with those who called Tatum a mere showman; "Those magnificent arpeggios, runs, and flurries, those supersonic turnbacks and contrary figures and thumb-driven bass walks aren't ornamental; they are the nerve center of his art, the jewels in his treasure box—an embarrassment of rewards."[84]

Isn't This a Lovely Day? (1935)—Fred Astaire (written by Irving Berlin)
Brunswick 7487
Recorded on June 27, 1935; *Pop Memories* debut Aug. 24, 1935 (peak #3)[85] (*APS*)

The warm, elegant *Isn't This a Lovely Day* was one of five hits that Irving Berlin provided for Fred Astaire in that most beloved of his pairings with Ginger Rogers, *Top Hat*. Astaire had been dancing on stage to Berlin songs ever since 1915, but they met for the first time during the making of this film, beginning a lifelong friendship.

In his Berlin biography *As Thousands Cheer*, Laurence Bergreen relates that Astaire used this song as the occasion for having some good-natured fun with the chronically worrying composer. Having learned the song from Berlin, choreographer Hermes Pan taught its first eight bars to Astaire. As Fred and Irving played gin rummy, the actor began to sing the brand-new song. Berlin was taken aback. "Fred, where did you hear that?" he asked. A nonchalant Astaire replied, "Oh, that? It's a tune from the *Hit Parade*." Just when Berlin began to panic that he had inadvertently plagiarized an existing song, Astaire burst out laughing and let him in on the joke.[86] *Top Hat* was a complete triumph, wiping out the memory of Berlin's previous unhappy experiences in Hollywood; made for $620,000, the film earned over $3 million—enabling the composer to take home $300,000 thanks to a profit-taking clause in his contract—and was universally hailed as a classic.

Just listen to the way Astaire sings the line, "As far as I'm concerned, it's a lovely day," and you can't help but smile, even without benefit of seeing him with Ginger. Johnny Green and his orchestra provide the accompaniment, with the leader on piano and the ensemble including clarinetist Jimmy Lytell. The singer's deft performance, writes James T. Morris, stands as one of the "enduring examples of Astaire's art."[87]

The Great Speckled Bird (1936)—Roy Acuff & His Crazy Tennesseans
Vocalion 04252, under title *The Great Speckle Bird*
Recorded on Oct. 20, 1936 in Chicago (*C&W-#51*)

Roy Acuff, the soon-to-be King of Country Music, began his journey to stardom with this song, the third number recorded at his debut session. Written by Reverend Guy Smith by about 1934 for the Church of God (although Vance Randolph in *Ozark Folksongs* noted unverified claims that it might date back some forty years before that), it was performed by Smith on radio in Springfield, Missouri, where he was known as "Uncle George." One text for the song, reports Randolph, was published anonymously in the March 26, 1936 *Aurora* (Missouri) *Advertiser*.[88] The song was initially heard by Acuff as performed in Knoxville (but never recorded) by a group called the Black Shirts. Its lyrics were based on Jeremiah 12:9: "Mine heritage is unto me as a speckled bird, the birds round about are against her; come ye, assemble all ye beasts of the field, come to devour"—a reference to the fact that believers in Christ were persecuted; accordingly, the song was adopted as an anthem by some Pentecostal groups such as the Assembly of God. In 1935, after hearing the song a number of times, Acuff asked the group's Charlie Swain to make a copy of the lyrics. It was copyrighted in 1937 several months after the Tennessee artist's recording, with the words credited to Smith and the music to Acuff.

Elizabeth Schlappi writes in her Acuff biography that a deep interest in this song sent William Calaway, the artists & repertoire man for the American Record Company, in search of Acuff. During one of Roy's WROL noon radio programs in Knoxville, an associate of Calaway was in the audience, and after he heard him perform *Great Speckled Bird*, ARC signed him to a recording contract (with his records being released on its Vocalion subsidiary). As Acuff would later say: "He wanted The Bird, he didn't want me!" A late-October 1937 Opry audition didn't go well when he nervously crooned the song instead of belting it out; when he got the opportunity to perform the tune in his normal fashion at a second audition on February 5, 1938, he earned a standing ovation, and

82. *Living With Jazz*, p. 419.
83. Schuller, p. 482–83.
84. *Visions of Jazz*, p. 442.
85. *Lovely Day* was Brunswick's second biggest selling record (behind *Cheek to Cheek*) for three straight months (August–October) as reported in *Variety*.
86. Bergreen, p. 348.

87. *American Popular Song* annotation, p. 53.
88. *Ozark Folksongs*, edited & abridged by Norm Cohen, p. 435.

two weeks later became a full-fledged Grand Ole Opry regular.[89] Strangely enough, the record didn't become a full-fledged hit until the fall of 1938.

Acuff's original 78 is actually entitled *The Great Speckle Bird* (lacking the "d"), but the missing letter was restored when he fashioned new lyrics for a sequel in March 1937, *Great Speckled Bird No. 2*. The original 1936 recording included Acuff's new second verse, written because he felt the opening verse needed some explanation. The same traditional British melody (which had itself been borrowed from the Carter Family's *I'm Thinking Tonight of My Blue Eyes* in 1929) was later used for Hank Thompson's *Wild Side of Life*, and Kitty Wells' *It Wasn't God Who Made Honky Tonk Angels* (the latter two both in 1952). Robert Cantwell describes the piece as "an ecstatic vision of the evangelist imagination, [which] acquired the status of a hymn in the holiness churches of the South."[90] Nick Tosches calls this "a great performance . . . one of the few truly mystical country records ever cut."[91] "But the great speckled bird in the Bible / Is one with the great church of God . . . I'll be joyfully carried to meet Him / On the wings of that great speckled bird."

Roy Acuff, courtesy of Library of Congress, LC-USZ62-124418.

89. Elizabeth Schlappi, *Roy Acuff, the Smoky Mountain Boy*, p. 33–36.
90. Robert Cantwell, *Bluegrass Breakdown: The Making of the Old Southern Sound*, p. 80.
91. Nick Tosches, *Country: The Twisted Roots of Rock 'n' Roll*, p. 142.

Bei Mir Bist Du Schoen (1938)—Andrews Sisters (music by Sholom Secunda; English lyrics by Sammy Cahn & Saul Chaplin)
Decca 1562
Recorded on Nov. 24, 1937; chart debut Jan. 1, 1938 (5 weeks at #1) (*World-#41, Trad-#44, GHF-#149, RR, DMDB*)

It began as a song in a musical during the 1932–1933 season at New York's Second Avenue Yiddish Theater, *I Would If I Could*, under the title *Bay Mir Bistu Sheyn* (To Me You Are Beautiful). The tune was performed in the show by the charismatic singer Aaron Lebedeff (who would remain a major artist for many years thereafter), with the great klezmer clarinetist Dave Tarras as featured accompanist, soloing on the song's bridge. Although (as klezmer historian Henry Sapoznik writes) the number "brought down the house" nightly, and the song sold out a sheet music printing of 10,000 copies within a few years, the show closed after a modest run.[92]

Sammy Cahn and Saul Chaplin heard the tune in 1935 at Harlem's Apollo Theater performed in Yiddish by two black singers billed as Johnny & George, and were startled to see how well it went over with an audience that couldn't understand a word of the lyrics. They filed it away for future reference. Two years later, when composer Sholom Secunda tried to break into Hollywood and offered *Bay Mir* to Warner Brothers, he was turned down; even actor/singer Eddie Cantor thought it was "too Jewish." "They had no idea how wrong they were," notes Sapoznik. Upon returning to New York, feeling that the song was played out, Secunda sold the rights to publishers Jack and Joe Kammen for the mighty sum of $30. The brothers promptly licensed the number to T. B. Harms, Warner Brothers' song publishing subsidiary. When agent Lou Levy came by for a visit with his clients the Andrews Sisters, the girls were intrigued.[93] The sisters persuaded Jack Kapp of Decca Records to let them record it, but he stipulated that they needed an English lyric. Cahn and Chaplin provided it, and all concerned simply hoped (as David Ewen put it) that "three gentile girls singing a Yiddish song might go over in New York City." The result was a nationwide phenomenon, the biggest-selling record ever by a female vocal group to that time. Benny Goodman's version (recorded a few weeks after the Andrews', with vocal by Martha Tilton) further expanded its popularity, and Goodman also performed it at his legendary February 1938 Carnegie Hall concert. It launched the careers of Patty, Maxene, and Laverne in their third recording session (the first two having produced no hits), also bringing a few other Yiddish-derived

92. Henry Sapoznik, *Klezmer! Jewish Music from Old World to Our World*, p. 128–31.
93. Levy would later marry Maxene Andrews.

tunes into the pop marketplace. "Secunda was mortified," reports Sapoznik, having sold one of the biggest hits of the era for just thirty bucks (although the Kammens eventually agreed to give him a portion of their share of the royalties). According to Michael Freedland (*So Let's Hear the Applause: The Story of the Jewish Entertainer*), the song's royalties ultimately totaled some $3 million by 1961.

By the account of Jack Gottlieb, the melody has ancestry in the Yiddish tune *Shuarts, bist du shaurts*.[94] When Patty Andrews first heard the tune, she asked if it was of Greek origin (the sisters were of Greek and Norwegian parentage). When the song broke through, it simply exploded; in a single week, it shot from nowhere on the *Billboard* Top 15 sheet music chart to #1 on January 8, 1938, a debut achievement matched by no other song during that period. Within a few weeks, over a dozen versions had been recorded, and the February 19 issue declared the Andrews' disc the most profitable record in coin-operated phonographs since *The Music Goes Round and Round* at the end of 1935. Gottlieb reports that in the 1990s, more than a half century after its initial heyday, the song became "the rage" in Japan, and it was featured in a Paul Taylor ballet score, *Company B*.

For the generation that came of age in the FDR era, Patty (born on February 16, 1920), Maxene (born January 3, 1918) and Laverne Andrews (born July 6, 1915, all in Minneapolis) came to symbolize America during World War II. The sisters made professional appearances as children in a revue at the Orpheum Theater in Minneapolis, began touring with the Larry Rich band in vaudeville as teenagers, moved up to clubs and theaters the next few years, and to radio appearances in 1937 until this record provided their breakthrough. The Andrews' high-spirited, lightly jazzy vocals (not as jazzy or inventive as those of their role models, the Boswell Sisters)[95] kept the folks on the home front entertained (both on their own and teaming with Bing Crosby), and to U.S. soldiers abroad they represented part of the America they were fighting for.

Although efforts to transform other Yiddish songs into pop hits in the wake of the phenomenon were generally not successful (the Andrews Sisters recorded Cahn's adaptation of the 1920s Yiddish hit *Yosl, Yosl* as *Joseph, Joseph* for their followup release, to only modest response), Benny Goodman scored big in 1939 when his trumpeter Ziggy Elman took a decades-old Yiddish tune with lyrics by Johnny Mercer as *And the Angels Sing*. Victor Greene: "The process by which the music of a single immigrant group became, by the end of the

Depression, an integral part of the nation's 'hit parade' reveals the emergence of a new segment of American culture."[96] Sapoznik declares that "the effect of *Bei Mir Bist Du Schoen* on the American Jewish community was huge." Although other Jewish songs had crossed over in a modest way, "this was the first to be adapted and accepted by the general public." The tune "became the anthem of second-generation Jews, who saw the song's acceptance as a symbol of their own."[97]

Tara's Theme (*Gone With The Wind*) (1939)—by Max Steiner

Film opened in Atlanta Dec. 15, 1939 (*NPR-100, AFI-#2, Trad-#61, RR-#74, GHF*)

Any list of the greatest composers of original motion picture scores must include Max Steiner in the highest echelon. During the early years of the sound cinema, his work helped establish the basic accepted structure of orchestral film music, serving as a model for a generation of Hollywood composers. While one can argue about what his greatest film score was, there can be no debate over which one had the most enduring impact. On an inflation-adjusted basis, *Gone With The Wind* remains, as of 2012, the biggest box office hit in Hollywood history, its unadjusted gross of $198 million translating to over $1.5 billion,[98] and Steiner's score matches its source as an undisputed classic.

Born in Vienna, Austria, on May 10, 1888, as a young prodigy Steiner graduated from Vienna's Imperial Academy of Music at thirteen, and the following year wrote the book and lyrics and composed the score for a musical that played for two years. After studying with Gustav Mahler, he began conducting at sixteen, and came to the U.S. in 1914. Years of conducting and orchestrating Broadway musicals served as the prelude for his Hollywood career starting in 1929 (following the advent of sound). *King Kong* in 1933 became his first score for a blockbuster success; he would go on to win Oscars for his scores for *The Informer* (1935), *Now, Voyager* (1942), and *Since You Went Away* (1945). As staff composer at Warner Brothers for nearly thirty years, Steiner became particularly associated with the films of Humphrey Bogart, including *Casablanca*, *The Big Sleep*, and *Treasure of the Sierra Madre*.

Steiner was amazingly prolific, and in 1939, he worked on twelve films—including *Gone With The Wind*, at the time the longest score (over three hours) ever written. As detailed by Tony Thomas, there were sixteen main themes in the score and over 300 separate musical segments. To complete the mammoth task in just twelve

---

94. Gottlieb, *Funny, It Doesn't Sound Jewish*, p. 57–61.

95. The Boswells had also recorded for Decca; they had recently broken up, giving the label an opening for a new sister act.

96. *A Passion for Polka*, p. 115.

97. Sapoznik, *Klezmer! Jewish Music*, p. 134.

98. As calculated by online service Box Office Mojo.

weeks (assisted by a team of five orchestrators who were all accomplished composers), he had a doctor supply him with Benzedrine so he could maintain a work schedule of twenty hours at a stretch.[99] [100] Of course what film lovers will always cherish above all is the central *Tara's Theme*, precisely the epic, sweeping romantic theme demanded for the biggest film ever. Startlingly, given both its musical quality and for a film that won eight Oscars, best score was not among them. But the American Film Institute rendered its historical judgment by selecting it as the second greatest film score ever behind John Williams' for *Star Wars*.[101]

Walking the Floor Over You (1941)—Ernest Tubb
Decca 5958

Recorded in Dallas on April 26, 1941 (*C&W-#23, GHF, NPR-300, HBN-#102, DMDB, SC*)

His rumbling bass-baritone wasn't exactly a thing of beauty as it occasionally wavered off key. But Ernest Tubb's voice possessed an earthy authority and warmth that invariably drew country music fans to him; he recruited some of the finest musicians ever to play in Nashville, always happy to share the spotlight with them; and generously assisted many other up and coming artists to get their first big breaks. For these reasons among others, he stands as one of the most beloved figures in country music history, and *Walking the Floor Over You* is his acknowledged classic.

Born on February 9, 1914, in the tiny farm community of Crisp in south-central Texas, later settling in the west Texas town of Benjamin, Ernest Tubb fell in love with the music of Jimmie Rodgers at fifteen, learned to play guitar, and began performing on San Antonio radio. It was Rodgers' widow Carrie who helped the young performer land his first two recording sessions for Bluebird in 1936–1937 (even lending him her husband's favorite guitar for good luck) and his first theater tour, singing in

Rodgers' blue-yodeling style, which was not well suited to his voice. It was not until he secured a new recording contract with Decca in 1940 that he began to find his own style—initially forced upon him when the removal of his tonsils in 1939 eliminated his ability to yodel. Still, his first Decca releases were modest sellers, and his future remained in doubt.

The story goes that Tubb's wife, Lois, had run up shopping charges that he couldn't pay, triggering an argument and Lois leaving with their son to visit her mother. Alone, angry, and depressed, he paced back and forth all night in the family's small apartment, then was inspired to pour out his feelings in a song.[102] *Walking the Floor Over You*, his seventh Decca single, was recorded at Bunny Briggs' tiny studio in Dallas, released in August 1941, and became his breakthrough, selling 400,000 copies in its first several months, an immediate honky-tonk anthem on jukeboxes across the South and Southwest.[103] [104] Label co-founder Dave Kapp preferred another number from the session for its first release, *I Wonder Why You Said Goodbye*, but deferred to the artist's insistence that this was the hit. When it was reissued after the war on a new coupling (Decca 46006), the record's total sales are said to have eventually topped one million.[105] Fay "Smitty" Smith, the staff guitarist at the Fort Worth station KGKO where Tubb had a regular program, was featured on electric guitar (standing in for Tubb's regular guitarist Jimmie Short, who couldn't make the session).[106] Although other country artists (most notably Bob Wills' guitar ace Leon McAuliffe) featured electric guitar, the sound of the electric pick-up attached to the conventional Martin guitar still provided the Tubb record with a distinctive sound and hastened its success.[107] By the time he joined the Grand Ole Opry in January 1943, he was universally known as E. T., the Texas Troubadour, and would remain one of the giants of country music until his death in 1984.

---

99. Thomas, *Music for the Movies*, p. 150–53. In his Warner Brothers career, Steiner provided the scores for nearly 150 films. Overall, "the general level of craftsmanship and the consistent understanding of the musical needs of motion-picture storytelling added up to an astonishing total contribution."

100. Among his other challenges, Steiner also clashed "bitterly" with David O. Selznick over the producer's editorial tinkering with his work. (Cooke, *A History of Film Music*, p. 73.)

101. The original *Gone With The Wind* soundtrack was commercially unavailable as an album for many years due to confusion over its ownership. In 1954 an all-new recording of soundtrack highlights, with orchestra conducted by Steiner, was released by RCA Victor and reached #10 in *Billboard* (it also charted again seven years later). Finally, in 1967, the legal issues were resolved, and the official soundtrack was released for the first time (by MGM), charting at #24, prior to a re-release of the movie (with the print expanded from 35 mm to 70 mm for widescreen viewing). The twenty-eight-year-old recording was remarkably good by modern standards because the large orchestra was totally covered, thanks to multiple miking which all went into one channel on the 35 mm strip of film. The sound did have to be balanced for stereo and electronically enhanced. (July 22, 1967, *Billboard*, p. 7.)

102. Ace Collins, *The Stories Behind Country Music's All-Time Greatest 100 Songs*, p. 40–41.

103. Article by Ronnie Pugh for the December *Journal of Country Music*, Vol. 7 #3 (1978).

104. *Walking the Floor* was cited as one of the country's biggest "folk" hits in ten different issues of *Billboard* from November 29, 1941, to October 17, 1942, an impressive eleven-month span; if the magazine had launched its country chart a few years earlier than the actual 1944 premiere, this would have been one of the decade's blockbusters. The May 30 issue remarked that his records were getting "terrific play in locations throughout the country," particularly the South. Bing Crosby's cover version was released in July 1942, which called still more attention to the original. The July 25 issue said two of the record's strongest markets were Des Moines and Philadelphia.

105. *Journal of Country Music*, Vol. 9 #1 (1981).

106. Peter Guralnick, in his chapter on Tubb in *Lost Highway: Journeys and Arrivals of American Musicians* (p. 30), writes that because Smith was a newcomer to the band and not comfortable with improvisation, "the accompaniment had to be learned note by laborious note."

107. Bill Malone, *Country Music, U.S.A.* (2nd revised ed.), p. 156–57.

The last of his ninety-one charted country hits was a new version of *Walking the Floor Over You* in 1979 accompanied by Merle Haggard and Charlie Daniels. *Walking the Floor* was ranked #15 among the top 100 country songs of all time by *Country America* magazine in 1992, and as #53 all time by Country Music Television in 2003.

Chattanooga Choo Choo (1941)—Glenn Miller & His Orchestra (written by Mack Gordon & Harry Warren)

Bluebird 11230

Recorded at Victor studios in Hollywood on May 7, 1941; chart debut Sept. 13, 1941 (9 weeks at #1)[108] (*MEM-#63, Trad-#83, Jazz-#114, GHF-#150, DMDB*)

Written for the band to perform in the film *It Happened in Sun Valley*, *Chattanooga Choo Choo* became the second biggest Glenn Miller hit of all only behind *In the Mood*. In the picture, the tale of the locomotive headed south from New York's Pennsylvania Station was performed not only by the band's vocalists Tex Beneke and Paula Kelly with the Modernaires, but also by the stunning Dorothy Dandridge with a wild dance routine by the Nicholas Brothers. Arranged by Jerry Gray,[109] *Chattanooga* was declared to be the first "official" million-seller since Gene Austin's *My Blue Heaven* over a dozen years earlier (the Miller record had gone over 1.2 million copies at that point); to commemorate the event, RCA Victor produced and presented him with a gold record—an idea picked up years later by the Recording Industry Association of America which began awarding gold records to artists who had a million-seller.[110] When, on October 30, 1941, ASCAP and the radio networks finally reached an agreement, thus enabling radio to once again play songs controlled by the songwriters' association after ten long months, *Chattanooga Choo Choo* was one of the first such numbers to be heavily featured.

The recording session came immediately after the band finished work on the picture, and during a three-week engagement at the Hollywood Palladium. Miller band member Chuck Goldstein recalled for biographer George T. Simon that when the band recorded the soundtrack, "Daryl Zanuck and the entire brass came in for a listen," and everyone was delighted with the musical results.[111]

Glenn Miller, courtesy of Library of Congress, LC-USZ62-136831.

The original music from the film was issued on LP in early 1959 by Twentieth Century Fox Records.[112] In the 1990s, soundtrack recordings of both *Sun Valley* and the Miller band's other showcase film, *Orchestra Wives*, were released in stereo for the first time, thanks to multiple microphones used on the Hollywood soundstage that allowed for a latter-day stereo mix, and the band sounded even better than it ever had on record.

"Since [soldiers abroad] were facing death, Miller reminded them of many feelings that they hoped to feel again if they survived," remarks William Howland Kenney. "*Chattanooga Choo Choo*, for example, reminded GI Joe of the excitement of entering Penn Station, ticket in hand for a trip home, getting a shine, hopping board and barely having time to read the latest magazine before arriving in Baltimore. He could swing into the dining car and eat and drink while watching the Carolina countryside flash by, and step out of the train in old Tennessee, looking sharp and feeling fine."[113]

Blues in the Night (1941)—Woody Herman & His Orchestra

Decca 4030

Recorded on Sept. 10, 1941; chart debut Dec. 6, 1941 (4 weeks at #1)[114] (*Trad-#193, NPR-300, BBC, DMDB*)

Although the Harold Arlen–Johnny Mercer masterpiece *Blues in the Night* was given its ultimate vocal

---

108. During much of its reign atop the *Billboard* chart, it was #1 in all four regions of the country. After twenty-three weeks on the market, it scored its biggest-selling week (January 17, 1942 *Billboard*, p. 13). *Chattanooga* also ranked as the #1 most popular number in coin machines in the December 1 and December 15, 1941, issues of *Down Beat* (published twice monthly), and remained in the top twelve through February 15.

109. Bill Conway arranged the vocal harmony and Hal Dickinson the verse.

110. The gold record was given as a surprise presentation to Miller during a live radio broadcast on February 10, 1942.

111. Simon, *Glenn Miller and His Orchestra*, p. 255.

112. In fact it was the very first LP ever issued by Twentieth Century Fox, also including the band's music from the film *Orchestra Wives*, along with some material cut from the pictures (January 22, 1959, *Down Beat*).

113. *Recorded Music in American Life: The Phonograph and Popular Memory, 1890–1945*, p. 199.

114. Also #1 on *Down Beat* March 1, March 15, and April 1, 1942, biweekly juke box charts.

performances years later by Frank Sinatra and Ella Fitzgerald, the man who introduced it on record was Woody Herman, and his rendition stands on its own terms as a classic.

Woodrow Charles Herman was born in Milwaukee on May 16, 1913, debuted in vaudeville as The Boy Wonder of the Clarinet, and got his music-industry start with the Tom Gerun band in late 1929. After stints with the Harry Sosnik and Gus Arnheim ensembles in 1932–1933, Herman first came to the attention of many as both sideman and vocalist with the Isham Jones orchestra from 1934–1936. He formed his own band in late 1936 with other Jones sidemen, and broke through in 1939 with his theme, *At the Woodchopper's Ball*. A first-rate if often underrated clarinetist, Herman was also a popular leader who commanded the loyalty of his musicians, with a special knack for recognizing new talent." Will Friedwald calls him "easily the most successful . . . talent scout in the history of jazz." And as a singer, Woody was equally outstanding, especially on ballads and the blues. George T. Simon in *The Big Bands*: "His phrasing was immensely warm and musical; he used his vibrato well, and his voice had both a sensuous and sensitive timbre."[115]

He brought these qualities to *Blues in the Night*. Surprisingly, he had originally planned to record it as an instrumental, but Mercer had just written lyrics to the tune, and taught them to Herman in the taxi en route to the recording session.[116] Composer Arlen also attended the session, and expressed his pleasure at the performance.[117] The song was introduced in the movie of the same name by Jimmie Lunceford's band (with vocal by William Gillespie as an incarcerated blues singer), but curiously Lunceford refused to record it until Jack Kapp of Decca Records applied some pressure; that band's year-end recording, spread across both sides of a 78, became a hit—but Herman had the chart-topping version. As a blues-rooted ballad using Mercer's wonderfully vernacular language ("My mama done tol' me . . ."), it played directly to Herman's strengths as a singer. The reputation of the Herman bands will always focus primarily on the forward-looking innovations of his "Herds" of 1945–1948 with brilliant arrangers and soloists, but to overlook the music of his early years, above all on this gem, would be to overlook considerable beauty.

I'll Be Seeing You (1944)—Bing Crosby (music by Sammy Fain, lyrics by Irving Kahal)[118]
Decca 18565
Recorded on Feb. 17, 1944; chart debut Apr. 22, 1944 (#1 for 4 weeks) (*HP-#2, Trad-#158, BBC*)[119]

Some songs, no matter how great, must await the proper moment before finding their audience. *I'll Be Seeing You* was written by Fain and Kahal for the short-lived 1938 Broadway musical *Right This Way*, but remained largely unknown until Bing Crosby recorded it six years later. (Frank Sinatra had recorded it in 1940 with Tommy Dorsey and his orchestra, but that recording didn't become a hit until after Bing's version was flooding the airwaves.) Suddenly this stunningly beautiful ballad, recalling a love affair in Paris, took on a deeper resonance in the midst of war. Its new meaning became that of a soldier who saw the image of his beloved in everything around him—if only in his mind's eye—and could cling tight to that thought until they were free to embrace again. "No other singer could so effectively portray so ineffable a sense of absence and loss," suggests Will Friedwald.[120] "Popular recorded music from home carried an exceptional power for those who heard it in such dire circumstances," notes William Howland Kenney in *Recorded Music in American Life: The Phonograph and Popular Memory, 1890–1945*. "To those who didn't know why they were fighting and had good reason to doubt that they would ever live through it," this song had a special meaning. Crosby was king of the music charts in 1944 (and also in Hollywood with his Oscar-winning performance that year in *Going My Way*), and this was his greatest recording since *White Christmas*.

I Can't Get Started (1945)—Dizzy Gillespie Sextet
Manor 1042
Recorded Jan. 9, 1945 (*Jazz-#118, SJ*)

Until January 1945, the great Vernon Duke–Ira Gershwin song *I Can't Get Started* was essentially owned by the late Bunny Berigan for his all-time classic 1936 and 1937 vocal recordings of the number. "From this recording onward," writes Martin Williams, the piece belonged to Dizzy Gillespie, as the bebop trumpeter crafted a masterful "dramatically sustained declamatory

115. Simon, p. 249.

116. Friedwald, *Biographical Guide*, p. 218. "What Herman achieved vocally with his big band . . . was remarkable."

117. Lees, *Leader of the Band*, p. 80. Herman had always credited Arlen (a band vocalist before he hit it big as a songwriter) as an early influence on his singing.

118. Born in New York City on June 17, 1902, Sammy Fain was a pianist-singer early in his career before focusing on songwriting. His long list of hits includes *That Old Feeling, Secret Love*, and *Love is a Many-Splendored Thing*. Irving Kahal collaborated with Fain on *You Brought a New Kind of Love to Me, When I Take My Sugar to Tea*, and *I Can Dream, Can't I?*

119. With ten weeks at #1 and seventeen weeks in the Top Five, it's the second biggest hit in *Your Hit Parade* history (1935–1955) behind only *White Christmas*.

120. *Biographical Guide*, p. 124.

exploration" of Duke's melody.[121] Gillespie biographer Alyn Shipton cites this performance as evidence of "his ability to construct a logical, powerful, and measured solo on a ballad sequence."[122]

John Birks Gillespie was born on October 21, 1917, in the small town of Cheraw, South Carolina, studied music early, played in the Philadelphia area starting by 1936, and landed his first regular job with Teddy Hill's band in 1937. A 1939–1941 stint with Cab Calloway demonstrated vast potential, which he began to further realize with Earl Hines in 1942–1943 alongside alto sax phenom Charlie Parker. Demonstrating his versatility by writing arrangements for Woody Herman and other bands, he became sideman/arranger/musical director for Billy Eckstine's trend-setting band of 1944. It was during late-night jam sessions at Minton's Playhouse in Harlem that Gillespie and Parker helped lay the foundations of what would become bebop. The year 1945 would announce to the world the arrival of bop with the trailblazing recordings of Diz and Bird, together and separately. Gillespie's good humor, the trademarked "beachball cheeks" popping out as he played, and the odd-looking custom-designed trumpet with an upturned bell might have led some to misinterpret him as merely a sidekick to the tortured genius of Parker, but the two men were equally responsible for a movement that transformed the nature of jazz.

"Few trumpeters have ever been blessed with so much technique," marveled Whitney Balliett in *Dinosaurs in the Morning*. "Gillespie never merely started a solo, he erupted into it." He "would hurl himself into the break, after a split second pause, with a couple of hundred notes that corkscrewed through several octaves, sometimes in triple time, and were carried, usually in one breath, past the end of the break and well into the solo itself . . . Gillespie's style at the time gave the impression—with its sharp, slightly acid tone, its cleavered phrase endings, its efflorescence of notes, and its brandishings about in the upper register—of being constantly on the verge of flying apart. However, his playing was held together by his extraordinary rhythmic sense."[123]

Dizzy had been playing *I Can't Get Started* for several years, with the first recorded instance being in his November 1941 New York stage debut with Benny Carter's band. January 9, 1945, marked Gillespie's first session under his own name, and it included his hugely influential novelty hit *Salt Peanuts*, a terrific rendering of Tadd Dameron's *Good Bait*, and a title theme for the new

school of jazz he and Charlie Parker were founding, *Bebop*. Shipton writes that Gillespie "treated the entire piece as a trumpet solo, and played throughout—an eight-bar introduction, the 32-bar AABA main theme, a two-bar tag, and a brief coda—the whole thing taken at a slow ballad pace."[124] Dameron provided the arrangement.[125] Trummy Young on trombone and Don Byas on tenor sax supplied long notes for the opening section prior to "the central channel, which has subsequently become the most widely adopted jazz harmonic sequence for the tune." (In Ira Gitler's *Swing to Bop,* Young explained that Byas came up with the tenor/trombone backing passage and taught it to him; Gillespie was so thrilled with it that he kissed them.)[126] Dizzy would re-use his ending of this recording for the February 1946 introduction of *'Round Midnight* (which would later influence Miles Davis' definitive version of the latter song).[127]

"Dizzy could have hardly chosen a better vehicle for his first session as a leader to announce that he had arrived at full maturity as a soloist," opined Shipton. "As the year went on, he was to restate this again and again, with a series of ever more accomplished solos, although few manage the delicate balance of imagination, modernity, and beauty that he achieved here." The performance was included on the *Smithsonian Collection of Classic Jazz.*

(Other personnel: Clyde Hart on piano, Oscar Pettiford on bass, Shelly Manne on drums)

Ornithology (1946)—Charlie Parker Septet (written by Charlie Parker & Benny Harris)
Dial 1002
Recorded in Hollywood on March 28, 1946 (*Jazz-#64, GHF-#79, RIA*)

One of the legendary jazz sessions of the 1940s, this very fruitful day's work included enduring performances of *Yardbird Suite, Moose the Mooche,* and the two classics that occupied opposite sides of one remarkable 78: Charlie Parker and cohorts cutting loose on *A Night In Tunisia,* and *Ornithology.* The latter song represents Bird's reworking of *How High the Moon,* and features what Ted Gioia calls his "whirlwind" 32-bar solo as its centerpiece. Nat "King" Cole had first shown Dizzy Gillespie the chord changes to *How High the Moon* at Kelly's Stable by around 1944. Ira Gitler writes that Dizzy then began playing the amended tune, "and it became the

121. Liner notes, *Smithsonian Collection of Classic Jazz,* p. 32.
122. *Groovin' High,* p. 84.
123. Article reprinted in *Collected Works: A Journal of Jazz,* p. 83–87.
124. Shipton, *Groovin' High,* p. 162.
125. Gil Fuller contended in Gillespie's autobiography (p. 224) that Dameron didn't actually write any charts for the band, and that they were all by Dizzy and himself.
126. *Swing to Bop,* p. 147–48.
127. Gillespie, *To Be or Not to Bop,* p. 135.

anthem of 52nd Street and the boppers."[128] (Its impact was broadened when an extended jam on *How High the Moon* was featured on Norman Granz's first commercially issued *Jazz At the Philharmonic* album in 1945.) Parker would take the song's reconstruction several steps further to produce something bold and new.

The roots of this song can be found still further back in a July 2, 1942, track that Parker recorded for Decca as a young sideman in Jay McShann's big band, *The Jumpin' Blues*; his chorus begins with an improvised phrase that he would expand (with the guidance of trumpeter Benny Harris) nearly four years later on this record. Parker is at the peak of his powers on this March 1946 date; when he returned to the studios less than three months later, his deepening drug addiction cut short the session and led to his institutionalization.

(Personnel: Parker on alto sax, Miles Davis on trumpet, Lucky Thompson on tenor sax, Dodo Marmarosa on piano, Alvin Garrison on guitar, Victor McMillan on bass, Roy Porter on drums)

Blue Moon of Kentucky (1946)—Bill Monroe & His Blue Grass Boys

Columbia 20370 (also issued on Columbia 37888)
Recorded on Sept. 16, 1946 (released on Sept. 22, 1947)
    (*C&W-#13, RR-#16, NPR-100, GHF, HBN-#40, RIA, TC, ACC, DMDB*)

The beloved theme song of the Father of Bluegrass came into being, so the story goes, when Bill Monroe was on tour driving north from Florida, and saw a particularly large full moon over the highway. It reminded him of the moons he had seen back home in Kentucky, so he used it as the point of departure for a love song, possibly about the married woman with whom he had recently fallen in love, Bonnie Lee Mauldin. Monroe had scored a Top Five country hit in 1945 with *Kentucky Waltz*, and *Blue Moon of Kentucky* seemed an ideal successor.[129]

Monroe's piercing tenor on this old-time waltz performance, writes Billy Altman, "virtually defines what would later be called bluegrass' 'high lonesome sound.'" This was the first recording session of the classic Monroe band, with the leader on mandolin, Lester Flatt on guitar, Earl Scruggs on banjo, and—opening up the record—Chubby Wise on fiddle. Modern Nashville fiddler Vassar Clements has declared that Wise "had the prettiest sound I ever heard." David Cantwell notes the hopeless feeling conveyed by Monroe as he sings of a blue moon that's not likely to stick around any longer than the girl he loves, and the crying quality of his mandolin solo.[130] The

ensemble had honed its sound by playing almost continuously on the road since spring.

Eight years later, a young Elvis Presley would transform *Blue Moon of Kentucky* into a giddy rockabilly raveup used for the B side of his historic debut release on Sun Records, *That's All Right*. Very soon after hearing Presley's recording, Monroe in September 1954 redid his classic (on Decca 9-29289) using three fiddles (Bobby Hicks, Charlie Cline, and Gordon Terry) instead of one, and switching gears dramatically from a waltz (in the beginning) to a rip-roaring 2/4 tempo, even faster than Presley's. He also urged the Stanley Brothers to cut their own version of the song (using a slower tempo)—a recording session that he even produced—in order to take advantage of the surge of publicity for the song. Decca released Monroe's new version two days after Presley performed it on the Grand Ole Opry. The songwriting royalties from Presley's version provided the most "powerful checks" (in his words) that the longtime icon had enjoyed in years.

One of the highlights of Monroe's life occurred in the mid-1980s when he and his band toured the Holy Land, including concerts in Jerusalem and Tel Aviv; despite his age and the stress of travel (as described by biographer Richard D. Smith), he savored every minute of the experience, leading the bus in singing gospel songs from Bethlehem to the Dead Sea. "Performing at the Sea of Galilee, a huge full moon shining behind him, he launched into *Blue Moon of Kentucky* and the crowd came to its feet. He encored seven times that night."[131]

Good Rocking Tonight (1947)—Roy Brown

DeLuxe 3093
Recorded in New Orleans in early July 1947; chart debut
    June 12, 1948 (#11 R&B) (*1001*)

For many aficionados, this is the record that started it all for rock 'n' roll. Roy Brown—the man who wrote and recorded one of the seminal rock classics—was born in New Orleans on September 10, 1925; his mother was of mixed Algonquin and black lineage. After stints in Los Angeles and Shreveport, Louisiana, he began singing blues at a Galveston, Texas, club in 1946. *Good Rocking Tonight* is based on a 1946 hit written for the Tommy Dorsey orchestra by Sy Oliver (who also did the vocal), *There's Good Blues Tonight*. Oliver based his piece on broadcaster Gabriel Heatter's nightly radio salutation, "America, there's good news tonight!" The Dorsey record begins with the call, "Hear ye! Hear ye! I've got good news tonight," then Oliver sings, "Oh yes, there's good blues tonight!" Jim Dawson and Steve Propes note that in both melody and message the Brown song resembles Oliver's—and that the

128. *Swing to Bop: An Oral History of the Transition in Jazz in the 1940s*, p. 136–37.
    129. Horstman, *Sing Your Heart Out, Country Boy*, p. 151.
    130. *Heartaches By the Number*, p. 25–26.

131. Smith, *Can't You Hear Me Callin'?*, p. 248.

melody was in turn based on that of a previous Oliver hit for Dorsey, 1941's *Yes Indeed.*[132]

Brown used Oliver's musical foundation, added a stronger, bluesier, rhythm, and in his new lyrics paid homage to characters from past popular songs and black folklore, including Elder Brown, Deacon Jones,[133] Caldonia (of Louis Jordan fame), Sioux City Sue, Sweet Georgia Brown, and Sweet Lorraine. While playing in New Orleans, Brown offered *Good Rocking* to his hero Wynonie Harris (who was also in town at the Rainbow Room), but Harris wouldn't hear it. However, Harris' musicians invited the kid on stage, and he belted out his new song to a big response. At the suggestion of a man at the club, Brown then took it to Cecil Gant (of *I Wonder* fame), who was playing down the street at the famous Dew Drop Inn. Gant flipped over the song, called DeLuxe records president Jules Braun in Linden, New Jersey, at four in the morning, and had Brown sing it over the phone to him. Braun quickly signed the twenty-one-year-old. The radio station that helped break the record was WJMR, New Orleans' first major station catering to a predominantly black audience; flooded with requests for the song from not only black listeners but also white teenagers after DJ Poppa Stoppa played it heavily, the station shot to new prominence due to its association with a 78 that was boldly suggestive for its time.

Brown's recording was just a moderate national R&B hit—ironically, Harris' harder-rocking cover version was bigger—but it took on more significance as Brown reeled off a series of R&B smashes from 1948–1953. Elvis Presley took *Good Rocking* to a whole new level with his historic 1954 waxing of the song for Sun Records. Unfortunately, Brown was unable to benefit from the rock explosion, scoring just a couple of minor hits after Elvis blew the doors open; he did enjoy a modest resurgence through concert performances in the 1970s before his death in 1981.

Per Oldaeus provided background to the Brown session in an article for *The Jazz Archivist.*[134] The bandleader for the date, New Orleans drummer Bob Ogden, got his first professional experience in 1937 with the *Darktown Scandals* road show starring blues artist Ida Cox, and subsequently played with the bands of Walter "Fats" Pichon and Oscar "Papa" Celestin. Ogden organized his

seven-piece combo in 1946, featuring tenor saxophonist Earl Barnes, and had first hired Brown to sing at a New Orleans gig around June 1947.[135] So it was natural that his band would accompany Brown for the historic session at Cosimo Matassa's J&M Recording Studio at the corner of Rampart and Dumaine Streets. Tony Moret (trumpet) designed the song's introduction, Barnes composed the riffs, and, Brown would recall, "I merely sang the song . . . It was a good rockin' thing, you know, and man, I just started singing . . . I felt real at ease."

Good Rocking begins like a Louis Jordan jump blues, and just keeps cooking, featuring an alto sax solo by O'Neil Jerome; also in the ensemble are Clement Tervalone on trombone, probably Walter Daniels on piano, and bassist Walter Spencer.[136] After the record took off, Syd Nathan, head of King Records, came down from Cincinnati and acquired the entire DeLuxe catalog, including Brown's contract. "Well, I heard the news, there's good rockin' tonight / I'm gonna hold my baby as tight as I can / Tonight she'll know I'm a mighty, mighty man / I heard the news, there's good rockin' tonight . . ."

Another noteworthy element of this performance discussed by Oldaeus is its blend of the clave rhythm (clave means "key" in Spanish, and is also the name of the double-stick percussion instrument on which the pattern is played in Cuban music) and the shuffle beat. *Good Rocking Tonight* offers an early version of what would become known as the Bo Diddley or "Hambone" beat, which he describes as a "two-bar rhythmic pattern of fixed asymmetrical accents . . . The New Orleans way of playing the clave beat pattern is to add an accent on the fourth beat in every second bar ('the big four')." The clave pattern has a long history in New Orleans music, including the "hold that tiger" part of *Tiger Rag* and Zutty Singleton's drumming on the 1929 Victoria Spivey–Louis Armstrong record *Funny Feathers*, among other examples, but it would fully flower with Roy Brown and then explode with Diddley.

Marianne (V-J Was the Holiday) (1947)—King Radio
Recorded in August 1947 (*World-#118*)

One of the founding fathers of Trinidadian calypso on record, the man known as King Radio was born Norman Span, and was a waterfront worker on the Port of Spain when he made his performing debut in 1929.[137] Six years

132. *What Was the First Rock & Roll Record*, p. 29–33 discussing the Wynonie Harris version.

133. Parson Brown and Deacon Jones were stock comic figures of sinful preachers who had (Nick Tosches discusses in *Where Dead Voices Gather*) been a part of the black songster tradition since the 1800s; Parson Brown appeared in the 1900 cakewalk composition *Foggy Jones*. Both men were major players (one of them dancing around "like a clown," the other rattling "them old bones") in the 1915 pop hit *Alabama Jubilee*. They were also featured in the 1945 Lucky Millinder smash *Who Threw the Whiskey In the Well*.

134. *William Ransom Hogan Jazz Archive*, Vol. XXI (2008).

135. Barnes, noted for his Lester Young–influenced playing, had been scheduled to play at a fateful April 23, 1940, engagement with Walter Barnes' band at the Rhythm Club in Natchez, Mississippi, but missed the bus for the job, and thus eluded the disastrous fire that killed some 200 people including ten of the twelve musicians.

136. *The Blues Discography, 1943–1970*, by Les Fancourt and Bob McGrath lists William Diamond as the bassist on the session.

137. Radio's years of experience as a stevedore may have proven valuable as a performer; socializing with crewmen on vessels from other

later his recording career was launched; within a short time, he stood alongside such other colorfully-named legends as Atilla the Hun, Lord Executor, Roaring Lion, and Growling Tiger at the forefront of popular music in Trinidad.[138] A charismatic performer, he often began on one side of the stage and would jump and bounce his way to the other side. Radio specialized in tales about the battle between the sexes, and his lighthearted style was sometimes accompanied by social commentary in the lyrics. When Harry Belafonte took his brand of calypso to the top of the American charts in 1956, it was the songs of King Radio that helped fuel his ascent, with outrageously infectious numbers like *Man Smart, Woman Smarter* (first recorded by Radio in 1936) and *Matilda* ("she take me money and gone Venezuela," originated by Radio in 1939).

Marianne is the original recording of the calypso classic later popularized in U.S. by Belafonte and the Hilltoppers. The lyrics depict Trinidad's nationwide celebration of the Allied victory over Japan, including a lament that FDR couldn't be alive to see it. But the central singalong refrain is the same as in the 1957 hit version: "All day, all night, Marianne / Down by the seaside, sifting sand / All the little children love Marianne . . ."

Radio popularized the song, but did not originate it. Another calypso artist, Lord Iere (real name Randolph Thomas), had performed *Marianne* in 1945, and claimed to have written it just after learning of Germany's surrender on May 7. The original lyrics, about an oversexed woman, were modified by Radio, and in his recording he indirectly acknowledges that the chorus is not his, preceding the familiar refrain with, "The leggo [chorus] was . . ."[139] Raymond Quevedo (known by his calypso title Atilla the Hun) reported that the tune had actually been introduced (minus the V-J Day verse) by Roaring Lion (Raphael de Leon) in 1944, although it didn't become popular until the following year.[140]

'Round About Midnight (1947)—Thelonious Monk Quintet

Blue Note 543

Recorded on Nov. 21, 1947 (*Jazz-#11, NPR-100, RIA-#37, GHF-#104, TG, TC, ACC*)

Originally recorded as *'Round Midnight* by Cootie Williams & His Orchestra on August 22, 1944 (for Major 7119),[141] the Thelonious Monk creation did not really begin its evolution into one of the defining classics of American jazz until Dizzy Gillespie rendered it on February 7, 1946 (as *'Round About Midnight*) for Dial. The composer finally got the opportunity to record it himself nearly two years later (under the latter title) with a small group that included drummer Art Blakey. While Miles Davis was to put his indelible stamp on the song in 1957, the beauty of Monk's own treatment carries a very distinctive power.

Thelonious Sphere Monk was born on October 10, 1917, in Rocky Mount, North Carolina, and grew up in New York City (the middle name came years later). Having played piano since age six, Monk plunged into the vibrant Harlem club scene of the early 1940s, and was house pianist at the legendary Minton's Playhouse where bebop was forged by Charlie Parker, Dizzy Gillespie, and cohorts in after-hours sessions. After playing with the bands of Lucky Millinder (1942) and Coleman Hawkins (1944), Monk established his reputation in sessions for Blue Note from 1947–1952, which introduced most of the compositions by which he became known, including *Straight No Chaser, Misterioso*, and *Criss Cross*. Because Monk's piano style was so idiosyncratic (specializing in "rhythmic displacement," unusual intervals, and dissonance) that it sounded strange to many listeners, he didn't receive wide public recognition until his albums for Riverside starting in 1955—and thanks in large part to Davis' popularization of *'Round Midnight*.

The tune was copyrighted on September 24, 1943, with lyrics by Thelma Elizabeth Murray as *I Need You So*; biographer Robin Kelley reports that he had been "noodling around" with the C-minor melody for at least a year. It was inspired by the young woman who would become his wife in 1948, Nellie Smith.[142] When Monk finally got to record his own classic, it was cut in a single take at WOR Studios; it became one side of his second 78 released by Blue Note a few months later.[143]

Gary Giddins points out that Monk "conducted his first record session at thirty, organized his first working band at forty, and dropped from sight at about fifty-five . . . he labored in solitude for much of his most creative period. His records were ignored, his compositions pilfered, his instrumental technique patronized, his personal style ridiculed. Yet no voice in American music was more autonomous and secure than Monk's, and no voice in

Caribbean islands, he sometimes learned foreign melodies and could adapt these into original numbers.

138. Maureen Warner-Lewis suggested that the colorful sobriquets or stage names for calypso artists provided a link with African custom: "These 'strong names' or 'praise names' proliferate in African epics and sacred verse." Keith Warner: "The sobriquet was a show of grandeur meant to inspire confidence, even fear, and so was prefaced either by 'the Mighty' or 'Lord' or 'King.'" *Kaiso! The Trinidad Calypso: A Study of the Calypso as Oral Literature*, p. 16–17.)

139. Liverpool, *Calypsonians to Remember*, p. 78–79. Iere, in classic calypso fashion, responded in 1946 to the appropriation of his song with a new, savagely satirical number, *Donkey City*.

140. Quevedo, *Atilla's Kaiso: A Short History of the Trinidad Calypso*, p. 85.

141. Williams added his name to the song as co-composer, based on his addition of a third section that was never recorded again after his original version.

142. Kelley, *Thelonious Monk: The Life and Times*, p. 87–88.

143. The flip side was another Monk standard, *Well You Needn't*.

jazz relied more exclusively on jazz itself for its grammar and vision."[144] Ira Gitler: "It's been said that Monk wrote *'Round Midnight* about 1939. And a lot of the tunes that he recorded much later were written in the early 1940s, but nobody heard them on record."[145]

Monk always tended to play his own compositions at a slower tempo than other interpreters did, and he approached *'Round About Midnight* as a "miniature concerto." Dan Morgenstern writes that Monk's original recording of the song "proves how much each note meant to Monk. He never wasted any—few players have been more economical than he . . . He was too conscious of the specific gravity and weight of each note he culled from the instrument, and its relationship to the next one." It's noteworthy that Monk had excelled in physics and mathematics at New York's demanding Stuyvesant High School. "His keen awareness of relationships was evident in everything he did." In his hands, *'Round About Midnight* "becomes a vehicle for new explorations of melody, harmony, rhythm, sound texture, and structural and spatial relationships . . . And how he knew to use space and silence!"[146]

(Other personnel: George Taitt on trumpet; Edmond Gregory on alto sax; Bob Paige on bass; Art Blakey on drums)

Boogie Chillen (1949)—John Lee Hooker (written by John Lee Hooker & Bernard Besman)
Modern 20-627
Recorded in Detroit on Nov. 3, 1948; chart debut Jan. 8, 1949 (#1 for 1 week on R&B chart) (*Blues-#3, RHF, GHF, R&B-#30, NPR-300, RR, RIA, FIR, TC, DEL, SB, ACC, DMDB*)

The record was billed as "John Lee Hooker & His Guitar," and indeed that's all it is. But the combination of guitar, vigorous foot-tapping, and the deep-blues groove he taps into made *Boogie Chillen*—from his debut recording session—a fiercely rhythmic performance and an immediate classic. It launched a half-century-long career that made Hooker a multi-generational icon.

Born on August 22, 1917, in Coahoma County near Clarksdale, Mississippi, John Lee Hooker was introduced to the blues by his stepfather, Will Moore, who was a locally popular guitarist who had occasionally worked with blues legend Charley Patton. Moore had grown up in Shreveport, Louisiana, and taught the youngster what Robert Palmer in *Deep Blues* calls "hypnotic, one-chord drone blues, with darkly insistent vamping, violent

treble-string improvisations, and songs that fitted both traditional and improvised lyrics into a loose, chant-like structure."[147] After spending most of the 1930s in Memphis, Hooker settled in Detroit in 1943, and played music on the side for five years at house parties and clubs. In 1948 he was introduced to Bernie Besman, a local record distributor, who recognized the artist's unique sound and had him record a demo at United Sound on Second Boulevard. He decided to record Hooker solo because his tendency to "jump time" made it difficult for a band to follow him. Bessman recalled for Michael Lydon that he amplified Hooker's guitar, and put a speaker in a toilet bowl next door to the little studio. "Then we put a mike under that so the sound would bounce off the water. I wanted that echo effect." A crucial final touch was engineer Joe Syracuse bringing in a plank board that Hooker's foot could tap time with, placing a microphone next to it to pick up the tapping.

It was near the end of the demo session after recording several slow blues numbers that Hooker laid down *Boogie Chillen*. Hooker describes walking down Detroit's Hastings Street, dropping into a music joint called Henry's Swing Club, liking what he hears, and shouting, "Boogie, chillen!" before launching into a guitar break. Then the record's famous dialogue: "One night I was layin' down. I heard Mama and Papa talkin'. I heard Papa tell Mama to 'let that boy boogie-woogie! 'Cause it's in him and it's got to come out!'"[148] Because Besman was Modern Records' Detroit distributor at the time, he sent the tape to the Los Angeles label run by brothers Jules and Saul Bihari; they loved it, and selected his demo performance of *Boogie Chillen* as his first release.[149] Gene Nobles, a top DJ at WLAC in Nashville (whose signal reached fifteen states and Canada), played the record ten times in a row one night, helping carry it to hit status.[150]

Hooker's music, with *Boogie Chillen* as a prime example, is discussed by Richard J. Ripani as blues utilizing so-called "static harmony" in which "the chords do not 'progress' from one to another in the Western music sense." This approach to harmony is seen as specifically African in origin, as much of African music is "based on cycles or clusters of cycles and a rhythmic relationship to body movement." Much as Blind Lemon Jefferson, Char-

---

144. *Visions of Jazz*, p. 309.
145. *Swing to Bop*, p. 120. Allen Tinney told Gitler: "When I came out of the Army, I was very hurt because Charlie Parker had become famous, Dizzy had become famous . . . and I said to myself, 'What happened to Monk?' because we were playing a lot of Monk's tunes."
146. *Living With Jazz*, p. 362.

147. Palmer, p. 243–44.
148. Hooker's lyric, remarks Gerard Herzhaft (*Encyclopedia of the Blues*, p. 460), borrows a bit from the old folk/blues chestnut *Mama Don't Allow* as recorded by Cow Cow Davenport in 1928.
149. A slightly different account was offered by Jules Bihari in an interview for the June 1970 *Blues Unlimited*, saying that Saul purchased *Boogie Chillen* along with some other Hooker masters while on a business trip to Detroit.
150. Published claims that the record was a million-seller are almost certainly exaggerated—Besman frequently denied such assertions—but thanks to Modern's strong distribution in the South, it was one of the era's defining blues hits.

ley Patton, and Skip James had done in the late 1920s and early 1930s, Hooker typically uses only one chord, and when a second chord is employed it "does not function in a typical Western manner"—meaning, in part, that the chords do not "resolve" in the way European-based music has led us to expect over the past two centuries.[151] Palmer describes it as "a rocking one-chord ostinato with accents that fell fractionally ahead of the beat." Unlike anything on the late-1940s R&B market, it was "a back-country, pre-blues sort of music—a droning, open-ended stomp without a fixed verse form that lent itself to building up a cumulative, trancelike effect." Ted Gioia: "Like those shamans of the non-Western world whose magical rhythms cause altered states of mind and a pathway to a higher . . . consciousness, Hooker seemingly channeled at will some powerful cosmic force, a primal boogie, that never let him down."[152]

Riders in the Sky (A Cowboy Legend) (1949)—Vaughn Monroe (written by Stan Jones)

RCA Victor 3411

Chart debut April 23, 1949 (12 weeks at #1); #1 (9 weeks) in England (*RIA, MEM-#15, Trad-#180, DMDB*)

Better known as *Ghost Riders in the Sky*, this flavorful Western story song was first recorded in early 1949 by folk singer Burl Ives, and made into one of the biggest pop hits of the decade by bandleader and authoritative baritone vocalist Vaughn Monroe. Born on October 7, 1911, in Akron, Ohio, Monroe was Wisconsin state champion trumpet soloist at fifteen, studied for opera at Carnegie Tech School of Music (now Carnegie Mellon University), and began performing in bands on trumpet and vocals in 1933. Organizing his own band in 1940, he achieved popular success quickly with chart-topping hits including *There I Go* (1940), *My Devotion* (1942), *Let's Get Lost* (1943), and *There! I've Said It Again* (1945). As time went on, his booming baritone increasingly became the focal point of his records, and 1947's *Ballerina* topped all his previous hits with 10 weeks at #1—until it too was surpassed by *Riders in the Sky*. It's a "cautionary ballad" about the ghosts of cowboys chasing the devil across the heavens, warning a cowpoke to mend his ways or he will end up like them.[153] The combination of its colorful, melodramatic story line and his rather overwhelming vocal style made it the subject of affectionate parody, but doesn't change the fact that this is a terrific pop record. The song quickly became a country music favorite as well, most notably by the Sons of the Pioneers.

Some Enchanted Evening (1949)—Ezio Pinza (music by Richard Rodgers, lyrics by Oscar Hammerstein II)

Columbia 4559

Chart debut Sept. 10, 1949 (reached #7); from the Broadway cast album of *South Pacific* (chart debut May 21, 1949, spent 69 weeks at #1) (*Trad-#71, NPR-300 for song, GHF & RIA for album; DMDB*)

Sixty-nine weeks at #1, roughly 250 weeks in the Top Ten, and 401 total weeks on the *Billboard* chart: those are the staggering statistics achieved by the original Broadway cast recording of *South Pacific*, making it the biggest hit album in chart history.[154] Topping all of the other unforgettable numbers from the classic Rodgers & Hammerstein score was its central love ballad, *Some Enchanted Evening*.

After their historic triumph with *Oklahoma!*, Richard Rodgers and Oscar Hammerstein scored another big hit (*Carousel*) followed by a disappointment (*Allegro*). Adapting James Michener's *Tales of the South Pacific*—a collection of nineteen stories based on his World War II Navy experiences on the islands of the New Hebrides and New Guinea, the 1948 Pulitzer Prize winner for fiction (the musical focused on two of these stories)—put them firmly back on the winning track.[155] The show opened on April 7, 1949, and had a spectacular run of 1,925 performances (exceeded up to that time only by, of course, *Oklahoma!*). The two songwriters and director Josh Logan won the 1950 Pulitzer Prize for Drama (only the second musical comedy to be so honored).[156]

For the male co-star to Mary Martin, the producers chose longtime opera star Ezio Pinza, portraying the much older, dashing French landowner Emile de Becque to Martin's Midwestern farm girl Nellie Forbush.[157] Born on May 18, 1892, in Rome, Pinza worked his way up from small opera roles to La Scala in Milan, where his powerful basso voice made a strong impression. Pinza made his Metropolitan Opera debut in 1926, and remained there for twenty-three years in such roles as Don Giovanni and Boris Godunov. When Rodgers & Ham-

---

151. *The New Blue Music: Changes in Rhythm & Blues, 1950–1999* (p. 34–37).

152. Gioia, *Delta Blues*, p. 245–47.

153. Hischak, *Tin Pan Alley Song Encyclopedia*, p. 300.

154. For weeks at #1, the only album that even comes within shouting distance of *Pacific* is the *West Side Story* soundtrack, with 54. Its weeks in the Top Ten far surpass all others; the *My Fair Lady* cast album is second with 173 weeks. While its total charted weeks have been topped by three LPs in the modern era, its 401 weeks in the Top 40 laps the field, followed (again) by *My Fair Lady* with 292.

155. Anticipation for the show ran so high that advance orders ranged from $300,000 to $500,000. The extent to which it met and exceeded all expectations is seen in the fact that nine months *after* it opened, the advance sale in January 1950 had risen to over $700,000. (Chapter on *Pacific* in Abe Laufe, *Broadway's Greatest Musicals*, p. 121–32.)

156. It also won seven Tony Awards, and was the Critics Circle choice for best musical.

157. While the popular appeal of Martin (already one of Broadway's most beloved leading ladies) and Pinza is undeniable—and their pairing represented perfect casting—*Pacific* continued playing to capacity houses long after they left the show. It was above all the story and the music that made it immortal.

merstein learned that he was about to leave the Met and was interested in Broadway, they moved swiftly to offer him the role. *Some Enchanted Evening* is the very definition of the big, sweepingly dramatic ballad, explaining the discovery of love through the grand gesture. The song established why the worldly de Becque would fall in love with a young, small-town girl. Perry Como had the chart-topping pop version of the song, but the massive success of the cast album made Pinza's original unsurpassable.

Mona Lisa (1950)—Nat "King" Cole (written by Jay Livingston & Ray Evans)
Capitol 1010
Recorded on March 11, 1950; chart debut June 10, 1950 (8 weeks at #1);[158] reached #2 in England (*GHF, HP-#32, Trad-#47, DMDB-#51, RIA-#109*)

In late 1949, Paramount Pictures asked Capitol Records to persuade Nat Cole to record the central ballad from its quickly-forgotten movie *Captain Carey, U.S.A.* Cole biographer Leslie Gourse reports that the singer initially felt the song (which was originally titled "Prima Donna" and was rejected by Frank Sinatra before a rewrite) was "too highbrow" to become a hit. But as a favor to his manager Carlos Gastel, he agreed to record it. With an arrangement by Nelson Riddle equal to the song's melodic beauty (although Les Baxter was credited with the orchestra accompaniment), *Mona Lisa* (an Academy Award best-song winner) became one of his most fondly remembered performances.

Cole was not alone in his doubts about the song's commercial potential. Gourse notes that like his 1948 smash *Nature Boy*, *Mona Lisa* was an out-of-tempo ballad, considered "experimental and risky," and Capitol didn't want to release it. But by that time Cole had become attached to the song, and he persuaded the company to issue it as the B side of an uptempo number, *The Greatest Inventor of Them All*. Disc jockeys ditched the latter song and helped make the "risky" ballad a smash. Nat was so pleased with Riddle's arrangement that the two men became regular collaborators (starting with *Unforgettable*), and they continued working together even after Frank Sinatra used Riddle for a series of classic albums.

"The slow tempo of this performance allows Nat to caress each word, to wrap his voice around it and to create a stylistic tour de force," opined Charles Wolfe. Duke Ellington told Cole he thought it was one of the best vocal arrangements he'd ever heard.[159] After *Mona Lisa* had

its run at #1 on the *Billboard* best-selling records chart, it spent a record-setting eleven consecutive weeks at #2. Capitol stated that *Mona Lisa* sold 1.5 million copies.[160]

Will Friedwald notes the careful design and consummate skill that lay beneath the surface of Cole's music. "He made accessibility his first priority; his was the art of the artless. Job one was hiding the hard work that it required to make his music so easy to listen to . . . Harder listening revealed layers of artistic mastery—the more attention you paid, the more you were rewarded. Ultimately, one finds in Cole's work a passion that bespeaks a design so accomplished that it seems the product of an inspiration beyond the quiet, unassuming man who created it."[161]

I'll Fly Away (1950)—James & Martha Carson (written by Albert E. Brumley)
Capitol 1415
Recorded c. late 1950 (released in March 1951) (*GOSP-#48*)

One of the most beloved of all hymns in both black and white churches, Albert E. Brumley's classic *I'll Fly Away* received perhaps its finest recording in this propulsively exciting performance. Born Irene Amburgey on March 19, 1921, in Neon, Kentucky, Martha performed with her sisters Bertha and Opal (all three gifted musicians as well as singers) as the Sunshine Sisters, then as the Hoot Owl Hollow Girls, on radio in Bluefield, West Virginia, (1939) and Atlanta (1939–1943). Martha married James Carson (real last name Roberts, the son of old-time fiddler Doc Roberts) in 1939, and throughout the 1940s the duo was a hugely popular act (the "Barn Dance Sweethearts") on Atlanta's powerful station WSB. They cut eight sides for White Church Records in 1947 and twenty-two more for Capitol in 1949–1950. The Carsons broke up professionally and personally in late 1950, and she launched her solo career; Martha also recorded some early-1950s singles with her sisters as Mattie, Marthie & Minnie or the Amber Sisters, including the high-powered bluegrass romp *We Can't Live With 'Em and We Can't Live Without 'Em*. Elvis Presley cited Martha as a major inspiration for his religious-themed performances.

Born into a tenant farm family near Spiro, Oklahoma, on October 29, 1905, Albert E. Brumley began writing songs around 1922, and his work was first published in 1927. Over the next half-century, he wrote over 600 published songs, nearly all designed with the goal of Christian evangelization through music. Brumley composed *I'll Fly Away* in 1929 but waited three years to publish it as part of a songbook, *Wonderful Message*. Bill Malone: "His visions

---

158. It was the decisive choice as best record of the past twelve months in the annual *Billboard* disc jockey poll (October 7, 1950), beating out *Goodnight, Irene*.

159. Peter J. Levinson, *September in the Rain: The Life of Nelson Riddle*, p. 81. Riddle was essentially working as an uncredited subcontractor or "ghostwriter" for Baxter, and Cole didn't learn that the arrangement was Riddle's until later.

160. Gourse, p. 124.

161. *A Biographical Guide to the Great Jazz and Pop Singers*, p, 99.

of a caring, personal Savior and of an abundant, pastoral Heaven where old acquaintances would be renewed were images especially satisfying in a world of deprivation."[162] Conveying the reassuring message that with death comes freedom from the burdens of life and eternal rest in heaven, it was inspired by Psalms 90:10: "The days of our lives are threescore years and ten; and if by reason of strength they be fourscore years, yet is their strength labor and sorrow; for it is soon cut off, and we fly away." [163]

According to the composer, the song first came to him as he worked in an Oklahoma cotton field, triggered in part by the Vernon Dalhart hit *The Prisoner's Song* and its line "if I had the wings of an angel."[164] It was first recorded by the Rev. J. M. Gates in February 1940 for Decca, also that year by evangelist Rex Humbard and the Humbard Family, and by several black gospel groups in the next few years, most notably the Selah Jubilee Singers (1941). The Brown's Ferry Four (the all-star teaming of Grandpa Jones, Merle Travis, and the Delmore Brothers) introduced it to a wider white country gospel audience in 1946, followed two years later by the Chuck Wagon Gang (a strong, soaring rendition quite comparable to the Carsons')[165], and then a fine 1951 version by the Maddox Brothers & Rose.[166]

James Carson sings lead and is on mandolin, with Martha on harmony and guitar, and they're accompanied by a small swelling choir (or possibly their own voices multi-tracked à la Les Paul and Mary Ford) on the big, rousing chorus. This rendition is included on the Dust to Digital boxed set *Goodbye Babylon*.[167] "Some glad morning, when this life is o'er / I'll fly away / To a home on God's celestial shore,/ I'll fly away . . . When I die, hallelujah, bye and bye / I'll fly away . . ."

So Long (It's Been Good to Know Yuh) (1951)—The Weavers with Gordon Jenkins' Orchestra (written by Woody Guthrie)
Decca 27376
Chart debut Jan. 13, 1951 (reached #4) (*Folk-#80*)

"On April 14, 1935, a great wall of blackness appeared to the north of town, late on an unseasonably hot Sunday afternoon. It extended as far as the eye could see to the east and west. There were red flecks at the upper edges of the blackness which led some of the faithful in town to believe that it was fire ('the fire next time') and this was Judgment Day, but it was dust. It was thousands of tons of dust from as far away as the Dakotas and Nebraska, dark topsoil and red clay, carried on winds of 45 to 70 miles per hour, and it was chewing up the countryside."[168] So writes Joe Klein in *Woody Guthrie: A Life* of the coming of the Great Dust Storm to Pampa, Texas. Twenty-three-year-old Woody Guthrie and his wife rode out the storm, had a baby that November, and—still uncertain about where his future lay—Woody began writing songs about what he had witnessed. One was a number he called *Dusty Old Dust*, setting his words to the melody (for the verses) of Carson Robison's *Ballad of Billy the Kid* (which Robison and Vernon Dalhart recorded for multiple labels in 1927 as simply *Billy the Kid*). Guthrie composed the chorus himself. When his travels brought him to New York and the opportunity to make records and appear on network radio, one of the songs he recorded on May 3, 1940, (issued on Victor 26622) was *Dusty Old Dust*. Woody

Weavers, PhotoFest.

162. Bill Malone, *Country Music, U.S.A.* (2nd revised ed.), p. 131. In *Southern Music/American Music* (p. 79), Malone and David Stricklin make the additional point that "Brumley's compositions, because of their simplicity and melodic beauty, were quintessentially southern in tone and theme."

163. The traditional South, remarked Charles Reagan Wilson with reference to this among other songs, "believed in a supernaturalism almost as pronounced as in medieval Europe, and one indeed sees the supernatural at work in country music. Ghosts haunt the music." (*You Wrote My Life*, p. 125.)

164. Charles K. Wolfe, *Classic Country: Legends of Country Music*, p. 245.

165. The Chuck Wagon Gang's version was issued on Columbia 20599 and 20701.

166. Perhaps the most exceptional black gospel rendition of *I'll Fly Away* was rendered in November 1951 by the Southern Sons Quartette for Lillian McMurry's Trumpet label.

167. Annotation by Dick Spottswood for *Goodbye Babylon*, CD 3, p. 5.

168. Klein, p. 70–71, 74–75. Guthrie dramatically recalled that fateful day as the song's inspiration in the June 1947 *People's Songs* newsletter.

also performed the song several times on the CBS Radio program *Back Where I Come From.*

When Pete Seeger and Lee Hays—with whom Guthrie had performed in the early 1940s as members of the Almanac Singers—hit it big in 1950 with Ronnie Gilbert and Fred Hellerman as The Weavers, it was only natural that they would turn to Guthrie for material. Woody, pressed for money as always, was happy to help; he personally revised the song known by now as *So Long, It's Been Good to Know Yuh*, sitting on the floor of orchestra leader Gordon Jenkins' suite at a midtown New York hotel (as Klein relates), writing down the words on a huge roll of wrapping paper. The rewritten version removed any references to the actual Dust Bowl setting.[169] Guthrie also attended the Weavers' recording session for his song, quite proud of the fact that his scruffy little creation was accompanied by a twenty-voice chorus and a thirty-piece orchestra. He received a $10,000 advance, enabling him to pay off his debts and the rent on the family's new apartment. And even under a schmaltzy arrangement, it was still Woody's defiant, vibrant song of survival, with the Weavers' voices ringing out strongly amidst the strings, and it was quite wonderful in the context of white-bread pop music in 1951.[170]

Cold, Cold Heart (1951)—Hank Williams & His Drifting Cowboys

MGM 10904

Recorded on December 21, 1950; chart debut March 17, 1951 (#1 for 1 week on C&W chart, 46 total weeks) (*C&W-#81, TC, TCHF, AL*)

Cold, Cold Heart, Hank Williams' response to the largely loveless marriage that he and Audrey had by the end of 1950, became the most lucrative composition of his too-short life, thanks to Tony Bennett's massively successful pop cover version. As outlined by his biographer Colin Escott, Williams, like so many other musicians, had frequent dalliances with other women when he was out on the road, and whenever he returned home had little left for Audrey. So she began taking lovers of her own. One version of the story is that she had a September 1950 abortion in part because the child might not have been Hank's. When she was in the hospital after developing an infection, she refused to let him kiss her, blaming

him for her situation, and he accused her of being cold-hearted. Audrey's version was that she found out about one of his affairs, he bought her some jewelry in atonement, she flung it back at him, and that stimulated him to write the song. The lyrics, that is, for the melody (notes Escott) were taken directly from the 1945 T. Texas Tyler recording *You'll Still Be in My Heart*, originally copyrighted by Ted West in May 1943 and shortly thereafter rewritten by Buddy Starcher.[171]

Williams' performance of the song ached with emotion, and in retrospect it's hard to imagine anyone not recognizing it as a certain hit. But MGM and Fred Rose, based on the experience of Williams' uptempo songs typically outselling his ballads, promoted a honky-tonk number written by Aubrey Gass, *Dear John*, as the A side, with *Cold, Cold Heart* merely as the flip side. *Dear John* did hit the country charts first, but within two weeks was decisively overtaken by Hank's genuinely heartsick classic.

Master country songwriter Harlan Howard offered a detailed analysis of Williams' lyric-writing craft to Dave Hickey. In the first verse, the eight short lines (summarized Hickey) "were invisibly held together by fifteen internal 'r' phonemes. There are triples in the first two lines, four pairs, and the terminal 'heart' that gives the verse closure." (". . . Some mem'ry from your lonesome past keeps us so far apart / Why can't I free your doubtful mind / And melt your cold, cold heart.") "Nobody notices this," remarked Howard. "That's the idea, but once the words are put together this way, they won't come apart." It was not that Williams worked this out on paper, but rather that he meticulously sang a composition-in-progress over and over "until they came out right"—and in his case, finally emerged as perfection.[172]

Cold, Cold Heart (1951)—Tony Bennett

Columbia 39449

Recorded on May 31, 1951; chart debut July 28, 1951 (6 weeks at #1) (*HBN*)

Tony Bennett had just released the record that would become his first #1 single *Because of You*, and with Columbia Records on the lookout for a suitable followup, Mitch Miller suggested a ballad by country music's reigning king Hank Williams, *Cold, Cold Heart*, which had recently topped the C&W charts. It was *Billboard* columnist Jerry Wexler (future Atlantic Records legend) who had alerted Miller to the song, just as the previous year Wexler had suggested to Patti Page's manager that she record *The Tennessee Waltz*. As a Tin Pan Alley and jazz purist, Bennett said he didn't think he could do a

169. Some folk purists criticized the Weavers' version for "emasculating" Guthrie's original. But Barry Kornfeld pointed out in the April 15, 1964, *Broadside* that not only had Woody personally done the rewrite for the group, but the new lyric is "a pretty darned good one—with just enough protest in it to mark Woody's work."

170. Seeger, and by extension the Weavers, were already under assault by the McCarthyite publications *Red Channels* and *Counterattack* for their activities on behalf of progressive causes, but their names had not surfaced publicly in this context. It would not be until summer 1951 that the blacklist reached out to strike them down. (Dunaway, *How Can I Keep from Singing? The Ballad of Pete Seeger*, p. 179.)

171. *Hank Williams: The Biography*, p. 138–40.

172. Dave Hickey essay in *A New Literary History of America*, p. 845–846.

country song. "He told me just to listen to the words and music, pointing out how beautiful the ending was," the singer recalled in his autobiography with Will Friedwald. Miller "convinced me, and I recorded it."[173] The result was a crossover success from county to pop so spectacular that it paved the way for many more to come.

David Cantwell writes in *Heartaches By the Number* that Bennett "set aside his prejudices and flat nailed the thing. Backed by a full string section and a loping rhythm arrangement (courtesy of Percy Faith), and belting his rough bel canto at the very top of his range, Bennett sounds desperate to know the answer to Hank's famous question. 'Why,' he asks, stretching out the word as he reaches for a note higher than any you'd have thought he could hit, 'can't I free your doubtful mind and melt your cold, cold heart?'"[174]

The record sold two million copies, and Williams called Bennett to thank him, good-naturedly cracking, "Tony, what's the idea of ruining my song?" Later, writes Bennett, "Hank's friends told me how much he loved my recording and said that whenever he passed a jukebox, he'd put a nickel in and play my version."

There Ain't No Grave (Gonna Hold My Body Down) (1953)—Brother Claude Ely with the Cumberland Four

King 5616[175]

Recorded on Oct. 12, 1953 (*GOSP-#39*)

It had been over twenty-five years since music from a Holiness church had been commercially recorded, but Brother Claude Ely made it worth the wait with this thrilling performance depicting transformation and the second coming of Christ. *Ain't No Grave* was first recorded (definitively) by black Mississippi Baptist Bozee Sturdevant for the Library of Congress in 1942, and five years later by Sister Rosetta Tharpe. By the late 1940s, reports Dick Spottswood, the song had become one of the most popular shouts of the Church of God in Christ.[176] Bringing to bear all the fearsomely emotional power of Pentecostal singing that filled white Southerners like Jerry Lee Lewis with the holy spirit—and adding strong new lyrics—Ely makes the song his own.

The Holiness movement arose during the 1800s in protest against what adherents regarded as the growing complacency of the established Methodist church, and eventually splintered into many smaller sects. "Speaking in tongues" became one of the trademarks of its services during the early 1900s. As described in *Holy Ghost Revival on Azusa Street: The True Believers: Eyewitness Accounts of the Revival That Shook the World* (edited by Larry Martin), central to the Holiness movement is belief in the blessing union of sanctification. "Originally the moment when the Holy Spirit made its presence felt, sanctification became understood as a flooding of holy power that leads to an immense sensation of spiritual cleansing, purity, and light." The movement achieved its greatest momentum through the Azusa Street Revival launched by African-American preacher William J. Seymour at a mission at 312 Azusa Street in Los Angeles from 1906–1909. During its early years the movement practiced a "radical racial harmony" in the belief (as one participant wrote) that the color line "was washed away in the blood" of Christ; this didn't last, and eventually missions began sorting out along racial lines.[177]

Although its churches were long segregated, from the start white Holiness services continued to be powerfully influenced by African-American religious musical styles, as exemplified in this recording. "In their music," writes Samuel A. Floyd, Jr., in *The Power of Black Music*, "the Sanctified and Pentecostal Church made extensive use of the hand-clapping and foot stamping that descended from the shout; they also used drums and tambourines, and their own distinctive songs were heavily laced with or based on call and response figures. From this tradition emerged the singing preachers of the Sanctified tradition."[178] A crucial inspiration for Ely was surely Leader Cleveland, a white Holiness singer whose 1929 recording of *Babylon Is Falling Down* (a song from the African-American church also famously performed by Reverend F. W. McGee) was clearly black-inspired, with guitar, harmonica, and shouted cries.[179]

Known as the Gospel Ranger, Ely (born July 21, 1922, near Pennington Gap, Virginia) had worked as a coal miner before a religious conversion led to his call to preach in 1949. He subsequently spent nearly thirty years as a minister throughout Appalachia from his native southwest Virginia to eastern Kentucky and eastern Tennessee.[180] This remarkable, hellfire and brimstone performance was made at the Free Pentecostal Church

173. Bennett acknowledged that Miller was right in this case. "We were always fencing," he told his biographer Will Friedwald (*Biographical Guide*, p. 43). "I always had the sword out."

174. *Heartaches By the Number*, p. 88–89.

175. The B side of King 5616 was *Holy, Holy, Holy*. The other best-known performance from this Ely session was *Little David, Play on Your Harp* (issued on King 5618), as cited in December 1966, *Blues Unlimited*.

176. Liner notes to *Goodbye Babylon*, CD 2, p. 1.

177. "The Azusa Street Revival," article by R. J. Smith in *A New Literary History of America*, p. 498–502.

178. Floyd, p. 63.

179. Elder Richard Bryant was another late-1920s role model for Ely as a fiery, freewheeling white Pentecostal recording artist with guitar and percussion accompaniment. One difference between Baptist services and those of the Sanctified and Holiness churches is that the latter regularly accompanied gospel songs with musical instruments, following Psalm 150:3: "Praise him with the sound of the trumpet . . . praise him with stringed instruments and organs . . ."

180. Biographical profile by W. K. McNeil, *Encyclopedia of American Gospel Music*, p. 116.

of God in Cumberland, Kentucky, where he was pastor, in a remote broadcast by WCTW radio in Whitesburg. Brother Claude and the Cumberland Holiness Congregation are accompanied by vigorous guitar, mandolin, and hand-clapping. King Records released two singles from the session; this is included on the Dust to Digital boxed set *Goodbye Babylon*.[181]

More than two decades after this performance, on March 16, 1976, Ely (as reported in the next day's *New York Times*), then affiliated with the Pentecostal Church of God in Cold Springs, Kentucky, presided over the service as the community of Benham, Kentucky, laid to rest the last of fifteen men killed in a coal mine explosion. He sang *There Ain't No Grave*, whose lyrics were quoted by *The Times*. "Those who are laid out on these hillsides . . . When there comes the sound of the trumpet, they will arise again."

Cherry Pink and Apple Blossom White (1955)—Perez Prado & His Orchestra (written by Louis Guglielmi)

RCA Victor 5965

Chart debut March 5, 1955 (10 weeks at #1); #1 for 2 weeks in England[182]; #1 (7 weeks) in Germany; #1 (3 weeks) in Australia (*BILLB-#18, HP-#36, World-#59, DMDB*)

The man known as "The King of the Mambo" was born Damaso Perez Prado in Matanzas, Cuba, on December 11, 1916. The organist/pianist/arranger led his first band from 1937–1944, gaining popularity with such outstanding vocalists as Miguelito Valdes. Ned Sublette writes that the first band to play the music that became known as the mambo was apparently Julio Cueva's band in 1944. "It's hard to give a precise definition for the mambo . . . It's an up-tempo, horn-driven dance music, but there are slower mambos. It's big band music, but you can play it with a [smaller] combo if you must." Big band mambo "polyrhythmicized the jazz band. It was characterized by a new way of treating the sax section," originated by Cueva's star arranger Rene Hernandez. "The sax section became independent from the other horns, and more rhythmic in function." The new Cuban arrangers "set the sax section in systematic counterpoint against the trumpets, giving the saxes a *sobremontuno*: a propulsive, repeating rhythmic part . . . the saxes connected the horns tightly to the rhythm, and created a new way of using the big band. In the mambo, once the saxes established

the sobremontuno, the trumpets would come in, blowing repeating figures to kick up the excitement."[183]

The word "mambo" first became known in 1938 when the Cuban band Las Maravillas de Arcano, led by Antonio Arcano, recorded a *danzon* by cellist "Macho" (Orestes) Lopez entitled *Mambo*; his brother, bassist "Cachao" (Israel Lopez), later to gain prominence in U.S. jazz, was a participant on the session. Isabelle Leymarie relates that the *nuevo ritmo* really took hold after Arcano's 1944 recording of *Arriba la Invasion*, the first time a piece was called a mambo on record or sheet music. But she agrees with Sublette that it was Prado "who truly invented the mambo as a distinct musical genre. Like Arcano, he used jazz and popular music elements in his danzones, but in a more systematic and extensive fashion, orchestrating them with trap drums, saxophones, and trumpets."[184]

"It was Perez Prado, with his unique sense of showmanship, combined with a taste for nervous, aggressive dissonance, who branded the mambo for all time," declares Sublette. However, because he favored arrangements that were considered outlandish for the time, he was blacklisted from working as an arranger. In response, he toured South and Central America before settling in Mexico City, where his band began releasing the first full wave of mambo records starting in 1949. "These records were scorchers. They don't sound like anything else in Cuban music, or anything else, period. His band had Cuban percussionists and a wind section of four saxes—deployed in their low register, playing rhythmically propulsive parts—along with five trumpets and one trombone. The second trumpet was Cuban, and pretty much everything else was Mexican, including the blistering high-note trumpet. The trumpets were a mile above the saxes, and having five of them made the ensemble seem to shriek at even higher tessitura than it really was." The intensity of Prado's music came in part from its Stan Kenton–like dissonance ("a controlled harmonic phenomenon obtained by sounding two pitches that are not closely related to each other"), but also from "its rhythmic tension, the clarity of his writing, the physical impact of its brilliant, forceful timbre, and the leader's sense of humor."[185] Prado's records became a sensation, including his 1950 hit *Mambo #5*.

Cherry Pink and Apple Blossom White began as a French song written in 1950, was recorded by artists including Jimmy Dorsey (for Columbia in 1951), and by Prado himself in 1951 (as *Cerazo Rosa*). When producers of the 1954 Jane Russell film *Underwater!* decided to use the tune as its theme, the bandleader was asked to

181. The records were sufficiently well received that Ely did another session in June 1954 at a courthouse in Letcher County, Kentucky, plus two studio sessions for King in 1962 and 1968. In 1993, the British label Ace reissued all of the 1953–1954 recordings, plus a few from 1962, on CD.

182. British trumpet star Eddie Calvert, best known for his U.K. smash recording of *Oh Mein Papa*, also hit #1 there with his cover version.

183. *Cuba and Its Music*, p. 507–9.
184. *Cuban Fire*, p. 114–15.
185. Sublette, *Cuba and Its Music*, p. 512, 558–62.

re-record it, and he also appeared briefly in the picture. Set at a medium mambo beat, it's a smoothly danceable instrumental featuring the melodramatic trumpet solos of Billy Regis. The drama is underlined when the tempo slows a few times with Regis' trumpet tailing off, then rising again as the brisker tempo returns. His big, showy final solo drives the record to a potent conclusion. John Storm Roberts praises the arrangement, as the trumpet solos, "screaming ensemble brass, exaggerated contrasts between saxes, trumpets, and trombones, and springy simplistic syncopation contributed to a witty whole."[186] Prado would enjoy one more chart-topping U.S. hit in 1958 with *Patricia*.

Why Do Fools Fall In Love? (1956)—Frankie Lymon & the Teenagers

Gee 1002

Recorded in spring 1955; chart debut Feb. 18, 1956 (#1 for 5 weeks R&B, #6 pop); #1 for 3 weeks in England[187] (*R&B-#50, RHF, GHF, DMDB-#93, RIA-#182, DM-#192, RS*)

The prototype for all the kid pop stars who would follow as the rock era unfolded, Frankie Lymon was rivaled in talent among this group only by Michael Jackson. Barely twelve years old when his trademark song was recorded, he was blessed with a high tenor (or castrano) for the ages and unlimited quantities of boyish enthusiasm and stage charisma. Although his life took a tragic turn, listeners in each subsequent generation can't help but smile when listening to his musical joyride on *Why Do Fools Fall In Love.*

Born on September 30, 1942, in New York City, Frankie's group was formed as the Premiers at junior high school in the Washington Heights section of the Bronx in early 1955. The story goes that while they were singing one night in a doorway, a tenant of the building handed them some poems written by his girlfriend. One was called "Why Do the Birds Sing So Gay," and they put it to music. Richard Barrett, leader of the R&B group the Valentines, heard them at the junior high that both groups used sometimes for rehearsals, and introduced them to the head of the Valentines' record label Rama-Gee, George Goldner. He agreed to give the kids a tryout. When (according to differing accounts) Herman Santiago (the group's usual lead singer) fell ill, or (as seems to have been the case) Goldner asked to see how the group sounded with Frankie in the lead, Frankie knocked the label owner out with his rendition of the new song. Goldner

signed the group, changed their name (at the suggestion of backing band leader Jimmy Wright), shifted the focus of the lyrics, and they recorded it at Bell Studios in spring 1955. The record stayed on the shelf as the kids entered high school, then was released the following January. It was an immediate smash, and triggered the formation of innumerable other young-teen pop groups, none of which even approached the success of the Teenagers. That summer it also became the first record by a black American vocal group to top the British singles chart.

While ostensibly the song is a description of heartbreak and the eternal question of why people enter into the "losing game" of love, Frankie's headlong gusto in evoking the innocent thrill of young romance is filled with joy rather than sadness. When he soars skyward on "tell me why," we know the answer. He may be a fool for falling, he seems to say, but the moments of happiness make it worth the pain.

The song was originally credited on the record label to Lymon and Goldner (with Santiago's name removed). When Goldner and music entrepreneur/publisher Morris Levy[188] had a dispute focused on Latin jazz star Tito Puente leaving Goldner's Tico Records for RCA Victor with Levy's help, Levy made amends by forming another record label with Goldner as A&R man, Roulette. In response, Goldner assigned to Levy's publishing company, Patricia Music, the copyright for the Lymon hit. This was, declares Tony Fletcher, "a gift that couldn't be measured in gold, for *Why Do Fools Fall In Love* proved arguably the greatest single of the vocal group era." Then in 1957, Goldner sold his three record labels, his publishing interests, and his share in Roulette to Levy and his partner for $250,000. At the same time, he also signed over his own songwriting credits. Fletcher: "In an act of audacity rarely rivaled in the history of the music business," Morris Levy promptly replaced Goldner's name on a number of hits including this one with his own.[189] The situation became the subject of a legendarily prolonged legal battle over an exceptionally lucrative property. The emergence of three different women, each claiming to be Lymon's widow, made it a legal circus, one that provided much of the basis for the 1998 movie named after the hit. Finally, in 1991, a judge ruled that the song rightfully belonged to surviving ex-Teenagers Herman Santiago and Jimmy Merchant.[190]

---

186. Roberts, *The Latin Tinge*, p. 133.

187. Lymon at fourteen became the youngest artist to reach #1 on the British chart, until 1972. He was also the youngest star to top the bill at the London Palladium, in 1957.

---

188. Levy's ties to organized crime have been characterized as "fairly undisguised" (Brian Ward, *Just My Soul Responding*, p. 60).

189. *All Hopped Up and Ready to Go*, p. 114–17.

190. The situation was an exact parallel to a legal tussle over the Mills Brothers' huge 1943 hit *Paper Doll*, when the three widows of the late composer Johnny Black each filed claims on the song's royalties (February 5, 1944 *Billboard*).

After four much smaller pop hits, Frankie and the other Teenagers went their separate ways by late 1957—and all immediately faded from public view. Frankie's solo career never took flight, especially after his voice changed, and soon he stumbled into drug addiction. With the help of a retired dancer in 1966, he cleaned up and seemed ready to mount a comeback attempt when he died from an overdose of heroin in February 1968, at age twenty-five.

Long Tall Sally (1956)—Little Richard
Specialty 572
Recorded in New Orleans on Feb. 10, 1956; chart debut Apr. 7, 1956 (#1 for 8 weeks R&B, #6 pop); reached #3 in England (*RS-#56, R&B-#57, RHF, GHF, DM-#278, AHR, ACC, DMDB*)

The followup to Richard's breakthrough hit *Tutti Fruti* was the equally scintillating *Long Tall Sally*. Producer Bumps Blackwell recalled that when some radio stations wouldn't play Richard's *Tutti* and instead put Pat Boone's pale cover version on the air, "we decided to up the tempo on the follow-up and get the lyrics going so fast that Boone wouldn't be able to get his mouth together to do it!" As Blackwell told the possibly apocryphal story to Richard's biographer Charles White, a female disc jockey known as Honey Chile called Blackwell asking him to help a teenage girl named Enortis Johnson who had walked all the way from Mississippi to sell a song to Richard. However, the "song" was nothing more than a few lines scrawled on a piece of paper, with no melody: "Saw Uncle John with Long Tall Sally / They saw Aunt Mary comin' so they ducked back in the alley." A dubious Blackwell, out of charity, brought it back to the studio. "We kept adding words and music to it . . . Richard started to sing it—and all of a sudden there was, 'Have some fun tonight.' That was the hook." They did several more takes, each one faster than the last, just to foil cover artists.[191] It worked; *Sally* quickly soared higher than *Tutti* had managed to and sold over a half million copies.

Interestingly, an early take of the song, with the same basic lyrics but under the title *The Thing*, was taken at such a slower tempo that at first it's almost unrecognizable as Little Richard. Perhaps it was only after he and Blackwell realized that this tempo would have been far too simple for Boone and others to cover that they decided to triple or quadruple the pace. Like nearly all of Richard's hits, remark David Dalton and Lenny Kaye, it features "notes slippin' and slidin' out of control in whoops and squeals, breathless hammering away with his percussive vocal at dizzying speed. His 'attack' on

a song gives the impression that *emotion itself*, shaking, wriggling . . . is forcing its own way through the words in its most elemental form."[192]

Accompanying the manic Little Richard presented special challenges for musicians. Tony Scherman writes in the Earl Palmer biography: "Earl may or may not have been literally the first, but he was easily the first widely heard drummer to streamline the shuffle beat of rhythm and blues into the prototypical rock-and-roll beat. As Earl says, he was only trying to match Little Richard's frenetic right hand (the Latin rhythms popular in the early Fifties and always an undercurrent in New Orleans music undoubtedly affected him, too.) Regardless, his achievement was to overhaul pop music's rhythmic foundation, discarding an 'old-fashioned,' jazz-based sound for something new: the headlong thrust of rock and roll."[193]

Dave Marsh: "*Long Tall Sally* is pure rock and roll, and Richard charges recklessly through it, shouting and jumping from the first note, rocketing at a pace exceeded in the Fifties only by Jerry Lee Lewis on *Whole Lotta Shakin'* . . ."[194]

(Other personnel: Lee Allen on tenor sax, Alvin "Red" Tyler on baritone sax, Edgar Blanchard on guitar, Frank Fields on bass)

Blue 7 (1956)—Sonny Rollins Quartet
Recorded on June 22, 1956, from the Prestige album *Saxophone Colossus* (*Jazz-#76, GHF, SJ*)

While John Coltrane rose to fame as the foremost jazz saxophonist of a new generation in the late 1950s, the one artist to win recognition as his peer was the Saxophone Colossus, Sonny Rollins. The song that symbolized Rollins' ascension was *Blue 7*. Born Theodore Walter Rollins on September 7, 1930, in New York City, he played local gigs as a teenager before making his recording debut in 1949 with Babs Gonzales, J. J. Johnson, and Bud Powell. Rollins worked regularly in the early 1950s with Miles Davis, Thelonious Monk, and Art Farmer, and after licking a drug problem recorded as a leader for the first time in 1955.

In contrast to other young musicians of the period who were exploring dissonance and free forms, Rollins (writes Ted Gioia) "focused on forging a classic solo style" rooted in jazz traditions, and above all in a deep commitment to improvisation showing his wide-ranging melodic imagination. At the time he recorded his most famous work, Rollins was working as a member of the Max Roach–Clifford Brown quintet.[195]

191. White, *The Life and Times of Little Richard: The Quasar of Rock* (originally issued with the subtitle *"The Authorised Biography"*), p. 60–63.

192. *Rock 100: The Greatest Stars of Rock's Golden Age* (1999 ed.), p. 13. Amusingly, the NBC censor declined to rule *Sally* obscene because he couldn't understand the words.
193. *Backbeat: Earl Palmer's Story*, p. 85.
194. *The Heart of Rock & Soul*, p. 196.
195. Gioia, *History of Jazz*, p. 309.

Blue 7 represented Rollins' gift in constructing solos through the manipulation of simple musical motives, as explored in a famous essay by Gunther Schuller. By taking melodic themes, restating, varying, and elaborating on them, said Schuller, the saxophonist combined an almost mathematical precision with instinctive creativity. The song's "structural cohesiveness—without sacrificing expressiveness and rhythmic drive or swing—one has come to expect from the composer who spends days or weeks writing a given passage. It is another matter to achieve this in an on-the-spur-of-the-moment improvisation." Martin Williams: "*Blue 7* is one of those rare improvised performances in which every part is related to every other part, adding up to a whole (of nearly eleven minutes) greater than the sum of those parts, with details so subtle and perfectly in place . . . yet Rollins made it all up in a recording studio as he went along. It is as if Rollins conceived of *Blue 7* as a whole all at once, although we hear him building it logically, from one phrase to the next."[196]

(Personnel: Sonny Rollins, Tommy Flanagan on piano, Doug Watkins on bass, Max Roach on drums)

You Send Me (1957)—Sam Cooke
Keen 34013
Recorded on June 1, 1957; chart debut Oct. 21, 1957 (3 weeks at #1 on pop chart; 6 weeks at #1 R&B); #1 (2 weeks) in Canada, #29 in U.K. (*R&B-#49, GHF, RHF, RS-#115, RIA, 1001, ACC*)

After six years as one of gospel music's greatest stars as lead singer of the Soul Stirrers, Sam Cooke felt he had gone as far as he could in the genre and was curious to see if he could cross over to the pop side. Leaving aside performers who mixed in some pop tunes with religious fare such as Sister Rosetta Tharpe, no gospel star had ever achieved a full transition—and the gospel faithful were fiercely resistant to the very idea. *You Send Me* was the mega-hit that enabled Cooke to become the first, thus paving the way for future gospel-turned-pop stars including Lou Rawls and Johnnie Taylor.

In December 1956, in between two Soul Stirrers engagements, Cooke quietly arranged his first pop music session in New Orleans, including the ballad *Lovable*. The song was released under the thinly veiled pseudonym Dale Cook at the end of January, and sold a modest 15,000 copies; not enough to make the charts, but enough to get some attention—some of it unwelcome, as gospel fans realized right away the singer was Sam, and were angry at the alleged sellout. Cooke decided that if he was going to make the change, he'd have to go all the way, and under his own name. After a final Soul Stirrers session on April 10, 1957, he sent producer Bumps

Blackwell a six-song demo in which he was accompanied only by guitar. Blackwell realized that at least one of the songs, *You Send Me*, had real potential. The piece was supposedly written by Sam's brother L. C., but in fact was penned by the singer.

Guitarist Cliff White, a jazz-influenced player who had toured with the Mills Brothers and had both blues and classical background, was recruited by Blackwell to accompany Cooke, and biographer Daniel Wolff described the guitarist's initial bafflement when Cooke introduced him to the song at a rehearsal. After scatting, "I know, I know, I know," Sam sang "Darling, you send me," repeated the phrase a few times, and followed it with eight bars of "you thrill me." "This dude must be out of his mind," White remembered thinking. New Orleans–born jazz and pop veteran Rene Hall fashioned the arrangement for the song; another New Orleanian, Harold Battiste, played on it and helped write the vocal arrangement.

In the June 1 recording session at Radio Recorders in Los Angeles, the industry veterans present "were amazed at how, on a standard set of chord changes, with a minimum amount of words, this man created a mood of young love, of 'infatuation,' which would soon appeal to millions," writes Wolff. "It was the timing of the line breaks; how he soared on the word 'you,' broke it into four syllables, and drew it across the beat; how he pulled the listener into his world from the first note . . . *You Send Me* may have been more singer than song, but what the veterans were missing was the grace of the melody, the way the bridge stuck in your mind and wouldn't leave, and how the comfortable, intimate feel of the tune suited the times. There's an extraordinary combination of reassurance and seduction in the gentle stroll of *You Send Me* that, in retrospect, mirrors the placid surface and strong undercurrents of the late fifties."[197]

But Specialty record chief Art Rupe didn't understand what he was hearing in the studio. In fact, he was furious and launched into a tirade against Blackwell, declaring that instead of the exciting gospel-fired singer he'd been expecting, he was getting a bland white-style balladeer. Charlie Gillett notes that a key reason for the label president's reluctance is that Specialty did good business in gospel, and he was wary of alienating that core audience.[198] Rupe made Blackwell what seemed like an outrageous proposition: if Bumps was so confident about Cooke, was he willing to relinquish his upcoming royalties on sessions he'd already produced for Little Richard in exchange for taking both Cooke and the masters Sam had just cut? Boldly, Blackwell replied,

196. Annotation, *Smithsonian Collection of Classic Jazz*, p. 39–40.

197. Wolff, *You Send Me: The Life & Times of Sam Cooke*, p. 146–49. Also see Peter Guralnick, *Dream Boogie: The Triumph of Sam Cooke*, p. 206–7, 211–12.

198. Gillett, *Making Tracks: Atlantic Records and the Growth of a Multi-Billion-Dollar Industry*, p. 73.

"you got yourself a deal." Blackwell later estimated that he'd given up some $50,000 in royalties on the Little Richard records (including *Good Golly Miss Molly* and *Jenny Jenny*). But he got *You Send Me*. Unbeknownst to Rupe, Bumps had already signed a deal with another label, Keen (located just down the street from Specialty in New York), started just four months earlier by Greek businessman and former Artie Shaw band member Bob Keane. Cooke wanted to sever all ties with Rupe, including a song publishing deal that split the royalties 3-to-1 in favor of the label owner, so he attributed the composition to his brother so he could benefit from a more generous arrangement with a different publisher. Rupe sued, and finally settled out of court.

During the week of September 9, after Sam had spent two months waiting anxiously and sleeping on a couch at Blackwell's apartment, *You Send Me* was released by Keen, initially as the B side of his reworking of the Gershwin classic *Summertime*.[199] For the first time, the man previously known as Sam Cook was billed as Sam Cooke—partly out of superstition (there were only seven letters in Sam Cook, and even numbers were considered lucky), and partly to symbolize a new beginning. After a promising start in the R&B market, Detroit DJ Casey Kasem (later Mr. "American Top 40") helped break the record big time in mainstream white radio. As it soared all the way to #1, the crossover was complete.

Tequila (1958)—The Champs (written by Chuck Rio) Challenge 1016

Chart debut Feb. 24, 1958 (#1 for 5 weeks); reached #5 in England; #1 (1 week) in Canada (*RHF, GHF, RIA, DMDB*)

One of the most irresistible instrumentals of the rock era, *Tequila* was launched onto the pop charts by a Los Angeles group including Danny Flores, known professionally as Chuck Rio, featured on sax), Buddy Bruce on lead guitar, Dave Burgess on rhythm guitar, Cliff Hils on bass, and Gene Alden on drums. Hollywood cowboy legend Gene Autry started Challenge Records in 1957, and hired Dave Burgess as music director. As related by Colin Escott in liner notes for Rhino's boxed set of 1950s rock, Burgess set out to create a line of instrumentals, and had already written the A side of the first single (*Train to Nowhere*) when Flores came back from a trip to Tijuana with a Latin riff in his head. They recorded it as the intended B side, *Tequila*, and issued it as "The Champs" in homage to Autry's horse, Champion.[200] *Train to Nowhere* was released on December 26, 1957, and as Fred Bronson

comments, "that's exactly where it went" at first. Then DJs began playing the flip side, and *Billboard* in its February 3, 1958, issue reviewed *Tequila* in two versions, with the competing version by saxophonist Eddie Platt's orchestra. The cover reached #20, while the Champs soared to the top.[201]

Gary Myers provided the record's full backstory in *Goldmine*. Burgess was an established if little-known songwriter including Ray Price's *I'll Be There*, and Margie Rayburn's Top Ten pop hit *I'm Available* (both 1957). Flores had been a busy session musician since 1950 on both sax and piano. The group was completing instrumental tracks for a Jerry Wallace album and there was time left over for that B side of Burgess's already-recorded selection. Flores had been using his Tijuana-inspired piece as his break number at club dates, and since he enjoyed drinking tequila, chose that as the title. Arranged on the spot with the title word spoken at the end of the bridge, the track was quickly recorded, and the musicians didn't even stick around to listen to the playback.[202]

Once you've heard that honking sax and chunky rhythm of *Tequila*, it's just about impossible to get it out of your mind.[203][204] The Champs had three other Top 40 hits through 1962 (most notably its followup record *El Rancho Rock*), and issued over two dozen singles through 1965 with multiple personnel changes, including stints by Seals & Crofts and Glen Campbell.

Chega de Saudade (1958)—Joao Gilberto (music by Antonio Carlos Jobim, lyrics by Vinicius de Moraes) Festa 6002

Original version recorded by Elizeth Cardoso & Gilberto in January 1958 for the album *Cancao do Amor Demais* (Song for an Excessive Love); solo version by Joao Gilberto recorded for Odeon on July 10, 1958 (*GHF, World-#15, Jazz-#112*)

The composition that would set the course for the cool breeze of bossa nova followed in the wake of *Orfeu da Conceicao (Black Orpheus)*, a theatrical drama with

199. Immediately upon its release September 9, the record was reported in *Billboard* as "breaking out" in Southern California, and on September 30 was formally listed as a territorial hit in Los Angeles.

200. Annotation to Rhino boxed set *Loud, Fast & Out of Control*, p. 71–72.

201. *The Billboard Book of Number One Hits*, p. 34.

202. Myers, August 1982 *Goldmine*. According to Larry Stidom in the September 1978 *Goldmine*, the group used up fifty-six minutes of the one-hour recording session for *Train to Nowhere*, and tossed off *Tequila* in the final few minutes.

203. A year after the record was a hit, bandleader Les Baxter filed suit seeking damages of $325,000 claiming that *Tequila* was "stolen" from Baxter's original calypso *De Rain*, first used in the film *Bop Girl Goes Calypso*, as reported in the April 2, 1959, *Down Beat*. It turns out that the melodies to the refrains of the two songs were identical, note for note. According to Burgess, Flores probably had seen the movie and unconsciously borrowed part of the tune. But Baxter himself may have picked up the tune from a traditional source while living in Mexico, and he agreed to settle the suit for $10,000 (Broven, *Record Makers and Breakers*, p. 313).

204. The R&B–based sax style of Flores aka Rio, influenced in part by the 1952 record *Pachuco Hop* by black saxophonist Chuck Higgins, and black saxmen Big Jay McNeely and Joe Houston, served as an inspiration to subsequent Chicano rockers.

songs composed by Antonio Carlos Jobim and poet-lyricist Vinicius de Moraes that opened in Rio de Janeiro on September 25, 1956, the prelude to the internationally renowned movie version. Shortly after the play finished its one-month run, they created the song (translating as "No More Blues"), which Jobim described as a kind of *samba-cancao* (a refined style of samba emphasizing melody over rhythm) in three parts, but with a *chorinho* flavor.[205] [206] Vinicius later said that writing lyrics for the song was one of his greatest challenges due to "the arduousness of trying to fit the words into a melodic structure with so many comings and goings."

Joao Gilberto, the definitive singer of bossa nova, was born on June 10, 1931, in Juazeiro, Bahia, Brazil. He fell in love with samba rhythms and American jazz as a teenager, and after moving to Rio de Janeiro began playing guitar on sessions for various artists, and made his solo recording debut in 1952.[207] His reputation was growing but he remained mainly a supporting player barely able to pay his rent when he accompanied singer Elizeth Cardoso on an album of songs by Jobim and de Moraes issued by a tiny label best known for poetry readings, Festa. Cardoso was a long-respected samba vocalist, but not a current hit-maker, and with Festa's modest distribution, the album's sales following its May release were minimal. But its impact, as the all-but-official first bossa nova recording, was something else again. Arnaldo DeScuteiro declares that "it had the impact of an atomic bomb on the Brazilian music scene."[208]

Cardoso offers a brief spoken introduction (an anachronistic carryover from the record announcements familiar from early twentieth century U.S. cylinders and 78s), and then carries the lead vocal with Gilberto's utterly distinctive guitar—a style that became known as *violao gago*, or "stammering guitar"—and backing vocal. It's warm and alluring, with brief trumpet and trombone solos, but with Joao's guitar always at the center, setting the gentle tempo behind her voice. Strings enter toward the end in the arrangement by Jobim.

Two months after the original record's release, Gilberto had the opportunity to record the song on his own, using a much-simplified version of Jobim's earlier arrangement, coordinated by the composer and drummer Milton Banana, with backing orchestra. Ruy Castro writes that

due to the singer's intense perfectionism—determined to create the definitive version of a great song on his first solo session in six years—it took nearly a month of careful preparations culminating in a few days of studio time. Released in August 1958, the record (issued on 78 rpm, a format retired for good that year in the U.S. but hanging on awhile longer in South America) got off to a slow start; Odeon's own sales director was initially baffled, asking, "what kind of damn rhythm was that?" But when it finally penetrated Brazilian radio, it became a sensation. Joao Gilberto, previously known only to Rio music insiders, "became a mini-phenomenon to the Sao Paulo public." By December, the single had sold 15,000 copies. When Gilberto's Odeon album, also titled *Chega de Saudade*, was released in 1959, it sold 35,000 copies in its early months, and ultimately, by one estimate, topped 500,000. The title track was, in Castro's phrase, "one minute and 59 minutes that changed everything."[209] [210]

There Goes My Baby (1959)—The Drifters (written by Benjamin Nelson, Lover Patterson, & George Treadwell)
Atlantic 2025
Recorded on March 6, 1959; chart debut June 1, 1959 (#1 for 1 week R&B, #2 on *Billboard* pop chart, reached #1 in *Cash Box*); #12 in Canada (*DM-#30, RHF, GHF, R&B-#70, RS-#196, ACC, DMDB*)

When Atlantic head of production Jerry Wexler first heard the Drifters' *There Goes My Baby*, he famously declared the record "a f***ing mess." Little wonder, perhaps, for nothing quite like this had been heard before, described by Gerri Hirshey as "a wild melange of kettle drums, strings, vocal bom-bom-boms, and Ben E. King's heartsick gospel wail on lead." But somehow, this crazy combination worked, and became a landmark R&B/pop hit.

The record marked the debut smash for the "new" Drifters; manager George Treadwell had disbanded the original Drifters in 1958 (three years after the departure of their most famous lead singer Clyde McPhatter), brought in the Five Crowns, and renamed them. The Crowns' lead singer joined the Army, and twenty-year-old Ben E. King—real name Benjamin Nelson—was brought in as the new lead singer. Songwriters Jerry Leiber and Mike Stoller, producing the session, were eager to try something new. Stoller explained: "The rhythm was *baion*, a Brazilian rhythm which we really loved. [They'd first been exposed to the rhythm through the title song of the Italian tear-jerking movie *Anna*, which was released in

205. The first samba to be commercially recorded is believed to be *Pelo Telefone* in 1916. (*MusicHound World*, p. 493.)

206. The chorinho and the maxixe were forms of dance-based Brazilian music popular in the early twentieth century; the maxixe briefly created an American sensation in 1914.

207. Castro, *Bossa Nova: The Story of the Brazilian Music That Seduced the World*, p. 39.

208. Liner notes, Motor Music compilation *A Trip to Brazil: 40 Years of Bossa Nova*. In May 1958, Gilberto—because of his mastery of the bossa beat (which at the time was difficult for other guitarists)—accompanied singer Os Cariocas on another version of *Chega de Saudade*.

209. Castro, *Bossa Nova*, p. 118–19, 126–39.

210. The historic significance of the record in Brazil was underlined when the year 2008 was packed with "festivals, concerts, panels, articles, and books" celebrating the fiftieth anniversary of bossa nova. (Giddins and Deveaux, *Jazz*, p. 525.)

the U.S. in 1953.] Then we started to orchestrate what was really done on a tom tom in Brazilian bands, with all kinds of percussion sounds." (The orchestration was done by Stan Applebaum, scoring it for four violins and a cello.)[211] Wexler raged about the timpani that seemed out of tune, and wondered whether audiences would accept an R&B record with a lavish string arrangement, then almost unprecedented.[212] (The Skyliners' *Since I Don't Have You* used a full string section a few months earlier.) Charlie Gillett in *The Sound of the City* noted that the violin section "played rocking riffs as saxophones had done in more conventional records." Atop everything else, Gillett remarks, the song "was virtually free form, almost unique at a time when rhyming lines were mandatory, no matter how tenuous" the rhyme.[213]

To at least one listener, the strings seemed to quote from, all of things, Tchaikovsky's *1812 Overture*. "It sounded like a radio caught between two stations," Wexler later wrote. The reason for this effect, explained Ed Ward in *Rock of Ages*, was the instrumental break the strings play halfway through, "a modal line unrelated thematically or harmonically to the rest of the song." Atlantic president Ahmet Ertegun also had doubts about the record, but gave Leiber and Stoller two hours to mix the song with master engineer Tom Dowd. "Maybe we ought to try and put it out," Ertegun finally decided after hearing the results.

Rising above it all, emphasizes Ward, is that "the performance was electrifying, from Ben E. King's distraught, haunted vocal" to the group's background chants, "swathed in echo to that weird string excursion. It was like no record ever made. Something new had been born."[214] Charlie Thomas was originally scheduled to sing lead on the number, but its wildly unconventional arrangement made him too nervous to perform. So Leiber & Stoller called on the song's principal composer King to take over the lead.

What "the arrangement really brought forward, by forcing King . . . to sing in a key well above his natural range and underpinning the result with so much pseudo-Tchaikovsky, was an air of abject hopelessness," writes Dave Marsh, ranking it #30 in *The Heart of Rock & Soul: The 1001 Greatest Singles Ever Made.* For all the seeming nuttiness of the combined elements, Leiber once said, "there was something magnificent about it."

Here's That Rainy Day (1959)—Frank Sinatra (written by James Van Heusen & Johnny Burke)
Recorded on March 25, 1959
From the Capitol album *No One Cares* (chart debut Aug. 24, 1959, #2 peak) (*APS*)

Frank Sinatra recorded five albums of strictly lovelorn, lonely ballads for Capitol from 1955–1959, and these sets included some of his most memorable performances. Biographer Will Friedwald writes that *No One Cares*, with conductor/arranger Gordon Jenkins, was inspired by Jenkins' collaboration with Nat "King" Cole on the hugely successful 1956 album *Love Is the Thing*, which included Cole's classic rendition of *Stardust*. The most indispensable song from this Sinatra album is *Here's That Rainy Day*.

The song was introduced in 1953 by Dolores Gray in the movie musical *Carnival in Flanders* and was little known until Sinatra made it a classic. Composer Jimmy Van Heusen began his career in the late 1930s, with hits including *Darn That Dream* and several Bing Crosby numbers. Then in the '50s and '60s he became one of Sinatra's favored songwriters (*All the Way, My Kind of Town*). Wrapping the singer's voice in sumptuous strings throughout the album, Jenkins (writes Friedwald) "disavows brass and reeds entirely," offering only judicious use of French horns and a handful of woodwinds to complement the army of violins. With supremely skillful if sugary arrangements and very slow tempos, Jenkins brought out "some of Sinatra's most compassionate performances ever."[215] This is undeniably true of *Rainy Day*, in which the singer captures every ounce of its sense of surprise at the end of a love affair and desolate feeling of loneliness.[216] Johnny Carson called it perhaps his all-time favorite song, and the usually ultra-composed host's eyes welled with tears when Bette Midler sang it directly to him on Carson's second to last *Tonight Show* broadcast in May 1992.

Shout (Parts 1 & 2) (1959)—Isley Brothers (written by O'Kelly Isley, Ronald Isley, & Rudolph Isley)
RCA 7588
Recorded July 29, 1959; chart debut Sept. 21, 1959 (#47 on pop chart) (*R&B-#47, RHF, GHF, RS-#119, RIA-#151, WASH-#49,*[217] *DM, 1001, ACC, DMDB*)

Just as Ray Charles' *What'd I Say* was cresting in the *Billboard* Top Ten soon after Labor Day 1959, that

211. As Leiber & Stoller discuss in their joint autobiography *Hound Dog* (p. 159–61), while understanding concerns about the record, they were convinced it was a potential smash. Wexler, still hating it, "refused to put it out for the longest time," but when finally released the producers' judgment was vindicated.

212. Robert Greenfield, in *The Last Sultan: The Life and Times of Ahmet Ertegun* (p. 154), reports that Leiber offered differing accounts of how Atlantic president Ertegun reacted to the record: either more diplomatic than Wexler though sharing his doubts, or flatly declaring to the composer, "You've got a hit record and you don't even know it."

213. Gillett, p. 193.

214. *Rock of Ages*, p. 201.

215. *Sinatra! The Song Is You*, p. 339–40.

216. Ted Gioia praises the song for its "impressionist" qualities, and musical ingenuity: "The radical harmonic movement in the first few bars is more suited to art song than pop hit, and serves as an inspiring underpinning for melodic improvisation." (*The Jazz Standards*, p. 142.) Over the years, Sinatra recorded eighty-five Van Heusen compositions.

217. *Shout* was voted the #25 all-time favorite oldie in eleven combined listener surveys (1994–2004) by WBIG-FM in Washington, D.C., including one year as #4.

classic's direct counterpart in completing the all-out fusion of gospel and rhythm & blues, the Isley Brothers' mighty *Shout*, exploded across radio airwaves. It is one of the ironies of the era that a record that helped define the very meaning of soul did not even make the R&B charts; no matter, for it made its way in history.

The "shout" has deep roots in black tradition as a physical manifestation of being possessed by the spirit, losing oneself in religious ecstasy. As outlined by Dena Epstein, the earliest known description of an African-American "shout," or sacred ring dance, was offered by Sir Charles Lyell as seen on New Year's Eve 1845 on a plantation in Hopeton, Georgia, following a Methodist prayer meeting. In reference to her 1850 visit to New Orleans, Fredrika Bremer wrote about the "tornado" of "shrieking and leaping, admonishing and preaching," which she saw as elements of "true African worship."[218] During the early years of the twentieth century many African-American houses of worship in the rural South, notes Barry Pearson, banned dance but "allowed rhythmic body motion if it adhered to certain arbitrary rules: if the feet never crossed and were seldom lifted, it wasn't dance, but a 'shout' or a 'ring shout.'"[219]

Seven years before the Isleys' classic, James Baldwin offered this depiction of the shout in his 1952 autobiographical novel *Go Tell It on the Mountain*: "They cried out, a long wordless crying, and, arms outstretched, like wings they began the shout. . . . the music swept on again, like fire, or flood, or judgment. Then, like a planet rocking in space, the temple rocked with the Power of God."[220]

The original quartet of Ronald, Rudolph, O'Kelly, and Vernon Isley formed a family gospel act in Cincinnati in 1954; after Vernon's death in a bicycling accident, the three remaining brothers went to New York City to record some unsuccessful doo-wop singles in 1957, with tenor Ronald as lead vocalist.[221] Clyde McPhatter was their biggest musical role model (the young Ronald sounded amazingly like him), and the ex-Drifters leader offered valuable encouragement. It was during a 1959 concert in Washington, D.C., that the group, while performing the Jackie Wilson hit *Lonely Teardrops*, interjected the line, "you know you make me want to shout," and got into a spirited back-and-forth with the

audience. An RCA executive in the house signed the Isleys to a contract, and suggested that they build a song around that catchphrase. The brothers responded with a song that—in the absence of any real lyrical content—consists of pure, unbridled passion, taking the frenzied call-and-response of black gospel into the secular realm.[222] The Italian-American duo of Hugo Peretti and Luigi Creatore, who had recently been hired by RCA as independent producers—the first such arrangement with a major label for an outside production group—was at the controls.[223] As Atlantic did with Brother Ray's breakthrough, RCA split *Shout* into two sides of a single: part one has the lyrics (such as they are), and on part two the boys just cut loose with such joy and energy it's hard not to chant along over the whole five minutes. This performance, remarks Elijah Wald, "was the era's defining dance-floor workout . . . It was pure rhythmic energy with hardly any tune—which helps explain why the white covers fell far behind the Isleys' original—and its ferocious power and raw vocalizing pointed the way to James Brown's [*Papa's Got*] *a Brand New Bag* and sounded the death knell for the old dance orchestras as surely as the twist killed the fox trot."[224]

The Isleys' greatest commercial success lay ahead of them, with the 1962 classic *Twist and Shout*, a Motown stint, and then a string of hits beginning in 1969 and carrying all the way into the new century; *Shout* was the foundation for all of it. Its featured role in the 1978 flick *Animal House* helped bring it before a new generation.

The Sky Is Crying (1959)—Elmore James & His Broomdusters

Fire 1016 (released as by "Elmo James & His Broomdusters")

Recorded in Chicago on Nov. 3 or 4, 1959; chart debut May 2, 1960 (#15 R&B); also recorded for Chess 1756 on Apr. 14, 1960 (*Blues-#35*, NPR)

Among the most electrifying blues recordings of the postwar Chicago era, Elmore James' *The Sky Is Crying* was a stirring testament by an artist who would be gone far too soon. Born Elmore Brooks on January 27, 1918, in Richland, Mississippi, the illegitimate son of a fifteen-year-old farmhand and raised in the Canton area, he acquired his last name from his stepfather, Joe Willie

218. *Sinful Tunes and Spirituals: Black Folk Music to the Civil War*, p. 208 & 211.

219. Pearson chapter, "Jump Steady: The Roots of R&B," in *Nothing But the Blues*, p. 172. "Ironically," he remarks, the Isleys' number "was an obvious church song sinfully tailored to secular rather than sacred ecstasy."

220. Quoted in *Freedom's Unfinished Revolution: An Inquiry into the Civil War and Reconstruction*, by William Friedheim with Ronald Jackson, p. 188.

221. Songwriter/arranger Richard Barrett, one of the era's leading talent scouts for doo-wop singers, discovered the Isleys performing on a New York street corner after their arrival.

222. The Isleys had worshipped at the First Baptist Church in downtown Cincinnati; their mother was the organist and taught the choir. As discussed in liner notes for the three-CD boxed set *It's Your Thing: The Story of the Isley Brothers*, gospel music filled their house.

223. Known as "Hugo & Luigi," the New York City natives had been writing songs together since the late 1940s, and had produced artists including Georgia Gibbs and the 1950s folk/pop star Jimmie Rodgers. They would go on to produce Sam Cooke, and to co-write such pop classics as *The Lion Sleeps Tonight* and Elvis Presley's *Can't Help Falling in Love*.

224. *How the Beatles Destroyed Rock 'n' Roll: An Alternative History of American Popular Music*, p. 220–21.

James. Inspired by two artists he met by 1937, Robert Johnson and Aleck "Rice" Miller (the second Sonny Boy Williamson), James soon became an accomplished guitarist, playing at local events. After Navy service from 1943–1945, he performed on Miller's popular radio program, and served as a sideman on Sonny Boy II's first recording dates for Lillian McMurry's Jackson, Mississippi–based Trumpet label in 1951. Later that year James made his own recording debut as a leader for Trumpet, and his exciting version of Johnson's *Dust My Broom* (a song he had been playing since at least 1938) became an R&B chart hit. Always restless, he spent the next several years moving around the country and recorded for other labels until Bobby Robinson offered him a contract with Fire Records in New York in 1959. He wouldn't stay for long, but while there recorded this classic. The combination of his great power as a performer and the aura of mystery that continues to surround him (he gave only one documented interview, and Gayle Dean Wardlow and Mike Leadbitter labored for a year to compile the basic facts of his life) has meant that, at least according to Wardlow, "the mythical stature given to James is quickly growing to equal that of Robert Johnson."[225]

A radio repairman by trade, James, writes Cub Koda, "reworked his guitar amplifiers in his spare time, getting them to produce raw, distorted sounds that wouldn't resurface until the advent of heavy rock amplification in the late 1960s. This amp on 11 approach was hotwired to one of the strongest emotional approaches to the blues ever recorded."[226] Elmore's best work of this period, declares Robert Palmer in *Deep Blues*, stands alongside the best of Muddy Waters, Howlin' Wolf, and just a few others as "the recorded pinnacle of Chicago blues." On his fervent blues ballads like *The Sky Is Crying*, writes Ted Gioia, his "sandpapery vocals, cracking and sometimes overwrought . . . could easily convince you that James had stopped weeping just moments before the session began."[227]

The Sky Is Crying, James' greatest original piece (with producer Bobby Robinson's assistance on the lyrics),[228] features him (in the definitive 1959 version) with a terrific Broom-dusters lineup: his own sizzling slide guitar plus J. T. Brown on tenor sax, Johnny Jones on piano, Elmore's cousin Homesick James on bass (and a solo art-

ist in his own right), and Odie Payne on drums. Jackson, Mississippi native Johnny Jones had played with Tampa Red and Muddy Waters among other artists before helping to assemble the Broomdusters. Unfortunately, this session would be the band's last as a unit; Brown, Jones, and Homesick James would return for the April 1960 Chess session, and Homesick for one more date in May. Elmore James would have only four more recording sessions after May 1960 (with different sidemen) until his death (after years of heart disease worsened by drinking) in May 1963. The song has become a blues standard, with noteworthy versions by his pal Rice Miller, Freddie King, Albert King, and Stevie Ray Vaughan among many others, but the original—cited by National Public Radio in 1999 as one of the 300 most important American musical works of the twentieth century—reigns supreme. Robert Santelli writes that the original 1959 performance "features the kind of stinging guitar notes that blister eardrums and a vocal delivery that creates a dark chamber of heartbreak and loneliness."[229]

Maria (1960)—Johnny Mathis (music by Leonard Bernstein, lyrics by Stephen Sondheim)
Columbia 41684
Recorded on Nov. 6, 1959; chart debut May 30, 1960 (#78 peak); from the album *Faithfully* (chart debut Jan. 18, 1960, reached #2)

West Side Story was a landmark in Broadway history for many reasons, ranging from its choreography to its provocative story line. Underlying it all was the music, remarkable songs that carry forward the narrative but also work brilliantly on their own outside the context of the show. *Maria* was arguably its greatest ballad, and Johnny Mathis gave the song its ultimate performance.

Director/choreographer Jerome Robbins and playwright Arthur Laurents had first discussed in 1945 the idea of updating Shakespeare's *Romeo and Juliet* as an interfaith romance in contemporary New York, and Leonard Bernstein came into the project before it was abandoned. A decade later, when urban racial gang wars involving newly arrived Puerto Ricans and native-born Americans as antagonists became big news, the idea was revived.

Leonard Bernstein (born in Lawrence, Massachusetts, on August 25, 1918) followed stints as assistant to Serge Koussevitzky at Berkshire Music Center and then assistant conductor at the New York Philharmonic (1943–1944) by becoming conductor of the New York Symphony (1945–1948). His first venture onto the Broadway stage was a major success with his score for the 1945

---

225. *Chasin' That Devil Music: Searching for the Blues*, p. 169.
226. *All-Music Guide to the Blues*, p. 132–33.
227. Ted Gioia, *Delta Blues*, p. 315.
228. Bobby Robinson offered his account of the song's genesis in liner notes for the Capricorn album *Elmore James: King of the Slide Guitar—The Fire/Fury/Enjoy Recordings*. The two men were kicking around ideas before the session. It had been raining all day, and they were standing at the window. James remarked, "It looks just like the sky is crying." Robinson suggested that he use that for a song. "Elmore worked with the band on the music, and I wrote the words. In a few minutes, we had it. The song was just a natural."

---

229. Robert Santelli, *The Best of the Blues: The 101 Essential Albums*, p. 44.

Playlist 7

musical *On the Town*, which became a hit movie four years later. Like no composer before him, Bernstein moved easily back and forth between the classical world (conducting the New York Philharmonic, and writing symphonies, works for piano and violin, and the ballet *Fancy Free*), Broadway (the 1953 hit musical *Wonderful Town*, the acclaimed 1956 show *Candide*), and Hollywood (his 1954 background score for *On the Waterfront*). *West Side Story* became his greatest Broadway triumph.

Bernstein started out writing lyrics as well as music for the show. But when it became clear help was needed, Laurents brought in Oscar Hammerstein's former protégé Stephen Sondheim—in his Broadway debut—as lyricist. Sondheim in turn recruited Harold Prince as co-producer (Prince would go on to produce many of Sondheim's classic musicals of the 1970s). *West Side Story* opened on September 26, 1957, and was immediately hailed as a masterpiece. Although its run of 732 performances was merely excellent and the show lost most of its Tony-nominated categories to *The Music Man*, its original-cast album reached #5 in *Billboard* and remained on the chart for 191 weeks.[230] Robbins' bold choreography, using ballet-inspired modern dance for dramatic purposes, set new standards and influenced a generation. And the 1961 movie version was nothing less than a phenomenon, winning ten Academy Awards including Best Picture, and its soundtrack remaining in the #1 position for a staggering fifty-four weeks, second in *Billboard* history only to the sixty-nine weeks of the *South Pacific* Broadway cast in 1949–1950.

Maria is the big love ballad sung by the white Anglo-Saxon Tony (played on Broadway by Larry Kert) to the Puerto Rican beauty of the song title (portrayed by Carol Lawrence) after he had met her at the gym.[231] Bernstein's gorgeous melody (which was perhaps inspired by the Mark Blitzstein song *Regina* from his 1937 show *The Cradle Will Rock*) and Sondheim's well-crafted lyrics are delivered impeccably by Johnny Mathis, with his impossibly perfect tone, breath control, and great range; when he returns from the orchestral chorus at mid-song, his high tenor seeming to glide directly from the heavens, it's a spine-tingling moment.

Only the Lonely (Know the Way I Feel) (1960)—Roy Orbison (written by Roy Orbison & Joe Melson)
Monument 421
Recorded on March 25, 1960; Chart debut June 6, 1960 (peak position #2); #1 (2 weeks) in England, #2 in

Canada[232] (*DM-#17, GHF, RS-#234, ACC-#142, AHR, TC, DMDB*)

Roy Orbison's brief career as a rock 'n' roller on Sun Records had yielded one minor hit (*Ooby Dooby* in 1956), and after writing songs for the Everly Brothers, Jerry Lee Lewis, and Buddy Holly, he signed with Fred Foster's new Monument Records. Session bassist Bob Moore (an investor in the new label) had heard that RCA Victor was letting Orbison go, and he convinced Foster to seize the opportunity. *Uptown* was a mild chart success, then Roy's writing partner Joe Melson showed him a fragment of a song he'd been working on, *Only the Lonely*. Colin Escott and Martin Hawkins: "They honed the song to perfection over a period of weeks and crafted an epic, the first song that truly probed the frightening potential of Orbison's voice."[233] Before recording it, the singer decided to stop off in Memphis and offer the song to his former Sun Records mate Elvis Presley. But Elvis was not up yet that morning, so Roy and Melson continued driving to Nashville—where they offered the song to the Everlys. However, Phil and Don in 1960 were determined to focus primarily on their own original material. Only then did Orbison—still lacking confidence as a performer despite his incredible vocal gifts—enter RCA's Nashville studio to record it himself.[234]

In this powerhouse performance which firmly established him as a singer with few equals, over producer Foster's lavish orchestration "soared his rich, supple voice, which rose to every occasion, such as the dazzling falsetto break on *Only the Lonely* during which the musicians fall silent as if in awe," writes Ken Emerson.[235] "Like the rest of Orbison's hits, *Only the Lonely* has tremendous dynamics (made possible by Orbison's near-operatic range) and a lyric that renders everyday heartbreak so universal that it acquires a tinge of the cosmic," declares Dave Marsh, ranking it at #17 in *The Heart of Rock & Soul*. "What's most remarkable, though, is at the very end Orbison shrugs off all the agony and asks only for the chance to lose his loneliness to love once again. This transcendental dismissal of the worst life has to offer should by itself earn Orbison a place in the pantheon of rock legends."[236]

---

230. After closing in New York in June 1959, the show went on a successful cross-country tour, and returned to Broadway on April 27, 1960, for an additional 249 performances.

231. One of the devices used by Bernstein was (writes Larry Stempel in *Showtime*, p. 402) a "three-note idea, formed by a tritone and a half step," serving (sometimes inverted) as a "seminal link" between Tony's songs *Maria* and *Something's Coming*.

232. #2 in New Zealand.

233. *Good Rockin' Tonight: Sun Records and the Birth of Rock 'n' Roll*, p. 152–53.

234. The song took just under thirty minutes to record, with Anita Kerr as arranger. (Ellis Amburn, *Dark Star: The Roy Orbison Story*, p. 92.)

235. *The Rolling Stone Illustrated History of Rock & Roll*, p. 129. Studio engineer Bill Porter, who worked on most of Orbison's Monument sessions, recalled that the singer knew exactly the sound he wanted for this song. For this and most of Roy's subsequent records, they started with the vocal and then all the instrumental parts were mixed down from that, a reversal of the standard procedure (*Journal of Country Music*, Vol. 18 #2 [1996]).

236. Marsh, p. 19.

Are You Lonesome Tonight? (1960)—Elvis Presley
(music by Lou Handman, lyrics by Roy Turk)
RCA 47-7777
Recorded on April 4, 1960; chart debut Nov. 14, 1960
(6 weeks at #1); #1 for 4 weeks in U.K., #1 (6
weeks) in Australia [237] (*GHF, BILLB-#131, AHR,
TC, DMDB*)

For the first time in his five-year tenure as manager
of the king of rock & roll, Col. Tom Parker asked Elvis
Presley to record a particular song. It had been a featured
number for the first artist Parker ever managed, 1920s
crooner Gene Austin, and it was the favorite tune of Parker's wife Marie. And so, at 4 a.m. in a marathon session
that had begun at 7:30 Sunday evening, Elvis recorded
one of the biggest and most unexpected hits of his career,
Are You Lonesome Tonight?

A moderately big hit in 1927 for female vocalist
Vaughn DeLeath and longtime recording star Henry Burr,
and also recorded by the Carter Family, *Are You Lonesome Tonight?* is the kind of sweet, sentimental ballad
the young Elvis liked to sing for his late mother, which
may explain why the old-fashioned number brought out
such an emotionally resonant performance. Earlier in the
session Presley had unleashed all of his vocal powers on
It's Now or Never; *Lonesome* enabled him to showcase
his gift with a quieter ballad. Biographer Peter Guralnick
relates that Elvis asked producer/guitarist Chet Atkins to
have all the lights turned down, and had all nonessential
persons leave the studio. It was just acoustic guitar, subdued drums and bass, gentle vocal backing by the Jordanaires, and Elvis, who had a copy of the Burr recording
and copied it exactly.[238] In just two complete takes, he
nailed the song including the dramatic if corny spoken
recitation in the middle that demonstrated more acting
ability than he was able to show in most of his films.
(Blue Barron's orchestra had done a 1950 version of the
song, which reached the Top 20, and which included a
very similar recitation—based on Jaques' "all the world's
a stage" speech in Act II of Shakespeare's *As You Like
It*—intoned by disc jockey John McCormick.)

"The romantic sadness of the lyrics is exaggerated by
the echo-laden vocals, which make Elvis sound as though
he is standing alone in the middle of a huge room," notes
Thomas Ryan. "Singing from a whisper to a bellow, he
manages to squeeze some nuance from the ancient material . . . outdated, and yet somehow beautiful and emotionally wrenching."[239]

Blue Rondo a la Turk (1960)—Dave Brubeck Quartet
Recorded on Aug. 18, 1959

From the album *Time Out* (chart debut Nov. 28, 1960, #2
peak, 164 total weeks); B side of single *Take Five*
on Columbia 41479 (Sept. 1961) (*Jazz-#42, TG*)

The jazz world's first exposure to Dave Brubeck's
Blue Rondo a la Turk came as a shock. From its opening
seconds it plunges the listener into a dense, furious 9/8
time signature, a million miles removed from the familiar
4/4 and related tempos, forbidding, exotic, and thrilling. Brubeck recalls that the group had frequently used
a "polyrhythmic approach" within its improvised solos,
and when on a State Department–sponsored 1958 tour in
the Middle East and India, and playing with native musicians who were accustomed to widely varying times, he
was particularly fascinated with the 9/8 pattern he heard
on the streets of Istanbul. In Bombay, the pianist tried to
play behind Abdul Jaffer Khan, a nationally known sitar
player. "His influence made me play in a different way,"
Brubeck wrote. "Although Hindu scales, melodies and
harmonies are so different, we understood each other."
In Ankara, Turkey, they jammed on stage with Turkish
bass, French horn, and drum players. "Combining the
Turkish 9/8 pattern with the classical rondo form and the
blues" resulted in *Blue Rondo a la Turk*.

After Brubeck and alto saxophonist Paul Desmond lead
the way on the opening section, the piece calms down to
a standard 4/4 with lovely soloing by both men rooted in
the blues, ultimately returning to the frenetic 9/8 for the
pounding finale. Mervyn Cooke in *Jazz* notes that the
piece emulates the "pseudo-Oriental" flavor of Mozart's
Turkish Rondo. "Departing from normal jazz textures,
Brubeck has all the instruments play [the unconventional
2 + 2 + 2 + 3] pattern simultaneously to intensify the
effect."[240] The climax of the opening section with percussively dissonant piano chords, he remarks, suggests the
influence of twentieth century classical modernists such
as Bartok and Stravinsky. It succeeds, writes Len Lyons,
"because of an inner tension between the unusual rigid
rhythms juxtaposed with the loosely swinging solos.
There is no denying that the alternation of 4/4 improvisations on *Blue Rondo* with the neatly arranged sections in
9/8 offers a pleasurable sense of release."[241]

From its late-1960 release the album *Time Out* was
the quartet's biggest seller to date, and then shot to an
entirely new level when Columbia released Desmond's
Take Five as a single the following fall, climbing all the
way to #25 in *Billboard* as one of the highest-charting
jazz singles in years, with *Blue Rondo* as the flip side.
The Brubeck combo was not the first to experiment with
unorthodox rhythms (Max Roach had already been noted
for his explorations), but they took it to a mass audience
with a boldly uncompromising approach.

---

237. It was also #1 in Chile, #2 in Japan, #5 in Spain, #6 in Italy, and
#7 in West Germany.
238. *The Unmaking of Elvis Presley: Careless Love*, p. 64–66.
239. *American Hit Radio*, p. 67.

240. Cooke, *Jazz*, p. 144.
241. Lyons, p. 208.

Runaway (1961)—Del Shannon (written by Del Shannon & Max Crook)

Big Top 3067

Chart debut March 6, 1961 (4 weeks at #1); #1 for 3 weeks in U.K., #1 (7 weeks) in Australia[242] (*RHF, GHF, PW, DMDB-#82, ACC-#102, DM, AHR, RS, TC*)

With a spectacular vocal featuring a soaring falsetto, a haunting minor-key melody, melancholy lyrics, and a startling Musitron solo (a variation on the electric organ), Del Shannon's *Runaway* sounded like nothing else on pop radio in 1961, and became one of the era's most memorable hits.

Born Charles Westover on December 30, 1934, in Coopersville, Michigan, Shannon (the stage name he adopted) had served a hitch in the Army, and was working at a furniture store by day and fronting a band in Battle Creek by night when an out-of-town DJ caught his act and arranged an audition that resulted in a record contract. When the first tracks he recorded in New York were deemed uncommercial, Shannon came up with a tune that his band had improvised in his stage act at Battle Creek's Hi-Lo Club. His organist Max Crook had played some wild chord changes with A minor followed by G, and Shannon was inspired to write lyrics to it the next day. While the final version of the song was about a girl, Shannon said that initially he was writing about himself, because he was regularly running away from relationships. When they recorded it—with Crook on an instrument that was a forerunner of the synthesizer, sounding positively futuristic in 1961—the result was magic. Released as his debut single, it shot straight to #1.

"You can break the performance down into a dozen or more component parts and each one—the organ solo, the falsetto warble, the nervous charming staccato beat, the melodic power of the final repeating phrase ('my little runaway, uh-run-run-run-run runaway')—seems a product of pure inspiration," writes Paul Williams in *Rock & Roll: The 100 Best Singles*.[243]

Shannon had fifteen more chart records the next five years, many (as Richie Unterberger describes it) exploring "brooding themes of abandonment, loss, and rejection."[244] After playing with a young British act on a European tour, he became the first American artist to cover a Beatles song with his 1963 minor-chart hit *From Me to You*.[245] He escaped from the oldies circuit to score a final Top 40 hit in 1981 produced by Tom Petty.

Lush Life (1961)—Nat "King" Cole (written by Billy Strayhorn)

Original version recorded March 29, 1949 for Capitol 57-606 (released in early September 1949), reissued in 1951 on Capitol C-677 and in 1953 on Capitol 1672

Superior version recorded for Capitol on April 20, 1961 (*Trad-#95, NPR-300, APS*)

When twenty-three-year-old pianist-composer Billy Strayhorn was introduced to Duke Ellington backstage at an Ellington concert in the youngster's hometown of Pittsburgh in December 1938, one of the greatest partnerships in jazz history was born. For the next three decades until Strayhorn's death in 1967, he served as Duke's musical alter ego, collaborating on songs and arrangements, and contributing several enduring compositions of his own. *Take the 'A' Train*, which became the band's immortal theme song soon after its introduction in 1941, was the most famous Strayhorn original, but in many ways the most compelling was *Lush Life*.

It was (along with *Something to Live For*) one of the songs Strayhorn auditioned for Ellington upon their first meeting. According to Strayhorn biographer David Hajdu, friends heard versions of the song as early as 1933 (when he was not yet eighteen); it was completed in 1936 and originally titled "Life Is Lonely." Yet not only did the orchestra never formally record it, but the song went unrecorded by any artist—and uncopyrighted—for thirteen years until Nat "King" Cole at last introduced it to the world at large in 1949. It's said that Billie Holiday wanted to record it in 1945, and indeed it could almost have been written for her, but sadly she never did. (The first time it was performed at a public venue seems to have been a November 13, 1948, Ellington concert, the last of his six annual programs at Carnegie Hall, when Duke invited Strayhorn to the piano to accompany Kay Davis' vocal.)[246]

Why would such a stunning piece of music stay hidden for so long? Perhaps because in part, Strayhorn enjoyed using the song as his surprise showstopper at cocktail parties; when invariably asked to play, he could astonish party-goers with a song rather unlike anything they'd ever heard. (His close friend Lena Horne said he would play it at every party she held in Los Angeles.) Also, its sheer musical and lyrical sophistication may have worked against it: the melody is intricate, minor-key, and distinctly melancholy, and the lyrics celebrate not only café society but the virtues of forgetting one's problems in a haze of alcohol. Like many in jazz, Stray-

---

242. *Runaway* was also #1 in Chile, #2 in Holland and New Zealand, and #3 in South Africa.

243. Williams, p. 49–50.

244. *All Music Guide to Rock*, p. 825.

245. In 1967 Shannon did a new live version of *Runaway* that was a regional hit in Seattle and reached #112 nationally; much more

successfully, three years later he produced Brian Hyland's smash remake of The Impressions' *Gypsy Woman*, with Crook on organ.

246. This landmark performance is included on the Vintage Jazz Classics CD *Carnegie Hall November 1948*. Davis' vocal is not on the Nat Cole level, but it's still an outstanding treatment, and the composer's soloing is gorgeous.

horn was no stranger to alcohol or drugs, and as a double minority—black and openly homosexual—his life was perhaps as lonely as the protagonist in his song. "I never intended for it to be published," he once said. "It was just something . . . that I liked for myself." How could such a young man compose something possessing such sophistication and depth? Strayhorn was an intensely serious student of both piano and harmony in high school, dazzling everyone (including his instructor) in 1934 with his performance of Edvard Grieg's *Piano Concerto in A Minor* with the Westinghouse student orchestra, and his early mastery of the basics of composition helped create the foundation of a masterpiece.

Lush Life, writes Hajdu, "is distinguished by a probing concerto-like exploration of its principal key (D-flat), some nicely surprising harmonic turns, melodic lines of often odd yet utterly natural-seeming duration, and virtually no repetition. Most impressively, the piece exquisitely weds words and music: A key change on 'everything seemed so sure' suddenly suggests optimism, and stress notes—for instance, the 'blue note' E-natural on the word jazz—fall precisely on the lyrics' points of drama."[247] David Jenness and Don Velsey remark of the melody: "The song attains an almost uncanny calmness, an alcoholic slowness, by the continuity of a bassline that simply oscillates (except for the release, and the remarkable last three bars) around chords that change only by a half-step."[248]

It was a 1949 album of six 78s produced by Norman Granz called *The Jazz Scene* that finally brought *Lush Life* from the shadows. Granz had fallen in love with the song at those cocktail party performances, and invited Strayhorn to record it for the album. As the composer cut the song on solo piano, Nat Cole—in the studio to do some retakes on an album he was making—was present, and told Strayhorn he'd love to record the number. As it turned out, Strayhorn's *Lush Life* was left off the Granz album—but he discovered that Cole had indeed recorded it as the B side to a pop tune called *Lillian*, released in fall 1949.[249] Normally mild-mannered, Strayhorn exploded in anger upon hearing Cole's take on the song; in part because the singer muffed some of the lyrics; in part because the vocal was accompanied not by piano but by a Pete Rugolo orchestral arrangement that the composer felt took too many liberties with the melody; but perhaps above all because his very private creation was suddenly quite public.[250] Just weeks after

this recording was released, Cole and his trio (making it a quartet) included *Lush Life* in a November 4, 1949, Carnegie Hall concert; in 2010, this performance—a stellar one minus the eccentricities of the Rugolo chart—was finally released (even Cole scholars hadn't known of the recording's existence) by Hep Records on *The Forgotten 1949 Carnegie Hall Concert*.

After the song was finally introduced by Cole, it still took quite awhile for the jazz/pop marketplace to accept it.[251] Cole's new 1961 recording—this time getting those finely-crafted lyrics right—became definitive. Yet Capitol didn't seem to know what to do with the masterpiece it had been handed; having recorded more than fifty songs in March and April, the artist had provided an oversupply of material, and *Lush Life* remained on the shelf. It was only in the fall of 1963, shortly after the splendid treatment of Strayhorn's gem by Johnny Hartman with John Coltrane, that Nat's finest rendition finally reached listeners. James Morris: "The easy use of

Nat King Cole, PhotoFest.

247. *Lush Life: A Biography of Billy Strayhorn*, p. 34–36.
248. *Classic American Popular Song: The Second Half-Century, 1950–2000*, p. 265.
249. According to Leslie Gourse in *Unforgettable: The Life and Mystique of Nat King Cole*, the singer may have already been aware of *Lush Life* before the Granz session, due to requests from patrons at the Trocadero who had heard Strayhorn perform it at parties.
250. Hajdu, *Lush Life*, p. 110–11.
251. Harry James recorded *Lush Life* in 1953 for Columbia, but by 1955 both this version and Cole's (which had drifted in and out of official listings for the previous few years) had been dropped from the list of active titles in *Popular Recordaid*. Sarah Vaughan and jazz pianist Bud Powell cut versions in 1956, followed by Sammy Davis, Jr., around the start of 1961.

natural speech inflections, the subtle shading of words, and the sensitivity to every musical turn place [Cole's] masterful performance at the pinnacle of artistry."[252]

Desafinado (1962)—Stan Getz & Charlie Byrd (written by Antonio Carlos Jobim & Newton Mendonca)
Verve 10260
Recorded on Feb. 13, 1962; chart debut Sept. 29, 1962 (peak position #15);[253] from the album *Jazz Samba* (1 week at #1, 70 charted weeks) (*World-#11, Jazz-#57, NPR, GHF*)

In 1960, guitarist Charlie Byrd and bassist Keeter Betts, having participated in previous State Department–sponsored goodwill tours of Europe and the Far East, were invited to South America. Playing in Brazil, they were entranced by the emerging sounds of bossa nova, whose burgeoning popularity had been fueled in part by the compositions of Antonio Carlos Jobim. Betts spearheaded a recording session at Pierce Hall in All Souls Unitarian Church on 16th Street in Washington, D.C., with Byrd and tenor saxophonist Stan Getz that would fully introduce America to the new music. Jobim's *Desafinado* began the stateside love affair with samba and bossa nova.

The samba had been around for quite awhile, emerging out of an urban dance believed to have derived from the *maxixe* (a Brazilian dance that burst into U.S. popularity during the 1910s). John Storm Roberts: "The word 'samba' itself, which is probably Congo-Angolan, is used for many different dances, found in many parts of Brazil. The version known overseas is the so-called 'carioca' form of Rio de Janeiro. This originally developed from the Afro-Brazilian ring-dance form still danced in the Rio slums to a battery of percussion, also the basis of most carnival dancing." Samba music grew steadily in popularity across Brazil during the next few decades until, by the 1940s, it had become a dominant force.[254] Through crossover artists such as Xavier Cugat and Carmen Miranda, samba also became well known in the U.S. Bossa nova was born as "a fusion of samba and jazz" (in Roberts' phrase), viewed by its creators as more progressive and liberating than the older form.

Gary Giddins and Scott DeVeaux: "Although detractors insisted that they were merely reinterpreting the traditional samba, Jobim and company insisted that bossa nova represented a break with tradition no less meaningful than bop's break with swing. The public agreed. Bossa nova incarnated a young, innovative attitude with poetic, sometimes self-mocking lyrics and melodies that, although occasionally melancholy, were almost invariably as gentle as a summer's breeze."[255]

"One minute and fifty-nine seconds that changed everything" (in Ruy Castro's phrase) was *Chega de Saudade* (No More Blues), the recording of an Antonio Carlos Jobim composition by guitarist Joao Gilberto in July 1958, issued in the antiquated 78 rpm format on the Odeon label.[256] Although it was not an immediate commercial hit, the record kicked off the bossa nova revolution. Audiences outside Brazil were first widely exposed to it through the 1959 soundtrack of *Black Orpheus*, and during the next few years the "sweet, soft sound" steadily gathered momentum until *Jazz Samba* took it to the next level.

Charlie Byrd was born in Suffolk, Virginia, on September 16, 1925, began studying guitar at age ten and pursued classical studies that included Spanish master Andres Segovia; after playing with various combos he led a group (including Betts) at his own club, the Showboat, in Washington, D.C., from 1957–1966. It was Washington, D.C.'s, most popular radio jazzman, Felix Grant (longtime host of WMAL's nightly show *The Album Sound*), who had told Byrd about the unique charms of Brazilian music based on his numerous trips there, and repeatedly urged the guitarist to go see for himself; when the opportunity finally came, jazz history was made.[257] Initially, Byrd was unable to interest an American label in a bossa nova album. Recruiting Stan Getz to co-headline *Jazz Samba* proved a master stroke. Getz had been one of the hottest young jazz saxophonists after establishing his reputation with the Woody Herman band in the late 1940s, and after a cold stretch rebounded with the acclaimed 1961 album *Focus*.

"With the success of *Chega de Saudade*, Jobim opened his drawer in one go, and out flew a flock of beautiful birds," writes Castro. Between mid-1958 and the end of 1959, he released a flurry of songs that would become standards, including *Desafinado* (Off-Key), *Samba de uma nota so* (One-Note Samba), and *Meditacao* (Meditation).[258] Pianist Newton Mendonca was his collaborator on these three songs among others, primarily as lyricist (although Castro suggests he may have also contributed to the music).[259] It was, once again, Joao Gilberto whose 78 rpm recording of *Desafinado* on November 10, 1958, popularized the tune in Brazil.[260] Lena Horne,

252. Liner notes, Smithsonian *American Popular Song*, p. 118.

253. Reached #14 in Canada, #16 Germany.

254. *The Latin Tinge: The Impact of Latin American Music on the United States*, p. 12–15.

255. Giddins and DeVeaux, *Jazz*, p. 520.

256. *Bossa Nova: The Story of the Brazilian Music That Seduced the World*, p. 126–29.

257. In 1964, Felix Grant was awarded the Order of the Southern Cross, Brazil's highest civilian honor, for promoting Brazilian music in the United States.

258. Castro, *Bossa Nova*, p. 164.

259. Mendonca died of a heart attack in November 1960.

260. Ted Gioia (*The Jazz Standards*, p. 79) calls the song "masterfully written," its intricate chord changes intriguingly contrasted with the deceptive simplicity of the tune."

and Sammy Davis, Jr. were the first American artists to perform bossa nova in 1960 during Brazilian visits, and at year's end Capitol released the album *Brazil's Brilliant Joao Gilberto* in the United States. (This was the album that Byrd gave to Getz as the saxophonist's introduction to the genre.)[261] Flutist Herbie Mann in 1961 became the first American jazzman to record an album in Rio using local musicians, and Dizzy Gillespie (always alert to the possibilities of Latin music) added *Desafinado* to his repertory that year. All of this paved the way for the breakthrough to follow.[262]

Betts' ingratiating bass vamp opens up *Desafinado*, and the wonderfully warm, sunny melody unfolds through the two leaders over the bubbling Brazilian rhythm. Gary Giddins praises Getz's "abiding economy, almost aphoristic in its precision," as evidenced by his "charging eight-bar exchanges" with Byrd.[263] Surpassing even the huge success of the Dave Brubeck Quartet the previous year, *Jazz Samba* became the first chart-topping jazz album in nearly a decade, and *Desafinado* (the Grammy winner as best jazz performance by a small group) the highest-charting jazz instrumental single since the early 1950s when the nearly six-minute album track was edited down to a mere two minutes. Getz went on to the still bigger triumph of *The Girl from Ipanema* in 1964, Byrd enjoyed a long career as a supremely skilled guitarist, and Betts served as accompanist for Ella Fitzgerald from 1964 until poor health forced her to stop performing in 1993.

I Can't Stop Loving You (1962)—Ray Charles (written by Don Gibson)
ABC-Paramount 10330
Chart debut May 5, 1962 (#1 for 5 weeks on pop chart;[264] #1 for 10 weeks R&B); #1 for 2 weeks in U.K.; #1 (4 weeks) in Australia;[265] from the album *Modern Sounds in Country & Western Music* (#1 for 14 weeks) (*GHF, BMI-#40, HBN-#44, DMDB-#63, C&W-#70,R&B-#79, RS-#164, AHR, DMDB*)

The already-established genius of Ray Charles blazed new trails with his landmark 1962 album. While hardly the first time that an R&B singer had recorded country

tunes, it was the first time one of his stature had tackled an entire album in the genre. And far from a crossover gimmick or artistic compromise, it demonstrated that a great singer can take quality songs from any field and make them work brilliantly. Country star Don Gibson wrote *I Can't Stop Loving You* and enjoyed a big hit with it in 1958;[266] brother Ray took it to a vast new audience. Whenever the strings and gooey white backup singers are a bit much, Charles' vocal mastery and the song's intrinsic beauty wipe away all musical obstacles.

Charles had been planning to do a country album for years; he'd listened to and loved the Grand Ole Opry as a kid alongside the blues, jazz, and pop, and had recorded a few country songs before, including the Hank Snow standard *I'm Movin' On* in 1959. "I was only interested in two things: being true to myself and being true to the music," he said in his autobiography with David Ritz. "I wasn't trying to be the first black country singer. I only wanted to take country songs and sing them my way."[267] Biographer Michael Lydon calls the album "an extraordinary work of art." On this song, he uses a device that became a trademark, allowing the chorus to lead the lyric, with his solo voice following. "Following the chorus gives Ray a roving independence over the musical flow. No longer the singer fixed in the spotlight, he cruises in and around the music as if on the wings, the Greek chorus no longer commenting on him, but he commenting on the chorus."[268]

In addition to its long tenure at #1, *Modern Sounds* spent thirty-three weeks in the *Billboard* Top Ten. When a "Volume 2" was issued and soared to #2 entering the holiday season, for a time Charles had four LPs in the top tier of the charts, with greatest-hits packages on both ABC and Atlantic. No one quite knew what to expect when the album was released; it became a phenomenon.[269]

Be My Baby (1963)—The Ronettes (written by Jeff Barry, Ellie Greenwich, & Phil Spector)
Philles 116
Recorded in July 1963; chart debut Aug. 31, 1963 (3 weeks at #2 pop, #4 R&B); reached #2 in Canada, #4 in U.K.[270] (*DM-#21, RS-#22, RR, GHF, RHF,*

261. Roberts, *The Latin Tinge*, p. 171.

262. Castro, p. 241–42. As the Byrd/Getz performance climbed the charts, early cover versions of *Desafinado* included Si Zentner, Julie London, Betty Carter, and Quincy Jones. Record company executives saw the sound as a possible commercial bonanza (October 13, 1962, *Billboard* feature: "Is the Bossa Nova the New Twist?")

263. *Visions of Jazz*, p. 412. Ironically, even though it was Byrd who had initiated the album project, his guitar solo was cut from the single version, so, remarks Roberts, he never received proper credit as the main source of the jazz-bossa fusion.

264. The August 18, 1962, *Billboard* reported that the record had surpassed 1.5 million in U.S. sales.

265. It was also #1 for 8 weeks in Belgium, 6 weeks in Israel, 4 weeks in Holland and New Zealand, for 1 to 3 weeks in Denmark and Ireland; #2 in Chile, Finland, and Hong Kong; and #3 in Japan and South Africa.

266. Gibson recalled writing it in a house trailer in Knoxville after setting out to pen a lost-love ballad; he also wrote his hit *Oh Lonesome Me* the same afternoon. (Horstman, *Sing Your Heart Out, Country Boy*, p. 165.)

267. *Brother Ray*, p. 222–23. According to the singer, he was unfamiliar with *I Can't Stop Loving You* before the label's A&R man Sid Feller included it among 100-plus songs offered for his consideration. (Guralnick, *Sweet Soul Music*, p. 68.)

268. *Ray Charles: Man and Music*, p. 215–19.

269. This was one of the early hits to feature the Fame studio band that fueled the legendary Muscle Shoals sound. The original great Fame band included David Briggs on piano, Norbert Putnam on bass, Jerry Carrigan on drums, Terry Thompson on guitar, and Dan Penn (engineer) on guitar.

270. #2 in New Zealand, #4 in Belgium, #9 Norway.

NPR, ACC-#10, R&B-#20, DMDB-#80, AHR, TC, 1001, RIA, NME)

"I knew that record was Number One from the minute I made it," declared producer Phil Spector of *Be My Baby*. "I believed it was a monster record." *Rolling Stone*, in ranking it as the #38 best single of the past twenty-five years in 1988, wrote, "*Be My Baby* is perhaps the quintessential expression of the single format: other songs may be more 'important,' others more catchy, but none has the muscular power that begins with the record's very first drum wallop or the evocative sass" of lead singer Veronica "Ronnie" Bennett (later Mrs. Spector, born on August 10, 1943, in New York City), her sister Estelle and their cousin Nedra Talley. Ronnie's multi-ethnic allure (half white, quarter black, and quarter Cherokee) was captivating. The Harlem-based trio had recorded two 1961–1962 singles for Colpix and three for the May label as Ronnie & the Relatives before Spector put them on a rocket ride to the top with this, their debut for his company.

Jeff Barry was born Joel Adelberg on April 3, 1938, in Brooklyn, raised in New Jersey, and after a stint in the Army reserves switched from engineering to songwriting, teaming with various collaborators on early hits including *Tell Laura I Love Her* (a 1960 hit for Ray Peterson). Ellie Greenwich, born in Brooklyn on October 23, 1940, began performing and writing songs while in high school, and became a Brill Building regular working with other writers in the Jerry Leiber–Mike Stoller publishing company Trio. She began her spectacularly successful association with Spector by co-writing the early-1963 hits *Why Do Lovers Break Each Other's Hearts* (Bob B. Soxx & the Blue Jeans) and *Today I Met the Boy I'm Gonna Marry* (Darlene Love). By that time she and Barry were married (wed in October 1962), and in mid-1963 they also became a songwriting team, starting with the Spector epics *Be My Baby* and *Da Doo Ron Ron*.

Although like all of Spector's classic hits for his own label *Be My Baby* was recorded at Gold Star Studios in Los Angeles, it was largely written in New York's Brill Building (and also at Spector's office on East 62nd Street and York Avenue) by Barry, Greenwich, and Spector. Barry recounted for *Vanity Fair* in 2001 that Spector would be at the piano crafting the chord progression while Barry focused on the lyrics and melody, and Greenwich on the song structure (she had the most technical experience of the three and could also translate ideas from the others onto the sheet music). "We just *got* Phil," said Greenwich. "We made him laugh. And we understood him. We accepted his idiosyncrasies." Spector's production drew upon what he had learned working with Leiber & Stoller, starting with the record's opening Brazilian-inspired baion drumbeat; but whereas that songwriting/production team (as Ken Emerson writes) "strove for a clean, clear sound in which every instrumental line was distinct," Spector went in the opposite direction by piling on multiple layers of instruments.[271] The backing singers included Darlene Love, Fanita James from the Blossoms, and a teenaged Cher (a fast friend of Ronnie's), who was then dating Philles promo man Sonny Bono.[272]

Ronnie Spector recalled in her autobiography that she and Spector had rehearsed *Be My Baby* in New York for weeks before he had her fly to California to record it. "Gold Star's Studio A was old and really tiny, but that was the only place he recorded anymore, because he knew he could get sounds out of that room that he couldn't get anywhere else . . . The room was so small, the sound seemed to bounce off the walls, creating a natural echo that made every song recorded there feel fuller."[273]

David Hinckley: "Some fans would deify Phil Spector had he made only one record: *Be My Baby*. From the first crash of the snare drums to the last 'Whoa-ho-ho-ho-ho,' *Be My Baby* painted rock 'n' roll's definitive romantic fantasy for adolescent males. It's so good they don't even mind that in real life Phil got the girl."[274] Ronnie, declares Tony Fletcher, "had a voice like a foghorn in heat."[275] Brian Wilson of the Beach Boys called it his all-time favorite song, and like other rockers of the era used the lush Spector sound as a "Rosetta stone" for his studio experiments.[276] Dave Marsh ranked *Be My Baby* at #20 in *The Heart of Rock & Soul*. The then-married Spector was in love with the innocent-but-sexy Ronnie, he notes, "and he built a rock and roll cathedral" around her. Hal Blaine's drum introduction "is one of rock's grand statements,"[277] and after the girls establish the mood of desperate teen longing, "there's the bridge, with its ranks of cellos, a mountainous mock-symphony that lasts for the rest of the record. Against all odds, Spector made an initially shaky proposition into what may be his greatest monument."[278]

---

271. Ken Emerson, *Always Magic in the Air*, p. 152.

272. As per usual for Spector, the arranger is Jack Nitzsche and the engineer Larry Levine. The annotation for the Spector *Back to Mono (1958–1969)* boxed set reveals that Ronnie is the only member of the Ronettes singing here. This was Spector's first session with a full string section at Gold Star Studios. In addition to Hal Blaine, Wrecking Crew regulars believed to be present include Tommy Tedesco and Glen Campbell on guitars, Nino Tempo on sax, Leon Russell on keyboards, and Carol Kaye on bass.

273. Ronnie Spector with Vince Waldron, *Be My Baby*, p. 49–56. Dave Thompson in *Wall of Pain* (p. 77), cites Darlene Love's comment that in his feverish work on this single, "he was not simply making a record. He was declaring his love for Ronnie."

274. Liner notes for *Back to Mono (1958–1969)*.

275. *All Hopped Up and Ready to Go*, p. 198.

276. *Rolling Stone 500 Greatest Songs* (2010), p. 32.

277. Oddly, Blaine's memoir doesn't say a word about the *Be My Baby* session, instead discussing his Spector/Wrecking Crew experiences only in general terms.

278. Marsh, p. 21–22.

My Guy (1964)—Mary Wells (written by Smokey Robinson)

Motown 1056

Chart debut April 4, 1964 (2 weeks at #1 on pop chart; #1 for 7 weeks on *Cash Box* R&B chart); reached #5 in England, #1 (2 weeks) in Australia[279] (*R&B-#58, RHF, GHF, RIA, AHR, DMDB*)

The team of Mary Wells as singer and Smokey Robinson as songwriter and producer was a powerful ingredient in the early rise of Motown. After combining forces for the 1962 hits *The One Who Really Loves You, You Beat Me to the Punch*, and *Two Lovers*, they scored their greatest triumph together with *My Guy*—not only an American chart-topper, but the first Motown record to become a top international hit.

In his autobiography, Motown founder Berry Gordy recalled that after writing *My Guy* but before even going into the studio, Robinson boasted that it was going to become a #1 pop hit. When Gordy suggested they make a bet of it, he pulled back a bit. After the prophecy was fulfilled, "he was sorry he hadn't bet!"[280]

A Detroit native born on May 13, 1943, Mary actually got her start as a songwriter at age seventeen, bringing *Bye Bye Baby*, a number she had written with Jackie Wilson in mind, to Gordy as Wilson's producer. (She got a friend of a friend, Motown chief engineer Robert Bateman, to introduce them.) Instead, upon hearing the teenager sing the number for him, Gordy signed her on the spot as an artist to his still-fledgling label, and the song became a moderate hit in early 1961. With a soft-voiced, gently sexy style and Smokey's writing and production prowess, Wells became Motown's first important solo female star. Whereas Gordy had pushed Wells too hard on her debut single, leaving her voice (as Nelson George writes) "sandpapery," "Smokey was sensitive enough to know that her malleable voice sounded best soft and soothing."[281]

My Guy is a warm, happy declaration of a girl's eternal loyalty to her man, with Mary backed by the mighty Earl Van Dyke–led Motown house band. Thomas Ryan notes that the record's featured horn phrase "was so obviously lifted from the melody of [the 1956 pop hit] *Canadian Sunset* that you can see the trace marks"—but with every musical ingredient falling perfectly into place, no one would dare complain. "Every girl wanted to find a boy she could feel this way about, and every boy wanted

his girl to be this true."[282] While James Jamerson was Motown's most celebrated bass player,[283] Carol Kaye (also a key contributor to Phil Spector's Wall of Sound) was the bassist on a number of Motown sessions, and she provides much of the rhythmic drive for *My Guy*.[284] Unfortunately, her biggest success was also to be Wells' virtual swan song. Lured by Twentieth Century Fox's extravagant promises and a $500,000 advance, the now-twenty-one-year-old singer won a court battle to have her Motown contract invalidated because it had been signed when she was underage. Recording for Fox and a series of other labels including Atco, Jubilee, Reprise, and Epic, she would never again approach the massive success she'd enjoyed with Gordy and Robinson, scoring only one minor Top 40 single after her departure.

Rock and Roll Music (1965)—The Beatles

Recorded on Oct. 18, 1964

From the British album *Beatles for Sale* and the U.S.-released Capitol album *Beatles '65* (chart debut Jan. 2, 1965, 9 weeks at #1)

John Lennon had been a hard-core Chuck Berry fan from the time he was introduced to rock 'n' roll, and in this no-holds-barred, frenzied lead vocal, the student may have even surpassed the master on Chuck's 1957 classic. The Beatles included *Rock and Roll Music* in their repertoire as early as 1960, so John had plenty of time to work his way up to this thrilling performance. The boys nailed it in just one take at the Abbey Road studio; good thing, for one wonders if Lennon's voice could have survived another such all-out assault. Ian MacDonald notes that Lennon's urgency is "remarkable after over eight hours in the studio [recording other songs including *I Feel Fine*], almost certainly prompted by his anxiety to do justice to a song he clearly regarded as virtual holy writ."[285]

Although not released as a single in the U.S. or England, it became a major international hit (indeed one of the group's biggest of the period), hitting #1 on the singles charts of Finland (8 weeks), Hong Kong (7 weeks), Luxembourg (6 weeks), Norway (4 weeks), West Germany (3 weeks), #1 in Malaysia; and also #2 in Australia, Holland, and Singapore, and #5 in Japan.

---

279. Also #1 in New Zealand.

280. Gordy, *To Be Loved: The Music, The Magic, The Memories of Motown*, p. 178–79, 185.

281. George, *Where Did Our Love Go? The Rise and Fall of the Motown Sound*, p. 43. "Under Smokey's guidance she sang sweetly, coolly, straightforwardly, sticking close to the melody line and the demonstration guide Smokey prepared for each song." She was Robinson's first non-Miracles production assignment.

---

282. *American Hit Radio*, p. 127.

283. Allan "Dr. Licks" Slutsky used *My Guy* as a point of departure for his analysis of Jamerson's style in *Standing in the Shadows of Motown: The Life and Music of Legendary Bassist James Jamerson*: "Gone were the two-beat, root-fifth patterns and post–*Under the Boardwalk* cliché bass lines that occupied the bottom end of most R&B releases. Jamerson had modified or replaced them with chromatic passing tones, Ray Brown style of walking bass lines, and syncopated eighth-note figures—all of which had previously been unheard of in popular music of the late Fifties and early Sixties."

284. Reder and Baxter, *Listen to This! Leading Musicians Recommend Their Favorite Artists and Recordings*, p. 383.

285. *Revolution in the Head*, p. 140.

Unchained Melody (1965)—Righteous Brothers (music by Alex North, lyrics by Hy Zaret)
Philles 129
Chart debut July 17, 1965 (#4 peak); #2 in Canada, #14 in England;[286] reissued as Verve Forecast 871882, chart debut Aug. 25, 1990 (#13 peak); #1 (7 weeks) in Australia[287] newly recorded 1990 version issued as Curb 76842, chart debut Oct. 6, 1990 (#19 peak) (*GHF, BBC-#5, WASH-#20, ASCAP, AFI-#27, DMDB-#40, AHR, RS, 1001*)

A big hit in 1955 for four different artists as theme from the film *Unchained*, most notably by big-voiced balladeers Al Hibbler and Roy Hamilton, *Unchained Melody* was taken to a still higher level in this blockbuster solo performance by Bobby Hatfield (fellow Righteous Brother Bill Medley sat this one out). This rendition, writes Thomas Ryan, "defined [the song's] greatness in a manner that eclipsed all previous versions. The beautiful license that Hatfield took to interpret the song transcended the already mellifluous melody . . . overwhelming." With Phil Spector's epic production and Hatfield's emotion-packed tenor soaring to stratospheric heights, it's a record designed to reduce anyone separated from the one they love to a "pile of mush."[288]

According to Bill Medley, on each Righteous Brothers album he and Hatfield would do one solo apiece. For their fourth album, both wanted to sing *Unchained Melody*. They flipped for it, and Hatfield won.

Of course its use as the love theme for Patrick Swayze and Demi Moore in the 1990 romantic smash *Ghost* triggered a massive revival in popularity, including two competing versions by the Righteous Brothers—the original versus a new performance—in the top echelon of the charts at the same time.[289] In eleven combined listener surveys by WBIG-FM in Washington, D.C. (1994–2004), *Unchained Melody* ranked as the #1 favorite oldie of all time (standing at #1 on the annual Top 500 countdowns in seven of those years).

19th Nervous Breakdown (1966)—Rolling Stones
London 9823
Recorded Dec. 3–8, 1965; chart debut Feb. 26, 1966 (3 weeks at #2); #1 (3 weeks) in England[290] (*DM-#190, AHR*)

Written by Mick Jagger and Keith Richards during the Stones' five-week U.S. tour and recorded during marathon December 1965 sessions at RCA Studios in Los Angeles, *19th Nervous Breakdown* reflected the sense of cynicism and dislocation the group was feeling during the period. Stones biographer Stephen Davis writes that it was cut to Bo Diddley's *Diddley Daddy* rhythm "with a clarion guitar flash" and lyrics representing "a Dylanesque take on an insane party girl." With Jack Nitzsche on piano, Ian Stewart on organ, and Brian Jones on harpsichord, the song featured "a bitter, lovelorn tone and a lot of echo," and concluded with Bill Wyman copying "the dive-bomber bass lick" from Diddley.[291] In lampooning the neurotic, self-obsessed rich, Jagger offers not a hint of sympathy. "The Stones at this point," writes Dave Marsh, "had a look and sound as lethal and streamlined as a Ferrari at full speed, with an engine [powered by Charlie Watts and Wyman] at least that efficient."[292]

Walk Away Renee (1966)—The Left Banke (written by Michael Brown)
Smash 2041
Chart debut Sept. 10, 1966 (#2 in *Cash Box*, #4 in *Record World*, #5 in *Billboard*); #1 in Canada[293] (*RHF, RS-#222, ACC*)

A pop song of rare beauty and delicacy, *Walk Away Renee* was called "an exquisite ode to love and longing" by *Rolling Stone* when the magazine named it one of the best 100 singles of the past twenty-five years in 1988. Michael Brown, keyboardist and co-founder of the Left Banke, wrote it at age sixteen. He helped form the group at the New York recording studio (World United Recording) owned by his father. The song was inspired by Renee Fladen, a young woman who had befriended the band. "It's not a love song about possession," Brown told *Rolling Stone*. "It's a song about loving someone enough to set them free." The song took about eight weeks to write and record—having the luxury of working on material at his father's studio enabled them to perfect their sound—and was rejected by ten major labels before Smash Records agreed to release it. "There's a certain purity to *Walk Away Renee*," said Brown, "and its purity comes from the idea that a dream lives, even if it's just a fantasy."[294]

Steve Martin's vocal is perfectly attuned to the minor-key, almost ethereal loveliness of the melody, with lyrics of melancholy romanticism, and Brown's harpsichord part and a flute solo add to the distinctly

---

286. #1 in Holland.
287. 1990: #1 (6 weeks) in New Zealand, #1 in Austria and Ireland, #2 in Belgium, #7 Germany.
288. Ryan, *American Hit Radio*, p. 175–76
289. The new version was of course no match for the original—Hatfield's control of his soaring upper range was a bit shakier—but it's nonetheless an impressive performance of an incredibly demanding song.
290. #1 in England according to *Billboard*; the charts used in the book *British Hit Singles* listed it at #2. *Nervous Breakdown* was also #1 for 2 weeks in W. Germany; #1 in Canada; #2 in Australia, Holland, Hong Kong, New Zealand, and Norway; and #3 in South Africa.

291. *Old Gods Almost Dead*, p. 150. Rob Bowman also calls attention to drummer Charlie Watts' dramatic cymbal crashes to mark the song's sections (*According to the Rolling Stones*, p. 101).
292. *The Heart of Rock & Soul*, p. 133–34.
293. Reached #5 in New Zealand.
294. September 8, 1988 *Rolling Stone*, p. 138–39.

European, quasi-classical flavor of the record. There was absolutely nothing like it on pop radio in 1966, and more than four decades later its sound still has few parallels. The Four Tops offered a fine cover version in 1968, and such artists as Cyndi Lauper and Rickie Lee Jones have added their interpretations; the original's peculiar magic remains in a class by itself. The Left Banke had one other sweetly enchanting Brown-penned hit, *Pretty Ballerina*, but broke up soon afterward. Brown was later a member of The Stories which scored a #1 hit in 1973 with *Brother Louie*.

I Never Loved a Man (the Way I Love You) (1967)— Aretha Franklin (written by Ronny Shannon)
Atlantic 2386

Recorded Jan. 24, 1967; chart debut March 4, 1967 (#1 for 7 weeks on R&B chart, #9 *Billboard* pop, #8 *Record World*); #15 in Canada (*RHF, PW, R&B-#89, RS-#189, DM-#201, AHR, ACC*)

Aretha Franklin's historic debut single for Atlantic Records was called "one of the great vocal performances of the century" by Paul Williams. In his book *Rock & Roll: The 100 Best Singles*, he wrote that the record "is so packed with emotional information a thousand computers couldn't hold it, even if they could find a way (other than Aretha's voice) to encode it."[295]

Brian Ward, in *Just My Soul Responding*, remarked on its complex, unsettling view of male-female relationships. The song begins with a fierce condemnation of her lover's infidelity ("you're a no-good heartbreaker"), "but later revealed masochistic undertones in describing acquiescence to such mistreatment. Franklin actually made a virtue out of her capacity to suffer and respond to her lover's cruelty with monumental, unshakeable love."[296]

This was the one and only track completed when producer Jerry Wexler (having just signed her to Atlantic following expiration of her Columbia contract) brought Aretha to record at the already-legendary Muscle Shoals, Alabama studio run by Rick Hall. Aretha worked out the rhythms for the song herself,[297] and played acoustic piano with Spooner Oldham on electric keyboards.[298] In true Muscle Shoals style, the track used a head arrangement with nothing written out; saxophonist Charlie Chalmers

set up the horn parts. "The minute Aretha touched the piano and sang one note, the musicians were captivated," wrote Wexler in his autobiography.[299] "They caught the fever and raced for their instruments." "I've never experienced so much feeling coming out of one human being," declared drummer Roger Hawkins. When the two-hour session wrapped, songwriter Dan Penn recalled: "It was a killer, no doubt about it. The musicians started singing and dancing with each other, giddy on the pure joy of having something to do with this amazing record."[300]

However, that night, Ted White and Rick Hall got into a ferocious argument that led to an actual fistfight. The following day, White took Aretha back to New York. Wexler knew they had a smash in *I Never Loved a Man*, and the dubs he sent to some radio stations generated a tremendous response, but its intended B side, Penn's *Do Right Woman—Do Right Man* had only a rhythm track without Aretha's vocals or piano; without it, he had no record to sell. The singer disappeared for two weeks (during a temporary split from White that later became permanent), with Atlantic executives going crazy, then returned to New York to cut a glorious *Do Right Woman*, enabling the company to release what became her breakthrough single.

Although this is "a song about a trapped victim," that's not the way she sings it, notes Williams. What "comes through more than anything is, confoundingly, the singer's strength and self-assurance . . . The power of her presence is awesome. I feel myself being given life." "Aretha isn't singing; she's practically praying, her every breath suffused with the spirit of what she's trying to convey, and no matter how secular the spirit, that's what it's all about," says Dave Marsh. "In the spaces between those breaths, there are those of us who would still swear you can hear the earth move a little bit . . ."[301] Matt Dobkin: "In the space of one three-minute song, Franklin graduated from singer to artist."[302]

I Can See for Miles (1967)—The Who
Decca 32206

Chart debut Oct. 14, 1967 (peak position #9); #1 in Canada, #10 in England; from the album *The Who Sell Out* (*DM-#40, PW, RS-#262, TC, ACC*)

"One of the best songs I've ever written," Pete Townshend would say (as quoted in his biography by Geoffrey Giuliano) of *I Can See for Miles*, the standout song from The Who's groundbreaking album *The Who Sell Out* and (remarkably enough) the group's only Top Ten U.S. single. "Quite a Wagnerian piece. I spent a lot of time

295. Williams, p. 111–12.
296. Ward, p. 387.
297. Shannon had been discovered by Aretha's then-husband Ted White in Detroit, and she'd been singing the tune at home for some time, accompanying herself on a Fender Rhodes. So, writes Matt Dobkin in his account of the album's creation (*I Never Loved a Man*, p. 120–23), in the studio "her sound was raw and earthy, but the vocal performance itself was polished." The other musicians' initial doubts about the song, based on an "awful" demo, disappeared when she launched into it.
298. Listening to the track again decades later, Wexler called Oldham the unsung "hero" of the track, for the way his Wurlitzer electric interfaces with Aretha's acoustic piano.

299. She saved her acoustic piano entrance for the second verse.
300. Wexler, *Rhythm and the Blues*, p. 210–13.
301. Marsh, p. 141.
302. Dobkin, p. 129.

working on the vocal harmonies and structuring it." The song was originally written in 1966 about jealousy, he explained, "but actually turned out to be about the immense power of aspiration. You often see what it is you want to reach, and know you can't get at it and say, 'I'm gonna try.'" Producer Kit Lambert decided to record it at Gold Star Studios in Los Angeles while the group was on tour, laying on multiple layers of Townshend's guitar, and Giuliano remarks that the site's "state of the art echo chamber greatly enhanced the track, drawing out [Roger] Daltrey's demanding vocals, and [Keith] Moon's drum-roll flourishes."[303] [304]

"The glory of the Who was its creation of a sound that was fundamentally physical—so loud it hurt, so big it was scary, as thick as it was sharp," writes Dave Marsh, ranking the song #40 in *The Heart of Rock & Soul*. "At best, the quartet performed like a single rough beast, grabbing its quarry by the throat and not stopping until blood ran." He calls *I Can See for Miles* the group's best of all: "thunderous Keith Moon drums, a Townshend guitar line that starts out like an earthquake and finishes like a razor. The record develops in surges of pure energy, drums and guitar crashing and slashing in a duel to the break, where they simply strip whatever rational sense the song makes to shreds, as if to say: If it doesn't hurt, it doesn't count."[305] [306]

"This is a song about jealousy and rage," declares Paul Williams in *Rock & Roll: The 100 Best Singles*. "The feelings it expresses are violent ones, and that violence is successfully captured and given voice in the music, slashing guitar chords and drums like windows shattering when attacked by fist or foot . . . There's an enormous smoldering power here that goes, I think, rather beyond nihilism." At times Williams hears a surface confidence that conceals "astonishing absence of hope." "Other times I hear this as an assertion of life, a visionary proclamation. 'I can see for miles.' A hymn to clarity and farsight."[307]

Stand By Your Man (1968)—Tammy Wynette (written by Billy Sherrill & Tammy Wynette)
Epic 10398

---

303. Giuliano, *Behind Blue Eyes*, p. 80.
304. Townshend told Dave Marsh (*Before I Get Old: The Story of The Who*, p. 273) that the demo for the song was so good, they deliberately held back on recording it as a single until they were certain Lambert was ready to do it full justice in the studio.
305. *Heart of Rock & Soul*, p. 33.
306. Marsh in his Who biography (p. 273–74): "Its ambition is virtually limitless, and everything it seeks is achieved." It's built around "drones and crescendos," creating an "ominous and hallucinatory" feeling—particularly in the ferocious, "chilling" opening punctuated by Townshend's powerful guitar figure and Moon's cymbal splashes: "I know you've deceived me . . ." "With the exception of *Like a Rolling Stone*, there is no other record in the world that starts so threateningly." The Gold Star echo chamber also gives Daltrey's voice a new depth.
307. Williams, p. 126–27.

Recorded August 26, 1968; chart debut Oct. 19, 1968 (3 weeks at #1 on C&W chart; #19 on pop chart); #1 for 3 weeks in England in 1975[308] [309] (*C&W-#2, NPR-100, HBN-#11, GHF, Juke-#21, DM, ACC, DMDB, SC*)

Stand By Your Man was never about a woman declaring total submission to a man; to its singer and co-writer Tammy Wynette it represented the romantic ideal that two partners in a marriage should do everything possible to make love work. A towering performance and production, the record established Wynette as one of the reigning queens of country music. Born Virginia Wynette Pugh on May 5, 1942, near Tupelo, Mississippi, she was raised by her grandparents after her musician father died when she was eight months old, moved to Birmingham as a teenager, married at seventeen and worked as a hairdresser and beautician. The couple divorced after three years and three children; to earn extra money, she began performing in clubs at night. Local TV appearances led to performing on Porter Wagoner's syndicated show, and in 1966 producer Billy Sherrill signed her to Epic Records. Her second single *Your Good Girl's Gonna Go Bad* became a major country hit in early 1967, and then *My Elusive Dreams* (a duet with David Houston) and *I Don't Wanna Play House* both shot to #1. Her mid-1968 country chart-topper *D-I-V-O-R-C-E* crossed over to the pop charts, setting the stage for her biggest triumph.

Billy Sherrill came up with the title *Stand By Your Man*, and Tammy poured her own feelings and experiences into the collaboration; the entire song was written during a twenty-minute break in a recording session. In her autobiography, Wynette said it was all about mutual emotional support: "Be willing to forgive him if he doesn't live up to your image of what he should be." "Jerry Kennedy's opening guitar figure sets a pregnant, yet intimate and conversational tone from the outset," writes Bill Friskics-Warren, ranking the song #11 in *Heartaches By the Number*. "The bruised, undulating notes he plays as the record begins conjure images of Tammy gulping hard before confessing to her sisters that, 'sometimes it's hard to be a woman,' the lump in her throat going absolutely nowhere. Then there's the pivotal phrase, 'If you love him, you'll forgive him,' which—judging by the catch in her voice and the way Pete Drake's steel [guitar] rains down tears with her—isn't so

---

308. Country records tended to fare poorly on the British charts in the 1960s (aside from a few artists such as Jim Reeves), and *Stand By Your Man* went nowhere in the U.K. in its original release. But six-and-a-half years later, its reissue became a stunning chart-topper. This led to successful British reissues of Wynette's previous U.S. hits *D-I-V-O-R-C-E* (reaching #12 in 1975), and *I Don't Wanna Play House*.
309. Following its remarkable U.K. reissue success, it also became a 1975 European smash, including #1 for 2 weeks in both Belgium and Holland.

much an injunction for her peers to follow as a statement of love's painful reality." It all builds to the final chorus: "amid a crescendo of voices, steel, and guitar, Tammy stretches out the penultimate line with palpable hurt, wailing, 'Keep giving all the love you can.' She isn't telling her long-suffering sisters to take whatever their men dish out, but rather encouraging them to give whatever love they can find it within themselves to give."[310]

Tammy knew all too well that her song's philosophy was no guarantee of a happy ending. At the time she recorded it, she was in her second marriage, which would end soon afterward. Her February 1969 marriage to fellow country superstar George Jones became legendary for its very public turbulence until their 1975 split, with a fourth divorce later to follow. She observed of this relationship in her autobiography: "There's no love in the world that can't be killed if you beat it to death long enough." Bill Malone: "Her clear, expressive, pleading voice tore at the emotions and pulled the listeners into her orbit of personal experience, making them feel that her songs of hurt and loneliness, which were somehow tempered by hope, mirrored their own and the singer's lives."[311] The record, her second Grammy winner, is reported to have sold two million copies, and was the biggest-selling single by a woman in country music history to that time. *Stand By Your Man* (which was further popularized in the 1970 Jack Nicholson film *Five Easy Pieces*) was declared the #21 biggest jukebox hit of all time in 1988 by the Amusement and Music Operators Association, and in 2003 proclaimed the #1 greatest song of country music by Country Music Television.[312]

Green River (1969)—Creedence Clearwater Revival
Fantasy 625
Chart debut Aug. 2, 1969 (#2 peak); #4 in Canada, #6 in Australia, #19 in U.K.;[313] from the album *Green River* (4 weeks at #1) (*PW, RHF, AHR, DM*)

In 1969 and 1970, Creedence Clearwater Revival had seven consecutive singles reach #4 or higher on the *Billboard* chart; every one of these—plus nearly all the B sides—were absolute gems, one of the most remarkable runs in rock history. *Green River*, a warm reminiscence of idyllic rural childhood days, stands proudly among them. It suggests that whenever any adult is too caught up in the complications of life and feeling that the "world is smoldering," he can always come back home—if only in his mind's eye—to the simpler pleasures of Green River.

"I always considered [the album] *Green River* a high-water mark in my musical life," said singer-songwriter-producer John Fogerty, "only because it felt so good. Here was the music closest to my musical center . . . *Green River* was where I lived from the sound of the record, the riffs, the setting which spills out onto the rest of the album . . . It's my most comfortable place." He called the track "a tip of the hat to the Sun Records sound," although not inspired by any particular song. John's brother Tom Fogerty said the song captured a part of the brothers' childhood, albeit in southern California rather than in Bayou country as some fans assumed. "It was exactly like the song describes it. There's one line, 'Up at Cody's Camp I spend my days.' Well, there was a place called Cody's Camp. That's where we used to stay. [The camp was in the small town of Winters about an hour's drive north of the Fogertys' home in El Cerrito.] There were cabins and we'd be there for two or three weeks every summer and swim in this really great creek. John, instead of calling it Putah Creek, called it Green River . . . Everything described in that song is real and actually happened."[314]

"His green river is alive with the noise of all the drowned souls it carries," writes Rob Sheffield, "the ghost cries of flatcar riders and crosstie walkers, Pharaohs and Israelites, husbands and gamblers." Fogerty "tapped into the deepest wellsprings of American music, sources of energy that refused to acknowledge the divisions that were tearing America apart during the years CCR was at its peak," declares Craig Werner. When Fogerty sings about Green River, "he was staking a claim to his corner of the mythic American soil where, if race doesn't go away, it at least doesn't keep us from hearing each other's voices."[315]

"If we define great poetry in terms of the strength and nature of its impact on the reader or listener . . . it follows as the day the night that John Fogerty/Creedence Clearwater Revival cannot be left off the list of 20th century masters of the art form," writes Paul Williams. "Listen . . . to the sound of the song in your mind . . . notice the extraordinary internal rhymes, onomatopoeia, notice the immediacy (simplicity/complexity) of the visual image before you as you listen, notice sounds, smell, touch of stone, air, water . . . Two verses of gloriously tangible images are instantly recast [in the third verse] as part of a story, and just in time (in the amazing economy of song

---

310. *Heartaches By the Number: Country Music's 500 Greatest Singles*, p. 8–9.

311. *Country Music, U.S.A.*, p. 310.

312. Among the song's other honors, it was cited as the #19 all-time country song by *Country America* magazine in 1992.

313. #5 in South Africa, #8 in Germany and Switzerland.

314. Hank Bordowitz, *Bad Moon Rising: The Unofficial History of Creedence Clearwater Revival*, p. 70–71. John Fogerty: "I learned how to swim there. There was a rope hanging from the tree." And as for the title: "You used to be able to go into a soda fountain, and they had bottles of flavored syrup. My flavor was called Green River," green and lime-flavored. (Werner, *Up Around the Bend: The Oral History*, p. 145–46.

315. *A Change Is Gonna Come: Music, Race, and the Soul of America*, p. 151.

structure, whole novels in the snap of a finger or blink of an eye) for the moral—'If you get lost, come on home to Green River.'"[316]

The Night They Drove Old Dixie Down (1969)—The Band (written by Robbie Robertson)

Capitol 2635

Uncharted B side of *Up On Cripple Creek* (chart debut Nov. 1, 1969); from the album *The Band* (reached #9) (*RHF, RS-#249, Time*)

A year after making rock history with their debut album *Music from Big Pink* including the classic *The Weight*, the Canadian-American assemblage known as The Band followed up with an album of equal quality; its centerpiece was the Civil War epic *The Night They Drove Old Dixie Down*. "Nothing I have read . . . has brought home the overwhelming human sense of history that this song does," declared critic Ralph Gleason. "The only thing I can relate to it at all is [Stephen Crane's] *The Red Badge of Courage*. It's a remarkable song, the rhythmic structure, [the vocal arrangement], make it seem impossible that this isn't some traditional material handed down from father to son straight from the winter of 1865 to today. It has that ring of truth and the whole aura of authenticity." Toronto-born (on July 5, 1944) Robbie Robertson wrote the song based on his fascination with the American South, and inspired by the work of Tennessee Williams. The piece took eight months to write (beginning in Woodstock, New York, and later completed in Hollywood), starting with the melody which he composed on piano, and then the much longer process of crafting the lyrics, including considerable library research. (According to its singer Levon Helm, he contributed to the lyrics, although Robertson gets sole copyright credit.) Looking at the war as an outsider allows a fresh perspective that deeply humanizes the song's Southern soldier and his profound sense of loss without implying any sympathy for the Southern cause.

Arkansas-born drummer Helm sings in the persona of Virgil Caine, a fictional Confederate ex-soldier who served on the Danville supply train until General George Stoneman's Union cavalry troops tore up the tracks.[317] The Richmond and Danville Road was the main supply route into Petersburg where Robert E. Lee's Army of Northern Virginia was holding a desperate defensive line to protect Richmond. The song vividly describes General Ulysses S. Grant's Union forces carrying out the final siege of Richmond from June 1864 to April 1865, leaving Lee's forces starving and beaten ("in the winter of '65, we were hungry—just barely alive"). When Virgil sings, "By May the tenth, Richmond had fell," he refers not to the actual fall of Richmond to Union forces (which had occurred five weeks earlier), but to the May 10 capture of former Confederate President Jefferson Davis, and President Andrew Johnson's announcement that day that armed resistance in the South had come to an end. Following the war, Virgil returns home to Tennessee; no longer able to make a living as a farmer, he's forced to hire himself out to chop wood and carry out various chores for others.

One line in the song that triggered much discussion occurs when Virgil recalls his brother being laid to rest in his grave, and declares sadly, "I swear by the mud below my feet / You can't raise a Caine back up when he's in defeat" (the double meaning of a man named Caine and the expression "raising cain"). Why would he swear by "mud" rather than by blood? Peter Viney and Art Dudley suggest that this word choice serves as the deliberate antithesis of the melodrama one would normally expect from the moment—after all, this tale is told by a weary man who accepts what has happened and is moving on, not by a man who's seeking vengeance—and also reflects the fact that Virgil is an earthy, simple man of the soil. It's also noteworthy that the line "they should never have taken the very best" suggests an antiwar sentiment, additionally appropriate given the background of Vietnam in 1969.

"It is hard for me to comprehend now any Northerner, raised in a very different war than Virgil Caine's, could listen to this song without finding himself changed," writes Greil Marcus. "You can't get out from under the singer's truth—not the whole truth, simply his truth—and the little autobiography closes the gap between us. The performance leaves behind a feeling that for all our oppositions, every American still shares this old event; because to this day, none of us has escaped its impact. What we share is an ability to respond to a story like this one."[318] Helm said that the song is not so much about the Civil War as it is about the way each American carries a version of that event within himself.

No one could have sung this song with the gritty integrity of Levon Helm, as his Caine struggles to make sense of a lost cause. Barney Hoskyns: "It was a vocal that drew from the great well of grief and defiance that still lingered on in the South after a hundred years, and to many young Americans it was simultaneously shocking and refreshing to hear."[319] As on *The Weight*, the close harmony singing of Levon Helm, Richard Manuel, and Rick Danko on the

316. *Rock & Roll: The 100 Best Singles*, p. 143–44.

317. Stoneman was in fact commander of the East Tennessee district, and led a Union raid across the Blue Ridge Mountains into North Carolina and southwest Virginia, including the destruction of miles of railroad tracks at the conclusion of the war; he would later serve as Governor of California. See website at http://theband.hiof.no/articles/dixie_viney.html

318. Greil Marcus, *Mystery Train: Images of America in Rock 'n' Roll Music*, p. 55–56.

319. Barney Hoskyns, *Across the Great Divide: The Band and America*, p. 175–77.

chorus lends the song an additional majesty. Garth Hudson contributes a harmonica-like Hohner melodica dubbed above his accordion-sounding Lowery organ behind the vocals, and the sound of a distant trumpet at the conclusion. Robertson is on acoustic guitar, Manuel on piano, Danko on bass, and Helm on drums. The number was recorded at a studio built in the pool house of an unoccupied Hollywood Hills home owned by, of all people, Sammy Davis, Jr. The powerful live versions on *Rock of Ages* and *The Last Waltz* add a horn section, and Helm's vocal on The Band's *Last Waltz* grand finale is especially impassioned. Joan Baez scored a Top Five 1971 single with her cover version (changing a few of the lyrics), but of course the original is definitive.

Fortunate Son (1969)—Creedence Clearwater Revival
Fantasy 634

Chart debut Nov. 1, 1969 (reached #4 in *Record World*, #6 in *Cash Box*, #14 in *Billboard*); #2 in Australia & Canada; from the album *Willy and the Poorboys* (#3 peak) (*RHF, RS-#99, ACC-#124, DM-#242, AHR, TC, DMDB*)

Fortunate Son was John Fogerty's cry of righteous fury at Richard Nixon, the Vietnam War, and all the children of privilege who were able to stay home while working-class kids were ground up by the military machine. At the time it was released, some 500,000 U.S. troops were stationed in Vietnam, and 34,000 had died there, exceeding total U.S. deaths during the Korean conflict. On November 15, 1969, as the record spread across the airwaves, the largest antiwar demonstration in U.S. history brought over 250,000 protestors to Washington, D.C. The song tapped into a well of deep generational anger. *Fortunate Son*, writes Craig Werner in his oral history of the band, "identifies the hypocrisy and violence underlying America's Fourth of July rhetoric as clearly as any political critique."[320]

Creedence Clearwater Revival's musical director, composer and lead singer Fogerty said he felt it was "a confrontation between me and Richard Nixon. The haves, the people who have it all . . . During the Vietnam war, these were the people who didn't have to go to war." With just the chord changes and the song title, "I went into the bedroom, sat on the edge of my bed with a yellow legal tablet and my felt-tipped pen. Out came the song. 'It ain't me, it ain't me, I ain't no fortunate son.' I was screaming inside, very intense, but not saying a word. Out it came, onto three sheets of legal paper." He told *Rolling Stone*: "It took about 20 minutes. It was like vroom—it just came right out."[321]

The band recorded the song and its cheerier flip side, *Down on the Corner*, at Wally Heider's studio in their hometown of San Francisco. A month after the session, Fogerty (also serving as producer) returned to the studio to do overdubs on the two songs. Because he first sang both background parts and the lead on *Down on the Corner*, by the time he got to *Fortunate Son* his voice was a bit raw. But that may have enhanced the power of the vocal, as its emotional, ravaged sound added to the fierce playing; drummer Doug Clifford sounds just as furious and inspired as Fogerty.

Rolling Stone named *Fortunate Son* the #8 single of the past twenty-five years in 1988. Dave Marsh remarks that Fogerty "rasps out the lyrics . . . in a voice filled with bile and uses his guitar as a weapon to run machine-gun stitches right through everybody who's ever abused a privilege."

Bridge Over Troubled Water (1971)—Aretha Franklin (written by Paul Simon)
Atlantic 2796

Recorded on Aug. 13, 1970; chart debut April 17, 1971 (#1 for 2 weeks on R&B chart; #6 on *Billboard* pop chart, #2 in *Cash Box*) (*DM*)

Aretha Franklin, daughter of Reverend C. L. Franklin, one of America's most famous Pentecostal preachers, "came to *Bridge Over Troubled Water* as if her historic mission was to restore the song's gospel roots," writes Dave Marsh. "She did the job audaciously," taking her time as the single runs over five-and-a-half minutes, "opening with about two minutes of meditative piano playing and undemonstrative call-and-response interchange with her backing singers, one of the most introspective interludes in the history of pop music." And when she finally reaches Paul Simon's lyrics, "they're damn near pulled apart by the surging release of tension."[322]

Of course it is Aretha herself on piano with Billy Preston on organ, Cornell Dupree on guitar, Chuck Rainey on electric bass, Ray Lucas on drums, the great tenor saxman King Curtis, and backing vocals by the Sweethearts of Soul and Cissy Houston. This won the Grammy for best R&B female vocal.

The Harder They Come (1973)—Jimmy Cliff
Single issued in England in July 1972 on Island 6139, and in U.S. in Feb. 1973 on Mango 7500

Featured on the 1973 motion picture soundtrack to *The Harder They Come* (originally released in late

---

320. Werner, *Up Around the Bend*, p. 100.
321. Bordowitz, *Bad Moon Rising*, p. 80–81. After performing *Fortunate Son* at an antiwar protest, and being congratulated by admirers backstage,

Fogerty told them, "Richard Nixon is a great inspiration." "The guy," he would later remark, "was obviously evil."
322. Marsh, *The Heart of Rock & Soul*, p. 364–65.

Feb. 1973;[323] chart debut March 22, 1975) (*RHF, World-#9, RS, TC, ACC*)

A key figure in the evolution of reggae from Jamaican folk music to a globally popular movement, Jimmy Cliff was born James Chambers in St. James, Jamaica, on April 1, 1948. He began performing in the Kingston ska scene at age fourteen in 1962, and recorded his first singles that year for the U.K. Island label and Leslie Kong, who would serve as his producer for the next nine years. Cliff enjoyed an international hit single at the end of 1969 with *Wonderful World, Beautiful People*; it was, along with Desmond Dekker's *Israelites* that same year, one of the earliest reggae hits in the United States. His antiwar song *Vietnam* also caused a stir (mainly in England) in 1970.

It was the 1973 film *The Harder They Come*, starring Cliff as a Jamaican country boy who comes to Kingston to make it as a singer but has to work with the city's vicious gangs, that not only made Cliff a top-level star but helped introduce reggae to a much wider American audience. The May 19, 1973, *Billboard* predicted that the film may "ignite a reggae fad," although it had been playing in scattered theaters for a few months with little impact. That began to change when, for the first time, it was given serious promotion, bringing the director to Boston in April for its local premiere and making him available for radio and print interviews. However, it didn't receive wide distribution in the U.S. until 1975, and that's when the film's (and the soundtrack's) following expanded beyond a devoted cult. The title song declares that even though "the oppressors are trying to keep me down," he forgives them, and will keep fighting for what he wants: "I'd rather be a free man in my grave / Than living as a puppet or a slave." Cliff has enjoyed a long subsequent career, although more with pop-oriented recordings and the 1986 movie comedy *Club Paradise* with Robin Williams; he scored a Top 20 hit with his 1993 remake of *I Can See Clearly Now*.

Midnight Train to Georgia (1973)—Gladys Knight & the Pips (written by Jim Weatherly)

Buddah 383

Chart debut Sept. 1, 1973 (#1 for 2 weeks pop, #1 for 4 weeks R&B); #10 in England (in 1976), #14 in Canada (*RIA-#29, R&B-#56, GHF-#69,*[324] *DM-#296, HBN, RS, TC, ACC, DMDB*)

When Gladys Knight & the Pips left the Motown-owned Soul label for Buddah in 1973, they were taking a calculated risk. The group not only had a seven-year

track record of hits with Motown, they were coming off one of their biggest smashes to date, *Neither One of Us*, in early 1973. But the family combo immediately made the move pay off as their first album for Buddah became their biggest seller ever, and produced perhaps their most memorable single of all, *Midnight Train to Georgia*.

The Jim Weatherly song had first been recorded by the composer, as *The Midnight Plane to Houston*. Cissy Houston (Whitney's mom) tackled it on her first solo album for Janus Records in 1971, after years as one of the top backing singers in the business for Aretha Franklin and others. She gave it a new title and modified the main chorus, with Weatherly's permission, and the single got some radio airplay, but with minimal promotion from Janus (a small indie label), Cissy's bid for solo stardom fell short.[325] Her misfortune became Knight's blessing. Dave Marsh writes that this tale of a husband who ends his quest for Hollywood stardom to return home to Georgia, with wife by his side, features "the best vocal performance of Gladys Knight's career." "'L.A.,' she begins, and then pauses while the orchestrated soul pumps on, 'proved too much for the man,' she continues. In that break in the action, you can feel the weariness and the inability to fathom new customs and regulations that might drive a man back to his homeland. . . . And when Knight again pauses, then draws a sharp breath, while singing the key line of the chorus—'I'd rather live in his world . . . than live without him in mine'—she makes you feel just how fateful such a choice can be." While listening to *Midnight Train*, "the thoughts of a million transplanted Southerners, black and white, turned to the places they—or their parents—had come from . . . What Knight, with aid from Weatherly, has done is capture beautifully what moved them to the effort."[326]

The conviction in Gladys' voice, writes Bill Friskics-Warren, is "that of a woman who, far from making a concession, knows what she wants and isn't afraid to make sacrifices in order to get and hang on to it. From the way she bites down on the line 'I got to go' as she rides out the final chorus, there's little chance she'll lose her nerve. Not as long as that choir of voices behind her (horns, strings, and the Pips) testifies to the possibilities—indeed, the freedom—inherent in commitment."[327]

Mother Russia (1974)—Renaissance

From the Sire album *Turn of the Cards* (chart debut Aug. 3, 1974)

323. The album was reviewed in the March 3, 1973, *Billboard*; that same week, Bob Marley & the Wailers' *Catch a Fire* was "bubbling under" the top 200 albums. The Cliff album itself spent three weeks "bubbling under" starting March 31, peaking at #215.

324. Selected for the Grammy Hall of Fame in its first year of eligibility.

325. Jeffery Bowman account in his Whitney Houston biography *Diva*. Weatherly himself offered a slightly different version when interviewed by *Songwriter* magazine (October 1975), saying that it was Cissy's producer Sonny Limbo who suggested the change of title, although Limbo may have been relaying Cissy's idea.

326. Marsh, *The Heart of Rock & Soul*, p. 210–11.

327. *Heartaches By the Number*, p. 135–36.

Aleksandr Solzhenitsyn, perhaps one of the greatest writers of the twentieth century and the recipient of the 1970 Nobel Prize for Literature, spent eight years (1945–1953) in prison and labor camps, and was twice exiled from his native Russia (1953–1956 and again in 1974), for his powerful criticisms of Stalinism and the Soviet Communist system. *Mother Russia* by the British symphonic-rock group Renaissance is a musically stunning tribute to the author and to all prisoners of conscience.

Renaissance was founded in 1969 by two former members of the Yardbirds (Keith Relf and Jim McCarty), Relf's sister and vocalist Jane Relf, and an ex-member of the Nashville Teens, pianist John Hawken. Its 1969 debut album was dominated by Hawken's piano and established the group's style fusing rock, folk, and classical music with Eastern themes. The group's second album (recorded in 1970 and released the following year) included two songs with lyrics by a friend of Jane Relf's, Cornish poetess Betty Thatcher, who was to become a key element in its evolution. Guitarist and songwriter Michael Dunford (another member of the Nashville Teens) had joined the group by this time. However, by the end of 1970, the original incarnation of Renaissance had split apart. Dunford and the group's new pianist, the brilliantly talented John Tout, began assembling (with the behind-the-scenes help of Keith Relf and Jim McCarty, even though both had left the group) a new Renaissance.

On New Year's Day 1971, Annie Haslam, a classically-trained soprano with a multi-octave voice, became its new vocalist. A year later, the first album with the reconstituted group, *Prologue*, was released with compositions by Michael Dunford and Betty Thatcher. (Bassist-singer Jon Camp and drummer Terry Sullivan were the other newcomers.) *Ashes Are Burning* in 1973 greatly expanded the audience for Renaissance; 1974's *Turn of the Cards* was its full breakthrough, earning the group a particularly intense following across the U.S. Eastern seaboard from Boston and New York to Washington, D.C. The group also had a fervent audience behind the Iron Curtain and in Israel, due in part to its strong Russian musical influence (not only in this song but a number of others).

Mother Russia represents the Renaissance sound in its full flowering. Dunford's melody is stunningly beautiful, slow and elegant; Betty Thatcher's lyrics express the theme of striving for freedom with her fine poetic touch; John Tout's piano virtuosity is dazzling, backed by a full orchestra; and Annie Haslam's vocal is crystalline in its purity. With its epic-length composition (the 9:18 length of this track was not at all unusual for them) radio airplay was a challenge outside of free-form FM stations, but in the song's meticulous construction and execution, Renaissance provided rich musical rewards.

Time Run Like a Freight Train (1975)—Eric Andersen

From the Arista album *Be True to You*, chart debut Apr. 19, 1975

An icon among lovers of introspective folk song-poetry, Eric Andersen was born in Pittsburgh on February 14, 1943, and served his apprenticeship in Greenwich Village.[328] Following his debut album *Today Is the Highway* for Vanguard in 1965, he guaranteed his reputation with the 1966 album *'Bout Changes 'n' Things* featuring such stunning songs as *Thirsty Boots* and *Violets of Dawn*. The next five years saw him fade from prominence including two lesser releases for Warner Brothers that mistakenly cultivated the rock audience, but this was only a prelude for his greatest album, 1972's *Blue River*. His followup was to be *Stages*, scheduled for release the following year, but, incredibly, Columbia Records lost the tapes (which were not recovered until over fifteen years later). The shattered performer left for Arista Records and re-recorded perhaps his finest creation of all, *Time Run Like a Freight Train*, as the centerpiece of *Be True to You*.

It began as a poem written by Andersen while looking out a hotel window on a rainy New York day. When Cary Raditz (a friend of Joni Mitchell's who was the inspiration for her song *Carey*) read the poem, he declared that Andersen had to put it to music. By dawn, recalled the composer, "it was written into a song, a personal spiritual anthem . . ."[329] It's a deeply reflective meditation on mortality and the ways in which tragedy, life experiences, and the nature of time and memory shape one's character; his grainy, expressive voice expresses the mingled emotions perfectly. The central image of the train taking one down the line of memory to see once again the pivotal experiences of a lifetime is poetic and moving.[330] The line "those who never asked to die and were too afraid to kill" of course refers to Vietnam. Its wordplay is supremely skillful—the lovers move "in green desire's light," "her mouth moves like a poem." "The poet who pawned his mystery in turn for some relief" depicts an artist relinquishing his greatest gift. During the early 1980s, Andersen moved to Norway, did a film score in Belgium, and an album partly recorded in Sweden. When the recovered *Stages* was finally released with the subtitle *The Lost Album* (including some new original material), it won the New York Music Award as Best Folk Album of 1991, and led to more new recordings. The original acoustic version of *Freight Train* is lovely, but the Arista

---

328. Tom Paxton (*The Last Thing on My Mind*) served as "my greatest teacher as a writer." (October–November 1992 *Dirty Linen*).

329. Liner notes to *Stages*.

330. Andersen would powerfully revisit the theme of looking back and searching for meaning, while also moving forward, in *Ghosts Upon the Road* (1989) and *Memory of the Future* (1999).

treatment that first reached the world, with a subdued string arrangement that quietly builds to the conclusion, conveys an emotional depth that's hard to top.

Luckenbach, Texas (Back to the Basics of Love) (1977)—Waylon Jennings (written by Bobby Emmons & Chips Moman)
RCA 10924
Recorded in Nashville's American Studios on Jan. 7, 1977; chart debut Apr. 16, 1977 (#1 for 6 weeks C&W, #25 pop); from the album *Ol' Waylon*[331] (*C&W-#110*)

The biggest country-chart hit of Waylon Jennings' career, *Luckenbach, Texas* is a warm, inviting celebration of down-home values and the eternal dream of getting away from the rat race to find happiness in the simple life. It's all an idyllic Texas state of mind, existing more in the realm of imagination than on terra firma, but as one relaxes and smiles upon hearing its soothing refrain, what a wonderful dream it is.

A native of Littlefield, Texas (born on June 15, 1937), Jennings spent a few years picking cotton before moving to Lubbock and getting a job at a radio station. There, he became a protégé of up-and-coming rock icon Buddy Holly, who taught him guitar licks, collaborated with him on songs, and produced Waylon's first record in 1958. Before anyone outside Lubbock knew his name, Jennings, while serving as temporary bass player for Buddy's combo, the Crickets, became an adjunct to tragic rock history as the man who gave up his place (to the Big Bopper) on the plane that took Holly to his death in February 1959. Waylon escaped from "footnote" status when he started hitting the country charts in 1965, and within a couple of years his sturdy baritone and rootsy honky-tonk style were making him a regular visitor to the C&W Top Ten. After winning creative control of his records in 1972, Jennings fully emerged as one of the heroes of the "outlaw" country movement along with Willie Nelson, remaining true to his musical heroes Hank Williams and Bob Wills while winning a legion of young rock fans for his strongly individualistic style. His black-and-white tooled-leather Fender Telecaster guitar was as central to his image as that rumbling voice.

Luckenbach, a tiny hill country hamlet located in south-central Texas near Fredericksburg, eighty miles west of Austin and north of San Antonio, had been established as a trading post in 1849, but was largely unknown to the world until a cast of colorful characters emerged in the early 1970s holding "hug-ins" and chili busts along with plenty of song picking. After Jerry Jeff Walker recorded his album *Viva Terlingua* in Luckenbach in 1973

to give the record a laid-back Texas atmosphere, the word really went out. Bobby Emmons and Chips Moman were inspired to write a musical tribute to the sleepy little town (which they had never visited), with Moman as producer.[332] No one could have been more ideally suited to sing it than Texas good ol' boy Waylon Jennings.[333] Pal Willie Nelson, by Jennings' account, "stumbled into" the studio while they were cutting the song, and he suggested that Willie sing lead on the final chorus. That impromptu contribution, remarked Waylon, was "inspirational."[334] He remarked in his autobiography written with Lenny Kaye: "It was making our own myth, only in a way that touched people who were themselves caught keeping up with the Joneses, whether drug-induced or materially possessed."[335] James C. Cobb sees it as a warmly romanticized narrative set against the background of the economic transformation of the South, and the concern that modern economic progress was being achieved at the cost of precious personal values.[336] Mark Coleman called it a "heart-shattering" song.[337]

(Other personnel: steel guitarist Ralph Mooney; guitarists Gordon Payne, Rance Wasson, & Reggie Young; bass guitarist Sherman Hayes; pianist Clifford Robertson; drummer Richie Albright; backing vocalist Carter Robertson)

Mainstreet (1977)—Bob Seger
Capitol 4422
Chart debut Apr. 23, 1977 (#24 in *Billboard*, #19 in *Cash Box*); from the album *Night Moves*

Heeding the aphorism "write what you know," raspy-voiced rocker Bob Seger made his breakthrough album *Night Moves* a collection of songs based on his years growing up in Ann Arbor, Michigan, just west of Detroit. The title song provided Seger's first Top Ten hit, and equally affecting is the followup single *Mainstreet*. It's an atmospheric rock ballad recalling his teenage nights of infatuation with a stripper who worked at a joint on Ann Street in Ann Arbor. As he related to Timothy White, the club was on the black side of town, and featured "this great band called Washboard Willie . . . It was a hard period for me, when my family had no money [his father had abandoned the family when Bob was ten, leaving

---

331. The album was #1 on the country chart for 13 weeks.

332. Moman had produced Elvis Presley's chart-topping *Suspicious Minds*; Jennings scored a hit with his cover version.

333. Oddly enough, according to Jennings he "never liked" the song, although "I'm glad I recorded it—it said some great things—but I never liked the 'movement' of it. The way you sing it, it just kind of lays there." (August 31, 1999, *Country Weekly* interview.) Fortunately, he was in a distinct minority with that view.

334. *Billboard Book of Number One Country Hits*, p. 195.

335. *Waylon: An Autobiography*, p. 256.

336. *You Wrote My Life: Lyrical Themes in Country Music*, p. 63–64, 75.

337. *The New Rolling Stone Album Guide* (2004), p. 428.

them virtually destitute], and as a young kid, on nights when I couldn't get WLAC on my radio, I'd walk over just to watch the dancers they'd have in the window of the club."[338]

His portrait of frustrated teen desire is rich with detail; we can picture her body swaying and the seedy crowd to which she performed, and feel that smoky beat. The interplay of guitar and organ is especially evocative, creating a mood of warm nostalgia and the power of memory to take one back in time and mentally relive those small but priceless moments. This album, noted Ben Edmonds of *Rolling Stone*, summed up Seger's musical strengths: "clarity, endurance, and heart." Half of the album, including this track (with Pete Carr on lead guitar),[339] was recorded at Muscle Shoals Sound Studios in Alabama, and that iconic studio's atmosphere can be felt here.

Album Personnel: Drew Abbott on guitar, background vocals; Peter Carr, Jimmy Johnson, Joe Miquelon on guitar; Alto Reed on alto, tenor & baritone saxophones, flute; Jerry Luck on accordion; Barry Beckett on piano, organ, ARP synthesizer, Clavinet, melodica; Robyn Robbins, Doug Riley on piano, organ; Chris Campbell on bass, background vocals; David Hood on bass; Charlie Allen Martin on drums, percussion, background vocals; Roger Hawkins on drums, percussion; Sharon Dee Williams, Rhonda Silver, Laurel Ward on background vocals.

Sorrow, Tears and Blood (1977)—Fela Kuti

From the MCA album *Opposite People/Sorrow, Tears and Blood*

As Nigerian music and pop-cultural icon Fela Kuti developed and refined the new sound of Afrobeat during the early 1970s, it soon (writes biographer Tejumola Olaniyan) "unequivocally captured the spirit of the age in all its mind-numbing contradictions. It remained the quintessential music of botched decolonization [with rampant government corruption and indifference to suffering in the aftermath of the country's 1967–1970 civil war] and ambiguous modernity."[340] Fela himself was at all times a walking contradiction: an unabashed playboy and womanizer who was at the same time fearless in confronting a belligerent Nigerian government. The symbol of the latter was a brutal 1977 government assault on his compound (which he had boldly expanded into what he intended to be an independent state). He wrote *Sorrow, Tears and Blood* as a tribute to those killed or injured in the assault. He also attacks political apathy: "My people we fear too much . . . we fear the things we don't even

see . . . We fear fighting for freedom, we fear fighting for justice . . . We always find a reason for fear." As per Fela's classic approach, the message is wrapped up in a highly danceable musical package, with blasting horns and pulsating rhythm. The government confiscated the tapes of this and other allegedly "seditious" songs, but Fela won a court order and released it on his own label.

"Star Wars" (Main Title) (1977)—John Williams & London Symphony Orchestra[341]

20th Century 2345

Chart debut July 9, 1977 (reached #10); album spent 3 weeks at #2 (*AFI-#1, Trad-#45, NPR-300, GHF*)

Declared the greatest motion picture score in history by the American Film Institute, John Williams' mighty *Star Wars* soundtrack almost single-handedly revived the venerable art of orchestral Hollywood music on the pop charts.[342] The stirring main theme became the first such instrumental soundtrack theme to become a Top Ten single since Ferrante and Teicher's string of successes in the 1960s, and the overall soundtrack was the biggest nonvocal score on the charts since *Doctor Zhivago* in 1966. Of course, its commercial success was enhanced by the record-shattering box office of the George Lucas film: The $461 million earned by *Star Wars*, including reissues, is equal to nearly $1.4 billion adjusted for inflation, ranking it #2 for all time behind only *Gone With The Wind*.[343] But Williams' thrilling musical creation richly earned its rewards.

The most honored film composer of the modern era, John Williams was born on February 8, 1932, in Long Island, New York. He began composing for TV in the late 1950s and for films in 1960; *Valley of the Dolls* (1967) placed him firmly into the big time. An Oscar winner in 1971 for his orchestration for *Fiddler on the Roof*, he began the most remarkable of all director-composer associations with Steven Spielberg for the latter's feature-film debut *The Sugarland Express* (1974), and

---

338. *Capitol Records Fiftieth Anniversary, 1942–1992*, p. 154. The young Seger would listen at night to WLAC—a 50,000-watt Nashville station—on his cheap transistor, soaking in the sounds of James Brown and other R&B favorites.

339. November 27, 1976, *Melody Maker*.

340. *Arrest the Music! Fela and His Rebel Art and Politics*, p. 57–58.

341. The music for the original three *Star Wars* films was recorded in London because portions of the movies were shot there, and Lucas did some of his post-production work there. Williams had previously done *Fiddler on the Roof* in London. It was Lionel Newman, musical director of Twentieth Century Fox, who suggested that Williams (as discussed in his interview with Craig Byrd) use the London Symphony Orchestra instead of freelance musicians as originally planned. The famed orchestra had played a symphony of Williams' under André Previn's direction a few years earlier, so he knew its principals well.

342. While the commercial success of Williams' soundtracks stands alone, Mervyn Cooke points out (*A History of Film Music*, p. 456) that other composers carried on the tradition of orchestral scores in the 1970s and 1980s, such as Elmer Bernstein and Jerry Goldsmith. Cooke remarked that Williams' *Star Wars* scores "imbued the films with a spirit of heroism in the face of threatened evil and humanized what had formerly been a genre marked by the calculated strangeness of electronics and atonality."

343. According to Box Office Mojo. Their closest inflation-adjusted competitors, both just over $1.1 billion, are *The Sound of Music* and the Williams-scored *E.T.: The Extra Terrestrial*.

a year later when his deliciously foreboding music for *Jaws* won the Oscar for original score. From that time on, just about every Spielberg film was taken to new levels by Williams' scores, including *Close Encounters of the Third Kind* (1977, its theme giving Williams a second Top 20 single), *Raiders of the Lost Ark* (1981) and its sequels, *E.T.* (1982, Oscar winner), *Jurassic Park* and his deeply moving Oscar-winning music for *Schindler's List* (both 1993), and *War Horse* (2011).[344] But his talent for crafting the perfect accompaniments to soaring adventure/fantasy epics has also extended to the films of other directors, including *Superman* (1978), the first three Harry Potter films, and above all Lucas' world-conquering series of films tracing a tale that began "a long time ago in a galaxy far, far away."[345]

Appropriately, it was Spielberg who recommended Williams to his good friend Lucas, who was then trying to find a composer for his picture. As Williams explained in an interview with Craig Byrd,[346] he didn't read the script, as per his usual practice. "I remember seeing the [rough cut of] the film and reacting to its atmospheres and energies and rhythms. That for me is the best way to pick up a film—from the visual image itself and without any preconceptions that might have been put there by the script." The film's opening "was visually so stunning" that it demanded music that "had to kind of smack you right in the eye and do something very strong." Considering its overall theme of a hero's journey, "I tried to construct something that . . . would have this idealistic, uplifting but military flare to it." The theme was centered in the brass instruments, and set in "the most brilliant register of the trumpets, horns and trombones so that we'd have a blazingly brilliant fanfare at the opening of the piece." That was followed by a contrasting second theme "that was lyrical and romantic and adventurous also." While the film was an outer-space saga, Williams followed Lucas' suggestion that the music be "emotionally familiar," timeless in quality, rooted in the nineteenth century operatic idiom and in "western cultural sensibilities." And timeless, in fact, the *Star Wars* score has proven to be.[347]

London Calling (1980)—The Clash
British chart debut Dec. 15, 1979 (reached #11)

From the Epic album *London Calling* (U.S. debut Feb. 9, 1980, #27 peak) (*GHF-#133, RHF, RS-#15, ACC-#34, DM-#173, 1001, TC, VIL, DMDB, DET*)

While their early punk-rock rivals the Sex Pistols crashed and burned after an explosive start, The Clash proved to have both more musical substance and a few years of additional staying power. *London Calling* is their anthem. The group was formed in 1975 in London by John "Joe Strummer" Mellor on vocals and Mick Jones on guitar, with Paul Simonon (who joined in 1976) on bass, and Nicky "Topper" Headon on drums. The relationship between Strummer and Jones, writes the band's biographer Pat Gilbert, "was the volatile chemical reaction that powered The Clash." Even amidst the tension with occasional fisticuffs, there was a deep bond between them. Both craved rock stardom from an early age, but in quite different ways; Strummer was a "middle-class hippy poet with a message for the world," choosing to live like a hobo even after stardom arrived, with Jones "the working-class guitar hero looking for a glamorous alternative to a dead-end life."[348] The Pistols were already winning a local reputation while The Clash were still getting their act together in 1976, and they couldn't have been more different in approach, with the Pistols' hatred for mainstream pop music, self-obsession, negativity, and penchant for violence contrasting with The Clash's fondness for pop (albeit in a hard-crunching rock context) and serious determination to change society. While the Pistols struck first with two hit singles by January 1977, The Clash made just as strong an initial impression in April 1977 with their debut album and its leadoff single *White Riot*. Just as the Pistols were unable to crack the American market, The Clash had to wait until early 1979 to even have an album released in the U.S. However, unlike their rivals, Strummer, Jones & Co. proceeded to hit it big in America, ultimately scoring five gold albums and a handful of hit singles.

London Calling began in mid-1979 with a "distinctive, strident" Jones guitar riff that was then developed by the group, with the two leaders going back and forth and guiding their bandmates, the lyrics revised as they went along. The first two albums had been U.K. hits, but they were still heavily in debt to CBS (which released the LPs on the Epic subsidiary), and success abroad remained elusive. Guy Stevens was enlisted to produce the third album, and the "manic intensity" that he brought was perfectly matched to the material.[349] Gilbert; "Guy's passion had the desired effect. He created an electric,

---

344. The composer's forty-seven Oscar nominations through 2011 place him second only to Walt Disney's fifty-nine.

345. Williams' menacing Darth Vader/Imperial March theme for *The Empire Strikes Back* (1980) places a close second to the original film's main theme in the franchise's musical pantheon.

346. January–February 1997 *Film Score Monthly*, interview reprinted in the Julie Hubbert–edited book *Celluloid Symphonies* (p. 414–22).

347. Among Williams' other distinctions, he succeeded Arthur Fiedler as conductor of the Boston Pops Orchestra from 1980–1993.

348. Gilbert, *Passion is a Fashion: The Real Story of The Clash*, p. 28–29.

349. Stevens had worked with Procol Harum and The Who among others, and did prison time on a drug charge.

unpredictable, exciting atmosphere that resulted in edgy, spirited performances."[350] Seeking to give fans the biggest bang for the buck, *London Calling* was released as a bargain-priced double album, and it became their worldwide breakthrough. *Rolling Stone* called the album and its title track "an SOS from the heart of darkness."[351] Set against the background of a Britain mired in soaring unemployment and racial conflict, the song is crackling with urgency as Strummer howls about real-life disasters (the 1979 Three Mile Island accident) and feverish fears of what might follow. Even while sounding as if the band "has looked the future in the face without flinching and understood that humanity is finished,"[352] it couples that feeling with humor and desperate determination to rage against the machine.

The Rose (1980)—Bette Midler (written by Amanda McBroom)
Atlantic 3656
Chart debut March 22, 1980 (reached #1 in *Cash Box* & *Record World*, #3 in *Billboard*); from the soundtrack album of *The Rose* (chart debut Dec. 22, 1979, peak #12) (*AFI-#83*)

This gorgeous, touching ballad served as the title song to a movie that took the multi-dimensional career of Bette Midler into a new direction. Born on December 1, 1945, in Patterson, New Jersey, and raised in Hawaii, Midler moved to New York in the 1960s, got a role in the Broadway musical *Fiddler on the Roof*, and by the start of the 1970s her musical/comedy nightclub act (developed over four years through a partnership with Barry Manilow) was attracting a growing audience. Bette's 1972 debut album for Atlantic, *The Divine Miss M*, became a surprise smash featuring her Top Ten revival of the Andrews Sisters' song *Boogie Woogie Bugle Boy*.[353] The movie *The Rose*, starring Midler as a fictionalized, self-destructive rock star based on Janis Joplin, elevated the charismatic performer to new heights with her Oscar-nominated performance.

Amanda McBroom, born August 9, 1946, in California, began as a TV actress with 1970s appearances in several *Hawaii Five-0* episodes as well as *Charlie's Angels* and *Lou Grant* among others, and had not yet begun a new career as a singer and songwriter when she was driving on the highway one afternoon and heard a song on the radio, *Magdalena*, written by Danny O'Keefe and sung by Leo Sayer. She was especially struck by one line:

"Your love is like a razor, my heart is just a scar." That got her thinking, what did she think love is? "Suddenly, it was as if someone had opened a window in the top of my head," she recalled. "Words came pouring in. I had to keep reciting them to myself as I drove faster and faster towards home, so I wouldn't forget them." Back home with her husband, she raced to the piano and completed *The Rose* in ten minutes. About a year later, a songwriter friend told her that the Bette Midler movie was in production, they needed a title song (the film's working title at that point was "The Pearl," Joplin's nickname, until Janis' estate said no), and suggested that she submit this one.[354] She did, but the producers hated it, because it wasn't rock & roll. But then Paul Rothchild, the music supervisor on the film and formerly Joplin's producer, asked them to reconsider, and mailed the tape to Midler. She loved the song, and the rest was history. McBroom recorded the widely-praised album *Growing Up in Hollywood Town* in 1980, and went on to a solid career as a cabaret singer and songwriter with several more albums.

Always at her best on sentimental ballads (such as her subsequent smashes *Wind Beneath My Wings* and *From a Distance*), Midler brought depth to the beautifully-crafted, heart-tugging theme song, sung by a character whose relationships have brought almost nothing but sorrow but is determined not to give up. *The Rose* earned McBroom the Golden Globe as best song from a motion picture, and Midler won the Grammy for best female pop vocal performance.

America (1981)—Neil Diamond
Capitol 4994
Chart debut Apr. 25, 1981 (#8 peak); from the soundtrack to *The Jazz Singer* (chart debut Nov. 29, 1980, #3 peak)

One can hardly imagine a more misbegotten notion than selecting, as the vehicle for the first movie starring role for musical non-actor Neil Diamond, a modernized remake of the 1928 Al Jolson blackface epic *The Jazz Singer*. And indeed, the film was rather embarrassing, making Diamond's acting career a one-shot deal.[355] However, he wrote a killer soundtrack that became the biggest smash album of his career, selling over five million copies (spending nearly five months in the Top Ten), and producing three Top Ten singles. The third, and best, was *America*, his genuinely stirring ode to the courageous

350. *Passion is a Fashion*, p. 234–39.
351. *Rolling Stone 500 Greatest Songs*, p. 26.
352. Marsh, *The Heart of Rock & Soul*, p. 120.
353. Biographical information from *Bette: An Intimate Biography of Bette Midler*, by George Mair.

354. By Mair's account (p. 132–38), the film project (which had been bouncing around Hollywood for a few years) had been renamed *The Rose* by 1977; filming began in April 1978.
355. As detailed by Diamond biographers Alan Grossman, Bill Truman, & Roy Yamanaka, the *Jazz Singer* project had been in discussions since 1977, and it was a troubled production with mid-filming change in directors and leading lady. But none of this affected the music.

immigrants (like his movie "father," Laurence Olivier as a Russian Jew) who helped make the country great. The film's concert finale, climaxing with *America*, was shot at the Pantages Theater in Hollywood. Diamond said that among all his hits, this one came the most quickly, and it's the song of which he's most proud, "because so many people are moved by it and feel an association with it."[356]

When American hostages were freed by Iran in January 1981, the song was used as a lead-in to news reports of the happy occasion. Diamond also performed it in front of the Statue of Liberty on the landmark's 100th anniversary, and at a Vietnam veterans "welcome home" concert. *Time* magazine called it an "uptempo celebration of the immigrant glories of American life." In 1984, presidential candidate Michael Dukakis achieved the high point of his campaign when he entered the Democratic convention to make his acceptance speech accompanied by the pounding, surging strains of Diamond's recording, generating a wave of excitement that his candidacy could never hope to match. "On the boats and on the planes, they're coming to America / Never looking back again, they're coming to America . . ."

(Produced by Bob Gaudio, arranged by Alan Lindgren. Richard Bennett & Doug Rhone on guitars, Tom Hensley & Lindgren on keyboards, Reinie Press on bass, Dennis St. John on drums, Vince Charles on percussion; backing vocals, Donny Gerard, Linda Press, Marilyn O'Brien, H.L. Voeker, Oren Waters, Luther Waters)

Shoot Out the Lights (1982)—Richard Thompson
From the Richard & Linda Thompson album (on Hannibal label) *Shoot Out the Lights* (released in April/ May 1982) (*VIL*)

Dark, intense, and compelling, the attributes of *Shoot Out the Lights* coincide with the attributes of Richard Thompson throughout his long career. Born on April 3, 1949, in London, he co-founded and recorded five albums with the British folk-rock group Fairport Convention as lead guitarist and songwriter (1968–1970), issued his debut solo album in 1972, then married and began working as a duo with Linda Thompson. *Lights* was the last of the Thompsons' several albums together (although the title song is a solo showcase). Their last two albums for Chrysalis had sold poorly, and they were at a career crossroads.

The road to the completed album was a tumultuous adventure. In autumn 1980, British pop star Gerry Rafferty (*Baker Street*), a Thompson admirer sympathetic to the artist's struggles with record company politics and trying to break through as a solo recording artist, offered his services as a producer. He and his co-producer Hugh

Murphy would underwrite the cost of a Richard & Linda album, then find the highest record-label bidder for an LP that would have behind it the clout of a currently hot performer. The album (more glossy and pop-oriented than the usual Thompson style) was recorded that September and October, amidst rising tensions, but it would never see the light of day. According to biographer Patrick Humphries, "they made the mistake of shopping it round to everyone at once," and everyone turned it down, even Rafferty's own label, United Artists.[357]

So Thompson went back to doing what he did best: recording live with an absolute minimum of overdubbing, no gimmicks. It was the exact same songs, but with a totally different approach, with Joe Boyd as producer. "Thompson felt that Rafferty had softened the sound of his songs and diluted the essence of his work, grafting on unnecessary sweetness where wormwood was required." Boyd got an agreement with Hannibal Records for a low-budget album, and they decided to cut it in four days on eight-track in late 1981, with total production (including mixing) taking a few weeks. By that time Linda was pregnant with the couple's third child, so Richard took on a larger share of vocals.

The LP has been described as "a harrowing portrait of a marriage gone bad," although this has been somewhat exaggerated; as Humphries points out, the same songs had been recorded in fall 1980, well before any marital problems had arisen. It wasn't until the album came out and they took it on the road that it became clear the marriage was in tatters.[358] They divorced not long after its release, and Richard devoted his next couple of albums to sorting out the psychological wreckage. The sense of raw immediacy in the Boyd-produced sessions is essential to the impact of the title track. It was actually written as his response to Russia's 1979 invasion of Afghanistan. As a follower of Islam, he supported the Muslim government that was overthrown by Brezhnev's armies. But the song clearly can be seen as having broader and deeper implications.[359] A tale of a killer so taut with coiled tension that it seems at the breaking point, it also features his most celebrated guitar solo (containing deliberate echoes of Link Wray's similarly menacing *Rumble*), setting off sparks with its anguished power. Hayden Childs: "This song is a sniper's bullet. It is the lash on a whip. It is sudden fury."[360]

Shoot Out the Lights was voted the #2 best album of 1982 in the *Village Voice* critics' poll, was selected as

356. Interview feature by David Wild, March 24, 1988, *Rolling Stone*.

357. *Richard Thompson: The Biography*. Humphries remarks that the Rafferty-produced version of the album came out as a bootleg, and wasn't that bad at all, although the official album packs more of a punch.

358. Richard told Humphries: "Whether it was remarkably prophetic songwriting or what, I don't know, or perhaps it's just a bunch of songs that I write anyway and maybe the songs fitted the interpretation."

359. *Richard Thompson: The Biography*, p. 202–5.

360. Childs, *Shoot Out the Lights*, p. 65.

one of the 500 all-time greatest albums in a 1998 Virgin poll of critics and fans, and similarly honored in a 2003 *Rolling Stone* poll of critics and music professionals. John DeVault in 1996 called it "one of the unquestionably great releases of the last 20 years, and the record on which Thompson forges a blazing union of his growing mastery of the old folk forms, his own brilliant musicality (both instrumental and compositional), and an impressive deepening of his artistic vision."[361]

Little Red Corvette (1983)—Prince
Warner 29746
Chart debut Feb. 26, 1983 (#6 on pop chart, #15 R&B, #17 Album Rock); #3 in Australia, #4 in Canada (*RHF, DM-#45, R&B-#105, RS-#109, ACC-#122, AHR, TC, DMDB, VIL*)

The breakthrough hit from Prince's fifth album and the first song recorded at the new 24-track studio built in the basement of his Minneapolis home, *Little Red Corvette* expanded his usual one-man band by adding keyboardist Lisa Coleman and Dez Dickerson on chorus vocals and Dickerson's guitar solo.[362] He wrote the lyrics in the back seat of Coleman's bright pink Ford Edsel. *Rolling Stone*, ranking it the #17 best single of the past twenty-five years in 1988, notes that Prince "concocted perhaps his tightest metaphor, getting double play out of clever horse and Trojan imagery to craft an ode to a speedy, gas-guzzling 'love machine.' The sexual motif is reinforced by the song's rhythmic structure, which builds from a mellow, pulsing synthesizer opening, then chugs into a lower-driven sing-along chorus."[363]

Timothy White—recalling that using the car as a sexual symbol dates back at least to Robert Johnson's 1936 debut *Terraplane Blues*—writes: "This foggy-windows rock raver pared the Robert Johnson personification of woman as hot car down to a sleek, hair-curling homily to internal combustion." Prince offered a guarantee: "I'm gonna try to tame your little red love machine." "As a graph of sexual excitement," declares Dave Marsh, "*Little Red Corvette* can't be beaten."[364]

Time After Time (1984)—Cyndi Lauper (written by Cyndi Lauper & Rob Hyman)
Portrait 04432
Chart debut Apr. 14, 1984 (spent 2 weeks at #1); #1 (3 weeks) in Canada, #3 in England, #6 in Germany;[365]

from the album *She's So Unusual* (chart debut Dec. 24, 1983, #4 peak, sold 6 million copies) (*GR, DM*)

One of the early queens of MTV, Cyndi Lauper ensured that her bouncy debut hit *Girls Just Want to Have Fun* didn't typecast her as a novelty act with the gorgeous followup ballad *Time After Time*. Born in Queens on June 20, 1953, and raised until age five in Brooklyn (with that accent, where else?), Cyndi dropped out of high school to sing in local bands, and became half of the duo Blue Angel that built a New York following; they released an unsuccessful album in 1980, and she filed for bankruptcy. After returning to the club circuit, she landed a contract with Portrait, and "overnight stardom" (including the Grammy for best New Artist despite her previous LP) ensued. The zany, playful personality she projected for MTV helped, but she backed it up with a strong collection of songs.

Time After Time, which Cyndi wrote with keyboardist Rob Hyman, was the last song added to *She's So Unusual*.[366] She told *Rolling Stone* (which ranked it the #66 greatest pop song in 2000) that the lyrics are largely autobiographical; her boyfriend and manager Dave Wolff had given her a loudly-ticking clock from his mother's house, and when she'd lie in bed "I'd hear the clock tick, and think of him."[367] It's an enormously touching, reflective ballad that's suffused with quiet longing. Among the listeners moved by it was jazz trumpet legend Miles Davis, who recorded a cover version. Dave Marsh notes that atop these virtues, "it's the gently desperate singing that clinches the deal."[368]

I Feel for You (1984)—Chaka Khan (written by Prince)
Warner 29195
Chart debut Sept. 8, 1984 (#1 for 3 weeks on both R&B and dance/disco charts, #3 pop); #1 (3 weeks) in England [369] [370] (*R&B-#169, DM-#335, 1001, VIL*)

"Talk about your supersessions," remarks Dave Marsh. *I Feel for You* was written by the best new black writer of the Eighties, produced by the guy who taught the Bee Gees how to boogie [Arif Mardin], rap assistance by Melle Mel, the proudest voice in Grandmaster Flash and the Furious Five, and harmonica solo by no less than Stevie Wonder."[371] And topped off by the mighty voice

---

361. July 5, 1996 *Washington City Paper*, p. 34.
362. Ronin Ro, *Prince: Inside the Music and the Masks*, p. 63. The husband-wife engineering team of David Leonard and Peggy McCreary helped him record and mix the songs.
363. September 8, 1988, *Rolling Stone*, p. 90.
364. Marsh, *The Heart of Rock & Soul*, p. 35–36.
365. #3 in Belgium, #5 in Austria & Holland, #9 in France.

366. Her label initially wanted this to be the album's leadoff single, but she felt *Girls* would provide listeners with a better introduction to her style. *Time* was "not your typical commercial song," and its chart-topping success came as a surprise (February 16, 1985, *Billboard*, p. 6).
367. December 7, 2000, *Rolling Stone*, p. 96.
368. Marsh, *The Heart of Rock & Soul*, p. 338.
369. Chaka's appeal in Britain is exemplified by the fact that her final hit with Rufus, *Ain't Nobody*, hit the Top Ten there twice five years apart, and her solo debut *I'm Every Woman* was a U.K. smash in both 1978 and 1989.
370. *I Feel* was also #1 in Canada & Ireland, #4 Germany, #6 Switzerland.
371. Marsh, *The Heart of Rock & Soul*, p. 233. Stevie's harmonica part was in part a sample from his 1963 chart-topper *Fingertips*, along with

of Chaka Khan, all the ingredients were in place for a sizzling R&B classic.

One of the most fervently soulful singers to emerge in the 1970s, the charismatic, voluptuous beauty was born Yvette Marie Stevens on March 23, 1953, in Great Lakes, Illinois, and grew up on the South Side of Chicago. She took her African name (in one dialect, Chaka means "fire" or "heat") while working in the Black Panthers' breakfast program in Chicago. After singing with local groups from age fourteen onward, Chaka hit it big as lead singer of the interracial band Rufus, kicking off a string of hits in 1974 with Stevie Wonder's *Tell Me Something Good*, and went solo in 1978. Blessed with a soaring, powerhouse voice, she has shown the versatility to convincingly perform high-powered dance/R&B, gorgeous ballads, and complex, demanding jazz pieces. Her busy schedule of collaborative work has included backing vocals for Stephen Bishop (1976 hit *Save It for a Rainy Day*), Ry Cooder's 1979 album *Bop Till You Drop*, and Steve Winwood's #1 smash *Higher Love* (1986).

Prince included *I Feel for You* on his second album in 1979;[372] it was reworked here, with the ear-grabbing addition of Melle Mel's raps of her distinctive name ("Chaka Khan, Chaka Khan, let me love you, Chaka Khan . . ."). The rap was added to the track by Mardin without her knowledge, and her first reaction was total embarrassment: "I said, 'Oh my God!' and I turned to Arif and asked him how he could do that to me! [Now] I just have fun with it when we perform."[373] It won the Grammy for best female R&B vocal. Mardin later told *Performing Songwriter*; "I look at that as one of the songs I'd like to take with me to a desert island."

Paper In Fire (1987)—John Mellencamp
Mercury 888763
Chart debut Aug. 15, 1987 (#9 pop, #1 for 5 weeks Album Rock); from the album *The Lonesome Jubilee* (peak position #6)

During the mid-to-late 1980s John Mellencamp had one of the three or four greatest rock bands in the business, and it was operating at full throttle on *Paper In Fire*. Razor-sharp guitars, powerful percussion, and—in keeping with his folk/heartland sensibilities during this period—fiddle, banjo, steel guitar, hammered dulcimer, autoharp, and mandolin, provided a unique sound. In this

tale of chasing a dream against much resistance, Lisa Germano's fiddle is especially crucial, driving the band forward, helping to generate a tremendous momentum on the chorus. The minute he heard Germano and acoustic guitarist John Cascella playing together in rehearsals for the song, Mellencamp told *Billboard*, "I knew that was a sound people hadn't heard before—or at least not with the parts we had them playing. The song came together in a few hours—"a sign of magic in the making," suggested biographer Heather Johnson.[374] The exciting, grittily realistic video was shot in a poor black neighborhood in Savannah, Georgia, with a number of longtime residents participating. According to Mellencamp, *Paper In Fire* is his tribute to his Uncle Joe, who had died the previous year, "and the family's ingrained anger." His uncle "wasted 53 years, and he only left himself another three to be a complete human being. I don't want that to be my story."

On *The Lonesome Jubilee*, Mellencamp told author Timothy White, "I want to create songs that include a lot of ordinary people, that raise their self-esteem." The album constituted his most ambitious attempt "to report on my boomer generation's bruised optimism . . . In the past, I've tried to sing about overlooked Americans. On the new album, I'm trying to speak for them." White noted that the songs' "heavily atmospheric musical settings have an eerie vividness that makes them more than topical." *Paper In Fire* "is the sound of a soul in desperate flight, running either from or toward its destiny. The choir of screaming fiddle, banjo, and squeezebox creates a chilling sense of suspense—but leaves the conclusion to one's imagination."[375]

(Other personnel: Mike Wanchic on guitar & dobro; Larry Crane on guitar; John Cascella on accordion & keyboards; Toby Myers on bass; Kenny Aronoff on drums; backing vocals by Crystal Taliafero, Mike Wanchic & Pat Peterson)

Free Fallin' (1989)—Tom Petty (written by Tom Petty & Jeff Lynne)
MCA 53748
Recorded in 1988; chart debut Nov. 4, 1989 (#7 peak);[376] from the album *Full Moon Fever* (RS-#179, RIA, 1001, VIL)[377]

The status of Tom Petty's *Free Fallin'* as one of the modern era's anthems for cutting loose of all fears and inhibitions in search of personal freedom was forever cemented by director Cameron Crowe's use of the

---

some newly-recorded soloing. *I Feel for You* was arranged by Reggie Griffin, from the hip-hop label Sugar Hill for which Grandmaster Flash also recorded.

372. Prince later contributed songs to Chaka's 1988 album *CK*, and performed her arrangement of *I Feel for You* live (*The 1001 Songs You Must Hear Before You Die*, p. 540).

373. Chapter on Chaka from David Nathan's *The Soulful Divas* (p. 211). The repetition of her name in the rap was actually a mistake, when Mardin's hand slipped on the sampler while recording Melle (he had intended to fit her name to the percussion); it worked so well that he kept it.

374. *Born in a Small Town*, p. 88–92.

375. Timothy White, *Rock Lives: Profiles and Interviews*, p. 595–604.

376. #10 in France.

377. *Rolling Stone* and MTV in December 2000 ranked it as the #72 best pop song from 1964 onward, and three years later VH1 placed it as the #39 top song of the past twenty-five years.

song in his 1997 film *Jerry Maguire*. Tom Cruise as the titular sports agent has just lost his lucrative job after writing an idealistic memo; as he drives out on the open California highway, feeling simultaneously liberated but afraid of what's ahead, he searches the radio airwaves for just the song to capture his mood. When the strains of *Free Fallin'* waft across the soundtrack, he breaks into a huge grin; at least for the moment, he feels, anything is possible.

Born in Gainesville, Florida (in the northern part of the state), on October 20, 1953, Petty dropped out of school at seventeen to form his first rock group Mudcrutch, which also featured guitarist Mike Campbell and keyboardist Belmont Tench, but the group split soon after moving to Los Angeles in search of a record deal. After a few years of working with various bands, Petty reconnected with Campbell and Tench in 1975; they were working with two others in a band called the Heartbreakers, and as Tom Petty & the Heartbreakers they released their debut album in 1976, which started slowly but soon became a hit with its roots-rock sound combining 1960s guitar rock with the leader's direct, Southern-tinged writing style. That success expanded with the second album, but it was followed by a fierce battle with their record company and a 1979 bankruptcy declaration by Petty. But late that year, with a new record deal, *Damn the Torpedoes* became the band's biggest album, and the hits flowed steadily in the years to come.

While working on *Full Moon Fever*, his first solo album apart from the Heartbreakers, Petty was given a new Yamaha keyboard as a gift from the band's roadie. Soon afterward, he recalled, he was sitting at the keyboard with producer Jeff Lynne (with whom he would shortly be working as members of the impromptu supergroup the Traveling Wilburys along with Bob Dylan, George Harrison, and Roy Orbison),[378] and "started playing a little lick, which turned into the three chords of the song. And I started to sing," ad libbing the first two verses. When he stopped, unsure where to go next, Lynne said, "free falling," and suggested Petty sing it an octave higher. And a hit was born. "We had a multitude of acoustic guitars. So it made this incredibly dreamy sound."[379] To Petty's astonishment, when he completed the album,

MCA didn't like it—indeed, "they didn't want to release it"—because executives didn't hear any potential hits on it. After saner heads prevailed, *I Won't Back Down* and *Free Fallin'* each hit the Top Ten, and the album would sell over five million copies, more than double what any of his previous LPs had done. "I loved the song . . . it's become synonymous with me, I guess."

I Fell in Love (1990)—Carlene Carter (written by Carlene Carter, Howie Epstein, Benmont Tench, & Perry Lamek)
Reprise 19915
Chart debut July 14, 1990 (reached #3 C&W); album *I Fell In Love* reached #19 C&W, 46 weeks[380]

This absolutely irresistible rockin' country song, giddy with the thrill of unexpected love, was the product of a gifted artist in a fortuitous collaboration with members of Tom Petty's Heartbreakers. The daughter of June Carter (thus she's Johnny Cash's stepdaughter) and country star Carl Smith, Carlene (born on September 26, 1955, in Nashville) worked with the Carter Family from the late 1960s to the early 1970s, then went solo and moved in a rock & roll direction; she was married for a time to British rocker Nick Lowe. The album *I Fell in Love* was a perfect marriage of traditional country influences with rock's energy. Howie Epstein of the Heartbreakers was Carlene's boyfriend at the time, and they wrote the title track together with fellow Petty bandmate Benmont Tench; Epstein served as producer. Albert Lee's lead guitar drives the band (with Howie Epstein on acoustic guitar, Benmont Tench on piano, John Ciambotti on bass, Eddie Baytos on accordion, Ed Greene on drums, and a stellar roster of backing vocalists that includes Dave Edmunds, Levon Helm, Jim Lauderdale, Jim Photoglo, and Kevin Welch). But atop it all is Carlene, cutting loose with a ferocious feistiness that recalls the likes of Wanda Jackson. Her followup album *Little Love Letters* (also produced by Epstein) featured a similarly flavorful C&W hit, *Every Little Thing*.

I Can't Make You Love Me (1991)—Bonnie Raitt (written by Mike Reid & Allen Shamblin)
Capitol 44729
Chart debut Nov. 23, 1991 (#18 peak); #50 in U.K.; from the album *Luck of the Draw* (chart debut July 13, 1991, reached #2, sold 7 million copies) (*1001*)

After nearly twenty years of grinding it out on the road as a slide guitarist and white blues singer with an intensely devoted following but only medium-level record sales,

---

378. The Wilburys album was recorded shortly after much of *Full Moon Fever*, but released a year earlier (in November 1988).

379. As discussed in *Conversations with Tom Petty* (by Paul Zollo, p. 114 and 232–33), it was the first song he and Lynne wrote together. After they'd finished most of it and Lynne went home, Petty came up with the final verse (about flying over Mulholland Drive). They recorded the song the following day, at Mike Campbell's bedroom studio. It was so small that, when jammed with recording gear, only the three principals (with Lynne on bass and Campbell as engineer) could squeeze into the room; microphone cables were run into the garage. It took only a little over one day to finish the track. A few days later, Petty and Lynne wrote Orbison's solo hit *You Got It*.

380. *The People's Almanac* (1999) selected it as one of the fifty best country albums.

Bonnie Raitt beat the odds by sweeping the Grammies and soaring to #1 with her 1989 album *Nick of Time*. That set the stage for her strong 1991 followup *Luck of the Draw* and its gorgeous ballad *I Can't Make You Love Me*, a poignant and deeply felt tale of a relationship's end.

The daughter of Broadway headliner John Raitt of *Carousel* and *Pajama Game* renown, Bonnie was born in Cleveland on November 8, 1949. She fell in love with the blues while a college student in Cambridge, Massachusetts, got to meet blues legends Mississippi Fred McDowell and Sippie Wallace, and quickly moved from the coffee-house circuit to blues and folk festivals around the country. From her 1971 debut album onward and with relentless touring, she built a fervent fan base with her terrific slide playing (inspired by McDowell and Son House) and soulful vocals. But after her ninth album for Warner Brothers in 1986, she was dropped by the label and faced a career crossroads—which she traversed with her epic 1989 comeback. *Something to Talk About*, Bonnie's biggest single ever, got the next album (produced by Don Was and Raitt) off to a tremendous start; this song fanned the flames still higher.

Pennsylvania-born Mike Reid, co-writer of Raitt's greatest song, was a defensive back at Penn State, and drafted in the first round by the Cincinnati Bengals, for which he played from 1970–1974 until injury forced his retirement. He launched an even more successful second career as a Nashville songwriter (including the 1983 Ronnie Milsap hit *Stranger in My House*) and performer. The ballad's other author, Allen Shamblin, has a number of other country successes to his credit, including *Don't Laugh at Me* by Mark Wills (1998). This song was inspired by a news account of a man accused of harassing his ex-girlfriend, leading the judge to admonish him, "You can't make someone love you."

"Ohhh, that's a great song," raved R&B great Ruth Brown (in *Listen to This! Leading Musicians Recommend Their Favorite Artists & Recordings* by Alan Reder and John Baxter). Legendary Motown songwriter Lamont Dozier calls it "a heartbreaking tale . . . about someone who doesn't want to be patronized but knows that the object of her desire will never love her." In *Time Out* magazine's book *1,000 Songs to Change Your Life*, Dozier recalls seeing Reid perform it in Nashville, "and I completely choked up. I was in tears, all over the place. Very embarrassing!"[381] Carole King told *Mojo* magazine: "It's torn from the depths of feeling, from that really horrible place where your love is unrequited."[382]

For this classic ballad, Bonnie sets her guitar aside to focus on some serious, straight-from-the-heart ballad

singing to the accompaniment of Bruce Hornsby's piano. It became the second biggest single of her career.

Take a Bow (1995)—Madonna (written by Kenny "Babyface" Edmonds & Madonna)
Maverick/Sire 18000
Chart debut Dec. 17, 1994 (#1 for 7 weeks); #1 (2 weeks) in Canada, #16 in England;[383] from the album *Bedtime Stories* (*BILLB*-#85)

The longest-running #1 single of Madonna's remarkable career, *Take a Bow* paired her as both co-writer and producer with Kenny "Babyface" Edmonds, one of the hottest talents of the era. Biographer J. Randy Taraborrelli notes that the album *Bedtime Stories* marked the first time since 1984's *Like a Virgin* (helmed by Nile Rodgers) that she had worked with a well-known producer. The first single from the album, *Secret*, was produced and co-written by Dallas Austin (of Boyz II Men and TLC fame); it was a hit, but the second single, *Take a Bow*, was a blockbuster.

It's a gorgeous, melancholy ballad of unrequited love, with the object of the singer's affection someone who hides behind a role-playing mask behind which only she can see. Her previous album *Erotica* had been fraught with controversy, and although that was normally her forte, she was concerned about taking things in too dark a direction, and wanted to shift gears to a more romantic vein.[384] There could be no better partner for that mood than the man known as Babyface (born Kenny Edmonds on April 10, 1959, in Indianapolis), who established himself as a master of smooth R&B through his work with Whitney Houston, Boyz II Men, and Toni Braxton among others, and his hits as a performer included the 1994 ballad *When Can I See You*. He makes *Take a Bow* virtually a duet with Madonna, echoing her words with his high tenor wafting dreamily behind her, and the song's minimalist arrangement is impeccably elegant. Adding to the aura of the song was a terrific music video shot over seven days in Ronda, Spain, with popular bullfighter Emilio Munoz playing the role of her lover, and a classic 1940s look.

Kiss Me (1998)—Sixpence None the Richer (written by Matt Slocum)
Squint CD single 79101
Chart debut Nov. 28, 1998 (#2 peak, 33 weeks); reached #4 in England, #1 (3 weeks) in Australia, #1 (3 weeks) on Canadian RPM chart[385]

---

381. *Time Out*, p. 125.
382. August 2000 *Mojo*, p. 80.

---

383. #1 in Brazil, Poland, Spain; #4 in Japan. Strangely, it was the first Madonna single (other than reissues) to fall short of the British Top Ten since 1984, ending a streak of 35 in a row.
384. O'Brien, *Madonna: Like an Icon*, p. 199.
385. #3 in Japan, #7 in Germany and Italy, and #1 (4 weeks) on the Hot 100 Recurrent Airplay chart.

This absolutely delightful midtempo pop ballad is a celebration of new love so giddy that it sweeps the listener up in its happiness, and possesses a timeless quality that's rare in contemporary pop.[386] Sixpence began in Austin, Texas, doing Christian-oriented material, then shifted to pop; it took seven years to achieve their breakthrough, including two years to escape a soured deal with their former label REX. The group was the first act signed to the start-up label Squint Entertainment in 1997, owned by producer-musician Steve Taylor, which provided strong promotional support, introducing the newcomers to radio programmers.[387] The group's guitarist/cellist Matt Slocum wrote *Kiss Me*; he's accompanied by Sean Kelly on rhythm guitar, bassist Justin Cary, and drummer Dale Baker. Lead singer Leigh Nash is huggably adorable—her entrancing vocal is warmly reminiscent of Harriet Wheeler on the British folk-pop group The Sundays' 1990 song *Here's Where the Story Ends*—and the musical arrangement (acoustic guitar-driven) and gorgeous melody match her appeal. VH1 featured the group upon the record's release in November 1998; the song was also on the soundtrack of the teen romantic comedy *She's All That*, and on TV's *Dawson's Creek*, along with *The Young & the Restless*. The La's sunny pop gem *There She Goes* provided Sixpence with a perfect followup hit.

Everything Is Everything (1999)—Lauryn Hill
Ruffhouse 79206
Chart debut June 19, 1999 (reached #35 on pop chart, #14 R&B); from the album *The Miseducation of Lauryn Hill*, chart debut Sept. 12, 1998, 4 weeks at #1)

The Miseducation of Lauryn Hill was one of the blockbuster albums of the past fifteen years in both sales (over seven million), quality, and pop-cultural influence. It combined hip-hop with classic R&B as seamlessly as any album has ever done, and showcased Lauryn Hill—singer, rapper, producer, and songwriter—as a multi-tasking artist of the highest order. Among all its outstanding selections, perhaps the finest was *Everything Is Everything*.

Born on May 26, 1975, in South Orange, New Jersey, Lauryn was singing and acting from childhood on, and began performing part-time with the hip-hop group the Fugees at age thirteen, taking time off for undergraduate studies at Columbia University and also acting (in a soap opera, the Steven Soderbergh film *King of the Hill*, and *Sister Act 2*). The group's six-million-selling 1996 album *The Score* (featuring their smash remake of *Killing Me*

Softly) gave her a national platform, and Lauryn seized the opportunity to make her first solo album. (Also in 1998, she co-wrote and produced the title track of Aretha Franklin's album *A Rose Is Still a Rose*, a Top 30 single.) Everyone knew she could sing and rap, but few were prepared for the prowess she demonstrated on *Miseducation* as songwriter, arranger, and producer—along with its sheer diverse scope. "The true theme of the album," writes Nevin Martell as VH1 ranked it as the #37 greatest album, "is one of questing—be that for love, artistic fulfillment, spiritual enlightenment, or personal well-being . . . a truly inspired album with a timeless sensibility."[388] "By turns socially engaged, personally revelatory, and, in the hip-hop tradition, a bit arrogant, *Miseducation* managed to filter hip-hop through a womanist lens, resulting in an album that appealed to an improbably wide spectrum of listeners," remarked Jon Caramanica in *Rolling Stone*.[389] The chart-topping leadoff single *Doo Wop (That Thing)* made clear that the album was headed for big things.

Everything Is Everything is a potent hip-hop statement of philosophy focused on pride and self-help to achieve personal dreams. She wrote it at the conclusion of her romantic relationship with Fugees' leader Wyclef Jean, a period that also marked the group's breakup and her loss of religious faith. "Let's love ourselves, then we can't fail / To make a better situation tomorrow, our seeds will grow / All we need is dedication . . ." She's backed on strings by the Indigo Quartet, and on piano by John Stephens (who would emerge several years later as an R&B singing star under the name John Legend).

Lauryn took home five Grammies for *Miseducation*, including Album of the Year. It was also voted the year's #2 album in the *Village Voice* critics' poll. Unfortunately she subsequently chose to recede from public view aside from an "MTV Unplugged" album and occasional public performances (alternating between thrilling and puzzling), making this set a glorious one-shot.[390]

Pastures of Plenty / Land / This Land Is Your Land (2001)—Lila Downs
Medley from the Narada album *Border / La Linea* (released on July 3, 2001)

One of Woody Guthrie's finest hours was the creation of twenty-six songs in twenty-six days during 1941 for the Bonneville Power Administration, written while driving along the Columbia River in Washington State while Bonneville was building the Grand Coulee Dam. The

---

386. The lyrics, describing romance at an old-time rural dance (amidst barley, "green, green grass," and dancing fireflies), could apply to 1899 as much as 1999.

387. August 14, 1999 *Billboard*.

388. *100 Greatest Albums*, p. 94–95.

389. One key decision she made with the album, setting it apart from most hip-hop releases, was to rely almost exclusively on live instruments, minimizing the use of samples and computer-generated sounds.

390. In 2012 Lauryn pled guilty to tax evasion but promised to record a follow-up album.

songs were part of a project (including a documentary) to promote the cause of rural electrification as an alternative to the big northeastern power companies. A few of the songs would become enduring folk standards, including *Roll On Columbia*, and above all *Pastures of Plenty*. Biographer Joe Klein describes it as "one of his most solemn pieces, almost a dirge," tracing the experience of migrant farm workers trying to support their families while roaming the countryside, all but unseen by most: "On the edge of your city you've seen us and then, / We come with the dust and we go with the wind."[391] Six decades later, Guthrie's anthem (set to one of the melodies associated with the folk standard *Pretty Polly*) would find an extraordinary new life.

Born on September 19, 1968, in Tlaxiaco, Oaxaca, Mexico, Lila Downs was born to a Mixtec (Native American) mother and British-American father, moved with her parents at fourteen to the United States, and two years later, following the death of her father, returned to Oaxaca with her mother. Blessed with a powerful voice and a passion for exploring the ethnic traditions of the Mixtec and of Mexico, she recorded her first album in 1994, and after two independent releases, began recording in 1999 for the larger Narada Productions, making her music more widely available in the U.S. and Europe. *Border / La Linea*, her third Narada release, featured her first songs in English, along with selections in Spanish and other native Mexican languages, and mixed traditional folk sounds with elements of hip-hop and rock.

Its centerpiece was a remarkable medley of two Guthrie classics and an original composition. Its opening is a mesmerizing a cappella first three verses of *Pastures of Plenty*, which segues (now accompanied by a combo) into *Land* (which she co-wrote with her husband, American saxophonist Paul Cohen), like Woody's an exploration of the migrant experience, but this time from the perspective of Mexican immigrants. Led by electric guitarist Ken Basman, she offers a portion of Guthrie's *This Land Is Your Land*, then returning to her own *Land*: "I really don't know who I am, but I will / I know there's a purpose, there's a reason for me to be here / Dust is to dust, hail thee memory / Even if they grind me, still dust I will be." Bringing it back for the conclusion to *Pastures of Plenty*, Woody's immortal couplet is now given a whole new resonance by what has come before. It's a very powerful, original creation. Lila has gone on to do further outstanding work, including a 2004 album focusing on a Mexican human rights defender, *One Blood*.

Hey Ya! (2003)—OutKast (written by Andre Benjamin)
Arista 54962

Chart debut Oct. 18, 2003 (9 weeks at #1 pop, reached #9 R&B); #1 (8 weeks) in Canada, #1 (2 weeks) in Australia, #3 in U.K., #6 in Germany;[392] from the album *Speakerboxxx/The Love Below* (7 weeks at #1, sold 10 million copies) (*2000s-#1, VIL-#2, BL-#15, ACC-#19, BILLB-#52, R&B-#135, RS-#182, Time, TO, GR, TC*)

Sometimes all it takes to achieve consensus between critics and fans is a booty-shaking dance floor gem that seems simple but is anything but, and that's what OutKast achieved with *Hey Ya*: the biggest single of 2003 and the year's across-the-board critical favorite. The duo of Andre 3000 (Andre Benjamin) and Antwan "Big Boi" Patton formed the hip-hop alliance OutKast in Atlanta in 1994, and after three increasingly successful albums, the 2000 release *Stankonia* was a four-million-selling smash. That set the stage for their biggest triumph of all, two solo CDs packaged as one album: Big Boi's *Speakerboxx* (including the #1 single *The Way You Move*), and Andre 3000's *The Love Below* (featuring *Hey Ya*).

"Even Prince at his most experimental never conceived a genre-smash as nutty as Andre 3000's electro/folk-rock/funk/power pop/hip-hop/neo-soul/ kitchen sink rave-up," declared *Blender* in calling *Hey Ya* the #15 best single of 1980–2005. "The sound is remarkable: Raucous acoustic guitar strumming collides with blipping synths, while Andre veers from tuneless shouts to gospel-style testifying. But beneath the sonic dazzle . . . lurks great confessional songwriting about love, sex, heartbreak and the impossibility of monogamy . . . All this, plus the 21st century's first great catchphrase: 'Shake it like a Polaroid picture.'"[393] Andre played almost all the instruments on a song voted the #1 single of the year in the *Village Voice* critics' poll, from the album voted #1 for the year by the same critics,[394] and winner of the Grammy as Album of the Year.

Built to Last (2007)—Melee (written by Chris Cron)
From the Warner Bros./WEA album *Devils & Angels* (released on April 3, 2007)

Most great pop songs are timeless: if it possesses the indefinable ingredients that, once heard, it becomes immersed deep in the listener's brain—and, more importantly, the listener wants to retain that pleasurable sensation—you can plop it into any decade, and regardless of passing trends, it simply works. *Built to Last* by Melee is such a song. After recording a 2003 EP for Hopeless Records and their first full-length LP a year later for Sub City, the California pop-rock quintet made its major-label

---

391. *Woody Guthrie: A Life*, p. 201–3.

392. #1 in Brazil, Italy, Norway, Spain, & Sweden; #2 on Eurochart and in Ireland, #4 in Austria, #7 France, #8 Japan.

393. October 2005 *Blender*, p. 90.

394. Taking into account percentage of the vote received, *Hey Ya* ranks second only to Arrested Development's *Tennessee* (1992) among all songs in *Village Voice* polls from 1974–2011.

debut in 2007, and while not reaching the charts, *Devils & Angels* left a powerful impression on nearly all who heard it. Its signature piece is the soaring mid-tempo rock ballad *Built to Last*, one of the most unforgettable pop tunes of the decade. Boasting a delicious, wide-ranging melody, warm lyrics, and piano-driven energy, it's an exhilarating love song showcasing the thoroughly engaging voice of singer-songwriter Chris Cron. One can call it a "formula" rock ballad in the 2000s-era mold of Maroon 5 or Daughtry, except that it's about ten times better in every respect (music, lyrics, and the fervor of the performance) than anything those bands have ever produced. Indicative of the fine songcraft at work is the introduction of emotionally vivid new lines just before ("walking on the hills at night") and within ("you are the sun in my universe") the concluding chorus. As his tenor flies heavenward on the final chorus, the sheer joy underlining the entire performance becomes unmistakable; it's all but guaranteed to bring a smile.

Girls In Their Summer Clothes (2008)—Bruce Springsteen

Hot 100 debut Feb. 2, 2008 (reached #95)
From the Columbia album *Magic* (chart debut Oct. 20, 2007; 2 weeks at #1)

Sounding unlike anything Bruce Springsteen has ever done, and yet fitting perfectly within a body of work that had reached thirty-five years by this point, *Girls In Their Summer Clothes* is the musical equivalent of a cool breeze on a hot August night, soft and oh so sweet. After a period in which the waits between new Springsteen albums seemed like an eternity to devoted fans (just three studio albums after 1987's *Tunnel of Love* through 2001), the New Jersey–born bard poured out four albums from 2002–2007, and after a pair of acoustic outings (*Devils & Dust* and the straight-folk *The Seeger Sessions*), *Magic* found him rocking out again with the E Street Band. It is, writes J. Freedom Du Lac, The Boss's "most musically accessible album since *Born In the U.S.A.*" in 1984, and *Girls In Their Summer Clothes* is arguably its high point.

This is a tale from the perspective of a guy who's rebounded from a shattered affair with a new love that "just saved my life." Brimming with warm nostalgia carried by an ingratiating melody, it is sung in a voice that seems entirely new to Springsteen: smooth, almost crooning, but still (even though initially almost unrecognizable) somehow Bruce. It's as if—like Bob Dylan on *Lay Lady Lay* four decades earlier—he was able to create an entirely new vocal sound that's absolutely perfect for the material. Chris Willman (*Entertainment Weekly*) called it "gloriously [Phil] Spectorian," a "glockenspiel-and timpani-adorned pop stunner."[395] Steve Van Zandt is on twelve-string guitar, and "the vocal harmonies, the chiming keyboards, Clarence Clemons' saxophone and Soozie Tyrell's violin combined to provide a lush orchestral cushion" for the artist as he "swooned through a lyric as unabashedly romantic as the song's title," writes A. O. Scott of *The New York Times*.[396] "I wanted one thing on the record that was the perfect pop universe," Springsteen remarked. "You know, that day when it's all right there; it's the world that only exists in pop songs, and once in a while you stumble on it."

"And the girls in their summer clothes / In the cool of the evening light / The girls in their summer clothes / Pass me by . . ."

---

395. October 5, 2007, Entertainment Weekly, p. 68–69.
396. September 30, 2007, *New York Times*, p. 24.

Playlist 8

Let the Good Times Roll, 1895–2011

The Band Played On (1895)—Dan W. Quinn (written by John E. Palmer)

Columbia 2045

Recorded in mid-1895; also for Berliner 961 on Nov. 3, 1895; also for New Jersey and Ohio 2400

Few songs of the 1890s remain as well-remembered today as *The Band Played On*, and the man who helped make it one of the pop sensations of the decade was Dan W. Quinn. John Palmer wrote it after hearing a German street band play in New York, and sold the number to vaudevillian and song publisher Charles B. Ward, who introduced it at Hammerstein's Harlem Opera House.[1] (On the original July 12, 1895, copyright Ward credited himself as composer with Palmer as lyricist, but subsequent accounts agree that Palmer was also almost entirely responsible for the music, with just minor "touch-ups" by Ward.)[2] The ballad's popularity was hastened by its vigorous promotion in the *New York World*, which published both words and music.

Born in San Francisco in 1859, baritone Dan Quinn was one of the first singers to achieve fame through phonograph records, which were still a novelty when he made his first cylinder tests in 1892. Working for a variety of companies including New Jersey, Columbia, and Edison, Quinn had the first recorded performances of many of the era's top song hits, including *The Bowery* (1893), *Daisy Bell* (1893), *The Sidewalks of New York* (1895), and *A Hot Time in the Old Town* (1896). He's reported to have recorded some 2,500 titles in a long career that largely ended in 1910, aside from a few final records in 1916–1918, virtually all in solo performances. The delightful, charming *The Band Played On* is sung with piano accompaniment at a medium tempo. Quinn's 1897 Berliner rendition is included on the Archeophone CD *The Phonographic Yearbook: The 1890s, Vol. 1: Wipe Him Off the Land.* "Casey would waltz with the strawberry blonde as the band played on . . ."

Arkansaw Traveler (1900/1901)—Len Spencer (written by Sandford Faulkner)

Columbia 11098

Pop Memories debut Nov. 3, 1900; biggest version recorded on Nov. 23, 1901, for Victor 1101, *Pop Memories* debut March 1, 1902 (#1 record of year); also issued on Columbia 21; also in 1902 for Edison Standard 8202 (*MEM-#32, DMDB*)

Arkansaw Traveler (the number's traditional spelling) is an ancient spoken comedy routine and accompanying fiddle tune that may have originated with Colonel Sandford C. Faulkner around 1850. The instrumental tune itself was published in sheet music form in 1847. A remarkable article by Henry Chapman Mercer in the March 1896 *Century Magazine*—four years before Spencer's initial recording—examined the history of both the tune and the humorous routine, "On the Track of the Arkansas Traveler."[3]

---

1. It was published in the June 30, 1895, *New York Sunday World* just prior to being copyrighted (Fuld, *Book of World-Famous Music*, p. 123).

2. Spaeth, *A History of Popular Music in America*, p. 283.

---

3. 1896 article reprinted in Summer 1970 *J.E.M.F. Quarterly*. Arkansas has been the object of more good-natured ribbing through song than any other state—*The State of Arkansas* (a traveler's tale of comic woe in his backwoods encounters) is particularly well-known—and at least in *Arkansaw Traveler* the ribbing goes both ways.

A prominent planter from Chicot County, Arkansas, Faulkner was supposedly inspired by a conversation with a backwoodsman in 1840. It's the tale of a traveler who's lost in the woods with night coming on, and seeks directions from a rural character who deflects all his questions with anecdotes and one-liners, and continually saws away on his fiddle. The yarn was popularized by six Currier & Ives lithographs in 1852 showing scenes from the comic narrative. The dialogue with music was first published in 1858 in Buffalo, with a Boston edition printed during 1861–1863. By 1865, when it was included in Frank B. Converse's *Banjo Instructor*, the complete piece was very well established. Arkansas historians report that although some folklorists have attributed the number to an Ohio Valley fiddler named Jose Tasso, Faulkner was so widely accepted as the author that before his death in 1874, the old St. Charles Hotel in New Orleans lettered "The Arkansaw Traveler" in gilt above the door of a room reserved for him. Also, in the year preceding his death, an Arkansas county was named after the colonel. Vance Randolph remarked that it "is by all odds the most famous fiddle tune in the rural South, and no fiddlers' contest is ever conducted without it."[4] [5] *Folk Songs of the Catskills* notes that "the core of the tale hinges upon the integration of a piece of music into the narrative," as signified by the term *cante-fable*, a story in which a musical quotation serves as a crucial ingredient.[6]

The routine was first recorded for Columbia in 1900 and credited to Len Spencer, although at least one historian (Tim Brooks) has suggested that the performer was actually Harry Spencer.[7] But it was indisputably Washington, D.C., native Leonard Garfield Spencer—one of the foremost recording artists of the age in a career that ran from 1890 to 1910 and encompassed ragtime-flavored songs, ballads, ethnic comedy, hymns, vaudeville and minstrel specialties, and even recreations of historical speeches—who recorded the most famous versions of *Arkansaw Traveler* for Victor in late 1901 and Edison the following year. He speaks the roles of both the exasperated traveler and the bemused Arkansas native who sits in front of his cabin giving witty answers; violinist Charles D'Almaine accompanies him. (Spencer also recorded a September 1903 version with banjoist Parke Hunter.) The

records became a popular sensation, further cementing Spencer's already considerable reputation.

On June 30, 1922, the very first authentic country music commercial recording was an instrumental performance of *Arkansaw Traveler* by Texas fiddler A. C. (Eck) Robertson (in a fiddle duet with Henry Gilliland) on the flip side of his fiddle solo *Sallie Gooden* for the Victor label. The record became such a hit that the already-familiar *Arkansas Traveler* (by this time typically using the state's correct spelling) was even more firmly established as a country fiddle classic, with recordings by Gid Tanner & Riley Puckett (1924), Earl Johnson & His Clodhoppers (1927), and Clayton McMichen & Dan Hornsby (1928), among many others. *Arkansas Traveler* served as the official state song of Arkansas from the late 1940s until 1963, and is now the official "state historical song" (separate from the state's "anthem" and two other "state songs").

Watermelon Party (1909)—Polk Miller & His Old South Quartette (written by James L. Stamper)
Edison Blue Amberol 2178
Recorded in Nov. 1909

Polk Miller's Old South Quartette was the first racially integrated group to both make records and tour (with white singer-guitarist and ex-Confederate soldier Polk Miller, physically present when Robert E. Lee surrendered at Appomattox, and his all-black backing group), and *Watermelon Party* is a further illustration of the passionate sound the group had demonstrated on its classic *Jerusalem Mournin'* from the same 1909 session in Richmond, Virginia. Tim Brooks writes in *Lost Sounds: Blacks and the Birth of the Recording Industry, 1890–1919* that although Miller's live performances presenting a highly romanticized vision of the pre–Civil War South through songs and stories (having studied the playing of slaves on his family's 1,300-acre plantation) had undeniably racist overtones, he "presented his material with respect, as a re-creation of earlier times."[8] He never used blackface, and often talked about the origins of a song before performing it. Unfortunately Miller's handful of recordings included his banjo playing on only one selection; one witness to his stage presentations declared that his playing represented "a compelling study of a direct transmission of black folk banjo styles from plantation slave banjo players to Polk Miller."

Written by the quartet's bass singer James L. Stamper, *Watermelon Party* has silly, light-hearted lyrics— "Watermelon's nice, hurry up and cut a slice / Watermelon's fine, hurry up and give me mine"—but is musically thrilling with the fervent call-and-response arrangement.

4. *Ozark Folksongs, Vol. 3* (p. 22–23).

5. In a vivid illustration of the tune's popularity, an "Old-Time Fiddlers' contest" in Terre Haute, Indiana, on February 17, 1899, opened with all 210 competing fiddlers on stage playing *Arkansaw Traveler* simultaneously (March 1899 *Metronome*).

6. Cazden, Haufrecht, and Studer, *Folk Songs of the Catskills*, p. 335–36.

7. *The Columbia Master Book Discography*, Vol. 1, p. 22. Harry Spencer did record some recitations for Columbia and other labels, and during the early years of the century served as Columbia's chief announcer, intoning the song title and artist name at the beginning of many cylinders and discs.

8. Brooks, p. 219.

Miller's guitar provides strongly syncopated accompaniment, and the entire piece has the feeling of an authentic folk/blues performance as opposed to a polished Tin Pan Alley number. Also, at the generous playing time of three minutes and forty seconds, the song is fully and satisfyingly developed. It's included on the Archeophone CD *Stomp and Swerve.*

Old Black Joe (1909)—Fisk University Jubilee Singers (written by Stephen Foster)
Victor 35097
Recorded Dec. 9, 1909

After a creatively fallow period from the mid to late 1850s, Stephen Foster composed his final flurry of important songs starting with the 1860 plantation ballad *Old Black Joe.* Ken Emerson in *Doo-Dah! Stephen Foster and the Rise of American Popular Culture* writes that the song "distills the world-weariness of many of Foster's previous songs, parlor ballads as well as blackface. Not only is *Old Black Joe* the singer of *Old Folks at Home* and the Uncle Tom figure [from *Uncle Tom's Cabin*] in *My Old Kentucky Home*, but take away the 'black' and an allusion to 'the cotton fields' and Joe could be white—the singer of [Foster's sentimental tune] *Old Dog Tray*, for example." It's a song that defies easy categorization. In one sense, notes Emerson, it "epitomizes Foster's racial condescension," as Joe can be viewed as having "a slave's cringing obedience." But the great black writer W. E. B. Du Bois, in *The Souls of Black Folk*, singled out *Old Folks at Home* and *Old Black Joe* for praise, calling them "songs of white America [that] have been distinctively influenced by the slave songs or have incorporated whole phrases of Negro melody."[9] Emerson agrees, saying that despite the tune's stereotypes, it "comes closest of Foster's famous songs to the African-American spiritual, and it approaches that tradition with sympathy and respect . . . Its soft melancholy and elusive undertone, rather than any formal musical correspondence, make *Old Black Joe* almost a spiritual."[10]

This association was powerfully underlined by the legendary black group the Fisk University Jubilee Singers' performance of *Old Black Joe* among the ten songs that they recorded in their historic December 8th, 9th, and 21st sessions for the Victor Talking Machine Company. A bass singer (most likely Alfred Garfield King, the first bass) takes the lead, and the quartet's classically trained voices bring out the beauty of Foster's melody. The rest of the group: leader John Wesley Work II (first tenor), James Andrew Myers (second tenor), and Noah Walker Ryder (second bass).

Manuelito (1912)—Lovey's Trinidad String Band
Columbia L-23
Recorded in New York on July 1, 1912[11] (*World-#26, RR*)

The music of Trinidad has enriched Western pop culture for generations, and it was captured on record for the very first time by a twelve-man ensemble led by violinist George R. L. Baillie (pronounced "Bailey"), aka "Lovey," in June 1912. A very popular group (including flute, clarinet, tiple, piano, two guitars, two cuatros, two violins, bass, and braga) regularly featured at social engagements at Port-of-Spain, Lovey's band sailed to America for a summer 1912 tour of northeastern Atlantic states, and during the trip stopped off in New York to make the historic recordings. On June 12 it performed the engaging *Trinidad Paseo* for the Victor label, and shortly thereafter made its finest recording, *Manuelito*, for Columbia.[12]

The dominant form of indigenous music in Trinidad and Tobago from the beginning of the twentieth century, the word calypso is either derived from the West African word "kaiso" (a shout of encouragement) or from the Spanish term for a tropical song, "caliso." However, Lovey's band recorded no calypsos, but waltzes and the 4/4 tempo dance numbers known as paseos.[13] *Manuelito* is a brisk, delightful instrumental described by musicologist Dick Spottswood as "a waltz of remarkable sophistication, modulating from major to minor through several keys, with an energy base consistent with the best Afro-American traditions."[14] It would be another two years before the group recorded again (for Columbia); it remained popular in Trinidad until the mid-1920s. Lovey died in 1937. In 2002, the Library of Congress named *Manuelito* (and the group's other 1912 recordings) as one of the original fifty selections for its National Recording Registry to be preserved in perpetuity. The performance can be found on the 1992 CD compilation by the Harlequin label, *Trinidad 1912–1941.*

Circus Day in Dixie (1916)—Versatile Four (written by Jack Yellen & Albert Gumble)
HMV C-645
Recorded on Feb. 3, 1916, in Hayes, Middlesex, England

Black bandleader and composer James Reese Europe became a virtual industry unto himself thanks to the

---

9. Du Bois, p. 197.

10. Emerson, p. 256–59. The song was copyrighted November 8, 1860 (Fuld, *Book of World-Famous Music*, p. 407).

11. The record was being advertised by mid-August (as cited in Bear Family's *West Indian Rhythm*), but Spottswood remarks that its American distribution was probably "negligible."

12. Richard Spottswood, *Ethnic Music on Records*, Vol. 5, p. 2913.

13. Until calypsos began to be extensively recorded by major labels like Decca in the 1930s, the music was regarded in Trinidad as primarily a seasonal treat to be enjoyed during carnival time early each year. Thus, bands like Lovey's had to be adept at playing a variety of other dance styles. The subsequent easy availability of calypsos on record made it more of a year-round music.

14. Liner notes to Harlequin CD, *Trinidad, 1912–1941.*

national fame he garnered as official bandleader for the internationally renowned dance team of Vernon and Irene Castle, and started many bands that operated under his management at home and abroad.[15] The Versatile Four was a Europe outfit that he sent to England in early 1916, and on their very first recording, created a musical marvel. David Wondrich describes it in *Stomp and Swerve: American Music Gets Hot, 1843–1924*: "with its minstrel themes transformed by pure musical testosterone, is one of the hottest records I've ever heard."[16] The group (as heard on Archeophone's *Stomp and Swerve* CD) consists of Gus Haston on banjo and brief vocal, Charlie Mills on piano, Tony Tuck also on banjo, and Charlie Johnson (or possibly George Archer) on trap drums. This is a fierce, passionate performance, the delightful looseness of its sound giving it a quasi-improvised feeling underlined by the shouts of encouragement reminiscent of the Europe orchestra's own magnificent *Down Home Rag* over two years earlier; the quartet recorded an exciting rendition of the latter tune during this same session. (The complete recordings of the Versatile Four and related combos were compiled by the Document label in *The Earliest Black String Bands, Vol. 2* covering 1916–1919.) The vocal, such as it is, is largely buried in the mix, and the trap drums are a bit heavy-handed, but these guys seem to be having the time of their lives and are wonderfully conveying that to the listeners. "Enjoy yourself" is one of the shouts heard, and at the conclusion, Haston calls out, "How's that?" Damn good, thank you very much.

Livery Stable Blues (1917)—Original Dixieland "Jass" Band (written by Nick LaRocca)

Victor 18255

Recorded on Feb. 25, 1917;[17] *Pop Memories* debut June 2, 1917 (#4 peak) (*Jazz-#151, TG*)

The first commercially issued, unquestioned jazz recording, *Livery Stable Blues* (with its flip side *Dixie Jass Band One-Step*) made the Original Dixieland Jazz Band an overnight sensation. No one outside of New Orleans (where black jazzmen such as Freddie Keppard, King Oliver and Kid Ory were introducing the techniques that

the white boys of the ODJB picked up) had ever heard music like this: raucous, frenetic, and thrilling. The ridiculously breathless tempo is due to the fact that the song ran too long to fit on a standard 78, and the band refused to drop a chorus, so they speeded everything up in order to fit. Although copyrighted by the band's cornetist/leader Nick LaRocca, the song's melody, or something very close to it, had been familiar in New Orleans at least a decade earlier under the title *Meat Ball*, according to Gunther Schuller.[18] LaRocca said the piece evolved from an improvisation on (ironically) Stephen Adams' sacred standard *The Holy City* (he changed one chord of Adams' original and deleted the last two measures).[19]

From a modern perspective, the playing here is raw and undisciplined, and the barnyard sound effects (a whinnying horse, crowing rooster, and braying donkey created on their instruments) a bit corny—the number was sometimes known as *Barnyard Blues*. The musicianship of group standouts Larry Shields on clarinet and Nick LaRocca would become more sharply focused within the next few years. But even with its flaws, this performance is exciting by any standard. Richard Sudhalter writes of LaRocca's early playing: "listening to the fierce drive he generates in the ensembles can be a heady experience."[20]

In previous years, sheet music had always been the primary means of marketing new songs, with recordings in a secondary role (as evidenced by the fact that in many cases no recordings were made of a new song until months after it had proven its commercial appeal through sheet music sales). This began to change in the 1910s, and Peter C. Muir cites *Livery Stable Blues* as an example. The recording was made in February and issued the following month, with several hundred thousand copies sold. There were two printed versions of the song (one instrumental, one with lyrics); these were copyrighted in June and November, respectively. So in these cases "the record clearly has primary, and the sheet music secondary, status."[21]

Clarinetist Alcide Nunez, who left the band shortly before its recording career began, filed a copyright claim on *Livery Stable* asserting that he co-wrote the song, triggering a lawsuit by the ODJB members seeking to enjoin its publication with any attribution to Nunez.[22] After heavily-publicized and sometimes wacky court-

15. In addition to his historic contributions as bandleader, composer, and the era's number one defender for the rights of black musicians, Europe (pointed out Ron Welburn in *Black Music Research Journal*, Vol. 7, 1987) was also a sophisticated early jazz analyst. His last published interview before his death, given to the *New York Tribune* in March 1919 and reprinted in *Literary Digest* as "A Negro Explains Jazz," was "the first published discussion of a music called 'jazz' by a practicing black musician."

16. Wondrich, p. 184–85.

17. The record's release was announced in the Victor supplement published in March, then the April 15 *Talking Machine World*, and a month later reported among Victor's top sellers. The May 15 issue also discussed the company's "attention-compelling" poster for retailers featuring the ODJB and Joseph C. Smith's orchestra.

18. William Russell and Stephen W. Smith, in their chapter on New Orleans music in the 1938 book *Jazzmen*, claimed that black New Orleans cornetist Freddie Keppard was playing *Barnyard Blues* before the ODJB picked it up. However, Schuller notes in *Early Jazz* (p. 181) that they offered no substantiation.

19. Bunn, *The Story of the Original Dixieland Jazz Band*, p. 70.

20. Sudhalter, *Lost Chords*, p. 16.

21. Muir, *Before "Crazy Blues," Volume I*, p. 75–76.

22. Nunez, unlike LaRocca, always acknowledged the inspiration for the music he played. After describing his contributions to *Livery Stable*, he noted: "All of this, however, was derived from the New Orleans blacks

room proceedings—Judge George A. Carpenter confided to friends that he was beginning to wake up at night and hear donkey cries and horse whinnies—Carpenter dismissed the case in October 1917, finding that if one stripped away all the improvised parts, there wasn't much left.[23] (The band also briefly filed suit against Victor in a side battle settled out of court.) David Wondrich: "For the first time on record, we can hear what happens when you promote the swerve from a means of coloring notes and phrases to an organizing principle—and it's not pretty. All blaring and braying, at first acquaintance these [early ODJB performances] are loud, ugly records that defy easy conceptions of musicality. They're ragtime gone feral, they're rock 'n' roll." [24] There's actually no improvisation here—each player wrote out his own part, and each chorus and verse is played the same way—but in the face of such thunder and lightning that hardly matters. Bix Beiderbecke, Mezz Mezzrow, and Eddie Condon are among the many young white musicians who used the record as one of the original inspirations for their careers.

Paul Whiteman none too gently poked fun at *Livery Stable* in his landmark 1924 "Experiment in Modern Music" concert that introduced Gershwin's *Rhapsody In Blue*, using it as an example of the silly side of jazz from which the music had since thankfully evolved. But Olin Downes of the *New York Times* was critical of this condescending approach, calling the ODJB song "a glorious piece of imprudence, much better in its unbuttoned jocosity and Rabelaisian laughter than other and more polite compositions that came later."[25]

Till We Meet Again (1919)—Henry Burr & Albert Campbell (music by Richard A. Whiting, lyrics by Raymond Egan)
Columbia 2668
Pop Memories debut Feb. 15, 1919 (9 weeks at #1) (*MEM-#77, DMDB*)

The Great War had just ended with the November 3, 1918, surrender of Austria-Hungary and Germany's signing of the armistice a week later; amidst relief that the terrible conflict had ended, it was a time of mourning for the fallen and longing for others who hadn't yet returned. *Till We Meet Again* tapped into these deep emotions, and

Henry Burr and Albert Campbell—two tenors who had been singing together as far back as 1904 as members of the Peerless Quartet—give the ballad a sweetly sentimental resonance. The song was first cited in the November 16, 1918, *Music Trades* immediately after the war's conclusion under the caption, "Ring Out, Sweet Bells of Peace!" *Till We Meet Again*, stated the publication, is "a major hit, [and] looks to be as big as [the 1918 smash ballad] *Smiles*." "Smile the while you kiss me sad adieu / When the clouds roll by I'll come to you / Then the skies will seem more blue . . . / So wait and pray each night for me / Till we meet again."

Leo Diamond in the June 1932 issue of *The Metronome* offered the back story to the song's climb to success. When the tune was first published by Jerome H. Remick & Co. on August 30, 1918, the firm had only about thirty-five outlets consisting of department and dry goods stores that had music counters, and the first printing drew little response. After about two months there was no demand for a second printing, so all leftover orchestrations and professional copies of the song were thrown out to make room for new contenders. But in November one of the Remick outlets sent in an order for 200 copies, stimulated because every time the store's pianist played the number, customers wanted to buy it. So songwriter and Remick executive Abe Holzmann decided to give *Till We Meet Again* another chance with a second printing and new promotional campaign, and the result, reported Holzmann, was orders coming in for a thousand lots at a time, and "one of the biggest overnight sensations we ever had, and mind you, we had almost forgotten about the number when it happened."[26]

The most prolific artist of the entire acoustic recording era, Henry Burr was born Harry McClaskey on January 15, 1882, in St. Stephen, New Brunswick, Canada. A burly man blessed with a beautiful tenor voice particularly suited to ballads and religious material, he was a soloist in his Methodist Episcopal Church, came to New York to study voice, and began his recording career for Columbia by early 1903, taking the last name Burr after one of his voice teachers. Within a year he was also recording for Victor and Edison, and subsequently worked for just about every American label at one time or another. On his Edison performances, he used the pseudonym of Irving Gillette. Burr recorded in virtually every format: solos (1905's *In the Shade of the Old*

and John Spriccio." (Lawrence Gushee, "The Nineteenth Century Origins of Jazz," Spring 1994 *Black Music Research Journal*, p. 2.)

23. Bunn offered a detailed account of the court case, p. 75–85. The September 29, 1917, *Music Trades* featured an ad regarding a temporary injunction issued against a "spurious" edition of *Livery Stable Blues*, proclaiming that "the only authentic edition" was published by the Leo Feist company. The October 20 issue reported the followup court finding that both Feist's *Barnyard Blues* and the Chicago-published *Livery* could be marketed.
24. *Stomp and Swerve*, p. 118–19.
25. February 13, 1924, *New York Times*.

26. This account is not quite consistent with an earlier one in the February 19, 1921, *Music Trades* by company president Remick himself. By this account, the firm paid $15,000 for rights to the song, exceptionally high for the era, but a bargain when it proved a "stupendous" seller. "Had we taken this song on a royalty basis we would have been compelled to pay more than $100,000 for it." Also, contrary to the implication of the Diamond article, Remick by 1918 was one of the biggest publishers in the business.

Apple Tree was one of his biggest successes), duets, trios (the Sterling Trio), groups (more than 20 years with the Peerless), and in the 1920s as guest vocalist with various dance bands. All told, he's said to have sung on some 12,000 recordings from 1903–1930.

Carolina Shout (1921)—James P. Johnson
Okeh 4495
Recorded Oct. 18, 1921 (released in Feb. 1922) (*Jazz-#120, TG*)

With musical roots in ragtime and a firm grounding in classical technique, James P. Johnson served as the model for a generation of jazz pianists—particularly Fats Waller, Willie "The Lion" Smith, Duke Ellington, and Count Basie—and through them, his influence would continue to be felt in future generations. Born on February 1, 1891, in New Brunswick, New Jersey, Johnson received early musical training from his mother and an Italian music teacher, played in Harlem rent parties as a youngster, and listened to both classical and early ragtime pianists. His professional career began in 1912 in New York clubs; he toured in shows and vaudeville, performed in England, and later in the decade accompanied future blues legend Bessie Smith (he would also accompany her on some subsequent records). In 1920–1921 he played with James Reese Europe's Hell Fighters Band (Europe himself had been killed in 1919), and this paved the way for his recording debut.

In an interview with Tom Davin published four years after the pianist's death in *The Jazz Review*, Johnson recalled *Carolina Shout* as one of several compositions that began during the early 1910s as a ragtime arrangement of a cotillion dance step at The Jungle Casino in New York.[27] As soon as he introduced it in local clubs, *Shout* became the test piece used by just about every New York rag-styled pianist, a supreme challenge of technique and skill, replacing Scott Joplin's *Maple Leaf Rag* in that capacity, particularly after it was made available on piano rolls in 1918.[28] One of the first published descriptions of a "shout" in black religious custom was in the May 30, 1867, *New York Nation*. Parishioners formed a ring, with some of the best singers and shouters at the center of the room, singing the body of the song as everyone else shuffled or danced around them. Shouts, which were described as a relic of African practices and particularly common in South Carolina and its Sea Islands, could last for hours into the middle of the night. Willie "The Lion" Smith observed that Johnson "played a 'shout' and

a shout was a stride. Shouts came about because of the Baptist Church and the way black folks sang or 'shouted' their hymns. They sang them a special way and you played them a special way, emphasizing the basic beat to keep everybody together."[29]

The third strain of the piece contains his keyboard version of a shout, described by Gunther Schuller as an "intensified elaboration of European-American hymn tunes. It is at the same time a call-and-response chorus in the old preacher-to-congregation relationship." One of Johnson's innovations was "his embodiment of improvisation within a broad compositional frame of reference." Schuller cites as examples the numerous different embellishments in his two recordings of *Carolina Shout*. "Johnson was famous in his day for the seemingly inexhaustible fertility of his imagination, which enabled him to produce variation upon variation on the same theme."[30] In this performance, write Rudi Blesh and Harrriet Janis, "one can literally hear the high shout of one worshipper and the answering outburst of the ecstatic congregation."[31] Samuel A. Floyd, Jr., in *The Power of Black Music* remarks that the piece "is replete with call-response tropes" constituting a modern treatment of African musical traditions: "call-and-response figures, riffs, straight bass with tricky reverses that create cross-rhythms, and much imitative hand-to-hand action."[32] A young Ellington learned it by following a Johnson piano roll set at slow speed; Waller in 1934 recorded a wonderful version of the song. David Jasen: "Like *Maple Leaf Rag*, it is a folk essence finely honed into a definitive masterpiece of its kind." The flip side of the landmark 78, *Keep Off the Grass*, was another of the 1920s' jazz classics.

King Porter (1924)—Jelly Roll Morton & King Oliver
Autograph 617
Recorded in Chicago in Dec. 1924 (*NPR-100, Jazz-#51*)

This classic duet between two of the reigning titans of 1920s jazz was not only a landmark because of its musical quality, but also as one of the first electrical recordings using then-experimental technology. By Morton's account, he wrote *King Porter Stomp* as a combination of three or four tunes in about 1905 during his original tenure in New Orleans, before he left the city in 1907 to become a pool shark, gambler, nightclub owner, and part-time piano player in various venues around the country. As he developed the piece on the road, write biographers

27. July 1959 *Jazz Review*, p. 13, from interviews done in 1953.

28. Jasen, *Ragtime: An Encyclopedia, Discography, and Sheetography*, p. 38. In *Rags and Ragtime*, p. 243, Jasen reported that Johnson's original piano roll performance of the song was issued in February 1918 on Artempo 12975.

29. Jasen and Tichenor, *Rags and Ragtime*. P. 240–44.

30. *Early Jazz*, p. 217–19. John Edward Haase in *Ragtime: Its History, Composers, and Music* calls *Sounds of Africa* "a spectacular example of the complexity and rhythmic drive of Eastern ragtime, as contrasted with the more sedate, 'not-to-be-played-too-fast' ragtime of the St. Louis ragtime fraternity."

31. *They All Played Ragtime*, p. 187.

32. Floyd, p. 110–11.

Howard Reich and William Gaines, one listener particularly taken by it was fellow piano player from Florida named Porter King, whom Morton came to admire, so he named the piece after him, inverting the title. (Rudi Blesh and Harriet Janis in *They All Played Ragtime* suggest that one or more of the themes was penned by King, based on the recollections of rag pianist Brun Campbell, who knew both men.)[33] Using the number as a sure-fire "ace up his sleeve" to defeat rival pianists in musical duels, he deliberately did not publish it to keep it for himself. The composition's "ferocious right-hand syncopations and relentless left-hand rhythms represented one of the first clear-cut distillations of swing rhythm, articulated almost a generation before Louis Armstrong gave this music galvanic new momentum in Chicago in the mid-1920s." An even bigger innovation was its third theme, in which he abruptly changed keys, from A-flat to D-flat. "With this radical gesture, the entire musical landscape of the piece shifted, from the hot, barreling swing pulse of the earlier sections to the sleekly understated rhythmic beat and cooler tone of the finale. In this single composition—a three-minute masterpiece if ever there were one—a composer at the dawn of the 20th century was pointing the way for at least two decades of musical evolution yet to come."[34]

By Morton's account, he submitted the piece to Scott Joplin, who returned it with the comment that it needed no improvement. (Ragtime authority David A. Jasen points out that the piece's B section uses a "Joplinesque" broken chord pattern, with Morton's variations. Jasen also remarks that the trio section is a "floating folk strain" recalled by rag pianist Charles Thompson as a musical interlude used by local pianists in contests between the tunes.)[35] The reason for writing something outside the realm of ragtime was practical: he was up against several New Orleans pianists whose high-speed virtuosity was, he felt, beyond his capability, so he needed to go in a different direction to distinguish himself from the competition.

Western Electric scientists Joseph Maxfield and H. Harrison, as explained by Andre Millard, came up with their system of electrical recording—using a condenser microphone to pick up the sound and change it into varying electric currents, an improvement on the way that the telephone turned speech into electricity—in 1920, and during the next few years began to make experimental recordings. When the company went to the Victor and Columbia studios in 1924 to cut some demonstration records, the record labels were impressed but hesitated to make the historic change, "loathe to abandon the old system and a massive inventory of acoustic machines and recordings." But as radio cut ever more deeply into the audience of the recording giants, sheer desperation finally forced the decision. The first test recordings were made in Columbia's New York recording laboratory in 1924 by Sam Watkins, a Western Electric engineer, and the Morton-Oliver recording was made very soon afterward.[36]

The small Autograph label, the first on the market with electric recording, operated out of Marsh Laboratories in Chicago under president Orlando R. Marsh. It was set up primarily to make records for other companies whose own studios were too far from Chicago to justify sending recording equipment there, but which had contracted artists doing engagements in the area.[37] Brian Rust remarks that this 78 is "quintessentially rare. The electric recording system could barely cope with the majestic power of Oliver's cornet."[38]

Morton initially recorded *King Porter Stomp* at his second studio session, and first for Gennett, on July 17, 1923, as a piano solo issued on Gennett 5289. King Oliver & His Creole Jazz Band had enjoyed success with Morton's composition *Froggie Moore* (aka *Frog-I-More Rag*) in 1923, so it was appropriate that when the cornet master made his first recording date outside a group context, he did it in a pair of duets with Morton in December 1924, *King Porter* and its companion piece *Tom Cat*. The pioneering electrical recording used a microphone twelve inches in diameter. The two jazz giants duet throughout the piece at a medium tempo, with both in excellent form.[39] Jelly Roll cut another solo piano version of his trademark song for Vocalion in April 1926, but never recorded the number with his Red Hot Peppers; Charles Creath's Jazz-o-Maniacs had cut the first group version in March 1925, and Fletcher Henderson's 1928 rendition helped pave the way for the many big bands that would record it in years to come. But to Morton's great frustration, as his creation reigned as one of the most familiar hits of 1935 through Benny Goodman's recording, he wasn't earning a dime from it; his publisher Walter Melrose wasn't paying him royalties, and the virtually all-white publishing association

33. *They All Played Ragtime*, p. 181. Another interesting element of the song: Morton's friend and fellow pianist/composer James P. Johnson recalled that Morton told him *King Porter* was originally inspired by cotillion dance music. (Cited by Johnson in a 1953 interview published six years later in the *Jazz Review*.)

34. *Jelly's Blues*, p. 36–38.

35. Jasen and Tichenor, *Rags and Ragtime*, p. 256–57.

36. *America on Record: A History of Recorded Sound*, p. 139–44.

37. Marsh also served as Paramount's recording engineer for Chicago sessions from 1923–1926. Stephen Calt, in his series of articles on the Paramount label, noted that because of the studio's proximity to the El (elevated trains), recording had to stop whenever trains passed (*78 Quarterly* #4 [1989], p. 28).

38. Rust, *The American Record Label Book*, p. 22.

39. Although Oliver confessed to being a poor sight reader, Terry Teachout notes in *Pops* (p. 399) that he unquestionably did read music, as he was reading from the written cornet part in the stock orchestration of *King Porter*.

ASCAP had denied him membership. The legend was scraping to get by and virtually out of music while everyone profited from his work but him.

The Stampede (1926)—Fletcher Henderson & His Orchestra
Columbia 654
Recorded on May 14, 1926 (*Jazz-#138, TG, SJ*)

Fletcher Henderson, who helped show the world how a big band could play jazz with fire that was comparable to a small combo in the 1920s, enjoyed one of his most memorable musical triumphs with *The Stampede*. Born in Cuthbert, Georgia on December 18, 1898, Henderson studied classical piano with his mother (a pianist, as was his father), earned a degree in chemistry and math from Atlanta University, but switched gears in 1920 to become a song plugger with the Harry Pace–W. C. Handy music publishing company. Pace hired Fletch as musical director at the black-owned Black Swan label, and he led groups backing its singers including Ethel Waters. While he gained national fame as bandleader at New York's Roseland Ballroom from 1924–1931, Henderson served as accompanist for Bessie Smith and other vocalists. His hiring of Louis Armstrong as featured soloist in 1924–1925 (after Satch left King Oliver) was a seminal event, as was the emergence of Don Redman as a pioneering arranger.

Martin Williams writes that the Henderson band's performance of his original *The Stampede* "shows the startling effects of Armstrong's influence" through the outstanding cornet work of future Duke Ellington star Rex Stewart (who has the opening and closing solos).[40] Joe Smith's longer solo around mid-song is praised by Donald Clarke as "pretty and perfectly constructed," and a fascinating contrast to Stewart's "ferocity."[41] The biggest star of the ensemble in 1926, tenor saxophonist Coleman Hawkins, offers a strong solo—considered to be his first classic improvisation—that also demonstrates some of the influence of Armstrong's boldness.[42] The song's arrangement by Redman "is almost an archetype of the big band score" with its written passages that separate the band by sections and variation-on-theme structure with room for solo improvisation.

Gunther Schuller joins in the praise for Stewart's "brash, lusty introductory solo that nails down the driving atmosphere of the entire performance." Schuller also cites a "spectacular" clarinet solo, apparently by Buster Bailey. The playing is so terrific that it renders the band's old-fashioned two-beat rhythm insignificant.[43] Ted Gioia contrasts this performance with the band's earlier work, noting that the "textures behind the soloists are no longer passive harmonic cushions, but extroverted lines that propel the improvisation with incisive counter-rhythms."[44] Henderson biographer Jeffrey Magee calls attention to the use of several "telltale" Redman trademarks. In the introduction, "the arranger creates a terraced, orchestrated crescendo—with an insistent rhythmic figure volleyed among parts of the band—spilling over into a clamorous improvisatory trumpet solo. With its quick shifts and solo-ensemble alternation, the passage evokes not just Redman in general, but also what might be called his 'Armstrong style'" as heard during Louis' tenure. In his *Stampede* solo, the twenty-one-year-old Hawkins employs a new "legato fluency," and "a relaxed rhythmic variety now takes the place of the jerky, breathless syncopations and flurries" he had previously employed. "In *The Stampede* we can hear Hawkins telling a story, working on the musical 'coherence' that made Armstrong's solos unique."[45] Despite its great innovations, the band would never quite break through with a national audience, but Henderson would make a profound mark on jazz history with his late-1930s arrangements for Benny Goodman.

Pretty Polly (1927)—B. F. Shelton
Victor 35838
Recorded in Bristol on July 29, 1927 (released Sept. 16)

Ralph Peer's recordings in Bristol, Tennessee, from July 25 through August 4, 1927, have lived in country music legend for more than eighty years as the sessions that introduced the world to the Carter Family and Jimmie Rodgers, and helped give birth to country music as an industry. But perhaps the most exceptional performance of all in Bristol belonged to neither icon, but instead was delivered by Benjamin Franklin (B. F.) Shelton.

A barber from Corbin, Kentucky, in Clay County, Shelton learned his two-fingered banjo picking technique in the area, and traveled to Bristol together with fellow Corbin resident Alfred G. Karnes, another of the sessions' unforgettable standouts (with evangelical numbers including *I Am Bound for the Promised Land*). Both men came as a result of a front-page story in the *Bristol News-Bulletin* evening edition for July 27, the third day of the sessions. He cut a handful of exceptional sides that July 29 that proved to be his only commercially issued recordings; slightly over a year later he had a session for

---

40. *Smithsonian Collection of Classic Jazz* (1973), p. 22.
41. *The Rise and Fall of Popular Music*, p. 166. Roy Eldridge recalled of Smith: "They talk a lot about Bix, but this cat was too much. Just listen to what he plays in the middle" of this performance (Dance, *The World of Swing*, p. 150).
42. Annotation by Phil Schaap, *Sony Music: Soundtrack for a Century*, p. 126.

43. *Early Jazz*, p. 264.
44. Gioia, *The History of Jazz*, p. 111–12.
45. *The Uncrowned King of Swing*, p. 111–14.

Columbia from which nothing was released at the time. Like the Carters, he had a deep knowledge of traditional songs. One side of Victor 35838 was his superb rendition of the folk standard *Darling Corey* (under the title *Darlin' Cora*), one of that song's earliest recordings. On the other was *Pretty Polly*. It was issued on a 12-inch 78 to provide more than four minutes of playing time, highly unusual for a "hillbilly" record.

Originally a British garland or broadside (as *The Gosport Tragedy*, or *The Perjured Ship Carpenter*), *Pretty Polly* is one of the many, frequently bloody English murder ballads handed down from one generation to the next in Appalachian families. The original 1750 version, in the form of a broadside and set in the English Channel town of Gosport near Portsmouth and the Isle of Wight, ran thirty-five quatrains;[46] J. Woodfall Ebsworth subsequently included it in *Roxburghe Ballads* in 1899.[47] John Harrington Cox in *Traditional Ballads* (1939) reported that the song in its American form may have derived from the murder of Polly Aldridge by William Chapman near Warfield, Kentucky, around 1820. The protagonist (a ship carpenter) and Polly are set to be married, but he suggests that they take a walk before they wed, and she quickly realizes that his intention is to kill her; Willie's motive is that he had gotten the unsuspecting girl pregnant, although this is typically left out in modern treatments. In the British version, the killer flees to Australia, but while en route Polly's ghost—with the baby to whom she was never able to give birth—rises up and seize him on the ship. (This supernatural revenge never appears in the Americanized versions, in which the killer is allowed to get away with the crime.) In the U.S., the song was in wide circulation by at least 1890. G. L. Kittredge discussed it in the *Journal of American Folklore*,[48] as did Cecil Sharp and Olive Campbell in *English Folk Songs from the Southern Appalachians* (1917).[49]

Polly was first put on record by Kentucky singer-banjoist John Hammond (no relation to the producer/talent scout) for the Champion label in 1925, then by the great Dock Boggs for Brunswick on March 10, 1927 (one day after he cut the immortal *Country Blues*). Shelton gives it an intense, compelling performance on solo vocal and five-string banjo that helped ensure the song would be a permanent part of the American folk reper-

toire. Noting that many early rural blues, both black and white, possessed a modal character (using the Medieval system of pitches that preceded modern tonalism with the latter's major and minor scales), Richard Nevins called Shelton's *Polly* a modal "masterpiece" that was "but a step away from its ancient antecedent."[50] Although the excellent 1938 version by the Coon Creek Girls is more widely known thanks to its inclusion on the Harry Smith folk music anthology, Shelton's rendition is definitive; the Stanley Brothers even credited him as the composer when they recorded it years later. The Shelton record was one of the first six Victor releases from the sessions. "Polly, pretty Polly, you're guessin' just right / I dug on your grave the biggest part of last night . . ."[51]

In his in-depth account of the Bristol sessions, Charles K. Wolfe declared that they were of immense significance for reasons other than Rodgers and the Carters. These were the first major field recordings that featured predominantly vocal performances, and provided wide-ranging "documentation of an emerging commercial art form in a bustling Southern city." Bristol in 1927, flanked by Johnson City and Kingsport (with collective Tri-Cities population of 32,000), was the largest urban area in Appalachia, situated on the Tennessee/Virginia border within easy driving distance from Kentucky, North Carolina, and West Virginia—a perfect location to record traditional performers. "Like a rock thrown into a still pond, the Bristol sessions would reverberate far beyond their time; they would send echoes down through the years, touching all kinds of people and their musics, and would emerge finally as the legend they deserve to be."[52]

Unzer Toirele (1928)—Abe Schwartz's Orkester
Columbia 8160-F
Recorded in Jan. 1928

In any history of American Jewish/klezmer recordings during the early decades of the twentieth century, the name of Abe Schwartz looms large.[53] Born in 1891 in Romania, he emigrated to America early in the new century and began a long and exceptionally prolific recording career in 1916, with multiple skills as fiddler, composer, arranger, bandleader, and behind-the-scenes organizer of ethnic music recording sessions. His earliest recordings of 1916–1917, as noted by Henry Sapoznik and Dick

46. Leonard Roberts, *In the Pine: Selected Kentucky Folksongs*.

47. Ebsworth, p. 142–45. Also see *Frank C. Brown Collection of North Carolina Folklore*, p. 234–35.

48. October–December 1907 *Journal of American Folklore*, 261–63. Another good discussion of the song's history is provided by Mellinger E. Henry, "Ballads and Songs of the Southern Highlands," July–September 1929 *Journal of American Folklore*.

49. Sharp and Campbell as song No. 49, under the title *The Cruel Ship's Carpenter*, but containing most of the central elements of *Polly*; in the 1952 reprint of the two-volume edition, p. 317 of Volume 1.

50. Liner notes to CD *Before the Blues: The Early American Black Music Scene*, Vol. 1, p. 3.

51. Rennie Sparks offers an extended analysis of *Pretty Polly* in *The Rose and the Briar*, p. 37–49. "The first time you hear *Pretty Polly*, you giggle nervously. The dark forest flowing with blood, the beautiful girl, the open grave—it makes you dizzy with a strange mix of horror and delight."

52. *Journal of Country Music*, Vol. 12 #2 (1989).

53. Liner notes by Henry Sapoznik for Sony CD *Abe Schwartz: The Klezmer King*. Schwartz's discography is found in Spottswood, *Ethnic Music on Records*, Vol. 3, p. 1497–1502.

Spottswood, "reveal the transition to small-group jazz in American music at large, presaging the influential groups of Ted Lewis, Wilbur Sweatman, King Oliver, and the Original Dixieland Jazz Band."[54] According to Dr. Martin Schwartz, his orchestra produced more recordings than any other American klezmer ensemble of the pre-1930 era.[55] One of his co-compositions was *Di Grine Kuzine*, later adapted into the Benny Goodman hit *My Little Cousin*.[56] Schwartz was noted for hiring terrific clarinetists, and after Naftule Brandwein (the "king of klezmer clarinet") left the band, his successor was the great Dave Tarras. Born in the Ukrainian town of Ternovka in 1897, Tarras made his arrival at Ellis Island in 1921, and got his professional start with Joseph Cherniavsky's Yiddish-American Jazz Band on the vaudeville circuit.[57] This led directly to his role as featured soloist with Schwartz, his technical brilliance unmatched in his field.[58]

Unzer Toirele, the leadoff selection in Yazoo's Dave Tarras compilation, is an exciting, vigorously uptempo instrumental with plenty of his clarinet soloing in an ensemble that also includes trumpet, trombone, piano, banjo, string bass, and drums. While drawing deeply upon European Jewish musical traditions, it also reflects American influences—not jazz, to be sure, but a compelling hybrid. Schwartz maintained a busy recording career through the 1930s (he died in 1963), and Tarras remained a hugely influential figure and mentor to other musicians until his death in 1989.

---

54. Annotation for *Klezmer Pioneers: European and American Recordings, 1905–1952*. Schwartz's 1917 recording of *Tants, Tants Yiddlekh (Dance, Dance Little Jews)*, a tune originally known as *Ma Yofus*, became a tremendous seller, reissued by Columbia several times (Sapoznik, *Klezmer!*, p. 88).

55. Liner notes for Arhoolie's *Klezmer Music: Early Yiddish Instrumental Music/The First Recordings, 1908–1927*.

56. Called by some "the biggest hit in the history of Jewish music," *Di Grine Kuzine*, possibly based in part on traditional themes, was first printed in 1917, and, writes Victor Greene (*A Singing Ambivalence: American Immigrants Between Old World and New, 1830–1930*) was such an "instant sensation" that it spawned numerous ballads about innocent young immigrants who were ground down in urban America. Even beyond European Jews in America, it became "one of the most popular songs of immigrant life in America."

57. The immigrant journeys of Schwartz and Tarras would become far less prevalent in America after President Coolidge on May 26, 1924, signed into law the Johnson-Reed Act, aka the Immigration Act of 1924, including the National Origins Act, which limited the number of immigrants who could be admitted from any country to 2 percent of the number of people from that country who were already living in the United States in 1890. Its purpose was to sharply restrict Southern and Eastern Europeans who had been coming to America in large numbers since the 1890s, while favoring northwestern Europeans, particularly those from Germany, Britain, and Ireland. In musical terms, the laws shut off large-scale Jewish and Slavic emigration to the U.S., narrowing the potential markets for traditional music from these ethnic groups. Still, the heavy immigration that had already occurred provided a large existing market for the ethnic music that record companies were producing in dramatically increasing numbers through the 1930s.

58. Biographical information, Sapoznik's liner notes for *Dave Tarras: Father of Yiddish-American Klezmer Music*.

She's a Great, Great Girl (1928)—Roger Wolfe Kahn & His Orchestra (written by Harry Woods)[59]

Victor 21326
Recorded March 14, 1928 (released on May 11)

For anyone who appreciates the hot dance-band jazz of the 1920s, Roger Wolfe Kahn's *She's a Great, Great Girl* is guaranteed to bring a smile.

A perfect case study of the proposition that sometimes money and art can be a winning combination, Kahn was born on October 19, 1907, in Morristown, New Jersey, the son of a nationally known steel magnate and art collector. Kahn was a jazz lover as a teenager; he played alto saxophone along with other instruments, but not quite well enough to make a living at it. His father agreed to buy out Arthur Lange's orchestra in late 1923, and Roger became a bandleader at age sixteen. Blessed with excellent taste and backed by his father's wealth, he began restocking the band with some of New York's finest jazzmen, and provided them with first-class arrangements and plenty of rehearsal time. The result was some of the best hot dance-band records of the era by an ensemble referred to by some as "the million-dollar band." When his band wasn't recording or headlining at New York's Biltmore Hotel, Kahn co-wrote some songs (including the pop standard *Crazy Rhythm*), and also owned a booking service and a nightclub. After recording prolifically from 1925 through 1932, Kahn left music to become an aviation consultant, served as a test pilot in World War II, and later worked at Grumman Aircraft.

She's a Great, Great Girl is a splendid, energetic instrumental with a happy vibe, featuring Jack Teagarden's classic trombone solo. Guitarist Eddie Lang and violinist Joe Venuti are among the other standouts in this all-star band; Venuti has an outstanding mid-song solo. Miff Mole couldn't make this record date as scheduled, so on short notice his place was taken (at the suggestion of another band member) by Teagarden. Just twenty-two at the time, Jack had made his recording debut only two months earlier after arriving in New York (with Johnny Johnson's orchestra), and this was his first important solo. According to Kahn, Teagarden arrived with little sleep and a "terrific" hangover—yet he not only played Arthur Schutt's hot arrangement perfectly, but cut loose with a full-chorus ad lib solo early in the record that became one of the great jazz moments of the 1920s.[60] Indeed, on the two takes of the song, he plays distinctively different and comparably terrific solos.

---

59. Harry Woods' list of major songs ranges from *I'm Looking Over a Four-Leaf Clover* and *Side By Side* to *We Just Couldn't Say Goodbye* and *What a Little Moonlight Can Do*.

60. Ross Wilby, liner notes to Jazz Oracle CD *Roger Wolfe Kahn: Recorded in New York 1925–1932*.

Although his solo is, remarks Richard Hadlock, "suggestive of Mole's approach and less positive than later Teagarden solos, [it] is unmistakably the work of a mature jazz trombonist with ideas well in advance of those of most of his contemporaries. Furthermore, he sets forth those ideas in the warm blues dialect of the South rather than in the more stilted ragtime-based phraseology of the Northeast. The effect is stunning."[61] Richard Sudhalter writes that the record created "a sensation" when it was issued.[62] From the 1980s to the present, this performance has served as the familiar theme song for Rob Bamberger's program *Hot Jazz Saturday Night* on WAMU-FM in Washington, D.C.

(Personnel: Jack Teagarden; Manny Klein & Tommy Gott on trumpet; Arnold Brilhart & Alfie Evans on clarinet & alto saxophone; Joe Venuti, Eddie Lang, Arthur Schutt; Arthur Campbell on bass; Vic Berton on drums)

Lucia di Lammermoor Sextet (Sextet from "Lucia") (Chi Me Frena?) (1928)—Giovanni Giovale

Victor V-21372

Recorded on April 3, 1928

In the opinion of musicologist Dick Spottswood, Giovanni Giovale was perhaps the greatest mandolin virtuoso (at least on commercial recordings) of the entire pre-Bill Monroe era. The Italian-American artist (born in November 1885, died in 1949) enjoyed a long career in vaudeville, and this selection from the Gaetano Donizetti opera *Lucia di Lammermoor* ("Chi Me Frena" translates as "What Restrains Me?") was his big show-stopper. Giovale plays all six parts of the sextet in a solo unaccompanied performance, and is quite remarkable, soaring and plunging, with dramatic tempo shifts. During the same exceptional session, he made a dazzling *Valse Brillante* accompanied by guitar; a comparably powerful record with his Giovale Trio (two mandolins and guitar), *Costumi Siciliani*; and a gorgeous trio waltz, *Idillio Primaverile*. They're all included on a Rounder CD assembled by Spottswood, *Italian String Virtuosi*.

Nicholas Tawa's book *A Sound of Strangers* documents the central role of music to most immigrants to America during the 1880–1930 era. "Whether for consolation [or] sheer joyousness . . . the settlers turned spontaneously to music, for music represented a significant dimension of their lives. To Americans this music may have been the sound of strangers. To immigrants the sound was an invigorating and life-sustaining force."[63]

Fishing Blues (1928)—"Ragtime Texas" Henry Thomas

Vocalion 1249

Recorded in Chicago on June 13, 1928 (released April 1, 1929) (*Folk-#99, Blues-#107, HS*)

It's doubtful that there has ever been a more jubilant, carefree ode to the joys of sitting on a lake with rod and reel in hand than this folk/blues classic—even if the song was originally designed to use fishing as a sexual metaphor. Born in 1874 in the Big Sandy area of eastern Texas (located near the bottomlands along the Sabine River in Upshur County), Henry Thomas couldn't abide the semi-feudal life of cotton farming in which his parents were trapped, and left home at an early age to perform on the streets of Dallas and at country dances; he rode the rails across Texas and beyond as a hobo and entertained the passengers. Growing up in the Reconstruction era and at least fifty-two when he made his recording debut, he's believed to be the oldest blues artist to make a significant number of recordings, and his enjoyably archaic style draws on various pre-twentieth century traditions. Tony Russell in *Blacks, Whites, and Blues* pointed out that Thomas was a black counterpart to country music pioneer Uncle Dave Macon: the two men were born less than four years apart (Macon in October 1870), both were songsters who were intimately familiar with a wide range of both black and white traditional material, and five songs were recorded by each.

Mack McCormick—who as a teenager met an old Houston street singer in 1949 whom he believed was Henry Thomas, and subsequently did years of research on the artist—compiled the definitive account of Thomas' life in his extraordinary liner notes for a 1975 Herwin LP assembling his complete recorded works. Ragtime Texas was, in his estimation, "a singular and important figure" whose body of recordings "represent one of the richest contributions to our musical culture."[64]

Thomas recorded twenty-three sides for Vocalion from 1927–1929, all solo performances on which he accompanies himself on guitar (which he strummed in the manner of a banjo to emphasize dance-like rhythms) and "quills"—a form of pan-pipe made from cane. The latter instrument, related to panpipes dating all the way back to ancient Greece, was commonly used by rural black performers in Mississippi, Louisiana, and Texas. Dena Epstein cites an 1811 slave uprising in St. John the Baptist, about fifty miles north of New Orleans, in which the participants were reportedly "goaded to a frenzy" by the beating of drums and iron kettles,

---

61. *Jazz Masters of the '20s*, p. 177–78.
62. *Lost Chords*, p. 125.
63. Tawa, p. 122. In his view (p. 24), the two immigrant groups to whom music was most crucial were Italians and Jews. These also happened to be

the two largest ethnic groups in U.S. immigration from 1880 to the 1920s (five million southern Italians, some 2.5 million East European Jews).
64. McCormick, "Henry Thomas: Our Deepest Look at the Roots," p. 1.

accompanied by the "shrill notes" of reed quills.[65] Norman R. Yetman in his study of slave narratives found an account by Bill Home, born in 1850, describing how he made quills as a child from willow stalk in Shreveport, Louisiana.[66] George Cable also discussed the instrument being used by black musicians in Louisiana in an 1886 article for *The Century Magazine*.

But because it was rarely recorded (bluesman Big Boy Cleveland had featured it on his instrumental *Quill Blues* in the spring of 1927, several weeks before Thomas's first recordings, and no other artist played it on record before 1950), its sound comes as a delightful surprise. David Evans suggests that the instrument brought commercially recorded 1920s blues quite close in form to the music's African roots.[67] On *Fishing Blues*, his vocal is warm and appealing, his guitar work strong and assured, and the quills greatly enhance the aura of innocent, carefree happiness, evoking a Tom Sawyer–like mental picture.

Texas collector Walter Prescott Webb published a song fragment "obtained from a Gatesville Negro named 'Rags'" called *If You Go Fishing* (in the *Miscellany of Texas Folk-lore* from the Frank Dobie–edited book *Coffee in the Gourd* issued by the Texas Folk-lore Society in 1923) that was virtually identical to *Fishing Blues*. Paul Oliver in *Songsters and Saints*, noting that Gatesville lies some fifty miles to the west of Marlin (where Thomas lived for a time), remarked that "it is tempting to think that 'Rags' was none other than 'Ragtime Texas' Henry Thomas."[68] McCormick suggested that the song came out of late 1800s minstrel shows, and that an early antecedent may have been *Gumbo Chaff* in the 1830s.[69]

Even before the song was introduced to a wider audience on Harry Smith's 1952 *Anthology of American Folk Music*, it was covered by Memphis Minnie in 1931, by Bumblebee Slim in 1935 as *Everybody's Fishing* (with Big Bill Broonzy on guitar), and carried into country music by Lew Childre's 1946 version. Veteran bluesman Sam Chatmon of Mississippi Sheiks fame recorded a version for Rounder in the 1970s (possibly an earlier variant from oral tradition) in which the song's double meaning is spelled out: "Early Sunday morning when the sun did rise / Ethan told his wife he'd been fishing all night. . . .

Listen, Mr. Ethan, you'd better understand / A woman's got as much right as a man . . . you say you're going fishing when you stay out late / Well, I'm going fishing, too!" Greil Marcus: "There is an almost absolute liberation in *Fishing Blues*—a liberation that is impossible not to feel, and easy to understand."[70]

The songs of Henry Thomas, writes McCormick, constitute "goodtime music reaching out from another era: anthems, stomps, gospel songs, dance calls, ballads, blues, and fragments compressed in a blurring glimpse of black music as it existed in the last century. It's the songs that came out of the shifting days when freedmen and their children were remaking their lives in a hostile nation."

My Daddy Rocks Me (With One Steady Roll) (1929)— Tampa Red's Hokum Jug Band, with Frankie "Half-Pint" Jaxon (written by J. Berni Barbour)
Vocalion 1274
Recorded in Chicago on April 13, 1929

The first rock and roll record? It would be hard to come up with an earlier plausible candidate than this delightfully salacious classic in its original September 1922 version as *My Man Rocks Me (With One Steady Roll)* for the Black Swan label by Trixie Smith, with a combo featuring Fletcher Henderson. Not only was BS 12147 apparently the first commercially issued record with both "rock" and "roll" in the title, but just about every rock and blues song with a "round the clock" theme, from *Rock Around the Clock* to Chuck Berry's *Reelin' and Rockin'*, can trace its ancestry back to the performance by twenty-seven-year-old Atlanta-born vaudeville performer Trixie.[71] It came in her fourth session for the Harlem-based label founded in January 1921 by Harry H. Pace, formerly W. C. Handy's music-publishing partner, as the first significant African-American-owned label with all black artists.[72] The Smith recording was a delicious tease, but with her thin, girlish voice something short of a classic, and the next several versions of the tune, including the Southern Quartet (1924), the Golden Gate Orchestra (1925), and Charles Creath's Jazz-O-Maniacs (1925), only slightly advanced the cause. Then came Tampa Red and his merry crew, and one can truly say that rock and roll was born.

65. Epstein, *Sinful Tunes and Spirituals*, p. 52. According to Robert D. Winan's study of WPA interviews with ex-slaves in the 1930s, there were thirty references to playing quills, indicating that during the pre–Civil War era, the instrument was used more frequently by black musicians than the guitar or piano.

66. Epstein, *Sinful Tunes and Spirituals,* p. 55. "The quills, or panpipes, apparently had wide currency."

67. Evans chapter, "Blues in Texas and the Deep South," *Nothing But the Blues*, p. 38.

68. *Songsters and Saints: Vocal Traditions on Race Records*, p. 131.

69. McCormick annotation, "Henry Thomas: Our Deepest Look at the Roots," p. 8.

70. Greil Marcus, *Invisible Republic: Bob Dylan's Basement Tapes*, p. 112.

71. See *Rock Around the Clock: The Record That Started the Rock Revolution*, by Jim Dawson, for a more detailed discussion of the Trixie Smith record (p. 13–16).

72. The Black Swan label enjoyed a few early successes, particularly the pairing of Ethel Waters' *Oh, Daddy* with Wilbur Sweatman's *Down Home Blues*, and issued an average of twelve records a month for a time. However, the negative impact of radio broadcasting among other factors cut into sales, and the company ceased active production in mid-1923, declared bankruptcy that December, and was purchased in April 1924 by Paramount.

Hudson Woodbridge, aka Tampa Red, was born on January 8, 1904, in Smithville, Georgia (his real name is often given as Hudson Whittaker, but Whittaker was the name of his mother's family, by whom he was raised in Florida), grew up in Tampa, Florida, and became a mainstay of the Chicago blues scene. Following his May 1928 recording debut, he was known as "The Guitar Wizard," whose slide work on steel National or electric guitar in later years left many stunned. It was his second recording session that October that made him a national figure with his wildly popular and erotic novelty *It's Tight Like That*, in partnership with pianist and future gospel composing great Thomas "Georgia Tom" Dorsey; the recording was made a few weeks after Tampa and Dorsey accompanied Ma Rainey on one of her last sessions. The song triggered many cover versions and answer records, including one by no less than Louis Armstrong. *My Daddy Rocks Me* is the best of his several followups along similar lines; but whereas *Tight* was merely good silly fun, *My Daddy* steams up the windows.

Frankie "Half-Pint" Jaxon (of *Christ Was Born on Christmas Morn* fame later in 1929) does his best falsetto female impersonation here, unleashing enough orgiastic moans and cries to get someone arrested, with Tampa on slide guitar, an unknown pianist (apparently not Dorsey), Bill Johnson on string bass, Herman Brown on washboard, and Carl Reid on horn. "I looked at the clock, the clock struck one / I said, 'Honey, let's have some fun!' . . . I looked at the clock, the clock struck three / I said, 'daddy, you're killin' me!' . . . I Looked at the clock, the clock struck four / I said, 'baby, let's have some more!' / My daddy rocks me with one steady roll . . ." Evidencing the record's success, Jimmie Noone's Apex Club Orchestra made a spicy cover version in July with vocal by May Alix.

Tampa's hokum material was but a small part of his repertoire during a career that spanned thirty years. He recorded extensively during the 1930s and 1940s with Big Bill Broonzy, and hit the R&B charts with the original versions of the blues standards *Let Me Play With Your Poodle* (1942) and *When Things Go Wrong With You* (1949), better known under the title *It Hurts Me Too*.

Pony Blues (1929)—Charley Patton

Paramount 15216

Recorded June 14, 1929 in Richmond, Indiana (*Blues-#7, NPR-300, GHF, RR, TC, SB, DEL*)

Perhaps the quintessential Delta country bluesman, Charley Patton constructed many of his songs from traditional folk blues material—borrowing melodies, guitar figures, and snippets of lyrics from a variety of sources and piecing them together in a way that made the result his own—and *Pony Blues* is the most renowned example

of his creative process. David Evans concluded on the basis of his interviews with many musicians who played in the Drew, Mississippi, area during the pre-1930 era (and those who saw them) that *Pony Blues* was a well-known piece locally long before it was ever recorded. Patton's biographers Stephen Calt and Gayle Dean Wardlow estimate its origins around the first decade of the twentieth century.[73] Minnie Franklin, one of the artist's several wives, said he was singing it when she met him in 1924; Howlin' Wolf learned it from Patton when he moved to Dockery's Plantation in 1926, and based on the recollections of others who knew Patton, he and frequent partner Willie Brown had already been playing it for a dozen years by that point. Indeed, by some accounts it was part of Patton's repertoire as early as 1907. The centerpiece of his debut recording session, it became his best-selling record, and most influential. On this remarkable date, Patton recorded fourteen selections, "something no traditional blues artist had ever done at a single session before" (noted Ted Gioia), and the quality of the material was so exceptional that even the B sides (*Banty Rooster Blues* was the companion to *Pony Blues*) were potent.[74]

Pony Blues, writes Robert Palmer, "depends for its musical effect on an extraordinary rhythmic tension. The guitar part strongly accents the first beat of each measure, while the vocal is just as strongly accented on beat four. Furthermore, Patton carries the note that begins on each accented fourth beat over into the next measure, producing the polyrhythmic effect of a three-beat measure followed by a five-beat measure over the clearly delineated four-beat measures of the guitar part." He compared these rhythmic devices to West African drumming, "and uses them in an African manner, stacking rhythms on top of one another in order to build up a dense, layered rhythmic complexity."[75] Calt and Wardlow agree: "The vocal accenting of *Pony Blues* was the most complicated of any dance blues song." Additionally, the piece "marked a level of melodic ambition that was otherwise unknown in the sphere of blues dance music," involving seven melodic strands.[76]

In his doctoral dissertation on Patton (published in book form in 1970), John Fahey remarked that the singer

73. *King of the Delta Blues Singers*, p. 81. Calt and Wardlow note: "In 1909, when Patton's song was likely to have been new, some two million horse-drawn carriages (as opposed to 80,000 automobiles) were manufactured in America."

74. Gioia, *Delta Blues*, p. 67.

75. *Deep Blues*, p. 63–64. His method of using single string picking to accompany a vocal line, as heard in segments of this song, "was exotic even for the 1920s," remark Calt and Wardlow (p. 65).

76. Calt and Wardlow, p. 99–100. In the February 1966 *Blues Unlimited*, Wardlow said the melody for *Pony Blues* is roughly the same as that used by Tommy Johnson for *Bye Bye Blues*, and Johnson was performing the latter song as early as 1921. Johnson is reported to have taught *Bye Bye Blues* to Patton around 1923.

usually selected his verses "at random from a large storehouse of them in his mind," and cited *Pony Blues* as an example. Evans suggests that Patton "was not the most coherent folk blues singer, but his blues were by no means unstructured, random compositions." He notes that Patton sings three different melodic strains and guitar parts, more than is typically found in blues, and that they have elements in common. Although the piece is "non-thematic," it deals in an emotionally relatable way with the problems of establishing and maintaining relationships with women. Patton would expand upon this in his 1934 version with new lyrics, *Stone Pony Blues*.[77]

"The sheer sweep and power of Patton's enduring classic is striking, and his originality and confident sense of self-expression were never on better display," declares Gioia. He notes the many complexities of *Pony Blues*: the eccentric five-beat introduction with an odd hesitation that he would employ on other songs; the use of three separate melodies with strikingly peculiar but expertly handled pauses between the sections; and the compelling vocal styling including dropping his voice to a whispering growl late in the performance.[78] With the release of this 78, country blues entered a new, classic era.

El Corrido del Agrarista (Parts 1 & 2) (1929)—Trovadores Tamaulipecos

Columbia 3689-x

Recorded in Aug. 1929

Among all the themes explored in Mexican-American *corrido* recordings, the one that dominates all others is the Mexican Revolution. Not only is it the most cataclysmic event in the nation's history, but it has all the characteristics beloved to the creators of narrative ballads: heroes, villains, epic military battles, class-based conflicts, the constant struggle to maintain national independence and dignity in the face of challenges by the great power to the north, and personal melodramas. One would be hard pressed to find a revolutionary corrido more powerful than *El Corrido del Agrarista* (roughly translated as "Tillers of the Land Under Agrarian Reform"). The name of the duo performing it, Trovadores Tamaulipecos, translates as troubadours or minstrels from Tamaulipas, a Mexican state located in the central/northeastern part of the federation near the Texas border.

Francisco Madero lit the fuse that became the Mexican Revolution with publication of a 1908 book advocating reform of the political system under the presidency of General Porfirio Diaz (who had held office ever since 1884). After he lost the 1910 presidential election to Diaz, Madero called for an armed uprising that began that November 20. Former bandit turned revolutionary

soldier Francisco "Pancho" Villa helped lead forces that defeated federal troops in May 1911, Diaz resigned, and Madero took office. But more turmoil followed, and in February 1913 Madero was deposed and assassinated. Villa again led revolutionary forces to a series of victories over the federal army, and when the United States recognized the latest Mexican government, Villa provoked several anti-American incidents in protest including cross-border raids in 1916. This led to an American expedition seeking to capture Villa, which failed. Violence subsided after Venustiano Carranza assumed the presidency in 1917, but three years later he was assassinated. Villa (who had previously laid down his arms) was murdered in 1923—an event marked just two months later by an August 1923 recording, *Corrido Historia y Muerte del Gral. Francisco Villa* (Corrido and Death of Gen. Francisco Villa)—and later that year there was an unsuccessful six-month revolt against the government. After four years of escalating tensions between the government and the Catholic Church, including armed insurrection by groups known as Cristeros (soldiers of Christ), President Alvaro Obregon was assassinated by a fervent Catholic in 1928. A settlement between church and state was finally reached in mid-1929.[79]

All of these events provide the background for *El Corrido del Agrarista*, which (in a two-part vocal and guitar duet across both sides of a 78, performed with great urgency) sketches a history of events since the rule of Diaz, from the specific perspective of poor farmers who suffered through multiple administrations and the relentless bloodshed. "This is the song of the poor who work in the fields / Of those of us who sweat to work our land / For a long time we have suffered the slavery of the vanquished / Until we finally could see our people together."[80] According to this account, conditions improved somewhat in the 1920s under the Obregon government thanks to redistribution of land, but this progress was cut short by more violence. "We want land and plows to cultivate the nation's fields," yearning for "hope, freedom and dignity." The chorus is passionate: "Ay, ay, ay, struggling for our dreams / Many of our brothers died, may God have them in heaven." The corrido concludes as it had begun, slowing the rapid tempo to a somber, determined march: "Let us march, agraristas, to the fields / To sow the seeds of progress / Let us march always united, without fail / Working for the peace of our nation."

This remarkable, intense musical manifesto was issued by a combo that made over seventy recordings from June

---

77. Evans, *Big Road Blues*, p. 146–49.

78. Gioia, *Delta Blues*, p. 68.

79. Guillermo Hernandez, annotation for Arhoolie CD *The Mexican Revolution*.

80. In a foreshadowing of the American coal mining epic *Sixteen Tons* a generation in the future, they sing: "Always work and more work / And always owing more to the company store / And when harvest time came, the sharecropper ended up losing . . . We lived like animals surrounded by wealth."

1928 through this final August 1929 session: the first three dates for Okeh, the others for Columbia.[81] Lorenzo Barcelata and Ernesto Cortazar are featured on the vast majority of the sides made by Trovadores Tamaulipecos, including this one; some of the earlier performances included other individuals. Whereas the vast majority of Mexican-American recordings during the period were made in Texas (primarily in San Antonio), this session was in New York. The corrido is a highlight of a four-record set by Folklyric/Arhoolie Records, *The Mexican Revolution: A Collection of Corridos from Early Historic Recordings*.

The Soul of a Man (1930)—Blind Willie Johnson
Columbia 14582
Recorded in Atlanta on April 20, 1930 (released on Feb. 28, 1931) (*GOSP-#85*)

Gospel at its best often deals with fundamental questions of the human condition and strips them down to their emotional core. That perfectly describes the finest song to emerge from the fifth and final recording session by the great Blind Willie Johnson, *The Soul of a Man*. Singing with the hypnotic urgency that was his hallmark, Johnson cries that he's traveled the world over, but still awaits the answer he desperately seeks. "Won't somebody tell me, answer if you can—what is the soul of a man?" Backed by female vocalist Willie B. Harris, he pounds home his message on guitar (as described by Samuel Charters) with his "driving, staccato thumb picking."[82] "I read the Bible often, I try to read it right / And far as I can understand— nothing but a burning light." One can hardly imagine a more eloquent summation—"nothing but a burning light"—of the salvation he sought through his religion, and achieved through his music. Columbia waited ten months to release the record; its manufacturing order (1,750 copies), small as it is, was actually higher than for most others in the race-record series during this period.

According to E. Franklin Frazier's *The Negro Church in America*, historically about 10 percent of black churchgoers have been, like Johnson, members of the Church of God in Christ, part of the Pentecostal movement. "Sanctified" religion, remarks Jeff Todd Titon in *Early Downhome Blues*, "fused African remembrance with evangelical Christian borrowings, creating a vital and unique church."

Following the last of his thirty recorded songs that would inspire generations of admirers, Johnson earned a meager living during the Depression singing on the streets of Beaumont, Texas, and performing for church benefits. Mark A. Humphrey writes in *Nothing But the Blues* that the artist's recordings for Columbia from 1927–1930 "constitute an incomparable body of work, at once universally expressive of African-American tradition and uniquely expressive of an extraordinary intuitive genius. Johnson's oeuvre may be the single most cogent and compelling exemplification of the black sacred music that evolved from the conversion of slaves up to the advent of professional gospel music in the 1930s."[83]

Politikos Manes (1930)—Kostas Karipis
Recorded in Athens on May 21, 1930

The Greek music scene was filled to overflowing with brilliantly talented performers during the 1920s and 1930s, and standing high among them was singer-guitarist Kostas Karipis. Born around 1880 in Constantinople, he came to Greece in 1922 following the horrendous violence in Smyrna due to the conflict between Greece and Turkey. By 1923 he was performing both solo and as a guitar accompanist to such other leading Greek artists as Dalgas (Andonis Dhiamandidhis), and began his recording career in 1925. During the next several years he was among the most prolific and admired of Greek recording artists, appearing on hundreds of 78 rpm sides. An extraordinary representation of his work is *Politkos Manes*.

This is a passionate, deeply melancholy performance in the undulating vocal style (known in Greece as Smyrnaic) particularly associated with his friend Dalgas, but more broadly utilized by various Turkish, Greek, and Middle Eastern artists. Central to the power of the song is the accordion accompaniment by the virtuoso known as Papatzis (Andonios Amiralis), who establishes the record's haunting tone with his introduction. "In the mountains, high mountains / There may your soul expire . . . And not a Christian there to be found to bury your body." Following another potent solo by Papatzis, he sings: "My Andonis, ach! . . . Your concertina has killed me, my Andonis!" It's included on the 1997 Rounder CD *Squeeze Play: A World Accordion Anthology*, compiled by Dick Spottswood.

Performances like this one (recorded specifically for the U.S. market) found a ready audience among Greek natives in the United States. After the 1900 Census showed just 8,500 Greek natives in the United States, there was a huge surge in immigration bringing that total above 100,000 in 1910 and to nearly 176,000 in 1920, before subsiding due to the anti-immigrant legislation adopted the next few years.[84][85]

81. Spottswood, *Ethnic Music on Records*, Vol. 4, p. 2317–19.
82. Liner notes, *The Complete Blind Willie Johnson*.

83. Humphrey, p. 119–20.
84. The 1940 census showed some 273,000 Americans whose mother tongue was Greek, a total including those born in the U.S. Pekka Gronow's analysis places them #13 in population among European ethnic groups; at least for Columbia, which issued more ethnic recordings than any other U.S. label, Greek records were disproportionately important in its catalog, ranking #5 in European ethnic releases in the U.S. from 1923–1952. (*Ethnic Recordings In America: A Neglected Heritage*, p. 23.)
85. The major record companies recorded very little Greek music in the United States after 1930, relying on imported records from Greece.

The Panic is On (1931)—Hezekiah Jenkins
Columbia 14585
Recorded Jan. 16, 1931 (released on March 14)

In January 1931, the Great Depression was bringing America to economic depths it had only imagined before in its worst nightmares. Unemployment had soared above the four million mark at the end of 1930, while reaching record levels in Europe. The failure of 608 banks in late 1930 made credit a desperately scarce commodity for businesses and individuals. It was at this moment that blues singer-guitarist Hezekiah Jenkins—an artist about whom virtually nothing was known until recently—offered one of the era's most vivid, documentary-like musical portraits of what was unfolding in the country. Jenkins had recorded four issued sides for Columbia in 1924–1925 (two of them with an unknown partner as Jenkins & Jenkins), and two for Gennett in 1926. This session, his first in four-and-a-half years, would also be his last. (His first name is misspelled on the label as "Hazekiah.") It's a country blues, with the artist on solo vocal and guitar. One of his suggested remedies was an end to Prohibition ("old Prohibition ruined everything").

Newman I. White, in his 1928 book *American Negro Folk-Songs*, quoted four song fragments collected from different individuals in Alabama and Mississippi in 1915–1916 built around the "Panic is on" theme, all inspired by the financial panic of 1908–1909. (Previous U.S. financial crises had been described with that word, most notably the "Panic" of 1893.) "Save up yo' money / Don't you buy no corn / 'Cause de panic's on," went one version heard in Lowndes County, Alabama. The Perrow, Mississippi, counterpart went in part: "A nickel worth of meal and a dime of lard / Will do while the panic's on."[86] Paul Oliver suggested at least an indirect connection between these song fragments and the Jenkins piece, which he included on an album based on his 1984 book. Oliver remarked that Jenkins echoed the "angry" tone taken by bluesman Kid Coley on his 1931 record *Tricks Ain't Walkin' No More* about tough times for a street hustler, but that *The Panic Is On* is "broader in its sweep."[87]

Blues great Furry Lewis made a 1927 recording with the same title for Vocalion, but it was unreleased and has never been found, and it's considered unlikely that it has any connection with this piece. Jenkins' performance was included on "Songs of War and History," Volume 10 of *Folk Music in America* by the Library of Congress in 1978. The artist's complete recordings were reissued as part of two albums on the Document label. The very Depression of which he sang ensured that his performance would be heard by few at the time; Columbia ordered a mere 649 copies of this record (as reported by Dan

Mahony in *The Columbia 13/14000-D Series: A Numerical Listing*). Just about all of the releases in Columbia's 1932 race-records catalog, most with production of only 350–400 copies each by that time, were still listed two years later, indicating (in the absence of new pressings) that even these small orders failed to sell out. Ted Gioia in *Delta Blues* says this suggests that "total demand in the United States for many race artists amounted to a little more than a dozen or so copies per month! The implication—as hard as it is to believe—is that a blues musician could reach a larger audience by playing in an obscure juke joint in the Delta than by recording for a major national label."[88] Central Kentucky guitarist/singer Eddie Pennington, known for his Merle Travis–inspired thumb-picking style, revived *The Panic is On* for his 2004 Smithsonian album *Eddie Pennington Walks the Strings*.

Previously an enigma, Hezekiah Jenkins' back story was discovered by Lynn Abbott and Doug Seroff in their 2007 book *Ragged But Right*. Jenkins was a veteran minstrel-show performer who was in the team of Overton & Jenkins before joining the troupe of Allen's New Orleans Minstrels in October 1914; after a brief departure, he returned the following April with a new partner, Clifford Brooks. Allen's Minstrels, founded in 1899, was one of the era's most successful black entertainment companies, a strong rival to the more celebrated Rabbit Foot Minstrels and the "Silas Green from New Orleans" troupe with a stellar array of performers. Billed as the "Originators of Tented Minstrelsy," write Abbott and Seroff, "they helped set the course for African American minstrel companies in the South, traveling by rail and showing under canvas." A July 1915 report in the black theatrical press said Jenkins was "screaming the house nightly" with his original songs, including *Poor Me, You're Mine*, and *My Own Rag*. Sometime in 1916, Jenkins and Brooks left to join Robinson's Old Kentucky Minstrels, causing "laughing riots nightly" with their sketch "Two Coons and a Razor."[89] How fascinating it is that Jenkins' personal journey from a broad comedic background would culminate with such a powerful social statement.

> "What this country is comin' to—I sure would like to
>   know
> If they don't do something bye and bye,
> The rich will live and the poor will die
> Dog-gone, I mean the panic is on.
>
> Can't get no work, can't draw no pay,
> Unemployment getting worser every day
> Nothing to eat and no place to sleep,
> All night long folks walkin' the street
> Dog-gone, I mean the panic is on . . ."

86. *American Negro Folk-Songs*, p. 350–51.
87. *Songsters and Saints*, p. 132–33.

88. *Delta Blues*, p. 133.
89. *Ragged But Right*, p. 239, 241–42.

Gold Watch and Chain (1933)—Carter Family (written by Thomas P. Westendorf)
Victor 23821
Recorded June 17, 1933

One of the Carters' most touching folk ballads is their reworking of an 1879 parlor tune originally known as *Is There No Kiss for Me Tonight, My Love?*[90] (Le Roy Anderson would record the song under its original title one month after the Carters' record.) Its author, Thomas P. Westendorf, is best known for writing the evergreen *I'll Take You Home Again, Kathleen* in 1875. A. P. and Sara Carter had separated in late February 1933, and Sara had moved across the mountain from the family's Poor Valley home in southern Virginia. Although Sara resisted the idea of making records again with her estranged husband, in the depths of the Depression it was still the best way to make a living. Finally she agreed, and the family loaded up the Chevrolet and headed for Camden, New Jersey, where they would make their first recordings since the split.

Gold Watch and Chain, a gorgeous tale of separated lovers in which the singer is longing desperately for her partner once again, was recorded against that background. "Whether A. P. and Sara's uneasy separation added a feeling to the song . . . is hard to know," write Carters biographers Mark Zwonitzer and Charles Hirshberg. "But both rancor and tenderness were left unspoken between them in 1933, their emotions joined only in music."[91] A. P. Carter, whose voice was frequently absent in Carters recordings, "basses in" here in support of Sara's contralto, with Maybelle's guitar as always providing impeccable accompaniment in her distinctive low tuning; Sara is on autoharp. Although the performance is a classic, it is a rarity for collectors; even the royalty of country music were selling very few records in the depths of the Depression.

"God, the first time I heard that song . . . I thought about my grandparents and I cried," said Emmylou Harris, who lovingly sang it on her 1980 album *Roses in the Snow*. "These are the emotional memories that maybe aren't even yours; they belong to your parents and your great-grandparents, and somehow it strikes a familiar chord in you . . . And I found the music very haunting."

Following the marathon recording session, the Carters set out to get paid by Ralph Peer the next day. But when the car broke down en route and they had to pay for repairs, they were left with 35 cents. Peer sent his limousine to pick them up and messengered over tickets to a Broadway show, but the Carters—the greatest stars in country music—were too proud to say that they had no money for food other than coffee and a doughnut.

State Street Rag (1934)—"Louie Bluie" (Howard Armstrong)
Bluebird 5593
Recorded in Chicago on March 23, 1934

For black musicians seeking to scratch out a career in entertainment during the Depression era, mastering multiple instruments and musical styles often meant the difference between success and poverty. Howard Armstrong exemplified this principle, and *State Street Rag* was his most wonderful musical legacy.

Born in Dayton, Tennessee, near Knoxville in 1909 (his family moved to nearby LaFollette when he was three), William Howard Taft Armstrong was raised in a musical family; his father (a laborer at a blast furnace and a part-time preacher) played the mandolin, and his mother was a fine singer. Teaching himself to play fiddle at age nine, he eventually became capable on twenty instruments, including mandolin, banjo, and viola. With his musical partner Carl Martin on string bass, he played on street corners and at dances, bars, silent-movie theaters, juke joints, bootleg and house rent parties, and medicine shows—anyplace where people would listen to him, he would say, all over the Smoky Mountains and around the South and Appalachia. Ted Bogan (guitar and mandolin) joined them by 1929.[92] Settling in Chicago by the early 1930s, he first recorded two sides for the Vocalion label during a Knoxville field session as a member of a trio called the Tennessee Chocolate Drops (along with brothers Carl and Roland Martin) in 1930; then he and Bogan recorded four titles for Bluebird at this March 1934 session. He used the name "Louie Bluie" after his name occasionally led him to be confused with Louis Armstrong, and a friend good-naturedly remarked, "you're no Louis Armstrong—you're just a little Louie Bluie!"[93]

State Street Rag is an exciting, turbo-powered instrumental with Armstrong on mandolin and Bogan on guitar, steadily escalating to an almost feverish intensity.[94] The flip side of this 78 recorded the same day, *Ted's Stomp* (in this case with Armstrong on fiddle and Bogan on guitar), is just as breathlessly scintillating. Bogan later recalled the session: "The guy told us if we played any faster, the thing could catch on fire!"[95]

---

90. Vance Randolph included the song as *Don't Forget Me, Little Darling* in *Ozark Folksongs* (Vol. 4, p. 207), and cited similar lines in *Old Virginny* as collected by Cecil Sharp and Maud Karpeles in *English Folk Songs from the Southern Appalachians*.

91. Zwonitzer, p. 168–69.

92. Armstrong feature by Terry Zwigoff, *78 Quarterly* #5 (1990), p. 41–49.

93. Zwigoff, part two of Armstrong's life story in *78 Quarterly* #6 (1991).

94. As Armstrong recalled for Rich DelGrosso (March–April 1988 *Living Blues*, p. 22), the piece was also known informally as *Mexican Rag* or *Mexicano Rag*.

95. Liner notes for Old Hat CD *Violin, Sing the Blues for Me: African-American Fiddlers, 1926–1949*, p. 23–24.

Dick Spottswood opines that the melody is one of the myriad variations on the tune known as *Draggin' the Bow*, and also owes something to the 1920s hit *I Wish I Could Shimmy Like My Sister Kate*. The latter song, as it happens, was actually created by Louis Armstrong in 1920 under the title *Get Off Katie's Head* and then sold outright to bandleader and music publisher Clarence Williams for fifty dollars, only to see Williams copyright the tune and rake in big profits.

Armstrong and Bogan continued performing together, along with Armstrong's son, and made some 1970s recordings as Martin, Bogan & Armstrong. Director Terry Zwigoff (of later *Ghost World* fame), who loved this record, tracked down Armstrong, and in 1986 made the documentary *Louie Bluie* about him. Performing once again with Bogan, they did everything from blues and jazz to Mills Brothers' standards and Hawaiian tunes, and we learned that Armstrong was also a talented artist and creator of bawdy poems (his journals were published after the release of the picture). "*Louie Bluie* peers into the areas where nothing is certain, except that these people live and strive and laugh and make music," wrote Roger Ebert. "It is a wonderful film." The film gave Armstrong a celebrity he had never enjoyed before, and he continued performing in the Boston area. In 2003 he was one of the recipients (along with Dolly Parton) of the Governor's Arts Awards in Tennessee. Not long after accepting the honor, he suffered a heart attack and died at ninety-four that July. Until his death, said his wife, she had no idea that the man she had married four years earlier was thirty years her elder.

What Would You Give In Exchange (for Your Soul)? (1936)—The Monroe Brothers Bluebird 6309 Recorded in Charlotte, NC on Feb. 17, 1936[96] (*C&W-#120*)

The very first recording session by one of country music's most legendary duos produced one of its most revered classics. Bill and Charlie Monroe made their first major appearances on the *WLS Jamboree* on WLS in Chicago starting in 1932, and two years later began touring to other states. After signing with Victor's Bluebird label, they immediately began making history. Bill Malone: "Bill and Charlie Monroe . . . were the most dynamic duet of the 1930s. Bill's high-tenor singing, Charlie's aggressive guitar runs, and their breakneck tempos all anticipated bluegrass music. Nevertheless, the Monroe Brothers' music

was still old-timey . . . [and] *What Would You Give* may have been their most beloved song."[97]

The lyrics to *What Would You Give* were written in 1912 by J. H. Carr (published in a shape-note songbook issued by the Trio Music Company in Texas, with F. J. Berry credited as co-author), and put to a revised melody in 1936 by John Hancock.[98] The title phrase in all likelihood was inspired by a Biblical phrase in Matthew 16:26: "What would it profit a man to gain the whole world but forfeit his soul?"[99] Wade Mainer and Zeke Morris recorded the song in the same studio two days before the Monroes (February 14, 1936), but the company didn't release their version (Bluebird 8073) until May 1939. The Prairie Ramblers also recorded it four months later for ARC. But it was the Monroes' intense performance—with superb brother harmonies and Bill's unmistakable mandolin—that stamped the song indelibly in country fans' minds after being released by Bluebird. Charles Wolfe: "The brothers had already been featuring the song on the radio, and the fans were ready when Bluebird made it the first Monroe Brothers release," in April 1936.[100] It proved so popular that they recorded three sequels as parts 2, 3, and 4 in October 1937 (Bluebird 7122, sides A and B) and February 1938 (Bluebird 7326). Tony Scherman calls this performance "slow and bone-sparse; unflashingly played, it sails aloft on the brothers' voices—Bill's especially, an eerie falsetto moan." Bill and Charlie parted ways shortly after the latter session; Bill went on to become the father of bluegrass, and Charlie enjoyed an outstanding if briefer solo career in his own right.

Robert Cantwell: "If the music of the Carter Family is a geological record of southern culture,[101] the Monroes' is a *vision* of it—one which partakes significantly of the documentary and regionalist mood which had overtaken American culture during the Great Depression, when, as Alfred Kazin wrote, America was 'hungry for news of

96. As outlined by Charles Wolfe in his June 1997 *Bluegrass Unlimited* feature on "the day they started their revolution," the session was held on the second floor of the Southern Radio Corporation Building. In six days producer Eli Oberstein recorded 137 masters by artists including Wade Mainer, Riley Puckett, and Cliff Carlisle; the Monroes arrived on the last day, interrupting a session by Arthur Smith and the Delmore Brothers.

97. Liner notes, *Smithsonian Collection of Classic Country Music*, p. 28. Malone remarks (*Country Music, U.S.A.*, p. 13) that while the song reflects a "folk fatalism" that Southern Christians shared with their British ancestors, it also shows a strain of anti-materialism and "even inchoate class consciousness."

98. The 1912 composition has two additional verses besides the two recorded by both the Monroes and Mainer/Morris, including these striking lines: "More than the silver and gold of the earth / More than all jewels thy spirit is worth / God, the Creator, has given it birth / What would you give . . . "

99. According to biographer Richard D. Smith (*Can't You Hear Me Callin'*, p. 42–43), the Monroes had learned the song at a church singing convention years earlier.

100. *Classic Country: Legends of Country Music*, p. 112. Wolfe notes that the tune appeared in a 1926 songbook issued by James D. Vaughan, probably the very book from which Bill learned to sing it as a teenager. Two other songs from this Vaughan collection were also recorded by the brothers.

101. The Carters didn't record this song commercially, but performed it on border radio.

itself.' . . . From the Monroe Brothers' records a kind of stylized picture of the Appalachian region emerges—not a picture which a social or labor historian would comfortably accept, but a romantic one, the musical equivalent of, say, a painting by Thomas Hart Benton, who drew heavily in his work upon mountain lore and folksong." Like the Blue Sky Boys, "the Monroe Brothers *simplified* Appalachian music. Through a consistent, homogenous style fired by heightened pitch and tempo, and a repertoire carefully culled of songs not conspicuously archaic, southern, and folk or folklike, the Monroe Brothers sought to sharpen the image of country music, to identify it more closely with the southern mountain tradition—a 'tradition' which stood out more plainly in the new urban perspective, and in a more pure and unified form than it had ever been in fact."[102]

I Believe I'll Dust My Broom (1936)—Robert Johnson
Vocalion 03475 (also issued on Conqueror 8871)
Recorded in San Antonio on Nov. 23, 1936 (*Blues-#65*)

This Robert Johnson classic about being away from the woman he loves and fantasizing about her, from his debut recording session, uses a melody first heard in Leroy Carr's *I Believe I'll Make a Change* (August 1934). The title verse had appeared in Kokomo Arnold's *Sagefield Woman Blues* (September 1934).[103] Elijah Wald writes that the song was a revelation because of his "stripped-down, driving guitar accompaniment. Though the revolutionary nature of what he played may [be] lost on modern listeners, it is still easy to get caught up in the way the fast high-note triplets alternate with a pulsing boogie beat. His choice to sometimes sing over the triplets, using the bass figure as an instrumental break, and sometimes to reverse this pattern increases the tension and energy of the performance—as does the fact that he expands and contracts the time, changing chords as inspiration hits, rather than keeping a regular count of twelve bars."[104]

That walking boogie bass line was adapted from boogie-woogie piano: "Lightnin' Hopkins, Jimmy Reed, and thousands of other guitarists have made this sort of solid guitar boogie their stock in trade, but it was brand-new when Johnson did it, and must have sounded astonishingly modern and exciting." Wald remarks that other guitarists including Blind Lemon Jefferson "had recorded boogie-woogie bass figures before this, but their versions did not have the steadily propulsive one-two beat that Johnson used." Postwar rhythm and blues

and early rock & roll would have been lost without this core musical element.

For this premiere session conducted in San Antonio, Johnson placed himself facing into a corner of the room—not out of shyness, Ry Cooder has suggested, but to take advantage of "corner loading," an acoustic principle designed to achieve the best possible tonality in the available space. While Johnson's intentions can't be known for certain, writes Peter Doyle, "it is clear that through corner loading as much as through instrumental technique, Johnson's voice and guitar gained 'supercharged' qualities that enabled a hugely enhanced dynamic range."[105]

Arthur "Big Boy" Crudup revived *Dust My Broom* on a March 1949 record for Victor, and two years later Elmore James brought the tune to its widest audience as a Top Ten R&B hit on the Trumpet label. This paved the way for it to become a standard in the 1960s blues revival, a song that became (notes Robert Santelli) "the template used by all subsequent slide guitarists."[106]

Golden Gate Gospel Train (1937)—Golden Gate Jubilee Quartet
Bluebird 7126
Recorded in Charlotte, NC, on Aug. 4, 1937 (*GOSP-#57*)

Talk about an auspicious debut: On their premier recording session for Victor's Bluebird subsidiary at Charlotte's Pope Hotel, the very first song committed to disk by the Golden Gate Jubilee Quartet was this blockbuster performance that would become a staple of their act for many years thereafter. Using trains as a metaphorical vehicle for the faithful to travel to the hereafter dates back to at least the 1850s, and no such journey could ever be so joyous as the one provided by the Gates (who would soon drop the "Jubilee" from their name). Their a cappella re-creation of locomotive sounds is so richly flavorful that even if Willie Johnson (lead vocal and baritone), Orlandus Wilson (bass), Henry Owens (first tenor), and William Langford (second tenor) had not followed up this first session with many more wonderful recordings to follow, their place in the Gospel Hall of Fame would have been secure. Mark A. Humphrey: "The Gates' 1937 Bluebird recordings presented a new development in spiritual singing, one which retained the style's folk roots while stepping in sync with the Swing era."[107]

In a 1995 interview, Wilson recalled that on the *Gospel Train*, "we were trying for an old rhythmic feeling and also to get the sound of what the train sounds like . . . the old coal burners or wood burners: 'wah-wah-wah-

102. *Bluegrass Breakdown*, p. 58.
103. The same basic tune had also been recorded by Carl Rafferty as *Mr. Carl's Blues* at his only known session in December 1933. (Timothy White, July 25, 1992, *Billboard*.)
104. Wald, *Escaping the Delta*, p. 136–38.

105. Doyle, *Echo and Reverb*, p. 76–80.
106. *The Best of the Blues*, p. 5.
107. Chapter "Holy Blues: The Gospel Tradition" in *Nothing But the Blues*, p. 137–38.

wah'—that kind of sound. That's why we didn't create a pump bass line, [which] wouldn't go with that. So we created a feeling instead like a bass-bass-sing: 'boom-boom-boom' something like a jazz bass tuba sound." It's included on the Dust to Digital boxed set *Goodbye Babylon*. Claudia Perry: "The Golden Gate Quartet, with its percussive and energetic vocals, changed quartet singing the way Charlie Parker revolutionized jazz." [108]

Bonaparte's Retreat (1937)—W. H. Stepp
Recorded for Library of Congress on October 28, 1937

The ancient Appalachian fiddle tune *Bonaparte's Retreat* originated eons ago in England; Gus Meade and Dick Spottswood report in *Country Music Sources* that its lower strain is based on the traditional *Bumble Bee in the Pumpkin Patch*, and it may also be a descendant of the Irish air *The Eagle's Whistle*.[109] Linda Burman-Hall suggests that one strain of the tune is a relative of the second strain of a Scottish reel, *The Lady's Breast Knot*, dating back to at least 1758.[110] George Pullen Jackson opined that it is "practically the same tune" as *I Love Jesus*, found in the 1868 hymnal *The Revivalist*.[111]

After being handed down through generations of players, the piece was first committed to record in March 1924 through A. A. Gray's fiddle solo for Okeh—utterly unlike the version we know today, Gray's treatment was slow and dignified like a concert violin piece. Gid Tanner & His Skillet Lickers (January 1930) and the Arthur Smith Trio (February 1936) were among the other artists to commercially record the tune; Bascom Lamar Lunsford rendered it for the Library of Congress in 1935. But it was the haunting solo fiddle rendition by W. H. Stepp for the Library in 1937 that made *Bonaparte's Retreat* immortal.

William H. (W. H.) "Bill" Stepp was born in April 1875 in rural Lee County, Kentucky, and began fiddling at local affairs in the mid-1890s, also later in Magoffin County where he relocated.[112] He made his living in the lumber business, rafting logs upriver from Beattyville to a sawmill in Royalton. As detailed by banjo-playing folklorist Stephen Wade, one month after his wife's death from a stroke, Stepp recorded seventeen tunes for Alan and Elizabeth Lomax in Salyersville, Kentucky, with Ruth Crawford Seeger (mother of Pete) transcribing the performance. The Lomaxes were in the final week of a Kentucky song-collecting expedition, which would produce over 800 recorded items, almost one-fifth of them involving the fiddle. It's little wonder that the piece inspired by Napoleon was among Bill Stepp's selections, because it was always the number he saved for last in local performances.[113] Wade: "*Bonaparte's Retreat* was usually played at a march tempo. But [Stepp] made a decision: He transformed this well-known tune from a march to a hoedown—and that made all the difference."[114] In Stepp's treatment, the tune "was reborn from a slow air into a dazzling example of instrumental virtuosity." The Library's fiddle-tune expert Alan Jabbour declared that Stepp's recording "is not just one more version, but a singular, racing breakdown."

The song was included in the 1941 compilation of songs from Lomax field recordings, *Our Singing Country*. That's where Aaron Copland discovered this recording while doing research at the Library in 1942, seeking traditional materials to use in his composition *Rodeo*, a work that had been commissioned to accompany a ballet choreographed by Martha Graham, much as Ludwig van Beethoven and Antonin Dvorak had drawn upon the traditional folk melodies of their people. Copland ultimately orchestrated Stepp's performance almost note for note for the famous *Hoedown* section of *Appalachian Spring* (a title he gave it only after completing the work); appropriately enough, the composition was given its premiere performance at the Library of Congress on October 30, 1944.[115] The melody would also be adapted with lyrics by Pee Wee King for the country and pop song *Bonaparte's Retreat*, a hit for Kay Starr in 1950. Stepp's simple gem was included on the CD *Treasury of Library of Congress Field Recordings*.

A Warrior on the Battlefield (Teach Me How to Watch and Pray) (1939)—Golden Eagle Gospel Singers
Decca 7682
Recorded in Chicago on Oct. 27, 1939 (*GOSP-#81*)

This compelling performance with a highly creative a cappella vocal arrangement using interweaving voices has a fascinatingly ancient feeling. The gospel group

108. "Hallelujah: The Sacred Music of Black America" in *American Roots Music*, p. 92.

109. *Country Music Sources*, p. 710.

110. "Tune Identity and Performance Style: The Case of *Bonaparte's Retreat*," selected reports in *Ethnomusicology*, Vol. 3 #1 (1978). Burman-Hall reported that American versions of the piece are often found in the "Bonaparte" group of titles, which includes several often applied to other airs, including *Napoleon, Napoleon Crossing the Rhine*, and *Bonaparte's Retreat from Moscow*. Stephen Wade (*American Music*, Vol. 18 #4 [Winter 2000]): "Napoleon Bonaparte's career touched the imagination of nineteenth-century America, making an impression that expressed itself in songs, set pieces, and marches wherever local militia drilled to the fife and drum."

111. *Spiritual Folk-Songs of Early America* (1937), p. 222.

112. The artist's name was initially reported by Lomax as "W. M." Stepp, and is thus found in early discographies, but his middle name was Hamilton.

113. Wade, "The Route of *Bonaparte's Retreat*: From 'Fiddler Bill' Stepp to Aaron Copland, *American Music*, Vol. 18 #4 (Winter 2000), p. 345–65. A friend of Stepp's recalled for Wade: "When he'd draw a bow, you couldn't just stand and listen . . . When he started playing, people drove like a bee to honey." A revised version of Wade's article served as the opening chapter of his 2012 book *The Beautiful Music All Around Us: Field Recordings and the American Experience* (p. 25–46).

114. Wade, November 1996–January 1997 *Sing Out!*, p. 66.

115. The other most famous theme from the Copland score was adapted from the traditional Shaker song *Simple Gifts* ("'Tis the gift to be simple, 'tis the gift to be free").

(sometimes known as the Golden Eagles of Chicago) with approximately five members, which first recorded for Decca in 1937, was led by Thelma Byrd and is believed to include Josephine Tillman and bass singer Leandrew Wauford. Paul Oliver opined that the group was probably from a Sanctified church, whereas most recording quartets of the era were Baptist.[116] Anthony Heilbut in *The Gospel Sound* noted that the group used "Dr. Watts' moaning polyrhythms, unusual harmonies triggered by the mixed membership," and was compared in its day with the mighty Golden Gate Quartet.[117] In 1997 this performance served as the title song of Rounder Records' compilation of *A Warrior on the Battlefield: A Capella Trail Blazers from the 1920s to the 1940s.*

Key to the Highway (1941)—"Big Bill" (Broonzy)
Okeh 06242
Recorded in Chicago on May 2, 1941 (*GHF, Blues-#76, BHF*)

One of the most prolific and enduring of all bluesmen, Big Bill Broonzy, born in Scott, Mississippi (on June 26, 1893), and raised in Arkansas, "helped shape the force that became Chicago blues" (writes David McGee).[118] [119] Broonzy began his recording career in 1927, and broke out as a top-level blues star within a few years through his forceful guitar style, strong vocals, and skillful songwriting. Until 1943, he almost never recorded under his last name, but simply as "Big Bill" or under pseudonyms such as Big Bill Johnson and Sammy Sampson. Some of his most popular early records came in 1930 and 1936–1937 as one of the Hokum Boys (the same name used for a number of 1928–1929 records by other artists, most notably the duo of Tampa Red & Georgia Tom Dorsey). White America "discovered" him at the 1938 Carnegie Hall *Spirituals to Swing* concert, and he remained a busy recording and concert artist right up until his death in 1958.

The blues classic *Key to the Highway* was first recorded by Chicago singer-pianist Charles Segar (on February 23, 1940, for Vocalion); its first widely successful version came on May 9, 1940 (Bluebird) by Bill "Jazz" Gillum, accompanied by Broonzy on guitar, and that record credited Gillum as composer. But the song's copyright was owned by its true author, Broonzy. Coming almost exactly a year after the Gillum recording, Broonzy's performance—with Gillum (returning the favor) on harmonica, and Bill's half-brother Washboard Sam on washboard—manages to surpass even the outstanding earlier renditions.

Broonzy's guitar style "represented the ideal marriage of city and country strains," writes Robert Santelli.[120] Amidst his vast body of work, few songs can match the enduring power of this one. Whitney Balliett's comment about the finest of blues lyrics—"they sometimes come close to the concision of rhythms, words, and imagery of genuine poetry"—applies perfectly here. "You haven't done nothin' but drive a good man away from home . . . I'm gonna roam this highway until the day I die."

Skylark (1942)—Harry James & His Orchestra, vocal by Helen Forrest (music by Hoagy Carmichael, lyrics by Johnny Mercer)
Columbia 36533
Recorded Jan. 29, 1942; chart debut May 2, 1942 (#11 peak)[121] (*APS*)

A ballad of shimmering beauty and yearning, *Skylark* was (writes his biographer Philip Furia) lyricist Johnny Mercer's statement of longing for Judy Garland, with whom he had recently had an affair broken off by the much-younger singer. It is yet another demonstration of the melodic ingenuity of Hoagy Carmichael, and provided Harry James with one of his most fondly remembered recordings.

Born in Albany, Georgia, on March 15, 1916, James spent much of his childhood traveling with his family (his father was a circus bandmaster) before the family settled in Texas, and that's where he began working professionally as a trumpeter with various bands in the early 1930s. A 1935–1936 stint with Ben Pollack's orchestra paved the way for his January 1937 debut with the nation's hottest bandleader, Benny Goodman; there, his full-throated, exciting solos and dapper looks made him a star. He left to form his own band in late 1938, but struggled for the first two years, despite employing a young, then-unknown singer named Frank Sinatra. From 1941–1947, James led one of the best-selling bands in the country[122] before changing musical tastes dimmed his popularity; his marriage to Betty Grable made them one of the top celebrity couples in show business. While not known as an innovator, James was never less than outstanding as a musician, made dozens of first-rate recordings featuring several superb vocalists, and surprised many by producing some fine latter-day, quite jazzy big band sessions in the 1950s and 1960s.

---

116. *The New Grove: Gospel, Blues, and Jazz*, p. 203. The group had been accompanied by piano, guitar, harmonica, and tambourine on its 1937 session, and in 1940 used blues harmonica player Hammie Nixon.
117. Heilbut, p. 44.
118. Discussing the big post–World War I flow of southern blacks to the city, record dealer George Leaner remarked to Arnold Shaw (*Honkers and Shouters*, p. 5): "The Illinois Central Railroad brought the blues to Chicago."
119. *New Rolling Stone Album Guide* (2004), p. 106.

120. *The Best of the Blues*, p. 123–26.
121. In different weeks, the James record reached #4 in the East and #8 in the South. The song hit #1 in radio plugs on April 18.
122. During the first quarter of 1942 alone, reported the September 28, 1942, issue of *Time*, James sold over 1.3 million records, four times what the band had sold in 1941's first quarter.

Skylark originated with a melody Carmichael gave to Mercer with the intention of using it in a musical he hoped to do about Hoagy's old friend and musical hero, Bix Beiderbecke. "Although the production never materialized, Mercer hung onto the music," relates Furia. Finally, after six months, he decided upon the title—having nothing to do with the Shelley poem (*To a Skylark*), he said—and then dashed off the lyrics in barely a half hour. "By the time he took the song to Carmichael, the composer had completely forgotten the music." Mercer's lyric matched the beauty of the melody. "The lyric expresses a yearning that ran even deeper than love, for someplace where he could find peace, fulfillment, happiness—Johnny Mercer's emotional equivalent of Garland's *Over the Rainbow*."[123]

When the James band added *Skylark* to its repertoire, Helen Forrest initially had such difficulty with the intricate melody (particularly the bridge) that she suggested to the bandleader that he do it as an instrumental. But knowing the quality of the lyric and the commercial value of her vocal, James came up with an alternate approach: she stood directly in front of him as he quietly played the melody, giving her the notes; this unusual but effective approach can be heard in the recording.[124]

James Morris writes that the song's opening melodic line "traverses an ear-catching path to the bridge, which is difficult, different, and very strong. The melody is loaded with chromatic shifts and changing emphases; the harmony is complex and daring." Forrest, one of the finest female big-band singers, was with James for only a period of months following her tenures with Artie Shaw and Benny Goodman (recording just nineteen titles with James due in part to the recording ban that started in August 1942), but enjoyed several fondly remembered hits with him. In Will Friedwald's view, Forrest "ranks with Bing Crosby and the Andrews Sisters as one of the definitive voices of the World War II era."[125] Here, she "rises easily to the song's challenges: its wide range, its large interval jumps, its chromatic path."[126]

Why Don't You Do Right? (1942)—Benny Goodman & His Orchestra, vocal by Peggy Lee (written by Joe McCoy)

Columbia 36652

Recorded July 27, 1942; chart debut Jan. 2, 1943 (#4 peak; also reached #4 R&B)

One of the greatest torch-song ballads of the Swing Era started its life as a blues called *Weed Smoker's Dream* by the Harlem Hamfats. Guitarist-vocalist Joe McCoy aka "Kansas Joe," ex-husband of blues great Memphis Minnie and a participant on many of her early records, wrote it for his Chicago-based (despite its name) group, which was a particular favorite of Al Capone, for whom they played on several occasions. The fine, moody melody for the song they recorded on October 2, 1936 (Decca 7234) is quickly recognizable, but the lyrics as sung by McCoy are quite different than the ones we know: "Why don't you do like the millionaires do / Put your stuff on the market, and make a million, too!" Herb Morand's evocative growling trumpet solo is a highlight.

Lil Green, a Chicago blueswoman who had spent time in jail for killing a man in a Texas roadhouse brawl, sang her way to freedom with a mixture of blues and gospel, and scored a hit from her debut May 1940 recording session with *Romance in the Dark*. Green was familiar with the Harlem Hamfats song, and McCoy reworked the number for her with new lyrics as *Why Don't You Do Right?*, which she recorded on April 23, 1941 (Bluebird 8714) with a quartet featuring guitarist Big Bill Broonzy.[127] The record's success enabled her to get a prestige engagement at New York's Café Society Downtown.

Among the biggest fans of the Lil Green record was Peggy Lee. Born Norma Jean Engstrom on May 26, 1920, in Jamestown, North Dakota, the Scandinavian-descended youngster started performing on Fargo radio at sixteen, and sang with the Will Osborne band starting in late 1940. It was while performing with a trio at Chicago's Ambassador East Hotel that she was hired by Benny Goodman, with whom she made her first recordings under her stage name, succeeding Helen Forrest as Goodman's girl singer, in August 1941. With a soft, sultry style most often compared to Billie Holiday's (Will Friedwald writes that her style actually owes more to Mildred Bailey and Lee Wiley, and Peggy herself said her number one early influence was Maxine Sullivan)[128] and an appealing blonde beauty, she made an immediate impression. Peggy was captivated by the Lil Green record (she had also seen Lil perform it live on multiple occasions at Café Society); biographer Peter Richmond notes that the "low-down, dirt-road, Deep South black blues" was "as emotionally and stylistically removed from the Northern Plains as it was geographically removed."[129] Lee took her windup phonograph with her

123. *Skylark: The Life and Times of Johnny Mercer*, p. 130–31. Commenting on Mercer's knack for constructing lyrics to fit "the space requirements of jazz licks," Wilfred Sheed in *The House That George Built* (p. 88) calls S*kylark* a "super suspension bridge."

124. Peter Levinson, *Trumpet Blues*, p. 117.

125. Friedwald, *Biographical Guide*, p. 593.

126. Annotation, Smithsonian's *American Popular Song*, p. 60–61.

127. A feature on Lil Green in the April 1943 *Metronome* noted that she learned the song directly from McCoy (his name erroneously cited as "Joe McCorry"), with his new lyrics.

128. *Jazz Singing: America's Great Voices from Bessie Smith to Bebop and Beyond*, p. 333–34.

129. *Fever: The Life and Music of Miss Peggy Lee*, p. 152–53.

everywhere, and this was one of her most frequently-played 78s. When the Goodman band returned to New York in May 1942 for an engagement at the Paramount Theatre, the venue's paper-thin walls between dressing rooms ensured that the bandleader heard her play it over and over. By some accounts the young singer begged him to let her record it, but according to Richmond, Benny, intrigued by her fascination for the number, asked her about it and then suggested that she do it with the band. Pianist Mel Powell wrote an arrangement (some sources have mistakenly attributed the arrangement to Eddie Sauter) that was somewhat brisker than Green's version, but still having "the undercurrent of an opium dream."

Mark Tucker observes that at age twenty-two Peggy had a limited voice and technique, but "got around her limitations by focusing on the emotional qualities of the lyrics."[130] Her phrases "float out like smoke rings, with only the slightest breath behind them." Peggy also had a dark vocal quality that was ideal for this most seductive of torch songs, suggesting vast romantic experience that certainly wasn't the case in real life. Gunther Schuller writes in *The Swing Era* that even though Peggy "appropriated" most of Lil Green's style, "down to the minutiae of individual vocal inflections and word enunciation, still somehow [turned] it into her own unique manner."[131] Richmond suggests that "the remarkable thing about Peggy Lee's version is the blackness of it. This isn't a half-white, half-black rendition; it's all black." Friedwald agrees that she "uses an African American–influenced style" informed by Ethel Waters as well as Holiday.[132] "It wasn't an imitation," the singer would later remark. "I understood that character. That was a woman who had a lot of bad times with that man. And yet it has some humor in it, too."[133]

The piece was recorded at the band's second to last session before the American Federation of Musicians' recording ban took effect at the end of July 1942. From August through October, the three major record labels (Victor, Columbia, and Decca) kept to their normal schedule of releasing from six to ten records apiece twice per month, based on expectations that the dispute between the AFM and the music industry would be short-lived. But as the legal battle dragged on into November and December, the pace of releases dwindled, and (as

the 1943 *Billboard Music Yearbook* put it) records "were issued one at a time, to maximum cash returns." Finally taken off the shelf shortly before Christmas, *Why Don't You Do Right* became a huge smash at the start of 1943, selling nearly a million copies. The song completed its journey into pop culture immortality when buxom Jessica Rabbit (in the singing voice of Amy Irving) utterly seduced a nightclub audience with her lascivious rendition in the 1988 animated classic *Who Framed Roger Rabbit?*

(Other personnel: Jimmy Maxwell, Lawrence Stearns, & Tony Faso on trumpets; Lou McGarity & Charlie Castaldo on trombones; Hymie Schertzer & Clint Neagley on alto saxes; Jon Walton & Leonard Sims on tenor saxes; Bob Poland on baritone sax; Mel Powell on piano; Dave Barbour on guitar; Cliff Hill on bass; Howard Davies on drums)

Blue Horizon (1945)—Sidney Bechet's Blue Note Jazz Men

Blue Note 43
Recorded Dec. 20, 1944 (*Jazz-#135, SJ, TG*)

The soprano saxophone is the instrument with which Sidney Bechet had become most closely associated during his previous quarter-century of jazz greatness, but in December 1944, in his first recording session in over a year, it was on clarinet that he delivered one of his most unforgettable performances on *Blue Horizon*. Born in New Orleans on May 14, 1897, Bechet played clarinet in the Crescent City bands of Bunk Johnson, Clarence Williams, and King Oliver, then headed north to Chicago, and from 1919–1921 was abroad including stints in London (where he played for the Prince of Wales at Buckingham Palace) and Paris. By the time he returned to the U.S. in late 1921 he was also frequently switching to soprano sax.

Bechet, writes Ted Gioia, became the most influential clarinetist of the 1920s, "pointing the way toward a more melodic, linear conception of the horn, and drawing on a more expansive palette of sounds. Much like King Oliver, Bechet developed a voice-like quality to his playing, and exhibited a rare sensitivity to the potential of timbre and phrasing."[134] The only jazz musician on any instrument who could rival his stunning virtuosity was Louis Armstrong, and the few occasions on which they played together—most notably a January 1925 session with the Clarence Williams' Blue Five on which the two men took turns making listeners' jaws drop—were invariably special events.[135] Bechet did some of his best work in the 1940s, mostly leading his own combo, and spent his

130. Annotation, Smithsonian's *Singers and Soloists of the Swing Bands*, p. 27.

131. Schuller, p. 39. Peggy's vocal is discreetly backed by Jimmy Maxwell on trumpet, who, notes George Simon, "throws in some plunger passages as a tribute to his idol, Cootie Williams." Simon (in liner notes to a Time-Life Goodman compilation) describes Benny's "little classic of a solo in a piercing, wailing, even outraged tone" preceding Peggy's final statement.

132. Friedwald, *Biographical Guide*, p. 289.

133. Richmond, *Fever: The Life and Music of Miss Peggy Lee*, p. 153.

134. Gioia, *The History of Jazz*, p. 58.

135. The two jazz icons had known each other in New Orleans, and Bechet always felt the sharp edge of rivalry with the younger musician.

last years performing in France from 1951 until his death eight years later.

On this gorgeous slow blues improvisation, Bechet is accompanied by mostly New Orleans veterans: Sidney De Paris on trumpet, Vic Dickenson on trombone, Art Hodes on piano, Pops Foster on bass, and Manzie Johnson on drums.[136] His tone is crystalline, with a rich fullness that could be mistaken for no one else. The performance, remarked Roger Pryor Dodge in the July 1945 *Record Changer*, "is like nothing I have ever heard. His vibrato is so pronounced that we nearly hear the rattle of it. There is nothing forced in his tone as this vibrato seems to flow of its own accord, especially on the deep low notes with which he usually ends his phrases."

Shaw 'Nuff (1945)—Dizzy Gillespie's All-Star Quintet with Charlie Parker (written by Dizzy Gillespie & Charlie Parker)
Guild 1002
Recorded on May 11, 1945 (*Jazz-#129, SJ*)

The bebop revolution in jazz that began with the issuance of the Dizzy Gillespie combo's Guild 1001 (*Groovin' High*) moved to the next level with the tremendous pairing of *Shaw 'Nuff* and *Lover Man*. The records, remarked Gillespie biographer Alyn Shipton, "defined the bebop small-group style once and for all, and they mark a turning point in jazz history."[137] The piece (which Charlie Parker later implied was his composition alone) is based loosely on the harmonies of *I Got Rhythm* in the key of B-flat, and it's an exhilarating performance by Hall of Fame artists at their peak. The title (like *Billie's Bounce*) refers to Parker's manager/booker Billy Shaw. After the themes are established by the full quintet, Gillespie on trumpet, Parker on alto sax, and pianist Al Haig each improvise a full chorus.[138]

Parker biographer Carl Woideck notes that the "frantic" quality of Bird's soloing provides much of the record's raw excitement.[139] Martin Williams: "This startling performance might be a classic if only for the superb unison passages between the two hornmen . . . It has leaping, ebullient, even humorous solos. And it offers, full-blown, a new jazz."[140] Gary Giddins: "Despite the velocity and rhythmic complexity of the theme, the trumpet and alto sax seem to breathe as one."[141] The Parker-Gillespie collaboration, writes Ingrid Monson, "radiated a musical

empathy articulated in fast, energetic, curlicued melodies played in unison with the most breathtaking precision. So magical was their ability to feel melodies together that Gillespie at times couldn't hear his own trumpet."[142] Said Diz: "Sometimes I couldn't tell whether I was playing or not because the notes were so close together."

Scott DeVeaux in *The Birth of Bebop* writes that on the bridge for this song, Parker uses virtually the same up-and-down arpeggiations he had used on the bridge for *Red Cross* in 1944 with Tiny Grimes.[143] This is one of only three Gillespie records issued by Guild before it went bankrupt. In this piece and *Hot House*, says DeVeaux, "the disjunct, asymmetrical passagework has become the theme [and not just as an interlude between conventional passages]. The package was now complete: virtuoso playing framed by original compositions, both startlingly new." Art Pepper, soon to become an important saxophonist in the 1950s, told Ira Gitler that when he first heard this record and Gillespie's *Salt Peanuts* while with the Army in Europe, it left him in a state of "shock" because "I had never heard anything like that. I said, 'My God, nothing can be like that.'"[144] Andre Hodeir: In his solos for *Shaw 'Nuff* and *Ko Ko*, "tranquil grace gives way to an angular, tormented phrase that has a restless beauty."[145]

(Other personnel: Al Haig on piano, Curly Russell on bass, Sid Catlett on drums)

Nuages (1940/1946)—Django Reinhardt/Quintet of the Hot Club of France (written by Django Reinhardt) (*GHF, Jazz-#60, TG*)
Originally recorded on Dec. 13, 1940 for Swing 88; greatest version on Jan. 31, 1946 (also for the Swing label)[146]

As amusingly but accurately depicted by Woody Allen in his film *Sweet and Lowdown*, Django Reinhardt was the one jazz guitarist who intimidated and awed just about every other guitarist alive during his career from 1934–1953. The French gypsy's most indelible contribution to the jazz canon was the gorgeous *Nuages* (Clouds).

Born in Liberchies, Belgium, on January 23, 1910, and raised in a gypsy settlement outside Paris, Jean Baptiste "Django" Reinhardt was a guitar phenom from an early age. In 1928, his left hand was seriously injured in a caravan fire, leaving him unable to use two fingers, but this

136. Dickenson and Foster were frequent sidemen to Armstrong.
137. *Groovin' High*, p. 167–68.
138. *Swing to Bop*, p. 144: Haig recalled to Gitler that when he first heard the combo play *Shaw 'Nuff*, just before he was hired to join (about two months before the recording), his reaction to the music is that it "was just incredible . . . It was just shocking."
139. Woideck, p. 109.
140. Annotation for *Smithsonian Collection of Classic Jazz* (1973), p. 32.
141. Giddins, *Visions of Jazz*, p. 267.

142. *A New Literary History of America* (p. 771). Monson describes the technically dazzling solos in this performance as "Parker cascading through the bridge of the rhythm changes like a kayak through a rapids and Gillespie proclaiming the glory of the flatted fifth in the opening motto at the same point in his chorus" (p. 774).
143. DeVeaux, *The Birth of Bebop*, p. 376–77.
144. Gitler, *Swing to Bop*, p. 152–53.
145. *Jazz: Its Evolution and Essence*, p. 105–6.
146. 1946 version first released in U.S. almost a year later (reviewed in January 15, 1947 *Down Beat*).

only provided a challenge to his musical ingenuity. Instead, writes Ted Gioia, "he forged a supple guitar technique notable for its speed and clarity of expression."[147] Richard Sudhalter: "Though initially inspired by [Eddie] Lang, he seemed to owe little direct debt to him or any of the other Americans: above all, his daredevil single-string solos, interspersed with rolls, glisses, rifle-shot punctuations, and biting chordal passages, seemed to reflect his gypsy heritage. Certainly his tone, vibrato, and attack bespoke that background: in his hands the guitar sang a passionate, rhapsodic song."[148]

When he met the brilliant French violinist Stéphane Grappelli, the two men formed the Quintette of the Hot Club of France with recordings beginning in 1934, and very quickly the group's reputation spread worldwide even though they never set foot that decade in the United States. After five years of dazzling performances, the combination of World War II and personal tensions split them apart while on tour in England in 1939; Grappelli decided to remain in London while Reinhardt returned to France, recording there with other musicians before and during the Nazi occupation.

Reinhardt first recorded his composition *Nuages* in December 1940 with a revised lineup featuring two clarinetists, Joseph Reinhardt's rhythm guitar, plus bass and drums. "Django's solo begins with eight bars of carefully measured harmonics, before opening out into characteristic double-time runs and flourishes," writes Sudhalter. Gioia sees the piece as reflecting the influence of Ravel, Debussy, and Gershwin imparting an "impressionist tinge" to Django's jazz, with an "exploration of whole tone scales" and "languorous beauty."[149] He recorded it again in 1942 with a large studio orchestra.

Perhaps the finest rendition came in his first reunion session with Grappelli in January 1946, accompanied by a second guitar and bass; even after more than six years apart, their magical chemistry together proved undiminished. The lovely, engaging melody is introduced by the violinist, then Django goes to work. On the more exciting of the two January 31 takes, describes Sudhalter, "he unleashes a torrent of ideas . . . compelling in its urgency." After additional 1947 and 1951 recordings of *Nuages*, another remarkable rendition came on March 10, 1953, this time on electric guitar, which he had taken up a few years earlier. "In its directness and simplicity, its avoidance of flourish, it is perhaps the most affecting of all," declares Sudhalter. Two months later, he would be dead of a cerebral hemorrhage at age forty-three.

Get Things Ready for Me, Ma (1946)—Grandpa Jones

King 545
Recorded in March 1946 in Hollywood

The recordings that brought together traditionalist singer and banjoist Grandpa Jones and virtuoso guitarist Merle Travis in the 1940s are among the undiluted pleasures of country music. Those who know Louis Marshall Jones only through his latter-day comic appearances on *Hee Haw* should know that he was a powerhouse performer whose contagious enthusiasm, the genuine joy he took in bringing old-time music to the people, and vigorous work on banjo made him a true musical treasure. Born on October 20, 1913, in Henderson County, Kentucky, Jones grew up in factory towns in Ohio and Kentucky; his father was a fiddle player and his mother a singer, and at age eighteen he was performing on radio as "The Young Singer of Old Songs." After moving to Chicago, he worked with folk singer Bradley Kincaid, who gave him the "Grandpa" nickname as a joke; Jones put on false whiskers and made it his stage persona. In the early 1940s, after a period in Wheeling, West Virginia, he, Travis, and Alton and Rabon Delmore began performing together at WLW in Cincinnati as the Brown's Ferry Four, which became one of the great country gospel groups. This paved the way for the enduring solo careers of Jones and Travis when both were signed by Syd Nathan to his fledgling King label, starting with the wonderful *It's Raining Here This Morning* (1944), Jones' debut accompanied by Travis.

Because by 1946 Travis was signed to Capitol Records and working in Los Angeles while Jones recorded for King in Cincinnati, they were able to work together as a duo only a limited number of times, but nearly all were memorable. *Eight More Miles to Louisville*, the leadoff number from the same Hollywood session, was also a classic; perhaps the most indelible of their performances (although it was only promoted as the B side to *East Bound Freight Train*) was *Get Things Ready for Me, Ma*.[150] Jones wrote the song during wartime service after he was stationed in Germany in late 1944; he was officially discharged on January 6, 1946, and returned to the recording studio two months later. The tune was inspired after Japan's surrender the previous September "as more and more of the boys finished their stints and started for

147. *The History of Jazz*, p. 172.

148. *Lost Chords*, p. 534–36. Biographer Charles Delaunay (*Django Reinhardt*, p. 26): "Django completely reinvented the role of the guitar in a jazz group, not only from the standpoint of melodic invention but also in regard to accompaniment."

149. Jackie Gleason was evidently an admirer of *Nuages*; he used it as the melodic basis for his famous *Honeymooners* theme *Melancholy Serenade*.

150. Feature on Jones by Charles K. Wolfe, *Journal of Country Music*, Vol. 8 #3 (1981). Wolfe found that King 545 sold nearly 59,000 copies, making it his fifth top pre-1950 seller (tops at 88,000 was the pairing of two Jones favorites, *Old Rattler* and *Mountain Dew*.)

the States."[151] After describing his two years working for Uncle Sam, "the hardest I have ever known," the song depicts a Southern boy who desperately missed that good home cooking and is counting the moments until he walks in the front door and sits down for a giant meal. The ferocious gusto with which Jones anticipates that return (enhanced by the swig of whiskey he had taken down in a single gulp at the outset of the session)—all but salivating over the thought of fried chicken, smoked ham, pumpkin pie, cornbread, possum, yam, turnip greens, biscuits buttered with sorghum molasses, and buttermilk, among other homemade delicacies—is particularly powerful given the historical context. His only accompanist is Travis, whose three-fingered electric guitar style (picking rhythm with the thumb and melody with the fingers) profoundly influenced a generation of players and is in prime form here.[152] "Get things ready for me, Ma—I'm comin' home!"

Let the Good Times Roll (1946)—Louis Jordan & His Tympany Five (written by Sam Theard & Louis Jordan as "Fleecie Moore")
Decca 23741
Recorded June 26, 1946; chart debut Dec. 21, 1946 (4 weeks at #2 on R&B chart) (*Blues-#69, GHF, R&B-#160*)

Louis Jordan could clown it up more entertainingly than any other bandleader of the 1940s on hits like *Caldonia*, but he could also sing the blues with equal aplomb, as he demonstrated on this superb midtempo number, light-hearted but reflective. It was written by veteran black comedian Sam "Spo-de-o-dee" Theard, whose previous credits included the Louis Armstrong favorite *I'll Be Glad When You're Dead, You Rascal You* (which Jordan would also record). According to Jordan biographer John Chilton, Theard outlined the song to the artist when they were working the Chicago club circuit in 1942, and Jordan fleshed it out to memorably record the number four years later. It was the flip side of *Ain't Nobody Here But Us Chickens* (which topped the R&B charts for 17 weeks). Not to be confused with the 1956 New Orleans romp of the same title by Shirley & Lee, the Jordan song was beautifully covered by Ray Charles in 1960.

Jordan's manager Berle Adams explained one key element in the artist's exceptional commercial success to Arnold Shaw: "When we walked into a studio to do a record date, we knew that the four songs would be hits—we had pretested the market. And everything we released was a smash because the public had already determined that they liked the song [from the band performing it on the road]. They had already judged them and waited for our recording."[153]

Blue Grass Breakdown (1947)—Bill Monroe & His Blue Grass Boys
Columbia 20552
Recorded Oct. 27, 1947 (released on March 14, 1949)[154]

Blue Grass Breakdown represents the ultimate country/bluegrass band in full cry, with Bill Monroe on mandolin, Earl Scruggs on banjo, Lester Flatt on guitar, Howard Watts on bass, and Chubby Wise on fiddle. It is, declares Billy Altman, "perhaps the definitive instrumental of the genre, with Monroe pushing the group into a frenetic pace that's positively jaw-dropping; featuring thrilling solos from him, Scruggs and Wise that would become the holy grail to countless generations of aspiring musicians." The leader takes the opening section, Wise follows with furious fiddling that kicks it to a still higher level, and after another Monroe solo, Scruggs (just over halfway into the record) cuts loose unforgettably—introducing some licks that he would expand upon two years later in the supreme Flatt & Scruggs classic *Foggy Mountain Breakdown*. There were three takes of the number, and the two alternate versions (made available years later), each one distinctively different, offer fresh insights into the combo's virtuosity. Dick Spottswood notes that the melody owes something to the folk standard *Lonesome Road Blues*, aka *Goin' Down the Road Feelin' Bad*, and suggests that there are also elements from a 1941 Monroe number, *Tennessee Blues*.[155] The originally issued treatment is included on the Sony bluegrass boxed set *Can't You Hear Me Callin'*. Robert Cantwell remarked of this breathless performance that Monroe "is less playing the mandolin than piloting it."[156] Some three decades after this sublime creation (as recounted by biographer Richard D. Smith), Monroe declared to his banjo player Butch Robins, "I never wrote a tune in my life." Asked for an explanation by the confused musician, he replied, "Those tunes are all in the air. I just happened to be the first one to pick them out."[157]

151. *Everybody's Grandpa: Fifty Years Behind the Mike*, p. 92–93.
152. Jones recalled that early in the session, Travis capoed his guitar "pretty high, and the strings were ringing a lot." Nathan, who had flown out with him to produce the session, was driving the artists a bit crazy, but once they nailed *Eight More Miles*, everything flowed smoothly (Jones and Wolfe, *Everybody's Grandpa*, p. 100–101).

153. *Honkers and Shouters*, p. 79–80.
154. Columbia followed a leisurely schedule of releases for Monroe's 1946–1947 recordings, holding back some for two years, and waiting nearly three years to issue one of the best-remembered performances, *Heavy Traffic Ahead*.
155. Although Monroe was originally credited as composer, it was long speculated that the tune was actually penned by Scruggs, which he confirmed in 2004. (Rosenberg and Wolfe, *The Music of Bill Monroe*, p. 66.)
156. Cantwell, *Bluegrass Breakdown*, p. 49–50.
157. Smith, *Can't You Hear Me Callin'?*, p. 234.

Bill Monroe, courtesy of Library of Congress (American Folklife Center, Corporate Subject file).

Tanga (1948)—Machito & His Afro-Cubans (with Charlie Parker) (written by Mario Bauza)
Clef MGC 511
Recorded in Dec. 1948 & Jan. 1949 (*World-#31*)

Regarded as the first Afro-Cuban jazz composition, *Tanga* was the trademark song of one of the unquestioned giants of the music, Francisco Raul Gutierrez "Machito" Grillo. Born in Havana on February 16 in 1908, 1909, or 1912 (all three years have been reported), the singer-maraca player came to New York in 1937 performing with a string-and-percussion group, Las Estrellas Habaneras, and violinist Alberto Iznaga's Orquesta Siboney. In addition to recording eight sides with Xavier Cugat, Machito in 1940 formed his own band with three saxes, two trumpets, piano, bass, bongo, and timbales. When trumpeter Mario Bauza (born April 28, 1911, in Havana) joined as musical director,[158] the Afro-Cubans became the genre's most influential band. Tito Puente was a member for a short time in the early 1940s, and the 1943 addition of Carlos Vidal—perhaps the first conga player to become a regular member of a New York group—was a crucial step. The arrangements

of Rene Hernandez were another key ingredient in the band's growing reputation.[159]

Bauza began composing *Tanga* on May 29, 1943, when he'd taken over the band after Machito (his brother-in-law) was drafted into the Army. While performing at La Conga, a club in midtown Manhattan, the band was taking a break, pianist Luis Varona began playing the introduction of the traditional tune *El Botellero*, and bassist Julio Andino joined in. This served as the inspiration for Bauza, and the next day he led the band through a performance of his new creation. Afterward, an audience member said the music was as exciting as *tanga*, what Cuban musicians called marijuana. Max Salazar: "This incident marked the beginning of Latinized jazz, Afro-Cuban jazz."[160] By 1947 *Tanga* was a centerpiece of all Machito concerts as his theme song, and late the following year it was given a defining performance.

Machito had long used some non-Latin players in the wind section to ensure a jazz-oriented sound, and for these two sessions his guest stars included the great Charlie Parker (alto sax) and Flip Phillips (tenor sax). Although Parker didn't have the same ongoing passion for Cuban music as his frequent partner Dizzy Gillespie, there was no musical setting in which he was less than brilliant, and this was a period in which he was actively looking for new sounds.[161] Combining (as Steven Loza suggests) a mambo-based structure with an Ellingtonian palette and Basie-like bluesy riffs, it's a thrilling performance with hot solos all around, brief vocals led by Machito, and powerful rhythms driven by four percussionists. Chico O'Farrill would later compose an extended variation of this 3:52 original, *Tanga Suite*.

Tanga, writes Ned Sublette, was "the first piece that we can unequivocally call Afro-Cuban jazz. . . . I don't mean the sit-down music that took over the jazz world a few years later. *Tanga* was one of the all-time dance hits of Latin New York."[162]

Other personnel: Frank Davilla, Bob Woodlen on trumpets, Gene Johnson, Fred Skerritt on alto sax, Flip Phillips, Jose Madera on tenor sax, Leslie Johnakins on baritone sax, Rene Hernandez on piano, Bobby Rodriguez on bass, Machito on maracas, Jose Mangual on bongos, Luis Miranda on congas, Ubaldo Nieto on timbales.

---

158. Bauza had gained fame as trumpeter and musical director with Chick Webb's orchestra (1933–1938), and then with Cab Calloway (1939–1941).

159. Roberts, *The Latin Tinge*, p. 101–2.

160. Liner notes, *Latin Jazz: La Combinacion Perfecta*, p. 6.

161. This was Parker's first recording with a big band since his last session with Jay McShann in 1942, and his first date after the second recording ban consumed nearly all of 1948. Carl Woideck (*Charlie Parker: His Music and Life*, p. 193) noted that working with Machito was a challenge for Bird, as the very simplicity of the Afro-Cubans' two-chord or one-chord harmonic/rhythmic vamps or *montunos* "can make it harder for the improviser to create the patterns of tension-and-release that are associated with modern jazz."

162. *Cuba and Its Music*, p. 472.

The Tennessee Waltz (1950)—Patti Page (written by
   Pee Wee King & Redd Stewart)
Mercury 5534
Recorded in Oct. 1950; chart debut Nov. 18, 1950 (13
   weeks at #1); #1 (9 weeks) in England[163] (*MEM-#5,
   HP-#21, RIA-#198, GHF, Trad-#38, DMDB-#41,
   UK-#48, BBC-#51, C&W-#77, HBN, DMDB*)[164]

It's just a simple, charming little 32-bar pop ballad, but
Patti Page's recording of *The Tennessee Waltz* became
one of the biggest-selling singles of all time, and one of
the most influential records of its era, by popularizing the
then-startling technique of multi-track overdubbing.

Pee Wee King & His Golden West Cowboys' original
version of *Tennessee Waltz* had been a medium-sized
country hit in early 1948, and the combination of his
RCA Victor record and Cowboy Copas' cover version
on King Records is reported to have sold some 380,000
copies.[165] King and his lead singer Redd Stewart had been
inspired to write the song—a variation on the tune they
were already using as their theme, *The No Name Waltz*—
after hearing Bill Monroe's *Kentucky Waltz* on the radio
while driving back to Nashville after a tour, which led
Stewart to wonder why no one had done a Tennessee
waltz. Jazz bandleader Erskine Hawkins recorded a version in 1950 with vocal by Jimmy Mitchell that, while
never hitting the charts, attracted attention. *Billboard*
columnist Jerry Wexler—later to make music history at
Atlantic Records—was alerted to the song by a version
on the Coral label by pianist Ace Harris. While looking
for story material at the Brill Building, Wexler recalled
in his autobiography, he bumped into Patti Page's manager Jack Rael, who mentioned that he needed a B side
for Patti's latest single, and suggested that she record the
song. She did, as the flip side of *Boogie Woogie Santa
Claus*, with no expectations.[166] Before Christmas 1950,
the record simply exploded all over the country. By May,
all combined versions of the tune had sold 4.8 million
copies (with Patti's accounting for the majority), and
ultimately topped six million.[167]

Born Clara Ann Fowler in Muskogee, Oklahoma, on
November 8, 1927, Patti Page grew up in Tulsa, performed on local radio, sang with the Jimmy Joy band on
Chicago radio in early 1947, then landed a contract with
Mercury and earned her first chart hit in mid-1948 with
Confess. Patti first recorded four-part harmonies with
herself on the 1949 record *Money, Marbles, and Chalk*,
and it was Columbia's musical director Mitch Miller who
devised the overdubbing, recording four separate vocals
on four separate acetates and then having the engineer
play them all together on a fifth and final acetate. The feat
was made possible by the relatively recent technique of
recording on magnetic tape. (The great guitar innovator
Les Paul had pioneered the technique at the start of 1948
with his recording of *Lover*, playing six overdubbed guitar parts.) Wexler credits Miller as "a bold innovator, a
model of the producer as artist rather than traffic cop."[168]

Page's recording opens with a trumpet obbligato
played by former Count Basie star Buck Clayton, and
Patti then unfolds the sad tale of watching the man she
loves fall for her best friend, in four-part harmony with
herself. Listeners were dazzled at hearing (as James
Miller describes it) "a delicate latticework of sound."
Fred Rose of the powerful Acuff-Rose firm often made
uncredited contributions to the songs he published, and
he supplied the bridge to the simple King-Stewart lyrics.[169] The music is simultaneously direct and ethereal,
plain yet highly ornamented, with an aura of childlike
magic, not unlike that once associated with music
boxes."[170] Patti would go on to collect more than eighty
chart singles (including *I Went to Your Wedding* and
Old Cape Cod) through 1968.

Un Poco Loco (1951)—Bud Powell Trio
Blue Note 1503
Recorded May 1, 1951 for the album *The Amazing Bud
   Powell*[171] (*Jazz-#31, GHF, NPR-300*)

The ultimate bop pianist, the astonishingly gifted but
perpetually troubled Bud Powell is shown at the height
of his powers on *Un Poco Loco*. "A little crazy" is an apt
phrase for the virtually frenzied—yet still controlled—
quality of his playing, and is also a wry acknowledgment
of the fact that, whether in or out of an institution, he

163. British sheet music charts in *Billboard*.

164. In 1958, New York's station WNEW declared *Tennessee Waltz*
one of the "Ten Greatest Records of All Time" (February 24, 1958,
Billboard). Fourteen years later, the Songwriters Hall of Fame inducted it
as one of ten historic standards (May 27, 1972, *Billboard*).

165. Charlie Gillett, in his Atlantic Record history *Making Tracks* (p.
29–30), relates the "probably apocryphal but nevertheless illustrative" story
that Copas, at the direction of King Records president Syd Nathan, had
purchased a batch of song copyrights in Nashville, but declined to buy the
rights to *Tennessee Waltz* because it was priced at what he considered an
outrageous fifty dollars. Nathan agreed: "There ain't no song in the world
worth fifty dollars."

166. *Rhythm and the Blues*, p. 66. Page was recording the Christmas
number at the request of Mercury's Philadelphia distributor. It was in Philly
that *Tennessee Waltz* first broke out (November 11, 1950, *Billboard*, p. 13).

167. The May 19, 1951, *Billboard* (p. 1), reporting these figures, said
the writers and Acuff-Rose had grossed about $330,000 from the song, and

suggested with some hyperbole that *Waltz* "possibly is the biggest song in
the modern history of the pop song business."

168. Wexler, *Rhythm and the Blues*, p. 67–68.

169. John W. Rumble, *Journal of Country Music*, Vol. 17 #1 (1994),
p. 61. Rumble also credits Rose and promotion man Mel Foree for "using
their broad network of connections" to aggressively promote Page's
recording, overcoming the fact that the firm's only office was in Nashville.

170. *Flowers in the Dustbin*, p. 46–47.

171. *The Amazing Bud Powell* was reissued in 1956, with three takes
of *Un Poco Loco*. The Sept. 1956 *Metronome* called these "a fascinating
example of how a jazz masterpiece is born."

was grappling with psychological problems that would ultimately shorten a brilliant career.

Born in New York City on September 27, 1924, Powell was raised in a musical family, received early training, and by fifteen had left school to become a professional musician. In the nightclubs of Harlem, he was present at the creation of bebop, and formed a friendship with fellow jazz keyboard pioneer Thelonious Monk, who served as house pianist at Minton's Playhouse which was the early center of the bop world. His first big opportunity came with the Cootie Williams orchestra, but when arrested in January 1945 for disorderly conduct during a road trip, Powell was severely beaten by Philadelphia police, and it was a triggering event; soon after his physical recovery, he was placed in a sanitarium, the first of several institutionalizations, in which he would be subjected to electroshock therapy. But after working with Dexter Gordon and Charlie Parker (1947), in 1949 he began producing dazzling recordings with Max Roach and Ray Brown, and from 1949–1951 his sessions for Norman Granz and for Blue Note would form the basis of his legendary status.

Powell's "right-hand lines suggested the alto sax, seemingly a magical transfer of Charlie Parker's searing, tortuous melodic concepts onto the keyboard," observes

Len Lyons. His compositions are "compelling examples of the bebop genre, full of delightful twisting, pausing, turning, and rhythmic shifting . . . Bud's improvising gushes forth at breakneck, nonstop pace, overflowing with ideas."[172] Powell's "reconfiguration of the jazz piano vocabulary would have a deep and lasting impact" on later pianists, declares Ted Gioia.[173]

On *Un Poco Loco*, an intense piece in Latin meter, Powell's telepathic musical relationship with Roach is crucial in establishing the piece as a classic. Alyn Shipton remarks that Powell's artistry is exemplified by the three takes of this song, "each of them more developed in complexity."[174] Before Bud, pianists in trios typically worked with guitar and bass, writes Gary Giddins; he "codified the now standard configuration of piano, bass and drums . . . The drums seemed to extend his palette, most conspicuously on the tantalizing *Un Poco Loco*, where the effect of Roach's clanging cowbell and cymbals is as bracing today as in 1951."[175] With Curly Russell on bass completing the trio, it's a mesmerizing, fiercely percussive performance.

His Eye Is on the Sparrow (1951)—Mahalia Jackson
(words by Civilla Martin, music by Charles H. Gabriel)
Apollo 246
Recorded July 17, 1951 (*GOSP-#5*)

A hymn with few equals in melodic and lyrical beauty, *His Eye Is on the Sparrow* was written in 1905 when lyricist Civilla Martin and her husband struck up a friendship during a stay in Elmira, New York, with a Mr. and Mrs. Doolittle. Mrs. Doolittle had been bedridden for twenty years and her husband was in a wheelchair, but both nonetheless seemed happy and hopeful. What was their secret, Mrs. Doolittle was asked. "His eye is on the sparrow, and I know he watches me," came her reply. "The beauty of this simple expression of boundless faith" fired Civilla Martin's imagination, she would relate, and became the inspiration for the song. She mailed the poem to Charles Gabriel, who put it to music.

Sparrow was first recorded by the Pace Jubilee Singers for Brunswick in April 1927, and five months later by the trend-setting Norfolk Jubilee Quartet for Paramount; the Soul Stirrers led by R. H. Harris waxed it for Aladdin in 1946. Long a fervent favorite in black Southern churches, it was introduced to a much wider audience by Mahalia Jackson, not only through this recording (with gorgeous vocal accompanied by Mildred Falls' combo with organ and piano) but her many performances of the number on

Tito Puente, PhotoFest.

172. Lyons, *The 101 Best Jazz Albums*, p. 196–97.
173. Gioia, *The History of Jazz*, p. 236.
174. *A New History of Jazz*, p. 362.
175. *Visions of Jazz*, p. 321.

radio and television. Equally identified with the song was Ethel Waters, who loved it so much that she made it the title for her autobiography. Seven years after Mahalia's Apollo performance, she delivered an equally memorable version for Columbia in August 1958. "I sing because I'm happy / I sing because I'm free / For His eye is on the sparrow / And I know He watches me."

Anthony Heilbut: "Ironically, the lady often cited by critics as an example of gospel dignity, was initially criticized for her physical gusto. From the start she was a 'stretch-out' singer, breaking all the rules, changing the melody and meter as the spirit dictated. Robert Anderson remembers, 'Mahalia took the people back to slavery times.'"[176]

"The black community's overwhelming affirmation of Mahalia's voice expressed a shared determination grounded in the unshakable knowledge that, in the eyes of God, their struggle was righteous," writes Craig Werner. "When Mahalia assured them that his eyes were on the sparrow, that he would calm the raging sea, it helped black folks gather their energy. When Mahalia called on her people to keep their hands on the plow, her voice helped them hold the plow, and each other, tight."[177]

It Wasn't God Who Made Honky Tonk Angels (1952)—Kitty Wells (written by J. D. Miller)

Decca 9-28232

Recorded May 3, 1952; chart debut July 19, 1952 (6 weeks at #1 on C&W chart) (*C&W-#6, HBN-#12, NPR-300, GHF, RR-6, SC, DMDB*)

Moving quickly as Hank Thompson's disapproving account of a free-spirited woman who loves the nightlife, *The Wild Side of Life*, rode the top of the country charts in 1952, Louisiana recording director/publisher/songwriter Jay Miller dashed off an answer song, *It Wasn't God Who Made Honky Tonk Angels*.[178] Like the Thompson song, it was built on the traditional melody used by both the Carter Family's *I'm Thinking Tonight of My Blue Eyes* and Roy Acuff's *Great Speckled Bird*. The first recorded version of the female response was by obscure female vocalist Al Montgomery.[179] But Decca producer Paul Cohen decided the piece would be perfect for a gifted singer who hadn't broken through yet: Kitty Wells, wife of

Johnny Wright (of the hit country duo Johnnie & Jack). Kitty made it the biggest smash by a solo country female artist since Patsy Montana's *I Want to Be a Cowboy's Sweetheart* seventeen years before, and launched one of the great country music careers.

Born Muriel Deason in Nashville on August 30, 1919, she sang with her sisters on a local radio station as the Deason Sisters in 1936. A year later, she married Johnny Wright, and they began performing together; he suggested her stage name in the early 1940s, taken from a folk song, *I'm a-Goin' to Marry Kitty Wells*. Kitty sang background vocals for Johnnie & Jack (Wright and his brother-in-law Jack Anglin) on some of their records for RCA Victor starting in 1949, and also recorded eight little-heard sides under her own name in 1949–1950 for RCA, then more or less retired to raise her three children until Cohen approached her to do *Honky Tonk Angels*.

She thought it was just an opportunity to collect the $125 union scale for the record session, but it became quite a bit more. The song "gave voice to the feelings of countless women living in postwar America," writes Bill Friskics-Warren. "When thousands of GIs marched off to war a decade earlier, women picked up the slack—and wore the slacks—entering the work force and gaining a measure of social and economic independence. But when the men came home, they tried to turn back the clock, expecting women to resume their roles as homebodies. Those who refused became scapegoats, their morals called into question by their newfound freedom." Thompson's record took the traditionalist male perspective, and found a ready audience. "So imagine their consternation when Wells' mournful whine pierced the airwaves that summer with the straightforward retort, 'It's a shame that all the blame is on us women.' Or when, on the chorus, with Shot Jackson's steel guitar bawling away in the background,[180] Wells charged, 'Too many times married men think they're still single / That has caused many a good girl to go wrong.'"[181] As Richard Crawford puts it, the song "uses one inequity to suggest a broader attitude of social discrimination: men may visit bars alone, but a woman who does so forfeits her claim to virtue. From the song's point of view, women are victims of the faithlessness and aggression of male desire."[182]

Because Kitty was merely empathizing with the free-living women, not condoning their lifestyle, the record was unthreatening—although at first she was forbidden from singing it at the Grand Ole Opry. But it had a tremendous impact; when *Honky Tonk Angels* sold over 800,000 copies, record labels that had all but ignored solo female artists scrambled to sign them. Wells would reign

176. *The Gospel Sound*, p. 62.
177. *A Change Is Gonna Come: Music, Race, and the Soul of America*, p. 7–8.
178. After hearing the Thompson song on the radio as he drove home, he pulled the car off Highway 90, took a tablet from his glove compartment, "and began to write the lyrics down as they came to my mind." (Horstman, *Sing Your Heart Out*, p. 223–24.) Aside from writing this song, Miller's other claim to fame was his prolific recording of Cajun, zydeco, and blues, all of it deeply marinated in traditional south Louisiana sounds based in Crowley.
179. The Montgomery original was on the Feature label, founded by Miller.

180. Paul Warren is on fiddle.
181. *Heartaches*, p. 9–10.
182. *America's Musical Life*, p. 741.

as "Queen of Country Music" with thirty-eight Top Ten country hits, the last in 1965. *Honky Tonk Angels* was called the #21 greatest song by *Country America* in 1992.

(Mama) He Treats Your Daughter Mean (1953)— Ruth Brown (written by Johnny Wallace & Herb Lance)

Atlantic 45-986

Recorded Dec. 19, 1952; chart debut Feb. 14, 1953 (#1 for 5 weeks R&B) (*RHF, Blues-#66, R&B-#127, DM, RH*)

This was the trademark hit for the woman who helped establish Atlantic Records as an industry powerhouse in the 1950s, and was the decade's definitive female R&B singer. Born Ruth Alston Weston in Portsmouth, Virginia, on January 30, 1928, she sang in the African Methodist Episcopal church growing up, won a 1944 Apollo Theater amateur talent contest, began to sing in local small clubs and USO shows, and after graduating from high school took gigs in other locales. It was a 1947 engagement in Detroit that brought her to the attention of Lucky Millinder, who hired her as the band's girl singer, until capriciously firing her. Singer and former bandleader Blanche Calloway, Cab's older sister, let the stranded and broke youngster sing at the Crystal Caverns, the Washington, D.C., club she ran, and then became her manager. Willis Conover of *Voice of America* (there with his guest Duke Ellington) saw her perform, and called Herb Abramson, then in the early stage of helping Ahmet Ertegun get Atlantic Records off the ground, saying he had to hear this girl; after a ten-month hospitalized recovery from a car accident, in May 1949 Ruth launched her historic tenure with Atlantic with the ballad *So Long*, the label's second hit record (after Stick McGhee's *Drinking Wine Spo-Dee-o-Dee*).

Mama, her seventh charted hit, showcases Ruth's sly sexiness as she complains about her man but despite it all seems to enjoy how he "drives me crazy . . . What's the matter with this man?" The song's central line was derived from Blind Lemon Jefferson's 1927 classic *One Dime Blues*, in which he sang: "Mother, don't treat your daughter mean / That's the meanest woman a man most ever seen . . ." Atlantic in 1949 had recorded a Blind Willie McTell session in which McTell did the song as *Last Dime Blues*. Her accompaniment includes Taft Jordan on trumpet, Mickey Baker on guitar, jazz drummer Connie Kay, and disc jockey Hal Jackson on tambourine.

Charlie Gillett notes that arranger Jesse Stone "had the drummer bash a tambourine close to the mike to make sure everybody noticed it was a dance song."[183] At the urging of Abramson, she works in her trademark squeal (which led her to be dubbed "The Girl With a Tear in Her Voice") at the end of such words as "mama," "man," and "understand." Ruth had listened to a lot of country music in her early years at the restaurant where her mother worked, and Chip Deffaa points out in *Blue Rhythms: Six Lives in Rhythm and Blues* that the C&W influence can be heard in the "hoo-ee" vocalizing she does at the end of this performance. The fact that she had been exposed to such a wide range of music, both white and black, helped her to connect with a multi-racial audience. Ruth had to endure some tough times after leaving Atlantic in 1961, but came roaring back by winning a Tony Award on Broadway in 1989 and recording a new series of acclaimed blues albums in the following years.

Crying in the Chapel (1953)—The Orioles

Jubilee 5122

Recorded June 30, 1953; chart debut Aug. 1, 1953 (#1 R&B for 5 weeks, #11 pop) (*GHF, RHF, R&B-#59, DM, HBN, 1001, DMDB, RH*)

The Baltimore-based vocal group that had helped give birth to doo-wop with their 1948 classic *It's Too Soon to Know* scored their biggest hit of all five years later. The Orioles, writes Philip Groia, interpreted white song material "in the style of black free harmony . . . [they] were the innovators of what became known as pure Rhythm and Blues four-part ballad harmony: a mellow, smooth, soft second tenor lead, a blending baritone featured as a 'gravel gertie' second lead, a floating high first tenor and a dominant bass."[184] A seventeen-year-old white country singer from Texas, Darrell Glenn, had first recorded this inspirational ballad (written by his father Artie Glenn) in the spring of 1953, and when Jubilee salesman Hy Weiss heard the song on a Southern trip, he convinced label owner Jerry Blaine to record it quickly. The Orioles' recording is virtually a solo showcase for lead singer Sonny Til, his expressive tenor soaring into falsetto in unforgettable fashion; his fellow Orioles (tenor Alexander Sharp, bass Johnny Reed, and group newcomers Gregory Carroll and Charlie Harris) offer gentle harmonies behind him. Getting an R&B record onto the pop charts was still a formidable achievement in 1953, and when the Orioles accomplished the feat, it helped pave the way for many more crossover smashes to follow for other artists. The crossover went the opposite direction in 1965 when Elvis Presley scored one of his biggest 1960s hits with a cover of *Crying* that was fondly patterned after the Orioles' version. Dave Marsh noted that it's a throwback to the early gospel tradition of jubilee singing, "a smoother, less testifying blend of spiritual

183. *Making Tracks: Atlantic Records and the Growth of a Multi-Billion-Dollar Industry*, p. 55.

184. *They All Sang on the Corner*, p. 15.

harmony" than the intense performances by groups like Claude Jeter's Dixie Hummingbirds.[185]

That's All Right (1954)—Elvis Presley (written by Arthur Crudup)
Sun 209 (billed as by "Elvis Presley, Scotty & Bill")
Recorded July 5, 1954; released on July 19 (*RHF, GHF, RS-#112, ACC-#73, DM-#300, FIR, DMDB, AL*)

It began at 7 p.m. on Monday evening, July 5. Having met the day before, nineteen-year-old Elvis Presley began his first formal session at Sun Records studio in Memphis with guitarist Scotty Moore and bassist Bill Black. Sam Phillips sat in the control room as the boys labored through multiple takes of ballads—*Harbor Lights, I Love You Because*. Phillips heard something special in the kid's voice, but the music just wasn't happening. Just when they were ready to quit for the night and try again the next morning, Presley remembered one of his favorite blues numbers by Mississippi-born, Chicago-based Arthur "Big Boy" Crudup (a non-hit on RCA Victor 2205 in 1946). Everything changed when he launched into *That's All Right*.

"All of a sudden," Scotty Moore would recall, "Elvis just started singing this song, jumping around and acting the fool, and then Bill picked up his bass . . . and I started playing with them." Phillips had the door to his control booth open, "and he stuck his head out and said, 'What are you doing?' And we said, 'We don't know.' 'Well, back up,' he said, 'try to find a place to start, and do it again.'"

Peter Guralnick: "They worked on it over and over, but the center never changed. It always opened with the ringing sound of Elvis' rhythm guitar . . . Then there was Elvis' vocal, loose and free and full of confidence, holding it together. And Scotty and Bill just fell in with an easy, swinging gait that was the very epitome of what Sam had dreamt of but never fully imagined." Moore recounted their reaction upon listening to the playbacks: "It sounded sort of raw and ragged. We thought it was exciting, but what was it? It was just so completely different. But it just really flipped Sam—he felt it really had something. We just sort of shook our heads and said, 'Well, that's fine, but good God, they'll run us out of town!'"[186]

The performance built on the foundation of musical explorations by Moore and Black with the country group Doug Poindexter's Starlite Wranglers in a Sun session several weeks earlier. At the encouragement of Phillips, Moore developed a bluesy style of finger-picking that would be taken to the next level accompanying Presley. Comparing the record with Crudup's original, Jim Dawson and Steve Propes in *What Was the First Rock 'n' Roll Record?* note that while for the most part he sticks closely to Crudup's text and style, Elvis altered the second half of the bluesman's lyrics.[187] Also, whereas Crudup used a drummer, Elvis had Scotty Moore playing "silvery runs" on his big hollow-body electric Echoplex. Black's bass-slapping gets "as much wood as bass notes." But Elvis's use of his guitar for syncopation, slapping the strings, followed the example set by Crudup.[188]

That Thursday night, having been blown away by the tape Phillips had played for him, Dewey Phillips, the hottest radio DJ in Memphis (no relation to Sam), played an acetate of *That's All Right* on his 9 p.m.-to-midnight show; the station was promptly flooded with dozens of phone calls. With a hard-rocking version of Bill Monroe's *Blue Moon of Kentucky* on the flip side, Phillips sent a review copy to *Billboard*, and in its August 7 issue the magazine included it among new country releases: "Presley is a potent new chanter who can sock over a tune for either country or R&B markets . . . A strong new talent."[189] The local furor the record generated didn't lead to any national chart action (although some stations in the Dallas area also picked up on the record, and it sold a reported 300,000 copies in the South overall)—but, with the trio's fusion of blues and hillbilly, the rock 'n' roll revolution had begun.[190] In 2002 the British magazine *Q* proclaimed *That's All Right* #1 among the 100 "Songs That Changed the World."

Gloria (1954)—The Cadillacs (written by Leon Rene)
Josie 765
Released in July 1954 (uncharted)

This achingly lovely harmony ballad, filled with longing, is one of the undisputed classics of doo-wop. Formed in P.S. 139 in Harlem in 1952 as the Carnations, the Cadillacs were led by the great Earl "Speedoo" Carroll, with Charles Brooks, Robert Phillips, Papa Clark and Earl Wade. "Known for their flashy outfits and superb dance routines," writes Bob Hyde, "the Cadillacs in their heyday could blow nearly any other group off the stage."[191]

185. Marsh, *The Heart of Rock & Soul*, p. 260.
186. *Last Train to Memphis*, p. 95–96.
187. Crudup's line "The life you're living, son, women be the death of you" was altered to "Son, that gal you're fooling with, she ain't no good for you." Sun historians Escott and Hawkins, *Good Rockin' Tonight* (p. 64): "The truly surprising thing . . . is how perfectly Presley, Moore, and Black retained the loose-jointed swing of the original."
188. Dawson and Propes, p. 155–58.
189. One week later, *Billboard* reported it as a hot R&B record in Memphis, alongside the latest releases by Muddy Waters (*Just Make Love to Me*), the Drifters, and the Midnighters.
190. *Blue Moon of Kentucky* was the bigger "hit" side in the *Billboard* territorial charts, reaching #1 on the Memphis C&W chart, and the Top Ten in New Orleans and Nashville. But *That's All Right* also appeared six straight weeks on the Memphis C&W Top Ten from September 4 through October 9 (peaking at #4), and reached #7 C&W in Nashville.
191. Liner notes, Rhino boxed set *The Doo Wop Box*, p. 36.

Indeed, they are regarded as the first R&B group to extensively use choreography in their stage routines.

Written by Leon Rene (also noted as founder of the independent R&B label Exclusive Records, which broke big with Joe Liggins' *The Honeydripper*), *Gloria* was first recorded by Johnny Moore's Three Blazers in 1946, and became a Top 20 hit for the Mills Brothers in late 1948. Esther Navarro, manager for the Cadillacs, reworked the song into the doo-wop format, with a different melody and a simplified version of the original lyrics depicting unrequited love. The opening seconds of the Cadillacs' record are unforgettable, as Carroll's voice enters delicately from a distance and then (writes Hyde) draws closer "to an almost in-your-face presence" singing, "Glo-or-eee-a . . . Glo-or-eee-a—It's not Cher-e-e-e . . . It's Gloria, but she's not in love with me . . ." Although this classic performance amazingly did not reach the *Billboard* R&B or pop charts, the group hit it big two years later with *Speedoo*; more than forty years later, Carroll was still a beloved presence on the oldies circuit with a reconstituted group.

Dr. Anthony J. Gribin and Dr. Matthew Schiff write in *Doo-Wop: The Forgotten Third of Rock 'n' Roll* that *Gloria* ranks third behind only *Over the Rainbow* and *A Sunday Kind of Love* among the songs most often recorded by doo-wop groups; other versions include the Five Thrills (also 1954), the Crowns (1956), Dee Clark with the Kool Gents (1957), and the Passions (1960). A survey of listeners by New York oldies station WCBS voted the Cadillacs' rendition the #8 favorite doo-wop record of all time. Philip Groia calls *Gloria* "the epitome of the street corner ballad that most reflects what has become known as 'The New York Sound.'"[192] The *Rolling Stone Album Guide* remarked that the "soaring, plaintive lead vocal . . . set a standard for all group harmony contingents aspiring to the pantheon."

Ain't That a Shame (1955)—Fats Domino (written by
Fats Domino & Dave Bartholomew)
Imperial 5348 (as *Ain't It a Shame*)
Recorded March 15, 1955; chart debut May 14, 1955 (#1 for 11 weeks R&B; reached #10 pop) (*R&B-#32, NPR-100, GHF, RHF, RS, DM, AHR, DMDB*)

The roly-poly piano man of New Orleans, gentle and unthreatening in contrast to his wild and crazy early rock & roll counterparts such as Little Richard and Jerry Lee Lewis, quietly racked up 65 million in record sales with a prolific array of fondly remembered hits with few equals in his era. Fats Domino had already been a major R&B star for five years before *Ain't That a Shame*; this

was the record that earned him crossover stardom that he would not relinquish.

Antoine Domino was born on February 26, 1928, in New Orleans, one of nine children in a musical family; his father was a well-known violinist. His brother-in-law Harrison Verrett, twenty-one years his senior (he had played in the bands of Papa Celestin and Kid Ory), taught the youngster to play piano, and would go on to serve as the guitarist in Domino's band. Quitting school at fourteen, Fats (nicknamed both for his bulk and after one of his musical heroes, pianist Fats Waller) went to work in a factory and began performing at local clubs. It was at the Hideaway club that he met trumpeter-bandleader Dave Bartholomew, then the local artists & repertoire man for the West Coast–based Imperial Records. Bartholomew arranged a record session backed by his own band, and the date produced Domino's first R&B smash, *(They Call Me) The Fat Man* in early 1950. The session was held in the back room of J&M Record Shop, owned by Cosimo Matassa, who also served as the recording engineer. The Domino-Bartholomew team would become an unbeatable team as hit songwriters and singer-producer tandem for the next two decades.

After twelve records that reached the rhythm & blues Top Ten, *Ain't That a Shame*—cut at Abraham "Bunny" Robyn's Master Recorders studio in Los Angeles while he was on tour, and released at just the time when white Top 40 radio was at last opening its airwaves to non-crooning black performers—smashed through the barriers. Domino biographer Rick Coleman reports that Bartholomew complained that the song was too simple and lacked a story line, but Fats wouldn't change it.[193] Peter Guralnick described the Domino sound as music "that is instantly recognizable, dominated by a warm vocal style and a thick, chunky, boogie-woogie-based New Orleans-flavored piano" that was influenced by Albert Ammons and generations of Crescent City pianists including Professor Longhair; right-hand triplets were central to his keyboard style. Fats' relaxed, ingratiating vocals were accompanied by Bartholomew's "clear, punchy" arrangements featuring riffing saxes, Herb Hardesty (trumpet/tenor sax),[194] the arranger/bandleader on trumpet, and steady, loping percussion.[195]

James Miller observes that the performance "featured a rolling bass line doubled by the electric guitar, and Domino's trademark eighth-note piano triplets, hammering home the beat. The main musical novelty was the staccato, stop-time arrangement (which Bartholomew

192. *They All Sang on the Corner*, p. 72.

193. *Blue Monday*, p. 102.
194. Hardesty, who solos here as on many of Domino's hits, had a softer, jazzier style than Fats' other best-known saxophonist, the hard-blowing Lee Allen.
195. *Rolling Stone Illustrated History*, p. 50–51.

patterned after the 1920s New Orleans Rhythm Kings jazz standard *Tin Roof Blues*), which broke up the easy swing of the performance, giving the song a lurching momentum" reminiscent of *Rock Around the Clock*. Papoose Nelson's guitar riff and Hardesty's sax solo contributed to the record's appeal. Pat Boone took a homogenized cover version of the song to #1 on the pop charts, but rather than hurting Domino's original, apparently helped it by making white listeners more curious about the source material.[196] Due credit for the record's commercial success must be given to Imperial owner Lew Chudd, who carried out furious promotion to overcome white radio stations' initial resistance to a powerfully rhythmic performance by a singer whose Creole accent baffled those hearing it for the first time.

Domino's piano here, writes Dave Marsh, "communicates so much joy, it never drowns the sadness of the lyric in its own sweetness."[197] "You made me cry when you said goodbye / Ain't that a shame, my tears flowed like rain . . ."

Coleman: "If Roy Brown supplied the name, the revelry, and the vocal fire of rock 'n roll, Domino and his producer Dave Bartholomew built its New Orleans rockhouse foundation with interlocking rhythms that would become the musical mainstream, which, like the Mississippi, everyone else would later ply."[198]

Feudin' Banjos (1955)—Arthur Smith & Don Reno
MGM 5202 & 12006; recorded in early 1955, released in May 1955

The original source for *Dueling Banjos* of cinematic *Deliverance* fame, *Feudin' Banjos* is a country/bluegrass instrumental classic by any standard. Born on April 1, 1921, in Clinton, South Carolina, Arthur Smith first recorded for Bluebird in 1938, and created his trademark song *Guitar Boogie* in 1945 for the Super Disc label. MGM's reissue of that song became a smash in late 1948, and made a strong impression on early rockabilly artists. Smith's guitar style also had jazz inflections adding another level of interest.

Don Reno, Smith's duet partner on this record, was born February 21, 1926, in Spartanburg, South Carolina. A multi-instrumental virtuoso, Reno began his successful partnership with Red Smiley in 1951, but during a period of inactivity from 1953 into 1955, Reno worked with Smith's Crackerjacks. On *Feudin' Banjos*, Smith is on four-string tenor banjo and Reno on the five-string; their musicianship is scintillating while still conveying the feeling of back-porch relaxation. Together with the

record's B side, *Bye, Bye, Black Smoke Choo Choo*—a loving homage to steam engine trains—this was one of the most exceptional double-sided country singles of the decade, even though it never showed up on the *Billboard* C&W chart. Its impact was suggested by a terrific 1957 cover version by Carl Story & the Rambling Mountaineers (featuring the Brewster Brothers) under the title *Mocking Banjo*.

James Dickey, author of the novel on which the film *Deliverance* was based and also a collaborator on the picture, loved the Arthur Smith record and played it for director John Boorman, who liked the song and decided to use it. Eric Weissberg and Steve Mandel scored a massive 1973 pop hit with their remake; as he explained years later, Weissberg had copies of both the Arthur Smith and Carl Story records, and as a member of the Tarriers in the early 1960s often shared the stage with the Dillards, who included the piece in their repertoire. The latter group also recorded it under the title *Dueling Banjos*. Warner Brothers, Weissberg noted, released the remake as a single without telling the performers, and also included it as an addition to a reissue of a 1962 album (*New Dimensions in Banjo and Bluegrass*) Weissberg had done with Marshall Brickman, marketing it as a *Deliverance* soundtrack—without bothering to list any songwriter credits.[199] The label simply assumed that the piece was traditional and therefore in the public domain. Smith, who had copyrighted his creation in 1955, filed suit with the financial assistance of Fred Foster, owner of Monument Records. As detailed by Ed Davis' profile of Smith, Warner Brothers' claim that Smith had simply adapted a traditional tune was shattered when experts found that there were no precedents in Barlow's dictionary of 10,000 musical themes, and Weissberg himself testified that *Feudin' Banjos* and *Dueling Banjos* were the same song. After a two-year battle, Smith received an out-of-court settlement granting him all the royalties (about $200,000 at the time) and credit as the author.[200]

Banana Boat Song (Day-o) (1957)—Harry Belafonte
(adaptation credited to Alan Arkin, Bob Carey & Erik Darling)
RCA Victor 6771
Recorded Oct. 20, 1955; chart debut on Jan. 12, 1957 (reached #5); #1 for 13 weeks in Germany[201]; #2 in England; from the album *Calypso* (chart debut June 16, 1956, 31 weeks at #1) (*GHF, World-#24, Folk-#42, RIA, AHR*)

196. *Flowers in the Dustbin*, p. 99–102.
197. *Heart of Rock & Soul*, p. 426.
198. Coleman, *Blue Monday*, p. 6.

199. Weissberg's letter to the editor, March 2006 *Bluegrass Unlimited*, p. 12–13.
200. Ed Davis article, February 1975 *Muleskinner News*.
201. Only eight records in the history of the German charts (1950s onward) held #1 for more weeks.

A tremendous force in expanding the mainstream popularity of folk music and introducing many Americans to the Jamaican sounds of calypso, Harry Belafonte was equally important for his tireless activism on behalf of civil rights and other causes. Just one phrase, the cry of "Day-o," elicits an automatic smile for Belafonte's most beloved classic, *Banana Boat Song*.

Born in Harlem to a Jamaican mother and West Indian father on March 1, 1927, Belafonte spent part of his childhood in Jamaica,[202] and upon returning to the U.S. joined the Navy for three years, studied acting alongside classmates including Marlon Brando and Tony Curtis, and then became a member of the American Negro Theatre. Although he had heard calypso music as a child, it was a meeting with Irving Burgie, an American (with a Barbadian mother) who performed West Indian songs as Lord Burgess and His Serenaders, that persuaded him to begin performing it. His performance of West Indian songs at the Village Vanguard in Greenwich Village led to a starring role in the 1954 film of Oscar Hammerstein's *Carmen Jones* opposite Dorothy Dandridge (who earned an Oscar nomination). Having already recorded several singles for RCA Victor in the early 1950s, this fresh acclaim persuaded the label to hustle Belafonte back to the studio to record full-length albums. Still, his concept of building the albums around calypso made label executives nervous, until company president George Marek gave his approval. It was his second album *Belafonte* in early 1956 that kicked off the calypso craze (and Belafonte adoration, based in part on his good looks and personal charisma as well as his music) into high gear as it topped the pop charts for six weeks, and just four months later *Calypso* soared still higher, becoming one of the biggest pop albums of the decade.[203]

Banana Boat Song is based on a Jamaican folk song (*Hill and Gully Rider*) brought to the U.S. in the late 1940s, with the singer's own improvisation that made it truly come alive.[204] It had appeared in print as early as 1952 in Tom Murray's *Folk Songs of Jamaica*.[205] After the Belafonte album became a phenomenon in summer 1956,[206] the folk trio the Tarriers (Erik Darling, Bob Carey, and future movie actor Alan Arkin) recorded a cover version that debuted on the charts in December and wound up reaching #4; somehow the Tarriers' names wound up on the song's lucrative copyright.[207] (Preceding both Belafonte and the Tarriers had been folk legend Bob Gibson, who was performing the song regularly in Greenwich Village's Washington Square Park.) But it was Belafonte's performance that defined for all time the song of Jamaican workers carrying, loading, and selling bananas. The arrangement is by the singer's musical director, Tony Scott, an acclaimed clarinetist who played at various times in the Duke Ellington and Tommy Dorsey bands and with such other jazz greats as Dizzy Gillespie, Thelonious Monk, and Billie Holiday.[208] Also featured is guitarist Millard Thomas.

Why did Belafonte's music become such a popular phenomenon in the U.S. when previous calypso stars—including those whose song catalogs were skillfully mined by Belafonte—had reached only a cult audience? Aside from his magnetic personal appeal, Ed Ward (*Rock of Ages*) suggests that another reason may be that his rhythms were "more Latin than Caribbean," and Latin music was very hot in the 1950s, as evidenced by the potent sales for Perez Prado and Tito Puente.

After selling many millions of more albums over the next decade, Belafonte's movie acting career continued (also directing a few films), as did his social activism, and in 1985 he was one of the key forces behind the USA for Africa *We Are the World* anti-hunger benefit. His recording of *Banana Boat Song* was amusingly used in the 1988 film *Beetlejuice*, and its chorus is often employed as a singalong chant at baseball games.

---

202. When the eight-year-old Harry was staying with his father for a time in Jamaica, he often watched the men load bananas at the Ocho Rios deepwater pier for the United Fruit Company boats (which also carried sugarcane, mangoes, and oranges). At the end of the school year, his father brought him back to New York on one of his banana boat runs. "Not by chance did that song become my signature; I knew of what I was singing," he remarked in his memoir *My Song* (p. 34).

203. Ed Ward in *Rock of Ages: The Rolling Stone History of Rock & Roll* (p. 139) notes that when RCA began promoting Belafonte, it was the first time a major label had seriously tried to promote calypso music to a broad national audience since Wilmoth Houdini, a long-popular Jamaican artist who was based in New York from the 1920s onward. The many other calypso stars of the 1930s and 1940s, such as Attila the Hun and King Radio, who were mostly signed to Decca, were primarily marketed to Caribbean immigrants in the U.S.

204. The original album's liner notes report that the number is based on the traditional work songs of the gangs who load the banana boats at night

in the Trinidad harbor. The cry of "Day-o" expresses the workers' longing for daybreak when they can return to their homes.

205. Norm Cohen, notes for Smithsonian's *Folk Song America*, p. 78.

206. A June 2, 1956, *Billboard* review confirms that *Day-o* was included on the original issue of the *Calypso* album, months before the Tarriers' single.

207. Arnold Shaw was the creative director of the song publishing firm Edward B. Marks Music, and he acquired the rights to the *Banana Boat Song* from Phil Rose under an arrangement in which the copyright was owned and jointly promoted by Rose's firm Bryden Music and E. B. Marks. But in Shaw's account in *Honkers and Shouters* (p. 427), he states incorrectly that Belafonte "rushed into the RCA Victor studios" to cut the song immediately after the Tarriers' version hit the charts, when in fact Belafonte had recorded the song over a year earlier, although the track wasn't released as a single until after the Tarriers' cover version. Rose filed suit against RCA Victor, which was handling pressings of the Arkin group's record, claiming that RCA was stalling on those pressings in order to give the Belafonte disc time to take command, but the assertion was not sustained by the courts.

208. Among Scott's other distinctions was composing music for short films featuring striptease artist Lili St. Cyr.

All Shook Up (1957)—Elvis Presley (written by Otis Blackwell)

RCA 47-6870

Recorded on Jan. 12, 1957; chart debut April 6, 1957 (9 weeks at #1); #1 for 4 weeks R&B;[209] #1 for 1 week C&W; #1 for 7 weeks in England;[210] #1 in Canada (*BILLB-#25, RS, TC, Juke-#35, DMDB*)

Elvis Presley arrived in Los Angeles by train on January 11, 1957, to begin work on the movie *Loving You*. He was not due at the Paramount studio for a few days, so on the twelfth he entered Radio Recorders in Hollywood for his first RCA session since September. The session's big highlight was *All Shook Up*.

Black songwriter Otis Blackwell, fresh from the recent success of his smoldering *Fever* for Little Willie John, got 1957 off to a big start with this smash, which would soon be followed by *Great Balls of Fire* for Jerry Lee Lewis. Born in Brooklyn (February 16, 1932), Blackwell won a talent contest at the Apollo Theater which led to a meeting with songwriter Doc Pomus, a source of encouragement in his career. It was Presley's massive success with Blackwell's *Don't Be Cruel* in 1956 that broke things open for him. Elvis continued to do well with subsequent Blackwell songs, including *Return to Sender* (1962); the songwriter's other hits included *Breathless* (Jerry Lee Lewis) and *Hey Little Girl* (Dee Clark).

The story goes that Blackwell's friend, songwriter Al Stanton, walked into his office one day shaking a bottle of Pepsi and challenged Otis to come up with a song called "All Shook Up." (In another version of the tale, Blackwell was in the office of publisher Goldie Goldmark, who told him, "you can write a song about anything, right? Write a song about this," grabbed a bottle of soda, and shook it.) Elvis gave the number an appropriately effervescent performance, and (as he'd done on *Don't Be Cruel*) slapped the back of his guitar to add a little extra spark. The record sold over two million copies, and was the King's second longest-running #1 hit.

Bye Bye Love (1957)—Everly Brothers (written by Boudleaux & Felice Bryant)

Cadence 1315

Recorded in March 1957; chart debut May 13, 1957 (#1 for 7 weeks C&W, 4 weeks at #2 on pop chart, #5 R&B); reached #2 in Canada, #6 in England (*RHF, GHF, C&W-#71, HBN-#104, RS-#210, DM-#235, AHR, TC, ACC, DMDB*)

A song turned down by more than thirty artists became the launching pad for one of the greatest vocal teamings in pop music history. Country music has a long history of brother acts—the Monroes, the Louvins, the Delmores, the Stanleys, the Bailes Brothers—and this is where Isaac Donald Everly (born February 1, 1937, in Brownie, Kentucky) and Phil Everly (born January 19, 1939, in Chicago), the sons of a Kentucky coal miner, trace their musical roots. Their dad, Ike Everly, was one of the guitarists who had taught the great Merle Travis the picking style that would be emulated by a generation of country and rock guitarists. The brothers were singing on local radio as children. Don wrote a minor country chart hit in late 1954 for Kitty Wells (*Thou Shalt Not Steal*), and the duo recorded one unsuccessful single for Columbia Records, which did not renew their option. Ike Everly asked his friend Chet Atkins to introduce his boys to publisher Wesley Rose, and it was Rose (subsequently their manager) who persuaded Archie Bleyer—who had turned them down once before—to listen to their tape again and sign them for the Cadence label.

Boudleaux Bryant and his wife Felice had been writing songs for over a decade and scored a few country and pop hits, but it would be their association with the Everly Brothers that elevated them to the top ranks of songsmiths. (Ike Everly had once been Boudleaux's barber!) Boudleaux originated the idea for *Bye Bye Love* and envisioned it as a vehicle for the country duo of Johnnie & Jack, because of the song's strong harmonies, their voices typically pitched a third apart. As detailed by Felice Bryant in Stephen Bishop's book *Songs in the Rough*, when the duo finished polishing the piece, they faced a long series of rejections; Johnnie & Jack did finally record it, but to little response. Archie Bleyer loved the song, and felt it would be perfect for the heavenly harmonies of Don and Phil. Their Cadence debut was an immediate smash, the first of the Everlys' thirty-plus hits.

Like the Louvin Brothers who served as role models, the Everlys possessed glorious voices that intertwined impeccably as only siblings can, could solo with equal aplomb, and were at home with either ballads or uptempo numbers. It is Don Everly's guitar lick that kicks off the record and sets a brisk, bouncy tempo (David Cantwell writes that he "chops away at the strings like an acoustic Bo Diddley," and indeed both Don and the Everlys' frequent accompanist Atkins were great admirers of Diddley), and their voices do the rest.[211] Franklin

209. The May 13, 1957, *Billboard* reported (p. 36) that Presley became the first "country-derived artist" (white) to win the magazine's Triple Crown Award for topping the R&B retail, jukebox, and disc jockey charts simultaneously.

210. *All Shook Up* was Presley's tenth British hit, but his first to reach #1. As related in *The Guinness Book of 500 Number One Hits*, almost immediately after the record's success, RCA Victor set up its own distribution network in the U.K., independent of its longtime partner HMV. RCA allowed that company to retain the iconic "Nipper the dog" trademark, "but this proved to be of little consolation for losing the rights to Elvis Presley."

211. *Heartaches By the Number*, p. 57. Interviewed by Colin Escott for the *Journal of Country Music*, Vol. 15 #2 (1993), Don Everly revealed that there are four guitars here: Phil played in regular tuning, Don with a guitar

Bruno reveals that this "spring-loaded" acoustic guitar introduction was imported (at Bleyer's suggestion) into the arrangement from an unreleased piece by Don Everly, *Give Me a Future*.[212] "The unearthly combination of Don and Phil Everly's voices was so perfect, so pure, that it seemed to emanate from a single source," writes Thomas Ryan.[213] Toby Creswell: "*Bye Bye Love* bounces along with an enthusiasm and joy that runs counter to the dark heartbreak sentiments, but it hardly matters. This is pure teenage joy."[214]

Chances Are (1957)—Johnny Mathis (music by Robert Allen, lyrics by Al Stillman)

Columbia 40993

Recorded June 16, 1957; chart debut Sept. 16, 1957 (1 week at #1); reached #3 in Canada (*GHF, Trad-#77, RIA, DMDB*)

"Feel like making love? Try Johnny Mathis. Millions have." So proclaimed a giant promotional billboard above Sunset Boulevard, report David Dalton and Lenny Kaye. "It is not the personality of Johnny Mathis, but the Voice, an almost disembodied sound, which has penetrated the ears of countless melting lovers around the world . . . This voice moves like a feathery wand, transforming tacky motel rooms and chintzy bedrooms into Arcadian boudoirs charged with sensuality . . . Sex at 33 RPM. Johnny Mathis is the master of pillowtalk crooning, an insinuating cupid who creates an ideal erotic ambiance."[215] One could hardly do better to illustrate that declaration than to listen to his swooning ballad classic *Chances Are*.

Born in San Francisco on September 30, 1935, one of seven children whose parents were domestic servants to a millionaire (one parent had also sung in vaudeville), Mathis studied opera from age thirteen. While attending San Francisco State College on a track scholarship (specializing in hurdles and high jump), he was invited to U.S. Olympic tryouts at nineteen, but decided to pursue a music career instead. George Avakian of Columbia Records signed him to a contract and initially viewed his pristine voice as an ideal jazz instrument, logically enough since he had developed his style singing in jazz clubs along the Bay City's North Beach area; but the label's artist & repertoire head honcho Mitch Miller shrewdly steered him toward pop. With his first two hits in early 1957, *Wonderful! Wonderful* and *It's Not for Me to Say* (both from his debut session with Miller), the Mathis sound was established: a multi-octave voice soaring and descending with the greatest of ease, smoother than velvet, caressing the lyrics with impeccable intonation, carried along in a cascade of strings that somehow never seem excessive but merely the perfect accompaniment for seduction. It was a sound dripping with vulnerability and soft, inoffensive, gender-less invitation.

Chances Are, Johnny's third hit, was arranged (like most of his early hits) by Ray Conniff. "He was a genius," declared the singer. "He did all of these songs with only eight or 10 musicians." However, the singer revealed that the basic piano arrangement was done by the tune's composer Bob Allen.[216] His early singles were recorded at Columbia's 30th Street Studio, an old renovated church on 30th Street and Third Avenue in New York City, and on average were completed in about thirty minutes each—amazingly economical considering their sumptuous sound. It appeared for the first time on an album with *Johnny's Greatest Hits* in 1958, one of the biggest albums of all time accumulating 490 weeks on the *Billboard* chart. One of the most delightful uses of *Chances Are* came in the Steven Spielberg film *Close Encounters of the Third Kind*; Mathis sings the opening lines "Chances are, I wear a silly grin the moment you come into view" just as a wide-eyed young boy is about to encounter the friendly extraterrestrials for the first time.

Summertime Blues (1958)—Eddie Cochran

Liberty 55144

Chart debut Aug. 4, 1958 (#8 peak); #10 in Canada, #18 in England (*RS-#74, RHF, GHF, RIA, ACC-#88, AHR, DM, 1001, DMDB*)

When Eddie Cochran recorded *Summertime Blues* in 1958, he was struggling to escape the tag of a one-hit wonder who looked the part of the rock idol in movies, but hadn't quite earned it in real life. Born on October 3, 1938, in Oklahoma City and raised in Albert Lea, Minnesota, Cochran began playing guitar at age twelve, recorded some country and rockabilly songs with the unrelated Hank Cochran (later a successful Nashville songwriter, including the Patsy Cline classic *I Fall to Pieces*) as the Cochran Brothers, and in 1955 began his association with songwriter Jerry Capeheart. In early 1957 he scored a Top 20 hit with *Sittin' in the Balcony*, and began landing appearances in rock & roll-related movies including *The Girl Can't Help It* and *Untamed Youth*. Buddy Holly biographer Ellis Amburn noted Cochran's reputation as a major-league chick magnet, "someone who could seduce a girl just by looking at her."[217] But his

open-tuned with a capo up on the neck, Nashville session man Ray Edenton played with the G string tuned up an octave, and Atkins contributed electric guitar fills.

212. Essay on Felice and Boudleaux Bryant for the *Oxford American* 12th Annual Southern Music Issue 2010, p. 30.

213. Ryan, *American Hit Radio*, p. 19–20.

214. Creswell, *1001 Songs*, p. 472.

215. *Rock 100*, p. 71–72.

216. Liner notes, Mathis boxed set *A Personal Collection*, p. 38.

217. Amburn, *Buddy Holly: A Biography*, p. 95.

followup singles were largely ignored, and the first day of a March 1958 session with Capeheart in Hollywood didn't produce anything promising. Then a guitar lick played by Cochran got Capeheart thinking: "I knew there had been a lot of songs about summer, but none about the hardships of summer. Of all the seasons, there'd never been a blues song about summer." They finished the tune in forty-five minutes, and cut it at the studio the following day, with a combo including drummer Earl Palmer. In his autobiography *Backbeat*, Palmer recalled being impressed by Cochran, who had the presence to rewrite Rene Hall's original arrangement for the song.[218]

Summertime Blues perfectly summarized teen attitudes in the new rock & roll era, and made Cochran a star. But he would have only one other Top 40 hit (the followup *C'mon Everybody*). The February 1959 death of his friend Buddy Holly was a hard blow. A tour of England and Europe in early 1960 was a huge success, helping to inspire a generation of rock fans there; George Harrison followed Cochran from town to town. But shortly before he was to fly back home from England, Cochran was killed in a car accident on April 17; fellow rocker Gene Vincent, sitting next to him in the taxi, survived.

Cochran's killer acoustic guitar riff is the heart and soul of the song, along with his overdubbed bass voice; intended to simulate adults who just don't understand (his father, his boss, his Congressman), it was inspired by the character of Kingfish on "Amos 'n Andy." Les Paul had pioneered the technique of overdubbing on record, and Cochran was an eager student; the record's multitracked percussion and guitar sounds accentuate its impact. The master tapes were remixed from four tracks down to two channels. The lyrics (primarily by Capeheart) are loaded with sassy attitude, and if they don't entirely make sense (asking his Congressman to take his problem to the United Nations), it could hardly matter less. Joel McIver sees the record, in its innocent way, as "giving voice to a generation of disgruntled youth. *Summertime Blues* was not exactly Rage Against the Machine, but at the time, when teens were just beginning to find their own identity, the song was cultural dynamite."[219] Blue Cheer and The Who later scored hits with the song. The original was included among the ten greatest protest songs cited by *Mojo* magazine in 2004.

Battle of New Orleans (1959)—Johnny Horton (written by Jimmy Driftwood)
Columbia 41339
Recorded in Nashville on Jan. 27, 1959; chart debut Apr. 27, 1959 (#1 for 6 weeks on pop chart; #1 for

10 weeks C&W); #1 for 6 weeks in Australia, #16 in U.K. (*GHF, C&W-#34, Folk-#43, BILLB-#112, RIA, SC, DMDB*)

On January 8, 1815, the War of 1812 came to a belated end with a lopsided American victory led by Andrew Jackson over British forces in New Orleans. A treaty ending the war had been signed two weeks earlier, but news hadn't yet reached the troops. The triumph was celebrated in song, including a fiddle breakdown called *The Eighth of January*, also known as *Jackson's Victory*. The fiddle tune was widely played at square dances and other locales throughout the South right up to modern days. This breakdown provided the basis for Johnny Horton's classic, rollicking country/pop story song, *The Battle of New Orleans*.

The first known recording of *The Eighth of January* was made in February 1928 by the Arkansas Barefoot Boys for Okeh (featuring Cyrus Futrell on fiddle), and a high-energy rendition was waxed two years later for the same label in San Antonio by the Fox Chasers, a fiddle-led string band.[220] Equally fine was a 1942 recording made for the Library of Congress by two black Nashville-area musicians, Frank Patterson (fiddle) and Nathan Frazier (banjo).

It was in 1955 that a Snowball, Arkansas, schoolteacher named James Corbett Morris, in an effort to make history lessons more interesting for his students, began writing lyrics to traditional tunes describing events in American history. One of these songs was his adaptation of *The Eighth of January* as *The Battle of New Orleans*. The number was so catchy that he recorded it in 1957 for a small label under the stage name Jimmy Driftwood.[221] The recording came to the attention of rising country star Johnny Horton, who invited Driftwood to edit the song down to a more radio-friendly length.[222] Three weeks later, Horton recorded it at Columbia's studios in Nashville.

Horton was born in Los Angeles (although a few sources claim Tyler, Texas) on April 3, 1929, continually moved with his family between Texas and California in an attempt to find migrant farm work, and after graduating from high school attended a Methodist seminary in preparation for a possible career in the church. Instead he left to begin traveling the country, and while living for a time in Alaska in 1949, working as a fisherman, began writing songs. The following year he won a talent contest in east Texas, and landed a recording contract in 1951.

218. *Backbeat*, p. 114.
219. *1001 Songs You Must Hear*, p. 93.

220. *Country Music Sources*, p. 766.
221. Driftwood was profiled by Irwin Silber for the Summer 1959 *Sing Out!*, p. 6–7. "My great grandfather came to Arkansas from the Smokies of Tennessee. I learned folksongs as a child from my parents, grandparents, and most anyone I could get to sing for me."
222. Steel guitar player Don Warden, the song's co-publisher (with country star Porter Wagoner), suggested it to Horton and his manager.

Hank Williams became a mentor to the young performer on the *Louisiana Hayride* show in 1952; after Hank's death, Horton married the legend's widow, Billie Jean, in September 1953. It was not until 1956 that Horton found success as a recording artist; appropriately for an artist who embodied the feisty qualities of honky-tonk country music with tinges of rockabilly, his first hit was *Honky Tonk Man*. The narrative ballad *When It's Springtime in Alaska* gave him fresh momentum in early 1959, and then came his biggest hit of all.

Horton's rendition of *Battle of New Orleans* (produced by Don Law) closely follows Driftwood's original, but his addition of emphatic downbeats, and a terrifically spirited, good-humored vocal, enabled the performance to leap off radios and cross over to become the second biggest pop hit of 1959 behind only Bobby Darin's *Mack the Knife*. It served as the model for a series of followup historical epics such as *Sink the Bismarck* and *North to Alaska*. At the height of his fame, Johnny Horton died following a car accident driving home from an Austin, Texas, concert to Shreveport, Louisiana, on November 5, 1960.[223]

Spoonful (1960)—Howlin' Wolf (written by Willie Dixon)

Chess 1762

Recorded in June 1960 (didn't chart) (*Blues-#17, RHF, NPR-300, R&B-#111, RS-#221*)

Spoonful is built around a rhythmic groove that is one of the most powerfully hypnotic by the Mississippi-born, Chicago-based blues legend who was born Chester Arthur Burnett but known to the world as Howlin' Wolf. Like many Wolf songs, it's loosely based on a number by his original mentor Charley Patton (the man who helped teach him how to play guitar in eastern Mississippi), in this case Patton's *A Spoonful Blues*, recorded at his original June 1929 session for Paramount, an account of cocaine addiction[224] with plenty of sexual overtones.[225] Papa Charlie Jackson actually recorded the number first as *All I Want Is a Spoonful* in 1925, with more coherent lyrics than Patton, who (suggests Paul Oliver in *Screening the Blues*) scrambled some lines in a manner indicating that

he had imperfectly learned the piece. The song had evidently circulated for some years earlier on the medicine show and black vaudeville circuits; Mack McCormick called it "one of the oldest and most venerated pieces of bawdy lore," and noted that it was cited by Gilmore Millen in his 1930 novel *Sweet Man* in describing early barrelhouse music.[226] Rewritten by Willie Dixon (who penned nearly everything Wolf recorded from 1960–1964), it becomes a vivid portrait of sexual desire and jealousy, given such urgency in Wolf's ferocious vocal that there could be no doubt he felt every word and emotion right down to his toes. Like Patton, write biographers James Segrest and Mark Hoffman, "Wolf dropped the word 'spoonful' from the end of many lines, letting Dixon's thumping bass substitute for the word."[227]

As on nearly all of Wolf's records from 1954 through the early 1960s, guitarist Hubert Sumlin helps drive the sound, as Cub Koda writes. "In what can only be described as an angular attack, Sumlin played almost no chords behind Wolf, sometimes soloing right through his vocals, featuring wild skitterings up and down the fingerboard and biting single notes."[228] Freddy Robinson provides a second guitar, with Otis Spann on piano and Fred Below on drums. "It could be a spoonful of diamonds; it could be a spoonful of gold / Just a little spoon of your precious love satisfy my soul." Willie Dixon: "The idea of *Spoonful* is that it doesn't take a large quantity of anything to be good. If you have a little money when you need it, you're right there in the right spot, that'll buy you a whole lot."[229]

Stolen Moments (1961)—Oliver Nelson & His Orchestra

Recorded Feb. 23, 1961

From the Impulse! album *Blues and the Abstract Truth* (*Jazz-#113*)

Largely unknown to the general public, Oliver Nelson (born on June 4, 1932, in St. Louis) had spent several years as a sideman (on alto and tenor saxophone and clarinet) in the bands of Louis Jordan, Erskine Hawkins, and Quincy Jones, and briefer stints with Duke Ellington and Count Basie, before stepping out as a leader in 1959. It was as composer, arranger, and recruiter of great young jazz talent that Nelson truly found his niche. *Blues and the Abstract Truth* became his greatest legacy, and *Stolen Moments* his most enduring creation.

---

223. Horton, who dabbled in spiritualism, had often predicted to his friend Johnny Cash and others that he was going to die soon, and that it would be a sudden death while on the road; the fatal accident occurred two weeks after his last such discussion with the singer (*Cash: The Autobiography*, p. 141; also see Colin Escott story on Billie Jean Horton, *Journal of Country Music*, Vol. 14 #3 1992).

224. The Memphis *Commercial-Appeal*, as cited by Calt and Wardlow, estimated around 1900 that close to 80 percent of the city's blacks used cocaine, which then sold for a nickel or a dime at pharmacies.

225. Stephen Calt and Gayle Wardlow discuss Patton's version in *King of the Delta Blues Singers*, p. 95–96. When it was recorded by Papa Charlie Jackson, it was regarded as a ragtime-tinged chestnut even then (Robert Wilkins recalled hearing it as a youth around 1904). Patton reworked it with a new melody and different rhythm, and Wolf followed his example.

226. Interestingly, Patton's record was announced in the same January 1930 Paramount monthly supplement as early versions of two other enduring classics, *Black Jack Davy* by Professor and Mrs. Greer, and *Tim Brook* (aka *Timbrooks and Molly*) by the Carver Boys.

227. *Moanin' At Midnight*, p. 173.

228. *All Music Guide to the Blues*, p. 123.

229. *I Am the Blues*, p. 148.

The song was first recorded in September 1960 by an ensemble led by tenor saxophonist Eddie "Lockjaw" Davis and including Nelson and Eric Dolphy, along with such other luminaries as Clark Terry (trumpet) and Jimmy Cleveland (trombone), on the Davis album *Trane Whistle*. Five months later, the composer gave the piece its finest showcase. The lineup on this album ranks with those of Miles Davis and John Coltrane as an all-star aggregation. Alto saxophonist Eric Dolphy was just beginning to establish his reputation when Nelson first used him in May 1960, and he performs double duty here, with some lovely soloing on flute for *Moments*. Hard-bop trumpeter Freddie Hubbard was not yet twenty-three when this album (his first with Nelson) provided a showcase for one of the next decade's most important jazzmen. Pianist Bill Evans was already universally known for his work with Davis and early solo gems, and bassist Paul Chambers was a fellow alumnus of Miles' *Kind of Blue*. Rounding out the ensemble were drummer Roy Haynes (another Miles veteran), George Barrow on baritone sax, and Nelson himself on tenor sax.

Stolen Moments opens with the gorgeous, elegant main theme played by the full ensemble, before moving into variations and solos. "The warm, clean quality he elicits from the horns is a triumph of craftsmanship and artistry," remarked Len Lyons.[230] Freddie Hubbard's mournful trumpet solo is a shiver-inducing moment. Eric Thacker cites the "preternatural lyricism" of Dolphy's flute here, and praises Nelson's own inventive solo. [231] Ted Gioia calls this "a consummate performance" which "belongs on any short list of the most important jazz tracks of the era."[232] The entire piece has a wonderfully inviting melodic quality, and with the subsequent addition of lyrics has been widely recorded by vocalists. After a handful of additional, well-regarded albums (particularly the ambitious *Afro/American Sketches*), Nelson became one of Hollywood's busiest studio arrangers and TV composers, and died in 1975 at forty-three.

Bring It On Home to Me (1962)—Sam Cooke
RCA 8036
Recorded April 26, 1962; chart debut June 23, 1962 (#2 for 4 weeks R&B, #13 pop) (*RHF, R&B-#134, DM-#366, AHR, TC*)

Bring It On Home to Me, one of Sam Cooke's finest achievements, is a song he tried to give away. Biographer Daniel Wolff writes that the singer, feeling the number was outside his normal pop range, offered it to his friend Dee Clark of *Raindrops* fame backstage at an Atlanta show, but Clark said it wasn't right for him. So approaching midnight in RCA's Los Angeles studio, after recording *Having a Party*, Cooke and the band members freely imbibed from a couple of jugs he had brought in, and, with everyone rather high and relaxed, they plunged into *Bring It On Home*.[233]

Peter Guralnick writes in *Dream Boogie* that the singer wrote the number under the influence of blues balladeer Charles Brown's *I Want to Go Home*, one of Sam's favorites; Brown's song in turn had been based on the old spiritual *Thank God It's Real*. The inspiration came to him while he was being driven to the Atlanta engagement in early April 1962 and he scribbled down the lyrics in the limo. He envisioned it as a piece whose call and response structure and lyrics suggested its spiritual origins, but with a refrain that made it secular.

The record opens with Ernie Freeman playing bluesy piano, and Cooke launches into a passionate vocal with lyrics pleading for forgiveness. It's a duet with Lou Rawls, the deep-voiced Chicago baritone who had made his reputation in gospel with the Pilgrim Travelers (1957–1959) and was trying to launch what would become an enduring pop and soul career. The two men had been friends for several years, and both were passengers in a November 1958 car accident that took the driver's life. Here, they are deeply locked into the same groove that harked back to their shared gospel roots; as they trade off cries of "yeah," it's impossible not to feel the intensity. The chorus on the first take also included J. W. Alexander, Fred Smith, and possibly the Sims twins (Bobbie and Kenneth); for the second and final take that we know today, Sam decided to use Rawls alone as the echoing voice. "Not since his Soul Stirrers days had Sam arranged a call-and-response structure this powerful, and he hadn't sounded this committed since sharing leads with Paul Foster," remarks Wolff. Guralnick: "What comes through is a rare moment of undisguised emotion, an unambiguous embrace not just of a cultural heritage but of an adult experience far removed from white teenage fantasy."[234]

We Shall Overcome (1963)—Pete Seeger
Recorded live at Carnegie Hall June 8, 1963

From the Columbia concert album *We Shall Overcome* (chart debut Dec. 14, 1963, reached #42, 36 weeks) (*Folk-#8, NPR-100, GHF, RR*)

It was in 1947 that Pete Seeger first encountered the song then known as *We Will Overcome*, as sung by striking workers at the American Tobacco Company in Charleston, South Carolina (starting in 1945), and taught to him by Zilphia Horton of the Highlander Folk

230. Lyons, *The 101 Best Jazz Albums*, p. 304.
231. *The Esssential Jazz Records, Vol. 2*, p. 549.
232. *The Jazz Standards*, p. 402–3.

233. Wolff, *You Send Me*, p. 248–49.
234. Guralnick, *Dream Boogie*, p. 393–95, 404–5.

School. Seeger loved it, and published it in the newsletter he helped run, *People's Songs*. After making several changes (such as shifting the time signature from 3/4 to 4/4, changing "will" to "shall," and dropping the old verses, making it a verseless song that was all chorus with a number of new lines to provide variety), in 1952 he taught it to Guy Carawan and Frank Hamilton.[235] Carawan made further slight modifications over the next several years, and in 1960 (by this time with a rewritten melody) introduced it to the founding convention of the Student Nonviolent Coordinating Committee (SNCC) at Raleigh, North Carolina. Seeger would recall: "A few months later across the entire South, it was not 'a' song [of the civil rights movement]. It was 'the' song."[236][237]

Whether the song had flowered from the seed of Rev. Charles Tindley's 1903 composition *I'll Overcome Some Day* (as generally believed) or whether Tindley wrote his European-style verses after hearing an older folk spiritual (as Seeger speculates may have happened),[238] by the time he stood on the stage of Carnegie Hall in June 1963, the tune had taken on a new life of its own.[239] Seeger was effectively blacklisted from network television appearances, but Carnegie Hall had long served as a favored venue even when his convictions had placed him in legal peril, such as The Weavers' celebrated concerts there in 1955 and 1960 that produced live albums. His 1963 performance (with the full-throated audience sing-along making it a collective experience, as always with Seeger), at a time when the civil rights movement was at its most intense and with President Kennedy preparing a major speech on the subject,[240] helped to bring the anthem to a much larger audience outside the movement.

---

235. It was Carawan's recollection that he learned the song from Hamilton.

236. Seeger, *Where Have All the Flowers Gone?: A Singer's Stories, Songs, Seeds, Robberies*, p. 32–35. Seeger credits Lucille Simmons as the activist who sang it on the picket line in very slow "long meter" style, and helped teach it to Zilphia Horton. Simmons also made the crucial change in the song's refrain from "I" to "we."

237. The song was published in 1960 under the names of Seeger, Carawan, Hamilton, and the late Horton, with all royalties and income going to a nonprofit, the We Shall Overcome Fund, which annually gives grants to advance African-American music in the South.

238. The older African-American spiritual may have been *I'll Be All Right*, a favorite of Mahalia Jackson, who often combined elements of the two songs in live performance.

239. Seeger's studio albums had been selling poorly, and Columbia Records—recognizing that (as biographer David King Dunaway notes) "he was the classic 'live' performer, whose electricity came from the crowd"—persuaded him to do a Carnegie Hall live album that might do well enough for the label to keep him. The LP proved a tremendous success, and he remained on Columbia for another ten years. (*How Can I Keep from Singing?*, 281–84.)

240. The President three weeks earlier had sent federal troops to help establish order in Alabama following white violence in response to a civil rights demonstration. On June 11, three days after the concert, two black students were enrolled at the University of Alabama under federal protection. Civil rights leader Medgar Evers was assassinated in Mississippi on June 15.

As explored in a 1988 PBS documentary by Jim and Ginger Brown on the song's evolution, it has resonated over the years among apartheid opponents in South Africa, peace activists in England, children in the Soviet Union, and farm workers in the American Midwest. Richard Harrington: "Quintessentially American, the song is not bound by any language, style or rhythm, except that of struggle, both for (civil rights, human dignity, peace) and against (racism, sexism, poverty). Anywhere in the world there is struggle, there is this song."[241]

Louie, Louie (1963)—The Kingsmen (written by Richard Berry)
Wand 143 (originally released on Jerden 712)
Chart debut Nov. 9, 1963 (6 weeks at #2);[242] #26 in U.K.[243]
　(*DM-#11, RHF, GHF, PW, RS-#54, NPR-300, Juke-#16, ACC-#18, DMDB-#30, TC, 1001, DET*)

"Really stupid, really great," writes Dave Marsh of *Louie, Louie*. "Not really dirty, but so what? *Louie Louie* is the most profound and sublime expression of rock and roll's ability to create something from nothing."[244]

Written by R&B singer Richard Berry (guest lead singer on the Robins' 1954 classic *Riot in Cell Block #9*, and the guy who sang the part of "Henry" on Etta James' response to *Work With Me, Annie*), the song's original version was issued by Berry and the Pharaohs on Flip Records #321 the week of April 13, 1957, as the reverse side of *You Are My Sunshine*; it was a calypso ditty sung by a sailor at sea yearning for his girl back in Jamaica. Berry borrowed the core rhythmic figure, a classic Cuban-style clave beat, from a Cuban song recorded for the GNP label in late 1955 or early 1956 by Los Angeles–based bandleader Rene Touzet, *El Loco Cha Cha Cha*.[245] The central riff we know from *Louie* is right there at the Touzet record's opening, and after the band takes the song in a different direction (using an unrelated, mellow melody) with lots of "cha cha cha's," it returns to that killer riff as the horns blast above it.[246] Ned Sublette says there's no doubt that this record was the source for the *Louie, Louie* lick: "It's the *tumbao*, or what Americans call the groove . . . You can jam on it as

---

241. August 27, 1988, *Washington Post*.

242. A 1966 reissue (using the same record number) reached only #97 nationally, but hit #4 in Detroit as reported in *Billboard*.

243. #1 in Canada, #2 in New Zealand.

244. *The Heart of Rock & Soul*, p. 12–15.

245. This was its Americanized title; Sublette reports that the Cuban pianist recorded it as *Amarren el Loco (Restrain the Madman)*. The tune's composer, Rosendo Ruiz, Jr., had written a 1954 smash hit for Ninon Mondejar's Orquesta America, *Rico Vacilon*, which helped launch the cha-cha-cha as a Cuban phenomenon.

246. The connection between the rock classic using a note-for-note riff taken from a quite obscure earlier record (Touzet's) is an eerily exact parallel to the way in which Glenn Miller's 1939 standard *In the Mood* was firmly rooted in the 1930 record *Tar Paper Stomp* by Barbecue Joe & His Hot Dogs.

long as you can keep the dancers excited, using a variety of musical devices that Latin musicians deploy as a matter of course."[247]

As for the lyrics and basic melody, Berry drew quite heavily for both from *Havana Moon* by the unrelated Chuck Berry,[248] with the same homesick-sailor story line and Caribbean accent (Richard relocated the center of the protagonist's longing from Havana to Jamaica). The Pharoahs record became a hit in the Pacific Northwest, where several bands included it in their live acts. Richard Berry's song is more rhythmically emphatic than Chuck's easy-loping calypso, and has the (literal) "duh-duh-duh, duh-duh" verbalization of the riff. The Seattle band The Wailers, with lead vocal by Rockin' Robin Roberts, did a rock & roll version in 1961; it starts out close to the Richard Berry original, but adds the "yeah yeah's" and the "let's give it to 'em right now!" cry. This was the record on which two other regional bands, the Kingsmen and Paul Revere & the Raiders, based their competing 1963 recordings.

Portland, Oregon, was the launching pad for the band that launched of the most ubiquitous songs in rock history. Producer Ken Chase, music director at local station KISN, recruited the Kingsmen to cut the song and urged them, in the small, acoustically awful Northwest Recorders studio, to perform it as they would on stage. Guitarist Jack Ely was the group's original lead singer and did the legendarily manic vocal on *Louie, Louie*. "I was yelling at a mike far away," Ely later told *Rolling Stone*. After it was initially issued in June 1963 on Jerden, nothing happened for over five months, then a Boston disc jockey began playing it. The somewhat larger Wand label licensed and marketed it nationally, and in November the single took off. The Raiders' version on Columbia was by far the more polished, but something about the muddy, nearly unintelligible Kingsmen rendition struck a chord. Certainly the FBI thought so when it launched a futile investigation into its purportedly naughty lyrics. After the record hit, drummer Lynn Easton took over leadership of the band and replaced Ely as lead singer.

Paul Williams, in *Rock & Roll: The 100 Best Singles*, justifies his inclusion of *Louie, Louie* partly on attitude, with "the persistence of the rhythm and the crude clarity of the sound and the sloppy, undeniable fluidity of the guitar solo and the way the singer says 'Okay, let's give it to 'em, right now!'"[249] Marsh: "Built up from a Morse

Code beat and a 'duh duh duh' refrain, with scratchy lead vocal, tacky electric piano, relentless rhythm guitar, and drums that sound like the guy who's playing 'em isn't sure what comes next, *Louie Louie* scales the heights of trash rock to challenge the credentials of all latter-day rockers: If you don't love it, you've missed the point of the whole thing." Marsh suggests, tongue only partly in cheek, that because singer Jack Ely got the song's beat wrong and thus the record was performed at an odd tempo, "in the process they helped invent reggae."

Christmas (Baby Please Come Home) (1963)—Darlene Love (written by Ellie Greenwich, Jeff Barry & Phil Spector)
Philles 119
Released in Nov. 1963 (didn't chart); from the album *A Christmas Gift for You* (DM-#22)

For two years, the gospel-fired voice of Darlene Love had become known to nearly all pop music fans as the anonymous lead singer on Phil Spector–produced hits even while her name remained unknown. Finally, she had her golden moment on one of the most thrilling performances and productions of the era—only to have Spector's legendary Christmas album buried in the avalanche of despair following the assassination of President Kennedy. But for nearly fifty years afterward she's been able to annually bask in the glow of reverence for this blockbuster recording.

Born Darlene Wright on July 26, 1938, in Los Angeles, Darlene (who changed her last name at Spector's suggestion, inspired by gospel singer Dorothy Love Coates) became lead singer of the Blossoms, which provided backing vocals on many 1960s records by Elvis Presley, Duane Eddy, the Mamas and the Papas, the Beach Boys, Dionne Warwick, and others. In late 1962, when Spector's girl group the Ronettes weren't following direction to his satisfaction, he had Darlene and the Blossoms secretly record two records under the Crystals name—which happened to be the #1 smash *He's a Rebel* and the Top 20–charting *He's Sure the Boy I Love*. Also in late 1962, Darlene and fellow Blossom Fanita James sang on the Top Ten remake of *Zip-a-Dee-Doo-Dah* by Bob B. Soxx & the Blue Jeans.

Spector had been promising an increasingly impatient Darlene that she'd get the chance to record singles under her own name, and at last the opportunity came in early 1963 with the Top 40 hits (*Today I Met*) *The Boy I'm Gonna Marry* and *Wait 'Til My Bobby Gets Home*. And then came the album Spector had planned as his masterwork—"his most grandiose gesture yet, an

247. "The Kingsmen and the Cha-Cha-Cha," Sublette chapter in *Listen Again: A Momentary History of Pop Music*. Ruiz told a Cuban journalist that the rhythmic lick itself was not part of his composition, so it may have been added by Touzet or an uncredited arranger.

248. *Havana Moon*, which didn't chart nationally, was released the week of Dec. 1, 1956.

249. Williams, p. 61–62. Roy Carr and Charles Shaar Murray, in the February 9, 1974, *New Musical Express*, noted that the song's riff—which

would be borrowed by a myriad of other rockers including the Kinks, the Troggs, the Who, and the Doors—"served as the basis for all of punk-rock."

album of rock 'n roll Christmas tunes that would pull out every sonic stop in his arsenal," writes biographer Dave Thompson.[250] Spector and Darlene were in charge of picking the songs, and she was allowed to select three for herself. Unexpectedly, a fourth song came her way, a number Spector had commissioned Ellie Greenwich and Jeff Barry to write for the Ronettes, but which they had been unable to handle. It was *Christmas (Baby Please Come Home)*.

Dave Marsh, ranking it #22 in *The Heart of Rock & Soul*, declares that Darlene Love "ranks just beneath Aretha Franklin among female rock singers, and *Christmas* is her greatest record . . . Spector's Wall of Sound, with its continuously thundering horns and strings, never seemed more massive than it does here. But all that only punctuates Love's hysterical blend of loneliness and lust. In the end, when the mix brings up the piano and the chorus to challenge her, the best the Wall's entire weight can achieve is a draw."[251]

The band includes four horns, five guitars (including Nino Tempo and jazzman Barney Kessel), three pianos, two bassists, drummer Hal Blaine, three other percussionists (including the album's arranger Jack Nitzsche), and the Johnny Vidor Strings. Spector was so thrilled with pianist Leon Russell's performance on the song, writes Thompson, that he leaped out of the control room and handed him a bonus check for $100 on the spot.

A Christmas Gift for You was scheduled for release in America on November 22, 1963, with Darlene's single release imminent. Then the news arrived from Dallas, and suddenly no one wanted to hear joyous Christmas music. The single was issued, but the album that had cost a then-whopping $55,000 to produce was released only in England, with U.S. copies left in warehouses awaiting destruction. The album would not see an official U.S. release until nine years later on the Beatles' Apple label.

However, it has lived on through radio airplay every subsequent December. And every holiday season since the late 1980s, fans of David Letterman's late-night show eagerly anticipate the program's tradition of bringing in Darlene Love, fronting a full gospel choir and a super-sized version of Paul Shaffer's band, to belt out what Dave always calls "the only Christmas song that matters," one more time. Darlene has enjoyed a nice post-Spector career, including portraying Danny Glover's wife in all the *Lethal Weapon* movies and starring in the off-Broadway show *Leader of the Pack*; this song (recalled anew in her 2011 induction to the Rock and Roll Hall of Fame) is her finest legacy.

I Saw Her Standing There (1964)—The Beatles
Capitol 5112

Recorded Feb. 11, 1963; chart debut Feb. 8, 1964 (peak position #14); #1 (7 weeks) in Australia, #1 in Canada;[252] from the album *Meet the Beatles!* (#1 for 11 weeks) (*DM-#64, RS-#140, AHR*)

One of Paul McCartney's most frenzied early rockers in the style of Little Richard (whose *Long Tall Sally* was the first song Paul ever sang on stage), he wrote the song (with a bit of help from Lennon on the lyrics) in Paul's living room while playing hooky from school, right after the Beatles had landed a record contract. The group performed it at early Liverpool gigs, and it was featured at the Star Club in Hamburg, Germany, in late 1962.[253] The song was first issued as the leadoff track on the British album *Please Please Me* (released on March 22, 1963, and topping the U.K. album chart). It was one of the six songs the Beatles sang during their second appearance on *The Ed Sullivan Show* on February 16, 1964. As the B side of *I Want to Hold Your Hand*, the number was a central part of early Beatlemania.

The furious energy of the performance as an expression of young male lust made it irresistible. And of course there was that outrageous opening: "One, two, three, FUH!" (At least it sounded outrageous; in fact, McCartney said it was just an out-of-breath "four.") Tim Riley: "The pauses that break up the playfully suggestive lines intensify the things that are left unsaid—the gaps in 'Well she was just—seventeen / You know—what I mean' punctuate the implications . . . the combined effect transforms the implied innocence into sexual bravado."[254] Dave Marsh, celebrating its "brilliant primitivism," ranked it #64 in *The Heart of Rock & Soul*. In early performances, the group would stretch the song for up to ten minutes, with multiple guitar solos; it provided George Harrison with his first solo on a Beatles record on his reverbed Duo Jet. Ian MacDonald calls it "an electrifying performance and proof that the 'charismatic powerhouse' which shook the Liverpool clubs during 1961–1962 was no myth." The record "sent a shock of earthy rawness through a British pop scene whose harmonic ethos had been shaped largely by the sophistication of Broadway." And lyrically, its use of blunt vernacular "socked rabid young radio listeners deliciously in the solar plexus. With the authentic voice of youth back on the airwaves, the rock-and-roll revolution, quiescent since 1960, had resumed."[255]

250. Thompson, *Wall of Pain*, p. 79–81.
251. Marsh, p. 21–22.

252. #1 (5 weeks) in Peru; #1 in Hong Kong, New Zealand and the Philippines; #3 Denmark.
253. Ray Coleman's Lennon biography estimated that the song was written in September 1962.
254. Riley, *Tell Me Why*, p. 50. Jonathan Gould in *Can't Buy Me Love* (p. 149) calls this "an innuendo worthy of Chuck Berry, whose spirit leers over the song."
255. MacDonald, *Revolution in the Head*, p. 68.

It's Over (1964)—Roy Orbison (written by Roy Orbison & Bill Dees)

Monument 837

Chart debut April 11, 1964 (#9 peak); #1 for 2 weeks in U.K.[256] (*DM*)

Roy Orbison at his most anguished, with that magnificent tenor voice in full flight. "Who else could have pulled off such a florid rock-bolero?" notes Dave Marsh. "With percussive guitars and riffing drums (and castanets) suggesting previously unsuspected flamenco nuances in Orbison's all-encompassing style, with the melody awash in strings and goosed by a ghostly chorus . . . *It's Over* is a record only one of the two greatest white voices in rock and soul history could have [managed]."[257]

His Top Ten predecessor to the biggest chart-topper of his career, *Oh Pretty Woman, It's Over* would be his next-to-last American Top Ten hit until his 1989 return. Ken Emerson: "It was not only the dramatic structure of his recordings and his thrilling vocal range that inspired comparisons to Caruso—it was also Orbison's passionate intensity . . . When Orbison's voice swelled at the close of *It's Over*, his love, his life, and, indeed, the whole world seemed to be coming to an end—not with a whisper but an agonized, beautiful bang."[258]

Walk On By (1964)—Dionne Warwick (music by Burt Bacharach, lyrics by Hal David)

Scepter 1274

Chart debut April 25, 1964 (peak position #6);[259] reached #6 in England[260] (*RS-#70, GHF, R&B-#87, Trad-#90, ACC-#103, RIA, DM, 1001, BBC, DMDB*)

For smooth, melodic, intelligently crafted, soulfully performed pop songs in the 1960s, the combination of Dionne Warwick and Bacharach & David was hard to top. They teamed for more than two dozen Top 40 hits from 1962–1970, and provided the model for a genre of pop music that is both of its time and also timeless. *Walk On By* represents the pairing at its very peak.

Marie Dionne Warrick (the original spelling of her last name) was born on December 12, 1940, in East Orange, New Jersey, sang with the Drinkard Singers gospel group, then formed the Gospelaires trio with sister Dee Dee Warwick and their aunt Cissy Houston. After working as a backup studio singer in the late 1950s, she got

together with Bacharach and David in 1962 (her backup singing on a Drifters record had impressed them), and after their debut record together *Don't Make Me Over* was a hit, she became the primary voice for their songs, the writers also serving as her producers on a long string of hits. After they went their separate ways, Dionne scored her first #1 single teaming with the Spinners in 1974 on *Then Came You*, then struggled for a few years before enjoying a new run of hits starting in 1979. The biggest record of her career came in 1985 as she led the all-star aggregation Dionne & Friends on the Burt Bacharach–Carole Bayer Sager song *That's What Friends Are For*.

Supreme songsmith Burt Bacharach was born in Kansas City on May 12, 1928, and came to New York with his family as a youngster. After studying composition at several institutions followed by Army service, he began writing songs for various artists, teamed with lyricist Hal David, and scored his first hit in 1957 with Marty Robbins' *The Story of My Life*. The following year he went on an extended tour as accompanist and arranger for Marlene Dietrich, returned in 1961, and re-teamed with David. While the majority of the duo's 1960s hits were performed by Warwick, they also scored with Jackie DeShannon's *What the World Needs Now Is Love* (1965), Herb Alpert's *This Guy's in Love with You* (1968), and their Oscar-winning 1969 score for *Butch Cassidy and the Sundance Kid*, among others. In later years Bacharach re-emerged as one of the coolest cats around, not only in his cameo in the second Austin Powers movie but on a collaboration with Elvis Costello that produced the remarkable *God Give Me Strength* (1996), and other special projects.

Walk On By has all the qualities we associate with the Dionne/Bacharach-David records: the sophisticated song construction, the piano-driven rhythm with a hint of Latin flavoring (in this case a bossa nova beat), tasteful strings and distinctive staccato flugelhorn interjections (a Bacharach trademark, producing a softer sound than a trumpet). An underappreciated contributor to the record's sound is drummer Gary Chester, whose playing with a stick in his right hand and a brush in his left had just the subtlety the composer wanted. Above all, it also has the gospel-trained urgency found in Warwick's best early records, conveying the sharp pain of lost love, underlined by the background vocals crying, "Don't . . . stop!" Thomas Ryan: "For the first time, Bacharach and David realized their ambition to create a soundscape. *Walk On By* is not just a song, but a fully developed concept. Warwick's cool, understated performance perfectly captures the hidden pain in David's lyric."[261] Florence Greenberg, head of Scepter Records, relegated *Walk On By* to the B side of the now-forgotten *Any Old Time of Day*, but

---

256. During this period of British chart dominance, *It's Over*—helped by Orbison's regular touring there—was the first record by a U.S. artist to top the U.K. charts in forty-four weeks, since Elvis Presley's *Devil in Disguise* in 1963. It was also #1 (3 weeks) in Ireland, #1 in New Zealand, #4 Belgium.

257. Marsh, p. 631.

258. *Rolling Stone Illustrated History of Rock & Roll*, p. 129.

259. #1 (3 weeks) on *Cash Box* R&B chart. *Walk On By* was recorded in the same three-hour studio session as her late-1963 classic *Anyone Who Had a Heart*.

260. #4 in New Zealand, #12 Canada.

261. Ryan, *American Hit Radio*, p. 130.

DJ Murray the K helped lead the way in flipping the 45 over.[262] Michaelangelo Matos calls this the "most quietly devastating record ever made; when the piano enters, quiet but hard, the bottom drops out as surely as the blast of distortion opens up *Smells Like Teen Spirit*."[263] Serene Dominic: "Warwick is able to walk the streets and refrain from bawling, until she sees the man who has forgotten her. Even her foolish pride, personified by the carefree flugelhorn, isn't enough to stop her crying. The circular piano figure and the tick-tock woodblock in the chorus simulate the eternity it will take for her old lover to turn the corner and be completely out of the picture."[264]

Rag Doll (1964)—Four Seasons (written by Bob Gaudio & Bob Crewe)

Phillips 40211

Chart debut June 20, 1964 (#1 for 2 weeks); #1 (4 weeks) in Canada, #2 in England[265] (*DM-#401*)

Four Seasons member and chief songwriter Bob Gaudio was inspired to create the group's most memorable hit one day while driving down the West Side Highway leaving New York City through the Holland Tunnel near 10th Avenue when, during a marathon three-minute stoplight, a young woman in tattered clothes came up to clean his windows, hoping for a tip. Finding nothing in his pockets smaller than a five-dollar bill (in some interviews it's a ten-dollar bill), he handed it to her, and, he recalled, "I could see her in the rear-view mirror, just standing in disbelief in the middle of the street with the five dollars. And that whole image stayed with me, a rag doll was what she looked like."

Lead singer Frankie Valli (born Francis Castelluccio in Newark, New Jersey, on May 3, 1937) recorded his first solo single as Frankie Valley in 1953, and two years later formed the Varitones, which became the Four Lovers and in 1956 hit the pop charts with *You're the Apple of My Eye*. Followup singles flopped, but in 1958 he met Bob Gaudio who was then a member of the Royal Teens, and out of the ashes of the Four Lovers, the Four Seasons were born in 1961. (The other two Seasons: Nick Massi and Tommy DeVito.) Their first single under the new name went nowhere, but *Sherry* in 1962 became the first of three straight Number One hits that showcased Valli's soaring falsetto on songs written by Gaudio and produced by Bob Crewe.[266] They were known for catchy

uptempo numbers; the heart-tugging *Rag Doll* became their first ballad smash. Its flip side, the gorgeous *Silence Is Golden*, would later become a Top Ten hit as remade almost note for note by the Tremeloes.

After Gaudio had written most of *Rag Doll*, he had trouble finishing the story of a guy in love with a girl from a poor family, so called Crewe for help, and they spent two weeks putting the finishing touches on it. The group was scheduled to leave town on tour, and eager to get the song out as a single—and unable to work in their regular studio on a Sunday—they recorded it in the basement of a demo studio on Broadway.[267] "The record they came up with is prototypical Four Seasons, with its crashing drum intro [provided by Buddy Saltzman] to the piercing glockenspiel and tambourine accoutrements, from Frankie Valli's wild falsetto to the bel canto doo-wop harmonies," writes Dave Marsh. "As a fantasy about love in America, it's certainly the best ever conceived at a stoplight." [268]

Baby, I Need Your Loving (1964)—The Four Tops (written by Eddie Holland, Lamont Dozier, & Brian Holland)

Motown 1062

Chart debut Aug. 15, 1964 (#11 pop, #4 on *Cash Box* R&B chart); #20 in Canada (*RHF, BMI-#8, R&B-#122, DM-#163, RS, AHR, DMDB*)

They'd been singing together for ten years, and making intermittent recordings for eight years. But in 1964, Levi Stubbs, Abdul "Duke" Fakir, Lawrence Payton, and Renaldo "Obie" Benson had yet to break through with a hit record. That came to an end with their debut single for Motown, *Baby, I Need Your Loving*.

All Detroit natives, the Tops formed in 1954, and two years later recorded one single each on the Grady label (now rare and worth up to $600 to collectors) and a less-scarce 45 for Chess; in 1960 came another unsuccessful single for Columbia, and in 1962 one more for Riverside. Four one-shots for different labels, four flops. But all the while, they were building a strong following in Detroit-area nightclubs, played Las Vegas, and toured with Billy Eckstine. Motown founder Berry Gordy recalls in his autobiography: "Their vocal blend was phenomenal . . . Smooth, classy and polished, they were big stuff. I wanted them bad."[269]

Motown's crack songwriting-production team of Holland-Dozier-Holland were just as taken with the group, and especially by the powerhouse voice of Levi Stubbs;

262. Warwick, *My Life, as I See It*, p. 45.

263. *Da Capo Best Music Writing 2004*, p. 178. Bacharach said this was the first time he used two grand pianos on a recording.

264. *Burt Bacharach: Song by Song*, p. 123.

265. Also #1 in New Zealand.

266. Two of the inspirations for Valli's falsetto were Peruvian singer Yma Sumac, who shot to U.S. stardom in the early 1950s with her five-octave voice, and jazz vocalist Little Jimmy Scott, renowned for his exceptional high natural voice. (Cote, *Jersey Boys*, p. 12.)

267. *Billboard Book of Number 1 Hits*, p. 152. The Four Seasons would take a different route to Broadway with the Tony-winning smash *Jersey Boys* paying tribute to their musical legacy.

268. Marsh, *The Heart of Rock & Soul*, p. 273–74.

269. *To Be Loved*, p. 149.

possessing a fierce beauty on ballads, that rough-edged voice and the fervor behind it could drive a rhythm piece with equal effectiveness. After a jazz-flavored Tops album fell flat, Gordy kept them busy contributing to other artists' records while waiting for just the right vehicle. After H-D-H wrote the irresistible midtempo soul ballad *Baby, I Need Your Loving*, they set it aside (according to Eddie Holland) for six months before realizing it was perfect for the Tops. Thomas Ryan relates that when Lamont Dozier told them about the song one night at a nightclub, they were so eager to get started that they headed right into the studio for a session that lasted from midnight into the wee hours.[270]

"With a vocal line that custom-fit Stubbs' gospel-tinged voice, and smooth harmony lines that simultaneously toned down and contrasted with the gruff edges of Stubbs; raspy vocal, *Baby, I Need Your Loving* suited the band from all angles," writes Ryan. Dave Marsh calls it "one of the definitive Holland-Dozier-Holland riffs, stated with a full ensemble of brass, drums, clunky gospel piano, and the sharpest finger-pop this side of 77 Sunset Strip."[271] Once this record hit big, the Tops were on a roll that didn't stop until more than a decade later. Broadcast Music, Inc. (BMI) ranks it as the #8 most played song of the past sixty-plus years with over nine million broadcast performances.

Song for My Father (1964)—Horace Silver Quintet
Recorded Oct. 26, 1964
From the Blue Note album *Song for My Father*; chart
    debut June 12, 1965 (#95 in *Billboard*, #82 in *Cash
    Box*) (*Jazz-#53*)

The records of Horace Silver, note Richard Cook and Brian Morton, "present the quintessence of hard bop."[272] His piano style is always strongly rhythmic and funky, rooted in blues and gospel; his sidemen regularly included first-rate soloists who were also able to lock firmly into the groove set by the leader; and his compositions are among the finest in post-1950 jazz. The most enduring of all is *Song for My Father*.

Born on September 2, 1928, in Norwalk, Connecticut (his father was of Portuguese heritage from the Cape Verde Islands off the north Atlantic coast of Africa), Silver made his recording debut in 1951 with Stan Getz, and after a year joined the all-star combo of drummer Art Blakey. Playing on the 1954 Miles Davis album *Walkin'* also elevated his profile. It was the album *Six Pieces of Silver* (recorded in late 1956), with the instant-standard *Senor Blues*, that established Silver as a combo leader and composer. Initially inspired by Bud Powell, Silver (writes Len Lyons) "works with short, finely chiseled

phrases that build upon one another."[273] His left hand is used percussively, and he "can almost make the lower register of the keyboard growl or bark," becoming almost drumlike in effect—not surprisingly, because he has acknowledged that playing with Blakey "definitely made me stronger rhythmically."[274]

Long interested in Latin rhythms, it was a South American trip that proved the starting point for his trademark song. "My dad was always after me to make a jazz arrangement of some of the Cape Verdean folk tunes he used to sing, but I was never really interested in them from a jazz point of view. I then came back from a trip to Brazil with that bossa nova beat in my head, and I started to write a tune around it. After awhile, I realized that while I was using that rhythm, the melodic context of the tune sounded more Cape Verdean, and I came up with *Song for My Father*."[275]

Dedicated to his father John Tavares Silver (whose photo appeared on the album sleeve), *Song for My Father* is a mesmerizingly gorgeous midtempo piece. Its infectiously rhythmic opening vamp on the lower end of the keyboard will be familiar to any fan of 1970s pop, because the jazz-loving Steely Dan quite consciously borrowed it, note for note, for the introduction to their hit *Rikki, Don't Lose That Number*. Tenor saxophonist Joe Henderson (a Blue Note mainstay of this era long before his own solo stardom, including the Lee Morgan hit *The Sidewinder*) first made a name for himself playing with Silver, and his soloing here is superb, particularly in his interplay with Carmell Jones on trumpet.[276] Anyone who complains that modern jazz lost interest in melody or musical "hooks" will find this a wonderful response; it is unfailingly tuneful, warm and inviting, moves along briskly, and the chorus is an irresistible "grabber." Its songlike quality was not lost on vocalists; with the addition of lyrics, it's become a favorite over the years, including a 1980s duet by Betty Carter and Carmen McRae.

Kenny Mathieson: "The tune, which employs a simple repeating camp-like two-note bass figure moving from F to C, and a 24-bar structure divided into three 8-bar sections, is in F minor, and that minor mood works against the usual gaiety associated with the bossa nova to create an unusual and striking effect. The fusion of elements evident in *Song for My Father* reveals a musician at the

270. Ryan, *American Hit Radio*, p. 139–40.
271. Marsh, *The Heart of Rock & Soul*, p. 114–15.
272. *Penguin Guide to Jazz on CD*, p. 1373.

273. Lyons, *The 101 Best Jazz Albums*, p. 193.
274. Mathieson, *Cookin': Hard Bop and Soul Jazz, 1954–65*, p. 36.
275. Mathieson, *Cookin'*, p. 41. Richard J. Ripani in *The New Blue Music* sees *Song for My Father* as one of the best representations of so-called "triplet swing" (songs in which each beat is, theoretically or actually, divided into triplets), and "the widespread incorporation of straight-eighth Latin and funk rhythms" in jazz.
276. In addition to Steely Dan's borrowing, Stevie Wonder appropriated the record's opening horn riff for his hit *Don't You Worry 'Bout a Thing*; no other jazz track had such an impact on 1970s pop.

height of his powers, comfortable with his materials, sure of his direction."[277]

(Other personnel: Teddy Smith on bass; Roger Humphries on drums)

I've Been Loving You Too Long (to Stop Now) (1965)—Otis Redding (written by Otis Redding & Jerry Butler)

Volt 126

Chart debut May 15, 1965 (#2 on R&B chart, #21 pop in *Billboard*, #15 in *Cash Box*) (*RR-#41, DM-#35, R&B-#82, RS-#111, ACC*)

Even though Otis Redding was already gaining recognition by spring 1965 with eight previous R&B chart hits, *I've Been Loving You Too Long* was his first song to crack the pop Top 40, and began the process of establishing him as a crossover superstar. It was the Iceman, Jerry Butler, who lit the fuse that became a soul classic. In January 1965 (as outlined by Redding biographer Scott Freeman) the two singers were both performing in Buffalo, staying at the same hotel, and Otis invited Jerry to hang out in his room. After Redding picked up his battered acoustic guitar and played a portion of a song he was writing, Butler responded by singing his own unfinished song, a slow, mournful melody: "I've been loving you too long to stop now / You are tired, and you want to be free." That was all he had: "I've been messing with this song for almost three years and can't get past that." Redding told him how much he loved it, and began plucking out the melody on his guitar. Two weeks later, Butler was in Detroit for a show, Redding tracked him down by phone and exclaimed, "Hey, man, it's a hit! I told you that song was a hit!" Butler was confused until Redding explained that it was the song they'd fooled around with in Buffalo—and that the record was already on the street. "It was his song—and it was a hit record for Otis?" But when he called Otis to have him play the record over the phone, writes Friedman, "his jealousy vanished. Otis had taken the song to places Jerry had never envisioned. The arrangement was so simple, yet so ingenious. And there was a magical quality in the feel that Otis had captured. The song was carefully crafted so that every single note, every nuance of the music, conveyed drama and emotion. There was an exquisite hesitation in Otis's voice as he sang the opening lines over the muted accompaniment. He might have been singing to a girlfriend. A wife in a troubled marriage. A woman in an illicit affair. Or a true lost love. That was the beauty of the lyrics: they were so universal that they struck an instant chord with almost anyone who heard them."[278]

I've Been Loving You Too Long is "the ultimate slow dance, a nonpareil seduction song . . . a song that will be covered as long as men and women want an excuse to hold each other tight in public," writes Dave Marsh. "Phrasing as though each line is coming to him only the instant before he sings it, quavering notes as if in the grip of an undeniably exquisite passion that must be consummated—now!—Otis tears the song up without showing a second's strain."[279] And his exceptional vocal is matched by the peerless Stax house band with guitarist Steve Cropper, bassist Duck Dunn, and drummer Al Jackson, and the horn section (directed by Wayne Jackson) that accentuated every emotion. His extended performance of the song at the 1967 Monterey Pop Festival helped ensure, said *Rolling Stone*, the single's "transition from hit to legend."

My Generation (1965)—The Who

Decca 31877

Recorded Oct. 13, 1965; British chart debut Nov. 4, 1965 (#2 peak); U.S. debut Jan. 15, 1966 (#74 peak)[280] [281] (*RS-#11, ACC-#11, RHF, GHF, RR, DMDB-#64, DM-#133, TC*)

Pete Townshend has offered various accounts of how he came to write the anthemic *My Generation*. According to one, he wrote it on his twentieth birthday (May 19, 1965) while riding a train from London to Southampton for a TV appearance, as the Who had recently scored their Top Ten British debut hit with *I Can't Explain*. His more colorful variation is that one day he had parked his car outside his flat only to find it gone the next morning; supposedly Britain's Queen Mother had seen it while driving each day from Clarence House to Buckingham Palace and decreed, "Have it removed!" Townshend, quoted in his biography by Geoffrey Giuliano: "I was outraged . . . That was the world I lived in, the world of imperious landlords . . . the Queen Mother who, with a flick of her finger, can have the first car you've ever bought removed from the face of the earth. That's where *My Generation* came from: I'd rather die than be like you people! I never want to be like you old fuckers. That's what I was saying."[282]

Based on a Jimmy Reed melody, the piece started as a talking blues, and evolved into what Who biographer Dave Marsh calls a "chunky, chugging blues."[283] It took months of arranging and re-recording before the song reached its final form, as producer Kit Lambert—sensing a major hit—prodded Townshend to further polish the

---

277. Mathieson, *Cookin'*, p. 48–49.
278. Scott Freeman, *Otis! The Otis Redding Story*, p. 115–18.

279. Marsh, *The Heart of Rock & Soul*, p. 29–30.
280. Reached #13 in Detroit (April 9, 1966 *Billboard*.
281. #5 in Holland, #12 Germany.
282. Giuliano, *Behind Blue Eyes*, p. 61–63.
283. Marsh, *Before I Get Old*, p, 181–83, 186–89.

number, including the addition of some Kinks-like progressive key changes. *Rolling Stone*, in ranking *My Generation* at #11 among its top 500 songs in 2010 (having previously placed it as the #16 greatest in 1988): "Bassist John Entwistle took the solo breaks with crisp, grunting aggression.[284] Roger Daltrey's stuttering vocal and the upward key changes created a vivid, mounting anxiety that climaxed with a studio re-creation of the Who's live gear-trashing finales, with Townshend spewing feedback all over Keith Moon's avalanche drumming."[285]

That Daltrey stutter, of course, became one of the record's defining characteristics. It happened (by one account) because the first time the singer performed the song as Townshend gave him the lyrics, he stuttered when he initially read them in the studio. Lambert heard it and suggested that he leave it in. More importantly, Marsh reports, the stammer was used because the song's character "was supposed to be a Mod blocked on pills—and amphetamine abusers stammered like mad." The BBC briefly banned the record because it feared that the stammering might be a cover for naughty language.

Nowhere to Run (1965)—Martha & the Vandellas
(written by Brian Holland, Lamont Dozier & Eddie Holland)
Gordy 7039
Chart debut Feb. 27, 1965 (#6 in *Record World*, #8 in *Billboard* pop, #5 R&B); #26 in England (*DM-#10, RS*)

The fourth pop Top Ten single by Martha Reeves and the Vandellas is a tale of a tortured love affair with a far darker tone than all but a few other Motown hits of the era. As Martha wails about running from a man who's "no good for me," being haunted by his face "every step I take" and whenever she looks in the mirror, and concludes there's "nowhere to run, nowhere to hide," this appears to be a portrait of an abused woman who can't bring herself to break free. It's disturbing, but compelling. For Reeves, the song evokes "how I felt after seeing 18- and 19-year-old kids coming back from Vietnam with injuries."[286]

Nowhere to Run, declares Dave Marsh in ranking it #10 in *The Heart of Rock & Soul*, "is one of the definitive Motown 45s: huge drums and popping bass propel a riffing horn section, while the frantic lead vocal recites straight pop verses with a gospel bridge." The production team of Holland-Dozier-Holland's "deployment of echo [and equalization] enables the record to begin at the height of excitement and sustain it all the way through." What especially makes the record stand out is its "shriek-

ing paranoia," hammered home by the mighty Motown rhythm section. "Bassist James Jamerson is justly celebrated today as one of the two or three most creative players on that instrument ever, and there's as much to be said for drummer Benny Benjamin . . . On *Nowhere to Run*, Benjamin simply explodes all over his tom-toms. Thanks to them, this relentlessly rhythmic record ranks with the most fearsome of all time."[287] [288]

Susan Douglas, echoing the view that this is "one of the greatest songs ever recorded," underlined its special significance to young female listeners: "In the face of our entrapment, Martha Reeves made us sweat, and celebrated the capacity of girls to love like women. She also articulated a sophisticated knowingness about how sexual desire overtakes common sense every time, even in girls."[289]

I Got You (I Feel Good) (1965)—James Brown & the Famous Flames
King 6015
Chart debut Nov. 13, 1965 (#1 for 6 weeks R&B, #3 *Billboard* pop, reached #1 in *Record World*);[290] #6 in Canada (*R&B-#77, RS-#78, RHF, RIA-#152, DM-#223, AHR, ACC, DMDB*)

Soul Brother Number One's followup to his blockbuster *Papa's Got a Brand New Bag* proved to be his biggest crossover pop hit. Dave Marsh says it "matches its predecessor by opening with a full-throated, cord-rupturing scream and, if it can't sustain quite that level of intensity, that may well be one of the reasons the record became Brown's biggest ever on the pop charts. Certainly, there's nothing conventional about the music, a thunderous melange of powerhouse horn riffs, jet-propelled drum bursts, and skittering guitar. And James sings the song as if God had called him to earth for the primary purpose of personifying sexual ecstasy."[291]

The original version of the song was an obscure, uncharted January 1962 recording called *I Found You* by Yvonne Fair, a singer with Brown's revue,[292] backed by the man himself on piano and JB's band. It's exactly the same as the hit we know, with slight word changes, a slower (rumba-beat) tempo, and far less charisma: "I

---

284. Entwistle soloed on a newly-acquired Danelectro bass, and went through multiple sets of strings as they broke under the stress of five separate demos of the piece.

285. *Rolling Stone 500 Greatest Songs*, p. 22.

286. Annotation for *Hitsville USA: The Motown Singles Collection, 1959–1971*.

287. Marsh, p. 12. Reeves writes in her autobiography (p. 123) that the instrumental track was recorded several months before the vocals, held until the group returned from touring. "Since we needed new product immediately, we had been rushed into the studio" with Brian Holland and Dozier. "I loved the lyrics from the moment I heard them," in part because they mirrored "the pace, urgency, and pressure" of the singers' lives during this period.

288. *Standing in the Shadows of Motown* by Allan "Dr. Licks" Slutsky is the definitive look at Jamerson and the other Motown sidemen. Other likely participants on this session include Earl Van Dyke on keyboards, Robert White, Eddie Willis, and/or Joe Messina on guitars.

289. *Where the Girls Are*, p. 94.

290. On the *Billboard* territorial charts, *I Got You* reached #1 on the pop charts of Baltimore, New Orleans (for several weeks), and Philadelphia.

291. Marsh, *The Heart of Rock & Soul*, p. 155–56.

292. She and Brown were also lovers, and she gave birth to his son.

feel good, I knew that I would," she begins. "So good, so good, that I found you . . . I feel nice, like sugar and spice . . ." She even does a few mini-shrieks during the song, which JB would dramatically amplify three years later.

In his autobiography, Brown recalled that the record was actually put out first by Mercury while that label was in a legal battle with King over the rights to his recordings, but due to an existing injunction had to withdraw it immediately. Finally, the courts resolved the dispute: Brown could do instrumentals on the Smash label, but all vocals had to be on King. Syd Nathan tore up his old contract to give Brown more favorable terms.[293] Jazz critic Stanley Crouch put Brown's musical achievement in genre-crossing terms by linking him with two of the most rhythmically innovative bands in jazz history, declaring that JB is "the Fletcher Henderson and Count Basie of rhythm and blues."[294]

Ain't No Mountain High Enough (1967)—Marvin Gaye & Tammi Terrell (written by Nicholas Ashford & Valerie Simpson)

Tamla 54149

Chart debut May 13, 1967 (#3 on R&B chart, #19 pop)
(*DM-#79, GHF, R&B-#109, RIA-#140, ACC*)

As Motown's foremost solo matinee idol during its early years, Marvin Gaye had been teamed with various female duet partners after he became an established star, most notably Mary Wells (on a double-sided 1964 hit) and Kim Weston (two hits in 1964 and 1967). He found his perfect match in Tammi Terrell. Born Thomasina Montgomery on April 29, 1945, in Philadelphia and married briefly to

James Brown & the Famous Flames, courtesy of Library of Congress, LC-USZ62-121427.

boxer Ernie Terrell, she first recorded for Wand in 1961, worked with the James Brown revue, and began hitting the charts for Motown in early 1966. Harvey Fuqua, Gaye's old boss with the Moonglows, put Marvin and Tammi together. The first and greatest of their collaborations was *Ain't No Mountain High Enough*.

Written by the husband-wife team of Nick Ashford and Valerie Simpson (who had recently joined Motown's staff) and produced by Fuqua with Johnny Bristol, *Mountain* is a joy from start to finish. The song itself could hardly be simpler as an expression of eternal romantic love, but it's the chemistry of Marvin and Tammi that makes it work. Her girlish voice was modest but pleasing, and the way she and Gaye bounce off each other and feed on the other's energy, truly seeming to enjoy one another's company, is a perfect simulation of the mutual devotion in the lyrics. Nelson George remarks that Gaye attacks the devotional lyrics with "a joyous, shouting, whooping vocal. Tammi is more reserved, and yet she has a vivacious warmth that really seems to inspire Marvin. He sounds as if he's ready to make love to Tammi the minute the song fades out (or that he might be doing it as we listen)."[295] Dave Marsh, ranking this #79 in *The Heart of Rock & Soul*, also pays tribute to the Ashford-Simpson role on the record: "In many ways, it's their production, especially the way they use bells, tambourines, and strings to create an ever-present trebly tension, that prods Gaye and Terrell to their heights of edgy urgency."[296] Of course the crack Motown studio band, powered from underneath by James Jamerson on bass, drives everything relentlessly forward. Gaye and Terrell would score seven Top 40 hits together, but the partnership was cut short when Tammi collapsed on stage in his arms in late 1967, and died three years later of a brain tumor. Diana Ross had a huge #1 pop hit with a more lavishly arranged version of *Mountain* in 1970; nevertheless, the song will always belong to Marvin and Tammi.

White Rabbit (1967)—Jefferson Airplane

RCA 9248[297]

Chart debut June 24, 1967 (#8 peak);[298] reached #4 in Canada;[299] from the album *Surrealistic Pillow* (chart

---

293. Brown, *The Godfather of Soul*, p. 159–60.
294. Crouch quoted by Nelson George, *Where Did Our Love Go*, p. 177.

295. *Where Did Our Love Go? The Rise & Fall of the Motown Sound*, p. 136. Harvey Fuqua and Johnny Bristol "provide one of those classic Motown intros, with bells, vibes, muffled strings, and the sound of drumsticks beat rapidly against the snare drum rim to captivate the ear."
296. Marsh, p. 57–58.
297. *White Rabbit* was prominently featured in Oliver Stone's 1987 Vietnam film *Platoon*, reflecting its popularity among soldiers. The song was reissued as a single on RCA 5156; the reissue also tied in with that year's compilation of the Airplane's early recordings, *2400 Fulton Street* (April 18, 1987, *Billboard*).
298. The album track was "forced out" as a single due to its heavy airplay by rock radio stations, noted the July 22 *Billboard*, while *Somebody to Love* was still riding high (peaking at #5 the week before *Rabbit* debuted).
299. Reached #3 in Holland (1970), #1 in France (1971).

debut March 25, 1967, #3 peak) (*RHF, GHF, RS, RIA, 1001, ACC, DMDB*)

Vaguely ominous guitar chords ring out, precise drumrolls out of Ravel's *Bolero* establish a steady and gradually escalating sense of coiled tension and foreboding, and Grace Slick enters with a twisted spin on *Alice In Wonderland*: "One pill makes you larger, and one pill makes you small / And the ones that mother gives you don't do anything at all . . ." The Jefferson Airplane's followup to its first smash hit *Somebody to Love* immediately established itself as equally extraordinary.

Slick had written *White Rabbit* while singing lead with the San Francisco band Great Society, and brought it with her when she came aboard for Jefferson Airplane's second album. Before writing the song, she confessed, "I took acid and listened to Miles Davis' *Sketches of Spain* album for 24 hours straight until it burned into my brain." She wrote in her autobiography that the lyrics allude in part to "the hypocrisy of the older generation swilling one of the hardest drugs [alcohol] known to man, but telling us not to use psychedelics." She "took at least five different kinds of drugs" while writing it. "You take a chemical, you get an adventure." The band's instrumental mix, featuring Jack Casady on lead guitar, Jorma Kaukonen on bass, Paul Kantner on rhythm guitar, and Spencer Dryden on drums,[300] carried the narrative to new dimensions. The British magazine *Q*, including it among its 100 Songs That Changed the World in 2003, noted with amazement that while other rock groups were getting into trouble with songs that gave the slightest hint of drug references, the Airplane soared right into the Top Ten with "a transparent eulogy to LSD, the psychedelic drug that was rapidly turning the world Day-Glo and San Francisco into hippie heaven." The fact that RCA was one of the industry giants, and also that they could point to the song's Lewis Carroll literary allusions as providing artistic license, perhaps accounted for its willingness to give the Airplane free rein.

But aside from the fact that the song openly advocated a drug that "promised instant liberation from normality," most important is that it lets the fable unfold with a concise elegance that reflects great clarity of musical vision. There's not a wasted word here, not a second of less than razor-sharp playing. It's a compelling musical journey.

I Heard It Through the Grapevine (1967)—Gladys Knight & the Pips

Soul 35039

Chart debut Oct. 21, 1967 (#1 for 6 weeks R&B, #2 on pop chart for 3 weeks); #47 in England

---

300. Kat Lister credits the way Dryden "snake-hipped the Spanish rhythm" (*1001 Songs You Must Hear*, p. 201).

Before Marvin Gaye defined the song for all time, Gladys Knight & the Pips established *I Heard It Through the Grapevine* as an R&B classic with a performance that was as brash and hard-driving as Gaye's was anguished. The Miracles, the Isley Brothers, and Marvin had all recorded the Norman Whitfield–Barrett Strong song before mid-1967, but none had yet been released when Gladys and the boys sent it to the top of the charts, selling a reported 2.5 million copies.

Blessed with a gritty, powerful, and gorgeous voice that's one of the shining jewels of pop music,[301] Gladys Knight (born on May 28, 1944, in Atlanta) won the grand prize on *Ted Mack's Original Amateur Hour* at age seven; she formed the group with her brother Merald "Bubba" Knight in 1957 when she was thirteen, and four years later they scored their first big hit, *Every Beat of My Heart*. From 1962 onward, the group was a quartet, with Gladys, Bubba, and cousins William Guest and Edward Patten. After Gladys got married and had a child in 1962, the group recorded only sporadically during the next few years. *Grapevine* became their second and biggest hit after signing with Motown (through its Soul subsidiary). Earl Van Dyke recalled for Nelson George that Gladys and the musicians had a special relationship. "We struck a groove right away."[302]

Barrett Strong would recall that "I came up with a little idea on the piano, the bassline figure," and the song just flowed from there. It was the recollection of Motown studio bandleader Earl Van Dyke that this version of *Grapevine* was cut about a month before Gaye's, although accounts of this sequence differ.[303] With Van Dyke on acoustic piano, James Jamerson on bass, and the Funk Brothers in peak form, the record has a relentless momentum, as Gladys lets her man know in no uncertain terms that she's not going to put up with his cheating ways.[304] In this performance, write Joe McEwen and Jim

---

301. B. J. Mason rhapsodized in an *Ebony* cover story: "Gladys, reaching back into time, pulled out the roots of black pain, black hope and black joy and described them in a revival-meetin' voice."

302. *Where Did Our Love Go*, p. 160. Knight said that Whitfield allowed the group to create the song's distinctive vocal arrangement. "We lived with that song at home, on the road, we ate, slept, everything with it for two months. We brought it back to Norman one day the way we had done it . . . He went into the studio that minute, put Smokey [Robinson] out so we could go upstairs and record! . . . We tore it apart, we did all the little things."

303. According to Berry Gordy's memoir *To Be Loved* (p. 273–74), after he shot down Gaye's version for single release in 1967, Whitfield got his permission to let him do the song with Gladys, and they proceeded to take it in an entirely different, gospel-tinged direction.

304. George (*Where Did Our Love Go?*, p. 169) writes that longtime Motown drummer Benny Benjamin by this time was weakened due to substance abuse problems, so the main rhythm on *Grapevine* was provided by Uriel Jones, with Benjamin merely adding "coloration" on cymbals. Benny died in 1969.

Miller, Gladys "was transformed into a fiery, hard-edge vocalist, unleashing her scorn with startling fury."[305]

Yesterday (1967)—Ray Charles
ABC/TRC 11009
Chart debut Nov. 11, 1967 (#9 on R&B chart, #25 pop)

Ray Charles' transformation of The Beatles' *Yesterday* was a mark of his distinctive genius, taking a song that was universally known and making it utterly his own. This is a powerful, emotionally ravaged interpretation. The Paul McCartney ballad is about love that is suddenly and devastatingly lost, and Charles (biographer Michael Lydon writes) decided to give it "the weight of age" by giving his voice an extra edge of hoarseness. When Sid Feller heard Ray rehearsing the number, he thought the singer had a cold, than realized it was intentional. "Ray was putting on a deliberate sound to speak for the character he was trying to create," said Feller.[306] When he sings, "Suddenly—I'm not half the man I used to be," he sounds like a man lost in genuine agony.

Scarborough Fair/Canticle (1966/1968)—Simon & Garfunkel
Recorded July 26, 1966
From the album *Parsley, Sage, Rosemary & Thyme* (chart debut Nov. 12, 1966, #4 peak, 145 charted weeks); after being featured on soundtrack of *The Graduate* issued as a single: Columbia 44465, chart debut March 2, 1968 (peak position #11)[307] (*Folk-#58*)

The tune that would later become known as *Scarborough Fair* dates back through its earliest known antecedent to a printed broadside in 1670. Generally known under the title *The Elfin Knight* (collected by Francis James Child as Child Song No. 2, and by Cecil Sharp as Sharp No. 1), it was also known as *The Lovers' Tasks*, one of many folk stories in which one person asks riddles or seemingly impossible tasks of the other. Child found comparable Turkish, Sanskrit, and Buddhist versions in addition to the numerous Scottish variants, and Russian translations of Greek tales derived from Arabic. The one who fails to find an answer, or to make an equally difficult counter-demand, has to submit to the will of the other (the stakes in these wagers could be high, extending to the risk of personal freedom, or as a means for the devil or a fairy to obtain the souls and bodies of mortals). *Gammer Gurton's Garland*, compiled by Joseph Ritson and posthumously published in 1810, provided the narrative text that would survive:

"Can you make me a cambric shirt / Parsley, sage, rosemary and thyme / Without any seam or needlework? / And you shall be a true lover of mine."[308] It was only in the mid-nineteenth century that it became associated with Scarborough Fair, an event held regularly in the small town of Scarborough on the coast of England, attracting traders and entertainers from around the country.[309] As the tune evolved, it was about a man trying to attain his true love, with herbs symbolizing desired virtues: parsley represented comfort, sage was strength, rosemary was love, and thyme was courage.[310] The July–September 1894 *Journal of American Folklore* reported U.S. versions of the song with the "parsley, sage, rosemary, and thyme" refrain.[311] [312]

Paul Simon was on tour in England when he first heard the song performed by folk singer-guitarist Martin Carthy (later a member of Steeleye Span, and an influence on Richard Thompson). Carthy had learned the old tune from an Ewan MacColl and Peggy Seeger songbook, and later included it on his 1965 album *Martin Carthy*.[313] It was also Carthy who had taught *Scarborough Fair* to Bob Dylan during the latter's December 1962 visit to London; Dylan used the melody during the following months for both *Girl from the North Country* and *Boots of Spanish Leather*. Todd Harvey finds that among print and recorded versions, Audrey Coppard's 1956 treatment was the only one besides MacColl's (1957) that utilized the melody performed, and handed down, by Carthy.[314] The British artist recalled for interviewers that, at Simon's request, he wrote the lyrics down for him. (By another account reported in Patrick Humphries' Simon biography, it was Art Garfunkel who learned the traditional song while visiting London and being taught to play guitar by a female friend.)[315]

Simon adapted the song for Simon & Garfunkel's third album, and this is one of the few S&G songs co-credited to Garfunkel; Art collaborated on the overall arrange-

305. *Rolling Stone Illustrated History of Rock & Roll*, p. 230.
306. Lydon, *Ray Charles: Man and Music*, p. 268.
307. At one point in June 1968, Simon & Garfunkel had the top two albums in the country (*The Graduate* and *Bookends*), a third in the Top Ten (*Parsley, Sage*), and a fourth in the Top 30 (*Sounds of Silence*).
308. Child, *The English and Scottish Popular Ballads*, Volume 1 (1962 ed.), p. 6–18.
309. Frank Kidson's *Traditional Tunes: A Collection of Ballad Airs* (1891) and *English County Songs* (1893 by Lucy Broadwood and J. A. Fuller) seem to be two of the earlier instances in which *Scarborough Fair* is used as the song's primary title.
310. Vance Randolph, *Ozark Folksongs*, Vol. 1, p. 38.
311. *Journal of American Folklore*, Vol. 12, "American Versions of the Ballad of the Elfin Knight," p. 228–32.
312. Phillips Barry (*Journal of American Folklore*, Vol. 30) found that it had been printed in an American songbook by about 1844, and as a Boston broadside a few years earlier.
313. MacColl's version was the basis for the song's presentation in the December 1962–January 1963 *Sing Out!*
314. *The Formative Dylan: Transmission and Stylistic Influences, 1961–1963*, p. 32–33.
315. After years of public resentment that Simon had not acknowledged his role in transmitting the song, Carthy ended the "feud" in 1998 when Paul, while performing in England, invited the British artist on stage to perform the number with him and, notes biographer Marc Eliot (*Paul Simon: A Life*), "graciously acknowledged Carthy's contribution to it."

ment and on the "Canticle" portion of the number. Simon borrowed the line "Remember me to one who lives there / She once was a true love of mine" from *Girl from the North Country*. Also, much of the "Canticle" section was taken from Simon's own early anti-war number *The Side of a Hill* that was included on his 1965 British solo album *The Paul Simon Songbook*.[316] [317]

When director Mike Nichols persuaded Simon & Garfunkel to provide music for *The Graduate*, the ever-perfectionist Simon didn't have much new material ready (even *Mrs. Robinson* was heard in the film only in an unfinished version), so Nichols made prominent use of earlier S&G songs, above all *Sounds of Silence* and *Scarborough Fair*. The latter song's haunting quality, the stunning close-harmony vocals, the intricate arrangement intertwining the traditional song with its countermovement "Canticle" (about a soldier on the battlefield)[318] and the delicately lovely acoustic guitar (deliberately evoking the tune's ancient folk roots) made it absolutely perfect for the mood of new college graduate Dustin Hoffman contemplating what he was going to do with his life. Columbia quickly released the year-and-a-half-old recording as a single, several weeks before coming out with the completed *Mrs. Robinson*. *Scarborough Fair* was unlike anything else on pop radio in 1968, or since.

Love Child (1968)—Diana Ross & the Supremes

(written by Pam Sawyer, R. Dean Taylor, Frank Wilson, Deke Richards, & Berry Gordy)

Motown 1135

Chart debut Oct. 19, 1968 (#1 for 2 weeks pop, #2 R&B); #1 in Canada, #15 in England[319] (*DM, AHR*)

As Motown transcended racial barriers to become "the sound of young America" during the 1964–1966, the record label's premier female group, the Supremes, could do no wrong, scoring #1 records seemingly at will. Most were written and produced by the trio of Eddie Holland, Lamont Dozier, and Brian Holland, which also churned out a series of classic records by the Four Tops. But when Holland-Dozier-Holland left Motown in the midst of a bitter legal/financial dispute, and other writers attempting to fill their shoes in providing the Supremes with hits came up short, the company was faced with a crisis.

In his autobiography *To Be Loved*, Berry Gordy recalls that the label had to turn to new writers for Supremes

material. He formed a new production unit for the group, "the Clan"; they assembled at Detroit's Pontchartrain Hotel, "where I told them we'd lock ourselves in until we came up with the right product."

"On about the second day of coffee and frustration, throwing ideas out in the air that nobody particularly liked, I started playing what felt like Holland-Dozier-Holland type chords—to get in the mood of what I was looking for. In the key of A minor I started playing with a sad, soulful feel. Soon everyone in the room was throwing out lyrics and melodies to match my chords."

"After what seemed like a mountain of mediocre ideas," Pam Sawyer (a white Englishwoman) came up with the concept for a song about a child born out of wedlock; the others thought it would be "too heavy" for the all-American Supremes. But Gordy encouraged her; as she came up with the bulk of the lyrics, "we all added and changed . . . refining and adapting as we continued to work. Ultimately, we arrived at a really touching story about a girl who herself was born out of wedlock and is telling her boyfriend that she doesn't want to go the wrong way with him and bring another love child into the world. We had managed to take a negative image and turn it around in a positive way. Now it was perfect for the Supremes." After Richards and Gordy polished the finished product, they left the Pontchartrain and went immediately to the studio to cut the track.[320] It became the fastest-selling Supremes record ever.

Gordy first encountered the quartet of Diane Ross (as she was then known, born on March 26, 1944, in Detroit), Mary Wilson, Florence Ballard and Betty McGlown in 1960 auditioning with a Motown exec in their lobby. He was impressed, but insisted that the high school seniors finish school before he could sign them. They'd come to Hitsville almost every day after school making friends with producers, trying to get gigs singing background for other artists. In January 1961 they signed with Motown, becoming a trio after Barbara Martin (who had replaced Betty McGlown) left. Until then they'd been singing as the Primettes, a sister group to the Primes, who would become the Temptations. Gordy said they needed a new name, and it was Florence who came up with the Supremes. "My belief in them sustained my hopes during three years of flop after flop." Finally, in 1964, *Where Did Our Love Go* opened the floodgates of what would become twelve chart-topping pop singles.

Underscoring the extent to which the Supremes had become a solo vehicle for Diana Ross, she recorded *Love Child* with unidentified background singers, as groupmates Mary Wilson and Cindy Birdsong (who had replaced Ballard) missed the session. She made it a full-

316. Kingston, *Simon & Garfunkel: The Biography*, p. 39–40, 64.

317. David Hartwell in the January 1967 *Crawdaddy* (p. 16) praised the intricate arrangement interweaving the original folk ballad with a new composition containing "an almost subliminal lyric [reflecting] the loneliness of the soldier. A song of real significance is created, greater than any of the parts or their sum."

318. In liner notes for the 1966 album, Ralph Gleason suggested that the song's quietly antiwar message is "signaled" by the electric bass.

319. #1 in New Zealand, #4 Australia.

320. Gordy, *To Be Loved*, p. 264–66.

fledged dramatic performance, acting out the role of the young woman facing a dilemma. It could easily have become overwrought melodrama, but instead is a triumph. Dave Marsh gives primary credit to the legendary Motown house band, which "makes you feel so intensely the potency of the predestination Diana is determined to deny."[321]

If I Can Dream (1968)—Elvis Presley (written by W. Earl Brown)
RCA 47-9670
Recorded June 23, 1968; chart debut Nov. 30, 1968 (#9 peak in *Record World*, #12 in *Billboard*); #2 in Australia, #7 in Canada, #11 in England;[322] from the TV special and album *Elvis* (#8 peak)

After nearly a decade of increasingly brain-dead movies featuring mostly assembly-line songs had relegated Elvis Presley to virtual irrelevancy in the contemporary pop marketplace, his career was transformed by the most unlikely vehicle of a Christmas special for NBC airing that December 3. It was Elvis's acceptance of the need to finally take a chance again, go in an entirely new direction with total emotional conviction, that made it a stunning triumph. The symbol of that turnaround was the song written especially for the show's finale, *If I Can Dream.*

As Presley turned in a series of electrifying performances taped for the show, everyone concerned realized it would be something special. Peter Guralnick writes in the second volume of his Elvis biography: "It was that very intensity, Elvis' whole emotional commitment in the act of recording, that brought home" to producers how essential it was for the show to have a powerful ending. Director Steve Binder approached the show's vocal arranger, Earl Brown, and asked him to write a song that would sum up "those things that he knew Elvis felt but could never fully express . . . a declaration of shared idealism." Brown went home and at seven the next morning called Binder to say: "I think I've got it. I think I've nailed the song." When Brown played it for Elvis, the singer quietly asked him to play it again, and then again—about six or seven times in all. Then, Binder recalled, "Elvis looked at me and said, 'We're doing it.'" Everyone was concerned that Presley's manager Colonel Parker would veto the brotherhood-and-understanding number for being too risky, and indeed (according to Joseph A. Tunzi), Parker initially scowled and told Brown, "That ain't Elvis's kind of song." But upon seeing Elvis' strong belief in the number, Parker had no objection— after making sure they had 100 percent of the copyright.

"I put him on the floor with a hand mike," recalled co-producer and engineer Bones Howe. "And he sang that song in front of the string section, complete with knee-drops. The string players were sitting there with their mouths open, they had never seen anything like this. Then he came back in, and we re-recorded the vocal. We turned off all the lights in the studio, and he sang it in the dark." Everyone else was sent home, and Elvis unleashed an intense performance in three or four takes in the darkened studio. What captivates the listener, writes Guralnick, is "the pain and conviction and raw emotion in Elvis' voice as he sings of a world 'where all my brothers walk hand in hand' and almost screams out the last line: 'Please / let my dream / come true / Right now!'" His voice so rough with down-to-the-bone feeling that one wonders if he'll make it to the end, "the words take on worlds of meaning, the melody soars, there is a thrill . . . in every listening." Binder recalled: "I think he was oblivious to everything else in the universe. When I looked out the window [of the control booth], he was in almost fetal position, writhing on the cement floor, singing that song."[323]

Darlene Love and the other members of the Blossoms, who sang backing vocals, told Brown "He really means this song more than any we've heard him do." On the composer's original sheet music, Elvis wrote: "My boy, my boy, this could be the one." Afterward, listening with enormous satisfaction to the playback perhaps fifteen times, Presley declared, "You know, I'll never sing another song that I don't believe in."[324]

In the Ghetto (1969)—Elvis Presley (written by Mac Davis)
RCA 47-9741
Recorded in Memphis Jan. 20, 1969; chart debut May 3, 1969 (#3 peak in *Billboard*; #1 in *Record World* & *Cash Box*); #1 (3 weeks) in Germany, #1 in Canada, #2 in England[325] (*1001, TC*)

Mac Davis, a twenty-seven-year-old Atlanta-born protégé of flamboyant rock entrepreneur Billy Strange, was an up-and-coming songwriter whose work had appealed to Elvis Presley since Elvis cut *A Little Less Conversation* in 1968. Biographer Peter Guralnick recounts that Strange had submitted a tape of seventeen Davis songs during the period immediately after the King's big Christmas comeback TV special, and the singer selected five—including the emotional ballad *Don't Cry, Daddy*—to record. Above all, there was *In the Ghetto*,

---

321. Marsh, *The Heart of Rock & Soul*, p. 257–58.
322. #7 in South Africa.

323. *Careless Love: The Unmaking of Elvis Presley,* p. 309–10.
324. Joseph A. Tunzi, *Elvis Sessions*, p. 129.
325. #1 (7 weeks) in both Norway and Sweden, 4 weeks in New Zealand, 2 weeks in Malaysia, #2 in Belgium and Switzerland, #3 Denmark, and #6 France.

and it shaped up as the most potentially controversial number he had ever put on record.

For the first time, Elvis was tackling a song of explicit social commentary, notes Guralnick, "detailing the inevitable consequences of ghetto poverty and societal indifference and pleading for compassion for black youth." Some in Presley's inner circle cautioned that he would risk alienating his fans. But Chips Moman, the producer of the 1969 Memphis recording sessions that would transform the legend's career, insisted that this was an important song that couldn't be passed over. Elvis was convinced, and at 9 p.m. on January 20 began a marathon session devoted to this one song, stretching into the early morning hours. Guitarist Reggie Young recalled how hard Presley worked, stopping several times because he felt he could do better. "It was like he was finally doing a song with some meaning to it, with some soul."[326] [327]

While working for seven years as a distribution man for Vee Jay and then the Liberty label, Mac Davis had been tinkering with the idea of writing a song called *The Vicious Circle* about people who find themselves trapped in a difficult situation. In the tumultuous year of 1968 (by which time he was working as a staff writer for a song publisher), news stories about the lethal cycle of ghetto life persuaded Davis that this should be the song's focal point. One day while hanging out with Freddy Weller, guitarist for Paul Revere & the Raiders, Weller played a guitar lick that triggered the songwriter's imagination as a perfect opening for the piece. He completed it that night, and called Weller at around 3 a.m. to play it for him; they both knew it was a hit.

"If you had never heard of Elvis Presley but were simply presented with the 23 meticulous takes of [*In the Ghetto*], it would be virtually impossible not to be won over," writes Guralnick. "The singing is of such unassuming, almost translucent eloquence, it is so quietly confident in its simplicity, so well supported by the kind of elegant, no-frills small-group backing that was a hallmark of [Moman's American studio] style—it makes a statement almost impossible to deny." There is a "tenderness" in Presley's singing recalling his earliest work, "offering equal parts yearning and social compassion."[328] The British magazine *Q*, ranking it the #5 all-time great-

est song in 1999, notes that "Elvis uses every trick in the book to get the tear ducts flowing in this plea for social justice. His downbeat delivery is both melancholy and thought-provoking, while steering the imagination away from thoughts of Las Vegas and white, tasseled jumpsuits."

When *In the Ghetto* was released as a single, no one quite knew what to expect. The two singles emerging out of his holiday special, *If I Can Dream* and *Memories*, had reached #12 and #35, respectively, in *Billboard*. Would audiences accept or reject this bold departure? Leaving such doubts in the dust, *Ghetto* became Presley's biggest smash in four years, and made it absolutely clear that this comeback was going to stick. In 2007, Lisa Marie Presley recorded a "duet" with her father on *In the Ghetto* (in the manner of Natalie and Nat Cole's *Unforgettable*) as a special online song (released on the thirtieth anniversary of her dad's death through Apple's iTunes) with all proceeds going to a New Orleans branch of Presley Place, a transitional housing facility for homeless families.

Israelites (1969)—Desmond Dekker & the Aces (written by Desmond Dekker & Leslie Kong)
Uni 55129
Chart debut May 17, 1969 (#6 in *Record World*, #8 in *Cash Box*, #9 in *Billboard*); #1 (1 week) in England, #1 (2 weeks) in West Germany[329] (*GHF, World-#12, ACC-#188, DM, AHR, TC, DET*)

Jamaica's first certified gold record and the first reggae performance to become a massive U.S. and international hit, Desmond Dekker's *The Israelites* carved out a small but important place in pop music history. Born Desmond Dacres in Kingston, Jamaica, on July 16, 1941, Dekker sang with a church choir as a youngster, and began his recording career in 1963 with the Jamaican hit single *Honour Your Father and Your Mother*. He soon began writing hit songs for other artists, and helped get future reggae legend Bob Marley—a boyhood friend—signed to producer Leslie Kong's label. Dekker earned his first international hit in 1967 with *007 (Shanty Town)*, which reached #14 in England and was later featured in the landmark film *The Harder They Come*.

The song that became his defining classic was first recorded in 1968 as *Poor Me, Israelites*, but its initial record release went nowhere. However, Graeme Goodall, the managing director of Pyramid Records, recognized the song's potential, remixed the master tapes, and reissued the record as *The Israelites* in 1969. It shot to #1 in England and the top echelon of the charts all over the world. This made it the first major reggae hit in the

---

326. The opening section of the record is virtually a voice-and-guitar duet. Young is playing the same old Gibson 440 he had played on Dusty Springfield's *Windmills of Your Mind*; Elvis' original guitarist Scotty Moore had traded the instrument to Moman.

327. Also key to the record's musical impact, remarks Roben Jones (*Memphis Boys*, p. 210) are the bass figure and "booming" tympani (bassist Tommy Cogbill's idea), "serving as punctuation, signaling each new paragraph in the story." Jones points out that the recording was made "in one of Memphis's seediest slums with the King assassination still fresh in everyone's mind."

328. *Careless Love*, p. 331–32.

---

329. #1 in Holland, South Africa, & Sweden, #2 in Canada & France, #3 in Australia.

U.S. (Millie Small's 1964 smash *My Boy Lollipop* had been the first American hit for dance-oriented Jamaican ska music, which modulated by 1966 into rock steady, de-emphasizing or dropping the horns and moving to a slower, sultry tempo, and then, as the bass became more dominant, into reggae.) Dekker went on to enjoy followup Top Ten hits in England with *It Mek* and *You Can Get It If You Really Want*, and amidst some career ups and downs remained a busy recording artist (including a 1980 album produced by rock star Robert Palmer) for decades thereafter, although he would have to settle for just the one moment of glory in the U.S. market.

It's entirely appropriate that *Israelites* became reggae's U.S. breakthrough, as Stephen Davis notes in *Reggae Bloodlines*, because it addresses the "archetypal reggae theme: Black Africans, the metaphorical lost tribes of Israel, sold into the bondage of a Caribbean Babylon." The song, like reggae as a whole, is rooted in Rastafarianism, the Jamaican religion rooted in the belief that blacks transported to the Western hemisphere were descended from Ethiopians, viewed as one of the twelve lost tribes of Israel.[330] Although American listeners who had difficulty understanding Dekker's Jamaican patois at first suspected wrongly that the song may have been anti-Semitic, in fact the singer, like other Rastafarians, identified deeply with the Jews, as one of God's chosen people. The song, notes Thomas Ryan, "tells a simple tale of trying to maintain respect and dignity in the face of poverty." More specifically, Dekker draws a parallel between Jews in bondage in Egypt, and the modern plight of Jamaicans.[331] The fact that it was accompanied by a brilliant, highly danceable rhythm track devised by producer Leslie Kong, laying the groundwork for the reggae hits to follow, ensured that even if the message wasn't grasped by listeners, the music would be. Ken Tucker called it "a mesmerizing chant that fully captured the lulling magic of reggae."[332]

Woodstock (1970)—Crosby, Stills, Nash & Young
(written by Joni Mitchell)

Atlantic 2723

Chart debut March 28, 1970 (#10 in *Record World* , #11 in *Billboard*);[333] from the album *Déjà vu* (reached #1, sold 7 million copies)

It began just after 5 p.m. on Friday, August 15, 1969, and concluded at mid-morning Monday, August 18; it created one of the nation's worst traffic jams, shutting down the New York Thruway; it was muddy and wild

and free (in every sense of the word). And the Woodstock Music and Art Fair at Max Yasgur's farm in the pastures of Sullivan County adjacent to Bethel, New York— "Three Days of Peace and Music"—attracted 450,000 people to the rock festival that defined (at least in legend) a generation.

David Crosby, Stephen Stills, Graham Nash, and Neil Young were there among the featured performers, so it was appropriate that when Joni Mitchell composed the song that further immortalized the event, they put it on record (with Stills on lead vocal).[334] This is doubly true considering that she could hardly have been more deeply intertwined with the group: Crosby had produced Joni's first album (and they had been lovers), Stills had played on it, she and Nash had an extended romantic relationship, and Young wrote the (unreleased) song *Sweet Joni* about her. Joni had been scheduled to play at Woodstock on Sunday night, but with the chaos surrounding the event by that point requiring a heroic effort even to get there, she had to regretfully cancel. "The deprivation of not being able to go provided me with an intense angle on Woodstock," she would recall, as quoted by biographer Karen O'Brien. "Woodstock, for some reason, impressed me as being a modern miracle . . . for a herd of people that large to cooperate so well, it was pretty remarkable and there was tremendous optimism. So I wrote the song *Woodstock* out of those feelings, and the first three times I performed it in public I burst into tears because it brought back the intensity of the experience and was so moving."[335] (She composed it at a New York hotel during the festival.)

Mitchell, Crosby, and Nash all appeared on *The Dick Cavett Show* following the festival, and they shared the flight back home to California. On the flight, Stills tried unsuccessfully to write a song about it. "Just as I was on the verge of getting it together, Joni came over and played us her song," he related. "I said I couldn't top it." It's all very idealized and romantic, of course, but it's a wonderful vision, and CSNY's performance is powerful.[336] [337]

---

330. *Reggae Bloodlines*, p. 2.
331. Ryan, *American Hit Radio*, p. 350–52.
332. *Rock of Ages*, p. 538.
333. Reached #2 in Canada, #6 Poland, #13 Australia.

334. In the group's authorized biography by Dave Zimmer (p. 111), Nash recalls that the first completed version of the song—one of the album's few tracks featuring all four members in the studio at once—was "magic," with a sensational Stills vocal. But Stills, never satisfied, later erased his vocal and replaced it with one that Nash felt "wasn't nearly as good."

335. O'Brien, *Joni Mitchell: Shadows and Light*, p. 109–11.

336. Michael Walker reveals in *Laurel Canyon* (p. 130) that the group's powerful manager David Geffen later "strong-armed" Warner Brothers into using CSNY's recording as the closing theme for the *Woodstock* movie by threatening to withhold the band's performances from the film.

337. Ironically, despite being one of their biggest hits, *Woodstock* was a number they rarely played during their 1970 tour, because, as David Browne notes in *Fire and Rain* (p. 236), "recreating the dense, multitracked harmonies of the studio version required a pinpoint accuracy they rarely managed over the din of electric guitars and drums."

Save the Country (1970)—The Fifth Dimension (written by Laura Nyro)

Bell 895

Chart debut June 13, 1970 (#20 peak in *Cash Box*, #27 in *Billboard*)

Within forty-eight hours after the assassination of Robert Kennedy on June 5, 1968, Laura Nyro wrote *Save the Country* in a surge of despair, fury, and desperate inspiration. Her recording of the song, rush-released on June 26 (Columbia 44592), was a hit on radio stations in Detroit and Los Angeles (L.A. radio station KRLA played it once an hour during the madness of the Democratic convention in Chicago in August), but not nationwide.[338] The following February she cut a sloweddown version that was released in January 1970, again without charting (Columbia 45089).[339] However, exactly two years after the original, the man who produced that Nyro session, Bones Howe, scored a memorable Top 40 hit with the song as performed by the Fifth Dimension.

Born Laura Nigro on October 18, 1947, in the Bronx, Laura attended Manhattan's High School of Music and Art, began performing in area clubs, and was signed by the jazz label Verve/Forecast. Although her 1967 debut album *More Than a New Discovery* was not a hit, its treasure trove of great original songs was to provide giant singles for other artists in the next few years: *Wedding Bell Blues* (a 1969 chart-topper for the Fifth Dimension), *And When I Die* (#2 smash for Blood, Sweat & Tears), and *Stoney End* (Top Ten for Barbra Streisand). Switching to Columbia in 1968, her second album generated more hits for others (including *Eli's Coming* for Three Dog Night), but also showed Nyro as a potent blue-eyed soulful performer in her own right. She demonstrated in 1971's *Gonna Take a Miracle* (accompanied by LaBelle) that she was absolutely terrific as an interpreter of other writers' 1960s soul gems. Intensely private and determined to follow her own path, Nyro retired from pop music at twenty-four, returned briefly four years later, and her subsequent appearances were too few for her cult-sized but passionate following.

No artists benefited more from Laura Nyro's songwriting prowess than the Fifth Dimension. Four of their previous 1968–1970 hits—*Stoned Soul Picnic, Sweet Blindness*, the aforementioned *Wedding Bell Blues*, and *Blowing Away*—were her creations.[340] But all were topped in musical power by *Save the Country*. Defying their reputation as safe, smooth popsters, Marilyn McCoo, Billy Davis, Jr., Florence LaRue, Lamont McLemore, and Ron Townson unleash gospel-fired passion (over a churchy organ) befitting the song. The record hurtles forward with great energy, and the momentum just keeps driving until the startling conclusion, as they sing in unison (the instruments dropping out at the end so that the voices ring out a cappella), "Save the country, save the country, save the country—NOW!" The final word hangs suspended in the air, like an urgent demand.

Take Me Home, Country Roads (1971)—John Denver & Fat City

RCA Victor 0445

Chart debut Apr. 10, 1971 (reached #2 pop in *Billboard*, #1 in *Cash Box*, #50 C&W);[341] [342] #12 in Canada (*Folk-#68, C&W-#102, GHF-#109, RIA-#160*)

Corny he may have been, but John Henry Deutschendorf (born on December 31, 1943, in Roswell, New Mexico) wrote and recorded some outstanding songs, of which this is the finest. Denver was a member of the Chad Mitchell Trio from 1965–1968, wrote the #1 smash *Leaving on a Jet Plane* for Peter, Paul & Mary (it was initially a track from his debut solo album, *Rhymes and Reasons*), and this is the record that sent his solo career skyward.[343] Bill Danoff and Taffy Nivert came up with the idea for the song through letters received from an artist friend who lived in the mountains of West Virginia, "reveling in the beauty of the countryside." The duo was driving to a family reunion of Taffy's relatives in Maryland, and the winding rural roads provided the additional impetus. Just before Christmas 1970, Denver visited their apartment after the last show at the Cellar Door, where he was headlining with Bill & Taffy as the opening act. He heard and loved the song, and they molded it into final shape (Denver wrote the bridge and helped revise the second verse) working on the piece until 6 a.m.[344] He premiered it at the Cellar Door on December 30; they recorded it a few weeks later. Bill & Taffy (as Fat City) sing backing vocals; they would later enjoy their own chart-topping success with Starland Vocal Band, on Denver's own Windsong label. *Country Roads* has such a pure, timeless folk-like simplicity and beauty that it will endure.[345] It was inducted into the Grammy Hall of Fame in 1998, in just its second year of eligibility.

338. Michele Kort, *Soul Picnic: The Music and Passion of Laura Nyro*, p. 65–66. A dramatic full-page ad for the record in the June 29 *Billboard* quoted the full lyrics, with rave reviews for Nyro.

339. William Brown, Columbia discography.

340. The group's 1967 breakthrough was Jimmy Webb's *Up, Up, and Away*.

341. Denver related in *Take Me Home: An Autobiography* that when the single initially struggled on the chart (entering *Billboard* at #99 and then falling off for two weeks), RCA was ready to give up on it, but he successfully urged the company to stick with a song he believed in.

342. Denver would later score three #1 country singles, to go with his four #1 pop hits.

343. Milton Okun, who had produced the Mitchell Trio's later records—and was the man who suggested Denver's professional name change—produced and arranged this and nearly all of Denver's hits.

344. Horstman, *Sing Your Heart Out, Country Boy*, p. 22–23.

345. Toots & the Maytals' reggae cover put a vibrant new spin on Denver's song.

Let's Get It On (1973)—Marvin Gaye (written by Marvin Gaye & Ed Townsend)

Tamla 54234

Chart debut July 14, 1973 (2 weeks at #1 on pop chart; 6 weeks at #1 R&B); #31 in England (*R&B-#95, DM-#140, RS-#168, GHF, TC, ACC, DMDB*)[346]

With its seductive vibe and well-placed moans and screams, *Let's Get It On* is one of the most erotic records ever made. "The singer is in a languorous rhythmic garden, and there's no evil in it," writes Gerri Hirshey. "Chastity doesn't stand a chance here, but still, it is a holy place. Serpent-soft, Gaye's voice wonders in a whisper whether the lady knows the meaning of being sanctified."[347]

Biographer David Ritz writes that the performance of *Let's Get It On*, and most of Gaye's songs from 1973 until the end of his life, was inspired by the woman who would become his second wife, Janis Hunter. She was sixteen years old when he met her while in the Motown studio recording the song. Janis was the daughter of jazzman Slim Gaillard of Slim & Slam fame (*Flat Foot Floogee*), a close friend of Gaye's producer and co-writer Ed Townsend. Marvin (age thirty-three then, married to a woman seventeen years older) was entranced by the beautiful teenager, and her presence spurred him to give a particularly impassioned performance. "*Let's Get It On* fit squarely in the metaphysical convention of lulling women—through extravagant imagery, sweet language, and philosophical logic—into sexual submission," remarks Ritz. The song is about the union of love and sex; sex isn't wrong, he sings, "if the love is true." He was struggling to overcome his Pentecostal upbringing, and seeking the ultimate goal not of mere physical satisfaction, but "spiritual fulfillment." "His growling and groaning, his shouts and whispers, were cries for understanding, not mere satiation." Gaye spent the last dozen years of his life trying "to integrate his two strongest sources of emotional enthusiasm—God and sex."[348] The album took two years to finish, fully justified by its huge success.

After a year and a half concentrating on making the Diana Ross film *Lady Sings the Blues*, Motown founder Berry Gordy, Jr., had a happy return to the music business when he walked in on this Gaye session. Gordy was blown away by the "raw" original tape, on which Gaye's voice was "fatter, fuller and sexier" than on the subsequent finished master (with more strings and horns). So at Gordy's urging, the "little 7 1/2" version was the one issued as a single.[349] *Rolling Stone* in 2004 called it "a masterpiece of erotic persuasion."

Hurricane (1975)—Bob Dylan

Columbia 10245

Recorded on Oct. 24, 1975; chart debut Nov. 29, 1975 (#33 peak); from the album *Desire* (5 weeks at #1) (*PW, TC*)

Rubin "Hurricane" Carter, a contender for the world middleweight boxing championship, was convicted of a 1966 triple murder in New Jersey on the basis of what turned out to be falsified evidence, fueled by racism. A national symbol of injustice, he wrote a best-selling autobiography, a copy of which he mailed to Bob Dylan. Moved by his story, Dylan visited Carter in prison, and the result was this song, boiling over with righteous fury.[350] The success of the song helped lead to the reopening of the case. In 1985, after a retrial and multiple appeals, Rubin Carter was at last set free, and thirteen years later became the subject of the Oscar-nominated film starring Denzel Washington.

In his first-ever sustained period of co-writing, Dylan had recently begun collaborating with theater director and lyricist Jacques Levy, and he was so pleased with *One More Cup of Coffee* and *Isis* that he suggested continuing, for what became the album's classic. Biographer Howard Sounes notes that Levy's theatrical sensibility heightened the song's drama, "opening the number like a movie" with pistol shots ringing out in the night.[351]

Hurricane is a fierce eight-minute epic, released on two sides of a single. The level of intensity never lets up from first moment to last, boosted further by Scarlet Rivera's fervent violin. Paul Williams named it one of the 100 best singles in pop music history. "If Dylan is a Picasso (as Leonard Cohen insists), then *Hurricane* is his *Guernica*—a major work, masterwork, by a mature artist, that is a cry of anger and pain loudly calling attention to what is happening to real people here in this political world right now," writes Williams. "*Hurricane* is superb rock and roll: passionate, innovative, great melody, great lyrics, great beat, incredible phrasing, wonderful instrumentation (violin, congas), and a drive that doesn't quit . . ."[352]

---

346. It was the #17 biggest hit on Los Angeles radio from 1956–1979, as compiled by Guy Zapoleon (*Book of Rock Lists*, p. 146).

347. *Nowhere to Run*, p. 215.

348. Ritz, *Divided Soul*, p. 182–86.

349. Gordy, *To Be Loved*, p. 326–27.

---

350. Dylan explained to Bill Flanagan (*Written In My Soul*, p. 99) that leaders of the movement to free Carter had written to him before the ex-boxer sent his book, "which really touched me." So after visiting the ex-boxer, by then convinced of his innocence, he brought it all to playwright Jacques Levy, who was serving as his collaborator on this album only, and said, "Why don't you help me write this song and see if we can do something?"

351. *Down the Highway*, p. 287–88. Andy Gill and Kevin Odegard (*Simple Twist of Fate*, p. 39) suggest that the influence of Dylan's art teacher Norman Raeben contributed to the cinematic "jump-cut" style of this song, "allowing him to reveal underlying truths" about the song's characters.

352. Williams, *The 100 Best Singles*, p. 163–64. There are quibbles one can have about aspects of the song: some awkward lines likely attributable to Levy; some debatable facts (Carter was not generally considered a likely "champion of the world"). But these are dwarfed by the intensity and power of the performance.

Deacon Blues (1978)—Steely Dan
ABC 12355
Chart debut Apr. 1, 1978 (#19 peak); from the album
  Aja (chart debut Oct. 10, 1977, #3 peak) (*GHF,*
  AHR, PIT)

More a concept than a band, Steely Dan provided two brilliantly talented but weird guys, singer-keyboardist Donald Fagen and bassist Walter Becker, with a vehicle for their deliciously off-kilter original songs, filled with wry, ironic humor, an array of literary and pop cultural lyrical references, and intriguing, sinuous melodies that had more in common with jazz than rock. One critic called the duo "a postmodern Rodgers & Hart." Fagen (a Passaic, New Jersey, native) and Becker (from Queens, New York) met at Bard College in New York in 1967, and found they shared similar tastes for jazz, Beat writers, and dry wit.[353] They began playing in various bands together, and formed Steely Dan (named after a dildo in William Burroughs' *Naked Lunch*) as the best available means to get their songs performed. Their 1972 debut *Can't Buy a Thrill* was a smash thanks to the Top Ten single *Do It Again*. After another four successful albums, they came up with their greatest work, *Aja*, and its indelible centerpiece *Deacon Blues*.

Fagen, Becker, and producer Gary Katz had always been obsessive perfectionists, often insisting upon numerous takes until each individual solo—played in some cases by a succession of different session musicians—met their very specific expectations. On *Aja*, this perfectionism reached its zenith; Becker attributed the album's success to the fact that they now had the luxury of being able to throw away everything that didn't work in the studio. Fagen explained *Deacon Blues* as being about "an alienated kid out in the suburbs who was looking for some sort of alternative values and turns to jazz and hip culture as something to grab on to." Of course, the kid was much like the song's creators. He's a "loser" by society's standards, "but the losers should have some sort of franchise as well. And the name which he has chosen which conveys a certain power is 'Deacon Blues.'"[354]

It is described by Thomas Ryan as "a song about insularity . . . [Fagen] nakedly recounts the tale of a misbegotten life, full of unrecognized accomplishments and misdirected choices. Wrapped in a cocoon of self-pity, the singer longs to embody the life of a romantic iconoclast. In his disillusionment, he envisions himself as a scotch-drinking, late-night jazzman who burns out before he fades away. In actuality, he accepts his fate, as well as his attitude of abandoned hope."[355] The intoxicat-

ing, intricate minor-key melody is unveiled by a killer studio band including guitarists Larry Carlton and Lee Ritenour, and backing vocalists including Clydie King. The horns are arranged and conducted by Tom Scott (also here on sax), and the featured, wailing tenor sax soloist is Pete Christlieb.[356] Chris Dahlen calls this the "pinnacle" of Steely Dan's work, the lush musicianship and glossy sound "making the song poignant even though you know better." The lyrics leave no doubt that the narrator is a decadent loser and he knows it, but "thanks to the bold and beautiful melody, the song achieved a suspension of disgust," and became a classic "for guys who wish they had something worth throwing away."[357]

Barry Walters writes of the album's "surreal sonic perfection, its melodic and harmonic complexity."[358] The listener is enveloped in a gorgeous sound collage, and the way Fagen presents his tale of a bohemian loser, it doesn't sound like such a bad life at all. *Aja* sold over five million copies, was inducted into the Grammy Hall of Fame in its first year of eligibility, and was voted one of the all-time top 300 albums by 100,000 fans in a 1998 Virgin poll. "My back to the wall, a victim of laughing chance / This is for me the essence of true romance / Sharing the things we know and love with those of my kind / Libations, sensations, that stagger the mind . . ."

I Will Survive (1979)—Gloria Gaynor (written by
  Dino Fekaris & Frederick Perren)
MGM 14508
Chart debut Dec. 16, 1978 (3 weeks at #1 on pop chart,
  #4 R&B), #1 (4 weeks) in England;[359] (*RIA-#89,*
  GHF, DMDB-#72, R&B-#110, RS, ACC)

One of the defining anthems of the disco era, *I Will Survive* is a song whose musical qualities and fierce spirit make it compelling even to those who otherwise disdain anything associated with glittering, spinning metal balls. Born on September 7, 1949, in Newark, New Jersey, Gloria Gaynor played her first professional engagement at eighteen, and after a few years of little success her group City Life gained a strong East Coast following. *Honey Bee* in spring 1974 gave her a hit in discos, and several months later her swirling dance remake of the Jackson 5 hit *Never Can Say Goodbye* carried her into the pop Top

353. Fagen would later play mainly keyboards, but during his first year at Bard he tried to learn saxophone; the protagonist in *Deacon Blues* declares he'll "learn to work the saxophone."

354. Brian Sweet, *Steely Dan: Reelin' In the Years*, p. 114–23.

355. Ryan, *American Hit Radio*, p. 496–97.

356. Christlieb was hired on the basis of his work in Johnny Carson's *Tonight Show* band.

357. *The Pitchfork 500*, p. 30.

358. A crucial contributor to the brilliant sound of this and other Steely Dan albums was Roger Nichols, a former nuclear engineer who became one of pop music's most gifted recording engineers. *Aja* earned him the Grammy for Best Engineered Recording. In addition to engineering just about everything the group ever recorded, he also worked with a wide range of other artists including Frank Sinatra, Natalie Cole, and Crosby, Stills & Nash.

359. #1 (4 weeks) in Ireland, #2 in Canada, #4 in Holland and Norway, #9 in Germany, #10 France.

Ten. After two years of both professional and personal hard times (in which she was hospitalized for spinal surgery following a fall), she teamed up with producers Dino Fekaris and Freddie Perren for a new album, *Love Tracks*.[360] *Substitute* was initially pegged as the A side of the leadoff single; Perren agreed to produce it if he could select its companion tune, which was then composed primarily by Fekaris.[361]

Gaynor recalled in her memoir that because of her strong feeling that *I Will Survive*, the B side, had hit potential, she made it the closing song of her live shows, and her husband took it to Richie Kaczor, the DJ at New York's Studio 54, who loved it. In short order other discos and radio stations jumped on the song, and it became a career-shaping smash.[362] Her mother had recently passed away, and she had to record *Survive* in a neck brace due to surgery on her spine a month earlier. "That's why I was able to record the song with such conviction." Sung from the perspective of a woman who's finally summoned the courage to leave an abusive lover, it speaks to anyone who's faced misfortune or tragedy and is determined to rise above it. *Survive* was cited by *Rolling Stone* in 2000 as the #56 greatest pop song.[363] In 2009, Gaynor celebrated the song's thirtieth anniversary with a new recording in English and Spanish.

Hot Stuff (1979)—Donna Summer (written by Pete Bellotte, Harold Faltermeyer & Keith Forsey)
Casablanca 978
Chart debut Apr. 21, 1979 (3 weeks at #1 on pop chart, #3 R&B, #1 for 7 weeks disco); #1 (2 weeks) in Canada, #1 (1 week) in Australia, #11 in England[364] (*RS-#104, DMDB, VIL*)

Queen of Disco Donna Summer went rock 'n roll on *Hot Stuff*, and she did it with a vengeance. This is one of the hardest-rocking singles of the 1970s, and one of the most salaciously sexual, as Donna's vocal positively drips with desperate desire and physical need; the lady wants it, and will not take "no" for an answer.

Born LaDonna Andrea Gaines in Boston on December 31, 1948, Donna took her name from Austrian actor Helmut Sommer (with an "o"), whom she married while living in Germany (later divorced) as a member of a traveling cast of *Hair* starting in late 1968. There

in 1973 she met Italian electro-pop producer/composer Giorgio Moroder, and the sixteen-minute heavy-breathing orgasmic workout *Love to Love You, Baby* (which they wrote together) at the end of 1975 launched her career just as disco was on the rise. Neil Bogart of Casablanca Records launched a massive promotional campaign that helped make her a worldwide superstar. She rode the disco wave the next few years with hits like *I Feel Love* and *Last Dance*, then hit a peak in 1979 with the back-to-back chart-toppers *Hot Stuff* and *Bad Girls*. The fact that her sultry beauty and provocative album cover poses matched the sensuality of her records certainly didn't hurt. Blessed with a voice more formidable and flexible than almost all of her disco competitors, Donna was able to survive the genre's decline to keep the hits coming through 1984, and after passing through the "where are they now" phase, scored a hit with a 1999 VH1 concert album.

Wayne Wadhams notes that *Hot Stuff* was "one of the first [rock songs] to voice the lust of a very horny, liberated woman. Listen to the musical package of *Hot Stuff*, its leering [synthesizer] hook licking into our ears with deep portamento. A heavy, butt-swinging bass and drum line stomps on the downbeat with each repeat of the words of the title." The "grim tonality" of its minor chords and relentless synth bass line "lends a modal, Middle Eastern aura, darkening the record's disco facade." And as for the vocal: "Summer's character is a cat in heat. She doesn't care who satisfies her need—any dude will do . . . A frenetic, almost atonal rock guitar solo writhes and screams like some beast caught in a trap . . . [this is] just unadorned animal instinct and desire."[365] The fact that Donna had gotten her professional start at age seventeen singing lead for a rock group, the Crow, meant that she was just as comfortable singing rock as she was dance or R&B material.[366]

"Setting a thumping kick-drum pulse against a raunchy guitar solo from Doobie Brother (and disco hater) Jeff Baxter," wrote *Rolling Stone* in ranking *Hot Stuff* #104 among its all-time top 500 songs, Moroder and Summer "paved the way for subsequent hybrids such as Michael Jackson's *Beat It*."[367] The performance won the Grammy for best rock female vocal.

Just Like Real People (1979)—The Kendalls (written by Bob McDill)
Ovation 1125
Chart debut May 5, 1979 (#11 C&W) (*DM*)

360. Freddie Perren had gotten his professional start at Jobete and then Motown, particularly as one of the co-writers of the Jackson 5's breakthrough hit, *I Want You Back*. Not long afterward, he and another ex-Jobete writer, Dino Fekaris, were "wooed away" (notes Motown historian Nelson George, *Where Did Our Love Go?*) to pen hits for the Sylvers and the Tavares.

361. *Billboard Book of Number One Hits*, p. 498.

362. Gaynor, *I Will Survive*, p. 135–37.

363. December 7, 2000, *Rolling Stone*, p. 92.

364. #1 in Switzerland, #2 in Norway, #3 in Austria and France, #6 in Germany.

365. *Inside the Hits*, p. 460–62.

366. Biographical information from Summer's autobiography *Ordinary Girl*. Oddly, although she discusses the making of the *Bad Girls* album (p. 171–73), she doesn't mention *Hot Stuff*.

367. *Rolling Stone 500 Greatest Songs*, p. 50.

Although too often neglected because of her relatively modest discography, Jeannie Kendall is one of country music's finest female vocalists of the past forty years, and *Just Like Real People* is her most powerful performance. Royce Kendall (born Royce Kykendall on September 25, 1934, in St. Louis) worked as half of the Austin Brothers in the late 1950s and 1960s with his brother Floyce. He formed a duo with daughter Jeannie (born on November 30, 1954, in St. Louis) when she was fifteen. Jeannie was a backing vocalist on Ringo Starr's 1970 country album *Beaucoups of Blues*. Steel guitar great Pete Drake signed them to Stop Records; after a few singles there, they moved on to Dot, United Artists, and finally Ovation. It was in 1977 that the Kendalls made their commercial breakthrough, having their greatest success with a long succession of cheatin' songs (like that year's country chart-topper *Heaven's Just a Sin Away*). Jeannie's crystalline voice is warmly reminiscent of Emmylou Harris and Dolly Parton; she basically solos on most songs, with her dad's harmonies, the most crucial exception being his showcase hit *Pittsburgh Stealers*. Royce died on May 22, 1998. It was more than four years later that Jeannie finally began performing once again.

This is a gorgeous, heart-wrenching ballad, as a woman who acknowledges making many mistakes confesses all of them to her new lover "before we go any further." From the emotion in her voice, she seems to feel this is her last chance for happiness. Dave Marsh: "Jeannie Kendall sings solo on this country restatement of the 'Let It Be' chords. The message isn't that far from the Beatles, either, since she's singing about self-acceptance, although from a much more desperate vantage point . . . The problem is a deep feeling of inadequacy (as if Jeannie can't hear the beauty of her own voice), based not in a lack of love but in a stoically detailed assessment of every mistake she's ever made." Royce isn't there to answer her, as in their other duets, because "there are no answers to what she's saying."[368]

He Stopped Loving Her Today (1980)—George Jones
(written by Bobby Braddock & Curly Putman)
Epic 50867
Recorded Feb. 6, 1980; chart debut April 12, 1980 (1 week at #1 C&W) (*C&W-#3, GHF-#99, RR, NPR-300, Time, HBN-#147, RS-#275, RIA, DM, TC, SC, ACC, DMDB*)[369]
Called the #1 greatest country song of all time by *Country America* magazine in 1992, the George Jones classic *He Stopped Loving Her Today* is declared a "Wagnerian

ode to undying love" by Bill Friskics-Warren. "We know how its gut-wrenching plot will unfold. We know that George's gloriously maudlin recitation will come after the first chorus, and we know that his measured, barely contained vocals will build to that chorus, and that [Billy] Sherrill's exacting arrangement will gradually unfurl on its way to sweeping up George's unbounded wail with a gust of swirling strings. Nevertheless, even after we've heard the record a hundred times, it can still render us defenseless." When the singer reveals the reason his friend is smiling for the first time in years, it has "the power to stand our every last nerve strand on end."[370] Pete Drake on steel guitar, Charlie McCoy on harmonica, and Millie Kirkham as the ghostly female voice heard during the recitation, contribute to the record's impact.

Bobby Braddock, best known for the Tammy Wynette classic *D-I-V-O-R-C-E*, brought the idea of a man who so loved his wife that his love only stopped the day he died to Curly Putman (also an established hit-maker including *Green, Green Grass of Home*). A number of artists passed on the song when they began shopping it around, other than Johnny Russell, who recorded it for two different labels starting with Mercury in January 1979 (but not issued as a single). When producer Billy Sherrill was given the composition (over two years after it was written), he made the crucial suggestion that the writers add a final verse at the funeral, and then gave it to Jones. Even then, the singer's first take was unimpressive. Then his ex-wife Wynette came into the studio, with her new husband, to watch from the booth. Braddock: "It was strange because, where she was sitting, a single light came down and illuminated her face. George Jones seemed riveted to that scene, and when he sang the song the second time, he never took his eyes off Tammy. It was like he was singing every word just for her."[371]

In his autobiography written with Tom Carter, Jones recalled that it took him eighteen months to record the song after the writers had first given it to him. Initially he waited because he felt strongly that it needed rewriting, to shift the death of his protagonist to later in the song. Then, when he finally tackled the number in the studio, he couldn't get Kris Kristofferson's *Help Me Make It Through the Night* out of his head, "so I sang Curly and Bobby's lyrics with Kristofferson's copyrighted melody." The next problem came with the spoken narration, the first time he had used one in years. "I couldn't get it. I had been able to sing while drunk all of my life. I'd fooled millions of people. But I could never speak

368. Marsh, *The Heart of Rock & Soul*, p. 378.

369. Winner of the Country Music Association award for best single of the year, in 2003 it was ranked (behind Wynette's *Stand By Your Man*) as the all-time #2 country music song by Country Music Television.

370. *Heartaches By the Number*, p. 79.

371. Ace Collins, *The Stories Behind Country Music's All-Time 100 Greatest Songs*, p. 250–51. Braddock said that upon listening to the tape a few days later, "It hit me that this was the perfect marriage of song, singer, and production."

without slurring when drunk." At last, he was able to complete the performance, and afterward told Sherrill: "Nobody will buy that morbid son of a bitch."[372] Never was he happier to be proven wrong. "*He Stopped Loving Her Today* did more for my career than all of the [other hits] combined." All of a sudden, the man whose appearance fees had plunged because promoters feared he wouldn't show up saw his fees skyrocket, in demand like never before. A "four-decade career had been salvaged by a three-minute song. There is a God."[373]

The Darkest Hour Is Just Before Dawn (1980)—Emmylou Harris with Ricky Skaggs (written by Ralph Stanley)

From the Warner album *Roses in the Snow* (chart debut May 24, 1980, #26 peak)

During the two decades in which the Stanley Brothers reigned as one of the great acts in bluegrass, it was Carter Stanley who was the primary focus of attention as lead singer, songwriter, and arranger. But in the years following Carter's death in December 1966, Ralph Stanley came into his own as a composer and one of the definitive voices of traditional Appalachian music. Perhaps his greatest original song, *The Darkest Hour Is Just Before Dawn*, a simple but deeply touching song of faith, was given a performance for the ages by Emmylou Harris.

The song's melody owes something to the Stanley Brothers' lovely 1949 record *The White Dove*, written by Carter. But Ralph's lyrics for *Darkest Hour* have a quietly earthy poetry all their own. In his autobiography, he recalled that the melody and some of the words came to him in a dream; he awakened at 4 a.m. and wrote it down so he wouldn't forget.[374] Stanley first recorded it on a 1971 gospel album for the tiny Jessup label, with lead vocal by Roy Lee Centers, and two future country stars in the lineup, Ricky Skaggs and Keith Whitley.[375]

Born on April 2, 1947, in Birmingham, Alabama, Emmylou spent much of her childhood in North Carolina, and began her serious musical education while attending the University of North Carolina. Her debut album in 1970 went nowhere, but while performing in the Washington, D.C., area she was hired as a vocalist by Gram Parsons, whose work with the Byrds and the Flying Burrito Brothers had forged a powerful fusion of country and rock. Just after completion of Parsons' second solo

album, *Grievous Angel*, he died of a morphine and tequila overdose in September 1973. Emmylou moved on from this tragedy to form her Angel Band, and record the album that would really launch her solo career, *Pieces of the Sky*.

Roses in the Snow was Emmylou's bluegrass album, her followup to the Grammy-winning *Blue Kentucky Girl*. Even though she'd earned six straight gold LPs, Warners was nervous about Harris doing back-to-back pure country albums, fearing that at a time when classic bluegrass was out of fashion, it made her less able to cross over to pop buyers. Indeed, she recalls that someone at the label warned that *Roses* would mean the end of her career. Instead, it became her fastest-selling release ever—"and that was supposed to be my 'kiss of death' record!"[376] From start to finish, it's a work of profound beauty. Featured throughout the album—and above all on this song—was Ricky Skaggs, a decade after he began his two-and-a-half years with Stanley starting at age fifteen. A phenomenal multi-instrumentalist as well as an outstanding singer, Skaggs (born on July 18, 1954, in Cordell, Kentucky) appeared on TV with Flatt & Scruggs at the age of seven, and after leaving Stanley and working the bluegrass circuit joined Emmylou's band in 1977. His duet vocal here (and taking the lead on the "like a shepherd out on the mountain" verse), along with the haunting loveliness of his multi-tracked work on mandolin, fiddle, and acoustic guitar, made *Darkest Hour* a singular treat. It helped provide the launching pad for Skaggs' solo career, still going strong over thirty years later.

(Also with the album's producer Brian Ahern on guitar,[377] Emory Gordy, Jr. on bass)

9 to 5 (1980)—Dolly Parton

RCA 12133

Chart debut Nov. 29, 1980 (2 weeks at #1 pop, 1 week at #1 C&W); #1 (2 weeks) in Canada[378] (*AFI-#78, C&W-#105, DMDB*)

Her outrageous flamboyance and showmanship have made her one of the best-known country music personalities ever outside the confines of Music City, but it is her indisputable gifts as a songwriter and singer who never lost sight of her roots that ensure Dolly Parton's place in music history. Born Dolly Rebecca Parton on January 19, 1946, in a cabin in Sevier Country, Tennessee, on the edge of the Smoky Mountains National Forest a few miles north of Gatlinburg, Dolly was the fourth of twelve children in a musical family (her grandfather was

---

372. Sherrill, convinced of the record's appeal, bet the singer $100 it would be a hit. "I won that one hands down." (*Billboard Book of Number One Country Hits*, p. 384.)

373. Jones, *I Lived to Tell It All*, p. 250–53.

374. *Man of Constant Sorrow: My Life and Times*, p. 381.

375. During the period (1970–1975) in which Skaggs and Whitley played with Stanley, the band recorded thirteen albums. Stanley would, in duet with Dwight Yoakam, record a new version of the song on his 1998 album *Clinch Mountain Country*.

376. Interview with Timothy White as she received the *Billboard* Century award for artistic achievement, in the magazine's December 4, 1999 issue.

377. *Roses* was one of eleven albums on which Emmylou worked with producer Ahern (from 1975–1983), to whom she was once married.

378. #5 in Austria and Belgium.

a fiddler and songwriter, and her mother and siblings also sang). Her father was a struggling tobacco farmer, and the family's living conditions were humble. The youngster's Uncle Bill Owens bought her a guitar at seven and helped get her regular appearances on a Knoxville radio show starting at ten. Dolly made her Grand Ole Opry debut in 1959, and her first record a year later. After several more unsuccessful records for small labels and becoming the first in her family to graduate from high school, she was signed to Monument Records by Fred Foster. A "bubbling under" pop single in 1965 was followed by *Put It Off Until Tomorrow*, a song written by Dolly and Bill Owens that became a Top Ten 1966 C&W hit for Bill Phillips. Dolly hit the country chart herself early the following year with *Dumb Blonde*, and after joining Porter Wagoner's syndicated TV series and switching to RCA she became a regular visitor to the top echelon of the C&W charts, both on her own and in duets with Wagoner. *Joshua* in early 1971 became her first country #1. Her pleasingly piercing high mountain-soprano voice, original songs of rural hard times softened by love (most notably *Coat of Many Colors*), warm Southern humor, and giant blonde wigs were all pure country.

Having already crossed over to the pop market with hits like *Here You Come Again* (1977) and with her innocently sexy beauty, voluptuous figure, and personal

Dolly Parton, PhotoFest.

appeal well established through TV appearances, the movies were the logical next step, and *9 to 5* was a perfect entree, a wickedly funny tale of three secretaries (Dolly, Jane Fonda, and Lily Tomlin) who band together against a piggish boss. For the title song, Dolly fashioned a feisty, empathetic ode to everyday working folks struggling to get by; as recalled in her autobiography, she wrote it on the set while shooting the film. "I remember writing the song on the back of my script and using my fingernails to create a rhythm as I sang it."[379] On record it's given an enormously catchy production by Gregg Perry (with pianist Larry Knechtel of *Bridge Over Troubled Water* fame setting the pace). The movie was a hit,[380] and the song became her second million-seller and a Grammy winner. Over two decades later Dolly wrote the score for a (relatively unsuccessful) Broadway musical built around the film and the song.

Being With You (1981)—Smokey Robinson
Tamla 54321
Chart debut Feb. 14, 1981 (5 weeks at #1 on R&B chart, 3 weeks at #2 on *Billboard* pop chart, reached #1 in *Record World*); #1 (2 weeks) in England, #3 in Canada[381] (*VIL*)

After slowly building momentum during the first six years of his post-Miracles solo career, Smokey Robinson achieved full flight with his 1979 Top Five smash *Cruisin'*, and Kim Carnes' 1980 Top Ten hit cover version of his classic Miracles composition *More Love*. Smokey proceeded to soar to the highest point of his "second act" with the achingly gorgeous ballad *Being With You*, a classic demonstrating that, as a crafter of unforgettable melodies, concisely poetic lyrics, and possessor of a glorious falsetto, very few rock-era artists can do a love song like Smokey Robinson. He actually offered *Being With You* to Carnes, but she realized immediately that the tune was far better suited to his elegantly sexy tenor than her husky alto, fortunately making possible one of his most indelible performances. It's a song that conveys utter romantic devotion with his trademark straight-to-the heart conviction. The mature Robinson, writes Gerri Hirshey, "can still pull a note like taffy and keep it sweet."[382]

---

379. Parton, *My Life and Other Unfinished Business*, p. 232–33. Every time she began working on the song, the women on the set gathered to listen. "Before long, I had created a whole section of backup singers made up of all the working women around me. Because of what the song had to say, I thought that was especially appropriate."

380. It premiered in Nashville on December 5, 1980, after the title song was already on the charts, and went nationwide two weeks later. Its $103 million box office made it the second biggest hit of 1980. In 1982, *9 to 5* became a short-lived TV series, with Dolly's sister Rachel Dennison.

381. #1 (4 weeks) in New Zealand, #2 in France.

382. *Nowhere to Run*, p. 130.

1999 (1983)—Prince
Warner 29896

Chart debut Oct. 30, 1982 (originally peaked at #44, re-
entered chart on June 4, 1983 and reached #12; #4
R&B); #8 in Canada, #25 in England (*GHF-#82,
RIA-#95, R&B-#71, RS-#215, DM-#227, VIL, ACC*)

Seventeen years before the Millennium and the darkness it represented to some, Prince declared that the only
response was to dance the night away, and the world
responded. "Two thousand, zero, zero, party over, out
of time / So tonight I'm gonna party like it's 1999." The
multi-instrumentalist singer-songwriter Prince Rogers
Nelson had grabbed attention with his 1978 album and
the following year's hit single *I Wanna Be Your Lover*,
and *1999* proved that his early promise was being fulfilled with his first unquestioned classic. After the song
stalled out short of the Top 40, his followup *Little Red
Corvette* became a smash, and renewed interest in the artist led *1999* to achieve its hit destiny a few months later.

During this period, Prince would work at the studio all
day and night, often without food. Much of the album was
finished, but his managers suggested it needed something
more, a title track with a main theme. Miffed at first, he
began writing a song about a nuclear "judgment day" with
a synthesizer line that (remarks biographer Ronin Ro)
some felt "unconsciously mimicked" the Mamas and the
Papas' *Monday, Monday*.[383] As detailed by Brian Morton
(*A Thief In the Temple*), he originally wrote the song's
verse in three-part harmony, but decided to split the vocal; the combined backing lines of Jill Jones, Dez Dick-

Prince, PhotoFest.

383. *Prince: Inside the Music and the Masks*, p. 63–64.

erson, and Lisa Coleman were promoted in the final mix.
Morton writes that this approach helped place the song's
"apocalyptic message in a familiar rock context." Calling it "one of the hottest dance tracks ever," Dave Marsh
notes: "Prince's vocal, a melding of whispers, squeals,
ejaculations, and groaning is buoyed on synth, relentless
bass drum, and chicken-scratch rhythm guitar, accented by
an occasional cymbal splash."[384] A reissue hit the charts a
year apart in early 1999 and upon the turn of the century.

If I Had a Rocket Launcher (1985)—Bruce Cockburn
Gold Mountain single 82013

Chart debut Feb. 9, 1985 (#88 peak); from the album
Stealing Fire (chart debut Aug. 25, 1984, #74 peak,
31 weeks) (*Folk-#129*)

In early 1983, Canadian folk singer-songwriter Bruce
Cockburn spent three weeks visiting a camp in southern
Mexico for refugees fleeing violence and government-
sponsored death squads in Guatemala. Part of a group
invited by the world hunger organization OXFAM,
Cockburn was already sensitized to the awful violence
in Central America that had begun with a right-wing
insurgency following the overthrow of the Somoza dic-
tatorship in Nicaragua in 1979, having read a report by
the Catholic human rights organization Pax Christi and
the poetry of Ernesto Cardenal. But he was shocked by
what he witnessed in the refugee camp, including attacks
on the refugees with strafing by Guatemalan helicopters.
Some refugees were kidnapped and murdered.[385] Even
though a born-again Christian pacifist, Cockburn was
driven by boiling fury over what he'd seen to write *If
I Had a Rocket Launcher*, perhaps the angriest social
protest song to hit the American pop chart since *Eve of
Destruction* (1965) and *Ohio* (1970). The fact that it was
released at a time when the Reagan administration was
still actively supporting some of the perpetrators of that
violence made its success all the more remarkable.

Born on May 27, 1945, in Ottawa, Ontario, Cockburn
began as a folk singer with his debut album in 1971,[386]
and after nearly a decade of building a Canadian audience, hit the U.S. Top 40 with *Wondering Where the
Lions Are* in 1980. Still, he was basically a cult artist
when his 1984 album *Stealing Fire* spread the word; he
has remained a prolific artist with a fervent core audience
ever since. *Rocket Launcher*, whose music video received MTV airplay, is (in the words of Brian Mansfield)

384. Marsh, *The Heart of Rock & Soul*, p. 159.

385. The April 9, 1983 *Billboard* reported on Cockburn's return from
Central America, after he generated Canadian headlines for declaring that
acceptance of U.S. policy in Guatemala "makes us participants in virtual
genocide."

386. He won the first of at least six Juno awards in 1971 as Canada's
Folk Singer of the Year.

"one of the most moving works of politically motivated rock ever created . . . shattering."[387] Cockburn's gifts as a guitarist, and his incorporation of world-beat rhythms, give the song a propulsive musical urgency accentuating the deep anger of the lyrics.

The Greatest Love of All (1986)—Whitney Houston
(music by Michael Masser, lyrics by Linda Creed)
Arista 9466
Chart debut March 29, 1986 (3 weeks at #1 on pop chart, #3 R&B); #1 (1 week) in Australia, #1 (1 week) in Canada, #8 in England;[388] from the album *Whitney Houston* (chart debut March 30, 1985, 14 weeks at #1)

The Greatest Love of All was originally the big ballad from the Muhammad Ali biopic *The Greatest*, starring none other than Ali himself, a #24 pop hit in 1977 for George Benson. Whitney Houston included it as a track on her blockbuster debut album in 1985, and made it the B side of the R&B hit *Thinking About You* later that year (Arista 9412). But when the song began generating heavy requests and radio airplay, the label released it as her fourth solo pop single, and was rewarded with the album's third straight chart-topper.

The daughter of soul/gospel singer Cissy Houston (who provided backing vocals for many soul and pop artists including Aretha Franklin and Dionne Warwick,[389] recorded as leader of the Sweet Inspirations, and made solo recordings during the 1970s including the first widely-heard version of *Midnight Train to Georgia*), Whitney Houston was born in Newark, New Jersey, on August 9, 1963. Blessed with a remarkable voice and willowy beauty to match (she modeled for teen and fashion magazines in the early 1980s), Whitney sang at the New Hope Baptist Church in Newark (where her mother was choir director) and in New York nightclubs. Signed by Clive Davis for his Arista label,[390] her debut album was a model of meticulously produced urban and adult pop, and it reached a massive audience.[391] After its leadoff single *You Give Good Love* reached #3 on the pop chart,

the smooth ballad *Saving All My Love for You* and the bouncy *How Will I Know* went to #1. *The Greatest Love of All* became her biggest hit yet, helping the album achieve total sales of more than 13 million copies—one of only about forty albums ever to achieve that level.

Michael Masser, producer and composer of *Greatest Love* (and also *Saving All My Love*), was best known for his hits with Diana Ross, including *Touch Me in the Morning*; lyricist Linda Creed co-wrote a string of hits for the Stylistics. It's an ode to self-discovery, attaining the realization of childhood dreams, and self-love (appropriate for the charmingly egotistical Ali), rooted in the idea of children learning to take pride in themselves. Whitney's mighty voice, with full orchestral accompaniment, makes it soaring and inspirational.[392] When she hits the big finish—"find your strength in love"—it's corny, but you can't help but believe.

Whitney Houston, PhotoFest.

---

387. *MusicHound Folk: The Essential Album Guide*, p. 165.

388. #1 in Brazil.

389. Cissy often took Whitney to the recording sessions; the youngster knew Aretha as "Auntie Ree," and they would record a duet together in 1989. Dionne, the daughter of Cissy's cousin, sang with her in the family gospel group the Drinkard Singers before her pop career.

390. Elektra had already offered to sign Whitney, but she went with Arista primarily because industry legend Davis had promised to personally supervise every detail of the debut album. The fact that Aretha and Dionne had experienced career revivals in association with Davis also weighed in his favor. (Jeffrey Bowman, *Diva*, p. 86–87.)

391. She signed with Arista in April 1983; Davis and the four producers he selected (handling three tracks each) took their time in selecting the songs and perfecting each number, and Arista spent several months vigorously promoting Whitney before any music from the album had been released.

392. Whitney had been performing the song since the early 1980s as part of her mother's nightclub act. Live, she had used it to showcase her gospel-trained vocal power, range, and soulfulness, but Davis instructed Masser to have her tone it down, smoother and with less melisma (Bowman, p. 104–5). In his memoir, *The Soundtrack of My Life* (p. 309), Davis recalls that upon seeing her perform for the first time, "I could not believe that a teenager could bring such overwhelming passion to *The Greatest Love of All*. I sat there awestruck."

The One I Love (1987)—R.E.M.

I.R.S. 53171

Chart debut Sept. 19, 1987 (#9 peak);[393] #51 in U.K.; from the album *Document* (#10 peak) (*PW, AHR, 1001, VIL, ACC*)

After five years of steadily building a fan base and critical admiration since their 1982 debut, the alternative rock group from Athens, Georgia, exploded into the top reaches of the pop chart with *The One I Love*. It's an intense, driving rock ballad that takes a decidedly dark look at love. While singing, "this one goes out to the one I love, this one goes out to the one I left behind," Michael Stipe then purports to view his significant other as nothing more than "a simple prop to occupy my time."

The band was amused to find fans failing to catch the bitterness seething beneath the song's surface. "It was strange to see couples mooning into each other's eyes when we were playing this spiteful number," remarked bass player Mike Mills. Stipe, said Mills, "really enjoyed the fact that it sounded like a sappy love song, but it was anything but." In fact, notes Tony Fletcher, "it was

R.E.M., PhotoFest.

a song of betrayal. 'The one I left behind was someone who had been rejected, cast off . . . If love had ever been expressed, it had never been meant. Final proof of deception came in the third verse . . . The singer had moved on to the next object, evidently with no more intention of longevity [than] with the previous one." Although Stipe claimed the lyric was so brutal that he was reluctant to record it,[394] "the sheer emotion of the performance ensured that it would always be a key track."[395]

It's the sound of *The One I Love* that makes it remarkable: the feverish, amped-up electric guitar-bass-drum arrangement, and Stipe's intermittent, stretched-out cries of "fire!"—the word itself carrying no particular meaning here, but its phonetic sound, and the emotion behind the way it is sung, conveying quite a bit. Paul Williams, including the record in *Rock & Roll: The 100 Best Singles*, admits that the "lyrics give me the creeps," but suggests that underneath the surface, the singer is expressing a form of self-hatred and "is raging at God (or himself) regarding his own inability to love." It "still feels like a love song," if a twisted one, and somehow manages to express a tremendous sense of longing.[396]

Have I Told You Lately (1989)—Van Morrison

Album cut, chart debut Sept. 9, 1989 (#12 on adult contemporary chart)

From the Mercury album *Avalon Sunset* (chart debut July 1, 1989)

Lyrically, it couldn't be more simple and direct; melodically, it's ravishingly beautiful. Add a fervent Van Morrison vocal and a shimmering piano and orchestral arrangement, and you have one of the most swooningly—and deeply felt—romantic love songs of recent decades.[397] The album title *Avalon Sunset* drew upon Celtic mythology, long a topic of keen personal interest. Like many songs by the Irish Catholic (but theologically flexible) Morrison,[398] it can be taken either as a statement from man to woman, or as a hymn to God.[399] Beyond his spiritual explorations, Morrison during the 1980s had come to believe more deeply in the power of music as a healing force (citing to a Dublin journalist the effect of different keys on people who were ill),[400] and it would

---

393. Reached #2 on Album Rock chart.

394. The song "was a little harsh," admitted Stipe. "I wanted to write a song with the word 'love' in it, because I hadn't done that before." (March 5, 1992, *Rolling Stone*)

395. *Remarks Remade: The Story of R.E.M.*, p. 151–52.

396. Williams, *The Best 100 Singles*, p. 227–29.

397. The title phrase had of course been used before: Scott Wiseman's *Have I Told You Lately That I Love You* was a 1946 country music smash for several artists, including Gene Autry.

398. Earlier in the 1980s, his spiritual exploration had included an interest in Scientology.

399. Much of *Avalon Sunset* is directly spiritual in nature, opening with *Whenever God Shines His Light* and *Contacting My Angel*.

400. Turner, *Too Late to Stop Now*, p. 149–50.

be difficult to find a song more healing than this one. Rick Clark, citing the album's "prayerful" quality, remarks that its rich orchestration "adds a quiet, dignified elegance and atmospheric unity not unlike the strings on Marvin Gaye's transcendent *What's Going On*."[401] Rod Stewart made *Have I Told You Lately* a #5 smash in 1993. Morrison's 1995 version teaming with Ireland's The Chieftains won the Grammy for Best Pop Collaboration with Vocals, topping the favored *One Sweet Day* by Mariah Carey and Boyz II Men. "Fill my heart with gladness, take away my sadness / Ease my troubles, that's what you do . . ."

Black Velvet (1990)—Alannah Myles (written by Christopher Ward & David Tyson)
Atlantic 88742
Chart debut Jan. 6, 1990 (2 weeks at #1); reached #2 in England[402]

There have been many musical tributes to Elvis Presley since his death in 1977, and all stand in the shadow of *Black Velvet*. The song began when Christopher Ward, as the first VJ for Toronto's music video channel MuchMusic, was sent to Memphis in 1987 to cover the tenth anniversary of the sad day, and (as related in *The Billboard Book of Number One Hits*) "I came to understand what the incredible passion was that these people had for this man, and what he really represented to them." He started to think about what it must have been like for Elvis to grow up in the South. A key line in the song—"a new religion that will bring you to your knees"—refers to the way southern fundamentalist preachers would exhort members of the congregation. "I realized in a flash that this was the same way Elvis exhorted his fans—that there was a real parallel between that power of religion and the power that he possessed in bringing rock and roll to the people."[403]

Alannah Myles, born on December 25, 1955, in Toronto and raised in Buckhorn, Ontario, began performing in Toronto coffeehouses as a teenager, met Ward when he was a performer, went on tour as his band's opening act, and they lived together for eight years. Her debut album was a Canadian smash before this single hit the U.S. She recorded *Black Velvet* on a 99-degree day in Toronto, in a basement studio with no air conditioning; she had to strip down to a swimsuit. Her powerful vocal (which becomes spine-tingling by the final verses) matches the richly atmospheric mood of the song; sultry, steamy as a summer day in Memphis, settling into a slow, intoxicating blues-rock groove. Alannah would have just one subsequent hit (*Love Is*),[404] but *Black Velvet* endures.

Jeremy (1992)—Pearl Jam
Released briefly as 45 rpm single on Epic/Associated 74745 in late 1991 (later charted Dec. 11, 1993, #70)
From the album *Ten* (chart debut Jan. 4, 1992, 4 weeks at #2, 250 charted weeks);[405] made Album Rock chart (debut Aug. 15, 1992, reached #5); issued as CD single on Epic 77935 (debut Aug. 12, 1995, #79 peak) (*NPR-300, RHF, DM, ACC*)

Jeremy is an anguished hard-rock ballad based on a real-life tragedy. On January 8, 1991, Jeremy Wade Delle, a troubled student at Richardson High School in the Dallas suburbs, was sent to the administrative office for a late-admittance pass, returned to his classroom with a .357 Magnum and killed himself. Eddie Vedder, leader of the emerging Seattle rock group Pearl Jam, was stunned by the accounts of the event. "I wrote the song that night, I think," he recalled. "I wonder why he did it. Richardson sounded to me like a decent suburb, middle- if not upper-class." Rather than intrude by getting into the details of the boy's life, Vedder drew upon his own experiences in creating one of the decade's most powerful songs.

Pearl Jam was formed out of the remains of another Seattle hard-rock group, Mother Love Bone, after that group's vocalist Andrew Wood died of a drug overdose. Guitarist Stone Gossard and bassist Jeff Ament launched a new band, recruiting Eddie Vedder (born December 23, 1964) as lead singer, Mike McCready on lead guitar, and Dave Krusen on drums. Pearl Jam recorded its debut album *Ten* in early 1991, and the album was released at the end of August; the breakthrough success of the Seattle grunge-rock group Nirvana (whose album *Nevermind* hit the charts in October 1991) helped open the doors for Pearl Jam to soar up the charts in early 1992, although the two groups were hardly friendly.[406] The album went on to sell more than 12 million copies, and in subsequent years, through personnel changes, legal battles, and personal travails, Pearl Jam has held strong as one of the most influential rock groups of the modern era.

Bristling with anger and hard-pounding, muscular energy, Pearl Jam were unabashed arena rockers, but possessing a combination of passion and integrity that

---

401. *All Music Guide to Rock* (1997 ed.), p. 631. Morrison self-produced the album; the string arrangements were by Fiachra Trench, with Gavin Wright as string section leader.

402. #1 in Norway & Switzerland, #2 in Austria & Belgium, #3 in France, Germany, Holland, & Sweden.

403. Bronson, p. 752.

404. *Love Is* had been her debut Canadian hit in 1989, but was her U.S. followup to *Velvet*.

405. The album had spent months on *Billboard*'s "Heatseekers" chart (for new acts) before finally cracking the main Top 200 in January 1992.

406. Both bands got their start with the Seattle indie label Sub Pop; both jumped ship to sign lucrative deals with corporate majors, while retaining their own fiercely independent credibility. Kurt Cobain "had it in for Pearl Jam big time," seeing them as corporate bandwagon-jumpers on the Seattle scene, although even he privately acknowledged the group's musical power. (Neely, *Five Against One*, p. 122–24.)

elevated them above bands that could arouse crowds without engaging their minds.

Vedder, wrote Johnny Black in *Blender*, drew on his recollection of junior high in San Diego, where a classmate once brought a gun to school and started firing. "I remember being in the halls and hearing it," said Vedder. "I had had altercations with this kid in the past . . . So [the song] is a bit about this kid named Jeremy, and also a bit about a kid named Brian who I knew."[407] When Vedder showed his lyrics to Jeff Ament, the bassist already had a piece of music that he had written on acoustic guitar with the intent of playing it on a new Hamer 12-string bass, and used this for *Jeremy*. The band taped a demo of the song, and developed it further in March at Seattle's London Bridge Studios. Arment: "This was big-time production, for us." In addition to Vedder's agonized vocal, McCready's wailing guitar soloing was another highlight of the piece. It wasn't one of the band's most inventive tracks musically, suggests biographer Kim Neely, "but it crackled with electricity once outfitted with haunting cello, new background vocals, and, especially, Eddie's lyrics."[408]

Although as a single *Jeremy* was not a hit, it was a centerpiece of their live shows, and the song's reputation was assured by the intense music video shot by Mark Pellington in London and Germany in June 1992 (several months after a much different, grungier video for the song by Chris Cuffaro, available only as a bootleg).[409] A year later, it won four MTV Video Music Awards, including Video of the Year. In 1995 MTV ranked it as the #8 top video ever. "The message of the video was a warning of what happened at Columbine," declared Ament. "Parents and teachers don't always pay attention to what's going on." In 2011 director Cameron Crowe—who had featured the group (while in the midst of recording the debut album) in his 1992 film *Singles*—paid tribute with an acclaimed documentary on the anniversary of *Ten*, *Pearl Jam Twenty*, demonstrating the unbreakable bond the band still has with its audience.[410]

---

407. The kid "had eyes like you wouldn't believe. They were just soulless and black, like a shark's." (Neely, *Five Against One*, p. 73.)

408. *Five Against One*, p. 73–74. "Whether he was expressing empathy for the disenchanted or mourning the battered psyche of an abused or neglected child, Eddie was clearly a writer who internalized everything he saw." Also, within months of launching the band's first major tour, Vedder had morphed from shy and withdrawn to a "whirling dervish with veins standing out on his forehead" on stage, his intensity frightening even his bandmates (Neely, p. 105).

409. *Alive* and *Even Flow* had been the album's first two singles in 1991/early 1992; neither was a hit, but such cult favorites that they later spent a record-demolishing 107 combined weeks "bubbling under" *Billboard*'s Hot 100.

410. That artist/audience bond is reflected in the fact that Pearl Jam in 2000 released the music from a staggering seventy-two different live shows—every concert from their world tour—at bargain prices, with excellent sound quality, and fourteen of those shows (plus three more from 2003) made the *Billboard* album chart.

Round Here (1994)—Counting Crows

Album cut, debuted on June 18, 1994 (reached #31 in radio airplay)[411]

From the DGC album *August and Everything After* (chart debut Jan. 1, 1994, reached #4, 93 weeks)

"The most important thing about this band is heart," declared Counting Crows' singer and primary songwriter Adam Duritz.[412] "That's where the songs come from: that's what I'd most want people to understand. What sounds good or looks good, that's nothing. The only worthwhile thing in art is seeing someone else's heart." Duritz's heart is on his sleeve in *Round Here*, the somber, deeply reflective acoustic ballad that became the second hit from the San Francisco–based group's debut album, its leadoff track, and perhaps its finest song.[413]

"With their angst-filled hybrid" of Van Morrison, the Band, and R.E.M., writes Stephen Thomas Erlewine, Counting Crows became an overnight sensation in 1994. Formed in San Francisco in 1991, Duritz, guitarist David Bryson, pianist Charlie Gillingham, bassist Matt Malley, and drummer Steve Bowman had the great benefit of the peerless roots-music guru T-Bone Burnett as producer for their debut album. *August and Everything After* sold over seven million copies and earned rock-critic accolades.[414] The despair underlying the song's story might become overwhelming if not for the glimmer of hope offered by the protagonist's intense powers of observation, empathy for the lost souls he meets, and apparent desire to survive.[415] "Catch me if I'm falling . . ."

I'm the Only One (1994)—Melissa Etheridge

Island 854068

Chart debut Aug. 6, 1994 (#6 peak); from the album *Yes I Am* (reached #15, 138 weeks, sold six million copies)[416]

The full-throated, guitar-driven roots rock of Melissa Etheridge culminated several years of steadily growing success by reaching its widest audience of all with her fourth album *Yes I Am*, and with the powerfully bluesy rock ballad *I'm the Only One*, her biggest single to date. Born on May 29, 1961, in the prison town of Leavenworth, Kansas, she went from four years of grinding away playing in southern California bars to major-label

---

411. #7 on Modern Rock chart, #11 Album Rock.

412. For this song, Duritz wrote the words to music composed by Dave Janusko, Dan Jewett, Chris Roldan & guitarist David Bryson.

413. *Mr. Jones*, the massively popular track from the debut album that introduced most listeners to the Crows, of course stands as their trademark song.

414. The Crows' second album *Recovering the Satellites* (1996) hit #1, and they have remained a top-level band in later years.

415. Edna Gundersen (November 16, 1999, *USA Today*) said of Duritz: "I'll take his bone-deep desolation over cheery veneer any day."

416. Etheridge's first eleven albums all reached the Top 25 in *Billboard*, including seven million-sellers.

stardom. Etheridge struck an immediate chord with her 1988 debut album, with vocals reminiscent of Janis Joplin and a knack for writing songs that played to her strengths as a passionate, charismatic live performer. Coming out as a lesbian didn't slow her ascent a bit.[417] *I'm the Only One*, like much of her best work, is a bold declaration of desire (in this case for her then-girlfriend Julie Cypher, with whom she would have two children), making it clear that nothing will stand in her way. It was one of her two Grammy nominees for 1994's top rock song (the other being *Come to My Window*); she didn't really mind losing the award to one of her heroes, Bruce Springsteen, and his AIDS-themed ballad *Streets of Philadelphia*. Melissa—an Oscar winner with her theme for *An Inconvenient Truth* (2004)—has rocked that much harder ever since beating breast cancer in 2005, symbolized by her inspirational anthem *I Run for Life*.

(Album personnel: Waddy Wachtel on electric guitar, Scott Thurston on keyboards, Pino Palladino on bass, Mauricio Fritz Lewak on drums)

Not Dark Yet (1997)—Bob Dylan

From the Columbia album *Time Out of Mind* (chart debut Oct. 18, 1997, reached #10)

At long last, the Grammy Awards bestowed its ultimate honor, Album of the Year, on Bob Dylan for *Time Out of Mind* (also the winner of two other Grammies, and the *Village Voice* critics' choice as best album). It was his first album of original material in seven years, and what a thrill it was to hear that at age fifty-six, the great master once again crafted a classic. *Not Dark Yet* is a haunting reflection on mortality that ranks with the finest work of his unparalleled career.

Like some other songs on the album, the circumstances of *Not Dark Yet* seem pre-twentieth century: there's no air conditioning; the time of day is measured by the sun. In part this reflects Dylan's career-long fascination with the American past, and his love for 1920s and 1930s blues, folk, and country, in effect placing himself in the shoes of his long-ago heroes. The protagonist is feeling a bone-deep weariness (imagining that his soul has turned to steel, with every nerve in his body vacant and numb) and a sense that the end is near, a feeling perhaps triggered by a woman who has left him. "Don't even hear the murmur of a prayer / It's not dark yet, but it's getting there."

Christopher Ricks sees the song as a modern recasting of John Keats' *Ode to a Nightingale*.[418] Alex Ross notes that "all the flourishes of his songwriting art come

together: slow, stately chords, swinging like a pendulum between major and minor; creative tweakings of the past, prickly aphorisms, and glints of biblical revelation . . . Like Skip James, the cracked genius among Delta blues singers, Dylan gives a circular form a dire sense of direction."[419]

Richard Harrington (*Washington Post*) called it "one of the best Dylan songs in decades; [it is] sad and sobering yet somehow uplifting. Built on a soft-spun martial cadence (the muffled drums evoke a funeral cortege), churchy organ and shimmering guitar harmonies, the song dissects the weight of experience and the burden of age with scalpel-sharp lyricism." Harrington notes that it is sometimes despairing in tone, but conveys that the narrator is "coming to terms with the inevitable with uncommon grace."

(Album produced by Daniel Lanois; also on guitar, mando-guitar. Personnel: Bucky Baxter on acoustic guitar & pedal steel, Robert Britt on guitar, Cindy Cashdollar on slide guitar, Tony Garnier on bass, Auggie Meyers on keyboards, Jim Keltner & Brian Blade on drums)

Crazy in Alabama (1998)—Kate Campbell (written by Kate Campbell & Kenya Slaughter Walker)

From the Compass Records CD *Visions of Plenty* (released on April 21, 1998);[420] new version on Compadre Records CD *The Portable Kate Campbell* (Aug. 2004)

Combining the observational powers of a short story essayist with a feeling for her native South and a deeply humanitarian outlook driven by religious faith, Kate Campbell has been a priceless if too often overlooked presence on the Americana/alt-country music scene since her first album in 1994. The daughter of a Baptist preacher from Sledge, Mississippi (population around 500 people, located near the northwest corner of the state, about fifty miles south of Memphis, and best known as the home of country star Charley Pride), Kate was born on October 31, 1961, in New Orleans, and spent much of her childhood in Sledge. After receiving a Masters degree in Southern history, she moved to Nashville to teach college history, and began writing songs. Getting her musical start as a staff writer at FAME (Florence Alabama Music Enterprises) in Muscle Shoals, she made a positive impression with her debut album *Songs from the Levee*. It was her second and third releases, *Moonpie Dreams* (1997) and *Visions of Plenty* a year later, that began generating comparisons through her bluesy-folk flavorings to Emmylou Harris and Lucinda Williams, and (given Kate's down-

---

417. *Yes I Am* was co-produced by Etheridge with Hugh Padgham, who went from engineer to superstar producer for artists including The Police, Genesis, Phil Collins, and Sting.
418. *Dylan's Visions of Sin*, p. 361–69.

419. May 10, 1999, *New Yorker*.
420. *Visions of Plenty* was nominated for folk album of the year by the Nashville Music Awards.

to-the-bone understanding of regional culture and faith) Southern gothic novelist Flannery O'Connor.

Many of Kate's songs deal with the civil rights movement, which she observed as a fascinated white child in a majority-black area that was a focal point of activism, and perhaps the most compelling is *Crazy in Alabama*. The narrative ballad burns with memories of witnessing a moment in history, and the eyes-of-a-child perspective has an enormously affecting quality reminiscent of *To Kill a Mockingbird*. Using a mysterious account of the neighbor's maid gone "crazier than hell" as a framing device, she launches into her tale, mingling the day-to-day issues of growing up (recalling the corner Dairy Dip's soft ice cream) with the drama of watching "the train of change" coming to her hometown. The original recording features harmony vocals by Emmylou Harris on the chorus; the 2004 remake is gorgeous in its own way, with Steve Conn's reflective piano adding graceful touches. This is musical storytelling at its best, a gently delivered moral parable.

Wide Open Spaces (1998)—Dixie Chicks (written by Susan Gibson)
Monument 79003
Chart debut Aug. 22, 1998 (#1 for 4 weeks C&W, #41 pop); from the album *Wide Open Spaces* (debut Feb. 14, 1998, reached #4, 134 weeks) (*RIA, C&W-#101, HBN-#214*)

Sisters Martie Seidel (fiddle and mandolin) and Emily Erwin (banjo and dobro) started their first bluegrass band as youngsters in their native Dallas in 1984. They formed the Chicks five years later, but after three well-liked but low-selling albums, a reconstituted Chicks—with vivacious new lead singer Natalie Maines (daughter of long-time stellar Nashville session musician Lloyd Maines) out front—suddenly became a crossover phenomenon in 1998. When Sony Nashville signed the trio, it revived the old Monument label, which had been moribund many years after Roy Orbison's glory days in the 1960s.[421] *Wide Open Spaces* exploded out of the gate, debuting on the pop chart at #17—the highest ranking for any country group in seven years—and just kept building from there, en route to selling a stunning 12 million copies, the fifth top-selling country album of all time.[422] Just when country music record sales had flattened out after the high-flying early-to-mid-1990s, the Chicks soared in to the rescue, bringing a whole new young, predominantly female audience (just as Taylor Swift would later do).

The title song of the gals' hello-to-the-world album is an inspirational number about a young woman setting out to find her place in the world.[423] With this album, the Chicks, writes Alanna Nash, created "the most organic amalgam of folk, country, pop, rock, and blues since Willie Nelson's breakthrough records of the '70s."[424]

(Produced by Paul Worley & Blake Chancey. Mark Casstevens on acoustic guitar, Lloyd Maines on steel guitar, George Marinelli on electric guitar, Bobby Charles Jr. & Joe Chemay on bass, Matt Rollings on keyboards, Greg Morrow on drums)

You'll Never Leave Harlan Alive (2001)—Patty Loveless (written by Darrell Scott)
From the Epic album *Mountain Soul* (chart debut July 14, 2001, reached #159 pop, #19 C&W, 81 weeks)

The career of Patty Loveless during its first fifteen years traveled a classic path: the Pikeville, Kentucky, native (born January 4, 1957) served her apprenticeship in Nashville (singing for three years with the Wilburn Brothers and writing songs for their publishing company); signed with MCA and began attracting attention with minor hits from 1985–1987; cracked the big time with the 1988 album *Honky Tonk Angel*, which generated five hit singles; scored twenty Top Ten country singles over the next decade including three chart-toppers; then began to lose some altitude (commercially, at least) by the end of the 1990s. What happened next departed delightfully from the traditional narrative: instead of slowly fading from center stage, she earned the biggest creative triumph of her career to date by returning to her Kentucky roots with her first-ever bluegrass album, featuring a song ensuring her place in contemporary music history, *You'll Never Leave Harlan Alive*.

Loveless had long been associated with the neo-traditionalist realm of country music, while not averse to mixing in some pop and rock touches like almost everyone in the 1990s Nashville mainstream. *Honky Tonk Angel* had included a few bluegrass elements, and she'd appeared on albums by Ricky Skaggs and Ralph Stanley, but *Mountain Soul* was her first headlong plunge into 100 percent acoustic music rooted in the Appalachian tradition. Pikeville, where she'd lived until age eleven until the family moved to Louisville, is a small mining town in southeastern Kentucky; bluegrass music is part of the local DNA. Throughout her childhood she'd heard her parents' Bill Monroe, Stanley Brothers, and Flatt & Scruggs records. So recording *Mountain Soul* (produced by her husband, Emory Gordy, Jr.) felt like going back

---

421. The *Spaces* album was the very first release since 1983 on the reactivated label, given a tremendous promotional campaign that was swiftly rewarded (January 17, 1998 *Billboard*, p. 15).
422. Garth Brooks has three albums that have sold over 14 million each in the U.S., and Shania Twain's *Come on Over* sold 20 million.

423. *Spaces* beat out Brooks and Twain to become the first of four consecutive Chicks studio releases to earn the Grammy for best country album.
424. September 10, 1999, *Entertainment Weekly*, p. 149.

home.[425] Indeed, one of its songs is a piece she had written at age fourteen, *Sounds of Loneliness*, so drenched in timeless mountain-style isolation that it also appeared on the soundtrack of *Songcatcher* (which is set in the pre-1920 Appalachians).

The song that helped ensure the album's classic status was written by another Kentucky native. Darrell Scott, born August 6, 1959, in London, Kentucky, is a singer/songwriter/multi-instrumentalist who recorded his first album in 1997, wrote the Dixie Chicks' Top Ten pop hit *Long Time Gone*, and has collaborated with a host of artists including Steve Earle and Emmylou Harris. *You'll Never Leave Harlan Alive* was on his 1997 album *Aloha from Nashville*; although raised in the Detroit area, Kentucky was never too far from his mind. His original version was powerful and moving; Patty took it to yet another level. The fact that her father had spent years as a miner, quitting when the coal dust caused him to contract black lung disease,[426] made its tale—of men trapped in a grim and hazardous life handed down from one generation to the next with little hope for escape—deeply personal. With its haunting a cappella introduction, banjo and dobro by Scott himself, the intense narrative set in "the deep dark hills of eastern Kentucky," the "place where I traced my bloodline," and her emotionally committed vocal, this is powerful stuff. Bill Friskics-Warren notes "the undeniably Appalachian quality" of her alto, a voice "as indelible" as fellow Pikeville native Loretta Lynn (a distant cousin).[427] Loveless told Phyllis Stark how important the album was to her: "This is a form of music that has been in my heart and blood and that I have carried with me all these years. It was something that was itching to come out."[428] By the conclusion—as the sun goes down with the narrator's somber realization that "you spend your life digging coal from the bottom of your grave / And you'll never leave Harlan alive"—the impact reverberates long after it fades to silence.[429]

(Other personnel: Jeff White on guitar, Emory Gordy, Jr., on bass, Tim Hensley on mandolin, Butch Lee on tremolo mandolin, Deanie Richardson on fiddle, Gene Wooten on dobro, Carmella Ramsey on backing vocals)

Where Were You When the World Stopped Turning (2001)—Alan Jackson

Hot 100 chart debut Nov. 24, 2001 (5 weeks at #1 on C&W chart, #28 pop);

from the Arista Nashville album *Drive* (sold 4 million copies)[430] (*C&W-#107, 2000s-#62*)

Just days after the shock of September 11, 2001, country music's most respected singer-songwriter of its past decade, Alan Jackson, responded with a song that reflected his core values of common-man populism and empathy. When he first publicly performed *Where Were You When the World Stopped Turning* at the Country Music Association (CMA) awards show in early November, the response was overwhelming. He recorded it in the studio days later, and as the piece generated a similar immediate reaction on country radio, the new album from which it came debuted at #1 on the pop chart and sold nearly a half million copies in its first week. In 2002 Jackson would sweep the CMA Awards, with male vocalist and entertainer of the year, *Drive* for best album, and *Where Were You* as single and song of the year.

Born on October 17, 1958, in Newman, Georgia, Jackson didn't start singing publicly until after high school, and wrote his first song at age twenty-three. He and his wife took the plunge of selling their home and moving to Nashville in 1985 so that he could try to make it in the industry, working part-time jobs and writing songs for Glen Campbell's publishing company while performing in local clubs. He was the first artist signed by Tim DuBois for Arista Records' Nashville office; in a short time the label was a powerful force in country music, with Brooks & Dunn, Diamond Rio, and Pam Tillis among others. He had his first charted single in 1989, his debut album early the following year, and by 1991 had become one of the most reliable hit-makers in country music.[431] The 1993 smash *Chattahoochee* marked his elevation to a superstar known to pop audiences as well as country, and he has retained that status ever since, without ever losing his down-home aura, quiet dignity, or his honky-tonk style that strongly evoked the country music traditionalists (such as George Jones and Merle Haggard) he unfailingly cited as heroes. Michael McCall noted that Jackson's virtues as a songwriter were evident from the start, particularly that he "fills the songs with images from real-life scenes anyone who's spent time in rural America will recognize."[432]

Bill Malone called the song "a sensitive and deeply felt meditation . . . a masterpiece of compassion."[433] There are criticisms of *Where Were You* that can be made; Bill Friskics-Warren noted its admission of ignorance about the

---

425. Gordy played bass for Elvis Presley, Neil Diamond, and Emmylou Harris among other artists, and began producing Patty before they married in 1989.

426. Her grandfather and uncles also worked in the mines.

427. July–August 2001 *No Depression*.

428. June 16, 2001 *Billboard*, p. 33.

429. In 2009 Loveless did *Mountain Soul II*.

430. *Drive* is one of seven Jackson albums to sell at least four million copies, and one of eight to stay on the country chart for at least 100 weeks.

431. Robert Oermann, in a feature on "Marketing the New Nashville" in *Journal of Country Music*, Vol. 14 #3 (1992), cited the role of Jackson's then-manager Barry Coburn for vigorous promotion that helped make the artist a top-level headliner.

432. *Journal of Country Music*, Vol. 17 #3 (1995), p. 21.

433. *Country Music, U.S.A.* (2nd revised edition), p. 430–31.

state of the world, "apparent lack of concern" about that ignorance, and dismissal of it with an invocation of religious faith in a manner that could be seen as "arrogance." All true up to a point; but these flaws are overwhelmed by the other qualities of the song, and the nature of the man. His words speak eloquently for the emotions of millions of Americans following 9/11, and seek to embrace shared values of humanity, the need for community and embracing one's family and friends, rather than seeking refuge in rage or vengeance. The fact that Jackson has represented quiet dignity and class from the outset of his career—in the same way that Bruce Springsteen's well-established persona enhanced the impact of his 9/11 response, *The Rising*—help to make the song's themes and his performance all the more resonant.

Dance Me to the End of Love (2004)—Madeleine Peyroux (written by Leonard Cohen)

From the Rounder album *Careless Love* (*Billboard* jazz album chart debut Oct. 2, 2004, reached #2; Pop album chart debut Jan. 29, 2005, reached #124); #5 peak on *Billboard* Internet sales chart

It's an irresistible story: a young American singer performing on the streets of Paris, recording an acclaimed debut album, disappearing for five years, and then returning to produce one of the finest vocal albums of recent years. Madeleine Peyroux, born January 1, 1973, in Athens, Georgia, and raised in southern California, moved to Paris at thirteen with her mother when her parents divorced, and with a precocious talent began singing on sidewalks and then cabarets around Paris. After moving to New York City, she was signed by Atlantic and her 1996 album *Dreamland* won raves. The pressure to follow up that success led her to step away from the business and travel for several years. And then came *Careless Love*, a remarkable collection showcasing her wide-ranging tastes from Billie Holiday and Bessie Smith to contemporary writers. "Peyroux's throaty alto carries uncanny echoes of Billie Holiday," noted Christopher Porterfield in *Time*. "She has the same knack of languorously lagging behind the beat, bending her notes into microtones of aching and yearning."[434]

The album's high point is Peyroux's compelling performance of *Dance Me to the End of Love*, a Leonard Cohen narrative that the Canadian artist had introduced on his 1985 album *Various Positions*. Born in Montreal on September 21, 1934, Cohen's literary reputation preceded him (through the first of his four collections of poetry in 1956, *Let Us Compare Mythologies*, his 1963 debut novel *The Favourite Game*, and the acclaimed *Beautiful Losers* three years later) when Judy Collins

introduced the world to his music in 1967 with *Suzanne*. Cohen began his own recording career the following year. In subsequent decades he has continued to enchant his legion of followers with songs like *Bird on the Wire, Hallelujah*, and *Song of Bernadette*, showcasing his unique quality of deep, romantic melancholy.

The song's genesis was an account he read about an orchestra of inmates who were forced by the Nazis to play as their fellow prisoners were marched off to the gas chambers. It would become a popular song at weddings, and in 1995 provided the title and words to a book of art and poetry utilizing the paintings of Henri Matisse.[435] It's an inherently haunting song that she takes to another level, caressing the poetic, seductive lyrics (envisioning children yet to be born, through a dance carrying the narrator to the very limits of tenderness and passion) with the sympathetic backing of a small piano-led combo. *Time Out*, including it among its *1000 Songs to Change Your Life*, called it one of Cohen's most emotionally engaging creations, and praised Peyroux's "airy, languid" interpretation.[436]

(Peyroux on acoustic guitar, Dean Parks on guitars, Larry Goldings on keyboards, David Piltch on bass, Jay Bellerose on percussion; album produced by Larry Klein)

Day After Tomorrow (2004)—Tom Waits

From the Anti-/Epitaph album *Real Gone* (chart debut Oct. 23, 2004, reached #28)

Thirty-one years following his debut album, and decades after leaving behind a lifestyle that might have killed a lesser man, grizzled song-poet Tom Waits created a song placing among his finest ever, *Day After Tomorrow*. With a froglike baritone, a world-weary, seen-it-all persona, and gift for narrative storytelling revealing the heart of a romantic, Waits has carved out his own unique niche in popular music over the past forty years. Born in Pomona, California, on December 7, 1949, he burst on the scene impressively with his debut album *Closing Time*. Once the listener got over the startling nature of that voice, the beauty of his melodies became clear, along with his knack for creating sharply-defined characters and visual images. Through all his career journeys including movie soundtracks, dabbling in musical theater, and character-acting roles, music has always been at the heart of it, dipping from the palettes of Tin Pan Alley, jazz, blues, country, mariachi music, and seemingly everything in between; erratic at times, but seldom less than compelling.

434. June 6, 2005 *Time*.

435. Sylvie Simmons, *I'm Your Man: The Life of Leonard Cohen*, p. 337. Simmons remarks (p. 343) that the minor-key melody "has a familiar Old European romance and gravity," but also a quality of modernity.

436. *1000 Songs to Change Your Life*, p. 146.

Never perceived as a political writer, Waits crafted *Tomorrow* against the background of the Bush administration's war in Iraq, although deliberately written in such a way that it could apply to any war; Tom Moon remarks that "it could be the voice of a Civil War soldier singing a lonesome late-night dirge."[437] The piece takes the form of a soldier writing to the folks back home of his utter exhaustion with battlefields and the stench of death, and how desperately he anticipates returning to his native Illinois two days hence. Waits himself has described it as an "elliptical" protest song about the Iraq war, but it is the composition's universal, timeless scope that provides its greatest power.

Leaving behind his musical experimentations, poetic metaphors, and the exoticism of his usually ravaged voice, Waits strips his language to the bone to replicate the voice of the homesick soldier, delivering the "letter" in a hushed voice accompanied by little more than acoustic guitar. Both his comrades and his adversaries in battle must pray to the same God, he speculates; if so, "how does God choose? Whose prayers does he refuse?" The centerpiece of the song resides in these simple but powerful lines: "I'm not fighting for justice / I am not fighting for freedom / I am fighting for my life / And another day in the world here." Thom Jurek describes *Day After Tomorrow* as "one of the most insightful and understated anti-war songs to have been written in decades. It contains not a hint of banality or sentiment in its folksy articulation."[438]

We Can't Make It Here (2005)—James McMurtry

From the Compadre album *Childish Things* (released Sept. 6, 2005)

"With a novelist's sense of detail and texture and a rocker's sense of rhythm, James McMurtry spins musical tales rich in imagery and emotion," writes Lynne Margolis.[439] Born on March 18, 1962, in Fort Worth, the son of legendary novelist Larry McMurtry, he shares his father's narrative brilliance rooted in the fertile storytelling soil of northeastern Texas. His greatest song, *We Can't Make It Here*, was originally made available for free on the artist's website shortly prior to the 2004 presidential election. It begins as a closely observed, mostly spoken account of a dying town over a country-rock background, and as it gathers steam, it becomes a furious attack on bloodless corporate honchos who ship jobs overseas, and Presidents who wage needless wars, without any regard for the human damage done. Sixteen years after

his powerhouse debut *Too Long in the Wasteland*, McMurtry created what Chris Willman called possibly the "protest song of the decade."[440] Pamela Murray Winters remarks that the story is told with "filmic elegance and efficiency," and as he "rhymes with the adeptness of a rapper and the passion of a doomsday evangelist, McMurtry's insistent diatribe leaves you no alternative but to pay attention."[441]

Empire State of Mind (2009)—Jay-Z & Alicia Keys

Roc Nation track, chart debut Sept. 26, 2009 (#1 for 5 weeks pop, #1 for 2 weeks R&B); #2 in England, #3 in Australia;[442] from the album *The Blueprint 3* (2 weeks at #1)[443] (*1001, 2000s-#58*)

He started as a small-time hustler, and wound up as a dominant force in the world of hip-hop and a place at the center of pop culture that virtually none of his competitors could match.[444] Born December 4, 1969, in Brooklyn, Shawn Carter moved from street life to founding his own label, Roc-A-Fella, with an auspicious 1996 debut album, *Reasonable Doubt*, showing off his verbal dexterity and deep understanding of the urban scene.[445] In live performance, he was also blessed with an astonishing memory for even the longest verses, enabling him to outdo even his toughest rivals. By the time of his Grammy-winning *Hard Knock Life* (1998) and critically adored *The Blueprint* (2001), he was firmly atop the rap field in both respect and sales. *Empire State of Mind* teams him with one of the queens of pop and R&B, Alicia Keys, to shout the praises of the city in which both artists had been raised. (They're accompanied by a piano riff based on The Moments' classic 1970 soul ballad *Love on a Two-Way Street*.) "These streets will make you feel brand new again," the Manhattan-born superstar sings. "These lights will excite you . . . There's nothing you can't do." Of course, Jay can't resist a bit of bragging, but the main focus is on tales of the city (the dark side as well as the light), and it's a compelling ride.[446] According to the artist, "It's about inspiration . . . it's about hope."[447]

---

437. www.anti.com/press.php?id=1&pid=501

438. www.allmusic.com album review

439. May 2008 *Paste* magazine.

440. September 23, 2005, *Entertainment Weekly*.

441. October 12, 2005, *Washington Post*.

442. #2 in Denmark & Ireland, #3 in France & Holland, #5 Norway.

443. *The Blueprint 3* became Jay-Z's eleventh #1 album, the most for any solo artist to that date.

444. That pop-culture status was only enhanced when he married fellow superstar Beyoncé Knowles in 2008.

445. As detailed by Dan Charnas in *The Big Payback* (p. 568–71), Roc-A-Fella was launched by Jay and partner Damon Dash with no real capital, gained credibility with Jay's first 12-inch single, and was able to gain financing for *Reasonable Doubt* while retaining creative control and ownership of the masters. Once the album broke big (followed quickly by Foxy Brown's debut on the label), he could write his own ticket.

446. A "Part 2" of *Empire*, by Alicia solo, was included on her album *The Element of Freedom* and was a European hit in early 2010.

447. *1001 Songs to Hear Before You Die*, p. 892.

Someone Like You (2011)—Adele (Adkins)

XL/Columbia track, chart debut July 16, 2011 (#1 for 5 weeks); #1 (5) in England, #1 in Australia;[448] from the #1 album *21*[449] (written by Adele & Dan Wilson) (*UK-#55*)

In an era of Auto-Tune–reliant fakery, sound-alike dance tunes and "American Idol"–imitating histrionics, Adele Adkins' marriage of a big, powerful voice and down-to-the-bone Everywoman honesty and emotional directness packs an extraordinary punch. The real-life experience of learning that her former love was newly engaged just a short time after their breakup, served as the basis for one of the era's standout ballads. The soulful British songstress—proclaimed by admirers "the new Queen of Heartbreak"—may be singing "I wish nothing but the best for you," but leaves no doubt about the darker feelings that boil just beneath the surface. Solo voice-and-piano records are a rarity on the modern pop charts (one reason why John Legend's *Ordinary People* had such impact), and *Someone Like You* was the first such song to reach #1 in many years. Stark, stripped down, devoid of pretenses, the performance drives straight to the gut. The second major breakout track from her blockbuster second album was a Grammy winner for best pop solo performance, one of her six wins that evening. Melissa Maerz: "This is music with so much heart, it hurts."[450]

---

448. #1 on Eurochart; #1 (9 weeks) in France; #1 (8 weeks) in Italy; #1 (4 weeks) in Ireland; #1 in New Zealand, Switzerland; #2 in Austria, Belgium; #5 Germany.

449. *21* remained in the U.S. Top Ten continuously for a year and a half from its March 12, 2011 debut, ultimately reaching 80 weeks, the longest run since Bruce Springsteen's *Born In the U.S.A.* (1984, 84 weeks). The last album to log 70+ weeks in the Top Ten was Alanis Morissette's *Jagged Little Pill* (1995, 72 weeks). (*Joel Whitburn Presents the Billboard Albums*)

450. *Entertainment Weekly* 2011 year-end special, naming *21* the year's best album.

Playlist 9

Wasn't That a Time? 1895–2006

The Sidewalks of New York (1895)—J. W. Myers
   (music by Charles Lawlor, lyrics by James Blake)
Recorded in early 1895 for Columbia; also recorded for
   Chicago 2609 and Ohio

Vaudeville buck-and-wing performer and amateur composer Charles Lawlor (born in Dublin and ultimately settled in New York) had come up with a catchy melody, and in need of some lyrics sought the help of James Blake, a New York City salesman in a hatter's shop who occasionally wrote verses. The result of their collaboration, *The Sidewalks of New York*, was introduced by Lottie Gilson at the Old London Theatre in the Bowery.[1] [2] The audience was so taken with it that they joined her in singing a repetition of the chorus; Gilson subsequently performed it at vaudeville houses around the country for years.[3] Music publishers Howley & Haviland were still struggling at the time—the songs of "silent partner" Paul Dresser (soon to achieve fame through *On the Banks of the Wabash*) hadn't yet caught on—and *Sidewalks* helped make the firm a staple of Tin Pan Alley.[4] It became a

sensation in sheet music sales,[5] and had two big recorded versions in 1895, by Dan Quinn and J. W. Myers.

John W. Myers was born in approximately 1864 in Wales, came to the U.S. at age twelve, became a theatrical manager in New York, and began recording for New Jersey Phonograph Company in 1892. The baritone ballad singer with the distinctive handlebar mustache became one of the top stars in the recording business, with his period of heaviest activity occurring from 1900–1905, specializing in sentimental numbers and venerable standards. *The Sidewalks of New York* would eventually become a virtual anthem for New York City, closely identified with Mayor James J. Walker, and then used as the theme song for the 1928 presidential campaign of New York's Al Smith (after he had first so used it at the 1924 Democratic convention). "East side, west side, all around the town . . ."

Down on the Old Camp Ground (1902)—Dinwiddie Colored Quartet
Victor 1714
Recorded Oct. 29, 1902

---

1. The song was copyrighted August 27, 1894. All of the names mentioned in the lyric were actual people Blake knew from his East 18th Street neighborhood.

2. Sigmund Spaeth (*A History of Popular Music*, p. 187) suggested that the 1879 Harrigan & Hart song *The Babies on Our Block* served as "the definite forerunner" for *Sidewalks* by offering a detailed picture of life in the humbler sections of the city.

3. Ewen, *Life and Death of Tin Pan Alley*, p. 41–42.

4. The June 11, 1927 *Music Trades* discussed the song's history. The firm then had only one room with a rented piano; the success of *Sidewalks*

enabled it to move to more spacious quarters on 32nd Street and Broadway. *Wabash*, and later *Bill Bailey, Won't You Please Come Home*, took Howley to the next level.

5. According to its publisher (September 29, 1900 *Music Trade Review*, p. 23), *Sidewalks* sold about 150,000 copies. Aside from *After the Ball* and *Hot Time in the Old Town*, no other 1890s songs are believed to have exceeded 600,000 in sales.

One of the highlights of the remarkable Dust to Digital 2003 boxed set *Goodbye Babylon* was its inclusion of one of just six songs recorded by the Dinwiddie Colored Quartet at its landmark October 29 and 31, 1902, sessions for the Victor Talking Machine Company in New York. While not the first black vocal group to record, it was the first to make discs instead of cylinders; only a few cylinders made by two black groups in the 1890s, the Unique Quartette and the Standard Quartette, have survived.

The Dinwiddies—from Dinwiddie County near Richmond in Virginia's coastal southern region—consisted of first tenor Sterling Rex, second tenor J. Clarence Meredith, first bass Harry B. Cruder, and second bass J. Mantrell Thomas. They were members of Ernest Hogan's and Billy McClain's Smart Set Company, a Philadelphia-based touring company. The quartet was formed to promote the John A. Dix Industrial School, the first private institution for black education in Dinwiddie County, founded in 1899; singing for two years in YMCA buildings, churches, and a wide range of public venues, they raised hundreds of thousands of dollars for the institution. Upon releasing the Dinwiddie records in 1903, Victor proclaimed them the "genuine Jubilee and camp meeting shouts." After a stint in vaudeville, the quartet disbanded in 1904; Sterling Rex went on to a prominent solo concert career in the Philadelphia area. Among the other a cappella recordings by the group was the first known recording of the spiritual *Steal Away*.[6]

Nearly three decades before the *Babylon* set, Dick Spottswood had also included this performance (of a song unrelated to the Civil War favorite *Tenting on the Old Camp Ground*) on the 1976 fifteen-record Library of Congress Bicentennial compilation *Folk Music in America*. There he described its significance as "part of a tradition of mixing churchly and secular sentiments in a loosely structured floating-verse scheme, an approach subsequently adopted in the blues. This distinctive and lasting musical form was still in its infancy when this recording was made."[7]

Come Take a Trip in My Airship (1905)—Billy Murray (music by George Evans, lyrics by Ren Shields)
Edison 8874 and Victor 2986
Recorded in Oct. 1904, released around year-end (#1 in *Pop Memories*)

The Ohio brothers Wilbur and Orville Wright made their celebrated first heavier-than-air flight in their own craft at Kitty Hawk, North Carolina, in December 1903, the longest lasting not quite a minute and covering 850 feet; by the following fall they had improved the plane to the point where they were able to fly over twenty-three miles. *Come Take a Trip In My Airship* is a jubilant celebration of that feat (seeing the new form of travel as a fresh opportunity for romance), and Billy Murray—just beginning to emerge as the era's greatest popular recording star—injects his trademark enthusiasm.

Vaudeville star George Evans and his writing partner Ren Shields had ensured their place in popular music history with *In the Good Old Summertime*, and *Come Take a Trip* provided a followup that was nearly as successful. The June 25, 1904, *Music Trades* noted that the new composition "is attracting a good deal of attention" among leading singers. The July 23 issue reported that Edna Wallace Hopper "has made a gigantic hit in vaudeville" featuring the tune.[8] The October 1 edition stated that when Evans sang it at Hammerstein's Victoria Theater, "he was compelled to repeat the chorus dozens of times at every performance." After noting on November 5 that is was being sung by "hundreds of well-known professional singers,"[9] the November 12 *Music Trades* summed it up nicely, declaring that *Airship* "is a great hit in the West, and is being sung, hummed, and whistled all over the streets of Chicago. This song will undoubtedly last for a great many years to come . . ."

"Come take a trip in my airship, Come sail away to the stars! / We'll travel to Venus, we'll sail away to Mars! . . ."

The Preacher and the Bear (1905)—Arthur Collins
(written by George Fairman & Arthur Longbrake)
Edison Standard 9000
Pop Memories debut June 3, 1905 (#1 hit of 1905)[10]
(*MEM-#31, DMDB*)

The first record purported to have sold two million copies (combined from multiple labels), and one of the most universally known songs of the pre-1920 era, *The Preacher and the Bear* was written by Front Royal, Virginia, native George Fairman in 1903, and sold outright for $250 to Joe Arzonia, owner of a café in which Fairman played piano;[11] Sigmund Spaeth reports that Arzonia "seems to have been merely a disguise" for the song's publisher, Arthur Longbrake.[12] Arthur Collins, already one of the top-selling performers in the record business ever since his 1898 debut, recorded the number first for Zon-o-Phone (issued in April 1905). Edison released its

---

6. Tim Brooks, *Lost Sounds*, p. 155–59.
7. Liner notes, Vol. 1 of *Folk Music in America*.
8. By early September, the publication said the song was being performed in at least fifty road company productions.
9. Ethel Robinson was another popular performer who featured it on stage. J. W. Myers had the most notable competing recorded version, for Columbia a few weeks after Murray's.
10. Also recorded for Columbia disc 3146 & cylinder 32720, Victor 4431, Zon-o-Phone 120, Indestructible 1087, & U.S. Everlasting 1092.
11. Fairman provided this information in a letter to acoustic-era historian Jim Walsh.
12. Spaeth, *A History of Popular Music in America*, p. 346. Longbrake, also a frequent patron of Arzonia's café, established the Eclipse Music Company; he in turn sold the tune to the Joe Morris Music Company. (*Popular American Recording Pioneers*, p. 69–70)

Collins recording in May, followed by Columbia a month later. The June 1905 issue of the latter label's in-house publication, *The Columbia Record*, declared that the record "is having a phenomenal sale, and should be in the home of every owner of a talking machine."

It's a comic number presenting a dilemma with which every listener could identify, and fit well into the vaudeville and minstrel tradition. Collins, with his combination of a pleasing baritone, strong rhythmic sense, gift for dialects, and gentle humor, was a perfect match of artist to material. "Oh Lord, didn't you deliver Daniel from the lion's den? / Also delivered Jonah from the belly of the whale and then three Hebrew chillun from the fiery furnace? / So the Good Book do declare. / Now Lord, if you can't help me, for goodness sakes, don't you help that bear!"

Maple Leaf Rag (1906)—United States Marine Band
Victor 4911

Recorded on Oct. 15, 1906; *Pop Memories* debut March 16, 1907

Five months before banjoist Vess Ossman rendered the definitive recording of Scott Joplin's *Maple Leaf Rag*, the U.S. Marine Band became the first artists to make a surviving commercial recording of ragtime's greatest classic. The famed orchestra was led at this time by Lt. William H. Santelmann, born in 1863 in Offensen, Germany, and trained in Leipzig, emigrated to the U.S. in 1887, enlisted in the Marine Band until 1895 when he left to form an orchestra of his own, and returned to become the director of "the President's own" in March 1898.[13] This brisk, engaging rendition, running just over two minutes, is included on the Archeophone CD *1907: Dear Old Golden Rule Days*.

One of the first notable published endorsements of ragtime was Rupert Hughes' "A Eulogy of Ragtime" in the April 1, 1899, *Boston Musical Record*. "It is young and unhackneyed and throbbing with life," wrote Hughes. "And it is racial." Noting the disparagement of the new music by stodgy academics and those with contempt for Negroes, he declared that such attacks had never succeeded "against a vital musical idea, and I feel safe in predicting that ragtime has come to stay . . ."[14]

Home, Sweet Home (1911)—Alice Nielsen (music by Henry Bishop, lyrics by John Howard Payne)
Columbia 5283

Released in June 1911 (reissued in Aug. 1915)[15]

Declared "the most popular song of the entire [nineteenth] century" by Charles Hamm,[16] *Home, Sweet Home* cast an imposing shadow over all other sentimental ballads of the 1800s as perhaps the definitive symbol of nostalgia for one's roots. The melody by Englishman Henry Bishop was first used to accompany other words in *Melodies of Other Nations* (1821), a piece entitled *To the Home of My Childhood*.[17] New York City–born poet John Howard Payne was in London writing plays and acting when he supplied the words of the song we know today, which first appeared in the opera *Clari or The Maid of Milan*, which opened in London on May 8, 1823. It was sung by Maria Tree at the end of the first act as a nostalgic recollection of her home, but came directly out of Payne's longings as he traveled restlessly throughout Europe.[18] Nicholas Tawa notes that in the wake of the song's massive popularity, other ballads about "home" proliferated,[19] perhaps none more familiar than Stephen Foster's *My Old Kentucky Home*. Legendary concert artist Jenny Lind made *Home, Sweet Home* a central part of her repertoire, singing it at the White House in 1850, an event to which the President invited Payne, two years before the latter's death.[20]

Richard Crawford suggests that "perhaps what gives *Home, Sweet Home* its enduring character is the way [its] simple elements construct a feeling of stability that manifests the idea of home." The melody has a range of just an octave, and the harmonic structure is equally simple, providing a sense of continuity. Its "home sonority" is in the tonic note E: "Like the walls of a house, the pitch E provides both the melody's upper and lower boundaries and the harmony's bedrock, domesticating any sense of restlessness" that the accompaniment might suggest. Payne's words match this plain, heartfelt approach; instead of trying for poetic eloquence, it states directly, "There's no place like home."[21]

13. He remained in that position until his retirement in April 1927.
14. Cited by Rudi Blesh and Harriet Janis in *They All Played Ragtime* (p. 131).
15. Columbia reissued eight of Nielsen's English-language records (sixteen sides) in August 1915. The reverse side of this disc was another perennial, Thomas Moore's *The Last Rose of Summer* (written in 1813).
16. *Yesterdays: Popular Song in America*, p. 165.
17. Ewen, *All the Years of American Popular Music*, p. 53. Bishop wrote or adapted some 100 stage productions during his lifetime, and conducted most performances of nearly all of them.
18. Fuld, *Book of World-Famous Music*, p. 274–75. The first American performance was on November 12, 1823. The *New York Mirror* called the tune "the most beautiful and tender we have ever heard."
19. *Sweet Songs for Gentle Americans*, p. 140. Because the song originated abroad, it could not be copyrighted in the U.S., so many American music publishers rushed their own editions into print in 1824–25.
20. Payne lamented that he spent much of his life hearing his words performed "without having a schilling to buy myself the next meal or a place to lay my head." He'd been promised $25 for the lyric, but apparently never received a penny. Years later a statue of Payne was erected in Prospect Park in Brooklyn with a thousand voices singing *Home, Sweet Home*.
21. *America's Musical Life*, p. 178–80. The simple elegance of the melody helps explain why, unlike most ballads of the early nineteenth century, it remained popular generations later. Popular recordings in 1955 by Hack Johnson & His Tennesseans (featuring banjoist Allen Shelton) and Don Reno & Red Smiley made the song a modern staple in bluegrass.

Innumerable commercial recordings were made of *Home, Sweet Home* dating back to the start of the industry, including John Yorke AtLee (1891), Harry Macdonough (1901), the Haydn Quartet (1902), Richard Jose (1906), and Alma Gluck (1912). One of the most enduringly popular was by Irish-American soprano Alice Nielsen (born June 7, 1872, raised in Kansas City), who started in vaudeville, and became enormously popular in light operas and concerts, particularly after her 1897 Broadway triumph in Victor Herbert's *The Serenade* (not the female lead, but it made her internationally known). A year after that success she formed her own Alice Nielsen Opera Company, with which she premiered Herbert's *The Fortune Teller*, playing three roles.[22] Nielsen sang with the Metropolitan Opera and from 1909–1915 in the company of the Boston Opera House, and recorded extensively from 1898–1928. During the 1910s she often sang in joint concerts with John McCormack. Her recordings such as *Home, Sweet Home* showcased a lovely, lilting soprano with a lighter texture than many operetta singers of her time, but a soaring range and pleasing quality, with orchestral accompaniment.

Dark Town Strutters' Ball (1918)—Arthur Collins & Byron Harlan (written by Shelton Brooks)
Columbia 2478
Pop Memories debut March 30, 1918 (reached #1)

Introduced in vaudeville by Sophie Tucker and on record (as an instrumental) by the Original Dixieland Jazz Band in 1917, *Dark Town Strutters' Ball* was unveiled in all its rowdy glory by the masters of minstrel/blackface–styled romps, Arthur Collins and Byron Harlan.[23] The duo had been recording together since 1901 (including the classic original 1911 version of *Alexander's Ragtime Band*), and this would be their last big hit together; Victor and Columbia stopped recording new numbers by the team later in 1918, except for one final Victor session in 1922, although they continued recording for Edison and smaller labels sporadically until 1924. Canadian-born Shelton Brooks, also the author of Tucker's mighty *Some of These Days*, was inspired to write this number by a social gathering he attended during San Francisco's Panama Pacific International Exposition in 1915.[24] This exuberant performance is the reverse side of Al Jolson's hit *I'm All Bound Round with the Mason Dixon Line.*

"We're gonna dance off both our shoes / When they play those jelly roll blues[25] / Tomorrow night at the dark town strutters' ball . . ." In 1972 it was one of ten songs honored by the Songwriters Hall of Fame as historic standards.[26]

Swanee (1920)—Al Jolson (music by George Gershwin, lyrics by Irving Caesar)
Columbia 2884
Recorded Jan. 9, 1920; *Pop Memories* debut May 8, 1920 (#1 for 9 weeks) (*Trad-#16, RR-#67, MEM-#74, RIA-#124, GHF-#188, DMDB*)

It was George Gershwin's first big hit, indeed the biggest-selling song the composer would ever enjoy— and probably the most un-Gershwin number one could imagine. Al Jolson had already been a top star for nearly a decade, and *Swanee* provided him with one of the signature songs of his career.

Dinty Moore's restaurant in New York was the birthplace for the song when Gershwin and lyricist Irving Caesar were having lunch to discuss song ideas. They decided to write a one-step dance number in the style of the recent hit *Hindustan*. Needing to give it an American setting—something like Stephen Foster's *Swanee River* (aka *Old Folks at Home*), suggested Gershwin—they had the idea for the song largely formed by the time they returned to Gershwin's apartment on Washington Heights. They completed it that afternoon in his living room while a poker game was in progress in the adjoining dining room.[27] Jack Gottlieb (*Funny, It Doesn't Sound Jewish*) notes that in its verse the song yearns for a kind of Promised Land, and suggests that the melody seems to "subconsciously recall a synagogue tune, *Hashivenu*." The piece was introduced by Muriel DeForrest in a lavish October 1919 production at New York's Capitol Theatre (sixty chorus girls with electric lights glowing on their slippers), but the number didn't go over, with sheet music sales poor. Then Gershwin played it at a party for the dynamic Jolson, who performed it in a Sunday night show at the Winter Garden in late December, and then added it to his long-running musical extravaganza *Sinbad*, making the tune a blockbuster.[28] "Jolson can take a song and make it do

---

22. Ironically, the only major song in the show that wasn't hers proved to be its biggest hit, *Gypsy Love Song*, performed by Eugene Cowles.

23. Tucker was pictured on the cover of the song's first edition as published January 18, 1917 (Fuld, *Book of World-Famous Music*, p. 193). The ODJB recording was from the band's May 31 session, after their big debut for Victor.

24. Spaeth, *A History of Popular Music*, p. 372. Despite its immediate San Francisco inspiration, the song is said to be about Chicago's State Street at a time when the black music scene was located near the Loop. (Donald Clarke, *The Rise and Fall of Popular Music*, p. 64.)

25. This can be seen as an indirect reference to Jelly Roll Morton's song *Jelly Roll Blues*, composed in 1905; stride piano great James P. Johnson saw him play it in New York in 1911, and the tune was published four years later. (Reich and Gaines, *Jelly's Blues*, p. 39–40, 45.) The lyrics also describe the singer and his sweetheart doing other dances including the buck & wing and Walking the Dog.

26. May 27, 1972, *Billboard*.

27. Ewen, *All the Years*, p. 230. Also see Rosenberg, *Fascinating Rhythm*, p. 38–40.

28. As discussed by Jolson biographer Herbert Goldman, the singer and composer had first met in Atlantic City in April 1919, where *Sinbad* was playing and Gershwin was preparing his show *La La, Lucille* for Broadway.

things its composers did not dream were in it," marveled Heywood Broun in the *New York World*.

This is just a big, brash vehicle ideally designed to be a show stopper for the most charismatic entertainer of the age. In addition to Jolson's best-selling record, it sold over a million copies of sheet music.[29] The May 1, 1920, *Music Trades* raved: "The very theme of the song is essentially and wholly American. *Swanee* stands for everything that sweet reminisce can conjure up, and this Jolson song is so fashioned that a fresh affection grips the heart for the ever-dear river of that country where the old folks were so much at home . . . [The song] sets a standard that is well worth while emulating, and its popularity over the length and breadth of the land is an encouraging commentary" on public tastes. Jolson would sing it again a quarter-century later for the 1945 Gershwin film biography *Rhapsody In Blue*, and a year later dubbed in the vocal for Larry Parks in the smash *The Jolson Story* that enabled Al to make a historic comeback.

The Shaskeen (1921)—Michael Coleman
Vocalion 14201
Recorded in April 1921

Called by some "Ireland's most influential traditional musician of the 20th century," Michael Coleman (born in 1891 in Knockgrania, located in County Sligo, Ireland) won fiddling competitions in 1909 and 1910, and sailed to America by 1913. Performing on the Keith Theatres vaudeville circuit starting not long after his arrival, he made some 150 recordings for various labels from 1920–36.[30] Nearly all are cut from the same tasty mold: brisk, thoroughly danceable reels, jigs, and hornpipes, normally accompanied by just a pianist or (on fewer occasions) a guitarist.[31]

One of his very first recordings, *The Shaskeen*, was also among his finest. A vigorous, exciting reel accompanied by pianist John Muller, the fiddling here is so powerful that one could swear there are two fiddlers, but actually it's all Coleman. The word "shaskeen" (we learn from *The Fiddler's Companion* by Andrew Kuntz) is derived from the Irish word "seisgeann" meaning either a marshy country, a truss of corn, or gleaned land. Shaskeen is also the name of a townland in County Sligo, Coleman's birthplace. The tune had been famously rendered on an Edison home recorder in 1904 by Irish uilleann pipes player Patrick J. "Patsy" Touhey, a performance that

Gaelic scholar Father Richard Henebry proclaimed with some hyperbole "a far bigger achievement" than the Homeric ballads and the then-new Brooklyn Bridge.[32] But Coleman's recording seventeen years later brought the tune to a much bigger audience. Listening to it, one is reminded of the recordings of Gid Tanner & His Skillet Lickers, one of country music's greatest string bands featuring two and sometimes three fiddlers furiously blazing away. The Skillet Lickers began recording in 1926, and knowing that the repertoire of early country string bands included many traditional Irish fiddle tunes, it wouldn't be surprising if the group members had been inspired by recordings like this one. Either way, it's a killer.[33] The piece is included on a two-CD compilation of Coleman recordings on the Gael-Linn label in Dublin.

Sounds of Africa (1921)—Eubie Blake
Emerson 10434
Recorded in July 1921; released on Paramount 14004 as *African Rag (AL)*

One of the great characters in popular music, Eubie Blake is best remembered today for a remarkable re-emergence as a pianist and raconteur in his eighties during the late 1960s and early 1970s, colorfully recalling a lost era of American pop culture. But he was a significant figure in his own right as a Broadway composer and first-rate ragtime pianist during the 1920s and 1930s, whose finest recording was this vivid, excitingly uptempo piano solo.

Born in Baltimore to former slaves on February 7, 1887,[34] Blake got his start in vaudeville, and by 1905 had become a featured performer in Atlantic City; future jazz piano great James P. Johnson saw him there, and regarded him as "one of the foremost pianists of all time." He began his famous collaboration with Noble Sissle in 1915. After World War I the two men worked together in James Reese Europe's orchestra, and then became a popular duo in vaudeville, featuring Blake's piano and Sissle's vocals. Their original score for the smash 1921 Broadway musical *Shuffle Along* (composed by Blake with Sissle's lyrics, including the standard *I'm Just Wild About Harry*) led to a series of black musical revues over

---

29. *Swanee* was first cited in the January 10, 1920, *Music Trades* just as Jolson recorded it, with predictions from publisher T. B. Harms that it will be "the best seller they have had in years."

30. The earliest verified commercially issued recordings by an Irish-American traditional musician (as distinct from Tin Pan Alley–styled Irish pop ballad singers) were the nineteen or more selections on cylinder made from 1899–1903 by uilleann piper James C. McAuliffe.

31. Dick Spottswood, *Ethnic Music on Records*, Vol. 5, p. 2743–47.

32. Touhey, as discussed by Paul F. Wells in his chapter on Irish music for *Ethnic and Border Music: A Regional Exploration* (p. 36), was regarded as the finest piper of his time, and performed at both the 1893 World's Columbian Exposition in Chicago and the 1904 St. Louis fair. Unfortunately the vast majority of the recordings he made were home-recorded cylinders made for particular customers, only a few of which survive in private collections, until he finally made some acclaimed 78s for Victor in 1919.

33. Pekka Gronow, *Ethnic Recordings in America* (p. 13), calls the performances of Coleman and other Irish violinists in the Columbia 33000-F series "among the finest examples of traditional music ever issued on commercial recordings."

34. Blake gave February. 7, 1883, as his birthdate, but his Social Security application and other documents later established 1887 as the correct year.

the next two decades. After entertaining for the USO during World War II, Blake kept a low profile until his dramatic return to a national stage at the 1969 Newport Jazz Festival and that year's wonderful album *The 86 Years of Eubie Blake*. He remained a national treasure until his death in 1983.

Gunther Schuller writes that *Sounds of Africa* provides a "good idea of Blake's prodigious technique and feel for a varied, chromatic continuity." "The three-part piece traverses three basic key areas . . . Within each strain there is a great deal of rhythmic variety in both the melodic right hand and the striding left hand." He notes that this performance "is an excellent example of piano music caught in the transition between ragtime and jazz."[35] In *Sounds of Africa*, writes Allen Lowe, "one can hear the beginnings of the modern idea of swing. This is an extraordinary and forward-looking performance, more substantial than that of the general run of novelty or show pianists."[36] A terrific representation of the Harlem stride piano style, the piece is also known under the titles *Charleston Shout* and *Charleston Rag*.

Joel A. Rogers' essay "Jazz At Home," included in Alain Locke's 1925 *The New Negro* anthology, suggested (in comments that apply to Blake's classic) that the "elementals" of jazz had "always existed" in worldwide dance forms, rooted in international folk culture: "It is in the Indian war dance, the Highland fling, the Irish jig, the Cossack dance, the Spanish fandango, the Brazilian *maxixe*, the dance of the whirling dervish, the hula of the South Seas, the *carmagnole* of the French Revolution, and the ragtime of the Negro."[37]

Froggie Moore (1923)—King Oliver's Creole Jazz Band (written by Jelly Roll Morton)
Gennett 5135
Recorded on April 6, 1923

The historic debut recording session by King Oliver's Creole Jazz Band in Richmond, Indiana, introduced several jazz classics, and one of its unquestioned standout performances was Jelly Roll Morton's *Froggie Moore* (sometimes known as *Frog-I-More Rag*). The Creole Jazz Band was by its very nature an ensemble that featured virtually no solos, but young Louis Armstrong as the group's second cornetist nevertheless is overpowering on his "quasi-solo" for *Froggie Moore*. Gunther Schuller praises the "wondrous luminous quality" of the opening section, the warmth of clarinetist Johnny Dodds adding "just the right sheen" to complement the horns of

Oliver and Armstrong.[38] Morton had very precise ideas about how his music should be recorded and was not given to easy praise, but he said that Oliver's was one of the few bands that presented his compositions the way he intended.

Oliver's original home base in Chicago starting in early 1920 was the Dreamland Café. Opened in October 1914 at 3520 South State Street, the Dreamland was celebrated as the grandest dance hall of its time on the city's South Side, with an 800-person capacity dance floor whose boards were laid in a circle; in June 1917 its "Original Jazz Band" was one of Chicago's first venues to spell "jazz" with two z's (as opposed to "jass").

Joe Oliver and Louis Armstrong, like Buddy Bolden before them, had attended Sanctified or Baptist church services in New Orleans, and Thomas Brothers in *Louis Armstrong's New Orleans* argues strongly that the church was the foundation for their music. One rhythmic quality that may have to come to jazz from the church, Brothers speculates, is the "four-beat style" or "flat 4/4," a steady background pulse of four undifferentiated beats per measure. Brothers further cites the importance of "congregational heterophony" in the black church (heterophony is the simultaneous singing or playing of two or more versions of a melody), and the classic New Orleans sound of the Creole Jazz Band can be seen as replicating the feeling of the congregation. "Collective improvisation may thus be read as a stylized and professionalized transformation of church heterophony."[39]

Because there is only one Louis Armstrong, there's a modern-day tendency to underrate Joe Oliver as a cornet player. Aside from the fact that he was a month shy of his thirty-eighth birthday at the time of these recordings and probably past his peak, his horn is nonetheless strong and vibrant here. He is believed to have been the first professional cornetist to mute his instrument, employing (as Samuel A. Floyd describes it in *The Power of Black Music*) "bottles, cups, and utensils constructed specifically for distorting the sound of his cornet, a uniquely African-derived" practice. (Village Africans, he notes, "traditionally have distorted and enhanced the natural sounds of musical instruments" through devices such as adding rattles to the heads of drums.)[40] And Armstrong himself never let it be forgotten that he modeled his playing after Oliver's; the man had been the king of New Orleans horn men before his protégé came into his own, blazing the path for Louis and others to follow. According to trumpet player Mutt Carey, who saw Oliver play on stage, he made his horn sound "like a holy roller meeting."[41]

35. *Early Jazz*, p. 215.
36. *American Pop*, p. 57–58.
37. *The New Negro: An Interpretation*, edited by Alain Locke; Rogers essay "Jazz At Home," p. 216–24.
38. *Early Jazz*, p. 84–85.
39. Brothers, p. 40–43.
40. Floyd, p. 124.
41. Shapiro and Hentoff, *Hear Me Talkin' to Ya*, p. 42.

King Oliver, courtesy of Library of Congress, Archeophone Records and Off the Record.

The Wreck of the Old '97 (1924)—Vernon Dalhart

Victor 19427[42]

Recorded on Aug. 13, 1924; released by Victor on Oct. 3, 1924 (*NPR-300, C&W-#76, SC*)

Train-wreck ballads were a big part of folk and country song repertoires during the first third of the twentieth century, and few were so ubiquitous as this one. As retraced by Norm Cohen in *Long Steel Rail*, the ballad describes what happened to Number 97, a fast mail train on the Southern Railway that ran between Washington, D.C., and Atlanta. On September 27, 1903, the train was running an hour late, an engineer unfamiliar with the route took over at Monroe, Virginia, and tried to make up for lost time; the train flew off the rails and plummeted into the ravine at Stillhouse Creek approaching Danville just north of the North Carolina border, killing all nine aboard. The Sunday-morning tragedy was witnessed or at least heard by many townsfolk, making news coverage of the event especially intense.[43]

Henry Clay Work's classic 1865 ballad *The Ship That Never Returned*, and the numerous parodies that gained popularity in the next few decades, provided the basic tune for several different songs that were written shortly after the tragedy. Robert Winslow Gordon, upon taking over the *Adventure* magazine column "Old Songs That

Men Have Sung," responded to a letter seeking information on a ballad the reader had once heard regarding the Old '97 wreck, printed one verse in the August 20, 1923, issue and solicited more from others. He received three responses, and in the January 30, 1924, issue printed a composite text of fourteen verses. The following year, after Harvard University appointed him a Sheldon Fellow for collecting folksongs, he obtained more information on the songs inspired by the wreck from residents in and around Greensboro, North Carolina, who claimed to have created them.

By that time the song had been recorded as *Wreck on the Southern Old '97* by Henry Whitter in December 1923,[44] and the popular success of his record helped unleash a seemingly unending flood of epic tales based on real-life disasters and tragedies, many of them crafted by Andrew Jenkins (*The Death of Floyd Collins*) and Carson Robison. The piece was soon covered by Ernest Thompson, mostly the same as Whitter's but opening with a different stanza.

Texas-born former light opera-turned-ballad singer Vernon Dalhart, an Edison recording artist since 1917 whose sales were on the downslide, was ready to try something new, and decided to copy Whitter's record for Edison in a May 14, 1924, performance accompanied by Hawaiian-style guitarist Frank Ferera;[45] as Cohen noted, he had difficulty making out some of the words sung by Whitter and delivered them as best he could (a much stronger vocal, though certainly less rootsy). The Edison disc was his best seller in years, enabling him to persuade Victor to let him record the piece for that label's vastly larger audience three months later (issued as part of its "Olde Time" series). Thanks in large part to its A side, *The Prisoner's Song*, Victor 19427 became a full-blown sales phenomenon, and Dalhart had a new career as hillbilly star and "master of disaster."

Although Victor, seeking to head off possible legal issues, paid Whitter and publishing house F. Wallace Rega for all their respective rights to the song, the company was sued by another copyright claimant, and in 1929 hired Gordon to provide his extensive research for a case that did not reach trial until two years later. He concluded that Concord, North Carolina, resident Fred Lewey had written the first version of the ballad, which was then picked up and revised by Charles Noell of Greensboro, and both men performed it locally. Frank Burnett heard them performing it as a duo, and around 1914 Henry Whitter learned it from Burnett; nine years later, he

---

42. Dalhart also recorded the song for Banner 1531, Edison Amberol 4898, Gennett 5588, & Regal 9829. In March 1926, Victor had Dalhart re-record *Old '97* and *Prisoner* using the new electrical process, the tunes reissued with the same record number.

43. Cohen, p. 197–222. Cohen's entry on the song was an expansion of his article in the January–March 1974 *Journal of American Folklore*, "Robert W. Gordon and the Second *Wreck of the Old '97*."

44. The flip side of Whitter's record, *Lonesome Road Blues*, became famous for its opening line, "Going down the road feeling bad."

45. Carter Family biographers Zwonitzer and Hershberg point out (*Will You Miss Me When I'm Gone?*, p. 185) that Ferera's guitar accompaniment on the Edison record was an early influence on Maybelle Carter.

made a few changes in it for his recording. Kelly Harrell, who recorded *Old '97* for Okeh in 1925, had learned it even earlier, as far back as 1904 from both Lewey and Noell. The March 1933 circuit court ruling oddly disregarded most of Gordon's findings and found in favor of copyright claimant David Graves George on the basis of dubious evidence (including apparently fabricated documents, opines Cohen), awarding George over $65,000. But after multiple appeals, this ruling was reversed, with the final petition denied by the U.S. Supreme Court in January 1940.

Beyond its vast popularity, its value as a symbol of the "event songs" that would dominate hillbilly music for years, and as a representative of songs with tangled oral-history backstories, *Old '97* would also find new life as the basis (along with Work's 1865 standard) for the Bess Hawes–Jacqueline Steiner 1948 parody *The MTA Song* protesting a proposed Boston subway fare increase, which would later become a pop hit for the Kingston Trio.

Odesser Bulgar Dance (1925)—Naftule Brandwein's Orchestra

Victor 78043
Recorded on April 1, 1925

The man known as "King of the Klezmer Clarinet," Naftule Brandwein was born in the Polish Galician town of Przymyzl in 1889, absorbed influences from his very musical family, and came to America in 1908. Billing himself with admirable chutzpah as the "King of Jewish Music," he built a local reputation performing in Yiddish theater in New York, then broke into commercial recordings thanks to Abe Schwartz, one of the most prolific klezmer bandleaders who also served as an A&R man for Columbia Records. After playing with Schwartz's orchestra and on his own for Columbia in 1922–1923, Brandwein switched to Victor and continued to record through 1927, then returning for a final session in 1941. Henry Sapoznik writes that with his passionate clarinet playing that made performances sound improvised even when they were carefully worked out, and his colorful personal style, Brandwein epitomized the klezmer scene of early twentieth century America perhaps more than any other single musician. Younger members of the Brandwein family remained active in music, and his nephew Nat Brandwynne attained prominence as a New York society pianist/bandleader who also made some popular recordings for Brunswick in the late 1930s.

The *bulgar* (as explained by Sapoznik in *Klezmer! Jewish Music from Old World to Our World*) is a traditional Jewish music form which originated in Bessarabia (located next to Romania), and produced the popular line dance of the same name, from the name *Bulgar-*

esti, or "in Bulgarian style." Sapoznik suggests: "What may have given rise to the name was the presence of an ethnic Bulgarian population in Bessarabia and Odessa [a major seaport located in southern Ukraine, and the fourth largest city in imperial Russia in the late 1800s] or the heavy interaction between klezmer and Moldavian Gypsy musicians in northern Bulgaria." By the end of the nineteenth century, among Jews who had emigrated to America, "the bulgars" had "become the descriptive for a far richer, old-time Yiddish dance repertoire that for the moment still flourished throughout Eastern Europe."[46]

The *Odessa Bulgar Dance*, write Rita Ottens and Joel Rubin in liner notes for the Wergo CD *Oytsres/Treasures/Schatze: Klezmer Music, 1908–1996*, is a very fast rendition of a bulgar dance melody" that was popular throughout the 1910s and 1920s among the New York klezmorim. The original melody is in the middle section; Brandwein either composed or added the opening and closing sections. Accompanied by Sam Spielman on trombone plus violin, piano, and traps, Brandwein really cuts loose in this exciting performance, and maintains the intense pace throughout the record's three-minute-plus length. "The 1920s may have been an era of rampant intolerance, anti-Catholicism, anti-Semitism, and racism," remarks Victor Greene, "but it was also a time when American corporations produced ethnic material that preserved and even promoted ethnic cultures."[47]

The Pearls (1926)—Jelly Roll Morton

Solo piano recordings on July 18, 1923 (Gennett 5323) and Apr. 20, 1926 (Vocalion 1020)
Recording with his Red Hot Peppers on June 10, 1927 (Victor 20948); definitive solo performance in Aug. 1938 later issued on Swaggie

Perhaps no Jelly Roll Morton song is more fascinating from the standpoint of both composition and its many layers of musical meaning than *The Pearls*. He wrote it in 1919 as a valentine to an unnamed waitress at the Kansas City Bar across the Mexican border in Tijuana, and, write biographers Howard Reich and William Gaines, "judging by its unflagging lyricism, he was smitten. The title refers to the way the piece is laid out, with each of several sections designed as an exquisite miniature unto itself, the sun glistening like perfect beads on a necklace. *The Pearls* was an ineffably poetic work, its phrases shaped as if they were short sentences with brief pauses set between them. Each time Morton restated a theme, he transformed it, uninterested in merely recapitulating familiar material. The filigree with which he embellished

---

46. Sapoznik, p. 27.
47. *A Passion for Polka*, p. 88. In the 1910s, close to 15 percent of the U.S. population was foreign-born, a percentage that was only slightly diminished by the 1920s.

each of the three main themes might be called operatic, except that no soprano could possibly articulate the runs, arpeggios, and other flourishes that the five nimble fingers on Morton's right hand could spin on the piano. With its meticulously composed jazz 'breaks' recalling New Orleans trumpet solos and its long-held coloratura trills marking the end of particular sections, *The Pearls* again drew upon New Orleans street music and European opera, the two primary sources of musical inspiration in Morton's youth."[48]

The opening section of the piece, remark David Jasen and Trebor Jay Tichenor in *Rags and Ragtime: A Musical History*, is "an adventurous harmonic conception." They call the 32-measure trio "one of Morton's most original strains, despite its reliance in the first few measures on a pop blues song, *Go Back Where You Stayed Last Night*." The authors praise "a lyrical, consistently moving melodic line, with great invention."

Morton's original 1923 solo piano version of the song immediately marked it as one of the master's classics; the 1926 solo for Victor was much better recorded and even more accomplished. The Red Hot Peppers version a year later was excellent, although perhaps not as satisfying as the solos. But possibly the greatest *Pearls* of all came in 1938. Very shortly after Jelly Roll made his historic May-to-July 1938 Library of Congress transcriptions for Alan Lomax (including a splendid performance of *The Pearls*), he made a handful of recordings in Baltimore of solos and small-combo pieces. Given full freedom to stretch out as he never could on 78s, Morton expanded upon the song's luscious themes across five minutes on solo piano, revealing aspects to the composition that had only been hinted at before. The acetate of this recording (and the others made at the time) was unknown to all but avid collectors until it was finally issued more than thirty years later by the Swaggie label.

Oj Kozacze Bilousyj (White-Mustached Cossack) (1926)—Pawlo Humeniuk

Columbia 27084
Recorded in November 1926

The four selections that Pawlo Humeniuk recorded at this November 1926 session in Chicago rank among the finest that the great Ukrainian-born violinist recorded in his long and prolific career. The piece translating as *White-Mustached Cossack* is an exciting, intensely fast-paced, brilliantly played four-part *kolomyika*, a folk dance based in the Carpathian Mountains area of southwestern Ukraine. "The King of Ukrainian Fiddle Players" is expertly accompanied by cymbaly (hammered dulcimer) and string bass. There were somewhat over half a million Ukrainians living in America in the 1920s, emigrating largely from the western regions of Ukraine, and settling primarily on the East Coast and Midwest where many found jobs in coal mines, steel mills, factories, and service trades. Census data show that Russian emigration to the U.S. soared during the thirty years before the 1924 statutory clampdown on immigration: whereas fewer than 36,000 Russian natives were in America in 1880, that figure climbed to 182,000 in 1890, nearly 424,000 in 1900, 1.2 million in 1910, and peaked at 1.4 million in 1920 before dropping back down thereafter.[49] For many of these people, Pawlo Humeniuk was a cultural hero, helping to remind them of their homeland and its traditions while trying to build a new life thousands of miles away. James D. Bratush: "The melodies and songs of the homeland" provided a 'common bond,' alleviated sadness and loneliness, and "enhanced the sense of belonging to an identifiable group."[50]

Match Box Blues (1927)—Blind Lemon Jefferson

Okeh 8455, recorded in Atlanta on March 14, 1927 (released on April 25)
Paramount 12474, recorded in Chicago in April 1927 (*Blues-#16, RHF, GHF, Folk-#27, SB*)

Before Blind Lemon Jefferson came along, virtually all commercial blues recordings were by female artists. From 1925 until his death five years later, Jefferson's nearly 100 recordings had a profound influence on a generation of artists in his vocal and guitar styles—although both were so distinctive that they defied imitation. He was truly the "king of the country blues," and *Match Box Blues* became his most enduringly popular creation.

Born blind (he may have had some residual sight) on July 11, 1897, in the rural town of Couchman, Texas, outside Wortham in Freestone County, Lemon Jefferson (his real name) learned to play guitar and began singing on street corners in cities including Galveston and Dallas during the 1910s, including a period teaming with Huddie Ledbetter (Leadbelly). As he also traveled to neighboring states, his fame as a street performer spread throughout the South. Black pianist Sammy Price, whose long career extended into the 1980s, had heard Jefferson for the first time around 1918 in Waco, and wrote to Paramount's recording director to recommend him. Paramount brought him into the recording studio for the

---

48. Reich and Gaines, *Jelly's Blues*, p. 66–67.

49. Whereas Ukrainians ranked as only the nineteenth most populous foreign-speaking European ethnic group in the United States in the 1940 census, the 430 records issued by Columbia in its Ukrainian series from 1923–1952 placed them seventh among all ethnic groups, according to Pekka Gronow (*Ethnic Recordings In America*, p. 23). Gronow notes that the records of Humeniuk "influenced ethnic recordings far beyond the field of Ukrainian-American music."

50. Bratush, *A Historical Documentary of the Ukrainian Community of Rochester, New York*, quoted by Tawa, *A Sound of Strangers*, p. 39.

first time around the end of 1925; his first two recorded sides were religious pieces under the pseudonym Deacon L. J. Bates. Within months he was among the best-selling of all blues artists, enabling him to live comfortably in Chicago. But memories of poverty and loneliness were never far from his mind, and ever-present in his songs.[51]

Match Box Blues describes having so little that all his possessions would fit inside a matchbox. It's in part a song about woman troubles, as he sings of his girl across town and asking who her manager (pimp) is. Paul Oliver: "When he sang it was with a deep pathos, a feeling that stemmed from the being of a man forever in darkness. His voice was high, lean and had a cutting edge that severed patience and bared the soul. With a natural command of nuance, he employed a range of vocal devices, striking a note with unerring accuracy, soaring up to it, letting his voice swell and fade, falling in cadence like a train whistle at night. Unlike that of Mississippi bluesmen, Lemon's singing, close to the holler, did not have an insistent beat; instead he would suspend the rhythm or hold a note to emphasize a word or line. By 'hammering' on the strings—using a quick release which produced a succession of open and fretted notes—by choking the strings and by dexterously picked arpeggios, Lemon used rapid phrases which extended the vocal line. For him the guitar was another voice . . ."[52] Robert Palmer remarks that Jefferson's "loose, improvisational, sometimes anarchic" single-string guitar style helped pave the way for the 1940s innovations of T-Bone Walker, who as a young man in Dallas would occasionally accompany Lemon on his walks around town.[53]

Jefferson first recorded *Match Box* for the Okeh label which tried to hire him away from Paramount after his 1926 recordings for the latter company had sold strongly. But when Paramount swept back in to lock up his services, Okeh didn't release the several other songs Lemon had waxed for them. The "rogue" session was fortunate for collectors; whereas Paramount (a subsidiary of a Wisconsin furniture company with little true interest in music) destroyed all of its masters, leaving behind only a scarce number of 78s for future generations, Okeh retained them, so its version of *Match Box* is sonically superior.[54]

An interesting element of this performance, pointed out by David Evans, is that at one point, he plays a variant of the eight-to-the-bar boogie-woogie bass figure, followed by a three-against-four piano ragtime figure. "This boogie-woogie figure, however, was not popularized on the piano" until Pine Top Smith's *Pine Top's Boogie Woogie* nearly two years later.[55] *Match Box Blues* was covered by Carl Perkins three decades later and then the Beatles.[56]

James Weldon Johnson in *Black Manhattan*: "Indeed, the blues are as essentially folk-songs as the Spirituals. In the one the Negro expresses his religious reactions to the hopes of a blissful life hereafter; in the other he expresses his secular and profane reactions to the ills of the present existence. In the Spirituals it is the exultant shout or the sorrow-laden cry of the group; in the blues it is always the plaint of the individual. It is my opinion that the blues are of more value as the repository of folk-poetry than of folk-music. Very often there is the flash of lines that have great primitive beauty and power."[57]

Dixie (1927)—Gid Tanner & His Skillet Lickers
Columbia 15158
Recorded in Atlanta on March 29, 1927 (released in Aug.)

Even before he wrote *Dixie* in 1859, Daniel Decatur Emmett had already secured his place in popular music history as founder of the Virginia Minstrels in 1843, cited by David Wondrich as "the first truly American band, playing American music."[58] While establishing the minstrel show as the dominant form of popular entertainment during the last half of the nineteenth century, they popularized folk tunes like *Turkey in the Straw*, and Emmett helped write others such as *Old Dan Tucker*.

Emmett wrote *Dixie* for the Bryant's Minstrels, a troupe he'd joined in late 1858, as musical accompaniment for a "walk around," the finale of the program. Hans Nathan, in his definitive study of Emmett, noted that the song had strong echoes both of an old German hymn and an English music hall song he used to sing. Robert Cantwell observes that it "had a happy Scots snap and an exhilarating melodic scope; but it caught something too of the folk tonality emerging in the South."[59] Within weeks after they introduced the number on April 4, 1859, at New York's Mechanics Hall, the tune was a citywide

51. Bob Groom, liner notes in Document Records' multi-volume series on his complete recordings.

52. Oliver, *The Story of the Blues*, p. 41–42.

53. *Deep Blues*, p. 107.

54. Jeff Todd Titon in *Early Downhome Blues* (p. 34–38, 99–100) noted differences between the lyrics in the three surviving takes by Jefferson as a means of analyzing the ways in which rural bluesmen pieced together "floating" folk stanzas (Ma Rainey's 1924 song *Lost Wandering Blues* included a line wondering if a matchbox could hold her clothes) along with a song's central components that establish its title and underlying themes. Even if the stanzas lack a chronological progression, he suggested, Jefferson achieved an "associative coherence."

55. Autumn 2000 *Black Music Research Journal* (p. 83–116) "Surely, if T-Bone Walker is the father of the modern lead guitar in the blues and its derivative genre, rock & roll, then Blind Lemon Jefferson is its godfather."

56. Perkins' version was inspired as much by Roy Newman's 1938 recording as by Jefferson's.

57. James Weldon Johnson, *Black Manhattan* (1991 edition of 1930 book), p. 228.

58. *Stomp and Swerve*, p. 21–22.

59. Nathan quoted by Cantwell in *Bluegrass Breakdown*, p. 124.

hit. A year later it was published under the title *I Wish I Was in Dixie's Land*. After minstrel companies throughout the North performed the song, its Southern popularity was triggered by its April 9, 1860, performance in New Orleans in the extravaganza *Pocahontas*, which led to a parody version as an anti-Lincoln piece during that year's presidential campaign.[60] With the start of the Civil War, it was appropriated—with new words—as the favorite war song of the South.[61] Unfortunately for Emmett, he had sold the publishing rights for just $100,[62] so was unable to profit from its escalating popularity. But he would continue to occasionally play fiddle and sing *Dixie* until his death in 1904.

Once the deep antagonisms of war had cooled, *Dixie* could be accepted on its own terms as simply a lovely, infectious regional anthem. First commercially recorded in 1896 by George J. Gaskin, it became a heavily recorded standard by many country and folk performers starting in the 1920s. Probably the best of all the early renditions was this one. Gid Tanner and the boys (by 1927 the record industry's supreme Southern rural string band) have three fiddles blazing away on this performance, with Bert Layne and the ever-spectacular Clayton McMichen, and they kick things up to a fever pitch. Even though vocalist-guitarist Riley Puckett seems to forget the lyrics at one point, he barrels ahead and the band doesn't miss a beat.

Big Road Blues (1928)—Tommy Johnson

Victor 21279

Recorded in Memphis on Feb. 3, 1928 (*Blues-#68, DEL*)

Tommy Johnson ensured his place in Delta blues legend with just one record, the two sides of his debut session cut at the Memphis Auditorium in February 1928. One side was the immortal *Cool Drink of Water Blues*; the other was the comparably powerful *Big Road Blues*. The intensity of his high-pitched vocal, with its leaps into falsetto in the final section, is matched by his fiery guitar style, ably supported by second guitarist Charlie McCoy. Not only did other blues artists directly cover *Big Road Blues*, but Johnson's guitar figures here were also copied by other performers, as in the Mississippi Sheiks' *New Stop, Look & Listen* (1932),[63] and—most importantly—Muddy Waters' 1956 classic *Smokestack Lightning* (which drew still more heavily on *Cool Drink*). Also, Tommy McClennan's *New Shake 'Em On Down* (1939)

borrowed the song's melody with new lyrics. However, Don Kent in the February 1966 *Blues Unlimited* speculated that some of Johnson's verses were "already floating [when he recorded them], and he may only be an intermediate figure. Artists such as Big Maceo and Bumble Bee Slim used verses of *Big Road Blues* with no apparent debt to Johnson." Robert Santelli writes that although Johnson is routinely linked to his mentor Charley Patton by blues historians, his sound is more closely related to another Mississippi blues great of the period, Skip James. "Like Johnson, James used a falsetto vocal style to accent despair and personal pain, which made his sound so completely his own that few bluesmen could copy it."[64] David Evans, who used the song as a book title, cited its wide influence, the intensity of Johnson's performance, and McCoy's second guitar work, "which becomes more complex and improvisational as the piece moves along," to conclude that the piece "must be considered one of the finest folk blues ever recorded."[65]

Frankie (1928)—Mississippi John Hurt

Okeh 8560

Recorded in Memphis on Feb. 14, 1928 (*Folk-#37, GHF, Blues-#79, HS*)

Ten months before he made the definitive recording of the folk-blues epic *Stack O'Lee Blues*, Mississippi John Hurt performed the same service for another classic folk tale based on a real-life murder of the 1890s in St. Louis, the song we know best as either *Frankie and Albert* or *Frankie and Johnny*, but which he recorded as simply *Frankie*. After midnight on October 16, 1899, a young black woman named Frankie Baker, a prostitute in her early to mid-twenties known for her beauty, shot her lover (and her pimp) Allen "Albert" Britt, age seventeen, after a quarrel about the fact that he'd been seen with another woman; he died three days later. In his history of the ballad in *The Rose and the Briar*, Cecil Brown reports that by the evening after the shooting, a "barroom bard" named Bill Dooley had already composed a song that became known as "Frankie Killed Allen," which spread throughout town, and before long throughout the region and beyond.[66] John Lomax included a 1909 version of *Frankie and Albert* from Texas sources in his 1934 book *American Ballads and Folk Songs*.[67] The most popular version of the tune was published in April 1912 as *Frankie and Johnny* by Tell Taylor with words by the Leighton brothers, and this is substantially the song most familiar to latter-day listeners.

60. On April 10, 1865, the day after Lee's surrender to Grant at Appomattox ended the war, Lincoln was serenaded at the White House. After brief remarks to the jubilant crowd, he said, "I have always thought *Dixie* one of the best tunes I have ever heard," and requested that the band "favor me with its performance."

61. Fuld, *Book of World-Famous Music*, p. 197–99.

62. In a *Philadelphia Press* interview reprinted in the July 1898 *Metronome*, Emmett said he sold the rights for $500.

63. The Sheiks' Walter Vinson also skillfully mimicked Johnson's haunting falsetto leaps/yodels.

64. Santelli, *Best of the Blues*, p. 280.

65. Evans, *Big Road Blues*, p. 268–77.

66. Brown chapter, p. 125–45.

67. Lomax also included a secondary version with stanzas obtained from Connecticut, North Carolina, Mississippi, Illinois, Tennessee, and Texas.

It should be noted that the basic structure of the song—the melody and some of the verses—apparently existed long before Frankie Baker killed Albert Britt. Carl Sandburg in *American Songbag* remarked that the song "was common along the Mississippi River and among railroad men as early as 1888." Thomas Beer, in *Mauve Decade*, took it back to 1850, and said that during the Civil War's siege at Vicksburg an Army officer wrote down twelve of the verses. Emerson Hough in *The Covered Wagon* traced it back still further to 1840.[68] Popular music historian Sigmund Spaeth cited the fact that in 1831 a woman whose first name was Frankie shot her husband Charles Silver at Toe River, North Carolina, and "this might have been the starting point for the entire saga."[69]

In hillbilly music, the song was first recorded as *Frankie Baker* in April 1924 by Ernest Thompson, and subsequently by Dykes Magic City Trio (*Frankie* in March 1927), Frank Crumit (*Frankie and Johnny* two months later), Emry Arthur (the man who did the first issued recording of *I Am a Man of Constant Sorrow*; *Frankie Baker* in June 1929), and the great Jimmie Rodgers (*Frankie and Johnny* in August 1929), among many others.[70] The first blues version was *Frankie* by Harry Frankel in January 1925. Then, just over three years later, came the superb rendition by Teoc, Mississippi–born John Hurt on one side of his first 78 release. This is the original folk version of the ballad, far more emotionally involving than the Leighton Brothers' vaudeville treatment. As in nearly all the variations, he portrays Frankie sympathetically as a decent woman driven by justifiable rage to take vengeance on her cheating man by shooting him three times. His gentle voice and lovely guitar accompaniment enable Hurt's performance to rise above the rest. Guitar wizard John Fahey declared this "one of the best vocal and guitar pieces ever, probably the best guitar recording ever."[71] Dick Spottswood points out that a portion of his guitar melody is drawn from the hymn *Dark Was the Night, Cold Was the Ground*, immortalized by Blind Willie Johnson's December 1927 recording; indeed, Hurt sings that title phrase at one point here.[72] (Even though Johnson's recording was made three months later, the song itself had been performed in Baptist church services in Texas since the early years of the twentieth century.)

Frankie and its companion piece *Nobody's Dirty Business* (aka *It's Nobody's Business What I Do*) were the only two of the eight recorded numbers released by Okeh, because they didn't obtain technically satisfactory masters on the others at the Memphis field session. The record sold well, so Okeh brought Hurt to New York for his classic second session in late December. This performance was included in Harry Smith's *Anthology of American Folk Music*.

In real life, Frankie Baker was arrested but the jury said that the killing was justifiable homicide in self-defense. Two months after Albert died, she heard the ballad for the first time and was so humiliated that she left St. Louis for Omaha, Nebraska. When the song reached Omaha, she moved to Portland, but before long the tune followed her there as well. She left prostitution while in Portland and became a chambermaid. After the 1935 Mae West–Cary Grant movie *She Done Him Wrong*, it became a matter of public knowledge that Frankie Baker was the actual woman behind the killing. She filed a $200,000 damage suit against Republic Pictures in 1938, and again three years later in response to another film called *Frankie and Johnny* starring Helen Morgan, losing both cases (the second one decided in February 1942) but providing court depositions that added to our knowledge of the event. Bill Dooley, the man who had created the iconic song and performed it on street corners throughout St. Louis, was one of the town's most prolific tunesmiths, primarily improvised ballads based on news events; he later became a street-corner preacher in Detroit, and was killed there in 1932.

Aidhinikos Horos (The Magic Fountain of Your Eyes) (1928)—Marika Papagika

Columbia 56100-F
Recorded in New York City c. Feb. 1928

Musicologist Dick Spottswood declares Marika Papagika "the Greek counterpart to Billie Holiday."[73] Born on the Greek island of Kos (just off the Turkish coast) on September 1, 1890, her family emigrated to Egypt when she was young, and she performed in nightspots there. Coming to the United States around 1915, she began her recording career in 1918, working with her husband Kostas (known as Gus, who plays cembalo, a regional variant of the harpsichord) and violinist Anthanasios Makedonas, and by the mid-1920s the couple owned their own nightclub in New York. In addition to recording Greek folk songs and other east European and Asia Minor repertoire, she specialized in the Smyrnaic style of the *rebetiko tragoudi*. This refers to the Rebetic

68. See Vance Randolph's capsule history of the song in *Ozark Folk Songs*, Vol. II, p. 125–27.

69. Spaeth, *A History of Popular Music*, p. 206–8. The legendary "Mama Lou" was reportedly singing an early variant of the song in St. Louis in the 1890s (Hischak, p. 111).

70. *Country Music Sources*, p. 63–64.

71. Liner notes, *Anthology of American Folk Music*, p. 10.

72. The tune as sung by Hurt, remarked Carter Family biographers Zwonitzer and Hershberg (p. 132), is also a close relative to that of the traditional blues *The Cannonball*, and Charlie Poole's *White House Blues*.

73. Spottswood details her discography in *Ethnic Music on Records*, Vol. 3, p. 1197–1204.

music of Smyrna, a Greek city seized by Turkey in the early 1920s; many songs of the genre describe the burning and destruction of the city. In all, she cut some 225 sides from 1918–1929 in New York and Chicago. Dr. Martin Schwartz: "That a small regionally based population like the Greek immigrants was able to support such a high level of recording activity speaks volumes about both Marika's popularity and about the importance of music in Greek life."[74] Rebetica music (sometimes spelled "rebetika" or "rembetica") became the dominant popular music of Greece from the 1920s until its demise by 1945. Typically slow and sad, the music is also complex; whereas Western music uses just two primary melodic modes, major and minor, Rebetica commonly uses thirty-five or more such modes, and the instrumentation has many complicated, rapid-fire ornaments.

Brendan Foreman: "Rembetica, the music of the Greek underground, has often been referred to as the 'Greek blues.' With its sensual sound and often unconventional, if not subversive, subject matters, including class struggle, forbidden love and drug use, rembetica was often a perfect soundtrack to the dispossessed and downtrodden of Greek and Turkish societies in the late Nineteenth and early Twentieth centuries, filling a musical hole similar to that which blues music filled for the American black community."[75]

Aidhinikos Horos features a beautiful vocal by Marika and exciting, fiery accompaniment by Athanasios Makedonas on violin, her husband on cembalo, and Markos Sifnios on cello. Prof. Martin Schwartz describes the piece (traditional with composer unknown) as a type of *karsilama*, a couples dance popular among Greeks from Asia Minor.[76] It's sung from the male perspective: "From your sweet eyes, beloved girl, immortal waters run / A drop to drink is all I asked, but you would give me none . . ." Fine as her vocal is, the recording is dominated by the musicianship; given a generous playing time of about 3:40, the three players blaze away at a furious tempo. Marika's recording career lasted until the late 1930s, and she died in New York in 1943.

Kassie Jones, Parts 1 & 2 (1928)—Furry Lewis
Victor 21664
Recorded in Memphis on Aug. 28, 1928 (*Folk-#50, Blues-#61, GHF, HS*)

The Casey Jones legend inspired a number of white and black song variations in the decades following the actual Illinois Central Railroad tragedy in 1900 at Can-

ton, Mississippi, and on the blues side none could top the epic two-part variation by Furry Lewis. Walter Lewis was born on March 6, 1893, (although varying years have been reported) in Greenwood, Mississippi, grew up in Memphis, and began playing a homemade guitar as a child, eventually developing a "Mississippi bottle neck" style (and credited by some with inventing the bottleneck style of guitar playing). He lost a leg in a 1917 railroad accident, began performing on Beale Street, played with traveling medicine shows, and also for a time with W. C. Handy's orchestra. On the medicine show circuit, he played with such formidable songsters as Jim Jackson, Will Shade, and Gus Cannon. His debut recording session in April 1927 for Vocalion was promising, but a second session that October was far better, including his rendition of *Billy Lyons and Stack O'Lee*, and the session's only unissued side: *Casey Jones*. He was working in the Memphis city garage when Victor's Ralph Peer invited him to participate in the label's August 1928 field session there.

Lewis had picked up *Casey Jones* from a middle-aged guitarist he knew as "Blind Joe," and by the time of this Victor session he'd been performing it for over a decade, honing and perfecting it with new verses. Bruce Eder: "By that time he had turned it into a guitar and vocal tour-de-force, a stripped-down epic that built in tension and excitement steadily for six minutes or more, and delighted the ear with all manner of wordplay as well." It included one stanza and parts of three others from the T. Lawrence Seibert-Eddie Newton *Casey Jones* that had been famously recorded by the American Quartet in 1910; the rest consisted of wonderfully original material. Part 2 is driven by Lewis' famous "on the road again" refrain that became one of the most familiar in blues annals. (Two weeks after the Lewis recording, the Memphis Jug Band recorded another *Casey Jones* variant called *On the Road Again*; it's possible that band members may have seen Lewis do his version in live performance, or that this phrase had simply attached itself to the railroad man's saga in the broader oral blues tradition since 1910.) Victor recognized the gem it had by issuing it across two sides of a 78, misspelled as "*Kassie*" Jones to avoid copyright charges.

After dropping out of music in the mid-1930s, Lewis worked as a laborer for the next two-and-a-half decades, while playing on the side for friends and neighbors. The inclusion of *Kassie Jones* on Harry Smith's *Anthology of American Folk Music* introduced the artist to the postwar generation; John Fahey, in the 1997 reissue of the anthology, called this "a masterpiece" and the "most surreal version of the Casey Jones theme" with "Freudian dream imagery." After blues scholar Samuel Charters rediscovered him, the man they called Furry returned to

74. Liner notes for *Marika Papagika: Greek Popular and Rebetic Music In New York, 1918–1929*.

75. November 1999 *Roots & Branches*.

76. Liner notes for the Arhoolie CD *Greek-Oriental Rebetica: Songs and Dances in the Asia Minor Style/The Golden Years, 1911–1937*.

the recording studios in 1961, still in fine form on vocals and guitar.[77] He made a tremendous hit in 1960s folk festivals, late-night talk shows, and even movie appearances (the blues-loving Rolling Stones insisted that he open their concerts twice in Memphis in the 1970s) until his death in 1981.

Bi-karar Olmakti sevmekten muradi gonlumen (c. 1927-1930)—Izak Algazi

Columbia 40002-F
Recorded c. 1927–1930

Called by Karl Signell and Dick Spottswood "probably the greatest Sephardic singer of the first half of the twentieth century," Izak Algazi (identified on many of his records as Izak El-Gazi) recorded at least thirty-two known sides during the 1923–1932 period, ensuring his reputation in Turkish and Jewish music. Born in Izmir, Turkey on April 24, 1889, he grew up immersed in Jewish religious music, and in his youth also learned Ottoman-Turkish music. At age nineteen he was appointed cantor to a local synagogue, from 1908–1911 was a member of the Izmir City Council, and in 1914 began teaching in Jewish schools. He and his family moved to Istanbul in 1923, and that year began his recording career. That part of his life concluded when he left Turkey in 1933 due to the professional difficulties he was increasingly facing as a result of his Zionist beliefs. Following a 1933–1935 tenure in Paris, he moved to Uruguay, where he helped to found the Latin American branch of the Zionist movement. In 1944 Algazi represented Uruguay in the World Jewish Congress meeting in New York regarding the Holocaust.

According to Bulent Aksoy's in-depth article on his life, twenty-five of his recordings were religious in nature, six were secular, and one was Zionist. The majority of his pieces were in free meter, ideal to employ his gift for improvisation. On *Bi-Karar*, Algazi sings his vocal lines without accompaniment showcasing his exceptionally expressive voice; an unidentified ud (a short-necked, unfretted lute) plays instrumental lines in between his vocal segments. Signell and Spottswood (in liner notes for the Rounder CD *Masters of Turkish Music*) remark that he "has no difficulty staying on pitch without the crutch of instrumental accompaniment." His performance accentuates the emotions of the lyrics: "My heart desired love's agony / You granted my wish, I am distraught now / I sought only happiness / My fate undone, I am lost . . ."

---

77. Norm Cohen (*Long Steel Rail*, p. 148–50) notes that from his 1928 original through his latter-day career, Lewis made ten recordings of the song, demonstrating that the ballad was "extremely fluid" in his mind, as he mixed and matched stanzas (out of a total of eighteen) in different ways each time.

Tom Dooley (1929)—G. B. Grayson & Henry Whitter

Victor 40235
Recorded in Memphis on Sept. 30, 1929 (*Folk-#121*)

When the Kingston Trio recorded *Tom Dooley* and made it a pop music phenomenon in 1958, they believed they were committing to disc for the first time a venerable Appalachian folk standard passed down through the generations. But in fact the song had been given a superb original recording twenty-nine years earlier, sung by a man related to one of the captors of Tom Dula himself.

Gilliam Banmon Grayson, born on November 11, 1888, in Ashe County, North Carolina, was one of the finest of all old-time hillbilly singers and a first-rate fiddler. He suffered serious eye damage as a baby that left him almost blind, but his exceptional musical gifts provided a livelihood. One of the first performers to merge the traditional Appalachian ballad singing style with contemporary instrument-backed vocals, he didn't have an opportunity to record until meeting William Henry Whitter at a 1927 fiddler's convention in Tennessee. Born on April 6, 1892, in Fries, Virginia, Whitter was actually the first country music vocalist to make a commercial recording, with some test pressings in March 1923 for the General Phonograph Corporation; however, these were left on the shelf until after Fiddlin' John Carson's breakthrough recordings three months later; Whitter was invited back to record in December, including the famous *Wreck on the Southern Old '97*. An outstanding harmonica player, Whitter was just fair as a singer and guitarist; his teaming with Grayson was to make country music history, as the duo cut the original versions of numerous songs that would live on as enduring country/bluegrass standards, such as *Going Down the Lee Highway, Train Forty-Five, Little Maggie*, and *Handsome Molly*.[78]

The Grayson-Whitter performance of *Tom Dooley*—at the sixth of their seven recording sessions—would seem very familiar to those who know the Kingston Trio's revival of the song; only a few of the lyrics are different. The song is based on the murder of Laura Foster, of Wilkes County, North Carolina, on May 25, 1866. Civil War veteran Tom Dula (who had served in the Confederate Army in Company K" of the 42nd North Carolina Infantry Regiment), known as a desperado and ladies' man, was having affairs with both Laura and her cousin Ann Melton, and had been engaged to marry Laura. (The relationship with Laura began when he returned from the war to discover that Ann, his former sweetheart, had married.) After Laura left home with Dula one night and never returned, her body was found in a shallow grave, stabbed through the heart. Dula was tried and convicted

---

78. See Norm Cohen's feature on Whitter's life and music, Summer 1975 *J.E.M.F. Quarterly*.

of the crime (twice, including a second trial on appeal), an event that drew reporters from as far away as New York, and was hung in the town of Statesville on May 1, 1868. Ann Melton was acquitted in November 1868 of being an accomplice in the murder.

The first known citation of the song was a paper read by Professor Frank C. Brown at the December 1914 meeting of the North Carolina Folklore Society on "Ballad-Literature in North Carolina." One of the ballads listed as having been collected, without further discussion, is *Tom Dooley* (as "Dula" had already been revised to "Dooley" for musical purposes). Brown was also responsible for collecting the song's earliest known recordings: at least seven separate versions rendered as cylinder recordings between 1915 and 1925 (as many as five coming from 1921), some under the title *Tom Dula (The Murder of Laura Foster)*. Thomas Smith from Zionville, North Carolina, offered a version on June 22, 1921, as *Tom Dooley*, with the refrain: "Oh, hang down your head, Tom Dooley / Oh hang down your head and cry / You killed poor Laura Foster / And now you are bound to die." This and other 1921 versions also include (with slight variations) the verse: "You met her on the hillside, supposed to be your wife / You met her on the hillside, and there you took her life." Mellinger E. Henry reported on a few of these versions in the January–March 1932 *Journal of American Folklore*, and printed them in full six years later in his book *Folk-Songs from the Southern Highlands*.[79] Charles K. Wolfe reported that some old-timers attributed the most popular version of *Tom Dula* to a local black banjo player named Charlie Davenport.[80]

Three of the 1920–1921 renditions for Brown and his researchers were offered by Mrs. Maude Minish Sutton, who said at least one of the versions was written in the period just after Dula's execution by Thomas Land, a Confederate soldier from Wilkes County who lived near the Fosters. Brown later related that Land (a journalist and occasional poet) left behind a book of verses, but nothing relating to the Dula ballad. Mrs. Sutton also reported hearing a tale that Ann Melton admitted killing Laura, a confession supposedly made to friends near the end of her life after seeing visions of the devil. A 1948 letter from Mrs. Orene West Burrell, a distant relative of Laura Foster, offered an account (found in the Brown compilation) suggesting that Dula and Ann Melton together had lured Laura away and killed her.

A central line in both the Grayson-Whitter and Kingston Trio records is: "If it hadn't been for Grayson, I'd-a

been in Tennessee." In fact, a relative of G. B. Grayson led the posse that captured Tom Dula: James W. M. Grayson, a former Lt. Colonel in the Union Army who in 1866 owned a farm in Watauga County south of Mountain City, near the Tennessee state line, on which Tom Dula, under an assumed name, briefly found employment after Laura Foster's death. As explained in a 1970 book by John Foster West (the younger brother of the aforementioned Mrs. Burrell), *The Ballad of Tom Dula: The Documented Story Behind the Murder of Laura Foster and the Trials and Execution of Tom Dula*, when Dula's whereabouts were discovered and he fled the farm, Col. Grayson assisted in the pursuit, and he joined with county deputies in capturing Dula on the road leading to Johnson City, Tennessee. West observed that the "if it hadn't been for Grayson" song lyric was therefore a "detail of unusual accuracy."[81] Just eleven months after this recording, G. B. Grayson was killed in an auto accident. "Hang down your head, Tom Dooley . . ."

Walk Right In (1929)—Cannon's Jug Stompers
Victor 38611
Recorded Oct. 1, 1929 (*Folk-#65, GHF, Blues-#78*)

Memphis was teeming with jug bands in 1929—Will Shade's Memphis Jug Band, Jack Kelly's South Memphis Jug Band, Jed Davenport's Beale Street Jug Band, etc.—but to many aficionados, Gus Cannon's combo was the finest of them all. Credit Victor A&R man Ralph Peer; when he recorded the Memphis Jug Band in February 1927, the 78s were such a hit that Peer set out to get other medicine-show entertainers to organize their own bands in the studio. Gus Cannon, a seasoned veteran of the tent-show circuit, was one of the first. Steve James: "A remarkable musician (he could play five-string banjo and jug simultaneously!), Gus Cannon bridged the gap between early blues and the minstrel and folk styles that preceded it."[82] Born on September 12, 1883, just north of Red Banks, Marshall County, Mississippi, he grew up with banjo and fiddle songs, as nearly all of his nine brothers played one or more instruments, and he began playing banjo seriously by age twelve. Working on the railroad in 1901, he said he made a recording for Columbia that year at Belzoni, Mississippi, although this is undocumented. He also worked on steamboats (as a roustabout) and on farms, playing music at every opportunity. In 1910 Cannon met mouth harp virtuoso Noah Lewis near Ripley, Tennessee; he performed on the medicine show circuit each spring and summer (known on stage as "Banjo Joe") from 1914–1929 (settling in Memphis

79. The most complete exploration of these early renditions came in *The Frank C. Brown Collection of North Carolina Folklore,* Vol. 2, published in 1952.

80. Wolfe, "The Legend of Tom Dooley," March–April 2000 *Tradition Magazine.* Another good discussion of the song's history was offered by Joe Wilson in Winter 1971 *J.E.M.F. Quarterly.*

81. Also see article on the song's history by Jim Grayson, great-grandson of James W. M. Grayson, in *Journal of Country Music*, Vol. 2 #2 (June 1971).

82. *All Music Guide to the Blues*, p. 44.

in 1916), often with Lewis and Hosea Woods. During a stint in Chicago with Dr. Benson's medicine show in fall 1927, a Paramount talent scout signed Cannon, and he made his first documented recordings as Banjo Joe accompanied on guitar by Blind Blake. With the jug band craze at its peak, Cannon's Jug Stompers were formed and began recording for Victor in January 1928.[83]

Walk Right In, the group's most famous song, is one of the most utterly relaxed, carefree records imaginable, consisting of only one verse and chorus, with Lewis' harmonica featured as always (Lewis would later serve as a mentor to blues mouth-harp greats John Lee "Sonny Boy" Williamson and Big Walter Horton) plus Hosea Woods on kazoo (taking the lead for a full chorus) and Cannon's banjo and jug, which he rigged around his neck so he could simultaneously pluck the banjo and blow into the jug.[84] At the end of the record someone in the studio is heard shouting encouragement; Samuel Charters suggests it was probably Sleepy John Estes, who was on hand preparing to record the next day. Thirty-four years later, the Rooftop Singers had a #1 pop smash with Cannon's composition, earning him substantial royalties and leading to the venerable artist recording an album for Stax around age eighty.[85]

Given Cannon's long experience as a "songster," Paul Oliver surmised that he may have been inspired to create the line "sit right down, and honey let your mind roll on" from an 1895 number by black minstrel and vaudeville icon Ernest Hogan called *Pas Ma La*, which included the dreamy image of putting your "hand upon yo' head, let your mind roll far." The Hogan piece was based on a French Creole dance known as the La Pas Ma La, and would be adapted by black medicine show singer Jim Jackson in *Bye, Bye, Policeman* in 1928 ("She puts her hand on her head and lets her mind rove on").[86]

Cannon's combo represented a venerable Southern tradition of full-service dance bands/entertainers who could play anything from waltzes and square dances to country hoedowns and gut-bucket blues, do comedy routines, and whatever else their audience demanded. The Jug Stompers rarely failed to please.

Blue Yodel No. 8 (Mule Skinner Blues) (1930)—Jimmie Rodgers
Victor 23503
Recorded in Hollywood on July 11, 1930 (*C&W-#134*)

One of the most famous songs ever created by "the father of country music" Jimmie Rodgers, best known to us as *Mule Skinner Blues*, would have its most legendary performance a decade later by Bill Monroe, but the 1930 original packs a terrific wallop, too. He based the song on his early experiences as a water boy on his father's railroad crew. David Cantwell: "The charm of Rodgers' original lay in its lazy, off-the-cuff sound; Jimmie is asking for work as a mule driver but you can tell he would just as soon pick and yodel his version of the country blues." His relaxed—but exuberant—approach is in marked contrast to that of Monroe, who "desperately wants the job." Accordingly, the famous cry of "Good morning, captain," serving as merely a respectful greeting in Rodgers' version, takes on an elongated intensity in the classic remake.[87]

The recording was made during a working holiday in California in which Rodgers cut over a dozen songs across two-and-a-half weeks, including his historic one-shot teaming with Louis Armstrong on *Blue Yodel No. 9*. Whereas he used backing groups on most of these sessions, this is a solo voice-and-guitar performance. Jimmie regularly borrowed bits and pieces of existing songs for his own purposes, and Jocelyn Neal remarks that all six of his verses here contain phrases that had been used on various blues recordings.[88] [89] However, he skillfully stitches them into a narrative that's more cohesive than most blues numbers.

An unabashed admirer, Bob Dylan wrote in liner notes to *The Songs of Jimmie Rodgers: A Tribute*: "If we look back far enough, Jimmie may well be 'the man who started it all' for we have no antecedent to compare him. His refined style, an amalgamation of sources unknown, is too cryptic to pin down."[90] Henry Pleasants wrote of Rodgers in *The Great American Popular Singers* that despite the technical limits of his voice, his ability to swoop beyond his range with his falsetto yodels and stay on pitch was impressive. "What grew on me was not so much the voice as what was being done with it—the phrasing, the coloring, the gentle slurring, the lightest and briefest of

83. Bengt Olsson, liner notes for Herwin's compilation of the Jug Stompers' complete recordings. The first organized jug bands developed in the Louisville area by 1905, typically featuring fiddle, banjo and/or mandolin, and guitar in addition to jugs made from clay. The Dixieland Jug Blowers began recording in December 1926, followed two months later by the Memphis Jug Band, and soon every record company had to have at least one jug band on its roster.

84. According to Samuel Charters (April–May 1963 *Sing Out!*), Cannon and Woods wrote the song during the early 1910s while they were on the medicine show circuit.

85. The Rooftop Singers initially claimed the song for themselves, but when Cannon filed a copyright claim, he quickly regained rights to the tune without having to go to court.

86. *Songsters and Saints*, p. 34.

87. *Heartaches By the Number*, p. 84.

88. *The Songs of Jimmie Rodgers*, p. 34–37. For example, the opening salutation recalled an obscure 1928 recording by Tom Dickson, *Labor Blues*: "It's good mornin', Captain, he said, good mornin', Shine . . ." The phrase "turn your damper down" had been used by Bessie Smith in *My Man Blues* (1923) and Blind Willie McTell in *Three Women Blues* (1928).

89. Years later, George Vaughan's name was added to the copyright as a "co-writer" for some sanitized new lyrics.

90. The multi-star tribute album was the first LP issued on Dylan's custom label Egyptian Records in 1997.

grace notes. Jimmie wanted the listener to get not only the words and the story they told, but also the feel of the story, [and to do so he would take] rhythmic liberties that are the very essence of jazz."[91] Although Rodgers was no guitar virtuoso, this performance features, notes Barry Mazor in *Meeting Jimmie Rodgers*, a prime example of his "surprisingly bold flat-picking chords and runs" in an atypically long instrumental break.[92]

Bill Malone: "Listening to the songs of the black gandy dancers (construction men) and muleskinners (mule drivers), [Rodgers] absorbed blues fragments and instrumental techniques which later appeared in his performances. Rodgers turns in a virtuoso performance on this recording. He yodels flawlessly, gives the lyrics the kind of boastful, mocking quality they need, and throws in, for good measure, one of the most exciting guitar breaks heard on early country recordings."[93] [94]

After reviewing decades' worth of *Mule Skinner Blues* cover versions in vastly different styles, from the Maddox Brothers & Rose (1949) and the Fendermen (1960) to Merle Haggard (1969) and Dolly Parton (1970), Mazor concludes that it "has clearly proven to be one sturdy and useful song . . . There was much that could be done with its combination of brazen, boastful aggression, a touch of workingman's contempt, and good-natured cockiness. It was, after all, really a song about a freelance worker primed to take on some extra work right now, with no obstacles about to get in his way, because he needs to rush home to his hot mama with extra cash and a bottle of booze."[95]

Goodnight Irene (1933)—Huddie Ledbetter (Leadbelly)

Original Library of Congress recording at Louisiana State Penitentiary, July 16–20, 1933; 2nd prison version on July 1, 1934; LOC version in Wilton, CT on Jan. 21, 1935; commercially unissued version for ARC on Feb. 5, 1935; multiple 1941 radio broadcast performances with Oleander Quartet; 1942 radio versions with Brownie McGhee & Sonny Terry; summer 1943 for Asch 343-2, later released on Atlantic 917 (*Folk-#4, RR-#34, NPR-100, GHF, RIA-#163, TC, BBC, SF*)

One of the greatest folk artists of the twentieth century, Huddie Ledbetter was forty-two and serving his third separate tenure in prison when John and Alan Lomax first encountered him at Angola, Louisiana, in 1933. On a mission to find vivid American folk songs on a grueling tour of Southern prisons, they found their living embodiment in Ledbetter, a man with a vast repertoire of traditional material and possessing such performing flair that, writes John Szwed, he "seemed to give off light when he sang." To the Lomaxes' delight, the man known as Leadbelly,[96] after being released from prison and launching into prolific recordings for the Library of Congress and the ARC label, "was presenting one-act dramas on country dances, work in the fields, and struggles of men and women to survive."[97] But the song that became his most beloved of all was a sweet, simple singalong ballad that would captivate the world, *Goodnight Irene*.

In Ledbetter's capable hands, the song that had begun as the sentimental waltz *Irene, Goodnight* by African-American composer Gussie L. Davis in 1886 had been reworked to fit his performing needs (accompanied as always by his Stella 12-string guitar), and served as a centerpiece of nearly all his public performances.[98] As discussed by his biographers Charles Wolfe and Kip Lornell, he had learned the tune around 1908 from his guitar-playing uncle Terrell from west Texas.[99] It was prominently featured in John & Alan Lomax's book *Negro Folk Songs as Sung by Lead Belly*, published in November 1936, and by the early 1940s was very familiar to everyone in the folk community. But it was of course The Weavers' recording of the song for Decca in 1950, several months after Ledbetter's death, that made it a pop hit for the ages; Pete Seeger had befriended Leadbelly, and knew how *Irene* could captivate an audience. Folk purists were sharply divided over the merits of the Weavers' version (some couldn't get past the violins and other orchestral touches provided by Gordon Jenkins), but everyone agreed that the venerable song as remolded by Leadbelly was a shining gem.[100] Ledbetter's version(s)

91. Pleasants, p. 116, 118.

92. Mazor, p. 19.

93. "For reasons unknown," remarks biographer Nolan Porterfield (p. 258), Ralph Peer's published version "bears no resemblance to the song Jimmie recorded."

94. Liner notes, *Smithsonian's Classic Country Music* (1990 edition), p. 25.

95. Mazor, *Meeting Jimmie Rodgers*, p. 317. In 1955, Rodgers' original recording of the song found new life when members of Hank Snow's Rainbow Ranch Boys, plus session leader Chet Atkins, expertly overdubbed their instrumental parts behind Jimmie's original 1930 recording, plus seven other Rodgers tracks.

96. During Ledbetter's lifetime, his stage name was generally spelled as two words ("Lead Belly"), most notably in the intensive press coverage of his public debut in 1935, the Lomaxes' 1936 book on the artist, and in John Lomax's 1947 book *Adventures of a Ballad Hunter*. During World War II, the name "Leadbelly" began to appear more often in print in contracted form, and from 1950 onward this became the norm.

97. *Alan Lomax: The Man Who Recorded the World*, p. 45, 68.

98. He sang *Irene* at the conclusion of a notoriously corny *March of Time* newsreel short made in early 1935, his vocal being heard over a close-up of the Declaration of Independence.

99. *The Life and Legend of Leadbelly*, p. 52–56. A Library of Congress recording in November 1936 of a Louisiana-raised singer named Gilbert Fike singing a variant of *Irene* called *The Girls Won't Do to Trust* (with the "Irene, goodnight . . . I'll kiss you in my dreams" chorus) indicated that Fike, like Ledbetter, probably "heard the song as it circulated among rural singers in Texas and Louisiana."

100. When the Weavers' managers approached Alan Lomax for clearance of the song, an agreement was reached dividing the royalties at

of the tune were in the second group of inductees to the National Recording Registry by the Library of Congress.

Stompin' at the Savoy (1934)—Chick Webb's Savoy Orchestra (written by Edgar Sampson)
Columbia 2926
Recorded on May 18, 1934 (*BBJ*)

One of the most exciting performances of the early Big Band Era, Chick Webb's *Stompin' at the Savoy* not only paid tribute to the legendary Savoy Ballroom in Harlem that served as the ensemble's home base, but helped establish the musical framework that legions of big bands would follow during the next decade. William "Chick" Webb was born on February 10, 1902, in Baltimore with a physical deformity described as tuberculosis of the spine. Refusing to let this hold him back, he came to New York in 1924, soon led a quintet at the Black Bottom Club, and in January 1927 formed the Harlem Stompers for the Savoy Ballroom. Quickly establishing himself as one of the most powerful drummers in jazz, Webb—the first drummer to lead a big band—recorded five sides in 1929 and 1931, then launched his fully developed recording career for Columbia in December 1933. Alto saxophonist Edgar Sampson (born on August 31, 1907, in Englewood, New Jersey) was crucial to the band's success as both composer and arranger. Trumpeter Taft Jordan, trombonist Sandy Williams, and bassist John Kirby were the group's other key members. Even before Ella Fitzgerald came aboard as its singer in June 1935, the Webb band was recognized as having few equals in musical imagination and thrills. As a drummer, Chick was renowned for both his driving power and remarkable control of bass drum and cymbals; Gene Krupa was just one of many musicians deeply influenced by his style. Sadly, just as the band was reaching a new peak of popularity thanks to Ella, Webb's health began to fail in 1938, and he died on June 16, 1939.

The Savoy Ballroom, opened on March 12, 1926, won international recognition as the symbol of Harlem nightlife below 110th Street, the demarcating line separating black Harlem from white New York.[101] Located at 596 Lenox Ave. a block south of the Cotton Club and extending a full block from 140th to 141st Street, the Savoy, writes Ted Gioia, "represented the new ethos at its highest pitch. It boasted a spacious dance floor of 250 by 50 feet, fronted by two bandstands, with a special section—the so-called 'Cats' Corner'—where the best dancers could display their moves."[102] Marshall and

Jean Stearns devote a chapter of their book *Jazz Dance: The Story of American Vernacular Dance* to the Savoy. The Lindy Hop, the jitterbug, and many other dance styles shot to popularity only after taking hold first at this iconic venue.[103]

Sampson wrote the piece in 1933 as a vehicle for trumpet star Rex Stewart (later with Duke Ellington) while both men were in Earl Magee's orchestra, and Magee used it as his theme while in residence at the Empire Ballroom until it broke up. It was also in 1933 that Sampson wrote his other best-known jazz classic introduced on record by Webb, *Don't Be That Way*.[104] The first solo on the Webb performance is by Cuban-born Mario Bauza on muted trumpet; when Sampson left the band in 1936, Bauza would become its musical director.

Although Benny Goodman enjoyed a far bigger hit in 1936 with *Stompin' at the Savoy* than Webb, using the same basic Sampson arrangement, Gunther Schuller calls the original far superior. "The gulf here between Webb and Goodman was a wide one, the former delivering [the song] with a raw excitement, rhythmic drive (faster tempos, too), and heated sonority; the latter with a neatly packaged cooled-off sound, bouncing along in a safe inoffensive manner."[105] While Schuller is too harsh in his assessment of the Goodman version, he's on target regarding Webb. (To Goodman's credit, he had the courage to face off against Webb in a May 11, 1937, four-hour "battle of the bands" at the Savoy, a fabled night in which 4,000 packed the hall and another 5,000 were turned away; of course, Webb emerged victorious.) Musically, *Stomping* is an utterly simple riff tune, but the way it relentlessly builds and surges never fails to delight.

Money Is King (1935)—Growling Tiger
Decca 17254
Recorded March 18, 1935 (*World-#85*)

As traced by performer and historian Raymond Quevedo (aka Atilla the Hun), the music we know as calypso—but initially known in Trinidad as "kaiso" (a West African word that's a corruption of *kaito*, an expression

---

50 percent for the song publishing company, World Wide, and the other 50 percent split between the Weavers and the Ledbetter and Lomax estates (Szwed, *Alan Lomax: The Man Who Recorded the World*, p. 249).

101. *Encyclopedia of New York City* (ed. By Kenneth T. Jackson), p. 1045.
102. Gioia, *The History of Jazz*, p. 124.

103. The dancers would stomp so frenetically at the venue billed as "The Home of Happy Feet" that management had to replace the burnished maple dance floor every three years; in 1936, with business at a peak, the ballroom was redecorated at a cost of $50,000. (Marshall and Jean Stearns, p. 321.)
104. The song's origins were discussed in the April 1937 *Metronome*. According to Rex Stewart in the April 7, 1966, *Down Beat* (reprinted in *Jazz Masters of the Thirties*, p. 31–32), the song was actually a collaboration between Sampson, trombonist Neldon Hurd, and himself. It was untitled and unrecorded at the time. "I was amazed" to later hear the tune on the radio, with no credit for his role. Sampson subsequently responded with a letter to the magazine saying he had "never accepted credit for material that I didn't write. It seems strange that after 30 years, Stewart and Hurd would have illusions that they composed *Stompin' at the Savoy*."
105. *The Swing Era*, p. 296. Webb's band roared through five full choruses of the piece in its furious performance, whereas Goodman's had time for not quite four.

of approval and encouragement similar to "bravo")—was brought by African slaves to the West Indies in the seventeenth century.[106] Its hallmarks were improvised songs with either flattering or satirical lyrics, often involving veiled social commentary. By the late 1800s kaiso was a prominent music of Trinidadian Carnival. The word "calypso" first appeared in 1900 to denote the winning Carnival song.[107] It was first commercially recorded by a U.S. record company (Victor) in 1914, and such calypso artists as Lionel Belasco (starting in 1915) and Wilmoth Houdini (1927 debut) recorded extensively. The music gained its greatest prominence in the U.S. starting with the ARC and Decca recordings of 1934–1935.

Born Neville Marcano in Trinidad in 1915, the artist known as the Growling Tiger was a celebrated young professional boxer (said to have won the national flyweight championship in 1929) before he turned to composing and performing calypso music in 1934. The following year he made his first recordings in New York for the Decca label along with Atilla the Hun and Lord Beginner. Calypso was becoming a powerful musical force through artists such as Atilla, King Radio, and the Roaring Lion, and all of these artists frequently combined buoyant, danceable music with barbed political commentary in the lyrics. Pekka Gronow and Ilpo Saunio: "When the Sa Gomes company in Port-of-Spain got the franchise for American Decca in 1935, it was natural that the company began regularly recording contemporary calypsos."[108] Decca technicians regularly visited Port-of-Spain for the next several years.

Money Is King, recorded three days after his U.S. debut, set the standard for other artists in its angry populist sentiments.[109] Like other Tiger songs of the period, it addresses the desperate economic straits in which the people of Trinidad were suffering, and makes clear his dark suspicions about the political forces underlying the Depression. The British colonial government that ruled Trinidad was hardly sympathetic to the plight of workers, and the colony would explode in June 1937 following a strike by oil workers, riots, and the iron-fisted response of the government seeking to shut down dissent through a controversial sedition law. He's accompanied by guitarist Gerald Clark & His Caribbean Serenaders.

Quevedo offered this reminiscence of 1935: "He came, he sang, and he conquered. From the very first *kaiso* he sang, Tiger became the most outstanding success I have

ever seen in kaiso. The song was *Money Is King*, and when it was over the cheering and the scene of jubilation it created were indescribable."[110] In 1939, Tiger earned another niche in history when, through his song *Labour Situation*, he won the first National Calypso King competition.

In 1962, when folklorist Alan Lomax came to Trinidad specifically to record the semi-retired artist, Tiger assembled a group of musicians skilled in the traditional brand of calypso he represented: fiddle, guitar, the small four-string guitar known as the cuatro, flute, bass, and percussion. One of the songs he recorded for Lomax was his original hit *Money Is King*. The session led to Tiger's performance at the 1966 Newport Folk Festival. In the Trinidad of the Depression years, he sings bitterly, if a man was poor, "a dog is better than you."

Honeysuckle Rose (1937)—Fats Waller & His Rhythm

(written by Thomas Waller & Andy Razaf)
Victor 24826 version recorded on Nov. 7, 1934
Best recording for Victor 36206 on April 9, 1937 (*Jazz-#35, GHF, Trad-#68, DMDB*)

One of Fats Waller's most universally known classics created for his 1928 revue *Load of Coal, Honeysuckle Rose* boasts a melody that is, writes Len Lyons, "exquisitely raggy."[111] Its melody may have been partly inspired (suggests Donald Clarke) by Vincent Youmans' *Tea for Two*.[112] Waller and his combo did a fine 1934 rendition of the song (with his vocal), but perhaps his greatest version came three years later, stretching out for a 12-inch disc. (It was issued in late September 1937 as part of Victor's historic *Symposium of Swing* multi-pocket album, eight 12-inch sides that also included Benny Goodman's *Sing, Sing, Sing* and Bunny Berigan's *I Can't Get Started*.) There's no vocal here, but the Rhythm is in peak form, with Herman Autrey's trumpet solo and distinctive touches provided on vibraphone by Slick Jones. The rest of the combo: Gene Sedric on clarinet/tenor sax, Albert Casey on guitar, and Charles Turner on string bass. The additional playing time afforded by the 12-inch format, remarks biographer Alyn Shipton, allowed them to develop variations in tone color and shading, and Fats' potent left-hand riff is a highlight of one of his best-ever piano solos in a band context.[113] In May 1941, Waller turned in a unique piano solo version of his classic, subtitled "a la Bach, Beethoven, Brahms and Waller," as he works in musical references to those composers, showing impressive classical chops, in a solo that runs close to four minutes.[114]

106. *Atilla's Kaiso*, p. 4.
107. Warner, *Kaiso! The Trinidad Calypso*, p. 8.
108. *An International History of the Recording Industry*, p. 78.
109. When the three calypsonians first arrived in New York, they were held at Ellis Island for three weeks by immigration officials until paperwork problems were resolved. (Hill, *Calypso Calaloo*, p. 128.) One wonders if that experience may have provided additional fuel for the emotion in this performance.

110. *Atilla's Kaiso*, p. 107.
111. Lyons, *The 101 Best Jazz Albums*, p. 56.
112. Clarke, *The Rise and Fall of Popular Music*, p. 335.
113. Shipton, *Fats Waller*, p. 157.
114. Hadlock, *Jazz Masters of the '20s*, p. 153: Waller enjoyed tossing in classical references on piano, but from a jazz perspective. "Whenever

Sedric, a key member of Waller's Rhythm for ten years, born in St. Louis on June 17, 1907, the son of ragtime pianist Paul "Con Con" Sedric, was, writes William Howland Kenney, "an integral part of the St. Louis jazz and riverboat jazz scene." He started in 1922 with Charles Creath's band, played for two years on the Mississippi River for Streckfus Steamers (including a stint with Fate Marable's combo), and from 1925–1931 was a member of Sam Wooding's Club Alabam Orchestra with the "Chocolate Kiddies" Review, including long tours around Europe and Russia, before joining Waller in 1932. He played with Waller for two years on Fats' Cincinnati WLW radio show, then in 1934 Fats brought the reedman with him to New York to begin the recording career of the Rhythm.

You Go to My Head (1938)—Billie Holiday (music by
    J. Fred Coots, lyrics by Haven Gillespie)
Vocalion 4126
Recorded May 11, 1938[115] (*Trad-#160, APS*)
One of the great ballads using the connection between the woozy effects of alcohol and love, *You Go to My Head* was given exceptional recordings some twenty years apart by Billie Holiday and Frank Sinatra (among other top artists), with Lady Day's rendition receiving the slight nod here. Brooklyn-born composer J. Fred Coots enjoyed a long list of hits over a career that ran from 1922 into the 1950s (including *Love Letters in the Sand, Santa Claus is Comin' to Town*, and *For All We Know*), and this was his most indelible melody. Lyricist Haven Gillespie, Coots' partner on the cited Christmas standard, hit it big in 1926 with *Breezin' Along with the Breeze*, and had his biggest-selling success twenty-three years later with *That Lucky Old Sun*.

Alec Wilder called *You Go to My Head* "a phenomenon" and "a minor masterpiece" in his book *American Popular Song*.[116] James R. Morris, in notes for the Smithsonian boxed set of the same title, remarked that it "succeeds through artful simplicity." A single repetitive syncopation "sets up and maintains a hypnotic spell." The harmony is "constantly in suspense" by shifting from major to minor tonalities. As "an introspective song, with restricted range and repeated notes that encourage singers to use their most personal intimate approach," it was ideally suited for Billie Holiday.[117] This was one of Billie's two 1938 sessions with pianist Claude Thornhill, and Holiday biographer Donald

Clarke notes that the "pastel" colors in the writing here are indicative of Thornhill's style.[118] The session occurred during the brief period in which Billie sang with Artie Shaw's band, and she would sometimes perform this number at live engagements with Shaw.

Holiday's "tart, knowing interpretation dispels any hint of excessive sweetness, and she toys with the melody and its rhythms, creating an atmosphere full of insinuation and nuance," writes Morris. In addition to Thornhill, she's accompanied by Bernard Anderson on trumpet, Buster Bailey on clarinet, Babe Russin on tenor sax, John Kirby on bass, and Cozy Cole on drums.

When the Saints Go Marching In (1938)—Louis
    Armstrong
Decca 2230
Recorded May 13, 1938 (*DMDB*)
A traditional spiritual rooted in slavery days, *When the Saints Go Marching In* (primarily known during its early years as *When de Saints Come Marchin' In*) possessed in its early complete versions the kind of apocalyptic quality found in other coded African-American hymns promising an end to suffering for the righteous, with references to the sun refusing to shine and the moon turning blood red. Ken Romanowski and Dick Spottswood explain that in this form, it referred to the end of time as described by John in the Book of Revelation. "The term 'saints' indicates a devout Pentecostal worshipper, as opposed to the official saints of the Roman church."[119] But over time these elements were stripped away as the song evolved into a joyous hymn, especially in New Orleans. The original legend of Crescent City jazz, Buddy Bolden, included *Saints* in his standard repertoire during the 1900–1906 period (as recalled by Kid Ory); a decade later Ory's combo (in which Louis Armstrong would subsequently play after World War I) also performed it regularly.

According to James J. Fuld, the song's written history begins with the June 1896 deposit of the song (as *When the Saints Are Marching In*) in Williamsport, Pennsylvania. Within the next few months, it was published in several song collections around the country. A somewhat different version was copyrighted in January 1908 by Harriet E. Jones and James D. Vaughan as *When the Saints March in for Crowning*. Fuld also suggests that the tune may have developed (or at least was known) in the Bahamas, based on a report that it was heard in Nassau in 1917.[120] *Saints* was finally published in its more familiar form in 1916 by song collector Edward Boatner, and first

---

you get stuck for a two-bar harmonic device," he explained, "you can always go back to Liszt or Chopin. Even so, it's all in knowing what to put on the right beat."
    115. The song reached #1 in radio airplay (just ahead of Ella Fitzgerald's breakthrough *A-Tisket, A-Tasket*) and #2 on the *Billboard* jukebox chart.
    116. Wilder, p. 497–99.
    117. Morris, p. 58.

    118. Clarke, *Wishing On the Moon*, p. 155.
    119. Annotation for Dust to Digital boxed set *Goodbye, Babylon*, CD 2, p. 28.
    120. Fuld, *Book of World-Famous Music*, p. 641–42. Alan Lomax suggests that melodically the song may have its roots in the white camp meeting hymn *The Old Ship of Zion*. (*Folk Songs of North America*, p. 449.)

recorded November 1923 by the Paramount Jubilee Singers (as *When All the Saints Come Marching In*), then one year later for Okeh by the Elkins-Payne Jubilee Singers. A number of blues and gospel artists covered it (including Barbecue Bob in 1927, Blind Willie Davis in 1928, and Memphis Minnie as "Gospel Minnie" in January 1935 under the title *When the Saints Go Marching Home*), but it remained relatively little known nationwide. In 1938, when Decca asked Armstrong to record some sides in the Dixieland tradition, he revisited some of his own 1920s classics such as *Struttin' With Some Barbecue*, and this hymn that he knew so well from his childhood. (Thomas Brothers reports that Louis began playing the song while staying in the New Orleans waifs' home in 1913–1914, because the camp's Maple Leaf Band played *Saints* every Sunday to accompany the delinquent boys in their procession to church, as an ironic comment.)[121]

Armstrong made the piece into a full production, light-heartedly declaring the studio a church for the occasion, with himself as the preacher. "Sisters and brothers, this is Rev. Satchmo getting ready to beat out this sermon for you," he announced. "My text tonight is *The Saints Go Marchin' In*. Here comes brother Higginbotham down the aisle with his trombone. Blow it, boys!" The nine-piece band then launches into it; Louis strips the number down to its celebratory first verse. Although the song had been a New Orleans staple for years, Dan Morgenstern notes that its "entry into the jazz repertory dates" from this Armstrong recording. The record proved so successful that Decca head honcho Jack Kapp had the artist record a series of spirituals backed by a white choir, including *Going to Shout All Over God's Heaven*. As the Dixieland revival gathered steam in the 1940s, *Saints* became its most universally known anthem; the fact that it became a cliché as overplayed by lesser bands should not diminish the potency of the original tune. Satch would record many new versions during the next three decades, and while other artists (such as the Weavers) waxed memorable versions, the piece would forever be associated with him.

(Personnel: Shelton Hemphill on second trumpet, J. C. Higginbotham on trombone, Rupert Cole on clarinet/alto sax, Charlie Holmes on alto, Bingie Madison on clarinet/tenor, Luis Russell on piano, Lee Blair on guitar, Red Callender on string bass, Paul Barbarin on drums)

God Bless America (1939)—Kate Smith (written by Irving Berlin)
Victor 26198
Recorded March 21, 1939; chart debut Apr. 8, 1939 (reached #10); returned to chart on July 27, 1940

(#5 peak)[122] (*RR-#6, Trad-#8, RIA-#19, GHF-#25, NPR-300, DMDB*)

Rivaled only by *This Land Is Your Land* and *America the Beautiful* as the most beloved of all American secular hymns, *God Bless America* was Russian-born Irving Berlin's tribute to his adopted country that he loved fiercely. The artist with whom it became permanently identified, Kate Smith, was born on May 1, 1909, in Greenville, Virginia. Known as the Songbird of the South, the large-proportioned soprano began performing in vaudeville as a teenager, rose to stardom with appearances at New York's Palace Theatre, came to Broadway in 1926, and made her recording debut the following year. National fame came in 1931 when she began a fifteen-minute radio show several nights per week, boosted by her warm, outgoing personality, and had a hit with her theme song, *When the Moon Comes Over the Mountain*. Through her program, recordings, and movie appearances, by 1938 she was one of the best-known entertainers in America.

Irving Berlin wrote *God Bless America* in late 1918, two decades before the world came to know it. Having already completed the score of his lavish revue honoring servicemen in World War I, *Yip! Yip! Yaphank*, as outlined by biographer Laurence Bergreen, he dashed off an unabashedly patriotic anthem with a soaring chorus. However, he was insecure about its originality. There were so many patriotic songs pouring out during that period, led by George M. Cohan's *Over There* along with many lesser efforts, adding one more seemed like overkill. Berlin also decided that the song was too solemn in contrast to the show's largely light-hearted score (including *Oh! How I Hate to Get Up In the Morning*). So he cut *God Bless America*, and filed it away for possible future use.[123]

In September 1938, Berlin sailed to England, ostensibly to resolve some business matters regarding English rights to his songs, but primarily to learn at close hand what was happening in Europe. He was there when British Prime Minister Neville Chamberlain made his fateful visit to Munich, and was horrified by the rapid spread of Hitler's Nazi forces, while at the same time detesting the thought of another war. Upon returning to New York the following month, he resolved to "write a great peace song"—this from a composer who had always avoided trying to shape public opinion through song. His first few attempts were unsatisfactory. "It then occurred to me to reexamine the old song, *God Bless America*." This would do nicely, he decided, although he made a couple of changes in the lyrics, which in

121. Brothers, *Louis Armstrong's New Orleans*, p. 102.

122. Reached #10 on the *Billboard* jukebox chart, and #7 for sheet music. The song enjoyed a resurgence in 1940 due to wartime patriotic sentiments, attaining a new peak, and again briefly soon after Pearl Harbor.
123. *As Thousands Cheer*, p. 156.

turn led to a slight revision of the melody. In the most important change reflecting his change in perspective, he dropped the 1918 line "Make her victorious on land and foam, God Bless America, my home sweet home," and it became: "From the mountains to the prairies to the oceans white with foam . . ."

The song completed, the next task, to find the right singer to introduce it, proved easy. Ted Collins, who managed Kate Smith, was looking for a patriotic number for Kate to perform during her Armistice Day broadcast—a song of peace. Berlin thought his revised *God Bless America* was such a song; and so the match was made. She introduced it on her November 11, 1938, radio broadcast, six weeks after Munich. "Within days of its belated debut, the song began to acquire the status of an unofficial national anthem," writes Bergreen. It was a rare instance for its time of a song becoming a massive hit without benefit of a Broadway show, movie, or aggressive song plugging. As performed by Smith, it "acted as a rallying point" for an American public deeply uneasy about events in Europe—as demonstrated by the panic over Orson Welles' *War of the Worlds* radio broadcast on October 30 over the same network (CBS) that broadcast her program. "The song's patriotic sentiments, which had seemed so cloying and overwrought two decades earlier, were now exactly right, and Americans clutched at them as if they were a prayer or a security blanket."[124] In much the same way, after the horror of September 11, 2001, another generation of Americans reached out for *God Bless America*, and the song became a regular feature of the seventh-inning stretch at major league baseball games. Although disparaged as jingoistic by some on the left—indeed, Woody Guthrie wrote *This Land* as an explicit response to Berlin—it actually stirred just as much vitriol from the right in its time, out of resentment that its composer was Jewish and the son of immigrants. The title phrase itself was a ritual saying of his Russian-born mother. The Ku Klux Klan even called for the song to be boycotted. Carl Sandburg responded in 1941, calling it "one of our national songs worth community singing no matter what the race of the author."

Air Mail Special (1941)—Benny Goodman & His Orchestra featuring Charlie Christian (written by Benny Goodman, Charlie Christian & Jimmy Mundy)

First version by Goodman & His Sextet for Columbia 36009 (March 13, 1941)

Full orchestra version for Columbia 36254 (May 5, 1941; released in early Aug.) (*Jazz-#140*)

In barely two years on the national music scene until his untimely death, Charlie Christian forged a legend as one of the most important guitarists in jazz history. The classic that he co-created for the Benny Goodman Sextet, *Air Mail Special*, provides a fine introduction to his genius.

Born in Dallas on July 29, 1916, and raised in Oklahoma City, Christian learned music early from his father, a blind guitarist, and was exposed to a wide range of sounds, from jazz and blues to Western swing and light classics, playing in his father's string band. He began to tour with territory bands, and arrived in New York by 1937, when Eddie Durham of Count Basie's band, impressed with the young man's prowess, introduced him to an early form of electric guitar. (Durham had played his first resonator-amplified guitar solo with the Jimmie Lunceford band in late 1935, shortly after Bob Dunn had pioneered the application of a homemade pickup and amplifier to the guitar with Milton Brown & His Musical Brownies.) In early 1939, producer and talent scout John Hammond, while supervising a record date for singer Mildred Bailey, was told by pianist Mary Lou Williams about the amazing young guitarist she'd heard back in Oklahoma City at the Ritz Cafe. Hammond flew to see him, was thrilled, and persuaded Goodman to send Christian the airfare to come to Beverly Hills where the band had a one-week engagement at the Victor Hugo restaurant in August. Benny was unimpressed at the sight of the black youngster in cowboy hat and purple shirt, but when Christian came on the bandstand with the Goodman Quintet for a jam session on *Rose Room* that kept going for forty-five minutes including some twenty choruses by the newcomer, Goodman hired him on the spot.

"With the advent of Christian, the guitar came of age in jazz," declared Leonard Feather.[125] Goodman biographer Ross Firestone: "Christian's astonishing technique, harmonic sophistication, unwavering sense of swing and limitless flow of ideas, drenched in the blues but also looking ahead to the modern jazz revolution of the decade to come, set the pace for every guitar player who ever heard him—and with the exposure he gained from Benny, all of them did."[126] Goodman called him "one of the most astounding musicians I think I've ever heard."

Having co-authored the riff classic *Flying Home* with Goodman and Lionel Hampton very soon after his arrival (first performed on radio in August 1939), Christian came up with another killer-diller here with Benny and arranger Jimmy Mundy. Utterly simple but totally

124. Bergreen, p. 370–72, 380–82. The song's unifying quality is exemplified by the fact that it was featured during the keynote ceremonies at both the Democratic and Republican conventions in 1940. Berlin arranged for all royalties from the song to go to the Boy Scouts and Girl Scouts of America; by 2000 this total had exceeded $10 million.

125. Firestone, *Swing, Swing, Swing*, p. 267.
126. Firestone, p. 264–69.

captivating, the piece—originally titled *Good Enough to Keep*—features thrilling solos by Goodman and Christian, with the band at this time also including Billy Butterfield and Cootie Williams on trumpets and Teddy Wilson on piano.[127] Tragically, by this time Christian had contracted tuberculosis, and after several months in a New York hospital died on March 2, 1942.

Guajira Guantanamera (1941)—Joseito Fernandez
Recorded for RCA Victor in 1941 (*World-#38, 1001*)

The song we've come to know as *Guantanamera*, the most famous tune in all of Cuban music, was (according to most accounts) composed in 1928 by Havana-born Jose Fernandez Diaz (stage name Joseito Fernandez), adapting a folk melody that had probably been sung by southeastern Cuban peasants going back to the turn of the twentieth century, and adding new lyrics. Fernandez began performing as a teenager in the early 1920s, sang with groups including Sexteto Bolona and a combo led by Raimundo Pia, and soon became popular on Cuban radio. As described by Ned Sublette in *Cuba and Its Music: From the First Drums to the Mambo*, he was one of the first *danzonete* singers (the danzonete was a danzon, or dance, that de-emphasized the cinquillo rhythm and included a vocal in the final section, during which the guiro player switched to maracas). After founding his own band, Fernandez debuted on station CMCQ in 1935, using as his theme *Guajira Guantanamera*.

The *guajira*, as a musical subgenre, is described by Peter Manuel as "a spin-off of the *son*," the musical style that had dominated popular culture in Cuba and much of the Spanish-speaking Caribbean since at least 1900. The guajira (also known as the *guajira-son*), as it had evolved by the 1930s, "fused a medium-tempo son rhythm [which itself incorporated Afro-Cuban features from rumba] with guitar-based backing and lyrics that praise the beauty of the Cuban countryside and the simple, happy life of the Cuban peasant, as imagined and romanticized by urban songwriters."[128]

"In a sense the tune was not so much a song as a genre unique to Fernandez, a sort of life support for his improvisations, sung in *decima* [a specialized Cuban rhyme scheme] in the guajiro tradition of an improvised lyric to an unwavering melody with a recurring chorus," writes Sublette. "The title has a double meaning: a guajira is both a style of music of country origin, and a woman from the country. A guajira guantanamera could be a style of country music from Guantanamo, or a girl from Guantanamo." As the number grew in popularity, he

recorded it in 1941, under the title *Mi biografia (My Biography)*. Every afternoon on his radio show from 1943 until 1957, Fernandez sang decimas improvising verses (often commenting on current events) to the melody of *Guantanamera*, "stamping the tune indelibly in the minds of a generation of Cubans."[129] As rendered by Fernandez, it served, writes Sue Steward, as "a heart-rending piece of nostalgia and nationalism that tears at the throat of every exile."[130]

As recorded by Fernandez, the song's lyrics describe a particular woman from Guantanamo with whom he had a romantic relationship, and who eventually left him. He also praises the gifts of the peasant women from that city's dance festival. But eventually new lyrics were added, drawn (in an adaptation by Julian Orbon) from the opening verse of the first poem of the collection *Versos Sencillos (Simple Verses)* by Cuban nationalist poet José Martí in the late 1800s. In July 1962, Pete Seeger learned the song at a summer camp from Cuban counselor Hector Angulo;[131] he crafted his own adaptation (as simply *Guantanamera*), which became a Top Ten U.S. hit in 1966 for the Sandpipers.

The Fernandez original with his danzon group, included on the Blue Jackal/Lightyear boxed set *Cuba: I Am Time*, takes the beautiful, familiar melody at a medium tempo with piano-led accompaniment, punctuated by the brass section. The tune arose from humble origins to become a national hymn.

I've Heard That Song Before (1943)—Harry James & His Orchestra, vocal by Helen Forrest (music by Jule Styne, lyrics by Sammy Cahn)
Columbia 36668
Recorded July 31, 1942; chart debut Jan. 16, 1943 (13 weeks at #1)[132] (*MEM-#6, DMDB*)

I've Heard That Song Before was introduced in the otherwise forgettable film *Youth on Parade* by Bob Crosby and his orchestra, and became one of the longest-running #1 hits of the 1940s with the perfect combination of Harry James' band and Helen Forrest's voice. Forrest was already one of the most popular female big band singers through her work with Artie Shaw (1938–1939, including *All the Things You Are*) and Benny Goodman (December 1939–August 1941, including *My Sister & I*), but after quitting Goodman "to avoid having a nervous breakdown," she got in touch with Benny's former

---

127. The sextet version was recorded a few weeks before Goodman entered the Mayo Clinic for a back operation, and the full-band treatment after his return.

128. Manuel, *Caribbean Currents*, p. 43–44.

129. Sublette, *Cuba and Its Music*, p. 488–90. The song also became a popular recording by Cuban artist El Indio de Nabori on the Panart label. John Storm Roberts (*The Latin Tinge*, p. 182–83) notes that it was "something of an anthem" for Fidel Castro's guerillas.

130. *Musica! The Rhythm of Latin America*, p. 39.

131. Dunaway, *How Can I Keep From Singing*, p. 262.

132. For the first several weeks of its run at the top, it was #1 on all four of the *Billboard* regional charts.

trumpet star James. It proved to be her happiest band experience, because while Shaw and Goodman had treated vocalists as just another instrument, James, writes George Simon, built "the arrangements around his horn and Helen's voice, establishing warmer moods by slowing down the tempo so that the two, instead of the usual three or more choruses, would fill a record."[133] (She and James also had a serious romantic relationship for about a year starting in late 1941.) The bandleader, according to biographer Peter Levinson, decided to speed up the tempo from the version composer Jule Styne had played for him, and as usual his judgment was on target.[134]

The recording was made at the band's final session the day before the American Federation of Musicians' strike took effect, and was held back from release for five months as Columbia carefully parceled out its stockpile. *I've Heard That Song Before* had just the aura of sentimental romanticism that people wanted to hear in the midst of wartime.[135] "Helen is absolutely tremendous" in this performance, raved Gordon Wright in the February 1943 *Metronome*; "what feeling and what a beat the girl gets!" The record sold so strongly that at one point Columbia announced that the wartime rationing of shellac prevented it from pressing more copies; during the early months of 1943 the record industry was allowed to use only one-fifth of its 1941 shellac allotment. Ultimately it sold 1,250,000 copies, making it (according to the July 1943 *Metronome*) the label's biggest hit ever to that point.[136] In Will Friedwald's view, "the most important hits of their time—the real substantial music of World War II that Forrest made immortal—were the sentimental songs of separation . . . No one ever sounded better at addressing absent lovers than Helen Forrest."[137]

Taking a Chance on Love (1940/1943)—Benny Goodman & His Orchestra, vocal by Helen Forrest (music by Vernon Duke, lyrics by John Latouche & Ted Fetter)

Columbia 35869

Recorded Nov. 29, 1940; chart debut April 24, 1943 (3 weeks at #1) (*APS*)

Introduced by Ethel Waters in the 1940 Broadway musical *Cabin in the Sky*, *Taking a Chance on Love*

was first released as a single by Benny Goodman in early 1941, but didn't go anywhere. It was the musician union's strike, preventing any new commercial recordings on Columbia or Victor from August 1, 1942, until 1944, that made possible the song's rise to smash-hit status (in conjunction with the release of MGM's film version of the musical). Limited to reissues or releases of stockpiled unreleased material, Columbia struck gold in an outstanding performance that should have made it big the first time around.

Taking a Chance on Love was added to the score of the Broadway show three days before its opening. Duke and Fetter had written an earlier version, "Fooling Around with Love," which Latouche, lyricist for the show, altered for *Cabin*. The song "ingratiates with its simply syncopated rhythmic structure and its buoyant melodic line," writes James R. Morris. In its eight-bar phrases, its "syncopated pattern is constant for the first six bars, then withheld in the seventh and eighth—a sure-fire device for establishing a finger-snapping swing that moves the song irresistibly forward."[138]

Goodman recorded it during an exciting period for the band shortly after Cootie Williams left Duke Ellington to lead Benny's trumpet section (this was Cootie's second session with the full Goodman ensemble). "Williams gave the band a trumpet spark it hadn't known" since Harry James had left in 1938, George T. Simon remarks in *The Big Bands*, with a "magnificent, rich tone and his spirited drive."[139] Bob "Cutty" Cutshall had just taken the place of Red Gingler, teaming with Lou McGarity to give Goodman (in the opinion of bio-discographers D. Russell Connor and Warren W. Hicks) Goodman's best-ever two-trombone team. Fletcher Henderson is the arranger. Helen Forrest had moved over from Artie Shaw to become Benny's girl singer in 1939, and on this song as on so many others, opines Morris, her "voice is lyrical and lovely, produced with an effortless grace and warmth that endeared her to several generations of listeners."

Alone Together (1944)—Jo Stafford (written by Arthur Schwartz & Howard Dietz)

Capitol 20052

Recorded on Nov. 22, 1944

Introduced as a dance number for Clifton Webb and Tamara Geva in the 1932 Broadway revue *Flying Colors*, *Alone Together* (aside from a fine 1939 recording by Artie Shaw's orchestra) didn't fully come into its own as a great pop standard until the 1940s, and it was the breathtakingly lovely recording by Jo Stafford that helped it reach that level.

133. Simon, *The Big Bands*, p. 270.

134. *Trumpet Blues*, p. 120.

135. Oddly enough in retrospect, almost no one expected much from this song upon its release, but as the February 27, 1943, *Billboard* noted, "Harry James has hit a stride where it seems every bit of the shellac he touches turns to gold."

136. In the first six months of 1943, James' record sales totaled $3.5 million, second only to Bing Crosby's and considered "staggering" for the era. *I've Heard That Song* was a chart-topper during the band's thirty-day engagement at New York's Paramount Theatre (selling out six or more shows a day) starting April 21, 1943, which generated pandemonium.

137. *Biographical Guide*, p. 595.

138. Morris, notes, Smithsonian's *American Popular Song*, p. 60.

139. Simon, p. 219.

One of the finest singers to emerge from the swing band era, Jo Stafford was born on November 12, 1920, in Coalinga, California, and sang on the radio with her two sisters as a youngster. Joining the vocal group the Pied Pipers (seven male singers plus Jo) in the late 1930s, she came with the group (reduced to four members) to perform with the Tommy Dorsey orchestra in 1940. They teamed with Frank Sinatra on the 1940 Dorsey smash *I'll Never Smile Again*; she had a hit duet with Sy Oliver on 1941's *Yes, Indeed!*, and soloed on the 1942 Dorsey success *Manhattan Serenade*. That set the stage for her solo career, signed by mentor Johnny Mercer to his label Capitol, with a long list of hits starting in 1944 leading to the chart-toppers *You Belong to Me* (1952) and *Make Love to Me!* (1954). Her crystalline soprano was ideal for ballads, but she also teamed with her husband, band leader Paul Weston, for a series of popular novelty records.

James Morris noted the exceptional qualities of *Alone Together*: "the long, sinuous lines of the melody, the brooding minor tension of the harmony, and the release in the final cadence which concludes in major tonality . . . The contrast in moods set out by Dietz's evocative lyric and Schwartz's melody is intriguing: the feeling is one of present or imminent sadness, as though to stress the 'alone' rather than the 'together.'" Jo Stafford's performance captures this contrast. "She sings so precisely at the center of the pitch, with so little vibrato, that there is a disembodied quality to her voice—a perfect tool for this occasion."[140]

Will Friedwald underlines the singer's unparalleled qualities: "It's apparent, from the very first note, that she's one of the greats, but her emotional approach to a song makes me think of her as the Mona Lisa of pop music, happy and sad at the same time. Even after years of listening closely, I find that it's almost as impossible to identify the source of her greatness as it is to deny the beauty of her voice and the haunting quality of her singing."[141]

Laura (1945)—Woody Herman & His Orchestra (music by David Raksin, lyrics by Johnny Mercer)
Columbia 36785
Recorded on Feb. 19, 1945; chart debut April 14, 1945
(peak position #4)
Laura is a film about a homicide detective's romantic obsession with a dead woman via her haunting portrait, and required a musical theme to match. David Raksin provided one for the ages, a ravishingly lovely melody with an undercurrent of mystery, and when matched with the lyrics of Johnny Mercer, the result was one of the era's unforgettable movie themes.

Unlike most film composers, David Raksin (born August 4, 1912, in Philadelphia) set out from the beginning of his career to write for the movies; his father had been the music conductor for silent films at the Metropolitan Opera House in Philadelphia, and imparted in him a fascination with the emotional impact of music for the cinema. After earning a degree in music at Penn University, Raksin began writing arrangements for dance bands, and at twenty-three was hired by Alfred Newman to do the arrangements for Charlie Chaplin's score for his 1936 film classic *Modern Times*. After several more films as either composer or arranger, Raksin landed the fateful assignment for the Twentieth Century Fox picture *Laura*. Originally relegated to B-movie status by the studio, it evolved into a film noir classic thanks in part to the direction of Otto Preminger. In the picture, detective Dana Andrews is investigating the murder of a beautiful young woman by a jealous lover; as he stares at her portrait and learns more about her, he falls in love with the image of ethereal Gene Tierney, and the illusion. The director initially wanted to use Duke Ellington's *Sophisticated Lady* as the recurring theme, but Raksin fought hard to provide his own theme. On a Friday, Preminger told him he would have to compose it immediately. "It came quickly, once it came," said Raksin. "I had from Friday until Monday morning to turn up with something immortal, and after all, you don't do something immortal every day."[142] The bittersweet theme was partly inspired by a Dear John letter he'd just received from his wife, actress Pamela Randell.

The film was a surprise hit and moviegoers loved the theme, so the studio and publisher Robbins Music clamored for the addition of a lyric. Alec Wilder recalled that he was present when the publishers played the melody of *Laura* before lyrics had been written, and there was unanimous agreement that "so complex a melody would be highly impractical to publish . . . And it is a very complex, however beautiful, melody. I believe that had a less lovely and loving lyric been written, the piece . . . would never have budged." The song is in C major, and Wilder notes that it begins on an A minor–dominant chord, is in G major by measure three, and continues to evolve in a highly unconventional way. The publishers presented two sets of lyrics to Raksin which he rejected, to their frustration. "I knew what I wanted and that was a lyric by Johnny Mercer, the Flying Wallenda of lyricists," said the composer. "I gave the melody to him, and he went off to meditate, or whatever marvelous thing he did, and the rest is history."[143]

140. Liner notes, Smithsonian boxed set *American Popular Song*, p. 71.
141. Friedwald, *Biographical Guide*, p. 436.
142. Tony Thomas, *Music for the Movies*, p. 210–14.
143. Wilder, *American Popular Song*, p. 514–15.

Mercer biographer Philip Furia: "The eerie resonance between film and lyric is all the more amazing given the fact that Mercer wrote the lyric without ever seeing the movie." He told an interviewer, "I simply absorbed the tune and let it create an atmosphere for me." "Mercer reasoned that if Raksin's melody had captured the mood of the film, his lyric could articulate that mood. Even before the words, however, came images, so that Mercer's lyric makes you see, hear, feel the emotional power in the music—the footsteps down the hall, the floating laughter, and Mercer's beloved train imagery." The composer was stunned and delighted. "I thought Johnny's achievement was amazing, that he should get that feeling into the lyric."[144]

The Woody Herman band recorded *Laura* at its first session for Columbia Records after leaving Decca, shortly after the end of the musicians' union recording ban. The story goes (as related by Will Friedwald) that Herman was all set to record the song as an instrumental, but Mercer, having just completed the lyrics, "taught them to Herman in the taxi en route to the session."[145] Pianist Ralph Burns provided the song with a brilliant, highly original arrangement well suited to Raksin's remarkable melody, the band (with such standouts as trombonist Bill Harris and saxophonist Flip Phillips) is in fine form, and Herman's vocal is wonderful. Vocalist Dick Haymes also had a hit with his excellent performance of *Laura*, but there's no topping what the Herman herd did with it.

(Other personnel: Ray Wetzel, Pete Condoli, Charlie Frankhauser, Sonny Berman, & Carl Warwick on trumpets; Ralph Pfiffner, & Ed Kiefer on trombones; Sam Marowitz, John LaPorta, Pete Mondello, & Skippy DeSair on saxophones; Marjorie Hyams on vibraphone; Billy Bauer on guitar; Chubby Jackson on bass; Dave Tough on drums)

La Piedrera (c. 1945)—Santiago Jimenez y Sus Valedores

Globe 2005, probably recorded in 1945 in Los Angeles (*World-#96*)

When Don Santiago Jimenez first stepped into a recording studio in February 1937, billed as "El Flaco y Sus Valedores" (The Skinny One and his comrades), Mexican-American *norteño* music built around the accordion was still in its formative period. Bruno Villareal, the first significant Tex-Mex accordionist, got his commercial recording start in January 1935, and Narciso Martinez, perhaps the finest of all norteño artists, debuted on record in October 1936. Born on April 25, 1913, in San Antonio, Jimenez learned to play accordion at an early age from his father Patricio, a successful dance-combo musician, and by age twenty was performing on local radio. His Decca sessions from 1936–1938 would establish El Flaco as the next great *conjunto* accordionist, and set the stage for a long, influential career.

The first accordion was built in 1822 by Friedrich Buschmann in Germany, and the instrument was first mass-produced (and given its name) in 1829 by Cyrill Damian in Vienna, Austria. According to Manuel Pena, it was introduced into Mexico by German immigrants by about 1860; Chris Strachwitz and others have postulated an alternate theory that Polish, German, and/or Czech immigrants settling in the San Antonio area during the 1840s may have brought the instrument into the Rio Grande border region.[146] In any event, by the 1890s the accordion was routinely heard throughout the Monterrey area and at southern Texas weddings, dances, and other festive occasions. Mexican-American recordings prior to 1930 were overwhelmingly either vocals with guitars, or *orquestas* (medium to large bands). It is surely no coincidence that the era of accordion-driven Tex-Mex recordings began in 1935 at the time when 1) the Depression had eased sufficiently to encourage record companies to resume more aggressive recording schedules, and 2) the rapid spread of juke boxes increased the importance of dance music featuring instruments—like the accordion—that could generate both volume and rhythmic punch.

When Victor, Columbia, and the other major labels largely abandoned large-scale ethnic recordings during the mid-to-late 1940s, small Mexican, south Texas, and California companies stepped into the vacuum with recordings that had modest distribution primarily limited to their home regions. Santiago Jimenez became one of the first artists to record for Globe around 1945, and also cut sides for Imperial and other small labels. The song that became his trademark, *La Piedrera*, was named after the barrio in which he was born (Manuel Pena explains that the name comes from *pedrera*, meaning a quarry).[147] It's a thoroughly engaging polka accompanied by Lorenzo Caballero on guitar and Ismael Gonzalez on bass, showing off Jimenez's dexterity with the double-row button accordion. Pena notes that Jimenez in 1937 was the first artist to introduce the contrabass, or *tololoche*, into the conjunto, which became standard by the late 1940s (although later replaced by the electric bass). Santiago's son Leonardo "Flaco" Jimenez (taking his dad's old nickname) began his recording career as a teenager in the 1950s, and eventually his fame would exceed that of his father; both men were featured in Strachwitz's acclaimed

144. Furia, *Skylark*, p. 150–53.
145. *Biographical Guide*, p. 218.

146. Strachwitz, liner notes for Arhoolie/Folklyric albums *Norteño and Tejano Accordion Pioneers* and *Texas-Mexican Border Music, Vol. 4*.
147. *The Texas-Mexican Conjunto*, p. 59–63.

1976 documentary *Chulas Fronteras*. (In the film Flaco's young son David is seen playing his grandfather's theme song.) The original version of *La Piedrera* was included on the New World Records LP *Old Country Music in a New Land* assembled by Dick Spottswood.[148]

Drifting Blues (1946)—Johnny Moore's Three Blazers (featuring Charles Brown)

Philo 112 (also released in Aug. 1946 on Aladdin 112)[149]
Recorded Sept. 11, 1945; chart debut Feb. 23, 1946 (#2 R&B, 23 weeks total) (*Blues-#34, RHF, R&B-#143, BHF, SB*)[150]

"Late night, lights down low, bottle of wine, someone to dream with, and Charles Brown, blues elegance personified—now there's a scenario suitable for any true romantic," writes David McGee.[151] Born in Texas City, Texas, on the Gulf Coast on September 13, 1922, Brown played piano for his Baptist Church and in his college band, earned a degree in chemistry, and was head of the science department at a Baytown, Texas, high school when he decided to take the full plunge into music (having received classical piano training) and relocated to Los Angeles in 1943. There, after winning an amateur talent contest at the Lincoln Theatre, he became one-third of Johnny Moore's Three Blazers (with Moore on guitar and Eddie Williams on bass), a bluesier version of the King Cole Trio. The combo attracted a growing audience; singer Frankie Laine was a fan, and hired the Three Blazers to back him on his first record (and theirs) in 1945, *Melancholy Madeline*.

His arrival in Los Angeles coincided with the historic moment when the city became the new center of blues and, more broadly, black American music. Los Angeles' black population more than doubled between 1940 and 1946, and as servicemen streamed back from war, it became the world symbolized by Walter Mosley's character of black detective Easy Rawlins. Writes Ken Emerson: "Melding the Kansas City swing of touring territory bands with the blues and boogie-woogie of migrants from Texas, Oklahoma, and Arkansas, R&B flourished in Central Avenue nightclubs like the Club Alabam and on local independent labels like Modern and Aladdin."

Brown was indeed the definitive after-hours blues balladeer, poised at his piano and gently recounting his sad tales of lost love or life's disappointments. *Drifting Blues* was the hit that started it all, a song Brown had written in high school under the title "Walkin' and Drif-tin'" During their engagement at the Copa Club, *Drifting Blues* became a featured and much-requested number. One night at the Copa, producers Sammy Goldberg and Eddie Mesner offered them $800 to record the piece, a flat payment with no royalties.[152] They signed the contract and cut the song, and even as the record became a smash hit, $800 is all they would earn from it, although the hit opened doors to high-paying engagements around the country. Johnny Otis sits in on drums. Chip Deffaa in *Blue Rhythms* calls it "an unforgettable expression of loneliness and alienation . . . When Moore sang with a touch of weariness how he was drifting, he seemed to be giving voice to the feelings of many blacks after World War II. Mingled feelings of disappointment, hope, uncertainty about the future—such things could be sensed in Brown's song." "I'm driftin' and driftin', like a ship out on the sea . . ."[153]

A Night In Tunisia (1946)—Charlie Parker Septet

Dial 1002
Recorded in Hollywood on March 26, 1946 (*TG*)

The exotically compelling *A Night In Tunisia* had been created by Charlie Parker's frequent musical cohort Dizzy Gillespie while playing with the Benny Carter band in 1942. The two men were playing together through much of 1945 and into early 1946 at the Three Deuces on 52nd Street plus other engagements including Town Hall, and *Tunisia* was one of their staples. Parker would carry out his friend's artistic vision in one of its finest renditions.

The great alto saxophonist's second session as a leader, this is one of his legendary dates that also produced classic performances of *Ornithology* (the flip side of *Tunisia*), *Yardbird Suite*, and *Moose the Mooche*. It came about when Gillespie took a group including Bird to Los Angeles to open at Billy Berg's nightclub in December 1945, and after Parker made his first of many appearances at Norman Granz's Jazz at the Philharmonic concert series on January 24 in Los Angeles. Gillespie returned to New York once the Billy Berg gig ended, but Parker stayed behind to play at other venues around town—and to cut this session for Dial.

Parker biographer Carl Woideck writes that during the first take of *Tunisia*, following the piece's introduction and an interlude, Bird filled a four-bar solo break "with a stunning fantasia in sixteenth notes. After the take, Parker said, 'I'll never make that break again.'" "Despite

---

148. Another version of the song by Jimenez, recorded circa 1953 in San Antonio, was included by Spottswood on a 1997 Rounder CD, *Squeeze Play: A World Accordion Anthology*.

149. Brown's subsequent solo version was recorded on August 26, 1953, for Aladdin 3209.

150. Winner of the *Cash Box* award as best R&B record of 1946.

151. *New Rolling Stone Album Guide* (2004), p. 107.

152. Eddie Mesner was vice president of the family-run Philo Records (which would change its name to Aladdin during 1946), with his brother Leo Mesner as president. The company's Santa Monica Boulevard offices were just a few doors away from another important independent label, Black & White, which would soon produce T-Bone Walker's *Call It Stormy Monday*.

153. Deffaa, p. 112.

Parker's claim, analysis of his solo breaks on this and the other two surviving takes of *A Night In Tunisia* show that he had already worked out his opening improvisational gambit: all three breaks are nearly identical. This lack of variation does not take away from the brilliance of his solo break; no other instrumentalist in jazz at the time would have conceived of and executed that passage."[154]

Parker's chorus in this performance was examined by Andre Hodeir in *Jazz: Its Evolution and Essence*. "It begins with a break of more than 60 sixteenth notes with embellishments that are hard to place exactly in such a deluge. Parker accents certain off-beat notes violently, in such a way that an inexperienced listener often loses the beat in this rhythmic complexity. However, it is all conceived and played with absolute strictness; at the end of this dizzying break, Parker falls right in on the first beat."[155]

Ted Gioia describes *Tunisia* as the highlight of this memorable session. Parker, he writes, uses that early four-bar break "to execute a mesmerizing double-time jazz cadenza. Few jazz reed players could approach the sheer speed of this passage, but even more impressive is the rhythmic phrasing in which coy accents, oddly placed in crevices between the beats, impart a bobbing, weaving quality to the horn line. Parker follows up with a sleek 16-bar solo, which for all its merits is overshadowed by the previous four-bar explosion."[156]

(Other personnel: Miles Davis on trumpet; Lucky Thompson on tenor sax; Dodo Marmarosa on piano; Alvin Garrison on guitar; Victor McMillan on bass; Roy Porter on drums)

Things to Come (1946)—Dizzy Gillespie & His Orchestra (written by Dizzy Gillespie & Gil Fuller)
Musicraft 447
Recorded July 9, 1946 (*Jazz-#144*)

A year after his revolutionary recordings with Charlie Parker that launched bebop as a full-blown new alternative to swing, Dizzy Gillespie formed his second big band, and this record set it into orbit. *Things to Come*, write Gunther Schuller and Martin Williams, "was the first full translation of Gillespie's and Parker's new bop language into big band terms. There isn't the slightest stylistic break between the solos and the arranged ensemble. The piece had the relentless speed, the frenetic emotional tension, all the new melodic and harmonic inventions that the boppers had developed in half a decade of small-group experimentation. Nothing like it had ever been heard before; it stunned the jazz world and, in its own curious and unstoppable way, spelled the end of the swing era."[157]

Gil Fuller, who had worked with Gillespie in the Billy Eckstine band of the early 1940s, served as musical director, and Ted Gioia remarks that his arrangement here "provided Gillespie with a suitably modernistic setting" to liberate his imagination.[158] In his Gillespie biography, Alyn Shipton declares: "This is playing of staggering virtuosity, with all the sections (and Milt Jackson on vibes) achieving a precision at a speed previously only attained by small groups, not to mention the extraordinary unison glissandi at the end of the arrangement."[159] Far too fast and complex to be danceable, it baffled most swing lovers, but thrilled a new generation of bop fanatics. Cuban bandleader/composer Chico O'Farrill was starting his career in a Havana big band, when a friend returned from a New York visit with recent American jazz records including *Things to Come*, and he recalled to Ira Gitler, "I was shocked. I said, 'If this is the shape of things to come, how in the hell am I going to cut it?' It was such a new thing . . . Here we were confronted with phrases that were asymmetrical." Gillespie, in constructing a big-band version of the composition he had recorded under the title *Be-Bop* with his small group a year earlier,[160] was using an "unusual harmonic concept that was so alien to what we had been doing . . . Frankly, for some time I was lost."[161] But like most of the jazz world, before long he was discovering a method, and great beauty, to the madness.

(Other personnel: Talib Daawud, Dave Burns, Raymond Orr, & John Lynch on trumpets; Gordon Thomas, Leon Cormenges, & Alton Moore on trombones; John Brown & Howard Johnson on alto sax; Ray Abrams & Warren Lucky on tenor sax; Pee Wee Moore on baritone sax; John Lewis on piano; Ray Brown on bass; & Kenny Clarke on drums)

Up Above My Head I Hear Music in the Air (1947)—Sister Rosetta Tharpe & Marie Knight
Decca 48090
Recorded on Nov. 4, 1947; chart debut Dec. 25, 1948 (reached #6 R&B) (*GOSP-#27*)

This thrilling performance, by the great gospel dynamo Sister Rosetta and her longtime partner Marie Knight, be-

154. Woideck, *Charlie Parker: His Music and Life*, p. 128–29.
155. Hodeir, p. 109.
156. Gioia, *The History of Jazz*, p. 219.
157. Liner notes, Smithsonian's *Big Band Jazz*.

158. *The History of Jazz*, p. 222.
159. Shipton, *Groovin' High*, p. 183–84. Calling it "an apocalyptic vision," Joachim-Ernst Berendt and Gunther Huesmann in *The Jazz Book: From Ragtime to the 21st Century* (p. 115) describe it as "a broiling, twitching mass of lava out of which, for a few seconds arise ghostly figurations, to disappear again at once. But above it all the clear and triumphant sound of Gillespie's trumpet. 'Music of chaos,' as some people said then, but also music about man's victory over chaos!"
160. Fuller in Gillespie's memoir *To Be or Not to Bop* (p. 225) recalls that they wrote the piece specifically because "we were trying to outdo Woody Herman's band . . . [it] was much faster than anything that they ever played."
161. Ira Gitler, *Swing to Bop*, p. 153.

came one of the few gospel records to crack the *Billboard* rhythm & blues charts. They trade off lines, drawing energy from one another and the potent accompaniment of Rosetta's powerfully bluesy guitar and the Sam Price Trio[162] (Price on R&B-flavored piano, George Foster on bass, and Wallace Bishop on drums), and drawing to a rousing conclusion.

Tharpe was born on March 20, 1921, in Cotton Plant, Arkansas, the daughter of Katie Bell Nubin, a mandolin-playing evangelist in the Church of God in Christ (COGIC) and gospel shouter known as "Mother Bell." A guitar-playing prodigy from the age of six, Rosetta began playing alongside her mother on the tent revival circuit with P. W. McGhee's troupe. In 1934, she married ukulele player Wilbur Thorpe (who later changed his name to Tharpe), although the union didn't stick. From an early age, remarks Jerma Jackson, she mastered the blues-based technique of making a guitar "talk" by "playing single notes rather than chords, turning the instrument into an extension of the vocal line and creating a second voice that made for a dynamic performance."[163] Rosetta created a stir in the gospel world and the Sanctified Church in particular when she performed at the Cotton Club with Cab Calloway's band in 1938, and became the first gospel artist signed by Decca Records other than Mahalia Jackson's one unsuccessful session for the label the previous year.[164] Her first recordings were made that October, with a mixture of sacred and borderline secular material, and *Rock Me* became a strong seller. At year's end her fame was spread by performing at John Hammond's "From Spirituals to Swing" concert at Carnegie Hall.[165] The combination of her superb musicianship, enthusiastic vocals, and charismatic personality made her a performer who transcended the gospel world, as evidenced when she recorded with Lucky Millinder's band in 1941, and made her first unabashedly secular recording in 1942, *I Want a Tall, Skinny Papa*. Her biggest solo hit was *Strange Things Happening Every Day* (1945).

Born Marie Roach on June 1, 1925, in Sanford, Florida, and raised in Newark, New Jersey, Knight became a gospel soloist in her late teens, and in the early 1940s

joined the revival team of Philadelphia evangelist Frances Robinson, traveling cross-country. In 1946, Tharpe invited Marie to join her as a duo, and they performed together on record and in tours (off and on) for nine years. Marie (sometimes billed in those years as "Madame Marie Knight") did the arrangements for most of their recordings, and her powerful contralto won a national reputation.[166] She would sing *Peace in the Valley* at Rosetta's funeral in 1973. Her faith was tested when a fire killed her mother and her two children. In the mid-1950s, she branched out into pop and blues. But she never lost her gospel roots; in 1973 Marie was ordained as an evangelist, two years later recorded her first solo gospel album, and in 2007 (!) released an album of new performances, *Let Us Get Together*.

Like *Strange Things*, *Up Above My Head* is an unmistakable precursor to rock and roll. Biographer Gayle Wald: "Especially in the instrumental bridge between verses, [it] leaves the Sanctified Church behind and charts a straight course toward rhythm and blues. Rosetta *works* the guitar, alternately plucking and strumming up a storm," and the record "had an undeniable energy that paralleled the collective optimism of black people in the postwar years . . . it captured people's budding hope that the late 1940s and early 1950s would bring about sorely overdue change."[167] Just as other spirituals and gospel songs such as *This Little Light of Mine* were adapted for the civil rights movement, so too was *Up Above My Head*. Betty Mae Fikes of Selma, Alabama, introduced her reworked version at the 1964 Freedom Conference in Atlanta: "Up above my head, I see freedom in the air . . . I really do believe, I said I really do believe, there's a God somewhere."[168] [169]

Early Autumn (1948)—Woody Herman & His Orchestra (written by Ralph Burns)
Recorded for Columbia 38367 on Dec. 27, 1947 as *Summer Sequence* (Part 4); then as *Early Autumn* in Dec. 1948 for Capitol 57-616 (*GHF, Jazz-#72*)

Ralph Burns wrote the three-movement *Summer Sequence* for the premiere of Igor Stravinsky's *Ebony Concerto* by the Woody Herman band at Carnegie Hall on March 25, 1946. While the Stravinsky piece drew a mixed reaction (it would win more acclaim in sub-

162. Price had been a ubiquitous session man and talent scout in blues and jazz since the early 1920s, and in the 1940s was a staff musician for Decca. Tharpe biographer Gayle Wald (*Shout, Sister, Shout!*, p. 67–68.) recounts that Rosetta and Price were regularly in conflict, partly because he considered himself the key musical partner on the records, whereas she regarded him as merely a skillful sideman on her sessions.

163. *Singing in My Soul*, p. 40.

164. She would remain an exclusive Decca artist until 1956.

165. "Making the guitar talk," writes biographer Gayle Wald, "had significance specific to Rosetta's position" coming from the COGIC. "In musical terms, it paralleled the religious practice of speaking in tongues." (*Shout, Sister, Shout!*, p. 72.) For all of Tharpe's great secular success, Knight recalled that the creative process for her partner was primarily a spiritual experience (Jackson, p. 101).

166. Knight's voice was darker than Tharpe's, and Horace Clarence Boyer remarks that "they made the perfect gospel duet" as heard here. On the chorus after Rosetta's solo, Marie "assumes the role of the male bass from gospel quartets, essaying her range from the top to the bottom" (*How Sweet the Sound*, p. 158–59).

167. Wald, *Shout, Sister, Shout!*, p. 86–87.

168. Guy and Candie Carawan, *Freedom Is a Constant Struggle*, p. 52.

169. On September 16, 1964, *Up Above My Head* served as the opening song for the premiere of the ABC youth music show *Shindig*, as performed in a "biracial choir" by artists including the Blossoms, Righteous Brothers, and Everly Brothers.

sequent years), Burns' work elicited wide enthusiasm. Herman broke up the band that December (the same fateful month that several other bands including those of Benny Goodman and Tommy Dorsey also at least temporarily broke up), but formed a new Second Herd several months later. Soon after re-forming, Herman asked Burns if he would write "a sort of extension," later viewed as an epilogue or fourth movement, to the suite. The reason is that the band was about to record its first ten-inch LP (*Sequence In Jazz*, released over a year later in January 1949), and the three movements (at eight-and-a-half minutes) weren't long enough to take up a full side. Tenor saxophonist Stan Getz had just joined the band, and the suite had nothing to feature him, so Burns wrote *Early Autumn*—Herman suggested the title—as a Getz showcase.

In its original recording as *Summer Sequence* (Part 4), writes Gary Giddins, Getz played "an ethereal eight-bar solo" and "a closing melody that promised more than was realized in that arrangement." A year later, this time for Capitol, the band returned to the studio to play Burns' new arrangement as *Early Autumn* built entirely on that "elusive closing melody," again with a ravishing Getz solo.

"One of the pleasures of 78s, and later 45s, was how they focused the attention of musician and listener alike," remarks Giddins. "Confronted with the three-minute limit, the former was pressed to undertake perfection—lapses permissible in a novel are less tolerable in a short story. In jazz, this meant training yourself, if you were an arranger, to make certain something colorful occurred in every measure. It forced soloists to maximize the few bars . . . they were assigned. Listeners, in turn, savored every detail. Today it is inconceivable that a musician could make his or her name in an eight-bar variation," but that is precisely what happened with Getz on this recording. Giddins notes that the performance underlined the dominant influence that Stan's idol Lester Young—with his "airborne melodies, smooth timbre, and advanced harmonies"—was to have on tenor saxophonists of the next decade.[170]

Woody's Second Herd featured one of the all-time great saxophone sections: three tenors (Stan Getz, Zoot Sims, and Herbie Steward), and a baritone sax (Serge Chaloff). Herman biographer Gene Lees writes that *Early Autumn* achieved its great fame in large part because Voice of America disc jockey Willis Conover used the recording as the theme for his *House of Sounds* radio show seven days a week for more than ten years. "Thus listeners in other countries [were] exposed to the piece more than 3,000 times."[171] Following the Capitol

release in 1949, *Early Autumn* made Stan Getz a star, and brought Herman one of his most admired recordings.

Ted Gioia praises Getz's "hauntingly delicate solo" on *Early Autumn*.[172] Ironically by the time the piece became a hit, the saxophonist had left Herman en route to his own long, successful solo career.

Wasn't That a Time? (1949)—The Weavers (written by Lee Hays & Walter Lowenfels)
Charter 503 (*Folk-#76*)

The period from late 1947 to late 1948 was a dark time for American progressives. "We're scared—and every day's paper makes us a little more scared," declared the lead editorial in the December 1947 *People's Songs*, co-founded by Pete Seeger. The Cold War had begun with a vengeance, and the House Un-American Activities Committee was lashing out at its perceived enemies, starting with the firing of ten Hollywood writers and directors. "We're scared as citizens of a country proud of its democratic heritage, and as cultural workers who know that the arts can only flourish in an atmosphere of freedom." The call went out for a musical response to this historic challenge: "We're looking for a song that can tell the American people about the danger the entire country is facing. We're looking for a song that can initiate action against the impending fascism which would mean death for all freedom in music." Several months later, that song arrived in the form of *Wasn't That a Time*.

"The days ahead will be as crucial as the days of Valley Forge, Gettysburg, Bataan," proclaimed the editorial in the November 1948 *People's Songs*. "These are times to try the soul of man. As the new song on page 3 says, these are times to free the soul of man as well." The new anthem was provided by Seeger's former colleague in the Almanac Singers, regular contributor to *People's Songs*, and starting in December 1948 his co-founder of The Weavers, the brilliant and fiery Arkansas-born populist Lee Hays, and his writing partner Walter Lowenfels, a renowned poet, journalist (editor of the Pennsylvania edition of the *Daily Worker* from 1938–1953), and activist in the labor and civil rights movements. *People's Songs* was founded in December 1945 by Seeger, Hays, Woody Guthrie, and Millard Lampell, and in addition to its monthly bulletin, the organization collected folk songs, published songbooks, taught classes, and organized concert tours. Hays, Lowenfels, and Seeger hurled themselves into Henry Wallace's Progressive Party campaign for President, and that experience (which included violence against Wallace supporters) helped inspire the song, whose four-line verse/four-line chorus structure was patterned after the labor rallying cry *Solidarity Forever*.

170. *Visions of Jazz*, p. 407–8.
171. Lees, *Leader of the Band*, p. 154–55.

172. *History of Jazz*, p. 285.

The American People's Chorus (under the direction of composer Elmer Bernstein) sang *Wasn't that a Time* that November 5 at Irving Plaza in New York.[173] Several months later it became one side of the first single ever issued by The Weavers (shortly before *The Hammer Song*, aka *If I Had a Hammer*), making it by definition a crucial song in folk music history. The piece speaks powerfully to the deep patriotism Seeger, Hays, Ronnie Gilbert, and Fred Hellerman felt in their bones even in the face of the era's profound travails.

In concert Seeger later recalled for audiences that one of his ancestors was on the Mayflower with Governor Bradford, one of the leaders of the Plymouth Community; one was a quartermaster and another a major on General Putnam's staff, and might have been at Valley Forge. "Those ancestors of mine were all subversives in the eyes of the established government of the British colonies. If they had lost the War of Independence, they might have each and severally been hung." His subsequent ancestors were ardent abolitionists; one of his great-grandmothers died after having to escape from Charleston after the firing on Fort Sumter. So the words of *Wasn't That a Time* were deeply personal, as was their relevance to the "terrible time" of McCarthyism that would ruin many American lives during the years following the release of this performance, and would also end the Weavers' all-too-brief career.[174]

One of the specific inspirations for the song was opposition to the so-called "thought control" represented by the Smith Act, enacted in 1940 to make it a crime to advocate overthrowing the government, to print, publish or circulate such ideas, or to belong to or "affiliate with" any organization espousing such doctrines. It was therefore a grim irony that on June 30, 1953, Walter Lowenfels was indicted on charges of "conspiracy to overthrow the United States government" under that statute. An unsigned editorial in the October 1953 *Sing Out!* attacked the indictment as evidence of "the increasing tempo of the attempt to impose fascism on our country," thus underlining the urgency of the ideals embodied in the song. He was convicted in 1954, but the conviction was subsequently overturned for lack of evidence; he returned to writing books of poetry (more than two dozen in all) and an autobiography. On August 17, 1955, the lyrics of *Wasn't That a Time* were a specific point of discussion in Seeger's testimony before the House Un-American Activities Committee. The panel's McCarthyite members thought it subversive; Seeger considered it patriotic and offered to sing it for them, an offer they declined before finding him in contempt.[175] At great personal cost, he finally succeeded in having the charge dismissed.

When the Weavers reunited one last time in November 1980 for the Carnegie Hall concerts that would serve as the basis for a celebrated PBS special, Ronnie Gilbert recalled how the song that provided the title for the documentary, *Wasn't That a Time*, always gave her chills.

> Our fathers bled at Valley Forge, the snow was red with blood
> Their faith was warm at Valley Forge,
> Their faith was brotherhood.
>
> Wasn't that a time, wasn't that a time?
> A time to try the soul of men,
> Wasn't that a terrible time?
>
> Brave men who fought at Gettysburg now lie in soldiers' graves
> But there they stemmed the slavery tide
> And there the faith was saved.
> . . .
> Isn't this a terrible time?
> Isn't this a time?
> A time to free the soul of men,
> Isn't this a wonderful time?[176]

Rudolph, the Red-Nosed Reindeer (1949)—Gene Autry (written by Johnny Marks)

Columbia 38610

Recorded June 27, 1949; chart debut Dec. 3, 1949 (1 week at #1 both pop and C&W); reached #3 in Dec. 1950 (*GHF-#40, BBC-#14, DMDB-#22, RIA-#31, Trad-#34, C&W-#88*)

One of the most monumental hit records of all time with eventual reported sales of over seven million copies,[177] *Rudolph* remains almost as ubiquitous as *White Christmas* every holiday season more than sixty years later. He was preceded by a few other Hollywood singing cowboys, but Gene Autry is the one who will be remembered the longest. Born Orvin Gene Autry on September 29, 1907 in Tioga Springs, Texas, Autry made his first recordings in 1929, and two years later scored one of the biggest C&W hits of the pre–World War II era with *That Silver-Haired Daddy of Mine*. He had his first starring big-screen role in 1935, and by 1937 was firmly established as one of America's biggest box office stars. After

173. December 1948 *People's Songs*. This proved to be the last regular issue of the newsletter, as People's Songs, Inc., was forced to shut down in March 1949 due to lack of funds. But one year later came its successor, *Sing Out!*, whose premiere issue in May 1950 featured—emblazoned across its front page—the lyrics to *The Hammer Song* by Seeger and Hays, later known as *If I Had a Hammer*.

174. Dunaway, *How Can I Keep from Singing*, p. 17–19.

175. *How Can I Keep from Singing*, p. 209–17.

176. Lyrics from David King Dunaway, *How Can I Keep from Singing?*, p. 18–19.

177. Murrells (*Million Selling Records*, p. 56) gives a U.S. sales figure of seven million, and Fuld cites collective sales by various artists topping 79 million copies. All figures are unverified.

more than a decade of Westerns for Republic came the hit that no one expected.

The character of Rudolph was created by Robert L. May, a Montgomery Ward ad copyrighter, as an illustrated poem handed out at the store's outlets during Christmas 1939 with a distribution of several million copies.[178] Songwriter Johnny Marks (born on November 10, 1909 in Mt. Vernon, New York) had written a handful of hit songs, mostly notably the 1939 Ink Spots hit *Address Unknown*, and drawing upon the inspiration from May's poem, produced a phenomenon that guaranteed a comfortable retirement. The song was given a vigorous multi-media promotion; a Max Fleischer animated short about Rudolph (actually made before the song existed) went into national distribution in December 1949, giving the song an extra boost.[179] By the close of that holiday season the Columbia pop pressing had sold 1.3 million copies in the U.S. alone, plus another 400,000 copies of the plastic "kid-disc" version.[180] (The latter ultimately became the first "kid-disc" ever to top the million mark in sales.)[181] Autry's record was one of the first fifty selections for the Grammy Hall of Fame. Marks' one subsequent smash returned to the holiday theme a decade later with Brenda Lee's *Rockin' Around the Christmas Tree*.

The Third Man Theme (1950)—Anton Karas
London 536
British chart debut Dec. 3, 1949 (10 weeks at #1);[182] U.S. debut Feb. 18, 1950 (11 weeks at #1) (*MEM-#19, UK-#26, Trad-#112, DMDB*)

Among the most remarkable of all one-hit artists, Anton Karas was born on July 7, 1906 in Vienna, Austria, learned to play the zither while young, and began playing professionally at eighteen. A stringed instrument consisting of a flat sound box over which are stretched from thirty to forty-five strings, the zither evolved in the Far East during the 1700s, became especially popular in the Austrian and Bavarian Alps, and was introduced in England by 1850; the four melody strings are stopped against frets on the finger board while they are plucked. The dulcimer (popular in the Appalachian area as well as Eastern Europe) is a type of zither. It was the expanding popularity of the piano that caused the zither to sharply decline in use during the late nineteenth

century, but the instrument remained popular in parts of Germany and Switzerland.

According to *The Encyclopedia of Recorded Sound* (edited by Frank Hoffman), the earliest known commercial zither recordings were fourteen cylinders made in 1898 by a "Professor D. Wormser" for the Bettini label; he went on to record for Edison and Columbia the following few years. The instrument had gathered enough of an American following for a North American Zither Players Association to be formed in Missouri in September 1912, the first musical body of its kind in the U.S.[183] Dick Spottswood also lists numerous zither recordings by German artists during the 1915–1929 period, with Henry Marchetti's 1920s discography the most notable.[184] But certainly for the American popular music market in 1950, the instrument qualified as highly exotic.

The director of the classic mystery thriller *The Third Man*, Carol Reed, was seeking music appropriate to postwar Vienna, found Karas, who was playing the zither in wine and beer gardens around the city, and commissioned him to write the music. The ominous zither motif he came up with is also known as *The Harry Lime Theme*, for the mysterious character played by Orson Welles who is pursued through the shadows of Vienna by Joseph Cotten. Karas based it on an eight-measure melody he found in a zither etude book. The record became a phenomenon selling a reported four million copies. The record first became a British smash in late 1949 soon after the film's release. But in the U.S., the single was held back by the insistence of its publisher, Chappell Music, that no record company be allowed to release versions prior to a designated date; indeed, the firm even filed suit against one company for trying to jump the gun.[185] Not surprisingly, its success was global in scope; Finnish author Pekka Gronow reports that it was a massive hit across Europe.[186]

(There'll Be) Peace in the Valley (for Me) (1951)— Red Foley (written by Thomas A. Dorsey)
Decca 46319[187]

178. Fuld, *Book of World-Famous Music,* p. 476. The song was copyrighted May 9, 1949.

179. December 17, 1949, *Billboard.*

180. January 21, 1950, *Billboard.* Subsequent reports placed the first-season sales at two million; another million were sold during the next Christmas season (Ewen, *All the Years,* p. 458).

181. November 24, 1951, *Billboard.* By that time, combined sales of the Autry disc in all formats had reached a reported three million.

182. *Billboard* U.K. sheet music chart, song listed as *Harry Lime Theme.*

183. September 28, 1912, *Music Trades.* The magazine's December 28, 1912, issue reported on the instrument's "renewed popularity" in New York.

184. *Ethnic Music on Records,* Vol. 1. In the U.S., Kitty Berger made recordings for Edison on harp-zither (May 23, 1914, *Music Trades*).

185. January 14 and 21, 1950, issues of *Billboard.* To get around the legal blockade, Art Mooney's band offered its own *Zither Serenade,* but it was a poor substitute for the real Karas article. On January 28, *Billboard* reported that after weeks of companies "champing at the bit" over the delay—which was partly at the behest of the film's producer David O. Selznick—Chappell finally gave the green light for legal releases. Guy Lombardo's cover version also proved a smash, but only the Karas original is remembered.

186. *The Recording Industry: An Ethnomusicological Approach,* p. 66.

187. Decca also simultaneously issued the record in its pop (#27856) and sacred (Decca 14573) series.

Recorded March 27, 1951; chart debut July 7, 1951 (#5 C&W) (*GOSP-#11, HBN-#38, Folk-#47, C&W-#56, RR-5, SC*)

Even during an era when there was limited crossover between black and white in country music, songs of faith always flowed freely across the racial divide. *Peace in the Valley* was copyrighted on February 1, 1939, by the greatest of all black gospel composers, Thomas A. Dorsey, and ever since had been a favorite of both black and white church-goers. However, curiously, it seems to have gone unrecorded for at least a decade. One of the first known renderings was by the Southern Sons Quartette for the Mississippi-based Trumpet label in early/mid-1950.[188] When a young Sam Cooke succeeded R. H. Harris as lead singer of the Soul Stirrers, *Peace in the Valley* was the very first song he and the group did for Specialty on March 1, 1951.[189]

Dorsey's inspiration came while traveling by train through southern Indiana en route to Cincinnati at a time of deep national worry over the threat of world war. Passing through a valley, he saw horses, cows, and sheep grazing near a gentle brook. "Everything seemed so peaceful with all the animals down there grazing together," he recalled. "It made me wonder what's the matter with humanity? Why couldn't man live in peace like the animals down there?"[190]

The tune's most renowned version was rendered by country superstar Clyde Julian (Red) Foley, a native of Blue Lick, Kentucky (born on June 17, 1910) who got his start on the WLS *National Barn Dance* from 1930–1937 and the *Renfro Valley Show* from 1937–1939.[191] Foley began hitting the country charts in 1944 (getting off to a huge start with *Smoke on the Water*, #1 for 13 weeks). With his strong baritone and sure sense of rhythm, he could perform either ballads or rollicking boogie numbers with equal skill. In addition to his mellifluous Bing Crosby–inspired crooning, Foley was familiar with the vocal techniques of black gospel vocal quartets, notes Bill Friskics-Warren in *Heartaches By the Number*. Perhaps inspired by the Dixie Hummingbirds' 1948 recording of the closely related Dorsey song *We Shall Walk Through the Valley in Peace* (which was itself, reports Anthony

Heilbut, an adaptation of a same-titled old spiritual),[192] Foley makes "liberal use of melisma, and the Sunshine Boys [on backing vocals] achieve a vocal weave more akin to the era's black quartets" than to white Southern gospel groups.[193] *Peace in the Valley* (with Grady Martin also featured on bluesy electric guitar) was by some accounts the first gospel song to become a million-seller.

Rocket 88 (1951)—Jackie Brenston & His Delta Cats
Chess 1458
Recorded March 5, 1951; chart debut May 12, 1951 (#1 for 5 weeks R&B) (*Blues-#43, R&B-#74, NPR-300, GHF-#207, 1001, TC, FIR, ACC, RH*)

It wasn't quite the first rock & roll record, coming five years after Arthur Crudup's *That's All Right*, and three years after Roy Brown's *Good Rocking Tonight*, but *Rocket 88* helped light the fuse that would soon blaze across the music world. The Delta Cats were actually Ike Turner's Kings of Rhythm, with his young cousin Jackie Brenston (born on August 15, 1930, in Clarksdale, Mississippi) the band's singer and saxophonist; since Brenston not only sang it but wrote it, his name wound up on the record label.[194] The number was not entirely original, as Colin Escott points out that it was "litigiously close" to Jimmy Liggins' 1947 R&B hit *Cadillac Boogie*, an ode to the Cadillac 8; and Liggins' song in turn was partly inspired by blues master Robert Johnson's 1936 recording *Terraplane Blues*. "Where it differed was in its explosiveness."

Ike Turner (born on November 5, 1931, also in Clarksdale) was a DJ on WROX in Clarksdale, Mississippi, just getting started as a hot session pianist (his style inspired by Pinetop Perkins) backing up various R&B artists, and releasing occasional records under his own name. B.B. King told Turner that the Memphis market would be good for him, and suggested that he audition for his producer, Sam Phillips. The Delta Cats date was one of the early sessions produced by Phillips at his Memphis Recording Service at 706 Union Avenue. Immediately after the session, he ran off dubs and, that same night, sent the dubs to the Chess brothers in Chicago.[195] Phillips, writes Escott, "gave the record a thunderous bottom end

---

188. It was one side of their second release, a year before their sensational treatment of *I'll Fly Away*.

189. The song was also a particular favorite of Sister Rosetta Tharpe (who recorded it in January 1952) and Clara Ward. Mahalia Jackson, who first came to prominence in association with Dorsey, has her name emblazoned directly underneath the song's title ("as sung by") on a September 1950 edition of the sheet music, but oddly she never recorded it commercially.

190. Horstman, *Sing Your Heart Out, Country Boy*, p. 58.

191. The first known country gospel version of *Valley* was by the Jordanaires for Decca on March 31, 1950; three days after that session, Foley did his hit *Birmingham Bounce* in the same Nashville studio. The Statesman Quartet cut it shortly before Foley in 1951, and the Harmoneers Quartet just after.

192. Heilbut, *The Gospel Sound*, p. 31.

193. *Heartaches By the Number*, p. 23–24. Foley recorded much religious material both solo and as a member of Brown's Ferry Four; *Just a Closer Walk with Thee* had charted for him in 1950. He later had a duet session with Sister Rosetta Tharpe.

194. It was always Turner's contention that the song was written by the entire group on the way to the session, as discussed in his interview for *The Oxford American*, Third Annual Double Issue on Southern Music (1999), p. 47.

195. Until this time, Phillips had an ongoing relationship with the Bihari brothers, recording B.B. King and other artists and leasing the performances to the Biharis' RPM label. But Leonard Chess was a frequent visitor to Memphis, and Phillips thought the label could provide him with a second outlet for recordings. When he leased *Rocket 88* to Chess, the

that came from pairing Ike's piano with Willie Kizart's guitar." Kizart's amplifier had fallen from the car on the way to Memphis, so Phillips stuffed some paper in the ruptured speaker cone "to conjure up the first fuzz tone."

Rocket 88 is a celebration of the 1950 Hydra-Matic Drive V-8 Oldsmobile 88, first on the market in 1949, billed as "the lowest priced car with the 'rocket' engine." GM advertised the engine as "Futurmatic" and described the sweeping contours of its "sleek Futuramic hood." Jim Dawson and Steve Propes remark that it was "a chrome-sparkled symbol of American postwar prosperity that even poor folks were getting a taste of at the time . . . Even a young black man in the segregated South could dream about driving a rocket, or as Brenston described it, 'movin' on out, oozin' and cruisin' along."[196] The band boasted that it was big enough to host a wild party with girls, booze, and the open road stretching out before them. "You women have heard of jalopies, you've heard the noise they make / Well, let me introduce my new Rocket 88 . . . baby, we'll ride in style!" With Turner's pumping boogie piano front and center, that fuzz-tone guitar (which Phillips deliberately over-amplified to enhance the boogie riff), and Raymond Hill's two wailing tenor sax solos ("Blow the horn, Raymond!" Brenston calls out), every listener wants to be along for the ride.[197]

Turner's resentment at being left off the record label credits on his own session led him to take his band to record for the Biharis, forcing Phillips and Brenston to hire other musicians.[198] General Motors gave Brenston a brand new Olds 88 in gratitude for the free advertising. But when his followup records went nowhere, he was ultimately rehired by Turner at minimum scale, and played on the Ike & Tina breakthrough hit *A Fool in Love* in 1960. The Delta Cats classic is included on two Rhino boxed sets: *The R&B Box* and *Loud, Fast & Out of Control*.

Sixty-Minute Man (1951)—The Dominoes (written by Billy Ward & Rose Marks)[199]
Federal 12022
Recorded on Dec. 30, 1950; chart debut May 26, 1951 (#1 for 14 weeks on R&B chart) (*RHF, R&B-#104, DM, FIR*)

Pianist-arranger Billy Ward (born on September 19, 1921 in Los Angeles, raised in Philadelphia) formed the Dominoes in 1950 from the ranks of the students he was teaching as a vocal coach in New York. With the soaring tenor of Clyde McPhatter as lead, the group (with the help of talent agent Rose Marks) took first place in Arthur Godfrey's *Talent Scouts* TV show in October 1950. Black arranger/guitarist Rene Hall saw the group's TV performance, and helped them land a contract with King's subsidiary Federal Records (owned by Syd Nathan). After their debut *Do Something for Me* was a moderate R&B hit, they soared into the stratosphere with this notoriously salacious number, recorded during the quartet's second session at the National Studios on 48th Street. Producer Ralph Bass, whose previous hits included Jack McVea's *Open the Door, Richard* and T-Bone Walker's *Call It Stormy Monday*, helmed the record date. The group's cover version of the ballad *Harbor Lights* was the initial single released from this session; only two months after that release did *Sixty-Minute Man* hit the market. Bill Brown's bass lead vocal described his romantic plans for the evening, including fifteen minutes each of kissin', teasin', pleasin', and "blowin' my top."[200]

The tale of Lovin' Dan traces back in part (as explained by Jim Dawson and Steve Propes in *What Was the First Rock 'n' Roll Record*) to a 1921 song called *The Lady's Man, Dapper Dan from Dixieland*, in which Dan, a Pullman porter, shouts out the names of passing towns on the railroad where he's got women stashed away. A sanitized version of that song became a pop hit in December 1921 for Frank Crumit as *Dapper Dan*. The jazz band the Black Dominoes (actually a white group featuring trombonist Miff Mole) recorded *Dancin' Dan* in 1923; six years later Bessie Smith (accompanied by pianist Clarence Williams and guitarist Eddie Lang) used the number as the basis for her delightfully naughty *Kitchen Man*. The next incarnation of the song was *Dan the Back Door Man*, recorded by Georgia White in 1937 (with young guitarist Les Paul offering some hot solos) and the Four Southerners (a Mills Brothers–like group with vocal impersonations of musical instruments) the same year.[201]

In *Big Beat Heat*, John A. Jackson suggested that Bill Brown's "braggadocio" is so "blatantly overstated" that white kids felt more amused than threatened, and this fact helped make possible the record's crossover to a pop audience.[202] Tony Fletcher partially agreed in *All Hopped Up and Ready to Go*, saying that *Sixty-Minute Man* "is,

---

Biharis cut him off and began recording King themselves. (See Escott and Hawkins, *Good Rockin' Tonight*, p. 23–25.)

196. *What Was the First Rock 'n' Roll Record*, p. 88–91.

197. In June 1951, Bill Haley cut a cover version of *Rocket 88*, which Robert Palmer (in DeCurtis, *Blues and Chaos*, p. 129) describes as "his first venture outside the strictures of conventional country & western music."

198. Turner's attitude was not brightened by the fact that, in typical fashion for the period, the band was paid in cash for both the recording and the publishing rights, with no royalties.

199. Rose Marks was manager of the Dominoes; Arnold Shaw in *Honkers and Shouters* (p. 282–83) said it was likely that Ward wrote the piece by himself.

200. King—"a company hardly prudish in its attitude to the raunchier side of R&B," as noted by Brian Ward in *Just My Soul Responding* (p. 35)—played it safe by recording a sanitized "radio version" of the Dominoes' hit.

201. Dawson and Propes, p. 91–95.

202. Jackson, p. 6–7.

for all its lyrical audacity, at heart a novelty record." It became one of the ten biggest hits in the history of the *Billboard* R&B charts.[203]

Cry (1951)—Johnnie Ray with the Four Lads (written by Churchill Kohlman)

Okeh 6840

Recorded Oct. 16, 1951; chart debut Nov. 24, 1951 (11 weeks at #1 pop, #1 for 1 week R&B); #2 in England[204] (*MEM-#21, GHF, HP-#25, Trad-#69, FIR, 1001, DMDB*)

When Johnnie Ray burst on the pop scene, no one quite knew what to make of him. A white singer with a vocal style rooted in black gospel, his over-the-top emotionalism was unlike anything heard before in mainstream white pop. But when that style was matched with a song to showcase it, *Cry*, the result was one of the most unexpected phenomena of the otherwise seemingly placid early 1950s pop scene. Born John Alvin Ray on January 10, 1927, in Dallas, Oregon, of Native American ancestry, Ray lost 50 percent of his hearing as a child and by age fourteen had to use a hearing aid. Inspired above all by the records of Billie Holiday, he sang in clubs starting in the mid-1940s, and in early 1951 landed a regular stint at the Flame Show Bar in Detroit (the only non-black performer featured there).[205] Biographer Jonny Whiteside remarks that he "wailed the blues with such conviction that he was quickly accepted, if not downright adopted," by the venue's regular performers, including LaVern Baker.[206] At the recommendation of local disc jockey Robin Seymour, he was signed by Okeh Records' head of A&R, Danny Kessler.[207] His debut single, the original R&B torch song *Whiskey and Gin*, didn't chart nationally, but showed enough promise (hitting #1 in Detroit and Buffalo, and generating a strong response in Cleveland) that Columbia A&R man Mitch Miller assigned him the song *Cry*.

Cry was written by forty-five-year-old Pittsburgh civil servant Churchill Kohlman (he penned it while moonlighting as a night watchman at a dry-cleaning plant), and recorded as a straight ballad by torch singer Ruth Casey in late summer 1951 on the Philadelphia–New York R&B label Cadillac Records. Miller placed Ray out front, with his vocal accompaniment (the Four Lads, later to become hit makers in their own right) and a combo including a glockenspiel and guitarist Mundell Lowe well in the background. Ray wailed, "If your sweetheart sends a letter of goodbye / It's no secret you'll feel better if you cry / If your heartaches seem to hang around too long / And your blues keep getting bluer with each song," holding out the consonants and seeming to weep, the intensity going closer to the edge as the song progresses. Buddy Weed on celesta is the one instrumentalist who stands out in the spare arrangement. "So let your head down and go on and cry!" The fervent intimacy carried across genres, and country legend Hank Williams remarked, "He's sincere and shows he's sincere. That's the reason he's popular—he sounds to me like he means it."[208] Jim Dawson and Steve Propes in *What Was the First Rock 'n' Roll Record* suggest that Ray's frenetic approach, crying and swooning, may be have been inspired in part by jazz singer Little Jimmy Scott through his 1950 record with Lionel Hampton's orchestra, *Everybody's Somebody's Fool*, in which he seemed "on the edge of hysteria."[209] Ray's live performances—tearing at his hair, falling to his knees, rolling on the floor, leaping back to his feet—generated their own hysteria among female fans. As he ran up a series of hits the next several years following the two-million-selling *Cry*, his success inspired comparable overt emotion on record by other male vocalists such as Clyde McPhatter. Whiteside's purple-prose tribute: "*Cry* stands as one of the most intense, empathetically powerful pop records ever made, a work of true interpretative genius. He took Kohlman's lyric soaring into blue strata of hopelessness, then plunged them into a vermillion pit of blood-churning emotion."[210]

How Many More Years (1951)—Howlin' Wolf

Chess 1479

Recorded in July 1951;[211] chart debut Dec. 8, 1951 (reached #4 on R&B chart) (*Blues-#117*)

The first and biggest R&B chart hit by the blues legend born Chester Arthur Burnett, *How Many More Years* is a raw, powerful performance announcing to the world the

---

203. Fletcher, p. 54.

204. Ray became enormously popular in England, including three #1 singles on the official U.K. charts (which were introduced in November 1952). *Cry* spent seven weeks at #2 on *Billboard*'s U.K. sheet music chart, kept out of the top spot by Nat King Cole's *Unforgettable*.

205. Motown founder Berry Gordy discussed the Flame Show Bar in his memoir *To Be Loved* (p. 73–74). Headliners such as Billie Holiday and Dinah Washington performed on a stage built right into the bar.

206. Whiteside, *Cry*, p. 52.

207. Okeh (an inactive label since 1942) had recently been reactivated by Columbia as a vehicle for "race records." Kessler, who also produced *Whiskey and Gin*, made his reputation with the Ray phenomenon. He went on to sign Joe Williams (*Every Day I Have the Blues*) and jazz pianist Ahmad Jamal.

208. Fellow Columbia artist Tony Bennett also served as one of Ray's biggest boosters at the outset of his career. The January 26, 1952, *Billboard* reported that Columbia had just enjoyed its biggest sales week in twelve years, shipping 1.2 million singles in seven days, with Ray accounting for nearly half the total and Bennett as the next biggest contributor.

209. Dawson and Propes, p. 98. Whiteside (*Cry*, p. 68) notes that like Scott, Ray "stretched out the words of a ballad so outrageously that he necessarily created his own meter . . . He was also phrasing on each individual syllable, something no one had ever done [on mainstream pop records], introducing a vocal delivery technique that became standard in rock and roll."

210. Whiteside, *Cry*, p. 80.

211. He did an unissued first take of the song at his debut May 14 session (decades later released on a Bear Family boxed set).

emergence of a new blues titan. He was already forty-one years old at this, his third recording session (he had cut rejected versions of the song along with a few other selections at May–June 1951 sessions), but having played juke joints around Mississippi since the late 1930s, and as an established radio personality in West Memphis, Arkansas since 1948, he would not waste any more time.

Producer Sam Phillips had just cut one of the first undeniable rock & roll records, *Rocket 88* by Ike Turner's band the Kings of Rhythm featuring front man Jackie Brenston, when he caught Wolf on the radio, and was knocked out. Told that if he would come down to Phillips' Memphis Recording Studio at his own convenience he'd be free to record whatever he wanted, the big man arrived at the studio a few days later, and made an immediate impression. "He would sit there with those feet planted wide apart, playing nothing but the French harp, and I tell you, the greatest thing you could see to this day would be Chester Burnett doing one of those sessions in my studio," Phillips later recalled for Robert Palmer. "God, what it would be worth to see the fervor in that man's face when he sang. He cut everything out of his mind and sang with his damn soul. I mean, his eyes would light up and you'd see the veins come out on the back of his neck."[212]

The number features Willie Johnson (who claims to have written the song on the way to the studio, although it was copyrighted by Wolf) on aggressive-sounding guitar, and Willie Steele on drums. The hard-rocking pianist was long believed to be Ike Turner,[213] but according to Phillips it wasn't, and the keyboardist's identity remains unconfirmed. Wolf biographers James Segrest and Mark Hoffman note that the band rode the boogie beat "for all it was worth—particularly Johnson, who romped along with slithering guitar runs and crunchy, distorted power chords."[214] Phillips sent the dubs to RPM/Modern (run by the Bihari brothers), which was prepared to sign Wolf. But due to the Biharis' dispute with Phillips over *Rocket 88*, Phillips sold Wolf's contract to Chess, and re-recorded *How Many More Years* and its hit flip side *Moanin' at Midnight* for that label. These would be Wolf's last recordings for Phillips, as the artist relocated to Chicago to record at Chess studios.[215] Robert Santelli writes that the piece "introduced Wolf's loud, craggy vocals, which quickly became the

most distinctive in all the blues. Often Wolf's voice sounded distorted and squirmed like a snake caught in the midday sun. It was mean-spirited. Sometimes it was ugly. But always it possessed the kind of emotional realism that has made the blues an accurate reflection of the human spirit."[216] Colin Escott and Martin Hawkins: "Phillips never found a bluesman to equal Howlin' Wolf. He has said that he would never have given up on him, that he would have recorded him until the day he died." The Sun founder even rated Wolf above Elvis Presley as his greatest discovery.[217]

Wolf's most widely-heard and seen performance of *How Many More Years* came on ABC's rock music show *Shindig* in 1965. The Rolling Stones made their appearance on the show contingent on having Wolf as their special guest, and he performed a thrilling version of his original hit with Mick and the boys sitting worshipfully at his feet. This performance exemplifies Albert Murray's description of the emotional essence of the blues: coming "back down from the cloudlike realms of abstraction and fantasy to the bluesteel and rawhide textures of the elemental facts of the everyday struggle for existence."[218]

The Things That I Used to Do (1954)—Guitar Slim & His Band

Specialty 482

Recorded in New Orleans Oct. 27, 1953; chart debut Jan. 16, 1954 (14 weeks at #1 on R&B chart)[219] (*Blues-#22, RHF, R&B-#119*)

The biggest one-hit artist in the history of the R&B charts, Guitar Slim was born Edward Lee Jones on December 10, 1926 in Greenwood, Mississippi, and chopped cotton as a youngster. He was a singer before he took up the guitar; blues singer-guitarist Robert Nighthawk was an early influence. He came to New Orleans by 1950, and after working as a dancer and guitarist with Willie Warren's group, made his solo debut as Guitar Slim at the Dew Drop Inn that August. Flamboyant Clarence "Gatemouth" Brown was another major influence on his emerging style. A young Ray Charles became Slim's frequent pianist starting in late 1951. For his second recording session, producer Johnny Vincent bailed Charles out of jail (there for a minor offense), and the group cut four sides in a session that ran from 5 p.m. until 7 a.m. the next day, including *The Things That I Used to Do*. Charles took charge of the session, dictating horn lines to trumpeter Frank Mitchell and doing what he could to keep Slim in line; the singer liked to wander

212. *Deep Blues*, p. 233–34.

213. *Blues Discography, 1943–1970* by Fancourt and McGrath (p. 239) credits Turner, as does the Smithsonian blues boxed set *Mean Old World*.

214. Segrest and Hoffman, p. 89–91.

215. As discussed by Escott and Hawkins in *Good Rockin' Tonight* (p. 31), Ike Turner simultaneously recorded Wolf doing a version of *Moanin' at Midnight* under the title *Morning at Midnight*, and that record made the R&B charts on RPM. Phillips and the Biharis resolved their differences in February 1952 in an agreement by which Chess kept Wolf and the Biharis kept another Phillips blues artist, Rosco Gordon.

216. Santelli, *Best of the Blues*, p. 24.

217. Escott and Hawkins, *Good Rockin' Tonight*, p. 31.

218. *Stomping the Blues*, p. 51.

219. Early reissues of the Guitar Slim classic featured overdubbed instrumentation, added at the behest of label owner Art Rupe; these overdubs were removed by the time of a 1984 reissue.

around the studio (and off mike) as he played his long-corded guitar. Charles' arrangement for this song, writes Robert Palmer, "proved that his comprehensive musical vision could also be highly commercial."[220]

Slim would tell friends that the song was given to him by the Devil in a dream. The song required (by at least one account) up to eighty takes, as the artist was often out of synch with the band. Charles biographer Michael Lydon: "Slim kept rushing the beat, trying to pull the band into his excitement, and Ray had to put on the brakes to hold the tempos steady." When we hear Charles shout "Hey!" at the end of the record, it's happiness because they had finally got it right.[221] With a memorable opening line borrowed from an old gospel number—"The things that I used to do, Lord, I won't do no more!"—Slim's gospel-style vocal and vigorous guitar break, Charles' piano right out of the church, and slow-rolling horn riffs (inspired by the 1952 Fats Domino record *Goin' Home*), the record was a knockout. Remarkably, when Vincent shipped the tape to Specialty owner Art Rupe in Los Angeles, Rupe thought it was worthless, and released it only as a favor. Superstar disc jockey Alan Freed helped it become a smash in Cleveland, and it kept growing to become a phenomenon, ruling the R&B charts during the first few months of 1954 and selling over a million copies.[222] Slim never had another chart hit (despite some other fine performances), and after years of grappling with a drinking problem, died of pneumonia in February 1959. Jerry Wexler called it "a timeless anthem of rue, reform, and regret."[223]

(Other personnel: Gus Fontenette on alto sax, Joe Tillman & Charles Burbank on tenor saxes, Lloyd Lambert on bass, Oscar Moore on drums.)

Joy Spring (1954)—Max Roach–Clifford Brown Quintet

Recorded for EmArcy on Aug. 6, 1954 (*Jazz-#44, NPR-300*)

From the time that trumpeter Clifford Brown hit the jazz scene in Philadelphia in 1948, write Gary Giddins and Scott DeVeaux, "word quickly spread that he 'had it all'—gorgeous tone, virtuoso technique, infallible time, and a bottomless well of creative ideas." Born in Wilmington, Delaware, on October 30, 1930, he was influenced by the trumpet style of Fats Navarro, and following Navarro's death in July 1950 was widely seen as his successor in the next generation of great horn men after Dizzy Gillespie. The fact that he was a clean-living departure from the drug

use that plagued so many jazzmen of the time made his potential seem all the more vast.[224] After a brief stint with drummer Art Blakey's combo including the famous February 1954 live album at Birdland, Brown formed a new quintet with drummer Max Roach.

Brown was at the peak of his powers during the too-short time of the quintet, with a brilliant array of compositions to match his remarkable playing, and Roach—known for his work as one of the first great bop drummers—simplified his approach to better fit his partner's gift for melody and emphatic staccato style. Alyn Shipton: "Brown's total technical command of the trumpet made him a very different kind of player from Miles Davis, and whereas he could produce a comparable beauty of tone in the middle register, he had far fuller control of the extremes of his range, and he was masterful at speed."[225] The group's August 1954 recordings included such gems as *Daahoud*, *Parisian Thoroughfare*, and *Delilah*, and topping them all was *Joy Spring*. Its vigor, warmth, and beauty marked the tune as an instant jazz standard and an inspiration to the "hard bop" movement, with the two leaders well supported by Harold Land on tenor sax, Richie Powell (Bud Powell's younger brother) on piano, and George Morrow on bass. Kirk Silsbee notes that the piece is "full of the optimistic ebullience that characterized [Brown's] playing.[226] Tragically, Brown was killed in an automobile crash (with Richie Powell) on June 26, 1956. Tenor saxophonist Benny Golson's ballad *I Remember Clifford* served as a moving homage.

When I Stop Dreaming (1955)—Louvin Brothers
(written by Ira & Charlie Louvin)

Capitol 3177

Recorded in Nashville on May 25, 1955; chart debut Sept. 10, 1955 (#8 on C&W chart) (*C&W-#157*)

Brother harmonies in country music just don't come any sweeter than those of the Louvin Brothers. Ira Loudermilk (born April 21, 1924) and brother Charlie (born July 7, 1927, both in Henagar, Alabama) began their careers on a small station in Chattanooga. They grew up in the same northern-Alabama hill country area that had also produced the Delmore Brothers. After World War II, having changed their last names to Louvin for professional purposes, they worked on Memphis and Knoxville stations, cut a single for Decca (1949, with one of their trademark ballads, *Alabama*) and a dozen songs for MGM (1951–1952) before Charlie was called up again for military service in Korea. After he got out of the Army, they began recording sacred material for Capitol (they'd been raised on shape-note "sacred harp" singing),

220. Liner notes for the 1991 compilation *Ray Charles: The Birth of Soul*, reprinted in *Blues and Chaos*, p. 172.

221. Lydon, p. 101.

222. It was first reported as a territorial hit on December 26, 1953, in several markets including Cleveland and New York.

223. *Rhythm and the Blues*, p. 96.

224. *Jazz*, p. 361–62.

225. *New History of Jazz*, p. 488.

226. Liner notes for Verve reissue, *Clifford Brown and Max Roach*.

but were still struggling until *When I Stop Dreaming* was released (their first secular number for the label), and became their career-defining smash.

A stellar Louvins original, *When I Stop Dreaming* "is superb as both a song and a performance," writes Bill Malone. "It is a perfect wedding of melody and lyric imagery, and the Louvins' high, clear, tension-filled singing of it is one of the great performances of recorded country music."[227] Ira Louvin's mandolin adds much to its appeal; Charlie's on acoustic guitar, and the combo also includes Chet Atkins on electric guitar. "The Louvins were actually in a class by themselves. No one in country music before or since achieved the kind of crisp, precise, and yet sky-high style of harmony heard in their music."[228] Charles K. Wolfe calls this performance "a masterpiece of hard country harmony."[229]

Charlie Louvin declared that they were "the first duet [team] to ever successfully use split harmonies. We didn't have to rehearse it. If the song was going to be too high for me to sing, then Ira would take the high lead, double whatever lead I was doing, and I would come in after him. We could switch two or three times in one line of a song because it was natural." Proudly and with good reason, he noted: "There would not have been an Everly Brothers if it weren't for the Louvin Brothers."[230]

After a string of country hits including the chart-topping *I Don't Believe You've Met My Baby* (1956), the brothers went their separate ways for solo careers in 1963. Ira was killed with his wife in a 1965 car accident. Their music went on to influence not only country and bluegrass performers, but also deeply affected such artists as Gram Parsons and Emmylou Harris. After Parsons' death, Emmylou—upon learning that most of the Louvins' albums were out of print in the mid-1970s—had the Country Music Hall of Fame make her a tape of their songs that she passed around Nashville. A Louvins tribute album (including Harris) won two Grammy Awards in February 2004, including best country album.

"Speaking to the woman who has broken his heart, Ira confesses a detail so private and intimate that it's hard to listen yet impossible to turn away—when she told him she was leaving, he wanted to die," writes David Cantwell. "Harking back to the Delmores and predicting the Everlys, [the Louvins'] harmonies embody the pain that arises when desire comes face to face with loss. If you were to claim that Ira and Charlie's harmonies were the closest anyone has come to catching all that hope and insecurity on tape, you might well be right. But you still wouldn't be doing them justice."[231]

Crazy Arms (1956)—Ray Price (written by Ralph Mooney & Charles Seals)
Columbia 21510
Recorded in Nashville on March 1, 1956; chart debut May 26, 1956 (#1 for 20 weeks on C&W chart, #67 pop) (*HBN-#6, C&W-#15, NPR, GHF, DM, SC*)

The onset of rock and roll had country music reeling in 1956, and in need of a fresh sound capable of attracting younger listeners while still remaining true to its proud heritage. Ray Price's response was the 4/4 Texas honky-tonk shuffle (deviating from country's standard 2/4 beat) with old-time fiddle but a great rhythmic vigor. "To fans of hard country music, *Crazy Arms* was an exhilarating experience and an indication that there was still great strength in the forms directly derived from tradition," writes Bill Malone.[232] With Van Howard on vocal harmonies, the record employed heavily bowed single-string fiddling by Tommy Jackson, pedal steel guitar by Jimmy Day, and at Price's suggestion, Buddy Killen's bassline was doubled up on both acoustic and walking electric bass. Floyd Cramer completed the ensemble on piano.

When Price began recording in 1949, he emulated the country crooning style of Eddy Arnold; after becoming a protege of Hank Williams, he consciously evoked Williams' phrasing, and after Hank's death recorded with the legend's band the Drifting Cowboys. It was only in late 1953 that he found his voice and forged his own style, forming a new band in 1954 with two fiddles and stronger rhythms suitable for honky-tonks. Tommy Jackson's fiddle style was modeled on the breakdown fiddling of Bob Wills, helping the band to swing. Jackson's open-string playing—using, again as suggested by Price, a capo (a metal clamp used on guitars to permit key changes while playing basic chords) and bending it—provided a unique sound. This evolution reached its peak on *Crazy Arms*.

The song was written by Charles Seals and West Coast steel guitarist Ralph Mooney.[233] Price heard an early recording of the tune and liked it, but decided to switch it to

227. Annotation, *Smithsonian Collection of Classic Country Music*, p. 45.

228. *Country Music, U.S.A.*, p. 215.

229. *Classic Country: Legends of Country Music*, p. 216. Prior to the Louvins, perhaps the most impeccable country harmony duo was the Blue Sky Boys. Wolfe describes the session in his Louvins biography *In Close Harmony* (p. 66–69). The song "set the tone for the classic Louvin style that was yet to come." Knowing that "their career might well be riding on this session," the brothers applied the lessons learned by performing the number live for the previous year, and the gospel-to-secular gamble paid off.

230. Interview with Louvin by Jimmy Guterman, *Journal of Country Music*, Vol. 12 #2 (1989).

231. *Heartaches By the Number*, p. 87–88.

232. Annotation, *Smithsonian Collection of Classic Country Music*, p. 44.

233. Mooney (who later served as Waylon Jennings' steel guitarist), recalls that the song was inspired by the time in 1949 when he was drinking heavily and his wife, having had enough, left him. "I sat down with my guitar and wrote, 'Blue ain't the word for the way that I feel, and a storm is brewing in this heart of mine.'" He sketched out most of the song in a few minutes, and few days later got his wife back. (*Sing Your Heart Out, Country Boy*, p. 157.)

the 4/4 beat—"we came up with it right there on the session," the singer would recall. Don Law was the producer, but he allowed Price to largely dictate the session, an approach that proved exactly right. Van Howard's high tenor harmonies alongside Price's sturdy baritone lead added to the record's appeal. With an amazing twenty weeks at #1 and forty-five total charted weeks, *Crazy Arms* became one of the ten biggest hits in the history of the *Billboard* country charts; he'd enjoyed six previous C&W Top Tens, but this was a quantum leap. "Price and company transformed the gutbucket country shuffle of the postwar era into a pop-wise rhythm that kicked as hard as big-beat rock and roll," declared Bill Friskics-Warren, ranking the song #6 in *Heartaches By the Number: Country Music's 500 Greatest Singles.*

Rich Kienzle writes that the record marked the culmination in the evolution of Price's sound, "summarized in one moving performance, magnificent in its fervor, combining drama and passion with the new, insistent rhythm . . . Its vocal and instrumental combination set a standard for honky-tonk records that remains nearly half a century later."[234]

Don't Be Cruel (1956)—Elvis Presley (written by Otis Blackwell)
RCA 47-6604

Recorded July 2, 1956; chart debut Aug. 11, 1956 (#1 for 11 weeks; #1 for 10 weeks C&W, #1 for 6 weeks R&B)[235] (*Juke-#1, HBN-#5, BILLB-#9, NPR-100, DMDB-#20, RIA-#68, GHF, BMI-#71,*[236] *C&W-#97, DM-#130, RS-#197, AHR, TC, 1001, BBC*)[237]

After a marathon session of eighteen takes had finally resulted in the classic performance of *Hound Dog* at the RCA Studios that July 2, Elvis Presley and associates broke for lunch and he began to sort through a stack of acetate demos submitted for him to consider recording. Peter Guralnick related in *Last Train to Memphis* that the second demo, R&B performer Otis Blackwell's *Don't Be Cruel*, grabbed Elvis immediately. Blackwell had originally given the song to a then-unknown group called the Four Lovers—only later to gain fame as the Four Seasons—but given the opportunity to submit it to Elvis, Blackwell persuaded the group not to record the song (instead he gave them *You're the Apple of My Eye*, which became their first minor chart success).[238] His composition

Fever had just been a smash hit for Little Willie John, and this one appeared to have similar potential. After listening to the song a couple of times, Elvis began working it out on guitar, sketched out a rough arrangement on the piano, and offered suggestions to lead guitarist Scotty Moore and drummer D. J. Fontana while backing singers, the Jordanaires, worked out their own arrangement. Twenty-eight takes later, Presley was finally satisfied.[239] Upon its release just five weeks later, the easy-loping, infectious *Don't Be Cruel* became not only a massive hit, but—with *Hound Dog* as its epic B side—the biggest double-sided smash in pop music history.

Ranking it #5 in *Heartaches By the Number*, David Cantwell writes that the song established "all the defining characteristics of the Nashville Sound" that would reshape country music within the next few years: "The spare instrumentation and restrained playing that left lots of open spaces; the at-ease yet crisply defined production with just a touch of echo; the singer's voice (and the bass) way out front in the mix; the backing bop-bop-bop vocals by the Jordanaires," and "the unmistakably warm, relaxed feel of the Nashville Sound. It was all there, and the result was a new kind of rock & roll, a new kind of pop, and the beginnings of what would be a new kind of country music."[240] Dave Marsh singles out Bill Black's virtual bass solo opening the song. The AMOA in 1988 ranked *Hound Dog* and *Don't Be Cruel* together as the #1 juke box single of all time.

Love Me Tender (1956)—Elvis Presley (written by Vera Matson)
RCA 47-6870

Recorded on Aug. 24, 1956, in Hollywood; chart debut Oct. 20, 1956 (5 weeks at #1); reached #3 on both C&W and R&B charts; #11 in England (*RHF, RS, WASH-#26*)

The title song of Elvis Presley's first feature film, *Love Me Tender*, was adapted from the 1861 parlor ballad *Aura Lee* (also known as *The Maid With the Golden Hair*), appropriately because the film was a drama about sons in a Southern family during the Civil War.[241] Although the quiet, elegant ballad was unlike anything Elvis had commercially recorded during his first whirlwind year as a star, it was, he told friends, the kind of music he'd grown up singing in church. Accompanied mainly by just Vito Mumolo strumming an acoustic guitar, with subdued vocal backing by the Jordanaires, Presley sings with earnest feeling. RCA Victor received over a million pre-orders for the single before it was released (thanks to

234. Kienzle, *Southwest Shuffle: Pioneers of Honky-Tonk, Western Swing, and Country Jazz,* p. 169.

235. *Hound Dog* was a #2 smash in England, but *Cruel* didn't officially chart.

236. BMI has certified it for four million broadcast performances.

237. Also the #1 biggest hit on Los Angeles radio from 1956–1979 (Marsh, *Book of Rock Lists,* p. 145).

238. Blackwell said he hadn't heard of Presley until his new publisher, Shalamar Music, told him of Elvis' interest in the tune (February 5, 1977, *Melody Maker* interview).

239. Guralnick, *Last Train to Memphis,* p. 378–79.

240. Cantwell, p. 4–5.

241. *Aura Lee* was sung by both Union and Confederate soldiers, and in later years became a barbershop quartet favorite for its harmonizing possibilities. (Hischak, *Tin Pan Alley Song Encyclopedia,* p. 23–24.

his performance of the tune on his first *Ed Sullivan Show* appearance on September 9, viewed by an astonishing 82.6 percent of the television audience), the first time this had ever happened. As a result, it made a sensational #2 debut on the *Billboard* Top 100, the highest debut since that chart had expanded to 100 positions the previous November; this would stand unsurpassed until the Soundscan era of the 1990s.[242]

Were You There (When They Crucified My Lord) (1957)—The Soul Stirrers featuring Sam Cooke

Specialty 907

Recorded in April 1957 in Chicago; released in 1958

In his final session as lead singer of the Soul Stirrers, Sam Cooke unleashed one of the most intense, gripping vocal performances of his life on a long-beloved gospel standard. *Were You There?* is one of those special songs, like *Amazing Grace, I'll Fly Away,* and *Peace in the Valley,* that had achieved equal popularity in both black and white churches. Among the many outstanding recorded versions, that of Cooke and the Stirrers topped them all.

A traditional hymn with unknown composer, one of its early appearances in print was John Wesley Work's *Folk Song of the American Negro* (1915). Odum and Johnson cited it in *The Negro and His Songs* (1929), and the 1927 edition of *Cabin and Plantation Songs as Sung by the Hampton Students* discussed a variant, *Did You Hear How Dey Crucified My Lord.*[243] R. Nathaniel Dett's *Religious Folk Songs of the Negro as Sung at Hampton Institute* (1929) has another variant, *Were You There When the Sun Refused to Shine*; George Pullen Jackson in *White Spirituals in the Southern Uplands* (1933) suggested that this song was related to the white hymn *While the Sun Refused to Shine,* which dates back to the 1820 supplement to the songbook *Kentucky Harmony.*[244]

In white country gospel, among the finest recordings of the song were by Wade Mainer (1938), Bill Monroe (1941), and Roy Acuff (1949). In black gospel and concert music, major artists who had recorded it included the Fisk University Jubilee Singers (1920), Paul Robeson (1925), the Pace Jubilee Singers (1927), the Golden Gate Quartet (1942), and Sister Rosetta Tharpe (1950).

The song tells the tale of two men walking the road to Jerusalem, as one asks the other if he saw the crucifixion. "The song hangs on the singer's ability to convince us that the answer is yes," writes Cooke biographer Daniel Wolff. Cooke adds to the piece with conversational

asides: "Tell me: did they really—did they pierce him in the side that morning?" As Sam cries, "sometimes it causes me to tremble," the group echoes his cries to perfection. "To say this is call and response is to understate what's going on here; it's the complicated, single beat of a heart, and the syncopated claps, [Leroy] Crume's jangly guitar, all underscore the testimony: yes, we were there."[245]

About two weeks later, Cooke sent a six-song demo tape of pop songs to producer Bumps Blackwell, severing his ties to gospel. One was *You Send Me*; the rest is pop music history.

Sweet Little Sixteen (1958)—Chuck Berry

Chess 1683

Recorded Jan. 6, 1958; chart debut Feb. 17, 1958 (3 weeks at #1 on R&B chart; 3 weeks at #2 pop); #1 for 2 weeks in Canada, #16 in U.K. (*DM-#180, RS-#277, DMDB*)

The biggest rock & roll chart hit of Chuck Berry's career (leaving aside the pre-adolescent novelty *My Ding-a-Ling*), *Sweet Little Sixteen* was inspired, says Berry in his autobiography, by an incident in the Ottawa Coliseum where he spotted a little girl, age seven or eight, running through the corridors trying desperately to get stars' autographs; most of the others at the show were in their mid-teens. "I was one year past thirty at the time . . . but somehow I could understand how they must have felt in their ambition to collect the signatures . . . The essence of the story is portrayed in the song for I was once sixteen and had the 'grown-up blues.'"[246]

Dave Marsh offers a rather different interpretation of Berry's inspiration, remarking that the artist had "the most finely articulated obsession with the passions of young girls since Lewis Carroll's. When he sings 'all the cats wanna dance with Sweet Little Sixteen,' he means to include himself, and he doesn't just mean dance."[247]

The record features one of Johnnie Johnson's hottest piano solos, as he tries to cut loose à la Jerry Lee Lewis; one writer compared the piano part to Jerry Lee riding a roller coaster. (Lafayette Leake was at the keyboards for Berry's December 1957 demo version of the song, as heard in Hip-O Select's 2008 boxed set of his 1950s Chess recordings, but stepped aside for the final version.) "I 'bout tore my thumbnail off trying to get the piano part where Leonard Chess wanted it," Johnson would recall. "He had me rippin' the keys up and down on the solo."[248] What makes the song interesting musically, writes Berry biographer Bruce Pegg, "is the tension created between

242. A week before it hit the chart, the October 13, 1956, *Billboard* (p. 42) reported that *Tender* "has chalked up an all-time record for first-week [sales] volume."

243. *Hampton Students*, 1927 edition, p. 106.

244. Copyright records show dozens of arrangements; perhaps the most notable is Harry T. Burleigh's, which was used for 1920s concert hall–styled recordings by Marian Anderson and Paul Robeson.

245. Wolff, *You Send Me*, p. 141.

246. Berry, p. 154.

247. Marsh, *The Heart of Rock & Soul*, p. 124–25.

248. Fitzpatrick, *Father of Rock & Roll*, p. 145–46.

the rhythm section and Berry's guitar. While the drums and bass play a swing shuffle, Berry plays his trademark straight four on guitar. Additionally, for the first half of the first verse and the whole of the second, the instruments drop out during the vocal line. The whole effect is to create a push-me-pull-you tension, perfectly capturing the girl's excitement."[249]

For Your Precious Love (1958)—Jerry Butler & The Impressions (written by Jerry Butler, Arthur Brooks & Richard Brooks)

Abner 1013 (released first on Falcon 1013; also on Vee-Jay 280)

Chart debut June 16, 1958 (#3 peak on R&B chart, #11 pop) (*R&B-#178, DM, RS, AHR, TR*)

For Your Precious Love—a song merging the reverential depth of emotion in gospel with the veneer of a romantic soul ballad—began its life as a poem lead singer Jerry Butler had written in high school. The song represented the Impressions' desperate last-ditch effort to secure a recording contract. Jerry Butler, Curtis Mayfield, Sam Gooden, Emmanuel Thomas, and brothers Richard and Arthur Brooks formed the Impressions as Chicago gospel-trained singers; both Butler and Mayfield had sung with the Northern Jubilee Gospel Singers. Their efforts to get signed by King Records (which had James Brown) and Chess (which had the Dells and the Moonglows along with its many blues acts) had produced rejections. They knew they had a jewel of a song in *For Your Precious Love* (which Butler and the Brooks brothers had put to music) but were wary of singing it due to fear a record company would steal the song without signing them. But when their audition with the other top R&B-related label Vee-Jay wasn't generating much enthusiasm with their other songs, the group decided (as Thomas recalled for author Craig Werner), "we gotta go for broke now, we already struck out twice." As they sang the ballad, Vee-Jay artists & repertoire man Calvin Carter's eyes lit up: "That's it! That's it! That's the one!"

There were some nervous moments before the group got to achieve their dream. When they entered Vee-Jay's studios, the great doo-wop group the Spaniels were there as well, and when Carter asked the Impressions to sing *Precious Love*, "there was a long pause as paranoia set in," Butler remembered. "Here comes the rip-off. He likes our song, and he wants them to record it." But the fears went unrealized. Two weeks later the Impressions recorded the song, and the results were so magical that the label rushed the disc into stores within days.

"A powerful bass line and softly strumming guitar provide a deceptively peaceful setting for Butler's sol-

emn testifying," describes Werner in *Higher Ground: Stevie Wonder, Aretha Franklin, Curtis Mayfield, and the Rise and Fall of American Soul*. "The call and response with the lead vocalist, whose baritone contrasts with Mayfield's sweet tenor, and the background chorus emphasizes the cut's gospel roots and points like a compass needle straight to the production techniques that would define Chicago soul."[250] The song is charmingly amateur, with lines of uneven length, but the melodic beauty and hushed fervency of the performance, at a glacially slow pace that emphasizes the intensity, overwhelm any technical flaws. It was, declares Joe McEwen, "a landmark record," representing "the music of a new generation that had spent its adolescence in [Chicago], synthesizing music from such diverse sources as the Soul Stirrers, the Ink Spots, the Dells, and, of course, the blues. The song can almost be considered the first soul record," providing inspiration for artists like Jackie Wilson and Solomon Burke.[251]

The record—released on Vee-Jay's subsidiary label Falcon—was an immediate hit. But when the group saw the hastily issued record, with Butler's name "written across the sky" and the Impressions in smaller type "under the magnifying glass" (as Thomas put it), the other guys were surprised and hurt. A sympathetic Butler asked if the company could reprint the label, but the cost would have been prohibitive. As the record soared up the charts, the group toured behind it, and then split up. Vee-Jay was perfectly happy to have Butler as a solo artist; Mayfield and the remaining Impressions would endure some hard times before beginning a long run of unforgettable hits in 1961 with *Gypsy Woman*.

Born in Sunflower, Mississippi, on December 8, 1939, Jerry Butler came to Chicago with his family, sang with Mayfield in the aforementioned gospel group, and became a member of the Roosters that would be renamed the Impressions. After going solo, the smash ballad *He Will Break Your Heart* in 1960 became the first of many hits on Vee-Jay (with Mayfield frequently serving as songwriter, producer, and/or harmony partner). His career reached a peak on the Mercury label with hits including *Only the Strong Survive* (1969). Butler later became a longtime Cook County Commissioner in Illinois, with music serving as a sideline to politics.

"The song is obsessive and blindly passionate," writes Thomas Ryan. "The consequences of love are not mentioned because it is only the love itself that matters. When a love is all-consuming and the song that expresses it is at your fingertips, the result is spine-tingling bliss." With the group supporting his lead like "pining angels, Butler

---

249. Pegg, *Brown Eyed Handsome Man*, p. 181–82.

250. Werner, p. 73–76.
251. *Rolling Stone Illustrated History of Rock & Roll*, p. 140.

sounds unearthly, as though his love has disembodied his voice. It comes from a place so deep inside, so personal . . . Only a handful of singers have allowed so much of their emotion to figure in a popular recording."[252]

Mambo Gozon (1958)—Tito Puente & His Orchestra
Recorded in 1958 for the RCA Victor album *Dance Mania!* (*World-#25, RR*)

"The genius of Tito Puente," writes biographer Steven Loza, "can be compared to the 20th century legacy of [Louis] Armstrong in strongly parallel fashion: Armstrong was American born, and so was Puente; Armstrong was African American, with all the cultural and social implications that heritage entails, and Puente was Latin American, with all the relative associations of that heritage; and Armstrong was a creative genius with regard to the contemporary values of individual artistry and African-connected improvisations, and so is Puente."[253] Among the 100-plus albums he recorded in a career span-

ning a half century, *Dance Mania!* was both the biggest selling and most enduring; *Mambo Gozon* is a perfect representation of his work.

Dance Mania, remarks Tom Moon in *1,000 Recordings to Hear Before You Die*, is "strikingly simple—verses followed by exchanges with a chorus of backing singers, followed by exciting, roof-raising instrumental mambos that make good use of then-novel stereo separations. Within that basic structure Puente and his musicians open up new worlds . . ."[254] Puente once described the mambo as differing from its antecedent, the rumba, "in that it concentrates more on the off-beat, the after-beat, like modern jazz—whereas the rumba is mostly on the beat."[255] As outlined by Loza, *Mambo Gozon* follows its orchestral break introduction with a solo piano *guajeo* (described by Ned Sublette as a repeating rhythmic cell that the piano plays in Cuban dance music, enabling the piano to serve as rhythmic percussion). At the seventh measure the saxophones . . . enter in the form of the *guajeo*," soon counterpointed

Fats Domino & band, courtesy of Library of Congress, LC-USZ62-126071.

252. Ryan, *American Hit Radio*, p. 34–35.
253. Loza, *Tito Puente and the Making of Latin Music*, p. xv–xvi.

254. Moon, p. 622.
255. Fletcher, *All Hopped Up and Ready to Go*, p. 83.

by the brass section of trumpets and trombones. The main *coro* (central melodic figure) enters immediately after this opening section. "Upon the opening *coros* of 'A gozar este rico mambo, a gozar' ('to enjoy this rich mambo, to enjoy')," Santitos Colon (aka Santos Colon) immediately begins his vocal *inspiraciones*.[256] The powerful mambo rhythms are driven throughout by Puente's timbales and his multiple percussionists, along with the surging horns. The repetitions and variations on the themes each culminate with a percussion solo, all the way to the end. *Dance Mania!* in 2002 became one of the fifty original inductees to the National Recording Registry.

The derivation of the term *mambo* is traced by Sublette to the Bantu people of central Africa, who came to the New World in the sixteenth century; "basically, mambo means a complex of things involving communication—all of which, in traditional Bantu culture, involved singing."[257] It was in the 1930s that Antonio Arcano's orchestra established the mambo in its modern musical form, as "a repeating instrumental figure over a *montuno*" (an undulating "melodic-rhythmic loop" of fixed pitches);[258] by the 1950s, with bandleaders such as Perez Prado and Puente, the genre achieved its zenith.

Flamenco Sketches (1959)—Miles Davis Sextet
From the Columbia album *Kind of Blue*
Recorded on April 22, 1959; *Cash Box* chart debut Oct.
    3, 1959 (reached #27) (*Jazz-#93*)
One of the undeniable gems on the ultimate Miles Davis classic album, *Flamenco Sketches* is a slow blues that seeps under the skin with repeated listenings. Reviewer Ronald Atkins remarked that "few recordings exude so hushed an air of solemnity—a feeling arising as much from the absolute perfection of the solos as from the slow tempo."[259] Gary Giddins has offered the view that while *So What* is the generally accepted masterpiece from the album, from a latter-day perspective, "*Flamenco Sketches* appeared more relevant, in challenging the soloists to play five scales, the duration of each to be determined by the improviser."[260]

In his book on the making of *Kind of Blue*, Ashley Kahn says that pianist Bill Evans is probably the song's primary composer. Just a few months earlier, Evans had recorded one of his best-known compositions, *Peace Piece*, which (says Kahn) contains the same "austere signature ostinato (an insistently repeated musical figure) bass pattern."[261] Davis told Evans that he had liked

Peace Piece and suggested that the sextet record it. Evans offered the alternate idea of expanding on the same approach by doing a series of five scales; he wrote it out in broad form on piano, and the other five musicians took it from there.

Kahn notes that the song refracts a wide range of influences—classical, impressionistic, exotic—"into a haunting, pan-cultural theme covering a wide emotional range." Perhaps the most striking scale used is Spanish or Andalusian scales, originating from Morocco, and very similar to the *hijaz*, a Middle Eastern mode; Dizzy Gillespie had explored these in some of his postwar recordings.[262]

It opens with Evans and bassist Paul Chambers setting a languid tempo; Kahn writes that drummer Jimmy Cobb's "almost inaudible brushwork provides more ambient texture than rhythm." Two brief runs through the primary theme lead to Miles' trumpet solo (using a Harmon mute), "pensive and floating." This is followed by John Coltrane's similarly meditative tenor sax solo, and Julian "Cannonball" Adderley's alto sax. Evans and Chambers serve as "modal traffic cops," directing or gently hinting at the transitions from one scale to another. "Miles' solo is a blend of opposites. Exceedingly calm yet impassioned, halting while still melodic . . ." Kahn also praises Coltrane's solo for its "emotional depth and subtlety. With hushed, tender nuance and a loose-knit approach prefiguring the spiritual intensity of his future recordings as a leader, he ranges from breezy and buoyant to somber, then bittersweet and melancholy, momentarily playing off the tune's plaintive Spanish sonority. It is impossible to be unaffected by his pristine passion."

"So powerful is the impact" of Davis's roughly two-minute solo, writes Richard Williams, "that the eight-second hiatus between the end of his improvisation and the start of Coltrane's is one of the most powerful anticipatory spaces in jazz, the rhythm section discreetly treading water" before Trane begins a solo "that matches the leader's for the patience of its pacing and even outdoes it in fidelity to the subtext of the harmonic material. When the tenorist's two minutes of carefully repressed drama end in a gently curling downward phrase, Adderley again supplies a leavening of joy to the prevailing astringency, adding a flush of color without disrupting the overall scheme."[263]

Len Lyons writes that Bill Evans' solo "recalls Bix Beiderbecke's famous piano solo *In a Mist* in its Debussy-influenced lush beauty. This track offers the improviser more freedom than any other on the album . . ." The song also benefits from John Coltrane's "strong sense of

256. Loza, *Tito Puente and the Making of Latin Music*, p. 156.
257. *Cuba and Its Music*, p. 53.
258. Sublette, *Cuba and Its Music*, p. 508.
259. Atkins quoted by Jack Chambers, *Milestones*, p. 308.
260. Giddins, *Visions of Jazz*, p. 349.
261. *Peace Piece* had been written while Evans was playing around with Leonard Bernstein's 1944 ballad *Some Other Time* and found himself "entranced" by the opening two chords.

262. *Kind of Blue: The Making of the Miles Davis Masterpiece*, p. 133–40. In its five-star review of the album, the October 1, 1959, *Down Beat* (p. 28) concluded: "This is the soul of Miles Davis, and it's a beautiful soul."
263. *The Blue Moment: Miles Davis's Kind of Blue and the Remaking of Modern Music*, p. 119.

dynamics."[264] Almost universally recognized as the greatest jazz album ever and inducted in the Grammy Hall of Fame in 1992, *Kind of Blue* was ranked as the #12 greatest album (by far the highest-ranking jazz LP) by *Rolling Stone* in 2003.

Last Night When We Were Young (1959)—Tony Bennett (music by Harold Arlen, lyrics by E. Y. Harburg)
Recorded Nov. 12, 1959
Issued on the 1960 Columbia album *To My Wonderful One* (*APS*)

Written in 1935 by two of the great masters of American popular song, *Last Night When We Were Young* was little known until the 1950s except for the dubious distinction of having been dropped from three movie soundtracks. Lawrence Tibbett performed it in 1936 for *Metropolitan*, Judy Garland in 1949 for *In the Good Old Summertime*, and Frank Sinatra (also in 1949) for *Take Me Out to the Ball Game*, but all three times the song was left out of the released film because it was deemed too depressing. (Sinatra subsequently recorded it for his classic 1955 album *In the Wee Small Hours of the Morning*, the version that introduced it to most listeners.) Tibbett's October 9, 1935, recording was issued on a 12-inch disc; two years later, sixteen-year-old Frances Ethel Gumm, the soon-to-be Garland, found a copy of the record, and it became one of her most beloved songs. The surviving video outtake of the adult Judy's emotional performance of the number is quite affecting.

When Arlen played the tune for George Gershwin and Jerome Kern, both composers warned him that it was too esoteric to become popular. Arlen biographer Edward Jabolonski says this was because "the underlying melancholy of the melody was accomplished with unexpected shifts of harmony and, in the release, octave jumps in the melody."[265] Harburg (whose lyrics came a year after the melody) told Deena Rosenberg that he had no idea where he got the title. "The juxtaposition of those two phrases is almost a whole world of philosophy," he said. "I don't know where it comes from . . . But I suppose the tune opened it up . . . the whole pathos of the human situation, of the human race, is in that musical phrase. Old Harold gave it to me. I rode in on the coattails of his genius."[266] Alec Wilder: "This is a most remarkable and beautiful

Tony Bennett, PhotoFest.

song. It is one which goes far beyond the boundaries of popular music."[267]

Finally, Tony Bennett established this deeply touching composition as an enduring standard. His performance (with orchestra conducted by Frank DeVol, including Tony's regular pianist Ralph Sharon) was included in the Smithsonian's *American Popular Song* boxed set. The Arlen melody is complex and haunting, the Harburg lyrics are introspective and melancholy, and in Bennett's hands the total impact is unforgettably powerful. Will Friedwald writes that in addition to drawing on the Italianate bel canto vocal tradition, Bennett's style also draws upon the Catholic Church's spiritual influence, which can be heard through his trademark big endings that constitute "part of his way of achieving a catharsis with his audience. In a traditionally Catholic way, every time Bennett does one of those amazing, gut-busting ballads [*Last Night* is introspective rather than "gut-busting," but the point remains pertinent from an emotional standpoint], he is, in a sense, symbolically dying and being resurrected."[268]

To the end of his life, whenever Arlen was asked to name his personal favorite song, this was his choice. "Last night when we were young, / Love was a star—a song unsung. / Life was so new, so real, so right / Ages ago, last night. / Today, the world is old / You flew away, and time grew cold . . ."

The Twist (1960)—Chubby Checker (written by Hank Ballard)
Parkway 811
Chart debut Aug. 1, 1960 (#1 for 1 week pop, #2 R&B); returned to chart Nov. 13, 1961 (#1 for 2 more

264. Lyons, *The 101 Best Jazz Albums*, p. 262–63.
265. Jablonski, *Rhythm, Rainbows & Blues*, p. 99–100.
266. Meyerson and Harburg, *Who Put the Rainbow in the Wizard of Oz?*, p. 96–98. The authors note that the lyric adapts ideas contained in a poem he had written in 1928, *Maturity*, referring to "last year, when I was young." "To Yip this [song] is the nearest thing to a Kaddish in the Arlen-Harburg songbook: it is a song about death—of romance, of belief. It is the only lyric Yip ever wrote about losing love irrevocably, and it came a year after his first wife had left him."

267. Wilder, *American Popular Song*, p. 266–67. Thomas Hischak (in *Tin Pan Alley Song Encyclopedia*, p. 204) commented on the series of descending triplets in each section.
268. Friedwald, *Biographical Guide*, p. 42.

weeks)[269] (*RIA-#32, RHF, GHF, RS, Juke-#35, R&B-#45, DMDB-#55, BILLB-#76,*[270] *ACC*)[271]

It all began with a dance, credited to Jo Jo Wallace and Bill Woodruff, members (incongruously enough) of the black gospel group the Sensational Nightingales, and a song they worked up to accompany it. Because as religious singers they were reluctant to record the number themselves, as Jim Dawson explains in *The Twist: The Story of the Song and Dance That Changed the World*, they offered it to R&B singers during the 1956–1957 period, one of whom was Hank Ballard.[272] Elijah Wald notes that the juxtaposition was not so unusual. "Just as the fervent singing styles of and complex rhythms of Clyde McPhatter, Ray Charles, James Brown, and the Motown stars were to a great extent adapted from gospel artists, steps that looked a lot like the mashed potato and the pony had been commonplace for decades in the less sedate black churches, where congregants seized by the spirit kicked out in footwork that the go-go dancers of the 1960s could only envy."[273] [274] The leader of the Midnighters rewrote it (to what extent is not clear), took sole composer credit, and recorded it as the flip side of the group's 1959 hit *Teardrops on Your Letter*. Just a catchy tune to fill a B side and attract a little action on its own (#16 on the R&B chart), and then forgotten, until Chubby Checker.[275]

He may not have gotten much respect from rock critics, but Chubby Checker certainly made an impression on record buyers. Born Ernest Evans on October 3, 1941, in Spring Gulley, near Andrews, South Carolina, and raised in Philadelphia, he changed his name at the suggestion of Dick Clark's then-wife because of his resemblance to a young Fats Domino. His novelty record *The Class* (which he'd initially recorded for Clark as an audio Christmas card sent to friends) was a mild hit in 1959, but *The Twist* made him a pop phenomenon. The dance—"round and round and up and down"—had become popular among black teenagers, done to medium uptempo songs (with a melody "outright stolen," as Charlie Gillett puts it, from the 1955 hit by Clyde McPhatter and the Drifters, *Whatcha Gonna Do*).[276] When the dance spread nationwide and became big on *American Bandstand*, Clark suggested to friends at the Philadelphia-based Cameo-Parkway label that Checker would be the perfect artist to bring the song to a wider audience. Fred Bronson reports that it took Checker thirty-five minutes and three takes to cut the song (copying Ballard's arrangement note for note, including Hank's familiar cry of "eee-yah"), backed by the vocal group the Dreamlovers.[277]

After he scored followup hits *It's Pony Time* and *Let's Twist Again*, the rapidly spreading dance craze, accelerated by a September 1961 article in the *New York Journal-American* about the local Peppermint Lounge noting that "you don't have to be a teenager to do the Twist," triggered an invitation for Checker to perform *The Twist* on Ed Sullivan's show on October 22, 1961. That led Parkway to re-release the original hit—and saw it return to the #1 position, the first record since Bing Crosby's *White Christmas* to accomplish this feat.

Black activist Eldridge Cleaver felt (albeit with a sense of irony) that Checker's breakthrough was an encouraging sign of white youths' interest in black music and dance, as he wrote in *Soul on Ice*. The twist, he suggested, had been "a guided missile, launched from the ghetto into the very heart of suburbia. The Twist succeeded, as politics, religion, and law could never do, in writing in the heart and soul what the Supreme Court could only write on the books."[278]

At Last (1961)—Etta James (music by Harry Warren, lyrics by Mack Gordon)

Argo 5380

Chart debut Jan. 16, 1961 (#2 on R&B chart, #47 pop) (*Blues-#37, GHF, RR, Trad-#86, R&B-#96, ACC, RH*)

It was known to the World War II generation as a swooning ballad recorded by Glenn Miller with vocal by Ray Eberle in 1942 (introduced in the Miller-led film *Orchestra Wives*), and in 1952 as a #2-charting smash for Ray Anthony's band. But ever since Etta James wrapped her voice around it nearly a decade later, *At*

---

269. According to the charts as reported in *Billboard*, *The Twist* was #1 for nine weeks in Australia and eleven weeks in France, and reached #5 in India. In England, it peaked at #44 in 1960, then #14 in early 1962.

270. During its two *Billboard* chart runs, *The Twist* accumulated twenty-five weeks in the Top Ten and thirty-three weeks in the Top 40, both figures easily topping any other #1 record of the 1955–1991 "pre-SoundScan" era. (*Joel Whitburn's Top Pop Singles*, 12th Edition; *Hot 100 Annual*, 2006.)

271. *The Twist* was also the #1 biggest hit on Los Angeles radio from 1956–1979, compiled by Guy Zapoleon of station KRTH, based on local sales reports and charts from three Los Angeles radio stations (*The Book of Rock Lists*, p. 145).

272. Ballard's version of the song's origin is that he saw his group work up a frantic, twisting dance routine on stage, and got the idea for *The Twist*.

273. *How the Beatles Destroyed Rock 'n' Roll*, p. 214–15.

274. Marshall and Jean Stearns in *Jazz Dance* (p. 98–99, 106–7) note that basic elements of the Twist can be found in the *Ballin' the Jack* routine, first experienced under that name by composer Perry Bradford in 1909, but itself incorporating steps that had been used for many years before that. In 1912, Bradford's song *Messin' Around* described the steps—hands on hips, with pelvis and backside twisting in a wide horizontal circle while the body bounces on the toes with each beat. Chris Smith's dance number *Ballin' the Jack* then became one of the biggest hits of 1913. The Black Bottom dance, very similar in most respects, became popular in the late 1910s, and gave rise to the DeSylva-Brown-Henderson song *The Black Bottom* in 1926.

275. Ballard told John Broven (*Record Makers and Breakers*, p. 429–30) that he made out very nicely from Checker's remake. "Oh yes, I've always gotten my royalties, big royalties!"

276. *Making Tracks*, p. 94.

277. *Billboard Book of Number One Hits*, p. 74.

278. Cleaver, p. 173–83.

Last has belonged solely to her, as a classic slice of romantic vocalizing.

Born Jamesetta Hawkins on January 25, 1938, in Los Angeles, Etta was singing gospel songs on Los Angeles radio with her Baptist church choir at age five, and began performing with two other girls with the Johnny Otis band in the early 1950s. Otis gave her the opportunity to record an answer song to the Hank Ballard & the Midnighters hit *Work With Me, Annie*, initially called *Roll with Me Henry*; Modern retitled it *The Wallflower*, a duet with Richard Berry (later of *Louie Louie* fame), and it became a #1 R&B hit in early 1955. After some strong late 1950s records flopped, Etta signed with Chess, and through its subsidiary Argo began an impressive run of hits starting in 1960.

Leonard Chess came up with the inspired idea of linking her gritty, soulful vocals with lush string orchestrations on standards with pop crossover potential.[279] *At Last* provided the template. Its composer, Brooklyn native Harry Warren, had a long list of enduring songs with Al Dubin (including *I Only Have Eyes for You* and the classic 1933 movie musical *42nd Street*), and teamed with Polish-born lyricist Mack Gordon on such hits as *Chattanooga Choo Choo, I Had the Craziest Dream*, and *At Last*. As was the case with Ray Charles' strings-laden ballad performances of the same period, Etta's voice soars above all the violins and really makes the sugary accompaniment work for her, and unlike Ray, she doesn't have to deal with any corny backup singers. Overcoming a long bout with heroin addiction that ended in 1974, James continued scoring hits into the early 1970s, and after a long absence made a dramatic comeback with a series of acclaimed blues albums from the early 1990s to today. This performance has been heard in a number of movies (including *Pleasantville* in 1998), and in 1993 Etta was inducted into the Rock & Roll Hall of Fame.

Running Scared (1961)—Roy Orbison (written by Roy Orbison & Joe Melson)
Monument 438
Chart debut April 10, 1961 (1 week at #1); reached #1 in
    Canada, #9 in England[280] (*DM-#323*)

Hot on the heels of his breakthrough hit *Only the Lonely*, Roy Orbison scored the first #1 single of his career with *Running Scared*, a song that neatly encapsulated the desperate paranoia of his musical persona, and oh my God, that voice. What is reality and what is merely a feverish nightmare as he envisions his beloved girl turning away from him to swoon before an ex-lover?

It is the combination of song structure, lavish production, and vocal majesty that makes *Running Scared*, like all of Orbison's classics, unforgettable. Bill Porter, Monument's recording engineer, recalled this record with particular pride for its exceptionally wide dynamic range (the difference between the softest and loudest notes), as it "started real soft, and built and built as the arrangement went on . . . from the very beginning of the song to the very end, there's a 25 dB [decibel] dynamic range," which was "unheard of" for a pop single.[281]

Ken Emerson points out that Orbison was "effectively his own producer. A sophisticated eclectic, he blended into his epics a little bit of everything. Latin rhythms, martial beats, reminiscences of classical music, keening steel guitars . . . Over everything soared his rich, supple voice, which rose to every dramatic occasion . . . [such as] the triumphant G-sharp to which the bolero beat of *Running Scared* leads inexorably. Hitting the final note in falsetto, he couldn't be heard over the instrumental Sturm und Drang. When he took a deep breath and reached it in his natural voice, the 30 musicians were literally too stunned to keep on playing."[282]

A Dying Man's Plea (1962)—Staple Singers
Recorded on Feb. 20, 1962 for Riverside

Few groups fused gospel, blues, and folk quite like the Staple Singers. Among all their recordings in many genres over the decades, perhaps none is as emotionally affecting as *A Dying Man's Plea*, in part because it provided a wonderful showcase for the patriarch, Roebuck "Pops" Staples. Born on December 28, 1914, in Winona, Mississippi, Roebuck Staples was a friend of blues great Charlie Patton (they worked at the same plantation), and became a supremely skilled blues guitarist in his own right.[283] Gravitating into gospel through his father's Methodist church, in 1937 he joined the Mississippi-based spiritual group the Golden Trumpets; upon moving to Chicago in 1940, he played and sang with the Trumpet Jubilees. Around 1949 his daughters Mavis and Cleotha, and his son Purvis, began performing with the man now known as Pops, as the Staple Singers.

From 1955–1960, the Staple Singers emerged as a potent force in gospel music with a series of superb recordings for Vee-Jay, including their rendition of the white gospel standard *Uncloudy Day*. Recording for Riverside from 1960–1963, they began to mix gospel with social-commentary songs, and this direction became more pro-

---

279. A model for this approach was provided by the still bluesier-voiced Big Maybelle with her hit 1956 version of another 1940s ballad, *Candy*.
280. Also #1 in New Zealand.

281. Porter interviewed by John Rumble, *Journal of Country Music*, Vol. 18 #2 (1996), p. 22–23. Harold Bradley starts the song playing acoustic guitar, then switches to electric bass guitar, which adds more depth to the low end.
282. *Rolling Stone Illustrated History*, p. 128–29.
283. By Staples' account, he introduced the guitar into Methodist churches, which had traditionally disdained musical instruments.

nounced after they went to Epic Records in 1964, with an emphasis on songs for freedom and equality. The incarnation of the Staple Singers that became most familiar to a mass audience was their work for the soul label Stax starting in 1968, landing them a series of pop hits in the 1970s, most memorably 1971's *Respect Yourself.*

A Dying Man's Plea is a slight reworking of Blind Lemon Jefferson's blues classic *See That My Grave Is Kept Clean* (recorded twice for Paramount in October 1927 and February 1928). Two early versions of the song had appeared as *Dig-a My Grave wid a Silver Spade* and *Angels Lookin' at Me* in *Negro Workaday Songs* by Howard Odum and Guy B. Johnson (1926), as collected in the South during 1924–1925. Samuel Charters stated in *The Bluesmen* (1967) that "the same folk melody and most of the original verses . . . were sung not only in Texas but in many other areas of the South."[284] Harold Courlander in *Negro Folk Music, U.S.A.* notes that some of the imagery (such as digging a grave with a silver spade and lowering the coffin with a golden chain) is derived from Anglo-American balladry. The Jefferson song is different from, but perhaps inspired by, the sentimental ballad *See That My Grave Is Kept Green*, which dates back to 1876 and was most famously recorded by the Carter Family in 1933.

Pop Staples' wondrously twangy, shimmering guitar is the song's defining sound; hearing just three seconds of that tremolo on his amplifier, you know it couldn't be anyone in the world but Pops. After opening with a brief spoken narration in the role of a dying man who's not afraid to go—"I don't want you to cry; don't you know we were born to die"—his lead vocal is gentle but moving, with Mavis's resonant voice in the background: "One kind favor I ask of you, one kind favor I ask of you . . . See that my grave is kept clean . . ." When Roebuck Staples died in 2002, no other performance could serve as a more fitting memorial.

Theme from *Lawrence of Arabia* (1963)—by Maurice Jarre

Colpix movie soundtrack album, chart debut March 2, 1963 (reached #2, 86 total weeks) (*AFI-#3*)

The 1955–1965 period was a golden age for motion picture soundtracks as dominant forces on the LP charts. While this mainly meant musicals, a number of orchestral soundtracks also fared remarkably well, including *Around the World in 80 Days* (#1 for ten weeks in 1956), the jazzy *Man With the Golden Arm* score (#2 that year), and *Ben-Hur* (#6 with ninety-eight charted weeks in 1960). Maurice Jarre's score for David Lean's sweeping epic *Lawrence of Arabia*—selected as the third greatest

movie score ever by the American Film Institute—is a powerful representation.

Foreign-born like so many of the top cinematic composers, Jarre was born September 13, 1924, in Lyons, France, wrote music for the concert hall, and provided scores for short films by various French directors before moving into international-production features in 1959. Lean's account of the life of T. E. Lawrence ran three hours and 40 minutes (not counting intermission), and with its many sumptuous vistas of desert (all in Super Panavision) and the story's mixture of grand adventure and mystery required a musical score running over two-and-a-half hours. Against tough competition (including Elmer Bernstein's sensitive score for *To Kill a Mockingbird*), Jarre's ravishingly romantic music was the Oscar winner for best score. After the film's success, the composer moved permanently to the U.S., and went on to work with many top American directors. He would also earn Oscars for his accompaniments to two more large-scaled Lean productions, *Doctor Zhivago* (1965) and *A Passage to India* (1984); another of his best-known works was *The Man Who Would Be King* (1975).[285]

Da Doo Ron Ron (When He Walked Me Home) (1963)—The Crystals (written by Ellie Greenwich, Jeff Barry & Phil Spector)

Philles 112

Chart debut Apr. 27, 1963 (#3 pop, #5 R&B); reached #5 in England[286] (*DM-#21, RHF-#69, RS-#114, ACC, AHR, TC, DMDB*)

One of the classic Phil Spector "wall of sound" productions, *Da Doo Ron Ron* was the Crystals' second biggest hit (after the previous fall's *He's a Rebel*), and their most memorable. Actually, both *Rebel* and its followup *He's Sure the Boy I Love* were recorded by a totally different group—Darlene Love & the Blossoms—under the Crystals' name; the girls had dared to question the mighty producer, so he replaced them, then brought them back.

The husband and wife team of Ellie Greenwich and Jeff Barry confessed that the title phrase meant nothing; they'd simply run out of words that fit, ad-libbed the phrase thinking that it would later be replaced, and in the end decided that it worked just fine if listeners simply imagined the meaning for themselves. Greenwich and Jack Nitzsche arranged the record, and Spector's all-star team of musicians unleashed some of their most exciting work. Darlene Love originally recorded the song with her fellow Blossoms, but Spector cancelled its release to have the girls instead record the old Disney number *Zip-A-Dee-Doo-Dah* under the name Bob

---

284. *The Bluesmen*, p. 178–79.

285. In all, Jarre wrote over 170 scores for film and television, as well as ballets, orchestral works, and operas.
286. #3 in Canada & New Zealand.

B. Soxx & the Blue Jeans. Then he brought back the original Crystals. Lead singer La La Brooks (backed by Barbara Alston, Dee Dee Kennibrew, and Patricia Wright), all of fifteen years old, had recently replaced the pregnant Mema Girard, and Spector biographer Dave Thompson writes that this change "completely rejuvenated" the group. "Her treatment of *Da Doo Ron Ron*, so different from Darlene Love's all-out assault, enchanted him . . . by the time he had it down on tape, it was mesmerizing."[287] Also, from a commercial standpoint, La La's voice was clearly girlish as opposed to Darlene's womanly vocal power, which served to accentuate the song's adolescence for the teen audience.

Most of the backing instrumental tracks were recorded in Los Angeles, then the tape was sent to New York for La La Brooks to record the lead vocal. It was all done on three tracks, due to Spector's deep distrust of stereo, yet the sound was monumental.

Dave Marsh, ranking it #21 in *The Heart of Rock & Soul*, writes, "basing the song in nonsense syllables can't disguise what it really is: teen desire incarnate. The battering [Hal] Blaine gives his drum kit (if anything he's the star of this show), the droning background 'ooo,' the sassy handclaps, and Steve Douglas's raging hormonal sax riff add up to more of the same. When Blaine hits his tom-toms after each line of the chorus, the effect is like moving up into overdrive—the song smoothly surges forward."[288] Thomas Ryan: "The frenetic tune has so many dense layers of instrumentation that it really is a wonder the central riff doesn't get stomped to death. Instead, it is the listener who gets stomped to death . . . [Blaine, Douglas and company] perform superbly, driving the triplets with as much energy as could possibly be expected (or expended). There is no way to escape the song's expansive yet claustrophobic production. Every space is filled."[289]

Ring of Fire (1963)—Johnny Cash (written by June Carter & Merle Kilgore)
Columbia 42788
Recorded March 25, 1963; chart debut June 8, 1963 (#1 for 7 weeks on C&W chart, #17 pop) (*C&W-#27, RS-#87, GHF, HBN-#94, RIA-#157, TC, ACC, DMDB*)
One of the biggest hits of Johnny Cash's career, *Ring of Fire* was written by his future wife June Carter (with help from Merle Kilgore) when she was falling in love with him after starting to perform with his show in December 1961 (joining his touring show full time two months later). "I was frightened by his way of life," June told *Rolling Stone*. This was, after all, a man who trashed hotel rooms, crashed several cars (including

June's new Cadillac) missed concerts due to his lethal mix of road weariness, amphetamines, tranquilizers, and alcohol, and in 1964 accidentally started a blaze while camping drunk that burned 500 acres of national forest in California (he would pay $125,000 for the damages).[290] "So I thought, 'I can't fall in love with this man, it's just like a ring of fire.'" There was another specific inspiration for the song: June had inherited from her father A. P. Carter (of the original Carter Family) an old book of Elizabethan poetry which A. P. had often used for ideas in the group's songs. A line in the book (never used for a Carters song) was underlined: "love is like a burning ring of fire."[291] She wrote much of the song after driving around aimlessly one night worrying about Johnny, and Merle Kilgore (of *Wolverton Mountain* fame) helped put the finishing touches on it. The pair had already written several songs together, but when her sister Anita asked for one more that she could record, June had the first verse and chorus, and called Kilgore (who lived nearby in Madison, Tennessee) to rush over. He came up with the

Johnny Cash, courtesy of Library of Congress, LC-USZ62-136863.

287. *Wall of Pain*, p. 78.
288. Marsh, p. 22.
289. Ryan, *American Hit Radio*, p. 100–101.
290. *Cash: The Autobiography*, p. 202–7.
291. Patricia A. Hall, *Journal of Country Music*, Vol. 7 #1 (January 1978). Also, June Carter told *Country Music* magazine (October–November 2000) that she had recently received a letter from a friend who had gone through a bad divorce, with the remark, "You know, love is like a burning ring of fire."

second verse, and together they finished it in ten minutes. Anita made the little-heard, folkish ballad recording as *Love's Burning Ring of Fire* in 1962. *Billboard* reviewed Anita's record in its January 12, 1963, issue: "A most unusual tune is sold in winning fashion."[292] When Johnny heard the record, he declared, "I want to do that song."

Bill Friskics-Warren writes that the song she composed "was a mix of desire and trepidation, the confession of a woman terrified of her passion burning out of control lest it, or its object, consume her. June, a devout Christian who disapproved of Johnny's bad habits even as she feared for his soul, had every reason to be wary of falling into a flaming pit with a hell-raiser like Cash—she could very well have been burned alive." In *Heartaches By the Number*, he and David Cantwell rank Cash's "swaggering" version—which "couldn't be more different from what June originally had in mind"—in their top 100.[293] The mariachi horns on the record were unlike anything heard in country music to that time; Cash said in his autobiography that he "heard Anita Carter singing the songs, with trumpets framing her verses, in a dream. It still sounded good in my head when I was awake," so he called producer Jack Clement (a fellow Sun records veteran who had written Johnny's hits *Guess Things Happen That Way* and *Ballad of a Teenage Queen*) to see if he could make it happen.[294] Clement recruited the trumpet players, fashioned the arrangement, and ran the session, although he wasn't credited (Don Law was). Trivia note: This is one of several Columbia hits for which Cash recorded a Spanish-language version atop the original instrumental track, *Fuego de Amor*.

Country Music Television declared it the #4 all-time country music song in 2003. Cash remarked: "The ring of fire that I found myself in with June was the fire of redemption. It cleansed."

Peace Be Still (1963)—Rev. James Cleveland with the Angelic Choir
Recorded for Savoy on Sept. 19, 1963 (*GOSP-#4, RR-#68, GHF*)

Creator of one of the most popular and influential gospel records ever, James Cleveland was born in Chicago on December 5, 1931, and was a soloist in Thomas A. Dorsey's Junior Gospel Choir at the Pilgrim Baptist Church. At fifteen he began an eight-year tenure with the Thorne Crusaders, and during that time began composing. His first major song (at sixteen), *Grace Is Sufficient*,

was recorded by the Roberta Martin Singers and became a gospel standard. He served as pianist and arranger for Albertina Walker's Caravans (with whom he also recorded), and performed with groups such as the Gospel Chimes. Having joined the Rev. Lawrence Roberts and his choir at the First Baptist Church in Nutley, New Jersey in 1960,[295] three years later he made his third album with this ensemble known as the Angelic Choir, featuring the landmark original piece *Peace Be Still*.

Cleveland sings the opening verses solo accompanied by piano, and the large choir takes it from there, also backed by organ (future solo star Billy Preston) and drums.[296] *Peace Be Still* (and nearly all of Cleveland's later work) was recorded live, due to his belief that the excitement of the music could only be captured in its natural element with the response of the congregation.[297] Anthony Heilbut notes the novelty of a 1960s song structured as "an 18th-century madrigal filled with archaic diction and imagery": "Master, the tempest is still raging, the billows are tossing high / The sky is o'er shadowed with blackness / No shelter or hope is nigh . . ." The choir is merely adequate, in his view, but the composition is strong, and Cleveland is "commanding." Still, no one could have expected its amazing appeal: the album sold over 800,000 copies to an exclusively black gospel audience. "No record ever," even *White Christmas*, "has so blanketed its market."[298] [299] Large gospel choirs had only begun to record in the late 1940s (most notably *God Be With You* by the St. Paul's Church Choir), and there were a few popular choir records in the 1950s; the enormous success of this performance made the large ensemble one of the most familiar formats for gospel recordings in subsequent years. In 1999 it became only the third gospel record inducted into the Grammy Hall of Fame. Cleveland (known by 1965 as "The Crown Prince of Gospel") would go on to one of the most celebrated careers in modern gospel, winning multiple Grammies, and in 1968 organized the Gospel Music Workshop of America, which by the 1980s would have several hundred thousand members with chapters around the country.

---

292. January 12, 1963, *Billboard*, p. 18. Further down the page is a review of Cash's record *Busted*.

293. *Heartaches By the Number*, p. 52.

294. *Cash: The Autobiography*, p. 268–69. Law and associate producer Frank Jones booked a double-long session to allow extra time for the horn players to learn their parts, which, in the absence of a written chart, had to be sung out to them by Cash.

295. Also in 1960, Cleveland scored a major hit leading a Detroit choir, the Voices of Tabernacle, on *The Love of God*. The large-ensemble performance established the model for *Peace*.

296. The choir features Eugene Bryant (first tenor), Diana Dickens (lead alto), and Odessa McCastle (second soprano).

297. Because Rev. Roberts' new church had not yet been completed, the album was recorded at a Seventh Day Adventist Church (Broughton, *Black Gospel*, p. 112).

298. *The Gospel Sound*, p. 212–14.

299. For a period in 1965, *Billboard* published gospel charts (they would not become a long-term feature until the 1980s), and *Peace Be Still*—over a year after its release—was #1 on the Hot Spiritual Singles chart almost continuously from January through June. Savoy Records reported the following year that the album had sold over 300,000 copies (March 5, 1966, *Billboard*).

Don't Worry, Baby (1964)—The Beach Boys (music by Brian Wilson, lyrics by Roger Christian)
Capitol 5174
Chart debut May 30, 1964 (reached #24) (*DM-#75, RHF, PW, ACC-#149, RS-#178, AHR, DMDB*)[300]

The B side of the Beach Boys' first #1 single *I Get Around*, *Don't Worry Baby* has proven to be the more enduring side of a classic 45. Brian Wilson originally wrote it for Ronnie Bennett and her Ronettes as a followup to that group's 1963 smash *Be My Baby*, but what began as an homage to the early Phil Spector sound became an unforgettable pop ballad in its own right.

"The Beach Boys' early singles caught the spirit of middle-class America in the pivotal stages of post–World War II affluence," suggests Dave Marsh. "Derived in equal measure from the romantic teen fantasies of Phil Spector, from the more mocking scenarios of Chuck Berry, and from harmony groups ranging from the straight pop of the Four Freshmen to the pure R&B of Frankie Lymon & the Teenagers, those songs were not only filled with telling details . . . but never ignored the downside of the dream." *Don't Worry Baby* "is lush with echo and gorgeous open-throated background harmonies that set off a sweet tenor lead vocal by Wilson himself." Hal Blaine—whose emphatic drumbeats set the tone for *Be My Baby*—provides the same service here, albeit in a gentler style. The male vulnerability Wilson reveals in confessing his constant sense of foreboding about his relationship with his girl "was probably unprecedented in rock and roll at that time, and one which laid the groundwork for every singer/songwriter confessional of the Seventies."[301]

"What on the surface seems to be a song about a guy who regrets opening his big mouth about his car in front of a bunch of hot-rodders is actually a song about comforting love," remarks Thomas Ryan. "The song becomes universal in scope, with its focused description of an insecure man-child who finds comfort in the arms and words of his girlfriend . . . less a character study than a description of the combination of love and fear that can afflict a teenager on the brink of adulthood."[302]

Wilson told *Rolling Stone* (which ranked it as the #31 best single of the past twenty-five years in 1988) that this song "has the best proportion of our voices and ranges." Carl Wilson called it "the easiest record we ever made."[303] Roger Christian, a disc jockey at KFWB who occasionally collaborated with Brian, penned the lyrics. The multi-part harmonies were done live in the studio without overdubs; Brian, Carl and Dennis Wilson, Mike Love, and Al Jardine all arranged around three microphones.

"*Don't Worry Baby* is one of the pinnacles of rock and roll artistry because of its utter unselfconsciousness, its innocent, unmatchable power and sincerity," declares Paul Williams. He celebrates what Wilson as producer achieved with the record's "layers of sound—primarily vocal (lead and harmonies) but there are extraordinary instrumental (percussive) inventions here, too—so human and real and unspeakably beautiful that one sinks into them as a cloudbank of heavenly reassurance, safety, harmony, love, surrendering all care, transported by the fullness and grace of those incomparable melodic and sonic textures."[304]

Good Lovin' (1966)—The Young Rascals (written by Rudy Clark & Arthur Resnick)
Atlantic 2321
Recorded Feb. 1, 1966; chart debut March 12, 1966 (1 week at #1); #1 (2 weeks) in Canada (*DM-#108, RHF, RS, TC, DMDB*)

The Compton, California-based R&B group the Olympics (of *Western Movies* fame) had recorded the original version of *Good Lovin'* in early 1965, and despite a nice, brassy arrangement the song got no higher than #81 on the pop chart (and was entirely absent from the R&B chart). Felix Cavaliere, singer and keyboardist for the up-and-coming group the Young Rascals, recalled for *Rolling Stone*: "I immediately heard how hot the song could be and said, 'Man, they're missing the boat on this.'"[305] In one of the infrequent occurrences of a white cover version clearly surpassing a black original in quality as well as sales, the Rascals' take on *Good Lovin'* became their breakthrough #1 smash and one of the top party records of the decade.

The Young Rascals (later to be known minus the "young") were formed in New York in 1964. Cavaliere, singer-guitarist Eddie Brigati and Canadian guitarist Gene Cornish had played with Joey Dee & the Starliters when Dee left the Peppermint Lounge to open his own club, the Starliter (Eddie's older brother David had been with the original group on Dee's #1 hit *Peppermint Twist*). Before playing with Dee, Cavaliere had been the only white member of the Stereos who had a Top 30 hit with *I Really Love You* in late 1961. The lineup of Italian-Americans was completed with the addition of drummer Dino Dinelli.[306] The musicians had all been immersed in

300. *New Musical Express* named it as the #4 greatest pop single in 1976.
301. Marsh, *The Heart of Rock & Soul*, p. 54–55.
302. Ryan, *American Hit Radio*, p. 133–34.
303. September 8, 1988 *Rolling Stone*, p. 104.

304. Williams, *The 100 Best Singles*, p. 65–66.
305. September 8, 1988 *Rolling Stone*, p. 143.
306. Toby Creswell in *1001 Songs* (p. 321): "The tradition of Italian R&B is a long and venerable one stretching back to Dion. If they lacked the cultural traditions of black Americans they had an equal intensity and theatricality."

the New York metropolitan area club scene, and Cavaliere recalled that the circuit was guided by one central rule: "If you don't get the people up and dancing, you don't get paid." Promoter Sid Bernstein saw them play at a floating discotheque at the Hamptons in Long Island, and got them signed to Atlantic after the label's engineer/producer Tom Dowd confirmed their potential. They had a medium-sized debut hit at the end of 1965 with *I Ain't Gonna Eat My Heart Out Anymore*. Its followup was *Good Lovin'*.

After Brigati had sung lead on the group's debut single, Cavaliere took over that role here. "The first time we did *Good Lovin'*, people jumped out of their seats and started dancing," he recalled for Tony Fletcher, so they entered the studio brimming with confidence.[307] The record explodes from the opening seconds, behind Cavaliere's "One! Two! Three!" count-off, fiery blue-eyed soulful lead vocal and hard-driving Hammond organ and the group's tight harmonies and relentless energy. Remarkably enough, Cavaliere thought the recording didn't fully capture the group's vitality and wanted to try another take, but listeners disagreed; this performance simply cooked. Co-producers Tom Dowd and Arif Mardin had set out to make the record as close to their live stage act as possible, and succeeded, right down to the fake-out ending and roaring finale. This was one of the first production jobs for Turkish-born Mardin, who had previously done arrangements and assisted other Atlantic producers.

Monday, Monday (1966)—The Mamas & the Papas
(written by John Phillips)
Dunhill 4026
Chart debut April 9, 1966 (3 weeks at #1); #3 in England, #1 (3 weeks) in Canada[308]; from the album *If You Can Believe Your Eyes & Ears* (1 week at #1, 105 total weeks)

When John Phillips was trying to launch the Mamas & the Papas out of the ashes of the former folk groups the Journeymen and the Mugwumps in 1965, he played his new groupmates a number he'd written, and afterward they told him he was crazy. "It's a stupid song about a day of the week!" declared Denny Doherty. John practically had to force the group to record it, and it was the last song they cut for their debut album. "Who knew? No one knew," Doherty would later ruefully confess about the song that would carry the group to #1, *Monday, Monday*.[309]

It wasn't an easy sell. Even the man who'd previously managed Phillips in the Journeymen, after being given a demo tape of the group by John Stewart of the Kingston Trio, refused to listen to it because John, for all his gifts as songwriter, arranger, and singer, was "a major pain in the ass." But up and coming Los Angeles producer Lou Adler was knocked out by the group when he heard them at a Barry McGuire recording session rehearsal, and so was America in 1966.[310] Thanks to the vast success of their first single *California Dreamin'*, the album was a smash by the time *Monday, Monday* was released, and the new single sold more than 150,000 copies on its first day in stores.

It's all about the harmonies. Doherty's lead vocal is warm and engaging, but it's the way Cass Elliott's mighty alto/soprano merges with Michelle Phillips' contralto and John's baritone that makes this performance—as with the group's other best work—truly shimmer. Even singing "ba-da, ba-da," it sounds glorious. The record won the Grammy Award for best contemporary group performance. *Rolling Stone*, ranking the debut album #127 for all time in 2003, gave as one of the prime reasons to "feast your ears: the luscious sadness of *Monday, Monday*."

Ironically, even as the Mamas & the Papas came to symbolize sunny Los Angeles folk-rock, the group was a real-life soap opera. John and Michelle's three-year-old marriage would soon be rocked by the willowy blonde's affairs with Doherty and Gene Clark of the Byrds. John knew about it, and even co-wrote *I Saw Her Again* specifically to bring the wayward-wife theme out in the open. But honesty was at the heart of his songwriting, and the four-part harmonies he crafted—inspired by the sophisticated arrangements of the Four Freshmen and the Hi-Lo's, but given a twangy new twist—were like nothing heard before.

Paint It Black (1966)—Rolling Stones
London 901[311]
Recorded March 8, 1966; chart debut May 14, 1966 (2 weeks at #1); #1 (1 week) in England[312]; from the album *Aftermath* (reached #2) (*RS-#176, 1001, AHR, ACC, DMDB*)

Musical adventurer Brian Jones had grown bored with the guitar by early 1966, and soon after the Beatles used a sitar on *Norwegian Wood* from the end-of-1965 album

307. *All Hopped Up and Ready to Go*, p. 225–26.

308. #1 (2 weeks) in Argentina and South Africa, #2 in Austria and West Germany, #3 in Australia, New Zealand, and Switzerland.

309. Unterberger, *Turn! Turn! Turn!*, p. 176–77.

310. Adler, in addition to his success as record producer, also produced the *Monterey Pop* documentary film on the landmark 1967 rock concert.

311. The record was officially titled *Paint It, Black*, with the comma inserted by someone at Decca, the odd punctuation arousing (notes Stephen Davis) much pointed comment.

312. After five consecutive #1 singles in England, the Stones had reached "only" #2 with *19th Nervous Breakdown*; *Paint It Black* put them back on top.

Rubber Soul, he purchased a new sitar at a music shop in downtown Suva while the group was on a brief vacation on the South Pacific island of Fiji. Rolling Stones biographer Stephen Davis reports that the fragile instrument quickly developed a large crack, but Jones taped it up and kept playing. Mick Jagger recalled proudly: "_Paint It Black_ is quite good and very different. It has that Turkish groove that was really out of nowhere . . . [the sitar] gave that record a particular flavor."[313] [314] _Paint It Black_—recorded when the group flew back to Los Angeles to complete the album _Aftermath_—provided Jones' first big sitar showcase. Sandy Pearlman, discussing the emerging trend of "raga-rock" in _Crawdaddy_, praised the Stones' approach on this record, remarking that the sitar "is used to help integrate the song through the impression of momentum, since this instrument can rapidly build up a gliding and continuous graduation of notes."[315] He's complemented by Bill Wyman on klezmer-tinged organ and Jack Nitzsche on piano. "There was nothing else like it on the radio," notes Davis. "This lurid tone poem seemed to describe a funeral procession amid haunting, existential self-doubt. Brian's sitar stated the melody with an otherworldly dolor, and pounding drums launched the song into a high-noir ambience of anxiety and hopelessness, desirous to see the sun blotted out from the sky."[316] Despite the aura of despair and the experimental instrumentation, the song became a chart-topper on both sides of the Atlantic.

Try a Little Tenderness (1966)—Otis Redding (written by Reg Connelly, Harry Woods & Jimmy Campbell) Volt 141

Recorded Sept. 13, 1966; chart debut Dec. 3, 1966 (#4 on R&B chart, #25 pop); from the album _The Otis Redding Dictionary of Soul_ (_RHF, R&B-#114, DM-#155, RS-#207, RH, ACC_)[317]

Tackling an ancient pop standard (popularized by Ted "Is Everybody Happy?" Lewis and Bing Crosby in 1933 and Frank Sinatra in the late 1940s), whose original lyrics are partly lost in translation, Otis Redding and the mighty Memphis Group house band created a most unexpected soul classic with _Try a Little Tenderness_. Redding had learned the song from Sam Cooke's version on his live Copacabana album; Cooke had used just two verses of

the song as part of a medley. Otis' manager Phil Walden suggested the song would be a perfect vehicle for him to cross over to a white audience, and pestered him about doing it for months.

Redding biographer Scott Freeman writes that as the band began "messing around" with the song, it started as a straight sentimental ballad, with a lovely three-horn introduction and hushed vocal by Otis with Isaac Hayes on piano, Booker T. Jones on organ, and gentle rhythmic backing.[318] "Then, on the second verse, Al Jackson unexpectedly began to tap out a double-time lick on his snare drum. Suddenly eyes began lighting up; everyone saw the song from a whole different perspective. What if they used Al's drum part as a springboard to take the song and build it from a soft ballad into a wild and frenzied ending?" "When Al did that drum thing, it just wailed everybody," bassist Donald 'Duck' Dunn recalled. We didn't know he was gonna do that."[319]

"The Stax studio," said Dunn, "would light up when Otis came in. He got everyone to play above their heads. He got performances out of us like no one else. He was an incredible creative spark, a life force that wouldn't quit." "I lived between Otis sessions," trumpeter Wayne Jackson told writer Rob Bowman. "Otis was the focus for everybody. You could feel the excitement when he was coming."[320] In addition to the four MGs, Hayes, and the Mar-Key horns (including Andrew Love on tenor sax), Gilbert Caple is also on saxophone; Stax co-owner Jim Stewart served as engineer.[321]

In _Rock & Roll: An Unruly History_, Robert Palmer cites as an example of the Stax ensemble at its finest Redding's "astonishing" reworking of _Tenderness_, in which Jackson's "metronomic tick-tock beat seems to operate on an entirely different rhythmic plane from the rest of the musicians and the vocal—at first. Gradually, the tempo begins to expand and contract, until suddenly the listener realizes that the band's rhythm and the drummer's have somehow meshed into a single, unstoppable groove. Far from calling attention to itself, this polyrhythmic legerdemain is employed entirely in the service of the song."[322] Walden noted proudly: "The interplay was pure alchemy."

313. _According to the Rolling Stones_, p. 93. Charlie Watts says the song's drum pattern may have been suggested by Jagger, or inspired by an R&B favorite such as the Miracles' _Going to a Go-Go_.

314. Keith Richards, _Life_ (p. 177): "I wrote the melody, [Mick] wrote the lyrics."

315. November 1966 _Crawdaddy_. As employed by the Stones, the sitar is "quite unobtrusive, whereas on _Norwegian Wood_, the instrument seemed "an arbitrary choice" merely to provide an "exotic accompaniment."

316. _Old Gods Almost Dead_, p. 164–65.

317. It was called the #49 best single of the past twenty-five years by _Rolling Stone_ in 1988.

318. Hayes, reports Rob Bowman in _Soulsville U.S.A._ (p. 105–7), was responsible for the three-part, contrapuntal horn line in the song's introduction, inspired by the strings on Cooke's _A Change Is Gonna Come_, and the cymbal break in the climax, which Hayes would later reuse on _Theme from "Shaft."_

319. Freeman, _Otis!_, p. 156–59.

320. _Soulsville, U.S.A._, p. 103.

321. Stewart, in liner notes for Rhino's 4-CD _Definitive Otis Redding_, called _Tenderness_ the one song above all others that summed up the artist. "That one performance is so special and unique that it expresses who he is." Al Bell, Stax's head of promotion, noted that Otis "had the entire arrangements in his head," and Jackson had the knack for locking into the singer rhythmically, staying with him through every shift in direction.

322. Palmer, p. 92–93.

When Redding sings "you won't forget it," writes Dave Marsh, "they cut loose, Booker T.'s organ shrieking them on, and the horns building to a crescendo until finally Otis releases himself in sweaty surrender to the heat they've generated . . ."[323]

Cold Sweat (Parts 1 & 2) (1967)—James Brown
King 6110
Chart debut July 22, 1967 (#1 for 3 weeks R&B, #7 pop)
   (*DM-#86, R&B-#183, 1001, DET*)

James unleashes one of his all-time greatest screams in this deeply influential soul monster. Dave Marsh: "On the evidence presented here, sometime in 1967 James Brown concluded that the most oppressive factor in music was the tyranny of the chord change, and so he decided to revolt by making music in which chord changes were superfluous. A result was the birth of modern funk, spread out over both the A and B sides of a 45. 'Give the drummer some' is the rallying cry, and that's all well and good but the constant activity emerges from Bernard Odum's bass, which assuredly moves the music along, popping and bopping. The result is dance music as skeletal as an X-ray and about as resistible as gravity."[324]

Declaring *Cold Sweat* one of the "40 Records That Shook the World" in *Details*, Will Hermes writes: "Its gunshot horn bursts and pugilist rhythm freaked out the R&B faithful," providing a classic showcase for Clyde Stubblefield, "whose snare might be the most sampled instrument on the planet . . . JB flowed directly into Parliament-Funkadelic and was echoed in Jamaican reggae, worshipped by Brazilian funkieros, and reimagined by Nigeria's Fela Kuti and Cameroon's Manu Dibango."[325] Cliff White and Harry Weinger write in liner notes for the Brown boxed set that fundamentally the piece was "just rhythm—barely any chord changes—with jazz intervals in the horn section," conceived by Alfred "Pee Wee" Ellis, a jazz tenor saxman who had been hired in early 1966 to succeed Nat Jones as the band's leader and arranger.[326] In his Brown biography, James Sullivan elaborates that Ellis "wrote *Cold Sweat* on a scrap of paper on the bus after listening to Brown wordlessly describe a fragment of an idea he had for a new tune. The riff, as the arranger points out, was directly influenced by Miles Davis's *So What*."[327]

In his autobiography, Brown explained that the song is a speeded-up version of a slow, bluesy album cut he'd recorded in 1962, *I Don't Care*. "It was good that way, but [by 1967] I was really getting into my funk bag now and

it became an almost completely different tune, except for the lyrics. It had the scratch guitar, the fast-hitting sound from the bass, and the funky, funky rhythms played by Clyde Stubblefield. *Cold Sweat* has a pattern that hasn't been duplicated yet."[328] A central element in the new funk style embodied by *Cold Sweat*, writes Richard J. Ripani, is that after many years in which jazz and R&B artists emphasized beats two and four, Brown in this record and thereafter emphasized beat one (and to a lesser degree, beat three). "To a modern ear it seems very normal to hear popular songs that accent the first beat of a measure, but in the context of the mid-1960s the concept was much more radical."[329]

Brown was the founding father of the music that became known as funk, and this record, as much as any other, helped point the way. Guthrie P. Ramsey, Jr.: "In my view, funk, or the 'in the pocket' groove, rivals in importance the conventions of bebop's complex and perhaps more open-ended rhythmic approaches. Each imperative—the *calculated-freedom* of modern-jazz rhythm sections and the *spontaneity-within-the-pocket* funk approach—represents one of the most influential musical designs to appear in twentieth-century American culture. The 'James Brown sound' inspired admiration, piqued the imaginations of black cultural nationalists interested in 'African origins,' and inspired contemporary dance crazes that swept across the country."[330]

"*Cold Sweat* deeply affected the musicians I knew," said Atlantic producer Jerry Wexler, soon to open a new chapter in soul history through his sessions with Aretha Franklin. "It just freaked them out. For a time, no one could get a handle on what to do next."[331]

Soul Man (1967)—Sam & Dave (written by Isaac Hayes & David Porter)
Stax 231
Chart debut Sept. 9, 1967 (7 weeks at #1 on R&B chart; 3 weeks at #2 on *Billboard* pop chart, #1 in *Record World*); #3 in Canada (*RHF, GHF, R&B-#60, RIA-#168, RS, DM, ACC, DMDB*)

"Ice-cold truth, told as much by trumpet and guitar as by the fabulous interplay of voices," describes Dave Marsh of this record. "In the history of braggadocio, few

323. Marsh, *The Heart of Rock & Soul*, p. 108–9.
324. Marsh, *The Heart of Rock & Soul*, p. 61.
325. November 1998 *Details*, p. 50.
326. Annotation for boxed set *Star Time*, p. 31.
327. *The Hardest Working Man in Show Business: How James Brown Saved the Soul of America*, p. 115–16.

328. James Brown with Bruce Tucker, *The Godfather of Soul: An Autobiography*, p. 173.
329. *The New Blue Music*, p. 93. Ripani also cites the surprising fact (p, 137) that *Cold Sweat* and Miles Davis' 1959 jazz classic *So What*—two songs seemingly from opposite ends of the musical spectrum—"use the same mode [an A dorian mode] and almost exactly the same riff—though performed on horns—played by the electric piano player" in the Dazz Band's 1982 hit *Let It Whip*.
330. Guthrie P. Ramsey, Jr., *Race Music: Black Cultures from Bebop to Hip-Hop*, p. 154.
331. *Star Time* annotation, p. 31.

have been so convincing."[332] The Memphis soul classic opens with Steve Cropper's guitar, with co-writer Isaac Hayes' low-register piano and Al Jackson a powerhouse on drums.[333] Bassist Donald "Duck" Dunn says that Hayes was responsible for "funkified rhythms" through counterpoint, such as the guitar-and-bass interplay. After Sam and Dave exclaim "I'm a soul man" four times, writes Rob Bowman, Cropper plays a slide guitar part "that has been buried deep into the collective consciousness of a generation." Hayes suggested, "give me some Elmore James"; Cropper didn't have a proper slide at hand, so he used a cigarette lighter to get the sliding effect. Sam Moore was so knocked out that he interjected, "play it, Steve!" "The excitement was so palpable that it was all left in."[334]

Soul Man was Sam & Dave's third Top 50 pop hit, following up *When Something Is Wrong with My Baby*, and their biggest.[335] At David Porter's urging, Moore unleashes his best "Bobby Bland squall," and the Memphis Horns top it all off.

By the Time I Get to Phoenix (1967)—Glen Campbell
(written by Jimmy Webb)
Capitol 2015
Chart debut Oct. 28, 1967 (#2 C&W, #26 pop); from
    the album *By the Time I Get to Phoenix* (#15 peak)
    (*BMI-#21, C&W-#61, GHF, RIA, HBN-#139, RS,
    AHR, DMDB*)[336]

For those who think of Glen Campbell only in terms of his slick TV and Las Vegas persona, let it not be forgotten that from 1967–1970, he was recording some of the most beautifully crafted pop songs of the era, true gems from the standpoint of composition, performance, and production. Jimmy Webb was responsible for most of those songs, and the one that got it all started was *By the Time I Get to Phoenix*.

Born in Delight, Arkansas, on April 22, 1936, Glen Campbell began playing guitar as a child and was playing with regional country bands by age fourteen. At twenty-two he moved to Los Angeles and became one of the most in-demand session musicians of the 1960s, playing on such hits as *Be My Baby* (the Ronettes), *You've Lost That Lovin' Feelin'* (Righteous Brothers), *Viva Las Vegas* (it's Glen's rapid-fire guitar licks on the Elvis Presley hit), *Strangers in the Night* (Frank Sinatra), and *I'm a Believer* (the Monkees). In his autobiography,

session drummer supreme Hal Blaine wrote that Campbell "incorporated country-style electric guitar into rock music, and his solos injected an uninhibited, savage, raw feeling into the records." Glen Campbell savage and raw? Indeed, he was a greatly admired and influential player before the public knew his name.

After Brian Wilson retired from public performing in 1965, Campbell became a touring member of the Beach Boys for several months, and played on *Good Vibrations* and the album *Pet Sounds*. Although he'd had a couple of modestly successful singles under his own name in the early 1960s, it was not until 1966 that he began to seriously pursue a solo career. His performance of John Hartford's *Gentle on My Mind* was his first important hit, and *By the Time I Get to Phoenix* soared still higher.

Jimmy Webb (born on August 15, 1946, in Elk City, Oklahoma, the son of a Baptist minister), then age eighteen, sent a tape of his songs to Johnny Rivers, who was so impressed that he bought the young composer's contract and all of his early copyrights. Rivers recorded this finely crafted kiss-off ballad as the leadoff track on his end-of-1966 album *Changes*, and considered releasing it as a single, but thought it might be too similar in its chord changes to his previous #1 hit *The Poor Side of Town*. Rivers arranged for pop crooner Tony Martin to record the song; that record went nowhere. In the meantime, he told *Goldmine*, "I'd given a copy of my new album to Al DeLory, who was Glen Campbell's producer. [DeLory had also played piano as part of the Wrecking Crew, including Campbell.] And the next thing I hear is Glen's version of it on the radio." Because Rivers owned the copyright, "it worked out great for all of us." Campbell first listened to the Rivers performance while on the road en route to his next gig, and recalled being so overcome with emotion that he promptly returned home to visit his folks.[337] "I changed *Phoenix* somewhat, amending the chord progression at the end," he remarked in his memoir. Having tinkered similarly with the many other Webb tunes he recorded, "Jimmy has always teased me that it's my obsession to tamper with his work," but the composer was delighted with the results.[338]

Campbell made it the first of his several definitive renderings of Webb songs. Guitar wizard James Burton (famous for the early Ricky Nelson hits and later work with Elvis Presley) plays on the song, and Leon Russell, a fellow veteran of the Spector sessions, is on piano. Broadcast Music, Inc. (BMI) ranks it as the #21 most-played song since 1940 with over five million broadcast performances.

332. Marsh, *The Heart of Rock & Soul*, p. 335.

333. Moore in the duo's oral history (*Sam and Dave*, p. 65): "Al Jackson was a genius, like a metronome."

334. Liner notes, *The Complete Stax/Volt Singles*, p. 33–34.

335. Even though it was a career song for him, Sam Moore never much cared for it, as seen in the oral history with Marsh.

336. *Phoenix* was a Grammy winner for best male vocal and Album of the Year.

337. Jeff Bleiel feature on Webb in December 20, 1996, *Goldmine*.

338. Campbell's recollection, in his autobiography *Rhinestone Cowboy* (p. 75), is that he discovered the song from listening to Rivers' album version during a break in a recording session, loved it, and suggested it to DeLory as his next single.

David Jenness and Don Velsey remark that the tune's "story is haunting, in a way that country songs about a man ditching a woman are generally not."[339]

Dance to the Music (1968)—Sly & the Family Stone
Epic 10256
Chart debut Jan. 27, 1968 (reached #8 on *Billboard* pop chart, #5 in *Record World*; #9 R&B); #7 in England, #20 in Canada[340] (*DM-#57, R&B-#65, RHF, GHF, RS-#225, TC, ACC, DMDB*)

The powerfully trend-setting debut hit by Sly & the Family Stone, *Dance to the Music*, embodied the group's qualities as outlined by Greil Marcus: "There was an enormous freedom to the band's sound. It was complex, because freedom is complex; sympathetic, affectionate, and coherent, like the reality of freedom. And it was all celebration, all affirmation, a music of endless humor and delight, like a fantasy of freedom."[341] Sylvester "Sly Stone" Stewart was born on March 15, 1944, in Dallas, recorded a gospel song with his family at age four, and moved with his family to San Francisco in the 1950s. He had a regional hit at age sixteen, studied music at Vallejo Junior College, and began playing in local groups. Sly (a childhood nickname) gained prominence as a radio disc jockey, which led to a job producing records for Autumn Records, and this enabled him to work with a variety of Bay Area acts, further broadening his musical horizons. He formed Sly & the Family Stone in early 1967, with his brother Freddie Stone on guitar, his sister Rosie Stone on piano and vocals, Cynthia Robinson on trumpet, Jerry Martini on sax, Sly's cousin Larry Graham on bass and vocals, and Gregg Errico on drums. Distinctive from the start with its multi-racial membership and eclectic musical style, the group had a local hit single on the small label Loadstone, leading to a contract with Epic Records and a debut album that flopped. But they bounced back quickly with this breakthrough smash.

Dave Marsh declares that other than James Brown's *Papa's Got a Brand New Bag*, "no great single has broken so many rules and reestablished them in its own image." In one sense the record could hardly be simpler, as Sly introduces each musician one at a time "to build up a powerhouse of psychedelic R&B, replete with call-and-response vocals, briefly interjected solos, interspersed cries of surprised glee, and a beat that bulldozes everything in its path. It's all so joyous[342] that it's easy to miss the 'message' declared by horn players Cynthia Robinson and Jerry Martini: 'All the squares go

home!'"[343] Other than Brown, no other artist wielded a deeper influence than Sly on the black popular music of the 1970s and into the 1980s.[344]

54-46 (Was My Number) (1968/1972)—Toots & the Maytals
Recorded for Beverly's (Jamaica) in late 1968
Released outside Jamaica in 1972 (*World-#8, DM-#76*)

Aside from Bob Marley and Jimmy Cliff, no name looms larger in reggae history than that of Frederick "Toots" Hibbert, born in 1946 in May Pen, west of Kingston, Jamaica. He moved in 1961 to Kingston, where he teamed up with Jerry Mathias and Raleigh Gordon to form a vocal trio. Toots was the lead singer, Mathias sang low harmony, and Gordon took the high. Their first single as the Maytals, *Hallelujah*, came out that year and reflected their common church backgrounds. The trio moved from gospel and R&B to ska music, then its successor rock-steady; and when rock-steady evolved into reggae, the Maytals found their fullest musical expression. (Indeed it was a Maytals dance record from 1968, *Do the Reggay*, that provided the new music with its name.) After recording dozens of singles, the group began to enjoy some success with Prince Buster and then Byron Lee (owner of Kingston's biggest studio, Dynamic Sound). Their progress came to a halt in 1966 when Toots went to prison on a ganja-dealing (marijuana) charge, for which he always insisted he was framed.[345] It was his eighteen months of jail time at Tamarind Farm that provided the basis for the Maytals' greatest classic.[346]

54-46 (Was My Number), recorded not long after his release with Jamaica's #1 producer Leslie Kong, is described by Dave Marsh as "almost folkloric, opening with a Leadbelly-like evocation of a guard's cry that's neatly poised on the edge of incoherence, then quickly seguing into tight, intense call-and-response dance music." The compelling narrative describes an armed stickup from the perspective of the prisoner who carried it out. Toots' central point about the eternal cycle of injustice in the prison system is heard in the chorus: "54 46 was my number / Right now someone else has that number." The trio's wordless chanting combines with (in Marsh's words) "a giddy organ part that is the closest reggae has ever come

---

339. *Classic American Popular Song: The Second Half-Century, 1950–2000*, p. 259.

340. Reached #3 in Malaysia.

341. *Mystery Train*, p. 70.

342. Martini, normally a saxophonist, is also on clarinet here (Selvin, *Sly and the Family Stone: An Oral History*, p. 61).

343. Marsh, p. 41–42. Richard J. Ripani in *The New Blue Music* (p. 94) writes that the record relies heavily on what he calls the "cyclic" form (using repeated riff patterns), and there "is no Western functional harmony" in the performance.

344. Rickey Vincent echoes this viewpoint in *Funk: The Music, the People, and the Rhythm of the One*. A major distinction between the two artists, he remarks, is that Brown was identified with the black community, while Sly "represented everyone else in the melting pot."

345. Davis, *Reggae Bloodlines*, p. 89–90.

346. "I wrote *54-46* to let people know I was innocent," declared Hibbert. "I wrote that song with all my heart." (Chang and Chen, *Reggae Routes*, p. 120–21.)

to psychedelia."[347] A few months later in 1969, the May-tals would record their other most famous track, *Pressure Drop*, which led to their signing by Island Records. The latter song's inclusion on the soundtrack of *The Harder They Come*, starring Cliff, ensured the Maytals' iconic status during the years to come.

Kevin O'Brien Chang and Wayne Chen: "*54-46* is not just a song about a man unjustly imprisoned, robbed of his humanity and reduced to a mere number. It's about his capacity not only to endure, but to thrive and grow amidst the hardships of injustice. It's the story of the Jamaican people writ small, a people who endured the unspeakable brutalities of slavery and yet maintained their dignity, vitality, sense of self-worth and, not least, an astonishing capacity for joy."[348]

Crystal Blue Persuasion (1969)—Tommy James & the Shondells (written by Tommy James, Ed Gray & Mike Vale)

Roulette 7050

Recorded in late 1968; chart debut June 7, 1969 (spent 3 weeks at #2; reached #1 in *Record World*); #1 (1 week) in Canada

The stunningly beautiful, impressionistic *Crystal Blue Persuasion* began much like Tommy James and the Shondells' previous chart-topping hit *Crimson and Clover*, by combining two unrelated phrases or words ("crystal blue"—representing truth—and "persuasion") and building a song around it. Born Thomas Jackson on April 29, 1947, in Dayton, Ohio, and raised in Niles, Michigan, Tommy James formed the pop group the Shondells at age twelve, and they recorded *Hanky Panky* on the Snap label in 1963. Two years later, with the group broken up, a Pittsburgh DJ suddenly started playing the song; Roulette acquired the master and re-released it, and as the record climbed to #1 James formed a new Shondells from an existing Pittsburgh group, the Raconteurs. After a strong run of additional hits, the group began to move toward a more mature sound with the early-1969 smash *Crimson and Clover* and its followup, *Sweet Cherry Wine*. *Crystal Blue Persuasion*—James' personal favorite among his records—carried that evolution to its zenith.

"The song came from the Bible," James later wrote in liner notes to his greatest-hits collection. "I was reading the Old Testament and those words—crystal blue persuasion—jumped out at me. They weren't connected; I just saw those words, and they sounded right.[349] The song really came from my heart. It was about the way we thought things were maybe going to change, and what they were going to change into. That song always reminds me of the magic summer of '69. In fact, it was peaking as Woodstock was taking place." The Shondells had been invited to play at the epic festival, but to their subsequent chagrin passed on the chance. James says in retrospect it was "the hardest record we ever made." The group's initial recording was overcrowded with rock instrumentation, and the track "did not match the song." So they went back in the studio and began "unproducing" the piece. "We kept extracting practically everything we had put in, and the more we took out the better it sounded."[350] The passionate idealism of the lyrics surges through James' vocal, and with the song's shimmering melodic beauty accompanied by gentle conga drum, acoustic flamenco guitar, tambourine, bass, and church-like organ, it's a record that has a singular capacity to produce a sense of spiritual peace.

I Want You Back (1969)—Jackson 5 (written by Freddy Perren, Deke Richards, Fonce Mizell, & Berry Gordy, Jr.)

Motown 1157

Chart debut Nov. 15, 1969 (1 week at #1 on pop chart, #1 for 4 weeks R&B); #2 in England & Canada[351] (*RHF, GHF, ACC-#29, R&B-#33, DM-#84, RS-#121, RIA, AHR, TC, DMDB*)

Motown founder Berry Gordy, Jr., recalled in his autobiography that the Jackson 5 came to Motown's attention after Bobby Taylor and his group the Vancouvers (including Tommy Chong) played on the same bill with them; the young brothers had previously recorded some sides for little Steeltown Records in their hometown of Gary, Indiana. Gordy had the foresight to videotape their July 1968 audition at the Motown building, which was dazzling.[352] It took several months to clear away some legal complications with the group's previous manager; in March 1969 the Jackson 5 were formally on board at Motown. Michael, then a few months shy of his eleventh

---

347. Marsh, *The Heart of Rock & Soul*, p. 55. He describes Hibbert as a Jamaican vocal counterpart to Otis Redding, albeit about a foot shorter.

348. The authors ranked the song at #1 on their all-time reggae Top 100 (p. 232).

349. In his autobiography *Me, the Mob, and the Music*, James offered a clarified account of the song's origin. At an Atlanta concert, a young fan gave James a poem he had written, a Christian poem inspired by the book of Revelation and containing the title phrase. He wrote the lyrics from that starting point, and Eddie Gray contributed the opening riff, "airy and ethereal with a Latin feel."

350. James, *Me, the Mob, and the Music*, p. 164–65. The idealism in the song was reflected in the artist's life at the time: the group had performed on behalf of Robert Kennedy's presidential campaign, was crushed by his assassination, and went on to participate in Hubert Humphrey's campaign.

351. Reached #8 in France, #9 in Japan.

352. Nelson George reports in *Where Did Our Love Go?* (p. 159–60) that even before this, in 1965, Gladys Knight & the Pips, after meeting the Jacksons at Chicago's Regal Theater, asked a Motown representative to check out the group's show, but no one came. Even when they praised the Jacksons to Motown on a second occasion, nothing happened. Gladys took this as one more piece of evidence that their opinion wasn't always given the weight it deserved at the label.

birthday, reminded Gordy of Frankie Lymon, and he wanted to come up with the perfect song to launch them.

As he had done with the Supremes' *Love Child*, Gordy put together a "creative commando team" to write and produce the song. "Once again, I was trying to have an anonymous, unified team where nobody's personal names or egos could get in the way." No one wanted a repeat of the Holland-Dozier-Holland situation with star songwriters who end up suing the company. So the group, including Motown staff producer Deke Richards, became the Corporation. Their song had originally been intended for Gladys Knight & the Pips under the title *I Want to Be Free*, but Gordy decided to retool it to introduce his new group. Gordy came up with the basic melody; Richards and the others recorded an instrumental track; and they worked together on the lyrics, using the Jackson 5 as their own demo singers, recording their voices right onto the master track. "So by the time the demo was done, we practically had a finished record." But it was an arduous process, as Gordy kept pressing everyone to make each element better, requiring take after take until he was satisfied.[353] The final session for the song ended at 2 a.m.; Richards said it may have been "the most expensive single in Motown history" to that point, costing about $10,000 at a time when most Motown singles cost around $2,000.[354]

Nelson George: "The resulting record was an explosive burst of youthful enthusiasm backed by immaculate, dynamic production and a clever lyric to which Berry had clearly contributed his expertise."[355] Jackson biographer Dave Marsh: "The record is almost perfect," the greatest debut disc by any pop or rock act.[356] Michael's alto, remarks Matthew Oshinsky, "revealed a musical and emotional intuition that most of our greatest adult singers never reach . . . only Michael Jackson could make heartbreak seem so perfectly blissful."[357] To launch the new group, Gordy had Diana Ross "present" their debut album, introduce them in public, and they opened for the Supremes in August at the Los Angeles Forum. The Jackson 5 "would be the last stars I would develop with the same intensity and emotional investment as I had with the earlier Motown artists. They would be the last big stars to come rolling down my assembly line."[358]

I Want You Back, recounted *Rolling Stone* in ranking it the #5 best single of the past twenty-five years in 1988, "kick-starts like a hot new model from the Motown assembly line: Freddie Perren and Fonce Mizell tool up a piano glissando; David T. Walker fuel-injects his guitar licks; Wilton Felder pumps out some liquid bass; and the Jacksons trade high-octane vocal lines with authority and electricity."[359] Little Michael's passionate lead vocal announced that a new star had arrived. Twelve years later, the magazine called it the #9 best pop song ever.

Your Song (1970)—Elton John
Uni 55265

Chart debut Nov. 28, 1970 (#8 in *Billboard*, #6 in *Record World*); #4 in Canada, #7 in England;[360] from the album *Elton John* (chart debut Oct. 3, 1970, #4 peak) (*GHF, RHF, WASH-#9, BMI-#37*,[361] *DMDB-#62, RS-#137, BBC*)

Direct, elegant, and beautiful, *Your Song* was the ballad that made Elton John a star, and over four decades later it still holds up as his best. The song was "about a young man's optimism," explained lyricist Bernie Taupin. "It was a simpler time, and it is a simple song. The thing about it is it's so wonderfully naive."

Born Reginald Dwight in Pinner, Middlesex, England, on March 25, 1947, Elton began playing piano at age four, and at eleven won a scholarship to the Royal Academy of Music. After studying for six years, he set out for a career in music; his band Bluesology backed American R&B stars touring in England, and in 1966 became Long John Baldry's touring band. In 1968, he began collaborating on songs with Taupin; his 1969 debut album *Empty Sky* was heard by relatively few at the time. For his second album he hired producer Gus Dudgeon, and arranger Paul Buckmaster (both men had worked on David Bowie's *Space Oddity*) worked up lavish string charts. After a smash engagement in August 1970 at the Troubadour in Los Angeles, dazzling audiences with his flamboyant showmanship (and triggering rapturous reviews), the album caught fire, selling 30,000 copies in just the next two weeks. The album's gospel-tinged leadoff single *Border Song* was just a moderate success, but then *Your Song* broke things wide open. John would go on to become the biggest-selling solo artist of the 1970s, and had at least one Top 40 hit every year from 1970 through 1995; after

353. Michael Jackson recalled in *Moonwalk* (p. 75–78) that the group was thrilled with the rough mix they'd recorded with Perren, Richards, Mizell, Taylor, and Hal Davis, only to find that Gordy still wasn't satisfied. "Berry insisted on perfection and attention to detail . . . This was his genius." Gordy "could identify the little elements that would make a song *great* rather than just good."

354. Taraborrelli, *Michael Jackson: The Magic, the Madness, the Whole Story*, p. 58–60.

355. George, *Thriller*, p. 186. "Once again, Berry had demonstrated his mastery of the increasingly anachronistic three-minute single."

356. *Trapped: Michael Jackson and the Crossover Dream*, p. 75–76, 86–87. Jon Landau in *Rolling Stone* called it "spellbinding . . . one of the most fortuitous events in the recent history of pop music."

357. *1001 Songs You Must Hear Before You Die*, p. 254.

358. Gordy, *To Be Loved*, p. 279–84. Michael reminded Gordy of Frankie Lymon, and he wanted the song to capture the feeling of youthful emotional release in *Why Do Fools Fall in Love*.

359. September 8, 1988, *Rolling Stone*, p. 66.

360. Reached #10 in Australia.

361. Over 7 million broadcast performances.

that remarkable streak finally ended, his 1997 revision of *Candle in the Wind* as a tribute to the late Princess Diana sold a staggering 14 million copies.

Elton John and Bernie Taupin wrote all the songs for that second album in the small apartment of Elton's mother in London's Northwood Hills. "There was an upright piano in the living room and bunk beds in a room in the back," Taupin recalled to *Rolling Stone*. "I'd sit on the bed, feverishly writing, and come out, give Elton an odd lyric or two, and he'd sit at the piano and work on them." *Your Song* was completed in about fifteen minutes at breakfast over coffee and eggs. The inspiration was said to be a girl on whom Taupin briefly had an unrequited crush. Producer Dudgeon was convinced the song was a hit from the time he heard the initial demo tape, but Uni (MCA's American subsidiary) wasn't as sure. "We actually thought *Your Song* might be a little bit too classy. When you consider the other records around at the time, it was an unusual record, to say the least." An early admirer of *Your Song* was the songwriters' ultimate pop hero, Brian Wilson of the Beach Boys; when Danny Hutton of Three Dog Night took them to Wilson's home following the Troubadour breakthrough, the reclusive genius introduced himself by singing the ballad's chorus.

Opening with Elton's unadorned piano chords and expanding behind him with a full orchestra, *Your Song* touched listeners with its loveliness and sense of yearning. His idiosyncratic style of phrasing combined with Taupin's charmingly awkward stream-of-consciousness lyrics added to the sense of believable earnestness.[362] Biographer Philip Norman: "Few songs have so perfectly suited their moment. After the long era of psychedelic pretentiousness, Bernie Taupin's simple lyric was a breath of fresh air that seemed almost revolutionary."[363]

Just My Imagination (Running Away With Me) (1971)—The Temptations (music by Norman Whitfield, lyrics by Barrett Strong)

Gordy 7105

Chart debut Feb. 6, 1971 (2 weeks at #1 on pop chart, 3 weeks at #1 R&B); #8 in England, #13 in Canada[364] (*RS, DM, AHR, DMDB*)

Eddie Kendricks' final lead vocal with the Temptations before launching his solo career features, writes Thomas Ryan, "the most mesmerizing and relaxed performance of his career . . . It was a dreamscape made in heaven. With the most sublime music to watch girls by, it is so languid that you can almost smell the heat rising off the sidewalk."[365] Norman Whitfield and Barrett Strong had written a succession of socially conscious songs for the Temps from 1968–1970, but as the novelty of that approach waned, it was time to go in a different direction. The team had sketched a rough outline of the ballad *Just My Imagination* a couple of years earlier, and upon returning to it in late 1970 were inspired to quickly complete the piece and get the group directly into the recording studio.[366] While there had been previous songs about a guy who imagined so fervently being with a particular lady that the fantasy became his own version of reality—see the Roy Orbison songbook—the utter lack of a dividing line between the two worlds and the swooning quality of his internal romantic vision places *Just My Imagination* in a realm of its own. Jerry Long fashioned a rich orchestration including tympani, an army of violins, and a harp, with the rhythmic support of James Jamerson's bass, and Jack Brokensha on vibes. The psychological makeup of the protagonist with the most tenuous hold on reality could perhaps land him in an institution; but we identify completely with his sweetly desperate yearning as he drifts into warm delusions.

Temptations biographer Mark Ribowsky observes that the song was a "throwback to the sound and flavor most people associated with the Temptations but that had lately been shunted aside: the pleas of real men who showed it was cool to cry, strong but vulnerable men shedding tears over women they imagined as perfect, who could turn them inside out with passion—and, in this case, almost pitifully, divert them into the shadows, able only to fantasize." The performance "reeked with shimmering beauty, class, and schmaltz." He calls attention to Paul Williams' interjection with strings and French horns rising, "Every night on my knees I pray," before Eddie finishes, "Dear Lord, hear my plea . . ."[367]

Nelson George called this "perhaps Whitfield-Strong's best single lyric and possibly their finest song. Paul Riser's string and horn arrangement was sublime, and the rhythm track was as supple as Kendricks' feathery falsetto."[368] Otis Williams of the Temps later wrote how the group was "totally knocked out" upon hearing the finished product. Kendricks—who was, they felt, very mindful that this would be his grand finale with the group—"did a wonderful job capturing the song's magical, dreamy sadness. It was, I think, Eddie's finest moment."

---

362. In a career-spanning interview with Timothy White in the October 4, 1997, *Billboard* (p. EJ-92) discussing his thirty years of collaboration with Taupin, Elton declared: "I think <u>the</u> [personal] favorite would have to be *Your Song*, because of the wonderful lyrics. I've sung it so many times and I've never really gotten fed up with singing it."

363. Norman, *Elton John: The Definitive Biography*, p. 157.

364. #10 in France.

365. Ryan, *American Hit Radio*, p. 396–97.

366. Bronson, *Billboard Book of Number One Hits*, p. 290.

367. Ribowsky, *Ain't Too Proud to Beg*, p. 222–23. Kendricks stayed in the studio all night with Whitfield getting the vocal right. The next day, Otis Williams wanted to tell Eddie how moved he had been by the performance, but the singer was unreachable, having firmly closed the door on his tenure with the group.

368. George, *Where Did Our Love Go?*, p. 173.

You've Got A Friend (1971)—Carole King

Recorded in Jan. 1971;[369]

From the Ode album *Tapestry* (chart debut Apr. 10, 1971, #1 for 15 weeks; 302 total weeks) (*GHF-#70, RHF, NPR-100, RR, RS, BBC*)

For over a decade, Carole King had composed the music and then-husband Gerry Goffin the lyrics for a long succession of pop music gems from *Up on the Roof* to *(You Make Me Feel Like) A Natural Woman*. *You've Got a Friend* was one of the first major songs for which she penned the lyrics as well, and it helped make *Tapestry* the biggest-selling album in pop music history to that time. With simple but masterful production by Lou Adler with engineer Hank Cicalo and a totally simpatico studio band,[370] it's an album that has held up over the decades creatively as well as commercially. It won the Grammy as Song of the Year, just as *Tapestry* won for best album; the LP was also inducted into the Grammy Hall of Fame in just its second year of eligibility. James Taylor, who is here on guitar and backing vocals, took the song to Number One with his own rendition that summer on the Warner label.[371]

James Perone remarks that the slow, reverent approach of the arrangement and its timeless theme enable it to achieve the "anthem-like qualities" of the previous year's *Bridge Over Troubled Water*.[372] The song was, King said, "as close to pure inspiration as I've ever experienced. The song wrote itself. It was written by something outside of myself, through me."[373]

Take It Easy (1972)—The Eagles (written by Jackson Browne & Glenn Frey)

Asylum 11005

Chart debut June 3, 1972 (#12 peak in *Billboard*, #6 in *Record World*, #9 in *Cash Box*); reached #2 in France, #12 in Canada; from the album *The Eagles* (#22 peak) (*RHF, BMI, DMDB*)

The California singer-songwriter movement of the 1970s—marked by reflective lyrics, ringing guitars, and easy-flowing harmonies—was kicked into high gear in the summer of 1972 by the Eagles' good-time debut smash *Take It Easy*. By the time it crested late in the decade with the Eagles and Fleetwood Mac (half British, half southern Californian) battling it out for top honors, the movement had helped shape a decade of American pop music.

Jackson Browne (born on October 9, 1948, on the U.S. Army base at Heidelberg, Germany, and raised in Los Angeles), still an up-and-coming songwriter in southern California clubs, was represented by future movie mogul David Geffen, and it was Browne who introduced Geffen to a friend on the Los Angeles rock scene, singer-guitarist Glenn Frey; the artist had met Frey when Glenn performed as a duo with J. D. Souther as Longbranch Pennywhistle. Drummer-singer Don Henley was performing with the country-rock group Shiloh, and while hanging out in Santa Monica Boulevard clubs got to know Browne, Souther, and Linda Ronstadt. Linda was looking for a backup band, and recruited Frey and Henley (the two men met at the fabled Los Angeles club the Troubadour).[374] Along with Bernie Leadon on banjo and mandolin and Randy Meisner on bass, the group backed Ronstadt on her 1970 album *Silk Purse*, but contrary to legend (writes Marc Eliot in the Eagles biography *To the Limit*), they only played one live date with her as a unit at Disneyland. During the rest of her 1971 tour, she used various combinations of musicians, with Frey and Henley as the main constants. The two men began to talk about forming a full-time band.

After the fateful introduction to Geffen, the Eagles signed a contract with Asylum in September 1971, and he had them hone their sound together at a trendy Aspen, Colorado, nightclub. Geffen recruited as producer of their debut album Glyn Johns, who had produced the Rolling Stones, the Who, and Led Zeppelin. Johns brought them to England's famous Olympic recording studio, and placed them on a fierce schedule, with sessions running until late at night. The album was completed in two "grueling weeks," recounts Eliot, partly because the group "couldn't wait to get out of England."[375] But the results are in the music, an album that generated three hit singles and launched a supergroup.

Take It Easy began as a not-quite-finished Jackson Browne composition. Frey offered several times to finish it up and Browne responded, no, I'll get around to it.[376] But Jackson finally gave in, Frey wrapped up the piece, and it became the Eagles' breakthrough hit, with Glenn's

---

369. The album was recorded in just five very efficient sessions (January 4 through 15) at A&M Studios in Hollywood, in what had been the old Charlie Chaplin Films lot on LaBrea Avenue off Sunset Boulevard.

370. Danny "Kootch" Kortchmar is on electric and acoustic guitar, Charles Larkey on string bass, Joel O'Brien and Russ Kunkel on drums, and Terry King on cello in addition to King on piano and Taylor. See King's discussion of the session in her memoir *A Natural Woman* (p. 210).

371. Taylor's album was recorded almost concurrently, from January 3 to February 27, with Danny Kortchmar once again on lead guitar for JT's treatment of this song (see Timothy White's Taylor biography, *Long Ago and Far Away*, p. 176–78).

372. *The Words and Music of Carole King*, p. 36–37. Perone cites King's recording as "fuller in texture" than Taylor's hit single.

373. *The Mojo Collection*, p. 231.

374. Michael Walker, *Laurel Canyon: The Inside Story of Rock-and-Roll's Legendary Neighborhood*, p. 147.

375. The members found Johns intimidating and sometimes antagonistic, although he had good reason to impose tight discipline, as Frey and Randy Meisner were smoking marijuana on the side, and studio time was lost while they were not at their best.

376. Frey was living in a dingy apartment above Browne's studio flat in Echo Park, and he'd heard Browne struggling to close out a number that clearly had the makings of a hit.

The Eagles, PhotoFest.

lead vocal. Eagles biographer Laura Jackson says Frey turned the narrative situation around, so that instead of a guy cruising for women, "it was the girl doing the cruising, boldly eying the song's protagonist in return—and that was [the song's] missing link."[377] (Browne later offered his own version on 1973's *For Everyman*.) It's a happy, easy-flowing rocker about hitting the road in search of peace of mind and maybe a little romance. Winslow, Arizona—a picturesque little town fifty miles east of Flagstaff, near the Painted Desert and with historic U.S. Route 66 running through its center—became a symbol of an idyllic place to kick back and leave your troubles behind. The song, suggests Barney Hoskyns, became "an anthem for every stringy, footloose youth at large in the Golden State."[378] Los Angeles music historian Dominic Priore: "*Take It Easy* was *Mr. Tambourine Man* for the next decade."[379]

Love Train (1973)—The O'Jays (written by Kenny Gamble & Leon Huff)
Philadelphia International 3524
Chart debut Jan. 20, 1973 (1 week at #1 on pop chart, 4 weeks at #1 R&B); #9 in England[380] (*GHF, RHF, R&B-#78, DM, ACC*)

"We were intentionally trying to put messages in the music about things we saw happening in the world," declared songwriter-producer extraordinaire Kenny Gamble. "When we wrote *Love Train*, we really thought we were talking to 'people all over the world.'" "We just wrote what we were seeing and hearing," added his partner Leon Huff. "Then we'd put it to some great music so people could dance while they listened to the message."[381] Message received; thanks to classics like

Love Train, Philadelphia replaced Detroit as the new center of American soul and dance music in the mid-1970s.

Possessing a staying power rivaled by few other groups, the O'Jays began in 1958 in Canton, Ohio, as the Triumphs, including Eddie Levert, Walter Williams, William Powell and two other members who would leave in succeeding years. They recorded as the Mascots for King in 1961, and after being renamed by Cleveland disc jockey Eddie O'Jay, scored their first minor chart hit in 1963 with *Lonely Drifter. I'll Be Sweeter Tomorrow* in 1967 put them in the R&B Top Ten for the first time, and the slow process of establishing themselves began to gather speed a couple of years later. It would be Gamble and Huff who put them over the top.

Kenny Gamble and Leon Huff met at a music publishing house where they both worked in the early 1960s. They eventually formed a group, and although it never had a hit, the members of Kenny Gamble & the Romeos would later become the core of the hit-making 1970s instrumental combo MFSB (Mother Father Sister Brother). After being rejected as songwriters by Motown in 1966, Gamble & Huff returned home to Philadelphia, and produced hits by Wilson Pickett, Dusty Springfield, and other artists for Atlantic. Their small label Gamble Records had hits with the Intruders—and sister label Neptune with the O'Jays (*One Night Affair* in 1969). Columbia Records, then headed by Clive Davis, struck a deal with the duo who formed Philadelphia International. One of the new label's first giant hits was the O'Jays' 1972 pop-crossover breakthrough *Back Stabbers*.

Whereas *Back Stabbers* was cynical, *Love Train* was bursting with idealism and hope, soaring harmonies, and an irresistible dance beat, extending the feeling of classic 1960s soul while offering a bridge to disco. After the writers sketched the outlines of the song through a give-and-take with a portable tape recorder rolling, the lyrics were finalized in the studio, recalled session guitarist Bobby Eli, "as the rhythm track was being laid down and before the O'Jays even got their hands on the song."[382] The song, writes Craig Werner, "celebrates an absolutely inclusive vision of human unity."[383] Gamble's spiritual beliefs would lead him to convert to Islam. Echoing the Impressions' *People Get Ready* in its imagery and Martha & the Vandellas' *Dancing in the Street* in feeling, it still managed to be distinct unto itself.[384] The Gamble & Huff production touch was impeccable; *Rolling Stone* declared, "the way that jazzy guitar line cuts through the

377. *Flying High*, p. 42–43.
378. *Hotel California*, p. 150–51. One of Frey's contributions was the pithy line "It's a girl, my Lord, in a flat-bed Ford."
379. Bud Scoppa predicted in *Rolling Stone* in 1972 that it would "stand proudly right next to the best recordings of the Byrds, the Buffalo Springfield . . . and the other premiere Los Angeles groups."
380. #10 in France, #17 Canada.
381. Mid-October 1997 issue of *USA Today* upon the release of the boxed set *The Philly Sound: Kenny Gamble, Leon Huff & the Story of Brotherly Love (1966–1976)*.

382. John A. Jackson, *A House on Fire: The Rise and Fall of Philadelphia Soul*, p. 123.
383. *A Change Is Gonna Come: Music, Race, and the Soul of America*, p. 200.
384. Stephen Holden, in annotation for *Sony Music: 100 Years/ Soundtrack for a Century*, called it "one of the last major hits to express an unalloyed hope for a transcendent reconciliation between America's black and white cultures."

layered vocals and swelling orchestration is so hypnotizing, so right."[385] The O'Jays would go on to score a long series of pop and R&B hits that stretched into the 1990s.

(Arranged and conducted by Thom Bell; Bunny Sigler on piano; Leonard Pakula on organ; Bobby Eli, Roland Chambers, Norman Harris, & Bunny Sigler on guitars; Ronnie Baker on bass; Earl Young on drums; Larry Washington on percussion; Vince Montana on vibes; strings and horns directed by Don Renaldo)

Killing Me Softly With His Song (1973)—Roberta Flack (music by Charles Fox, lyrics by Norman Gimbel)

Atlantic 2940

Chart debut Jan. 27, 1973 (5 weeks at #1 on pop chart; 4 weeks at #2 R&B); #1 (5 weeks) in Australia, #1 (3 weeks) in Canada, #6 in England[386] (*GHF-#59, BMI-#11,*[387] *DMDB-#58, R&B-#132, RS, TC, BBC, DMDB*)

When singer Lori Lieberman saw Don McLean (of *American Pie* and *Vincent* fame) performing at the Troubadour in Los Angeles in 1971, she was overwhelmed by his poetic musical narratives (*Empty Chairs* was the song that particularly moved her), and wrote a poem about it, "Killing Me Softly with His Blues." Songwriters Charles Fox and Norman Gimbel (in 1973 they would co-write the Jim Croce hit *I Got a Name*, and Gimbel had penned the lyrics to many previous songs including Peggy March's #1 hit *I Will Follow Him* and the English words for Antonio Carlos Jobim's *The Girl from Ipanema*), who were writing songs for her new album, used her poem as the basis for the ballad *Killing Me Softly With His Song*, which she recorded for Capitol single 3379.[388] Fresh from her chart-topping success with *The First Time Ever I Saw Your Face*, pop/jazz singer-pianist Roberta Flack heard the Lieberman recording while on a TWA flight from Los Angeles to New York, loved it, and decided to record it. Working in the studio with producer Joel Dorn, she labored obsessively on the song for three months, experimenting with different background vocals, determined to make the most of a piece she knew was special.[389] It paid off with a stunningly lovely recording containing much

of the hushed emotional intimacy of her first hit (including an ear-grabbing a cappella introduction), but within the framework of a fuller pop production.

In addition to becoming her second of three #1 singles, *Killing Me Softly*, like its predecessor, was also an unstoppable force at the Grammy awards, winning top honors for Record and Song of the Year, and best pop female vocal. When the Fugees revived the song with a Top Ten version in 1996, they featured Roberta in their video, seated at the piano as if she were teaching the number to Lauryn Hill. In 1999, her original classic was inducted into the Grammy Hall of Fame in its first year of eligibility.

Jason King rhapsodized about the "spellbinding vibe" created by Flack in her early years, and derived the title for his essay ("The Sound of Velvet Melting") from a chapter on Roberta by Linda Jacobs for a children's book series called *Women Behind the Bright Lights*. "Her voice was rich and warm, like thick purple velvet," described Jacobs. "It slipped easily between soft and loud, high and low, always flowing. If velvet could melt, that's how it would sound . . ."[390]

Soul Makossa (1973)—Manu Dibango
Atlantic 2971

Chart debut June 23, 1973 (reached #22 pop in *Cash Box*, #35 in *Billboard*; #21 R&B) (*World-#33*)

One of the first African jazz musicians to gain international renown, Emmanuel "Manu" Dibango was born February 10, 1934, in the town of Douala in Cameroon, a republic in western central Africa bordering Nigeria to the west, and with a coastline along the Atlantic Ocean. Ronnie Graham explains that the urban music of Cameroon began to take shape after World War II. "Foreign influences from Cuba and Zaire were grafted onto indigenous growths like the makossa beat [accompanying a native dance] and the rhythms of bikutsi, mangambe, and assiko. Cameroon had a long tradition of guitar playing but after the war the instrumental base was enlarged with the importation of other western instruments."[391] Still, the nation's recording industry was modest until Manu Dibango.

After music studies in France he started playing in clubs in Brussels in 1957; by 1960, the alto saxophonist began to earn a reputation, played on over 100 singles for Decca—then the only company with distribution throughout Africa—during a 1961–1965 tenure in Zaire (which had recently achieved independence), and starting in 1965 returned to Paris.[392] Even though he was

385. *Rolling Stone Album Guide* (1992 ed.), p. 519. Leon Huff, interviewed in the January–February 2009 *American Songwriter* (p. 61), said the key quality that distinguished the Philadelphia Sound was the orchestration. "I played in bands, and Gamble was always into orchestration. We started using the tympani, vibes and French horns in our music. We loved strings—cellos and violas. We incorporated all of that into our orchestration."

386. #1 (4 weeks) in New Zealand; #1 in Brazil and Singapore; #2 in Hong Kong and Mexico; #3 in Holland; #5 in France.

387. The song has had over five million broadcast performances.

388. In an interview for the June 1979 *Songwriter* magazine, Fox said that while Lori's experience served as a partial point of departure, most of the lyric came from Gimbel's "lyric writing book . . . It just happened that Lori could relate to it."

389. Bronson, *Billboard Book of Number One Hits*, p. 329.

390. Chapter on Flack, *Listen Again: A Momentary History of Pop Music*, p. 175.

391. Ronnie Graham, *The Da Capo Guide to Contemporary African Music*, p. 165.

392. Graham, p. 167–68.

spending little time in his home country, he made his first makossa record in 1964 (*Nasengina*) specifically for the home market, combining elements of the Nigerian highlife sound with those of Central African/Congolese music.[393] He was also inspired by American soul and jazz, citing records by Booker T. and the MGs, jazz organist Jimmy Smith, James Brown, and especially tenor saxophone great King Curtis (after Curtis was killed in 1972, Manu recorded *Tribute to King Curtis*).

As detailed by Graeme Ewens, in 1972 Dibango persuaded the Cameroonian government to sponsor a record in praise of the national football team then hosting the African Nations Cup tournament. On one side of the record was the football anthem *Mouvement Ewondo*; on the other was the original version of *Soul Makossa*. The "connection between the dance and the music [of his native country] gave me the idea to compose, not exactly makossa but *Soul Makossa*; my vision of the makossa which is a traditional dance," he explained. Cameroonian officials liked the praise number but were dismissive of the other; still, Manu, realizing its potential, returned to Paris and recorded a new version.[394]

In early 1973 the swirling rhythm number he had recorded the previous year for a small international label came to the U.S. as an initially obscure import, and was soon creating a sensation. David Mancuso at the trend-setting New York City discotheque known informally as the Loft, having discovered the record as an import, decided (writes Tony Fletcher) that its "gently vibrating soul-funk rhythm, tribal vocals, and punchy brass riffs" were perfect for the Loft dance floor, and began playing it regularly; that lit the fuse. Frankie Crocker, a radio DJ at WBLS, picked up on it, and other clubs quickly followed suit. Due to the record's scarcity, copies were selling for up to ten dollars each, and various labels began issuing cover versions to meet the demand.[395] Seeing an opportunity, Atlantic Records acquired distribution rights to the Dibango original, and it became one of the most exotic hit singles of the era.[396] Tim Lawrence, in his study of 1970s dance music, sees *Soul Makossa* as a landmark because it was the first hit that was specifically launched by New York club DJs, and as a forerunner of the dance culture/disco craze that was about to explode.[397]Tom Ter-

rell and Gary Graff: "*Soul Makossa* was truly massive: though more of a jazz-funk jam than a *makossa* (Cameroonian pop) beat, the song also had a major influence on the emerging salsa scene."[398] Dibango's sax wails over a churning, compelling beat with multiple percussion instruments and a driving horn section; he raps occasional lines in an African language (Cameroon's official languages are French and English, but it has numerous other linguistic groups), and a vocal group chants the title phrase at various intervals. For many Western listeners unaccustomed to African sounds, the record had a rather hypnotic effect. Although this would be his only U.S. hit, Dibango released more than twenty albums on various labels, and scored another international hit in 1985 with *Abele Dance*. One of the many Americans apparently entranced by the record was Michael Jackson; on his 1983 Top Ten hit *Wanna Be Startin' Somethin'* from the history-making album *Thriller*, late in the song his backing group begins chanting repeatedly, "ma-ma soul, ma-ma soul, ma-ma makossa."

Part of the Plan (1975)—Dan Fogelberg
Epic 50055
Chart debut Feb. 1, 1975 (#24 in *Cash Box,* #31 in *Billboard*); from the album *Souvenirs* (chart debut Dec. 7, 1974, #17 peak)

The mid-1970s was the final phase of a golden age for pop singer-songwriters; with disco arriving and punk rock on the way, the lyrical ruminations of introspective solo artists would soon exit center stage. But before that happened, Dan Fogelberg introduced himself with a superbly crafted piece honoring a rich tradition, *Part of the Plan*.

Peoria, Illinois, native (born on August 13, 1951) Fogelberg began playing piano at fourteen, switched to guitar, and played local coffeehouses while majoring in art at the University of Illinois. Relocating to Los Angeles, he played the folk circuit, served as a session musician, and did a tour backing Van Morrison. His 1972 debut album for Columbia, *Home Free*, featured some gorgeous acoustic ballads showcasing his pristine tenor voice, but was not a hit.[399] Thanks to his manager Irving Azoff, whom he'd met in college, he snagged ex–James Gang leader Joe Walsh (soon to join the Eagles) as producer and lead guitarist. The resulting album, *Souvenirs*, was an impeccable blend of ballads and (gentle) rockers, and

---

393. Even before 1973, Dibango had also found an audience among expatriate Africans in England and Europe, with *Soma Loba* his best known pre-*Makossa* song.

394. Graeme Ewens, *Africa O-Ye!: A Celebration of African Music*, p. 115.

395. A cover version by the Los Angeles studio band Afrique debuted in *Billboard* two weeks before Dibango's, and reached #47. The May 26, 1973, *Billboard* reported (a month before Dibango's chart debut) on the radio airplay received by the battling cover versions.

396. *All Hopped Up and Ready to Go: Music from the Streets of New York, 1927–77*, p. 286.

397. Lawrence, *Love Saves the Day: A History of American Dance Music Culture, 1970–1979*, p. 114–16. He cites an influential September 13, 1973,

Rolling Stone essay by Vince Aletti on the record's impact; three weeks later, *Billboard* (October 6, 1973) ran an abridged version of Aletti's article, titled "Discotheques Break Singles."

398. *MusicHound World: The Essential Album Guide*, edited by Adam McGovern, p. 219.

399. After being reissued in 1982, *Home Free* became a long-running smash on the *Billboard* Pop Catalog chart (#2 peak, ninety-seven total weeks).

would become a two-million-selling smash. This song was its centerpiece.

Walsh had Fogelberg write down a wish list of musicians he'd like to get for the album; the first was drummer Russ Kunkel (from James Taylor's third album), and Walsh got him. Fogelberg wrote *Part of the Plan* when he lived outside Nashville in 1973. After recording the basic track (with Walsh on acoustic and electric twelve-string guitars) and while the producer was on the road, Fogelberg kept working in the studio, adding a second guitar solo. When Walsh heard and loved it, he persuaded Graham Nash to drive over and sing harmonies on the song.[400]

It's a thoughtful, reflective midtempo rocker with a razor-sharp arrangement and production driven by the multi-tracked guitars, and a philosophy of "be who you must" and "someday we'll all understand." The soaring chorus is absolutely irresistible, with Nash's harmonies adding to its impact. This would be the first of seven consecutive platinum albums for Fogelberg. "All of the answers you seek can be found / In the dreams that you dream on the way . . ." It provided the launching point for the artist's string of hits into the 1980s, including the enduring ballad *Longer*.

(Recorded at Record Plant and Elektra Studios, both in Los Angeles; Fogelberg on acoustic & electric guitars, piano & organ; other personnel: Kenny Passarelli on bass, Joe Lala on percussion)

Kashmir (1975)—Led Zeppelin

From the Swan Song album *Physical Graffiti* (chart debut March 15, 1975, 6 weeks at #1; sold 15 million copies) (*RS-#141, DMDB*)

Guitarist Jimmy Page originally composed the mysterious Arabic-sounding melody he called "Driving to Kashmir" inspired by a long, deserted stretch of road connecting Goulimine and Tantan in the Moroccan Sahara, an area where he had vacationed. It was a road that (writes Richard Cole) he had "driven several times, always with the feeling that it would never end. There was no scenery other than an occasional camel and its rider to break the monotony." As he traveled the northwest African desert, he imagined himself driving all the way to Kashmir. The other-worldly lyrics are apparently the work of both Page and Robert Plant.[401] Bassist John Paul Jones had spent many boyhood hours listening to Arab music on a short-wave radio that picked up North African stations; Plant was "constantly surrounded by Indian film music" as a teenager, in the East Indian area of London

where his girlfriend lived, and had also been exposed to Egyptian pop. So the group as a whole had a deep fascination with the music of that region.

Page began recording *Kashmir* on his Danelectro guitar, and "worked and reworked the song's now famous riff, drawing upon a guitar cycle that he had created years before." Page was obsessed with its structure, continually fine-tuning it. John Paul Jones added an ascending bass riff and a compelling string arrangement that added to the piece's impact. Regarding the "cascading, descending phrase for massed guitars" that defines the piece, the guitarist told Robert Palmer: "I had this idea to combine orchestra and mellotron and have them duplicate the guitar parts. Jonesy improvised whole sections with the mellotron and added the final descending riff, whereby the song fades." With Plant's intense vocal and the crunching drums of John Bonham, the structure was complete.[402] Palmer calls the song "about as perfect a blend of lyric, of music, tradition, and innovation as one could imagine." Second only to *Stairway to Heaven* among Zep's boatload of classic-rock favorites, *Kashmir* was declared "the definitive Led Zeppelin song" by Plant in 1988.[403] "The song was bigger than me. I was petrified. I was virtually in tears."[404]

The Immigrant (1975)—Neil Sedaka (written by Neil Sedaka & Phil Cody)

Rocket 40370

Chart debut March 29, 1975 (reached #22); from the album *Sedaka's Back*

While he was cranking out thirteen Top 40 hits from 1958–1963 including the #1 smash *Breaking Up Is Hard to Do*, Neil Sedaka was synonymous with happy, carefree pop tunes geared to the teen market. But after he returned to the pop charts following an eight-year absence, he achieved a career musical peak with a moving, deeply felt ballad about the ideals that America is supposed to embody but had suddenly forgotten, *The Immigrant*.

Brooklyn-born on March 13, 1939, Sedaka was a piano prodigy who seemed destined for a career in classical music with training at Juilliard, but the advent of rock & roll was a siren call he couldn't resist. After singing with an early doo-wop version of the Tokens, he began scoring hits as a songwriter in 1958 in partnership with lyricist Howard Greenfield, working alongside the fabled

400. Liner notes, Fogelberg boxed set *Portrait*, p. 18–19.

401. Although band biographer Richard Cole attributes the lyrics to Page, Robert Palmer credited them to Plant in his liner notes to the Led Zeppelin boxed set (reprinted in *Blues & Chaos*, p. 238–47). Both men had driven that desolate Sahara road.

402. *Led Zeppelin Uncensored*, p. 240–41. Biographer Mick Wall (*When Giants Walked the Earth*, p. 322): "*Kashmir* encapsulated Zeppelin's multi-strand approach to making rock music (part rock, part funk, part Himalayan dust storm) as completely as *Stairway*, but is arguably an even greater achievement."

403. Interview in March 24, 1988, *Rolling Stone*. Plant: "It's the quest, the travels and explorations that Page and I went on to climes well off the beaten path." They got a glimpse into how Berber tribesmen lived in the northern Sahara, and he tried to capture some of that in his lyrics.

404. *Rolling Stone 500 Greatest Songs of All Time* (2010), p. 57.

tunesmiths of New York's Brill Building, including pal Carole King. His own hits on RCA Victor, all sung in a sunny, multi-tracked high tenor, included six Top Tens. When the hits ran dry with the British Invasion, he continued writing, earned early 1970s comeback hits in England, and after landing a new U.S. recording contract with Elton John's label Rocket, shot to #1 with the late-1974 ballad *Laughter in the Rain*. That led to a nice run of several additional hits through 1980, both for himself and other artists (The Captain & Tenille made his *Love Will Keep Us Together* a massive chart-topper in 1975).

The Immigrant was inspired by John Lennon's battle with U.S. immigration officials who were trying to deport him from his new home in New York due to a marijuana bust and (more particularly) his active opposition to U.S. war policies in Vietnam. The song declared this (in broad poetic terms) as a betrayal of the American tradition of welcoming foreigners from all lands. With a passionately idealistic message, soaring melody, and Sedaka's fervent vocal (perhaps his best ever), it packed a musical wallop. Very soon after its release, the song took on a still deeper resonance. After the frenzied U.S. evacuation of Saigon on April 29, 1975 (just as *The Immigrant* was climbing the charts), 140,000 refugees from South Vietnam were flown to the U.S., with thousands more to follow, and many faced open hostility (including physical attacks in some cases) from the American communities in which they tried to carve out new lives. The song's lyrics were entered into the *Congressional Record* as a statement of true, open-armed American values. "It was a time when strangers were welcome here / Music would play, they tell me the days were sweet and clear . . ."

At Seventeen (1975)—Janis Ian
Columbia 10154
Recorded on Sept. 17, 1974; chart debut June 14, 1975 (reached #3); from the album *Between the Lines* (chart debut March 22, 1975, spent 1 week at #1) (*GHF, Folk-#61*)

Both as a songwriter with a gift for unfolding deeply introspective narratives, and as a performer with a voice of hushed intimacy, Janis Ian is an artist who takes listeners inside the minds and hearts of her characters with an immediacy matched by few others. This has made her beloved among her fans to a degree far exceeding her record sales. *At Seventeen* is both her biggest hit and most representative creation.

Born Janis Eddy Fink in New York City on April 7, 1951, Janis (the daughter of a music teacher) studied piano as a child, wrote her first songs at twelve, entered Manhattan's High School of Music and Art, and began performing on the city's folk circuit. *Society's Child*, a tale of interracial romance written at age fifteen, became a much-discussed Top 20 hit in 1967 after Leonard Bernstein invited her to perform it on a network TV special. At first she was unable to follow up her early success, with four albums that were heard by few. Then her 1974 album *Stars* attracted strong notices, boosted when Roberta Flack had a hit with its ballad *Jesse*. That was vastly exceeded by her next album, *Between the Lines*, and its surprise smash *At Seventeen*.

In her autobiography, Ian recalled that the song's initial inspiration was a magazine article in which a woman talked about her coming-out debutante party and what a letdown it was, with the opening line, "I learned the truth at eighteen." Because the words didn't quite match the samba lick she was exploring on guitar, which needed another syllable, she changed it to, "I learned the truth at seventeen." "Writing *At Seventeen* took a long time"—in part because she was so determined to make it "truthful to my own life" (citing her short stature, her physical imperfections, always feeling apart from the crowd) even if some individual details weren't autobiographical, "I became increasingly shy about singing it to anyone." The feeling even reached the point where "I decided I'd never sing it in public." After she set the song aside for a few weeks came a turning point: "Why not suddenly look at it from a different point of view entirely and bring them in on it? So I started my last verse by assuming that somewhere out there, there was at least one person who'd been through what I'd been through." ("To those of us who knew the pain / Of valentines that never came . . .") The conclusion transformed a sad and deeply personal song into one that had a universal message and "hope and redemption."[405]

The pain of feeling unattractive and different slices like a knife in her words and performance; but easing the pain is the realization that "it was long ago and far away," and the winners and losers in high school often find their positions reversed as life goes on. It wasn't just self-proclaimed "ugly girls" who could identify with the experiences and feelings she describes. The touching performance won the Grammy for best female pop vocal, and paved the way for strong followup albums including *Miracle Row* (1977) and *Night Rains* (1979). When she lost her record deal in the early 1980s, Janis stepped back from the limelight but continued writing; her moving ballad *Some People's Lives* became the title song of Bette Midler's two-million-selling 1990 album. The superb 1993 album *Breaking Silence* launched a new phase of Janis Ian's career.

---

405. Janis Ian, *Society's Child*, p. 152–55. She recounted the recording sessions for the album at CBS' New York studios in which she worked "the morning shift," Bruce Springsteen at night, and Melanie in between (p. 160–62).

Birdland (1977)—Weather Report (written by Joe Zawinul)

From the Columbia album *Heavy Weather* (chart debut April 2, 1977, #30 on pop chart; 2 weeks at #1 on jazz chart) (*Jazz-#26, SJ*)

One of the groups at the forefront of jazz-rock fusion in the 1970s, Weather Report, was formed in December 1970 under the leadership of saxophonist Wayne Shorter (who served as musical director of Art Blakey's Jazz Messengers from 1959 to early 1964 before achieving renown with Miles Davis' legendary ensemble of 1964–1970), and Joe Zawinul. Born in Vienna, Austria, Zawinul came to the U.S. in 1959, accompanied Dinah Washington for two years, then joined Cannonball Adderley and remained with him as pianist and primary composer until 1970. In 1967 the Adderley combo scored a crossover pop smash with Zawinul's *Mercy, Mercy, Mercy*; he also wrote the title track of Davis' *In a Silent Way* (1969), and played on both that and Miles' hugely influential next album *Bitches Brew*. Bassist Miroslav Vitous was the other original co-leader. Weather Report's 1971 debut album was successful, but it was 1972's *I Sing the Body Electric* that really established them as one of the decade's top jazz combos. By 1974 their albums were cracking the top fifty of the pop chart, and *Heavy Weather* became their biggest seller of all. Shorter and Zawinul were the only continuous members as the group underwent regular personnel changes. A crucial addition in 1976 was Jaco Pastorius (regarded as the best electric bassist of the era),[406] and he became the group's third co-leader; the other members at this point were Alejandro Acuna on drums and Manolo Badrena on percussion. From 1976 onward, writes Len Lyons, their albums "acquired a nearly orchestral density, provided by Zawinul's masterful use of the polyphonic, or multi-voiced, synthesizers."[407] The group's commercial success also made it a lightning rod for criticism from jazz purists, but even amidst its pop-rock textures, use of electronic instruments, and borrowings from other genres such as world music, its music remained rooted in jazz traditions, particularly bebop.

Zawinul's *Birdland*—named for the legendary jazz club on Broadway that had in turn been named for Charlie Parker—not only became Weather Report's trademark song, but was rivaled only by Herbie Hancock's *Chameleon* as the most popular jazz track of the 1970s.[408] It's a jubilant, enormously infectious number that garnered much AM radio airplay. Jose Bowen notes that *Birdland* draws heavily upon Count Basie's classic riff style, constructed from a series of very short, punchy themes that repeat with variations, as a single riff is passed from player to player.[409] Shorter on soprano and tenor sax and Zawinul are the featured soloists.

Vivan los Mojados! (Long Live the Wetbacks) (1977)— Los Tigres del Norte (written by Jesus Armenta)

Recorded for the 1977 Discos Fama album *Vivan los Mojados!* (*World-#99*)

For more than 35 years, the dominant force (both commercially and creatively) in Mexican-American *norteña* music—made by and primarily for Mexican immigrants to the southwestern United States—was Los Tigres del Norte, "The Tigers of the North." The group attained its greatest fame (or infamy, in some eyes) for establishing the wildly popular subgenre of *narcocorridos* (narrative ballads about the border-crossing, drug smuggling underworld). But their music is ultimately a broader celebration of the Mexican-American immigrant, and their most celebrated song in this vein is *Vivan los Mojados*.

The story of the "Little Tigers," writes Cathy Ragland in *Musica Norteña: Mexican-American Migrants Creating a Nation Between Nations*, has become "part of Mexican immigrant folklore and still gives hope to all who cross the border seeking work and a better life." The four Hernandez brothers left the small town of Rosa Morada in the western state of Sinaloa, Mexico, crossing the border into California to make a little money playing music in 1968; the oldest brother, Jorge, was just fourteen, and a border control agent nicknamed them the "Little Tigers." After making their way to San Jose, the brothers soon began recording for Fama Records, and their first three albums were well received but reached only a narrow audience. Then came their breakthrough song in 1973, *Contrabando y Traicion* (Smuggling and Betrayal), a *corrido* about a woman and her partner who smuggle marijuana from Mexico to Los Angeles. It became such a phenomenon that it triggered not only an outpouring of additional *narcocorrido* recordings over many years, but also films on the same theme, many of these featuring Los Tigres. From that point onward, notes Ragland, they "introduced innovative stylistic and

---

406. Berendt and Huesmann even suggest that Pastorius' bass work "is comparable to Charlie Parker's importance for the saxophone" (*The Jazz Book*, p. 462).

407. Lyons, *The 101 Best Jazz Albums*, p. 365–69. Zawinul on the Oberheim polyphonic synthesizer "stacked up voices like horn sections of a big band." For *Heavy Weather* in particular, he achieved "impeccable" separation of voices that "brings the rich texture of this music to life."

408. Zawinul saw shows at Birdland almost daily after coming to the U.S., and during that period it was "the most important place in my life."

409. *Jazz: The Smithsonian Anthology*, p. 162–63. Pastorius' ability to play melodically on the bass at one point enables him to take the lead while the synthesizer plays the bass line, and there is "constant interplay" between bass and keyboards.

compositional elements" that would significantly change the sound of *norteña* music, in part building upon the emotion and working-class ideology of a key predecessor group, Los Relampagos del Norte. "They also fused their own regional musical and cultural influences with a direct way of speaking (and singing in) the language of working-class Mexicans."[410] In his book *Narcocorrido*, Elijah Wald calls Los Tigres "the kings of *norteño*," remarking that in the world of Spanish speakers in the United States, "Los Tigres are like Willie Nelson and the Rolling Stones combined, the enduring superstars of down-to-earth, working-class pop."[411]

Songwriter Jesus Armenta provided the group with the song that took its music in a new direction and transformed its career. *Vivan los Mojados* is a *cancion-corrido* about the American public's growing dependence on Mexican laborers and what could happen if they were sent back home. Performed at a danceable tempo with accordion, *bajo sexto*, electric bass guitar, and snare drum, Jorge Hernandez and his brothers sing about the futility of U.S. anti-immigration laws in the face of mojados' fierce determination to cross the border. These immigrants, as described by Ragland, are "now beginning to create a distinctly Mexican immigrant space and an identity that is no longer helpless, fragile, or susceptible to the forces that kept the community marginalized."[412] Musically simple and lyrically direct, it takes a stance of bold defiance and cultural pride—one that remains as provocative and relevant well over thirty years later.[413]

Rapper's Delight (1979)—Sugarhill Gang

Sugar Hill 542

Chart debut Oct. 13, 1979 (#4 R&B, #14 disco, #36 pop); #1 (2 weeks) in Canada, #3 in England[414] (*NPR-100, RHF, R&B-#39, RIA-#162, RS-#251, ACC-#158, DM, 1001, DET*)

For the world at large, hip-hop was born with *Rapper's Delight*, the first commercially successful record in the genre's history. But in the Bronx, according to Jeff Chang, it came along at a time when hip-hop as a local fad was "passing." The South Bronx was in desperate straits during the 1970s, with the loss of 600,000 manu-

facturing jobs and youth unemployment topping 60 percent. "The downward spiral created its own economy," and one offshoot was the emergence of a new music. It all began with a soon-to-be-legendary West Bronx party at the end of August 1973, with music provided by teenager Clive Campbell, who had been DJ-ing house parties for three years. Growing up in Jamaica, he was familiar with the sound systems that were transforming dance music there. Kingston studio owner Lee "Scratch" Perry, with his cheap four-track mixing desk, "whirled and bopped and twiddled the knobs, imbuing the recordings with wild crashes of echo, gravity-defying phrasing, and frequency-shredding equalization."[415] Campbell—known forever after as DJ Kool Herc—applied some of the same principles to his own sound system, using two amplifiers, two turntables, an echo chamber, and as the soul, funk, and dancehall discs rocked the apartment house, he further ramped up the energy level by grabbing the mic and adding his own shouted interpolations.

Seeing that the response was wildest during the "break" segment of a record when the drums or percussion took over, he got two copies of the same record (most often James Brown) and cut back and forth between them "to prolong the break or sonic climax," as described by S. H. Fernando, Jr. "Unwittingly, Herc had stumbled upon the breakbeat, the starting point for much hip hop, dance, techno, and [drum & bass] today."[416] The sensation he created quickly led other local DJs to follow his example, but Herc ruled the scene with regular parties all over the Bronx the next few years, assembling his own crew of DJs, dancers, and rappers. Peaking by early 1977, he saw his audiences begin to decline.[417] But for hip-hop as a genre, it was only the calm before the storm.

Sylvia Robinson's original claim to fame had been as half of the soulful duo Mickey & Sylvia with Mickey Baker, whose series of hits included the 1957 smash *Love Is Strange*. Even on that record, her sensual speaking voice had been showcased, and in 1973 she scored a surprise million-seller by erotically half-purring, half-rapping *Pillow Talk*. She and her husband Joe Robinson enjoyed some success with their small label Stang, including the Moments' *Love on a Two-Way Street* and her own hit, but soon settled down into a modest operation (later as All-Platinum Records) focusing on New York black neighborhoods. By 1979 the local hip-hop scene was focusing on the creative raps of MCs, and the Robinsons were so impressed that they decided to make it the focal point of their rechristened Sugar Hill Records,

---

410. Ragland, *Música Norteña*, p. 142–43.

411. Wald, p. 1–2.

412. Ragland, p. 167. The music and cross-national appeal of Los Tigres was also analyzed by Steven Loza in *Ethnic and Border Music: A Regional Exploration*.

413. Showing their staying power, Los Tigres were featured in a May 2011 *MTV Unplugged* broadcast from the Hollywood Palladium, the first time that series had ever showcased a regional Mexican act. As of that date, the group had sold 4.1 million albums in the United States, with three albums certified gold (March 19, 2011, *Billboard*).

414. #1 in Holland, #2 in Norway and Switzerland, #3 in France and Germany.

---

415. Chang, *Can't Stop Won't Stop*, p. 29.

416. *The Vibe History of Hip Hop*, p. 15.

417. Chang, *Cant' Stop Won't Stop*, p. 67–85.

named after one of the most famous sections of Harlem.[418] That August, they assembled a trio of rappers—Michael "Wonder Mike" Wright, Henry "Big Hank Bank" Jackson, and Guy "Master Gee" O'Brien—who went to work over a constantly repeated four-bar musical phrase from the recent chart-topping disco hit *Good Times* by Chic (led by Nile Rodgers and Bernard Edwards). The raps were pretty silly ("Heeyip-hop-heeyip-hop," "skippidy-be-bop," indeed), but when matched to the rhythm track it grabbed hold of any listener. The track ran all of fifteen minutes, which led Joe Robinson to insist on the need for a radio-friendly edit. But Sylvia declared, "We're going to keep every word," and she was vindicated when the record became the phenomenon of New York clubs. Before long it went national, and ended up selling (by some unverified accounts) one to two million copies.[419] At the time it seemed like a wacky novelty; time would prove that conclusion wrong.

Holding Back the Years (1986)—Simply Red (written by Mick Hucknall & Neil Moss)
Elektra 69564
Chart debut April 5, 1986 (1 week at #1); reached #2 in England,[420] #6 in Canada

This gorgeous, introspective ballad introduced us to a group that would be a consistent hit maker in England for the better part of two decades even while enjoying just a handful of U.S. hits.[421] Simply Red was formed in 1984 in Manchester, fronted by lead singer/songwriter Mick "Red" Hucknall (born June 8, 1960, his red hair furnishing the group's name), and their debut album provided one of the decade's most satisfying singles. Hucknall had written the song, which he called autobiographical, at age nineteen several years earlier with the guitarist of his band at the time, the Frantic Elevators.[422] His soaring, evocative, blue-eyed soulful voice made it unforgettable. The melancholy in the lyrics—recalling childhood fears and yearnings, ruminating that "I've wasted all my tears, wasted all those years"—plays against the sense of fervent hope conveyed in the vocal, culminating with the determined declaration, "I'll keep holding on." The

group would top the U.S. charts again three years later with their revival of Harold Melvin & the Blue Notes' *If You Don't Know Me By Now*.

Guitar Town (1986)—Steve Earle
MCA 52856
Chart debut June 21, 1986 (#7 C&W)

Just when country music was once again settling back into the profitable but creatively sterile complacency of Nashville's Music Row, along came a fiercely individualistic roots rocker who couldn't be tamed, and was just too good to ignore. Steve Earle was born on January 12, 1955, in Fort Monroe, Virginia, raised near San Antonio, Texas, and by age thirteen was a good enough guitarist to win a school talent contest. Dropping out of school at sixteen, he settled in Houston, and was befriended by country-outlaw greats Townes Van Zandt and Jerry Jeff Walker. After moving to Nashville, Earle worked blue-collar jobs by day while writing songs and playing bass with Guy Clark's band by night. He appeared briefly in Robert Altman's classic 1975 film *Nashville* and got his songs recorded by a few artists, but soon returned to Texas. After scoring his first hit song with Johnny Lee's 1982 recording of *When You Fall in Love*, Earle recorded his first EP as a performer, then cut some singles for the Epic label that went nowhere.

It was his debut album for MCA Records, *Guitar Town*, that broke things wide open in 1986. The title track in particular combined the "new traditionalist" style shared with Dwight Yoakam (who also debuted that year) with the populist-rock outlook of Bruce Springsteen. Earle freely acknowledges the impact of the Boss, whom he saw in concert during the *Born In the USA* tour: "I think it had a big influence on the way I ended up putting *Guitar Town* together." With its twangy Duane Eddy–style guitar featuring Richard Bennett,[423] restless open-road imagery, and rock 'n' roll self-mythologizing in the tradition of *Johnny B. Goode*, *Guitar Town* has a timeless quality rooted as much in the 1950s as in the 1980s. Voters in the "Virgin All-Time Top 1,000 Albums" poll selected it as one of the top 500 albums ever (1998), and a year later the *People's Almanac* picked it as one of the fifty best country albums. Having survived horrendous personal problems including drug and alcohol dependency that led to a prison sentence and drug rehab during the early 1990s, and rejection by Nashville

418. Veteran music impresario Morris Levy—a major (and controversial) industry figure since the 1950s—gave Sugar Hill instant credibility as an investor.

419. Dan Charnas, *The Big Payback: The History of the Business of Hip-Hop*, p. 28–45. There had been a few rap records prior to *Rappers' Delight*, including *Rhymin' and Rappin'* by Paulette and Tanya Winley a few months before, but none had received more than localized action.

420. Peaked at #51 in its original November 1985 release, then broke big upon returning to the U.K. chart in May. *Holding Back* also reached #1 in Ireland, #3 in Holland.

421. The group scored five #1 albums in England (including 1991's *Stars*, #1 for 11 weeks with 134 total weeks), and three others that reached #2.

422. Bronson, *The Billboard Book of Number One Hits*, p. 640.

423. Bennett, a Los Angeles session guitarist on many records dating back to Neil Diamond and Billy Joel sessions of the early 1970s, shifted to country music in the 1980s, his style inspired by Grady Martin. After serving as associate producer on the *Guitar Town* LP (with Emory Gordy, Jr. and Tony Brown), he later produced albums by Emmylou Harris, Marty Stuart, and many others (*Journal of Country Music*, Vol. 14 #3 (1992)).

for his leftist politics, Earle has produced a steady stream of quality albums since 1995 confirming the rich promise of this classic performance.

I Still Haven't Found What I'm Looking For (1987)— U2
Island 99430
Chart debut June 13, 1987 (#1 for 2 weeks); reached #6 in England;[424] from the album *The Joshua Tree* (9 weeks at #1) (*RS-#93, RHF, RIA-#120, ACC, DMDB*)

A song of deep spiritual doubt, *I Still Haven't Found What I'm Looking For* was inspired when lead singer Bono listened to classic gospel recordings by the Swan Silvertones, the Staple Singers, and Blind Willie Johnson. In writing a song rooted in gospel, Bono sensed, according to Niall Stokes, that "the theme was big enough to allow him to go for broke, to write an anthem."[425] An Irish Catholic who took his faith seriously in speaking out against violence and (in later years) on behalf of debt relief for Africa and the fight against AIDS, Bono was saying that his spiritual quest was just beginning.

It started out as a "one-note groove" on which Adam Clayton, Larry Mullen, Jr., and The Edge were jamming; they assembled a basic mix for Bono to fashion a melody and lyric. Producer Daniel Lanois was also a contributor to the song, humming a traditional melody to Bono that inspired him. "That's it! Don't sing any more," he said, and went off to write the melody for this song. The Edge recalls that "he just nailed this fantastic melody that came out of a classic soul tradition." As he listened to "this incredible song emerging out of the fog," he remembered a possible song title that he had written in a notebook, handed it to Bono as he sang, and Bono took it from there.[426] Thomas Ryan called it "one of the most eloquent statements about confusion that I have ever heard. Looking for truth in a dogmatic world, Bono was being pushed and pulled, and he willingly played out his passion play on record."[427] As *The Joshua Tree* became the #1 album of 1987 (and won the Grammy as Album of the Year), *I Still Haven't Found* followed in the footsteps of *With or Without You* to the top of the singles chart.

Tunnel of Love (1987)—Bruce Springsteen
Columbia 07663
Chart debut Dec. 5, 1987 (reached #9); from the album *Tunnel of Love* (1 week at #1)

The album *Tunnel of Love* and its title song explored a romantic relationship plagued with whole universes of doubts and uncertainties. Biographer Christopher Sandford writes that its allegory of love as a carnival thrill ride viewed it as "juddering up sheer gradients or swooping down, turning blind corners along an inky, waterlogged rail towards a light (that of the oncoming train) at the end of the line. What singled it all out was Springsteen's bewildering balance: on the one hand a native, quixotic faith that dreams are there to grab, like roses; on the other, an alien cynicism that the bloom, once picked, will prick." The chorus of *Tunnel of Love* "was one of Springsteen's best—sunny and dark, at the end of his vocal tether."[428]

Dave Marsh saw Nils Lofgren's guitar "surging out of the mix like the louder voice in a bickering couple's terminal argument. The singing is all portent and turbulence; the lyrics fill in the shadows without illuminating any of the details." The song, like much of the album, "dashes the whole idea of romantic love."[429] Springsteen, in the book *Songs*, writes that this and other tracks on the album "uncovered an inner life and unresolved feelings that I had carried inside me for a long time . . . For twenty years, I'd written about the man on the road. On *Tunnel of Love* that changed, and my music turned to the hopes and fears of the man in the house."[430]

Make Me Lose Control (1988)—Eric Carmen (written by Eric Carmen & Dean Pitchford)
Arista 9686
Chart debut May 21, 1988 (#3 peak)

A few months after his soundtrack song from *Dirty Dancing, Hungry Eyes*, brought him back to the Top Ten, ex-Raspberries leader Eric Carmen scored even higher with the glorious pop extravaganza *Make Me Lose Control*. A proud descendant of the great tradition of Beatles-esque pop, he was born in Cleveland (on August 11, 1949) and hit it big as lead singer/songwriter of the Raspberries from 1970–1974, including the Top Ten smash *Go All the Way*. The group having run its course, Carmen was signed as a solo artist by Arista president Clive Davis. His 1975 debut album produced three deliciously melodic hits including *All By Myself* and *Never Gonna Fall in Love Again*. After *It Hurts Too Much* (actually his most exciting solo creation yet) mysteriously fell short of hit territory in 1980, he slipped off the pop-cultural radar screen and was without a record deal until Jimmy Ienner (producer of all the Raspberries hits and Carmen's solo debut), assigned to work on the music for *Dirty Dancing*, invited his old pal to participate. That

424. #1 in Ireland, #2 in Poland, #6 in Sweden.
425. Stokes, *U2 into the Heart*, p. 64–65.
426. *U2 by U2*, p. 226–27.
427. Ryan, *American Hit Radio*, p. 564.
428. Sandford, *Point Blank*, p. 283.
429. *Two Hearts*, p. 654–55. Springsteen's 1985 marriage to actress Julianne Phillips would end in separation in April 1988, and later divorce.
430. *Songs*, p. 190–91.

track's success led Carmen and Ienner to team once more for this all-new blast from the past.[431]

It marked his return to the Arista label after a period on Geffen. He's looking back from an adult perspective at teen days of pursuing romance to the soundtrack of 1960s pop, and finds that those giddy thrills of youth can be recaptured once more. Co-writer Dean Pitchford also co-wrote such hits as *Fame* (Irene Cara), *Footloose* (Kenny Loggins), and *Let's Hear It for the Boy* (Deniece Williams). The intense imagery ("the city's the color of flame in the mid-summer heat") is matched by his inspired performance with soaring tenor vocal. Sixteen years after his Raspberries breakthrough, Carmen can still hit the stratospheric high notes. David Wild of *Rolling Stone* called the song "an infectious hymn to the seductive powers of pop," and indeed "hymn" is an appropriate word. It's exhilarating, sexy, and possesses an irresistibly powerful drive, but above all it regards pop music with a deep reverence while reveling in its joys. "Turn the radio up . . ."

The Majesty of the Blues (The Puheeman Strut) (1989)—Wynton Marsalis

Recorded Oct. 27 & 28, 1988

From the Columbia album *The Majesty of the Blues* (chart debut July 8, 1989, 5 weeks at #3 on jazz chart)

After all these years it's easy to take Wynton Marsalis for granted. He's the one jazzman of the post-1980 era who is universally familiar even to non-jazz fans, ubiquitous on public television, NPR, the greatest jazz educator of his generation, and the first jazz artist honored by the Pulitzer Prize. All of this recognition sometimes triggers jealousy and suspicion, but the man has backed it up with an exceptional body of music. Born in New Orleans on October 18, 1961, the son of esteemed jazz pianist Ellis Marsalis, he showed his trumpet virtuosity at an early age, attended Juilliard School of Music, and had a celebrated if brief tenure with Art Blakey (1980–1981). He exploded on the scene as a leader in 1982 with an acclaimed quartet album, which proved to be just a prelude for the wonders of 1983–1984: winning double Grammies both years for jazz <u>and</u> classical albums, an unprecedented feat.[432] After all the jazz-rock fusion explorations of the late 1960s and 1970s led some to fear the essentials of jazz were being lost, Marsalis' combination of dazzling technique with adherence to the "classic" post-bop, pre-fusion jazz combo sound seemed like a breath of fresh air, even

though it represented a back-to-basics approach. Some felt Marsalis was leading jazz into an excessively conservative direction, his unquestioned technical command of his instrument linked with a certain chilliness and lack of feeling. But as his playing (and also his composing) continued to evolve by the late 1980s, he was stretching out in interesting directions. And by decade's end it had led him back to the blues.

The very young Marsalis hadn't been particularly interested in the deep traditions of his own home town, or in the blues, but that all changed. He embraced those traditions and recorded a series of albums steeped in the blues, with *The Majesty of the Blues* a fitting representation. To set the stage for the album, Wynton used New Orleans' Second Line (funeral) tradition as a symbol for the death and resurrection of the blues and jazz. The title track is a fourteen-minute original—minor-key and thoroughly bluesy—showcasing that amazing technique, but this time emphasizing the growl and wah-wah approaches associated with early Crescent City hornmen. The brilliant blind pianist Marcus Roberts, the one holdover from his previous combo, has plenty of solo space (using some bebop harmonies), as do Todd Williams on tenor and soprano sax and Wes Anderson on alto sax. Roberts called this "a very important, definitive song" that helped lay the groundwork for the epic *Blood on the Fields*, Marsalis' 1997 Pulitzer-winning oratorio.[433]

Nothing Compares 2 U (1990)—Sinead O'Connor (written by Prince)

Ensign/Chrysalis 23488

Chart debut March 17, 1990 (4 weeks at #1); #1 (11 weeks) in Germany, #1 (8 weeks) in Australia, #1 (5 weeks) in Canada, #1 (4 weeks) in England;[434] from the album *I Do Not Want What I Haven't Got* (6 weeks at #1) (*RS-#165, Time, VIL-#15, DMDB-#57, AHR, 1001, TC, DM*)

It was an obscure song that the ever-prolific Prince had tossed off on a 1980s side project for his protégé group The Family; his original version was heard by few until a 1993 compilation of B-sides and unreleased tracks. Idiosyncratic but gifted Irish singer Sinead O'Connor made *Nothing Compares 2 U* an unforgettable ballad performance and international smash. Rock manager Fachtna O'Ceallaigh (her then-lover in an affair that was winding down) gave her a tape of the song in 1988, and it struck a chord. Thomas Ryan called it "vividly intense . . . O'Connor moves from a soothing whisper to a hair-raising howl in an instant, and she

431. April 7, 1988, *Rolling Stone*.

432. Ulrich Olshausen: "No other trumpeter in the world today has the technical resources that Marsalis has. A talent like his probably doesn't come along more than once or twice in a century." (Berendt, *The Jazz Book*, p. 163.)

433. Gourse, *Skain's Domain*, p. 161–62.

434. #1 (5 weeks) on Eurochart, #1 in Austria, Belgium, Holland, Ireland, Japan, New Zealand, Norway, Poland, Spain, Sweden, and Switzerland.

does it without any of the forced melodrama or arty pretensions of other singer/actresses."[435]

Born on December 12, 1966, in Dublin, O'Connor (writes Rick Clark) "came onto the music scene in 1987 with a powerful image of a woman who could express great sensitivity while not losing any qualities of inner strength" with her debut album *The Lion and the Cobra*.[436] The album went gold, but no one was quite prepared for the impact of its 1990 followup. After an initial attempt to record the song with Soul II Soul producer Nellee Hooper proved unsatisfactory, O'Connor and O'Ceallaigh went off by themselves to Eden Studios in West London where the finished product was crafted.[437]

In the compelling video that helped break the song wide open on MTV, as described by Mikal Gilmore, for nearly five minutes, "O'Connor holds the camera—and therefore the viewer—with a heartsick gaze, and tries to make sense of how she lost the one love that she could never afford to lose. One instant she tosses out sass, the next, utter desolation, until by the song's end, the singer's grief has become too much for her, and she cries a solitary tear of inconsolable loss." "I didn't intend for that moment to happen," she confessed, "but when it did, I thought, 'I should let this happen.'"[438] The tears, it turns out, were for O'Ceallaigh and the end of their affair and also the end of their business relationship; by the end of 1989 she had dropped the devoted but intensely controlling and controversial O'Ceallaigh as her manager.[439] Toby Creswell: "This is a song of obsessive love and O'Connor finds its centre. She tries to do nothing but slowly lead herself through the modal arrangement. Mostly, though, it's just O'Connor. She holds her singing back as though there's a huge body of emotion behind her voice and she's just keeping it in check."[440] The song shot O'Connor to a level of stardom she didn't really want, given her defiant and individualistic style, and subsequent albums played to a far smaller audience but served her artistic sensibilities.

Biographer Jimmy Guterman calls her performance "the most all-encompassing song of unrequited love since *Layla* by Derek and the Dominos." In Sinead's hands, the song is "as bereft of hope as Hank Williams' *Lost Highway* or Robert Johnson's *Love in Vain*, but she sings it with such phenomenal lung power that it is impossible to conceive of her as someone as drained as she claims to be."[441] Described by critic Ann Powers

as "a gospel of hurt," the ballad is taken to unforeseen places by O'Connor's (in Bill Friskics-Warren's phrase) "otherworldly soprano." "O'Connor turns the song into a monument to estrangement that is as harrowing as Robert Johnson's *Stones in My Passway*, or the Stanley Brothers' *Rank Strangers*."[442]

Our Town (1992)—Iris DeMent

From the Philo/Rounder album *Infamous Angel* (released on Oct. 7, 1992),[443] reissued by Warner Bros. in 1993

Critics were bowled over by the remarkable debut album *Infamous Angel* by a young woman with a heart-tugging soprano (reminiscent of Emmylou Harris and Nanci Griffith) and an evocative storytelling style of songwriting. Born the youngest of fourteen (!) children in a farming family on January 5, 1961, in the town of Paragould, located in the northeast corner of Arkansas (near the Tennessee and Missouri borders), Iris moved at age three with her family to California, where several times a week they worshipped at a charismatic Pentecostal church; she would later record some of the gospel songs she grew up singing. After college, she moved to Nashville where she began writing songs; rather than pitch them to a publishing company, she did secretarial and other work on the side while performing in clubs.[444] Record producer and folksinger Jim Rooney (who had produced three of Griffith's early albums)[445] was impressed, and signed on to produce her debut album, recruiting a stellar group of Nashville studio musicians.[446] Emmylou Harris became her biggest early booster;[447] 10,000 Maniacs recorded a song from her debut, *Let the Mystery Be*. After *Angel* established her reputation, its 1994 successor *My Life* earned still wider acclaim. Within a musical context of folk/bluegrass string-band simplicity, her songs, writes Greg Kot, "celebrate the commonplace with uncommon eloquence."[448] As for her pristine soprano, Kevin Brockmeier declares: "It is capable of carrying so much exultation on the one hand and so much sorrow on the

435. Ryan, *American Hit Radio*, p. 579–81.
436. *All Music Guide to Rock* (2nd ed.), p. 670.
437. December 7, 2000, *Rolling Stone* (p. 73), ranking *Nothing Compares* as the #16 "greatest pop song."
438. *Night Beat*, p. 312.
439. Jimmy Guterman, *Sinead: Her Life and Music*, p. 77–78.
440. Creswell, *1001 Songs*, p. 691.
441. Guterman, p. 92–94.

442. *I'll Take You There*, p. 77.
443. While not charting nationally in the U.S. or Britain, the album reached #3 on the monthly charts of the British magazine *Folk Roots* (based on a survey of U.K. specialist and general record dealers) for July 1993 (published in the September issue), remaining in the Top Ten from May through August.
444. Interview by John Tobler, August 1993 *Folk Roots*.
445. Rooney has also produced albums by such top singer-songwriters as John Prine and Townes Van Zandt.
446. The album's lineup includes Stuart Duncan on fiddle, mandolin, Jerry Douglas on Dobro, and Roy Huskey, Jr., on upright bass, along with Iris on acoustic guitar. Performances at the 1992 Newport and Philadelphia Folk Festivals, after opening for Griffith on her *Other Voices, Other Rooms* tour, generated word of mouth about the newcomer.
447. Seeing Emmylou perform at a Lake Tahoe casino where Iris was working as a waitress had first inspired her to pursue her musical ambitions. Harris sought her out to sing harmonies on Emmy's 1990 album *Brand New Dance*. It was right around this time that she signed with Rounder.
448. *New Rolling Stone Album Guide* (2004), p. 228.

other, with so little costumery or ornamentation, that it can seem as if she has lived an entire life inside every note she delivers."[449]

Our Town, Iris' finest song, was also her first composition that she felt had something special (written around 1986). A poignant lament for a beloved hometown—recalling first kisses, babies being born, and walking down Main Street in the cold morning mist—it was inspired when she drove through a seemingly deserted small town in Oklahoma. "I write about the people that have been in my life, and about memories and where I come from," she told Craig Harris.[450] Stephen Betts: "DeMent's most singular quality seems to be an ability to present a mass of contradictions—joy mingling with sorrow, faith hand-in-hand with uncertainty, directness tinged with irony."[451] Appropriately, this irony-free gem was used in 1995 under the concluding montage for the final episode of the classic series *Northern Exposure*. "And you know the sun's settin' fast, / And just like they say, nothing good ever lasts. / Well, go on now and kiss it goodbye, But hold on to your lover, 'cause your heart's bound to die. / Go on now and say goodbye to our town, to our town . . ."

Until I Fall Away (1994)—Gin Blossoms
A&M 0862

Chart debut May 14, 1994 (reached #21 in radio airplay, 43 weeks; #13 on Modern Rock chart)

From the album *New Miserable Experience* (debut May 1, 1993, #30 peak, 102 weeks)

For fans hungry for richly melodic guitar-rock in the R.E.M. vein as an alternative to all the grunge, rap, and metal on the airwaves in 1993–1994, The Tempe, Arizona-based Gin Blossoms were a blessedly welcome arrival on the music scene. With deliciously infectious songs primarily written by guitarists Doug Hopkins and Jesse Valenzuela, the appealing lead vocals of Robin Wilson, and a guitar-driven pop/rock sound in the Beatles/Byrds tradition—musically optimistic if at times lyrically melancholy—the Gin Blossoms' debut EP *Up & Crumbling* in 1992 scored big on the college radio scene, paving the way for the tremendous success of their first full album. *New Miserable Experience* (co-produced by John Hampton with the band), with the smash singles *Hey Jealousy* and *Found Out About You*, sold more than four million copies and stayed on the charts for two years.

It was the album's third big song, *Until I Fall Away* (penned by Wilson and Valenzuela), that demonstrated the group's gifts most vividly. It's a gorgeous rock ballad with a thoroughly compelling melody, those jangly guitars, and Wilson's strong delivery of a song expressing a mixture of fear, uncertainty and longing about whether a current romantic relationship can survive. Even if the lyrics don't entirely hold up on paper, the emotions come across. The Gin Blossoms overcame the departure and subsequent suicide of Hopkins to record a solid though less popular followup album in 1996, but unfortunately broke up not long thereafter. *New Miserable Experience* ranked halfway up the Virgin All-Time Top 1,000 Albums poll of fans and critics in 1998.

I Don't Want to Wait (1997)—Paula Cole
Warner 17318

Chart debut Nov. 1, 1997 (reached #11, 56 total weeks); #43 in England; from the album *This Fire* (chart debut Feb. 22, 1997, reached #20, sold 2 million copies)

Born on April 5, 1968, in Rockport, Massachusetts, Paula Cole graduated from the Berklee College of Music where she studied jazz singing and was a member of the gospel choir, and after being signed by Imago records was invited to perform on Peter Gabriel's 1992–1993 world tour. Her 1994 debut album *Harbinger* was poorly distributed and the record company went out of business. Moving to Warner Brothers, she broke through with the 1997 album *This Fire*, combining thoughtful, introspective songwriting with passionate vocals. After hitting the Top Ten with the album's leadoff single *Where Have All the Cowboys Gone*, Paula scored a still more memorable hit with *I Don't Want to Wait*, a vivid narrative of a woman who comes of age during World War II, with a timeless message of reaching out for all that life has to offer. The song took on a second life as the opening theme for the hit WB series *Dawson's Creek*, making it an anthem for youthful yearning and hope. Paula won the Grammy for Best New Artist (even though this was her second album) and toured with the first Lilith Fair. Her followup album *Amen* (1999) received praise for its strong R&B flavor, and showed her multi-instrumental flair (on piano and clarinet), and after an eight-year absence returned with *Courage* (2007).

Smooth (1999)—Santana featuring Rob Thomas
Arista 13718

Chart debut July 31, 1999 (12 weeks at #1, 58 charted weeks);[452] #1 (1 week) in Canada, #3 in England,

---

449. Writing in the *Oxford American*, reprinted in *The Oxford American Book of Great Music Writing*, p. 142.

450. February–March 1993 *Dirty Linen*.

451. Artist feature in *Journal of Country Music*, Vol. 17 #1 (1994), p. 7–9.

452. In addition to its long run at #1, *Smooth* spent thirty weeks in the *Billboard* Top Ten, more than any other #1 single of the rock era. (*Torn* by Natalie Imbruglia in 1998 had thirty-two weeks in the Top Ten of the *Billboard* radio airplay chart, but as a non-single was not eligible for the Hot 100.) Also, its fifty weeks in the Top 40 was unsurpassed in the latter category (except for two other airplay-only hits, *Don't Speak* by No Doubt in 1996 and *Iris* by the Goo Goo Dolls in 1998, each with fifty-two

#4 in Australia;[453] from the album *Supernatural* (12 weeks at #1, sold 15 million copies)[454] (*BILLB-#10, RIA, GR, DMDB, VIL*)

One year after his induction into the Rock & Roll Hall of Fame, Carlos Santana at age fifty-two scored the biggest hit of his career, and one of the supreme comebacks in pop music history, with the album *Supernatural*. Perhaps only Al Jolson's return in 1947 with the soundtrack of *The Jolson Story* after a decade and a half away from center stage could compare in its combination of a great artist's long absence followed by a massive new success. Seventeen years after he last reached the Top 40 of either the album or singles charts, *Supernatural* gave the legendary San Francisco guitarist the third #1 hit of his career (and the first since 1971's "Santana III"), and his first chart-topping single ever with *Smooth*. It reached #1 on October 23, 1999, thirty years to the week after Santana's first chart single, *Jingo*, debuted.

The man who helped make it possible, singer-songwriter Rob Thomas, was born in Orlando on February 14, 1972. His group Matchbox Twenty's 1997 debut album *Yourself or Someone Like You* sold a whopping 11 million copies, but despite its success was regarded as amiable lightweights by most critics. *Smooth* gave Thomas not only a career-defining hit but the credibility he'd been lacking. The melody was written in one weekend by pop/dance composer Itaal Shur, who'd written for Maxwell among other artists but his lyrics were deemed too sexual. EMI Music Publishing called Thomas and asked him to work with Shur on the song. He came up with a new chorus, and with Shur reworked the rest of the song and cut a demo. Arista president Clive Davis—who had signed Santana to Columbia thirty years earlier and was determined to make his album a hit with contemporary guest singers—still had George Michael in mind for the vocal. But producer Matt Serletic thought Thomas should perform his own song, Davis agreed, and Santana (who, chuckled the singer, "had no idea who the hell I was") concurred.[455] The combination of his grainy voice with Santana's ever-elegant and incendiary guitar soloing and a slinky rhythm proved perfect. *Smooth* sent *Supernatural* into the stratosphere (the song's thirty weeks in the Top Ten set a rock-era record to that point), and together Santana and Thomas swept the Grammy Awards with Record and Song of the Year honors, in addition to the Mexico-born titan's Album of the Year. *Rolling Stone* in 2000 named *Smooth* the #31 top pop song ever.

Eminem, PhotoFest.

Cleanin' Out My Closet (2002)—Eminem

Aftermath album cut, Hot 100 chart debut Aug. 3, 2002 (reached #4 pop, #11 on R&B/Hip-Hop chart); #3 in Germany, #4 in England;[456]

From the Aftermath album *The Eminem Show* (debut June 8, 2002, 6 weeks at #1, sold 8 million copies)

A deeply autobiographical rap number that's boiling over with anger and bitterness, *Cleanin' Out My Closet* is at times grating for its self-justifying venom as Eminem lashes out at his mother, his wife, and seemingly everyone with whom he comes into contact—yet, for all its nastiness, is also a powerful, revealingly honest performance. David Stubbs: "Jeff Bass's intricate, reggae-fied backbeat indicates that this is Eminem in thoughtful, serious mode, staring into the flickering embers, brooding intensely on his grievances."[457] Counterbalancing the venom is the tenderness expressed for his daughter, and the touching, apologetic chorus (which he actually sings). As vexing a personality as he can frequently be, Marshall Mathers' talent is too vast to be denied.

Get Busy (2003)—Sean Paul

VP/Atlantic 88020

Chart debut Feb. 22, 2003 (3 weeks at #1 on pop chart); #1 (1 week) on R&B chart; #3 in Germany, #4 in England & Australia;[458] from the album *Dutty Rock* (chart debut Nov. 30, 2002, reached #9) (*BL-#219*)

Jamaican dancehall music made one of its biggest breakthroughs on the U.S. music charts with the huge

---

weeks), until topped in 2011–2012 by Adele's *Rolling in the Deep*. (*Joel Whitburn's Top Pop Singles*, 12th edition; *Hot 100 Annual*, 2006)

453. #1 in Brazil and Poland, #6 Japan.

454. The album's reported worldwide sales are 27 million.

455. Clive Davis, in his memoir *The Soundtrack of My Life* (p. 429–30), writes that some negotiation was required to clear a path for Thomas (an exclusive Atlantic artist) to record with Santana, but a "win-win" agreement was reached.

456. #4 in Norway, #5 Switzerland, #6 Sweden.

457. Stubbs, p. 101–2. As he lashes out against his mother, it's "painful, awful, fascinating." While Eminem's language is hardly up to the bard's, "there is something Shakespearian about the venomous, tear-streaked, inter-familial rage here."

458. #1 (7 weeks) in Italy, #1 in Holland, #2 in Norway and Switzerland, #3 on Eurochart, #4 Japan and Sweden.

success of Sean Paul's *Get Busy*.[459] Born Sean Paul Henriques on January 8, 1973, in St. Andrew, Jamaica, with a multi-racial heritage (part Portuguese and Chinese), he played for the Jamaican national team in water polo before becoming a DJ and beginning to write songs. His debut single *Baby Girl* was a hit in 1996, and three years later he had a U.S. rap hit with *Hot Gal Today*. His debut album in 2000 (a compilation of his Jamaican singles) didn't chart, but served as a prelude for his American breakthrough with the album *Dutty Rock*. Mixing singing and rapping over an irresistible dancehall beat (spitting out the rapid-fire lyrics with great agility), *Get Busy* is a pure good-time party song with just one thing on its mind as it urges women to shake their booties. In addition to its chart-topping status, it was voted the year's #20 best single in the *Village Voice* critics' poll. "*Get Busy* even sounds like sex, with a click-clack rhythm and melodies that spiral down like beads of sweat," remarked *Blender*. "Who cares if you can't understand what he's saying?"[460] Paul returned to #1 later in 2003 with a guest appearance on Beyoncé Knowles' smash *Baby Boy* (taking off from his own debut hit).

The Black Horse and the Cherry Tree (2006)—KT Tunstall

Album cut, Hot 100 debut March 25, 2006 (#20 peak); reached #1 (10 weeks) on Adult Top 40; #28 in England

From the Relentless/Virgin album *Eye to the Telescope* (chart debut Feb. 25, 2006, #33 peak)

It's all about the beat: a soulful, pleasantly raspy voice singing over a driving, stimulating staccato rhythm provided entirely by her own acoustic guitar looped through an effects pedal. *Black Horse and the Cherry Tree* gave singer-songwriter KT Tunstall her first pop hit and one of the most memorable singles of 2006.

The biological daughter of a part-Chinese dancer and a traveling Irish singer, KT (no initials, merely short for Katie), born on June 23, 1975, in Edinburg, Scotland, was adopted by the Tunstalls when she was two weeks old, raised in St. Andrews, and earned a degree in drama and music at the University of London's Royal Holloway College. Having mastered classical piano and flute before teaching herself guitar and bass, she performed for several years in bluegrass and folk groups, formed a three-piece rock band, then in late 2002 hooked up with producer Steve Osborne, whose credits included U2; this

led to a recording contract with Virgin. She had finished recording her debut album when an unexpected call arrived in October 2004 to appear on a popular BBC live music TV show on which the performers also included Anita Baker, Jackson Browne, and the Cure. She performed *Black Horse*, a song she had only written after the album was done; her only accompaniment was her guitar and an Akai E2 Headrush Delay and Phrase Sampler Pedal, which allowed her to loop her own voice and guitar. The performance was a sensation, and the song was hastily added to the album. *Eye to the Telescope* became the United Kingdom's biggest-selling album of 2005 by a female artist, topping one million copies. Released in the U.S. in January 2006, the album started slowly, then quickly gathered steam as its showcase song garnered airplay. Its momentum was vastly accelerated after Katharine McPhee, the eventual *American Idol* first runnerup, made the song one of her most successful numbers before a TV audience of more than 25 million.

Lyrically, *Black Horse* is all metaphors and/or dream images in describing a reluctance to commit to a relationship: "I said, no, no . . . you're not the one for me." Musically, it's a one-woman show, with Tunstall's guitar and bass multi-tracked, and generating plenty of adrenaline in its short 'n' snappy 2:51 playing time. Tunstull would score an equally big hit with her followup, *Suddenly I See*, featured on the soundtrack of *The Devil Wears Prada*.

Resurrection (2006)—Ray Wylie Hubbard (written by Al Grierson)

Originally on Philo album *Dangerous Spirits* (released Aug. 1997)

Best version on Sustain Records album *Snake Farm* (released June 27, 2006)

Tales of personal redemption don't come in much tastier musical packages than Ray Wylie Hubbard's *Resurrection*. Born on November 13, 1946, on a small farm in Hugo, Oklahoma, in the southeastern part of the state, Hubbard moved with his family in the mid-1950s to the Dallas suburb of Oak Cliff, where he learned to play guitar and later formed a folk group with future country star Michael Martin Murphey. Befriended by such emerging Texas icons as Jerry Jeff Walker and Ramblin' Jack Elliott, Hubbard performed with two other short-lived groups, then achieved a measure of fame in the progressive country movement when his song *Up Against the Wall, Redneck Mother* was recorded by Walker in 1973. John T. Davis: "Hubbard seemed fully formed in the mid-to-late 1970s, with a river-bottom baritone, a mordant and irreverent sense of humor, a touch for vividly lyrical storytelling," and a "booze-fueled romantic fatalism."[461]

459. Although the roots of Jamaican dancehall music date back far earlier, the "dancehall" label fully took hold in 1983, signifying music in which the deejay, not the singer, was dominant. (Of course singers such as Marcia Griffiths and Sean Paul remained important.) Another aspect of dancehall, write Chang and Chen (*Reggae Routes*, p. 59–66) is an emphasis on drum machines to set the rhythm.

460. October 2005 *Blender*, p. 116.

461. May–June 2003 *No Depression*.

A 1975 album with his group the Cowboy Twinkies went nowhere, but three solo albums from 1978–1984 showed promise. After several years of relentless touring (and dealing with alcoholism), Hubbard entered into the most prolific and acclaimed phase of his career in 1992, and since that time has released at least nine more albums. Hubbard's original songs during his recent period have included such gems as *The Messenger* and *Conversation with the Devil*, but perhaps his finest recording of all is a piece by a close friend, Al Grierson, *Resurrection*.

A native Canadian born in 1948 and raised in the Vancouver suburb of New Westminster, British Columbia, Grierson worked as a newspaper editor, railroad worker, and even a Zen Buddhist monk while developing his skills as a songwriter, inspired by Jack Kerouac and the classic generation of "beat" poets. He released his first album in 1995 while living in Oregon, then two years later moved to Austin, Texas, where he ran his own "armadillo farm" near the iconic town of Luckenbach. There he was befriended by like-minded Texas artists including Hubbard, whose personal struggles preceding a stronger-than-ever "second act" to his life may have helped inspire Grierson's masterpiece, *Resurrection*. It's the tale of a man at the end of his physical and emotional resources, who finds new life through a woman's love. The Christian metaphors are explicit (comparing the character's darkest moments to "the face of Jesus in his final agony" and the haunting refrain "he was gone when they rolled away the stone"), but it's a gritty, down-to-earth account of one tough Texan. No one could have delivered it with earthier conviction than Hubbard, with his craggy, world-weary voice and his bottleneck resonator slide guitar utterly perfect for the material.[462] The original 1997 recording was superb in its own right (although its brisk uptempo arrangement seemed a bit too slick for such a personal piece), but better by far is the singer's 2006 version on the album *Snake Farm*, with a much slower, broiling blues/gospel-driven arrangement and performance.[463] "This one comes from somewhere on the desert horizon," remarks Thom Jurek (*All Music Guide*, online). The superb blues/roots-music singer Ruthie Foster's backing vocals on the refrain "add a late-night gospel feel to the band's spectral blues." It's a fitting tribute to Grierson, who died in November 2000 when he was swept away in a Texas flash flood. The song's narrator wonders if the protagonist "ever much believed in God, or God believed in him / But they both believed in a woman and the truth that set him free . . ."

---

462. Hubbard told Vernell Hackett (June 9, 2001, *Billboard*, p. 35) that his songs revolved around "redemption and hope"—precisely the themes that form the core of *Resurrection*.

463. Guitarist Gurf Morlix (a master at creating a dark, turbulent sound, as also heard on his productions for Lucinda Williams and Robert Earl Keen) co-produced the album with Hubbard.

Playlist 10

Memories of You, 1889–2012

Electric Light Quadrille (1889)—Issler's Orchestra
Recorded for Edison in 1889

Thomas Edison's introduction of the phonograph was the culmination of a communications revolution that included the telegraph in 1850 and Alexander Graham Bell's invention of the telephone in 1876. After more than a year of research at his Menlo Park laboratory, Edison in July 1877 devised an indenting stylus connected to a diaphragm, which in turn was attached to a telephone speaker, with a strip of paraffin-coated paper placed underneath the stylus, and the sound waves from his shouted voice created marks on the paper that played back his voice as the strip was pulled back under the stylus. Five months later, his laboratory workers constructed the first working phonograph: a cylinder attached to a long feed screw turned by a hand crank, a sheet of tinfoil wrapped around the cylinder, with a funnel-like mouthpiece connected to a thin metal diaphragm, to which a steel stylus was attached. "Shouting into the funnel vibrated the diaphragm and moved the stylus, which incised the spiral analog of the sound waves onto the soft metal foil as it was turned. On the other side of the cylinder, a playback reproducer of stylus and diaphragm was run back over the indentations in the foil to vibrate the diaphragm in the same way that the recording had been made. The listener had to pay close attention to discern the faint noises coming from the vibrating diaphragm."[1] Crude though it was, the December 6, 1877, demonstration at the office of the *Scientific American* created a popular sensation. But as he was distracted by work on other inventions, it would be another decade before he took the next crucial step.

By the time Edison announced in the summer of 1888 that he had "perfected" the phonograph, he was under intense pressure from other inventors exploring alternate means of recording sound, most notably Emile Berliner. Edison had founded the Edison Speaking Phonograph Company in 1878, and in 1887 established the Edison Phonograph Works in West Orange, New Jersey, to assemble talking machines. It was with the introduction of automatic, coin-operated machines in 1889, dropping a nickel in the slot to hear one play of a cylinder record, that the musical entertainment possibilities of the phonograph emerged as an actual business model. And so it was that Edison began making his earliest musical recordings for commercial sale.[2]

Edward Issler was hired by Edison Laboratory's chief recording engineer A. Theo E. Wangemann in mid-1889 as Edison's regular pianist for commercial recordings. In addition to piano accompaniments, Issler also formed a small orchestra, initially consisting of piano, cornet, flute, and a violin. The recordings of Issler's Orchestra are among the earliest surviving musical recordings, and one of the best of these early efforts was *Electric Light Quadrille*. It's a pleasant dance number with spoken dance calls ("now, promenade"), and midway through there's an announcement paying tribute to Edison's other most famous invention besides recording, the carbon filament incandescent electric light bulb patented in late 1879: "Issler's Orchestra will give a free concert at Keystone Hall where the electric light will be used for the first time!" The Issler band continued to record extensively for Edison for more than a decade.[3] This performance—with

Thomas Edison, courtesy of Library of Congress, LC-USZ62-67878.

surprisingly sharp fidelity considering its age—is included on a Mark 56 Records LP from 1984, *The World's First Entertainment Recordings, 1889–1896*.

Turkey in the Straw (1891)—Billy Golden (lyrics by Daniel Decatur Emmett to traditional melody)
Recorded c. summer 1891 for Columbia; Golden recorded many subsequent versions, including Dec. 19, 1896 for Berliner, 726

"This is the classical American rural tune," wrote Carl Sandburg in 1927's *American Songbag* of *Turkey in the Straw*. "It has been sung at horses and mules from a million wagons. It has a thousand verses, if all were gathered. In the solitude of tall timbers it has been the companion of berry pickers in summer and squirrel hunters in fall time. On mornings when the frost was on the pumpkin and the fodder in the shock, when nuts were ripe and winter apples ready for picking, it echoed amid the horizons of the Muskingum River of Ohio and the Ozark foothills of Missouri . . . It is as American as Andrew Jackson, Johnny Appleseed, and Corn-on-the-Cob."[4]

Few other songs were as universally performed in minstrel shows during the years following its publication in 1834 as *Turkey in the Straw*, originating as a simple two-strain fiddle tune that shared its melody with *Zip Coon* (as copyrighted on March 29 that year). Dan Emmett, later the co-founder in 1843 of the trend-setting Virginia Minstrels, wrote new comic lyrics to the familiar folk melody (the tune sometimes attributed to Bob Farrell and/or George Washington Dixon), and as minstrelsy swept the country in the 1840s, the song became ubiquitous nationwide, although it wasn't copyrighted under the name *Turkey in de Straw* until 1861.[5] (Josiah Combs sug-

1. Described by Andre Millard in *America on Record*, p. 23–27.
2. Welch and Burt, *From Tinfoil to Stereo*, p. 19–27.
3. The Edison-owned United States Phonograph Co. declared in its 1895 catalog: "We are the only manufacturer of the genuine Issler's Orchestra. Their success has filled the market with imitations of same name and titles."

4. *The American Songbag*, p. 94.
5. Fuld, *Book of World-Famous Music*, p. 591.

gested in his 1915 book *All That's Kentucky* that the tune was "stolen from" the British folk air *The Jolly Miller*, a play-song.)[6] A blackface troupe called the Ethiopian Serenaders performed at the White House in 1844, the Virginia Minstrels toured the British Isles, and within a year countless minstrel troupes were crisscrossing America, most of them headquartered in New York City.

Billy Golden, born William B. Shires on June 9, 1858, in Cincinnati and raised in St. Louis, as a child sang and danced on steamboats traveling from St. Louis to New Orleans. He began doing a blackface act in vaudeville in 1874, and within the next few years (under his new stage name) made *Turkey in the Straw* a part of his act while a member of Bailess & Kennedy's "Brightlights" vaudeville troupe. Golden was both a comedian and dancer (supposedly he originated the "cane pat" that became standard among buck dancers), and his vocals were serviceable enough in getting across the dialect-driven comedy. He also worked in traveling medicine shows which, instead of charging admission, sold medicine, salves, and tonics. The shows were packed with entertainment, including theatrical performances, magicians, ventriloquists, contortionists, trapeze artists, black-face comedians, jugglers, and the charismatic pitches of the "doctors" themselves.

Turkey in the Straw was Golden's first great success upon starting to make recordings for Columbia in 1891, and he would record fresh versions for just about every other company in the next fifteen years; although the piece was recorded by many other artists, it would long be indelibly associated with Billy Golden. On his December 1896 version for Berliner (included on the Archeophone CD *The Phonographic Yearbook: The 1890s, Vol 1: "Wipe Him Off the Land"*), accompanied by piano, he intersperses energetic delivery of the lyrics with a big, guffawing laugh. Golden remained a popular recording artist (even though his singing increasingly gave way to mainly dialogue comedy routines) and vaudeville entertainer until shortly before his death in January 1926.

"Black and white music in [the pre-1920 era] were not two separate portfolios," writes Tony Russell. "There was a huge common stock of songs and tunes that everybody sang and played: dance tunes like *Turkey in the Straw*, the story-songs of *John Henry* and *Casey Jones*, minstrel-show favorites like *I Got Mine*." Before record producers began to impose orthodoxy on artists to record

material that fit into established genres, "musicians put their personal songbooks together from all the musics that floated in the air about them."[7]

Simon J. Bronner, in an article for the May 1979 *Journal of Country Music*, suggested a case could be made that the early recordings of old-time music by the Edison Phonograph Company, specifically including Billy Golden's versions of *Turkey in the Straw* for Edison in 1898 and 1899, "should be considered as a significant part of the history of country music." As Roderick R. Roberts put it in another issue of the same publication, "The insistence on the primacy of the Eck Robertson-Henry Gilliland recordings [in 1922] as the first hillbilly recordings may have blinded scholars to the existence of traditional material recorded by [earlier] artists lacking the hillbilly image." So, perhaps, one more distinction for Billy Golden: country music pioneer?[8]

You've Been a Good Old Wagon But You Done Broke Down (1896)—Len Spencer (written by Ben Harney)
Columbia 7209
Recorded in 1896 (#2 in *Pop Memories*); later recorded for Berliner 0145, and in 1902 for Lambert 989

The man who was more responsible than anyone else for making ragtime the rage of New York in the 1890s, Ben Harney was born on March 6, 1871,[9] in Middlesboro, Kentucky, played piano in saloons and brothels in Kansas City and then around the West, and in 1896 came to New York with his minstrel troupe. He soon established a name for himself as pianist and singer, getting star billing at Tony Pastor's Music Hall, and touring vaudeville houses in the East and Midwest. Harney's greatest fame came with his piano rags, "ragging" semi-classics by Mendelssohn and other composers, and in 1897 published the genre's first tutorial volume. "Beyond doubt the sheet-music novelty of last season was the *Ben Harney Rag-time Instructor*," declared the March 4, 1899, *Music Trades*. "To say that it met with favor is putting it mildly." The twelve-page publication "is one of the best money makers on the market." A light-skinned African-American who often passed as white (his race was long a topic of disagreement, but Eubie Blake said he was unquestionably black), Harney

---

6. Paul F. Wells opined in *Ethnic and Border Music*, that the melody of *Zip Coon* was a variant of the traditional Irish tune *The Rose Tree* (popular since at least 1785), before it spawned such fiddle numbers as *Turkey in the Straw* and *Sugar in the Gourd*. George Pullen Jackson called *Turkey* a variant of *The Rose Tree* in his 1933 book *White Spirituals in the Southern Uplands* (p. 166).

7. *Blacks, Whites, and Blues*, p. 26–28. Underlining the song's cross-racial appeal is the fact that *Turkey* was the most frequently cited song title in the WPA's 1930s interviews with ex-slaves, as culled by Robert Winans for a snapshot of Southern black music-making before the Civil War. (Spring 1982 *Black Music Research Newsletter*)

8. The song's country music credentials were proven anew when Carson Robison provided new patriotic wartime lyrics to the old tune and scored a smash hit with *1942 Turkey in the Straw*, on jukeboxes for nearly a full year starting in spring 1942.

9. As there are no official birth records, the exact year is uncertain.

was also a successful songwriter; his biggest hits were *Oh, Mister Johnson, Turn Me Loose* (1896) and *You've Been Good Old Wagon, But You Done Broke Down.* Len Spencer, one of the decade's top stars and a specialist in partly syncopated "coon" songs, had popular recordings of both songs for Columbia.

Although the latter song was first widely circulated in 1896 through its publication by Witmark & Sons, it had originally been published in January 1895 in Louisville by Bruner Greenup (according to Rudi Blesh and Harriet Janis), who sold it to Witmark. This makes it, the authors argue, "the first song scored as ragtime ever to appear, and it makes Benjamin Robertson Harney the first of the ragtime pioneers." "Besides the patent fact that the words of the song are in definite blues imagery," remark Blesh and Janis, "the piano accompaniment and the concluding instrumental 'dance' section are bona fide, if elementary, ragtime."[10] The lyrics ostensibly relate to the dummy line, or small construction and logging-camp railroads. However, its subtext, notes Philip Furia, is that the singer's "wagon"—his woman—has lost her sexual drive.[11] Lynn Abbott and Doug Seroff, adding detail to a citation by Blesh, point out that a partial precedent for the song was in George Evans' *Standing on the Corner, Didn't Mean No Harm*, first cited in the February 10, 1894, *New York Clipper.* The two songs are "structurally, if not melodically related," and both make use of the "standing on the corner" verse. Evans' version went: "Standing on the corner, didn't mean no harm / With my Susan Ann Melinda / Up came a coon, and he grasped her by de arm."[12] In July 1930, Jimmie Rodgers used a variant of this couplet to open *Blue Yodel No. 9*, the one record on which he was accompanied by Louis Armstrong.

David Wondrich in *Stomp and Swerve: American Music Gets Hot, 1843–1924* calls Spencer's 1902 performance of *Good Old Wagon* for Lambert "one of the hottest of all coon records, complete with vamping piano breaks."[13] This version (included on the Archeophone companion CD for the book) is one of the very few original ragtime recordings featuring piano; all but a few of the other pre-1920 rag records were either band performances or banjo features. There's a piano introduction, and several energetic piano solo breaks as Spencer sings in minstrel/blackface style (using the "n" word twice). Bessie Smith revived the song at the same January 1925 session accompanied by Louis Armstrong that included her immortal version of *St. Louis Blues.*

Hello Ma Baby (1899)—Arthur Collins (written by Joseph Howard & Ida Emerson)

Edison 5470

Recorded in Jan.–March 1899; released in April 1899, #1 in *Pop Memories*; later recorded for Berliner 01004

The performing-songwriting team of Joseph E. Howard and Ida Emerson (then married) performed in vaudeville before becoming established stars in Chicago and New York starting in 1895. *Hello Ma Baby*, their most celebrated song, was also in the first wave of mainstream popular songs using ragtime-styled syncopation.[14] Howard would go on to co-author other hits including *I Wonder Who's Kissing Her Now.* Len Spencer recorded a popular version in 1899; Arthur Collins' performance, issued at about the same time, was the finest. It's one of at least 227 solo two-minute cylinders the prolific Collins made for Edison from 1898 to 1912.

Based on the frequency with which it's mentioned and also the strength of those citations in *The Music Trades* during 1899, *Hello Ma Baby* can safely be called the #1 popular hit of that year. The February 18 issue declares that it "is voted by those who have heard it to be one of the best coon songs that [has] been published in a long time." The tune's sales have been "phenomenal," stated the March 11 edition, and publisher Alex Harms remarked that it had "sold more rapidly than any other song that they had published."[15] May 6: The song "is selling east, north, west and south in large numbers." On May 20, the magazine remarked that Joe Howard's classic "can be heard in every flat in Harlem where there's a piano, and on the street corners you can hear *Hello Ma Baby* being sung by the boys who congregate there, and whistled to beat the band." When bands played it in New York's Decoration Day parade, said the June 10, 1899, issue, "the boys and girls on the sidewalk gave vent to their feelings by singing the words, which only goes to show how popular this song is."[16]

The genre of coon songs, though typically held in low regard from a modern perspective, has historical significance, argued Peter C. Muir in his 2004 dissertation for the City University of New York.[17] It was, he writes, "the first genre to develop in the commercial mainstream that makes extensive use of secular black music, for while

---

10. *They All Played Ragtime*, p. 95–96, 211–12.

11. Philip Furia article, *A New Literary History of America*, p. 509.

12. *Out of Sight: The Rise of African American Music, 1889–1895*, p. 336.

13. *Stomp and Swerve*, p. 100.

---

14. While its rhythmic pattern is suggestive of ragtime without being a genuine example of that genre, *Hello Ma Baby* was released with a piano sheet music version labeled "Rag-Time March." (Hamm, *Yesterdays*, p. 318.

15. Vaudeville performers the Beaumont Sisters reported in the April 8, 1899, *Music Trades* that it was "their biggest hit": "Encore after encore had to be responded to, and even after the Beaumont Sisters left the stage the audience clamored for more of *Hello, Ma Baby.*"

16. According to its publisher, the song sold 150,000 copies of sheet music by mid-1900 (September 29, 1900, *Music Trade Review*).

17. *Before 'Crazy Blues'*, p. 204–5.

minstrelsy . . . satirized black culture, it had not borrowed extensively from it. The coon song, however, began to borrow directly from the African-American musical vernacular during the 1890s." The earliest such song may have been *Push Along, My Honey, Push Along* (1893) by Dave Reed, Jr., whose melody draws heavily from the spiritual *Joshua Fit the Battle of Jericho. Hello, Ma Baby* finds the genre at its peak.

As heard on the Archeophone CD *The Phonographic Yearbook: The 1890s, Vol. 2*, the piece has a comic opening before Collins launches into the half-sung, half-spoken vocal, accompanied by piano. Thoroughly infectious with a rousing chorus ("hello ma baby, hello ma honey, hello ma ragtime gal . . ."), it's also one of several 1890s songs with the telephone in a central role.

Creole Belles (1901)—Columbia Orchestra (written by
    J. Bodewalt Lampe)
Columbia 330 & Columbia 31688
Recorded in August 1901
Creole Belles, one of the most influential cakewalks of the turn-of-the-twentieth century era, was written by Ribe, Denmark-born, Buffalo-based J. Bodewalt Lampe, with a copyright date of October 16, 1901. It was recorded by the Metropolitan Orchestra (October 1901), Sousa's Band (January 1902), and banjoist Vess Ossman (February 1902). Additionally, the earliest known recording of piano ragtime was made on *Creole Belles* by C. H. H. Booth, a house pianist for Victor, in November 1901—a historic performance that, unfortunately, has never been found. The very first recorded version of the standard was billed on the label simply as by "Orchestra," but this is almost certainly the in-house Columbia Orchestra directed by Charles A. Prince (a pianist on recordings as early as 1891 and the label's studio conductor from shortly after 1900 until 1923). As heard on the Archeophone CD *Real Ragtime* as re-recorded by basically the same band a few months later in 1902, it's a thoroughly catchy midtempo performance, very danceable, although unfortunately a bit short (1:48). In addition to its significance in ragtime history, *Creole Belles* was also a hugely popular composition. "Oh, what a hit!" raved the January 4, 1902, *Music Trades*, which would subsequently declare the song multiple times (initially on February 8) as "the biggest instrumental hit since *At a Georgia Camp Meeting*" (Kerry Mills' 1897 classic).[18]

The August 1, 1903, issue reported that it sold over 500,000 copies of sheet music.

The turn-of-the-century boom in ragtime triggered a backlash that led the national Musicians Union at its 1901 meeting in Denver to declare a "crusade" against the music, calling for the restoration of "the better class of wholesome, clean and instructive music." The group formally resolved that its members "shall henceforth make every effort to suppress and to discourage the playing and publishing of such musical trash . . ." The May 25, 1901, *Music Trades* responded to this tirade by calling the campaign "rather quixotic. There are ears to which 'rag-time' is more fascinating than grand opera, and ears of this sort are more numerous."

Saint Louis Rag (1904)—Arthur Pryor's Band (written by Tom Turpin)
Victor 2783
Recorded on March 23, 1904; new version recorded on
    April 20, 1906[19]
One of the first important ragtime composers, Thomas M. J. Turpin was born in Savannah, Georgia, in 1873, and played piano at Babe Connors' celebrated Castle Club in St. Louis, where several popular songs of the 1890s (including *Hot Time in the Old Town* and *Bully of the Town*) were launched. Seven years after opening his first bar in 1893, his new Rosebud Bar became (writes ragtime historian David A. Jasen) "the mecca for all underground ragtime musicians." He and his brother Charlie were the first significant black politicians in St. Louis, running gambling houses, dance halls, and sporting houses. *Harlem Rag* in 1897 introduced Turpin as a formidable composer, followed by *A Ragtime Nightmare* (1900). *Saint Louis Rag*, published in November 1903, was written to celebrate the Louisiana Purchase Exposition. The piece "features typical Turpin fireworks, beginning with a beautifully syncopated and very pianistic A section. There are breaks in both B and C sections (another pioneering feature in ragtime by the composer). D is the final display, sparked with a blaze of ascending chromatic runs, a fitting overture to 'that splendid summer' in St. Louis." The song's first mention in *Music Trades* came in the October 8, 1904, issue, stating that Sol Bloom had published the tune's orchestral arrangement "in compliance with many demands from all over the country."[20]

Arthur Pryor, John Philip Sousa's leading trombone soloist and assistant conductor for eleven years before he left to form his own band in late 1903, was both a brilliant performer/conductor of rag-based material and an outstanding composer of such works, including *Can-*

---

18. January 11, 1902, *Music Trades*: "*Creole Belles* is selling largely all over the country. It unquestionably leads all other instrumental pieces in sales at the present time." The February 1 issue cited reports of the song being played in Brooklyn, Boston, and Detroit. According to the June 7 *Music Trades*: "Nearly every band that marched down Fifth Avenue on Decoration Day played Lampe's *Creole Belles*."

---

19. Remained in Victor catalog with same record number.
20. Jasen and Trebor, *Rags and Ragtime: A Musical History*, p. 28–29.

hanibalmo Rag among many others. Rudi Blesh and Harriet Janis, comparing Pryor to his fellow featured soloist in the Sousa band, cornetist Herbert L. Clarke: "Where Clarke's cornet was a serious-minded and romantic instrument, Pryor's trombone spoke in a humorous folk dialect. From this tendency came a whole line of band pieces called trombone smears [featuring upward and downward trombone glissandi] . . . These are authentic Americana preserving the flavor of the bands that once paraded the streets to advertise minstrel shows and circuses as well as electoral candidates." Pryor's ensemble "played with far more syncopation than any other brass band."[21] His was the first band to record the *Saint Louis Rag*, and the performance is technically impeccable as well as thoroughly catchy. It's included on the French RCA two-record LP *Ragtime (1900–1930)*.

Periodically after ragtime became the national rage, skeptics would declare that it had run its course, only to be proven wrong. The *Music Trades* in its February 1, 1902, issue reprinted a letter to a Cincinnati newspaper by song publisher Phil Kussel declaring that the continuing demand for ragtime "is really astonishing. It has not nearly reached its zenith . . . The reason that rag-time music has become so popular is not because it is a lower class of music, but because it has catchy, ringing, swinging rhythm, easily memorized, and which is a source of pleasure to the tired."

Listen to the Mocking Bird (1904)—Corinne Morgan & Frank C. Stanley (written by Septimus Winner and Richard Milburn)

Edison 8715

Recorded in mid-1904 (#3 in *Pop Memories*); later recorded for Columbia 1833 & 32531, and Victor 4080 & 31316

Listen to the Mocking Bird, written in 1855 by Septimus Winner (at least officially), was one of the most monumentally popular songs of the nineteenth century, by some (wildly exaggerated) accounts selling an amazing 20 million copies of sheet music.[22] Winner, born in Philadelphia on May 11, 1827, became one of the city's best-known musical figures, running a music shop, giving lessons on several instruments, and preparing some 200 instruction books for twenty-three instruments. He arranged more than 2,000 compositions for violin and piano, wrote articles on music for a magazine edited by Edgar Allan Poe, and somehow found time to found the venerable Philadelphia Music Society.

However, several published accounts (including James Weldon Johnson's) make clear that the tune's actual composer was Richard Milburn, a Negro barber in Philadelphia who was a guitar player and renowned whistler.[23] Milburn played and whistled it under that title at several public events, including a concert at St. Thomas' Church, the city's main black Episcopal church. Winner wrote down the melody (and perhaps provided the words) after Milburn performed it for him, and indeed the title page of the song's original April 17, 1855, copyright credits it as follows: "Sentimental Ethiopian Ballad . . . Melody by Richard Milburn—written and arranged by Alice Hawthorne." (The latter was Winner's mother's name, under which he published some of his work.) However, within the next year, Milburn's name had been erased from the credits, never to return.

According to Septimus Winner biographer Charles Eugene Claghorn, Abraham Lincoln likened the song to the "laughter of a little girl at play."[24] Another noteworthy element of *Listen to the Mocking Bird*, cited by Charles Hamm in *Yesterdays: Popular Song in America*, is that it helped to popularize the verse-chorus structure in popular songs, which would soon become almost universal.

"Artistic whistler" John Yorke AtLee attained brief stardom in the early 1890s with his rendition of the song, but perhaps its finest recording was by the duo of bass-baritone Frank C. Stanley (later the leader of the Peerless Quartet) and contralto Corinne Morgan (born Corinne Morgan Welsh in circa 1875). Corinne began recording in 1902, with her greatest successes coming in her several duets with Stanley and collaborations with the Haydn Quartet (including the 1906 hit *How'd You Like to Spoon With Me?*), and also worked with the Edison Sextet, the Metropolitan Mixed Quartet, and the Mendelssohn Mixed Quartet. On this performance (included on the tinfoil.com CD *Two-Minute Wax Cylinder Phonograph Recordings: Popular Songs*), the two dramatically contrasting voices mix pleasingly, with accompanying bird whistling.

The Bully (1907)—May Irwin

Victor 31642

Recorded May 20, 1907

The Bully, argues Peter C. Muir in his 2004 dissertation *Before 'Crazy Blues'*, is "the first known commercial composition to use the twelve-bar [blues] form that can be convincingly linked to proto-blues culture." [25] The song had been circulating for some time before it

---

21. *They All Played Ragtime*, p. 151.
22. That oft-quoted number is totally unverified, but the tune's popularity is undisputed; the January 24, 1903, *Music Trades* stated that the copyright, which Winner sold for a reported five dollars, netted over $100,000.

23. *Black Manhattan*, p. 112.
24. Quoted by David Ewen, *All the Years of American Popular Music*, p. 54.
25. *Before 'Crazy Blues,'* p. 255.

crossed over to national popularity. W. C. Handy in his autobiography recalled it as being popular among black stevedores along the Mississippi River levees of St. Louis when he was stranded there for a time in 1893. The earliest known contemporary reference to the song was in a Kansas City black newspaper, the *Leavenworth Herald*, on December 8, 1894, as discovered by Lynn Abbott and Doug Seroff. [26]

It would not be until eleven months after this reference that the song was published. There were actually six different copyrighted versions within a six-month period, the first on November 12, 1895, as *Looking for a Bully*, followed by three in January 1896 (*Dat New Bully, The New Bully*, and *De New Bully*), and the final one in April again as *The New Bully*, all with different authors and various different lyrics or musical elements. [27] The one that hit it big was Charles Trevathan's song, published on February 19, 1896, under the title *May Irwin's Bully Song*. Based on the black Southern rural version transcribed by Howard W. Odum in 1908 and published three years later in the *Journal of American Folklore*, Muir believes the original black folk song used a straight 12-bar structure without the 16-measure chorus that is found in five of the six copyrighted treatments including Irwin's, and which was probably added for commercial purposes. [28] He also views *The Bully* as "an early manifestation" of the *Frankie & Johnny* song family, and cites a number of similarities in phrase structure and harmony between it and *Stack-o-Lee Blues*. [29]

Another striking element is that the Trevathan song, unlike any of the other "Bullies," contains a couplet that would become very familiar in later years: "When you see me comin', hist your windows high / When you see me goin', hang your head and cry." This "floating folk strain" had previously been collected by Gates Thomas in 1892 as the last verse of a black folk song; later it turned up in many songs, including a 1928 record by "Ragtime Texas" Henry Thomas, *Texas Easy Street Blues*, and the 1941 Count Basie/Jimmy Rushing hit *Goin' to Chicago Blues*. Despite all this, *The Bully* is not a blues, but G. Malcolm Laws (in *Native American Balladry*) classified it as a "Negro ballad" in the tradition of bad-man tales. [30]

J. W. Myers was perhaps the first artist to record it as *The New Bully* for Berliner on April 18, 1896. [31]

Born Ada Campbell in Whitby, Ontario, Canada, on June 27, 1862, May Irwin performed at Tony Pastor's theater in New York, and became a Broadway star in the end-of-1893 show *A Country Sport*. She introduced her trademark song in the production *The Widow Jones*, which opened in February 1896. Irwin happened to be traveling by train when she saw sportswriter Trevathan entertaining passengers by singing an early, bawdy version of the number (which he had, in turn, learned from Pullman porters); she encouraged him to develop it into a full song. According to blues scholar Paul Oliver, Trevathan may have picked up the number from traveling black songsters; a St. Louis brothel singer known as Mama Lou is said to have performed it in the mid-1890s at Babe Connors' club. Sigmund Spaeth makes the point that the song was "not as raggy as some of the other syncopated tunes of its day, but it had the spirit of unfettered rhythm." Its lyrics, though simple, had "something of the belligerent mood" of that raw early American classic by minstrel man Dan Emmett, *Old Dan Tucker*. [32]

The year 1896 was big for May Irwin for another reason, as she made history by repeating for the Edison motion picture cameras a kissing scene from *Widow Jones* with her stage partner John C. Rice; *The Kiss* gained national renown and controversy, denounced as immoral by some religious leaders. May became particularly associated with ragtime-style numbers, most notably Ben Harney's *Mister Johnson, Turn Me Loose*, which she unveiled in the December 1896 show *Courted in Court*. More than a decade after she first performed the song, May finally recorded *The Bully* at her debut session for Victor in 1907 (one of just six songs she would record). As was unfortunately the custom for "coon songs" of the time, it briefly uses language that would soon be unacceptable ("I'm a Tennessee nigger . . ."). "I'm looking for the bully of the town . . . I'm looking for the bully and I'll make him weep!"

Kleftico Vlachiko (1908)—Orchestra Goldberg

Odeon 5470

Recorded in Istanbul in 1908

Klezmer recordings from the first third of the twentieth century are fascinating because they are often comprised from bits and pieces of music from a wide range

---

26. *Out of Sight, 1889–1895*, p. 448.

27. One variation of the song, *The New Bully Two-Step* by "G. Donigan," was cited as a strong sheet music seller in the March 23, 1896, *Music Trade Review*. As outlined in subsequent articles (April 18, August 1 and November 14, 1896), Trevathan's publisher filed suit for copyright infringement over both this version and another (*De New Bully*) credited to John W. Cavanaugh. A court held that Trevathan was the song's author, and permanently enjoined others from offering "any colorable imitation" of the composition.

28. *Journal of American Folklore*, July–September 1911, p. 293.

29. Muir, *Before 'Crazy Blues'*, p. 307–10, 319–20.

30. The complex of racial elements in *The Bully* was explored by Karl Hagstrom Miller in *Segregating Sound* (p. 42–46). As the song was first

---

heard by most whites, the title character is murdered, and the killing of an African-American man goes unpunished. But as the song evolved in the black community, it became a tale of the character taking heroic action to end indiscriminant violence against African-Americans.

31. Myers' recording can be found on the Archeophone CD *The 1890s: "Wipe Him Off the Land."*

32. Spaeth, *A History of Popular Music*, p. 286.

of ethnic folk traditions. The word "klezmer" originally referred to musical instruments (it stems from a Yiddish word meaning "vessels of song" or musical instrument), and was later extended to the musicians who perform secular Jewish music. According to Dr. Martin Schwartz, *Kleftico Vlachiko* begins as a *doina* (a kind of "slow, intense, non-metrical improvisation" associated with rural Romanian music) that may be Moldavian in origin. This section is followed by a well-known Bessarabian dance tune (another term for the geographical region also known as Moldavia, which became part of Romania). During the pre–World War I period, many Romanian, Greek, Jewish, Croatian, and other songs and instrumentals using this tune appeared in Europe. The tune for this second section became identified with Jews in the United States, and elements of it were used for a number of songs, including *Palesteena* which was popularized by the Original Dixieland Jazz Band (1920) and Eddie Cantor.[33] Schwartz explains that the title "Kleftico Vlachiko" is made up of the Greek words for a Romanian "regional non-rhythmic heroic ballad."[34] We don't know the identity of the musicians here, but the performance features a classically trained cornetist who skillfully navigates the technically demanding melody while the orchestra provides a drone-like background, producing a haunting quality. For the final minute, the tempo sharply accelerates. The Goldberg ensemble made only two known discs for Odeon; the flip side is a Greek *sirto*, and its other known record consisted of two Turkish fanfares, attesting to the "cosmopolitan nature" of the European klezmorim.

El Garrotin (c. 1913)—Orquesta Pablo Valenzuela

Columbia C-1072; recorded in New York[35]

The Cuban *danzon* emerged in the 1870s from its predecessor the *contradanza*, based, like the merengue and the bolero, on the *cinquillo* rhythm (meaning quintuplet), and in Havana its leading exponents were two bandleading brothers, Pablo and Raimundo Valenzuela.[36][37] According to Ned Sublette, Raimundo, who was playing professionally by 1864, "practically invented the Cuban school of dance-band trombone," until his death in 1905. Pablo (1859–1926) was the first great Cuban king of the cornet, and with his recordings starting when he took over his brother's band, the *danzon* became (write Dick Spottswood and Cristobal Diaz Ayala) "the first African-American musical form to be recorded in depth."[38] Victor's subsidiary company Zon-o-Phone made its first expedition to Havana in 1905, producing over eighty recordings by Valenzuela's orchestra; Edison and Columbia arrived the next year with a wide variety of recordings, followed by Victor itself in 1907.[39] Chris Strachwitz notes that the instrumentation of the early Cuban bands was similar to that of the New Orleans groups of the same period, with front lines of cornet, trombone, clarinet, and one or more violins; the Cuban rhythm sections were driven by the timbale (kettle drum), serving a function similar to the American bass drum.[40]

El Garrotin, one of the most exceptional of Pablo's surviving recordings, is an adaptation of an Andalusian melody, a vibrant four-minute instrumental that was issued on a 12-inch disc. Spottswood and Diaz remark that his playing "is quite strong for a man of 54; it's startling to realize that he was born fully 18 years before the unrecorded Buddy Bolden."[41]

There's a Long, Long Trail (1915)—James Reed & James F. Harrison (music by Zo Elliott, lyrics by Stoddard King)

Victor 17882

Recorded Sept. 29, 1915; *Pop Memories* debut Dec. 18, 1915 (reached #1)

One of the most famous anthems of the First World War was written in 1913, a year before the conflict began, by two seniors at Yale University, for a fraternity banquet. The following fall, when Zo Elliott entered Trinity College at Cambridge, England, he submitted *There's a Long, Long Trail* to a small publisher who accepted it only after Elliott agreed to pay the expenses for the first printing, with the money refundable if the song was profitable. As outlined by David Ewen, when the war broke out in Europe in 1914, Elliott was traveling in Germany; when he was able to get to Switzerland, he discovered the song had become a hit in England and was earning him substantial royalties. Upon returning to America later in 1914, Elliott got M. Witmark and Sons to publish the song, but for over a year the sales were modest. As the war heated up in late 1915 (with an Allied offensive against German forces beginning in late September, amid

---

33. See discussion by Sapoznik in *Klezmer!*, p. 77–78.

34. Liner notes for the Arhoolie CD *Klezmer Music: Early Yiddish Instrumental Music*.

35. Spottswood says the recording *may* have been made in Havana in 1909; pinning down discographical details for Valenzuela is difficult.

36. The *danzon*, which was the dominant Cuban music form for nearly a half-century until the *son* boom of the 1920s, remained popular through the 1940s, and led directly to the mambo and the cha-cha-cha in the 1950s (Sublette, *Cuba And Its Music*, p. 247–48).

37. Diaz defines the *danzon* as a series of dance strains whose primary theme is often restated as a chorus in ABACAD fashion. It came to prominence during the same era as the tango, habanera, and ragtime, "each with elements echoing the danzon."

38. Liner notes, Arhoolie's *The Cuban Danzon: Before There Was Jazz*.

39. The pre-1910 recordings in Havana were made primarily for that country's domestic market and elsewhere in Latin America, with little distribution in North America, making them rarities for collectors. The other two pioneering Cuban bands on record were also led by cornetists, Enrique Pena and Felipe Valdes.

40. *The Cuban Danzon: Before There Was Jazz*, p. 4; see footnote 36.

41. Liner notes, Harlequin's *Hot Music from Cuba, 1907–1936*.

Memories of You, 1889–2012

heavy casualties), and American sympathies for the British and French despite official neutrality, interest grew in the ballad. While not a "war song" as such, *Trail* had been embraced by British listeners longing for their loved ones, and this feeling carried across the Atlantic. [42]

The song's recording was by two artists working under pseudonyms. "James F. Harrison" was actually baritone Frederick Wheeler, born on October 10, 1877, in Boone, New York, who began recording for the Edison label in 1904, primarily in duets with Albert Campbell (a 1904 recording of *You're the Flower of My Heart, Sweet Adeline*) and Harry Anthony, and specializing in religious and art songs along with sentimental ballads. Billed as "The Golden-Voiced Baritone," he was also a member of the Knickerbocker Quartet, and within a few years was also recording for Victor and Columbia. "James Reed" was tenor Reed Miller, born on February 29, 1880, in Anderson, South Carolina. Miller earned a reputation in concert recitals, and starting in 1910 recorded under his own name for Victor and Columbia. "Harrison and Reed" began a successful series of duets for both of those labels in early 1915, and *There's a Long, Long Trail* was the biggest. The superb performance is included on the Archeophone *Phonographic Yearbook* CD for 1916. "There's a long, long trail a-winding into the land of my dreams / Where the nightingales are singing and the white moon beams . . ."

This is one of the rare instances during the early years of the century of a song becoming a successful commercial recording well <u>before</u> hitting big in sheet music sales. It was not until slightly over a year after this recording that *Long, Long Trail* was discussed by *Music Trades*, but by that time it had already come a long way. The song, stated the November 11, 1916, issue, can be heard "in every concert hall and every vaudeville house in America." A list of performers singing it "would look like a telephone directory." In its February 17, 1917, issue, the magazine reported that the song "has quietly forged its way" to the front "until to-day it is one of those ballads that the whole English-speaking world is singing and talking about. In Britain, it is the universal hit . . . [It is] a remarkable song in every way." More accolades came in the March 17 issue, as the song "is carrying all before it . . . has both Europe and America in its pleasant grip." The tune "is second to none in both popularity and sales of any ballad written." A partial explanation for the time lag is that due to its wartime associations (in emotional impact though not in its lyrics),

the song, as explained by the *Trades*, was "the reigning hit in Britain for many months" from the end of 1915 through 1916, and then expanded to become ubiquitous "in Allied trenches in Europe." Finally, as war tensions rose in the U.S. in early 1917 and President Wilson went before a joint session of Congress that April 2 to request a declaration of war against Germany, *Long, Long Trail* also exploded in the U.S. The April 14 *Trades* declared it "an epoch-making song—there is no room for doubt on that point"; Witmark was "overwhelmed by the demand for it from every corner."

Seeking to explain the phenomenon, several weeks later *Music Trades* remarked that when King and Elliott composed the tune it was presented as a conventional ballad. But when the wartime classic *It's a Long, Long Way to Tipperary* had run its course, *Trail* was taken up by British soldiers (becoming known as the anthem of "Kitchener's Army") and the public. On one occasion, when a British transport off the coast of Africa was struck by a mine and in danger of sinking, the soldiers reportedly lined up and broke into the song "as they faced what appeared to be certain death." The ship survived, and newspapers on both sides of the Atlantic played up the event. Although it had become a war song, the composition "contains no word or sentiment that can be considered as either martial or jingoistic, or indeed, anything but poetically expressed sentiments." The tune, concluded the publication, "represents an international song success second to none that modern song history has revealed."[43]

Rose Room (1919)—Art Hickman's Orchestra (written by Art Hickman & Harry Williams)
Columbia 2858
Recorded Sept. 19, 1919; *Pop Memories* debut May 1, 1920 (reached #5)

Although little remembered today except for historians and collectors, Art Hickman played a key role in the evolution of the American dance band by establishing the basic instrumentation and style that would be further developed and popularized by Paul Whiteman. Born on June 13, 1886, in Oakland, he moved with his family to San Francisco around the turn of the century, and listened eagerly to black musicians in hop joints and honky-tonks. The earthquake of 1906 temporarily shut down all the city's entertainment venues, but when they reopened he became a manager at more than one vaudeville house. He formed his first band while serving as entertainment director for the spring training camps of the baseball minor league team the San Francisco Seals. As recounted

42. Ewen, *All the Years of American Music*, p. 233. Fuld, *Book of World-Famous Music*, (p. 573) clarifies that the song was published in London in February 1914; U.S. publication by Witmark came later that year. The most popular British recording of the song was made in 1916 by tenor Ernest Pike for Zon-o-Phone.

43. May 26, 1917, *Music Trades*. The ballad remained an active topic over a year later; the December 14, 1918, issue called it "the song of destiny."

by Bruce Vermazen, a 1913 news story about the camps referred to the band as playing "jazz," an early published use of the word regarding music. However, it stemmed back to an April 2, 1912, story in the *Los Angeles Times* in which a Portland Beavers pitcher said he called his new curveball "the Jazz ball because it wobbles and you simply can't do anything with it"—one of the first known examples of the word "jazz" in print. (The first documented use of the word "jazz" on record, reports Nick Tosches, goes back still further to 1909 on a comedy record for Columbia by the great monologist Cal Stewart, *Uncle Josh in Society*.) This led to players calling out, "come on, let's jazz it up," and then to the word being applied to Hickman's spring training camp band. This brought him the opportunity to organize a band for dancing at the St. Francis Hotel in its Rose Room ballroom (hence the song title) in 1914 and serving as the hotel's amusement director until the end of the decade. For the first time ever in the city, there was scheduled public dancing in hotels thanks to the appeal of his ensemble. Despite published accounts that Ferde Grofe (active in San Francisco musical circles at the time) played a role in the band's arrangements, Vermazen says there is no evidence for this, and that Hickman deserves the credit.[44]

Hickman was first approached by the Victor Talking Machine Company to make records in 1917, but the deal was called off when the federal government took over much of Victor's production capacity to manufacture armaments for the Great War.[45] With war's end, Columbia signed Hickman and brought the band to New York. The band poured out twenty-two issued sides within nine days in September 1919. Upon their release in early 1920, the records made a strong impression with their quality and variety, with shifting leads among the instruments in the ten-man ensemble. Joshua Berrett: "Hickman's innovation was far-reaching in its effect in that the military-band, Dixieland model of cornet lead, trombone countermelody, and clarinet obbligato was modified in favor of a warmer and more varied texture. All of this was made possible by the dividing of the brass and reeds into sections, having countermelodies accompany statements by the brass, and inserting orchestrated 'breaks'— that is, disruptions of the established rhythm, often filled with syncopated saxophone figures."[46]

Rose Room, certainly the most famous Hickman recording, derived the core of its melody from the third strain of William H. Tyers' 1896 composition *Toscha: A Cuban Dance*. But, writes Vermazen, "the chorus is one of Hickman's best inventions, a simple melodic-rhythmic idea of four bars repeated eight times with graceful changes of color and harmonic setting, good enough to last as a jazz standard into a new century." The highlight is a piano duet between Hickman and Frank Ellis; the record's conclusion is a double cadence featuring Walt Roesner's "flutter-tongued" trumpet.[47] *Rose Room* would become a staple of the Swing Era, with versions by Artie Shaw, Duke Ellington, Benny Goodman and other bands; its chord progression also served as the initial inspiration for Ellington's 1940 classic *In a Mellotone*. Unfortunately, by that time Hickman had been dead for ten years. Hickman's complete recordings were reissued on CD by Archeophone.

Chimes Blues (1923)—King Oliver's Creole Jazz Band
Gennett 5135
Recorded in Richmond, Indiana on April 6, 1923 (*GHF-#151, Jazz-#96*)

Chimes Blues is noteworthy in jazz history because it contains Louis Armstrong's first recorded cornet solo, in a performance called "an astonishing piece of work" by his biographer Laurence Bergreen. It was the fifth number attempted during the landmark debut recording session for the Oliver ensemble, and released as the flip side of another enduring Oliver standard, *Froggie Moore*. "The song contains both the past and future of jazz," writes Bergreen. "Although the musical technique is far from perfect, the song ticks along nicely, with Johnny Dodds' clarinet weaving in and out of the predictable rhythm." It is near the end of the song (its fourth strain) that Armstrong "suddenly fast forwards into the twentieth century. His bold, ascending, trilling, metallic notes streak over the creaky proceedings like a comet. Louis demonstrates great presence; as soon as you hear his horn—jarring, jagged, and sinuous—you know he has it. His horn sounds twice as loud as the rest of the musicians put together, and his subtle, suspenseful rhythmic shifts, combined with fleeting grace notes where least expected, impart drama to the song. The confidence with which Louis attacked *Chimes Blues* suggested that, unlike his older, stodgier colleagues, he instantly grasped the possibilities of recordings."[48] Armstrong was so much more powerful in tone that he had to stand much farther back

44. Liner notes, Archeophone CD *Art Hickman's Orchestra: The San Francisco Sound*.

45. According to the December 20, 1919, *Music Trades*, nearly 90 percent of Victor's production was turned over to war work by late 1918, resulting in an "almost total disappearance of Victrolas from the market." The Armistice was signed in November 1918, but it was not until the following March that Victor could clear its plant of war work, and it took an additional four months to return to normal production levels.

46. Berrett, *Two Kings of Jazz*, p. 15–16.

47. Vermazen CD liner notes, p. 16. The publication of *Rose Room* was reported in the March 22, 1919, *Music Trades*, six months before Hickman recorded it.

48. Bergreen, *An Extravagant Life*, p. 218.

from the acoustic recording horn (by some disputed accounts, as far back as twenty feet) than Oliver.

Gunther Schuller remarks of Armstrong's solo here: "It was unusual for the Creole Jazz Band in that it was accompanied only by the rhythm section. Yet it is a solo only in the sense that it takes place alone; it is not yet fully a solo in character and conception. It might easily have been one part of a collectively improvised chorus lifted from its background. But it is clearly headed in the solo direction, and it is not a thematic variation."[49]

Gary Giddins says of this performance by Armstrong: "He doesn't improvise at all, but the declaratory tone and rhythmic dash are unmistakable, unlike anything recorded up to that time."[50] Along with a few New Orleans Rhythm Kings originals such as *Tin Roof Blues*, *Chimes Blues* was one of the first jazz compositions issued in sheet music form by the Melrose Brothers Music Co. in Chicago. Jelly Roll Morton's quartet piece *Mournful Serenade* was based in part on this performance.

Countin' the Blues (1924)—Ma Rainey & Her Georgia Jazz Band
Paramount 12238
Recorded Oct. 16, 1924 (*Blues-#135, SB*)

Recorded at the same session as her classic *See See Rider Blues*, *Countin' the Blues* finds Ma Rainey accompanied by the mighty ensemble of Louis Armstrong on cornet, Charlie Green on trombone, Buster Bailey on clarinet, and Fletcher Henderson on piano, plus Charlie Dixon on banjo and Kaiser Marshall on drums. She opens the piece by calling everyone to kneel in prayer, and the performance is steeped in the sounds of the black church, with a call and response structure as her voice is answered by individual instruments. Robert Santelli notes that "Rainey's style was to work with her backing musicians, not compete with them, and this resulted in a more unified, cohesive sound than many of her contemporaries possessed."[51] Rudi Blesh rhapsodized in *Shining Trumpets*: "Gertrude Rainey was a great person, a deeply human and articulate one, and the song she made is great art."

Inasmuch as Rainey was one of the original blues performers in the early years of the twentieth century, this is an appropriate place to note that, as discussed by essayist Whitney Balliett, novelist Washington Irving seems to have been the first to use the term "the blues" in print, in 1807, as a synonym for melancholy: "He conducted his

harangue with a sigh, and I saw that he was still under the influence of a whole legion of the blues." This usage was a shortening of "the blue devils" (Robert Burns: "In my bitter hours of blue-devilism"), a synonym, writes Balliett, "for a baleful presence that goes back at least to Elizabethan times, when blue apparently became associated with being down in the dumps."[52] Ma Rainey helped give the term a still deeper meaning.

The Titanic (1925)—Ernest V. Stoneman
Okeh 40288
Recorded Jan. 8, 1925; new version recorded as *Sinking of the Titanic* for Edison 5200 on June 22, 1926 (*C&W-#170, SC*)

When the mighty White Star oceanliner the Titanic hit an iceberg off Cape Race, Newfoundland, on its maiden voyage from Southampton, England, to New York City and sank on April 14, 1912, killing more than 1,500 persons, it stirred deep reactions around the world, and—like so many tragedies before it—stimulated ballads to tell the tale and draw moral lessons from it.[53] According to Guthrie T. Meade, Jr., over 160 such songs were copyrighted and/or published during the next several months. None of these compositions immediately emerged to strike a chord with the public, but a dozen years later, one did become a country music classic.

Ernest Van Stoneman, born on May 25, 1893, in Monarat in Carroll County, Virginia, of Scots-Irish ancestry, helped make his home region (in the Blue Ridge Mountains near the town that would become Galax) one of the most renowned centers of old-time country music. He was working as a carpenter in Bluefield, West Virginia, in 1924 when he heard Henry Whitter's first record—the two men had worked in textile mills together—and, convinced he was a better singer, wrote to Columbia and Okeh asking for the chance to record. As detailed by Graham Wickham and Eugene Earle,[54] both companies responded positively; after raising enough money and rehearsing material, that September 1 he went by train to the Columbia offices in New York. He turned down the label's offer of just $100 for up to twenty sides, and made a better deal with Okeh at $25 per side. Producer Ralph Peer had to wait three days for his engineers to return from an Atlanta field trip, and upon their return Stoneman (on solo vocal, harmonica, and autoharp) re-

49. *Early Jazz*, p. 83. David Metzer remarks (Autumn 1997 *Black Music Research Journal*) that *Chimes Blues* incorporates the refrain from the white hymn *The Holy City* and transforms it into a 12-bar blues, as Duke Ellington would later do with the same source material in *Black and Tan Fantasy*.

50. *Visions of Jazz*, p. 81.

51. Santelli, *Best of the Blues*, p. 237.

52. Balliett, *Collected Works*, p. 67.

53. James C. Cobb called the song "a latter-day parable of the Tower of Babel," representing God striking back at Man as "the all-but-inevitable result of attempting to construct a ship billed as 'unsinkable.'" (*You Wrote My Life*, p. 69.).

54. In their biographical feature for the September 1967 *J.E.M.F. Newsletter*. Also see *The Early Recording Career of Ernest V. "Pop" Stoneman*, p. 3–4.

corded *The Titanic* and *The Face That Never Returned.* Upon listening to the playback both men agreed that he'd played the pieces too fast, so he returned to Bluefield, practiced the numbers at half the speed, and returned not quite four months later to successfully re-record both plus two other tunes. The debut release became one of the biggest-selling discs in early hillbilly music (although it was certainly not a million-seller as sometimes reported), establishing the foundation for a great career including more than 200 sides for various labels (also including Victor and Gennett) through 1934. After more than a dozen years struggling to raise a family in poverty and hoping to return to music, Stoneman with his family won a 1947 talent contest at Constitution Hall in Washington, D.C., leading to six months of local television appearances. From 1956 until his death on June 14, 1968, "Pop" (as he was then known) and the Stoneman Family (including his most gifted son, fiddler Scotty Stoneman) enjoyed a prolific period of new recordings, TV and radio appearances, and concerts, solidifying his legend.

Stoneman learned *The Titanic* as a poem printed in the May 23, 1912, *New York Clipper.* He started humming a tune to it, and by 1914 "I'd play it wherever I went" at parties.[55] George Pullen Jackson reported in *Spiritual Folk-Songs of Early America* that the tune utilizes "practically the same melodic trend" as a traditional hymn known as *Dulcimer* or *Beloved,* a melody attributed to Freeman Lewis (1780–1859). That tune, in turn, bears some similarity to British ballads in the *Lord Lovel* song family. Variants of the Stoneman number were also recorded by "master of disaster songs" Vernon Dalhart (under four slightly different titles for different labels from 1925–1928) and William and Versey Smith (*When That Great Ship Went Down* in 1927), among others. The Stonemans' new 1963 recording of the song introduced it to another generation.

When the Work's All Done This Fall (1925)—Carl T. Sprague (written by D. J. O'Malley)

Victor 19747

Recorded Aug. 5, 1925 (released on Oct. 1) (*C&W-#158*)

Carl Sprague was not the first recorded cowboy singer of Western songs, but his rendering of *When the Work's All Done This Fall* was a historic landmark as the record that triggered widespread interest in commercial recording of Western material, and helped pave the way for the era of Hollywood singing cowboys. Born on May 10, 1895, near Houston to a farming and ranching family, Sprague went on cattle drives with his uncles and worked as a ranch hand. He recalled that "we'd make camp all night right there on the open prairie where there wasn't

anything but cattle, horses, and stars. That was where I first learned my songs, from real cowboys." He led a band at Texas A&M which he began attending in 1915. After service in France he returned to graduate from A&M in 1922, and was hired by the school's athletic department where he worked as an assistant coach for fifteen years. In 1925 he began doing a weekly sixty-minute program on the campus radio station.[56]

It was the massive popular success of Vernon Dalhart (a fellow Texan) with *The Prisoner's Song* that inspired Sprague in August 1925 to travel to Camden, New Jersey, and record six cowboy songs for the Victor Talking Machine Company. Charles Nabell had preceded him as the first cowboy singer to make records, for Okeh in November 1924, but Sprague was the first to make a powerful popular impression.[57] The first issued 78, *When the Work's All Done This Fall* (which had previously been recorded by Fiddlin' John Carson in March 1924 as *Dixie Cowboy*) coupled with *The Bad Companions,* became a surprise hit, by several accounts selling several hundred thousand copies. Although he was paid a flat fee of just $75 per side for most of his recordings, for this song he also received both a half-cent performing royalty and an additional royalty because he put some personal writing/arranging touches on the number. He would go on to record an additional eighteen sides for Victor and its subsidiary Bluebird through 1929.

Published in October 1893 (initially as a poem for the *Stockgrower's Journal*), *When the Work's All Done* is the tragic tale of a cowboy who, while trying to return home to see his mother, is killed in a night stampede. The song was chronicled by John and Alan Lomax in *Cowboy Songs and Frontier Ballads.* John Lomax learned the song from a Fort Worth, Texas, correspondent who reported that it had originated on the Spotted Wood Trail, 140 miles out of Deadwood, South Dakota, based on an actual incident. Sprague gives a sincere, affecting performance in a solo vocal accompanied only by his own guitar. His subsequent work was almost entirely in the same Western vein, including *O Bury Me Not on the Lone Prairie, Here's to the Texas Ranger,* and *The Last Great Round-Up.* Gene Autry and all the other singing cowboys who galloped across the silver screen in the 1930s and 1940s could tip their Stetsons to Sprague as the man who showed the way. This performance was included on the original Smithsonian *Collection of Classic Country Music,* and the boxed set *American Pop: From Minstrel to Mojo.*

---

55. Horstman, *Sing Your Heart Out,* p. 89.

---

56. John I. White feature on Sprague, Spring 1970 *J.E.M.F Quarterly.*

57. The Victor monthly supplement announcing the record remarked that Sprague had "a repertoire of cowboy songs that would turn a collector green with envy."

Valencia (A Song of Spain) (1926)—Paul Whiteman & His Orchestra (music by Jose Padilla, lyrics by Lucien Jean Boyer & Jacques Charles; English lyrics by Clifford Grey)

Victor 20007

Recorded March 30, 1926; *Pop Memories* debut June 26, 1926 (#1 for 11 weeks) (*MEM-#28, DMDB*)

Paul Whiteman's dominant position in the world of recorded dance band music was consolidated with every passing year since his 1920 blockbuster hit *Whispering*. His triumphant 1923 European tour and hero's welcome back home; the massively successful February 1924 Aeolian Hall concert introducing *Rhapsody In Blue*; his self-promotional but popular 1926 book *Jazz*; and above all the unending string of big-selling records for Victor deepened the hold that the genial Buddha-like big man had on popular music. The 1926 smash *Valencia* proved anew that he had a virtually unparalleled knack for taking a good musical idea and developing it into something that resonated with a massive audience.

Valencia is a terrifically danceable number in brisk 6/8 tempo by Spanish composer Jose Padilla, and originally given French lyrics. It was introduced in Paris by an artist simply named Mistinguett, and then taken to the U.S. by Hazel Dawn and the cast of the show *Great Temptations*. As always, Whiteman and arranger Ferde Grofé maximized the potential of the insinuating melody, with a dramatic vocal chorus by Brooklyn-born tenor Franklyn Baur (accompanied by trumpeter Walter Holzhaus and trombonist Boyce Cullen). It was one of the featured pieces of the band's 1926 European tour, including a memorable April 11 concert at London's Royal Albert Hall in which all 8,000 seats were filled with another 5,000 turned away at the door.[58]

"As a musical formula," remarks Richard Sudhalter, the Whiteman style "worked, and well. The orchestra as heard on this [mid-to-late 1920s] series of Victor records played with a polish, euphony of sound and engaging musical lift which . . . made people listen to popular music—jazz included—as well as dance to it. On record after record . . . the sheer quality of sound and balance are to be deeply admired—as they were by most musicians of the day, regardless of color or stylistic persuasion." In one decade, suggests Elijah Wald, "Whiteman had not only become America's best-known musician and sold more records than anyone alive, but he had also transformed dance music, transformed the world's attitude toward jazz, and transformed popular singing [by hiring and effectively showcasing Bing Crosby]. Whether he had transformed them for the better remains a matter of opinion, but it is hard to argue that any artist before or since has had a greater impact."[59]

Engancha Carretero (Hitch Up, Oxcart Driver) (1928)—Sexteto Matancero

Recorded in Havana, Cuba on Feb. 7, 1928

The *son* (deriving from sonar, to sound) is the most fundamental form of twentieth century Afro-Cuban popular music, and during the early years of Cuban commercial recording the vast majority of sons were recorded by small combos, sextetos and septetos. Ned Sublette explains in *Cuba And Its Music: From the First Drums to the Mambo*: "The genre called *son* is a Cuban synthesis: Bantu percussion [the Bantus were a subfamily of the Niger-Congo family in West Africa, particularly from the present nations of Nigeria and Cameroon, who emigrated in significant numbers to Cuba], melodic rhythm, and call-and-response singing, melding with the Spanish peasant's guitar and language."[60] The genre evolved over a long period of time and existed in some recognizable form by the 1860s, and accelerated by the 1880s with the abolition of slavery in Cuba, but fully came into its own in the early years of the twentieth century. The first *son* sextet recordings were made in 1918, and during the next decade and a half a huge number of small-combo *son* recordings were made. John Santos: "Combined with the introduction of radio in Havana (1922), the *son* caught on like wild fire, replacing the *danzon* as Cuba's most popular dance and music."[61] One of the best was *Engancha Carretero*.

A central element in son recordings is the *tres*, a guitar variant that is, writes Sublette, "likely an adaptation by Africans of the *bandurria*, a small, pear-shaped, double-string instrument" popular among guajiros. The *tres* is "metal-strung, tuned high and tight. Smaller than the modern guitar, it has three pairs of double strings, not adjacent to but widely spaced from each other. This spacing allows the tresero room to get some throw with his wrist as he whacks each pair of strings with his pick."[62] Among the finest treseros of his time was Isaac Oviedo, best known for his work with the Sexteto Matancero (which by the early 1930s was a septeto). Oviedo was the first *tresero* to take a solo on record. Santos: "He was the Jimi Hendrix, so to speak, of the Cuban *tres*," converting it to a solo instrument and not merely a component of the ensemble. On *Engancha Carretero*, Oviedo imitates the sound of an approaching locomotive's "choo-choo" whistle and bell; he is also the lead singer atop the group

58. Rayno, *Paul Whiteman: Pioneer in American Music*, p. 134–35.

59. *How the Beatles Destroyed Rock 'n' Roll*, p. 83.
60. Sublette, p. 333.
61. Liner notes, Arhoolie/Folklyric CD, *Sextetos Cubanos: Sones, Vol. II*.
62. Sublette, *Cuba and Its Music*, p. 337.

vocal. The singing is nothing special, but his soloing is genuinely spectacular, far ahead of his time, with some virtuoso effects. This is the second to last selection on the Arhoolie compilation *Sextetos Cubanos: Sones, Vol. II.*

He Manao Healoha (Thoughts of Love) (1928)—Kalama's Quartet

Okeh 41023

Recorded in March 1928

A Hawaiian group led by steel guitarist and tenor falsetto singer Mike Hanapi (born on March 18, 1898, in Honolulu), and also featuring William Kalama on tenor voice and ukulele, Kalama's Quartet recorded thirty or more titles from 1927–1932. Sandy Miranda: "There is a deep, almost eerie spiritual quality to their unforgettable four-part harmonies, and no other group has even come close to sounding like them. Their songs are so full of musical inventiveness, humor, and intense emotion that they are truly in a class by themselves, singing about the balmy trade winds, beautiful women, and places that they love." [63]

The music of the islands came to commercial records when Columbia in 1901 issued two cylinders of Hawaiian music by uncredited performers. Victor made its first recordings in Hawaii in 1905, with about fifty songs issued in its foreign catalog. The Panama Pacific Exposition in San Francisco (February 20 to December 4, 1915), in honor of the recently opened Panama Canal, featured hula dancers from Hawaii and native guitarists, and a nationwide craze for Hawaiian music began, kicking into high gear in 1916 with Tin Pan Alley hits like *Hello, Hawaii, How Are You* and *On the Beach at Waikiki*. By 1917 Victor alone had 175 Hawaiian titles in its catalog; Portuguese-Hawaiian steel guitarist Frank Ferera was the era's most popular Hawaiian musician on record and in vaudeville. [64]

Kalama's Quartet first recorded instrumentals in 1926–1927 as the Hanapi Trio, then became a vocal quartet in late 1927; their last records as a group were made in January 1932. Mike Hanapi became a member of the Royal Hawaiian Band in 1940, playing first saxophone until his death in 1959. *He Manao Healoha* features one of Hanapi's most renowned falsetto vocals; Bob Brozman calls this "an overwhelmingly deep three minutes." [65]

K. C. Moan (1929)—Memphis Jug Band

Victor 38558

Recorded in Memphis on Oct. 4, 1929 (*Folk-#81, Blues-#124, HS*)

A train song with a gently haunting quality, *K. C. Moan* is a perfect representative of genuine folk blues handed down by oral tradition over a number of years before the blues, as such, even existed. It was first reported by Howard W. Odum in two 1911 articles for the *Journal of American Folklore*, with several similar versions centered in Newton County, Georgia, all very close to the song that would debut on record sixteen years later, as *Thought I Heard That K. C. Whistle Blow*. Odum observed that it is sung from the perspective of a laborer waiting at a station to carry him or her back home—or watching it carry his woman away—and hearing the train whistle "blow lak' she never blow befo'." [66] [67] The same song was collected in Alabama in 1915–1916 (from a singer who had first heard it in Georgia) and reported by Newman I. White. [68] The tune was first recorded as *K. C. Railroad Blues* in 1927 by the Georgia-based black father-and-son duo (or uncle-and-nephew, depending on the account) of Andrew & Jim Baxter. Charley Patton sang slightly altered versions of the opening verse on two 1929 records, *Pea Vine Blues* and *Green River Blues*; a variation on its melody would later be recorded as *Lonesome Road Blues* by Kokomo Arnold (1936) and Big Bill Broonzy (1940). Also, Roy Acuff's band borrowed the song's central lyric for *Steamboat Whistle Blues* in 1936 ("I thought I heard that steamboat whistle blow / Blowed like she never blowed before"). But it's hard to top this performance by the Memphis Jug Band.

Tony Russell writes about the role of Memphis as one of the "hothouses" of Southern music to which Northern talent scouts flocked in the late 1920s, as "the river city at the junction of Tennessee, Mississippi and Arkansas. Thanks to cotton, highways and railroads it was one of the busiest commercial centers in the South. There was money in Memphis, and ways to spend it, especially on Beale Street—shows at the Palace Theater, gambling at the Monarch, prizefighting at the Vintage," and—as Will Shade recalled—"sportin' women" running "up and down the street all night long." [69] And everywhere, there was music.

Leader Will Shade is on harmonica with Tewee Blackman on guitar and Ben Ramey on kazoo, and Blackman

63. *MusicHound World*, p. 358.

64. See Norm Cohen and Paul F. Wells chapter, *Ethnic Recordings in America* (p. 184).

65. Brozman, liner notes to Arhoolie CD, *Kalama's Quartet: 1927–1932*.

66. *Journal of American Folklore*, July–September 1911, p. 287, and October–December 1911, p. 360–62, "Folk-Song and Folk-Poetry As Found in the Secular Songs of the Southern Negro." The same traditional line also turned up in *Train Forty-Five* by G. B. Grayson & Henry Whitter in 1927.

67. Titon notes in *Early Downhome Blues*, p. 25 that the song variants as reported by Odum are in the three-line, AAB stanza blues format, although in a non-blues eight-bar form.

68. *American Negro Folk Songs*, p. 273.

69. *The Blues: From Robert Johnson to Robert Cray*, p. 23.

leads the vocal trio, supported by Ramey and guitarist Charlie Burse. Blackman had been Shade's old guitar teacher, and this was his only session with the group. Robert Cantwell in *When We Were Good: The Folk Revival* sees the piece as "the inward ruminations of a man in a workgang" listening to the distant train whistle and lost in thoughts of his woman while drowning his sorrows with a fraternal quartet. "The blue notes seem gradually to fade out of existence as the song draws to a close—and with them a world lapses behind us, a door closes, an old dispensation runs out, [and] a new land opens up . . ."[70]

Norm Cohen in *Long Steel Rail* notes: "There have been so many railroads running through Kansas City with that city as part of their name that one would be hard pressed to pick a single referent for the song lyrics." But perhaps the likeliest candidate, he suggested, is the Kansas City Southern, incorporated in 1900, the biggest of the "KC" railroads.[71] Samuel Charters remarked of the Memphis Jug Band: "They were a rough, noisy group, but there was an intense sadness in some of the slower blues."[72] *K. C. Moan* was reissued in 1952 on Harry Smith's landmark *Anthology of American Folk Music*.

"The train may on occasion serve as witness of the grief of a folk songster," wrote Dorothy Scarborough of *K. C. Moan* in *On the Trail of Negro Folk Songs* (1925). "The headlight of an engine can see a great deal—has looked down on many griefs. If it wept over all the woes it witnesses, the tracks would be flooded."[73]

> I thought I heard that K.C. when she moaned, I thought I heard that K.C. when she moaned . . .
> She moaned like my woman's on board.
> When I get back on that K.C. road, when I get back on that K.C. road . . .
> I'm going to love my baby like she's never been loved before.

Barbara Allen (1930)—Bradley Kincaid
Vocalion 02685[74]

Recorded Jan. 24, 1930; also recorded for Supertone 9211 (on Feb. 27, 1928) (*Folk-#90, SC*)

The most universally known traditional folk song in the English language, the tale of "Bar'bry" Allen dates back in print to at least 1666 in England;[75] it was well

known in colonial America, and the melody was first published in the U.S. (with different lyrics) in 1780 as a patriotic song called *Sergeant Champe*. Abraham Lincoln is reported to have sung it as a boy.[76] Francis James Child collected many British versions, and the tune was No. 84 in his epic compilation. Vance Randolph called it "perhaps the most popular of all the traditional ballads" in America, with over 200 different versions collected all over the country from 1883[77] to the 1940s.[78] The narrative is simplicity itself, a lament of unrequited love: boy loves girl, she fails to return his affections, and he dies of a broken heart, as townspeople condemn his beloved forever as "hard-hearted Barbara Allen." The kicker is that she dies of remorse, instructs her mother to bury her alongside poor William in the church graveyard, and the rose and the briar from their respective graves grow to ultimately entwine in a lovers' knot. Dave Marsh: "It's that last image that drives the whole song, for me," a mystical and poetically appropriate image that explains why people have sung the ballad for half a millennium.[79]

Born on July 13, 1895, in Garrard County, Kentucky, Bradley Kincaid was a sensationally popular radio performer of traditional folk songs, many of which he collected in rural communities in the Appalachian mountains. In addition to recording under his own name, Kincaid cut records under such pseudonyms as Dan Hughey, John Carpenter, and Harley Stratton, and is estimated to have sold up to 400,000 copies of his twelve song folios.[80] Billed as the Kentucky Mountain Boy, he was a regular on the *National Barn Dance* show on Chicago's WLS from 1926–1930, a top concert attraction throughout the 1920s and '30s, and heard on other radio programs through 1950, including a 1944–1947 stint as a *Grand Ole Opry* regular.[81] Kincaid's solo acoustic version of *Barbara Allen*—which proved so popular that reportedly he sang it every Saturday night on the *Barn Dance* for four years—helped to define the song for a generation.[82]

One of Kincaid's most important contributions to country music was his 1936 discovery of a young singer and banjo player named Lewis Marshall Jones, whom he renamed Grandpa Jones. After thirteen years of semi-retirement, he recorded 162 songs over four days in 1963,

70. Cantwell, p. 229.
71. Cohen, p. 408–10.
72. *The Country Blues*, p. 113.
73. Scarborough, p. 242.
74. This recording was also issued on Melotone, Conqueror, & Panachord.
75. Before being mentioned in Pepys' *Diary* (January 2 and 6, 1666), it's believed to have been a Scottish-originated favorite for another century or more, and was included in Percy's *Reliques* (1765).

76. According to Beveridge's 1928 Lincoln biography. (Citation made by Vance Randolph, *Ozark Folksongs*, p. 41 of single-volume abridged edition.)
77. William Wells Newell (*Games and Songs of American Children*, 1883) found *Barbara Allen* being used as a game song in New England.
78. Randolph, *Ozark Folksongs*, Vol. 1, p. 126–27.
79. Marsh chapter on the song in *The Rose and the Briar*, p. 9–17.
80. Kincaid's first folio, *Favorite Mountain Ballads and Old-Time Songs*, came out in April 1928 and went through six printings (Spring 1977 *J.E.M.F. Quarterly*).
81. See Loyal Jones' profile of Kincaid in the Spring 1977 *J.E.M.F. Quarterly*.
82. Charles Wolfe, *Classic Country*, p. 126.

providing material for at least seven albums of *Mountain Ballads and Old-Time Songs*.

The House Carpenter (1930)—Clarence (Tom) Ashley
Columbia 15654
Recorded April 14, 1930 (*Folk-#97, HS*)

The centuries-old Anglo-Irish folk story song *The House Carpenter* is described by Kip Lornell as "a parable about inescapable punishment that follows a deep moral error about class, love, and marriage." Out of the 305 ballads from England and Scotland that Harvard English professor Francis James Child assembled from 1882 to 1898, Norm Cohen and Guthrie Meade reported that this (Child No. 243) was among the fifteen most often collected and published tunes. The ballad has its roots in the same ancient myth that inspired Richard Wagner's opera *The Flying Dutchman*, in which a young woman "sails endlessly with an other-worldly mariner until she shows remorse and breaks the magical spell."[83] According to Vance Randolph's *Ozark Folksongs*, elements of the song—also known as *The Daemon Lover* and *James Harris*—can be traced back to seventeenth century manuscripts; one of the earliest collections to include it was Walter Scott's *Minstrelsy of the Scottish Soldier* (1812).[84] Clinton Heylin has suggested (in *Dylan's Daemon Lover*) that the song was brought to America in the mid-eighteenth century through the Scots who emigrated to the southern Appalachians. Cecil Sharp and Olive Campbell (1917) found the ballad to be well known in North Carolina, Kentucky, and Tennessee; Arthur Kyle Davis printed twenty-eight Virginia texts in 1929.[85]

In an article for *The Sociological Review Monograph*, Dave Harker went back still further than Child to identify what seems to have been the song's first reference in print as *A Warning for Married Women*, registered with the Stationers' Company of London on February 21, 1657. The broadside may have been published the following year, was included as part of the *Samuel Pepys Collection*, which dated it to the 1686–1688 period, and turned up (almost always under its 1657 title) on broadsides and in garlands at least a dozen times from that point to the end of the eighteenth century. *The Euing Collection* describes it as the tale of Mrs. Jane Reynolds from Plymouth who exchanged vows of marriage with a seaman (James Harris) who was pressed into service as a sailor and after three years reported as dead, was afterwards married to a carpenter by whom she bore three children, and is finally carried away by a spirit who calls himself James Harris. (In early-twentieth century American

versions collected by folklorists, the returning lover is generally human, not spirit, although "ghostly overtones" can be detected.) The song's originator is believed to be Laurence Price, a London native who wrote or compiled over 200 known ballads between 1628 and 1680, with his best-known works dating from 1655–1657. Harker sees *The House Carpenter* as a reflection of Price's attitudes about the subservient place of women in society as compared to the sexual freedom of men.[86]

The song was first recorded under the title *Can't You Remember When Your Heart Was Mine?* in 1928 by the Carolina Tar Heels, of which Clarence "Tom" Ashley was a member (although he wasn't the vocalist on that performance). Six months after recording his classic (and comparably ancient) *The Coo Coo Bird*, Ashley performs it on solo vocal and five-string banjo. "They say you're married to a house carpenter, and your heart will never be mine." He persuades her to leave her husband and baby and they go out to sea, as she weeps with the knowledge that she'll never see her child again; they die when the ship sinks. The Ashley performance is very true to most traditional versions, including the opening verses ("Well met, well met, said an old true love . . . I'm just returning from the salt, salt sea, and it's all for the love of thee . . ."). The tune gained fresh currency with new cover versions during the folk revival.

In his extended commentary on the Harry Smith anthology, Greil Marcus remarks that *The House Carpenter*, "a ballad in which earthly lust is ended with unearthly punishment, is as suffused with religious awe as the Reverend J. M. Gates' sermon *Must Be Born Again*."[87]

John the Revelator (1930)—Blind Willie Johnson
Columbia 14530
Recorded in Atlanta on April 20, 1930 (*GOSP-#58*)

John the Revelator, the second to last song recorded by Blind Willie Johnson at his final session,[88] introduced one of gospel music's sturdiest classics. It's the tale of John, the last surviving Apostle of Jesus, drawn from chapter 5 of the Revelation of St. John the Divine, which, writes Harold Courlander, "with all its spectacular, visionary, and poetic effects, evidently made a deep impression on the creation of the Negro spiritual songs. Its free, cosmic, and often wild and primitive imagery provided rich opportunities for sermons and for conveying, through musical statements, a spirit of wonder and awe."[89] The Bessemer Sunset Four had cut an unissued version of the song in September 1928. The great south-

83. Child, *The English and Scottish Popular Ballads*, p. 360–69.
84. Randolph, *Ozark Folksongs, Vol. 1*, p. 166.
85. *English Folk Songs from the Southern Appalachians*, p. 119 and 328 in 1917 edition; p. 244 and 420 in 1932 edition.

86. *Sociological Review Monograph* 34, p. 107–59. Also see Todd Harvey's discussion of the song's history in *The Formative Dylan*, p. 44–48.
87. *Invisible Republic*, p. 104.
88. It's included in the Harry Smith folk music anthology.
89. Courlander, *Negro Folk Music, U.S.A.*, p. 66.

eastern Texas singer-guitarist is in typically ferocious voice as he shouts out, "Who's that writing? What's John writing?" The female answering calls of Willie B. Harris, as she responds to each question, "John the Revelator," sound pale by comparison (but then, almost any mere human in 1930 sounded pale compared to Blind Willie). The Golden Gate Quartet recorded the song in January 1938; also the Dixie Hummingbirds in the 1940s; veteran bluesman Son House did a powerful rendition after his early-1960s rediscovery; and in 2003 John Mellencamp brought it to a new generation.

My Black Mama, Parts 1 & 2 (1930)—Son House
Paramount 13042
Recorded in Grafton, Wisconsin, on May 28, 1930 (*Blues-#142*)

A first-generation Delta blues master whose strong influence was heard in Robert Johnson and Muddy Waters, and therefore by extension to future generations of blues-based rockers, Eddie "Son" House, Jr., was born on March 21, 1902, near the village of Lyon, Mississippi, about two miles from Clarksdale. He began preaching at age fifteen, and by twenty was pastor of a small Baptist church until an affair with an older woman ended his tenure. He took up the guitar in his twenties, and gained a local reputation. In 1928 he shot and killed a man at a drunken house party (acting in self-defense, he said), and was sentenced to fifteen years for manslaughter at the state penal farm at Parchman; after a little less than two years a judge reexamined his case and had him released. Seizing the opportunity, in May 1930 he accompanied the already legendary Charley Patton and two other Delta blues artists to Grafton, Wisconsin, for a remarkable recording session for the tiny Paramount label. The handful of performances he recorded that day were powerful, but with the label's minimal distribution sold poorly. He returned home to work in a variety of jobs (including tractor operator, railroad porter, and cotton picker) and perform at juke joints and house parties. Eleven years later Alan Lomax sought him out for Library of Congress field recordings that made an impression on all who heard them. However, his original Paramount recordings had been heard by very few postwar collectors until Pete Whelan and Bill Givens reissued both parts of *My Black Mama* on their Origin Jazz Library LP *Really! The Country Blues* (one of the earliest blues reissue compilations following Columbia's landmark Robert Johnson LP) in 1963.[90] His rediscovery in the folk revival resulted in some exceptional new recordings.

Peter Welding was among many listeners in awe of House's 1960s performances, declaring that he "summons up an almost unbelievable force and intensity." Although he was no guitar virtuoso, his playing "is profoundly moving, passionate and intense . . . House's rhythms throb with a tense emotionality that threatens to swallow up the words he sings." As for his singing, Welding described the "near-brutal force and raw power" of his voice. The interaction of his voice and guitar generated a suspense that was "simply astonishing," one of the most "unforgettable musical experiences in the world today."[91] Ted Gioia: "His throbbing, spasmodic guitar sound is the stuff of legend. Did a guitarist ever do more with less?"[92]

My Black Mama, which he learned from his musical mentor James McCoy, is a song House would perform live with different verses for different occasions. It was a favorite of Robert Johnson, who would incorporate parts of it (along with House's *Walkin' the Blues*) for his own *Walkin' Blues*. House's slashing slide guitar style influenced the eager student Johnson. One of its lines would gain a special measure of fame when Kokomo Arnold borrowed it a few years later for *Milk Cow Blues*: "If you see my milk cow, tell her to hurry home / I ain't had no milk since that cow been gone." The slow, fervent performance runs over six minutes and 20 seconds across both sides of the Paramount 78. Greil Marcus remarks that the song ends "almost mystically"; the woman who was in trouble in Part 1 is dead in Part 2, as he's summoned to see her body. "When he sings, in his last verse, his deep voice seemingly deepening with every syllable, 'I fold my arms and walked away,' you can feel him walk off the earth."

Memories of You (1930)—Louis Armstrong & His Sebastian New Cotton Club Orchestra (written by Eubie Blake & Noble Sissle)
Okeh 41463
Recorded in Los Angeles on Oct. 16, 1930 (*NPR-300, Trad-#131, Jazz-#134*)

Louis Armstrong made his first trip to California in late summer 1930, as he was booked into Frank Sebastian's Cotton Club in Culver City for a seven-month engagement. For most of the gig, he fronted Leon Elkins' band (soon taken over by Les Hite), featuring a young drummer and occasional pianist named Lionel Hampton. One week after Armstrong waxed his classic rendition of *Body and Soul* in October, he returned to the studio to cut a song from the Eubie Blake–Noble Sissle hit score for the musical *Blackbirds of 1930*. *Memories of You* became

---

90. Simon Napier in the August 1964 *Blues Unlimited* discussed the sensation provided by the reissue of *My Black Mama*; even Samuel Charters in his influential *The Country Blues* had only briefly acknowledged House, until Whelan brought the original recordings to his attention.

91. Welding in February 1966 *Blues Unlimited*.
92. *Delta Blues*, p. 99.

one of his most fondly-remembered ballad performances, with considerable help from the then-unknown Hampton.

It seems that Armstrong happened to spot a vibraphone in the corner of the studio (which was primarily used by the National Broadcasting Company) and pulled it out. NBC had been using it simply to play the three notes symbolizing the radio network, and as chimes serving as an intermission signal. The xylophone-like instrument (distinguishing itself by the vibrato it produced by rotating electrically operated fans at the upper ends of the resonator tubes) had only been around for about a decade, and was unknown to jazz. Hampton recalled in his autobiography that as the musicians waited while technicians fixed some malfunctioning equipment, Armstrong asked Hamp if he could play the instrument. "Sure," he replied with youthful bravado, although he had never tried before. They plugged in the vibes, and Hampton utilized the mallets to reproduce Satch's solo on *Cornet Chop Suey*. Delighted, Armstrong declared, "Come on, we're going to put this on a record."[93]

And so it was that in the first recorded vibe solo in jazz history, Hampton provided a gorgeous, shimmering introduction that offered a perfect complement to Armstrong's warm, wistful vocal and trumpet soloing. (Les Hite's alto sax is also prominent.) After the leader's concluding horn lines, the vibes return to get the last "word." Incidentally, according to Richard Hadlock, the melody borrows a few phrases from the 1929 Fats Waller–Andy Razaf song *Black and Blue* (made famous on record by Armstrong) with the help of Razaf himself.[94] Benny Goodman, Rosemary Clooney, and Frank Sinatra were just two of the many artists who later rendered wonderful versions of the song, but *Memories of You* will always belong to Satch and Hamp.

One Step d'Oberlin (1930)—Amédé Ardoin & Dennis McGee
Brunswick 495
Recorded in New Orleans on Nov. 20, 1930 (*World-#82*)

After two-and-a-half years in which commercial recordings of French Cajun music brought the previously strictly local folk music of south Louisiana to the attention of a wider audience, the first era of Cajun recording came to a conclusion—but a glorious one—with this session by the genre's greatest team, black accordionist/singer Amédé Ardoin and white fiddler Dennis McGee. After this date, there would be no further Cajun recordings until the same duo waxed new sides for Bluebird on August 8, 1934.[95]

Ardoin was the towering giant of early Cajun music, a passionate vocalist, powerful accordionist, and also a composer; *One Step d'Oberlin* is one of his finest originals. Barry Jean Ancelet calls it "an exceptional example of virtuosity in singing, in timing and improvisation." While the main focus is on Ardoin, McGee's fiddling "holds the song together."[96] Jared Snyder notes that while McGee basses a single chord, Ardoin "layers triplets and thickly syncopated runs, making extensive use of the technique of bouncing from low to high notes."[97] Ryan Andre Brasseaux: "Although the lore surrounding Ardoin's life and career is as grandiose as legends cloaking the escapades of such seminal American musical figures as Buddy Bolden and Robert Johnson, Ardoin's influence on Cajun music cannot be overstated . . . [He] formulated the equation for all of the accordion-based Cajun arrangements that would follow."[98]

Basin Street Blues (1931)—Charleston Chasers (written by Spencer Williams)
Columbia 2415 (billed as by "Charleston Chasers under the Direction of Bennie Goodman")
Recorded Feb. 9, 1931; Reached #14 in *Pop Memories*

The "Charleston Chasers" is one of several noms de plume that were adopted by jazz studio groups of constantly shifting memberships during the 1920s and early 1930s; Red Nichols and Miff Mole recorded a number of 78s under the name from 1925–1929. The most acclaimed record of all under the Chasers banner was the very last one of the era: this thrilling all-star aggregation led by a young Benny Goodman.

Basin Street Blues was one of the great jazz standards of the 1920s, a warm tribute to the music and spirit of New Orleans. Composer Spencer Williams (born in New Orleans on October 14, 1889) also has such enduring songs as *I Ain't Got Nobody, Royal Garden Blues*, and *I've Found a New Baby* to his credit. It was introduced on record by the December 4, 1928, performance by Louis Armstrong's ensemble with Earl Hines; Armstrong would later sing it in three films. Clarinetist Benny Goodman, all of twenty-one years old, was playing in the Broadway pit orchestra for the George & Ira Gershwin musical *Girl Crazy* when he led the Chasers session,

---

93. Hampton, *Hamp: An Autobiography*, p. 37–38.
94. *Jazz Masters of the '20s*, p. 157.
95. During 1929 alone, record companies produced 176 sides of Cajun music, a figure that plummeted to just thirty-two in 1930. Small accordion-driven dance bands represent an overwhelming 62 percent (174 recordings) of the instrumental arrangements during the early commercial era of 1928–1934, according to Ryan Andre Brasseaux (*Cajun Breakdown*, p. 56–58).
96. *The Makers of Cajun Music*, p. 23.
97. Liner notes to Arhoolie compilation of Ardoin recordings, *I'm Never Comin' Back*. Brunswick made the November 19 and 20 recordings on inferior equipment resulting in overmodulation and distortion, but the performances still shine through. The company rented out a floor of New Orleans' Roosevelt Hotel for their portable studio.
98. Brasseaux, *Cajun Breakdown: The Emergence of an American-Made Music*, p. 83.

a date he recalled fondly as the first time "I put across something like a style of my own." He recruited some of the same musicians (associated with Red Nichols) with whom he'd played on recent sessions for the Melotone label, including trombonist Glenn Miller, Charlie Teagarden on trumpet, and drummer Gene Krupa. A crucial addition was young trombone virtuoso and Charlie's brother Jack Teagarden. Miller biographer George T. Simon noted that this is one of eighteen sides Glenn cut for Goodman in 1931 alone;[99] the two men had also played together with Ben Pollack's band (1926–1928), and were good friends.

For *Basin Street Blues*, as related by Ross Firestone, Miller worked out a new arrangement and, with Jack's assistance, added lyrics and a verse ("Won't you come along with me / To the Mississippi . . .") that would quickly become standard parts of the song. Jack Teagarden "was in inspired form that day and dominates the proceedings" with a wonderful vocal and two splendid solos; Goodman also gave himself two solos, including a passionate full-chorus blues solo with a growl.[100] In years to come the song would become indelibly associated with Teagarden, who would probably perform it thousands of times (including more than a dozen recorded versions)—never better than on this occasion. Richard Sudhalter also calls attention to Dick McDonough's imaginative guitar work here, using an adapted version of the drummer's accented "press roll" behind Teagarden's trombone.[101] The flip side of the 78, quite appropriately, was *Beale Street Blues*, also sung by Teagarden. "A really good record," Goodman later said with pride.

(Other personnel: Charlie Teagarden on trumpet; Sid Stoneburn on alto sax; Larry Binyon on tenor sax; Arthur Schutt on piano; Harry Goodman on string bass)

Pidkamecka Kolomyjka (1931)—Josef Pizio
Columbia 27297-F
Recorded Sept. 24, 1931

Some of the most remarkable violinists making non-classical recordings during the 1920s and 1930s could be found on the rosters of Victor's and Columbia's catalogs designed for east European ethnic audiences in U.S. urban markets, and shining most brightly in that genre were artists who emigrated from Ukraine. Pawlo Humeniuk was the reigning superstar among Ukrainian fiddlers recording in America, and a brilliantly talented counterpart was Josef Pizio, who came to the U.S. shortly before World War I. He had only two sessions

for Columbia (the other in 1933), and the standout of the first date was the excitingly uptempo dance number *Pidkamecka Kolomyjka*. Dick Spottswood, author of a massive multi-volume discography of ethnic recordings in the U.S., notes that unlike Humeniuk, Pizio didn't read music, so he relied upon superbly executed improvisations, this one in the centuries-old Ukrainian kolomyika form, a simple structure with "endless possibilities" for embellishment (he cites *Yankee Doodle* as an American equivalent of the kolomyika). Pizio is accompanied by two additional violins and string bass, and we hear occasional bird whistles and yelps as added touches; the record remained in print for nearly two decades.[102] This performance was included by Spottswood on Volume 5 ("Dance Music: Ragtime, Jazz, & More") of the Library of Congress Bicentennial compilation *Folk Music in America*, and also on his *Ukrainian Village Music* CD for Arhoolie. "Pizio's compelling fiddle sound is one of the most dynamic on record."

Dinah (1931)—Bing Crosby & the Mills Brothers
(music by Harry Akst, lyrics by Sam Lewis & Joe Young)
Brunswick 6240
Recorded Dec. 16, 1931; *Pop Memories* debut Jan. 9, 1932 (#1 for 2 weeks)

It is often forgotten that during his early years before he became America's most popular crooner, Bing Crosby was a masterful jazz singer with few early peers outside of Louis Armstrong and Connee Boswell, and perhaps no recording better displays this quality than his teaming with the Mills Brothers on *Dinah*. When both Bing and the brothers (Herbert, Harry, John, and Donald Mills) were booked for three weeks at Brooklyn's Paramount Theatre in late summer 1931, they got to know one another, and after the shows they would jam together. Crosby was delighted by the group's gift for using their voices to mimic an entire orchestra.[103] Although both Crosby and the Millses participated in an October two-sided record, *Gems from "George White's Scandals,"* along with the Boswell Sisters, the arrangement allowed no interaction between Bing and the brothers, and biographer Gary Giddins writes that "Bing was determined to rectify that."

99. *Glenn Miller and His Orchestra*, p. 56, 58. Goodman was in heavy demand for session work at Paramount Studios on Long Island, and he regularly recommended Miller.
100. *Swing, Swing, Swing*, p. 71.
101. *Lost Chords*, p. 543.
102. One of the driving forces for the dissemination of ethnic music in America during this period was the rapid expansion of radio stations that offered programming in foreign languages. Starting in 1927, an increasing number of stations—particularly in cities with large ethnic populations such as New York, Cleveland, and Philadelphia, but also elsewhere—provided daily programs in Italian, German, Yiddish, Polish, Ukrainian, Lithuanian, and more. Such stations became even more important when the record industry collapsed in 1930–1933. (See Greene, *A Passion for Polka*, p. 180–83.)
103. The Millses (born in Piqua, Ohio) had perfected their techniques on Cincinnati radio in the late 1920s, and rocked the jazz and pop worlds with their October 1931 recordings of *Tiger Rag* and *Nobody's Sweetheart*.

Crosby made a point of being at the Brunswick studios during the Mills Brothers' next scheduled session two months later, and dropped in for this performance. They worked out a routine on *Dinah*, which was associated with Ethel Waters through her classic October 1925 recording.[104] Bing scats convincingly and swingingly around the Millses (accompanied by bandleader Bennie Kreuger's sidemen), and there's the unmistakable feeling that these guys are really having fun as they rip through this loose-limbed rendition of one of the 1920s' favorite standards.[105] After the Millses sing a unison double-time chorus, Donald Mills briefly scats and then Bing unleashes a 16-bar improvisation. He would never again sound quite so musically liberated as he does here. Nat Hentoff remarks that this performance "is a short course on the essentials of the jazz vocal.[106] The instrumental phrasing, the hot scat singing over the flowing rhythm section that was the Mills Brothers; and the last chorus, on which Bing sounds like a joyful, driving cornet."[107] "Dinah, is there anyone finer . . ."

Moten Swing (1932)—Bennie Moten's Kansas City Orchestra (written by Buster Moten & Bennie Moten)
Victor 23384
Recorded Dec. 13, 1932 (*Jazz-#145, SJ*)

For most of the decade following its 1923 recording debut, Bennie Moten's orchestra was one of the most popular in the Midwest, solid record sellers and a hot live attraction. But the Depression devastated its audience, and the December 13, 1932, session at Victor's Camden, New Jersey, studio was to be its last. It would also produce the band's greatest recording, *Moten Swing*.

Born on November 13, 1894, in Kansas City, Bennie Moten played piano in local bands before forming his band in the early 1920s. Kansas City was a thriving hotbed of jazz, aided by the city's free and easy style (its Pendergast machine–protected gambling revenues averaged around $100 million a year during the 1920s) and its musical tradition as one of the key centers for ragtime.[108] Moten's would be the first significant jazz band hailing from Kansas City, soon to be rivaled only by Walter Page's Blue Devils. By the end of the decade most of Page's stars had switched over to Moten, including Count Basie, Eddie Durham, Hot Lips Page, and Jimmy Rushing. But just as it was becoming a greater

musical powerhouse than ever, the ruined economy sent the band's fortunes going in the same direction as its biggest 1920s hit: *South*.

Martin Williams described the desperate circumstances of that day, as the men of the Moten band "were demoralized, literally hungry," and the marathon session was to be its final act. As the musicians didn't have any money, someone got them a rabbit and four loaves of bread, and (clarinet and alto sax soloist Eddie Barefield recalled) "we cooked rabbit stew right on a pool table. That kept us from starving, and then we went on to make the records." Afterward, they got back on a rickety old bus and returned to Kansas City. Yet, writes Williams, "there is nothing either in the music or in the frequently joyous way it's played . . . to indicate that the band was in such straits at the time."

Moten Swing, declared Williams, showcased "a large jazz orchestra which could swing cleanly and precisely according to the manner of Louis Armstrong—a group which had grasped his innovative ideas of jazz rhythm and had realized and developed them in an ensemble style." He praises the song's "rather sophisticated chord structure"—a series of variations based on the chords of the 1930 pop hit *You're Driving Me Crazy* (particularly as recorded that year by Louis Armstrong)—and Count Basie's vigorous Fats Waller–style piano solo.[109] Hot Lips Page's trumpet soloing is another standout feature. Arranger Eddie Durham, notes Allen Lowe, was "one of the first to successfully conceptualize the large jazz band as a rhythmically streamlined entity, to employ the smooth four-beat flow of Southwestern swing as a function of orchestration as well as of basic ensemble swing."[110] Less than three years after his swan song and crowning achievement, Bennie Moten died in 1935, and his former sidemen would form the core of the mighty Basie band. *Moten Swing* was included on both the *Smithsonian Collection of Classic Jazz* and the Smithsonian's *Big Band Jazz* compilation.

Hula Girl (1934)—Sol Hoopii & His Novelty Quartet
Brunswick 6768
Recorded c. Jan.–Feb. 1934

For most of the first thirty-plus years of the twentieth century, the worldwide standard setters when it came to steel guitar were the instrumental masters of the Hawaiian islands. Virtually all of Western Swing's first generation of great steel guitarists in the 1930s (most notably Bob Dunn from Milton Brown's Musical Brownies and Leon McAuliffe of Bob Wills' Texas Playboys) fell in love with the instrument through exposure to Hawaiian

104. Thomas Hischak (*Tin Pan Alley Song Encyclopedia*, p. 84) calls it "arguably the most famous song to come from a nightclub show," originally written for the floorshow *Plantation Revue* where Waters introduced it.

105. The tune was selected as one of Tin Pan Alley's ten greatest songs in a February 1937 *Down Beat* poll of forty musicians including Louis Armstrong and Duke Ellington.

106. Crosby would also sing *Dinah* on screen in *The Big Broadcast* of 1932.

107. Hentoff, *Listen to the Stories*, p. 59.

108. See *Kansas City and All That's Jazz*, p. 3, 25–29.

109. Liner notes, RCA Victor compilation of Bennie Moten, reprinted in notes to *Smithsonian Collection of Classic Jazz* (1973, p. 23).

110. *American Pop from Minstrel to Mojo*, p. 135.

music. There were a number of Hawaiian steel guitar virtuosos on record during those early years, but none achieved greater fame and more enduring admiration than Sol Hoopii.

By most accounts, in 1885 an eleven-year-old boy named Joseph Kekuku on the North Shore of Oahu, then a student at the Kamehameha School, was experimenting with his traditional guitar when he discovered that by sliding certain objects (such as a hair comb or a steel cylinder) across the strings, his guitar began to produce a distinctively different, "sweet" sound. He soon refined the technique by using a heavy metal bar, fingerpicks, and raised action of the strings. Kekuku's innovation quickly spread through Hawaiian schools, and by 1905 (writes Bob Brozman) "the first generation of Hawaiian steel guitarists was performing, touring, and recording."[111] Frank Ferera was the most acclaimed of the early guitar greats, recording over 1,000 sides from 1912 to 1931.

Born in 1902 in Honolulu, Sol Hoopii (pronounced "Ho-oh-pee-ee") played the ukulele as a child, and by his teen years was winning a local reputation on Hawaiian steel guitar. In 1919 he and two friends stowed away aboard an ocean liner, and made such an impression on passengers with their music that a collection was taken up to pay their fares. After arriving in San Francisco, he played in clubs, moved to Los Angeles, and made his first recordings for a small label in 1925. His broader fame began with recordings for Columbia starting two years later (fronting his "Novelty Trio," including another soon-to-be-famous guitarist, Lani McIntyre). From very early his lead soloing showed great comfort with jazz and blues stylings, although most of the trio's repertoire was pop-oriented material in a Hawaiian or pseudo-Hawaiian mode. Switching to Brunswick in 1933, he added a bassist for quartet performances, and Brozman remarks that his playing (on the National brand of Hawaiian steel) "reached new heights of technical bravado and imagination, with very complex chordal and phrasing ideas."[112] Hoopii's fame also led to movie appearances as both musician and actor.

Hula Girl is an outstanding representation of his style, a vigorous uptempo number with mostly English vocal (singing feather-light lyrics), but the overwhelming emphasis is on his wonderfully propulsive, jazz-tinged soloing, accompanied by ukulele, rhythm guitar, and bass. By 1935 Hoopii had switched permanently from acoustic to electric lap steel guitar, and continued recording regularly into 1938, when he became a born-again Christian. After nearly a decade away from the studio, he made some additional recordings (along with preaching) until his death in 1953. At his best during those early years, writes J. Poet, the Hoopii combos "sounded like a stripped-down Hawaiian version of the Quintette of the Hot Club of France."[113]

St. Louis Blues (1935)—Milton Brown & His Brownies
Decca 5070
Recorded in Chicago on Jan. 27, 1935 (*SC*)

The co-creator (with Bob Wills) of that tasty fusion of hillbilly music and jazz known as Western swing, Milton Brown was born on September 8, 1903, in Stephenville, Texas, southwest of Fort Worth. Singer Brown and fiddler Wills worked together in a medicine show trio in 1930, began performing on radio as the Wills Fiddle Band, and both became founding members of the Light Crust Doughboys in early 1931, performing daily on local radio, soon branching out to become syndicated statewide. Brown struck out on his own late the following year to form his Musical Brownies (often shortened on later records to just the Brownies), and began recording in April 1934. By the time Wills launched his own bandleading career on record with the Texas Playboys in September 1935, the basic parameters of Western swing—combining the fiddles and other instrumentation of country music into a larger ensemble and a repertoire that included heavy doses of blues and pop—had been established by the Brownies; Wills would take that model still further. Brown biographer Cary Ginell notes that during the early years of Western swing, the genre "bore little similarity to country music"; the Brownies "would have felt more comfortable" playing alongside the Quintette of the Hot Club of France than on the stage of the Grand Ole Opry.[114] "With his husky, virile voice, Milton Brown set a standard which other Western swing vocalists found difficult to equal," writes Bill Malone.[115]

This is the best of all country versions of the W. C. Handy blues classic, a condensed three-minute version of an arrangement so popular that the band played it twice each Saturday night at the Crystal Springs ballroom.[116] It features Brown's vocal, jazz-flavored piano by Fred "Papa" Calhoun (the first pianist to play professionally with a C&W band), Cecil Brower on fiddle (playing in "slow-drag" tempo), and the "revolutionary" horn-like steel guitar sound of Bob Dunn, just months after he became the first country guitarist to electrify the instru-

---

111. Annotation, Rounder album *Vintage Hawaiian Music: Steel Guitar Masters, 1928–1934*.

112. Liner notes, Rounder's *Sol Hoopii: Master of the Hawaiian Guitar*, Vol. 2.

113. *MusicHound World*, p. 323.

114. *The Founding of Western Swing*, p. xxii.

115. *Country Music, U.S.A.*, p. 163. Kevin Reed Coffey, in the *Journal of Country Music*, Vol. 17 #1 (1994), p. 56–60: "His rhythm, tone, and lack of stylistic affectation made Milton Brown a startlingly modern singer in 1935." Even from the perspective of six decades later, he "still sounds great."

116. Ginell, *The Founding of Western Swing*, p. 131.

ment.[117] [118] Dunn (born February 5, 1908, near Braggs, Oklahoma), who was in his first month of recording with Brown, is called by Nick Tosches "the lord of the steel guitar. In the 1930s, he wrought a music full of electric wonders . . . Three years before Django Reinhardt made his first records, Dunn had a style as subtle and involved as Reinhardt's would be, but Dunn had a daring, febrile energy" that virtually no one else could comprehend.[119] Brown sings an entirely different set of lyrics from W. C. Handy's aside from the final verse. This performance is from the band's first session for Decca after recording for Bluebird in 1934. Ginell with Roy Lee Brown chronicled the artist in the oral history *Milton Brown and the Founding of Western Swing.*

(Additional personnel: Ocie Stockard on tenor banjo; Derwood Brown on guitar; Wanna Coffman on string bass)

After You've Gone (1935)—Benny Goodman Trio
Victor 25115
Recorded July 13, 1935

The first recordings of the Benny Goodman Trio teaming the clarinetist with Teddy Wilson on piano and his regular drummer Gene Krupa made jazz history, with two classic performances on one 78: *Body and Soul* and *After You've Gone.* "With Krupa's drums as the only other instrument, Benny and Teddy work together . . . alternating solos, splitting choruses, interweaving phrases, exchanging breaks, clearly having a wonderful time with each other as they negotiate the routines they worked out in the studio to give shape to their ongoing dialogue," writes Goodman biographer Ross Firestone.[120]

The trio setting had some precedents in jazz before 1935, but not many. Goodman himself had recorded a pair of trio sides in 1928, and Jelly Roll Morton and Johnny Dodds had recorded in duets and trios with piano and clarinet leading one or two rhythm instruments. But it was nonetheless a gamble for a musician who in mid-1935 was not yet an established star; his first big network radio showcase, *Let's Dance,* had lasted twenty-six weeks before being dropped in May 1935. The fact that he had such a brilliantly gifted partner as Wilson (who also made the recording debut of his own orchestra that same month) to share the melodic burden, cutting

loose on a beloved 1919 pop standard, made all the difference.[121]

I Want to Be a Cowboy's Sweetheart (1935)—Patsy Montana & the Prairie Ramblers
Vocalion 03010
Recorded Aug. 16, 1935; reissued on Columbia 37602 in June 1947 (*NPR-300, GHF, HBN-#31, C&W-#37, SC*)

Country music was a man's world during the 1920s and early 1930s. Sara and Maybelle Carter defined the sound of the Carter Family, and female artists were occasionally heard on record, but no female headliner had scored a major country hit until this Patsy Montana classic.[122] Born Ruby Blevins on October 30, 1914, in Hot Springs, Arkansas, she learned to yodel (inspired by Jimmie Rodgers) and play several instruments as a child. After moving to California in 1930, she won a talent contest and began appearing on local radio as "Ruby Blevins, the Yodeling Cowgirl from San Antone." Performing on the air with Stuart Hamblen as part of the Montana Cowgirls, she had the opportunity to record four songs for Victor in November 1932 at a Jimmie Davis session, and took the name Patsy Montana (the other reason for the stage name is that she had toured with a troupe led by rodeo cowboy performer Montie Montana). In 1933 she became a regular on the *National Barn Dance* broadcast out of WLS Chicago, with the Prairie Ramblers (featuring fiddler Tex Atchison) as her backup band. Even though times were still tough for the record industry at mid-decade, the American Record Company's Art Satherley believed in her talent, and provided the opportunity for the landmark session.

Patsy made an unissued trial recording of *I Want to Be a Cowboy's Sweetheart* in February 1935; the keeper came six months later. Hamblen's popular *Texas Plains* had become her signature song as *Montana Plains,* which she recorded with the Prairie Ramblers for Bluebird on December 6, 1933.[123] Then she adapted it with new lyrics for *Cowboy's Sweetheart,* coupled with a jaunty polka rhythm (which helped make the record popular in northern cities). David Cantwell, ranking it #31 in *Heartaches By the Number,* writes that the performance demonstrated a feisty independence not typically seen in women of the time, "In the first verse she says she wants to be a

117. Dunn admired jazzman Jack Teagarden, and modeled his steel guitar improvisations on Tea's trombone. (Ginell, *The Founding of Western Swing,* p. 112.)

118. In addition to the historic roles of Dunn and Calhoun, Brown's other contributions to the evolution of Western swing included the introduction to this genre of the slapped bass and the use of twin fiddles.

119. *Country: The Twisted Roots of Rock 'n' Roll,* p. 180–81.

120. Firestone, *Swing, Swing, Swing,* p. 139. "The swing addicts will go 'cuh-razy'" for this pairing, declared the September 4, 1935, *Variety,* calling it an "ultra-modern" recording.

121. Goodman years later remarked of this performance to George Simon: "I wonder how many musicians could do it today. It's just about impossible unless you can find a pianist with a left hand like Teddy's and a drummer with taste like Gene's."

122. Robert Coltman, in his article for Winter 1978 *J.E.M.F. Quarterly,* found that only three percent of recorded country music singers from 1922–1942 were women.

123. Their initial attempt at *Montana Plains* was rejected by Victor a year earlier (November 4, 1932).

cowboy's sweetheart, but she proceeds to sing longingly and at length about her heart's real desires: roping and riding on the plains, hearing the coyote's howl, watching the setting Western sun . . . What Patsy really wants is to *be* a cowboy. Free and self-sufficient, unbound." When she unleashes her exuberant Jimmie Rodgers–influenced yodels, she indeed sounds totally free.[124] Patsy went on to make many more recordings, and was featured in the 1939 Gene Autry movie *Colorado Sunset*. In 1966 she made an album for Starday, *Cowboy's Sweetheart*, with Waylon Jennings on lead guitar, reviving her most famous song as a "honky-tonk yodel."

Robert K. Oermann and Mary A. Bufwack: "In her songs and stage presence, she rewrote the myth of the American cowboy to include women, providing a new option for women country singers, and popularizing an innovative, independent female image." Musically, the performance "appealed to the dance spirit that was sweeping the country" following the December 1933 repeal of Prohibition. Lyrically, the song is "a story of freedom and companionship which is at once down to earth and independent."[125]

El Tren (1937)—Mariachi Vargas de Tecalitlan
Peerless 1113
Recorded in Mexico City in 1937

The tradition of mariachi bands in Mexico dates back to at least the 1840s in the region surrounding Tecalitlan (a small city and municipality in the state of Jalisco in central-western Mexico), typically consisting of violin, harp, and *guitarra de golpe* (a five-string guitar variant).[126] The most famous of all early Mexican mariachis, Mariachi Vargas, was formed in Tecalitlan in 1897 with that same instrumentation by Don Gaspar Vargas, a master of the guitarra (or mariachera). As detailed by Jonathan Clark, Silvestre Vargas joined his father's group as a second violinist in 1921. Silvestre took over leadership of the combo in 1932, and soon recruited as new members the Quintero brothers, Rafael on violin and Jeronimo on guitar. When violinist Santiago Torres joined in 1933, bringing the membership to eight, and Trinidad Olivera switched from violin to *guitarron* (a variety of acoustic bass guitar), the classic lineup of Mariachi Vargas was complete. The group began winning Mexico City mariachi contests in 1934, and then was hired as the official mariachi of the Mexico City Police Department, providing entertainment in the city's

parks and gardens. Appearing in the 1937 film *Asi es Mi Tierra*—the first of some 200 motion pictures in which they eventually turned up—coincided with their first commercial recordings that year.

El Tren, one of its first recordings for the small Peerless company (before the band began a long-term association with RCA Victor Mexicana), is also perhaps its most celebrated performance, lovingly imitating through the musicians' instruments the whistles, rumbling, and chugging of a steam locomotive journey, from the conductor's announcement at the outset and slowly gathering speed while pulling away from the station until finally reaching the destination. The brisk tempo is driven by the vigorous front line of fiddlers. The vocals are by Gaspar Vargas and Rafael Quintero, with a fantasy vision of a train that "carries men across the ocean." While other mariachis came and went over the years, Mariachi Vargas survived to become a national institution (with evolving membership)—remaining a string band at heart even after adding the now-standard trumpet in 1941—and reached a new American audience in 1988 joining Linda Ronstadt for her album *Canciones de mi Padre*. *El Tren* is included on the 1992 Arhoolie CD *Mariachi Vargas de Tecalitlan: Their First Recordings, 1937–1947*.

The Commission's Report (1938)—Atilla the Hun
Decca 17350[127]
Recorded Feb. 26, 1938

Although it was little noted outside the West Indies, one of the most tumultuous political events on the Caribbean island colony of Trinidad in the 1930s was a 1937 oil field strike that thrust into a glaring spotlight the deep divisions between the people and the government, against the background of the Depression. As documented by musicologist Dick Spottswood, the event and its aftermath inspired a remarkable flurry of calypso recordings that traced this history, and demonstrated the capacity of popular music to properly capture it. One of the finest in this group of recordings was this performance by the artist known as Atilla the Hun.

Raymond Quevedo, aka Atilla, was born (of half-Venezuelan ancestry) on March 24, 1892, in Trinidad, began performing in 1911, and first achieved prominence in 1926. Virtually all calypsonians adopt colorful stage names, and Quevedo fashioned himself after the warrior who led an army of Barbarians in attacks on the Roman Empire in the fifth century. (The warrior's name was spelled "Attila," but Quevedo's was spelled as seen here.) This was appropriate, remarked Hollis Urban Liverpool in *Kaisonians to Remember* ("kaiso" being the original

---

124. *Heartaches By the Number*, p. 19–20.
125. Patsy Montana feature, *Journal of Country Music*, Vol. 8 #3 (1981).
126. The earliest significant mariachi recordings were made in 1908–1909, when all three major U.S. companies—Victor, Columbia, and Edison—recorded the Cuarteto Coculense in Mexico; see Jonathan Clark's liner notes for that group's Arhoolie compilation.

127. On most of his 1937–1941 records he was billed simply as "The Atilla."

name for calypso), because he "became the scourge of many calypsonians" as he "attacked them mercilessly" in the "war" and "picong" songs that constituted Trinidad's early version of rap music's battles.[128] The principles of picong and rap wars were much the same, in each case depending on the ability to create and perform improvised pieces seeking to crush musical rivals with often savage satirical wit. Atilla quickly established himself as one of the most ingenious and charismatic of the island's performers, and in 1930 won the first open competition held at the calypso tents. He began his prolific recording career four years later.

After several years of growing worker unrest (symbolized by a 1934 hunger march), labor activists organized a sit-down strike of oil workers in June 1937, in defiance of colonial law. Leading the campaign was Grenadian-born Tubal Uriah "Buzz" Butler, who had worked in Trinidad oil fields since 1921. A pro-labor rally led to a police crackdown and rioting; Butler went into hiding until he was promised the opportunity to testify at hearings of the Forster Commission, established by the Crown to investigate the crisis. Butler was found guilty of sedition and sentenced to two years in prison. When he returned in 1939 to resume his activism, wartime regulations led to a more prolonged imprisonment. Nevertheless, his impact was considerable on Trinidad's road to independence.[129]

All calypsos during this period had to go through colonial government censors, and although some of the songs inspired by the events of 1937 were either banned or toned down, the records surviving the process constitute a fascinating body of work. In songs such as *The Strike* and *Where Was Butler?* Atilla traced the sequence of events; his piece *The Governor's Resignation* lamented the forced departure of Sir Murchison Fletcher as governor of Trinidad when British authorities found him too sympathetic to worker grievances. *The Commission's Report* remarks that the Forster Commission criticized British authorities for inciting unrest. At the same time Atilla gently attacks the report for also blaming Butler while condoning the police "shooting people down." Read through its pages, he sings, and "there is no mention of capitalistic oppression." Despite its innocuous title, Spottswood notes that this was considered an "incendiary" record that was banned on the island (although commercially released in the U.S.), "perhaps because it

comes closer than any of the other 1938 Butler songs to reflecting the sense of anger and frustration felt by a major portion of the working population." According to Atilla, authorities also blocked him from receiving any royalties for the song. It exemplifies Errol Hill's statement that Atilla, more than any other artist, "held fast to the ancient role of the calypso as the poor man's newspaper and the voice of the people."[130]

Calypsonians had been prominent figures in the island's politics for years, but Quevedo was the first calypso artist to hold public office, elected to the Port-of-Spain City Council in 1946, and then to the Legislative Council of Trinidad and Tobago four years later, he also became one of the foremost historians of the music he performed; his book *Atilla's Kaiso* (written with John La Rose) was published in 1983, twenty-one years after his death.

Beer Barrel Polka (1939)—(Will) Glahe Musette Orchestra

Victor V-710

Recorded in Germany in late 1935/early 1936; *Billboard* debut May 6, 1939 (4 weeks at #1)[131] [132] (*World-#40*)

Originating as a Czech peasant dance developed in Eastern Bohemia and introduced into the ballrooms of Prague in 1835,[133] polka music had been a presence on commercial recordings virtually since the dawn of the recording industry.[134] It became more significant in the last half of the 1920s as major companies like Victor and Columbia greatly expanded their recordings of ethnic music. But in the United States it was marketed overwhelmingly to immigrants from Poland, Germany, Czechoslovakia, and other European countries. (Polkas also became a major part of Mexican-American combos' repertoire on record from the 1920s onward.) Perhaps the best-known early artists recording polka were Chicago's Polish-American fiddler Franciszek (Frank) Dukla, who

128. Liverpool, p. 41 (originally published under the title: *Kaisonians to Remember*).

129. Spottswood, in liner notes for the Arhoolie album *Calypsos from Trinidad: Politics, Intrigue, and Violence in the 1930s*, remarked that Butler's work "helped to develop a new sense of worth and power among the disenfranchised working classes of Trinidad and Tobago and channeled sentiments which were to coalesce into a successful movement toward independence from England in 1962." This song and the other calypsos surrounding the oil strike are also discussed in Donald R. Hill's *Calypso Calaloo*, p. 197–202.

130. Hill, Foreward to *Atilla's Kaiso.*

131. #1 (4 weeks) on *Billboard*'s jukebox chart, and the year's official #1 hit on that chart, it was also a huge sheet music seller (in the Top Three for fifteen weeks), and was declared Victor's #1 biggest seller of 1939 in the January 6, 1940, issue. Describing the record's success, the July 5, 1939, *Radio & Television News* remarked: "Today's polka craze is unique in the annals of . . . popular music favorites in that radio played no part in its beginning. While the leading dance bands blanketed the airwaves with swing and 'sweet' music, coin-operated phonographs were sending the polka on its spectacular rise to fame."

132. Long after falling off the charts, the Glahe record was frequently reported to remain a big number on jukeboxes, including the *Billboard* issues of April 13, 1940 (still going strong in Kansas City), June 15 (in Chicago), and July 27, 1940 (Philadelphia).

133. *New Grove Dictionary of Music and Musicians*. Polkas were introduced as sheet music in 1837, and brought to Vienna by a Bohemian military band around the same time.

134. For example, Paul Charosh's discography of the Berliner company's disk records from 1892–1900 lists well over a dozen polka performances, and John Philip Sousa did numerous polkas for multiple labels from 1895 onward.

recorded from 1926–1929 (mainly Polish village-style music with polka elements), and Baca's Czech Orchestra, a family band based in Texas (the family patriarch formed the band in Fayetteville, Texas, by the 1870s) whose long recording career began in 1929. And then came *Beer Barrel Polka*, transforming a venerable ethnic tradition into a national craze.

Will Glahe, born on February 12, 1902, in Elberfeld, Germany, formed his own band in 1932, and quickly became one of the country's most popular accordionists and bandleaders. The explosion in popularity of jukeboxes from 1934 on, causing record companies to produce more dance-oriented music, expanded the potential market for polka. Also making the cultural atmosphere more receptive to the music were the numerous 1930s ethnic folk festivals, and the increasing number of radio stations airing ethnic music programs. When the Andrews Sisters scored a massive early-1938 hit with the Yiddish-derived *Bei Mir Bist Du Schoen*, it demonstrated that ethnic music could sell on a national scale. *Beer Barrel Polka* took things to a whole new level.

The melody began as a Czech tune called *Modranska Polka* written in either 1927 or 1929 by Jaromir Vejvoda, a young musician living just outside of Prague, and performed by his father's brass band. As outlined by Victor Greene, it became locally popular and was published in 1934 by a Prague publishing house, Hoffman and Widow. The publishers hired Vaclav Zeman to add lyrics, and it was issued under the revised title *Skoda Lasky* (Unrequited Love). It became popular in Europe under a variety of titles; in Germany, it was known as *Rosamunde* ("Pinkmouth," a German female nickname). Tin Pan Alley lyricist Lew Brown was struck by the tune, and teamed with Vladimir Tinn (real name Tetos Demetriades, a Victor Records staffer who later headed its International Division) to give it an English title and lyrics, as *Beer Barrel Polka*.[135]

Glahe and his small combo recorded it as an instrumental by early 1936 under that title. When RCA Victor decided to release the record in the U.S., everyone seemed to think that *Hot Pretzels* was the side with commercial potential. But in early 1939 jukebox operators discovered that it was the record's flip side that was generating ever-increasing plays, and that spring it basically took the country by storm. The Andrews Sisters (repeating their success with *Bei Mir*) recorded a cover version on May 3, 1939, that reportedly sold 350,000 copies by September. ("Jolly Jack" Robel cut an instrumental version for Decca about five weeks before the Andrews, also reported to have sold briskly.) However, some months after this record's release, Decca leader Jack Kapp imposed a ban on radio airplay of his company's releases by disc jockeys (out of the same self-destructive impulse that would lead to the musician union's subsequent recording ban), and *Billboard* suggested that the action was responsible for Glahe's version ultimately out-selling the Andrews' with total sales over 400,000.[136]

Dick Spottswood: "*Beer Barrel Polka* suited everybody's mood exactly. Not only was it possible to buy full-strength beer legally again, but more and more people had the means to do so. The tune was simple and catchy, and Glahe's recording of it was loud and forceful enough to be easily heard over the din in a noisy tavern. In popular locations the record had to be replaced frequently because copies rapidly wore out."[137]

The Glahe performance is simplicity itself, as the leader's accordion, accompanied by piano and electric steel guitar (in somewhat Hawaiian style) in the forefront, lay out the utterly infectious and danceable melody. Glahe went on to score several other U.S. chart hits, including *Woodpecker* (1940), *You Can't Be True, Dear* (1948), and finally a surprise Top 20 hit in 1957 with *Lichtensteiner Polka*. A *Billboard* poll of jukebox operators (in its January 22, 1949, Jukebox Supplement) ranked *Beer Barrel Polka* as the ninth most popular song of the previous decade.

Holy Babe (1939)—Kelly Pace & Group
Recorded in May 1939 for the Library of Congress at Cumins State Farm in Gould, Arkansas (*GOSP-#87*)

The first full-length recording of the Christmas standard we know best as *Children, Go Where I Send Thee* is a marvel of precision vocalizing—all the more remarkable for the fact that it was recorded in prison.[138] Kelly Pace leads a group consisting of Aaron Brown, Joe Green, Matthew Johnson, and Paul Hayes in a beautifully rendered, unaccompanied performance of a very intricate song that takes them through twelve stanzas, each stanza rolling back through the previous ones. Even though John Lomax used reel-to-reel tape which allowed for a longer recording time, the song still had to be broken up into two parts to get it all in. (The year 1942 has been given for this recording, but *Blues and Gospel Records, 1890–1943* reports that Cumins State Farm was not visited that year by Lomax.) In 1934, Pace had made an important early recording of *Rock Island Line* for Lomax at the same prison. Robert Kelly Pace, born on January

---

135. *A Passion for Polka*, p. 131–33.

136. March 30, 1940, *Billboard*. The record's staying power was exceptional. The September 20, 1941, *Billboard* reported (p. 71) that it was still selling 10,000 to 15,000 copies a month after being on the market for three years.

137. "Eighty Years of Polish Music in Chicago," chapter in *Ethnic Recordings in America*, p. 150.

138. An abbreviated version of the song had been recorded in 1936 for ARC by Dennis Crumpton & Robert Summers as *Go I'll Send Thee*.

2, 1913, spent over half his life behind bars, as detailed by Stephen Wade, serving two separate terms totaling almost six years for burglary between 1931 and 1938, followed by a conviction for grand larceny that kept him in Cummins State Farm for sixteen years until his release in 1955.[139] This number was first released in 1943 on the Library of Congress album (a package of 78s) *Negro Religious Songs and Services*.[140]

This is a song with a vast history and many variants, traced by William Wells Newell in the July–September 1891 *Journal of American Folklore*, Vol. 4 #14. *The Carol of the Twelve Numbers*, as it was then most often known, began (as collected in 1889) "come and I will sing you," with the response, "What will you sing me?" This is followed by an enumeration including the twelve apostles (Vance Randolph's *Ozark Folksongs* cited it under the title *The Twelve Apostles*), eleven of whom were saints who went to heaven (excluding Judas), the Ten Commandments, etc. It was included by Davies Gilbert in 1823's *Some Ancient Christmas Carols*. J. Sylvester's *A Garland of Christmas Carols* (1861) has a variant called *A New Dial*, which, according to Sylvester, bears a date of 1625, taken from an old almanac preserved in the British Museum. Latin forms of the "number-song," writes Newell, predate 1602. In Germany, the song, by 1649, was altered into a hymn, as also occurred in England, and before long was found across Europe. Each country tended to use different citations for the numbers; for example, a German version sung as part of the Jewish Passover service in 1768 had the number two meaning the table of Moses, three the fathers (Abraham, Isaac, and Jacob), twelve representing the tribes of Israel, etc. Newell's conclusion: "There cannot be much doubt the song was well known in Europe as early as" the fifteenth century. One can hardly imagine a more timeless rendition than that of the remarkable Pace group.

Black Jack David (1939)—Cliff Carlisle & His Buckle Busters

Decca 5732

Recorded July 26, 1939

Black Jack David is an American variant on the traditional ballad *The Gypsy Laddie*, published as Child number 200 by Harvard professor Francis James Child in *The English and Scottish Popular Ballads* (1883–1898), which can be traced back to at least 1630. It appeared in many landmark early song collections including James Johnson's *The Scots Musical Museum No. 2* (1788) and Joseph Ritson's 1794 Scottish song compendium, under various titles such as *The Wraggle Taggle Gipsies*. In the original song, a band of gypsies stopping by the dwelling of an absent nobleman sings so sweetly that his wife falls in love, runs off with one of them, and is then pursued by her husband. Child printed eleven different versions, drawing on Scottish, English, Irish, and American sources. The names of the husband and the gypsy change from version to version; in several, the husband finds his woman and hangs the gypsies; in others, she regrets her change in status.[141] In Bertrand Bronson's four-volume *The Traditional Tunes of the Child Ballads* (1959–1971), some 130 versions of *The Gypsy Laddie* appear. Child dismissed the claim (widely published in nineteenth century accounts, including William Motherwell's *Minstrelsy* in 1827) that a real historical figure, the wife of the Earl of Cassalis in the 1640s, was the ballad's heroine. The apparent inspiration for the ballad was Johnny Faa, a "notorious Egyptian and chieftain" who was condemned to death in 1616, several years after gypsies were expelled from Scotland.[142] Some of the many early American versions collected were discussed by Olive Dare Campbell and Cecil Sharp in *English Folk Songs from the Southern Appalachians* (1917).[143]

Born in Taylorville, Kentucky, on May 6, 1904, Cliff Carlisle recorded over 300 sides for a variety of labels during the 1930s; originally known for Jimmie Rodgers–style yodeling, he also became recognized for helping to pioneer the use of the dobro steel guitar in country music, as on this record.[144] Carlisle learned the song from T. Texas Tyler, who copyrighted *Black Jack David* in 1939 and recorded it himself several years later (for Four Star 1052). A decade earlier, a duo billed as Professor & Mrs. I. G. Grier (Prof. Grier was a singer in the formal parlor-room style and also a song collector) had first recorded *Black Jack David* across two sides of a 78 for Paramount in October 1929; years later the Griers would make some recordings for the Library of Congress. Carlisle gives it (writes Bill Malone) "the kind of cocksure reading the song deserves." His brother Bill accompanies him on Spanish guitar. Judith McCulloh pointed out that one deviation Carlisle makes from the traditional song is that it is Black Jack David, not the girl, who puts on, rather than removes, the high-heeled "boots of Spanish leather."[145] It was of course that lyrical reference that later inspired

139. Wade, *The Beautiful Music All Around Us*, p. 66.

140. Six decades later, *Holy Babe* was included on the Spottswood-produced 2004 Dust to Digital CD *Where Will You Be Christmas Day?* He compares the introductory wordless vocalizing to the Southern tradition of sacred harp singing.

141. *The English and Scottish Popular Ballads*, Vol. 4, p. 61–74.

142. Also see Davis, *Traditional Ballads of Virginia*, p. 423.

143. *English Folk Songs from the Southern Appalachians* (1917), p. 112 and 327; 1932 edition, Vol. 1, p. 233 and 419.

144. Carlisle in his early period was also a master of double-entendre songs; Charles K. Wolfe noted that his "blues sounded so authentic that some of his records were released in the 'race' series (aimed at an African-American audience)."

145. Judith McCullough, "Some Child Ballads on Hillbilly Records," from *Folklore and Society: Essays in Honor of Benjamin A. Botkin* (1966).

Bob Dylan's *Boots of Spanish Leather*. The song was recorded in 1940 by the Carter Family, and a year later (as *The Gypsy Davy*) by Woody Guthrie.

You Are My Sunshine (1940)—Jimmie Davis
Decca 5813
Recorded on Feb. 5, 1940 (*RIA-#14, Folk-#27, C&W-#29, GHF, HBN, DMDB, SC*)

One of the most enduringly popular songs in country music history was written by Paul Rice and recorded by his Louisiana group the Rice Brothers' Gang (on September 13, 1939, for Decca), the Pine Ridge Boys (about three weeks earlier on August 22, 1939, for Bluebird), and Bob Atcher (on January 17, 1940, for Vocalion/Okeh). By this time Jimmie Davis was an established country star and a rising political power in Louisiana. Rice was in need of cash, so he sold all rights to the song to Davis for a price that has been variously stated at between $17.50 and $500. Davis reworked the tune, including revised lyrics, recorded and published it as his own, and his version was quickly followed by Gene Autry's and Bing Crosby's recordings. Its simple singalong quality has made it universally familiar to generations of schoolchildren. Davis made *Sunshine* his theme song in successful campaigns for the Louisiana governorship in 1944 and 1960, saw it become a smash once again by Ray Charles in 1962, and continued to perform it for more than fifty years until his death.

Born in Beech Grove, Louisiana, on September 11, 1902, Davis earned a master's degree from Louisiana State University and taught history at a small college in Shreveport before launching his recording career in 1928. He recorded over seventy sides the next five years for Victor, many emulating the style of his musical hero Jimmie Rodgers, and including some rather bawdy blues-based numbers. His breakthrough record was *Nobody's Darlin' But Mine* in 1934 after he moved to Decca, and he soon became one of the top attractions in country music. Surprisingly, however, his version of *You Are My Sunshine* was only the fourth most popular in the country/folk field as chronicled in *Billboard*'s hillbilly "hits of the month" listings; Gene Autry's was indisputably the biggest (racking up at least twenty-one unofficial weeks at #1 in 1942), after versions by Atcher and then the Airport Boys had topped the folk lists in 1940. (*Billboard* reported that Davis' version finally began gathering significant jukebox play in late 1943 after he launched his first gubernatorial campaign.)[146] Davis had other records cited as country hits by *Billboard* (starting with *Two More Years and I'll Be Free* in 1939), but his treatment of *Sunshine* was overlooked at the time.[147] But of course,

in subsequent years, Davis took full possession of the song. *Sunshine* was ranked as the #14 song of the century by the Recording Industry Association of America, and as the #35 all-time C&W song by *Country America*.

Shango Dance (1940)—The Lion
Recorded for Decca in Port-of-Spain on Feb. 10, 1940

The grim legacy of slavery on the island nation of Trinidad, from the age of Spanish colonizers starting in the early 1500s until the abolition of the slave trade a decade after British rule began in 1797, left an enduring mark in many respects, including its culture and music. "Calypsonians are mainly men of African descent," notes historian Keith Warner. Because men were powerless for many years to carry out their traditional role as protectors, "they used calypso to reassert their manhood," with songs as a vehicle for boasting of their prowess, much as in hip-hop.[148] But another aspect of this African heritage is religion; the Yoruba religion, historically based in southwestern Nigeria and its neighboring regions, found its way into Trinidadian tradition. This can be heard in the song *Shango Dance* by one of the legends of calypso, Rafael de Leon, known as Roaring Lion, or simply as The Lion.

Born on February 22, 1908, in the Caura Hills of northern Trinidad, de Leon began his performing career at sixteen and rose to fame in the early 1930s, known for his ability to improvise lyrics on any subject. Described by his occasional singing partner Atilla the Hun (Raymond Quevedo) as "a tall, slim man of African descent with a volatile disposition and the temperament of a prima donna,"[149] he began his recording career in March 1934. In short order, he assumed his place among the royalty of calypso. The Lion's many celebrated performances included 1934's *Marry an Ugly Woman* (also recorded as *Ugly Woman*), which three decades later became a U.S. #1 by Jimmy Soul as *If You Wanna Be Happy*, the fascinating *Fall of Man* (1936), and the surprisingly serious *Death* (1939).

The Yoruba religion had been a recurring topic of the Lion's ever since his debut session; *Shango* in 1934 described, with amusement but a careful eye for detail, Yoruba ceremonies. His 1937 piece *Ho Syne No Day* further portrayed the Shango dance, and *African War Call* (1938) offered a medley of Yoruba chants. Shango, sometimes known as Xango or Chango in Latin America, is the god of thunder and lightning in the Yoruba tradition, originally the third king of the Oyo Kingdom. All

146. November 5, 1943 *Billboard*.
147. Driven mostly by the Crosby version, *You Are My Sunshine* reached #11 on the *Billboard* sheet music chart in September 1941. At the

same time, Autry had the nation's two biggest hillbilly hits with *Sunshine* and *Be Honest with Me*. Davis' highest-placing record on the late-1941 hillbilly listings was *I'm Sorry Now*.
148. *Kaiso! The Trinidad Calypso*, p. 115–27.
149. *Atilla's Kaiso*, p. 104.

of the faith's major initiation ceremonies are based on the Shango ceremony of Ancient Oyo; Africans carried these traditions through the Middle Passage and spread them wherever they were brought as slaves.[150] The topic was also regularly addressed by other calypsonians; two other songs entitled *Shango* are by the Keskidee Trio (Atilla, Lord Beginner, and the Growling Tiger) in 1935, and by The Caresser in 1938.

Shango Dance, the best of these Yoruba-based numbers, is compelling in part because it is so different from the majority of calypsos. Recordings of calypso artists in the 1930s and 1940s were generally bright, bouncy, danceable, and humorous in tone, although frequently the breezy musical surface covered lyrics with a serious underpinning. By contrast, *Shango Dance* begins a cappella, and thereafter is simply vocals accompanied by a variety of drums and bongos. It's sung entirely in native tongue, whereas most calypsos on record are either in English or a part-English patois. The performance has a compelling, primitive feeling akin to a Lomax field recording, conveying to the listener a mental picture of the Yoruba ceremony. It's included on the Rounder compilation *Shango, Shouter & Obeah: Supernatural Calypso from Trinidad, 1934–1940*.

Vula imbobo (1940)—Zulu Wandering Singers

One year after Solomon Linda and His Original Evening Birds recorded their historic *Mbube*, only a generation later known as *The Lion Sleeps Tonight*, another black South African group recorded this gem. The Linda record was the biggest-selling record in black African history before the 1950s, and the Zulu Wandering Singers show his influence (although of course both groups drew upon similar folk traditions, most notably the "isikhunzi" vocal style) in this haunting a cappella performance recorded in Johannesburg, including some stellar falsetto crooning.

The first recordings of traditional African music were made on cylinders during the 1900–1905 period, primarily by German companies. African recordings were rare until Edison Bell began making discs in West Africa in 1927, followed a year later by the British label Broadcast. Regal started recording in southern Africa in 1930, then Brunswick a year later. The Gallotone label, which became the most important in black Africa with the region's only permanent, well-equipped studio, was founded by Eric Gallo in Johannesburg in 1931. A cappella (although occasionally with very light accompaniment in the back-

ground) vocal music, which for years meant only male choral groups, was the most heavily-recorded style of southern African music, as heard on the Rounder album *Mbube Roots: Zulu Choral Music from South Africa, 1930s–1960s*.[151] *Ina Ma Wala* (He Is Exaggerating) by the Fear No Harm Choir is a lovely 1934 example. The Zulu harmonies became legendary to aficionados of the genre, sometimes quite intricate, and usually marked by soaring falsetto leads.

Perdido (1942)—Duke Ellington & His Famous Orchestra (written by Juan Tizol)
Victor 27880
Recorded in Chicago on Jan. 21, 1942 (released in late May)

Perdido (meaning "lost" or "strayed") is one of the great jam-session favorites of the big band era. Valve trombonist Juan Tizol fashioned the piece out of the simple *Tea for Two* chord structure, and it serves as a wonderful vehicle for hot, straight-ahead soloing by Harry Carney on baritone sax, Ray Nance on two trumpet solos, Rex Stewart on cornet, and Ben Webster on tenor sax. Gunther Schuller in *The Swing Era* writes that the piece "swings deeply, powerfully, and builds to a grandly sustained climax. Carney and Stewart are the outstanding soloists here," and he also cites the "powerful walking bass lines" Alvin 'Junior' Raglin contributes, not long after Raglin replaced the late great Jimmy Blanton in the band.[152] Albert Murray, in discussing Ellington's mastery at playing his orchestra "as if it were a single instrument," cited *Perdido* as a prime example, with "the tearful hoarseness of the shouting brass ensemble in the call-and-response outchorus" of the song.[153] The main theme, suggests Donald Clarke in *The Rise and Fall of Popular Music*, is "a riff which summed up jazz composition for a whole generation."[154]

John Henry (1942)—Josh White
Keynote 541
Recorded c. early 1942 (*Folk-#74*)

The iconic American folk ballad *John Henry* had become almost universally familiar by the early 1940s, and one of the artists who became most closely identified

---

150. Some 9,000 indentured Yorubans came to Trinidad in the mid-1800s. The Shango ceremonial heritage has remained particularly strong in Cuba, Puerto Rico, and Venezuela in addition to Trinidad, although there are significant differences in the songs and rhythms of the Yoruba-derived music of each location.

151. Kip Lornell has suggested that Zulu and Xhosa choral music was strongly influenced by a black minstrel troupe led by Orpheus Myron McAdoo, the Virginia Jubilee Singers from Hampton, Virginia, during an eighteen-month tour of South Africa starting in June 1890. "It is ironic that this genre of African American minstrelsy, spiritual music, should return across the Atlantic Ocean to inform indigenous music in South Africa." (*From Jubilee to Hip Hop: Readings in African American Music*, p. 13–14.)
152. Schuller, *The Swing Era*, p. 139. Eddie Lambert in *Duke Ellington: A Listener's Guide* (p. 104) praises the way Webster comes out of the middle eight into the last part of the chorus with "such supple swing."
153. *Stomping the Blues*, p. 114.
154. Clarke, p. 194.

with the classic was Josh White. About a year after he had first recorded the song teaming with the Golden Gate Quartet for the Library of Congress in December 1940, White rendered a powerful solo voice-and-guitar version, on a 78 coupled with his treatment of the Billie Holiday protest anthem *Strange Fruit*. The recording was reissued a few years later as part of an album (three 78s packaged together) by Mercury, a collection that also included his influential performance of *House of the Rising Sun*.

Born on February 11, 1914, (or, by some accounts, 1908) in Greenville, Mississippi, the singer-guitarist began his recording career in 1932 as a blues artist in the East Coast "Piedmont" style (sometimes recording as "Pinewood Tom") who also did gospel material as "Joshua White, the Singing Christian." By 1940 his repertoire had shifted firmly into the folk vein, and the combination of his skills, good looks, and stage charisma made him an enduring legend on the folk-club circuit, and later an inspiration to the post-1950 folk generation.

Scott Reynolds Nelson concluded in his history of the classic that *John Henry* arose out of the Chesapeake & Ohio (C&O) Railway's effort to dig tunnels from the Allegheny Mountains near Richmond to the Ohio River before the end of 1872 by leasing convicts (including a young black man from New Jersey named John William Henry, serving time in the Virginia State Penitentiary after being convicted in 1866 for stealing several dollars worth of goods from a shop) along with steel drills, and driving many to their deaths. Records indicate that approximately 10 percent of the hundreds of Virginia Penitentiary workers leased to the railroad died during the 1870s, many from the silica dust they had inhaled in the tunnels. Under the contract between the state and the C&O, the bodies of all prisoners who died working on the tunnels were shipped back to the "white house" (cited in many versions of the song) and buried on the grounds of the penitentiary; if they were not sent back, the C&O faced a $100 fine per man. "Nearly 100 men came back between 1871 and 1873, most of them dead," Nelson reported. The story of terrible exploitation was conveyed through the coded message of song, just as blacks had done in slavery times. "In societies where everyday life is closely regulated, language goes underground . . . They crafted the story as a plaintive chant, broken up by hammer blows and structured inside a much older ballad tradition." He notes that the song's structure was influenced by the ancient Anglo-American ballads which black coal miners and railway workers would have heard all their lives. A roundhouse cook named Cal Evans, who cooked for workers on the Lewis Tunnel (on which Henry had worked) and then the nearby Big Bend Tunnel, was widely known for telling stories about John Henry into the 1920s, and was probably one of those who had immortalized him in song.[155]

The first published mention of the song was in a 1909 folklore journal by Louise Rand Bascom, a Wellesley student who was searching for colloquial songs and quoted a line from a ballad she'd heard sung in southwestern North Carolina about a "Johnie Henry" who "died with a hammer in his hand."[156] Four years later, Eber Carle Perrow transcribed from memory a John Henry song he had heard in east Tennessee in 1905, and a longer version he'd acquired in 1912 in Kentucky.[157] From the mid-1920s onward, no published compilation of American folk songs—Carl Sandburg's *American Songbag*, Benjamin Botkin's *Treasury of Southern Folklore*, and John and Alan Lomax's *Our Singing Country* among many others—was complete without *John Henry*.[158]

In being transmitted from old-timers to young workers, writes Nelson, *John Henry* became "an early bragging song among African-American men, structured as a ballad that could be spoken, shouted out at a worksite, or even sung with a guitar. In such songs the men described were free, powerful, and angry"[159]—a comforting piece of folklore quite different from harsh realities.

As the song evolved over many years and countless variations, it "carries a message from the supposedly voiceless, illiterate railway workers of the nineteenth century whom no one expected to leave a trace. *John Henry* is a tale of the terrible betrayals of the postwar South, about black workingmen's race to the bottom, and about where the bodies were buried." And it is also "a story of a man robbed of his dignity and his life, who in death claimed victory."[160]

Straighten Up and Fly Right (1944)—King Cole Trio
Capitol 154
Recorded on Nov. 30, 1943; chart debut April 15, 1944 (10 weeks at #1 on R&B chart; reached #9 on pop chart) (*RR-#95, GHF, R&B-#81, Jazz-#84*)

"Straighten up and fly right" was the phrase that Nat Cole's reverend father would regularly call out in his sermons, writes biographer Leslie Gourse, "urging people to cling to their Christian beliefs no matter how precarious their lives were." In 1943 the King Cole Trio, while

155. *Steel Drivin' Man: John Henry, The Untold Story of an American Legend*, p. 73–92.
156. *Journal of American Folklore*, April–June 1909, p. 247.
157. *Journal of American Folklore*, April–June 1913, p. 163–65.
158. The earliest commercial recordings of *John Henry* were by country artists such as Fiddlin' John Carson and Gid Tanner (both 1924). The most significant early blues versions were by Henry Thomas (1927) and Mississippi John Hurt (*Spike Driver Blues*, 1928).
159. Nelson, p. 112.
160. *Steel Drivin' Man*, p. 40.

drawing loyal audiences to their southern California shows, had not yet broken through as recording artists, and Cole used the phrase as the theme for an original song. *Straighten Up and Fly Right* created a metaphorical story line built around the African-American symbol of the "signifying monkey," which (in the opinion of Samuel A. Floyd in *The Power of Black Music*) was an urban version of the traditional African folk tale "Why Monkeys Live in Trees." In its modern form, that myth—explored in depth by Henry Louis Gates in his book *The Signifying Monkey: A Theory of African-American Literary Criticism*—had inspired such previous songs as Big Maceo's 1940 blues classic *Can't You Read*. And songs about monkeys and baboons as representatives of quarrelsome people have a long history in black music, including *The Monkey and the Baboon* by Lonnie Johnson and Spencer Williams (1930). Cole took the song to music publisher Irving Mills, whose brother Jack Mills bought it for fifty dollars, and—in a practice common for the era—placed Irving's name on the copyright. In fact, initially, Mills' name alone appeared on the copyright, meaning that Cole did not receive any royalties as composer; he filed suit against Mills and lost, but eventually the song was generally credited jointly to Cole and Mills Music.

The cleverness of the lyric (including a lot of musicians' jive lingo) and Cole's star quality leads most modern listeners to focus mainly on the vocal. But the great rhythmic agility and seamless quality of the Trio—the great Oscar Moore on guitar, Wesley Prince on string bass, and the effortless swing of Nat on piano—is central to the record's effectiveness. The first song recorded under Cole's new contract with Capitol (following the trio's early work for other labels, not widely heard), it became both a "race records" and pop smash, and by early 1945 the King Cole Trio was one of America's hottest acts.[161] "Cool down, papa, don't you blow your top—fly right!"

Strange Things Happening Every Day (1945)—Sister Rosetta Tharpe

Decca 8669

Recorded Sept. 22, 1944; chart debut April 28, 1945 (2 weeks at #2 on R&B chart) (*GOSP-#26*)

One of the giants of gospel music history and among the finest guitarists (male or female) of her time, Rosetta Tharpe had won national renown performing with the bands of Cab Calloway (1938) and Lucky Millinder (1939–1942) in addition to her own sensational solo work. Those experiences set the stage for her first full-fledged solo hit, *Strange Things Happening Every Day*. The song, remarked Bil Carpenter, was "a sly slap at the church hypocrites who sought to besmirch Tharpe's name for performing gospel outside the four walls of the church."[162] This was her first of many collaborations with veteran blues pianist Sam Price (Decca's session supervisor and staff pianist/arranger since 1937) and his small combo (bassist Abe Bolar and drummer Harold "Doc" West). We learn from Gayle Wald's biography that Price "disliked Rosetta and found her difficult to work with," partly because he couldn't adjust himself to her unique guitar style, until she agreed to use a capo (the bar that sits across the fingerboard of a guitar and changes its pitch); the capo enabled her to play in what Price considered a "normal jazz key," rather than the open tuning that she and many Delta blues guitarists used. Wald suggests that a more significant reason for Price's conflict with Tharpe on this session was that *Strange Things* might be considered one of the first rock & roll records. Its sound "is thoroughly modern, not quite gospel, but gospel becoming rhythm and blues."[163] [164] Briskly paced and funky, it kicks off with Rosetta's guitar in vibrant form (later throwing in some fancy riffs and arpeggios) before Price enters in boogie-woogie mode, "like an Arizona Dranes of the dance hall,"[165] and she launches into her strong, emotionally direct vocal, backed by the call-and-response of the musicians. In addition to the power of the performance, the impressionistic lyrics, which indirectly refer to those who claim holiness and yet live in sin, also seemed to have broader application at the time: "In 1945, there were indeed strange things happening, some wonderful, some horrific." Germany's April 1945 surrender occurred while this record was on the airwaves, and with all the vast social changes coming with the end of war, these were, truly, remarkable times.

Will Friedwald points out Rosetta's performances in a series of "soundies" (three-minute film shorts made for video jukeboxes) in 1941 is which she "is positively radiant, standing there with her guitar, feet planted firmly on the ground and wailing away, her eyes blazing with the Holy Spirit. She's so exuberant, so extravagant, so

---

161. Paul Grein, *Capitol Records Fifitieth Anniversary, 1942–1992*, p. 22.

162. *Uncloudy Days*, p. 406.

163. *Shout, Sister, Shout!*, p. 67–68. *Strange Things*, in contrast to the "big and brassy" Millinder records, "is dance music pared down to its essentials, stripped of everything but a rhythm section and a powerful voice." Jerry Lee Lewis (whose background in the white Pentecostal church exposed him to musical influences similar to Tharpe's) loved this song, which he played at his Sun Records audition for Sam Phillips, and saw Rosetta perform in Mississippi.

164. The "unique element" in this performance, remarks Horace Clarence Boyer, is that in her elongated guitar phrasing of single tones, "where one single tone would normally suffice, Tharpe uses four. For each beat, then, she plays four notes, giving each bar 16 different tones. This is no easy task for any guitarist." (Boyer, p. 156)

165. Arizona Dranes was a remarkable gospel pianist/singer of the late 1920s, from the Holiness church; Rosetta saw her perform multiple times, and her guitar style was in some ways inspired by Dranes' powerfully rhythmic piano technique.

charismatic, that she doesn't make me think of even Louis Jordan, Mahalia Jackson, or almost any artist of her era—she really seems like an exact prototype for Chuck Berry or Elvis . . . If Elvis was Jesus, Sister Rosetta was John the Baptist."[166]

The Honeydripper (Parts 1 & 2) (1945)—Joe Liggins & His Honeydrippers (written by Joe Liggins)
Exclusive 207
Recorded April 20, 1945; chart debut Aug. 11, 1945 (18 weeks at #1 on R&B chart) (*Blues-#88, R&B-#154, FIR, AL*)

One of the biggest hits in the history of the *Billboard* rhythm & blues chart,[167] *The Honeydripper* has been called by some the first "true" R&B record, and launched the career of singer-pianist-bandleader Joe Liggins, born on July 9, 1916, in Guthrie, Oklahoma. Based in Los Angeles from 1939 on, Liggins played with various bands including the California Rhythm Rascals, and in 1942, when the band needed a tune to go with a new dance called the Texas Hop, Liggins came up with something he initially called "Cripple Joe." When girls would come up to him at the piano, the drummer commented, "Man, you drip a lot of honey. Hey, you're a honeydripper!" So Liggins added some lyrics to fit the idea. Later, after Liggins formed his own combo also featuring Little Willie Jackson (alto and baritone sax), his performances of the song generated such a buzz that Leon Rene, founder of Exclusive Records, went to see him at the Samba Club at 5th Street and Towne Avenue in Los Angeles. Leon Rene (born in Covington, Louisiana, writer of such hits as *When It's Sleepy Time Down South, When the Swallows Come Back to Capistrano,* and *I Sold My Heart to the Junkman*) and his brother Otis Rene had ventured to Los Angeles in 1925, and started their respective record labels (Excelsior for Otis) in 1943.[168] Rene went up to the bandstand and asked Liggins to play *The Honeydripper,* but was told he'd have to wait until 11:45; there was a wartime curfew, with lights out at midnight, and the band always saved the fifteen-minute piece as the finale. When Rene finally heard it, he was quickly convinced.

The phrase "honey dripper," referring to a virile male, goes back a number of years, and stimulated several blues recordings, including three versions of the erotic *Honey Dripper Blues* by Edith Johnson in 1929, unrelated to Liggins' tune other than the theme ("He treats me so mean, just comes to me sometimes / But the way he spreads his honey, he will make me lose my mind . . ."). Pianist Roosevelt Sykes, who played on the first Johnson record, adopted the number as his theme, and was billed as "The Honey Dripper" on most of his numerous Decca recordings starting in 1936.[169]

At Liggins' urging, the number was recorded across both sides of the 78; Part 1 with the vocal, the continuation mainly instrumental. For the record, Liggins added a drummer and replaced his regular bassist with young jazzman Red Callender (besides the leader and Little Willie Jackson, the others are tenor saxman James Jackson and guitarist Frank Pasley). The leader kicks it off with an infectious piano riff, the combo digs a deep jump-blues groove, and after about a minute he launches into the bragging lyrics: "Boy, he's a honeydripper, he's a killer, the honeydripper. He's a solid gold cat, he's the height of jive . . . he's a riffer, the honeydripper . . ." Jim Dawson and Steve Propes point out that the song is built on the bass line of the folk tune *Shortnin' Bread,* and on part two Little Willie Jackson, having previously soloed on alto sax, plays a verse from the children's favorite on clarinet.[170]

Johnny Otis, king of the Los Angeles R&B scene in the 1945–1952 period, described the record's sound as "a hybrid of big-band jazz and bebop, small group and good-time swing, country blues and basic boogie woogie . . . amplified and squashed down for public dancing." Barney Hoskyns: "This was Texas/Oklahoma cornbread blues relocated in smoggy, sunburned Watts."[171]

With this one record, Leon Rene's little business suddenly became quite big. Peter Grendysa writes that in these days before the existence of an independent distribution network, Rene (who had only Southern California distribution) used Pullman car porters, who would carry dozens of copies of Exclusive records to Chicago, St. Louis, and other major cities along the rail lines, to be sold in those cities at premium prices, up to $10 a copy.[172] Despite the obstacles, the record sold over a million copies, one of the first discs on an independent label to become an out-and-out smash. Rene tried to open distribution in New York at considerable cost, but failed, and Exclusive folded in 1948. Liggins signed with Art

166. Friedwald, *Biographical Dictionary*, p. 792.
167. It's ranked as the all-time #1 biggest hit on the *Billboard* R&B charts in *Joel Whitburn Presents Top R&B Singles 1942–1999*, p. 640.
168. Exclusive issued its first records in July 1943, and for most of its first two years the label was used almost exclusively to showcase compositions by the brothers.
169. Oliver, *Screening the Blues*, p. 218.
170. Dawson and Propes, *What Was the First Rock 'n' Roll Record?*, p. 5–8.
171. *Waiting for the Sun*, p. 21–22.
172. Interviewed by Arnold Shaw for *Honkers and Shouters* (p. 154–55), Leon Rene recalled: "We had great difficulty getting pressings because Allied Records was the only independent pressing plant in Los Angeles, and each customer was limited to only 200 records a week." Exclusive had to scrounge all over town to buy old records, re-heat them at their own one-press plant, and make enough additional copies to meet demand. In his article on Liggins for the *Oxford American Southern Music Issue* (2006), p. 53, Tom Piazza remarks that the record "was reportedly bootlegged by the Mob for their jukeboxes."

Rupe's Specialty label, and cut a new version of *Honeydripper* that—because it remained continually in catalog—eventually became the most-heard version. Liggins went on to score thirteen more R&B chart hits through 1951, including the chart-topping *Pink Champagne* in 1950.[173] *The Honeydripper*, write Dawson and Propes, "was a hit booming from every record store, shoeshine stand, barber shop and barbecued chicken shack on Los Angeles' famed Central Avenue as many thousands of G.I.s returned from the Pacific, hungry for nightlife and new civilian experiences . . . *The Honeydripper* and the southern California that spawned it gave black and white Americans a taste of the postwar culture to come."

The Tramp on the Street (1946)—Molly O'Day with the Cumberland Mountain Folks (written by Grady & Hazel Cole)

Columbia 37559 (record credited simply to "The Cumberland Mountain Folks")

Recorded in Chicago on Dec. 16, 1946 (released on July 7, 1947) (*C&W-#124*)

Even though she never had a record on the *Billboard* charts, Molly O'Day is regarded as one of the most important female performers in country music history, and *The Tramp on the Street* was her classic. Born Lois LaVerne Williamson on July 9, 1923, in the remote Appalachian community Pike County, Kentucky, she grew up admiring cowgirl singers like Patsy Montana, and began singing and playing guitar in a string band with her two brothers. After brother Skeets began performing on a West Virginia radio station in 1939, she soon followed. In 1940, under the stage name Dixie Lee Williamson, she joined guitarist Lynn Davis' band the Forty Niners, and they married the following year. The band toured the South extensively, and by the time they settled in Louisville in 1946, she was known as Molly O'Day. Writer/publisher Fred Rose signed her that year to Columbia, and she became the first important artist to record the songs of a young unknown named Hank Williams, including *Six More Miles to the Graveyard*.

It was Williams who had introduced her to *The Tramp on the Street* when she saw him sing it in Montgomery in 1942,[174] and it was the leadoff song at her debut recording session, and her first release. Based on a poem put to music by Addison Crabtree in 1877 (as *Only a Tramp*), the song was recorded under that title in 1933 by Uncle

Pete & Louise for Conqueror, then was revised and copyrighted by Grady and Hazel Cole of Rome, Georgia, who recorded it under the more famous title for Bluebird in August 1939.[175] But it was Molly's deeply touching performance—using a substantially different melody—that made it famous. A powerful musical statement making the connection between the sufferings of Christ and those of a homeless derelict, it shows off her "soulful, gut-wrenching" vocal style (in Jason Ankeny's phrase), unvarnished and plainly Appalachian.[176] In addition to her own guitar she's accompanied by husband Lynn on harmonies and guitar, brother Skeets Williamson on fiddle, Speedy Krise on dobro, and future country star Mac Wiseman on bass.[177] Just as this song reflected her Christian beliefs, Molly included much religious material in her repertoire, and left show business in 1951 to focus on performing in churches; in 1954 Davis became an ordained minister with the Church of God, and the couple did full-time evangelistic work for years in West Virginia. O'Day returned to record for small gospel labels in the 1960s. *The Tramp on the Street* was included in the Smithsonian's *Collection of Classic Country Music*. Bill Malone calls the song "one of the great pleas for Christian compassion found in country music."[178] "He was some mother's darlin', he was some mother's son / Once he was fair, and once he was young / And some mother rocked him, her darlin' to sleep / But they left him to die like a tramp on the street . . ."

Colonel Fraser / My Love Is In America / Rakish Paddy (Medley of Reels) (1947)—Johnny Doran

Widely recognized as one of the great Irish bagpipers even though he never made any formal commercial recordings, Johnny Doran was born in 1907 in the village of Rathnew near Wicklow town. His father was an accomplished piper, and his great-grandfather a celebrated piper named John Cash.[179] [180] From his early twenties

---

173. In March 1950, Hollywood record man Harry Fox was granted the right to press and distribute nationally the masters of the defunct Exclusive label, including *The Honeydripper*, meaning that Liggins' 1945 original returned to circulation at least for awhile.

174. The song was included in the first song book sold by Molly and Lynn, printed in Louisville in January 1944. It was her summer-1946 performance of *Tramp* on station WNQX that led Rose to contact and sign them.

175. *Country Music Sources*, p. 302.

176. *All Music Guide to Country*, p. 341.

177. As discussed by Robert Cogswell in the Summer 1975 *J.E.M.F. Quarterly*, Wilma Lee & Stoney Cooper recorded the song for Rich-R-Tone in 1947 (Wilma Lee's vocal style was similar to Molly's) with the intention of making it their third release for the label, but the Cumberland Mountain Folks record came out first.

178. *Country Music, U.S.A.* p. 131–32.

179. Although some recordings of Irish traditional music were made as early as 1899, including by uilleann piper James C. McAuliffe, record companies only began to seriously explore the commercial market for such music starting in 1916. Within a few years, record catalogs were increasingly packed with old-time Irish instrumentals, particularly by fiddlers. Oddly enough, relatively few early recordings were made by pipers; the most notable was Chicago-born Tom Ennis, who recorded over sixty sides from 1917–1929.

180. The Uilleann or "Union" pipes were introduced in the sixteenth century as a bellows-born variation on the older mouth-blown war pipes; the Gaelic word "uilleann" ("elbow") which describes the method of inflation by an under-arm bellows was probably later corrupted to "Union."

onward Doran made a living as an itinerant musician, traveling with his family around Ireland in a horse-drawn caravan and playing at fairs and sporting events. Fiddler John Kelly first saw him play at horse races in 1932, and became a friend and frequent playing partner. In 1947 Kelly, concerned about Doran's health and feeling strongly that his friend's artistry should be preserved for posterity, contacted a representative of the Irish Folklore Commission, who very quickly arranged for him to be recorded. (According to Paul F. Wells, no 78 rpm recordings of American uilleann pipers were made from 1929 until the modern era.)[181] Doran recorded nineteen tunes and airs, using a concert pitch set of Leo Rowsome uilleann pipes, on nine 12-inch acetate disks.[182] This medley of three traditional reels demonstrates his brilliant fluency and speed, playing for some five-and-a-half minutes until the disk ran out of space. Sadly, plans for additional recordings would never be realized; on January 30, 1948, while his caravan was parked in Dublin's Cornmarket area and he was standing outside, a powerful gust of wind caused a brick wall to collapse on the caravan, paralyzing him from the waist down. The tragedy led to further health problems, and he died on January 9, 1950. All of his recordings were issued decades later on an Irish LP from Claddagh Records called *The Bunch of Keys*.

La Valse du Pont d'Amour (Love Bridge Waltz) (1948)—Iry LeJeune

Opera 105[183]

Recorded c. late 1948, probably released in 1949 (*RR, World-#18*)

After the original "golden age" of French Cajun music spanning the years from 1929 (when Joseph Falcon made the historic first successful Cajun recordings) to 1942, the vibrant brew of south Louisiana traditional sounds was in danger of nearly disappearing back into the tiny regional genre it had once been. The major record labels stopped recording Cajun (just as they largely abandoned other types of ethnic music) after 1942, leaving the field wide open for small independents with limited distribution. But then came the phenomenon of Harry Choates scoring a national hit in early 1947 with *Jole Blon*, and suddenly everyone was jumping on the Acadian bandwagon, if only on a modest scale. Regional record company entrepreneurs like George Khoury, J. D. Miller, Eddie Shuler, and Floyd Soileau gave Cajun artists a fresh chance to

reach an audience,[184] and one of the first artists to benefit from this postwar boom was Iry LeJeune.

A nearly blind accordionist-singer from Acadia Parish, born on his father's small farm on the outskirts of Church Point, Louisiana, on October 28, 1928, LeJeune (whose name has sometimes been spelled "Lejune") was influenced by his cousin Angelas LeJeune (an important early Cajun recording artist) and the 1930s string bands such as Leo Soileau's. Above all, he was influenced by Amédé Ardoin, perhaps the greatest of all Cajun performers during his too-brief 1929–1934 recording career. Ardoin was black and LeJeune white, but Iry was one of the few singers of his time to recapture the "crying" emotional urgency that marked Ardoin's singing. After moving to Lacassine, a small town near Lake Charles, he began performing with local bands. He happened to meet Virgil Bozman's Oklahoma Tornadoes after that band's performance in Evangeline; the Tornadoes were about to travel to Houston to record for Floyd LeBlanc's Opera label, and he persuaded the members to let him come along. Mike Leadbitter: "His recording of *Love Bridge Waltz* was the turning point in his life and in French music. It was a strong seller, at a time when accordion-driven music had fallen out of style in favor of the fiddle, "and for the first time in 10 years the accordion wailed from juke boxes in Cajun country."[185] It's a simple medium-tempo number, one of the first accordion records in the era's dancehall style,[186] made special by the desperately earnest quality in a voice steeped in loneliness, and the squeeze box evoking generations of Acadian tradition. Ryan Andre Brasseaux reports that the melody to *Alone At Home*, a tune recorded in November 1929 (but not released until 1940) by accordionist Delin Guillory and fiddler Lewis LaFleur, "served as the basis" for *Love Bridge Waltz*.[187]

After six months in Houston, he returned to Louisiana. Goldband Records president Eddie Shuler recalled first meeting LeJeune coming up the street with his accordion in a flour sack. Most of their recordings were made at the artist's home south of Lacassine. "We would take the tape recorder (after they came out) and set it on the table in the kitchen." The artist, notes Louisiana-based longtime *American Routes* radio host Nick Spitzer, became known to admirers as "the Cajun Hank Williams."

181. *Ethnic and Border Music*, p. 42.

182. Dublin-born Leo Rowsome, known as "the king of the Pipers," was a celebrated uilleann pipe virtuoso from the 1920s until his death in 1970. Uilleann pipes, the standard bagpipe of traditional Irish music, are distinguished from Scottish and other bagpipes by their tone and wide range of notes; the chanter has a range of two full octaves.

183. The record's B side also became popular, *Evangeline Special*.

184. The companies run by these four men were all based in Louisiana and east Texas, and that's also where the lion's share of their record sales were made. The only national labels showing even a slight interest in Cajun music during the 1947–1953 period were Modern (in Los Angeles) and DeLuxe (New Jersey).

185. Liner notes for Goldband's *The Legendary Iry LeJeune*, Vol. 1.

186. Kevin Fontenot describes the dancehall sound, consisting of "a driving, swinging accordion" accompanied by the fiddle, drums, guitar, and a "crying" steel guitar. The music was amplified "to cut through the noise of the dancehall." (*Ethnic and Border Music*, p. 10.)

187. *Cajun Breakdown*, p. 196–97.

Tragically, LeJeune died just shy of his twenty-sixth birthday following an auto accident in October 1954. His son Eddie went on to an enduring career carrying on in Iry's trademark style. Brasseaux sees LeJeune's music as a crucial step in the birth of Cajun honky-tonk.[188] Pierre Daigle: "In my opinion, the highest point of Cajun music was reached in this man's music."[189]

Santa Barbara (Que Viva Chango!) (1948)—Celina Gonzalez

Recorded in November 1948 (*World-#77*)

Called "the undisputed queen" of Cuban "musica campesina," a kind of "roots salsa," Celina Gonzalez was born in the town of Jovellanos and grew up in Santiago de Cuba. At fifteen, she began performing with Reutilio Dominguez, a singer of guajira music (soon to become her husband), and in 1947 she was given a shot at a daily program on Radio Cadena Oriental in Santiago. Ned Sublette writes in *Cuba and Its Music* that, a natural poet, she would take letters from listeners and make up rhymes about them. In early November 1948, Celina and Reutilio were given a one-week opportunity on Radio Suaritos in Havana. On the third day of the program, Celina awoke at 5 a.m. and wrote a song of devotion to the Catholic saint Santa Barbara, and a Yoruba deity named Chango.[190] The number quickly became known by its tag line, "Que viva Chango (Long Live Chango)."

"At that time, the country music of Cuba was off in a corner by itself, apart from the rest of Cuban musical scene, with little African influence, at a time when Cubans wanted to dance," explains Sublette. "Celina and Reutilio brought it into the fold, making it more danceable and more a part of mulatto culture." According to Diaz Ayala, "the effect was not unlike mixing gospel, blues, and country music."[191] A huge hit across Cuba in 1949 and the most famous song of Celina's career, the tune became a symbol of merged Afro-Cuban religion. Years later, it would be remade as a salsa hit for Celia Cruz.

With Celina on lead vocal and Reutilio on second vocal and guitar, the performance is introduced by the horn section, then a duet vocal on the chorus with Celina solo on the verses. The highly danceable number also features his nice guitar solo at mid-record. In liner notes for the Blue Jackal/Lightyear boxed set *Cuba: I Am Time*, Al Pryor, Jack O'Neil, and Nina Gomes note that *Santa Bar-*

bara epitomized how Africans in Cuba had disguised the gods of their native religion behind figures of Catholic saints. "But no one had ever dared mention Santa Barbara and Chango in the same song!"

But Not for Me (1950 and 1959)—Ella Fitzgerald
(music by George Gershwin, lyrics by Ira Gershwin)
Recorded for the Decca album *Ella Sings Gershwin* on Sept. 12, 1950[192]
New version for the Verve album *The George & Ira Gershwin Songbook* on March 26, 1959.

Nine years apart, Ella Fitzgerald rendered two of the most impeccable versions of the gorgeous Gershwin ballad *But Not for Me*. Whether with solo piano or backed by full orchestra, it's wonderful.

Written for the 1930 Broadway musical *Girl Crazy* (in which it was introduced by Ginger Rogers), *But Not for Me*—unlike the other big ballad from that show, *Embraceable You*—was not an immediate hit, and had not been widely recorded before the Harry James band had a moderate hit with the song in 1942. It was during the postwar era that it fully emerged as a great standard. Alec Wilder called it "a masterpiece of control and understatement from beginning to end, verse and chorus. Because everyone knows the song and its author, it is hard to realize that it is not by any means typical of Gershwin's most characteristic style." Simple in structure with a range of only one note over an octave and minimal syncopation, explains Wilder, its verse uses Gershwin's favored repeated-note device, "but contrasts it with moving lines. As a verse it couldn't be better. The entire song is Gershwin at his purest."[193]

Ella Fitzgerald was already one of America's best-loved singers in 1950, but she was not satisfied with the quality of material she was being given by Decca Records. Will Friedwald writes, "she was getting better and what she sang was getting worse." With the help of producer Milt Gabler, she finally persuaded the label to allow her to record an eight-song, ten-inch album of Gershwin songs, with the solo piano accompaniment of the superb Ellis Larkins, and it proved to be a landmark in her career.[194] Fans who had associated her with silly rhythm or novelty pieces discovered what her admirers

188. *Cajun Breakdown*, p. 159.
189. *Tears, Love, & Laughter*, p. 86.
190. Also known as Shango; see the essay here on *Shango Dance* by The Lion.
191. Sublette, p. 563–65. Sue Steward remarks in *Musica! The Rhythm of Latin America* (p. 39) that Gonzalez "has done more than any other artist to bring *guajira* music into towns and cities." But this, her trademark hit, was a sacred homage sung in the guajira style, and created in the standard *campesina decima* format.

192. *Ella Sings Gershwin* with Larkins, which was originally her first album of newly-recorded material issued in the new 33 1/3 rpm format (the songs were also released separately in 78 rpm), was reissued in late 1956 (reviewed, January 1957 *Metronome*).
193. *American Popular Song*, p. 149. Deena Rosenberg noted in *Fascinating Rhythm*, p. 177–78) that "the refrain melodies of *The Man I Love* and *But Not for Me* are similar in rhythm and shape: both start off the beat and pivot around a single note in a similar way." While the singer in *But Not for Me* is sad, she remarks, its music, clearly in major key, "seems to imply that all is not lost."
194. *Jazz Singing*, p.145–46.

already knew, as biographer Stuart Nicholson writes of her performance on this album:

"She sings with confidence and a total lack of artifice, without flights of virtuosity or exercises in complexity . . . she does not attempt to impose an emotional dimension on what she sings, throwing the subjective interpretation fairly and squarely into the listener's corner . . . The success of these numbers lies in the way they sound detached yet at the same time intimate. Ella achieves this through a combination of impeccable diction (in which she took great pride), the clarity and purity of her voice, and precise intonation that allowed her to project her voice quietly into the microphone, totally confident of pitch."[195] And as for Ellis Larkins' accompaniment, Wilder declared: "Technically he is a marvel, accomplishing his infinitely fine musical embroidery by means of wholly relaxed fingers, a musical mind, and a loving heart."

After the universal acclaim for Ella's Cole Porter, Rodgers & Hart, Duke Ellington, and Irving Berlin *Songbooks* for Verve from 1955–1958, George & Ira Gershwin were the next recipients of the Ella treatment, and this one was an epic: a five-disc, 53-song compilation with the finest arranger in 1950s American pop music, Nelson Riddle. Friedwald says it "amounts to an opera" covering "the widest range of human situations. The

Ella Fitzgerald, PhotoFest.

early ten-inch *Ella Sings Gershwin* stands to this monument as a Picasso sketch does to his epic *Guernica*."[196] [197]

Eyesight to the Blind (1951)—Sonny Boy Williamson II (Aleck "Rice" Miller) (written by Aleck Miller)
Trumpet 129
Recorded in Jackson, Mississippi on March 12, 1951 (*Blues-#102*)

The man who called himself the second Sonny Boy Williamson was actually born nearly fifteen years before the first Sonny Boy, on December 5, 1899, in Glendora, Mississippi, raised in Arkansas, and would become just as important a bluesman as his namesake. (His early years remain shrouded in mystery, and even his real name is disputed; some say he was born Aleck Ford.) By the mid-1930s, he was performing across the Delta under the alias of Little Boy Blue; the great Robert Johnson was one of his playing partners, a list that also included Robert Nighthawk, Robert Jr. Lockwood, and Elmore James. It was during the early 1940s that he achieved fame as the star of America's first live blues radio show, KFFA's *King Biscuit Time*, and that's when he assumed his new name: His sponsor, the Interstate Grocery Company, persuaded him to pose as the nationally renowned Tennessee-born, Chicago-based blues harmonica wizard Sonny Boy Williamson (whose many blues classics included *Good Morning Little Schoolgirl*). Although Miller was also a blues mouth harpist and singer, his style was nothing like the original Sonny Boy. But the ploy worked, and when John Lee Williamson was murdered in 1948, Rice Miller became the one and only Sonny Boy Williamson.

Despite Miller's great success on radio, it was not until 1951 that he began his recording career, and Lillian McMurry, the owner of the fledgling Trumpet Records in Jackson, Mississippi, had to track the artist down at a nearby boarding house to persuade him to finally enter the studio. His very first Trumpet release, *Eyesight to the Blind*, was an instant classic, although (partly due to Trumpet's limited distribution) it didn't reach the national R&B charts.[198] Accompanied by a tight combo, he cries out the tale of a woman whose lovemaking prowess can work miracles, punctuated regularly by

195. Nicholson, *Ella Fitzgerald: Biography of the First Lady of Jazz*, p. 133–34.

196. Friedwald, *Jazz Singing*, p. 149–50.

197. Ted Gioia points out (*The Jazz Standards*, p. 50) that Ella's version was featured in the 1959 Clark Gable film titled after the song, and that the movie's debut coincided with the release of the singer's Gershwin songbook.

198. Darryl Stolper chronicled the story of Trumpet Records, including this session, in the January 1972 *Blues Unlimited*. Lillian McMurry and her husband owned a furniture store in Jackson which bought out a record store. She fell in love with the blues, acquired thousands more records, and, she recalled, "pretty soon it was all records and no furniture, and we became the biggest record store in Mississippi." She started Trumpet Records in 1950.

his short bursts on the harp. "You've been talkin' 'bout your woman, I sure wish you could see mine . . . Every time that girl starts to lovin', she brings eyesight to the blind . . ." Robert Santelli, comparing Sonny Boy II to the 1950s' king of mouth harpists, Little Walter: "Where Walter was the unquestioned master of tone and dynamics, Williamson had a greater reach and often played his harp as if it were a wailing saxophone. Walter was about finesse; Sonny Boy possessed raw percussive ferocity . . . [his] unpredictable spirit and spontaneity gave his songs a verisimilitude only the best blues artists could summon at will."[199] Within a few years Williamson would move to the era's dominant blues label, Chess, in Chicago (through its subsidiary Checker), enabling him to score a few national R&B hits, most notably *Don't Start Me to Talkin'* (1955). He cut a new, somewhat less intense version of *Eyesight* for Checker in 1957 under the title *Born Blind. Eyesight to the Blind* would be covered by many other bluesmen, including B.B. King, and it received a special honor as the only non-original song included in The Who's rock opera *Tommy.*

(Other personnel: Either Dave Campbell or Willie Love on piano, Joe Willie Wilkins on guitar,[200] Cliff Givens on bass, Joe Dyson on drums)

Earl's Breakdown (1951)—Lester Flatt, Earl Scruggs & the Foggy Mountain Boys
Columbia 20886
Recorded Oct. 24, 1951[201] (*C&W-#79*)

The second most famous Flatt & Scruggs bluegrass instrumental dazzler is based on the melody of their former employer Bill Monroe's *Bluegrass Ramble*, from Monroe's first recording session for Decca in February 1950. Like their earlier classic *Foggy Mountain Breakdown*, this is an exciting Earl Scruggs virtuoso five-string banjo showcase, with Howdy Forrester also given ample solo space on fiddle, Everett Lilly on mandolin, and Flatt on guitar. Neil Rosenberg writes that on this piece Scruggs used his new "tuners" (later called "Scruggs pegs"), devices that "allowed him to produce striking effects by accurately retuning two strings of his banjo while playing."[202] Within the decade, *Earl's Breakdown* was one of the tunes that every aspiring banjoist tried desperately to master, though no one could do it like Earl.

The Earl Scruggs banjo style, explains Robert Cantwell, "consists of a chain of eighth notes in 4/4 time played by the thumb, index, and middle fingers in a series of variable three-finger sequences or 'rolls' . . . in a continual mutual interplay. This provides for an unhesitating and often astonishingly rapid delivery of notes, since each finger has a full beat to recover itself for the next strike, and, since the bar always occurs in the middle of a roll, ties measures together in an unbroken chain." At its basic level this technique is "a series of ascending and descending arpeggios . . . Altogether it is a rangy, treasonous, brilliant sound, a sound full of the South."[203]

Hello Young Lovers (1951)—Mabel Mercer (music by Richard Rodgers, lyrics by Oscar Hammerstein II)
Atlantic 402
Recorded Nov. 17, 1951 (*APS*)

Richard Rodgers and Oscar Hammerstein II ruled the musical theater world at mid-century as 1949's *South Pacific* had surpassed even the massive popular and critical acclaim for *Oklahoma!* and *Carousel*. That status was further deepened by the success of *The King and I*. Margaret Langdon's novel *Anna and the King of Siam* (made into a popular movie in 1946) was seen by longtime star Gertrude Lawrence as an ideal vehicle for her return to the musical stage. Cole Porter declined the project, but then Rodgers and Hammerstein accepted her invitation to write and produce the show.

Set in Bangkok in 1862, the story relates how an adventurous Englishwoman named Anna is hired to serve as governess and tutor to the king's many children, and despite great cultural differences and strong disagreements, she and the king come to respect and care for one another. The show opened on March 29, 1951, ran for 1,246 performances, and made an overnight star of the previously unknown Yul Brynner as the king. Lawrence enjoyed a career-capping triumph as Anna; she died while the show was going strong in 1952. Its Broadway cast album spent fifty-four weeks in the *Billboard* Top Ten, and the movie version in 1956 (again starring Brynner) was a smash.

Hello Young Lovers follows Anna's observation of the deep love between Tuptim and Lun Tha, and her recollection of how much she had loved her late husband Tom. Alec Wilder in *American Popular Song* calls the chorus "enormously touching, beautifully written, harmonically colorful and . . . indeed, one of Rodgers' finest waltzes."[204] David Jenness and Don Velsey remark that it "manages to be both deliberate in its main beats and light" in tone, as in "All my good wishes are with you tonight."[205]

Born on February 3, 1900, in Birmingham, England, Mabel Mercer got her start in British musical comedies, was a long-running success in Paris, and enjoyed her

199. *The Best of the Blues*, p. 72.
200. Fancourt and McGrath (*The Blues Discography, 1943–1970*) additionally list Elmore James on guitar for this session.
201. The song appeared on Columbia's first Flatt & Scruggs LP, *Foggy Mountain Jamboree* (1956).
202. Rosenberg, p. 104.
203. Cantwell, *Bluegrass Breakdown*, p. 101.
204. Wilder, p. 221.
205. *Classic American Popular Song: The Second Half-Century, 1950–2000*, p. 78.

greatest acclaim as an unsurpassed cabaret singer with multi-year engagements in top New York venues starting in 1941. Signed to Atlantic Records in 1951, her first sessions were produced by Ahmet Ertegun, resulting in an EP later expanded into the 10-inch LP *Songs by Mabel Mercer*. Frank Sinatra, Peggy Lee, and Nat "King" Cole were among her many admirers, all influenced by her style. Known for her intimate, quietly emotional delivery, she is accompanied here only by piano, bass, and drums. "Her reading of the lyric is very personal and touching," writes James R. Morris. "Few singers could make more of the line 'I've been in love, like you,' and the lines in the bridge, 'I know how it feels' through 'not really by chance' are an object lesson in lyric interpretation. In the verse, beginning with 'When I think of Tom,' she uses every color and nuance that the words afford to paint a memorable picture." Rodgers ends the song on a climbing scale—"a very apt choice, for it leaves us with no feeling of resolution but with a lingering touch of the nostalgia that permeates the whole piece."[206] Will Friedwald points out that many of Mercer's songs were done in three-quarter time, perfect for songs such as this one in which she regresses to young girlhood, setting up her trademark sophistication "expressly so she can . . . dispense with it"; it becomes all about how she "transports us back to another time, another place . . . The waltz is the time signature of the fair and the merry-go-round, saturating these songs with a feeling of innocence and naivete by harking back to a time when the world was so much younger than we and merry as a 3/4 carousel."[207]

Moody's Mood for Love (1952)—King Pleasure
Prestige 924
Recorded in Feb. 1952; chart debut May 17, 1952 (reached #2 on R&B chart) (*Jazz-#131*)

The art of "vocalese"—crafting new lyrics and vocally re-creating a great instrumental jazz solo—can be traced back to the late 1920s. There were a few recordings that can be seen as precursors, such as Ethel Waters' 1928 treatment of *West End Blues* a couple of months after Louis Armstrong's classic, but without attempting to specifically mimic Satch's solo. Perhaps the first true vocalese performance was an obscure 1929 recording of *Singin' the Blues* in which vocalist Bee Palmer imitated (through lyrics written by Ted Koehler) the solos of Bix Beiderbecke and Frankie Trumbauer.[208] But the form was largely unexplored until the pioneering 1950s recordings

of King Pleasure, Jon Hendricks, and Eddie Jefferson. Pleasure was born Clarence Beeks on March 24, 1922, in Oakdale, Tennessee, and launched his career after winning the Apollo Theater's amateur contest in November 1951. His award-winning song, *Moody's Mood for Love*, also became his breakthrough jazz/R&B hit in 1952, opening up whole new horizons for jazz singers.[209]

It's based on alto saxophonist James Moody's instrumental solo improvising on the chord changes to the 1930s standard *I'm In the Mood for Love*, but with Pleasure's new lyrics: "There I go, there I go . . ."[210] The accompanying combo led by Teacho Wiltshire includes Gerald Wiggins on piano, Harold Land on tenor sax, and Cecil Payne on baritone sax, and at the end female vocalist Blossom Dearie duets with him briefly. Readers of *Down Beat* voted it the 1952 Record of the Year. Within a few months of this left-field hit, vocalese records by Jefferson and *Farmer's Market* by Annie Ross were released, ensuring that the new subgenre had firmly taken root. Pleasure made a modest number of other terrific records—particularly an unforgettable vocal treatment of *Parker's Mood* by Charlie Parker—but his star soon faded, even though his "voice was as flexible as a saxophone and as mellow as a cello."[211] "James Moody, you can come on in and blow now if you want to—we're through!"

Too Close to Heaven (1953)—The Bradford Specials
Specialty 852
Recorded on June 19, 1953 (*GOSP-#16, DM*)

Professor Alex Bradford was one of the top gospel stars of the immediate postwar era, and a major influence on Ray Charles. Born January 23, 1927, in Bessemer, Alabama, by age thirteen he had his own gospel group, and a year later his own local radio show. Based in Chicago after World War II, he joined the Willie Webb Singers in 1949, and one year later formed his own group. He'd written songs for Roberta Martin and other gospel artists, but it was when he joined Art Rupe's Specialty Records in 1953 (as both artist and talent scout) that Bradford became

206. Annotation, Smithsonian's *American Popular Song* boxed set, p. 82.

207. Friedwald, *Biographical Guide*, p. 326–27.

208. Her performance was accompanied by Beiderbecke and Trumbauer—replicating the solos they had first cut two years earlier—with a small-group contingent of Paul Whiteman sidemen; strangely, despite its high quality, the recording was not commercially issued at the time.

209. Jon Hendricks himself declared: "*Moody's Mood for Love* struck a chord in my soul" (Friedwald, *Biographical Guide*, p. 691). Ralph Gleason wrote in the October 13, 1960, *Down Beat* that both *Moody's Mood* and *Parker's Mood* by Pleasure "have already entered into the folk mythology of jazz."

210. The James Moody track, recorded in Sweden in late 1949, had been given only limited distribution in the U.S. before 1952. Much like sampling on rap records decades later, vocalese raised copyright issues, and the composer of *I'm In the Mood for Love*, Jimmy McHugh, publicly objected after Pleasure's record hit.

211. *Biographical Guide*, p. 691–92. Will Friedwald remarks that that despite the talent that created "one of the most enduring of all pop records," Pleasure proved too eccentric and limited to be a long-term star. Jefferson later claimed to have written the lyrics to *Moody's Mood*, and although many have accepted the claim (Bill Milkowski asserts in *Swing It! An Annotated History of Jive* (p. 121–22) that Beeks saw Jefferson perform the song in Cincinnati shortly before Beeks did it at the Apollo), Friedwald says flatly, "there's not a shred of evidence to support this contention."

a star in his own right. This was his first session for the label after two 1951–1952 dates for Apollo. His trademark composition *Too Close to Heaven* was first recorded (as *I'm Too Close*) by Eugene Smith with the Roberta Martin Singers in November 1952, and around the same time there was a tremendous version for the Gotham label by the Davis Sisters featuring Ruth Davis.[212] Anthony Heilbut writes in *The Gospel Sound* that Bradford's performance is reported to have sold a million copies and established him as "the Singing Rage of the Gospel Age. His huge, rough voice shook listeners," in combination with the group's colorful choreography.[213] As he sang and Little Joe Jackson answered his calls, they'd swirl off together, while the other five Specials would similarly dip in unison. Robert Darden calls this recording "a tour de force that sounds remarkably fresh today," particularly dramatic when his husky baritone "suddenly shoots to a true high C in falsetto—and back again."[214] Bradford carries the lead vocal on this moderately slow-tempo number, supported by the group and accompanied by piano, organ and light percussion. "I'm too close to heaven, I can't turn around . . . I can almost see God's face."

Just Make Love to Me (1954)—Muddy Waters (written by Willie Dixon)
Chess 1571
Recorded April 13, 1954 in Chicago; chart debut June 5, 1954 (#4 R&B) (*TC*)

The song we know as *I Just Want to Make Love to You* is one of the defining classics of 1950s electric Chicago blues. Little Walter Jacobs' powerful mouth harp playing and Otis Spann on piano combine with Muddy Waters delivering Willie Dixon's simple but erotically charged lyrics with emphatic authority, accompanied by his potent slide guitar, to produce a musical powerhouse. "There was quite a few people around singing the blues," remarked Dixon. "But most of 'em was singing all sad blues. Muddy was giving his blues a little pep, and I began trying to think of things in a peppier form."[215] Toby Creswell remarks on the combination of pride, confidence, and lust in the performance. "There's a touch of the gospel in the way Muddy seduces his prey; there's the promise of epic lovemaking in the gradual build. There's the pressure of desire that can barely be contained by the band."[216] "Fred Below's backbeat and Otis Spann's clever piano licks clearly give the music a sense of progression and drama earlier blues combos lacked," notes Robert Santelli. "Waters recalled the raw, rural feel of

Muddy Waters, courtesy of Library of Congress, LC-USZ62-123600.

the Mississippi Delta blues in his singing, without losing sight of the fact that he now lived in the big city, where new sounds swirled around him."[217]

The Wind (1954)—Nolan Strong & the Diablos
Fortune 511
Released in fall 1954 (*DM-#67, 1001*)[218]

Among the greatest of all doo-wop records, *The Wind* is also among the eeriest pop records ever made. It is an utterly compelling, atmospheric ballad, with an ethereal feeling. In *The Heart of Rock & Soul*, Dave Marsh ranked it as the #67 single of all time: "A guitar and bass chime the intro with *Twilight Zone* melodrama,[219] and then the bass voice announces 'Wind, wind—blow, wind.' A falsetto trills wordless notes over the top. At last an unbelievably high, slightly quavering male voice begins, measuring the cadence like a man conserving heartbeats:"

When the cool summer breeze sends a chill down my
    spine
When I long for my love's sweet caress
I know she has gone, but my love lingers on
In a dream that the winds bring to me.

212. Bessie Griffin would later make *Too Close* her trademark song, with passionate live renditions that often ran 20 minutes.

213. Heilbut, p. 154.

214. *People Get Ready! A New History of Black Gospel Music*, p. 263.

215. Gordon, *Can't Be Satisfied*, p. 123.

216. Creswell, *1001 Songs*, p. 32.

217. Santelli, *Best of the Blues*, p. 11.

218. The Diablos' debut single, *Adios My Desert Love* (Fortune 509), was reported as a territorial hit in their native Detroit in late May 1954. On December 25, *The Wind* was also cited as a breakout in Detroit.

219. The "shimmering chord work" (in Terence McArdle's phrase) is by guitarist Johnnie Bassett, who later played on recordings of Smokey Robinson's Miracles.

After the second verse, the music begins to drop out "until all that's left is the bass chanting 'wind, wind' underneath the corniest recitation you've ever heard. Strong speaks in a surreally wimpy voice that nevertheless possesses a certain kind of power." "Darling, when a star falls, I want you to remember," he declares. "If [this record] had arrived in a meteorite shower, and there are times when you swear it should have, it couldn't be any spookier."[220] Sophie Harris remarks that when Strong begins to sing, "it's a true goosebump moment."[221]

The cousin of Motown songwriter/producer Barrett Strong, Nolan Strong formed his group—with his brother Jimmy, Willie Hunter, Quentin Eubanks, and guitarist Bob "Chico" Edwards—while they were attending Detroit's Central High School. As detailed by Philip Groia, the group's name was inspired by a book Nolan had read in school, *El Nino Diablo* (The Little Devil). He had written *The Wind* while the group was hanging out on Hudson and Tilghman Streets. Central High just happened to be across the street from the studios of Fortune Records, located in a garage behind Jack and Devora Brown's record store. Strong had been a vocal student of Billy Ward (leader of the R&B group The Dominoes); Fortune signed them after an audition. Groia: "Perhaps that is how he learned the lead phrasing and harmony patterns that were so reminiscent of the Dominoes and the Drifters" (the latter during the early period led by Clyde McPhatter, a clear influence on Strong, as was Sonny Til of The Orioles).[222]

The Diablos never reached the *Billboard* chart; this was the second of the twenty-one singles they released, all on Fortune, the last new title coming in 1964. Smokey Robinson has acknowledged this record as an inspiration for his classic falsetto sound.[223] In 1960, the Jesters recorded a similarly wonderful version of *The Wind*, but it's tough to top the strange magic of the original.

Reconsider Baby (1954)—Lowell Fulson
Checker 804
Recorded in Dallas on Sept. 27, 1954; chart debut Dec. 4, 1954 (reached #3 R&B) (*GHF, Blues-#49, SB*)

One of the foremost bluesmen of the immediate postwar era, Lowell Fulson was born on March 31, 1921, on an Indian reservation in Tulsa, Oklahoma, to a highly musical family, began singing and tap dancing at an early age, and played guitar at picnics and country dances as a teenager. In 1940, based by this time in Texas, he served as accompanist to blues singer Texas Alexander at juke joints around their respective native states. After World War II service, he made his first recordings in Oakland in 1946, and began hitting the R&B charts two years later. His 1950–1951 recordings for the Swing Time label established him as a star, especially *Everyday I Have the Blues* (originally by Memphis Slim, later by B.B. King) and Lloyd Glenn's *Blue Shadows*. Arnold Shaw: "Mastery of the electric guitar helped make him a pivotal figure in the transformation of the Texas blues of Blind Lemon and Lightnin' Hopkins into West Coast R&B."[224]

It was Fulson's first release after switching to the Chess/Checker label, *Reconsider Baby*, that would prove his greatest. Made at Sellers Recording Studios in Dallas with a superb band including three saxmen (David "Fathead" Newman on tenor, Julian Beasley on alto, and Leroy Cooper on baritone sax), with Stan Lewis as producer, this is postwar urban blues at its best. Fulson's crisp guitar adds to the impact of his strong vocal. Elvis Presley was listening, and later cut his own cover version.

Django (1954)—Modern Jazz Quartet (written by John Lewis)
Recorded for Prestige on Dec. 24, 1954 (*Jazz-#27, NPR-100, RIA, SJ, TG*)

Pianist John Lewis first heard the great Belgian-born Gypsy guitarist Django Reinhardt during World War II while on a weekend pass, and was awestruck. After listening intently to his classic 1930s records with the Quintette of the Hot Club of France, he got to know the guitar virtuoso's music still better when Reinhardt came to the U.S. in 1947 to play with Duke Ellington. When Django came down to the club where Lewis was playing on New York's 52nd Street, "we played overtime to make a good impression." By the time of his death in May 1953, Reinhardt was one of the world's most beloved musicians. Lewis' musical tribute to the icon became the defining song for his group, the Modern Jazz Quartet.

Born on May 3, 1920, in LeGrange, Illinois, Lewis, after his discharge from military service, became pianist and arranger for Dizzy Gillespie's big band (1946–1947), including his charts for *Emanon* (issued on 78 as the flip side of the Gillespie classic *Things to Come*), *Two Bass Hit*, and *Minor Walk*. In addition to playing with Illinois Jacquet (1948–1949), and playing and arranging for the influential Miles Davis Nonet (1949, including the arrangements for *Move* and *Budo*), he freelanced with Charlie Parker among other artists (soloing on the 1948

---

220. Marsh, p. 48–49.
221. *1001 Songs You Must Hear*, p. 60.
222. *They All Sang on the Corner*, p, 32–33.
223. Berry Gordy tried to sign the Diablos to Motown, but Fortune outbid him to retain the group into the 1960s, and refused to license their recordings to other companies with better distribution, thus consigning them to regional cult status.

224. *Honkers and Shouters*, p. 96. In an interview with author Arnold Shaw (p. 104), the artist explained the different spellings of his last name used on record: "My name is sometimes spelled with an 'm' [at the end] and sometimes with an 'n.' My grandfather used *m*. My mother changed it to an *n*."

masterpiece *Parker's Mood*). Then in 1951–1952 he joined the Milt Jackson Quartet, with vibraharpist Jackson, bassist Ray Brown, and drummer Kenny Clarke; the four men had served as the rhythm section for Gillespie's band, and were regularly given their own quartet features in concerts. By the end of 1952 (with Percy Heath replacing Brown) it was renamed the Modern Jazz Quartet. The combination of Lewis' classically-structured arrangements, Jackson's virtuosity, and the chamber-jazz quality of the group's presentation, made the MJQ one of the era's most influential combos.

Django opens and closes with an elegant dirge-like melody (designed as a funeral processional with elements of both consolation and celebration, a nod to New Orleans and early jazz tradition) played in a slow, free tempo; the main body of the piece offers a series of choruses over which Jackson and Lewis solo. "*Django* is one of the few truly sustained 'extended' performances in recorded jazz," wrote Martin Williams.[225] "The subtle range of feeling it encompasses would be an achievement all by itself." Len Lyons calls it "sublime . . . possibly Lewis's best composition."[226] The MJQ received the Prix du Disque for its 1954 recording of *Django* at the American Embassy in Paris. Ted Gioia: "The MJQ's music captured an intimacy and delicacy, and a sensitivity to dynamics, that was closer in spirit to the great classical string quartets than anything in the world of bop or swing. But unlike their classical world counterparts, the MJQ thrived on the tension—whether conscious or subliminal—between their two lead players."[227] Jackson's improvisations offered a compelling contrast to Lewis' intricate designs.

Gary Giddins opines that the definitive performance of *Django* was delivered at the quartet's famous "last concert" in 1974. (Seven years later, the MJQ reunited for new live performances and recordings.) "Here all the elements of Lewis's skill and the MJQ's interpretive power are as one: the evocative Gypsy feeling in the main theme, recalling the *Adagio* of Mendelssohn's Octet; the eloquently stout bass motif; the congruence of delicacy and force, discipline and spontaneity, tragedy and joy."[228]

Rag Sindhu Bhairaui (1955)—Ali Akbar Khan

From the Angel album *Music of India: Morning and Evening Ragas*, recorded in April 1955

Declared "the greatest musician in the world" by violinist Yehudi Menuhin, Ustad Ali Akbar Khan was

born on April 14, 1922, in Shibpur in East Bengal (now Bangladesh). He is the master of the sarode, a 25-string, lute-like Indian instrument, and was introduced to music early by his parents—his father was a classical cellist and his mother a pianist. Khan was a featured performer on Indian radio from his teen years, became a court musician for the Maharaja of Jodhpur, and then achieved fame composing music for films in Bombay. In 1955, he was invited to America by Yehudi Menuhin, whom he had met when his parents accompanied the great violinist on All India Radio. After performing at New York's Museum of Modern Art, Khan that year recorded the first long-playing album of Indian classical music ever produced.[229] *Raga Sindhu Bhairavi* is a centuries-old raga of late morning, but commonly played as the last selection of an all-night concert. It's a lovely nineteen-minute piece with gradually building intensity, also featuring Chatur Lal on tabla, the two-headed Indian drum. He returned to India, made more than eighty albums, and taught thousands of students at the Ali Akbar College of Music in Calcutta. In 1967 he also founded a college of music in Berkeley, California, where his students included Carlos Santana. In 1971 Khan and Ravi Shankar were featured at George Harrison's Concert for Bangladesh at Madison Square Garden.

Ay-Tete-Fee (1955)—Clifton Chenier

Specialty 552

Recorded in Los Angeles; released in late summer/early fall 1955 (*World-#42, NPR, Folk-#70*)

A postwar phenomenon emerging out of Cajun music with primarily African-American variations—as accordion-driven rhythm & blues with a focus on accompaniment for dancing—zydeco first blossomed in Texas cities such as Port Arthur, Beaumont, Galveston, and Houston, not far from the Louisiana border.[230] The word "zydeco" itself first appeared in Houston during the late 1940s, and it quickly took hold in Cajun country as well.[231] John Minton calls it "a unique confrontation between African-American and African-French traditions indigenous to southeast Texas" (often played by musicians who are neither black nor French), with roots in

---

225. *The Jazz Tradition*, p. 175–77.

226. Lyons, *The 101 Best Jazz Albums*, p. 211.

227. Gioia, *The History of Jazz*, p. 285. In *The Jazz Standards* (p. 82), Gioia remarks: "*Django* sounds deceptively simple to the casual listener: indeed, there is a certain innocent, childlike quality to this composition that contrasts markedly with its arcane structural underpinning."

228. *Visions of Jazz*, p. 647.

229. *MusicHound World*, p. 376–78.

230. Many French Creoles had moved to Houston where jobs were more plentiful, and in the oil refineries and shipyards of Port Arthur.

231. The word "zydeco" is generally believed to derive from the phrase "les haricots" (pronounced *layzarico*) from an old song, *L'Haricots Sont Pas Sales* (The Snap Beans Aren't Salted), an allusion to hard times. The phrase was first documented in a 1934 performance of Louisiana *juré* music (from the French *jurer*, to testify or swear) recorded for the Library of Congress by Alan Lomax. A "zydeco" also meant a country party or dance, as in, "Let's go to the zydeco!" (Nyhan, Rollins, and Babb, *Let the Good Times Roll! A Guide to Cajun & Zydeco Music*, p. 13.)

Louisiana's colonial era.[232] The crucial artist who paved the way for the emergence of modern zydeco (which was commonly known by other names before the 1950s such as "la-la" music) was the great African-American accordionist-singer Amédé Ardoin with his recordings from 1929–1934. Texas bluesman Lightnin' Hopkins, having been exposed to the music of Louisiana Creoles in Houston's Fifth Ward, sang "Let's zydeco a little while for you folk" in the late-1949 recording *Zolo Go* (the title apparently the record label's misunderstanding of "zydeco"), on which he mimicked the sound of the accordion on a Hammond electric organ.[233] Clarence Garlow's *Bon Ton Roula* (translating from the actual French phrase "*laissez les bons temps rouler*" to "let the good times roll," a perfect slogan for the music)—a national Top Ten R&B hit in early 1950 for the Houston-based Macys label—was the first widely heard recording with the essential characteristics of zydeco,[234] [235] followed by Boozoo Chavis' *Paper In My Shoe* (1954). It was Clifton Chenier who gave the music its first superstar.

Born June 25, 1925, near Opelousas, Louisiana, Chenier was a self-proclaimed "black Frenchman" with French Creole heritage. After moving in 1947 to Lake Charles where he worked at an oil refinery, he began performing when he was off work, and made his recording debut in a 1954 session at Lake Charles radio station KAOK, consisting of all English selections.[236] But his first commercially released single was the record that became a zydeco classic, *Ay-Tete-Fee* (a phonetic spelling of "*eh, petite fille*"). Recorded at Specialty Records' Los Angeles studio and working with Bumps Blackwell (later renowned as Little Richard's producer), it's a delightfully exuberant performance with lyrics opening and closing in French, with an English chorus in between ("Oh, little girl, I wish you were mine") driven by his piano-key accordion, and backed by James Jones on piano, Philip Walker on guitar, and unknown bass and drums. This is a record that can get any dance floor

rocking. Oddly enough, despite the success of this disc, he would record almost nothing but R&B material (with minimal sales) for the next several years until moving full-time into zydeco in 1964. From that time until his death in 1987, Chenier reigned as the undisputed king of zydeco, playing to packed houses around the world and recording extensively; his most acclaimed album was *Bogalusa Boogie* (1976).

The Great Pretender (1955)—The Platters (written by Buck Ram)
Mercury 70753
Recorded in Sept. 1955; chart debut Dec. 17, 1955 (2 weeks at #1 on pop chart; #1 for 11 weeks R&B); reached #5 in England[237]; #1 (3 weeks) in Australia (*NPR-100, R&B-#35, GHF, RHF, DM-#154, RS, DMDB*)

The most sensationally successful pop group of the 1950s, the Platters got their start when Tony Williams ventured from Elizabeth, New Jersey, (where he was born on April 5, 1928) to Los Angeles in 1952, and was recruited to become the fledgling group's lead singer. The group's original 1954–early 1955 records for Federal were flops. Then they were taken under the wing of veteran songwriter/arranger/artist manager Samuel "Buck" Ram, who got the Chicago-based Mercury label to sign them as a package deal with another group he managed, the Penguins (of *Earth Angel* fame). Fourteen-year-old Zola Taylor was added as the group's girl singer, joining holdover members David Lynch (tenor), Alex Hodge (baritone), and Herb Reed (bass). Ram made Williams, with his soaring tenor lead, the centerpiece of the group, and emphasized their strength in big, dramatic ballads with a doo-wop heart but lavish pop production values. *Only You*, a song the group had first cut for Federal, became its breakthrough smash in summer 1955 through a new version made for Mercury.

The Great Pretender—like *Only You* a Ram original—was the quintet's second release for Mercury. The Platters were performing eight shows a night at the Flamingo in Las Vegas when Mercury president Irv Green called for them to hustle back to Los Angeles to record the song; Zola Taylor recalled them driving out in Reed's 1949 Ford "on four flat tires." Williams had just gotten over a touch of tonsillitis.

Dave Marsh suggests that it "touches the core of social and personal dysfunction, and that's no joke . . . Sure, the presumption is that Tony Williams is singing about the loss of romantic love. But what the song's really about is alienation."[238] ("Too real is this feeling of make believe

---

232. Minton article, "Houston Creoles and Zydeco: The Emergence of an African American Urban Popular Style," *American Music*, Vol. 14 #4 (Winter 1996).

233. Alan Govenar, *Lightnin' Hopkins: His Life and Blues*, p. 50–51. Hopkins was also the man who helped revive Chenier's career in 1964 when he brought Chris Strachwitz to see the zydeco master perform, leading to a new recording contract.

234. Garlow sang, "If you want to have fun, now, you got to go / Way out in the country to the zydeco. / Well, let the bon ton rouler . . ."

235. It was folklorist Mack McCormick who helped popularize the word "zydeco" as a generic term for the music on his two-LP 1960 anthology *A Treasury of Field Recordings*, by folk musicians in Houston. Nick Spitzer, best known as longtime host of the Louisiana-based public radio series *American Routes*, discovered through fieldwork among rural Creole musicians additional roots for the term "zydeco" in various West African languages.

236. Louis Jordan and Fats Domino were his biggest R&B influences. See Ben Sandmel's interview feature on Chenier from his book *Zydeco!* reprinted in *From Jubilee to Hip-Hop*, 221–36.

237. Released in U.K. in late 1956 with *Only You* as the B side.

238. Marsh, *The Heart of Rock & Soul*, p. 108.

/ Too real when I feel what my heart can't conceal.") Everything builds to Williams' melodramatic, soaring-to-the-heavens climax, setting the standard for so many Platters hits to come.

Pithecanthropus Erectus (1956)—Charles Mingus & His Orchestra

Recorded on Jan. 30, 1956

From the Atlantic album *Pithecanthropus Erectus* (*NPR-300, Jazz-#123*)

Pithecanthropus Erectus was composer/bassist Charles Mingus' musical conception of no less than mankind's struggle out of chaos, evolving to a position of supremacy, and then its self-destruction back into chaos due to committing the sin of pride. According to Gary Giddins, it "established Mingus's place in the jazz vanguard . . . The thematic material is striking—a mysterious, modal melody propelled by a throbbing bass walk, climaxing with a three-beat rest, and resuming, with a sudden shift in dynamics, as a 32-bar extension played with steadily increasing polyphony. Its most startling feature in 1956 was not the modality or the break or the uncommon structure, but the intensity that resulted from employing the most extreme registers of the saxophone."[239] Mervyn Cooke remarks in *The Chronicle of Jazz* that the piece's passages of free improvisation foreshadow the "free jazz" movement to be led by Ornette Coleman a few years later. Paul Evans (*Rolling Stone*) notes that it "showed how Mingus often wrote music to illustrate a very specific, often elusive emotional state. And the playing, with its gospel influence, its whoops and hollers, displayed the characteristic Mingus exuberance." This work, says Len Lyons, "epitomizes his creativity on several counts: varying tempos; extended form; virtually atonal collective improvising; and the use of pedal-point tonality instead of chord changes . . . his first major successful piece."[240]

(Jackie McLean on alto sax; J. R. Monterose on tenor sax; Mal Waldron on piano; Willie Jones on drums)

On the Street Where You Live (1956)—Vic Damone

(lyrics by Alan Jay Lerner, music by Frederick Loewe)

Columbia 40654 (chart debut April 21, 1956, reached #4)

One of the landmark shows in the history of the Broadway musical, *My Fair Lady* featured a score so packed with wall-to-wall gems that initially it's difficult to single out just one. But in the midst of such standards as *I Could Have Danced All Night, I've Grown Accustomed to Her Face, With a Little Bit of Luck,* and *Wouldn't It*

Be Loverly, On the Street Where You Live emerged as the biggest, most beloved ballad of all, and its leading pop rendition was by Vic Damone.

Lyricist Alan Jay Lerner was born in New York City on August 31, 1918, and grew up on the songs of the American musical theater. Composer Frederick Loewe, born on June 10, 1904, in Vienna, Austria, was (notes the duo's biographer Gene Lees) raised on Viennese operetta, and remained "Viennese to the day he died." "Thus Lerner and Loewe combined in their work two important musical strains,"[241] both of which had contributed to the Broadway tradition (as such previous composers as Victor Herbert, Jerome Kern, and Kurt Weill had come from backgrounds similar to Loewe's). Loewe wrote his first European hit at fifteen, came to the U.S. in 1924, and had minimal success in the next decade and a half as a pianist and composer (writing a short-lived 1938 Broadway musical with lyricist Earle Crooker). He teamed with the younger Lerner (whose previous work had been writing radio scripts) starting with the 1943 musical *What's Up*; one more flop later came their breakthrough in 1947, the classic *Brigadoon*, followed by the 1951 hit *Paint Your Wagon.* Then came the show that would define them for all time.

My Fair Lady, a musical adaptation of the George Bernard Shaw play *Pygmalion*, had a timeless Cinderella theme (Henry Higgins' transformation of working-class Eliza Doolittle into a lady of society), but the play's absence of romance and its deeply British nature presented the writers with a challenge. They met it brilliantly, with a dazzling score and the matchless pairing of Rex Harrison and Julie Andrews. From its March 15, 1956, opening, it was an instant blockbuster (the *New York Times'* review proclaimed it the "show of the century"), running for over 2,700 performances, shattering the seemingly unbreakable record of Rodgers & Hammerstein's *Oklahoma!* It was also a phenomenon on the *Billboard* album chart: fifteen weeks at #1, 173 weeks in the Top Ten (second only to the *South Pacific* cast album), 292 weeks in the Top 40 (also second for all time), and 480 total weeks.

Born Vito Farinola in Brooklyn on June 12, 1928, Vic Damone made his chart debut in 1947, had a #1 smash two years later with *You're Breaking My Heart*, and had his greatest success in the 1950s with movie appearances (including *Kismet* and *Meet Me in Las Vegas*) and his own 1956–1957 TV series. Will Friedwald praises his "beautiful voice, the light clear sound, the precise articulation, the impeccable phrasing." His style was in the classic "bel canto" mold, strongly Sinatra-influenced, with moderately slow love ballads his specialty. *On the Street Where You Live* (sung on stage by John Michael King

239. *Visions of Jazz*, p. 447–48.
240. Lyons, *The 101 Best Jazz Albums*, p. 275.
241. *Inventing Champagne*, p. 4.

as Eliza's suitor Freddy) was tailor made for Damone. After his long tenure on the Mercury label (1947–1955), *Street* was his debut hit for Columbia—appropriately, as Columbia had invested heavily in *My Fair Lady* and reaped spectacular profits from it. He and producer Mitch Miller selected the song from the score, but Friedwald remarks that the choice "seems predestined," so ideally is it suited to both his voice and (through its warmly romantic naiveté) to his approach of "utter sincerity."[242]

Uncloudy Day (1956)—Staple Singers (written by the Rev. Josiah K. Alwood)
Vee-Jay 224
Recorded in Chicago on Sept. 11, 1956 (*GOSP-#14, GHF*)

The second single on Vee-Jay released by Roebuck "Pops" Staples and his family group featuring the wondrous voice of seventeen-year-old Mavis Staples, *Uncloudy Day* became the record that established the Chicago-based group's national reputation. Their debut for the label, *If I Could Hear My Mother Pray Again*, had sold barely 300 copies, but *Uncloudy Day* turned things around in a hurry, reportedly selling well over 100,000. Written in 1890, for many years the inspirational song was largely a staple of white sacred and country performers, including versions under the title *The Unclouded Day* by Homer Rodeheaver (1914), the Old Southern Sacred Singers (1927), Smith's Sacred Singers (1928), Cliff Carlisle & His Buckle Busters (1939), and the Maddox Brothers & Rose (1950). Roebuck "Pops" Staples fashioned a new arrangement with a "dirge-like" tempo. "With Pops' Delta-influenced guitar tuning, Pervis's falsetto, and Cleotha's high notes contrasting with Mavis's lusty contralto," writes Bil Carpenter, "the Staples created a unique sound that made them instant gospel celebrities."[243] Anthony Heilbut in *The Gospel Sound* cited Mavis' "deep, erotic lead" in this performance.[244]

I Can't Quit You Baby (1956)—Otis Rush (written by Willie Dixon)
Cobra 5000
Recorded in Chicago c. July 1956; chart debut Oct. 13, 1956 (reached #6 on R&B chart) (*Blues-#46, RHF*)

Standing in the forefront of the great postwar Chicago blues guitarists even though his fame would never match his musical prowess, Otis Rush was born in Philadelphia, Mississippi, on April 29, 1934, came to Chicago with his family in 1948, formed his own band in 1955, and blues songwriter/maestro Willie Dixon helped him land a contract with Eli Toscano's Cobra Records. His very first recording—and Cobra's maiden release—*I Can't*

Quit You Baby, would become his only charted record and his enduring masterpiece.[245] It's a searingly powerful performance that Bill Dahl calls "startlingly intense."[246]

Robert Palmer described it as "a medium-slow, steady-rocking shuffle, with Otis shouting the gospel blues and playing rapid-fire bursts of high-note guitar paced by bass-string riffs that still retained a little of the Muddy Waters feel." Indeed, this was one of the earliest major blues recordings that featured the new innovation of electric bass, played by Greenwood, Mississippi, native Willie D. Warren, playing (as Palmer writes) "bass lines on the bottom four strings of his regular guitar before Fender began marketing the four-stringed bass guitar."[247] The rest of the ensemble: Walter Horton on harmonica, Red Holloway on tenor sax, Lafayette Leake on piano, Wayne Bennett on guitar, and Al Duncan on drums.

This session and the launching of Cobra was important for Willie Dixon, who—having already made his name at Chess Records—had full creative control for the first time. He recalled in his autobiography that Toscano was begging for a hit. "I told him, 'This record will sell,' because Otis was a helluva good singer with a lot of expression. We were fooling around in the studio and I figured the best idea was to dim the lights to get Otis in the mood." When Rush really cut loose after a few takes, Dixon looked at Toscano in the booth: "That must be the first time I ever saw anybody's hair stand straight up on their head." When the number was done, the label founder was crying with joy.[248]

Brown Eyed Handsome Man (1956)—Chuck Berry
Chess 1635
Chart debut Oct. 20, 1956 (#4 R&B) (*RS, DM*)

Brown Eyed Handsome Man, writes Chuck Berry biographer Bruce Pegg, "boasts an extraordinary set of lyrics that, if not for the first time in a popular song, then certainly for the first time in a rock-and-roll song, expressed pride in being black. The title indicates brown eyes, and—but for the times—it could equally well have said 'brown-skinned,' so overt was its message." In its dramatic opening stanza depicting harassment in the legal system, his protagonist finds himself "arrested on charges of unemployment"—"a wonderful phrase that in

242. *Biographical Guide*, p. 129–30.
243. Carpenter, *Uncloudy Days*, p. 389.
244. Heilbut, p. 278–79.

245. In liner notes for *The Cobra Records Story* (p. 8), Howard Bedno, who helped Toscano create the label, recalled being at this session held at Boulevard Studios, located (behind Toscano's record shop) near the intersection of Jackson and Wabash in downtown Chicago. "Otis was very young and bashful. He didn't say much, so when he would open his mouth and start to sing, it was just astounding."
246. *All Music Guide to the Blues*, p. 229.
247. *Deep Blues*, p. 266–67.
248. *I Am the Blues*, p. 107–8. According to Dixon, before the label pressed records for the performance, he and Toscano brought a dub to Chicago disc jockey Big Bill Hill, who played it on station WOPA, and the station's switchboard "lit up like a Christmas tree."

just five words manages to describe both the social and economic inequalities" facing blacks in America.

"But Berry had an even more radical, even subversive message for his listeners," continues Pegg. "Many of the verses describe women of some social standing, presumably blue-eyed themselves, in pursuit of the brown-eyed man."[249] And then of course there is the indelible final verse that's become warmly embedded in baseball history, describing a game-winning home run by a brown-eyed handsome man—a description that in 1956 probably meant either Willie Mays or Jackie Robinson. Perhaps in part because of the song's lyrical boldness, the record failed to make the pop chart even while scoring big on the rhythm & blues chart.

Brian Ward, in *Just My Soul Responding*, notes that Berry "proudly celebrated the historical potency and allure of black men and mocked white racial and sexual taboos by explaining how the Venus de Milo—the quintessence of white female beauty" had "lost both her arms in a wrestling match / To win a brown-eyed handsome man."

Summertime (1957)—Louis Armstrong & Ella Fitzgerald

Recorded in Aug. 1957 for the Verve album *Porgy and Bess* (*Jazz-#110*)

The three albums teaming Louis Armstrong and Ella Fitzgerald (all recorded in 1956–1957) gave us two of the twentieth century's supreme musical legends who, if perhaps not perfectly matched in their very distinctive styles, nonetheless provided some magical moments. Among the most magical was their rendition of the George Gershwin masterpiece *Summertime*. This gorgeous performance opens with a French horn introduction, then Armstrong's trumpet (backed by strings) playing the first half of the melody. Ella enters the record to sing the first sixteen bars solo, followed by Louis singing the last sixteen bars. Fitzgerald returns to the start of the lyric, this time with a vocal obbligato by Satch, and they duet on the final half-chorus. "Armstrong and Fitzgerald are utterly majestic," writes Will Friedwald, "particularly their final half-chorus together, which ends with Fitzgerald jumping around to E and F sharp rather than simply going to the tonic B as written."[250] Dan Morgenstern praises the "luxurious" production of the album, arranged and conducted by Russ Garcia, with production by Norman Granz. Richard Cook and Brian Morton write that *Summertime* "is turned into a profoundly moving meditation, and the closing bars of this version are as transcendent as anything in the work of either Ella or Louis."[251]

Theme from *Vertigo* (1958)—Bernard Herrmann

Soundtrack album released on Mercury; film released on May 9, 1958 (*AFI-#12*)

For many film fanatics, *Vertigo* stands as the ultimate Alfred Hitchcock picture. Among its many cinematic virtues—the profound mystery of its psychological explorations, dazzling visuals, (twisted) romance, and the lead performances of James Stewart and Kim Novak—the original score composed by Bernard Herrmann is among its greatest. The film's opening credits, as scored by Herrmann evoking an overwhelmingly eerie sense of dark foreboding, rank among the most spine-tingling sequences in movie history.

Born to a non-musical family in New York on June 29, 1911, Herrmann studied composition at New York University and Juilliard, and by age eighteen had already written a ballet for a Broadway show and had formed and conducted a chamber orchestra. He joined CBS in 1933 as composer-conductor for dramatic and documentary radio shows, and conducted original concert pieces with the CBS Orchestra. Among the many radio programs he scored were programs directed by the young Orson Welles, and it was Welles who hired Herrmann for the film score that launched his Hollywood career: *Citizen Kane*.[252] After films including *Jane Eyre* (1944), *The Ghost and Mrs. Muir* (1947), and *The Day the Earth Stood Still* (1951), Herrmann began his association with Hitchcock on *The Trouble with Harry* (1955) and *The Man Who Knew Too Much* (1956), and continued with *North by Northwest* (1959) and *Psycho* (1960). Topping them all was his score for *Vertigo*.

The tale of traumatized San Francisco detective Scottie Ferguson (Stewart) and his obsession with mystery woman Madeleine (Novak), *Vertigo* opens with the amazing credits sequence designed by Saul Bass, filled with swirling spiral figures and kaleidoscopic images, rendered far more extraordinary by the music of Herrmann. Page Cook described it: "The credit music, in an invention of major thirds, accompanies some dizzy optical effects, and the prelude begins with a huge basso ostinato upon which a solid horn figure startlingly appears. We then hear, for the first time, the melody, written in the key of D major, which is the clue to Madeleine's obsession about her dead grandmother. The melody's first use grows in intensity—the orchestration is quite bizarre—and achieves grim crescendo, which leads, after a harrowing drop, to a sustained note in the double bass. The harmonies are abstract but never cacophonic."[253]

Jay Alan Quantrill: "Bernard Herrmann's music is rooted in traditional tonalities, but under the influence of

249. Pegg, p. 67–68.
250. *Stardust Melodies*, p. 337–38.
251. *Penguin Guide to Jazz*, p. 57–58.

252. Tony Thomas, *Music for the Movies*, p. 186–94.
253. Career profile on the composer in *Films in Review*. The *Vertigo* score attained the stature to be performed in concert halls.

such a modernist as Charles Ives, he developed a palette of harmonies based mainly on the triads (the basic three-note chord in its various permutations and positions). He constructed polytonal harmonies by combining triads, such as the E flat minor/D minor combination that is the major feature of the *Vertigo* score. This polytonality gives his music its tension, its unresolved 'resolutions' which are unsettling and therefore quite appropriate to Hitchcock's style of cinema—which is consistently unresolved (sometimes even at the end)." Quantrill notes that in the opening sequence, Herrmann's use of "a triadic figure, ascending and descending, punctuated by phrases and chords . . . expertly captures the emotions of the title." The music he devised "to create the feeling of vertigo with its throbbing hot-cold sweat of fear is perfectly captured in the contours of the music."[254]

Mi Unico Camino (My Only Path) (1958)—El Conjunto Bernal

Recorded in late 1958, title song of album for Ideal Records (*World-#84*)

Accordion-led *conjuntos* with male harmony vocals had been a dominant force in Mexican-American border music for about twenty years by the time the group originally known as Los Hermanitos Bernal was formed in 1952, and it seemed that the longtime genre's glory days had come and gone. But the combo proved that there was plenty of vigor still left in the music, and the symbol of that renewal became *Mi Unico Camino*. When the major record labels largely abandoned Tex-Mex music (along with other ethnic genres) after 1942, regional labels tried to fill the void, and one of the most noteworthy was Ideal, founded in 1946 by Armando Marroquin of Alice, Texas, and Paco Betancourt of San Benito. After scoring early successes with vocal duets by Carmen y Laura (the owner's wife and her sister), Ideal recorded accordion legend Narciso Martinez, Tony de la Rosa, Valerio Longoria, and (starting in the mid-to-late 1950s) Flaco Jimenez and Freddy Fender. El Conjunto Bernal would be the label's biggest act of all.

Born in Raymondville, Texas, on June 22, 1939, accordionist-singer Paulino Bernal was thirteen years old when he began playing dances with his older brother Eloy on bajo sexto and vocal harmonies in 1952. Paulino's strengths as both singer and instrumentalist, and eventually as a songwriter, helped the brothers build a steadily growing audience in south Texas, and another major asset was powerful high tenor vocalist Ruben

Perez; their first important single was *Mujer Paseada* (Traveled Woman) in 1955. *Mi Unico Camino*, a *ranchera* (a traditional Mexican vocal music rooted in the times of the Mexican Revolution of the 1910s) in *vals* (waltz) tempo, was their breakthrough. Manuel Pena writes that the song was "an unparalleled success, the more impressive because it marked the first time a conjunto had ever incorporated three-part harmonies." Such harmonies had been used in other forms of Mexican music, but their use in the conjunto format added "a new dimension" and a jolt of electricity to the music. Central to its impact here is the slow, intensely romantic arrangement employing dramatic pauses before the three voices soar to an emotional peak, a show-stopping device that packs a wallop. Pena: "I believe it is safe to say that in El Conjunto Bernal" during its early years, "the most ideal conjunto sound had been achieved."[255] Paulino Bernal launched his own record label (Bego) in 1963, and the group remained popular through the end of the decade. *Mi Unico Camino* earned a new distinction in 1996 when it was used as the opening song in John Sayles' acclaimed film *Lone Star* whose story was set amidst the ethnic tensions of south Texas.[256]

Lonely Teardrops (1958)—Jackie Wilson (written by Berry Gordy, Jr. & Billy Davis)

Brunswick 55105

Recorded Oct. 15, 1958; chart debut Nov. 17, 1958 (#1 for 7 weeks R&B; #7 pop); #11 in Canada (*DM-#42, GHF, R&B-#100, RS, AHR, TC, DMDB*)

"Jackie Wilson opened his mouth and out poured that sound like honey on moonbeams, and it was like the whole room shifted on some weird axis." So said Dick Jacobs, the Brunswick artists & repertoire man who co-produced the Detroit dynamo's early records, and *Lonely Teardrops*—his third charted record and first giant hit—introduced much of the world to that sound.

Budding Detroit songwriter and soon-to-be Motown founder Berry Gordy had co-written Wilson's first successes *Reet Petite* and *To Be Loved*. He related in his memoir: "When I started writing another song for Jackie I decided to do something different. Convinced he could do anything, I created a story about a guy crying, begging a lost love to come back." Dick Jacobs heard the demo and arranged for Gordy to make his first trip to New York to ensure that Wilson would capture the song's feeling. "The give-and-take between Dick and me was wonderful. Together, we worked out the tempo to his great calypso-type arrangement without losing the feel and drama. Everybody in sync: the horns, the strings, the flutes, the

---

254. Liner notes to the soundtrack CD. Kathryn Kalinak (*Movie Music, The Film Reader*, p. 1–22) remarks that Herrmann set out to create a score that "exploits harmony for disturbing effect." For the opening theme he did this through "alternately descending and ascending arpeggiated chords played in contrary motion in the bass and treble voices."

255. *The Texas-Mexican Conjunto*, p. 89–92.

256. It also serves as the title song of a 24-track group history issued by Arhoolie (1992).

bells. And a harp. All this music over the speakers surrounding me felt like I was in a concert hall . . . I knew that this was the way great records should be made."[257]

Wilson in October 1957 had become one of the first black artists to perform on *American Bandstand*, and he (like Gordy) was determined to reach the predominantly white teenage audience. Toward that end, *Teardrops* employs a danceable cha-cha rhythm done to a modified calypso beat, and a perky white backing vocal group. But it's the vocal pyrotechnics of Wilson that makes it soar. It was also the last song Jackie Wilson ever performed on stage; while in the middle of the number at the line "my heart is crying" at a New Jersey casino in 1975, he collapsed and fell into a coma from which he never recovered. Often compared to James Brown and Sam Cooke, Joe McEwen remarked that "the comparison is not unflattering: as a showman, Wilson was the equal of Brown, while as a vocalist, he could match Cooke's range and then some."[258]

Lonely Woman (1959)—Ornette Coleman
Recorded May 22, 1959 for the Atlantic album *The Shape of Jazz to Come* (released in November 1959) (*Jazz-#73*)

Ornette Coleman was the most widely-discussed, controversial jazz artist of his time: to his supporters a visionary whose work pointed the way to an exciting future, to his detractors an undisciplined and often unmusical experimenter. Born March 19, 1930, in Fort. Worth, Texas, he played tenor sax with local bands as a teenager (later switching mainly to alto), and the next few years worked mainly with R&B groups including Pee Wee Clayton's. After moving to Los Angeles, he studied harmony and theory (self-taught) as he developed a style departing from the traditional concept of improvisation based on chord patterns. His 1958 debut album (*Something Else!*) on the Contemporary label, followed in early 1959 by *Tomorrow Is the Question*, stirred enough interest (and debate) for Atlantic to sign him. His first LP recorded for the label, *The Shape of Jazz to Come*, left no doubt through its title about the audacious scope of his ambition, and the music largely backed it up.

Called by Martin Williams "perhaps the most powerful of a series of magnificent dirges that he has recorded," *Lonely Woman* is a haunting, rather tortured jazz ballad. In *The Jazz Tradition*, Williams remarks that it is "remarkable both in plan and in execution," opening with bass and drums, then the horns entering in a slow tempo setting forth the "stark" theme. Coleman's alto solo features "freely accented individual phrases and an adroit use of implied double-time [that] give an immea-

surable complexity and richness to the performance."[259] His combo is a huge asset to the piece: trumpeter Don Cherry (the only musician to also appear on his first two albums), bassist Charlie Haden, and drummer Billy Higgins. Giving the album a 4-star review in the December 10, 1959, *Down Beat*, John S. Wilson compared the "shock" provided by the quartet's music to that of Dizzy Gillespie and Charlie Parker in the 1940s, and suggested that Coleman and Cherry possessed a similar musical chemistry.[260] Ted Gioia notes that his early music continued to use standard 32-bar and 12-bar structures and familiar chord changes, but exemplified a "purging" of other traditions. "It was . . . as though all of the clichés and hoary riffs accumulated over a half-century of jazz music were thrown overboard, lightening the load and opening up the horizon."[261] [262]

While Coleman's unconventional approach meant that only a small portion of his repertoire was picked up by other jazzmen until wider acceptance arrived by the 1980s, the raw beauty of *Lonely Woman* eventually made it something of a modern jazz standard. *Change of the Century* further expanded his growing influence, and 1960's *Free Jazz*—even if it didn't quite meet the artist's bold claims that he was breaking free of the music's outmoded traditions—became, along with the later work of John Coltrane (a Coleman admirer), an enduring symbol of modern jazz. As he continued his restless explorations into the twenty-first century, Coleman continued to embody the observation of Richard Cook and Brian Morton: "No jazz musician—possibly ever—has so comprehensively and irredeemably divided [critical] opinion." Whatever one's opinion of his improvisations, Gary Giddins is among those who marvels at Coleman as a composer, calling *Lonely Woman* "incomparably poignant."[263]

Cloudburst (1959)—Lambert, Hendricks & Ross
(music by Leroy Kirkland, lyrics by Jon Hendricks)
Recorded on Aug. 6, 1959 for the Columbia album *The Hottest New Group in Jazz* (released in early 1960)[264] (*TM*)

---

257. *To Be Loved*, p. 96–97.
258. *Rolling Stone Illustrated History of Rock*, p. 118.

259. Williams, p. 242. He also praises the "textural richness" of drummer Billy Higgins' work.
260. Wilson: "*Lonely Woman*, on which Coleman makes formidable use of his interest in paralleling his instrument with the human voice, achieves a lamenting wail that is strikingly similar to the New Orleans dirges" as recorded by such ensembles as the Eureka Brass Band.
261. Gioia, *The History of Jazz*, p. 342–43.
262. John Litweiler (*The Freedom Principle: Jazz After 1958*, p. 37) suggests that if the quartet had played *Lonely Woman* in a slow tempo, "self-pity would have resulted. But with the fast drums of Higgins and Haden's bass suspended in irregular double stops, the setting is ambiguous and the slow theme emerges as pity, sorrow, and resignation in unevenly measured strains"; ultimately, "the woman becomes a breathing, sexual being."
263. *Visions of Jazz*, p. 470.
264. The album was reviewed in the March 3, 1960, *Down Beat*. The small combo backing LHR features Harry Edison on trumpet and Ike Isaacs on bass.

Dave Lambert, Jon Hendricks, and Annie Ross had each done pioneering work exploring the still-evolving field of vocalese before they joined forces to become the most influential and popular group in the entire genre. Dave Lambert (born June 19, 1917, in Westport, Connecticut) first made his mark singing with Gene Krupa's band in 1944–1945, making the first bop vocal record, *What's This*, and leading the Dave Lambert Singers in the early 1950s. Jon Hendricks (born September 16, 1921, in Newark, Ohio) began working as a songwriter in 1951, and the following year made an acclaimed vocal version of the Woody Herman band's *Four Brothers* (arranged by Lambert). Annie Ross, born in Mitcham, England, on July 25, 1930, came to the U.S. with her aunt, singer/actress Ella Logan, and burst on the scene with her dazzling vocal records of Art Farmer's *Farmer's Market* (late 1952) and Wardell Gray's *Twisted*.

After first working together on *Four Brothers*, Jon Hendricks and the Dave Lambert Singers teamed in May 1955 for *Cloudburst*, based on a previously obscure early 1950s jazz instrumental by "Claude Cloud & His Thunderclaps," led by the tune's composer, guitarist Leroy Kirkland. The 1955 performance was released as a Decca single, and paved the way for the formation of Lambert, Hendricks & Ross (LHR). The trio made a big splash with their 1956 verve album *Sing a Song of Basie*, featuring Hendricks' rapid-fire lyrics to Count Basie instrumental classics. After two more albums, LHR switched to Columbia for the album generally regarded as their greatest. The trio's new version of *Cloudburst* surpassed the previous version: Hendricks cuts loose with breathtakingly rapid-fire vocalizing based largely on the tenor sax soloing of Sam "The Man" Taylor on the "Claude Cloud" original, packing a lot into just two minutes and eighteen seconds. Tom Moon: "Through choruses taken at breakneck speed, he rattles off crazed, not-quite-nonsense syllables that romanticize, and also humanize, the feats of the music's great instrumentalists."[265] LHR remained a winning team until Ross's departure in 1962; Lambert died four years later, and Hendricks and Ross remained titans of vocalese for decades thereafter.

"Before Lambert, Hendricks & Ross, there were certain preconceived notions of what the human voice could do and what instruments were supposed to do," writes Will Friedwald. "LHR showed how an instrumental, big band performance could be translated into vocal terms—not only with voices, but with words."[266] Years later, whenever Jon Hendricks performed live with his group Jon Hendricks & Company, he would announce that "we are dedicated to the perpetuation of the sound of Lambert, Hendricks & Ross, the greatest vocal group

ever to perform on the planet Earth." As he related with a chuckle to Nat Hentoff: "After I say that, I wait for someone to contradict me. And it never happens."[267]

Akiwowo (Chant to the Trainman) (1960)—Babatunde Olatunji

From the Columbia album *Drums of Passion* (*World-#36, RR*)

The Western pop music world had not yet gotten hip to the wonders of African music in 1960. Some musically astute folks had heard Solomon Linda's 1939 South African classic *Mbube* (still a year away from being reworked as *The Lion Sleeps Tonight*), and an elite group of British and American listeners had some exposure to Hugh Tracey's long series of 1940s and 1950s field recordings for the International Library of African Music. The one album that dramatically hastened the process was Babatunde Olatunji's *Drums of Passion*.

Born in 1927 in the small West African town of Ajido, Nigeria, the son of a fisherman, Olatunji had an early fascination with musicians at village festivals. As detailed by Craig Harris, he came to America in 1950 to attend Morehouse College in Atlanta, and while there produced a multi-media show on the music and culture of his native land. After continuing his studies in New York starting in 1954, he burst into wider prominence through an extended 1957 engagement at Radio City Music Hall, performing a medley of African songs with a sixty-six-piece orchestra.[268] Legendary producer and talent scout John Hammond was deeply impressed, and after he completed his tenure at Vanguard Records and returned to his former home at Columbia, he signed the artist and arranged for him to record *Drums of Passion*.

The music on this landmark album was inspired by the multiple drums regularly used in Nigeria to proclaim the arrival of a local dignitary. This was tied to the long tradition of "talking drums" throughout West Africa. The entire LP is compelling, and the opening track, *Akiwowo*, is electrifying. The barrage of drums is designed in part to suggest the rhythmic beat of a freight train, and the piece has a powerful, surging drive.[269] It is, along with the rest of the album, the ancestor of such "drum orchestras" as the black Brazilian group Olodum, as heard on Paul Simon's *The Obvious Child* twenty-nine years after this recording. Although it did not appear on the *Billboard* chart, *Drums of Passion* received such widespread exposure that it was an early world music counterpart to *Buena Vista Social Club*. John Storm Roberts called the

265. Moon, *1,000 Recordings to Hear Before You Die*, p. 439.
266. *Biographical Guide*, p. 280.

267. Hentoff, *Listen to the Stories*, p. 63.
268. *MusicHound; World*, p. 570–71.
269. He plays the ngomo drum, ashiko drum, the djembe (played without sticks, it's become one of the most popular non-European instruments in the West), and shekere (dry gourds covered with a net of shells), with other musicians contributing additional percussion instruments.

album a symbol of the "Africanization of jazz."[270] Its success—by one (probably exaggerated) account it sold five million copies worldwide—paved the way for Olatunji to compose the score for the Broadway and film productions of *A Raisin in the Sun*, and to record followup *Drums of Passion* albums for the Rykodisc label in the 1980s arranged by Grateful Dead drummer Mickey Hart, who credited the Nigerian with inspiring his interest in drums.[271] In 2004 the original classic was one of the third group of recordings selected by the Library of Congress for the National Recording Registry.

Runaround Sue (1961)—Dion
Laurie 3110

Chart debut Sept. 25, 1961 (2 weeks at #1); reached #1 in
    Canada, #11 in England [272] (*DM-#111, GHF, AHR,*
    RIA, TC, ACC, DMDB)

When Dion DiMucci split from the Italian-American doo-woppers the Belmonts to forge his own solo career, he carved out a new persona (as described by David Dalton and Lenny Kaye: "a freewheeling, restless character caught in perpetual motion. He was the moody stranger, gone before you knew he'd arrived, leaving a chain of broken hearts and wishful dreams in his turbulent eddy."[273] The hit that helped establish that classic image was *Runaround Sue*.

Born in the Bronx on July 18, 1939, DiMucci first recorded in 1957 as Dion & the Timberlanes on the Mohawk label. Finding three new musical partners from the pool halls and streets of his neighborhood, Dion & the Belmonts (after Belmont Avenue in the Bronx) began scoring hits on the Laurie label in 1958 with the street-corner harmony charmer *I Wonder Why*, but after several more hits he went solo to pursue a more rock & roll direction in late 1960, while the Belmonts continued to make doo-wop recordings on their own. His first few solo records were not memorable; then came this breakthrough.

Ernie Marseca, who had written the Belmonts' second hit *No One Knows*, wrote *Runaround Sue* with Dion, and had penned its smash successor *The Wanderer* a few years earlier. To recapture the vocal group feeling of the Belmonts but with a more rock-oriented attitude, producer Gene Schwartz teamed the artist with the Del-Satins. In *The Billboard Book of Number One Hits* by Fred Bronson, Dion recalled that although he married a woman named Sue, the song was written about a girl named Roberta. "The song was put together in a schoolyard. We used to hang out and just bang on cardboard boxes and get these riffs going that you could sing to.

That was one of those things that worked, and I put some words to it."[274] DiMucci's early records, writes Anthony DeCurtis, "are masterpieces of pop attitude. Dion's falsetto soaring and his intensely rhythmic phrasing—now lingering behind the beat, now racing ahead of it—rival Sinatra's." After several more hits, Dion vanished from the scene for a few years while conquering a drug addiction; the emotional homage to fallen leaders *Abraham, Martin and John* gave him a big comeback hit in 1968, and in subsequent years he cheered longtime fans with strong albums reconnecting him to his New York street-corner roots.

Runaround Sue is the tale of a cheating girlfriend, warning other guys to "stay away from that girl—you don't know what she'll do," and epitomized by his cocky certainty that in ditching her, he was making himself available for the next doll worthy of his charms. In his macho world, it was fine for the guy to play the field, but woe to the girl who tried to exercise the same freedom. Charlie Gillett noted in *The Sound of the City* that the record's party-time group chant and instrumental arrangement were "shamelessly copied" off the Gary "U.S." Bonds hit *Quarter to Three*, but that Dion probably arrived at this approach by imitating the demo made by Marseca. (Part of the melody also owes much to the Bonds record, and litigation over the matter resulted in an out-of-court settlement.)[275] "Normally a cultured-sounding singer, Dion adopted a rough-and-ready growl which sounded as if it was sliding out of the corner of his mouth; suddenly the street hoodlums of New York had a voice of their own . . ." Dave Marsh writes that on this performance Dion emerged as "one of the great Italian-American tenors of the post-Sinatra era," scatting and swinging with zest and conviction.[276]

They Say It's Wonderful (1963)—Johnny Hartman &
    John Coltrane (written by Irving Berlin)
Recorded March 7, 1963; from the Impulse album *John
    Coltrane & Johnny Hartman*

The career of the great black baritone balladeer Johnny Hartman was, to quote the title of a Fletcher Henderson compilation, a study in frustration. Possessing a gloriously rich, lustrous baritone that made him a worthy counterpart to Billy Eckstine, Hartman rarely received the kind of attention to which Mr. B was accustomed, and sometimes went several years without recording. But he made the

270. Roberts, *Black Music of Two Worlds*, p. 256.

271. He was frequently featured in Hart's *Planet Drum* live performances during the 1980s and early 1990s.

272. #1 in New Zealand

273. *Rock 100*, p. 70–71.

274. Bronson, p. 99.

275. Gillett, p. 116. Marseca acknowledged to Wayne Jones in the November 1980 *Goldmine* that the song was in part a direct takeoff from the Bonds record; the latter artist was on the LeGrand label, for which Dion's Laurie Records was handling national distribution. Dion said in his 1988 memoir (p. 103) that "some after-hours song-swapping" with Bonds had helped inspire *Sue*. But, as noted above, Dion's cocksure style gave his performance a very different feeling.

276. Marsh, *The Heart of Rock & Soul*, p. 81.

most of his prime opportunity in the limelight, turning in career-defining performances on this classic album with tenor saxophone great John Coltrane. One of the finest was their gorgeous rendition of *They Say It's Wonderful*.

Born in Chicago on July 13, 1923, Hartman made his recording debut in 1947, and worked with Earl Hines (1947) and Dizzy Gillespie (1948–1949), but didn't receive wide attention until two acclaimed 1956 albums, which came after five years away from recording studios. And these fine collections were followed by six years in which he waxed only one little-heard LP. It was producer Bob Thiele who came up with idea of having Coltrane—blazing hot following the success of *Giant Steps* and *My Favorite Things*—do a full album with a singer for the first time. Trane had admired Hartman's work for years; the singer had toured and recorded with Gillespie just before Coltrane joined Dizzy, and they appeared on the same bill with Diz in March 1950. The remarkable collaboration, remarks Will Friedwald, "has become, along with Sinatra's *Songs for Swingin' Lovers* and [Nat] Cole's *After Midnight*, the *Kind of Blue* of vocal albums. It would be hard to think of a vocalist of the past 40 years . . . who hasn't been profoundly influenced by this classic record."[277]

Working with the peerless Coltrane combo of pianist McCoy Tyner, bassist Jimmy Garrison, and drummer Elvin Jones, Hartman wraps his velvety-smooth tones around one of Irving Berlin's finest latter-day ballads, written for his smash 1946 Broadway musical *Annie Get Your Gun*. Perry Como had the big hit single with the song and Dick Haymes (whose vocal style was not unlike Hartman's) gave it a splendid performance, but the Hartman-Coltrane pairing puts all other versions in the shade. (Coltrane had recorded an instrumental version with his quartet on November 13, 1962.) This is sophisticated ballad singing of the highest order; listen to the way he swoops down slowly to the bass-baritone depths on his final statement of the word "wonderful" and appreciate the man's beautifully honed musical instrument and intelligent handling of lyrics. The universal acclaim for this album finally put Hartman on the career track he'd long deserved, and by the time of his death in 1983 he was one of America's most respected jazz vocalists. No one admired him more than Clint Eastwood, who used several Hartman performances for the soundtrack of his hit 1995 movie romance *The Bridges of Madison County*.

Watermelon Man (1963)—Mongo Santamaria (written by Herbie Hancock)
Battle 45909
Recorded Dec. 17, 1962; chart debut March 16, 1963 (reached #10); from the album *Watermelon Man* (#42 peak) (*GHF-#197, World-#22, Jazz-#48*)

There are few parallels to the career of Herbie Hancock: from brilliant young jazz virtuoso/composer in the 1960s to the leader in jazz/rock fusion in the 1970s, to funk/pop explorations in the 1980s, and helping to bridge the gap between classic jazz and mainstream pop in the early twenty-first century. Born April 12, 1940, in Chicago, the precocious pianist played a Mozart concerto with the Chicago Symphony at eleven, and began his jazz career playing with Lee Morgan, Hank Mobley, and Coleman Hawkins while still in college. It was his work with Donald Byrd's combo that brought him to the attention of Blue Note founder Alfred Lion. His first session as a leader in May 1962, *Takin' Off* included the composition that would first make his reputation, *Watermelon Man*.[278]

The song was based on memories of Chicago's South Side and streetside vendors hawking their wares.[279] The gospel-tinged piece in its original performance (also with a hard-bop flavor) features a powerful trumpet solo by fellow star-in-the-making Freddie Hubbard, and intense playing by the great tenor saxophonist Dexter Gordon, about a year after his return from a long career break. (Hancock would win the Oscar for composing the score of the 1987 film that earned Gordon an Oscar nomination as an actor, *Round Midnight*.) Richard Cook and Brian Morton call the album an "astonishingly mature and poised" debut.[280] It would be the first of many triumphs for Hancock, including the brilliant albums *Maiden Voyage* (1964) and *Cantaloupe Island* (1965), a star-making 1963–1968 residency with one of Miles Davis' greatest ensembles, the sensational success of his 1973 fusion album *Headhunters*, the crossover pop hit *Rockit* (1983), and pulling one of the all-time Grammy Award upsets by winning Best Album honors for *River: The Joni Letters*, his 2007 tribute to Joni Mitchell.

A key figure in Latin-jazz-pop fusion, Ramon "Mongo" Santamaria was born in Havana on April 7, 1922 ("Mongo" in Senegalese means "chief of the tribe"), became an accomplished percussionist with Chano Pozo as his role model, and played in Cuban clubs until leaving in 1948 for Mexico and by 1950 the U.S. Experience working with Perez Prado, George Shearing, and Tito Puente (recording six albums from 1951–1957 with the mambo king, including *Puente in Percussion*) led to a celebrated tenure (1957–1961) with Cal Tjader, who was more deeply involved than any U.S. jazzman of his time (other than perhaps Dizzy Gillespie) with Cuban-based jazz. During that period he also began recording as a

---

277. Friedwald, *Biographical Guide*, p. 204.

278. The composer's own version charted briefly (at #121) at the same time Santamaria's was climbing the Hot 100 in March 1963.

279. Hancock: "I remember the cry of the watermelon man making the rounds through the back streets and alleys . . . The wheels of his wagon beat out the rhythm on the cobblestones."

280. *Penguin Guide to Jazz*, p. 672.

leader, including a 1959 album for Fantasy that included his most famous composition, *Afro-Blue*, later recorded by John Coltrane. All of this was prelude to his big pop crossover with *Watermelon Man*. It was Byrd who suggested that Hancock play the piece for Santamaria, and it was a perfect match of material to artist.

Santamaria's opening beats on *Watermelon Man*, declares Ed Morales, "are as distinctive and awe-inspiring as any laid down by a conga player in the history of recorded music. When he is joined by Hancock's grooving piano and a teasing horn section [the track's only solo is by trumpet player Marty Sheller], you can hear a whole new style coming into being."[281] Francisco "Kako" Baster sets a cha-cha beat on timbalero, and drummer Ray Lucas establishes the backbeat. The Cuban-jazz hybrid also served as one of the starting points for boogaloo (or *bugalu*), a combination of Afro-Cuban rhythms with R&B that became a hot subgenre during the next few years.[282] In 1998 the performance became the first Latin jazz inductee to the Grammy Hall of Fame.

Detroit City (1963)—Bobby Bare (written by Mel Tillis & Danny Dill)
RCA Victor 47-8183
Recorded April 18, 1963; chart debut July 6, 1963 (#6 C&W, #16 pop)[283] (*C&W-#66, HBN-#66, DM-#337, SC*)

This is a tale of a Southern boy who comes to the big city to work in an automobile plant, and gets more than he bargained for, co-written by future country star Mel Tillis with Danny Dill. He writes the folks back home about what a great time he's having, but they're all lies. "By day I make the cars / By night I make the bars / I wish that they could read between the lines—I want to go home." Tillis had written the melody and part of the lyric, and Dill (co-writer of the Lefty Frizzell classic *Long Black Veil*) suggested fleshing out the story line based on his experience playing bars in Detroit and seeing Southerners who had left home to make good money in Ford and Chevy plants but became so homesick they drank away their paychecks.[284] The song was first recorded in late 1962 by Billy Grammer as *I Want to Go Home*, and

got to #18 on the country chart. When Chet Atkins heard the record, he brought it to the attention of Bobby Bare, his new RCA Victor act; it turned out that Bare had loved the Grammer record as well. They retitled the song *Detroit City* to make it seem new.

David Cantwell sees it as a compelling description of a historically significant development, the waves of southerners leaving home in the postwar years to find work in northern or western factories and assembly lines. By 1950, seven million black and white southerners had moved, a figure growing to 10 million a decade later. "By 1960, one in every six white people born in the South had left the region."[285] To them, *Detroit City* was more than a song; it was the story of their lives.

Born April 7, 1935, in Ironton, Ohio, Bare moved past a difficult childhood through music, and soon after going to Los Angeles scored a 1958 pop smash with the talking-blues *The All-American Boy* (miscredited to the song's co-writer Bill Parsons). After military service, he scored a series of pop/country hits with a strong folkish tinge starting in 1962; the biggest was the followup to this record, *500 Miles Away from Home*. Also noteworthy is his 1966 hit *Streets of Baltimore*, another tale of a rural southerner who moves to the urban north and ends up regretting it.[286] He would continue hitting the country charts well into the 1980s. Dave Marsh: "Bare sounds like a mean and mournful drunk; he hits the bars not even for kicks but to assuage his nostalgia."[287] Charlie McCoy's lead guitar (replicating Grammer's string-bending effect) is another key contributor to the track's power.[288] A Grammy winner for best C&W recording, the record was ranked as the #61 all-time C&W song by *Country America* magazine.

Luck Be a Lady (1963)—Frank Sinatra (written by Frank Loesser)
Recorded July 24, 1963
From the Reprise album *Sinatra '65* (chart debut July 3, 1965, #9 peak)[289]

The 1955 movie version of Frank Loesser's classic Broadway musical *Guys and Dolls* was regarded as a disappointment due to the miscasting of Marlon Brando as Guy Masterson and a less than stellar acting performance

281. *The Latin Beat*, p. 176–77.
282. Ray Barretto's *El Watusi* (1962) was another early building block for boogaloo, which was symbolized for many by Joe Cuba's 1966 hit *Bang Bang*. During his 1964–1969 tenure on Columbia, Santamaria was a major part of this movement; his band for a time featured pianist Chick Corea and flutist Hubert Laws.
283. #2 in Bavaria.
284. *Sing Your Heart Out, Country Boy*, p. 10–11. The Tampa, Florida-born, Tillis (who would score over seventy-five country chart hits as a performer) brought a similar experience to the song's creation, having heard many friends in military service talk about finding work in automobile plants when they returned home. "It got into the back of my mind."

285. *Journal of Country Music*, Vol. 23 #2 (2003), p. 38–44.
286. Melton McLaurin remarks that each of these "exile" songs, from the perspective of displaced southerners seeking a better life but feeling something lost in the process, "mirrored the realities of daily life for Dixie's white working class." (*You Wrote My Life*, p. 20–22.)
287. Marsh, *The Heart of Rock & Soul*, p. 235.
288. Bare recorded the song's spoken segment live in the studio, with no overdubs (*Journal of Country Music*, Vol. 18 #1 (1996)).
289. *Put Your Dreams Away: A Frank Sinatra Discography* reports that two different versions of the song were issued: a severely edited 2:25 rendition (on Reprise 2F/2FS 1016), and the full-length 5:15 treatment (Reprise FS-2016) that is the best-known classic.

by Frank Sinatra as Nathan Detroit, the proprietor of the "oldest established permanent floating crap game in New York." *Luck Be a Lady*, introduced on Broadway by Robert Alda,[290] was sung in the film by Brando; finally, eight years later, the Chairman got to tackle a song tailor-made for him.[291] This collaboration with arranger Billy May on *Luck Be a Lady*, writes biographer Will Friedwald, "became legendary, due to Sinatra's swaggeringly jocular combination of a gambler's flamboyance and the tight, even swing of May's streamlined aggregation." May had originally written it at a breakneck pace, but the singer suggested a somewhat more leisurely tempo, and his instinct proved flawless.[292]

The song is a perfect fit for Sinatra not only because it matches his persona but also due to its impeccable structure. David Jenness and Don Velsey cite the Loesser composition as an example of songs in which "the metrical fitting of words or phrases to a given melodic contour follows the natural prosody of spoken English." Specifically, in the opening phrase: "The emphases are on the first word, *luck*, the grammatical subject, and then on the strong syllable of the word 'la-dy,' which completes the first statement of the governing metaphor for the entire song: luck should be a good girl, not a bad one." Loesser also achieved another central quality of classic popular song in that the lyrics are concise, "in a familiar mode, without fancy touches or straining for effect." The character of Masterson is direct and emphatic, and Sinatra hammers the message home: "Stick with me, baby, I'm the guy that you came in with / Luck be a lady tonight . . ."[293]

Night Life (1963)—Ray Price (written by Willie Nelson)
Columbia 42827
Recorded Feb. 22, 1963; chart debut Oct. 5, 1963 (#28 on C&W chart); new version recorded on Jan. 29, 1968 for Columbia 44505 (*HBN-#53, C&W-#200*)

The all-time Willie Nelson classic *Night Life* was introduced to most listeners through this definitive performance by Ray Price, in whose band Willie had played bass while trying to build a career as a songwriter. "Honky-tonk doesn't get any better than this," declares David Cantwell, ranking it #53 in *Heartaches By the Number*. Nelson had written the song about four years earlier, and recorded it in 1960 for a small Houston label under the pseudonym Paul Buskirk & His Little Men featuring Hugh Nelson. (Buskirk was a guitarist-mandolinist for whom he worked at the time, and, pressed for cash, he sold half the rights to the song to Buskirk and partners for $150.)[294] Price and his stellar ensemble clearly understood the deeply bluesy, reflective nature of the song, taking their time in unfolding the narrative. "Buddy Emmons' bluesy, horn-like pedal steel swaps sad tales throughout with Pig Robbins' weary piano, and their smoky, jazz-inspired conversations lend the record a decidedly uptown feel . . . And the cut's driving force— the brushwork of Buddy Harman—bears witness to the lessons he'd learned studying Buddy Rich, Gene Krupa, and other jazz drummers."[295]

Nelson wrote the song against the background of his struggling life in Houston in the late 1950s, giving guitar lessons, performing, and writing music along with other odd jobs. Biographer Joe Nick Patoski relates that the "long, lonely commutes on the Hempstead Highway, the Gulf Freeway, and Eastex Freeway provided close to an hour's worth of quality time to think and create every night . . . The twinkling lights and pungent odors of oil and chemical refineries, paper mills, and factories turned private thoughts into poetry," and the songs flowed like never before.[296]

Born on January 12, 1926, in Perryville, Cherokee County, Texas, Price cut his first record in 1949, worked with Lefty Frizzell, came to the Grand Ole Opry thanks to his friendship with Hank Williams, and began hitting the country charts in 1952 after landing a contract with Columbia. After a few years of slowly growing success, Price's embrace of the rhythmically intense 4/4 shuffle beat starting with the 1956 blockbuster *Crazy Arms* made him one of the foremost stars in country music. He also hit the top of the country charts with *My Shoes Keep Walking Back to You* (1957), the Bill Anderson classic *City Lights* (1958), and *The Same Old Me* (1959).

Rich Kienzle: "Price poured passion and humanity into his performance, exceeding his usual fervor and revealing a flair for the blues . . . Emmons and Grady Martin, who played a pivotal role in creating the band's arrangements in the studio, wrapped his vocal in some of the finest accompaniment the Cherokee Cowboys/A-team alliance ever created." Emmons' intimate steel guitar intro was inspired by one of his jazz favorites, Lionel Hampton's *Midnight Sun*.[297] Ray Benson of Asleep at the Wheel

---

290. The show, based on stories and characters by Damon Runyon, opened on Broadway on November 24, 1950, and ran for 1,200 performances.

291. In concert, Sinatra recalled that it "wasn't my good fortune" to sing this number in the film because producers had chosen "that world-famous baritone from the Met," Brando, to perform it. "Holy Jeez," he jibed sarcastically. In fairness, he noted, singing "wasn't his racket—it's mine." The Chairman described the song's subject as a love affair between "a guy and his dice."

292. *Sinatra! The Song Is You*, p. 299.

293. Jenness and Velsey, *Classic American Popular Song: The Second Half-Century*, p. 9–10.

294. According to biographer Joe Nick Patoski (*Willie Nelson: An Epic Life*, p. 99), Buskirk bought *Night Life* for $100 and *Family Bible* for $50.

295. *Heartaches By the Number*, p. 32.

296. Patoski, p. 98.

297. *Southwest Shuffle*, p. 173. A couple of years earlier, Emmons had become the first pedal steel guitarist to record a jazz album.

declared this record among the crucial discs that "turned my head around and kept me out of medical school."[298] [299] *Night Life* was the B side of Price's #2 C&W smash ballad *Make the World Go Away*. Rusty Draper's version reached #57 on the pop chart at exactly the same time, but Price's performance, powerful and understated, cannot be topped. By the 1990s *Night Life* had become a true American standard, recorded by close to 100 artists and appearing on a reported 30 million records. "Oh, the night life, it ain't no good life / But it's my life . . ."

Mississippi Goddam (1964)—Nina Simone
From the Colpix album *Nina Simone in Concert* (chart debut Sept. 19, 1964)

The murder of Medgar Evers and the bombing of the Birmingham Sixteenth Street Baptist Church in 1963 resulted in what Nina Simone in her autobiography called her political "road to Damascus . . . it came in a rush of fury, hatred and determination. In church language, the Truth entered me." She channeled her anger into this, her first explicitly political song.[300] Brian Ward in *Just My Soul Responding: Rhythm & Blues, Black Consciousness, and Race Relations*: "With its bold gospel-jazz chording and stentorian vocals, Simone's song perfectly captured the same mood [along with Martin Luther King's "Letter from Birmingham Jail"] of mounting impatience with white prevarication and false promises." For many activists, *Mississippi Goddam* (taken from her Carnegie Hall concert album) became an anthem in the 1964 Mississippi Freedom Summer Project, for which Simone headlined a benefit concert for SNCC. Civil rights activist Stanley Wise declared: "I mean everybody in the Movement just took that as a tribute to the Mississippi [Freedom] Summer Project," even though it had been written several months earlier. It was, notes Ward, "a good example of the ways in which the meanings of a particular song could be amplified, manipulated or simply imposed thanks to acts of creative consumption by listeners."[301]

A performer with no true counterpart in her ability to span musical genres from jazz and traditional pop to blues, folk, gospel, and classical, she was born Eunice Waymon February 21, 1933, in Tryon, North Carolina. A classical piano prodigy, she attended Juilliard, then (given the lack of professional opportunities for black classical pianists) began working as a pianist-singer in Atlantic City. Her recording career was launched in 1957 with trio sessions released on two albums by Bethlehem Records. One of those tracks, her haunting vocal treatment of George and Ira Gershwin's ballad from the folk opera *Porgy & Bess—I Loves You, Porgy*—became a Top 20 pop hit in late 1959, a stunning achievement for a delicate jazz piano trio rendition of a twenty-four-year-old tune. Will Friedwald notes that the one constant in Simone's music is intensity; "every single number, even when she's having fun, is as serious as your life."[302]

That quality is certainly heard in *Mississippi Goddam*—"and I mean every word," she declares during the quietly incendiary song—and the other classic social-protest original from the same live album, *Four Women*.[303] Showing admirable audacity, Colpix released *Mississippi* as a single, which was quickly banned from Southern radio stations. Former Freedom Singers member, Movement activist, and scholar Bernice Johnson Reagon remarked that Simone—through her active and conspicuous involvement, willingness to discuss black issues, and the way in which she comported herself in general—gave her special status in the movement. "Simone helped people to survive," she recalled. "When you heard her voice on a record it could get you up in the morning . . . She could sing anything, it was the sound she created. It was the sound of that voice and piano . . . Nina Simone captured the warrior spirit that was present in the people. The fighting people."[304]

You Really Got Me (1964)—The Kinks
Reprise 0306
Chart debut Sept. 26, 1964 (reached #7); #1 (2 weeks) in England[305] (*RHF, GHF, RS-#80, PW, ACC-#21, DMDB-#49, RIA, DM*)

Lead singer Ray Davies' rewrite of the Kingsmen's *Louie Louie* gave his British rock band the Kinks their giant debut hit.[306] In the British Invasion of 1964, the

---

298. *Listen to This!* by Alan Reder and John Baxter, p. 53. Price once likened Martin's guitar artistry to that of Andres Segovia's classical work.

299. Daniel Cooper, in a study of Price's career for *Journal of Country Music*, Vol. 14 #3 (1992), p. 22–31, calls the *Night Life* sessions the culmination of the Cherokee Cowboys' 1956–1963 "golden era." Emmons had recently replaced Jimmy Day as steel guitarist, providing here "some of the spookiest slide steel tracks ever laid down on record." According to Emmons, they got the sound by plugging his steel into Martin's amplifier and letting Martin play with the amp's tremolo while Emmons soloed. Alluding to Price's classic 1958 hit, Cooper remarks: "The narrator of *Night Life* is the hero of *City Lights* five years later, having cynically succumbed to the bright array."

300. The Evers assassination occurred June 11, 1963, and the Mississippi church bombing just over three months later. She composed the song on September 15, the same day she learned about the latter crime, and first publicly performed it soon thereafter at the Village Gate. (David Brun-Lambert, *Nina Simone: The Biography*, p. 111–12.)

301. Ward, p. 301.

302. *Biographical Guide*, p. 413.

303. *Mississippi* was featured in the April 30, 1964, issue of the folk/topical-song periodical *Broadside*.

304. Ward, *Just My Soul Responding*, p. 302, Bernice Johnson Reagon interview with the author.

305. #2 in New Zealand, #13 Canada.

306. Andrew Weiner noted in *New Musical Express* (November 10, 1973) that of all the bands that based their sound on *Louie Louie*, "no one got more mileage out of that riff than the Kinks." After their breakthrough

Beatles represented the most finely polished pop sensibilities; the Rolling Stones stood for young white rockers' absorption of blues influences; The Who symbolized rowdy working-class alienation. It was left to the Kinks to embody a rock 'n' roll variation on the English music-hall tradition, as filtered through the creative mind of lead singer, songwriter, and guitarist Ray Davies (born on June 21, 1944, in London). Davies formed the band in 1963 with brother Dave on guitar and vocals, bassist Pete Quaife, and drummer Mick Avory. Although Davies would soon shift his focus to loftier concerns as reflected in songs like *Waterloo Sunset*, at the outset the band's emphasis was squarely on adolescent lust.

The group's first two singles had flopped after they became the first rock act signed by Mo Ostin for Reprise (the label founded by Frank Sinatra in 1960), and they decided the reason was that they were too pristine. "The world's trashiest guitar riff" was provided by Ray's seventeen-year-old brother Dave Davies, who, according to a 1966 *Melody Maker* interview, had "ripped up the speakers of his cheap amplifier [taking a razor to the speaker cone] and hooked it directly into the Vox amplifier—essentially inventing an electronic version of the fuzz box" that Link Wray had created mechanically in his 1958 classic *Rumble*.[307] In his semi-novelistic memoir, Ray Davies offers a simpler explanation for the sound: Dave was playing as loud as possible through amplifiers that were not equipped for the volume, and this produced screeching feedback.[308]

Davies originally conceived the piece as a blues, "indirectly inspired" by the central riff of *Train and the River* by jazzman Jimmy Giuffre. It became a crunching hard rocker when Dave began playing his guitar part. They doctored the speakers in order to replicate the raw sound of favorite Chuck Berry tracks.[309]

Paul Williams: "Here is the anguished, joyous, claustrophobic, liberating, beat-your-head-against-the-door, ultimately unspeakable essence of adolescence . . . Rock and roll at its best is the raving, gleeful self-expression of the terminally inarticulate, and we all recognize ourselves in its mumbled shrieks."[310]

---

hit, follow ups *All Day and All of the Night* and *Tired of Waiting for You* were also clever variations on the same theme. Charles Shaar Murray in *NME* called *You Really Got Me* "the first heavy metal record of all time."

307. *Rock of Ages*, p. 285–86.

308. *X-Ray*, p. 101–2. As Davies light-heartedly recalls, "The engineer screamed and ran out of the building" until Dave finally turned down his amp (somewhat).

309. A young, pre–Led Zeppelin Jimmy Page is reputed to have contributed a bit of "sweetening" to the machine gun-like guitar sound, but by most accounts Page (for whom Ray Davies had played a demo of the song) didn't play here but did some rhythm guitar on a later Kinks album.

310. Williams, *The 100 Best Singles*, p. 69–70.

River Deep, Mountain High (1966)—Ike & Tina Turner (written by Ellie Greenwich, Jeff Barry & Phil Spector)

Philles 131
Chart debut May 28, 1966 (#88 peak); #3 in England[311] (*RS-#33, RHF, GHF, PW, ACC-#22, R&B-#64, TC, DMDB*)

After nearly four years as the "Titan of Teen" whose mega-productions had made him an unstoppable force in pop music, Phil Spector had been absent from the upper level of the music charts since his end-of-1964 masterpiece with the Righteous Brothers, *You've Lost That Lovin' Feelin'*. Ever the showman, he was determined that if he was going to exit center stage, it would be with a finale the world would never forget: his biggest production ever featuring one of the most thrilling voices he had ever encountered, Tina Turner. *River Deep, Mountain High* proved a commercial disaster that hastened his semi-retirement, but (small consolation) it was just as unforgettable as he'd envisioned.

Clarksdale, Mississippi–born, Ike Turner grabbed an early piece of rock history in 1951 as session leader and pianist on Jackie Brenston's *Rocket 88*, and during the next several years was a relentlessly busy sideman on both piano and guitar, first at Sun Records and then other labels, backing bluesmen from Howlin' Wolf and Elmore James to Otis Rush and also producing sessions of his own. His career shifted to a higher gear in 1959 when he met Anna Mae Bullock (born on November 26, 1938, in Nutbush, Tennessee), and hired the dynamic youngster as lead singer for his Kings of Rhythm. Soon married and renamed, the team of Ike & Tina Turner began hitting the charts in 1960 with *A Fool in Love*, 1961's *It's Gonna Work Out Fine*, and one of the most electrifying live stage shows in all of rock. But they'd never had a defining hit worthy of their talents. Spector was captivated with Tina's voice and sensuality, and saw her as a perfect vehicle for his ambitions. He leased Ike & Tina from their label, Warner Brothers, for $20,000, much as he had previously "rented" the Righteous Brothers from Moonglow. To his relief, he found that Ike Turner didn't mind being on the outside looking in (indeed, contractually required to stay out of the studio) if the end result was a hit; the record would read "Ike & Tina Turner," but in reality it was only Tina, Phil, and his Wall of Sound.

Spector came to New York to work with Jeff Barry and Ellie Greenwich (who had recently divorced), and in less than a week they completed three songs. Given the tensions between all three writers, reports Ken Emerson, they contributed disparate elements to *River Deep*:

---

311. #1 in Spain, #9 Holland.

Greenwich provided the melody of the verse, Spector that of the chorus, and Barry most of the words.[312] Spector biographer Dave Thompson: "The end result would be born of no less than three separate tunes, superimposed atop one another to create an almost discordant whole, which Turner would—and she alone could—bind together through the sheer force of her vocal."[313] Nearly two dozen musicians were required at three separate sessions (or five sessions by another account) in February and March 1966 at Los Angeles' Gold Star Studios to record the instrumental track: four drummers, four guitarists, four bassists, three keyboards, two percussionists, and a brass section, even before adding strings and a veritable army of backup singers including the great Darlene Love. Initially Spector wanted Turner to sing live with the massive ensemble, but she was so overwhelmed by its size and confused by the song that she couldn't sing. A week later she returned to provide her vocals with no one in the studio but Spector and engineer Larry Levine, and arranger Jack Nitzsche testified that her passionate performance kicked up the intensity of the musicians another notch. Levine recalled that Tina—her blouse soaked with sweat as she was called upon to sing take after take—"was electric. And she couldn't swing the song with all her clothes on, so she took her blouse off and sang it just wearing a bra. It was unbelievable, the way she moved around." Record company executive Bob Krasnow agreed: "Your hair was standing on end. It was like the whole room exploded."

Spector and his cohorts were convinced that *River Deep, Mountain High* was his ultimate masterpiece. But Barry and Greenwich were shocked upon hearing the acetate, feeling that Spector's monumental production had overwhelmed the song. Levine concluded that the producer had "tried to go beyond the scope of what we could do" technically. The advance buildup for the single was tremendous. When it came out, however, the record barely scraped the bottom of the charts before vanishing. The fact that the single became a smash in England could hardly cushion the blow. Still, the general U.S. rejection of his epic didn't drive Spector out of the music business; it just provided an excuse to take a sabbatical as he had already intended. The eccentric genius would return after three years, but only for occasional special projects that didn't carry his personal imprint; *River Deep* provided the final blast of full-tilt Spector.

The record "manages to be lovable and playful even as it overwhelms," remarks Paul Williams. Set aside the corniness of the lyrics, he suggests, to focus on remarkable details such as the "swoop of Tina's voice from vulnerable little girl to passionate man-eater." When she moves from "my love has grown" to "and it gets stronger," she "changes the sound of her voice, violently, abruptly, invariably sending a shot of adrenaline through the listener's veins." It all builds to metaphorically create a "link-up between lovemaking and memory and the awe we feel in contemplating our trembling existence, depths of the firmament spread below us and the heights of heaven rising above. The singer personalizes this: tells her lover what he stirs up in her." Finally, at the conclusion, there is "catharsis," as a transported Tina is all but singing in tongues.[314]

"Phil Spector sets out to express the sensation of a love that's as profound as it is skyscraping with a musical bliztkrieg that ranges from super-quiet . . . to an all-out orgiastic shriek," described the British magazine *Q* in 1999. "I think when it came out, it was just like my farewell," Spector told *Rolling Stone* in 1969. "I was just saying goodbye, and I just wanted to go crazy for . . . four minutes on wax."

When Something Is Wrong With My Baby (1967)— Sam & Dave (written by Isaac Hayes & David Porter)

Stax 210
Chart debut Feb. 25, 1967 (#2 on R&B chart, #42 pop) (*DM-#65*)

It's amazing to look back at *Billboard* chart history and see that before *Soul Man* in fall 1967, the nuclear-powered duo of Sam & Dave had reached the pop Top 40 only once—and that the emotion-packed soul ballad *When Something Is Wrong With My Baby* stalled just short of that mark. No matter; this is a performance that is remembered long after its higher-charting competitors have faded into obscurity.

The song—their only ballad hit—was written at a time when David Porter was deeply unhappy in his marriage. "I got up out of bed and went downstairs and said, 'If I was in love with somebody, then the relationship should be such that if something is wrong with her, something is wrong with me,'" he recalled. "It was about 2:00 in the morning and I wrote the whole song." Following an introduction (as described by Rob Bowman) by four ringing guitar chords followed by bass, understated snare, and piano triplets, Sam Moore sings the opening lyric "in a quavering high voice wracked with melismas." The second half of the verse, accompanied by swelling organ, drums and fuller guitar and piano, is sung by Dave Prater.[315] Isaac Hayes wrote out the harmony parts for the two men to sing together, but as they unleashed every ounce

---

312. *Always Magic in the Air*, p. 235–36.
313. *Wall of Pain*, p. 113–16.
314. Williams, p. 97–99.
315. *Soulsville, U.S.A.*, p. 114.

of emotion in the chorus, what was written on paper was all but forgotten in the intensity of the moment, and it all worked. (It should be noted that the song's central lyric may owe something to Tampa Red's 1949 blues classic *It Hurts Me Too:* "When things go wrong with you, it hurts me, too"). The track required thirty-six takes,[316] but persistence paid off.

Moore: "When we performed, we had church. On Sundays the minister would preach and the people in the pews would holler back to him. This is what we started doing. I arranged the parts between Dave and me so that one of us became the preacher and would say 'Come on Dave' or 'Come on Sam' . . . That was our style."[317]

Moore and Prater could barely stand one another by the late 1960s, but "no duo ever harmonized better than these two," writes Dave Marsh, ranking this song #65 in *The Heart of Rock & Soul.*[318] Aretha Franklin would borrow the horn chords from the record a few months later for her own *Respect.*

Brown Eyed Girl (1967)—Van Morrison
Bang 545
Chart debut July 15, 1967 (reached #10) (*RHF, GHF, PW, DMDB-#39, WASH-#50, BMI-#57, ACC-#98, RS-#110, RIA-#131, DM, AHR*)

After the demise of his rock group Them, Van Morrison teamed with producer Bert Berns (who had produced Them's biggest hit *Here Comes the Night*) to create the sunniest pop song of his career (and one of the best depictions of teenage infatuation), *Brown Eyed Girl.* After twenty-two takes of the number, reports biographer Steve Turner, Berns "achieved a satisfying balance between his own pop instincts and Van's allegiance to rhythm and blues."[319] Its original title was *Brown Skinned Girl*; the piece was recorded in New York City, with Berns contributing background vocals. "What a great performance!" exults Paul Williams. "Such easy, happy music, guaranteed to brighten the heart and bring a smile absolutely every time you hear it, something Latin in the rhythms, fabulous bass solo break in the middle, Van's voice so open and radio friendly."[320] It is, writes Geoffrey Cannon in *Melody Maker*, "a perfect song, the music's pace is delicate, its spaces timed to haunt the ear." Dave Marsh praises its "lubricious imagery conveyed atop a melody that seems the perfect breath of innocence."[321]

Classical Gas (1968)—Mason Williams
Warner 7190
Chart debut June 22, 1968 (2 weeks at #2); #2 in Canada, #6 in Australia, #9 in U.K.

It all began with an ingenious film short for the Smothers Brothers' comedy/variety show on CBS. The piece offered an overview of human history racing by in three minutes of dizzying, rapid-fire images. All that was needed was a music track. Mason Williams, on staff as a music and comedy writer for the show, was called upon to provide it. Williams had already been working on a composition for classical guitar, which happened to work perfectly with the film. He later told Christopher Feldman that he thought of the piece "simply as repertoire or 'fuel' for the classical guitar, so I called it 'Classical Gasoline.'" The title was inadvertently abbreviated by a copyist into *Classical Gas.*[322]

Born on August 24, 1938, in Abilene, Texas, Williams came to Los Angeles and performed folk music in clubs when he was introduced to Tommy Smothers. The ensuing friendship led to his hiring when the Smothers' show began in fall 1967. Immediately after the film aired, CBS was flooded with inquiries about the thrilling, intricate classical guitar theme. Expanded with the addition of an orchestra and a propulsive arrangement, *Classical Gas* became one of the most delightfully original and memorable instrumental hits of the rock era. It won Grammies for best pop instrumental, best instrumental theme, and best instrumental arrangement. In 1968, he came up with the idea of running the Smothers' deadpan comedian Pat Paulsen for President. After a stint putting his imagination to work as a conceptual artist, Williams served as head writer for one year on *Saturday Night Live*, and in 1987 teamed with Mannheim Steamroller for a new rock/orchestral treatment of his trademark song. Soon thereafter it was declared by BMI to be the publishing group's most popular instrumental ever.

Born to Be Wild (1968)—Steppenwolf (written by Dennis Edmonton)
Dunhill/ABC 4138
Chart debut July 13, 1968 (3 weeks at #2); #1 in Canada, #30 in England;[323] from the album *Steppenwolf* (chart debut March 9, 1968, reached #6) (*RHF, GHF, Juke-#15, AFI-#29, RS-#130, RIA, DMDB-#65, DM, AHR, TC, ACC*)

It will always be associated with the image of Peter Fonda and Dennis Hopper roaring down the highway atop Harley-Davidsons living out their version of re-

316. *Sam and Dave: An Oral History*, by Moore and Dave Marsh, p. 68–69.
317. Portia Maultsby chapter on Soul in *African American Music: An Introduction* (edited by Mellonee Burnim and Maultsby), p. 281. Moore remarked in the duo's oral history (p. 47): "I had *always* wanted to be a preacher."
318. Marsh, p. 47.
319. Turner, *Too Late to Stop Now*, p. 76.
320. Williams, *The 100 Best Singles*, p. 122–23.
321. Marsh, *The Heart of Rock & Soul*, p. 282.
322. Feldman, *Billboard Book of Number Two Singles*, p. 102.
323. Reached #18 in 1999 U.K. reissue. Also #3 in France, #4 Holland.

bellious freedom in *Easy Rider*.[324] But Steppenwolf's *Born to Be Wild* had already established its status as a rock classic a year before it reached the big screen. Lead singer/guitarist John Kay (born Joachim Krauledat in Germany on April 12, 1944, and raised in Canada) formed the hard-rock outfit in Los Angeles with Michael Monarch on guitar, John "Goldy McJohn" Goadsby on keyboards, and Jerry "Edmonton" McCrohan on drums; all but Monarch were initially members of a Canadian band called Sparrow. The name Steppenwolf was taken from a 1927 Hermann Hesse novel.

Recording their debut album for Dunhill/ABC, the group was offered the song *Born to Be Wild* by another former Sparrow, Jerry Edmonton's brother Dennis (the former group's lead guitarist, he used the pseudonym "Mars Bonfire" for the songwriting credit), who had recorded a demo that was sluggish and unimpressive. But as the members played around with the arrangement, something very different emerged, galvanized by Monarch's aggressive lead guitar, a furious "buzz-saw stomp" tempo (in Thomas Ryan's phrase), and Kay's powerful, throaty rasp. It was the third single released by the group, but when it came out the previous flops were forgotten. The debut album was recorded in four days—"mixing included" in a converted restaurant, recalled Kay, done on an eight-track machine.[325] By the time the song served as the ultimate cinematic biker anthem, it had burned the phrase "heavy metal thunder" into the pop-cultural landscape. Steppenwolf's heyday wasn't long, with two other Top Ten singles (although the second was also a classic, *Magic Carpet Ride*), but this song guaranteed their place in rock history. *Born to Be Wild*, became, declared Kay with pride, "the anthem for the motorcycle individual anywhere on the globe."

Mama Tried (1968)—Merle Haggard
Capitol 2219
Chart debut July 27, 1968 (#1 for 4 weeks C&W) (*C&W-#22, HBN-#22, GHF, NPR-300, TC, SC*)

Mama Tried is country music as only slightly dramatized autobiography. A native of Bakersfield, California (born on April 6, 1937), Merle Haggard learned all about hard times from the beginning, as he moved with his parents from Oklahoma to California during the Great Depression, converting an old boxcar into a home. His father (who died when Merle was nine) had played fiddle in honky-tonk bars, and Merle taught himself to play guitar at twelve. Several years of constant rebellion

and trouble followed, and in an effort to straighten him out his mother placed him in several juvenile detention centers. Haggard recalled in a *Billboard* interview with Bob Eubanks, "She had a boy who was more than wild . . . Mama certainly did try." Meeting country star Lefty Frizzell before a concert, he sang the artist a couple of songs and made such an impression that Frizzell had the kid come on stage to do a few numbers, to an enthusiastic response. But after a first attempt to make it in country music left him still virtually broke, he committed a robbery and was sentenced to fifteen years at San Quentin in 1958, serving three years.[326] Following his release, talent and persistence enabled him to begin hitting the country charts in late 1963 after serving a valuable apprenticeship in Wynn Stewart's band, and fully emerging as a top star three years later, a status he would never relinquish thereafter. He also began to blossom as an important songwriter who drew upon the experiences of a hard life, the most original writer among country performers since Hank Williams. This is best exemplified by *Mama Tried*.

Written for an obscure movie in which he appeared (ironically enough, as a cop), *Killers Three*, *Mama Tried* is the somber tale of a man who plunged deeper into darkness than Haggard himself, being sentenced to life without parole, and understanding too late that there's only one person responsible for his plight. It's a powerfully rendered narrative, produced by Ken Nelson and boosted by the potent electric guitar of Roy Nichols and the backing vocals of Merle's occasional duet partner, Buck Owens' ex-wife (and then Haggard's) Bonnie Owens.[327] *Mama Tried* was ranked #22 in *Heartaches By the Number*, and as country music's #30 greatest song by *Country America* magazine in 1992.

Bad Moon Rising (1969)—Creedence Clearwater Revival
Fantasy 622
Chart debut May 3, 1969 (#2 in *Billboard*, reached #1 in *Record World*); #1 (3 weeks) in England, #1 (1 week) in Canada, #3 in Australia;[328] from the album *Green River* (4 weeks at #1) (*DM-#198, RS, Juke-#27, AHR, TM, ACC, DMDB*)

With *Proud Mary* near the top of the charts, John Fogerty took Creedence Clearwater Revival back into the

---

324. In fall 1968, Fonda and Hopper contacted the band's management company, and after the members attended a screening of the film, they agreed to allow the use of *Born to Be Wild* and *The Pusher*.

325. Interview feature on Kay by Michael Buffalo Smith, May 26, 2006, *Goldmine*.

326. Haggard in *Sing Me Back Home* (p. 157): "I survived prison not because it taught me a lesson—though I learned a lot—but because I had to prove I could survive. I believe I got my life together in spite of prison, maybe even in defiance of it."

327. According to Tom Roland (*Billboard Book of Number One Country Hits*, p. 12), Glen Campbell is also on guitar. Nelson, one of the architects of the West Coast "Bakersfield sound," headed Capitol's country department from 1950–1976, producing most of Buck Owens' hits and other artists such as Ferlin Husky and the Louvin Brothers.

328. #1 in Ireland, New Zealand and South Africa, #2 in Israel, Norway, Singapore, and Sweden.

studio to record a new single, *Bad Moon Rising*. It was a dark song for dark times, with the Vietnam war raging and Richard Nixon in power—but all set to a bouncy, jangly beat; a vision of Doomsday with a smile. "The lyrics are thoroughly at odds with the joyous melody and tempo, [but] they perfectly capture the fine line between exhilaration and fear," suggests Thomas Ryan. He also points up the sometimes-overlooked perfection of Creedence as a band, with the crisp economy of drummer Doug Clifford, bassist Stu Cook, and Tom Fogerty as rhythm guitarist alongside John's lead. "There is nothing extraneous on a CCR record; every sound is integral."[329]

Fogerty designed *Bad Moon Rising* as an homage to Elvis Presley's Sun Records sound, inspired particularly by Scotty Moore's guitar licks. According to Fogerty, its imagery came from the 1941 movie *The Devil and Daniel Webster*, in which the devil protects Daniel Webster because of a deal they'd made. "There's one great scene where there's a huge storm, and the neighbor's corn crop was completely knocked down. But next door . . . you can see Daniel Webster's corn still standing tall in a straight row, six feet high. The contrast represented a very strong image for me. I took it in a Biblical sense, meaning hurricanes and lightning . . . Scary, spooky stuff."[330] Craig Werner: "Sounding like something out of the Old Testament prophets, Fogerty's poetic images tap a power similar to that of Robert Johnson's classic Delta blues."[331]

Rivers of Babylon (1970)—The Melodians
Recorded for Trojan Records (*World-#29, Time, DM*)

Religious faith and the Rastafarian identification with the lost tribes of Israel is a central underpinning of early reggae, as beautifully represented by *Rivers of Babylon*. A free adaptation of Psalm 137:1–4 ("By the rivers of Babylon we sat and wept . . .") plus a bit of Psalm 37:11 and 20 ("The meek shall inherit the earth . . . The wicked shall perish . . ."), the song is given a lovely, earnest vocal harmony treatment by the Melodians: Brent Dowe, Tony Brevett, and Trevor McNaughton, in a performance produced by Leslie Kong.[332] Dowe and McNaughton are credited as composers. The rivers of Babylon are the Euphrates river, its tributaries, and the Chebar river. Under Rastafarian beliefs, Zion refers to Africa, from which their fathers were captured and taken as slaves to the New World represented by Babylon. Note that the group changes the reference in the traditional line "How shall we sing the Lord's song in a strange land?" to "King Alpha's song"—King Alpha being, in Rasta eyes, Ethiopian Emperor Haile Selassie. In 1972 its place in reggae history was assured by inclusion in the soundtrack of the landmark film *The Harder They Come*. In 1978 the partly-Jamaican group Boney M scored a massive worldwide hit with a slightly disco-tinged version of the song,[333] but the Melodians' original—included on the Island Records boxed set *Tougher Than Leather: The Story of Jamaican Music*—is the one that's stood the test of time. "By the rivers of Babylon, where we sat down / And there we wept, when we remembered Zion . . ."

I'll Be There (1970)—The Jackson 5 (written by Bob West, Berry Gordy, Hal Davis, & Willie Hutch)
Motown 1171
Chart debut Sept. 19, 1970 (spent 5 weeks at #1 on pop chart, 6 weeks at #1 on R&B chart); #2 in Canada, #4 in England, #10 in France[334] (*BILLB-#95, DM-#306, AHR*)

After soaring to #1 with their first three Motown releases, Michael Jackson (just turned twelve when this hit the charts) and his brothers topped themselves as *I'll Be There* became their longest-reigning chart-topper of all. Label founder Berry Gordy, Jr., noted in his memoir that a big, dramatic ballad made a perfect change of pace after three happy uptempo numbers (*I Want You Back, ABC*, and *The Love You Save*). Bob West wrote the song in its original form, then Gordy called on producer Hal Davis and songwriter Willie Hutch to further polish it.[335] Jackson recalled in his memoir that the song "grabbed me from the moment I heard the demo."[336] Marveling at Michael's precocious performance, Dave Marsh remarks: "What's startling about *I'll Be There* is the perfect aplomb he brings to material that ought to be both more romantic and more dramatic than he could possibly comprehend."[337] Michael's promises of "I'll be there to protect you" are answered by Jermaine's "I'll be there with a love that's strong—I'll be your strength, I'll keep holdin' on."

329. Ryan, *American Hit Radio*, p. 347–48.

330. Bordowitz, *Bad Moon Rising*, p. 59–60.

331. *A Change Is Gonna Come*, p. 155–56. Fogerty: "I've literally been trying to write *Bad Moon Rising* since 1957 . . . when I learned my first chord on guitar." (*Up Around the Bend*, CCR oral history by Werner, p. 144–45.)

332. Formed in 1965 for a local singing contest, the Melodians' second best known song was *Swing and Dine*, covered in 1968 by The Gaylads. The Sanctuary Records CD *Rivers of Babylon: The Best of the Melodians, 1967–1973* covers their career.

333. The Boney M remake was one of the biggest hits in British chart history (#1 for 5 weeks, 40 weeks total, and only the second record ever to sell two million copies in the U.K.), also #1 for 16 weeks in West Germany, 16 weeks in Switzerland, and 6 weeks in Australia.

334. According to Jackson biographer J. Randy Taraborrelli (*The Magic, the Madness, the Whole Story*, p. 81), the record sold close to 3.2 million copies worldwide (Motown claimed 4 million); the label reported that it surpassed even Marvin Gaye's *Heard It Through the Grapevine* as the biggest Motown seller to that date.

335. Gordy, *To Be Loved*, p. 287–88.

336. *Moonwalk*, p. 86–87. The single (with lush arrangement including harpsichord) was produced by co-writer Hal Davis, assisted by Suzy Ikeda.

337. Marsh, p. 216. In Marsh's *Trapped* (p. 126), he remarks that Michael "simply turned in a stunning, airy tour de force," while brother Jermaine ably handles the tune's "earthier inflections."

Coal Miner's Daughter (1970)—Loretta Lynn

Decca 32749

Recorded on Oct. 1, 1969; chart debut Oct. 31, 1970 (1 week at #1 on C&W chart, #83 on pop chart) (*NPR-100, C&W-#14, GHF-#123, RIA-#185, HBN-#78, Time, TC, DMDB, SC*)

The song that provided the title for Loretta Lynn's best-selling autobiography and the 1980 movie that earned Sissy Spacek the Oscar as best actress for portraying the country music legend, *Coal Miner's Daughter* has taken on almost mythic connotations for embodying her life and as a snapshot of the broader postwar Appalachian experience. It lives up to the billing as a simple but powerful narrative. Born on April 14, 1934, in Butcher Hollow, Kentucky, indeed the daughter of a coal miner, she sang in church and local concerts, but after marrying at age thirteen she moved with her husband to Washington state where they raised four children. After ten years she began performing again, and signed a contract with Zero Records which released her debut single in 1960, *I'm a Honky Tonk Girl*, which reached #14 on the country chart, thanks in part to tireless promotional efforts by Loretta and her husband. The Wilburn Brothers invited her to tour with them; after arriving in Nashville she signed with Decca, and began a long run of hits on that label in 1962. In addition to her earthy honky-tonk–rooted vocal style that established an emotional connection with listeners, Loretta also emerged as a gifted songwriter with feisty numbers such as *You Ain't Woman Enough, Fist City,* and *Don't Come Home A-Drinkin'*. Most of her original songs reflected elements of her experiences, but of course none as deeply as *Coal Miner's Daughter*.

As explained in her autobiography, Loretta began to write her anthem while sitting around the television station at WSIX, waiting to rehearse a show. "I'd always wanted to write a song about growing up, but I never believed anybody would care about it . . . I went off to the dressing room and just wrote the first words that came into my head." The narrative was "nothing but the truth," having to work a bit harder only on the rhymes. "In a couple of hours, I had nine of the best verses I ever wrote." But once the tune was recorded, it sat on the shelf for a year. The released version excised three verses adding further details about childhood days, which "just about broke my heart." Deeply proud as she was of her creation, she was amazed at its popular success, and of the new vistas it opened up for her.[338] While there had been many previous country story songs retracing rural southern lives, Melton McLaurin argues that Lynn broke new ground, going farther than previous artists in "praising her family roots and rural origins. She is the first southern country music artist to proclaim her pride in her origins."[339] [340]

Owen Bradley, known for his elegant pop/country fusion productions for Patsy Cline, showed his versatility by providing a polished yet suitably down-home setting for Loretta. David Cantwell points out that while Bradley "strips the music down to a foot-stomping beat and a relaxed, front-porch banjo," he also helped Lynn pare down the song from nine to six verses.[341] The arrangement has the record open with Harold Rugg's pedal steel guitar, then places Bobby Thompson's overdubbed banjo in the spotlight as Loretta retraces her Kentucky youth, before returning the pedal steel at the conclusion as her tale comes back to the present. In 2003 it was called the #13 greatest song of country music by Country Music Television.

Many Rivers to Cross (1972)—Jimmy Cliff

Originally from the A&M album *Wonderful World, Beautiful People* (late 1969)

Released as single in 1972 on Island WIP 6139 (*RHF, World-#6, RS-#325, DM, 1001*)

Among the most hauntingly lovely of reggae hymns, *Many Rivers to Cross* reached its widest U.S. distribution on the 1973 soundtrack of the film in which Jimmy Cliff starred, *The Harder They Come*. An original composition of faith and determination in the face of obstacles ("It's only my will that keeps me alive"), it's performed with organ-led accompaniment, accentuating its religious implications. (Cliff is a Muslim, but the song is a comfortable fit for Rastafarians, or indeed for adherents to any other faith.) The character he plays on screen may be a gangster dope dealer, but the song is pure, spine-tingling gospel. Cliff was undergoing a spiritual awakening at the time, and Jim Harrington remarks that he "sang each word as though his soul depended on it."[342] Colin Escott calls it a "transcendently great performance of a transcendently great song."[343]

Spain (1972)—Chick Corea/Return to Forever

From the Verve album *Light as a Feather* (recorded in Oct. 1972)

Chart debut April 7, 1973 (#6 on jazz chart) (*TG*)

338. Lynn, p. 159–60.

339. *You Wrote My Life: Lyrical Themes in Country Music*, p. 23. In the author's view, it was only after the success of this record that country music saw an outpouring of songs proclaiming fierce pride (sometimes crossing the line into chauvinism, a flaw certainly not present in Loretta's utterly personal classic) in southern rural origins.

340. Predecessors in a similar vein were Frankie Miller's 1959 classic *Black Land Farmer*, and Bill Anderson's 1961 Top Ten country hit *Po' Folks*.

341. *Heartaches By the Number*, p. 45–46.

342. *1001 Songs You Must Hear Before You Die*, p. 237.

343. *This is Reggae Music* annotation, p. 33. Leslie Kong produced the record.

"Jazz/rock fusion" was a loaded term for many jazz purists during the 1970s, but, remarks Len Lyons, "no musician has used the fusion concept with more variety, intelligence, and unimpeachable taste than Chick Corea." Born in Chelsea, Massachusetts, on June 12, 1941, pianist-composer Armando Anthony Corea studied with his father (a music professor), and worked with Mongo Santamaria (1962), Willie Bobo (1963), and Blue Mitchell (1964–1966), then began recording under his own name, while also playing with Stan Getz (1966–1968). Corea was thrust into the limelight in 1968 by joining Miles Davis just when the trumpet icon was creating a wider audience through the use of electronic instruments and rock rhythms on a series of hugely influential albums including *In a Silent Way* and *Bitches Brew*. (Davis happened to be the artist who had inspired him to drop out of Columbia University in 1959 to pursue a jazz career after seeing Miles perform at Birdland.) The pianist struck off on his own in 1970, and became one of the leaders in the fusion movement after forming the group Return to Forever with Joe Farrell on flute and soprano sax; Stanley Clarke on bass; and the Brazilian husband-wife duo of Airto Moreira on drums and percussion and vocalist Flora Purim. The early-1972 album *Return to Forever* got the ball rolling; *Light as a Feather* became the group's most acclaimed success.

Alyn Shipton describes the 1972 Return to Forever as "a relatively gentle Latin-oriented group" possessing an "airiness and grace,"[344] and these are qualities that accurately describe Corea's greatest original, *Spain*.[345] The piece opens with an allusion to *Concierto de Aranjuez* by Spanish composer Joaquin Rodrigo, and (writes Lyons) "evolves into an intensely rhythmic second theme and a joyous, hand-clapping celebration—Corea's most effective emotional mood." The performance succeeds "because its joy is so infectious."[346]

Candle in the Wind (1973/1987)—Elton John

Originally released on MCA album *Goodbye Yellow Brick Road* (chart debut Oct. 20, 1973, spent 8 weeks at #1, sold 7 million copies); #11 in England (1974)

New live version released as single on MCA 53196 (chart debut Nov. 7, 1987, reached #6); #5 in England (1988)

She was the foremost pop-cultural icon of the twentieth century, her name and physical image serving as symbols of timeless Hollywood glamour and the particular tension between sexuality and innocence that marked America

in the 1950s. Yet even at the peak of her fame she was also a haunted young woman terrified of performing and desperately uncertain of the very qualities that had made her a legend. Few entertainers have provided pleasure to more people over the past half century than Marilyn Monroe, and fewer still left behind a sadder story. Marilyn's combination of sensual beauty, aching vulnerability, saucy humor, and aura of joy emerging out of sorrow left us a wondrous and singular legacy. Elton John and Bernie Taupin perfectly captured that poignancy in their original classic *Candle in the Wind*.

As introduced on John's greatest album, the song, written from the perspective of a "young man in the 22nd row" dazzled by Marilyn's image and haunted by her tragedy, impeccably conveys the feeling that generations of fans have shared: the wish that we could have known her and somehow helped to give her the confidence and sense of self-worth that she lacked, thereby enabling her story to have a happy ending. The electric guitar figure played by Davey Johnstone following the title phrase rings out as a somber, sympathetic elegy. MCA had planned to release it as a single, but DJs began playing *Bennie and the Jets* so heavily as an album cut that the much less compelling though popular *Bennie* got the nod instead.

After fourteen years as a beloved favorite on classic-rock stations, *Candle in the Wind* finally received its due as a Top Ten single through Elton's fervent live performance with the eighty-eight-member Melbourne Symphony Orchestra; while lacking the sheer perfection of the original, it was an undeniably strong rendition. The emotion driving it had a special edge: his voice worn down through a long tour (for which this was the final night), he had recently been told by a doctor that his vocal cords were ruined and might never recover. He believed that this concert (nationally televised across Australia) might be his last. Fortunately, therapy and rest enabled his voice to fully recover. In 1997, the song would make pop history in a new form.

Candle in the Wind 1997 (1997)—Elton John
Rocket 568108

Chart debut Oct. 11, 1997 (14 weeks at #1); #1 (43 weeks) in Canada, #1 (7 weeks) in Germany, #1 (7 weeks) in Australia, #1 (5 weeks) in England[347] [348] (*BILLB*-#5, *DMDB*-#18)

---

344. Shipton, *New History of Jazz*, p. 620.

345. Charles Shaar Murray remarked of the group's music in the October 21, 1973, *New Musical Express*: "It's the most peaceful, happy music imaginable, exuding an air of enormous serenity and tranquility despite its strength, the musical equivalent of a cool drink on a hot day—a Bacardi and peppermint, perhaps."

346. Lyons, *The 101 Best Jazz Albums*, p. 355.

347. *Candle* shattered all records for longevity in Canada. It remained almost continuously in or near the Canadian Top Five from September 1997 into 1999, selling an "unprecedented" two million copies nationally as reported in the April 17, 1999, *Billboard*. Due to its unique nature as a Diana tribute, it sold not only in record shops but in "nontraditional" venues like grocery and drug stores. After holding the #1 position for 42 non-consecutive weeks from October 1997 through October 1998, it returned to #1 in 2002!

348. #1 in Europe (6 weeks at #1 and 12 weeks at #2), Denmark (18 weeks at #1), Austria (17 weeks at #1), Spain (13 weeks at #1), Switzerland (11 weeks), Belgium, Netherlands, and Sweden (7 weeks each), France

Elton John had come to know the Princess of Wales, the former Diana Spencer, and like everyone else was shocked by her death on August 31, 1997, following an auto accident in France. Because of their friendship, Diana's family asked him to perform at her funeral. Elton called on Bernie Taupin to write new lyrics to their 1973 Marilyn Monroe tribute *Candle in the Wind* in honor of Diana, and John performed it at her September 6 funeral at Westminster Abbey. The event was telecast around the world, and the response to the song was so overwhelming that John recorded it. One of the biggest pop music events of the era, the record soared quickly to #1 (although a quirk in *Billboard* policy caused the far less noteworthy B side, *Something About the Way You Look Tonight*, to be listed first during most of its chart run,[349] an error corrected by Joel Whitburn in his Record Research books that list *Candle* first), selling a confirmed 11 million copies in the U.S. and a reported 33 million worldwide.[350] (Its total weeks at #1, as reported in *Billboard*'s "Hits of the World" charts, were at least 190 weeks, an astonishing figure not even approached by any other record.) This placed it alongside Bing Crosby's *White Christmas* (over 31 million) and Bill Haley & the Comets' *Rock Around the Clock* (over 25 million) as one of the three biggest-selling singles of all time. The performance also won the Grammy as best pop male vocal.

Long Yellow Road (1974)—Toshiko Akiyoshi—Lew Tabackin Big Band
Recorded April 4, 1974 for RCA album *Long Yellow Road* (*SJ*)

Overcoming a host of obstacles as an Asian woman in jazz, Toshiko Akiyoshi has enjoyed an impressive career as composer, pianist, and bandleader, and *Long Yellow Road* represents her talents well. Born in Dairen, Manchuria, December 12, 1929, to Japanese immigrant parents, she moved with her family to Japan in 1946, began playing with combos there in 1949, and was heard by piano great Oscar Peterson during a 1953 Japanese visit, leading to recordings for Norman Granz. After earning a reputation as Japan's leading jazz pianist, she came to the U.S. in 1956, steadily built her stateside credentials, and in 1970 debuted as a composer-conductor. Toshiko's greatest fame came after she married American tenor saxophonist Lew Tabackin; the sixteen-member orchestra they formed in 1973 (with all compositions

by Akiyoshi) soon attained international success. *Long Yellow Road* shows her gift for, in Jose Bowen's words, "exotic melodies and delicate orchestration," and her Ellington-like gift for writing to the strengths of her musicians.[351] The saxophone section is prominently featured, leading to a strong Tabackin solo; other soloists are Gary Foster on alto and Bobby Shew on trumpet. In both 1978 and 1979 she won the *Down Beat* readers' polls for top band and arranger, and earned second place as composer. Peter Rothbart: "The concentration required to perform Akiyoshi's music makes the band look almost like a symphony orchestra,"[352] given her penchant for changing meters several times per piece, but, as here, her music swings admirably.

Song of the Soul (1975)—Cris Williamson
From the Olivia album *The Changer and the Changed*

An icon of the women's music movement, Cris Williamson was born in 1947 in Deadwood, South Dakota, the daughter of a forest ranger, and grew up in the Black Hills of South Dakota, Colorado, and Wyoming. A precocious songwriter, pianist, and guitarist as well as singer, she recorded her self-titled debut album in 1971, and it sold 11,000 copies on a tiny label.[353] Called "the original spark that ignited the women's music revolution," *The Changer and the Changed* became a phenomenon soon after its release in 1975, the all-time best seller for the women's music label that she co-founded, Olivia, influencing a generation of performers. The album was packed with passionate acoustic gems like *Waterfall, Sweet Woman*, and *Shooting Star*; its centerpiece was *Song of the Soul*, a joyous anthem of spiritual uplift. It opens with a prayer-like a cappella intro, then ushering in a band that includes fellow Olivia stars Meg Christian on classical guitar and Margie Adam on piano as the tempo becomes bouncy reflecting the piece's giddy optimism, and the soaring chorus features a choir of more than two dozen female voices. Williamson has recorded at least fifteen more albums over the years, and this will always be her trademark song. "We can sing for a long, long time . . ."

Ponta de Lanca Africano (Umbabarauma) (1976)— Jorge Ben
From the album *Africa Brasil* (*World-#62*)

When a song is firing on all musical cylinders—melodically, rhythmically, vocally, instrumentally, and emotionally—sometimes it just doesn't matter what it's "about." *Ponta de Lanca Africano* is a celebration of a soccer hero,

---

and Norway (6 weeks each), Ireland and Italy (5 weeks each), Finland (3 weeks), Japan (2 weeks); also #1 in Poland.

349. *Something* was listed ahead of *Candle* starting on November 1, 1997, because it ranked higher in radio airplay, without regard to the fact that the single's massive retail sales were driven almost entirely by *Candle*, as *Billboard* made clear in its news articles throughout late 1997 and early 1998.

350. *Guinness World Records* 2001, p. 100.

351. *Jazz: The Smithsonian Anthology* (2010), p. 155–56.
352. August 1980 *Down Beat*.
353. *MusicHound: Folk*, p. 849.

but even those who couldn't care less about the sport can hardly fail to be thrilled by this propulsive, powerful fusion of Brazilian and African musical influences.

Jorge Ben (born Jorge Duilio Menezes on March 22, 1945, in the Rio de Janeiro slum of Madureira)[354] burst upon the Brazilian music scene in 1963, the country's first important black composer since the emergence of bossa nova a few years earlier. Fellow Brazilian artist Caetano Veloso remarked that "he was also, and most importantly, the first to make that blackness the determining stylistic element," incorporating African sounds and linking himself with the American black movement. He "became a symbol, a myth, a master for us."[355] Ben's song *Mas Que Nada* became an international hit for Sergio Mendes in 1966, and his music continued to evolve, adding rock (electric guitar), jazz, R&B, and funk elements.[356] *Samba esquema novo* (New Style Samba) was the popular name for the multi-genre fusion he created. Jorge's best concerts, writes Chris McGowan, "are like tribal celebrations in which the entire audience dances almost to the point of a trance" through his fervent guitar and the dense rhythms of his band, Ze' Pretinho.[357]

The complete centrality to Jorge Ben of rhythm over everything else is exemplified by *Ponta de Lanca Africano*. From the opening seconds onward, the listener is immersed in a complex, turbulent world of rhythms, as his guitar plus driving bass and multiple percussion instruments send the piece hurtling ever forward underneath his sometimes-chanted lead and strong female backing vocals. David Byrne, leader of the Talking Heads, was dazzled by the number, and made it the leadoff track of his 1989 multi-artist Brazilian compilation *Beleza Tropical*. A delightfully colorful animated video for the song by British illustrator Susan Young carried it onto MTV and VH1;[358] the fact that it came out at precisely the time that albums by the Gipsy Kings and the Bulgarian State Radio & Television Female Vocal Choir were captivating many U.S. listeners heightened its popular impact. This new American visibility led to his 1994 album at Prince's Paisley Park Studios, *World Dance*.

Anarchy in the U.K. (1976)—Sex Pistols

EMI single, British chart debut Dec. 11, 1976 (reached #38)

From the Virgin album *Never Mind the Bullocks, Here's the Sex Pistols* (British debut Nov. 12, 1977, #1 for 2 weeks); U.S. debut Dec. 10, 1977 (#106 peak) (*ACC-#7, RS-#56, RHF, PW, DM-#100, 1001, TC, DMDB*)

Punk rock's moment in the musical sun was brief, but it was incendiary, and the snarling face of the movement was the Sex Pistols. With Johnny "Rotten" Lydon's screeching vocals accompanied by Steve Jones on guitar, Sid Vicious on bass, and Paul Cook on drums, the Pistols began playing local gigs in November 1975; their breakthrough was on April 18, 1976, playing before a packed house of 150 at a seedy little Soho strip club called El Paradise. But they were then banned from a succession of venues because "their name was synonymous with trouble, obscenity, and violence." Their cult following expanded after their appearance at the September 21 and 22 Punk Rock Festival.[359] From nearly the outset of their public performances, *Anarchy in the U.K.* was one of their trademark songs, with their "instantly identifiable, evisceral splurge" driving fans wild, as described by Caroline Coon.[360] As the British rock magazines frantically hyped the group, a front-page story in the November 6, 1976, *Melody Maker* announced the imminent release of the single, with the band set to launch its first major tour at month's end. Upon its issuance, Coon declared, "it was difficult to imagine how the band could recapture all that [live] excitement on vinyl. They HAVE done it, though." The record, she gushed, "is the epitome of their sound, at the group's most furious, venomous, best. The song is a threat, a malediction."[361] At its conclusion, Johnny Rotten screamed, "Destroy!"[362]

That is precisely what the group swiftly proceeded to do—to itself. An obscenity-drenched appearance on Thames television was a quickly legendary disaster; just as the single was generating airplay and sales, radio stations moved to ban it in the face of angry phone calls, their planned tour fell apart with a wave of cancellations, and just after New Year's, EMI terminated its contract with the band and withdrew the single from stores. The Pistols came roaring back by signing with Virgin and hit-

---

354. He adopted the stage identity from his Ethiopian mother (Ben was her maiden name). In 1989 he changed it to Jorge Benjor after discovering royalties lost to jazzman George Benson because of confusion over their names.

355. Veloso, *Tropical Truth: A Story of Music and Revolution in Brazil*. Gilberto Gil, another of Brazil's most gifted artists, was so deeply moved by Ben that for a time he stopped writing original songs, feeling they could not measure up. The two artists would team up for the acclaimed 1975 album *Gil e Jorge*.

356. The melodic line of Jorge's 1972 song *Taj Mahal* was adapted by Rod Stewart into his 1979 smash *Do Ya Think I'm Sexy*; when he sued, Stewart acknowledged the borrowing, and donated his royalties to the United Nations Children's Fund.

357. *The Brazilian Sound*, p. 95–96.

358. February 18, 1989, *Billboard*.

359. Caroline Coon in her history of the group for the November 27, 1976, *Melody Maker*.

360. October 2, 1976, *Melody Maker*.

361. November 27, 1976, *Melody Maker*. The group scrapped its first version of the single, then re-recorded it with producer Chris Thomas. This time they nailed it, "and their care and attention pays dividends, totally destroying the myth that U.K. punk rock revels in untuned instruments and sloppiness."

362. Paul Williams (p. 167–68): "The first 50 seconds are sheer ecstatic release: the thundering bass intro, the timing and energy of Rotten's opening words ('Right. Now!') . . .." The record is "sarcastic, baiting, contemptuous, hate-filled . . . It is joyous. It is liberating. It is big noise."

ting #1 with their album, including the smash *God Save the Queen*. It was to be their only proper album (a much-later, ill-conceived reunion produced only a dismal live LP), as their brand of punk-rock nihilistic anger didn't translate to baffled U.S. record buyers, and they completed their inevitable implosion. However short-lived, the Pistols had left their mark on rock history. In *Anarchy in the U.K.*, proclaimed Coon, Rotten "is not advocating anarchism. He <u>is</u> anarchy."

Go Your Own Way (1977)—Fleetwood Mac (written by Lindsey Buckingham)
Warner 8304
Chart debut Jan. 8, 1977 (#10 peak); #16 in Canada, #38 in England;[363] from the album *Rumours* (31 weeks at #1) (*RHF, GHF, RS-#120, RIA, DM, 1001, TC, ACC, DMDB*)

The *Rumours* commercial juggernaut that would reign supreme atop the charts for most of 1977 was triggered by its first single, a brilliant pop creation whose sunny sound belies angry lyrics inspired by the two recent romantic breakups within Fleetwood Mac: between Buckingham and Stevie Nicks, and John and Christine McVie. "Like everything else on *Rumours*, it was very, very autobiographical," said Buckingham.

"I remember writing it in a bunch of Holiday Inns," while the band was on the road doing colleges, he told *Rolling Stone*. "It was at a time when both Christine and Stevie wanted to move on. It was a feeling they encouraged in one another." When Stevie first heard the lyric, "she objected quite vehemently to the brutal honesty of it, or what she thought was exaggeration, but to my mind it wasn't." The propulsive energy of the record came despite the fact that drummer Mick Fleetwood elected to use a different rhythm than the one originally written. "It moves along, like a train building up speed."[364] The album took eleven months to complete (six months in the studio, five months of mixing and editing), which in the pop world of the 1970s seemed an eternity; Warner Brothers could afford to be patient, since the band's previous album was still selling in huge numbers. Remarkably, as discussed in Bob Brunning's Mac history, the label was afraid that the 1975 album had been a fluke, and (not yet having heard any of the new material) executives initially didn't plan to issue a single from *Rumours* because if it bombed, it might hurt the LP's sales. Then Mick Fleetwood met with Mo Ostin and other Warners officials, and played *Go Your Own Way*. Immediately,

the fears were erased, and the pop phenomenon was launched.[365]

Rumours—one of the ten biggest albums ever with sales over 19 million in the U.S.—won the Grammy for Album of the Year, and was inducted into the Grammy Hall of Fame in its first year of eligibility. Dave Marsh: "*Go Your Own Way*, with its churning guitar, heavy-footed bass drum, and Buckingham's keening lead vocal . . . is as close to the heart of rock and soul as [anyone else has] come in the post-Beatles period."[366]

(What's So Funny 'bout) Peace, Love and Understanding (1979)—Elvis Costello (written by Nick Lowe)
Columbia 1172 (uncharted single);[367]
From the album *Armed Forces* (chart debut Jan. 27, 1979, #10 peak) (*RS-#290, DM*)

Nick Lowe (born on March 25, 1949, in Suffolk, England) wrote *Peace, Love and Understanding* in the mid-1970s while he was a member of the pub-rock band Brinsley Schwartz before his solo career; when he produced Elvis Costello's first six albums, it was a natural for Elvis to record. It became the most unforgettable of Costello's early recordings which established him at the vanguard of British rock's "new wave."

A Liverpool native born Declan McManus on August 25, 1955, Costello led the country-rock band Flip City in 1976 before signing a solo record deal under his new stage name. Two singles in 1977 (including the ballad *Alison*) didn't become hits but generated enough interest to help make his debut album, *My Aim Is True*, an immediate British success in summer 1977, followed at year's end with its release in the U.S. Ironically enough considering the idealistic subject matter of this song, Stephen Thomas Erlewine notes that "his bristling cynicism and anger linked him with the punk and new wave explosion."[368] His main connection with the punks was "his unbridled passion," which—coupled with his intelligent lyrics and (starting with his second album) the hard-rocking band the Attractions—made Costello a powerhouse performer. He was also prolific; his first three albums (*Armed Forces* was the third and biggest-selling) had their U.S. releases within a fourteen-month span. The new album was recorded over six weeks in August–September 1978; while Lowe again produced, Elvis at that point was increasingly assertive and, by

363. #1 (4 weeks) in Belgium, also #1 in Holland, #2 in France; oddly enough, none of the singles from *Rumours* cracked the Top 20 in England.
364. September 8, 1988, *Rolling Stone*, p. 124.

365. Brunning, *The Fleetwood Mac Story: Rumours and Lies*, p, 117–18.
366. *The Heart of Rock & Soul*, p. 319.
367. The song was initially released in Britain only as a B side, not on the U.K. version of the album.
368. *All Music Guide to Rock* (1997), p. 215.

Lowe's account, "had the final say." Keyboardist Steve Nieve worked closely with Lowe on the arrangements.[369]

Costello "transformed *Peace, Love and Understanding*," writes Dave Marsh. Recorded at a time "when hope still tempered his misanthropy, Costello eradicated Lowe's cynicism and replaced it with joyous acceptance and thinly veiled remorse. [It is] Costello's most openly emotive record . . . though what he reveals is anything but peaceful—he's angry, choking on tears of rage . . ." Marsh remarks that this is "also the hottest rock and roll his band, the Attractions, ever made." Pete Thomas' "cascading drum rolls" combine with a Costello guitar line "as fierce as his vocal."[370] Costello's most celebrated early live performance of the song (just after the album was wrapped up) was as the thematically appropriate closing number at a show organized by the Anti-Nazi League attended by 150,000 people in London's Brockwell Park. Thanks to performances like this explosively exciting track, *Armed Forces* was voted the #5 album of 1979 in the *Village Voice* critics' poll.

The Devil Went Down to Georgia (1979)—Charlie Daniels Band (written by Charlie Daniels, Fred Edwards, Jim Marshall, Charlie Hayward, Tom Crain & Taz DiGregorio)
Epic 50700
Recorded at Nashville's Woodland Studios on Dec. 5, 1978; chart debut June 30, 1979
(#1 for 1 week C&W, #3 pop) (*C&W-#54, RIA, DMDB, SC*)

A record that brings old-time fiddling into an exciting rock & roll context, *The Devil Went Down to Georgia* interweaves an original narrative with elements of fiddle themes that reach back generations.[371] *Hell Broke Loose in Georgia* was recorded by Fiddlin' John Carson in both 1925 and 1927,[372] and in 1930 (as *Hell's Broke Loose in Georgia*) by that furious-fiddling Atlanta group Gid Tanner & His Skillet Lickers.

Fiddler/guitarist/singer Charlie Daniels, born in Wilmington, North Carolina on October 28, 1936, had written a hit in 1964 for Elvis Presley, *It Hurts Me*, and launched his own performing career with his country-rock band in 1973. Bob Dylan, with whom he played on the *Nashville Skyline* album (1969), wrote admiringly in his book *Chronicles, Vol. One* of Daniels "coming up with a new form of hillbilly boogie that was pure genius." Here he creates an exciting, compelling pop classic in spinning the tale of a fiddle duel for the ages between a country boy and the Devil, with young Johnny's soul hanging in the balance. Daniels' scorching fiddling lives up to the challenge.[373]

By the artist's account, the song was created "just about by accident. We were doing the album *Million Mile Reflections*, when I realized we had gone without a good fiddle song. We literally stopped recording, went into the rehearsal studio and wrote the song that afternoon." The band's keyboard player, "Taz" DiGregorio, came up with the bridge, and Tommy Cain wrote the guitar parts. "Once we got into the recording of it, we felt we had something."[374] The tale about dueling with the devil for a musical prize was inspired by the 1925 Stephen Vincent Benet poem *Mountain Whippoorwill: How Hill-Billy Jim Won the Great Fiddler's Prize*, which he recalled reading in high school.[375] *Devil* was named one of *Country America* magazine's all-time top 100 C&W songs, and honored as the CMA's Single of the Year and the Grammy winner for best C&W group vocal. BMI reports that the song has received over two million broadcast performances. "The sound hasn't dated at all, [and] the subject matter, about good versus evil, never goes out of style, either."

Once in a Lifetime (1980)—Talking Heads (written by David Byrne)
From the album *Remain in Light* (chart debut Nov. 1, 1980, #19 peak)
British single reached #14 (1981); live version of song released in 1986 from the soundtrack of *Stop Making Sense* as single on Sire 29163 (#91 peak) (*NPR-100, RHF, ACC-#129, 1001, TC, DET*)

An epic of surrealism that is no less fascinating for its self-conscious nature, *Once in a Lifetime* is perhaps the song that best defines David Byrne and Talking Heads. Rod Serling could have constructed a nifty episode of *Twilight Zone* out of this one.[376] Singer-guitarist Byrne, bassist Tina Weymouth, and drummer Chris Frantz

---

369. *Complicated Shadows*, p. 100–2.

370. Marsh, *The Heart of Rock & Soul*, p. 385–86. With its thundering drums and droning piano, said *Rolling Stone* admiringly in its top 500 ranking (p. 83), it's "like Abba playing punk rock."

371. The ancient *Village Hornpipe* is the ultimate source for some of the themes (as outlined in *Country Music Sources* by Meade and Spottswood, that tune's subsequent variations included *The Eighth of January*, later evolved into *The Battle of New Orleans*).

372. *Hell Broke Loose in Georgia* was also one of the fiddle standards performed in the heavily-publicized fiddle competition held in January 1926 in Nashville sponsored by the Ford Motor Company.

373. The band recorded two versions, which Daniels referred to as the Methodist version and the Baptist version. In the latter, Johnny's reference to the devil as "son of a bitch" is overdubbed as "son of a gun." (*Billboard Book of Number One Country Hits*, p. 239.)

374. Interview, August 24, 1999, *Country Weekly*, p. 38–39. Producer John Boylan's long association with Daniels began with this record. He told Eric Olsen, "I was the first person [at Epic Records] to think it was a single" (*Encyclopedia of Record Producers*, p. 85).

375. *Sing Your Heart Out, Country Boy*, p. 380–81. Benet is best remembered for his 1937 short story *The Devil and Daniel Webster*, which was adapted into a folk opera and then a celebrated 1941 film.

376. Indeed, it's wonderfully evocative of an episode from the first season of *Twilight Zone*, "A World of Difference" (aired in March 1960), in which a man discovers that the life he thinks he's been living (job, wife,

formed the group after they met in the early 1970s at the Rhode Island School of Design, began to earn a following in 1975 at the New York punk club CBGB's, and were joined in 1976 by keyboardist Jerry Harrison. Its 1977 debut album made the band a favorite of critics for Byrne's edgy lyrics and vocals and (as described by Stephen Thomas Erlewine) its "nervous energy, detached emotion, and subdued minimalism." With the production of Brian Eno, it was the Heads' second album that took it to the next level of both critical and popular success. *Remain in Light* was the band's third and last teaming with Eno, and the zenith of their collaboration. Byrne and Eno had both begun to explore African music and its trance-like qualities achieved through playing multiple rhythms (most dramatically heard on their 1983 hit *Burning Down the House*). As Eno described it, his perception of the song's rhythm was fundamentally different from the musicians', and "there was this tension between my picture of the song and theirs" that actually served to make the track more compelling.[377] It was selected by *Rolling Stone* in 1988 as the #69 best single of the past twenty-five years.

Nansi Imali (Here Is the Money) (c. 1981–1983)—Ladysmith Black Mambazo

From the Gallo Records album *Phansi Emgodini* (*World-#88*)

Already the most celebrated vocal group in all of black Africa by the early 1980s, Ladysmith Black Mambazo was catapulted to worldwide iconic status by Paul Simon's *Graceland*, a status backed up by more than four decades of great music. Joseph Shabalala was born August 28, 1941, in Thukela in the district of Ladysmith, located in the province of Natal in South Africa. The original edition of his group was known as the Durban Choir, which he joined in January 1960, but during the next few years music could only be a sideline, as he had to work on a white man's farm under the terms of a contract so that his family could continue living on the homestead. By 1964, now known as Ladysmith Black Mambazo (Zulu translation: "The Black Axe of Ladysmith"), he was training the group with his original songs, and soon they began performing on radio; a surviving 1967 radio performance, *Umama Lo* (It Is Mama), shows their a cappella vocal style already well developed. The group was building upon an ancient tradition of vocal harmonizing by Zulu male groups, represented on records since the early 1930s, but adding its own distinctive touches. There was frequent turnover in group personnel, with Shabalala the only constant. By 1972, they were successful enough

that members could quit their day jobs and focus solely on music. Recordings began for Gallo Records—the same company for which Solomon Linda's Evening Birds had done their legendary *Mbube* in 1939—and in 1977 Mambazo received its first of many gold records for selling over 50,000 copies of *Ukusindiswa*.[378]

Nansi Imali served as the opening track for the album *Phansi Emdogini*, and the closing number on the multi-artist South African compilation that introduced many Westerners to this music, *The Indestructible Beat of Soweto*. It's a superb representation of the group's impeccable a cappella mastery—tightly disciplined, yet rich with feeling—based on *iscathamiya*, the traditional singing style of South Africa's miners.[379] "Here is the money dug by the men in the mines / Where the fainthearted will not go / We congratulate our men for their bravery . . ." Shabalala and Mambazo proceeded to make history in 1986 with Simon, through the group's unforgettable performances on *Homeless* and *Diamonds on the Soles of Her Shoes*, followed by a rousing international tour with Simon, and their own Grammy-winning 1987 album *Shaka Zulu* (produced by the singer). Subsequent decades have only deepened their artistry and reputation, with one highlight being their 1994 performance at the inauguration of Nelson Mandela as South Africa's first black president. In 2011 they reunited with Simon for a twenty-fifth anniversary concert in South Africa presented in the acclaimed documentary *Under African Skies*.

(Other personnel: one alto, one tenor, and seven bass vocalists, including Jabulani Dubazana, Abednego Mazibuko, Albert Mazibuko, Russell Mthembu, Headman Shabalala, Jockey Shabalala)

Sexual Healing (1982)—Marvin Gaye (written by Marvin Gaye, Odell Brown & David Ritz)

Columbia 03302

Chart debut Oct. 16, 1982 (10 weeks at #1 on R&B chart; #3 pop); #1 (3 weeks) in Canada, #4 in U.K. & Australia[380] (*RHF, R&B-#83, RS, DM, ACC, DMDB*)

Five-and-a-half years after his last Top 40 pop hit, Marvin Gaye scored his one and only hit away from his twenty-year home at Motown, the gently but intensely seductive *Sexual Healing*. He made the decision to leave in early 1981, seeking a fresh start, and a year later finalized a lucrative new deal with Columbia. The late 1970s had been a battlefield for the soul legend, with the end of his second marriage, drug addiction, big debts to the IRS, and depleted creative energy. When he divorced Berry Gordy, Jr.'s, sister Anna, a court ordered that he carry out a financial settlement under which he

family) is a lie: he's merely an actor on a movie soundstage, and when it is disassembled, his only connection to the world he knows will vanish.
    377. *Encyclopedia of Record Producers*, p. 217–18.

    378. Information from biography by Alex Thembala & Edmund Radebe.
    379. *MusicHound: World*, p. 416.
    380. #1 (6 weeks) in New Zealand, #3 in Belgium and Holland.

was to record two albums and surrender all resulting money to Anna. Gaye fulfilled the deal by recording the strange, and relatively poor-selling, 1979 double album *Here, My Dear*. Having concluded his obligations to Motown, he made the move to Columbia, which purchased his contract for two million dollars.

But by 1982 he felt rejuvenated, physically, spiritually, and musically. Biographer David Ritz proved to be a contributor to the song that enabled Gaye to come back with a vengeance. Visiting the singer's new home in Belgium (after Gaye's three years in England), Ritz took note of his extensive collection of pornography, including books on sadomasochism, and the author suggested that Marvin needed sexual healing. Gaye seized on the concept to overcome a case of writer's block. For months he'd been listening to a reggae-styled instrumental track written by one of his sidemen, Odell Brown, and now he was inspired to write matching lyrics. He recorded the album at Katy Recording Studio in the village of Ohaine a few miles from Brussels. Marvin's original mentor Harvey Fuqua (with whom he had sung in the Moonglows back in 1959–1960, and also his former brother-in-law) served as (uncredited) co-producer and contributed vocal harmonies, along with Gordon Banks.[381]

Like his 1973 classic *Let's Get It On, Sexual Healing* explores (as Thomas Ryan phrases it) "the sanctified element of sex. Eroticism is expressed as liberation of the soul."[382] The record's huge success—his longest-running #1 single ever on the R&B charts, and a certified million-seller—looked like the beginning of a Gaye revival, but it turned out to be the coda of an amazing career. On April 1, 1984, suffering once again from an ongoing depression, he was fatally shot by his father after a violent quarrel in Los Angeles, one day before his forty-fifth birthday.

Jump (1984)—Van Halen
Warner 29384

Chart debut Jan. 14, 1984 (5 weeks at #1); #1 (2 weeks) in Canada, #7 in England;[383] from the album *1984* (5 weeks at #2, sold 10 million copies) (*DM-#28, RHF, RIA-#119, ACC, TC, DMDB, VIL*)

They had already conquered the world of hard rock, but Van Halen expanded to at least briefly rule the rest of the pop world with *Jump*. Formed in Pasdena, California, the group consisting of virtuoso lead guitarist Eddie Van Halen, flamboyant singer David Lee Roth, Eddie's brother Alex Van Halen on drums (both brothers were born in

the Netherlands and moved to California in 1967), and bassist Michael Anthony, exploded on the rock scene in 1978 with a debut album that ultimately sold 10 million copies, and their next four albums sold a combined 13 million. Between Eddie's dazzling guitar technique and Roth's showmanship, the group had few rivals in its field. It was Eddie's discovery of electronic synthesizers, giving the group a more melodic, slightly softer sound while still rocking out as before,[384] that helped them move to the next level. Another key ingredient was Eddie's guitar solo on Michael Jackson's 1983 chart-topper *Beat It,* which not only helped the album *Thriller* conquer the world, but also exposed Van Halen to a new audience.

Jump was the first song the group recorded at the 16-track studio built on the grounds of Eddie Van Halen's new home in the hills just beyond Hollywood. Eddie had written the song on synthesizer, but the group had rejected it for the 1982 album *Diver Down* because he didn't play guitar on the original version. After he laid down a new demo, producer Ted Templeman and the band were blown away.[385] The song is "a stunningly catchy pop-rocker" driven by Eddie's surging synth work (and of course a killer guitar solo), wrote *Rolling Stone* in ranking it as the #47 greatest pop song in 2000.[386] Dave Marsh, citing *Jump* as #28 in *The Heart of Rock & Soul,* says its riff is a "direct descendant" of The Who's *Won't Get Fooled Again,* "but with a sweeter, more cogently stated melody."[387] The music video, featuring Roth's swaggering charisma[388] and Eddie's telegenic smile, was one of the first undisputed classics that defined MTV.

Theme from *The Natural* (1984)—Randy Newman
Warner Brothers soundtrack album (didn't chart);[389] movie premiere May 11, 1984

After making his reputation in the 1970s as a pop singer-songwriter with an exceptional melodic gift and a uniquely skewed lyrical perspective, it was only natural (so to speak) that Randy Newman would turn his hand to writing for movies—particularly as the nephew of two of Hollywood's most admired composers, Alfred and Lionel Newman.[390] Randy had composed for three films

---

381. Richard J. Ripani in *The New Blue Music* notes that *Healing*—a quintessentially sensual "quiet storm" jazzy ballad, is set at the moderately slow yet funky groove of 95 beats per minute. This was one of the early known uses of an electronic drum machine, a Roland TR-808 which created multilayered drum parts.

382. Ryan, *American Hit Radio*, p. 520–21.

383. #3 in Germany, #4 in Switzerland, #5 in Austria, #8 France.

384. The group had made its first use of keyboards on *The Cradle Will Rock* (1980). Eddie had taken years of piano lessons before focusing on guitar, and often wrote songs on piano.

385. For the keyboard section, he played an Oberheim OB-Xa. The band recorded *Jump* in a single take. (Ian Christie, *Everybody Wants Some: The Van Halen Saga*, p. 94–97.

386. December 7, 2000, *Rolling Stone*, p. 88.

387. Marsh, p. 26.

388. Roth dedicated *Jump* to Benny Urquidez, the kickboxer who trained him three hours a day for months before the band's 1984 tour, evidenced by his leaping ability in the video.

389. Newman also conducted the orchestra, with orchestration by Jack Hayes. The soundtrack album was produced by Lenny Waronker.

390. Alfred Newman won nine Academy Awards. Eight were in the capacity of leading a team of arrangers and orchestrators for Twentieth

early in his career (1970–1971), but his breakthrough as a major film composer was with his Oscar-nominated score for the 1981 Milos Forman film *Ragtime*. His next screen assignment would be arguably his greatest (and certainly his most enduring), for Barry Levinson's adaptation of the Bernard Malamud novel *The Natural*, starring Robert Redford as Roy Hobbs. The character of Hobbs possessed extraordinary gifts that seemingly destined him for greatness, until one youthful near-fatal error in judgment sent him into oblivion for seventeen years before his career could even begin, until launching a last-ditch bid to fulfill a dream. Newman's entire score was rich and varied, but of course it is the closing theme that became immortal.

It begins with the stirring, soaring fanfare theme we had initially heard when Hobbs first proved what he could do at Wrigley Field ("Knock the Cover Off the Ball"), and is taken to a still grander scale with the final home run. Christian Clemmensen: "This triumphant and deliberate brass theme, aided by the magic of tingling percussion and electronic bass enhancements, has become an anthem for sporting perseverance in the decades since."[391] [392] This theme itself showed the influence of Aaron Copland, and also that of Vangelis' immensely popular theme from *Chariots of Fire*, although possessing a richness and grandeur that places it on another level. But elevating the closing theme still higher is Newman's entirely new melody (as part of *The Final Game*), a slow, deeply emotional and romantic orchestral theme that conveys everything running through Hobbs' mind as he rounds the bases—not just athletic victory and redemption, but his love for the woman who had always believed in him, Iris (played by Glenn Close), and his discovery of the son he never knew he had. Little wonder that the score would earn Newman another Oscar nomination, and a Grammy victory as best original motion picture score. Over his career Newman has earned twenty Oscar nominations and two wins (so far); the staying power of this theme tops them all.

Walk This Way (1986)—Run-DMC with Steven Tyler & Joe Perry
Profile 5112

Century Fox (he served as the studio's music director for twenty years starting in 1940); his one award for composing was the score for the religious drama *Song of Bernadette* (1943). Lionel Newman supervised and orchestrated scores for more than 250 films, and won an Oscar for his work on *Hello, Dolly*!

391. Clemmensen for website *Filmtracks*.

392. Perhaps the most unforgettable non-movie use of Newman's fanfare theme was on October 16, 1988, to begin NBC's coverage of Game 2 of the World Series, to commemorate a hobbled Kirk Gibson's bottom-of-the-ninth-inning home run that gave the Los Angeles Dodgers a stunning come-from-behind victory over the Oakland Athletics the previous night.

Chart debut July 26, 1986 (#4 pop, #8 R&B), #4 in Canada, #8 in England, #9 in Australia;[393] from the album *Raising Hell* (#3 peak) (*RHF, NPR-300, RS, VIL-#17, R&B-#80, ACC-#94, DM*)[394]

When Aerosmith made *Walk This Way* its second Top Ten hit in early 1977, it solidified the Boston-based group as one of the hottest rock ensembles on the scene. But the group could not have anticipated that the song would enjoy an even more spectacular second life a decade later, a collaboration that would help complete the crossover hip-hop music was making, to become as familiar among white suburban teenagers as it already was with black kids.

Singer Steven Tyler, lead guitarist Joe Perry, guitarist Brad Whitford, bassist Tom Hamilton, and drummer Joey Kramer carried their Rolling Stones-inspired riffs and stagecraft to double-platinum status with their 1973 debut album. Although they didn't crack the pop singles market until *Dream On* hit the Top Ten in its 1976 reissue, their first five albums (led by their blockbuster third LP *Toys in the Attic*) sold over 21 million copies combined. The hard-rocking *Walk This Way*, featuring Tyler's rapid-fire, partly spoken-rather-than-sung lyrics with a horny-teenager narrative, failed to chart in its original 1975 release on Columbia 10206, but in its November 1976 reissue on Columbia 10449 climbed to #10. The group fell apart over the next several years with drugs and other excesses, then enjoyed a rebirth starting with the 1987 album *Permanent Vacation*, and reaching a peak with the chart-topping, seven-million-selling 1993 album *Get a Grip*. It was a comeback kicked off by this record.

One of the most influential rap acts ever, Run-DMC—a trio from Queens, New York, with rappers Joseph "Run" Simmons and Darryl "D.M.C." McDaniels plus DJ Jason "Jam Master Jay" Mizell—came on the hip-hop scene in 1983 at a time when artists like Grandmaster Flash & the Furious Five were showing the creative possibilities of rap. Their debut album was both a commercial and critical hit, with *It's Like That* a trademark track, but the second album was not as well received. All doubts were removed by their third album, *Raising Hell*. Rick Rubin, who had co-founded the Def Jam label in 1984 with Russell Simmons, with LL Cool J serving as their breakout artist), served as co-producer (with Simmons) of *Raising Hell* with the intent to capture something "raw, musical, and ferocious." The album was nearly done when he came up with the idea of doing *Walk This Way* as a "kicker" to the project. Initially Run-DMC

---

393. #1 (7 weeks) in New Zealand, #2 in Holland, #7 in Italy, #8 in France.

394. *Q* magazine (2003) ranked it #8 among "Songs That Changed the World."

wanted to just sample the original record's beat and write a new original song around it, but Rubin sold them on the idea of a collaboration. Since Aerosmith was still in its "down" period, he had no problem persuading Tyler and Perry to re-create their classic in a new musical setting. Rubin saw the teaming as a way to open the white public's ears to rap, and it proved a winning bet, thanks in part to the video's saturation airplay on MTV.[395] It was the biggest smash yet enjoyed by hip-hop, the album sold three million copies, and Aerosmith was on its way to its lucrative second life. Run-DMC scored a handful of other hits, though nothing comparable to this breakthrough, but the trio had paved the way for many who would follow. Sasha Frere-Jones: "Run-DMC were rap's Moses, parting the pop waters simply, but profoundly, to reveal that hip hop was there."[396]

Sweet Child o' Mine (1988)—Guns N' Roses
Geffen 27963
Chart debut June 25, 1988 (#1 for 2 weeks); #6 in
    England;[397] from the album *Appetite for Destruc-
    tion* (chart debut Aug. 29, 1987, #1 for 5 weeks,
    sold 15 million copies) (*RS-#198, RIA-#210, BL-#3,
    DMDB-#45, ACC-#90, DM*)

It's a song about a love affair that later resulted in a 1990 marriage lasting barely three weeks between Guns N' Roses lead singer Axl Rose and Erin Everly (daughter of Don Everly), from one of the most famously dysfunctional groups in rock history. But *Sweet Child o' Mine*—boasting a remarkable opening guitar solo and Rose's passionate vocal—is a power ballad that soars above it all.

Guns N' Roses was formed in Los Angeles in 1985 by singer William "Axl Rose" Bailey, guitarist Saul "Slash" Hudson, guitarist Jeffrey "Izzy Stradlin" Isbell, bassist Michael "Duff" McKagan, and drummer Steven Adler. They recorded their first EP in 1986, earning them a contract with Geffen and their debut album in late 1987.[398] It started slowly, expanded through buzz from their live shows, climbed into the Top Ten in April 1988, and then exploded as MTV gave heavy airplay to the video for the single. "While Slash and Izzy Stradlin ferociously spit out dueling guitar riffs worthy of Aerosmith or the Stones, Axl Rose screeched out his tales of sex, drugs, and apathy in the big city; [McKagan and Adler] were a

limber rhythm section that kept the music loose and powerful," writes Stephen Thomas Erlewine. Guns N' Roses' music was "basic and gritty, with a solid hard, bluesy base; they were dark, sleazy, dirty and honest—everything that good hard rock and heavy metal should be."[399]

Slash's pyrotechnic opening guitar solo "establishes the record as an elegy—an ode to lost innocence, and a spur to the quest to recover that feeling," writes Dave Marsh. The song "has the enormous power of the simple promises extended from one kid to another: Confidences will be kept, feelings respected, hopes and dreams preserved in privacy."[400] Rose and the band would implode within a few years, but the tenderness expressed here showed the heart behind the destructiveness.

Follow the Leader (1988)—Eric B & Rakim
Uni 50003
Chart debut July 16, 1988 (#16 R&B)[401] (*VIL*)

The rapid-fire, verbally deft performance of Eric B & Rakim's often poetic lyrics, in Dave Marsh's opinion, "revolutionized the art of rapping." Dan Charnas: "Hip-hop fans were mesmerized by the intricate lyrics and low-key delivery" of Rakim, "because they were the antithesis of the Def Jam aesthetic [that ruled rap at the time], where beats boomed and mouths roared."[402] The singles *Eric B is President* and *I Know You Got Soul* established the duo's credentials, and their debut album *Paid In Full* proved that they had plenty more to offer. William "Rakim" Griffin (from Long Island, New York) served as the MC, with Eric Barrier (from Elmhurst, New York) the DJ/producer. After switching from the indie label 4th & Broadway to Uni, *Follow the Leader* was their leadoff major-label release, and it became their biggest hit (aside from their supporting role on Jody Watley's 1989 pop smash *Friends*). While (like *I Know You Got Soul*) it can be characterized as an extended boast to Rakim's supremacy as a rapper, the genuinely dazzling ingenuity and craftsmanship prove his point. To paraphrase Muhammad Ali, it's not bragging if you can back it up. After proclaiming that he can "go on for days and days / with rhyme displays that engrave deep as x-rays," he envisions a journey "at magnificent speeds around the universe," and offers socially conscious advice: "You're not a slave / 'cause we was put here to be much more than that." Sasha Frere-Jones remarks that Rakim was "the first MC to cross the bar line and let his rhymes scan in idiosyncratic, rhythmic clumps, just like Thelonious

395. Jake Brown, *Rick Rubin in the Studio*, p. 33–37. Also in 1986, Rubin produced the Beastie Boys' nine-million-selling album *Licensed to Ill*, the first rap disc to hit #1.

396. *The Vibe History of Hip Hop*, p. 65.

397. #1 in Brazil, #10 in France.

398. The album was produced with panache by Mike Clink, whose approach (writes band biographer Stephen Davis, *Watch You Bleed*, p. 138–39) was "to capture the ferocity of the band in full manic episode, not tame the music for commercial release."

399. *All Music Guide*, p. 401. The album excluded all of the band's ballads (like *November Rain*), making it, writes Davis, "the hardest hard rock album since Led Zeppelin's blistering *Physical Graffiti* in 1975."

400. Marsh, *The Heart of Rock & Soul*, p. 255–56.

401. Reached #5 on Hot Dance Music/maxi-singles sales chart, #11 for dance music/club play.

402. *The Big Payback*, p. 180.

Monk had done years before."[403] Matthew Horton praises the way in which the beats and James Brown samples are layered in "to emulate an orchestra of the apocalypse . . . evoking danger with every stab of brass, every rat-a-tat of machine-gun bass, every word of Rakim's relentless onslaught."[404] The act split after 1992's *Don't Sweat the Technique*. Rakim soared to #4 on the pop chart with his 1997 debut solo album, *The 18th Letter*. The duo was nominated for 2012 induction to the Rock & Roll Hall of Fame"; although they fell short, the Hall of Fame seems the inevitable destination for a team that profoundly influenced hip-hop acts from Public Enemy to Eminem.

Erghen Diado (Song of Schopsko) (1988)—Bulgarian State Radio & Television Female Vocal Choir

From the Nonesuch album *Le Mystère des Voix Bulgares* (The Mystery of Bulgarian Voices), released in 1987, chart debut Dec. 17, 1988 (*World-#101*)

One of the most exotic (to Western ears) albums to make the *Billboard* pop chart since Yma Sumac in the 1950s, *Le Mystère des Voix Bulgares* introduced the outside world to the extraordinary multi-layered vocals of Bulgarian female choirs. In liner notes for this album, Ingram Marshall notes some of the striking characteristics of this music: "Scales not based on major-minor tonality, melodies of limited range yet with expressive power, harmonies which incorporate 'dissonant' intervals as freely as consonant ones, and timbres, both vocal and instrumental, which seem more akin to Asian than European traditions." One reason for the latter is although modern Bulgaria is almost 100 percent Slavic, the original Bulgars came from southern Asia starting in the seventh century, and later the nation was dominated for 500 years by the Ottoman Turks. Bulgarian composer Philip Koutev organized a national ensemble for folk songs and dances (using his original compositions based on traditional Bulgarian melodies) that began decades of touring the world in 1952, including a 1964 U.S. tour. The album *Music of Bulgaria* was recorded for EMI around the late 1950s, and when the masters were licensed to Elektra several years later,[405] the album became a surprise success, greatly admired by U.S. musicians; David Crosby said it influenced the vocal harmonies of Crosby, Stills, & Nash.[406] Musicologist Marcel Cellier built on that foundation with female choirs starting in the early 1970s.

The Bulgarian State Radio & Television Female Vocal Choir (produced by Cellier and under the direction of Koutev and Krasimir Kyurkchiyski) is a tremendous representative of this long musical tradition.[407] Most of the album presents their intricate vocals without instrumental accompaniment, but *Erghen Diado* is a dramatic exception, featuring a powerful bass drum and clicking/clapping percussion underneath those heavenly voices (along with some unusual vocal effects), creating a thrilling contrast. Tom Moon praises the group's talent for creating "delicate shares of otherworldly yearning," a trait well evidenced in this performance.[408]

Hammer and a Nail (1990)—Indigo Girls (written by Emily Saliers)

From the Epic album *Nomads-Indians-Saints*, chart debut Oct. 13, 1990 (#43 peak)

A year after bursting upon the folk and pop scene with their major-label debut album featuring the breakthrough hit *Closer to Fine*, the Georgia-based acoustic duo of Emily Saliers and Amy Ray returned with a comparably powerful knockout of a song. *Hammer and a Nail* suggests that one way to make life emotionally fulfilling and not a purely intellectual exercise is to get down to some good-old physical labor. In the process, it also (in true Indigos fashion) declares the need for social responsibility, and the soaring hope that everyone has something to offer: "If I have a care in the world, I have a gift to bring." Mary Chapin Carpenter joins in the rip-roaring chorus.[409] *Hammer and a Nail* won the Grammy for best contemporary folk recording.

Ashokan Farewell (1990)—Jay Ungar & Fiddle Fever

Originally from the 1983 Fiddle Fever album *Waltz of the Wind* for Flying Fish Records

Popularized on 1990 Elektra Nonesuch soundtrack to *The Civil War* (series debuted Sept. 23, 1990; *Billboard* debut Dec. 22, 1990, reached #76)[410] (*Folk-#64, NPR-300*)

Perhaps never in the history of public television has one piece of music become so universally familiar as a direct result of its TV exposure there as Jay Ungar's

---

403. *New Rolling Stone Album Guide* (2004), p. 281.

404. *1001 Songs You Must Hear Before You Die*, p. 607.

405. Elektra reissued the album on its new Nonesuch label, which would also release *Le Mystère*.

406. Elektra founder Jac Holzman recalled in his memoir *Follow the Music*: "Its vocal layers, with their soaring harmonies and open-throated exuberance, turned many sets of ears towards the richness of world music, though that term was not yet in common use."

407. Amy Gibson (June–July 1992 *Dirty Linen*) remarked that the tonal brittleness of the group's sound, "produced by throwing the voice forward into the palate and nasal passages, with an almost jarring lack of vibrato, combines with harmonic fourths and fifths to create an Arabic sound, not unlike that heard in a Mosque. The tonal effect is more reminiscent of the Eastern flavors and colors of Greece" than modern urban Bulgaria.

408. Moon, *1,000 Recordings to Hear Before You Die*, p. 130–31.

409. Produced by Scott Litt; the ensemble includes Kenny Aronoff on drums and Benmont Tench of Tom Petty's Heartbreakers on "fake accordion".

410. The *Civil War* soundtrack spent ten weeks at #1 on *Billboard*'s Classical Crossover chart in early 1991. It sold over 200,000 copies by the end of January 1991; also, *Ashokan Farewell*, issued as a single, received airplay on some country stations (February 4, 1991, *Time*, p. 62).

Ashokan Farewell. Bronx-born fiddler/composer Jay Ungar came to love traditional American music at a young age, got his start performing in Greenwich Village coffeehouses, and traveled through North Carolina and Tennessee to link up with like-minded musicians to play old-time acoustic tunes. In the late 1970s at a rural New York club he met Washington state–born Molly Mason, a bass player with the same musical tastes.[411] When he formed the band Fiddle Fever with fellow violinists Evan Stover and Matt Glaser plus guitarist Russ Barenberg, she came aboard, and (later as husband and wife) they've performed together ever since. During this period Ungar began the Ashokan Fiddle & Dance Camps for adults and families, designed to carry on traditions of American music and dance.

Ungar wrote *Ashokan Farewell* in 1982 (Molly suggested the name), and Fiddle Fever recorded it a year later as part of the band's second album. As the composer explains, the song (and his camps) were named after a village that is now largely covered by water, the Ashokan Reservoir, located in the Catskill Mountains near Woodstock, New York, which provides drinking water for New York City a hundred miles to the south. Ashokan first appeared as a place name in seventeenth century Dutch records, and may have been a corruption of a local Lenape Indian word meaning "a good place to fish." He was feeling "a great sense of loss and longing" after his fiddle & dance camps had finished the season, and he had to return from the pristine woodland camp to routine modern urban life. "By the time the tune took form, I was in tears. I kept it to myself for months, unable to fully understand the emotions that welled up whenever I played it," he has written. "I had no idea that this simple tune could affect others in the same way." *Ashokan Farewell* "was written in the style of a Scottish lament. I sometimes introduce it as, "a Scottish lament written by a Jewish guy from the Bronx."[412]

In 1984, Glaser and Barenberg were working with young filmmaker Ken Burns on his documentary *The Brooklyn Bridge*, and gave him a copy of *Waltz of the Wind*. He fell in love with the song, used it on his next documentary about former Louisiana governor Huey Long, *Huey*, and Jay and Molly became regular participants in his projects. So when Burns launched his PBS masterpiece *The Civil War* in 1990, he knew from the outset that *Ashokan Farewell* would serve as its musical touchstone. The original waltz-tempo Fiddle Fever recording—introduced by Ungar's solo fiddle, with Barenberg's elegant guitar solo, string parts by Evan Stover, and Molly's upright bass—is heard at the beginning of the PBS series, and this and other versions are heard twenty-five times for a total of more than fifty-nine minutes across the course of the eleven-hour series. The soundtrack renditions include three fiddles (the others being Matt Glaser and Evan Stover) and the two guitars. Joe F. Compton called the theme a "compelling leitmotif for the human sacrifices intrinsic to this clash of cultures . . . [they] perform the elegy with considerable grace."[413] Jay, Molly, the other members of Fiddle Fever, and pianist Jacqueline Schwab also played much of the nineteenth century music used in *The Civil War*. The soundtrack won a Grammy, and *Ashokan Farewell* earned an Emmy nomination.

Since signing with Angel Records in 1991, Ungar and Moore have recorded a wide range of traditional music (including an album of Stephen Foster songs and a collection of old-time fiddle music from both American and international traditions), and composed original works including *The Lovers' Waltz* and a twenty-minute orchestral piece, *The Harvest Home Suite*. All of this is in addition to continuing the fiddle & dance camps, held at the lakefront Ashokan Field Campus of the State University of New York at New Paltz.

Ashokan Farewell has been recorded by scores of other artists, and one can hardly imagine a concert of traditional-style acoustic music with a featured fiddler that does not include it.

Walking in Memphis (1991)—Marc Cohn
Atlantic 87747

Chart debut March 30, 1991 (reached #13, 23 total weeks); from the album *Marc Cohn* (reached #38, 63 total weeks)

Blessed with a fine narrative songwriting style and a gritty, arresting baritone, Marc Cohn made a lasting impression with his breakthrough hit *Walking in Memphis*. Born July 5, 1959, in Cleveland, he developed his talents as singer, writer, and pianist by his college years, moved to New York City, and fronted a fourteen-piece swing band that performed at Caroline Kennedy's wedding. Cohn landed an Atlantic recording contract with the demo tape that provided the basis for his debut album. *Walking in Memphis*, the smash that helped earn him the Grammy as best new artist, is a compelling story song steeped in a reverence for the musical traditions of the subject city, from W. C. Handy to Elvis Presley, and with a gospel choir at the conclusion. Making the tribute to the town's blues and gospel roots all the more convincing is his fervent performance that embodies roots-music qualities. Although pop radio didn't embrace Cohn's subse-

---

411. During the mid-1970s Ungar had occasional "teach-in" articles in *Sing Out!* on playing traditional fiddle.

412. Ungar's comments from the couple's website www.jayandmolly .com.

413. April–May 1991 *Dirty Linen*, p. 74.

quent releases, his 1993 and 1998 albums earned strong reviews, and after surviving being shot in the head in an attempted carjacking in 2005, the artist has remained a potent live attraction, with admirers that include Bonnie Raitt and David Crosby. "Not since Randy Newman has there been a songwriter as inherently gifted as Marc Cohn, and not since Joe Cocker a more soulful and sincere, physically powerful singer," declared songwriting legend Jimmy Webb.

Something to Talk About (1991)—Bonnie Raitt (written by Shirley Eikhard)
Capitol 44724
Chart debut July 20, 1991 (#5 peak); from the album *Luck of the Draw* (#2 peak, 120 weeks) (*RHF, RIA, Folk-#88, Blues-#139*)

Just like the vintage blueswomen she admires, Bonnie Raitt has always made an undercurrent of sly sexuality a key part of her repertoire, conveyed as much by her wicked slide guitar as her vocals—B.B. King has called Raitt his favorite slide guitarist—and that quality comes across delightfully in *Something to Talk About*. She's definitely looking for love, but is also mindful of the humor beneath the desire. It's an easy-rolling performance (with elements of Memphis soul and Delta blues) demonstrating why she was inducted into the Blues Hall of Fame in 2010. Riding on the momentum from her Grammy-sweeping album *Nick of Time*, *Luck of the Draw* became her biggest seller (its seven million copies topping its predecessor's five million), and featured Bonnie's highest-charting single. The Rock & Roll Hall of Fame song about friendship blossoming into romance later provided the title of a Julia Roberts movie.

(Produced by Don Was and Bonnie Raitt; with James Hutchinson on bass, Stephen Bruton on acoustic guitar, Scott Thurston on keyboard, Ricky Fataar & Curt Bisquera on drums, Debra Dobkin on percussion, and backing vocalists Sweet Pea Atkinson, Harry Bowens, & David Lasley)

Why We Sing (1994)—Kirk Franklin & the Family
Album cut, chart debut Dec. 24, 1994 (#28 R&B, 25 weeks)
From the GospoCentric album *Kirk Franklin and the Family*; chart debut March 12, 1994 (reached #58 on pop chart, 36 weeks);[414] #1 for 37 weeks on gospel chart (*GOSP-#49*)

The 1993 release *Kirk Franklin and the Family* became the biggest-selling gospel album since Aretha Franklin's *Amazing Grace* twenty-one years earlier. Born on January 26, 1970, in Fort Worth, Texas, Franklin was just twenty-two when the album was recorded on July 25, 1992 live at Grace Temple Church in his home town. After debuting in July 1993 on the *Billboard* gospel chart and reaching #1 six months later (with over 120 total charted weeks), it became the first black gospel recording to cross over to the Contemporary Christian chart, where it would spend at least 68 weeks into late 1995. Called "the biggest phenomenon since *Oh Happy Day*," the LP became the first gospel album to be certified platinum as a million-seller. *Why We Sing*, its breakthrough hit, was winner of two Black Gospel Music Clef Stellar Awards, and two Dove Awards from the predominantly white Gospel Music Association. Its remarkable success helped make Vicki Mack Lataillade's GospoCentric label (founded only a few months before the Franklin album's release) one of the top five-selling gospel labels.[415]

Why We Sing uses the text of the 1905 gospel standard *His Eye Is on the Sparrow*, later popularized by Mahalia Jackson and Ethel Waters. As described by Mellonee Burnim, Franklin then "completely transformed the original composition by creating a new melody; establishing a different meter, rhythmic treatment, and form; and . . . changing the harmony."[416] He leads a call and response with the seventeen-member choir: "I sing because I'm happy / I sing because I'm free / His eye is on the sparrow / That's the reason why I sing . . ." The resulting song "skillfully contextualizes and affirms African American musical and cultural values . . . *Why We Sing* has also become a standard in the African American church, crossing demographic boundaries of denomination, geography, and class." It was among the classics included in the 2001 *African American Heritage Hymnal*. Franklin's spectacular career in subsequent years included crossing over more aggressively for a three-million-selling 1997 album leading the funk-rap-gospel collective God's Property that included the hit single *Stomp*, and the two-million-selling *Nu Nation Project* in 1998.[417]

You Oughta Know (1995)—Alanis Morissette (music by Alanis Morissette & Glen Ballard, lyrics by Alanis Morissette)
Hot 100 chart debut June 17, 1995 (reached #13 in radio airplay, 32 weeks); #22 in England;[418]
From the Maverick album *Jagged Little Pill* (#1 for 12 weeks) (*VIL-#95, DM, 1001, DMDB*)

---

414. Reached #6 on R&B album chart, 108 weeks.

415. Gospel music held between 2.5 percent and 4 percent of annual U.S. record sales during the late 1980s and early 1990s, but climbed to a peak of 6.3 percent by 1998, and Franklin was the genre's #1 star during this period (April 3, 1999, *Billboard*).
416. *African American Music: An Introduction*, p. 419–20.
417. In 2011, Franklin's *Hello Fear* became his tenth consecutive album to reach #1 on the *Billboard* gospel charts dating back to his 1993 chart debut.
418. Reached #6 in Japan.

The leadoff hit from one of the biggest-selling albums of all time, *You Oughta Know* is, remarked one critic, "the sound of a formerly pliant girl giving way to her inner banshee as she ambushes her ex at dinner." Fierce and angry, it's also a razor-sharp piece of rock writing and singing; the breakthrough by Alanis Morissette enabled a new wave of young female singer-songwriters to gain entry into the pop marketplace.

The Ottawa, Canada, native (born on June 1, 1974) made a far less auspicious debut in 1991 with the teen pop-dance album *Alanis*, which sold 100,000 copies in Canada but was ignored elsewhere; its followup a year later made few converts. But moving to Los Angeles and collaborating with savvy songwriter-producer Glen Ballard (a former member of Quincy Jones' studio team who had worked on albums by Michael Jackson, Barbra Streisand, and Wilson Phillips),[419] opened her up creatively with strongly autobiographical lyrics and an edgy, jittery new rock sound. Madonna's new label Maverick Recordings signed her after hearing the duo's demo, and they cut the album at Westlake Studios in Hollywood. The stellar band includes Flea and Dave Navarro of the Red Hot Chili Peppers, and keyboardist Benmont Tench of Tom Petty's Heartbreakers. No one could have anticipated the commercial tsunami unleashed by *Jagged Little Pill*; as *You Oughta Know* was followed by a stream of other hits, the album sold more than 16 million copies in the U.S., placing it among the fifteen biggest-selling albums ever. *You Oughta Know* won Grammies for best rock song and best female rock vocal (the *Village Voice* critics' poll also voted it the #2 single of the year, behind only *Gangsta's Paradise* by Coolio), and *Jagged* earned top honors as Album of the Year.

Don't Speak (1996)—No Doubt (written by Gwen Stefani & Eric Stefani)

Album cut, debut on Hot 100 Airplay chart Oct. 19, 1996 (#1 for 16 weeks);[420]

From the Trauma/Interscope album *Tragic Kingdom* (chart debut Jan. 20, 1996, 9 weeks at #1) (*BILLB-#3, DMDB*)

Formed as a ska/new wave band in Anaheim, California, in 1987, No Doubt followed a long journey to multi-platinum success, as its 1992 debut album flopped and a self-produced followup won good notices but had little distribution. But it all came together on *Tragic Kingdom*, as the combination of Gwen Stefani's winsomely appealing vocals and an energetic collection of songs enabled it to sell more than 10 million copies. Gwen's kittenish *Just a Girl* was the album's first hit; it was the ballad *Don't Speak* that made it one of the decade's foremost smashes. She wrote the song with her brother Eric before he quit the group in 1994, inspired in part by her recent breakup with her boyfriend of eight years, No Doubt bassist Tony Kanal. *Rolling Stone*, ranking this among the 100 greatest pop songs: "Stefani moaned the song's lovelorn vocal like an injured diva, recounting the end of the two most important relationships in her life."[421]Stefani (born October 3, 1969, in Fullerton, California) went on to great solo success in her own right starting in 2004 with hits including the chart-topping *Hollaback Girl*, until No Doubt reunited in 2011.

Torn (1998)—Natalie Imbruglia

Track from the RCA album *Left of the Middle*; chart debut Feb. 14, 1998 (11 weeks at #1 on *Billboard* radio airplay chart); #1 (5 weeks) in Spain, #2 (3 weeks) on Eurochart, #2 in England & Australia, #4 in Germany[422] (*BILLB-#22, DMDB, VIL*)[423]

The most pleasantly inescapable song on pop radio in 1998, *Torn* was originally recorded by an alt-rock group called Ednaswap, whose version was probably heard by a few dozen people, and made into a pop juggernaut by Natalie Imbruglia. Born on February 4, 1975, in Sydney, Australia, the dazzlingly beautiful brunette began as an actress, achieving a measure of fame on the popular Aussie soap *Neighbours*, then moved to London and had two years of scraping by. Natalie began writing songs, which enabled her to land a recording contract, and hit the jackpot with her debut album thanks to this song (virtually the only one on the album she didn't have a hand in writing). Voted the #10 best song of 1998 in the *Village Voice* critics' poll, it's the tale of a romantic breakup, from the disappointed but clear-eyed perspective of a woman who's come to realize that the magic she thought was there, isn't: "Illusion never changed into something real." Her voice of "guileless sweetness" (as phrased by *Rolling Stone*) is perfect for the tale, and the chorus—"I'm all out of faith"—rolls over the listener like a mighty wave.

419. Ballard recorded most of the album on Alesis ADAT modular digital multitrack (MDM) recorders, and after Morissette's huge success, the format's combination of affordability and high quality helped make MDM one of the industry's hot technologies of the late 1990s. (*Encyclopedia of Record Producers*, p. 30.)

420. *Don't Speak* was not issued as a single, and under *Billboard*'s rules at the time doesn't qualify for the Hot 100 "record book." However, its sixteen weeks at #1 on the radio airplay chart was topped by only one other song (the similarly airplay-only *Iris* by the Goo Goo Dolls in 1998, with eighteen weeks), and its fifty-two weeks in the Top 40 tied for the highest total ever until Adele exceeded it in 2011 with *Rolling in the Deep* (fifty-four weeks).

421. December 7, 2000 *Rolling Stone*, p. 104.

422. #1 (5 weeks each) in Belgium, Denmark, and Sweden; #3 in Austria, Italy, Netherlands, and Switzerland; #4 in France.

423. Its thirty-two weeks in the Top Ten set a new record for #1 hits of the rock era (*Joel Whitburn Presents the Billboard Hot 100 Annual*, p. 858), although this doesn't count in the "official" Hot 100 records since the track was not issued as a single.

Scarecrow (1999)—Melissa Etheridge

From the Island album *Breakdown* (chart debut Oct. 23, 1999, #12 peak)

The horrific gay-bashing 1998 murder of twenty-one-year-old Matthew Shepard in Laramie, Wyoming, served as the basis for this strongly rocking cry of outrage by Melissa Etheridge. As a gay activist who had long been politically active, and who was about to have a son with her partner, she was not only infuriated by the murder but fearful. Pouring everything into the song "possessed me," she told *Billboard*. "It became a song without me trying . . . Recording it was one of the more emotional experiences of my career."[424] She combined her rage at ignorance and hatred with her life-affirming instincts of tolerance and love, and the result was an unforgettably powerful song.[425] It was a focal point of the Human Rights Campaign's 2000 "Equality Rocks" concert in Washington, D.C. In 2001–2002, the Rock & Roll Library held a "Scarecrow Song Lesson Contest" in which teachers around the country built lesson plans around the song, concluding with a visit by Etheridge to the school of the winning teacher. When Melissa performs the song in concert, usually as the finale, she and the audience repeat the word "love" over and over—the one way, she explains, to stop the cycle of intolerance.

Somebody Hurt You (2004)—A Girl Called Eddy
(written by Erin Moran)

From the Anti Records album *A Girl Called Eddy*, released on Aug. 10, 2004

The girl's name is actually Erin Moran, a Neptune, New Jersey-born, singer-songwriter who moved to Sheffield, England; she chose the pseudonym to avoid confusion with the *Happy Days* actress. Following a 2001 EP, *Tears All Over Town*,[426] her 2004 debut full-length album struck a chord with listeners as (in Robert Borrow's words) "an album of elegance and depth . . . music made by grown-ups for grown-ups."[427] Former Pulp guitarist and solo artist Richard Hawley co-produced the album and assembled an acoustic band with occasional jazz-flavored touches. *Somebody Hurt You* is a gorgeous ballad expressing deep empathy for a fellow shattered soul, promising that she would never do to him what his previous lover had done. "You're lonely like only the broken can know / Aching for love but afraid to show . . . Boy, someone might hurt you / But it would never be me . . ." The delicate beauty of the melody and arrangement show

the artist's self-described admiration for Burt Bacharach. Her performance, like the lyric, is emotionally direct with a hushed, intimate quality, drawing us in to the feelings behind the words. Emphasizing her blue-eyed soul connection to Dusty Springfield, Ben Ratliff called her "Dusty's latest daughter."[428] David Browne praised the album's "elegant pop craftsmanship,"[429] and the *Wall Street Journal* called it one of the ten best of 2004.

Life Ain't Always Beautiful (2006)—Gary Allan (written by Cyndi Goodman & Tommy Lee James)

Chart debut Jan. 21, 2006 (#4 on C&W chart, #62 pop)

From the MCA album *Tough All Over* (chart debut Oct. 29, 2005, #3 on pop chart)[430]

During the several years that followed his 1999 masterpiece *Smoke Rings in the Dark*, California honky-tonker Gary Allan continued to build on his country music stardom with strong-selling, well-regarded albums. Then came his 2005 CD *Tough All Over*, the most exceptional collection of songs in his career to date. It came against the background of personal tragedy: the suicide of Allan's wife in October 2004. In addition to co-writing four selections on the album (most notably *I Just Got Back from Hell*), the singer selected several powerful songs with protagonists who came through devastating experiences and grappled with how to move on with their lives. None was more compelling than the deeply somber, but movingly life-affirming, *Life Ain't Always Beautiful*. Allan's gritty baritone is vividly expressive of what he'd been through, and his determination to rise above it. The lyric's evocation of Nietzsche is fitting: "The struggles make you stronger, and the changes make you wise." "Sometimes chilling, always heartbreaking songs" such as this, remarked Brian Mansfield, "show scars of grief just as plain as the tattoos on Allan's arms. Few country singers travel so far down that lost highway Hank Williams once sang about; fewer still make it far enough back to sing, 'Life ain't always beautiful, but it's a beautiful ride.'"[431]

Hips Don't Lie (2006)—Shakira featuring Wyclef Jean

Epic 84467

Chart debut April 1, 2006 (2 weeks at #1); 8 weeks at #1 on Hot Latin Songs;[432] #1 (15 weeks) in Europe, #1 (9 weeks) in Australia, #1 (5 weeks) in England, #1 (3 weeks) in Germany[433] (*2000s-#26*)

424. September 4, 1999 *Billboard*.

425. Richard Harrington remarked (April 28, 2000, *Washington Post*) that the "disquieting" song's emotionally cathartic impact is similar to that of Peter Gabriel's tribute to a murdered South African activist, *Biko*.

426. Another track she released on a multi-artist 2001 CD, *Soundtrack of Your Life*, received TV exposure on *Dawson's Creek*.

427. Borrow, review on www.amazon.com.

428. August 15, 2004, *New York Times*.

429. August 13, 2004, *Entertainment Weekly*.

430. *Tough All Over* was Allan's first #1 country album, but his fourth to log seventy or more weeks on that chart.

431. October 11, 2005, *USA Today*. Roger Holland (*PopMatters*) called it a "slow and heartfelt statement of heartbreak and deliverance."

432. #1 (8 weeks) on Pop 100 Airplay.

433. #1 (9 weeks) in Ireland and Spain; #1 in Belgium, Holland, New Zealand, Sweden, Switzerland; #2 in Austria, Norway.

One of the biggest international hits of the past twenty years, *Hips Don't Lie* is an irresistible slice of contemporary dance-pop by one of the established queens of Latin rock. Shakira Isabel Mebarek Ripoll was born February 2, 1977, in Barranquilla, Colombia, got her first record contract at age thirteen, and soon became Colombia's—and Latin America's—#1 pop star. She burst onto the Western scene in 1998 with the album *Donde Estan Ladrones?* (Where Are the Thieves?), which was not only a #1 hit on the *Billboard* Latin charts but also a gold album. Her vibrant contralto, songwriting chops, openly emotional style, sensual beauty, and charisma as a live performer began grabbing fans outside the Latin pop world. Shakira's first English-language album,[434] *Laundry Service*, became a three-million-selling smash in late 2001 with the Top Ten singles *Whenever, Wherever* and *Underneath Your Clothes*. Teaming up with Haitian-born singer/rapper Wyclef Jean (who had moved from great 1990s success with the Fugees to solo hits including *Gone Till November*) brought her biggest success of all. Known for her hip-gyrating dance moves on stage (she started belly dancing as a child), the title phrase came from one of her regular expressions: "My hips don't lie." Wyclef's spoken cries of "Shakira, Shakira!" set off her vocal undulations to a killer dance track.

The Long Way Round (2006)—Badly Drawn Boy
(written by Damon Gough)

From the EMI/Astralwerks album *Born in the U.K.* (released on Oct. 16, 2006)

A man of many talents, singer/songwriter/guitarist/pianist Damon Gough was born on October 2, 1969, in Bolton, Lancashire, England, and first came to wide attention for writing and performing the soundtrack music for the 2002 Hugh Grant film *About a Boy* under his alias, Badly Drawn Boy. His fifth studio album, *Born in the U.K.,* featured perhaps his finest song to date, the shimmering pop ballad *The Long Way Round*. It's a stunning piano-driven piece in which the protagonist emerges from the disappointment of a failed relationship ("I assumed you would be my strength / Oh, how wrong I was") to realize that he is stronger for the experience and the lessons learned. Like Joni Mitchell in *The Circle Game*, he comes to see life as a carousel-like ride, and taking the long way around—"See the sights, hear the sounds"—is better than the direct route that may be quicker and more painless, but also with fewer potential rewards. Gough has declared his great affection for the work of Burt Bacharach, and one can hear it in this song, with its rich melody and elegant horn-punctuated arrangement. *The Long Way Round* is a very touching,

life-affirming pop gem about the eternal mystery of the human journey, offering hope in a time of sadness: "Where you'll go, nobody knows." If you venture out, he concludes, "take the long way round / You'll be lost, then found / It's a long way home, but you're not alone."

Falling Slowly (2007)—Glen Hansard & Marketa Irglova

From the Canvasback/Sony Music soundtrack *Once* (chart debut June 16, 2007, reached #7, 52 total weeks);[435]

Falling Slowly Hot 100 debut March 15, 2008 (reached #61; #20 peak on Hot Digital Songs), released on Overcoat Recordings[436][437]

In the annals of Academy Award winners for best song, *Falling Slowly* occupies a niche virtually all its own. Most Best Song winners are either big pop hits from major commercial releases, or themes from one of that year's biggest or most prestigious films. *Falling Slowly* is an intimate acoustic ballad from a scruffy little Irish independent film. Its victory was a symbolic triumph for exactly the kinds of outsiders and underdogs that the picture itself celebrated.

Born April 21, 1970, in Ballymun, Dublin, Ireland, Glen Hansard quit school at thirteen to begin busking on Dublin streets. He formed the folk-rock band The Frame in 1990, which released its first album a year later, then appeared in the 1991 Alan Parker film *The Commitments*, which became a surprise international hit, with its soundtrack a Top Ten, two-million-selling smash. The next decade was devoted to writing songs and singing lead for the Frames. Then John Carney, former bassist for that band, wrote the screenplay for a film built around a character not unlike Hansard, and asked his friend to write the songs and contribute anecdotes about busking in Dublin. As the project was developed in cooperation with the Irish Film Board, Hansard finally emerged as the film's star (directed by Carney), with Czech-born musician Marketa Irglova as female lead. It was shot in Dublin over seventeen days on a budget of just $160,000. The tale of an Irish musician scuffling to make ends meet while pursuing dreams of a record contract, and finding possible love with a woman he encounters while singing on the street, struck a deep chord with moviegoers, and following its March 2007 release, it earned over $20 million in the U.S.

Falling Slowly was written by the two performers, while bearing the octave-leaping melodic quality already associated with Hansard's songs. In the film we hear it

---

434. She taught herself English by listening to Leonard Cohen and Bob Dylan songs (November 12, 2009, *Rolling Stone*).

435. During its initial 2007 chart run, *Once* reached #60. After the Oscar nomination, the soundtrack jumped back onto the chart in January 2008, and soared into the Top Ten.

436. Reached #56 on Pop 100.

437. #2 in Ireland.

first soon after the characters meet; they go into a Dublin music shop, he teaches her the ballad on guitar, and she joins him on piano. It's a song of aching heartbreak based on the character's split with his ex-girlfriend, and the sense of yearning in the soaring melody and fervent lyrics is palpable. Near the conclusion of the film, as they're able to get a bank loan to finance a demo recording session, we hear the fully developed version of the song. As the film was shot and awaited release, versions of the tune were released on the Frames' album *The Cost*, and by Hansard & Iglova as the Swell Season (both in 2006), but 99 percent of the world heard it first in *Once*. They were a real-life romantic couple for a time, but even when the romance ended, they continued performing together as the Swell Season. Four-and-a-half years after the movie, *Once* came to Broadway (with the film's original songs), and in June 2012 swept the Tony Awards with eight trophies, including Best Musical.

F*** You (Forget You) (2010)—Cee-Lo Green

Elektra/RRP track, chart debut Sept. 11, 2010 (reached #2); #1 (2 weeks) in England, #5 in Australia;[438]

From the album *The Lady Killer* (*VIL-#18, 2000s-#61*)

Just as he had done as half of Gnarls Barkley with the instant-classic *Crazy* four years earlier, Cee-Lo Green (born Thomas Burton in Atlanta on May 30, 1975) crossed genre boundaries with one of the most talked-about hits of recent years, the song ultimately known as *Forget You*. A symbol of digital times, it burst on the pop-cultural scene on YouTube as a viral video smash that generated over three million views barely over a week after first being uploaded on August 20, 2010. The profanity was really secondary to the song's Motown-style, retro-soul glory, the sheer exuberance with which Green (with the help of hot-selling singer Bruno Mars, who also co-wrote and co-produced)[439] hurls himself into telling off an ex-girlfriend. For all the glee he conveys in telling her how he no longer needs her, he quickly reveals that he still desperately wants her back, and it's the combination of his surface bravado with his whimpering neediness that makes the song hit home. Once the edited *Forget You* hit the airwaves, there was no stopping it, as it remained on the chart for nearly a year, and was voted the #1 song of the year in the *Village Voice* critics' poll. As Jody Rosen wrote in reviewing the album, Cee-Lo is "a showman with a penchant for scrambling a variety

of sounds—rock, soul, hip-hop . . . into something deliciously strange."[440]

Firework (2010)—Katy Perry

Capitol track, chart debut Nov. 6, 2010 (4 weeks at #1); #1 (1 week) in Canada, #3 in Australia & Germany, #4 in U.K.;[441]

From the album *Teenage Dream* (debut Sept. 11, 2011, 1 week at #1)

Lady Gaga may be more outrageous, but Katy Perry is the #1 poster girl for contemporary dance-pop, for good or ill. Her records can be overflowing with giddy, girlish joy, or annoying with flashy gimmicks and vapid superficiality. Ultimately one must simply take Katy on her own terms: "I want to make music that's fun and has feeling and emotion to it."[442] A perfectly noble goal when it comes to pop music, and she has certainly achieved it, and more. Born Katheryn Elizabeth Hudson on October 25, 1984, in Santa Barbara, California, she was raised by traveling evangelical ministers, went to Nashville at age fourteen where she got a record contract as a Christian artist but didn't get much farther, then moved to Los Angeles where two more record contracts (including a brief 2004 tenure on Columbia), and two more failures, followed. By that time she was a self-proclaimed "wild one," breaking away from her sheltered upbringing with a vengeance. Finally she was signed to Capitol Records (adopting her stage name then), and the fourth try proved the charm. *I Kissed a Girl* in 2008 was her breakthrough (#1 for 7 weeks), and from that point on there was no stopping her. One smash hit followed another without a pause, and her combination of mild exhibitionism (having whipped cream spurting from the tassels of her barely covered breasts) with a sunny, innocent smile enabled her to seem like a good girl even when she was being rather naughty.

In 2011 she matched a feat only attained by Michael Jackson by notching her fifth #1 song from a single album. Even more impressively, she became the first artist since Elvis Presley to remain continuously in the Top Ten of the *Billboard* Hot 100 with at least one tune for a full calendar year, then going beyond it.[443] *Firework* is an ideal representation of her repertoire: utterly simple as a bouncing, danceable celebration of new love, belted out

---

438. #1 on Euro Digital chart.

439. Born Peter Gene Hernandez in Honolulu October 8, 1985, Bruno Mars scored his first hit as vocalist and co-writer of the B.O.B. hit *Nothin' on You* (2009), and in late 2010 began his own string of smashes with *Just the Way You Are*.

440. November 10, 2010 *Rolling Stone*.

441. #1 in New Zealand, #2 in Norway, #3 in Austria, Ireland and Sweden; #4 France, #5 Italy, #7 Mexico.

442. July 7–21, 2011 *Rolling Stone*, p. 72.

443. From June 5, 2010, through September 17, 2011, sixty-nine consecutive weeks. Elvis ran off fifty-two straight weeks in the Top Ten (April 7, 1956, through March 30, 1957), was out of the Top Ten one week, then ran off another streak (April 13 through September 30, 1957), giving him seventy-eight of seventy-nine weeks in the Top Ten.

in her soaring contralto, amidst the Auto-Tune–assisted vocal hiccupping. In addition to topping the charts, it won Video of the Year at the MTV Video Music Awards.

This Is Why We Fight (2011)—The Decemberists
From the Capitol album *The King Is Dead* (chart debut Feb. 5, 2011, 1 week at #1)
Song debuted on Rock Songs chart Feb. 26, 2011 (#41 peak); reached #10 on Triple A chart, #21 on Alternative chart

The early 2000s may have been a difficult period for mainstream rock, given the chart and radio dominance of dance-pop and hip-hop, but the rise of the Decemberists offers cause for hope that rock remains very much alive. The Portland, Oregon–based, group was formed in 2000 by lead singer/songwriter/guitarist Colin Meloy, bassist Nate Query, and keyboardist/multi-instrumentalist Jenny Conlee, soon joined by guitarist Chris Funk, and in 2001 released its five-song debut EP.[444] Three albums on the Kill Rock Stars label from 2003–2005 earned the Decemberists a growing cult following; its inspirations and musical ambitions were symbolized by the 18 1/2-minute track *The Tain*, based on an Irish mythological epic. This set the stage for the group to move into major-label territory with its 2006 debut album on Capitol, *The Crane Wife*, which would be voted NPR listeners' favorite release of the year (appropriately for this proudly "nerd-rock" band). *Hazards of Love* (2009), which was originally planned as a stage musical (with all the songs built around an original mythological tale), built on this success, reaching #14 in *Billboard*.[445]

The King Is Dead carried the Decemberists to a new creative and commercial peak. R.E.M. had long been one of the group's musical role models, and with the legendary Georgia band's guitarist Peter Buck appearing on three tracks, the album was suffused with R.E.M.'s melodic and guitar-driven folk/rock sound, plus the sense of purpose and social commitment shared by both. Among its many standout tracks, *This Is Why We Fight* perhaps stands tallest. It's an intense, crisp, hard-driving rocker, its narrative set against the background of war, declaring a fierce determination to unite and sacrifice all ("with our arms unbound") for a worthy cause, building to a stirring conclusion. Its tale was underlined by an April 2011 music video depicting teenagers living in a post-apocalyptic society and ready to battle the king and his forces. *Rolling Stone* reviewer Will Hermes: "What's remarkable is how much richness and beauty the group has folded into the 40-minute album."[446] Meloy's debut novel was published in late 2011, and his theatrical aspirations seem destined to wind up with a Broadway rock musical that, based on what has come before, will likely be worth the wait.

Stronger (What Doesn't Kill You) (2012)—Kelly Clarkson (written by Jorgen Elofsson, Ali Tamposi, David Gamson & Greg Kurstin)
19/RCA track; chart debut Jan. 7, 2012 (3 weeks at #1); #3 in Canada, #8 in England, #9 in Europe[447]
From the album *Stronger* (chart debut Nov. 12, 2011, reached #3)

The impact of *American Idol* on the pop music scene has included many negatives, including its encouragement of a lot of over-singing by would-be vocalists who substitute shrill, mindless melisma in place of honest emotion and originality. But amidst the mediocrity, it has brought forward a few first-rate talents, such as country superstar Carrie Underwood, Oscar winner Jennifer Hudson, and the show's first and biggest discovery, Kelly Clarkson. Born April 24, 1982, in Fort Worth, Texas, Kelly got *Idol* off to a roaring start as the winner in 2002 of its inaugural season. Her initial chart-topping hit *A Moment Like This* was unmemorable, but her 2003 debut album *Thankful* showed promise, and better still the following year was *Breakaway*, which sold 12 million copies worldwide, featuring the inspirational title song. By this time she had proven comfortable with a range of material from big ballads to rock, R&B, and catchy dance-pop (co-writing a number of songs by her third album), and soon was also occasionally branching out into country music. *Stronger*, the title song of her fifth album, her tenth Top Ten hit and third #1, showcases Clarkson's virtues as an artist: that mighty, tear-down-the-walls soprano voice, of course, but also a feisty spirit of empowerment and a message of resilience in the face of setbacks,[448] all set to a pounding, dance-floor-ready beat. The track sold over 3.6 million digital copies. Melissa Maerz called it "a throbbing glitter-disco tribute to believing that it really does get better."[449]

---

444. The group's name derives from the 1825 Decembrist revolt in Imperial Russia.
445. By this time John Moen was on board as the group's drummer.

446. David Fricke called the collection "the most immediately charming album the Decemberists have ever made" (March 31, 2011, *Rolling Stone*, p. 34–35).
447. #1 in Belgium, Denmark, and Poland; #4 in Ireland.
448. The title was inspired by Friedrich Nietzsche's famous aphorism: "That which doesn't kill us makes us stronger."
449. October 28, 2011, *Entertainment Weekly*.

Bibliography

GENERAL U.S./WORLD HISTORY

The Blue and the Gray: The Story of the Civil War As Told by Its Participants, Volumes 1 and 2, edited by Henry Steele Commager (The Fairfax Press, 1982 edition).

Chronicle of the 20th Century, edited by Clifton Daniel (Chronicle Publications, 1987).

The Culture of Time and Space: 1880–1918, by Stephen Kern (Harvard University Press, 1983).

Dancing in the Dark: A Cultural History of the Great Depression, by Morris Dickstein (W. W. Norton & Co., 2009).

The Fifties, by David Halberstam (Fawcett Columbine, 1993).

Freedom's Unfinished Revolution: An Inquiry into the Civil War and Reconstruction, by William Friedheim with Ronald Jackson (The New Press, 1996).

The Glory and the Dream: A Narrative History of America, 1932–1972, by William Manchester (Bantam Books, 1975).

A History of American Life, edited by Mark C. Carnes (Scribner, 1996).

Home Fronts: A Wartime America Reader, edited by Michael S. Foley and Brendan P. O'Malley (New Press, 2008).

Lincoln and the Music of the Civil War, by Kenneth A. Bernard (The Caxton Printers, Ltd., 1966).

A New Literary History of America, edited by Greil Marcus and Werner Sollors (Belknap Press of Harvard University Press, 2009).

Only Yesterday: An Informal History of the 1920s, by Frederick Lewis Allen (Perennial Library, 1959 edition).

The Oxford Companion to United States History, edited by Paul S. Boyer (Oxford University Press, 2001).

Random House Historical Dictionary of American Slang, Vol. II, edited by J. E. Lighter (Random House, 2011).

Since Yesterday: The 1930s In America, by Frederick Lewis Allen (Perennial Library, 1972 edition).

The Sixties: Years of Hope, Days of Rage, revised edition, by Todd Gitlin (Bantam Books, 1993).

The Sounds of Slavery: Discovering African American History Through Songs, Sermons, and Speech, by Shane White and Graham White (Beacon Press, 2005).

The Unfinished Nation: A Concise History of the American People, by Alan Brinkley (McGraw-Hill, 2000).

CITY/STATE/REGIONAL STUDIES

Chicago Jazz: A Cultural History, 1904–1930, by William Howland Kenney (Oxford University Press, 1993).

Detroit: see Rhythm & Blues

Geographical Studies, General*: The Sounds of People and Places: A Geography of American Music from Country to Classical and Blues to Bop,* fourth edition, edited by George C. Carney (Rowman & Littlefield, 2003).

Kansas City and All That's Jazz, Kansas City Jazz Museum (Andrews McMeel Pub., 1999).

Los Angeles: *Waiting for the Sun: A Rock 'n Roll History of Los Angeles,* by Barney Hoskyns (Backbeat Books, 2009 edition).

Louisiana: *South to Louisiana: The Music of the Cajun Bayous,* by John Broven (Pelican Publishing Co., 1987).

Memphis: *Goin' Back to Memphis: A Century of Blues, Rock 'n' Roll, and Glorious Soul,* by James Dickerson (Prentice Hall International, 1996).

New Orleans: *Bayou Underground: Tracing the Mythical Roots of American Popular Music,* by Dave Thompson (ECW Press, 2010).

Up from the Cradle of Jazz: New Orleans Music Since World War II, by Jason Berry, Jonathan Foose, and Tad Jones (University of Georgia Press, 1986); also see Jazz.

New York: *All Hopped Up and Ready to Go: Music from the Streets of New York, 1927–77,* by Tony Fletcher (W. W. Norton, 2009).

Black Manhattan, by James Weldon Johnson (Da Capo Press, 1991 edition of 1930 book).

The Encyclopedia of New York City, edited by Kenneth T. Jackson (Yale University Press, 1991).

52nd Street: The Street of Jazz, by Arnold Shaw (Da Capo Press, 1971).

Terrible Honesty: Mongrel Manhattan in the 1920s, by Ann Douglas (Farrar, Straus & Giroux, 1995).

ALBUM GUIDES

Note: See album guides under Blues, Country, Ethnic and World Music, Jazz, and Rock.

The All Music Guide: The Experts' Guide to the Best CDs, Albums & Tapes, edited by Michael Erlewine, Vladimir Bogdanov, Chris Woodstra, and Stephen Thomas Erlewine (Miller Freeman, 1997); all genres.

The New Rolling Stone Album Guide/Completely Revised and Updated 4th Edition, edited by Nathan Brackett and Christian Hoard (Fireside/Simon & Schuster, 2004).

The Rolling Stone Album Guide, edited by Anthony DeCurtis and James Henke with Holly George-Warren (Random House, 1992).

The Rolling Stone Record Guide, edited by Dave Marsh and John Swenson (Random House/Rolling Stone Press, 1979).

ALL-TIME GREAT RECORDS

Acclaimed Music: "The All-Time Top 3000 Songs" (www.acclaimedmusic.net/).

Albums: The Stories Behind 50 Years of Great Recordings, various contributors (Thunder Bay Press, 2005).

American Film Institute: "100 Years . . . 100 Songs" (greatest songs from the movies) (www.afi.com/100years/songs.aspx).

American Hit Radio: A History of Popular Singles from 1955 to the Present, by Thomas Ryan (Prima Publishing, 1996).

ASCAP Top 25 Songs of the Century (www.ascap.com/press/songs-122799.html).

BBC Radio 2: Top 100 Songs of the 20th Century (www.bbc.co.uk/radio2/soldonsong/songlibrary).

The Best Rock 'n' Roll Records of All Time: A Fan's Guide to the Stuff You Love, by Jimmy Guterman (Citadel Press, 1992).

Blender, October 2005, "The 500 Greatest Songs Since You Were Born" (1982–2005).

BMI Top 100 Songs of the Century (www.bmi.com/musicworld/news/archive/199912/1999121488.asp).

Dave's Music Database Presents: The Top 100 Songs of the Rock Era, 1954–1999, by Dave Whitaker (Dave's Music Database: CreateSpace, 2011).

Dave's Music Database: The DMDB Top 1000 Songs of the 20th Century (davesmusicdatabase.blogspot.com/2012/12/the-top-1000-songs-of-all-time.html).

Dave's Music Database: "The Top 100 Songs of the 21st Century (2000–2009) (davesmusicdatabase.blogspot.com/2011/10/top-100-songs-of-21st-centuryso-far.html).

Grammy Hall of Fame (www.grammy.org/recording-academy/awards/hall-of-fame):

Details, November 1998, "The 40 Records That Shook the World," by Will Hermes.

The Heart of Rock & Soul: The 1001 Greatest Singles Ever Made, by Dave Marsh (Da Capo Press, 1999 edition of 1989 book).

Listen to This! Leading Musicians Recommend Their Favorite Artists and Recordings, by Alan Reder and John Baxter (Hyperion, 1999).

Mojo, August 2000, "The 100 Greatest Songs of All Time."

The Mojo Collection: The Greatest Albums of All Time, edited by Jim Irvin (Mojo Books, 2000 and 2003 editions).

Mojo, June 2007, "100 Records That Changed the World."

National Recording Registry (Library of Congress) (www.loc.gov/rr/record/nrpb/registry/nrpb-masterlist.html).

1,000 Recordings to Hear Before You Die: A Listener's Life List, by Tom Moon (Workman Publishing, 2008); primarily albums, from classical and jazz to pop.

1001 Songs: The Great Songs of All Time, by Toby Creswell (Thunder's Mouth Press, 2006).

1001 Songs You Must Hear Before You Die, edited by Robert Dimery (Universe, 2010).

The Pitchfork 500: Our Guide to the Greatest Songs from Punk to the Present, edited by Scott Plagenhoef and Ryan Schreiber (Fireside/Simon & Schuster, 2008).

Popular Song: Soundtrack of the Century: The Most Influential Songs of the Last 100 Years, by Alan Leusens (Billboard Books).

Q magazine, February 1999, "The 100 Greatest Singles of All Time."

Q magazine (early 2003), "100 Songs That Changed the World."

Q magazine (undated special issue, c. 2004–2005), "1001 Best Songs Ever."

Rock and Roll: The 100 Best Singles, by Paul Williams (Carroll & Graf, 1993).

Rolling Stone, September 8, 1988, "The 100 Best Singles of the Last Twenty-Five Years."

Rolling Stone, December 7, 2000, "100 Greatest Pop Songs."

Rolling Stone, December 11, 2003, "The 500 Greatest Albums of All Time."

Rolling Stone, December 9, 2004, "The 500 Greatest Songs of All Time."

Rolling Stone, December 24, 2009–January 7, 2010, "The 50 Best Songs of the Decade."

Rolling Stone: 500 Greatest Songs of All Time (Special Collectors Edition) (RollingStone, 2010).

Singles: Six Decades of Hot Hits and Classic Cuts, by Johnny Black (Thunder Bay Press, 2006).

"Songs of the Century," Top 365 Songs of the Twentieth Century as announced by the Recording Industry Association of America (RIAA) and the National Endowment for the Arts (NEA) (www.theassociation.net/txt-music5.html).

Stranded: Rock and Roll for a Desert Island, edited by Greil Marcus (Da Capo Press, 1996 edition).

Time Entertainment: "All-Time 100 Songs" (since the beginning of *Time* magazine, 1923–2011) (entertainment.time.com/2011/10/24/the-all-time-100-songs/).

Time Out: 1000 Songs to Change Your Life, by the editors of Time Out (Time Out Guides, Ltd., 2008).

The Top 100 Rock 'n' Roll Albums of All Time, by Paul Gambaccini (Harmony Books, 1987).

VH1's 100 Greatest Albums, edited by Jacob Hoye (Pocket Books, 2003).

The Virgin All-Time Top 1000 Albums, by Colin Larkin (Virgin Books, 1998).

Zagat Survey Music Guide: 1,000 Top Albums of All Time (Zagat Survey, 2003).

DISCOGRAPHIES

Note: Most discographies are listed under specific musical genres and Record Label Histories.

The American Dance Band Discography, 1917–1942, by Brian Rust, two volumes (Arlington House, 1975).

American Dance Bands on Record and Film, 1915–1942, compiled by Richard J. Johnson and Bernard H. Shirley, five volumes (Rustbooks Publishing, 2010).

Cakewalks, Rags and Novelties: The International Ragtime Discography, 1894–1930, by Allan Sutton (Mainspring Press, 2003).

Complete Entertainment Discography: From the Mid–1890s to 1942, by Brian Rust (Arlington House, 1973).

Goldmine Price Guide to 45 RPM Records, by Tim Neely (Krause Publications, 1999).

GENERAL MUSIC HISTORY

Note: See Recording Industry, General Histories.

All the Years of American Popular Music, by David Ewen (Prentice-Hall, 1977).

America on Record: A History of Recorded Sound, by Andre Millard (Cambridge University Press, 1995).

American Popular Music Business in the 20th Century, by Russell Sanjek and David Sanjek (Oxford University Press, 1991).

Best Music Writing 2010, edited by Daphne Carr and Ann Powers (Da Capo Press, 2010).

Black Music Research Journal (periodical covering jazz, blues, R&B, etc.), issues from 1987–2000, as well as earlier issues published under the title *Black Music Research Newsletter.*

The Complete Encyclopedia of Popular Music and Jazz, 1900–1950, five volumes, by Roger Kinkle (Arlington House, 1974):

Volume 1: Music Year by Year, 1900–1950.

Volume 2: Biographies A through K.

Volume 3: Biographies L through Z.

Volume 4: Indexes and Appendices.

Da Capo Best Music Writing 2003: The Year's Finest Writing on Rock, Pop, Jazz, Country & More, edited by Paul Bresnick and Matt Groening (Da Capo Press, 2003).

Da Capo Best Music Writing 2004: The Year's Finest Writing on Hip-Hop, Jazz, Pop, Country & More, edited by Paul Bresnick and Mickey Hart (Da Capo Press, 2004).

The Faber Companion to 20th-Century Popular Music, by Phil Hardy and Dave Laing (Faber & Faber, 1990).

The Grammys, by Thomas O'Neil (Perigee, 1993).

Guinness World Records, 2001 edition (Guinness).

Hole in Our Soul: The Loss of Beauty and Meaning in American Popular Music, by Martha Bayles (Maxwell Macmillan Canada, 1994).

How the Beatles Destroyed Rock 'n' Roll: An Alternative History of American Popular Music, by Elijah Wald (Oxford University Press, 2009).

Jazz Dance: The Story of American Vernacular Dance, by Marshall and Jean Stearns (Da Capo Press, 1994 edition of 1968 book).

Lissauer's Encyclopedia of Popular Music in America: 1888 to the Present, by Robert Lissauer (Paragon House, 1991).

Million Selling Records from the 1900s to the 1980s, by Joseph Murrells (Arco Publishing, 1984).

The New Grove Dictionary of Music and Musicians, second edition (Grove/MacMillan Publishers, 2001).

Popular Recordaid; artist and song listings, many monthly supplements from 1948 to 1960s (Recordaid).

The Rise and Fall of Popular Music, by Donald Clarke (St. Martin's Press, 1995).

Since Records Began: EMI, The First 100 Years, by Peter Martland (Amadeus Press, 1997).

Sony Music 100 Years: Soundtrack for a Century, twenty-six-CD boxed set with accompanying book, song recordings from 1890s to 1990s (Sony, 1999).

33 Revolutions Per Minute: A History of Protest Songs, from Billie Holiday to Green Day, by Dorian Lynskey (Ecco/HarperCollins, 2011).

Variety Presents the Complete Book of Major Show Business Awards, edited by Mike Kaplan (Garland, 1985).

The Virgin Encyclopedia of Popular Music, edited by Colin Larkin (Virgin/Muze, 1997).

AMERICAN POP CHARTS

Note: See Country, Rhythm & Blues.

The Billboard Albums (Top Album charts, 1956–2005), sixth edition, by Joel Whitburn (Record Research, 2006).

The Billboard Book of Number One Albums, by Craig Rosen (Billboard Books, 1996).

The Billboard Book of Number One Hits, fifth edition, by Fred Bronson (Billboard Books, 2003).

The Billboard Book of Number Two Singles, by Christopher G. Feldman (Billboard Books, 2000).

The Cash Box Album Charts, 1955–74, compiled by Frank Hoffman and George Albert, with Lee Ann Hoffman (Scarecrow Press, 1988).

Cash Box Pop Singles Charts, 1950–1993, by Pat Downey, George Albert, and Frank Hoffman (Pat Downey Enterprises, 1994).

Joel Whitburn's Album Cuts, 1955–2001, compiled from *Joel Whitburn's Top Pop Albums* (Record Research, 2002).

Joel Whitburn's Billboard Music Yearbooks, annual chart updates (Record Research, 1983–2004).

Joel Whitburn's Hot Dance/Disco, 1974–2003 (Record Research, 2004).

Joel Whitburn's Pop Hits 1940–1954: Singles and Albums (Record Research, 2002).

Joel Whitburn Presents A Century of Pop Music: Year by Year Top 40 Rankings of the Songs and Artists That Shaped a Century, 1900–1999 (Record Research, 1999).

Joel Whitburn Presents the Billboard Hot 100 Annual, 1955–2005 (Record Research, 2006).

Joel Whitburn's Rock Tracks: Album Rock, 1981–1995/Modern Rock, 1988–1995 (Record Research, 1995).

Joel Whitburn's Top Adult Contemporary, 1961–2001 (Record Research, 2002).

Joel Whitburn's Top Pop Singles 1955–2008, twelfth edition (Record Research, 2009).

Pop Memories 1890–1954: The History of American Popular Music, by Joel Whitburn, with Steve Sullivan (Record Research, 1986).

Popular Songs of the Twentieth Century, Volume 1: Chart Detail & Encyclopedia, 1900–1949, by Edward Foote Gardner (Paragon House, 2000).

Your Hit Parade and American Top Ten Hits: A Week-by-Week Guide to the Nation's Favorite Music, 1935–1994, by Bruce C. Elrod (Popular Culture Ink, 1994).

BRITISH AND INTERNATIONAL CHARTS

All Music Guide to Hit Albums (Top 10 U.S. and British charts, 1960–1994) (Miller Freeman Books, 1995).

Billboard Magazine, British charts (1945–1952) and "Hits of the World" section, 1960 onward.

British Hit Singles, by Paul Gambaccini, Jonathan Rice, and Tim Rice (Guinness Publications/Billboard Books, 1991).

The Complete Book of the British Charts: Singles and Albums, by Neil Warwick, Jon Kutner, and Tony Brown (Omnibus Press, 2004).

The Guinness Book of 500 Number One Hits, by Jo and Tim Rice, Paul Gambaccini, and Mike Read (GRRR Books, 1982).

Tsort.info/music, website whose data on international chart performance filled gaps in the above sources.

1800s–1940s: POPULAR MUSIC, GENERAL

Note: See Recording Industry Histories, Record Label Histories, Jazz, other genres.

All the Years of American Popular Music, by David Ewen (Prentice-Hall, 1977); from 1700s onward.

America the Beautiful: The Stirring True Story Behind Our Nation's Favorite Song, by Lynn Sherr (Public Affairs, 2001).

America's Musical Life: A History, by Richard Crawford (W. W. Norton & Co., 2001); from pre-1800 to modern era.

American Pop from Minstrel to Mojo: On Record 1893–1956, by Allen Lowe (Cadence Jazz Books, 1997).

Archeophone Records CD series: *The Phonographic Yearbook: The 1890s* (Vols. 1 and 2), 1907, 1908, 1912, 1913, 1915, 1916, 1920, and 1921.

Art Hickman's Orchestra: The San Francisco Sound (CD, notes by Bruce Vermazin; Archeophone Records, 2004).

The Ballad of America: The History of the United States in Song and Story, by John Anthony Scott (Grossett & Dunlap, 1967).

The Banjo on Record: A Bio-Discography, edited by Uli Heier and Rainer Lotz (Greenwood Press, 1993).

Before "Crazy Blues," Volume I: Commercial Blues in America, 1850–1920, PhD dissertation by Peter C. Muir (City University of New York, 2004).

Billboard; selected years from 1890s–1934; all issues, 1935–1943; partial, 1944–1949.

Book of World-Famous Music: Classical, Popular, and Folk, fourth edition, by James J. Fuld (Dover Publications, 1995); covers from 1700s onward.

Brown Wax Cylinder Phonograph Recordings (series of 14 CDs) by www.tinfoil.com covering 1888–1912, notes by Glenn Sage (1996–2003).

"Bully Song: Court Ruling on May Irwin's Song," November 21, 1896 *Music Trade Review.*

"By the Light of the Silvery Moon Will Go Over 1.5 Million Copies," April 9, 1910 *Music Trades.*

Cakewalks, Rags, and Novelties: The International Ragtime Discography, 1894–1930, by Allan Sutton (Mainspring Press, 2003).

Columbia Records catalogs, 1890 to 1920s.

"Creole Belles is the Biggest Hit Since *Georgia Camp Meeting,"* January 4, 1902 *Music Trades.*

"Dardanella is One of the Biggest Successes in Years," February 7, 1920 *Music Trades.*

Edison Disc Artists and Records, 1910–1929, compiled by Raymond R. Wile (APM Press, 1990 edition).

Edison Phonograph Monthly, 1903–1910 issues.

"Hello Ma Baby Can Be Heard in Every Flat in Harlem," May 20, 1899 *Music Trades.*

A History of Popular Music in America, by Sigmund Spaeth (Random House, 1948); covers from 1700s onward.

Hit Songs, 1900–1955: American Popular Music of the Pre-Rock Era, by Don Tyler (McFarland and Company, 2007).

Hobbies magazine, many articles on pioneer recording artists by Jim Walsh, 1942–1972.

"Hot Time in the Old Town is Defiant, Full of Hope," August 6, 1898 *Music Trade Review.*

Jukeboxes: The Golden Age, by Vincent Lynch and Bill Henkin (Lancaster-Miller, 1981).

Lost Sounds: Blacks and the Birth of the Recording Industry, 1890–1919, by Tim Brooks (University of Illinois Press, 2004); and two-CD companion by Archeophone.

Metronome (monthly periodical), 1885–1901; twice-monthly issues, 1927–1928; see Jazz for later coverage of *Metronome.*

The Music Trade Review (weekly industry publication), all issues, 1894–1901; also 1925–1929.

The Music Trades (weekly industry publication), nearly all issues, 1899–1933.

"On the Trail of the *Arkansas Traveler*," by Henry Chapman Mercer, March 1896 *Century Magazine*; article reprinted in Summer 1970 *J.E.M.F. Quarterly*.

Out of Sight: The Rise of African American Popular Music, 1889–1895, by Lynn Abbott and Doug Seroff (University of Mississippi Press, 2002).

"*Over There,* Phenomenal Hit, Purchased by Leo Feist," November 10, 1917 *Music Trades*.

Phonogram (record industry periodical), 1890–1893.

Phonoscope (monthly lists of top records), 1896–1899.

The Piano in America: 1890–1940, by Craig H. Roell (University of North Carolina Press, 1989).

"'Play That Barber Shop Chord': A Case for the African-American Origin of Barbershop Harmony," article in Fall 1992 *American Music* by Lynn Abbott.

Popular American Recording Pioneers, 1895–1925, by Tim Gracyk with Frank Hoffman (Haworth Press, 2000).

Ragged But Right: Black Traveling Shows, "Coon Songs," and the Dark Pathway to Blues and Jazz, by Lynn Abbott and Doug Seroff (University of Mississippi Press, 2007).

Rags and Ragtime: A Musical History, by David A. Jasen and Trebor Jay Tichenor (Seabury Press, 1978).

Ragtime: An Encyclopedia, Discography, and Sheetography, by David Jasen (Routledge/Taylor and Francis Group, 2007).

Ragtime: Its History, Composers, and Music, edited by John Edward Haase (Schirmer Books, 1985).

Real Ragtime: Disc Recordings from Its Heyday, with notes by Richard Martin and Meagan Hennessy (Archeophone compilation, 2001).

Recorded Music in American Life: The Phonograph and Popular Memory, 1890–1945 by William Howland Kenney (Oxford University Press, 1999).

Recorded Ragtime, 1897–1958, by David A. Jasen (Archon Books, 1973).

"*School Days* Continues to Be the Reigning Hit Throughout the Entire Country," September 21, 1907 *Music Trades*.

"*Shine On, Harvest Moon* is Being Featured by Hundreds of Performers," June 5, 1909 *Music Trades*.

So Let's Hear the Applause: The Story of the Jewish Entertainer, by Michael Freedland (Vallentine, Mitchell, 1984).

Spreadin' Rhythm Around: Black Popular Songwriters, 1880–1930, by David A. Jasen and Gene Jones (Prentice Hall, 1998).

Steamboatin' Days: Folk Songs of the River Packet Era, by Mary Wheeler (Books for Libraries Press, 1944).

Stomp and Swerve: American Music Gets Hot, 1843–1924, by David Wondrich (Chicago Review Press, 2003); and accompanying CD on Archeophone.

"The Sousa Marches are Now the Musical Craze of the Civilized World," March 11, 1899 *Music Trades*.

"*Stars and Stripes Forever,* Sousa's New March," June 19, 1897 *Music Trade Review*.

Stories of Our National Songs, by Ernest K. Emurian (W. A. Wilde & Company, 1957).

"*Stormy Weather* Such a Hit That It Peps Up Whole Industry," July 1933 *Metronome*.

The Story of the House of Witmark: From Ragtime to Swingtime, by Isidore Witmark and Isaac Goldberg (Da Capo Press, 1976 edition of 1939 book).

Sweet Songs for Gentle Americans: The Parlor Song in America, 1790–1860, by Nicholas E. Tawa (Bowling Green University Popular Press, 1980).

Talking Machine News (monthly British periodical), 1903–1905.

Talking Machine World (monthly U.S. record industry periodical), 1905–1930.

Tantalizing Tingles: A Discography of Early Ragtime, Jazz, and Novelty Syncopated Piano Recordings, 1889–1934, by Ross Laird (Greenwood Press, 1995).

"*There's a Long, Long Trail:* The Whole English-Speaking World is Singing and Talking About It" (February 17, 1917 *Music Trades*).

They All Played Ragtime, by Rudi Blesh and Harriet Janis (Oak Publications, 1971 edition of 1950 book).

"'They Cert'ly Sound Good to Me': Sheet Music, Southern Vaudeville, and the Commercial Ascendency of the Blues," article by Lynn Abbott and Doug Seroff in *American Music* (Winter 1996).

"*Till We Meet Again:* Ring Out, Sweet Bells of Peace" (November 16, 1918 *Music Trades*).

Variety magazine, selected years, 1905–1928; all issues, 1929–1935.

Variety Music Cavalcade: Musical-Historical Review, 1620–1969, third edition, by Julius Mattfield (Prentice-Hall, 1971).

Victor Talking Machine Co. record catalogs and monthly supplements, 1901 to 1930s.

The Way to Tin Pan Alley: American Popular Song, 1866–1910, by Nicholas E. Tawa (Schirmer Books, 1990).

"*Whispering*: The Biggest Western Hit Ever Published" (September 11, 1920 *Music Trades*).

Yesterdays: Popular Song in America, by Charles Hamm (W. W. Norton & Co., 1979); covers from 1700s onward.

Yodel-Ay-Ee-Oooo: The Secret History of Yodeling Around the World, by Bart Plantenga (Routledge, 2004).

Biographies/Bio-Discographies

Stephen Foster: *Doo-Dah! Stephen Foster and the Rise of American Popular Culture,* by Ken Emerson (Da Capo Press, 1997).

Al Jolson: *Jolson: The Legend Comes to Life*, by Herbert G. Goldman (Oxford U. Press, 1988).

Scott Joplin: *Dancing to a Black Man's Tune: A Life of Scott Joplin,* by Susan Curtis (University of Missouri Press, 1994).

Scott Joplin and the Ragtime Era, by Peter Gammond (St. Martin's Press, 1976).

Billy Murray: The Phonograph Industry's First Great Recording Artist, by Frank Hoffman, Dick Carty, and Quentin Riggs (Scarecrow Press, 1997).

Nathaniel Shilkret: Sixty Years in the Music Business, by Nathaniel Shilkret, edited by Niel Shell and Barbara Shilkret (Scarecrow Press, 2005).

John Philip Sousa: *The Incredible Band of John Philip Sousa,* by Paul Edmund Bierley (University of Illinois Press, 2006).

The Sound of Sousa, compiled by Walter Mitziga (South Shore Printers, 1988).

The Sousa Band: A Discography, compiled by James R. Smart (Library of Congress, 1982).

Wilbur Sweatman: *That's Got 'Em! The Life and Music of Wilbur C. Sweatman,* by Mark Berresford (University Press of Mississippi, 2010).

Paul Whiteman: Pioneer in American Music, 1890–1930, Volume 1, by Don Rayno (Scarecrow Press, 2003).

AFRICAN-AMERICAN MUSIC: HISTORY AND ANALYSIS

Note: See Blues.

African American Music: An Introduction, edited by Mellonee Burnim and Portia Maultsby (Routledge, 2006); from pre-1800 to modern era.

African Banjo Echoes in Appalachia: A Study of Folk Traditions, by Cecelia Conway (University of Tennessee Press, 1992).

Black Culture and Black Consciousness: Afro-American Folk Thought from Slavery to Freedom, by Lawrence W. Levine (Oxford University Press, 1977).

"Black Instrumental Music Traditions in the Ex-Slave Narratives," by Robert D. Winans, *Black Music Research Journal* (Spring 1990).

The Book of American Negro Poetry, edited by James Weldon Johnson (Harcourt, Brace & World; 1958 edition of 1922 book).

From Jubilee to Hip Hop: Readings in African American Music, edited by Kip Lornell (Prentice Hall, 2010).

The Harlem Renaissance: A Historical Dictionary for the Era, edited by Bruce Kellner (Greenwood Press, 1984).

The Music of Black Americans: A History, by Eileen Southern (Norton, 1983).

The Negro and His Music: Negro Art, Past and Present, by Alain Locke (1969 Arno Press and New York Times edition of 1936 book).

The Negro Church in America, by E. Franklin Frazier (Schocken Books, 1964).

Negro Folk Music, U.S.A., by Harold Courlander (Columbia University Press, 1963).

The New Negro: An Interpretation, edited by Alain Locke (Johnson Reprint Corp., 1968 reprint of 1925 book.)

The Power of Black Music: Interpreting Its History from Africa to the United States, by Samuel Floyd, Jr. (Oxford University Press, 1995).

The Signifying Monkey: A Theory of Afro-American Literary Criticism, by Henry Louis Gates, Jr. (Oxford University Press, 1988).

Sinful Tunes and Spirituals: Black Folk Music to the Civil War, by Dena J. Epstein (University of Illinois Press, 1977).

Slave Culture: Nationalist Theory and the Foundations of Black America, by Sterling Stuckey (Oxford University Press, 1987).

Soul on Ice, by Eldridge Cleaver (McGraw-Hill, 1968).

The Souls of Black Folk, by W. E. B. Du Bois (Gramercy Books, 1994 edition of 1903 book).

AMERICAN ROOTS MUSIC

American Roots Music, edited by Robert Santelli, Holly George-Warren, and Jim Brown (Rolling Stone Press, 2001).

Anthology of American Folk Music, edited by Harry Smith (originally issued in 1953, Smithsonian Folkways reissue, 1997).

Anthology of American Folk Music, musical commentary edited by John Dunston and Ethel Raum (Oak Publications, 1973).

Bossmen: Bill Monroe and Muddy Waters, by James Rooney (Da Capo Press, 1971).

Chasing the Rising Sun: The Journey of an American Song, by Ted Anthony (Simon & Schuster, 2007).

Country: The Twisted Roots of Rock 'n' Roll, by Nick Tosches (Da Capo Press, 1996).

The Early Years of Folk Music: Fifty Founders of the Tradition, by David Dicaire (McFarland & Co., 2010).

Feel Like Going Home: Portraits in Blues and Rock 'n' Roll, by Peter Guralnick (Vintage Books, 1981 edition).

Folk Music in America, fifteen-volume series of albums of recordings from 1890s to 1970s, selected and annotated by Dick Spottswood (Library of Congress, 1976).

The Formative Dylan: Transmission and Stylistic Influences, 1961–1963, by Todd Harvey (Scarecrow Press, 2001).

Good for What Ails You: Music of the Medicine Shows, 1926–1937, two-CD set, annotation by Marshall Wyatt and Bengt Olsson (Old Hat Records, 2005).

Hard Times Come Again No More: Early American Rural Songs of Hard Times and Hardships, Vols. 1 and 2, notes by Don Kent and Richard Nevins (Yazoo compilations, 2000).

"Iris Dement Sails Outside of the Mainstream," by Stephen Betts, *Journal of Country Music,* Vol. 17 #1 (1994).

Invisible Republic: Bob Dylan's Basement Tapes, by Greil Marcus (Henry Holt & Co., 1997).

J.E.M.F. Quarterly (John Edwards Memorial Foundation, 1965–1976); all issues and all reprints.

Long Steel Rail: The Railroad in American Folksong, by Norm Cohen (University of Illinois Press, 2000 edition).

Lost Delta Found: Rediscovering the Fisk University and Library of Congress Coahoma County Study, 1941–1942, by John W. Work, Lewis Wade Jones, and Samuel C. Adams, Jr. (Vanderbilt University Press, 2005).

Lost Highway: Journeys and Arrivals of American Musicians, by Peter Guralnick (D. R. Goldine, 1979).

Musical Traditions (British periodical), issues from 1983–1986, selected issues thereafter.

My Rough and Rowdy Ways: Early American Rural Music/Badman Ballads and Hellraising Songs, Vols. 1 and 2, notes by Don Kent and Richard Nevins (Yazoo compilations, 1998).

Mystery Train: Images of America in Rock 'n' Roll Music, by Greil Marcus (Plume, 1997 edition).

The New Encyclopedia of Southern Culture: Music, edited by Bill Malone (University of North Carolina Press, 2008).

Only a Miner: Studies in Recorded Coal-Mining Songs, by Archie Green (University of Illinois Press, 1972).

"Out of the Past" (feature on Emmylou Harris), by Daniel Cooper, *Journal of Country Music,* Vol. 18 #2 (1996).

Oxford American Southern Music Issues, 1997 through 2010.

The Oxford American Book of Great Music Writing, edited by Marc Smirnoff (University of Arkansas Press, 2008).

Roots 'n Blues: The Retrospective, 1925–1950, boxed set and book (Columbia Legacy, 1992).

Segregating Sound: Inventing Folk and Pop Music in the Age of Jim Crow, by Karl Hagstrom Miller (Duke University Press, 2010).

Southern Music/American Music, by Bill Malone and David Stricklin (University Press of Kentucky, 2003 edition).

Steel Drivin' Man: John Henry, the Untold Story of an American Legend, by Scott Reynolds Nelson (Oxford University Press, 2006).

Times Ain't Like They Used to Be: Early American Rural Music/Classic Recordings of the 1920s and '30s, Volumes 1–6, notes by Richard Nevins (Yazoo compilations, 1997).

Violin, Sing the Blues for Me: African-American Fiddlers, 1926–1949, notes by Marshall Wyatt (Old Hat compilation, 1999).

Where Dead Voices Gather, by Nick Tosches (Little, Brown & Co., 2001).

BLUES

Note: See African-American Music, American Roots Music, Rhythm & Blues.

Afro-American Spirituals, Work Songs, and Ballads, edited by Alan Lomax (1942).

All Music Guide to the Blues, edited by Michael Erlewine, Vladimir Bogdanov, Chris Woodstra, Cub Koda (Miller Freeman Books, 1996).

Barrelhouse Blues: Location Recordings and the Early Traditions of the Blues, by Paul Oliver (Basic Civitas Books, 2009).

Before "Crazy Blues," Volume I: Commercial Blues in America, 1850–1920, PhD dissertation by Peter C. Muir (City University of New York, 2004).

Best of the Blues: The 101 Essential Albums, by Robert Santelli (Penguin Books, 1997).

Big Road Blues: Tradition and Creativity in the Folk Blues, by David Evans (Da Capo Press, 1982).

Blacks, Whites, and Blues, by Tony Russell (Studio Vista, 1970).

The Blackwell Guide to Blues Records, edited by Paul Oliver (Basil Blackwell Ltd., 1989).

Blues: An Anthology, Complete Words and Music of 53 Great Songs, by W. C. Handy, with historical and critical text by Abbe Niles (Da Capo Press, 1985 edition of original 1926 book).

Blues and Gospel Records, 1890–1943, by Robert M. W. Dixon, John Godrich, and Howard W. Rye, fourth edition (Oxford University Press, 1997).

The Blues Discography, 1943–1970, by Les Fancourt and Bob McGrath (Eyeball, 2006).

Blues Fell This Morning, by Paul Oliver (Collier Books, 1960); 1972 new edition as *The Meaning of the Blues.*

The Blues from Robert Johnson to Robert Cray, by Tony Russell (Schirmer Books, 1997 edition).

The Blues Line: Blues Lyrics from Leadbelly to Muddy Waters, edited by Eric Sackheim (Thunder's Mouth Press, 1969).

Blues Lyric Poetry: A Concordance (3 volumes), by Michael Taft (Garland Publishing, 1984).

Blues: 100 Essential CDs/The Rough Guide, by Greg Ward (Rough Guides, 2000).

The Blues: A Smithsonian Collection of Classic Blues Singers, annotation by W. K. McNeil (Smithsonian Collection of Recordings, 1993).

The *Blues* Foundation: Blues Hall of Fame Inductees, Classics of Blues Recordings, Singles, and Album Tracks (inducted recordings, 1982–2012) (www.blues.org/halloffame/inductees).

Blues People: Negro Music in White America, by Leroi Jones (Amiri Baraka) (Harper Perennial, 2002 edition of 1963 book).

Blues Unlimited, all issues, 1963–1972.

The Bluesmen: The Story and the Music of the Men Who Made the Blues, by Samuel Charters (Oak Publications, 1967).

Broadcasting the Blues: Black Blues in the Segregation Era, by Paul Oliver (Routledge, 2006).

Chasin' That Devil Music: Searching for the Blues, by Gayle Dean Wardlow (Backbeat Books, 1998).

Coley Jones and the Dallas String Band: Complete Recordings in Chronological Order, annotation by Paul Oliver (Matchbox Records, 1983).

The Country Blues, by Samuel B. Charters (Da Capo Press, 1975 edition of 1959 book).

"*Crazy Blues* is a Smash," January 22, 1921 *Music Trades.*

Deep Blues, by Robert Palmer (Viking Press, 1981).

Delta Blues: The Life and Times of the Mississippi Masters Who Revolutionized American Music, by Ted Gioia (W. W. Norton & Co., 2008).

The Devil's Music: A History of the Blues, by Giles Oakley (Da Capo Press, 1997 edition of 1976 book).

Early Downhome Blues: A Musical and Cultural Analysis, by Jeff Todd Titon (University of North Carolina Press, 1994 edition of 1977 book).

Encyclopedia of the Blues, by Gerard Herzhaft (University of Arkansas Press, 1992).

Escaping the Delta: Robert Johnson and the Reinvention of the Blues, by Elijah Wald (Amistad/HarperCollins, 2004).

"Finding Son House," by Bernard Klatzko, September 1964 *Blues Unlimited.*

"Folk-song and Folk-Poetry as Found in the Secular Songs of the Southern Negroes," parts 1 and 2, by Howard W. Odom, *Journal of American Folklore* (July–September 1911 and October–December 1911).

The History of the Blues: The Roots, the Music, the People, by Francis Davis (Hyperion, 1995).

In Search of the Blues, by Marybeth Hamilton (Basic Books, 2008).

The Land Where the Blues Began, by Alan Lomax (The New Press, 1993).

Living Blues (periodical), issues from 1970–1974, selected issues thereafter.

Ma Rainey and the Classic Blues Singers, by Derrick Stewart-Baxter (Stein & Day, 1970).

Mean Old World: The Blues from 1940 to 1994, annotation by Lawrence Hoffman (Smithsonian Collection of Recordings, 1996).

Memphis Blues and Jug Bands, by Bengt Olsson (Studio Vista, 1970).

"Notes on Negro Music" by Charles Peabody (the first published discussion of the music that would become known as the blues), *Journal of American Folklore* (July–September 1903).

Nothing But the Blues: The Music and the Musicians, edited by Lawrence Cohn (Abbeville Press Publishers, 1993).

Recording the Blues, by Robert M. W. Dixon and John Godrich (Stein & Day, 1970).

Re-Engaging Blues Narratives: Alan Lomax, Jelly Roll Morton, and W. C. Handy, PhD dissertation by Vic Hobson (University of East Anglia, 2008).

Savannah Syncopators: African Retentions in the Blues, by Paul Oliver (Stein & Day, 1970).

Screening the Blues: Aspects of the Blues Tradition, by Paul Oliver (Da Capo Press, 1989 edition of 1968 book).

78 Quarterly (periodical), all issues, 1967–1968, 1988–1994.

Songsters and Saints: Vocal Traditions on Race Records, by Paul Oliver (Cambridge University Press, 1984).

Stomping the Blues, by Albert Murray (McGraw-Hill, 1976).

The Story of Boogie-Woogie: A Left Hand Like God, by Peter J. Silvester (Scarecrow Press, 2009).

The Story of the Blues, by Paul Oliver (Northeastern University Press, 1997 edition of 1969 book).

Sweet As the Showers of Rain: The Bluesmen, Vol. II, by Samuel Charters (Oak Publications, 1977).

"Unknown Bards: The Blues Becomes Transparent About Itself," by John Jeremiah Sullivan, November 2008 *Harper's Magazine.*

Urban Blues, by Charles Keil (University of Chicago Press, 1966).

When the Sun Goes Down: The Secret History of Rock and Roll, series of classic-blues CDs (Bluebird/RCA Victor, 2003).

"Who Was Geechie Wiley?" by Greil Marcus, *The Oxford American Southern Music Issue* 1999.

Biographies

Howard Armstrong: "Louie Bluie: The Life and Music of William Howard Armstrong," by Terry Zwigoff, *78 Quarterly* #5 (1990); and part 2, *78 Quarterly* #6 (1991).

Perry Bradford: *Born With the Blues: Perry Bradford's Own Story* (Oak Publications, 1965).

Willie Dixon: *I Am the Blues: The Willie Dixon Story,* by Dixon with Don Snowden (Da Capo Press, 1989).

W. C. Handy: Father of the Blues, An Autobiography (Macmillan Company, 1941).

W. C. Handy: The Life and Times of the Man Who Made the Blues, by David Robertson (Alfred A. Knopf, 2009); also see Handy, *Blues: An Anthology.*

Lightnin' Hopkins: His Life and Blues, by Alan Govenar (Chicago Review Press, 2010).

Howlin' Wolf: *Moanin' At Midnight: The Life & Times of,* by James Segrest & Mark Hoffman (Pantheon Books, 2004).

Albert Hunter: A Celebration in Blues, by Frank C. Taylor and Gerald Cook (McGraw-Hill, 1987).

"Mississippi John Hurt," feature by Richard K. Spottswood, August 1963 *Blues Unlimited.*

Skip James: *I'd Rather Be the Devil: Skip James and the Blues,* by Stephen Calt (Chicago Review Press, 1994).

Blind Lemon Jefferson, entire issue devoted to artist, including articles by Alan Govenar and David Evans, *Black Music Research Journal* (Autumn 2000).

Robert Johnson: *Searching for Robert Johnson: The Life and Legend of the "King of the Delta Blues,"* by Peter Guralnick (Dutton/Penguin Group, 1992).

Robert Johnson: Feature by Stephen Calt and Gayle Dean Wardlow, *78 Quarterly* #4 (1989).

B.B. King: *Blues All Around Me: The Autobiography of B.B. King,* by B.B. King with David Ritz (Avon Books, 1996).

Blues Boy: The Life and Music of B.B. King, by Sebastian Danchin (University Press of Mississippi, 1998).

The Little Walter Story: Blues with a Feeling, by Tony Glover, Scott Dirks, and Ward Gaines (Routledge, 2002).

Charlie Patton: *Charley Patton,* by John Fahey (Studio Vista, 1970).

King of the Delta Blues Singers: The Life and Music of Charlie Patton, by Stephen Calt and Gayle Wardlow (Rock Chapel Press, 1988).

Ma Rainey: *Mother of the Blues: A Study of Ma Rainey,* by Sandra R. Lieb (University of Massachusetts Press, 1981).

Bessie Smith: *Bessie,* by Chris Albertson (Yale University Press, 2003 edition of 1972 book).

Bessie Smith: The Complete Recordings, Vol. 2, two CDs, notes by Chris Albertson (Columbia, 1991).

Henry Thomas—"Ragtime Texas": Complete Recorded Works, 1927 to 1929, in Chronological Order, annotation by Mack McCormick (Herwin double album, 1974). [Note: McCormick's extensive liner notes constitute a mini-biography of Thomas.]

Ethel Waters: *His Eye is On the Sparrow: An Autobiography,* by Ethel Waters with Charles Samuels (Doubleday and Company, 1951).

Muddy Waters: *Can't Be Satisfied: The Life and Times of Muddy Waters,* by Robert Gordon (Little, Brown & Co., 2002).

COUNTRY MUSIC

Note: See American Roots Music, Bluegrass.

All Music Guide to Country, edited by Michael Erlewine, Vladamir Bogdanov, Chris Woodstra, and Stephen Thomas Erlewine (Miller Freeman Books, 1997).

"America's Blue Yodel," by Lynn Abbott and Doug Seroff, *Musical Traditions* 11 (1993).

The Best of Country Music, by John Morthland (Doubleday & Company, 1984).

The Billboard Book of Number One Country Hits, by Tom Roland (Billboard Books, 1991).

The Billboard Book of Top 40 Country Hits: Complete Chart Information about the Most Popular Country Music Songs and Artists, 1944–2006, by Joel Whitburn (Billboard Books, 2006).

"A Biblio-Discography of *White House Blues,*" by Neil Rosenberg, June 1968 *J.E.M.F. Quarterly.*

Classic Country: Legends of Country Music, by Charles K. Wolfe (Routledge, 2001).

Country Music Originals: The Legends and the Lost, by Tony Russell (Oxford University Press, 2007).

Country America, October 1992, "Top 100 Country Songs of All Time."

Country Music Records: A Discography, 1921–1942, by Tony Russell (Oxford University Press, 2004).

Country Music Sources: Biblio-Discography of Commercially Recorded Traditional Music, by Guthrie T. Meade, Jr. with Dick Spottswood and Douglas S. Meade (University of North Carolina at Chapel Hill Libraries, 2002).

The Country Music Story, by Robert Shelton (Bobbs-Merrill Company, 1966).

Country Music Television: "100 Greatest Songs of Country Music" (2003) (www.cmt.com).

Country Music, U.S.A., second revised edition, by Bill Malone (University of Texas Press, 2002).

Country: 100 Essential CDs/The Rough Guide, by Kurt Wolff (Rough Guides, 2000).

Definitive Country: The Ultimate Encyclopedia of Country Music, by Barry McCloud (Perigee, 1995).

"*Detroit City:* The Anatomy of a Record," by David Cantwell, *Journal of Country Music,* Vol. 23 #2 (2003).

Don't Get Above Your Raisin': Country Music and the Southern Working Class, by Bill Malone (University of Illinois Press, 2002).

Grand Ole Opry: The Complete Story of a Great American Institution and Its Stars, by Chet Hagan (H. Holt, 1989).

Heartaches By the Number: Country Music's 500 Greatest Singles, by David Cantwell and Bill Friskics-Warren (Vanderbilt University Press, 2003).

"Hillbilly Music: Source and Symbol," by Archie Green, *Journal of American Folklore* 78 (July–September 1965).

A History and Encyclopedia of Country, Western, and Gospel Music, second edition, compiled by Linnell Gentry (Clairmont Corp., 1969).

"I Owe My Soul to the Company Store: The Saga of 'Sixteen Tons,'" by Merle Travis, *Sing Out!,* Spring 1956.

"An Introduction to the Study of Hillbilly Music," by D. K. Wilgus, *Journal of American Folklore* 78 (July–September 1965).

Joel Whitburn's Top Country Albums, 1964–1997 (Record Research, 1998).

Joel Whitburn's Top Country Singles, 1944–1997 (Record Research, 1998).

The Journal of Country Music, all issues, 1971–1992; most issues, 1993–2006.

"The Legend That Peer Built: Reappraising the Bristol Sessions," by Charles Wolfe, *Journal of Country Music,* Vol. 12 #2 (1989).

Linthead Stomp: The Creation of Country Music in the Piedmont South, by Patrick Huber (University of North Carolina Press, 2008).

Listen to the Stories: Nat Hentoff on Jazz and Country Music, by Nat Hentoff (HarperCollins, 1995).

Old-Time Fiddle Classics, Volume 2, 1927–1934, liner notes by Richard Nevins (County Records LP, 1973).

Old Time Music (British periodical), first fourteen issues, 1971–1974.

"The Prisoner's Song," article by Riley Barnes, *Old Time Music* 32 (1979).

"Roots of the Country Yodel: Notes Toward a Life History," by Robert Coltman, Summer 1976 *J.E.M.F. Quarterly.*

Sing Your Heart Out, Country Boy, by Dorothy Horstman (Country Music Foundation, 1986 revised edition).

"The Singing Cowboy: An American Dream," by Douglas B. Green, *Journal of Country Music* (May 1978).

"The Skillet Lickers: A Study of a Hillbilly String Band and Its Repertoire," by Norman Cohen, *Journal of American Folklore* 78 (July–September 1965).

The Smithsonian Collection of Classic Country Music, selected and annotated by Bill Malone (original edition 1981; revised edition in 1990).

Southwest Shuffle: Pioneers of Honky-Tonk, Western Swing, and Country Jazz (by Rich Kienzle, Routledge, 2003).

The Stories Behind Country Music's All-Time 100 Greatest Songs, by Ace Collins (Boulevard Books, 1996).

Three Chords and the Truth: Hope, Heartbreak, and Changing Fortunes in Nashville, by Laurence Learner (HarperCollins, 1997).

Tom Dooley: The Story Behind the Song, by Jim Grayson, *Journal of Country Music,* Vol. 2 #2 (June 1971).

Traditional Country Hall of Fame, list of inducted songs (www.talentondisplay.com/kicINsongs.html).

"Vernon Dalhart and 'The Prisoner's Song,'" by Walter Darrell Haden, Winter 1971 *J.E.M.F. Quarterly.*

"'*You Are My Sunshine*': A Question of Authorship," by Toru Mitsui, Winter 1990 *Old Time Country,* Vol. 6 #4.

You Wrote My Life: Lyrical Themes in Country Music, edited by Melton McLaurin and Richard A. Peterson (Gordon & Breach, 1992).

Biographies/Bio-Discographies

Roy Acuff, the Smoky Mountain Boy, by Elizabeth Schlappi (Pelican Publishing Co., 1993 edition).

Milton Brown and the Founding of Western Swing, by Cary Ginell with Lee Roy Brown (University of Illinois Press, 1994).

Glen Campbell: *Rhinestone Cowboy: An Autobiography,* by Glen Campbell with Tom Carter (Villard Books, 1994).

Fiddlin' Georgia Crazy: Fiddlin' John Carson, His Real World, and the World of His Songs, by Gene Wiggins (University of Illinois Press, 1987).

Carter Family: *Will You Miss Me When I'm Gone?: The Carter Family and Their Legacy in American Music,* by Mark Zwonitzer with Charles Hirshberg (Simon & Schuster, 2002).

Johnny Cash: The Autobiography, by Johnny Cash with Patrick Carr (Harper, 1997).

Johnny Cash: The Songs, edited by Don Cusic (Thunder's Mouth Press, 2004).

Patsy Cline: *Honky Tonk Angel: The Intimate Story of Patsy Cline,* by Ellis Nassour (St. Martin's Press, 1993).

The Patsy Cline Collection, annotation by Paul Kingsbury, boxed set (MCA Records, 1991).

Patsy: The Life and Times of Patsy Cline, by Margaret Jones (Da Capo Press, 1994).

Patsy Cline: The Making of an Icon, by Douglas Gomery (Trafford, 2011).

"Patsy Cline's Recording Career: The Search for a Sound," by Joli Jensen, *Journal of Country Music,* Vol. 9 #2 (1982).

Ted Daffan: "Indelible Ink: The Life and Times of Songwriter Ted Daffan," by Kevin Reed Coffey, *Journal of Country Music,* Vol. 16 #2 (1994).

Vernon Dalhart: First Star of Country Music, by Jack Palmer (Mainspring Press, 2005).

Take Me Home: An Autobiography, by John Denver with Arthur Tobier (Harmony Books, 1994).

Dixie Chicks, by Brett Michaels (Rosen Pub. Group, 2009).

"Steel Colossus: The Bob Dunn Story," by Kevin Reed Coffey, *Journal of Country Music,* Vol. 17 #2 (1995).

Merle Haggard: *Sing Me Back Home: My Story,* by Merle Haggard with Peggy Russell (New York Times Books, 1981).

Merle Haggard's My House of Memories: For the Record, with Tom Carter (Cliff Street Books, 1999).

Waylon Jennings: *Waylon: An Autobiography,* by Waylon Jennings with Lenny Kaye (Warner Books, 1996).

"George Jones: The Grand Tour," by Nick Tosches, *Journal of Country Music,* Vol. 16 #3 (1994).

I Lived to Tell It All, by George Jones with Tom Carter (Villard Books, 1996).

Grandpa Jones: *Everybody's Grandpa: Fifty Years Behind the Mike,* by Louis M. "Grandpa" Jones with Charles K. Wolfe (University of Tennessee Press, 1984).

Louvin Brothers: *In Close Harmony: The Story of the Louvin Brothers,* by Charles Wolfe (University Press of Mississippi, 1996).

Loretta Lynn: *Coal Miner's Daughter,* by Loretta Lynn with George Vecsy (Vintage Books/Random House, 2010 edition of 1976 book).

Wade Mainer: *Banjo on the Mountain: Wade Mainer's First Hundred Years,* by Dick Spottswood (University Press of Mississippi, 2010).

"Grady Martin: Unsung and Unforgettable," by Rich Kienzle, *Journal of Country Music,* Vol. 10 #2 (1985).

Bill Monroe: *Can't You Hear Me Callin'?: The Life of Bill Monroe, Father of Bluegrass,* by Richard D. Smith (Da Capo Press, 2000).

The Music of Bill Monroe, by Neil V. Rosenberg and Charles K. Wolfe (University of Illinois Press, 2007).

"Patsy Montana and the Development of the Cowgirl Image," by Robert K. Oermann and Mary A. Bufwack, *Journal of Country Music,* Vol. 8 #3 (1981).

Willie Nelson: An Epic Life, by Joe Nick Patoski (Back Bay Books/Little, Brown & Company, 2008).

Molly O'Day, Lynn Davis, and the Cumberland Mountain Folks: A Bio-Discography, by Ivan M. Tribe and John W. Morris (John Edwards Memorial Foundation, Special Series No. 7, 1975).

Dolly Parton: *Dolly: My Life and Other Unfinished Business,* by Dolly Parton (HarperCollins, 1994).

Ralph Peer: "His Years at Victor," feature by Nolan Porterfield, *Journal of Country Music* (December 1978).

Charlie Poole: *Rambling Blues: The Life and Songs of Charlie Poole,* by Kinney Rorrer (Old Time Music, 1982).

"Being Ray Price Means Never Having to Say You're Sorry," by Daniel Cooper, *Journal of Country Music,* Vol. 14 #3 (1992).

Marty Robbins: Fast Cars and Country Music, by Barbara J. Pruett (Scarecrow Press, 1990).

Eck Robertson: "What Ever Happened to Country Music's First Recording Artist? The Career of Eck Robertson," by Charles K. Wolfe, *Journal of Country Music,* Vol. 16 #1 (1993).

Jimmie Rodgers: The Life and Times of America's Blue Yodeler, by Nolan Porterfield (University of Illinois Press, 1992 edition).

Meeting Jimmie Rodgers: How America's Original Roots Music Hero Changed the Pop Sounds of a Century, by Barry Mazor (Oxford University Press, 2009).

The Recordings of Jimmie Rodgers: An Annotated Discography, by Johnny Bond (John Edwards Memorial Foundation, 1978).

The Songs of Jimmie Rodgers: A Legacy in Country Music, by Jocelyn R. Neal (Indiana University Press, 2009).

The Hank Snow Story, by Hank Snow with Jack Ownbey and Bob Burris (University of Illinois Press, 1994).

"Carl T. Sprague, The Original 'Singing Cowboy,'" by John White, Spring 1970 *J.E.M.F. Quarterly.*

Ernest Stoneman: *The Early Recording Career of Ernest V. "Pop" Stoneman: A Bio-Discography* (John Edwards Memorial Foundation, 1968).

"The Recording Career of Ernest Tubb," by Ronnie Pugh, *Journal of Country Music,* Vol. 9 #1 (1981).

Porter Wagoner: *A Satisfied Mind: The Country Music Life of Porter Wagoner,* by Steve Eng (Rutledge Hill Press, 1992).

Hank Williams: The Biography, by Colin Escott (Little, Brown & Co., 1995).

Hank Williams: The Complete Lyrics, edited by Don Cusic (St. Martin's Press, 1993).

Bob Wills: *San Antonio Rose: The Life and Music of Bob Wills,* by Charles R. Townsend (University of Illinois Press, 1986).

Bluegrass (subset of Country Music) Biographies

Lester Flatt: *The Good Things Outweigh the Bad: A Biography of Lester Flatt,* by Jake Lambert with Curly Seckler (Jay-Lyn Publication, 1982).

Bill Monroe: see listing under Country.

Ralph Stanley: *Man of Constant Sorrow: My Life and Times,* by Ralph Stanley with Eddie Dean (Gotham Books, 2009).

Bluegrass: A History, by Neil V. Rosenberg (University of Illinois Press, 1993 edition).

Bluegrass Breakdown: The Making of the Old Southern Sound, by Robert Cantwell (University of Illinois Press, 1984).

Bluegrass Unlimited (periodical), all issues from 1966–1970, selected issues thereafter.

Can't You Hear Me Callin': Bluegrass: 80 Years of American Music, boxed set (Sony Music, 2004).

"An Introduction to Bluegrass," by L. Mayne Smith, *Journal of American Folklore* 78 (July–September 1965).

ETHNIC AND WORLD MUSIC/ INTERNATIONAL RECORDING INDUSTRY

Africa

Africa O-Ye! A Celebration of African Music, by Graeme Ewens (Da Capo Press, 1992).

African Biographies

Fela Kuti: *Arrest the Music: Fela and His Rebel Art and Politics,* by Tejumola Olaniyan (Indiana University Press, 2004).

Ladysmith Black Mambazo: *The Life and Works of Bhekizizwe Joseph Shabalala and the Ladysmith Black Mambazo,* by Alex Thembala and Edmund Radebe (Reach Out Publishers, 1993).

Bob Marley: Lyrical Genius, by Kwame Dawes (Bobcat Books, 2002).

Catch a Fire: The Life of Bob Marley, Timothy White (Henry Holt & Company, 2006 edition).

Black Music of Two Worlds: African, Caribbean, Latin, and African-American Traditions, by John Storm Roberts (Schirmer Books, 1998).

The Da Capo Guide to Contemporary African Music, by Ronnie Graham (Da Capo Press, 1988).

"In the Jungle," by Rian Malan (history of Solomon Linda, *Mbube,* and *The Lion Sleeps Tonight*), May 25, 2000 *Rolling Stone.*

Music Is the Weapon of the Future: Fifty Years of African Popular Music, by Frank Tenaille (Lawrence Hill Books, 2002).

"Savannaphone: Talking Machines Hit West Africa," by Paul Vernon, August 1993 *Folk Roots.*

Stern's Guide to Contemporary African Music, by Ronnie Graham (Pluto Press, 1988).

The World of African Music: Stern's Guide to Contemporary African Music, Vol. 2, by Ronnie Graham (Pluto Press, 1992).

Brazilian

Bossa Nova: The Story of the Brazilian Music That Seduced the World, by Ruy Castro (Chicago Review Press, 2000).

Brazilian Popular Music and Globalization, edited by Charles Petrone and Christopher Dunn (University Press of Florida, 2001).

The Brazilian Sound: Samba, Bossa Nova, and the Popular Music of Brazil, by Chris McGowan and Ricardo Pessanha (Temple University Press, 2009 edition of 1991 book).

A Trip to Brazil: 40 Years of Bossa Nova (Motor Music compilation, 1998).

Tropical Truth: A Story of Music and Revolution in Brazil, by Caetano Veloso (Da Capo Press, 2002).

Cajun/Zydeco

Amédé Ardoin: *I'm Never Comin' Back,* CD with notes by Michael Doucet and Michael Tisserand (Arhoolie/Folklyric, 1995).

Amédé Ardoin: His Original Recordings 1928–1938, CD liner notes by Michael Doucet (Arhoolie).

Cajun Breakdown: The Emergence of an American-Made Music, by Ryan Andre Brasseaux (Oxford University Press, 2009).

Cajun Music: A Reflection of a People, edited by Ann Allen Savoy (Bluebird Press, 1984).

"Cajuns and Creoles: The French Gulf Coast," article by Nicholas Spitzer in "Long Journey Home: Folklife in the South," special issue of *Southern Exposure* (1977).

"Houston Creoles and Zydeco: The Emergence of an African-American Urban Style," article by John Minton, *American Music,* Vol. 14 #4 (Winter 1996).

Le Gran Mamou: A Cajun Music Anthology: The Historic Victor/Bluebird Sessions, 1928–1941, CD with notes by Charlie Seeman (Country Music Foundation, 1990).

Let the Good Times Roll: A Guide to Cajun and Zydeco Music, by Pat Nyhan, Brian Rollins, and David Babb (Upbeat Books, 1997).

The Makers of Cajun Music, by Barry Jean Ancelet (University Of Texas Press, 1984).

Pioneers of Cajun Accordion, 1926–1936, album with notes by Barry Jean Ancelet (Arhoolie, 1989).

South to Louisiana: The Music of the Cajun Bayous, by John Broven (Pelican Publishing Co., 1983).

Tears, Love, and Laughter: The Story of the Acadians, by Pierre V. Daigle (Acadian Publishing Enterprise, 1972).

Calypso Music/Trinidad

Atilla's Kaiso: A Short History of the Trinidad Calypso, by Raymond Quevedo ("Atilla the Hun") (University of the West Indies, 1983).

Calypso Calaloo: Early Carnival Music in Trinidad, by Donald R. Hill (University Press of Florida, 1993).

Calypso Pioneers: 1912–1937, CD with notes by Dick Spottswood (Rounder Records, 1989).

Calypsonians to Remember, by Hollis Liverpool (Juba Publications, 1987).

Calypsos from Trinidad: Politics, Intrigue & Violence in the 1930s, CD, edited and annotated by Dick Spottswood (Arhoolie, 1991).

"The Golden Age of Calypso," by Richard Noblett, *Musical Traditions* 4 (1985).

Kaiso! The Trinidad Calypso: A Study of the Calypso as Oral Literature, by Keith Q. Warner Passeggiata Press, 1999 edition).

Shango, Shouter & Obeah: Supernatural Calypso from Trinidad, 1934–1940, CD with notes by Dick Spottswood (Rounder Records, 2001).

Trinidad 1912–1941, CD with notes by Dick Spottswood (Harlequin compilation, 1992).

Cuban

Cuba and Its Music: From the First Drums to the Mambo, by Ned Sublette (Chicago Review Press, 2004).

Cuban Fire: The Story of Salsa and Latin Jazz, by Isabelle Leymarie (Continuum, 2002).

Cuba: I Am Time, four-CD set (Blue Jackel, 2004).

The Cuban Danzon: Before There Was Jazz: 1906–1929, CD, liner notes by Dick Spottswood and Cristobal Diaz Ayala (Arhoolie, 1999).

Cuban Music: From Son and Rumba to the Buena Vista Social Club and Timba Cubana, by Maya Roy (Markus Wiener Publishers, 2002 English translation of 1998 French book); also see Latin American, and Latin Jazz.

Hot Music from Cuba: 1907–1936, CD, liner notes by Cristobal Diaz and Dick Spottswood (Harlequin, 1993).

Ethnic Recordings (General)

Ethnic and Border Music: A Regional Exploration, edited by Norm Cohen (Greenwood Press, 2007).

Ethnic and Vernacular Music, 1898–1960: A Resource and Guide to Recordings, by Paul Vernon (Greenwood Press, 1995).

Ethnic Music on Records: A Discography of Ethnic Recordings Produced in the United States, 1893 to 1942, by Richard K. Spottswood, seven volumes (University of Illinois Press, 1990): *Volume 1: Western Europe (Dutch, French including Cajun, German, Italian)*; *Volume 2: Slavic (including Bohemian, Polish, Russian, Ukrainian)*; *Volume 3: Eastern Europe (including Greek, Hungarian, and Jewish)*; *Volume 4: Spanish, Portuguese, Philippine, Basque*; *Volume 5: Mid-East, Far East, Scandinavian, English Language, American Indian, and International*; and *Volumes 6 and 7: Appendices.*

Ethnic Recordings in America: A Neglected Heritage, with chapters by Dick Spottswood, Pekka Gronow, Norm Cohen, etc. (American Folklife Center, Library of Congress, 1982).

Italian String Virtuosi, with notes by Dick Spottswood (Rounder compilation, 1995).

La Zampogna in Italia (The Bagpipe in Italy), LP (Albatros, 1972).

Squeeze Play: A World Accordion Anthology, with notes by Dick Spottswood (Rounder compilation, 1997).

European Ethnic Music

Old-Country Music in a New Land: Folk Music of Immigrants from Europe and the Near East, LP, annotation by Richard Spottswood (New World Records, 1977).

A Passion for Polka: Old-Time Ethnic Music in America, by Victor Greene (University of California Press, 1992).

A Singing Ambivalence: American Immigrants Between Old World and New, 1830–1930, by Victor R. Greene (Kent State University Press, 2004).

A Sound of Strangers: Musical Culture, Acculturation of the Post-Civil War Ethnic America, by Nicholas Tawa (Scarecrow Press, 1982).

Greek

Dalgas: Andonios Dhiamandidhis, 1928–1933, CD, notes by Charles Howard (Heritage, 1997).

Greek-Oriental Rebetica: Songs and Dances in the Asia Minor Style/The Golden Years, 1911–1937, CD with notes by Prof. Martin Schwartz (Arhoolie/Folklyric compilation, 1991).

Marika Papagika: Greek Popular and Rebetic Music from New York, 1918–1979, CD with annotation by Prof. Martin Schwartz (Alma Criolla Record Company, 1994).

Mourmourika: Songs of the Greek Underworld, 1930–1955, notes by Charles Howard (Rounder, 1999).

Rembetica: Historic Urban Folk Songs from Greece, with notes by Charles Howard (Rounder compilation, 1992).

Irish

Hugh Gillespie: Classic Recordings of Irish Traditional Fiddle Music, CD, notes by Tony Engle and Tony Russell (Green Linnet, 1992).

Irish-American Dance Music and Songs: Early Recordings from the Late 1920s, notes by Bill Healy (Folklyric Records, 1977).

Leo Rowsome: The King of the Pipers, CD (Shanachie Records, 1992).

Michael Coleman, 1891–1945: Ireland's Most Influential Traditional Musician of the 20th Century, two-CD set (Gael-Linn, 1992).

Klezmer/Traditional Jewish Music

Beyond Hava Nagila: A Symphony of Hasidic Music in 3 Movements, by Velvel Pasternak (Tara Publications, 1999).

Funny, It Doesn't Sound Jewish: How Yiddish Songs and Synagogue Melodies Influenced Tin Pan Alley, Broadway, and Hollywood, by Jack Gottlieb (State University of New York/ Library of Congress, 2004).

Klezmer! Jewish Music from Old World to Our World, by Henry Sapoznik (Schirmer Trade Books, 2006 edition).

Klezmer Music: Early Yiddish Instrumental Music/The First Recordings, 1908–1927, with notes by Dr. Martin Schwartz (Arhoolie/Folklyric compilation, 1997).

Klezmer Pioneers: European and American Recordings, 1905–1952, CD, notes by Henry Sapoznik and Dick Spottswood (Rounder Records, 1993).

"Klezmerized: Simon Broughton's History of Klezmer Music," by Simon Broughton, July 1992 *Folk Roots.*

Oytsres-Treasures: Klezmer Music, 1908–1996, with notes by Rita Ottens and Joel Rubin (Wergo compilation, 1999).

"A Quick Cantor: The Early Days of Recording Jewish Music," by Paul Vernon, January–February 1994 *Folk Roots*.

Hawaiian

Hawaiian Steel Guitar Classics, 1927–1938, CD, notes by Bob Brozman (Arhoolie/Folklyric, 1993).

Kalama's Quartet: Early Hawaiian Classics: 1927–1932, CD, notes by Bob Brozman (Arhoolie/Folklyric, 1993).

Legends of the Hawaiian Steel Guitar, CD (Hana Ola, 2006).

Sol Hoopii: Master of the Hawaiian Guitar, Volume Two, CD, notes by Bob Brozman (Rounder Records, 1987).

Vintage Hawaiian Music: Steel Guitar Masters, 1928–1934, CD, notes by Bob Brozman (Rounder Records, 1989).

Latin American

Black Music of Two Worlds: African, Caribbean, Latin, and African-American Traditions, by John Storm Roberts (Schirmer Books, 1998).

The Latin Beat: The Rhythms and Roots of Latin Music from Bossa Nova to Salsa and Beyond, by Ed Morales (Da Capo Press, 2003).

Latin Jazz: *Afro-Cuban Jazz,* by Scott Yanow (Miller Freeman Books, 2000).

Latin: 100 Essential CDs/The Rough Guide, by Sue Steward (Rough Guides, 2001).

The Latin Tinge: The Impact of Latin American Music on the United States, by John Storm Roberts (Oxford University Press, 1999).

Musica! The Rhythm of Latin America: Salsa, Rumba, Merengue, and More, by Sue Steward (Chronicle Books, 1999).

Tito Puente and the Making of Latin Music, by Steven Loza (University of Illinois Press, 1999).

Mexican

Lydia Mendoza's Life in Music/La Historia de Lydia Mendoza, by Yolanda Broyles-Gonzalez (Oxford University Press, 2011).

Corridos y Tragedias de la Frontera, boxed set, annotation by Chris Strachwitz (Arhoolie, 1994).

The Mexican American Orquesta: Music, Culture, and the Dialectic of Conflict, by Manuel H. Pena (University of Texas Press, 1999).

Mexican Border Ballads and Other Lore, edited by Mody Coggin Boatwright (Texas Folklore Society, 1946).

The Mexican Revolution: La Revolucion Mexicana, A Collection of Corridos from Historic Early Recordings, boxed set, annotation by Prof. Guillermo Hernandez (Folklyric, 1994).

Musica Norteña: Mexican Migrants Creating a Nation Between Nations, by Cathy Ragland (Temple University Press, 2009).

A Texas-Mexican Cancionero: Folksongs of the Lower Border, by Americo Paredes (University of Texas Press, 1995).

Texas-Mexican Border Music, Volumes 2 and 3, album liner notes by Philip Sonnichsen (Arhoolie, 1975).

The Texas-Mexican Conjunto: History of a Working-Class Music, by Manuel H. Pena (University of Texas Press, 1985).

"With His Pistol In His Hand": A Border Ballad and Its Hero, by Americo Paredes (University of Texas Press, 1958).

Reggae/Jamaican Music

Caribbean Currents: Music from Rumba to Reggae, by Peter Manuel and Kenneth Bilby (Temple University Press, 2006 edition); covers Jamaica, Trinidad, Cuba, Puerto Rico.

Reggae Bloodlines: In Search of the Music and Culture of Jamaica, by Stephen Davis (Da Capo Press, 1992).

Reggae, Rasta, Revolution: Jamaican Music from Ska to Dub, edited by Chris Potash (Schirmer Books, 1997).

Reggae Routes: The Story of Jamaican Music, by Kevin O'Brien Chang and Wayne Chen (Temple University Press, 1998).

This Is Reggae Music: The Golden Era, 1960–1975, boxed set, annotation by Colin Escott (Trojan/Sanctuary, 2004).

Tougher Than Tough: The Story of Jamaican Music, boxed set, annotation by Steve Barrow (Mango, 1993).

Ukrainian

Pawlo Humeniuk: King of the Ukrainian Fiddlers/New York, 1925–1927, The Early Years, notes by Dick Spottswood (Arhoolie compilation, 1993).

Ukrainian Village Music: Historic Recordings, 1928–1933, notes by Dick Spottswood and Anisa Sawyckyj (Arhoolie compilation, 1994).

World Music Album Guides

MusicHound World: The Essential Album Guide, edited by Adam McGovern (Visible Ink, 2000).

World Music: 100 Essential CDs/The Rough Guide, by Simon Broughton (Rough Guides, 2000).

World Music: The Rough Guide, Vol. 2—Latin and North America, Caribbean, India, Asia and Pacific, by James McConnachie and Mark Ellingham (Rough Guides, 2000).

FOLK MUSIC

Note: See separate lists for Folk Song Collections, Folk-Rock/Americana, and American Roots Music.

Adventures of a Ballad Hunter, by John A. Lomax (MacMillan, 1947).

All This for a Song, edited by Norm Cohen (Southern Folklife Collection, University of North Carolina, 2009).

American Fiddle Tunes, liner notes by Alan Jabbour (Library of Congress, 1971).

American Troubadours: Groundbreaking Singer-Songwriters of the '60s, by Mark Brend (Backbeat Books, 2001).

Anglo-American Ballads, edited by Alan Lomax (1942).

Anglo-American Folksong Scholarship since 1898, by D. K. Wilgus (Rutgers University Press, 1959).

Anglo-American Shanties, Lyric Songs, Dance Tunes, and Spirituals, edited by Alan Lomax (Library of Congress album, 1942).

The Anthology of American Folk Music, edited by Harry Smith (Smithsonian Folkways Recordings, 1997).

Anthology of American Folk Music (book exploring the songs in the Harry Smith Anthology), edited by Josh Dunson and Ethel Raum (Oak Publications, 1973).

The Ballad Mongers: Rise of the Modern Folk Song, by Oscar Brand (Funk & Wagnalls, 1962).

"Ballad-Literature in North Carolina," by Frank C. Brown (first published citation of *Tom Dooley*), paper presented at Fifteenth Annual Session of the North Carolina Folk-Lore Society (December 1914).

Ballad of America: The History of the United States in Song and Story, by John Anthony Scott (Grosset & Dunlap, 1967).

The Beautiful Music All Around Us: Field Recordings and the American Experience, by Stephen Wade (University of Illinois Press, 2012).

Blowin' in the Wind, cover of *Broadside* #6, late May 1962.

"Bob Dylan—A New Voice Singing New Songs," by Gil Turner, *Sing Out!,* October–November 1962.

Broadside, all issues from 1962–1968.

Folk Music in America, fifteen-LP collection, compiled and annotated by Dick Spottswood (Library of Congress, 1976–1978).

Folk Music: More Than a Song, by Kristin Baggelaar and Donald Milton (Thomas Y. Crowell Co., 1976).

Folk Song America: A 20th Century Revival, annotation by Norm Cohen (Smithsonian Collection of Recordings, 1990).

"'Frankie and Johnnie': The Trial of Frankie Baker," by John R. David (*Missouri Folklore Society Journal*, Vol. 6 (1984).

Journal of American Folklore (periodical), all issues, 1888–1965; selected issues thereafter.

Making People's Music: Moe Asch and Folkways Records, by Peter D. Goldsmith (Smithsonian Institution Press, 1998).

MusicHound Folk: The Essential Album Guide, edited by Neal Walters and Brian Mansfield (Visible Ink, 1998).

"'Must Be Born Again': Resurrecting the *Anthology of American Folk Music,*" by Katherine Skinner, *Popular Music,* Vol. 25 #1 (2006).

"Never Quite Sung in This Fashion Before: Bob Dylan's 'Man of Constant Sorrow,'" by Todd Harvey, *Oral Tradition,* Vol. 22 #1 (2007).

The NPR Curious Listener's Guide to American Folk, by Kip Lornell (Grand Central/Perigee, 2004).

"The Original Man of Constant Sorrow: The Mystery of Emry Arthur," by Charles Wolfe. *Bluegrass Unlimited,* April 1992.

People's Songs (periodical), all issues, 1946–1949.

"'Poor Wayfaring Stranger': Early Publications," by John F. Garst, *The Hymn,* April 1980.

"The Price You Pay: An Introduction to the Life and Songs of Laurence Price," by Dave Harker (history of *The House Carpenter*) *Sociological Review Monograph* 34 (1992).

Railroad Man's Magazine, articles on the song "Casey Jones" in March 1908, May 1908, December 1911, and April 1912 issues.

The Rainbow Sign: A Southern Documentary, by Alan Lomax (Duell, Sloan & Pearce, 1959).

The Rose and the Briar: Death, Love, and Liberty in the American Ballad, edited by Sean Wilentz and Greil Marcus (W. W. Norton & Co., 2005).

Sing Out! (periodical), most issues, 1950 onward.

"Singing for Freedom: Music and the Integration Movement," by Robert Shelton, *Sing Out!,* December 1962–January 1963.

"Some Child Ballads on Hillbilly Records," by Judith McCullough, in *Folklore and Society: Essays in Honor of Benjamin A. Botkin* (Folklore Associates, 1966).

"'Streets of Laredo' and 'St. James Infirmary': Case History of a Folk Song," by Irwin Silber, *Sing Out!,* Fall 1957.

"'Ten Broeck and Molly': A Race and a Ballad," by D. K. Wilgus, *Kentucky Folklore,* July–September 1956.

Transforming Tradition: Folk Music Revivals Examined, edited by Neil Rosenberg (University of Illinois Press, 1993).

Treasury of Library of Congress Field Recordings, CD, annotated by Stephen Wade (Rounder Records, 1997).

When We Were Good: The Folk Revival, by Robert Cantwell (Harvard University Press, 1996).

"A Who's Who of 'The Midnight Special,'" by Mack McCormick, *Caravan: The Magazine of Folk Music* 19, January 1960.

Biographies

Joan Baez: *And a Voice to Sing With: A Memoir,* by Joan Baez (Simon & Schuster, 2009 edition).

Harry Belafonte: *My Song: A Memoir,* by Harry Belafonte with Michael Shnayerson (Alfred A. Knopf, 2011).

Judy Collins: *Sweet Judy Blue Eyes: My Life in Music,* by Judy Collins (Crown Archetype, 2011).

Trust Your Heart: An Autobiography, by Judy Collins (Houghton Mifflin Co., 1987).

Woody Guthrie: *Bound for Glory,* by Woody Guthrie (E. P. Dutton, 1976 edition of 1943 book).

Woody Guthrie: A Life, by Joe Klein (Delta, 1999 edition).

Leadbelly: *The Life and Legend of Leadbelly,* by Charles K. Wolfe and Kip Lornell (HarperCollins, 1992).

Negro Folk Songs as Sung by Lead Belly "King of the Twelve-String Guitar Players of the World" by John Lomax and Alan Lomax (MacMillan, 1936).

"Notes on the Songs of Huddie Ledbetter ('Leadbelly')," undated manuscript by John Lomax at Library of Congress.

Lightfoot: If You Could Read His Mind, by Maynard Collins (Deneau, 1988).

Alan Lomax: The Man Who Recorded the World: A Biography, by John Szwed (Viking, 2010).

Pete Seeger: *How Can I Keep from Singing? The Ballad of Pete Seeger,* by David King Dunaway (Villard Books, revised 2008 edition).

Folk Song Collections/Studies of Traditional Folk Songs

Afro-American Folk Songs, by Henry Edward Krehbiel (Frederick Ungar Pub. Co., 1975 edition of 1914 book).

All That's Kentucky: An Anthology, compiled by Josiah Henry (J. P. Morton, 1915).

American Balladry from British Broadsides: A Guide for Students and Collectors of Traditional Song, by G. Malcolm Laws, Jr. (American Folklore Society, 1957).

American Ballads and Folk Songs, by John A. Lomax and Alan Lomax (MacMillian Company, 1934).

American Folksongs of Protest, by John Greenway (Octagon Books, 1970).

American Mountain Songs, compiled by Ethel Park Richardson (Greenberg Publishers, 1927).

American Negro Folk Songs, by Newman I. White (Folklore Associates, 1965 edition of 1928 book).

American Negro Songs: A Comprehensive Collection of 230 Folk Songs, Religious and Secular, by John Wesley Work (Howell, Soskin & Co., 1940).

The American Songbag, by Carl Sandburg (Harcourt, Brace & World, 1927).

Ballads and Songs Collected by the Missouri Folk Lore Society, edited by H. M. Belden (University of Missouri, 1955 edition of 1940 book)

"Ballads and Songs of Western North Carolina," by Louise Rand Bascom (the first published citation of "John Henry"), *Journal of American Folklore* (April–June 1909).

Ballads, Carols, and Tragic Legends from the Southern Appalachian Mountains, by John Jacob Niles (Schirmer, 1937).

Calhoun Plantation Songs, collected and edited by Emily Hallowell (AMS Press, 1976 reprinting of 1907 first edition).

Cecil Sharp's Collection of English Folk Songs, edited by Maud Karpeles (Oxford University Press, 1974); two volumes covering songs collected from 1903–1923.

Chanteys and Songs of the Sea, songbook edited by Walter Goodell (Hall & McCreary, 1939).

Coffee in the Gourd, edited by J. Fred Dobie (Southern Methodist University Press, 1969 edition of 1923 book).

Eighty English Folk Songs from the Southern Appalachians, by Cecil Sharp (Faber & Faber, 1968 edition).

The English and Scottish Popular Ballads, by Francis James Child, five volumes in three books (Cooper Square Publishers, 1962 edition of 1882–1898 books); also see *Traditional Tunes of the Child Ballads*.

English County Songs, collected and edited by Lucy E. Broadwood and J. A. Fuller Maitland (Leadenhall Press, 1893).

English Folk Songs from the Southern Appalachians, by Cecil Sharp, Olive Dame Campbell, and Maud Karpeles (Oxford University Press, original 1917 edition with 122 songs; and 1952 reprinting of the two-volume 1932 edition with 274 songs).

Folk Hymns of America, collected and arranged by Annabel Brown Buchanan (J. Fisher & Bros., 1938).

The Folk Song Abecedary, by James F. Leisy (Hawthorn Books, 1966).

Folk Song of the American Negro, by John Wesley Work (Negro Universities Press, 1969 edition of 1915 book).

Folk Song USA: The 111 Best American Ballads, collected by John A. Lomax and Alan Lomax (Duell, Sloan & Pearce, 1947).

Folk-Songs from the Southern Highlands, collected and edited by Mellinger Henry (J. J. Augustin, 1938).

The Folk Songs of North America in the English Language, by Alan Lomax (Dolphin Books/Doubleday, 1975 edition of 1960 book).

Folk Songs of the Catskills, edited and annotated by Norman Cazden, Herbert Haufrecht, and Norman Studer (State University of New York Press, 1982).

Folk-Songs of the South, collected by the West Virginia Folklore Society and edited by John Harrington Cox (Folklore Associates, 1963 edition of 1925 book).

Folk Songs of the Southern United States, 1925 doctoral dissertation by Josiah H. Combs, edited by D. K. Wilgus (University of Texas Press, 1967).

The Frank C. Brown Collection of North Carolina Folklore, collected by Frank C. Brown from 1912–1943 in collaboration with the North Carolina Folklore Society, seven volumes, Henry M. Belden and Arthur Palmer Hudson, eds. (Duke University Press, 1952–1964):

Volume 2: Folk Ballads from North Carolina.
Volume 3: Folk Songs from North Carolina.
Volume 4: The Music of the Ballads.
Volume 5: The Music of the Folk Songs.

Freedom Is a Constant Struggle: The Story of the Civil Rights Movement Through its Songs, by Guy and Candie Carawan (Sing Out Corp., 1968); same book reprinted in 1990 under the title *Sing for Freedom.*

Games and Songs of American Children, by William Wells Newell (Dover Publications, 1963 edition of 1883 book as updated by the author in 1903).

Robert Winslow Gordon Manuscripts/American Folk-Song Collection (Archive of American Folklife, Library of Congress, 1921–1930).

In the Pine: Selected Kentucky Folksongs, collected by Leonard Roberts, music transcriptions by C. Buell Agey (Pikesville College Press, 1978).

Lonesome Tunes: Folk Songs from the Kentucky Mountains, Vol. 1, by Loraine Wyman and Howard Brockway (H. W. Gray Company, 1916).

Minstrelsy, Ancient and Modern, by William Motherwell (Singing Tree Press, 1968 reprint of 1827 book).

Native American Balladry: A Descriptive Study and Bibliographical Syllabus, by G. Malcolm Laws, Jr. (American Folklore Society, 1964 edition of 1950 book).

The Negro and His Songs: A Study of Typical Negro Songs in the South (by Howard W. Odum and Guy B. Johnson (University of North Carolina Press, 1964 reprint of 1925 book).

Negro Folk Rhymes, Wise and Otherwise, by Thomas W. Talley (University of Tennessee Press, originally published in 1922; second edition 1949; new 1991 edition).

Negro Workaday Songs, by Howard W. Odum and Guy B. Johnson (Negro Universities Press, 1926).

The New Lost City Ramblers Song Book, by John Cohen and Mike Seeger, musical transcriptions by Hally Wood (Oak Publications, 1964).

Notes and Sources for Folksongs of the Catskills, by Cazden, Haufrecht, and Studer (State University of New York Press, 1982).

On the Trail of Negro Folk-songs, by Dorothy Scarborough (Folklore Associates, 1963 edition of 1925 book).

Our Singing Country: A Second Volume of American Ballads and Folk Songs, by John A. Lomax (The MacMillian Company, 1941).

Ozark Folksongs, four volumes, compiled by Vance Randolph (University of Missouri Press, 1980 editions of 1946–1950 books): *Volume 1: British Ballads and Songs*; *Volume 2: Songs of the South and West*; *Volume 3: Humorous and Play-Party Songs*; and *Volume 4: Religious Songs and Other Items.*

Ozark Folksongs, one-volume, abridged, edited by Norm Cohen (University of Illinois Press, 1982).

Publications of the Texas Folklore Society, edited by J. Frank Dobie (Folklore Associates, 1926).

Singing America: Song and Chorus Book, edited by Augustus Zanzig (C. C. Brichard & Co., 1953).

Some Current Folk-songs of the Negro, by W. H. (William Henry) Thomas (Folk-lore Society of Texas, 1936 reprint of 1912 booklet).

A Song Catcher in Southern Mountains: American Folksongs of British Ancestry, by Dorothy Scarborough (Columbia University Press, 1937).

"Songs and Rhymes from the South," by E. C. Perrow (with early citations of many key folk songs including "Careless Love"), *Journal of American Folklore* (April–June 1915).

Songs of the Cattle Trail and Cow Camp, by John Lomax (Forgotten Books, 2012 reprint of 1919 book).

Songs of the West: Folk Songs of Devon and Cornwall, Collected from the Mouths of the People, by S. Baring-Gould, H. Fleetwood Sheppard, and F. W. Bussell, edited by Cecil J. Sharp (Methuen & Co., 1913 edition, originally published in 1890).

Spiritual Folk-Songs of Early America: 250 Tunes and Texts, by George Pullen Jackson (J. J. Augustin, 1937).

Steamboatin' Days: Folk Songs of the River Packet Era, by Mary Wheeler (Books for Libraries Press, 1944).

A Syllabus of Kentucky Folk Songs, by Hubert Shearin and Josiah Combs (Northwood Editions, 1977, reprinting of Transylvania Printing Co. 1911 book).

Traditional American Folk Songs from the Anne and Frank Warner Collection, edited by Anne Warner (Syracuse University Press, 1984).

Traditional Ballads of Virginia, by Arthur Kyle Davis (University Press of Virginia, 1969 edition of 1929 book).

The Traditional Tunes of the Child Ballads, with Their Texts, According to the Extant Records of Great Britain and America, four volumes, edited by Bertrand Harris Bronson (Princeton University Press, 1959–1972).

Treasure Chest of Home Spun Songs (Treasure Chest Publications, 1935).

A Treasury of Southern Folklore: Stories, Ballads, Traditions, and Folkways of the People of the South, edited by B. A. Botkin (Bonanza Books, 1980 edition).

Twenty Kentucky Mountain Songs, collected by Loraine Wyman and Howard Brockway (Oliver Ditson Co., 1920).

Victorian Songhunters: The Recovery and Editing of English Vernacular Ballads and Folk Lyrics, 1820–1883, by E. David Gregory (Scarecrow Press, 2006).

Where Have All the Flowers Gone?: A Singer's Stories, Songs, Seeds, Robberies, by Pete Seeger (Sing Out Publications, 1993).

FOLK-ROCK/AMERICANA

Are You Ready for the Country? Elvis, Dylan, and the Roots of Country-Rock, by Peter Doggett (Penguin Books, 2001).

The Best of No Depression: Writing about American Music, edited by Grant Alden and Peter Blackstock (University of Texas Press, 2005).

Dirty Linen (periodical), issues from 1988–1994.

Eight Miles High: Folk-Rock's Flight from Haight-Ashbury to Woodstock, by Richie Unterberger (Backbeat Books, 2003).

Folk Roots (British periodical), most issues from 1986–1995.

Hotel California: The True-Life Adventures of Crosby, Stills, Nash, Young, Mitchell, Taylor, Browne, Ronstadt, Geffen, the Eagles and Their Many Friends, Barney Hoskyns (John Wiley & Sons, 2006).

Laurel Canyon: The Inside Story of Rock-and-Roll's Legendary Neighborhood, by Michael Walker (Faber & Faber, 2006).

No Depression (periodical), many issues from 1995–2008.

Paste (periodical), issues from 2002–2009.

Stand and Be Counted: Making Music, Making History/The Dramatic Story of the Artists and Events That Changed America, by David Crosby and David Bender (Harper San Francisco, 2000).

Turn! Turn! Turn! The '60s Folk-Rock Revolution, by Richie Unterberger (Backbeat Books, 2002).

Biographies

The Byrds: Timeless Flight Revisited: The Sequel, by Johnny Rogan (Rogan House, 1998).

Crosby, Stills, and Nash: The Authorized Biography, by Dave Zimmer (St. Martin's Press, 1984).

Bob Dylan: *The Ballad of Bob Dylan: A Portrait,* by Daniel Mark Epstein (Harper Collins, 2011).

Behind the Shades Revisited, by Clinton Heylin (Harper Entertainment, 2001).

Down the Highway: The Life of Bob Dylan, by Howard Sounes (Grove Press, 2001).

Bob Dylan by Greil Marcus: Writings, 1968–2010 (Public Affairs, 2010).

Bob Dylan in America, by Sean Wilentz (Doubleday, 2010).

Bob Dylan: The Recording Sessions, 1960–1994, by Clinton Heylin (St. Martin's Press, 1995).

Chronicles: Volume One, by Bob Dylan (Simon & Schuster, 2004).

The Dylan Companion, edited by Elizabeth Thompson and David Gutman (Da Capo Press, 2001).

Dylan's Visions of Sin, by Christopher Ricks (Eco, 2003).

The Formative Dylan: Transmission and Stylistic Influences, 1961–1963, by Todd Harvey (Scarecrow Press, 2001).

Keys to the Rain: The Definitive Bob Dylan Encyclopedia, by Oliver Trager (Billboard Books, 2004).

Like a Rolling Stone: Bob Dylan at the Crossroads, by Greil Marcus (Public Affairs, 2005).

No Direction Home: The Life and Music of Bob Dylan, by Robert Shelton (Backbeat Books, revised 2010 edition).

A Simple Twist of Fate: Bob Dylan and the Making of "Blood on the Tracks," by Andy Gill and Kevin Odegard (Da Capo Press, 2004).

Song and Dance Man III: The Art of Bob Dylan, by Michael Gray (Continuum, 2000).

Joni Mitchell: Shadows and Light: The Definitive Biography, by Karen O'Brien (Virgin, 2001).

Simon & Garfunkel: The Biography, by Victoria Kingston (Fromm International, 1998); also see Paul Simon, Pop Music).

Richard Thompson: The Biography, by Patrick Humphries (Schirmer Trade Books, 1997).

GOSPEL/SPIRITUALS/SACRED MUSIC

Amazing Grace: The Story of America's Most Beloved Song, by Steve Turner (Ecco, 2002).

Black Gospel: An Illustrated History of the Gospel Sound, by Viv Broughton (Blandford Press, 1985).

Black Religion: The Negro and Christianity in the United States, by Joseph Washington (University Press of America, 1984).

Blues and Gospel Records, 1890–1943 (see Blues).

The Book of American Negro Spirituals, including The Second Book of Negro Spirituals, by James Weldon Johnson and J. Rosamond Johnson (Da Capo Press, 1977 reprint of books published in 1925 and 1926).

The Christian Harmony, by William Walker (Christian Harmony Publications, 1958 revised edition of the 1866 first edition).

"The Coming of 'Deep River,'" by Wayne D. Shirley, *American Music,* Vol. 15 #4 (Winter 1997).

The Complete Blind Willie Johnson, double CD with annotations by Samuel Charters (Columbia Legacy, 1993).

The Dett Collection of Negro Spirituals, edited by R. Nathaniel Dett (Hall & McCreary, 1936).

Encyclopedia of American Gospel Music, edited by W. K. McNeil (Routledge, 2005).

Folk Hymns of America, collected and arranged by Annabel Brown Buchanan (J. Fisher & Bros., 1938).

Folk Music of the United States: Negro Religious Songs and Services from the Archive of American Folk Song (Library of Congress album, 1934–1942).

Forty-Two Popular Spirituals, edited by Walter Goodell (Schmitt, Hall & McCreary, 1939).

The Good Old Songs, a choice collection of the good old hymns and tunes as they were Sung by our fathers and mothers, by Elder Claud H. Cayce (Dover Publications, 1963 edition of 1913 book).

Goodbye, Babylon, boxed set and book, edited by Dick Spottswood and Steven Lance Ledbetter (Dust to Digital, 2003).

Gospel Records 1943–1969: A Black Music Discography, two volumes, by Cedric J. Hayes and Richard Laughton (Record Information Services, 1993).

The Gospel Sound: Good News and Bad Times, by Anthony Heilbut (Limelight Editions, 1989 edition).

Happy in the Service of the Lord: African-American Sacred Vocal Harmony Quartets in Memphis, by Kip Lornell (University of Tennessee Press, 1995).

Holy Ghost Revival on Azusa Street: The True Believers: Eyewitness Accounts of the Revival That Shook the World, edited by Larry Martin (Christian Life Books, 1998).

How Sweet the Sound: The Golden Age of Gospel, by Horace Clarence Boyer (Elliott & Clark Publishing, 1995).

Jubilee Songs as Sung by the Jubilee Singers of Fisk University, no credited author (Biglow and Main, 1872).

Jubilee Songs of the United States of America, by Henry Thacker Burleigh (G. Schirmer, 1916).

Kings of the Gospel Highway: The Golden Age of the Gospel Quartets, CD with notes by Anthony Heilbut (Shanachie, 2000).

The Life and Ministry of William J. Seymour and a History of the Azusa Street Revival, by Larry Martin (Christian Life Books, 1999).

The Missouri Harmony: A Collection of Psalm and Hymn Tunes and Anthems, by Allen D. Carden (University of Nebraska Press, 1994 edition of the ninth edition from 1840).

Negro Religious Field Recordings, 1934–1942, CD (Document Records, 1994).

The New Grove: Gospel, Blues, and Jazz, by Paul Oliver, Max Harrison, and William Bolcom (W. W. Norton & Co., 1986).

People Get Ready! A New History of Black Gospel Music, by Robert Darden (Continuum Press, 2004).

Religious Folk Songs of the Negro as Sung at Hampton Institute (Hampton University Press, 1972 edition of original 1874 book, with additions from 1909 and 1927 editions; 1927 edition edited by R. Nathaniel Dett).

"Religious Folk-Songs of the Southern Negroes," by Howard W. Odom, *American Journal of Religious Psychology and Education* 3 (July 1909).

Repercussions: A Celebration of African-American Music, edited by Geoffrey Haydon and Dennis Marks (Century Publ., 1985); covers world music, gospel, etc.

The Sacred Harp, by Benjamin White and E. J. King (Broadman Press, 1968 reproduction of an 1860 imprint of the third edition from 1859).

Singing in My Soul: Black Gospel in a Secular Age, by Jerma Jackson (University of North Carolina Press, 2004).

Slave Songs of the United States: The Complete Original Collection, 136 songs compiled by William Francis Allen,

Charles Pickard Ware, and Lucy McKim Garrison (Oak Publications, 1965 reprinting of the 1867 book).

The Southern Harmony and Musical Companion, by William Walker (University Press of Kentucky, 1987 fourth printing of the 1854 edition).

Spiritual Folk-Songs of Early America: 250 Tunes and Texts, by George Pullen Jackson (J. J. Augustin, 1937).

Spreading the Word: Early Gospel Recordings, four-CD set, notes by Keith Briggs (JSP Records, 2004).

The Story of the [Fisk] Jubilee Singers, With Their Songs, by J. B. T. Marsh (Houghton, Osgood, 1971 reprinting of 1887 book).

Testify! The Gospel Box, three-CD set, annotation by Opal Louis Nations and Lin Woods (Rhino, 1999).

Twelve Folk Hymns from Old Shape Note Hymnbooks, edited by John Powell (unknown binding, 1934).

Uncloudy Days: The Gospel Music Encyclopedia, by Bil Carpenter (Backbeat Books, 2005)

Universal Songs and Hymns: A Complete Hymnal, edited by A. E. Brumley, W. O. Cooper, and R. S. Arnold (Albert E. Brumley & Sons, 1949).

We'll Understand It Better By and By: Pioneering African American Gospel Composers, edited by Bernice Johnson Reagon (Smithsonian Institution Press, 1992).

When Gospel Was Gospel, CD, multi-artist compilation, notes by Anthony Heilbut (Shanachie, 2005).

White and Negro Spirituals: Their Life Span and Kinship, by George Pullen Jackson (Da Capo Press, 1975 reprint of 1943 book).

White Spirituals in the Southern Uplands: The Story of the Fasola Folk, Their Songs, Singings, and "Buckwheat Notes," by George Pullen Jackson (Dover Publications, 1965 reprinting of original 1933 book).

Biographies

Dixie Hummingbirds: *Great God A' Mighty! The Dixie Hummingbirds: Celebrating the Rise of Soul Gospel Music,* by Jerry Zolten (Oxford University Press, 2003).

Thomas Dorsey: *The Rise of Gospel Blues: The Music of Thomas Dorsey in the Urban Church,* by Michael W. Harris (Oxford University Press, 1992).

Mahalia Jackson: *Got to Tell It: Mahalia Jackson, Queen of Gospel,* by Jules Schwerin (Oxford University Press, 1992).

Just Mahalia, Baby: The Mahalia Jackson Story, by Laurraine Goreau (Word Books, 1975).

Sister Rosetta Tharpe: *Shout, Sister, Shout! The Untold Story of Rock and Roll Trailblazer Sister Rosetta Tharpe,* by Gayle F. Wald (Beacon Press, 2007).

Clara Ward: *How I Got Over: Clara Ward and the World-Famous Ward Singers,* by Willa Ward-Royster as told to Toni Rose (Temple University Press, 1997).

"Rev. Robert Wilkins: An Interview," feature by Richard K. Spottswood, *Blues Unlimited,* July 1964.

JAZZ (AND RAGTIME)

Note: See 1700s–1940s and Tin Pan Alley.

All Music Guide to Jazz, second edition, by Valdimir Bogdanov, Chris Woodstra, Michael Erlewine, and Scott Yanow (Miller Freeman Books, 1996).

"'And the Angels Sing' Voted Best Record of 1939," *Down Beat* (January 1, 1940).

Best of the Big Bands: Claude Thornhill, CD, notes by Will Friedwald (Columbia, 1990).

Big Band Jazz: From the Beginnings to the Fifties, selected and annotated by Gunther Schuller and Martin Williams (Smithsonian Collection of Recordings, 1983).

Big Band Renaissance: The Evolution of the Jazz Orchestra, The 1940s and Beyond, boxed set with annotation by Bill Kirchner (Smithsonian Collection of Recordings, 1995).

The Big Bands, fourth edition, by George T. Simon (Schirmer, 1981).

The Biographical Encyclopedia of Jazz, by Leonard Feather and Ira Gitler (Oxford University Press, 1999).

The Birth of Bebop: A Social and Musical History, by Scott DeVeaux (University of California Press, 1997).

"Buddy Bolden's Blues," by Vic Hobson, *The Jazz Archivist: A Newsletter of the William Ransom Hogan Jazz Archive,* Vol. XXI (2008).

"'Body and Soul': Hawk Ends Year in Blaze of Glory with 64-Bar Solo," by Barrelhouse Dan *Down Beat* (January 1, 1940).

The Chronicle of Jazz, by Mervyn Cooke (Abbeville Press, 1997).

Classic Ragtime: Roots and Offshoots, CD, notes by Dick Spottswood (RCA, 1998).

"The Clave of Jazz: A Caribbean Contribution to the Rhythmic Foundation of an African-American Music," by Christopher Wasburne, *Black Music Research Journal* (Spring 1997).

Collected Works: A Journal of Jazz 1954–2001, by Whitney Balliett (St. Martin's Griffin, 2002).

Cookin': Hard Bop and Soul Jazz, 1954–65, by Kenny Mathieson (Canongate, 2002).

The Creation of Jazz: Music, Race, and Culture in Urban America, by Burton Peretti (University of Illinois Press, 1992).

Dinosaurs in the Morning: 41 Pieces on Jazz, by Whitney Balliett (Phoenix House, 1964).

Down Beat (periodical), most issues, 1934–1960; selected issues thereafter.

Down Beat: 60 Years of Jazz, edited by Frank Alkyer (Hal Leonard, 1995).

Down Beat: The Great Jazz Interviews: A 75th Anniversary Anthology, edited by Frank Alkyer (Hal Leonard, 2009).

Early Jazz: Its Roots and Musical Development, by Gunther Schuller (Oxford University Press, 1986 edition of 1968 book).

The Essential Jazz Records, Vol. 1: Ragtime to Swing, by Max Harrison, Charles Fox, and Eric Thacker (Da Capo Press, 1984).

The Essential Jazz Records, Vol. 2: Modernism to Postmodernism, by Max Harrison, Charles Fox, and Stuart Nicholson (Mansell Publishing, 2000).

The Freedom Principle: Jazz After 1958, by John Litweiler (Da Capo, 1990).

Giants of Jazz: Benny Goodman, liner notes by George T. Simon (Time-Life Records, 1979).

The Guide to Classic Recorded Jazz, by Tom Piazza (University of Iowa Press, 1995).

The Harmony Illustrated Encyclopedia of Jazz, by Brian Case and Stan Britt (Harmony Books, 1987).

Hear Me Talkin' to Ya: The Story of Jazz As Told by the Men Who Made It, by Nat Shapiro and Nat Hentoff (Dover Publications, 1966).

The History of Jazz, by Ted Gioia (Oxford University Press, 1997).

"I Went Down to St. James Infirmary," online blog essay by Robert W. Harwood (from a prospective book on the song's history).

In the Mood: "Manone Says 'In the Mood' is His Tune," *Down Beat* (January 1, 1940).

Jazz, by Gary Giddins and Scott DeVeaux (W. W. Norton & Co., 2009).

Jazz: A History of America's Music, by Geoffrey Ward and Ken Burns (Knopf, 2000).

Jazz: The American Theme Song, by James Lincoln Collier (Oxford University Press, 1993).

Jazz: Its Evolution and Essence, by Andre Hodeir (Grove Press, 1956).

Jazz: 100 Essential CDs/The Rough Guide, by Digby Fairweather and Brian Priestley (Rough Guides, 2001).

Jazz: The Smithsonian Anthology, produced by James Burgess (Smithsonian Folkways Recordings, 2010).

Jazz: The Story of America's Music, five-CD set edited by Ken Burns (Columbia, 2000)

Jazz and Ragtime Records (1897–1942) by Brian Rust, edited by Malcolm Shaw (Mainspring Press, 2002); revised two-volume version of original Rust jazz discography.

The Jazz Book: From Ragtime to the 21st Century, seventh edition, by Joachim-Ernst Berendt and Gunther Huesmann (Lawrence Hill Books, 2009).

A Jazz Lexicon, by Robert S. Gold (Aldred A. Knopf, 1964).

Jazz Masters of the '20s, by Richard Hadlock (Da Capo Press, 1988 edition of 1965 book).

Jazz Masters of the '30s, by Rex Stewart (Da Capo Press, 1982 edition).

Jazz Masters of the '40s, by Ira Gitler (Da Capo Press; 1984 edition of 1966 book).

Jazz Masters of the '50s, by Joe Goldberg (Da Capo Press, 1965).

Jazzmen: The Story of Hot Jazz Told in the Lives of the Men Who Created It, edited by Frederic Ramsey, Jr. and Charles Edward Smith (Limelight Editions, 1985 edition of 1939 book).

Jazz on the River, by William Howland Kenney (University of Chicago Press, 2005).

Jazz 101: A Complete Guide to Learning and Loving Jazz, by John F. Szwed (Hyperion, 2000).

Jazz Piano: A Smithsonian Collection, annotation by Dick Katz and Martin Williams (Smithsonian, 1989).

Jazz Records, 1897–1942, two volumes, compiled by Brian Rust (Storyville Publications, 1975 edition).

The Jazz Revolution: Twenties America and the Meaning of Jazz, by Kathy J. Ogren (Oxford University Press, 1989).

The Jazz Standards: A Guide to the Repertoire, by Ted Gioia (Oxford University Press, 2012).

The Jazz Tradition, second edition, by Martin Williams (Oxford University Press, 1993).

Let Freedom Swing: Collected Writings on Jazz, Blues, and Gospel, by Howard Reich (Northwestern University Press, 2010).

Listen to the Stories: Nat Hentoff on Jazz and Country Music, by Nat Hentoff (Harper Collins, 1995).

Living With Jazz: A Reader, by Dan Morgenstern (Pantheon Books, 2004).

Living With Music: Ralph Ellison's Jazz Writings, edited by Robert G. O'Meally (The Modern Library, 2001).

Lost Chords: White Musicians and Their Contribution to Jazz, 1915–1945, by Richard Sudhalter (Oxford University Press, 1999).

Metronome, most issues, 1930–1957.

A New History of Jazz: Revised and Updated Edition, by Alyn Shipton (Continuum, 2007).

New Hot Discography: The Standard Directory of Recorded Jazz, by Charles Delaunay (Criterion, 1948).

"New Orleans Jazz and the Blues," by Vic Hobson, *Jazz Perspectives* 5 (2009).

"The Nineteenth-Century Origins of Jazz," by Lawrence Gushee, *Black Music Research Journal* (Spring 1994).

The 101 Best Jazz Albums: A History of Jazz on Records, by Len Lyons (William Morrow & Co., 1980).

The Penguin Guide to Jazz on CD, by Richard Cook and Brian Morton, fourth edition (Penguin Books, 1998).

"Post-War Jazz: An Abitrary Road Map," by Gary Giddins, *Village Voice* (June 5–11, 2002).

RCA Victor Jazz: The First Half-Century: The Twenties Through The Sixties, five CDs, notes by Dan Morgenstern (RCA, 1992).

The Record Changer (jazz periodical), issues from 1943–1947.

Riding on a Blue Note: Jazz and American Pop, by Gary Giddins (Da Capo Press, 2000 edition).

Roger Wolfe Kahn: Recorded in New York, 1925–1932, CD, notes by Ross Wilby (Jazz Oracle, 2000).

The Rolling Stone Jazz and Blues Album Guide, edited by John Swenson (Random House, 1999).

Satchmo Blows Up the World: Jazz Ambassadors Play the Cold War, by Penny Von Eschen (Harvard University Press, 2004).

"Shadow Play: The Spiritual in Duke Ellington's 'Black and Tan Fantasy,'" by David Metzer, *Black Music Research Journal* (Autumn 1997).

Shining Trumpets: A History of Jazz, by Rudi Blesh (Alfred A. Knopf, 1949).

"'Sing, Sing, Sing' Voted Best Recording of 1938," *Down Beat* (January 1939).

Singers and Soloists of the Swing Bands, boxed set with annotation by Mark Tucker (Smithsonian Collection of Recordings, 1987).

The Smithsonian Collection of Classic Jazz, selected and annotated by Martin Williams (W. W. Norton & Co., original 1973 and 1987 revised editions).

The Story of Jazz, by Marshall Stearns (Oxford University Press, 1972 edition of 1957 book).

Storyville (British periodical), issues from 1965–1971.

Strange Fruit: The Biography of a Song, by David Margolick (Ecco Press, 2001).

Swing Changes: Big Band Jazz in New Deal America, by David W. Stowe (Harvard University Press, 1994).

The Swing Era: The Development of Jazz, 1930–1945, by Gunther Schuller (Oxford University Press, 1989).

Swing It!: An Annotated History of Jive, by Bill Milkowski (Billboard Books, 2001).

Swing to Bop: An Oral History of the Transition in Jazz in the 1940s, by Ira Gitler (Oxford University Press, 1985).

Swingin' the Dream: Big Band Jazz and the Rebirth of American Culture, by Lewis Erenberg (University of Chicago Press, 1998).

Visions of Jazz: The First Century, by Gary Giddins (Oxford University Press, 1998).

We Called It Music: A Generation of Jazz, by Eddie Condon with Thomas Sugrue (Da Capo Press, 1992 edition of 1947 book).

The World of Swing: An Oral History of Big Band Jazz, by Stanley Dance (Da Capo Press, published 1974, 2001 edition).

Biographies/Artist Discographies

Louis Armstrong: All of Me: The Complete Discography by Jos Willems (Scarecrow Press, 2006).

The Complete Hot Five and Hot Seven Recordings, boxed set, annotation by Phil Schaap (Sony, 2000).

Louis Armstrong: An Extravagant Life, by Laurence Bergreen (Broadway Books, 1997).

Louis: The Louis Armstrong Story, by Max Jones and John Chilton (Little, Brown & Co., 1971).

Louis Armstrong and Paul Whiteman: Two Kings of Jazz, by Joshua Berrett (Yale University Press, 2004).

Louis Armstrong: Portrait of the Artist as a Young Man, 1923–1934, four CDs, annotation by Dan Morgenstern and Loren Schoenberg (Sony, 1994).

Louis Armstrong, In His Own Words, edited by Thomas Brothers (Oxford University Press, 1999).

Louis Armstrong's Hot Five and Hot Seven Recordings, by Brian Harker (Oxford University Press, 2011).

Louis Armstrong's New Orleans, by Thomas Brothers (W. W. Norton, 2006).

Pops: A Life of Louis Armstrong, by Terry Teachout (Houghton Mifflin Harcourt, 2009).

Satchmo: The Genius of Louis Armstrong, by Gary Giddins (Da Capo Press, 1988).

Satchmo: My Life in New Orleans, by Louis Armstrong (Da Capo Press, 1986 edition of 1954 book).

Satchmo: The Wonderful World and Art of Louis Armstrong, by Steven Brower (Abrams, 2009).

Count Basie: A Bio-Discography, by Chris Sheridan (Greenwood Press, 1986).

Count Basie: Good Morning Blues: The Autobiography, by Count Basie as told to Albert Murray (Primus, 1985).

The World of Count Basie, by Stanley Dance (C. Scribner's Sons, 1980).

Sidney Bechet: *Treat It Gentle: An Autobiography,* by Sidney Bechet (Da Capo, 1978 reprint of 1960 first edition).

Bix Beiderbecke: *Bix: Man and Legend: The Life of Bix Beiderbecke,* by Richard Sudhalter and Philip R. Evans, with William Dean-Myatt (Arlington House, 1974).

Bunny Berigan: *Mr. Trumpet: The Trials, Tribulations, and Triumph of Bunny Berigan,* by Michael P. Zirpolo (Scarecrow Press, 2011).

Buddy Bolden: *In Search of Buddy Bolden, First Man of Jazz,* by Donald M. Marquis (Louisiana State University Press, 1978).

Cab Calloway: *Hi-De-Ho: The Life of Cab Calloway,* by Alyn Shipton (Oxford University Press, 2010).

John Coltrane: His Life and Music, by Lewis Porter (University of Michigan Press, 1998).

Coltrane: The Story of a Sound, by Ben Ratliff (Picador, 2007).

Miles Davis: *The Blue Moment: Miles Davis's Kind of Blue and the Remaking of Modern Music,* by Richard Williams (W. W. Norton & Co., 2009).

Kind of Blue: The Making of the Miles Davis Masterpiece, by Ashley Kahn (Da Capo Press, 2000).

Miles: The Autobiography, by Miles Davis with Quincy Troupe (Simon & Schuster, 1989).

Milestones: The Music and Times of Miles Davis, by Jack Chambers (Da Capo Press, 1998).

Tommy Dorsey: Livin' In a Great Big Way, A Biography, by Peter Levinson (Da Capo Press, 2005).

Duke Ellington: *Beyond Category: The Life and Genius of Duke Ellington,* by John Edward Haase (Omnibus Press, 1993).

Duke Ellington, by G. E. Lambert (Cassell, 1959).

Duke Ellington, by Barry Ulanov (Da Capo Press, 1975 edition of 1946 book).

Duke Ellington and His World, by A. H. Lawrence (Routledge, 2001).

Duke Ellington: A Listener's Guide, by Eddie Lambert (Scarecrow Press, 1999).

The Duke Ellington Reader, edited by Mark Tucker (Oxford University Press, 1993).

Duke Ellington's America, by Harvey G. Cohen (University of Chicago Press, 2010).

"Duke Ellington's 'Black, Brown and Beige,'" (entire issue), edited by Mark Tucker, *Black Music Research Journal* (Autumn 1993).

Duke Ellington: *Music Is My Mistress,* by Edward Kennedy Ellington (Doubleday & Company, 1973).

James Reese Europe: *A Life in Ragtime: A Biography of James Reese Europe,* by Reid Badger (Oxford University Press, 1995).

Ella Fitzgerald—see Tin Pan Alley.

Pops Foster: *The Autobiography of Pops Foster, New Orleans Jazzman*, as told to Tom Stoddard (Backbeat Books, 2005 edition of 1971 book).

Dizzy Gillespie: *Dizzy: To Be or Not to Bop: The Autobiography of Dizzy Gillespie*, by Dizzy Gillespie with Al Fraser (Quartet Books, 1982).

Groovin' High: The Life of Dizzy Gillespie, by Alyn Shipton (Oxford University Press, 1999).

Benny Goodman and the Swing Era, by James Lincoln Collier (Oxford University Press, 1989).

Benny Goodman: Listen to His Legacy, by D. Russell Connor (Scarecrow Press and Institute for Jazz Studies, 1988).

Benny Goodman's Famous 1938 Carnegie Hall Jazz Concert, by Catherine Tackley (Oxford University Press, 2012).

BG on the Record: A Bio-Discography of Benny Goodman, by Russell Connor and Warren W. Hicks (Arlington House, 1973 edition of 1969 book).

Swing, Swing, Swing: The Life and Times of Benny Goodman, by Ross Firestone (W. W. Norton & Co., 1993).

John Hammond on Record: An Autobiography, by John Hammond with Irving Townsend (Ridge Press, 1977).

Lionel Hampton: *Hamp: An Autobiography*, by Lionel Hampton with James Haskins (Warner Books, 1989).

Coleman Hawkins: *Song of the Hawk: The Life and Recordings of Coleman Hawkins*, by John Chilton (University of Michigan Press, 1990).

Fletcher Henderson: *The Uncrowned King of Swing: Fletcher Henderson and Big Band Jazz*, by Jeffrey Magee (Oxford University Press, 2005).

Woody Herman: *Leader of the Band: The Life of Woody Herman*, by Gene Lees (Oxford University Press, 1995).

Milt Hinton: *Playing the Changes: Milt Hinton's Life in Stories and Photographs*, by Milt Hinton, David G. Berger, and Holly Maxson (Vanderbilt University Press, 2008).

Billie Holiday: *Billie's Blues: The Billie Holiday Story, 1933–1959*, by John Chilton (Da Capo Press, 1975).

Billie Holiday: Wishing On the Moon, by Donald Clarke (Viking, 1994).

Harry James: *Trumpet Blues: The Life of Harry James*, by Peter Levinson (Oxford University Press, 1999).

Jimmie Lunceford: *Rhythm Is Our Business: Jimmie Lunceford and the Harlem Express*, by Eddy Determeyer (University of Michigan Press, 2006).

Wynton Marsalis: Skain's Domain: A Biography, by Leslie Gourse (Schirmer Trade Books, 1999).

Glenn Miller and His Orchestra, by George T. Simon (Da Capo Press, 1974).

Moonlight Serenade: A Bio-Discography of the Glenn Miller Civilian Band, by John Flower (Arlington House, 1972).

Thelonious Monk: The Life and Times of an American Original, by Robin D. G. Kelley (Free Press, 2009).

Monk, by Laurent de Wilde (Marlowe, 1997).

Jelly Roll Morton: *Jelly's Blues: The Life, Music, and Redemption of Jelly Roll Morton*, by Howard Reich and William Gaines (Da Capo Press, 2003).

Mister Jelly Roll: The Fortunes of Jelly Roll Morton, New Orleans Creole and "Inventor of Jazz," by Alan Lomax (University of California Press, 1973 edition of 1950 book).

King Joe Oliver, by Walter C. Allen and Brian A. L. Rust (Sidgwick & Jackson Ltd., 1958).

Original Dixieland Jazz Band: *The Story of the Original Dixieland Jazz Band*, by Harry O. Brunn (Louisiana State University Press, 1960).

Charlie Parker: His Music and Life, by Carl Woideck ((University of Michigan Press, 1998).

Les Paul: In His Own Words, by Les Paul and Michael Cochran (Gemstone Publishing, 2008).

Django Reinhardt, by Charles Delaunay (Da Capo Press, 1982 edition of 1961 book).

Artie Shaw: His Life and Music, by John White (Continuum, 2004).

Artie Shaw, King of the Clarinet: His Life and Times, by Tom Nolan (W. W. Norton & Co., 2010).

The Trouble with Cinderella: An Outline of Identity, by Artie Shaw (Da Capo Press, 1952).

Nina Simone: The Biography, by David Brun-Lambert (Aurum Press, 2009).

Billy Strayhorn: *Lush Life: A Biography of Billy Strayhorn*, by David Hajdu (North Point Press, 1996).

Ain't Misbehavin': The Story of Fats Waller, by W. T. Ed Kirkeby with Duncan Schiedt and Sinclair Traill (Peter Davies, 1966).

Fats Waller: The Cheerful Little Earful, by Alyn Shipton (Continuum, 2002 edition of 1988 book).

MOVIE MUSIC

Celluloid Symphonies: Texts and Contexts in Film Music History, edited by Julie Hubbert (University of California Press, 2011).

The Film Encyclopedia, by Ephraim Katz (Harper Perennial, 1994 edition).

"Have You Seen . . . ?" A Personal Introduction to 1,000 Films, by David Thomson (Alfred A. Knopf, 2008).

A History of Film Music, by Mervyn Cooke (Cambridge University Press, 2008).

The Hollywood Film Music Reader, edited by Mervyn Cooke (Oxford University Press, 2010).

Knowing the Score: Film Composers Talk about the Art, Craft, Blood, Sweat and Tears of Writing Music for Cinema, by David Morgan (Harper Entertainment, 2000).

Movie Music, the Film Reader, edited by Kay Dickinson (Routledge, 2003).

Music for the Movies, by Tony Thomas (Silman-James Press, 1997).

POP MUSIC, 1955 ONWARD

Note: See Rock, Folk-Rock/Americana, Recording Industry, Rhythm & Blues

Always Magic in the Air: The Bomp and Brilliance of the Brill Building Era, by Ken Emerson (Viking, 2005).

Behind the Muse: Pop and Rock's Greatest Songwriters Talk about Their Work and Inspiration, by Bill DeMain (Tiny Ripple Books, 2001).

Billboard (weekly periodical), hundreds of issues each decade, 1950s–2000s.

The Billboard Book of American Singing Groups: A History, 1940–1960, by Jay Warner (Billboard Books, 1992).

The Brill Building Sound: Singers and Songwriters Who Rocked the '60s, four CDs, notes by Greg Shaw and Dawn Eden (Era Records, 1993).

Fire and Rain: The Beatles, Simon and Garfunkel, James Taylor, CSNY, and the Lost Story of 1970, by David Browne (Da Capo Press, 2011).

Girl Groups: Fabulous Females That Rocked the World, by John Clemente (Krause Publications, 2000).

Girl Groups: The Story of a Sound, by Alan Betrock (Delilah Books, 1982).

Girls Like Us: Carole King, Joni Mitchell, Carly Simon, and the Journey of a Generation, by Sheila Weller (Washington Square Press, 2008).

Goldmine (periodical), many issues from 1977 through 1990s; selected later issues.

Hitmaker: The Man and His Music, by Tommy Mottola with Cal Fussman (Grand Central Publishing, 2013).

I'll Take You There: Pop Music and the Urge for Transcendence, by Bill Friskics-Warren (Continuum, 2005).

Inside the Hits: The Seduction of a Rock and Roll Generation, by Wayne Wadhams (Berklee Press, 2001).

Listen Again: A Momentary History of Pop Music, edited by Eric Weisbard (Duke University Press, 2007).

Memphis Boys: The Story of American Studios, by Roben Jones (University Press of Mississippi, 2010).

Off the Record: Songwriters on Songwriting: 25 of the World's Most Celebrated Songs, by Graham Nash (Andrews McMeel Pub., 2002).

Playing from the Heart: Great Musicians Talk About Their Craft, edited by Robert L. Doerschuk (Backbeat Books, 2002).

The Poetry of Rock, edited by Richard Goldstein (Bantam Books, 1969).

Record Makers and Breakers: Voices of the Independent Rock 'n' Roll Pioneers, by John Broven (University of Illinois Press, 2010).

Rock 'n Roll Gold Rush: A Singles Uncyclopedia, by Maury Dean (Algora Publishing, 2003).

Singer-Songwriters: Pop Music's Performer-Composers, from A to ZEvon, by Dave DiMartino (Billboard Books, 1994).

Songbook, by Nick Hornby (Riverhead Books, 2003).

Songs in the Rough: From Heartbreak Hotel to Higher Love, Rock's Greatest Songs in Rough Draft Form, by Stephen Bishop (St. Martin's Press, 1996).

Songwriter Magazine, issues from 1975–1980.

The Twist: The Story of the Song and Dance That Changed the World, by Jim Dawson (Faber & Faber, 1995).

Where the Girls Are: Growing Up Female with the Mass Media, by Susan J. Douglas (Times Books/Random House, 1995).

RECORDING INDUSTRY, GENERAL HISTORIES

Note: See Record Label Histories.

America on Record: A History of Recorded Sound, by Andre Millard (Cambridge University Press, 1995).

American Popular Music Business in the 20th Century, by Russell Sanjek and David Sanjek (Oxford University Press, 1991).

Echo and Reverb: Fabricating Space in Popular Music Recording, 1900–1960, by Peter Doyle (Wesleyan University Press, 2005).

The Encyclopedia of Record Producers, by Eric Olsen, Paul Verna, and Carlo Wolff (Billboard Books, 1999).

The Encyclopedia of Recorded Sound, two volumes, second edition, edited by Frank Hoffman (Routledge, 2005; 1993 first edition edited by Guy A. Marco).

From Tinfoil to Stereo: The Acoustic Years of the Recording Industry, 1877–1929, by Walter L. Welch and Leah Broderick Stenzel Burt (University Press of Florida, 1994 edition).

An International History of the Recording Industry, by Pekka Gronow and Ilpo Saunio (Cassell, 1998).

Million Selling Records from the 1900s to the 1980s, by Joseph Murrells (Arco Publishing, 1984).

The Music Goes Round, by F. W. Gaisberg (The MacMillan Company, 1942); on the recording industry from 1890s onward.

The Patent History of the Phonograph, 1877–1912, by Allen Kroenigsberg (APM Press, 1990).

The Recording Industry: An Ethnomusicological Approach, by Pekka Gronow (University of Tampere, 1996).

Recording the 'Twenties: The Evolution of the American Recording Industry, 1920–29, by Allan Sutton (Mainspring Press, 2008).

Biographies/Musical Histories

Christina Aguilera: A Biography, by Mary Anne Donovan (Greenwood, 2010).

Burt Bacharach: *Song by Song: The Ultimate Burt Bacharach Reference,* by Serene Dominic (Schirmer Trade Books, 2003).

Beach Boys: *Brian Wilson and the Beach Boys: The Complete Guide to Their Music,* by Andrew G. Doe and John Tobler (Omnibus Press, 2004).

Good Vibrations: Thirty Years of the Beach Boys, boxed set, annotation by Mark Linett, David Leaf, and Andy Paley (Capitol Records, 1993).

Surf's Up! The Beach Boys on Record, 1961–1981, by Brad Elliott (Pierian Press, 1982).

Wouldn't It Be Nice: Brian Wilson and the Making of the Beach Boys' Pet Sounds, by Charles L. Grenata (Chicago Review Press, 2003).

The Beatles: The Authorized Biography, by Hunter Davies (McGraw-Hill, 1968).

Rolling Stone: The Beatles 100 Greatest Songs, special edition (Rolling Stone Magazine, 2010).

Beatlesongs, by William J. Dowlding (Fireside, 1989).

Can't Buy Me Love: The Beatles, Britain, and America, by Jonathan Gould (Harmony Books, 2007).

A Day in the Life: The Music and Artistry of The Beatles, by Mark Hertsgaard (Delacorte Press, 1995).

Revolution in the Head: The Beatles' Records and the Sixties, third edition, by Ian MacDonald (Chicago Review Press, 2007).

Shout! The Beatles in Their Generation, by Philip Norman (Fireside/Simon & Schuster, 1981).

Tell Me Why: The Beatles: Album by Album, Song by Song, by Tim Riley (Knopf/Random House, 1988).

The Ultimate Beatles Encyclopedia, by Bill Harry (Hyperion, 1992); also see John Lennon, George Martin, Paul McCartney).

Bee Gees: The Authorized Biography, by Barry, Robin, and Maurice Gibb as told to David Leaf (Dell Pub., 1979).

Hal Blaine and the Wrecking Crew: The Story of the World's Most Recorded Musician, by Hal Blaine with Mr. Bonzai (Rebeats Publications, 2003).

Eva Cassidy, Songbird, by Rob Burley and Jonathan Maitland (Orion, 2001).

Harry Chapin: *Taxi: The Harry Chapin Story*, by Peter M. Coan (Lyle Stuart Book/Carol Publishing Group, 1987/1990).

Leonard Cohen: *I'm Your Man: The Life of Leonard Cohen*, by Sylvie Simmons (Ecco, 2012).

Clive Davis: *The Soundtrack of My Life*, by Clive Davis with Anthony DeCurtis (Simon & Schuster, 2013).

Neil Diamond: *Diamond, A Biography*, by Alan Grossman, Bill Truman, and Roy Oki Yamanaka (Contemporary Books, 1987).

Dion: *The Wanderer: Dion's Story*, by Dion DiMucci with Davin Seay (Beech Tree Books, 1988).

Everly Brothers: "Teenage Idyll: An Everly Brother Looks Back," by Colin Escott , *Journal of Country Music*, Vol. 15 #2 (1993).

Four Seasons: *Jersey Boys: The Story of Frankie Valli and the Four Seasons*, by David Cote (Broadway Books, 2006).

Whitney Houston: *Diva: The Totally Unauthorized Biography of Whitney Houston*, by Jeffery Bowman (Harper, 1995).

Janis Ian: *Society's Child: My Autobiography*, by Janis Ian (Jeremy Tarcher/Penguin, 2008).

Michael Jackson: The Magic, the Madness, the Whole Story, by J. Randy Taraborrelli (Grand Central Publishing, 2010 edition).

Michael Jackson: Moonwalk, by Michael Jackson (Harmony Books, 2009 edition of 1988 book).

Thriller: The Musical Life of Michael Jackson, by Nelson George (Da Capo Press, 2010).

Trapped: Michael Jackson and the Crossover Dream, by Dave Marsh (Bantam Books, 1985).

Tommy James: *Me, the Mob, and the Music*, by Tommy James with Martin Fitzpatrick (Scribner, 2010).

Billy Joel: The Life and Times of an Angry Young Man, by Hank Bordowitz (Billboard Books, 2006).

Elton John: The Definitive Biography, by Philip Norman (Simon & Schuster, 1993).

Carole King: *A Natural Woman: A Memoir*, by Carole King (Grand Central Publishing, 2012).

The Words and Music of Carole King, by James E. Perone (Praeger Publishers, 2006).

Hound Dog: The Leiber and Stoller Autobiography, by Jerry Leiber and Mike Stoller with David Ritz (Simon and Schuster, 2009).

John Lennon: The Life, by Philip Norman (Ecco/HarperCollins, 2008).

Lennon: The Definitive Biography, by Ray Coleman (Harper Perennial, 1992).

Madonna: An Intimate Biography, by J. Randy Taraborrelli (Berkley Books, 2002 edition).

Madonna: Like an Icon, by Lucy O'Brien (Harper Entertainment, 2007).

Mamas and Papas: *California Dreamin': The True Story of the Mamas and the Papas*, by Michelle Phillips (Warner Books, 1986).

George Martin: All You Need Is Ears, by George Martin with Jeremy Hornsby (St. Martin's Press, 1994 edition).

Paul McCartney: *Fab: An Intimate Life of Paul McCartney*, by Howard Sounes (Da Capo Press, 2010).

Paul McCartney: Many Years from Now, by Barry Miles (H. Holt, 1997).

Bette Midler: *Bette: An Intimate Biography of Bette Midler*, by George Mair (Carol Pub. Group, 1995).

Laura Nyro: *Soul Picnic: The Music and Passion of Laura Nyro*, by Michele Kort (Thomas Dunne Books, 2002).

Roy Orbison: *Dark Star: The Roy Orbison Story*, by Ellis Amburn (Carol Pub. Group, 1990).

Paul Simon: A Life, by Marc Eliot (John Wiley & Sons, 2010).

Paul Simon: Still Crazy After All These Years, by Patrick Humphries (Doubleday, 1989).

Phil Spector: *Wall of Pain: The Biography of Phil Spector*, by Dave Thompson (Sanctuary, 2003).

Ronnie Spector: *Be My Baby: How I Survived Mascara, Miniskirts, and Madness, or My Life as a Fabulous Ronette*, by Ronnie Spector with Vince Waldron (Harmony Books, 1990).

James Taylor: Long Ago and Far Away: His Life and Music, by Timothy White (Omnibus Press, 2002).

Dionne Warwick: My Life, as I See It: An Autobiography, by Dionne Warwick with David Freeman Wooley (Atria Books, 2010).

RECORD LABEL HISTORIES/ DISCOGRAPHIES

The American Record Label Book, by Brian Rust (Arlington House Publishers, 1978).

American Record Labels and Companies: An Encyclopedia (1891–1943), by Allan Sutton (Mainspring Press, 2000).

Atlantic: *Making Tracks: Atlantic Records and the Growth of a Multi-Billion-Dollar Industry*, by Charlie Gillett (E. P. Dutton & Co., 1974).

Capitol Records Fiftieth Anniversary, 1942–1992, by Paul Grein (Capitol, 1992).

Chess: *Spinning Blues into Gold: The Chess Brothers and the Legendary Chess Records,* by Nadine Cohodas (St. Martin's Griffin, 2000).

Columbia: *The Label: The Story of Columbia Records,* by Gary Marmorstein (Thunder's Mouth Press, 2007).

The Columbia Master Book Discography, Vol. 1, by Tim Brooks (Greenwood Press, 1999).

The Columbia Records (U.S.) 35000–40000 Series: Popular Singles Discography, 1939–1974, compiled by William Brown (William Brown Productions, 1996).

The Columbia 13/14000-D Series: A Numerical Listing (Record Handbook No. 1), by Dan Mahony (Walter C. Allen, 1966).

Sony Music 100 Years: Soundtrack for a Century, twenty-six CDs covering Columbia Records history from 1890–1999 with accompanying book by Phil Schaap, Arthur Levy, Billy Altman, Didier Deutsch, Mitchell Cohen, Bruce Dickinson, Virginia Prescott, and Al Quaglieri; Sony Music, 1999).

360 Sound: The Columbia Records Story, by Sean Wilentz (Chronicle Books, 2012).

The Decca Labels: A Discography, six volumes, compiled by Michael Ruppli (Greenwood Press, 1996): *Vol. 1: California Sessions, 1934–73*; *Vol. 2: Eastern and Southern Sessions, 1934–42*; *Vol. 3: Eastern Sessions, 1943–56*; *Vol. 4: Eastern Sessions, 1956–73*; *Vol. 5: Country Recordings, Classical Recordings, and Reissues*; and *Vol. 6: Numerical listings and artist index.*

Duke/Peacock Records: An Illustrated History with Discography, by Galen Gart and Roy C. Ames (Big Nickel Productions, 1990).

Edison Blue Amberol Recordings, 1912–1914, by Ronald Dethlefson (APM Press, 1980).

Edison Blue Amberol Recordings, Vol. 2, 1915–1929, by Ronald Dethlefson (APM Press, 1981).

Edison Cylinder Records, 1889–1912, with an Illustrated History of the Phonograph, by Allen Koenigsberg (Stellar Productions, 1969).

Edison Disc Artists and Records, 1910–1929, compiled by Raymond R. Wile (APM Press, 1990).

Edison, Musicians, and the Phonograph: A Century in Retrospect, edited by John Harvith and Susan Edwards Harvith (Greenwood Press, 1987).

Elektra: *Follow the Music: The Life and High Times of Elektra Records in the Great Years of American Pop Culture,* by Jac Holzman and Gavan Daws (First Media Books, 1998).

EMI: *The First 100 Years/Since Records Began,* by Peter Martland (Amadeus Press, 1997).

Gennett: *Jelly Roll, Bix, and Hoagy: Gennett Studios and the Birth of Recorded Jazz,* by Rick Kennedy (Indiana University Press, 1999).

The King Labels: A Discography, two volumes, compiled by Michel Ruppli with Bill Daniels (Greenwood Press, 1985).

Little Labels—Big Sound: Small Record Companies and the Rise of American Music, by Rick Kennedy and Randy McNutt (Indiana University Press, 1999); Gennett, Paramount,

Dial, King, Duke-Peacock, Sun, Riverside, Ace, Monument, and Delmark.

Motown: *Standing in the Shadows of Motown: The Life and Music of Legendary Bassist James Jamerson,* by "Dr. Licks" (Dr. Licks Publishing, 1989).

To Be Loved: The Music, the Magic, the Memories of Motown, An Autobiography, by Berry Gordy, Jr. (Warner Books, 1994); also see Rhythm & Blues.

Paramount's Rise and Fall: A History of the Wisconsin Chair Co. and Its Recording Activities, by Alex Van der Tuuk (Mainspring Press, 2003).

Stax: *Soulsville U.S.A.: The Story of Stax Records,* by Rob Bowman (Schirmer Trade Books, 1997).

Sun: *Good Rockin' Tonight: Sun Records and the Birth of Rock 'n' Roll,* by Colin Escott with Martin Hawkins (St. Martin's Press, 1992).

Victor: *The Encyclopedic Discography of Victor Recordings: Pre-Matrix Series (1900–1903),* by Ted Fagan and William R. Moran (Greenwood Press, 1983).

The Encyclopedic Discography of Victor Recordings, Matrix Series (April 1903 to January 1908), by Ted Fagan and William R. Moran (Greenwood Press, 1986).

RECORD LABEL CATALOGS/ RECORD LISTINGS

Columbia: Oct. 1, 1890 record listing (one page, only U.S. Marine Band selections), Jan. 26, 1892 catalog (17 pages).

The Columbia Record (Columbia's in-house publication), all monthly issues, 1904–1907; Columbia monthly supplements, 1911–1914.

New Jersey Records: Oct. 7, 1892 catalog.

North American: June 18, 1890 record listing (no artists credited), Dec. 1, 1893 catalog.

Ohio Phonograph Co.: 1890s record listing (undated).

Paramount monthly record supplements, 1929–1930.

Victor monthly supplements, 1911 through 1935.

RHYTHM & BLUES

The Billboard Book of Number One Rhythm & Blues Hits, by Adam White and Fred Bronson (Billboard Books, 1993).

Bim Bam Boom ("The Magazine Devoted to the History of Rhythm and Blues"), issues from 1971–1972.

Eminem: *Cleaning Out My Closet: The Stories Behind Every Song,* by David Stubbs (Thunder's Mouth Press, 2003).

Lauryn Hill: *Heart of Soul: The Lauryn Hill Story,* by Elina and Leah Furman (Ballantine Books, 1999).

Kanye West: A Biography, by Bob Schaller (Greenwood Press, 2009).

Can't Stop Won't Stop: A History of the Hip-Hop Generation, by Jeff Chang (Picador/St. Martin's, 2005).

Hip Hop America, by Nelson George (Penguin Books, 2007).

"'Most of My Heroes Don't Appear on No Stamps': The Dialogues of Rap Music," by Elizabeth Wheeler, *Black Music Research Journal* (Autumn 1991).

The Source (periodical), issues from 1999–2006.

Vibe (periodical), issues from 1993–2004.

The Vibe History of Hip Hop, edited by Alan Light (Three Rivers Press, 1999).

"The Black Authentic: Structure, Style and Values in Group Harmony," by Stuart Goosman, *Black Music Research Journal* (Spring 1997).

Blue Rhythms: Six Lives in Rhythm and Blues, by Chip Deffaa (University of Illinois Press, 1996).

Blues and Rhythm (British periodical), first twenty issues, 1984–1986.

"Central Avenue Blues: The Making of Los Angeles Rhythm & Blues, 1942–1947," by Ralph Eastman, *Black Music Research Journal* (Spring 1989).

A Change Is Gonna Come: Music, Race, and the Soul of America, by Craig Werner (Plume, 1999).

The Chitlin' Circuit and the Road to Rock 'n' Roll, by Preston Lauterbach (W. W. Norton & Company, 2011).

Dancing in the Street: Motown and the Cultural Politics of Detroit, by Suzanne E. Smith (Harvard University Press, 1999).

The Death of Rhythm and Blues, by Nelson George (Penguin Books, 1988).

The Fire/Fury Records Story, two CDs, notes by Diana Reid Haig and John Morthland (Capricorn, 1993).

First Pressings: The History of Rhythm & Blues, 1950, compiled by Galen Gart (Big Nickel Publications, 1993).

First Pressings: The History of Rhythm & Blues, 1953, by Galen Gart (Big Nickel Publications, 1989).

First Pressings: The History of Rhythm & Blues, 1954, by Galen Gart (Big Nickel Publications, 1990).

First Pressings: The History of Rhythm & Blues, 1955, by Galen Gart (Big Nickel Publications, 1990).

First Pressings: The History of Rhythm & Blues, 1956, by Galen Gart (Big Nickel Publications, 1991).

First Pressings: The History of Rhythm & Blues, 1957, by Galen Gart (Big Nickel Publications, 1993).

Funk: The Music, the People, and the Rhythm of the One, by Rickey Vincent (St. Martin's Griffin, 1996).

Higher Ground: Stevie Wonder, Aretha Franklin, Curtis Mayfield, and the Rise and Fall of American Soul, by Craig Werner (Crown Publishers, 2004).

Hitsville USA: The Motown Singles Collection, 1959–1971, boxed set, liner notes by Leo Sacks, Elvis Mitchell, and Nelson George (Motown, 1992).

Honkers and Shouters: The Golden Years of Rhythm and Blues, by Arnold Shaw (Collier Books, 1978).

A House on Fire: The Rise and Fall of Philadelphia Soul, by John A. Jackson (Oxford University Press, 2004).

Joel Whitburn Presents Top R&B Singles, 1942–1999 (Record Research, 2000).

Joel Whitburn's Top R&B Albums, 1965–1998 (Record Research, 1999).

Just My Soul Responding: Rhythm & Blues, Black Consciousness, and Race Relations, by Brian Ward (University of California Press, 1998).

Love Saves the Day: A History of American Dance Music Culture, 1970–1979, by Tim Lawrence (Duke University Press, 2003).

MusicHound R&B: The Essential Album Guide, by Gary Graff, Josh Freedom du Lac, and Jim McFarlin (Visible Ink, 1998).

The New Blue Music: Changes in Rhythm & Blues, 1950–1999, by Richard J. Ripani (University Press of Mississippi, 2006).

Nowhere to Run: The Story of Soul Music, by Gerri Hirshey (Da Capo Press, 1994).

The Original Johnny Otis Show, double album, notes by Pete Welding (Savoy/Arista, 1978).

The R&B Box: Thirty Years of Rhythm & Blues, boxed set, annotation by Gary Peterson (Rhino, 1994).

Race Music: Black Cultures from Bebop to Hip-Hop, by Guthrie P. Ramsey, Jr. (University of California Press, 2003).

Songs in the Key of Black Life: A Rhythm and Blues Nation, by Mark Anthony Neal (Routledge, 2003).

Soul: 100 Essential CDs/The Rough Guide, by Peter Shapiro (Rough Guides, 2000).

The Soulful Divas: Personal Portraits of Over a Dozen Divine Divas, by David Nathan (Billboard Books, 1999).

Sweet Soul Music: Rhythm & Blues and the Southern Dream of Freedom, by Peter Guralnick (Little, Brown & Co., 1999).

Walking to New Orleans: The Story of New Orleans Rhythm & Blues, by John Broven (Flyright, 1977).

Where Did Our Love Go? The Rise and Fall of the Motown Sound, by Nelson George (University of Illinois Press, 2007).

Biographies/Artist Histories

James Brown: The Godfather of Soul, by James Brown with Bruce Tucker (Thunder's Mouth Press, 2002 edition).

The Hardest Working Man in Show Business: How James Brown Saved the Soul of America, by James Sullivan (Gotham Books, 2008).

Ray Charles: *Brother Ray: Ray Charles' Own Story,* by Ray Charles and David Ritz (Da Capo Press, 2003 revised edition).

Ray Charles: Man and Music, by Michael Lydon (Riverhead Books, 1998).

Sam Cooke: *Dream Boogie: The Triumph of Sam Cooke,* by Peter Guralnick (Little, Brown & Co., 2005).

You Send Me: The Life and Times of Sam Cooke, by Daniel Wolff with S. R. Crain (W. Morrow, 1995).

Fats Domino: *Blue Monday: Fats Domino and the Lost Dawn of Rock 'n Roll,* by Rick Coleman (Da Capo Press, 2006).

The Drifters: *Save the Last Dance for Me: The Musical Legacy of The Drifters, 1953–1993,* by Tony Allan with Faye Treadwell (Popular Culture Ink, 1993).

Ahmet Ertegun: *The Last Sultan: The Life and Times of Ahmet Ertegun,* by Robert Greenfield (Simon & Schuster, 2011).

Aretha Franklin: *Aretha: From These Roots,* by Aretha Franklin with David Ritz (Villard Books, 1999).

I Never Loved a Man the Way I Love You: Aretha Franklin, Respect, and the Making of a Soul Music Masterpiece, by Matt Dobkin (St. Martin's Griffin, 2004).

Marvin Gaye: *Divided Soul: The Life of Marvin Gaye,* by David Ritz (Da Capo Press, 1991).

Gloria Gaynor: *I Will Survive,* by Gloria Gaynor (St. Martin's Press, 1997).

Al Green: Take Me to the River, by Al Green with Davin Seay (Harper Entertainment, 2000).

Michael Jackson—see Pop Music.

Little Willie John: *Fever: Little Willie John: A Fast Life, Mysterious Death, and the Birth of Soul: The Authorized Biography*, by Susan Whitall and Kevin John (Titan Books, 2011).

Louis Jordan: *Let the Good Times Roll: The Story of Louis Jordan and His Music,* by John Chilton (University of Michigan Press, 1992).

Alicia Keys, by Terrell Brown (Mason Crest Publishers, 2007).

Beyoncé Knowles: A Biography, by Janice Arenofsky (Greenwood Press, 2009).

Otis Redding: *Otis! The Otis Redding Story,* by Scott Freeman (St. Martin's Press, 2001).

Martha Reeves: *Dancing In the Street: Confessions of a Motown Diva,* by Martha Reeves and Mark Bego (Hyperion, 1994).

Smokey Robinson: *Smokey: Inside My Life,* by Smokey Robinson with David Ritz (McGraw-Hill, 1989).

Diana Ross: *Memoirs: Secrets of a Sparrow,* by Diana Ross (Villard Books, 1993).

Sam and Dave: An Oral History, by Sam Moore and Dave Marsh (Avon Books, 1998).

Sly and the Family Stone: An Oral History, by Joel Selvin (Avon Books, 1998).

Donna Summer: *Ordinary Girl: The Journey,* by Donna Summer with Marc Eliot (Villard Books, 2003).

The Temptations: *Ain't Too Proud to Beg: The Troubled Lives and Enduring Soul of the Temptations,* by Mark Ribowsky (John Wiley & Sons, 2010).

Jerry Wexler: *Rhythm and the Blues: A Life in American Music,* by Jerry Wexler and David Ritz (St. Martin's Press, 1994).

Stevie Wonder: *Signed, Sealed, and Delivered: The Soulful Journey of Stevie Wonder,* by Mark Ribowsky (John Wiley & Sons, 2010).

Stevie Wonder, by John Swenson (Plexus, 1986).

Doo-Wop (as subset of Rhythm & Blues)

The Doo Wop Box: 101 Vocal Gems from the Golden Age of Rock 'n' Roll, boxed set, annotation Bob Hyde (Rhino, 1993).

The Doo Wop Box II: 101 More Vocal Group Gems, annotation by Bob Hyde (Rhino, 1996).

Doo-Wop: The Forgotten Third of Rock 'n' Roll, by Anthony Gribin and Matthew Schiff (Krause Publications, 1992).

Encyclopedia of Rhythm & Blues and Doo-Wop Vocal Groups, by Mitch Rosalsky (Scarecrow Press, 2000).

They All Sang on the Corner: A Second Look at New York City's Rhythm & Blues Vocal Groups, by Philip Groia (Dee Enterprises, 1983).

Rap/Hip-Hop (as subset of Rhythm & Blues)

The Big Payback: The History of the Business of Hip-Hop, by Dan Charnas (New American Library, 2010).

ROCK

Note: See Pop Music, Folk-Rock/Americana.

All Music Guide to Rock, by Michael Erlewine (Miller Freeman Books, 1997).

Big Beat Heat: Alan Freed and the Early Years of Rock and Roll, by John A. Jackson (Schirmer Books, 1995).

B-Sides, Undercurrents, and Overtones: Peripheries to Popular in Music, 1960 to the Present, by George Plasketes (Ashgate, 2009).

Blues and Chaos: The Music Writing of Robert Palmer, edited by Anthony DeCurtis (Scribner, 2009).

The Book of Rock Lists, by Dave Marsh and Kevin Stein (Dell/Rolling Stone Press, 1981).

Christgau's Record Guide: The '80s, by Robert Christgau (Pantheon Books, 1990).

Cowabunga! The Surf Box, boxed set, annotation by Gary Peterson (Rhino, 1996).

Crawdaddy (The Magazine of Rock 'n Roll), issues from 1966 through 1972.

The Day the Music Died: The Last Tour of Buddy Holly, the Big Bopper and Ritchie Valens, by Larry Lehmer (Omnibus Press, 2003).

Flowers in the Dustbin: The Rise of Rock and Roll, 1947–1977, by James Miller (Simon & Schuster, 1999).

The Illustrated Discography of Surf Music, 1961–1965, compiled by John Blair (Popular Culture, Ink, 1995).

The Illustrated Encyclopedia of Rock, by Nick Logan and Bob Woffinden (Harmony Books, 1977).

Lillian Roxon's Rock Encyclopedia (Tempo Books/Grosset & Dunlap, 1971 and 1974 editions).

Loud, Fast, and Out of Control: The Wild Sounds of '50s Rock, boxed set, annotation by Colin Escott (Rhino, 1999).

The Mansion on the Hill: Dylan, Young, Geffen, Springsteen, and the Head-on Collision of Rock and Commerce, by Fred Goodman (Times Books, 1997).

Melody Maker (British periodical), issues from 1976–1980.

MusicHound Rock: The Essential Album Guide, edited by Gary Graff (Visible Ink, 1996).

The New Book of Rock Lists, by Dave Marsh and James Bernard (Fireside/Simon & Schuster, 1994).

New Musical Express (British periodical), issues from 1972–1974.

Night Beat: A Shadow History of Rock & Roll, Collected Writings, by Mikal Gilmore (Doubleday, 1998).

Race, Rock, and Elvis, by Michael T. Bertrand (University of Illinois Press, 2000).

Rock & Roll: An Unruly History, by Robert Palmer (Harmony Books, 1995).

Rock Around the Clock: The Record That Started the Rock Revolution, by Jim Dawson (Backbeat Books, 2005).

Rock Lives: Profiles and Interviews, by Timothy White (Holt, 1991).

Rock of Ages: Rolling Stone History of Rock & Roll, by Ed Ward, Geoffrey Stokes, Ken Tucker (Rolling Stone Press/ Summit Books, 1986).

Rock 100: The Greatest Stars of Rock's Golden Age, by David Dalton and Lenny Kaye (Cooper Square, 1977–1999).

Rock: 100 Essential CDs/The Rough Guide, by Al Spicer (Rough Guides, 1999).

Rockin' Bones: 1950s Punk & Rockabilly, boxed set, annotation by Colin Escott (Rhino, 2006).

Rockin' In Time: A Social History of Rock and Roll, by David P. Szatmary (Prentice Hall, 1991).

Rolling Stone (periodical), issues from 1967 onward.

The Rolling Stone Encyclopedia of Rock & Roll, third edition, edited by Holly George-Warren and Patricia Romanowski (Fireside, 2001).

The Rolling Stone Illustrated History of Rock & Roll, edited by Jim Miller (Rolling Stone Press, 1976).

The Rolling Stone Interviews, edited by Jann Wenner and Joe Levy (Back Bay Books, 2007).

Rolling Stone: The 100 Greatest Artists of All Time (Special Collectors Edition), by Nathan Brackett (Jann S. Wenner, 2011).

The Sound of the City: The Rise of Rock & Roll, by Charlie Gillett (Pantheon Books, 1983 revised edition).

Spin (periodical), issues from 1988–1992; selected issues thereafter.

That Old-Time Rock & Roll: A Chronicle of an Era, 1954– 1963, by Richard Aquila (Schirmer Books, 1989).

There's a Riot Going On: Revolutionaries, Rock Stars, and the Rise and Fall of '60s Counterculture, by Peter Doggett (Canongate, 2007).

What Was the First Rock 'n' Roll Record? by Jim Dawson and Steve Propes (Faber & Faber, 1992).

Written In My Soul: Rock's Great Songwriters Talk About Creating Their Music, by Bill Flanagan (Contemporary Books, 1986).

Biographies/Artist Discographies

The Band: *Across the Great Divide: The Band and America,* by Barney Hoskyns (Hal Leonard, 2006 revised edition).

Chuck Berry: *Brown Eyed Handsome Man: The Life and Hard Times of Chuck Berry,* by Bruce Pegg (Routledge, 2002).

Chuck Berry: *The Autobiography,* by Chuck Berry (Fireside/ Simon & Schuster, 1988).

Eric Burdon: *I Used to Be an Animal But I'm All Right Now,* by Eric Burdon (Faber & Faber, 1986).

Eric Clapton: *Clapton: The Autobiography,* by Eric Clapton (Broadway Books, 2004).

Crossroads: *The Life and Music of Eric Clapton,* by Michael Schumacher (Hyperion, 1995).

The Clash: *Passion Is a Fashion: The Real Story of The Clash,* by Pat Gilbert (Da Capo Press, 2005).

Elvis Costello: *Complicated Shadows: The Life and Music of Elvis Costello,* by Graeme Thomson (Canongate, 2004).

Creedence Clearwater Revival: *Bad Moon Rising: The Unofficial History of Creedence Clearwater Revival,* by Hank Bordowitz (Schirmer Books, 1998).

Up Around the Bend: The Oral History of Creedence Clearwater revival, by Craig Werner (Spike, 1998).

Dick Dale: *Surf Beat: The Dick Dale Story,* by Stephen McFarland (C Music Books, 2000).

Bo Diddley: Living Legend, by George R. White (Castle Communications, 1995).

Fats Domino—see Rhythm & Blues.

The Doors: A Guide, by Doug Sundling (Sanctuary, 2003).

The Doors: A Lifetime of Listening to Five Mean Years, by Greil Marcus (BS/Public Affairs, 2011).

Bob Dylan—see Folk-Rock.

The Eagles: Flying High, by Laura Jackson (Portrait, 2006).

To the Limit: The Untold Story of The Eagles, by Marc Eliot (Little, Brown & Co., 1997).

The Fleetwood Mac Story: Rumours and Lies, by Bob Brunning (Omnibus Press, 2004).

Fleetwood: My Life and Adventures in Fleetwood Mac, by Mick Fleetwood with Stephen Davis (Morrow, 1990).

Peter Gabriel and Genesis: *Turn It On Again: Peter Gabriel, Phil Collins, and Genesis,* by Dave Thompson (Backbeat Books, 2005).

Grateful Dead: *The American Book of the Dead: The Definitive Grateful Dead Encyclopedia*, by Oliver Trager (Simon & Schuster, 1997).

Guns N' Roses: *Watch You Bleed: The Saga of Guns N' Roses,* by Stephen Davis (Penguin Group, 2008).

Jimi Hendrix: Electric Gypsy, by Harry Shapiro and Caesar Glebbeek (St. Martin's Press, 1992).

Room Full of Mirrors: A Biography of Jimi Hendrix, by Charles R. Cross (Hyperion, 2006 edition).

Buddy Holly: A Biography, by Ellis Amburn (St. Martin's Press, 1995).

Johnnie Johnson: *Father of Rock & Roll: The Story of Johnnie "B. Goode" Johnson,* by Travis Fitzpatrick (Thomas, Cooke & Co., 1999).

Janis Joplin: *Buried Alive: The Biography of Janis Joplin,* by Myra Friedman (Harmony Books, 1992).

The Kinks: *X-Ray: The Unauthorized Autobiography,* by Ray Davies (Overlook Press, 2007).

Mark Knopfler: An Unauthorized Biography, by Myles Palmer (Sidgwick & Jackson, 1991).

Led Zeppelin: When Giants Walked the Earth, by Mick Wall (St. Martin's Griffin, 2008).

Stairway to Heaven/Led Zeppelin Uncensored, by Richard Cole with Richard Trubo (Harper Entertainment, 2002).

Jerry Lee Lewis: *Hellfire: The Jerry Lee Lewis Story,* by Nick Tosches (Dell, 1982).

Little Richard: *The Life and Times of Little Richard/The Quasar of Rock,* by Charles White (Harmony Books, 1984).

John Mellencamp: *Born in a Small Town: John Mellencamp/The Story,* by Heather Johnson (Omnibus Press, 2007).

Van Morrison: Too Late to Stop Now, by Steve Turner (Viking, 1993).

Nirvana: *Kurt Cobain,* by Christopher Sandford (Carroll & Graf, 2004).

Nirvana/Teen Spirit: The Stories Behind Every Song, by Chuck Crisafulli (Simon & Schuster, 2003).

Earl Palmer: *Backbeat: Earl Palmer's Story,* by Tony Scherman (Smithsonian Institution Press, 1999).

Pearl Jam: *Five Against One: The Pearl Jam Story,* by Kim Neely (Penguin Books, 1998).

Tom Petty: *Conversations with Tom Petty,* by Paul Zollo (Omnibus Press, 2005).

The Police: *Walking on the Moon: The Untold Story of The Police,* by Chris Campion (John Wiley & Sons, 2010).

Elvis Presley: *Careless Love: The Unmaking of Elvis Presley,* by Peter Guralnick (Little, Brown & Co., 1999).

Elvis: The Biography, by Jerry Hopkins (Plexus, 2010 edition).

Elvis: From Nashville to Memphis: The Essential '60s Masters, boxed set, liner notes by Peter Guralnick (RCA, 1993).

Elvis: The King of Rock 'n' Roll: The Complete '50s' Masters, boxed set, liner notes by Peter Guralnick (RCA, 1992).

Elvis: Walk a Mile in My Shoes: The Essential '70s Masters, boxed set, liner notes by Dave Marsh (RCA, 1995).

Elvis Sessions: The Recorded Music of Elvis Aron Presley, 1953–1977, by Joseph A. Tunzi (JAT productions, 1993).

Last Train to Memphis: The Rise of Elvis Presley, by Peter Guralnick (Back Bay Books, 1994).

Prince: A Thief in the Temple, by Brian Morton (Canongate, 2007).

Prince: Inside the Music and the Masks, by Ronin Ro (St. Martin's Press, 2011).

Queen: *Is This the Real Life? The Untold Story of Queen,* by Mark Blake (Da Capo, 2010).

R.E.M.: *Remarks Remade: The Story of R.E.M.,* by Tony Fletcher (Omnibus Press, 2002).

Rolling Stones: *According to the Rolling Stones,* by Mick Jagger, Keith Richards, Charlie Watts, and Ronnie Wood, edited by Dora Loewenstein and Philip Dodd (Chronicle Books, 2009).

Heart of Stone: The Definitive Rolling Stones Discography, 1962–1983, by Felix Aeppli (Pierian Press, 1985).

Life, by Keith Richards with James Fox (Little, Brown & Co., 2010).

Old Gods Almost Dead: The 40-Year Odyssey of the Rolling Stones, by Stephen Davis (Broadway Books, 2001).

Rick Rubin in the Studio, by Jake Brown (ECW Press, 2009).

Bob Seger: *Travelin' Man: On the Road and Behind the Scenes With Bob Seger,* by Tom Weschler and Gary Graff (Wayne State University Press, 2009).

Sinead: Her Life and Music, by Jimmy Guterman (Grand Central Publishing, 1991).

Bruce Springsteen: *Songs,* by Bruce Springsteen (Harper Entertainment, 2003 edition).

Bruce Springsteen: Two Hearts: The Definitive Biography, 1972–2003, by Dave Marsh (Routledge, 2004).

Glory Days: Bruce Springsteen in the 1980s, by Dave Marsh (Pantheon Books, 1987).

It Ain't No Sin to Be Glad You're Alive: The Promise of Bruce Springsteen, by Eric Alterman (Little, Brown & Co., 1999).

Runaway Dream: Born to Run and Bruce Springsteen's American Vision, by Louis P. Masur (Bloomsbury Press, 2009).

Springsteen: Point Blank, by Christopher Sandford (Da Capo Press, 1999).

Bruce Springsteen: *Racing in the Street: The Bruce Springsteen Reader,* edited by June Skinner Sawyers (Penguin Books, 2004).

Steely Dan: Reelin' In the Years, by Brian Sweet (Omnibus Press, 1994).

Rod Stewart: Vagabond Heart, by Geoffrey Giuliano (Carroll & Graf, 1994).

Richard Thompson: The Biography, by Patrick Humphries (Schirmer Books, 1997).

Richard and Linda Thompson's Shoot Out the Lights (33 1/3), by Hayden Childs (Continuum, 2008).

Pete Townshend: *Behind Blue Eyes/The Life of Pete Townshend,* by Geoffrey Giuliano (Dutton, 1996).

U2: An Irish Phenomenon, by Visnja Cogan (Pegasus Books, 2007).

U2 by U2, by Bono, The Edge, Adam Clayton, Neil McCormick, and Larry Mullen, Jr. (It Books, 2006).

U2 into the Heart: The Stories Behind Every Song, by Niall Stokes (Thunder's Mouth Press, 2002).

Van Halen: *Everybody Wants Some: The Van Halen Saga,* by Ian Christie (John Wiley & Sons, 2008).

The Who: *Before I Get Old: The Story of The Who,* by Dave Marsh (Plexus, 1983).

Neil Young: *Shakey: Neil Young's Biography,* by Jimmy McDonough (Anchor Books, 2003).

TRADITIONAL POP/ TIN PAN ALLEY AND BROADWAY

"Alexander and His Band," by Charles Hamm, *American Music* (Spring 1996).

American Musical Theater: A Chronicle, by Gerald Bordman (Oxford University Press, 1978).

American Musical Theater: Shows, Songs, and Stars, annotation by Dwight Blocker Bowers (Smithsonian Collection of Recordings, 1989).

American Popular Song: The Great Innovators, 1900–1950, by Alec Wilder (Oxford University Press, 1990 edition of 1972 book).

American Popular Song: Six Decades of Songwriters and Singers, annotation by James R. Morris (Smithsonian Collection of Recordings, 1984).

American Singers: 27 Portraits in Song, by Whitney Balliett (Oxford University Press, 1988).

The American Songbook: The Singers, the Songwriters, and the Songs, by Ken Bloom (Black Dog & Leventhal, 2005).

The Artistry of Marion Harris, liner notes by Bill Tynes (Take Two Records, 1984).

Beautiful Mornin': The Broadway Musical in the 1940s, by Ethan Mordden (Oxford University Press, 1999).

A Biographical Guide to the Great Jazz and Pop Singers, by Will Friedwald (Pantheon Books, 2010).

Broadway's Greatest Musicals, by Abe Laufe (Funk & Wagnalls, 1977).

Classic American Popular Song: The Second Half-Century, 1950–2000, by David Jenness and Don Velsey (Routledge, 2006).

Coming Up Roses: The Broadway Musical in the 1950s, by Ethan Mordden (Oxford University Press, 1998).

The Concise Oxford Companion to American Theatre, by Gerald Boardman (Oxford University Press, 1987).

Easy to Remember: The Great American Songwriters and Their Songs, by William Zinsser (David R. Godine, 2002).

The Great American Popular Singers, by Henry Pleasants (Victor Gollancz, Ltd., 1974).

The House That George Built: A History of the Golden Age of American Popular Music, by Wilfred Sheed (Random House, 2007).

It's a Hit! The Backstage Book of Longest-Running Broadway Shows, by David Sheward (Back Stage Books, 1994).

The Jazz Singers: A Smithsonian Collection, boxed set with annotation by Robert G. O'Meally (Smithsonian, 1998).

The Jazz Singers: The Ultimate Guide, by Scott Yanow (Backbeat Books, 2008).

Jazz Singing: America's Great Voices from Bessie Smith to Bebop and Beyond, by Will Friedwald (Da Capo Press, 1996 edition).

The Life and Death of Tin Pan Alley, by David Ewen (Funk & Wagnalls, 1964).

The Melody Man: Joe Davis and the New York Music Scene, 1916–1978, by Bruce Bastin with Kip Lornell (University Press of Mississippi, 2012 edition).

The NPR Curious Listener's Guide to Popular Standards, by Max Morath (Perigee, 2002).

The Poets of Tin Pan Alley: A History of America's Great Lyricists, by Philip Furia (Oxford University Press, 1990).

Showtime: A History of the Broadway Musical Theater, by Larry Stempel (W. W. Norton & Co., 2010).

Show Tunes: The Songs, Shows & Careers of Broadway's Major Composers, 1905–1991, by Steven Suskin (Limelight Editions, 1992).

Stardust Melodies: A Biography of 12 of America's Most Popular Songs, by Will Friedwald (Pantheon Books, 2002).

The Tin Pan Alley Song Encyclopedia, by Thomas S. Hischak (Greenwood Press, 2002).

White Christmas: The Story of an American Song, by Jody Rosen (Scriber, 2002).

Biographies (Arrangers and Producers)

Norman Granz: The Man Who Used Jazz for Justice, by Tad Hershorn (University of California Press, 2011).

Nelson Riddle: *September in the Rain: The Life of Nelson Riddle,* by Peter J. Levinson (Billboard Books, 2001).

Biographies (Songwriters)

Harold Arlen: *Rhythm, Rainbows & Blues,* by Edward Jablonski (Northeastern University Press, 1996).

Irving Berlin: *As Thousands Cheer: The Life of Irving Berlin,* by Laurence Bergreen (Penguin Books, 1991).

Hoagy Carmichael: *Stardust Melody: The Life and Music of Hoagy Carmichael,* by Richard Sudhalter (Oxford University Press, 2002).

George and Ira Gershwin: *Fascinating Rhythm: The Collaboration of George and Ira Gershwin,* by Deena Rosenberg (1991, Dutton).

The Gershwin Years, by Edward Jablonski and Lawrence Stewart (Doubleday, 1973).

Gershwin: His Life and Music, by Charles Schwartz (Bobb-Merrill Co., 1973).

The Memory of All That: The Life of George Gershwin, by Joan Peyser (Simon & Schuster, 1993).

Ira Gershwin: The Art of the Lyricist, by Philip Furia (Oxford University Press, 1996).

Lyrics on Several Occasions, by Ira Gershwin (Limelight Editions, 1997 edition of 1958 book).

Oscar Hammerstein: *Getting to Know Him: A Biography of Oscar Hammerstein,* by Hugh Fordin (Random House, 1977).

E. Y. Harburg: *Who Put the Rainbow in the Wizard of Oz?: Yip Harburg, Lyricist,* by Harold Meyerson and Ernie Harburg (University of Michigan Press, 1993).

Jerome Kern: *His Life and Music,* by Gerald Boardman (Oxford University Press, 1980).

Lerner and Loewe: *Inventing Champagne: The Worlds of Lerner and Loewe,* by Gene Lees (St. Martin's Press, 1990).

Johnny Mercer: *Skylark: The Life and Times of Johnny Mercer,* by Philip Furia (St. Martin's Press, 2003).

Cole Porter: *A Biography,* by William McBrien (Vintage Books, 1998).

Richard Rodgers and Oscar Hammerstein: *Rodgers and Hammerstein,* by Ethan Mordden (Harry N. Abrams, Inc., 1992).

Biographies/Discographies (Singers)

Fred Astaire: A Wonderful Life, by Bill Adler (Carroll & Graf, 1987).

Steps In Time: An Autobiography, by Fred Astaire (Harper Entertainment, 1959).

Tony Bennett: *All the Things You Are: The Life of Tony Bennett,* by David Evanier (John Wiley & Sons, 2011).

Forty Years: The Artistry of Tony Bennett, boxed set, notes by Will Friedwald, Ralph Sharon, Leonard Feather, and Jonathan Schwartz (Columbia Legacy, 1991).

The Good Life, by Tony Bennett with Will Friedwald (Pocket Books, 1998).

Rosemary Clooney: *Girl Singer: An Autobiography,* by Rosemary Clooney with Joan Barthel (Doubleday, 1999).

Nat King Cole, by Daniel Mark Epstein (G. K. Hall & Co., 1999).

Unforgettable: The Life and Mystique of Nat King Cole, by Leslie Gourse (St. Martin's Press, 1991).

Bing Crosby: *Bing: His Legendary Years, 1931 to 1957,* four CDs, annotation by Will Friedwald (MCA Records, 1993).

Bing Crosby: A Pocketful of Dreams: The Early Years, 1903–1940, by Gary Giddins (Little, Brown & Co., 2001).

Bing Crosby: A Bio-Bibliography, by J. Roger Osterholm (Greenwood Press, 1994).

Doris Day: *Considering Doris Day,* by Tom Santopietro (Thomas Dunne Books, 2007).

Ella Fitzgerald: A Biography of the First Lady of Jazz, by Stuart Nicholson (Da Capo Press, 1994).

First Lady of Song: Ella Fitzgerald for the Record, by Geoffrey Mark Fidelman (Carol Pub. Group, 1994).

Judy Garland: *Get Happy: The Life of Judy Garland,* by Gerald Clarke (Random House, 2000).

Judy Garland: Beyond the Rainbow, by Sheridan Morley and Ruth Leon (Arcade/Time-Warner, 1999).

Billie Holiday: *Billie's Blues: The Billie Holiday Story,* by John Chilton (Day Books, 1978).

Billie Holiday: Wishing On the Moon, by Donald Clarke (Da Capo Press, 2002 edition); also see *Strange Fruit: Biography of a Song.*

Lena Horne: *Lena: A Personal and Professional Biography of Lena Horne,* by James Haskins with Kathleen Benson (Stein & Day, 1984).

Stormy Weather: The Life of Lena Horne, by James Gavin (Atria/Simon & Schuster, 2009).

Peggy Lee: *Fever: The Life and Music of Miss Peggy Lee,* by Peter Richmond (Picador/Henry Holt & Co., 2006).

Johnnie Ray: *Cry: The Johnnie Ray Story,* by Jonny Whiteside (Barricade Books, 1994).

Frank Sinatra: *Put Your Dreams Away: A Frank Sinatra Discography,* by Luiz Carlos do Nascimento Silva (Greenwood Press, 2000).

Sinatra! The Song Is You: A Singer's Art, by Will Friedwald (Scribner, 1995).

Barbra Streisand: *Barbra: The Way She Is,* by Christopher Andersen (William Morrow, 2006).

Hello, Gorgeous: Becoming Barbra Streisand, by William J. Mann (Houghton Mifflin Harcourt, 2012).

Sarah Vaughan: A Discography, by Denis Brown (Greenwood Press, 1991).

Sassy: The Life of Sarah Vaughan, by Leslie Gourse (Da Capo Press, 1994).

Title Index

Note: This index contains song titles, album titles, titles of Broadway musicals, plays, films, and TV shows. Songs with full essays are in capital letters, and the page numbers for a song's essay are **bold**.

Subject & Name Index

Note: Full essays on songs by the credited artist (including lead singer or featured soloist) & songwriters are in **bold**.